Contemporary
Literary Criticism

Guide to Gale Literary Criticism Series

When you need to review criticism of literary works, these are the Gale series to use:

If the author's death date is:	You should turn to:

After Dec. 31, 1959
(or author is still living)

CONTEMPORARY LITERARY CRITICISM

for example: Jorge Luis Borges, Anthony Burgess,
William Faulkner, Mary Gordon,
Ernest Hemingway, Iris Murdoch

1900 through 1959

TWENTIETH-CENTURY LITERARY CRITICISM

for example: Willa Cather, F. Scott Fitzgerald,
Henry James, Mark Twain, Virginia Woolf

1800 through 1899

NINETEENTH-CENTURY LITERATURE CRITICISM

for example: Fedor Dostoevski, Nathaniel Hawthorne,
George Sand, William Wordsworth

1400 through 1799

LITERATURE CRITICISM FROM 1400 TO 1800
(excluding Shakespeare)

for example: Anne Bradstreet, Daniel Defoe,
Alexander Pope, François Rabelais,
Jonathan Swift, Phillis Wheatley

SHAKESPEAREAN CRITICISM

Shakespeare's plays and poetry

Antiquity through 1399

CLASSICAL AND MEDIEVAL LITERATURE CRITICISM

for example: Dante, Homer, Plato, Sophocles, Vergil,
the Beowulf Poet

Gale also publishes related criticism series:

CHILDREN'S LITERATURE REVIEW

This series covers authors of all eras who have written for the preschool through high school audience.

SHORT STORY CRITICISM

This series covers the major short fiction writers of all nationalities and periods of literary history.

ISSN 0091-3421

Volume 60

Contemporary Literary Criticism

Excerpts from Criticism of the
Works of Today's Novelists, Poets,
Playwrights, Short Story Writers, Scriptwriters,
and Other Creative Writers

Roger Matuz
EDITOR

Cathy Falk
Mary K. Gillis
Sean R. Pollock
David Segal
Bridget Travers
Robyn V. Young
ASSOCIATE EDITORS

 *Gale Research Inc.* • DETROIT • NEW YORK
WASHINGTON, D.C. • CHICAGO • LONDON

STAFF

Roger Matuz, *Editor*

Cathy Falk, Mary K. Gillis, Sean R. Pollock, David Segal,
Bridget Travers, Robyn V. Young, *Associate Editors*

John P. Daniel, Tina N. Grant, Michael W. Jones, David Kmenta,
Susanne Skubik, Allyson J. Wylie, *Assistant Editors*

Jeanne A. Gough, *Production & Permissions Manager*
Linda M. Pugliese, *Production Supervisor*
Suzanne Powers, Maureen A. Puhl, Linda M. Ross, Jennifer VanSickle, *Editorial Associates*
Donna Craft, James G. Wittenbach, *Editorial Assistants*

Victoria B. Cariappa, *Research Manager*
H. Nelson Fields, Judy L. Gale, Maureen Richards, *Editorial Associates*
Paula Cutcher, Alan Hedblad, Jill M. Ohorodnik, *Editorial Assistants*

Sandra C. Davis, *Permissions Supervisor (Text)*
Josephine M. Keene, Kimberly F. Smilay, *Permissions Associates*
Maria L. Franklin, Michele Lonoconus, Camille P. Robinson,
Shalice Shah, Denise M. Singleton, Rebecca A. Stanko, *Permissions Assistants*

Patricia A. Seefelt, *Permissions Supervisor (Pictures)*
Margaret A. Chamberlain, *Permissions Associate*
Pamela A. Hayes, Lillian Quickley, *Permissions Assistants*

Mary Beth Trimper, *Production Manager*
Marilyn Jackman, *External Production Assistant*

Art Chartow, *Art Director*
C. J. Jonik, *Keyliner*

Laura Bryant, *Production Supervisor*
Louise Gagné, *Internal Production Associate*

The paper used in this publication meets the minimum requirements
of American National Standard for Information Sciences—Permanence
Paper for Printed Library Materials, ANSI Z39.48-1984. ∞™

Copyright © 1990
Gale Research Inc.
835 Penobscot Bldg.
Detroit, MI 48226-4094

Library of Congress Catalog Card Number 76-38938
ISBN 0-8103-4434-3
ISSN 0091-3421

Printed in the United States of America

Published simultaneously in the United Kingdom
by Gale Research International Limited
(An affiliated company of Gale Research Inc.)

Contents

Preface   vii

Acknowledgments   xi

Authors Forthcoming in *CLC*   xvii

Preface

Named "one of the twenty-five most distinguished reference titles published during the past twenty-five years" by *Reference Quarterly*, the *Contemporary Literary Criticism (CLC)* series has provided readers with critical commentary and general information on more that 2,000 authors now living or who died after December 31, 1959. Previous to the publication of the first volume of *CLC* in 1973, there was no ongoing digest monitoring scholarly and popular sources of critical opinion and explication of modern literature. *CLC*, therefore, has fulfilled an essential need, particularly since the complexity and variety of contemporary literature makes the function of criticism especially important to today's reader.

Scope of the Series

CLC presents significant passages from published criticism of works by creative writers. Since many of the authors covered by *CLC* inspire continual critical commentary, writers are often represented in more than one volume. There is, of course, no duplication of reprinted criticism.

Authors are selected for inclusion for a variety of reasons, among them the publication or dramatic production of a critically acclaimed new work, the reception of a major literary award, revival of interest in past writings, or the dramatization of a literary work as a film or television screenplay. The present volume of *CLC* includes:

☞ Harper Lee—whose work *To Kill a Mockingbird* is the most widely studied contemporary novel in American high schools, according to *A Study of Book-Length Works Taught in High School English Courses* (1989), which was published by the Center for the Learning and Teaching of Literature, a research and development organization located at the University of Albany, State University of New York.

☞ Umberto Eco—whose work *Foucault's Pendulum* was widely read in several languages and was the best-selling novel among American college students during the 1989–90 academic year, as reported in *The Chronicle of Higher Education*.

☞ Annie Dillard and James Michener—who prove consistently popular among critics and readers with each new work.

Among other writers represented in the present volume are Carlos Fuentes, a major figure in contemporary literature whose novel *The Old Gringo* was recently adapted for film, and Ishmael Reed, a leading American experimental writer.

Perhaps most importantly, works that frequently appear on the syllabuses of high school and college literature courses are represented by individual entries in *CLC*. Kurt Vonnegut's *Slaughterhouse-Five* and Peter Shaffer's *Equus* are examples of works of this stature in *CLC*, Vol. 60. Attention is also given to several other groups of writers—authors of considerable public interest—about whose work criticism is often difficult to locate. These include mystery and science fiction writers, literary and social critics, foreign writers, and authors who represent particular ethnic groups within the United States.

Format of the Book

Altogether there are about 500 individual excerpts in each volume—with approximately seventeen excerpts per author—taken from hundreds of book review periodicals, general magazines, scholarly journals, monographs, and books. Entries include critical evaluations spanning from the beginning of an author's career to the most current commentary. Interviews, feature articles, and other published writings that offer insight into the author's works are also presented. Students, teachers, librarians, and researchers will find that the generous excerpts and supplementary material provided by *CLC* supply them with vital information needed to write a term paper, analyze a poem, or lead a book discussion group. In addition, complete bibliographical citations facilitate the location of the original source and provide all of the information necessary for a term paper footnote or bibliography.

A *CLC* author entry consists of the following elements:

- The **author heading** cites the form under which the author has most commonly published, followed by birth date, and death date when applicable. Uncertainty as to a birth or death date is indicated by a question mark.

- A **portrait** of the author is included when available.

- A brief **biographical and critical introduction** to the author and his or her work precedes the excerpted criticism. The first line of the introduction provides the author's full name, pseudonyms (if applicable), nationality, and a listing of genres in which the author has written. Since *CLC* is not intended to be a definitive biographical source, *cross-references* have been included to direct readers to these useful sources published by Gale Research: *Short Story Criticism* and *Children's Literature Review*, which provide excerpts of criticism on the works of short story writers and authors of books for young people, respectively; *Contemporary Authors*, which includes detailed biographical and bibliographical sketches of nearly 95,000 authors; *Something about the Author*, which contains heavily illustrated biographical sketches of writers and illustrators who create books for children and young adults; *Dictionary of Literary Biography*, which provides original evaluations and detailed biographies of authors important to literary history; and *Contemporary Authors Autobiography Series* and *Something about the Author Autobiography Series*, which offer autobiographical essays by prominent writers for adults and those of interest to young readers, respectively. Previous volumes of *CLC* in which the author has been featured are also listed in the introduction.

- The **excerpted criticism** represents various kinds of critical writing, ranging in form from the brief review to the scholarly exegesis. Essays are selected by the editors to reflect the spectrum of opinion about a specific work or about an author's literary career in general. The excerpts are presented chronologically, adding a useful perspective to the entry. All titles by the author featured in the entry are printed in boldface type, which enables the reader to easily identify the works being discussed. Publication information (such as publisher names and book prices) and parenthetical numerical references (such as footnotes or page and line references to specific editions of a work) have been deleted at the editor's discretion to provide smoother reading of the text.

- A complete **bibliographical citation** designed to help the user find the original essay or book follows each excerpt.

New Features

Beginning with Vol. 60, *CLC* has incorporated two new features designed to enhance the usability of the series:

- A list of **principal works**, arranged chronologically and, if applicable, divided into genre categories, notes the most important works by the author.

- A **further reading** section appears at the end of entries on authors who have generated a significant amount of criticism other than the pieces reprinted in *CLC*. In some cases, it includes references to material for which the editors could not obtain reprint rights.

Other Features

- A list of **Authors Forthcoming in *CLC*** previews the authors to be researched for future volumes.

- An **Acknowledgments** section lists the copyright holders who have granted permission to reprint material in this volume of *CLC*. It does not, however, list every book or periodical reprinted or consulted during the preparation of the volume.

- A **Cumulative Author Index** lists all the authors who have appeared in *CLC, Twentieth-Century Literary Criticism, Nineteenth-Century Literature Criticism, Literature Criticism from 1400 to 1800, Classical and Medieval Literature Criticism,* and *Short Story Criticism,* with cross-references to these Gale series: *Children's Literature Review, Contemporary Authors, Contemporary Authors Autobiography Series, Contemporary Authors Bibliographical Series, Dictionary of Literary Biography, Something about the Author, Something about the Author Autobiography Series, Yesterday's Authors of Books for Children,* and *Authors & Artists for Young Adults.* Readers will welcome this cumulated author index as a useful tool for locating an author within the various series. The index, which lists birth and death dates when available, will be particularly valuable for those authors who are identified with a certain period but whose death date causes them to be placed in another, or for those authors whose careers span two periods. For example, Ernest Hemingway is found in *CLC*, yet a writer often associated with him, F. Scott Fitzgerald, is found in *Twentieth-Century Literary Criticism*.

• A **Cumulative Nationality Index** alphabetically lists all authors featured in *CLC* by nationality, followed by numbers corresponding to the volumes in which they appear.

• A **Title Index** alphabetically lists all titles reviewed in the current volume of *CLC*. Listings are followed by the author's name and the corresponding page numbers where the titles are discussed. English translations of foreign titles and variations of titles are cross-referenced to the title under which a work was originally published. Titles of novels, novellas, dramas, films, record albums, and poetry, short story, and essay collections are printed in italics, while all individual poems, short stories, essays, and songs are printed in roman type within quotation marks; when published separately (e.g., T.S. Eliot's poem *The Waste Land*), the title will also be printed in italics.

• In response to numerous suggestions from librarians, Gale has also produced a **special paperbound edition** of the *CLC* title index. This annual cumulation, which alphabetically lists all titles reviewed in the series, is available to all customers and will be published with the first volume of *CLC* issued in each calendar year. Additional copies of the index are available upon request. Librarians and patrons will welcome this separate index: it saves shelf space, is easy to use, and is disposable upon receipt of the following year's cumulation.

A Note to the Reader

When writing papers, students who quote directly from any volume in the Literary Criticism Series may use the following general forms to footnote reprinted criticism. The first example pertains to material drawn from periodicals, the second to material reprinted from books:

[1]Anne Tyler, "Manic Monologue," *The New Republic* 200 (April 17, 1989), 44-6; excerpted and reprinted in *Contemporary Literary Criticism,* Vol. 58, ed. Roger Matuz (Detroit: Gale Research, 1990), p. 325.

[2]Patrick Reilly, *The Literature of Guilt: From 'Gulliver' to Golding* (University of Iowa Press, 1988); excerpted and reprinted in *Contemporary Literary Criticism,* Vol. 58, ed. Roger Matuz (Detroit: Gale Research, 1990), pp. 206-12.

Suggestions Are Welcome

The editors welcome the comments and suggestions of readers to expand the coverage and enhance the usefulness of the series. Please feel free to contact us by letter or by calling our toll-free number: 1-800-347-GALE.

Acknowledgments

The editors wish to thank the copyright holders of the excerpted criticism included in this volume, the permissions managers of many book and magazine publishing companies for assisting us in securing reprint rights, and Anthony Bogucki for assistance with copyright research. We are also grateful to the staffs of the Detroit Public Library, the Library of Congress, the University of Detroit Library, Wayne State University Purdy/Kresge Library Complex, and the University of Michigan Libraries for making their resources available to us. Following is a list of the copyright holders who have granted us permission to reprint material in this volume of *CLC*. Every effort has been made to trace copyright, but if omissions have been made, please let us know.

COPYRIGHTED EXCERPTS IN *CLC*, VOLUME 60, WERE REPRINTED FROM THE FOLLOWING PERIODICALS:

The Alabama Review, v. XXVI, April, 1973 for "The Romantic Regionalism of Harper Lee" by Fred Erisman. Copyright © 1973 by The University of Alabama Press. Reprinted by permission of the publisher.—*America,* v. 129, December 8, 1973. © 1973. All rights reserved. Reprinted with permission of America Press, Inc., 106 West 56th Street, New York, NY 10019.—*The American Book Review,* v. 10, January-February, 1989; v. 11, March-April, 1989. © 1989 by *The American Book Review.* Both reprinted by permission of the publisher.—*Analog Science Fiction/Science Fact,* v. CVI, July, 1986 for "So Long, and Thanks for All the Fish" by Tom Easton; v. CVIII, February, 1988 for "Dirk Gently's Holistic Detective Agency" by Tom Easton. © 1986, 1989 by Davis Publications, Inc. Both reprinted by permission of the respective authors.—*Art in America,* v. 76, June, 1988 for "Dancing with Baudrillard" by Suzi Gablik. Copyright © 1988 by Art in America, Inc. Reprinted by permission of the publisher and the author.—*Artforum,* v. XXII, April, 1984 for "From Imitation to the Copy to Just Effect: On Reading Jean Baudrillard" by Kate Linker; v. XXVII, October, 1988 for "Here, There & Otherwise" by John Welchman. © 1984, 1988 Artforum International Magazine, Inc. Both reprinted by permission of the publisher.—*Arts Magazine,* v. 61, September, 1986 for "The Politics of Art" by Jeremy Gilbert-Rolfe. © 1986 by the Arts Digest Co. Reprinted by permission of the author.—*The Atlantic Monthly,* v. 163, January, 1939 for "Two Second-Generation Americans" by James T. Farrell. Copyright 1939 by The Atlantic Monthly Company, Boston, MA. Reprinted by permission of the Literary Estate of the author./ v. 164, December, 1939 for "John Fante vs. John Selby" by E. B. Garside; v. 264, November, 1989 for "The Novel as Status Symbol" by Alexander Stille. Copyright 1939, 1989 by The Atlantic Monthly Company, Boston, MA. Both reprinted by permission of the respective authors.—*Belles Lettres: A Review of Books by Women,* v. 4, Fall, 1988. Reprinted by permission of the publisher.—*Best Sellers,* v. 41, January, 1982. Copyright © 1982 Helen Dwight Reid Educational Foundation. Reprinted by permission of the publisher.—*The Black Scholar,* v. 18, May-June, 1987. Copyright 1987 by *The Black Scholar.* Reprinted by permission of the publisher.—*The Bloomsbury Review,* v. 9, May-June, 1989 for an interview with Douglas Adams by Marc Conly. Copyright © by Owaissa Communications Company, Inc. 1989. Reprinted by permission of Marc Conly and Douglas Adams.—*Book World—Chicago Tribune,* February 20, 1972 for "Way Out in the East" by Audrey C. Foote. © 1972 Postrib Corp. Reprinted by permission of *The Washington Post* and the author.—*Book World—The Washington Post,* April 13, 1969 for "Nice Niece" by Leo L. Barrow. © 1969 Postrib Corp. Reprinted by permission of *The Washington Post* and the author./ January 29, 1978; April 4, 1982; December 5, 1982; January 2, 1983; July 17, 1983; June 2, 1985; September 29, 1985; March 16, 1986; May 1, 1988; July 3, 1988; November 13, 1988; June 25, 1989; August 20, 1989; August 27, 1989; September 24, 1989; November 12, 1989. © 1978, 1982, 1983, 1985, 1986, 1988, 1989, *The Washington Post.* All reprinted by permission of the publisher.—*Books,* London, n. 23, February, 1989. © Gradegate Ltd. 1989. Reprinted by permission of the publisher.—*Books,* New York, August 6, 1961. Copyright 1961 I. H. T. Corporation. Reprinted by permission of the publisher.—*Boston Review,* v. XIV, February, 1989 for a review of "Dictionary of the Khazars" by Fred Miller Robinson. Copyright © 1989 by the Boston Critic, Inc. Reprinted by permission of the author.—*The Centennial Review,* v. XX, Summer, 1976 for "Time, Uncertainty, and Kurt Vonnegut, Jr.: A Reading of 'Slaughterhouse-Five' " by Charles B. Harris. © 1976 by *The Centennial Review.* Reprinted by permission of the publisher and the author.—*Chicago Sunday Tribune Magazine of Books,* September 10, 1961 for "Witty Sermonizing" by Genevieve Casey.—*Chicago Tribune—Books,* September 13, 1987 for "Childhood Relived" by Catherine Petroski; October 11, 1987 for "The Flame Flickers" by Beverly Fields; November 6, 1988 for "A Novel of Intricate, Disorienting Pleasures" by Douglas Seibold; July 2, 1989 for "A Stagey, Readable Leftover from Michener's 'Alaska' " by Peter C. Newman; August 6, 1989 for "Living between the Lines" by William Logan. © copyrighted 1987, 1988, 1989, Chicago Tribune Company. All rights reserved. All reprinted by permission of the respective authors./ October 22, 1989. © copyrighted 1989, Chicago Tribune Company. All rights reserved. Used with permission.—*College Literature,* v. 1, Spring, 1974. Copyright © 1974 by West Chester University. Reprinted by permission of the publisher.—*Commentary,* v. 81, May, 1986 for "Montezuma's Literary Revenge" by Fernanda Eberstadt. Copyright © 1986 by the American Jewish Committee. All rights reserved. Reprinted by permission of the publisher and the author.—*Commonweal,* v. CIII,

COPYRIGHTED EXCERPTS IN *CLC,* VOLUME 60, WERE REPRINTED FROM THE FOLLOWING BOOKS:

Authors Forthcoming in *CLC*

Nicholson Baker (American novelist)—Baker has received critical praise for his debut novel, *The Mezzanine,* a contemplative, detail-oriented work in which an escalator ride inspires revelations on the unexamined, seemingly trivial aspects of daily life.

Malcolm Bradbury (English novelist and critic)—A prolific author, Bradbury writes satirical novels about British and American university life in which he examines themes of social dislocation and liberalism.

Gillian Clarke (Welsh poet)—Considered an important new voice in contemporary Welsh poetry, Clarke utilizes traditional Celtic metrics that resonate throughout her primarily meditative verse. Clarke often employs these subtle sound and rhythmic patterns to explore the nature of female experience.

Maria Irene Fornés (Cuban-born American dramatist)—Winner of six Obie awards, Fornés is a leading off-Broadway dramatist. Although unconventional, her humorous, intelligent plays reflect such traditional concerns as human relationships and social and political corruption.

Larry Gelbart (American scriptwriter and dramatist)—Chief writer for the first five years of the television series "M*A*S*H," Gelbart has recently garnered praise for his comic plays *Mastergate*, a satire on the Iran-Contra scandal, and *City of Angels*, a parody of 1940s detective films.

Ernest Hemingway (American novelist and short story writer)—Recognized as one of the preeminent American authors of the twentieth century, Hemingway wrote powerful, terse narratives of disillusionment, personal loss, and stoic resolve in the face of an apparently meaningless world. Critical commentary in Hemingway's entry will focus upon his acclaimed novel, *The Sun Also Rises*.

Zora Neale Hurston (American novelist and short story writer)—Regarded as an important writer of the Harlem Renaissance, Hurston is respected for works that provide insights into black culture and the human condition. Hurston's entry will focus on her novel *Their Eyes Were Watching God*, which is enjoying renewed popularity through Women's Studies courses.

Jack Kerouac (American novelist)—Kerouac was a key figure in the artistic and cultural phenomenon known as the Beat Movement. This entry will focus on his novel *On the Road*, considered a quintessential work of Beat literature for its experimental form and its portrayal of a rebellious, hedonistic lifestyle.

Stephen King (American novelist and short story writer)—King is a prolific and popular author of horror fiction. Nonsupernatural in emphasis, King's recent novels include *Misery*, in which a bestselling writer is held captive by a psychotic nurse, and *The Dark Half*, about a pseudonymous author attempting to shed his false persona who finds that his submerged alter-ego seeks revenge.

George F. Walker (Canadian dramatist)—Closely associated with the Factory Theatre, a group that promotes alternative drama in Toronto, Walker writes social satires in which he employs black humor and a variety of unconventional theatrical devices. His recent play, *Nothing Sacred*, for which Walker received his second Governor General's Award, was popular in regional theaters in the United States and Canada.

Martin Amis (English novelist, critic, and short story writer)—Amis employs a flamboyant prose style in satirical novels that castigate hedonism in contemporary society. Criticism in this entry will focus on *Einstein's Monsters*, a short story collection, and *London Fields*, which is widely considered Amis's most ambitious novel.

John Berryman (American poet and critic)—A key figure in the group of American poets known as the "Middle Generation," Berryman expanded the boundaries of post-World War II poetry with his intense, confessional verse and his imaginative adaptations of various poetic forms and personae. The recent publication of Berryman's *Collected Poems* has revived interest in the work of this influential poet.

Anthony Burgess (English novelist, essayist, and critic)—Considered among the most important novelists in contemporary literature, Burgess is a prolific writer best known for his dystopian novel *A Clockwork Orange*. His work, which covers a vast range of topics, frequently explores the conflict between free will and determinism and the role of the artist in society.

Henry Dumas (American short story writer and poet)—Considered an author of extraordinary talent, Dumas did not achieve critical recognition until after his death in 1968. His posthumously published collections *Ark of Bones* and *Goodbye Sweetwater* emphasize the African heritage of black Americans as he chronicles their divergent experiences in the rural South and the industrial North.

Lorraine Hansberry (American dramatist)—The first African-American woman to win the New York Drama Critics Circle Award, Hansberry is best known for *A Raisin in the Sun*. This acclaimed play about a black working-class family's attempt to move into a white neighborhood will be the focus of entry.

Tony Hillerman (American novelist)—Valued for their accurate and evocative depictions of Native American life on reservations of the Southwest, Hillerman's popular and critically respected mystery novels feature Navajo tribal policemen who employ both modern crime-fighting methods and ancient Navajo philosophy.

Margaret Laurence (Canadian novelist and short story writer)—One of Canada's most prominent contemporary writers, Laurence is respected for her "Manawaka" works, a series of four novels and a volume of short stories that examine Canadian social and historical issues through their evocation of small-town Manitoba life.

Cynthia Ozick (American short story writer and novelist)—Ozick is praised for her intricate, poetic fiction that incorporates magical elements within narratives concerning Jewish identity. This entry will focus on Ozick's recent works, *The Messiah of Stockholm* and *The Shawl*.

Sylvia Plath (American poet and novelist)—Considered one of the most powerful poets of the post-World War II era, Plath examined conflicts relating to her familial, marital, and career aspirations. This entry will concentrate on her autobiographical novel *The Bell Jar*, which portrays a young woman's struggles with despair and her attempts to assert a strong female identity.

Thomas Pynchon (American novelist and short story writer)—A preeminent author of postmodern works best known for his celebrated novel *Gravity's Rainbow*, Pynchon has attracted renewed critical interest with the publication of *Vineland*, his first novel in seventeen years.

Douglas Adams

1952-

(Born Douglas Noel Adams) English novelist and scriptwriter.

Adams is best known for the series of interrelated books he began with his highly popular first novel, *The Hitchhiker's Guide to the Galaxy.* Mixing deadpan humor, absurdism, black comedy, and satire, these works utilize elements from the science fiction genre to portray a chaotic universe populated by such entities as chattering objects and bizarre alien creatures with ridiculous names. Originally written as a series of radio scripts that were broadcast on British Radio, *The Hitchhiker's Guide to the Galaxy* has proved immensely popular, generating a theater production, a television series, audio recordings, and four sequels to the novel. Although some critics have concurred with Mat Coward's contention that Adams is "a genuine [science fiction] writer, despite his irreverence for the genre," Adams has asserted that he is a "comedy writer" who merely uses "the devices of science fiction to send up everything else. The rest of the world . . . is a better subject to take than just science fiction."

Upon receiving his honors degree in English Literature from Cambridge University in 1974, Adams began writing scripts for radio and television. He stated that the idea for his first novel came while he was "lying drunk in a field in Innsbruck and gazing at the stars" and realized "that *somebody* ought to write a hitchhiker's guide to the galaxy." Described by David N. Samuelson as "Monty Python in Outer Space," *The Hitchhiker's Guide to the Galaxy* depicts the adventures of Englishman Arthur Dent and his extraterrestrial guide to the galaxy, Ford Prefect of Betelgeuse, after the Earth is scheduled to be destroyed by aliens to make room for an intergalactic highway. Initially compared by reviewers to the works of Lewis Carroll, Jonathan Swift, and Kurt Vonnegut, *The Hitchhiker's Guide to the Galaxy* proved highly popular not only with adolescent and college readers but also, according to Philip Howard, "among those normally impervious to the mechanical charms of science fiction." Ensuing novels in the series include *The Restaurant at the End of the Universe,* in which Dent and Prefect travel to the perimeter of the cosmos to visit a chic restaurant where celebrities and press agents have gathered to observe the evening's entertainment, featuring the apocalypse; *Life, the Universe, and Everything,* in which Dent and Prefect once again avert the destruction of the universe, while a computer known as Deep Thought determines that the answer to the mystery of existence is equal to forty-two; and *So Long, and Thanks for All the Fish,* in which Arthur returns home to find that the Earth was not actually destroyed. Although occasionally faulted as sophomoric or uneven, these works garnered largely positive reviews for their irreverent and offbeat treatment of modern existence.

With his next novel, *Dirk Gently's Holistic Detective Agency,* Adams draws upon science fiction elements to portray the adventures of Richard MacDuff, a character similar to Arthur Dent. MacDuff is unwittingly forced to save humanity from extinction with the help of Reg, a time-traveler and aged Cambridge professor who can no longer remember where he

came from, and Dirk Gently, a psychic who bases his work as a private detective on "the interconnectedness of all things." In a related novel, *The Long Dark Tea-Time of the Soul,* Adams satirizes the epic by focusing on Gently's inadvertent confrontation with a group of people whose violent tendencies and dissatisfaction with the modern world are revealed to express their true identities as Norse Gods. Marc Conly commented: "[*The Long Dark Tea-Time of the Soul*] is sometimes absurdly funny, and provides an interesting insight into Adams' previous work."

(See also *CLC,* Vol. 27; *Contemporary Authors,* Vol. 106; and *Dictionary of Literary Biography Yearbook: 1983.*)

PRINCIPAL WORKS

NOVELS

*The Hitchhiker's Guide to the Galaxy   1979
*The Restaurant at the End of the Universe   1980
*Life, the Universe, and Everything   1982
*So Long, and Thanks for All the Fish   1984
Dirk Gently's Holistic Detective Agency   1987
The Long Dark Tea-Time of the Soul   1988

OTHER

The Original Hitchhiker's Radio Scripts 1985

*These works were published in Great Britain as *The Hitchhiker's Guide to the Galaxy: A Trilogy in Four Parts* and in the United States as *The Hitchhiker's Quartet* in 1986. The first three volumes were also published as *The Hitchhiker's Trilogy* in 1983.

SUE MARTIN

Douglas Adams is a . . . NUT. And not of the macadamian variety. Not satisfied with a reputation that has become a by-word in science fiction (a word not mentionable in polite society) or for creating a rush on hotel towels—and oh, yes, ***The Hitchhiker's Guide to the Galaxy,*** a must for those extra-terrestrial minded. *Noooo*—he has to go write yet a *fourth* book in his aforementioned trilogy [***So Long, and Thanks for All the Fish***] and extend his reputation (and career) even further.

When last we dealt with the peripatetic Arthur Dent (Our Hero) in ***Life, the Universe and Everything,*** he was left with the information that on a certain planet was God's Last Message to His Creation. The message is NOT the title to the book. . . .

Arthur Dent returns to Earth, to his favorite village pub, confused but glad to be here, since as last he knew, the planet had been previously destroyed by the Vogons to make way for an inter-galactic freeway.

Things grow more complicated. Dent meets the girl of his dreams, Fenchurch. He gets his job back with the BBC. He learns how to fly without the aid of a plane or glider, and—all the dolphins have disappeared, but they have left a clue behind. Dent and Fenchurch have an important voyage to make, to read God's Last Message, etc. etc. and well, that *would* be telling. . . .

There is much more wonderful, inventive Adams humor let loose between the innocent pages of this book in his wild, whiplash style and short chapters. I must give you an example, from the *Guide*'s entry on San Francisco, we find:

> A good place to go. It's very easy to believe that everyone you meet there is also a space traveler. Starting a new religion for you is just their way of saying 'hi.' Until you've settled in and got the hang of the place it is best to say 'no' to three questions out of any given four that anyone may ask you. . . .

I, for one, am grateful that we haven't seen the end of Arthur Dent (or the universe for that matter), and I sincerely hope that there is even a *fifth* book [in the series]. . . .

> *Sue Martin, "A Trilogy Transformed to New Lengths," in* Los Angeles Times Book Review, *February 3, 1985, p. 14.*

PAUL M. LLOYD

[In ***The Hitchhiker's Guide to the Galaxy***], the Earth was supposed to have been demolished to make way for a new hyperspace bypass (progress, you know), and our hero, Arthur Dent, has been bumming around the galaxy for eight years. [In ***So Long, and Thanks for All the Fish***], he finds himself back on Earth, which seems to be none the worse for wear after having been blown to smithereens. No one on Earth seems to realize what happened, except for Arthur's hearthrob, the lovely Fenchurch. Everyone thinks Fen is nuts, while Arthur realizes that she is right but it doesn't matter anyway. All that matters is that he loves her madly. They manage to fly through the air more or less by denying that gravity has any effect on them. Meanwhile, back in space, another of our heroes, Ford Prefect, continues to zoom around from here to there in the galaxy.

Good natured silliness is fine in its place, and in fairly small doses, and science fiction parodies can be amusing at times. Unfortunately, I think this book is likely to provoke more yawns than smiles. Adams would have done well to stop while he was ahead. Maybe now he could turn his hand to something less fluffy.

> *Paul M. Lloyd, "The Hitchhiker Runs Down," in* Fantasy Review, *Vol. 8, No. 4, April, 1985, p. 14.*

ALLEN VARNEY

[***So Long, and Thanks for All the Fish***] takes its title from a joke in [Adam's earlier book, ***The Hitchhiker's Guide to the Galaxy***]: All dolphins vacated Earth with this exit line just before the planet was destroyed. The reference, like the entire story, will be incomprehensible to those who haven't read the first book and its sequels, ***The Restaurant at the End of the Universe*** and ***Life, the Universe, and Everything.***

As with most bestsellers, reviewing this book is pointless. Either you've already bought it or you won't; whether it's good is irrelevant. In fact, this book is very bad, which has had no effect on its sales. And that's worth talking about.

The book-buying public, most especially including SF fandom, seems sequel-happy, series-happy. Authors who have done good work in the past—even one good story—have a free meal ticket for the rest of their careers. People will line up for all their future work, no matter how banal, boring or bad. They want to recapture that original thrill, or maybe they're lazy-minded and want to return to a familiar fictional background, where they don't have to make the effort to meet new characters or see new places or think about new ideas. . . .

Thus the recent work by our aging giants of the field and thus Douglas Adams. Perhaps tuckered out by the strain of inventing an entire hilarious cosmos in previous books, Adams stays mainly on a recreated Earth in this book. The hapless Arthur Dent falls in love, wanders around some, tells an anecdote that Adams has told on talk shows, and basically treads water for 150 pages (200 in paperback). There are two or three good lines, but the inventiveness is gone.

No novel provokes universal agreement, but I honestly can't see much in this lame isometric exercise that would appeal to readers who liked the previous books in this series. I've reviewed them all, . . . but I'm bowing out with this one. Still, it's a bestseller; I daresay Adams' future books will be as well. People keep lining up . . .

There's nothing we can do about this. Authors are either willing to give good weight or they aren't, and negative feedback seems to have no effect. All we can do is vote with the pocket-book and stop buying the new novels. But there always seem to be new readers to take our places—so many new readers, in fact, that there must be one born every minute.

> *Allen Varney, in a review of "So Long, and Thanks for All the Fish," in* Science Fiction Review, *Vol. 15, No. 2, May, 1986, p. 57.*

TOM EASTON

How many people are being introduced to SF by Douglas Adams's Hitchhiker books? They're colossal bestsellers, so the tally must be immense. With luck, their readers will even turn to such as Asimov, in hopes of getting another fix.

Alas, Adams's readers are doomed to disappointment. Adams's books are a unique brand of utter, unmitigated, un-alloyed, loony, foolish, trivial tripe. In past books, he had the Earth destroyed for a hyperspatial bypass, while Earthling Arthur Dent roams the galaxy with the aid of that marvelous electronic encyclopedia, *The Hitchhiker's Guide to the Galaxy,* complete with electronic, saucer-stopping Thumb, and *Guide* researcher and writer Ford Prefect bumbles along from crisis to crisis.

In *So Long, and Thanks for All the Fish,* we find the Earth mysteriously restored. Dent returns home with odd talents. Prefect bumbles some more. And we learn just a little about the dolphins that were the sole sentients rescued from Earth's destruction. . . .

And that's it. *Sui generis.* Tongue-in-cheek, cock-eyed, ridiculous tripe. Fun, too.

> *Tom Easton, in a review of "So Long, and Thanks for All the Fish," in* Analog Science Fiction/Science Fact, *Vol. CVI, No. 7, July, 1986, p. 182.*

MAT COWARD

It must be quite a tough gig, being Douglas Adams. As a young man, you have this really marvellous idea for a radio show. What's more, you can still remember it when you sober up. Not only do you persevere with the idea until it is finished, and not only does the BBC buy it, but it also turns out to be the most original, acclaimed and thoroughly satisfactory use of the medium since Spike Milligan had his first breakdown. As if that wasn't enough, you then make the obviously suicidal move of adapting your radio scripts into book and TV form, and confound the doubters by succeeding brilliantly again. A decade after *The Hitch-Hiker's Guide to the Galaxy* first hit the airwaves you are still quite young, and your marvellous idea has been translated into every imaginable medium, including computer games and bath towels. . . . The difficulty, of course, is what do you do with the rest of your life?

The answer that Douglas Adams has come up with is to start all over again, only missing out the radio stage this time round. [*Dirk Gently's Holistic Detective Agency*] is, as before, a science fiction comedy in which the human race is saved from total extinction by a slightly wet hero and his bizarre friends. Instead of Arthur Dent we have Richard Mac-Duff, a computer software whizz, who becomes unwittingly involved in matters of a cosmic and life-threatening nature. His comrades in this are Reg, a time-travelling Cambridge

professor, who is so vague and so many centuries old that he can't remember who he is or where he comes from; and Gently, a psychically gifted pal of Richard's from student days, now working as a private detective specialising in 'the interconnectedness of all things'—which is handy, since of course, this is just what Adams himself specialises in.

The author's other specialism is that, like Shakespeare, almost every line he writes instantly transforms itself into a quotation. Indeed, there are probably more people in this country who could tell you who said 'I never could get the hang of Thursdays' than 'Out, damned spot'. Dirk Gently continues the tradition, describing the 'absurdly thin' Mac-Duff as 'a sort of pleasant genial mantis that's given up preying and taken up tennis instead.' . . .

As well as having a good radio writer's ear for a snappy, jolting gag, Adams also possesses an enthusiasm for eccentric ideas and 'What if . . . ?' speculations, as befits a former *Dr Who* script editor. He is, in other words, a genuine SF writer, despite his irreverence for the genre. This novel contains some wonderful wonderings and fascinating inventions, such as the Electric Monk, a labour-saving device from a decadent civilisation, which saves you the bother of believing in things, just as a VCR 'watched tedious television for you, thus saving you the bother of looking at it yourself'. Adams also explores the common idea that people become ghosts if, at death, they have left some important business unfinished. In part, this book is a genuinely eerie and haunting spook story.

All in all, this is a hugely entertaining novel, albeit a bit long. When science fiction and comedy come together, what they produce is insight into the human character and condition, and here they certainly do, much more so than in Adams's previous work. The characters, their reactions and motives, are much more real and affecting. Perhaps because of this, though, *Dirk Gently* is finally less satisfying than [*The Hitch-Hiker's Guide to the Galaxy*]; the plot is less symmetrical and less of a fable, and in the end I was a little puzzled, unsure whether I had fully followed all its twists and turns. This was perhaps explained by the last words in the book: 'to be continued'. If he's serious about that, then clearly the problem I mentioned earlier—'what does Adams do next?'—has yet to be dealt with, and he has allowed his commercial instinct (to produce another best-selling saga) to overrule his writer's instinct (to write a real, self-contained novel). I worry that Douglas Adams may have suffered the worst possible fate for a writer who doesn't die before 30: that he wrote his best book first.

> *Mat Coward, "Connections," in* The Listener, *Vol. 117, No. 3017, June 25, 1987, p. 29.*

TOM EASTON

The new book is *Dirk Gently's Holistic Detective Agency.* It opens with a scene of primeval desolation; switches to an Electric Monk, a robot designed to believe in things, who passes through a plain white door from his world to ours; gives us Professor Urban Chronotis at an Oxford look-alike, who seems to have nothing to do on campus but accomplishes the most astonishing magic tricks; and tells us that Coleridge actually did not fail to complete "Kubla Khan."

And here we begin to twig: The professor has to be a time traveler, the Coleridge clue reveals that here is an alternate world, and *something* will happen to bring the novel onto the timeline more familiar to us.

The story's protagonist is Richard MacDuff. His employer, shot by a mysterious assailant, becomes a ghost of baffling difficulties. MacDuff, driven by his own problems, falls into the clutches of old acquaintance Dirk Gently, once a youth of apparent precognitiveness, now a private detective with quantum mechanical leanings and a tendency to rip off his old-lady clients. And then there is Michael Wenton-Weakes, a very Wodehousian upper-crust nitwit, who is possessed by a spirit that wishes to change the dank and dusty past from which it comes.

And it all falls together, rather more neatly than ever it did for the *Hitchhiker,* and with the kind of anticipated click that makes us enjoy some of the best detective stories. It's wacky, yes, but given the premises, it has all the inevitability of a boulder rolling downhill. (pp. 187-88)

> Tom Easton, in a review of "Dirk Gently's Holistic Detective Agency," in Analog Science Fiction/Science Fact, Vol. CVIII, No. 2, February, 1988, pp. 187-88.

CHRIS BIDMEAD

Years before 'graffiti' had become an English word in common use, bored actors would scribble their bons mots on the trundling wooden doors on wheels that provide sound effects in BBC radio studios. It was on the battleship grey side of one of these affable cabinets thirty years ago that I came across one of the best jokes of my early life. 'Reggie Smith,' someone had scrawled, naming a much-loved radio producer famous for his intimate acquaintance with the local hostelries, 'is a legend in his own lunchtime.'

With *The HitchHiker's Guide to the Galaxy* Douglas Adams built a career on essentially the same joke. Bathetic substitution doesn't carry you very far—certainly not to the Restaurant at the End of the Universe—unless it has the cracked tinkle of truth about it, and the changes are rung with literary dexterity. Adams achieved all this and more in the early *HitchHiker* satires on high-street existence, and there are stretches that for my money match *Tristram Shandy*.

You can flog this kind of thing to death, as Adams found after—or perhaps even during—the writing of *So Long and Thanks for All the Fish,* described on the blurb rather too tellingly as 'part four of the *HitchHiker Trilogy*'. But it was a dead theme he couldn't bury. His public liked the strain too much, and publishers forced huge sums on him to get back behind the keyboard of his Apple Macintosh.

With *Dirk Gently's Holistic Detective Agency,* Adams abandoned the *HitchHiker* format and characters and resurrected his inspiration along more novelish lines. The book is a re-working of *Doctor Who* material that never made it to the screen during his stint as script editor of that programme in the late Seventies. To it he adds, significantly, a central character who spends much of the first part of the story wandering around as a ghost.

> Some of the less pleasant aspects of being dead were beginning to creep up on Gordon Way . . . The idea of walking through walls frankly revolted him . . . He had instead been fighting to grip and

grapple with every object he touched in order to render it, and thereby himself, substantial . . .

The newest arrival in the Adams canon, a sequel to *Dirk Gently,* has a title that reverts plonkingly to the bathetic substitution joke, and you might wonder what naivety, lofty arrogance, or divine aplomb allowed him to call it *The Long Dark Teatime of the Soul.* The cover illustration exhumes another old chestnut in depicting a flying saucer, complete with tea-cup.

Within the tired old wrapping is prose that wriggles like something not quite dead. But *Teatime* is a multi-layered confection: a detective story centring on a Faustian contract, iced with Mills and Boon sugar and interleaved with a fairly silly sword-and-sorcery theme about Nordic gods striding the earth. What carries it through, although not perhaps altogether *off,* is that the entrails Adams is boiling in the pot are genuinely his own: the amusing tinkle of truth in his earlier prose now drowns under the toxin of his own deep and gloomy sense of the essential Supermarketness of Life. . . .

In the world of the gods, curiously superimposed on ours in a way that has Valhalla sharing co-ordinates with St Pancras station, immortality does not spare them from extinction. Mortals' 'guilty secrets' and 'things not dealt with properly' are spreading a divine plague called 'the onx'. As Thor explains, 'In the final stages you simply lie on the ground and after a while a tree grows out of your head and then it's all over . . . You eventually emerge as a great pure torrent of water, and like as not get a load of chemical waste dumped into you. It's a grim business being a god these days, even a dead god.'

> Chris Bidmead, "A Bathetic Fallacy," in The Listener, Vol. 120, No. 3086, October 27, 1988, p. 34.

CATHLEEN SCHINE

The Long Dark Tea-Time of the Soul is a clever and funny novel about an English detective, an American girl in a bad mood and a Norse god who sells his soul to an advertising executive. . . .

[Early in the book, Dirk Gently] sleeps through an appointment with a client. Gently's client is found later that day seated on one side of his parlor while his severed head spins at 33 r.p.m. on the turntable across the room. Meanwhile, Kate Schechter, an American with an exquisite sensitivity to life's little bothers, gets stuck behind a large, obstinate blond man arguing hopelessly with the willfully obtuse check-in clerk at an airport ticket counter. The ticket counter, and the check-in clerk, are suddenly consumed by a giant fireball.

"The usual people tried to claim responsibility," Mr. Adams writes of the explosion.

> First the IRA, then the PLO and the Gas Board. Even British Nuclear Fuels rushed out a statement to the effect that the situation was completely under control . . . that there was hardly any radioactive leakage at all, and that the site of the explosion would make a nice location for a day out with the kids and a picnic, before finally having to admit that it wasn't actually anything to do with them at all.

The devastating fireball is finally designated an "act of God," which, actually, it is—the act of a large, obstinate blond god (his name is Thor) stuck at an airport check-in counter without a credit card. Inconvenience, for Douglas Adams, is a powerful force.

Dirk Gently is a detective interested in the "interconnectedness" of things. And indeed Mr. Adams's vision of the world is of a tangled unity, the unifying force being not God or fate or biological destiny, but this same potent inconvenience. There has always been a form of humor that celebrates things going so wrong that they turn out right. What Mr. Adams does is expand disgruntled comic bungling to cosmic proportions—he is *The Whole Earth Catalog*'s Kingsley Amis. It is an odd combination, at least to American readers—we like our prophets earnest. But Mr. Adams creates a universe of urgent trifles that add up to an astronomical farce.

His world is so unrelentingly trivial, perverse and irritating that even the sun is offended:

> The sun crept slowly across the bedclothes, as if nervous of what it might find among them, slunk down the side of the bed, moved in a rather startled way across some objects it encountered on the floor, toyed nervously with a couple of motes of dust, lit briefly on a stuffed fruit bat hanging in the corner, and fled.

The gods, too, are caught in this grand web of petty frustrations. They appear matter-of-factly, introduced into the novel without fuss, amusing cranks, rather like stuffy English tourists unable to find tea in Palermo.

Only Odin, father of the gods, seems comfortable in the modern world, a one-eyed old man comfortably stretched out in an exclusive, luxurious nursing home where he sleeps the days and nights away. . . .

Odin has found his Valhalla on earth and it is a land not of heroes but of clean, unruffled linens (changed daily) and lack of consciousness. In the past, there was "lots of big talk of things being mighty, and of things being riven, and of things being in thrall to other things, but very little attention given, as I now realize, to the laundry." Sleep is the only revered activity in *The Long Dark Tea-Time of the Soul.* For Mr. Adams, to be alive (and awake) is to be annoyed. Kate, reflecting on Thor and the obnoxious check-in clerk, thinks: "There had been something oddly noble in his perverse bloody-mindedness." The trivial is epic, the epic trivial, all leveled by a sensibility that is essentially "cross," one of Mr. Adams's favorite words.

Mr. Adams is sometimes compared to the Monty Python troupe, presumably because he is English, silly and literate. But the engine that drives Monty Python is very different—a playful joy in baroque inefficiency. Douglas Adams's vision is more conventional—the modern world is dehumanized by technology; and worse, the technology doesn't even work. His humor, crisp and intelligent, and his prose—elegant, absurdly literal-minded understatements or elegant, absurdly literal-minded overstatements—are a pleasure to read. But there is something, finally, unsatisfying about his work. His books are too limited, temperamentally and intellectually, to be serious novels. At the same time, his world is more a novelty than it is the genuinely bizarre, personal universe of a comic master like Mr. Amis or P. G. Wodehouse—or Monty Python, for that matter. In spite of all the nimble plots, the skillful writing and the underlying wit of his work, Mr. Adams is a bit banal.

Cathleen Schine, "Dirk Gently, Holistic Detective," in The New York Times Book Review, *March 12, 1989, p. 11.*

DOUGLAS ADAMS   (INTERVIEW WITH MARC CONLY)

The kind of fiction Adams' fans have come to love and expect doesn't fit into any genre very neatly. In *The Long Dark Tea Time of the Soul,* Adams has thrown a smattering of Norse mythology, a pinch of detective fiction, and a good helping of fantasy into a stew of satire and sardonic observation that the fans of *Hitchhiker's Guide to the Galaxy* will easily recognize. This is Adams' second book featuring Dirk Gently, introduced in *Dirk Gently's Holistic Detective Agency,* although this is not a sequel.

The book is sometimes absurdly funny, and provides an interesting insight into Adams' previous work. At one point during Dirk Gently's explanation of his working method as a detective, he says that he disagrees with Sherlock Holmes' statement that once the impossible is ruled out, whatever remains, however improbable, must be the truth. Gently's contention, which is apparently Adams' working hypothesis in all his novels, is that the impossible has what he calls an "integrity," whereas the improbable is merely commonplace. So, you can assume, with delight and a delicious rubbing of your hands together, that in Adams' most recent book, the impossible will assert itself with hilarious regularity. . . .

What Gently is trying to get to the bottom of is the murder of his only client. He teams up with a girl named Kate, who has had a close encounter of the electric kind with Thor, the Norse god of thunder, who is extremely angry about the way Odin, in his dotage, is treating the old gang back at Valhallah.

Adams' plot is tightly constructed, and he enjoys poking fun at the inconsistencies in religion and the smug self-satisfaction of the modern sellout. Occasionally, it seems that a desire to be constantly witty forces Adams to resort to formula; and when he tries to address the issue of the homeless and ties it together with the sad fate of the ancient gods of our world, he approaches self-righteousness.

However, it is his inventiveness and his sudden turns to absurdity, that make Adams so readable. His social awareness and the accuracy of his barbs keep the narrative of *The Long Dark Tea Time of the Soul* from becoming too frothy. Douglas Adams is a dismayed idealist in jester's clothing. His portrayal of modern society, and his unrelenting dissection of the modern style of self-centeredness, make us think, make us laugh, and make us look forward to his next book. . . .

• • • • •

[Marc Conly]: *What are you doing these days?* . . .

[Douglas Adams]: I'm spending a year on the road, doing research for a wildlife project. I'm taking a year off from doing novels and writing a wildlife book and doing a radio series as well. (p. 16)

Are there more novels in the works?

No. Basically, it used to be you'd have an idea for a novel and work from there. Now what happens is your agent has an idea for a contract, and so you do a contract—say, for a two-book deal. We've done that. At the end of the work on this project, . . . I then sit down and start working on two new novels. I'm deliberately not thinking about them until I get there, because I've been writing novels for a while, and it's quite good, you know, to step back from them and look where you think you're going.

I wondered how you would make the transition from the **Hitchhiker** *series to the mystery form.*

Well, I think that somebody who is a die-hard detective novel fan would feel that this did not adhere to what they expected from a mystery novel.

Although you say you're not thinking about the novels, is there any future for Dirk Gently?

I don't know, I might do some more or I might not, or I might do something different and come back to him. With the **Hitchhiker** books, it was a continuous story in one sense, and these two are not. This one (**The Long Dark Tea Time of the Soul**) is by no means a sequel to the other (**Dirk Gently's Holistic Detective Agency**); it just happens to have the same main character. So I'm free to pick it up or put it down as I like. I feel, having done one four-book trilogy, maybe I ought to redress the balance by leaving this as a two-book trilogy.

I see. That's fair.

But I don't know. Part of me is waiting for the next book. Although I tend to be a person who thinks seriously about things, I tend not to put that up-front in the books, but write the books purely as entertainment, and to write what I find funny. Obviously, what I find funny is going to reflect what I think about in that regard. The serious aspects of it come up of their own accord.

Is it difficult to write funny books?

I think that it is very, very difficult to write funny books, and certainly the authors I admire the most tend to be authors who are good at being funny, because I know how difficult it is. But I wonder if I mightn't try and be a bit more deliberate next time. Because very often, you know, going for the joke will be an escape route from confronting something that maybe you should confront.

To be honest, I've had a bit of a year of emotional crises, and am suddenly realizing that there are all sorts of areas in myself that I've never drawn on at all in writing books, and maybe I ought to look at some of them.

Is it a little scary to take yourself seriously as an author?

Well, it can be. Absolutely. When the book is meant to be primarily funny, it's very easy, as I say, to duck behind the joke when you want to be a little ambiguous. Actually, I tell you, one of the books I admire the most, one of the books I would most—you know, if one could choose to have written another book—a book that would be very high on my list would be *A Handful of Dust* by Evelyn Waugh, which seems to me to do magnificently the job of being simultaneously a comedy and a real tragedy. And that, I think, would be a good high-water mark to aim at. So, I suppose what I've been doing so far, in a sense, is . . . looking after the comedy and letting the tragedy take care of itself. And maybe I should shift gears slightly.

The thing is, I think you actually have got to constantly find new challenges for yourself, and I think that would be an interesting way to do it. As far as the reader's concerned, very often when I'm setting off in a new direction and setting myself a new set of challenges, what actually emerges at the other end of the mangle is something that the reader nevertheless finds extremely familiar in terms of what I've done before. And it's largely because each time you write a book, you set yourself specific problems, and what emerges is a result of your grappling with those problems. It's the process of grappling that produces the book rather than the original idea.

Like life itself.

Yeah.

In the Dirk Gently novels you had Dirk base his working method on a contradiction of Sherlock Holmes' famous statement about the impossible and the improbable. One does sometimes get the impression that, for you, the fun of writing is to create a situation which is tacitly impossible, and then find your way around it somehow.

Yes, 'tis true. I actually said that half as a joke, and then I expanded it in here (**Tea Time**) and realized that I meant something serious by it.

The Sherlock Holmes thing was, once you've eliminated the impossible, then whatever's left, however improbable, must be the case. When I turned it 'round, I suddenly realized that, in fact, very often the impossible actually has a greater ring of truth to it than the improbable, because the improbable means that you're seriously off-beam, whereas the impossible suggests you're at a hundred and eighty degrees from it. And something that's a hundred and eighty degrees from the truth is often as true as something that is more obvious.

At the very beginning of **Tea Time,** *Kate is on the highway on the way to the airport, in a hurry, and you wrote:*

> . . . she was finding it increasingly easy to believe that God, if there was a God, and if it was remotely possible that any godlike being who could order the disposition of particles at the creation of the universe would also be interested in directing traffic on the M4, did not want her to fly to Norway either.

So, on the one hand you sprinkle a novel full of statements dismissing, or at least making pointed jabs at, conventional wisdom or at religion, and yet all your books revolve around a presumption of the interconnectedness of all things.

What I was having a jab at there, pretty obliquely, is that people will very often and very easily, and in a self-serving way, invoke the idea that God is in some way directing their lives, in order to achieve a certain object. And remember, the moment you start doing that, you effactually turn your intelligence off. And, very often, if you assemble a picture of a person who would do all the things that people say God does, he would actually come over as a rather juvenile, petty, and ratty little person; and that, I think, does tend to support the idea that we create God in our own image.

And I think that if there is any consciousness inherent in the structure of the universe—let's call it that—then again, I think that the idea he'd be trying to direct traffic on the M4 is something that I would look at rather skeptically.

Was the fourth book of the **Hitchhiker** *series,* **So Long, and Thanks for All the Fish,** *in mind when you wrote the others?*

No, to be honest, that book was a mistake. I had sworn that

I would not do another *Hitchhiker* book, and what happened in the meantime was that I'd gone to California to work on the movie of *Hitchhiker*—what movie, you may ask, and that's a very pertinent question.

What movie?

Yes, well, I'm waiting for the answer to that question myself. Basically, what happened to it was Hollywood. And so I spent most of 1983 living in Los Angeles working on this, and it was a terrible experience. At the end of it, I felt I'd hit my first major failure of my career. I felt very disoriented by it. I went back to England, because people were constantly asking me to write another *Hitchhiker* book; and you'd say "No-way" ninety-nine times, and you'd say "Yes" once, and, of course, you're committed. I was running for shelter a bit, agreeing to do another book while I wanted to write something else.

Knowing that the public would respond to it?

Right.

. . . no matter what you did.

And so I was writing it on the one hand resenting the fact that I was doing another *Hitchhiker* book, and trying to do something else, and falling between the two stools. [*So Long, and Thanks for All the Fish* is] not a book I'm happy with, and it certainly was a very miserable experience writing it.

I have to remark on your courage in **Hitchhiker's Guide to the Galaxy** *in destroying the Earth utterly. I thought that was a very gutsy thing to do.*

Yeah, that got that one out of the way.

It surprised me when you brought it back.

Yeah. No, again, I think that was probably all part of the same running for shelter thing. (pp. 16-17)

In Chapter 30 of **The Long Dark Tea Time of the Soul,** *where Draycott is trying to negotiate with Dirk Gently, there is a mordancy in the writing that you allowed yourself, which ordinarily you'll gloss over with a little humor; yet, in that circumstance, Dirk's "drop dead" reaction is totally humorless.*

Yeah. It was a very strange experience writing that chapter actually, because there's a sort of very accelerated process I get into at the end of a book, usually because it's some sort of terrible panic deadline coming up. But also, it really winds you up, and the flywheels start to move, and you don't go to bed for several nights. Actually, I think for about the last four days of writing the book, I didn't go to bed at all. Everytime

I really felt tired, I would go and sort of work on the exercise cycle—eight minutes and twenty three seconds, which is the length of the third movement of Mozart's 23rd Piano Concerto, which is a very invigorating and bracing piece of music.

I started that chapter knowing somehow that I had to reveal the whole of what Draycott had been up to, and I had no idea how I was going to do it. I just knew I had to get the information across, and I also had to get the character across. So, I thought, "Well, I'll just start with him speaking and see what happens." And then it sort of got into this complete fit, where I was just writing and writing and writing—and suddenly, the whole chapter was a monologue.

And I thought, "Well, this is insane, how can you make a whole chapter a monologue?" And I looked at it again, and thought, "You can, it works." What I liked about it was that Dirk, apart from the end of the scene, has just one interjection throughout the whole thing, and you can hear the whole tone of the silence in which he listens from the one remark he makes in the middle. I was actually quite proud of that.

It worked so well for you that you felt no need to slip out the back door of humor at all.

Yeah. Yeah, yeah. But it was such a curious experience, writing that. (p. 17)

Douglas Adams and Marc Conly, in an interview in The Bloomsbury Review, *Vol. 9, No. 3, May-June, 1989, pp. 16-17.*

FURTHER READING

Crichton, Douglas. "Douglas Adams Explains *Life, the Universe and Everything*—Mice Included—in a Sci-Fi Trilogy." *People* 19, No. 1 (10 January 1983): 33-34.

Irreverent portrait in which Adams comments upon his third novel.

Crichton, Jennifer. "Douglas Adams's Hitchhiker Trilogy." *Publisher's Weekly* 223, No. 2 (14 January 1983): 47-8, 50.

Incorporates publishing and publicity details surrounding the publication of Adams's first three novels with comments by the author.

Jean Baudrillard

1929-

French sociologist and philosopher.

A preeminent postmodern theorist, Baudrillard is best known for his application of semiotics, the study of language as a system of signs, to Marxist concerns. The term "post-modernism," as applied to literature and other art forms, refers to a philosophical position that denies the existence of rational order in the universe beyond the random play of elements on the surface of reality. As applied to economic and social institutions, "postmodern" or "post-industrial" describes a technology-driven society dominated by white-collar and service-industry employment rather than manufacturing or agriculture. Although some commentators consider his language alarmist and obscurantist, Baudrillard is generally viewed as an important social critic. Steven Helmling commented: "If culture-bashing must go on, . . . then Baudrillard is as satisfying a culture-basher as we presently have. To read his impassioned denunciations of advertising, consumerism, . . . TV, and the conduct of politics in a media age, is to see everything you most despise about our culture trashed in the manner that it deserves."

Although Baudrillard utilizes the language of various disciplines in his works, his application of semiotics to the structure of society is widely considered his most significant contribution to social theory. Semiotics distinguishes between the signifier, usually a word or an image, and the thing itself, known as the signified, or referent. According to Baudrillard, the culture of late capitalism is dominated by simulacra, floating signifiers cut off from their referents, that create a hyperreal effect and destroy the possibility of true knowledge. Kate Linker remarked that simulacra "register that irony of contemporary existence—that what we accept as reality is already simulated, a massive fabrication of effects which stands in for reality's absence." Baudrillard often cites examples from television, advertising, the news media, and politics to illustrate this phenomenon.

Baudrillard's first two works, *Le système des objets* and *La société de consommation,* attempt to augment Marx's studies of the means of production with a semiological interpretation of the status of commodities, the products of a post-industrial society. Baudrillard directs his semiological model against Marxism itself in *Pour une critique de l'économie politique du signe* (*For a Critique of the Political Economy of the Sign*) and *Le miroir de la production: ou, l'illusion critique du matérialism historique* (*The Mirror of Production*). In these works, Baudrillard examines Marxism as an historical phenomenon that in some ways mirrors the constructs of capitalism, which arose during the same period. In *L'échange symbolique et la mort,* Baudrillard attempts to characterize the structure of communication in the media of postmodern society through a detailed analysis of its commodities. Karlis Racevskis remarked: "[*L'échange symbolique et la mort*] irrepressibly tears away at the cultural discourse with which Western societies have woven their history. Baudrillard's purpose is to trace a genealogy of the simulacra and the value systems that constitute civilization, thus unveiling the pretense, the deceits, and the tautologies on which it rests."

In his next major work, *Oublier Foucault* (*Forget Foucault*), Baudrillard examines French philosopher Michel Foucault's epistemology and contends that it colludes with the traditional power structures that Foucault purportedly critiques. In *De la séduction,* Baudrillard asserts the dominance of hyperreality and consequently denies the efficacy of theories, including psychoanalysis and Marxism, which profess to decipher the reality beneath appearances. Baudrillard's next collection of essays, *Simulacres et simulation,* extends his emphasis on the hegemony of simulacra. Mark Poster defined a simulation as "different from a fiction or lie in that it not only presents an absence as a presence, the imaginary as the real, it also undermines any contrast to the real, absorbing the real within itself." In *Les stratégies fatales* and *La gauche divine,* Baudrillard describes the postmodern condition as characterized by manipulation and victimization by the code, the system of simulacra. Baudrillard proposes complete passivity as the only form of resistance that the code cannot appropriate. In *Cool Memories, 1980-1985* and *L'autre par lui-même* (*The Ecstasy of Communication*), Baudrillard summarizes and inverts ideas promulgated in his earlier works, attempting to discover how these have become part of the system that they critique. Although poorly received by many critics, *Amérique* (*America*) is Baudrillard's most widely reviewed book to date. In this work, Baudrillard's travels across the

United States allow him to view myriad manifestations of his theories in action in the ultimate postmodern culture.

PRINCIPAL WORKS

ESSAY COLLECTIONS

Le système des objets 1968
La société de consommation 1970
Pour une critique de l'économie politique du signe 1972
  [*For a Critique of the Political Economy of the Sign,* 1981]
*Le miroir de la production; ou, L'illusion critique du matérial-
  ism historique* 1973
  [*The Mirror of Production,* 1975]
L'échange symbolique et la mort 1976
Oublier Foucault 1977
  [*Forget Foucault,* 1987]
A l'ombre des majorités silencieuses ou la fin du social 1978
  [*In the Shadow of the Silent Majorities,* 1983]
De la séduction 1979
Simulacres et simulations 1981
  [*Simulations,* 1983]
Les stratégies fatales 1983
La gauche divine 1985
Amérique 1986
  [*America,* 1988]
L'autre par lui-même 1987
  [*The Ecstasy of Communication,* 1988]
Cool Memories, 1980-1985 1987
Jean Baudrillard: Selected Writings 1988

SUSAN WILLIS

We in the United States have for a long time acknowledged the fact that we live in a "consumer society." Our bodies are permeated and surrounded with consumer goods, our minds infused with consumer vocabulary. Yet our understanding of consumer society in no way equals our ability to invent commodity terminology. Although we may possess an abundance of commodities, we lack a systematic study of commodity culture.

So for us Jean Baudrillard's *Le Système des Objets* is a useful tool in that it provides an account of consumer society as system. That is, Baudrillard does not base his study on production, nor does he employ the language of economics. Instead he evolves his analysis by observing the things with which we have become the most familiar—the objects of commodity culture. Thus Baudrillard's project becomes one of imposing limits on a seemingly limitless field.

In choosing his classificatory criterion, he rejects two traditional models. First he refuses to use empirical categories which would treat objects as reified museum pieces by classifying them according to material, size, weight, age, color, shape. Instead he seeks a dynamic model which would see objects in practice. Yet he denies also the ability of Marxism to deal with the phenomena of consumer society. Essentially what he is looking for is a method of analysis which will incorporate the notion of a dynamic and at the same time penetrate the system of relationships which operate under commodity culture—and he finds such a model in semiotics. It

remains then for us to determine if this bold application of semiotics fulfills the task of categorizing and, in particular, analysing the phenomena of advanced Capitalism.

Baudrillard's debt to structural linguistics is evident from the first. In his introduction to *Système des Objets,* he proposes to evolve a classificatory system on the basis of the linguistic distinction between *parole* (here taken to mean the behavior patterns manifested through our relationship with objects) and *langue* (here the underlying system of production, distribution, consumption). Baudrillard works, then, at two levels: he responds first to objects at the surface level of description—the *signifié* of the semiotic sign, then he integrates this information into a system of formal analysis—the level of *signifiant.* The book illustrates the great degree of contemporary investment in objects by describing, first, the ways in which we relate to, arrange, and collect them; second, the various types of object—antique or gadget; and, third, the phenomena associated with objects—production, credit and advertising. Throughout, Baudrillard is most interested in superstructural considerations—the evidence gathered at the level of *parole.* Essentially he has reversed the Marxian priorities; here the description of superstructure provides the terms for penetrating the infrastructure of production.

Nonetheless, Baudrillard is concerned with factors which have traditionally shaped Marxian analysis, and, in particular, he directs his attention to process (which we may see as a semiotician's abstraction of praxis.) He looks not at objects in their pure form, but in practice: the indicators of man's active social life. Again we notice that his attention is focused on the most "super" of superstructural considerations; objects, he indicates, serve to define social relationships—social relationships, in turn, are used to interpret relationships of production.

By seeing objects as indicators of social relationships, Baudrillard points to an important contradiction which he will develop throughout the book. He finds that in consumer society our relationship to objects is always one of "arranging"—choosing colors, grouping furniture—all of which connotes great activity. But he goes on to show that this "active" relationship with objects is in fact grounded in passivity. All arrangement is a sterile operation whose end product is nothing more than the creation of a pleasant "ambiance." Here I think we can appreciate the value of Baudrillard's analytical dichotomy. He is at once aware of the *appearance* of consumer society—its activity and variety; yet at the same time he can turn the information of appearance back on itself to emphasize the underlying stagnation of the system. Thus, Baudrillard's method is initially descriptive, and finally demystifying.

But the aspect of consumer society most emphasized in *Système des Objets* is the process of abstraction. Again, this is a problem traditionally treated in Marxian analysis. The notion of abstraction, it would seem, represents a semiotic extrapolation of what Marxian terminology calls "alienation." But according to Baudrillard's reasoning, alienation is a term constrained by its reference to political economy and is therefore grounded in production. It serves to define man in relation to his labor, just as that other Marxian category, reification, describes man only in relation to the product of labor. For Baudrillard, neither alienation nor reification can explain the relationship of the consumer to commodities. Thus he has chosen the term "abstraction" to correspond to all levels—defining all social relationships, and at the same time connoting the fragmentation of consumer society while denoting the logic of Capitalism itself. Furthermore, the process of abstraction is integrally bound to the theory of the linguistic sign. Here Baudrillard's analysis, itself a process of theoretic abstractions, also seeks to explain the notion of abstraction as a phenomenon of commodity consumption. As he sees it, everything that enters into the consumer system is cut off from the constraints of its traditionally meaningful referent and re-incorporated as an infinitely functional integer—a *sign*. So, for example, color, once infused with traditional or even allegorical meaning, has been liberated. Red no longer signifies passion nor does blue signify tranquility; instead, both have become functional abstractions capable of entering into various combinations in conformity with man's project to create ambiance.

Once again, though, Baudrillard finds that the way consumer society manifests itself in "emancipated" superficial phenomena only serves to mask the rigidity of its underlying intent. For under advanced Capitalism, each movement toward systematic abstraction has been coupled with a compensatory desire on the part of the individual to experience objects as personalized. Colors, once systematically abstracted to become empty signs, are made to take on personalized values and are characterized as either "warm" or "cold" tones. Yet this process of personalization serves only as a compensation for that deeper process which produces functionally interchangeable sign-units through abstraction. This notion of compensation is defined more specifically by the term "alibi" in Baudrillard's system. Essentially, all that Capitalism takes out of an object is put back, but in a degraded form, in the same way that synthetic additives are thrown into processed foods. The additive then functions as an "alibi" both for the lost quality and for the empty product. (pp. 231-33)

[Not] all of Baudrillard's analysis is derived by focusing on active relationships with objects. A major portion of *Système des Objets* is devoted to the "discours subjectif," or our relationship to "non-functional" objects. And here Baudrillard's choice of objects as well as the logic of his argument seems to correspond with the practice of psychoanalysis. He singles out those objects that consumer society overtly condemns as marginal: antiques, collections, or perversions such as gadgets and robots—in much the same way that psychoanalysis focuses our attention on what society sees as misfits. And here, just as in analysis, these marginals become the means of penetrating and knowing the system which works to exclude them.

It is important to note Baudrillard's recourse to psychoanalysis, as this whole section involves not only the logic but the language of analysis. For Baudrillard, the inclusion of psychoanalytic interpretation allows him to offer explanations which semiotics alone cannot provide. Here we come to realize the limitations of pure semiotic analysis. It allows us to put raw or culturally processed material into perspective, to organize and categorize. But as *Système des Objets* shows, because semiotics has no content—and particularly, no history—it has no means by which it can make interpretations— hence Baudrillard's borrowings from companion fields.

Once more Baudrillard is concerned with abstraction. In dealing with the non-functional gadgets, he finds that the notion alone of an object's functionalism permits its abstraction and thus allows it to enter the system as a sign. However, these "non-functional" objects prove to possess the most *fonctionnalité* and so, represent the highest level of abstrac-

tion. (We remember that functionalism in Baudrillard's definition should not be taken in an economic sense. Instead it belongs to the imaginary level of connotation.) Furthermore, all objects in consumer society are the loci of imaginary investment with the least practical, often the most technologically advanced—the gadgets and robots—lending themselves to the highest degree of cathexis. As Baudrillard explains, the notion that an object is "functional," corresponding as it does to Capitalism's project to reinvent the world according to a technological principle, is sufficient to endow that object with autonomy. And the autonomy of the object choice is what enables the cathexis of libidinal energy. It is not surprising then that consumer society has manufactured in the robot the most highly evolved substitute phallus—a sex without a sex, and, consequently, a slave. Here Baudrillard's evaluation of the robot corresponds with Victor Tausk's analysis of the "Influencing Machine" in schizophrenia. Tausk's study establishes the relationship between machine and phallus and traces this symbolic attachment to the childhood stage of narcissism. So the robot, typifying the unsexed world of narcissism, represents at once the dominated phallus and the wishfulfillment for ego control. However, abstracted into repression, cathexis proves unsatisfactory. There is always the theoretical possibility that the alienated factors (implicit in the master/slave relationship) will culminate in revolt, the threat that man's domesticated sexuality might one day turn against him. (pp. 233-34)

As [Baudrillard] sees it, Capitalist production is based on the relationship of model to series, or ideal object to massproduced commodity (the Dior original made into thousands of copies, those copies further reduced by cheap imitations). And for Baudrillard this model-series syndrome of production re-evokes the robot theme. In the same way that the robots of [Karel Capek's play] *R.U.R.* turned against their human models, so commodities turn on and obliterate their more perfect models.

At this point Baudrillard can't help but raise an essential question: why, given Capitalism's tremendous technological evolution, does production systematize itself on the faulty model-series relationship with its characteristic impermanence and fragility? (Baudrillard uses the word "fragilité," for which English does not provide a precise equivalent. The awkward term "indurable" would offer a closer approximation, signifying both shoddiness and obsolescence.) Is the system the "détraquée machine désirante" envisioned by Deleuze and Guattari in *l'Anti-Oedipe*; or, in Baudrillard's own terms, is it "dysfonctionnel"? Does it survive not in spite of, but because of, its internal contradiction? The previous technologues of society (the Lewis Mumford of *Technics and Civilization*) have chosen to avoid the marked term "contradiction." They see the problem as one which will be ironed out once technology stabilizes itself through progress. But Baudrillard, in line with a more Marxian tradition, seizes the notion of contradiction and finds that the system exists because it operates on the basis of disparity.

Rather, though, than completing his analysis in economic terms, Baudrillard again has recourse to psychoanalysis. As he explains it, humans have made it their project both to tame external natural forces and at the same time to harness internal libidinal energy. The resultant technological evolution is then characterized by a double risk: first, that their sexuality will be neutralized in technique; second, that the technological order will itself be endangered by pent up cathected energy. It is then only in the desire for fragility that the system's inherent contradiction finds resolution. Thus, for Baudrillard, fragility has nothing to do with weakness. Rather, it is the multi-purpose binding force of Capitalism, capable of satisfying the contradictory demands of the death-wish (which extinguishes sexual anxiety by replacing sexuality with a perfectly functioning machine), and the Eros instinct (which surfaces in the recurrence of production). The Capitalist mode of production, based on the model-series relationship, reflects then the need to constantly reproduce fragility, a situation Baudrillard sees as tragic because it responds to an all-consuming fatalism in which man's project becomes nothing more than the desire to constantly re-experience that fragility. For Baudrillard, the revolt of the robot, along with all the other representations of machines turning on their creators, provides a certain shock value which we accept and willingly experience not out of masochism but out of the contingent gratification offered by its implicit reference to fragility. An infallible creation would in fact produce far more anxiety, standing as it would for the total absorption of sexuality. Only in the gaps provided by man's fragile creation does sexuality renew itself. (pp. 234-35)

Baudrillard re-examines the internal contradiction of Capitalism and shows the logic of its relation to commodity consumption. Yet he does so by side-stepping economic theory, incorporating instead psychoanalytic evaluations. But most essentially his analysis corresponds to the logic of the linguistic sign. Hence he defines consumption as the practice of consuming the sign of a social relationship rather than consummating a real relationship. In the end, consumer-society individuals contradict the label of "materialistic" which has been the by-word of commodity culture; in fact, they practice supreme idealism. And this idealism is supported by the conservative function of the myths of consumer society: the objects. Here Baudrillard's analysis coincides with Lévi-Strauss' evaluation of myths—they dissolve the tension of systemic contradiction in imaginary resolution and so provide the society with a counter-revolutionary force. Baudrillard's description of objects shows that consumer myths have reached counter-revolutionary perfection. Consumer society, which makes a sign of everything, realizes itself in empty consumption (how can we approach satiety or even experience gratification if all we consume are signs?). At the same time it provides for the complete tolerance of opposites, hence political stagnation (how can there be conflict if signs correspond to an interchangeable formal homogeneity?). Again Baudrillard's intent is to reveal the disparity between the lived experience of consumer society and its structural reality. The myriad inessential changes of each model-year, the accumulated nuances of color and brand-name products: both seem to connote social mobility. But, as *Système des Objets* reveals, these surface changes function to hide the total inertia of the system, which operates on the basis of a dichotomy between the appearance of consumer society's imaginary project and the reality of Capitalism's repressive logic.

In the end, Baudrillard's *Système des Objets* must be seen as successful in its attempt to systematize the phenomena of commodity culture. And to a certain extent, it refers us to the total organization of consumer society. On both counts the book provides a useful model for Americans who seem bent on avoiding the problematics of consumer society, perhaps in an attempt to avoid reliving the trauma of its advent. Yet I think we should read this book within the context of Baudrillard's more recent work. For the *Système des Objets* repre-

sents his first attempt to come to grips with advanced Capitalism. It is significant that this book was written prior to May '68. It represents the naive possibility of dealing with consumer society on its own terms. For the most part the analysis remains at the level of the object relationships it sets out to define. However, the events of May '68 apparently caused Baudrillard to re-examine his initial analysis. Significantly, his later books go far beyond objects, leaving behind these symptomatic manifestations of consumer society, to focus instead on Marxian theory. Here I am referring to *Pour Une Critique de l'Economie Politique du Signe* and *Miroir de la Production,* where Baudrillard works to penetrate the logic of Capital by, as he would put it, demystifying Marxian theory. Marxists will of necessity take a hard stand on these two books, whose combined intent is a systematic critique of the most basic of Marxian premises—use-value, exchange-value, need—in fact, the whole notion of production. *Système des Objets* seems less objectionable, but by omission, since it does not include Marxian theory among the consumer objects it categorizes. But we should not dismiss Baudrillard's earlier work, for the same laws we found operative at the level of objects are, in his later books, shown to determine Marx's political economy—namely, the necessity for Capitalism to divorce sign from object, or, in economic terms, use-value from exchange-value, or production from consumption.

I think, though, we should question the privileged position ascribed to semiotics. Why should semiotics rather than Marxian analysis provide the means for understanding Capitalism? For Baudrillard the answer is easy: the political economy of Marx occupied a privileged position during the nineteenth-century consolidation of Capitalism. But because it evolved during the rise of Capitalism its theory is symptomatic of the forces involved in Capitalist production. Today the privileged position is occupied by semiotic theory. Yet again the logic of advanced Capitalism has permeated its theoretical discourse. Hence much of Baudrillard's own analysis is constantly turned back on itself in what he admits is a futile attempt to disengage the theory of the sign from the code of Capitalism.

We are aware of the limitations of semiotic theory in *Système des Objets,* where Baudrillard's recourse to psychoanalysis supplies interpretative content not present in the model. We become more aware of these limitations in the later books where Baudrillard works to meta-criticize his own theory. Some of the reason for the convoluted nature of semiotic analysis can be attributed to what is fast becoming a tradition is semiotics—using semiotics to talk about semiotics. A lot of this convolution represents the semiotician's interest in closed systems and his or her failure to cope with exterior phenomena, a problem which Marx, emphasizing production and praxis as he did, never had. But because Baudrillard's analysis steps outside the safe confines of the text and is grounded in an interest in society, he is to a certain extent able to avoid this tendency to inward-directedness.

I think we can best understand Baudrillard's work if we see it as an attempt to create a meta-language. For in Baudrillard's definition of advanced Capitalism, there are no more protagonists of historical change—social classes no longer exist as a determining category. In a sense we have been catapulted out of historical materialism to the rarified level of advanced Capitalism where only the organizational code of Capitalism functions. So for Baudrillard, revolutionary praxis is moved to the abstracted level of meta-language, hence his own grappling with theoretical discourse and his failure to completely work out his notion of the *symbolique.* A convenient category which lurks in the background of all his analyses, it seems to represent the opposite of Capital, a state of anti-production where relationships are patterned on human relationships of demand and response rather than the value-determined categories of use and exchange.

Yet Baudrillard has raised some important questions. Does Capitalism as Marx defined it continue to operate today? Is traditional Marxist analysis capable of handling the problems of consumer society? And if Marxism can no longer deal with economic concerns, can it be expected to solve the problems voiced by feminists, racial minorities, and the Third World? Baudrillard's answer is predictable: "Something has radically changed in the Capitalist sphere, to which Marxist analysis no longer responds."

Marxists should take Baudrillard's position as a challenge. But rather than refuting him through ideological rebuttals, Marxists must meet these demands through praxis—a two-pronged praxis, one directed toward real political activity, the other toward the formulation of a coherent analysis of production under the conditions imposed by advanced Capitalism. One plan of attack would be a systematic confrontation between the theories evolved by the Frankfurt School (who also saw the need for an analysis of culture) and Baudrillard's theory. Yet I think the most fruitful project would not involve criticism of Baudrillard's theory, but would focus our attention on the object of his study. Rather than recycling Marx through the optic of commodity consumption, we must re-Marxianize our analysis. (pp. 236-38)

> Susan Willis, *"Should We Recycle Marx?" in* Praxis, *Vol. 1, No. 2, Winter, 1976, pp. 231-38.*

KARLIS RACEVSKIS

Western civilization has entered the age of hyperreality, a state of existence that is characterized by the domination of codes. We live in an era of simulation, of simulacra that refer to one another in an unending play of duplication and of reflections. The only way out, the only hope, is to push these systems to their limit, to the point where they appear in their hollow absurdity and collapse. This, briefly, is the apocalyptic vision that Baudrillard evokes in *L'Echange symbolique et la mort,* a work that irrepressibly tears away at the cultural discourse with which Western societies have woven their history. Baudrillard's purpose is to trace a genealogy of the simulacra and the value systems that constitute civilization, thus unveiling the pretense, the deceits, and the tautologies on which it rests.

Baudrillard's critique is self-consciously radical and displays itself as a theoretical terrorism. At the same time, it voids all other radicalisms, past and present, considering them only as revolutions in the cyclical sense of the term. The epistemological history of our culture is, for Baudrillard, a spiral-like evolution of three distinguishable stages, each new circle simply being a reflection, a repetition on a higher level of the system below. Accordingly, the second level is the locus of theoretical critiques of the social realm, the determinisms, objectifications, and dialectics that purport to explain linguistic, economic, conscious, and subconscious subjects. The third, to which we have acceded, uses the second-level systems as its referents and is thoroughly dominated by codes which have

become its principles of reality. We have been ushered into the era of simulation, of undecidable, commutable values, where distinctions of "the beautiful and the ugly in fashions, of left and right in politics, of truth and falsehood in all the messages of the media, of the useful and the useless at the level of objects, of nature and culture at all levels of signification" are all erased as are "all the great humanistic criteria of value." (*Echange*), God, Man, Progress, History, have all died for the benefit of the code, transcendence has given way to immanence, it is now "the discontinuous indeterminism of the genetic code that governs life—the teleonomical principle" (*Echange*). Dialectical teleologies have given way to molecular play, ideological models have been replaced by the aleatory strategies of both electronic and micro-biological cells.

The new strategies have, at the same time, made possible new techniques of control, newer and more efficient modes of socialization. But the new systems do not admit they exist for purposes of social management since "any system, in order to become an end in itself, must put aside the question of its true ends" (*Critique*). The new order therefore relies on referents of the second level:

> There have always been Churches to hide the death of God, or to hide that God was everywhere—which is the same thing. There will always be animal and Indian reservations to conceal that they are dead, and that we are all Indians. There will always be factories to conceal that work is dead, that production is dead, or that it is everywhere and nowhere (*Echange*).

Economic and political systems are falling into a binary pattern, thus making possible an illusion of bipolar oppositions and insuring a stability and durability that monopolies, single political parties, or lone super-powers would not possess standing by themselves alone. The dual form of our logic is characteristic of the fundamental code that regulates our society; it allows for distinction, opposition, and exclusion, and determines the processes of simulation that dominate our culture.

The mechanism of these processes is the subject of Baudrillard's *Pour une critique de l'économie politique du signe,* in which he shows that the binary articulations, together with a strategy of dissimulation, characterize the development of all social systems, beginning with the signifying process itself. He further elucidates these themes in *Le Miroir de la production,* which is in the main a critique of Marxist epistemology but which also provides a fuller account of the social and historical implications of the signifying practices that have evolved in Western civilization. For Baudrillard, these practices are governed by a metaphysics of abstraction and conceptualization that institutes the rationality of all systems of knowledge. Western epistemology is marked by a tautological process which consists of first positing concepts and then universalizing them, thus making them into absolutes, into "truth referents." Beginning at the most fundamental level, we can thus see that in the domain of semiology, the signified and the referent both come into being thanks to the signifier, they are both "implicated in the logic of the sign" (*Critique*). (pp. 34-5)

The proliferation of codes in modern society has led to a "fetishism of the signifier," an obsession with signifying systems that are fascinating because they provide an "abstract coherence that stitches all contradictions and divisions" (*Critique*).

At the same time, as we noted above, the signifier requires the justification of a signified, a "natural" foundation that provides a rational, moral, or ideological alibi. Carrying this analysis to the economic level and considering society in Marxist terms, Baudrillard demonstrates that it is exchange value which is the determining motivation and use value is no more than a post-facto rationalization. In Western societies, the first to be instituted are value systems, which then call forth the necessary, concrete referents; the latter are subsequently presented as the motivations and the needs that found humanity. In such a system of political economy, "there is not only a quantitative exploitation of man as productive force by the *system* of capitalistic political economy, but a metaphysical overdetermination of man as producer by the *code* of the political economy" (*Miroir*). As for Marxism, it has only succeeded in perpetuating the myth on which Capitalism is founded; since it resorts to a similar metaphor of production, it appeals to "the same fiction, the same naturalization, which is to say, to a convention just as arbitrary, a model of simulation destined to encode all human material, all possibility of desire and exchange in terms of value, of finality and of production" (*Miroir*). Marxism fails to provide an alternative to Capitalism because Marx failed to see the collusion that links the order of production to that of representation in Western society. A radical critique of Western Capitalistic society is possible only if it recognizes that exchange value and the signifier are "the ultimate 'Reason,' the structural principle of the whole system," and that "it is the rational abstraction of the exchange value system and the play of signifiers that rule the whole" (*Critique*). As a consequence, it is the capacity to control codes and to manipulate signs that grants political and economic power in our society. This circumstance, in turn, permits the continuous process of accumulation and exploitation that takes place under the aegis of a metaphysics of reason: "The whole repressive and reductive strategy of systems of power is already in the internal logic of the sign, as it is in the internal logic of exchange value and of political economy" (*Critique*). Therefore, to put an end to the terrorism of rationality that permeates our culture, "the only strategy is a *catastrophical* one, and not at all dialectical. Things must be pushed to their limit, where quite naturally they reverse themselves and collapse" (*Echange*). The poetic mode must be enhanced at the expense of rationality, ambiguity must replace the tyranny of sense, of things that "make sense," reversibility must take the place of linearity and accumulation; to these ends, the Symbolic must be reinstated so as to terminate the hegemony of the sign and of value. (p. 35)

Baudrillard's intention to discredit Michel Foucault [in his ***Forget Foucault***] . . . has to be viewed in terms of a strategy aimed at the imperialism of discourses that support the Imaginary and that consolidate phantasms. Such, for example, are the theoretical constructs of Freud and of Marx, whose systems are fundamentally tautological: their claim to truth is founded on an excision made in the Symbolic field, on a carefully selected area that has subsequently been privileged with an original and originating status—as primary process or as mode of production. Subjects, however, are nothing but discursive constructs and just as there never has been a linguistic subject, "there has never been an *economic subject,* a homo œconomicus: this fiction has never been inscribed anywhere but in a code. Likewise, there has never been a *subject of consciousness,* and likewise there has never been a *subject of unconsciousness*" (*Echange*). It must be admitted, however, that in this light, the attempt to link Baudrillard's critique of Fou-

cault to that of other discursive imperialisms becomes subject to a paradox. On the one hand, we realize that Baudrillard intends to criticize Foucault on the same grounds as the others since "the coherence and transparency of *homo sexualis* has never had more reality than that of *homo œconomicus*" (*Oublier*). But we are also aware of Foucault's own accomplishments as a demystifier of Western humanistic discourse. Indeed, the concerns of Foucault appear to have a striking similarity with those of Baudrillard. One of Foucault's principal purposes has been to discredit the anthropocentric foundations of our society and to show that Western man is inextricably enmeshed in the discourse he utters about himself. He has therefore submitted this discourse to an "archeological" scrutiny and in announcing the "death of man" and the "death of the author" he is proclaiming the advent of a new era in which man will be free from the myths that have given rise to his consciousness of words and things. (pp. 37-8)

From the perspective of Baudrillard's analysis, Foucault is to be seen as a generator of signs engaged in an impressive but futile codifying strategy that fits into an particular political economy of signs. He must be perceived as a mystifier because "there is mystification from the moment when there is a rationalization in the name of whatever instance it might be. When the sexual is sublimated and rationalized in the political, social, or moral—but just as well when the symbolic is censured and sublimated in a dominating sexual discourse" (*Echange*). The discourse of Foucault, thus supported by a "metaphysics of rationality," is bound to a fetishism of the signified: to a fascination with an "abstract coherence that stitches all contradictions and divisions" (*Critique*). Foucault is not only fascinated by a "decoy of power" ("le leurre du pouvoir"), but has been caught by it, since he "unmasks all the final or causal illusions pertaining to power, but he tells us nothing *about the simulacrum of power itself*" (*Oublier*). He is a mystifier because his discourse takes place entirely in the realm of the Imaginary where "we only grant meaning to that which is irreversible: accumulation, progress, growth, production, value, power, and desire itself are irreversible processes." At the level of the Imaginary, power does exist, but only as exploitation, and it is precisely the Imaginary that produces exploiters and the exploited; here power wants to be irreversible, cumulative, and immortal, "it shares all the illusions of the real and of production, it wants itself to be the order of the real and thus tumbles into the imaginary and into a superstition of itself (with the help of theories that analyze it, even with the purpose of contesting it). Ultimately therefore, Foucault's discourse is self-referential: it generates its own substance and produces its own subject, it is "a discourse which, essentially, firmly describes the only true spiral, that of its own power."

Though imaginary, the power of Foucault's discourse is, however, far from negligible. From Baudrillard's standpoint, there is something insidious in the way Foucault's writings have established their cultural domination. Far from representing a break with traditional epistemology, the discourse of Foucault provides a propitious reference-alibi for traditional systems of power operative in Western capitalistic society. Baudrillard finds that Foucault's discourse on power and sexuality produces new simulacra that lend further support to the signifying practices of a society that exerts its domination with signs, "just as political economy and production know their full scope only with the sanction and the blessing of Marx." Furthermore, though they appear to contradict traditional analyses, his writings only serve to animate or reanimate referents that are on their way out, visibly disintegrating all around us, that are, in one word, *révolus*. Only in this sense is Foucault's discourse revolutionary—it marks the end of a cycle and therefore manifests itself as a paroxysm, since "the immanent death of all the great referentials (religious, sexual, political, etc.) manifests itself as an exacerbation of the forms of violence and of representation which characterized them." The intense nature of Foucault's prose may give it an appearance of originality, but in the spiral of epistemological evolution his discourse is only a reflection, a representation of the cycle that is ending, it is a simulacrum empty of content, a form pretending to be content. In this sense, Foucault is one of those contemporary thinkers who "are still playing at linear revolution while it has already rolled back upon itself to produce its simulacrum." In this sense also, Foucault's undertaking is construed as a threat by Baudrillard and is ranked with those forces in contemporary society that are fundamentally antihuman.

By producing a discourse whose principal merit is to reproduce concepts that no longer make sense, have lost their representational dimension and are carried along by a superstitious belief in themselves, Foucault's project epitomizes the general tendency of the age—a fascination with the hyperreality of codes and of simulation. Baudrillard therefore ranks Foucault with the advocates of today's scientology which is the new religion of an age when "everyone wallows [. . .] in the molecular as if it were something revolutionary." These molecules and the spirals of the ADN are an ever-present temptation for intellectuals who are eager to "rediscover as a mechanism of desire that which cyberneticists have described as a codifying and controlling matrix." By increasing the prestige and efficacy of a teleonomical power, Foucault "will have contributed to putting into place a power which will be of the same order of functioning as desire, just as Deleuze will have put into place a desire which is of the order of future powers." Therefore, suggests Baudrillard, let us forget them both.

The image of Foucault as an accomplice in a grand design of cybernetic control is doubtless outrageous and should perhaps be viewed as a caricature. But outrageous parody, we must remember, is still within Baudrillard's admitted strategy aimed at discrediting the realm of the Imaginary. He therefore wishes to pursue the logic inherent in a simulacrum to its absurd limits: "Against a hyperrealistic system, the only strategy is pataphysical, in a manner of speaking—'a science of imaginary solutions'—that is to say a science fiction of the reversal of the system against itself, at the extreme limit of simulation, of a reversible simulation in a hyperlogic of destruction and of death" (*Echange*). It is natural to suspect such destructive urges of not being completely gratuitous, and Baudrillard's basic thesis, just as his attack on Foucault, does seem to be motivated by certain axiological prejudices. It is possible to read, between the lines of Baudrillard's writing, a nostalgic partiality for a primeval, "acultural" world, or at least for a social system that valorizes reversible relations, where humans are no longer bound by codes, no longer defined, identified, signified. The relations between humans would no longer be circumscribed by systems of knowledge that derive their authority from the truths they themselves promulgate. These kinds of systems still predominate today; fortunately, they are doomed, according to Baudrillard: their foundations are slowly being eroded by manifestations of the Symbolic and it is only a matter of time before we realize that

there has always been something that goes through these models of simulation, which are all *rational* models—there has always been a radicalness that was absent from all these codes, from all these 'objective' rationalizations, which at bottom have given rise to but one great subject: *the subject of knowledge,* whose form is shattered from now on, from this moment on, by symbolic language ['la parole indivise']. After all, anybody always knows more than Descartes, than Saussure, than Marx, than Freud. (*Echange*)

The accumulation of systems of knowledge, the generation of signifying practices simply amount to a grand obfuscation, they have only succeeded in concealing something essential and valuable—a common and authentic experience of our humanity.

If the underlying premise of Baudrillard's work sounds almost trivial, his strategy remains radical. While the discourse of Foucault represents an advanced level of sophistication in the evolution of signifying practices, that of Baudrillard is a dramatic and provocative attempt to reveal the gratuitous nature of these practices. His critique is particularly adept at disclosing the complicity these discourses unwittingly entertain with capitalistic society, with "this machine of truth, of rationality, of productivity, which has no objective end, no reason" (*A l'ombre des majorités silencieuses ou la fin du social*). In accordance with the basic principle of binary opposition, whereby antithetical terms are recognized to exist as mutual supports, the condemnation of a society simply serves to preserve it: "This counter-discourse, failing to institute any *real* distance, is as immanent in a consumer society as any one of its other aspects. This negative discourse is the secondary residence of the intellectual. Just as the society of the Middle Ages founded its equilibrium on God and on the Devil, ours does it on consumption and on its denunciation" (*La Société de consommation*). Furthermore, since signifying systems are always and inevitably recuperated in a consumer society—made into articles of consumption—they end up forming a discursive layer that shields us from a "pre-discursive" reality, that is to say, from one that has not been codified and signified. In today's world, the only satisfactory, consumable reality is that of signs.

Obviously, Baudrillard also engages in a signifying practice, yet his discourse is meant to avoid recuperation, to escape consumption, because it constitutes a challenge to the system; it is a *défi* "from that which has no meaning, no name, no identity, to that which prides itself of a meaning, a name, an identity—it challenges meaning, power, truth to exist as such, to pretend to exist as such. Only such a reversal can put an end to power, to meaning, to value" (*A l'ombre*).

The basic intention of Baudrillard is then to undermine sense, to discredit those who "make" sense. Society, man, have no need for sense, for definitions and rationalizations that will supposedly help them find themselves: "Every man is present in his entirety at every moment. Society, also, is present in its entirety, at every moment" (*Miroir*). They have only to be left alone to allow them to fully realize themselves in the Symbolic. This means that Baudrillard's project is, in the main, a quarrel with the intellectuals, a group that he considers as a class or caste continuously engaged in socializing, politicizing, acculturating the masses, but, fortunately, to no avail. The masses, Baudrillard finds, are becoming immune to sense; they consume only signs and reject meaning, suspicious of the "terrorism of simplification which is behind the ideal hegemony of sense" (*A l'ombre*). As a result, society today is on the brink of an inward collapse, a cataclysmic implosion that will bring an end to the social hyperreality of production. This event, warns Baudrillard, can only be "violent and catastrophical, because it results from the *failure* of the system of explosion and directed expansion that has been our Western scheme for several centuries." Since for Baudrillard the symbolic destruction of culture is a process that is well on its way, his critical violence can be understood to belong to this general process of disintegration. His writing does not have the purposeful, direct quality of imaginary critiques but is, in effect, implosive; such indeed is the injunction of **Oublier**: it calls for a disappearance, for an aspiration of systems of knowledge into an epistemological black hole.

Such an eventuality would mark the end of a civilization and the beginning of a new era when subjects, "cast free from their identities, like words, are dedicated to social reciprocity in laughter and in an existence of pleasure [la jouissance]" (**L'Echange**). Baudrillard's vision thus implies a utopian aspiration and, in this context, his discourse finds itself in a serious predicament. If it is not recuperable as a contribution to contemporary thought, it is no more than the prophetic vision of a Cassandra. At the same time, Baudrillard's texts have an evident intellectual appeal, they *make* sense—too much sense to be ignored. Now intellectual and utopian constructions both depend upon the Imaginary, one for concepts, the other for ideals and values. Therefore Baudrillard's attempt to set himself apart from intellectual enterprises such as those of Foucault and Deleuze does not appear to be very successful. Furthermore, seen from a more pragmatic level, the distinction between the Symbolic and the Imaginary as a way of differentiating the approach of Baudrillard from that of Foucault becomes even less convincing. Baudrillard celebrates the authentic world of a primordial existence, Foucault thrives on the inauthentic world of simulacra: however, their cerebration takes place at a level that suggests less the distance that separates them both than the distance that separates them from the reality of average existences. The rejection of culture is a privilege that is not enjoyed by many: while our mental health and human integrity would probably benefit from such a rejection, as ordinary social beings, most of us simply cannot afford the consequences of this drastic a step. We are subject to a "double bind" dilemma familiar to psychiatric therapists: "For the 'average' person in our culture—with house, family, car, children, credit-rating, and job, and without the degrees of freedom enjoyed by intellectuals and the more privileged classes—any true 'cure' would amount to an injunction to 'go crazy,' as that is defined by the culture, and you can't feed your children that way" (Wilden, *System and Structure*). When all is said and done, both Baudrillard and Foucault appear as members of a highly privileged class—the class of intellectuals, poets, and professors.

Dramatic differences, even clashes between intellectuals, poets, and professors are inevitable as they engage in the games of words that constitute their universe, but the violence of these confrontations is mostly rhetorical and does not constitute a serious issue if viewed from the down-to-earth level of real violence. Yet there are discourses, such as Foucault's that in one way or another are responses to the kind of violence which is not abstract, which singles out specific subjects, not symbolic, not imaginary, but children, men, and women. Obviously, Baudrillard is also affected by dehumanization, brutalization, and exploitation, but in this regard

he can only offer the hope of "brutal irruptions and of sudden disintegrations which, in an equally unpredictable but certain way as those of May 1968, will come to break up this white mass," that is, the promise of an upheaval that will destroy this society saturated with its own myth (**La Société de consommation**). Seen in this light, and for those of us steeped in the Imaginary, the relative security offered by the Imaginary might well appear more attractive than this primordial spontaneity set loose by the Symbolic. (pp. 39-42)

Karlis Racevskis, "The Theoretical Violence of a Catastrophical Strategy," in Diacritics, *Vol. 9, No. 3, Fall, 1979, pp. 33-42.*

MARK POSTER

Baudrillard's early works, **Le Système des objets** (1968) and **La Société de consommation** (1970) took their inspiration from the problematics of the critique of everyday life developed by Baudrillard's teacher Henri Lefebvre and from Roland Barthes' semiology. Under advanced capitalism, Baudrillard maintained, consumerism had come to dominate the various aspects of everyday life. At this stage of his thinking Baudrillard was happy to place the regional analysis of consumption within the broader Marxist critique of capitalism. The experience of the events of May 1968 had dramatized changes in the structure of capitalism, such as the importance of everyday life, that required analysis and critique. Where Baudrillard differed from traditional Marxism was in his use of semiological theory to make intelligible in a new way the features of consumerism.

Like Habermas, Baudrillard was unwilling to accept language theory—in this case structuralist semiology—in its dominant versions. Saussure's structural linguistics, as employed by Lévi-Strauss, Lacan, and Barthes, enables the investigator to examine phenomena at a new level of complexity. An object can be dissected into its binary oppositions, revealing a play of rules and patterns of formation, without resorting to a concept of consciousness or subjectivity. Social experience is open to analysis at a level of internal articulation: myths, kinship systems, fashion magazines, consumer objects each constitute a structured world of meaning that derives its intelligibility from its likeness to language. Yet the use of structural linguistics in social theory bears a certain cost: the formalism of linguistics, when carried over into social science, implies a dehistoricization and a weakening of critical powers. Structural linguistics mandates that phenomena be studied synchronically, outside time, and without reference to normative evaluations.

Baudrillard was probably the first thinker in France to attempt to employ semiology both historically and critically. The thesis of **Consumer Society** was that in advanced capitalism a new structure of meanings had emerged whose effectiveness was based on a logic of differentiation that was subject to analysis only by a semiological theory. "The social logic of consumption," Baudrillard wrote, "is not at all that of the individual appropriation of the use value of goods and services . . . it is not a logic of satisfaction. It is a logic of the production and manipulation of social signifiers." But Marxism missed its analytical boat if it rested on demonstrating that capitalism generated these signifiers to manipulate the masses into unwanted acts of consumption. The point was rather that the signifiers themselves, not the products, had become objects of consumption that drew their power and fascination from being structured into a code. The code, in turn, could be deciphered not by the logic of capital but by the logic of semiology.

Baudrillard's analysis of consumption was thus fully historical because it subordinated semiology to critical theory: the production of commodities had entered a new stage that was accompanied by a new structure of signs, a new linguistic apparatus. Once this new structure of meanings was analyzed semiologically, revealing its structured code, an argument could be developed that radical change must focus on the code, develop a practice to dismantle it and a strategy to create a new order of symbolic exchange with a new system of signs. Baudrillard's intent was double: to revise semiology so that its formalism and ahistoricity were tamed to the needs of critical theory; and to revise Marxism so that its productivism was tamed to the needs of cultural criticism. The result would be a new critical theory that captured the interdependence of technology and culture, production and symbolic exchange.

The System of Objects and *Consumer Society* carried out these goals by demonstrating the advantages of semiology over the Marxist concept of needs in the analysis of consumerism. If commodities are conceptualized as deriving their value from labor and their use from need, the extraordinary expansion of consumerism since World War II remains a mystery. Why would workers exhaust themselves in labor only to purchase the dubious products that capitalism places on the market? According to Marx, human needs are not fixed, but alter with changes in the mode of production. If that is true, capitalism has successfully instituted an infinite cycle of production and consumption. But Marx's analysis overlooked, according to Baudrillard, the function of social exchange. Limited to the metaphor of production in the analysis of social practice, Marx missed the force of the social exchange of meanings that envelope commodities in a nonproductivist logic. If, on the other hand, society were seen as a system of symbolic exchange, the power of the code would reveal its force.

Under advanced capitalism, Baudrillard contends, the masses are controlled not only by the need to labor in order to survive but by the need to exchange symbolic differences. Individuals receive their identity in relation to others not primarily from their type of work but from the meanings they consume. Taking his cue from Veblen and certain anthropological theories, Baudrillard asserts the importance of commodities as social signifiers, not as material objects. But he avoids the dangers of such theories of emulation by rooting his analysis firmly in the soil of the current social epoch. The shift from the primacy of production to the primacy of exchange has been facilitated by the development of new technologies, such as radio and television. The cultural significance of these technologies is that they emit a single message and constitute a new code: "the message of the consumption of the message." The new media transform the structure of language, of symbolic exchange, creating the conditions in which the new code of consumerism can emerge.

From the vantage point of semiology, the new code is easy enough to decipher. An ad for Pepsi-Cola, for example, pictures a community of all ages, sexes, and races enjoying a drink together. The message is clear if subliminal: to drink Pepsi-Cola is not so much to consume a carbonated beverage as to consume a meaning, a sign, that of community. In this ad, a value that capitalism destroys (community) is returned

to society through the ad. In another example, the code operates not as utopian realization but as pressure to conform. Brut cologne is associated with aggressive manhood. Again, to use the product is to consume the meaning, in this case a stereotype of masculinity. The implication of the ad is that those who do not use Brut will not be manly, losing out in the game of sexual conquest.

Although opposite in their strategy, both ads illustrate the mechanism of the code. The product itself is not of primary interest; it must be sold by grafting onto it a set of meanings that have no inherent connection with the product. The set of meanings, subject to semiological analysis, becomes the dominant aspect of consumption. Unlike Habermas, who sees meanings as scarce in advanced capitalism, Baudrillard discovers a profusion of meaning in the system of consumption. This difference in the two thinkers speaks to the relative value of their sources: the elitist pessimism of the Frankfurt school, which, failing to find "authentic" values in mass society, rejects popular culture out of hand, and the semiology employed by Baudrillard, which grants the validity of popular culture long enough to carry out a trenchant analysis of it.

In *Pour une critique de l'économie politique du signe* (1972) Baudrillard endeavored to correlate systematically his critical semiology with Marx's critique of political economy. Still remaining within Marxist framework, at least nominally, he tested the general principles of Marx's analysis of the commodity with that of semiology's analysis of the sign. Just as Marx decomposed the commodity into use value and exchange value, so semiology deciphered the sign as signified and signifier. Baudrillard discovered a homology between the sign and the commodity: the signifier is to exchange value what the signified is to use value. The parallelism at the formal level, however, masks a certain misrecognition or ideology which is the effect both of the structuralist concept of the sign and the Marxist notion of the commodity.

The structuralist concept of the sign naturalizes or universalizes what is in fact, according to Baudrillard, a historically based semiological formation. The sign, split off from the referent and intelligible only at the level of the relation of signifier to signifier, is actually a drastic reduction of the symbolic. In a universe of symbols, signifier, signified, and referent are integrated in acts of communication. Symbols are characterized by an ambivalence of meaning as they are exchanged from one person to another. The sign, on the contrary, is full, positive, univocal. It is not an inevitable truth about language, but a product of a specific semiological epoch. Programmed by industry and bureaucracy, the sign is part of the strategy of power. Removed from the web of mutual reciprocity, the sign is a unilateral message, a communication without a response. Signs are made possible by the new technologies of the media in which signifiers flash by potential consumers. Once signifiers have been separated and abstracted in this way, floating free, so to speak, in communicational space, they can be attached to particular commodities by the arbitrary whim of advertisers. Thus a new structure of meaning is instituted that collaborates with the requirements of advanced capitalism.

Marx's concept of the commodity never attains this level of analysis. He neglects the process of transformation by which exchange value becomes a sign. Because the conceptual apparatus of Marxism is modeled on production and labor, it cannot make intelligible "the social labor of producing signs," which is based on a different logic. The circulation of signs itself produces surplus value, one based not on profit but on legitimacy. At this time, Baudrillard was content to argue that his analysis of the message was parallel to Marx's analysis of the commodity. Just at the point where Marxism became "ideological" because it could not decode the semiology of the commodity, Baudrillard stepped in to enrich and improve upon historical materialism, updating it to the circumstances of advanced capitalism.

Hints of a coming break with Marx were nonetheless present in *Pour une critique.* The point of divergence with Marx centered on the question of the logic of production versus the logic of exchange, the materiality of commodities versus the ideality of the sign. In rejecting the structuralist separation of the sign from the world, Baudrillard argued that the world "is only the effect of the sign." If individuals consumed meanings rather than products, the center piece of social theory was symbolic exchange, not the production of goods. Value was created, therefore, not in the labor process but in the communicational structure. In *Pour une critique,* Baudrillard's emphasis was on revising Marx rather than supplanting him but the seeds of post-Marxist critical theory were already planted.

The break with Marx came only a year later with the publication of *The Mirror of Production.* Here Baudrillard presented in no uncertain terms his critique of the notion of labor, systematically deconstructing the apparatus of the critique of political economy:

> A specter haunts the revolutionary imagination: the phantom of production. Everywhere it sustains an unbridled romanticism of productivity. The critical theory of the *mode* of production does not touch the *principle* of production. All the concepts it articulates describe only the dialectical and historical genealogy of the *contents* of production, leaving production as a *form* intact.

The Marxist concept of labor, Baudrillard proposes, is too close to the liberal notion of *homo economicus* to provide a radical critique of political economy. Like the liberals, Marx reduces practice to labor and society to production. Marx discovered in use value the radical basis for the critique of the liberal notion of exchange value. The labor that goes into the commodity constitutes for Marx its true worth, not the amount for which it is exchanged. The notion of exchange value reduces all labor to one level; it obscures concrete differences between human acts, Marx complains.

Baudrillard responds that to uncover the human essence of labor behind the capitalist shroud of exchange value is not enough. Marxism only "convinces men that they are alienated by the sale of their labor power; hence it censors the much more radical hypothesis that they do not have to be the labor power, the 'unalienable' power of creating value by their labor." Like liberalism, Marx conceptualized the social field in the mirror of production, presenting back to capitalism its own image, only in an inverted form. A radical critique must rather locate the field that is obscured by liberals and Marxists alike—that of symbolic exchange.

Baudrillard locates the point at which Marxist theory becomes complicit with capitalist productivism by reviewing the stages of the relation of production and exchange presented by Marx in *The Poverty of Philosophy.* During stage one, before capitalism, production was for use by the produc-

ers and only the surplus was exchanged. In stage two, that of classical capitalism, all production by industry was exchanged. In stage three, fully developed capitalism, not only industrial production, but everything—"virtue, love, knowledge, consciousness"—is placed on the market for possible exchange. Marx views the spread of capitalist principles beyond the area of production as a "corruption" or a time of "universal venality." For Marx, stage three involves the reflection of the base in the superstructure, a secondary effect of the mode of production. Thus the basic shift for him is from stage one to stage two, stage three being conceived only as the logical working out of the system, its general extension to all social relations.

In his critique Baudrillard wavers not between supplementing Marx and rejecting him but between rejecting him only for the analysis of stage three or rejecting him for the entire genealogy of capitalism. In the weaker critique Baudrillard argues that Marx obscures the significance of the shift to stage three because of his productivist metaphor. Social exchange in stage three, from the semiological perspective outlined above, reveals a structurally new type of domination generated by the code or the sign, a type of domination that cannot be made intelligible through the concept of production. In this case, Marxism becomes inadequate as a critical theory only with the advent of the sign as the general principle of communication. In the stronger critique Baudrillard maintains that the sign and the commodity arose together at the beginning of the process of the birth of capitalism and that the critique of the political economy of the sign is more radical than the critique of political economy from the outset. As a critical category, the mode of signification should perhaps take precedence over the mode of production.

The tendency to give priority to symbolic exchanges rather than labor is found in the recent work of both Baudrillard and Habermas. The question of whether they have strayed too far from traditional Marxism cannot be answered within the scope of this essay. What can be said is that both have enlarged the scope of critical theory to encompass the phenomenon of language and that both have placed technology in a closer relationship with culture than Marx did. The mode of signification becomes as central to critical theory as the mode of production. The ideal speaking situation for Habermas and symbolic exchange for Baudrillard become the new basis of revolutionary theory. The problem of transforming the mode of production must share the attention of criticism with the problem of transforming the world of meaning, culture, and language. By taking critical theory in this direction both Habermas and Baudrillard provide a ground for incorporating into the revolutionary perspective a locus of radicality outside the workplace. Women, minorities, gays, criminals, all the oppressed subcultures, may now take part in the process of social transformation on a footing equal to that of the proletariat. Although neither Baudrillard nor Habermas systematically addresses the question of the relation of these subgroups to the mode of signification, there is the clear implication in their thought that this issue is high on the agenda of critical theory.

Although the similarities in direction of the ideas of Baudrillard and Habermas are striking, there remain fundamental differences between them. These divergences can be clarified by comparing their relationship to the Left of the late 1960s. In Germany Habermas became a focus of criticism by the New Left, who saw his notion of a public sphere as insufficiently radical. For his part Habermas viewed the students as bourgeois children protesting paternal authority and sexual repression. The significance of their revolt was that they forced into public attention areas of life that hitherto had remained private. They had successfully broken through the shell of bourgeois ideology revealing the absence of democracy throughout society. In the advanced societies the main problem, however, was that of technology and its undemocratic character. Here the issue could be resolved only through resort to an ideal speaking situation. (pp. 467-74)

Baudrillard was far more enthusiastic than Habermas about the radicalism of the late 1960s. May 1968 was for him an apocalyptic smashing of the repressive code. Against the monologue of the TV, May 1968 presented a festival of symbolic exchange. The streets and walls of Paris shouted down the abstract murmurs of the sign. A new mode of signification was realized in everyday life, if only briefly. The seemingly unconquerable power of the code dissolved in a volley of chatter from students and workers. The new mode of signification was created not through the dialectical maneuvers of the class struggle but in a simple explosion of expressive communication. Like graffiti, the force of symbolic exchange erupted in the semiological field in a sudden burst of meaning. The events of May 1968 confirmed for Baudrillard the poverty of the Marxist notion of revolution. It shattered in one brilliant display of semiological fireworks the notion of the party with its intellectuals, its theory, its cadre, its careful organization and strategy, its duplication of the bourgeois world that it would supplant. The theory of symbolic exchange in Baudrillard's version thus implies a very different world from that of Habermas. The new mode of signification depends not on a new notion of the subject or a new realization of rationality. It denotes instead a new structure of communication in which signifiers would be generated directly in the course of exchange, connected closely to both signified and referent.

Although Baudrillard's critical semiology permits a deeper analysis of the communication structure of advanced capitalism than that of Habermas and avoids undue reliance on concepts of the subject and rationality, it too misses, finally, a satisfactory resolution of a theory of technology and culture. The danger in Baudrillard's notion of the code is that it accepts too easily the omnipotence of the semiological structure; it totalizes too quickly the pattern of communication that it reveals. As opposed to Habermas' subjectivism, Baudrillard's analysis errs in the direction of objectivism. In his view floating signifiers pervade the social space without adequate recognition or theoretical account of the continuous disruptions of it by subjects. Baudrillard convincingly theorizes one side of the question—the emission of the signals—but the reception of the signals remains beyond the ken of his semiology. For reception is also an act and it is one that is discontinuous with emission, especially during the epoch of the sign. Revolt against the sign takes place not only in the exceptional collective outburst, such as that of May 1968. Protest and transgression are repeated daily by women who refuse to douse themselves in seductive perfumes, by gays who overtly display their threatening sexuality, by prisoners who do not accept the discipline of the panopticon, by workers who sabotage the smooth flow of the production line, by everyone who draws a line through or erases or marks over the imperatives of the code.

If critical semiology enables critical theory to make intelligi-

ble the domination inherent in the mode of signification, it displaces the locus of revolt, failing to present a theory of subjectivity that would account for the gaps and fissures within the system. When Baudrillard argues that escape from the code is found only in death, when meaning finally is not reincorporated into the nightmare of signs, it becomes plain that his objectivism has led to a retreat to a distant desert. Nonetheless, Habermas and, more especially, Baudrillard have carried critical theory far beyond the boundaries of the mode of production to a more fertile theoretical field in which a resolution of the question of technology and culture can be pursued. (pp. 475-76)

Mark Poster, "Technology and Culture in Habermas and Baudrillard," in Contemporary Literature, *Vol. 22, No. 4, Fall, 1981, pp. 456-76.*

KATE LINKER

The 20th century has observed a striking reduction in the notion of the imagination. What was once the shaping power of thought, the purveyor of meaning, has become a kind of cybernetic machine, its overloaded circuits programmed to spew out scintillating visual forms. "Sheer" images, "pure" surfaces emanate from the image mechanism, only to slither in the glamor of the void that constitutes consumer society, their external enchantments compensating for the loss of substantive matter. These seductive, inherently spectacular forms are not, as before, glosses of meaning; they do not hint at inner depths, silhouetting intent. As phantasmatic phenomena, dispersed throughout contemporary culture and defining its allures, they suggest similarities to the shimmering masks of absence that go by the name of simulacra.

From their conceptual origins, simulacra were instruments of illusion. Although the simulacrum's dictionary definition stays constant as a "mere image, a specious imitation or likeness," the concept has shifted through time according to social relations and systems of power, and the signifying practices they imply. In the most extensive treatment of the subject to date, Jean Baudrillard [in *L'échange symbolique et la mort*] distinguishes three orders of simulacra. The first, he writes, that of the counterfeit, was born with the Renaissance in a sign finding value in emulation of nature, posing the metaphysical question of reality against appearance. Based on imitation, it was structured on the natural law of value; with industrial development, it receded before the productivist order, patterned on market law. In this second order, corresponding to the modern period, signs no longer refer to nature but to human production; its models are the machine, energy, and the system of labor itself. The avatar is not the crafted analogue of nature, singular in form, but the plural, reproducible forms of series—forms reflecting the growing importance of technique. The industrial simulacrum, however, diminishes on entry to our period, the postindustrial period, characterized by "simulacra of simulation" dominated by the code, the model, and the operational practices of the cybernetic world.

As Baudrillard indicates, this shift from the stucco angel to computer graphics and synthetic hues is not fortuitous: it is historically determined, reflecting changes whose impact is felt in culture, politics, and economics. Most importantly, however, these changes mirror mutations in the structure of representation, which register the gradual loss of the real or objective world and with it of the notion of reference. Thus the Renaissance counterfeit invoked the terms of the philosophy of representation, of the original, of *ressemblance* and faithful imitation. Its structure corresponded to the classic sign, composed of signifier and signified, repeating its doubled arrangement in the substitution of reality's image for the real. Nature underlies this configuration as the ultimate referent, and it was the aim of creating a parallel universe, echoing the natural world, that haunted the period, inspiring the great theatrical interiors and other examples of trompe l'oeil. The emblem of *ressemblance* was the automaton, conceived as the mechanical counterpart, the ideal figure, the "perfect double" of man.

To the automaton the second order opposed the robot, a figure whose emergence is more than the signal of industrial connotations. For the robot is regulated not by likeness but by equivalence; it is not man's analogue, conceived in his image, but his functional or "operative" adjunct. The equivocations between truth and falsity or reality and appearance that had sustained the preindustrial simulacrum are absorbed by the liquidation of reality through the system of production, and with it, of reproduction. For the industrial simulacrum is not a counterfeit, but a product—since the image is fabricated, it has no referent in the world. With this period, signs no longer refer to specific objects, but to the meanings with which they are invested, resulting in the "arbitrariness" or "abstraction" that was cited by Ferdinand de Saussure. Furthermore, the period also marks the beginning of serial production, for the absorption of the question of origin opens the possibility of a potentially infinite number of identical objects—objects that are equivalent and interchangeable in market terms. The process witnesses the sign's devaluation from conformity to natural law to the market law of value, the system of exchange: "Only the extinction of the original reference permits the generalized law of equivalence, meaning the *possibility of production.*"

This shift in representation is evident in the visual arts in the Modernist suspension of the referent so as to stress the purity of the visual signifier, or rather, in the substitution of function and modes of facture as the meanings of cultural modernity. The sense of form as content—or of formal principles as artistic significance—pervades the period within the framework of the productivist esthetic; we find the equivalent of the labor theory of value in the concept of form produced either through manufacture (as in painting, modeling, welding, or carving) or, in the case of Minimalism, through industrial labor. But it is in the photograph that pure serial production finds its apogee; Walter Benjamin's noted axiom that "to ask for the 'authentic' print makes no sense" would phrase the photograph as the very "type" of industrial simulacrum, as one in an endless number of identical copies. Indeed, the increasing circulation of such simulacra in society testifies to reproduction's role as the core of industrial capital. As Baudrillard observes of the decisive shift inaugurated by technique, "We know today that it is on the level of reproduction—fashion, media, publicity, information, and communications networks—on the level of what Marx negligently called the false cost of capital . . . meaning, in the sphere of simulacra and code, that the total processes of capital are knit together." But as he notes, this stage of serial reproduction is short-lived, receding before a third stage corresponding to postindustrial development, and to its rampant technology. . . . In this third stage, the signifier becomes detached from the signified, estranged from its "natural" pretension to meaning. Reality is now subservient to the signifi-

er: it is produced by the latter, or rather, by the varied modes of signification. In such self-regulating systems, the signifiers are related "digitally," by distinctive oppositions: they no longer reflect "the law of equivalence, but the commutation of terms—no longer market law, but the structural law of value." With these structures of coded oppositions we pass into a world of forces and tensions, moving far from the provisions of natural law and from the representational structure of the classic sign. We move away from the society of production into that of consumption. And we arrive at the regulating power of the signifier, and at the recognition of its tyranny, as the latter motivates contemporary epistemology and, in particular, that branch of reflection characterized as postmodern thought.

Within this universe in which the simulacrum precedes reality, the double the original, the robot's analogue is the computer, a machine programmed to produce reality according to its codes. As with the paradigm of the modern period, such regulation is all-pervasive, establishing correspondences between production, language, and the other structuring instances of society. Its radicality can be grasped by comparison with the earlier model, based on production and labor, which permeates the early and high capitalist period and finds its climax in the Bauhaus. The structuring of modern society corresponds to a utilitarian paradigm: to each thing, a use; to each form, a meaning. To the extent that functionalism imposes itself as "the *dominant rationality,* susceptible to giving an account of everything and to directing all process," function serves as the "transcendental 'signified' " of signs. In each case, the coherence of two elements insures the structure of meaning, binding form to content, object to use, and ending to motive force. This sense of "objective determination" informs the functionalism of period architecture, the notion of style, and the ideology of progress. And it finds expression in the teleological structure of Modernism, by which the totality of art is directed toward an encompassing ending, toward fulfillment of an inner logic.

To this vertical paradigm of interiority recent theory has responded with a horizontal model, based on the lateral play of signifiers. This is a historical mutation which Baudrillard has described in a simple structural opposition, invoking a clear inversion of terms. The 19th century, he writes, [in *Simulacres et simulations*], was characterized by the destruction of appearances to the profit of meaning, by a general activity, dispersed through criticism, representation, and history, of the world's "disenchantment" by interpretation. However, the 20th-century postmodern period has witnessed the destruction of meaning and the hollowing-out of criticism, the elevation of system, structure, and surface. Gone is the aim of hermeneutics: signs no longer refer to a "subjective or objective 'reality,' " but to themselves, and to the reticulation of their networks. The signifier becomes its own referent, in a tautological repetition of itself. And gone are the illusions of utilitarianism, for rationality is transferred to the system's own self-defining closure. Within such contemporary production, the signs for reality come to replace reality, registering the eclipse of reference: these "simulated" forms generate an unreal real, a real without origin, foregrounding their superficial, supplementary, surface status.

Artificial sunsets and Technicolor hues, glossy finishes, plastic wood and hyped-up special effects fall within the compass of such "hyperreal" production, to say nothing of Disneyland or Great Adventure, which purports to evoke the jungle consigned by civilization to the past. Such production does not conform to the structure of representation for, as Baudrillard notes, there is no reality left to re-present. Unlike "true" or "classic" simulacra, simulated forms do not imitate reality in an illusory manner; as opposed to the copy, the double, or the mirror, they precede and formulate the real. They register that irony of contemporary existence—that what we accept as reality is already simulated, a massive fabrication of effects which stands in for reality's absence. And although such hyperreality has been described as attesting to the "falsification of social life," the grounds for objective truth have been annihilated with the destruction of reference and, with it, all means for imputing the "false." What simulation discloses, then, is a world beyond truth, reference, and casuality, an artificial universe without meaning.

Central to the productions of this period, as Frederic Jameson has observed, is the decline of *affect*, the passionate investment of anxiety that characterized the Modernist period, and its replacement by effect, the alternately jarring and fascinating lures of technological incandescence. A sheer pleasure in surfaces, in a "look"—in shimmering synthetics that flaunt their artificial origins—effect has given rise to a whole new object world and to a distinctive cultural style. It is a style determined by and reflective of the complexity of new technology, which has moved beyond simple serial repetition to dazzling virtuoso effects. As Jameson notes, this phenomenon is a historical one, a function of a specific moment in late capitalism when "it is very precisely those older vehicles of production which have been subsumed under the radically different industrial dynamic of the computer, of nuclear energy and of the media." Yet it is also a style with moral and epistemological implications: much as the discourse of interiority would abolish appearances, so this empty discourse of surfaces, in its annihilation of meaning, leads to the erosion of all coordinates of value, resulting in the equivalence of images experienced in the media's cool, dispassionate regime. "The era of simulation," Baudrillard writes,

> begins with the commutability of terms that were once contradictory or dialectically opposed. . . . In politics, of the left and the right; in the media, of true and false; in objects, of utility and uselessness, and of nature and culture on every level of signification. All the great humanist criteria . . . have been effaced in our system of images and signs. Everything becomes undecidable—this is the characteristic effect of domination by the code, which rests on a principle of neutralization and indifference.

Within such "decentered" production, it is no longer possible to envision an expressive self as referent for a private, personal style. Nor is it possible to entertain once-elemental distinctions between authentic and inauthentic, original and copy. "Reality" is constructed by the codes of society, by the "already written," by the received languages and conventions that assume the subject's place. (pp. 44-6)

> *Kate Linker, "From Imitation to the Copy to Just Effect: On Reading Jean Baudrillard," in* Artforum, *Vol. XXII, No. 8, April, 1984, pp. 44-7.*

JEREMY GILBERT-ROLFE

I am interested here in what seem to be the implications of the thinking of Jean Baudrillard for the practice and recep-

tion of art, the latter being a term to which I am for these purposes prepared to give as wide a definition as any reader may wish. In particular I am concerned with what one might extrapolate from his writings as to the matter of art, the art world, and Ideology.

Baudrillard's name has been around the art world for a little while now. . . . He is both popular and unpopular, and a great deal has been written about and against his ideas as a result.

But it seems to me that much that he has to say has gone essentially unremarked. Baudrillard, whose interests are in many respects similar to those of Marshall McLuhan and Walter Benjamin, is concerned with how we live through and in a world of signs, where it is understood that the world is nothing but that. He is a social science professor who investigates the functioning of the sign. This sign-form, his term for the complete sign, *i.e.,* the signifier seen together with its signified, the image together with the idea to which it is made to refer, is for him a term covering everything from the bundles of signs given to us by television programming to the sign which is the television set itself, which announces its owner's possession of access to what it can provide. Before owning a television became common-place, possession functioned as a sign of privileged access, of status. His studies have led him to bring Nietzsche to bear on Marx, a clue to which is to be found in his insistence that in our world "everything is dead and risen in advance," in other words, everything implies a model for itself which preceded it, but to which it cannot be reduced. This idea, however distantly, is related to Nietzsche's idea of the external return—that recognition is somehow that, re-cognition, the re-knowing of something already known—and it renders the sign uncontrollable in a manner which can only bring Baudrillard into conflict with a very important element in contemporary art and criticism, namely that which seeks to make work, and to think about it, in the terms set by what is known as Critical Theory.

Critical Theory is the name given to that critical practice, the foremost living exponent of which is Jürgen Habermas, which is derived from the method put forward by the Frankfürt Institute, a collective of scholars inaugurated before the Second World War by T. W. Adorno and Max Horkheimer, who sought to make social-critical method out of Marx (the social macrocosm) and Freud (the family as social microcosm). . . . (p. 21)

Critical Theory sees the symbolic order as directly continuous with the world of things, so that for Habermas, meaning is social meaning, and is to be found through regarding the work as something which is both produced and about production. At the level of the symbolic, or as praxis (the meeting of theory and practice,) the meaning of the work lives in its usefulness (its use-value) as a laying bare of reality, of a sort which can be experienced as a model for personal-social action (the self-realization of the social self, the self as an element in a collectivity, the work as the symbolic exploration of the idea of collectivity).

Here is where Critical Theory and Baudrillard come into direct conflict. For Baudrillard one has not exhausted the sign when one has reduced (or returned) it to the conditions of its production. On the contrary, it is in the course of such reduction that the sign comes into its own, is seen to turn into another kind of sign-form, and, from the point of view of Critical Theory, or any other, becomes uncontrollable. The idea is an aesthetic, as opposed to moral, one, and central to Baudrillard's theory of the sign's final incarnation as simulacrum, its function in the world it makes for itself. That is a world which signs refer not (or rather not only) to reality but rather to one another, and in that intra-referentiality obscure or obviate the sign's alleged reference to the real. When the sign has reached the point of engaging in simulation it is no longer interested in representation, it has departed from the path set by its precedent model, to which it continues to refer but no longer in any way which allows it to be reduced to its origin in the sense that the original can be said to contain the meaning now redolent in the simulacrum. Here too one finds Baudrillard echoing Nietzsche, but more importantly this is an idea which begins with a reading of Marx in which Baudrillard chooses to locate the meaning of the sign elsewhere than in the realm of man the producer. For Marx, there is man the maker and then the man that man the maker makes. *Homo faber,* man the maker, allows man to be that being who has time to think: *homo otiosis,* man at leisure, man the producer of non-production, *i.e.,* reflexivity instead of action, the symbolic, in a word, cultural production.

The two postulates, the idea of the simulacre and the idea that the cultural sign should be read as a sign of *homo otiosis* rather than *homo faber*—as a sign not reducible to any model of material production—leads Baudrillard to a position which can only cast grave doubts on the enthusiasms of, say, Peter Bürger. In Baudrillard's terms the art which Habermas-Bürger might see as offering promise because of the kind of attention to the historical significance of artistic practice which it exhibits, is for precisely those reasons no more than an exercise in self-deception, a self-deception founded on a wholly inadequate notion of the relationship of the sign to anything called reality. Rather than challenging anything, in Baudrillard's terms such works (Haacke, Buren, the collaborative and feminist practices espoused by Bürger) do exactly the opposite. As Baudrillard himself says: "Everything is metamorphized into its inverse in order to be perpetuated in a changed form." The socially critical work adds to what it pretends to abolish and diminishes its self-proclaimed task of clarification as it does so. It can do nothing else because of its failure to grasp the sign's indifference to the real on the one hand, and its consequent dependence on a spurious idea of the relationship between the meaning of the sign and the conditions of its production on the other.

I have called Baudrillard's notion of the simulacre aesthetic and shall illustrate it through an aesthetic example. What is threatening for Critical Theory in Baudrillard is his insistence that what is said in the following example about poetic meaning is true of all images, of the culture as a whole.

In his book *Text Production,* Michel Riffaterre uses Baudelaire to demonstrate how misleading it is to attempt to locate meaning in poetry by pursuing the usual meaning of the images it manipulates; *i.e.,* by reducing the poem to the real. He takes the example of a bit of poetry by Baudelaire which is about a bat flapping clumsily around in a dungeon, and shows that one will learn nothing about the poem by considering the bat as a bat. Roman Jakobson, who sees Baudelaire reconstituting the flutter of bat's wings in the choice of palato-alveolar and sibilant consonants, is for Riffaterre obviously barking up the wrong tree. As is anyone who cares to prattle on about Baudelaire's characterization through poetic enunciation of the zigzagging flight of the bat, or for that matter anyone who points out that bats have a radar which prevents

them from bumping into things. All this is beside the point, because Baudelaire's bat is not a bat. It is an image which Baudelaire has taken over from Hugo, where it exists as an opposition to the image of a bird. Like Hugo's, Baudelaire's bat is an anti-bird. As Baudelaire internalizes and simultaneously undermines Hugo's Romanticism, so he internalizes and represents as a doubled image the bat as anti-bird, now flying in a cellar—a milieu recognizably Gothic, and also an inversion of the latter's predilection for towers and garrets, and therefore Romantic—and in that an anti-bird which has the double referent of both a bird free to fly and its antinomy, a bird encaged.

There is more of course, but this much of Riffaterre's argument will serve to show how it is that the poem performs an act which goes way beyond representation and invents a life for the word 'bat' which is quite apart from its ordinary, or *real,* meaning, while still being continuous with ordinary connotation to the extent that we are obliged to think of a bat, but then further obliged to see the bat specifically as an anti-bird. Normally we don't need to think of birds at all when we see bats. Meaning here is then a meaning generated by a use of the word bat, of such a sort that we cannot get at this newly generated meaning by asking ourselves or the poem any questions about bats. Meaning has become detached from the ordinary use-value of the word 'bat,' and cannot be reduced to it.

Baudrillard wants to say that not only poetic images, but in fact all images, work like that. This can only land him in trouble with Habermas-Bürger, because it proposes the production of meaning which is in every sense out of control, not reducible to use-value (and thus the moral project) because it cannot be seen either as a negation of use-value, or as any other form of the latter in which it is possible to say that the new meaning remains in the original, but instead has to be seen as a meaning which is independent of that which made it possible. Not only independent of it, but another thing which is seen to be more: to offer another kind of meaning, than its apparent referent. If it is more and other than that which gives rise to it, then it will never do to see it as a recoding of a narrative, the constituents of which are already known: History, for example. For Baudrillard, it is rather that the uncontrollability of the sign, calls into question the mastery of the Master Narrative. The freedom of the signifier renders the signified unstable.

Baudrillard's model is itself an historical one, in which the present condition of the sign contains its earlier selves as subsumed conditions or states, although it is not a consequence or product of them. So it is hardly a question of Baudrillard's being ahistorical. Actually, it seems to me that Baudrillard's developmental scheme is historical in a manner which might best be thought of as scientistically naturalist. The development of the sign, its transformation of itself and therefore of the sign-form, is reflected in historical periodicity but is like the formation of vision, in which infantile formations which replaced one another—passive vision giving way to looking in which the infant takes sides—are also still present in adult looking, not merely as opportunities for regression, but as subsumed possibilities necessary to the functioning of the whole. However, inasmuch as it is unable to admit to what has happened to the sign-form (or what is happening to it), Critical Theory must in Baudrillard's terms be said to be engaged in what is alas a regression and nothing more. Stuck at the level of the representational, Critical Theory, like the

Generals of 1914 and 1939, is thoroughly ready to fight the last war. Here is what Baudrillard says:

> These would be the successive phases of the image:
> —It is the reflection of a basic reality
> —It masks and perverts a basic reality
> —It masks the absence of a basic reality
> —It bears no relation to any reality whatever: it is its own pure simulacrum.

The passage is one from representation to simulation, in the course of which representation slips away and becomes something else. A new sign-form is constructed which parallels, but in that parallelism obviates, its original.

The importance of this in the present discussion resides in what it is that the final state of the sign displays. Baudrillard introduces the distinction between *homo faber* and *homo otiosis* in order to deal with display of a very basic sort, the display of prestige. The display of prestige, as he explains at first through the example of the potlatch ceremonies of the native Americans of the Pacific North-West, is a concern of (also a definition of) man at leisure. The destruction of the precious is a celebration of the possession of a surplus, of the possession therefore of power. This is a conversion of use-value into what Baudrillard calls prestation-value, the sign's value in the display of prestige. In Capitalism such prestation always survives democratization. Now that everyone has one, the television set no longer represents the ownership of that which all do not own. Instead, it tells the lie, that all have equal access to information, in fact the double lie, that such access is also access to power. This is an ideological formation where ideology is in every sense something other than "a sort of cultural surf frothing on the beachhead of the economy."

The situation leads to a further simulation, that of the sense of real power over the television, which comes from seeing that the lie is a lie, which gives rise to the image of the conscious consumer.

In addition to which there of course remains the question of the cheap or expensive television set, which itself returns one to the display not only of wealth but of taste. (pp. 21-2)

I propose that the work of art, or any kind of art practice, cannot escape functioning as a sign of prestation in some sense. The work flatters those who already know enough to be able to enjoy it because it confirms their mastery of complexity. It is in some way an object of special knowledge, to enter an art gallery is *still* an act which sets the gallery-goer apart from the others—and when this is no longer the case the very nature of the art work guarantees that no equality will be achieved, because there are still likely to be those who 'get more' out of waht they see or read. It seems to me that normally this is in effect a harmless component of the work's appreciation, even a beneficial one, insofar as it encourages seriousness on the part of the viewer. You can enjoy Don Judd without knowing much (anything?) about art, but you can enjoy it much more if you know much more and perhaps it doesn't do any harm to be aware of that. But for the political work it is a component whose effect is like that of cancer, an inescapable and destructive condition generated by the work's own terms, a web woven by the fly. To apply the ideas available in Minimalism to a putatively "increasingly complex system of analysis in which the aesthetic work would obtain a more operative, functional dimension of use-value (as opposed to the 'merely' aesthetic, disinterested structures) within the various parameters of historical determin-

ism. . . ." is to appeal to the prestige-value of two codes, but it is not quite there that the work is doomed to display nothing but the *cachet* latent in the possession of its terms (and conceivably of a relationship between them.) It is in its inescapable commitment to self-congratulation, a commitment which is for the most part involuntary, that the political work can be nothing except what it does not want to be, an élite object exhibiting, or encouraging, with the work as simulation. As simulation, the ideological affect of the work is exactly the one not intended. It absolves its audience of complicity in what it depicts, and therein lies its hopeless fate as prestation, a display of self-congratulation.

To demonstrate this I shall discuss a piece of Hans Haake's. . . . (p. 23)

The piece of Haake's which I wish to discuss is *Metromobilitan,* 1985: a schematic replica of the front of the Metropolitan Museum, three banners such as often adorn that and every other museum, one a reproduction of a banner advertising a show of Nigerian Art sponsored by Mobil and the other two banners displaying compromising quotes by the Mobil Corporation about its involvement in South African industry, behind these, black people.

In regard to this work, I propose to restate Baudrillard's successive phases of the image as follows:

> —It is a representation of the state of things (Mobil, Africa, and the culture business)
> —It obscures, through simplification, the state of things (proposing a determined relationship between Mobil etc.)
> —It conceals, through the illusion of determination, the arbitrariness of the relationship it proposes.
> —It functions as a poetic text in which its terms are sufficient to its own message. No longer reducible to its alleged context, it functions as an item of prestation.

A fuller statement of which would be: The work is about Mobil's involvement in the culture industry and Africa (South Africa and also ex-colonial Nigeria and its precolonial art.)

The work, in proposing that connection, suggests an equivalence between its referents (Mobil and Africa and the Metropolitan Museum) which is both persuasive and not true.

The work, having thus disturbed the reality of that relationship (which it never presents except as a distortion, an artificial equivalence), and concealed it beneath a thoroughly simplistic model of direct correlation as opposed to the web of uncontrollable complicity which actually characterizes the relationships between Africa and Mobil and the Metropolitan Museum, thus conceals also that as Baudrillard says there is no basic reality, no one relationship between Mobil and the Met, but rather an elaborate series of exchanges which ultimately reveal Capitalism as a predatory, asocial, force rather than a conspiratorial, social, one.

The work bears no relationship to Mobil at all, the complexity of which it couldn't address if it wanted to but is in its simplicity an interesting use of the apparatus of Pop Art and Conceptualism (two sides of the same coin). As such it also functions as an object of prestation, which replaces its alleged function as a political act, subsuming the latter into a display of prestige which symbolically distances its consumers from that which it purports to represent.

Using the gallery as a ready-made, the work involuntarily celebrates the gallery-as-ready-made's capacity to absorb any kind of content (a celebration already performed in tandem by Pop Art and Conceptualism.) This celebration is involuntary in that, in a number of obvious ways, the gallery is Capitalism. (pp. 23-4)

The political work cannot in its own terms be the occasion for a genuinely alienating symbolic enterprise of the sort offered by Baudelaire's use of the word 'bat.' That it desires to present itself as exemplary practice precludes it from doing so. Here too it demonstrates its ideological insecurity. The Haacke show we all remember with great fondness is the one which caused the Guggenheim to actually close its doors. An exquisitely Habermasian use of artistic practice, that show, in which Haacke proposed to exhibit photographs of New York slum property accompanied by the names of the properties' landlords, who were trustees of the Guggenheim, was successful precisely because it didn't take place. But what if, instead of losing their nerve, the landlord-trustees had not called off the show but had rather decided to call the artist's bluff? A show in which, as one stood on the Guggenheim's sloping floor and contemplated the images of decay and wickedness presented by pictures of slums and the names of their owners, the immense and predatory arrogance of power demonstrated by the latter's willingness to let the show go on could only have been in some sense affirmed even as it stood denounced.

Needless to say it made no difference, as far as I know, to the slum dwellers of New York whether the show went on or not, but that is of course not the point. It is to the point, though, that, as Haacke at the Guggenheim demonstrates, the political work must claim to begin and end in use-value of some sort, either or both as an irritant to the ruling class or as an agent of self-instruction (preferably both), and to do that it must stop thought: stop it from going astray, stop it from turning into something else. In practice, the extent to which the political work fails to arrest its own development is the degree to which it cannot remain true to its task. (p. 24)

It is pretty safe to assume that virtually no one who saw *Metromobilitan* was in favor of Apartheid, or of American or any other oil companies supporting it. As display . . . it gives us pictures of what we ourselves would not do. As irritant, it has essentially no one to irritate—perhaps a few collectors who recall having a few shares here and there. As instruction it works only if one has internalized a certain model of determination. If not, it might read a bit differently. If Capitalism is a truly asocial force, as Baudrillard proposes it to be, then it can intervene anywhere, at will rather than of necessity. One is obliged to once again remember South Africa's neighbor Angola, where Gulf Oil's refineries—on which Angola's people depend—are guarded by Cuban and East German troops against Jonas Savimbi's guerillas, who are funded by the C.I.A. South Africa needs Capitalism and so does Nigeria, one might say, but Capitalism only needs them if it pays it to need them. It is only arbitrarily that one may declare either the masses whom Haacke counterpoises to the work's audience, or the Yuppie socialists who make up that audience, to have escaped absorption by that which the gallery represents. Even as a representation, in other words, the work cannot guide the instruction it wants to perform. As simulation, it is at once uncontrollable and a failure in its own terms.

Which is to say that having made no sustainable argument about the necessity of the historical relationship between Mobil, the Metropolitan, and/or South Africa *Metromobilitan* also cannot generate a fully satisfactory articulation of its own poetics, because these become curiously confused as a result of the simplicity of the piece. For example, the theme given by the banners is that Mobil publicizes its involvement in Nigeria while keeping its operations in South Africa relatively quiet. Openness as a way of concealing something else, then, a theme echoed in the rest of the work. But the force of the Nigerian banner is surely of a different, more complex, order than that of those on either side of it. The Nigerian banner advertises a show of Nigerian art. Mobil makes it possible for the Metropolitan to present to New York the artifacts of the past of that present-day oil-producing nation which is Nigeria.

Mobil seeks to appropriate Nigeria's past. But seen as such this banner is, once again, an image of arbitrariness rather than determination. Mobil can appropriate anything, it doesn't have to be involved anywhere. When, which is probably soon, it can make more money displaying non-involvement in South Africa than it can from being circumspect about its involvement there, it will doubtless do so. As a thoroughly asocial force it will even, on occasion, as with Nixon recognizing the Chinese People's Republic, do what's right. The Nigerian banner is of an order of ambiguity such as to call into question what is surely meant to be *Metromobilitan*'s presiding sentiment: that the situation in South Africa is somehow determined by Capitalism.

What is actually called into question, then, is precisely what the work doesn't want to question at all, the supposed dependence of Capitalism on Apartheid—rather than the mere dependence of Apartheid on Capitalism, which is not in doubt—and therefore on keeping its involvement in South Africa secret. The poetics of the piece give us instead a Capitalism which, like a bird or if you like a bat, perches where it pleases. And is free to leave when its feet get hot or it starts to rain. A Capitalism which, like the gallery, can absorb anything: the political, the non-political, the racist republic, the republic of self-determination. A Capitalism, perhaps, whose secrets are more a matter of good taste than of urgent necessity. Out of control, the Haacke as simulacre provides a simulation in which Capitalism is so pervasive as to be continuous with diction itself. Seen as exemplary production, *Metromobilitan* is a collage which seeks to contrast disparities which are in effect unintentionally overwhelmed by that which is meant to keep them apart. As exemplary production, the work seeks to subsume all to the moral. What it instead exemplifies is a capacity, like Capitalism's, to render dissimilarities similar. Unlike Capitalism, it does not obviously benefit from the loss of meaning which results.

On the other hand, when considered as prestation *Metromobilitan* displays a doubly-privileged good taste. It is morally good to be against Apartheid and intellectually or spiritually good to be at one with the practices of contemporary art. It is a final good to reconcile the one with the other in a manner which allows for the appearance of, or belief in, mutual clarification. Thus may one come to see *Metromobilitan* as a celebration of the ability (predestined, and infinitely *post*-ordained) of the historical narrative, the ultimate locus of the truth, to subsume all significance and give it meaning. It is in this sense that one sees in Haake's work the absolute confirmation of what such art must consciously at all costs seek to avoid. The reduction of the notion of opposition to that of the complement. As a work which cannot re-examine (afford to destabilize) its dependence on an agreed-upon moral base, *Metromobilitan* complements the entirely amoral enterprise (which will cheerfully destabilize anything) to which it seeks to be opposed, and in that confirms the latter in every respect. For Baudrillard, complementarity is a condition of the age of the simulacre. Two World Trade Center towers, not one against all, or one difference among others, as with the Chrysler building or the Empire State, but instead a sign of self-cancelling equivalence, in which as he says the final triumph of monopoly is seen in its becoming binary: the original and its replication in the same thing, the equivalence of complements. As he also says, in the age of the simulacre it is the complementariness of instituted power which unites precisely mirrored adversaries, the U.S. and the S.U., in their mutual concern to maintain an equilibrium in which each superpower has its own role as complement of the other. Baudrillard's example is of the Vietcong, whom he says both the Russians and the Americans insisted should be brought under the control of the regular North Vietnamese forces before the superpowers could permit the war to end.

Such a dependence as *Metromobilitan*'s on a secret recognition of its role as complement has been a characteristic of Avant-Garde practice as a display of prestige for a long time. In our own period this has required that the consumer of advanced art be an accomplice to a quite highly developed hypocrisy at every level of her or his engagement with the work. The performance artist who denounces the gallery system, and all that it produces or accommodates, as corrupt, and in that denunciation celebrates her freedom from it, has a freedom guaranteed by her tenure as a professor which we are asked not to take into account. We are similarly familiar with the "independent" (*i.e.,* grant-supported) film whose very claim to seriousness is predicated on the absence in the film of the facilities provided by commercial cinema. One might say that moral hypocrisy has been a prerequisite of the enjoyment of the counter-culture at least since Brecht and with a renewed vengeance since the great liberation of the nineteen sixties. What Baudrillard allows us to see is that the language of Critical Theory itself, once subsumed into that of the art world, is no more than another tool in the hands of those privileged élites from whose hands Habermas for one would like knowledge-power to be wrested. Worse, the hypocrisy is not willed. It is the result of sincerity. (pp. 24-5)

Jeremy Gilbert-Rolfe, "The Politics of Art," in Arts Magazine, *Vol. 61, No. 1, September, 1986, pp. 21-7.*

MEAGHAN MORRIS

'Everything disappears faster and faster in the rear-vision mirror of memory . . . '

In Baudrillard's *Amérique,* a driver's experience of the acceleration and disappearance of images becomes something like an allegory of Life. At least, of Life in modern America as observed by Jean Baudrillard. But the same comment might just as well serve as an allegory of the experience of reading Baudrillard's books—faster and faster to get through, harder and harder to retain. A few hours after closing *Amérique,* little remains beyond a few blurred images of freeways and deserts and telescreens flickering in empty rooms, an insistent

echo from the rhythms of his prose, and a nagging sense of malaise.

An effect like this might be just what the author was seeking. After producing over a dozen hefty books and a number of furious pamphlets in some 20 years as the professional *enfant terrible* of French sociology, Baudrillard has began to work equally hard at playing the Disappearing Theorist. He has progressively and deliberately abandoned the protocols of systematic research, scrupulous argument, thesis formulation, 'critique'—in favour of a style of personal *jotting* (and jaunting) about the world. For some, the result represents the emergence of a writer and thinker of great originality, while for others it epitomises the defeat of analysis by burble in the fashion-field of postmodernism.

Either way, Baudrillard's trajectory is now taking him straight toward the standard romantic genres of adventure and discovery—travel writing, the *carnet de voyage* (*Amérique, L'autre par lui-même*) and, more recently, the Writer's Notebook (***Cool Memories***). With a gesture appropriate to any writer heading in that direction, all three books announce Baudrillard's renunciation of the Academy. Henceforth, he'll be a travelling man, a Ricky Nelson of theory—gazing out as he goes at the 'desert of the real', reading the world, not the library.

Baudrillard makes a distinction between '*le travelling*', the modern practice of pure circulation, driving for driving's sake, and '*le voyage*', the old-fashioned habit of seeking a destination, and arriving. *Amérique* is about travelling. *L'autre par lui-même*—Baudrillard's formal defence of his academic achievements—is presented as an 'imaginary voyage'. The only way to 'simulate' arriving at the end of a coherent project is, says Baudrillard, to discover his own works as though they were documents of some lost civilization which he tries to reconstruct.

However, anyone who looks to this slim volume for a summation of Baudrillard's *oeuvre* will be sadly disappointed. In fact, most of it reads more like a word-processed assemblage of offcuts, out-takes and second-hand sentences from ***Les stratégies fatales*** (1983) and ***De la séduction*** (1979). There are brief, static rundowns on the buzzwords of the late Baudrillardian thematics—ecstasy, communication, obscenity, metastastis, indifference, seduction. Only in the last two chapters is there any sense of a voyage, any hint that Baudrillard's project might have changed in the past 20 years. All trace of that phase of his work still of most interest to radical social theory today—the critiques of Marxism and semiotics in ***For A Critique of the Political Economy of the Sign*** (1972) and ***The Mirror of Production*** (1973)—has been rigorously removed.

It's often said that Baudrillard's work can be divided into two distinct phases. The first was a systematic study of the commodity form in so-called consumer society, followed by an abrasively argued attack on the labour theory of value and on the work-ethic enshrined in Marxist concepts of 'production'. (pp. 28-9)

A different note begins to emerge with *L'exchange symbolique et la mort* (1976). Notions of consumption give way to models of 'simulation'. Contemporary reality is now seen to be generated in the image of an Image, as more real than real (hyperreal, like retouched corpses in funeral 'homes'). . . . The value of *reversibility* begins to replace that of *opposition* to theorise a method of action. It comes in two different techniques: simulation (the parodic aggravation of an existing state of affairs, the ecstasy of making things worse) and seduction (the provocative practice of fatal allure, the art of 'survival make-up'). Both are used by Baudrillard as techniques of writing.

This kind of schematic division easily creates shorthand myths of a Good and Bad Baudrillard—the radical critic of neo-capitalism on the one hand, the post-political fashion figure on the other. It also ignores a number of continuities in his work.

L'autre par lui-même discusses one of these, the interest in a theory of Objects (rather than 'the subject'). *Le système des objets* (1968) was in many ways the book that some still wish that Roland Barthes had written instead of *Mythologies*. Heavily influenced by Barthes, it combined a study of the mythic 'speech' of objects with a social theory of technology *and* of consumer practice. By the time of *Les stratégies fatales* (1983), Baudrillard was expounding an ironic myth of something like what my mother used to call the Object Conspiracy—objects are actively hostile to humanity, and lose themselves on purpose. For Baudrillard, the flight of the object from the subject's search for meaning offers exemplary hope—in a warped sort of way—for escape and survival in the world of simulation.

Two other points of convergence between Baudrillard's early and late work might be described as temperamental, rather than theoretical. One is a profound suspicion of the effectiveness of 'critique'. In his second book, *La société de consommation* (1970), he was already arguing that the 'morose and moralising' discourse of critical opposition was in fact a necessary component of consumer mythology. His own move to methods of simulation and parody is probably a logical extension of, rather than a break with, his early radicalism. The other point is a fascinated ambivalence for much of the contemporary culture that he claims to describe. Parts of *Les stratégies fatales* on the wet, steaming, pornographic, promiscuous obscenity of the world of videos, racial mixity and sexual liberation should count as some of the most ghastly pages of cultural criticism produced since Adorno's shell-shocked comments on American popular culture.

One of the novelties of *Amérique* is that this rhetorical dislike of the excessiveness of moist, messy things is absorbed by a myth of America, and of modernity, as a 'desert'—natural, social, cultural. Baudrillard's is a *dry* America—a collage of images of harsh light, infinite distance, endless horizontal circulation, political indifference and, of course, simulation. The chapter on New York is the most perfunctory in the book, with routine notes on its verticality and centrifugal force, and stray comments of the order of 'he who eats alone is dead'. The real energy of *Amérique* is elsewhere, in the 'expurgated' and 'exalting' vision that the West allows of 'the desertification of signs and men'.

'Desertification' really means the disappearance of European values. For, in a clever twist, *Amérique* is written by a fictional Parisian, an inhabitant of the capital of the 19th century, abroad in America's 'realised utopia'. Baudrillard presents himself as a new De Tocqueville, and his *Amérique* is fundamentally a book about France. Its explicit central question is 'How can one be European?'

His stance as fuddy-duddy Frenchman allows Baudrillard to recycle some astounding museum-piece arguments about whether America is 'uncultured', 'vulgar', 'stupid'—voicing,

for example, ancient anxieties about television destroying conversation and family relations. It's another exercise in simulation ('in a naive country, you have to be naive'), and sometimes it still produces those luminously cold descriptions of oddness in everyday life that can make even the worst of Baudrillard's writing so entertaining—like his pages on the 'toothpaste effect' of smile-politics under Reagan, and on yuppy culture as an integrated freeway circuit (POOR PEOPLE MUST EXIT). . . .

The method of argument is by Catch-22. Thus, Old Europe is defined as *the* culture of History, Ideology, Politics—the 'scene' of reality and difference. Hyperreal, ob-scene, thoroughly modern America is, by definition, post-historical, liberated, utopian, and indifferent after the orgy of desire in the 1970s. Consequently, any signs of historical thinking, political opposition, or critical spirit in America today can simply be treated as throwbacks—an embarrassing 'aping' of European ways by insecure American intellectuals. There's no way out of that one, and it's easy to see why Baudrillard's itinerary depends on an assiduous avoidance of conversation with flesh and blood Americans on—or off—the freeway.

The trouble with this is not that a sense of grim acquiescence in the status quo is the logical effect of the method. Baudrillard does try to see new passions and new modes of being emerging in the desert. He also argues that the greatest threat to America today is the apparent collapse of the ideologies of contestation—the 'antibodies' of democracy—that once sustained its moral power. . . .

The really awful, depressing feature of *Amérique* is the intellectual complacency that requires this flattering yet mortifying image of the fabulous American Other. There's a touch of self-loathing to it, though most of the loathing is directed towards Baudrillard's intellectual Others in France. But, above all, *Amérique*'s anti-academic discovery of the weird post-political wasteland depends precisely upon a comfortable academic insulation.

Baudrillard describes certain American campuses as 'foetal' security spaces—nice people, nice trees, nice radicalisms all growing together in isolation from the rest of society. It's a biting image, with a certain sting of truth. Yet Baudrillard's car on the freeway has its own foetal effect and, as he rolls along watching the landscape fleeing from his rear-vision mirror, he raves about the spectacle with the monomania of the lonesome hero who hears no other voice but his own.

But this travelling man is no Mad Max. There's no sense in Baudrillard's glass bubble that anything nasty might happen, or impinge, if it does, on him. His America is 'desert-ed' not only of people, but of incidents—no accidents on the freeway, no dramas in the motel, no strangers in the car. Disasters happen distantly, as data or as television: so many symptomatic images of the curious fate of other people. . . .

[Baudrillard's] adventuring intellectual is always watching the news, never caught in the war. His car, alas, remains an armchair. (p. 29)

> *Meaghan Morris, "Asleep at the Wheel?" in* New Statesman, *Vol. 113, No. 2935, June 26, 1987, pp. 28-9.*

JANE GALLOP

A good number of us have, in recent years, been swept away

by something both charming and dangerous which, for lack of an honest name, I will call French Theory. One of the peculiar things about this particular intersection of Seduction and Theory is that, according to local mores, seduction can function as a positive term. . . . The possibility of valorizing seduction occurs either through some sort of equation between seduction and femininity, or at least through casting seduction as a threat to the uprightness of phallogocentrism.

At this point in time, I would like to consider a book entitled *De la séduction* (Of Seduction), published in 1979 and written by Jean Baudrillard. Baudrillard is, by discipline, a sociologist and, by stance, a very provocative thinker. . . . His work is quite interesting, if totally outrageous to a liberal humanist sensibility. I introduce him here, however, not to give you yet another French theorist whose works you must tackle, but because he is the French theorist who has written a book called *Of Seduction,* because I want to talk about seduction as we find it in French theory.

The form of the title—*De la séduction,* which I translate as "Of Seduction"—is reminiscent of one of the best-known monuments of contemporary French theory—Jacques Derrida's *De la grammatologie,* which Gayatri Spivak translated as "Of Grammatology." Derrida's book makes the point that, although writing appears to be a secondary form, mediating speech, there is actually a kind of writing or difference primary within speech. The secondary form that would appear to adulterate the original is exposed by Derrida as actually more fundamental than, as constitutive of, the so-called "original." *De la séduction* makes a similar sort of point. Although we think of seduction as a secondary adulteration of truth, production, or sexuality, Baudrillard contends that seduction is a primary, constitutive form.

"We were led to believe that everything was production. . . . Seduction is only an immoral, frivolous, superficial . . . process, of the order of signs and appearances. . . . And what if everything, contrary to appearances . . . if everything marched to seduction?" Not only does Baudrillard, like Derrida, promote a secondary something to the rank of primary, but there seems to be a kinship between the two causes championed. According to Baudrillard, "seduction is superficial, of the order of signs and appearances." Writing is precisely of the order of signs and appearances, the surface which mediates pure spirit or thought or logos. And just as there is a certain paradoxical logic to thinking of writing as anterior to speech, to Derrida's use of the term writing to designate something ordinary, so "seduction" must always connote a leading away (*se-ducere*) from something else which would be logically anterior. Both French theorists choose to promote terms that must necessarily connote something secondary and adulterated.

In the quotation I just read you from Baudrillard, he is caught up in just such contradictory logic. On the one hand he says that "seduction is of the order of appearances," on the other hand he asks "and what if everything, contrary to appearances, marched to seduction?" In promoting seduction, throughout the book, he frequently valorizes the realm of appearances. Yet here he asserts that there might be a hidden order "contrary to appearances," and that seduction might be that hidden order. In fact, right after he writes "contrary to appearances," he adds a parenthetical correction, cognizant of the contradiction. The actual sentence with its parenthetical insertion reads: "And what if everything, con-

trary to appearances—in fact according to the secret rule of appearances—if everything marched to seduction?"

What does it mean for something to be both "contrary to appearances" and at the same time "according to appearances"? What would be a "secret rule of appearances" if not something precisely hidden, some aspect of appearance which does not appear? Similar contradictions are constantly at work in *De la séduction.* For example, seduction is supposed to, everywhere and at all times, undermine truth, and yet Baudrillard is announcing the truth (he even uses the word) that everything is seduction. And then, of course, there is the enormous problem that—although he announces the superiority of seduction over truth and distinctions and categories—the book operates by assertions, by setting up categories and distinctions. In other words, the writing itself is far from seductive.

Now these sorts of contradictions are by now familiar to those of us who have strayed down the path of French theory, where the rule is the breakdown of metalanguage, the impossibility of theorizing about something without the theory itself being nastily entangled in the very problematic on which it would like to pronounce. Every theory, however masterful it would be, has always already been seduced, including and especially the theory of seduction. (pp. 111-13)

Nonetheless, Baudrillard's contradictions seem less subtle than those of other practitioners of such theory, since he remains within a classical theoretical rhetoric of assertion, category, logic. If Baudrillard's case is interesting to me, it is, first of all, because of the blatant enormity of the contradictions which are better hidden by the stylistic charms of a Derrida or a Lacan. And second of all (this second reason being for me the primary one—my hidden agenda, in fact), because the contradictions seem linked to a rather rabid attack Baudrillard makes on feminism. Many of us have seriously wondered about the effect of French theory on feminism's health. Baudrillard is, to my knowledge, the male French theorist who most explicitly and most frontally adopts an adversarial relation to feminism.

I would like to quote you a passage from the first chapter of *De la séduction* where the theoretical contradiction occurs within Baudrillard's pronouncement of the proper course for women:

> Now, woman is only appearance. And it's the feminine as appearance that defeats the profundity of the masculine. Women instead of rising up against this "insulting" formula would do well to let themselves be seduced by this truth, because here is the secret of their power which they are in the process of losing by setting up the profundity of the feminine against that of the masculine.

When he writes "insulting formula," he puts the word "insulting" (*injurieuse*) in quotation marks. He does not consider it an insult to say that woman is only appearance. Baudrillard is writing against the history of writing against appearances. He is for appearances, and against profundity, so that when he says that "woman is only appearance" it should be taken as a compliment.

Nonetheless, when I read this passage, as a woman, I feel insulted. Baudrillard would have it that my feeling of offense is a great error which stems from my inscription within the sort of masculinistic essentialist thinking which condemns appearances as misleading mediations of essences, realities, and truths.

Yet, in considering the passage carefully, I decide that it is not what he says about "woman" that offends me so much as what he says about "women": "Women would do well," he advises, "to let themselves be seduced by this truth." It is the phrase "would do well" (*feraient bien de*) that irks me. Although he puts "insulting" in quotation marks, he uses the word "truth" (*vérité*) straight. He knows the truth—the profound or hidden truth, I might add—about women, and women "would do well to let themselves be seduced" by the truth he utters. He speaks not from the masculine or masculinist position (which he identifies as against appearances and for profundities) but from a position that knows the truth of the feminine and the masculine and can thus, from this privileged position beyond sexual difference, advise women how best to combat masculine power. It is his assumption of this position of superiority, of speaking the truth—more than any content of "truth" that he may utter—which offends me. Women, he warns, are in danger of losing their power, but if they would only let themselves be seduced by what he says . . . A line if ever I heard one. (pp. 113-14)

As opposed to truth, which is necessarily irreversible (the opposite of the truth cannot be true), seduction, as Baudrillard understands it, is the very principle of reversibility. Hence the very best "technique" for seduction turns out to be that which can never be simply a technique at all. As Baudrillard puts it: "To be seduced is yet again the best way to seduce. . . . No one, if he is not seduced, will seduce others." Truth cannot seduce; only seduction seduces. Baudrillard cannot seduce feminism with his truth, because he protects his truth from being seduced by feminism.

Throughout the book he persists in seeing feminism as stupid, wrong, mistaken. Only at one point does he even come close to imagining a reversal of that judgment. This in a book where he reverses almost every judgment, where he is championing seduction as a generalized principle of reversibility. At one point he writes: "Even the most anti-seductive figures can turn back into figures of seduction," and he immediately adds the following parenthesis: "(it has been said of feminist discourse that it rediscovers, beyond its total nonseduction, a sort of homosexual seduction)."

He is announcing the reversibility of seduction itself (the opposite of seduction can seduce). This is, I contend, the central moment of the book, the moment when seduction itself must be seduced so that reversibility rather than a new truth will reign. And at the very moment when seduction as truth would be seduced, feminism appears. If antiseduction can seduce, than surely even feminism could be seductive. Yet there is one, and to my knowledge only one, reversal he cannot allow himself. The reversal of the negative judgment of feminism is not a complete 180 degrees. "It has been said . . . ": Baudrillard cannot assert feminism's seduction but only reports something to which he does not add his assent. And what he reports is only "a sort of seduction." And besides, it is homosexual; it is not for him. Baudrillard cannot imagine—except through the defenses of a triple mediation—finding feminism seductive. Feminism can only be an adversary, forcing him away from seduction's reversibility into the strategy of irreversible truth, the very position he has designated as weaker, stupider, inferior. (pp. 114-15)

Jane Gallop, "French Theory and the Seduction of

Feminism," in Men in Feminism, *edited by Alice Jardine and Paul Smith, Methuen, 1987, pp. 111-15.*

SUZI GABLIK

We are experiencing in our culture a sudden radical break with the will-to-meaning which until now has always been understood as a fundamental drive of human life. "I have seen many people die," wrote Albert Camus, "because life for them was not worth living. From this I conclude that the question of life's meaning *is* the most urgent question of all." If it is true that the creation of meaning is vital to life itself, then how are we supposed to respond to the undermining of the very legitimacy of meaning itself, implicit in the work of the French deconstructionist philosophers? The loss of meaning I am talking about involves two quite different levels, only one of which concerns the way that signs may be deconstructed to destabilize the symbolic order. I am referring also to the greater loss of a basic ground of meaning: that belief in a fundamental psycho-spiritual truth that transcends institutional assumptions and socio-historical circumstance.

Deconstructionists claim as obsolete any necessary union of a signifier and a signified; this emancipation of the sign (or image) releases it from any "archaic" obligation it might have had to embody a single, immutable meaning. Mobile or "floating" signifiers maintain no fixed relationships—they can break with any given context and engender an infinity of new contexts—which is exactly what we experience in the paintings of David Salle. In the layered and slippery space of postmodernism, images slide past one another, dissociated and decontextualized, failing to link up into a coherent sequence. When the Surrealists juxtaposed disjunctive and decontextualized images, they wanted to shatter the parameters of the rational, everyday world, and to spark off new and unexpected poetic meanings. Salle does not seem to me to be doing this, however, since his images function more like Warhol's—neutral in their isolation of cultural logos that "perform" without expressive or manipulative intent. The nonreciprocal interactions among the images in Salle's paintings offer the illusion that something is taking place, but it's not clear what that might be. "Strictly speaking," to quote Jean Baudrillard, "nothing remains but a sense of dizziness, with which you can't do anything."

Because the unifying presence of a transcendental order no longer exists in our culture, the implication is that works of art can no longer offer a unifying vision of the world either. So it is not just the loss of any referent or signifier that is at stake; there is also the loss of wholeness and coherence of vision, the bonding power which holds everything together. One thing you can't address through deconstruction is a spiritual need; it is the established dogma of leading postmodernist theorists that there is no sacred order now, if ever there were any, to which anyone can belong. . . .

In the paradigm shift away from the utopian visions of the avant-garde, many postmodern artists have simply given up idealizing. Since strategies of protest are no longer seen to be effective, only a rearguard action is possible, according to Peter Halley, "of guerrilla ideas . . . eccentric ideas that seem innocuous . . . doubtful ideas that are not invested in their own truth and are thus not damaged when they are manipulated, or nihilist ideas that are dismissed for being too depressing."

Since many artists today have come to believe that there is no release from the oppressive socio-economic forces of contemporary life, having faith in the transcendent power of art is, for them, self-deluding. In the absence of any possibility of fulfilling heroic cultural ideals, it is felt that the artist or intellectual facing the system today has no choice but to cover up his tracks and slip into elusiveness. What is revolutionary, in the opinion of Lyotard, is to hope for nothing. In his view, the very notion of hope (in the sense of hoping for change) is one more pointless variation on a theme which has been heard too often, as he states in *Driftworks.* Thus to criticize the system is to play right into its hands—to engage in a parody of rebellion. Drift is the only form of subversion that doesn't reinforce the status quo—that is to say, the withdrawal of cathexis, letting the energy drain away. . . .

Rather than protesting, or trying to resuscitate the betrayed ideals of avant-garde art, the postmodern artist will often disguise his or her intentions in a way that makes it impossible to know what position is being taken. So we have art that looks just like the thing which it supposedly challenges: with Simon Linke's paintings of commercial gallery advertisements copied straight from the pages of *Artforum,* we cannot really know if this is radical criticism or inspired clowning. Linke doesn't attempt to resolve the contradictions of the marketplace; his art simply embodies them in its innermost structure. Declaring its pointlessness openly, his art baits us with its indifference; the artist openly adopts the posture of a charlatan, a sort of trickster who is not going to get us out of the mess we're in, but who will engage in the only legitimate cultural practice possible for our time, which is, in the words of Baudrillard, "the chance, the labyrinthine, manipulatory play of signs without meaning."

For Baudrillard, the second great revolution of the 20th century, the revolution of postmodernity, is the immense process of the deconstruction of meaning as it is traditionally understood—which is equal to the earlier deconstruction of appearances. The paintings of David Salle are certainly the setting around which this particular way of thinking, this esthetic style and mood, are expressed. Salle's pictures deal with spectacle, and to interpret them is to make a false move; we are warned by Baudrillard that it is dangerous to unmask images in general, since they dissimulate the fact that there is nothing behind them. (p. 27)

The liquidation of all coherent referentiality is based upon the principle of equivalence, whereby everything is reduced to the same thing and is de-realized into what Baudrillard describes as an "event without consequences—like [Robert] Musil's man without qualities." Salle's ironic detachment seems to suggest that his choice of images implies no particular commitment or consequences, close in a way to Roland Barthes's notion that meaning is not communication (information) or signification (symbolism), but is lived experience, always in play, always different. Unbalancing the message is the only way of avoiding "the tyranny of correct meaning." (Barthes goes so far as to claim that language is quite simply fascist—"for fascism is not the prohibition of saying things, it is the *obligation* to say them.")

If the creation of meaning implies that one is carrying out intentions, making choices and influencing others, to apply these standards to work that declares its own lack of engagement and that has willfully withdrawn from signification becomes highly problematical. As the previous distinctions of original/copy, authentic/inauthentic become blurred, this in-

determinacy brings with it an impossibility of choice. We are all implicated in this unfolding dilemma of debilitating choices, made numb with endless variety, and the whole issue of having to make choices, of even knowing what one wants, is really a bore. According to Baudrillard, choice is a burden that, deep down inside, no one wants any part of. To illustrate this hermetic wisdom, he recounts a story about Beau Brummel, who, when traveling in a region of Scotland that has many lakes, each more beautiful than the other, turned to his manservant and asked, "Which do I prefer?" "That people are supposed to know, themselves, what they want—I think we have pressed beyond that point," Baudrillard adds, "beyond truth, beyond reality." How can one not fall for the deranged wit of this man, for whom all secrets are contained in the art of giving in, of not resisting?

By not resisting, we need no longer be trapped in an obsolete avant-gardism tied to out-of-date projects of critical engagement. With the infiltrator or double-agent situation, we are never sure whether the artist is the accomplice or the opponent of consumer culture, which promises that it is possible to have everything we want and need as long as we accept and conform to the system. Rather, the artist merely intensifies an already unsatisfactory situation by pushing things a little further. We are faced with a curious syndrome, where meaning has become so detached from itself that its central collapse is what defines much of the art of our time—to the point where the "will" to meaning often courts meaninglessness and even finds satisfaction in it.

Nowhere, for instance, are the "beautiful effects of disappearance" better illustrated than in the paintings of Allan McCollum, which simultaneously dramatize and thwart our desire to look at pictures. On close scrutiny, McCollum's paintings reveal themselves as simulacra—pseudo-artifacts in which picture, mat and frame are all one seamless object, molded in plaster—but there is nothing to see. In place of any communicating image there is a dark, thick substance, like pitch—a pure screen of black, whose emptiness would seem to express the posthumous condition of culture and art. (pp. 27, 29)

"If only art could accomplish the magic act of its own disappearance!" states Baudrillard. "But it continues to make believe it is disappearing when it is already gone."

Since in an age of simulacra nothing separates true from false, how can we assess the reaction of the power structure to a perfect simulation? By feigning a violation, suggests Baudrillard, and putting it to the test. "Go and simulate a theft in a large department store," he has written. "Or organize a fake hold-up. . . . How do you convince the security guards that it is a simulated theft?" You won't succeed, because the web of artificial signs will be inextricably mixed up with real elements (a police officer will really shoot on sight, or a customer will faint from fear). Likewise, how do you convince an art dealer that McCollum's pictures are not "real" works of art, but simulations? You won't succeed, because collectors will buy them, dealers will show them and critics will write about them; even simulations cannot escape the system's ability to integrate everything. And so it is that art survives its own disappearance: somewhere the real scene has been lost, but everything continues just the same.

How does one deal with cultural inauthenticity if one's own means and materials are indistinguishable from those of the cultural reality one is attempting to expose? "Aware that our culture is excessively artificial, and even meaningless, we choose to live in it. We will at times use irony, mimicry, and even mockery, in order to identify the position we are in," Haim Steinbach stated recently, in a symposium on "Avant-Garde Art in the '80s." . . .

Since commodity fetishism is the distinguishing mark of our culture, the artist's consciousness has been fatally enriched with this knowledge. "It is one thing to speak about this situation, it's quite another matter to recognize how we participate emotionally in this ecstasy, how we should monitor it," Steinbach also stated at the same symposium. "We live in a culture of pornography, we are engulfed by it, contained in it. We are not standing by the riverbank watching this excess of shit flow by, rather we are flowing with it, in it." . . . Steinbach dissolves the difference between our desire for commodities and our desire for art. In the distortions of the market, where culture is itself disseminated as a product, these distinctions, rather than being polarized, now cancel each other out. . . .

Thus it is that postmodern parody does not claim to speak from a position outside the parodied. For these artists, their works function in total complicity with the context they are confronting and become indistinguishable from it. Duplicity is the virulent, if disenchanted, strategy the new artists have adopted to replace the old one of antagonism and critical engagement. All objects must be consecrated to the ideology of consumerism and, under its false dynamic, enjoy the same prestigious status.

"It is a thoroughly vulgar metaphysic," states Baudrillard. "And contemporary psychology, sociology and economic science are all complicit in the fiasco. So the time has come to deconstruct all the assumptive notions involved—object, need, aspiration, consumption itself . . .," which is what this art tries to do. The work of these artists becomes the cheerful orchestration of collapse, the cracked mirror of a culture where products must continually replicate other products, where artists become the author of someone else's work, and everything competes within the same marketing system of seductive senselessness. "Don't buy us with apologies," goes the slogan on one of Barbara Kruger's photomontages. "I shop therefore I am," states another. "Buy me," commands another, "It will change your life." Kruger sends back to the system its own dubious logic intensified and brilliantly exposed. Irony now forms a reality principle unto itself, no longer dynamic but the inert substance of the matter, what Charles Newman refers to in *The Post-Modern Aura* as the "rhetoric of terminality": the deep suspicion, which postmodernism harbors, that we have only unpleasant choices—that we may already have seen the best civilization has to offer.

Is there, then, no way out of the alliance between capitalism and culture? Is deconstruction the only answer—cultivating paradox and leaping, as it were, over one's own shadow? "I think an understanding of the limits is less paralyzing than going off on some silly campaign based on false assumptions," says Peter Halley in *Artscribe*. "To me, that would be really paralyzing." Implosive strategies demand going to extremes—or doing nothing—until the system devours its own empty forms, absorbs its own meaning, creates a void and disappears. And so, this policy of going nowhere, of not occupying a position, becoming nothing, having no positive horizons, no goals, no constructive alternatives—"right away people ask, 'What can you do with that?' " writes Baudril-

lard. But, apparently, that is just the point: there is nothing to be had from it. The only thing you can do is to let it run, all the way to the end. (p. 29)

Suzi Gablik, "Dancing with Baudrillard," in Art in America, *Vol. 76, No. 6, June, 1988, pp. 27, 29.*

SIMON FRITH

Baudrillard, more than any other philosophy star, is defined by the commodity system he himself describes, his *aperçus* circulating as analytic signs rather than meeting analytic needs, an important but elusive figure, read for the manner rather than the substance of his thought but admirable as the first person to articulate theoretically the gut feeling that mass culture is not a subject for despair (or celebration) but simply describes the world in which we live. Politics (and this is a point that has had particular resonance for radical artists) is no longer a matter of utopianism or negation, but has now to be restricted to a fatal *irony*. . . .

In an intelligent mix of book extracts and articles, previously translated and untranslated work, [Mark Poster, the editor of *Jean Baudrillard: Selected Writings,*] offers a history of Baudrillard's thought and brings to light two aspects of it which help explain his impact, particularly in the USA. First, it is fascinating to realise how much of Baudrillard's understanding of consumer society comes not from European theory but from American social science; second, it becomes clear that Baudrillard's own mode of thought is a ruthless rationalism, the pursuit of every consequence of his starting premise that classic Marxist thought can't make sense of consumption. If his later work is unconvincing, it is not because he is illogical but because (unlike Roland Barthes) he is rather unimaginative.

In his first writings—*System of Objects,* 1968 and *Consumer Society,* 1970—Baudrillard's understanding of post-war capitalism is clearly taken from late 1950s American left liberals like J. K. Galbraith. He shares their penchant for pseudo-empiricism; he reads adman's copy as documentary evidence; his deliberate exaggeration of consumer trends is reminiscent of sf writers like Frederik Pohl and Cyril Kornbluth. But if at times this makes one want to shout out the British Marxist response to the *embourgeoisement* thesis—"a washing machine is a washing machine is a washing machine"—there's also no doubt that Baudrillard is a much more determined thinker than the socio-psycho babblers from whom he takes his lead.

What begins as a methodological point—"a washing machine *serves* as equipment and *plays* as an element of conformity, or of prestige, etc. It is the field of play that is specifically the field of consumption."—thus becomes Baudrillard's intellectual project: to understand this field of play both in its own terms and according to its human consequences. If consumption is not just the satisfaction of needs, not just a material practice, if it involves the manipulation of the object-as-sign and is thus a discourse, then what is necessary to analyse it is a critique of materialism and a theory of signs.

Baudrillard provides both in his most important book, 1972's *Towards a Critique of a Political Economy of Signs.* This remains necessary reading, if only for its assault on the concept of real (versus false) needs and the subsequent application of the critique to the concept of use value. Baudrillard argues convincingly that human needs are not biological or anthropological givens but define the relationship between person and object set up by the commodity system itself. The point is not simply that each market object produces its own subject (as Marx argued), but that the capitalist system of objects produces a *system* of subjects. That system (stoked by desire disguised as need) can only be understood in terms of signification. (p. 23)

Marx got things the wrong way round when he suggested that human need invests goods with the use value on which the successful realisation of exchange value depends. Rather, commodity production makes necessary social exchanges which work by defining us as "needing" subjects. Use value is thus the *ideological* guarantee of exchange value and Baudrillard goes on to apply the same argument to the central use value in Marxist theory, labour power itself. By placing labour at the centre of its critique:

> Marxism assists the cunning of capital. It convinces men that they are alienated by the sale of their labour power, thus censoring the much more radical hypothesis that they might be alienated *as* labour power . . .

For Baudrillard the era of political economy (of which Marxism was an effect) is over. We are now in the era of symbolic economy and so his work since 1972 has meant theorising the experience of symbolic exchange, first through a critique of structural linguistics and then through what we might call a metaphorics, an attempt to get at the contemporary meaning of the market through metaphors for it: seduction, simulation, death. The philosophical (and literary) problem is how to describe events which are exactly what they seem to be, to record conversations in which there are no referents, to assess deals in which nothing changes hands. The basic categories of meaning (truth and reality) can't indicate anything outside this sign system; they are the (hysterical) effects of it.

I find much of Baudrillard's recent work difficult to follow (it leans too heavily on the multiple meanings of words that don't translate) but he remains an important thinker for two reasons. First, the questions he asked from the start about consumption are now at the heart of British political debates—and I'm not just referring to designer socialism here. The problem of consumption faces Thatcherites too. How to police desire? How to make greed responsible? Second, however wilfully sweeping or shallowly provoking are Baudrillard's ideas, they do confront the difficulty of cultural *production* (which explains why he has had such an impact on the art world—the questions he asks are theirs: what oppositional strategy is left when *everything* is symbolically equivalent?). (pp. 23-4)

Simon Frith, "What Is a Washing Machine?" in New Statesman, *Vol. 115, No. 2984, June 3, 1988, pp. 23-4.*

JOHN WELCHMAN

America has been subject to representation by a whole phalanx of out-siders and other-continentals—romantic prophets and the mawkishly curious, intellectual imperialists and political spectators, moral fanatics and doomsayers, discoverers, conquistadors, and social fantasists, from Chateaubriand and Tocqueville to Reyner Banham and Jean Baudrillard. These attentions have usually already begun their particular labor of interested misrepresentation in the utterance of their

very first syllables, which so often collapse the body of the Americas into the short hand of "America," *the* America, for which read the United States of America—another place altogether, both inside and outside its relation with the continental whole. (p. 10)

Disguised as the opposite of what it pretends it isn't, Baudrillard's [*America*] infallibly loops back upon itself, inexorably returning to the discourses of primitivism and sublimity with which it dissembles to contend. In the process, of course, enough paradox, enough aberrationism, enough contradiction circulates within this archipelago of essentialisms as to render them all doubtful—if well-used (*merci bien*).

In the beginning was the desert. Recurrent as symbol, mytheme, and rhetorical trope throughout the text, this extra-urban space is, for Baudrillard, a "miraculous geological" dance of particles, "magically" stacked or "ineluctably eroded" by a "cataclysmic" nature into the rapturous spectacles of the American Southwest. But the desert is also a literal pulverization of landform into "pure . . . abstraction," the final repository of a dissolution of cultural practices and social meaningfulness (the "unculture" of the desert), the bland reductio and ultimate referent of all signage—the way station for its dazzling reflection in(to) the simulacrum. "Desertification" in the last analysis is erasure—the disappearance, the blocking out, of "culture, politics . . . sexuality. . . . Even the body."

Graphic though it is, this writing-out of "America" as desert is an ultimately self-defeating inscription of geosocial nihilism. The complex historical formation of the United States' preferred expansionist consciousness was elaborately managed not through the metaphor of the desert (though it crept in, and was subsumed) but through the allied concepts of frontier and "wilderness." . . . The wilderness, imagined as compounds of prairie and forest, mountain and desert, was the governing locus of a specifically "American" national development, the great signature of national self-awareness, from the Puritan typologists who saw the travails of Old Testament peregrinations in their westward musterings through the pragmatic forest-taming of woodsmen like Daniel Boone, the transcendentalism of Thoreau and Emerson, the painters and writers of the wilderness such as Thomas Cole and Frederick Church, Washington Irving and James Fenimore Cooper, the protoenvironmentalism of state and national parks in the late 19th century, up to the conceptual transference of the wilderness into the "urban jungle" (Upton Sinclair, etc.) and sundry Modernistic wastelands. "American culture," then, emphatically cannot be said to be "heir to the deserts." Ignoring or eclipsing the wilderness, this other and dominant construction, this particular reckoning of nature-versus-culture that has tracked across the making of "America" with all the ideological gravity of a small historical moon, Baudrillard favors instead the fey après-post-Modern evaporation ("dryness"—*sécheresse*—and "denutrition," says he), the cute reductivist s(embl)able, of the desert. In doing so he sacrifices any and all notions of history to the meager acuities of theoretical voy(ag)eurism.

Then there are the inhabitants of *America,* who come in three assortments. First are the chimeric phantasms (*"Ghost towns, ghost people"*) of the kind that will appear on the stool next to the author in a bar in Santa Barbara ("Foucault, Sartre, and Orson Welles"), or flicker on-screen en route over Greenland (Catherine Deneuve), or be appealed to in-text as (somehow) knowing witnesses of the New World order of things—

Ernest Mandel, Jean François Lyotard, Hieronymus Bosch, "I. Huppert," . . .—or as Old World simile figures to facilitate the explication of Americanistic imagery, such as the Bjorn Borg–faced Christs of Salt Lake City. Secondly there are streams, nay floods, of generic types chorusing across the text and imaged on a dime. Marathon runners and rap gymnasts, word-processing Californian academics and "biosocial mutants," . . . a whole litany of the *"surhumanité"* of the "anti-Ark" (Noah's), in which "tribes, gangs, [and] mafia families" replace the erstwhile two-step of (normative) coupledom. There are Chicano guides, feebly configured Indians, "rich-living, puritanical" Mormons, the "sublime and animal . . . beauty" of black and Puerto Rican women. Junkies, druggies, alkies, drop-outs, yuppies. The scintillating NY crowd with its "Pre-raphaelite" or "Afro" hair-dos. A galaxy of quickly glimpsed dramatis personae stranded in the consumptive logic of the prof. *en vacance,* and no better defined than the faint protagonists of cereal-pack animation.

And then there are some individual Americans. Mostly bit parts here . . . except, that is, for the gipper, who is thoroughly (and convincingly) caricatured and sign-typed as the epigone of the age of narcissism and perpetual repetition. Respecting, then, his characterization, we might say of Baudrillard, as Tzvetan Todorov claimed of Columbus, that he "speaks about the men he sees because they too, after all, constitute a part of the landscape." Grains of sand in the desert. "In Columbus' hermeneutics human beings have no particular place"; there is a "preference for land over men."

The records of the New World gazes of Columbus and Co., as reconstructed by Todorov, and Baudrillard's interconference entr'acte in *America* reveal further unexpected homologies. The much-remarked physical nakedness of the Native Americans as the boats pulled up finds its counterpart in Baudrillard's designation of the cultural nudeness of the American scene, the void signage of the desert, the abstraction and simulation of Old World values, the whole *mise à nue* of counterfeits and distractions in the iterated American affliction of "hyperreality." Similarly, as Columbus directed his naturalist enthusiasm toward the newfound finery of American avifauna (especially parrots), so Baudrillard reproduces the curio-seeking attachment of the po-mo enthusiast to deviant or remark-able regimens. Metaphysical souvenirs and scintillating critical aperçus have replaced the tangible tokens of in situ frippery. . . . Then, the "splendid naiads" excitedly spotted onshore by the Spanish sailors, telescopes atremble, reveal a torrid lust for the other that Baudrillard rather crudely recapitulates (even as its sexuality is denied) in his black and Puerto Rican sightings. There are even, dare I say it, flourishes of sheer Buffo(o)n-ery, as when Baudrillard, in noticing the neutered and insufficient aspects of American sexuality—its "collective asexual obsession"—seems to follow the reactionary environmental determinism of the 18th-century Comte de Buffon, who, in his *Natural History,* described the recently evolved geomorphology of the New World as "still humid and noxious"; found its inhabitants possessed of small and insufficient "organs of reproduction," with no hair, and no sexual "ardor"; and pronounced them a disgrace to nature.

Both Baudrillard and the Spaniards negotiate their sheer astonishment at an alien social and cultural order through a recourse to the language of fables and romances, and to the conundrums of their available metaphysics. But the armadaless and unmissionary modern-day theorist, more at home in Santa Cruz than Veracruz, is constrained to compel only by fanfare and display; only thus can the inscrutable rite-bound cycles of exemplary capitalist order be deregulated, remystified, and opened out. What we have here (among other things) is an extraordinary reinscription of primitivist discourse back onto the body of America, which is made to epitomize the regression of modernity in the teeth of the future. Said to be staged on the "primitive" scene of the desert, claimed to be unfolding a "brutal naiveté," a kind of "drive-in" recidivism, Baudrillard attempts in *America* to play Prospero at the interface of the Old World and the New. But his charms, though still potent, are fading; the would-be glamor and wisdom of his European sentences are giving way to a panoply of assertive essentialisms, a new metaphysics, and an egregious neo-primitivism, mellifluous groans from an imaginary cynic-cure to an ignoble new world. (pp. 10-11)

John Welchman, "Here There & Otherwise," in Artforum, *Vol. XXVII, No. 2, October, 1988, pp. 10-11.*

JOHN THACKARA

Baudrillard argues that in the age of television, film and advertising, the production of images and symbols has created a new form of consumption, a state of 'hyper-reality' in which we experience reality as one more special effect. Modern men and women, says Baudrillard, are awash in a sea of private languages, no longer even interested in politics and morality. In today's black hole of universal images we have lost our sense of progress.

Although he speaks the language of the critic, much of Baudrillard's audience appears to revel in 'hyper-reality': in these narcissistic times we appear to *enjoy* the perceptual vertigo induced by the simulated experiences that surround us. Baudrillard's popularity, among people not otherwise inclined to philosophy, derives in part because he makes nihilism and superficiality respectable. . . .

For Baudrillard, the images we see on television are 'simulacra': they *look* realistic, but it is their very realism that makes them perverse. The modern viewer cultivates a knowing, ironic fascination with television; we *allow* ourselves knowingly, we think, to be seduced. But this sophisticated irony, argues Baudrillard, conceals a fatal strategy of conformity.

> Television cools and neutralises the meaning of events. The cold light of television is inoffensive to the imagination, even that of children, because we no longer "see" it as an image at all. The television image has become a miniaturised terminal locked in your head, and you are the screen. We no longer differentiate between it and reality—nor do we want to!

Satellite broadcasting has convinced Baudrillard that images are being produced by an epidemic process which no one can control. Television radiates oblivion, obliterates discussion and exterminates understanding of the context of events.

One is surprised to discover, given such views on television, that Baudrillard is an unrestrained film buff. 'Film is the last great myth of our modernity,' he says, 'the idolatry of stars, the cult of Hollywood idols, they all help the cinema life with a mythical ambience.' The technological mass media are driven by our appetite for images that appear to refer to a real world, when none of them do. 'Cinema is different, it does not even try to masquerade as real.' . . .

Although he concedes that many of his readers appear to enjoy their immersion in hyperreality, Baudrillard is contemptuous of what he calls

> the generation that has come from the Sixties and Seventies, but has rid itself of all nostalgia for, all bad conscience about, even any subconscious memory of, those wild years. They have excised the last traces of marginality as if by plastic surgery—a new focus, new fingernails, glossy brain cells—the whole topped off and tousled with software. All they are contemplating, on their word processors and exercise bikes, is the operation of their own brain cells.

Mindful, perhaps, that this last accusation might not unfairly also be levelled at himself, Baudrillard has taken to the road in recent years, driving around America in a Chrysler, like the James Dean of postmodern philosophy. The result, a book called **America,** mixes insight with unintentional hilarity. More thinker than traveller, he feels compelled to philosophise on everything he encounters, from joggers to hamburgers. Hence, 'On Jogging':

> Decidedly, joggers are the true Latter-day Saints and the protagonists of an easy-does-it Apocalypse. Nothing evokes the end of the world more than a man running straight ahead on a beach, swathed in the sounds of his Walkman, cocooned in the solitary sacrifice of his energy, indifferent even to catastrophes since he expects destruction to come only as the fruit of his own efforts, from exhausting the energy of a body that has in his own eyes become useless.

(p. 45)

America, for Baudrillard, is 'the only great primitive society of modern times; it is a country where the image has become the ultimate sex object that, alone, satisfies human needs and desires'. The irony is that Americans lap all this up: if America invented this vast new market for images, critics seem to say, then the market, banal or not, must be OK. Baudrillard, too, seems mesmerised by it all. 'Take Disneyland: what a play of illusions and phantasms—a deep-frozen, infantile world conceived by a man who awaits his own resurrection at minus 180C' (Walt Disney was a great believer in cryogenics). 'Disneyland is the *real* America: it's presented as imaginary in order to make us believe the rest is real, when it's not.'

For all the playfulness of his arguments, Baudrillard does not appear really to enjoy the travelling of modern life. 'My reason for travelling is that driving is a spectacular form of amnesia, but I discovered that the car is no longer an object of psychological sanctuary.' He once speculated that the car would become 'a kind of capsule, its dashboard the brain, the surrounding landscape unfolding like a television screen.' Today, he seems less enamoured of the social isolation that such developments imply. 'Space, and cities, are no longer experienced horizontally; cities have become *subterranean;* we can no longer speak of public life, but of *publicity* life. We don't relate to where things happen, but to where they're looked at. All travelling achieves is an awareness of social isolation; it takes you further into the mental desert.'

Baudrillard is even more downbeat about the future. Convinced that the intellectual history of this century ground to a halt during the Seventies, he sees the 1990s as a 'dead zone—of some use, perhaps, as a time in which to prepare for the next century, but no more'. Does he feel superfluous to requirements? 'In the old days, it was left to the philosophers, alone, to ask questions about the reality of the real; today, such questions have become a feature of the system itself.' (p. 46)

John Thackara, "Jogging Cool Memories," in The Listener, *Vol. 120, No. 3091, December 1, 1988, pp. 45-6.*

ZYGMUNT BAUMAN

In one of his essays George Orwell recalls the long-extinct American journal *The Booster,* which used to advertise itself as "non-political, non-ethical, non-literary, non-educational, non-progressive, non-literary, non-consistent, and non-contemporary". I think of *The Booster* whenever I try to visualize the world as portrayed by Jean Baudrillard, professor of sociology at Nanterre and, for the past decade or more, one of our most talked-about social analysts. Like the obscure journal, though with much more sound and fury, Baudrillard patches together the identity of his world out of absences alone. The world according to Baudrillard is like a party notable mostly for the extraordinary number of people we knew and thought highly of who have, alas, failed to turn up. He writes of what has gone missing, what is no more, what has lost its substance or foundation. The major characteristic of our times, he insists, is disappearance. History has stopped, so has progress, if there ever was any. The things we live with today are mostly vestiges: once parts of a totality which gave them a place and function, but today fragments condemned to seek a meaningful design in vain.

So far, I admit, there is nothing here to shock a seasoned reader of the many biographies of our contemporary "postmodernity", a term which means little more than an end or disappearance. How after all can one write about a change which is still happening and is far from complete? But the change Baudrillard writes about is no ordinary one, it is a change that puts paid to change itself, a change, as a result of which we can no longer speak of change, and even the words "no longer" lose their sense.

Change implies solidity: before it can alter its identity, an object must first have one, must possess clear boundaries and unmistakable features of its own. It must differ, too, from images and representations of it. The world in which once we confidently spoke of change and renewal, of trends and directions, was a solid one in which we could tell the difference between an idea and its referent, a representation and what it represented, the image and the reality. But now the two things are hopelessly confused, says Baudrillard. Our language, however, implies still that there are objects "out there", which occupy their own sites in space and time. No wonder that once we use such a language to speak of Baudrillard's world, whatever we may say will sound clumsy and confused.

Take the most important of his concepts: that of simulation ("feigning to have what one hasn't"). Simulation, you might think, consists in pretending that something is not what it in fact is; this does not alarm us because we feel that we know how to tell the pretence from reality. Baudrillard's simulation is not like that, however; it effaces the very difference between the categories of true and false, real and imaginary. We no longer have any means of testing pretence against reality, or know which is which. Nor is there any exit from this quandary. To report the change involved, we must say that "from now on" the "relationship has been reversed", that the map, as it were, precedes the territory, or the sign the thing. Yet such talk is itself illegitimate, for with simulation rampant, even the words that we use "feign to have what they haven't", ie, meanings or referents. In fact we do not know the difference between the map and the territory, and would not know it even if we had our noses pressed up against the thing itself. Where our ordinary concept of "simulation" upholds the reality principle, Baudrillard's "simulation" undermines it. All simulation is a deception, but his is doubly so: "It is no longer a question of a false representation of reality (ideology), but of concealing the fact that the real is no longer real", or at least no more real than whatever feigns it. What we face is simulation to the power of two, or to use Baudrillard's own favourite prefix, *hyper*simulation.

In his world everything is "hyper": we live in a hyperreality, "more real than real", in that it no longer sets itself against something else, which is illusive or imaginary. Everything can now claim to be real. What is real politics, for instance? Smiling faces on the television screen emitting headline-catching one-liners, or the profound visions and great deeds that they simulate? In hyperreality, truth has not been destroyed, it has been made irrelevant. . . .

In these *Selected Writings* Mark Poster gives us a brief yet comprehensive intellectual biography of Baudrillard, together with a selection from his various books, from *Le Système des objects* (1968) and *La Société de consommation* (1970), in which he attempted to fit tired Marxist jaws with new, high-tech teeth, to *L'Echange symbolique et la mort* (1976) and *De la séduction* (1979), which are remarkable mainly for the post-revolutionary gloom and despondency they exude. More recently, *Les Stratégies fatales* (1983) and *La Gauche divine* (1985) have introduced us to the Baudrillard vision Mark II, with its exuberant obscenity and intemperance, and revealed their author's latest synthesis of his own early hopes and subsequent resignation. Now he tells us that the bovine immobility of the masses is the best form of activity we have, and the highest form of "resistance".

But there is another way of looking at Baudrillard's world. The world he paints is the one likely to be seen by someone permanently glued to the television screen, someone who has no windows in his house and whose attention is at its sharpest during the commercial breaks. More than a century ago another Frenchman, Baudelaire, suggested that the right way to observe and make sense of the modern world is to stroll along the streets of the metropolis and past the shops. The *flâneur* of the metropolis, he proposed, has the best idea of the essence of modernity. Baudrillard's *flâneur,* however, no longer strolls, he sits in front of his television set, he has become a watcher.

In *America,* his most recently translated book, he embarks on the search for "l'Amérique sidérale", which can only be found "in the indifferent reflex of television, in the film of days and nights projected across the empty space, in the marvellously affectless succession of signs, images, faces, and ritual acts on the road". Even when he watches the scene through the window of his fast-moving car, what he sees looks like a television film, and can be understood only in the terms set by a television film. And when Baudrillard's *flâneur* starts his car, it is not to explore the promenades of the city

centre, he drives into the desert, looking for the most prominent mark of our times: the *disappearance*. Postmodernism is at its fullest bloom in the desert, "for the desert is simply that: an ecstatic critique of culture, an ecstatic form of disappearance". For the same reason, one would guess, Baudrillard is fascinated by America: for the genius it has shown "in its irrepressible development of equality, banality, and indifference".

America is a postmodern record of a postmodern world: the world is postmodern because it is not fully translatable, the record because it is not a full translation. Much as the Third World would never make Western capitalism and democracy its own, so Europe, burdened with its history and its memories of class, could never become as thoughtlessly equal or as effortlessly indifferent as America. Among the many things which have disappeared here, the hope of universality is perhaps the most salient. To replace the vision of an increasingly orderly garden of humanity, Baudrillard offers us an image of a chaotic site split into many tiny allotments, each with its own mini-order. To scan them all, one needs a fast car, or a fast flow of pictures on the television screen, and such scanning is entertainment, an endless play of simulation. It is also freedom from responsibility, and from the need to be serious.

But one suspects, *pace* Baudrillard, that there is still life beyond television, and many people for whom it is anything but "simulation". For them, reality remains what it always was, solid, resistant and often harsh. It becomes a philosopher and an analyst of his time, like Baudrillard, to use his feet now and again.

Zygmunt Bauman, "Disappearing into the Desert," in The Times Literary Supplement, *No. 4472, December 16-22, 1988, p. 1391.*

MARK POSTER

Baudrillard has developed a theory to make intelligible one of the fascinating and perplexing aspects of advanced industrial society: the proliferation of communications through the media. This new language practice differs from both face-to-face symbolic exchange and print. The new media employ the montage principle of film (unlike print) and time-space distancing (unlike face-to-face conversation) to structure a unique linguistic reality. Baudrillard theorizes from the vantage point of the new media to argue that a new culture has emerged, one that is impervious to the old forms of resistance and impenetrable by theories rooted in traditional metaphysical assumptions. Culture is now dominated by simulations, Baudrillard contends, objects and discourses that have no firm origin, no referent, no ground or foundation. (p. 1)

Baudrillard began his writing with *The System of Objects* (1968) and *Consumer Society* (1970) as an effort to extend the Marxist critique of capitalism to areas that were beyond the scope of the theory of the mode of production. He gradually abandoned Marxism, a process that is traced in the pages of [*Jean Baudrillard: Selected Writings*] developing his position along lines that have affinities with post-structuralists like Foucault and Derrida. Baudrillard found that the productivist metaphor in Marxism was inappropriate for comprehending the status of commodities in the post-war era. Only a semiological model, he argues, can decipher the meaning structure of the modern commodity. But the commodity embodies a communicational structure that is a departure from the traditional understanding of the sign. In a commodity the relation of word, image or meaning and referent is broken and restructured so that its force is directed, not to the referent of use value or utility, but to desire.

Like the post-structuralists, Baudrillard rejects traditional assumptions about referentiality. . . . In Baudrillard's terms, "hyperreality" is the new linguistic condition of society, rendering impotent theories that still rely on materialist reductionism or rationalist referentiality. In these respects, Baudrillard's work is important to the reconstitution of critical theory, and, more generally, appeals to those who would attempt to grasp the strange mixture of fantasy and desire that is unique to late twentieth-century culture. (pp. 1-2)

In *The System of Objects* (1968) Baudrillard initiated a comprehensive rethinking of the thesis of consumer society from a neo-Marxist perspective, one that relied on both Freudian and Saussurean themes. He explores the possibility that consumption has become the chief basis of the social order and of its internal classifications. He argues that consumer objects constitute a classification system that codes behavior and groups. As such, consumer objects must be analysed by use of linguistic categories rather than those of Marxian or liberal economics, Freudian or behaviorist psychology, anthropological or sociological theories of needs. Consumer objects have their effect in structuring behavior through a linguistic sign function. Advertising codes products through symbols that differentiate them from other products, thereby fitting the object into a series. The object has its effect when it is consumed by transferring its "meaning" to the individual consumer. A potentially infinite play of signs is thus instituted which orders society while providing the individual with an illusory sense of freedom and self-determination. *The System of Objects* went beyond earlier discussions of consumer society by systematically imposing linguistic categories to reveal the force of the code.

In *Consumer Society* (1970) Baudrillard provided numerous concrete examples of consumer objects as a code. He also undertook a critique of discussions of consumer society in the fields of economics and sociology. These disciplines were unable to capture the novelty of consumerism because economics was burdened by a doctrine of *homo economicus,* the free individual acting in the marketplace, and sociology was hampered by a notion of individual taste and a determinist concept of society. Against these positions Baudrillard effectively shows that a semiological analysis reveals that consumer objects constitute a *system of signs* that differentiate the population. This system of signs cannot become intelligible if each sign is related to each object, but only through the play of difference between the signs. In some of the most remarkable pages he has written, he indicates how consumer objects are like hysterical symptoms; they are best understood not as a response to a specific need or problem but as a network of floating signifiers that are inexhaustible in their ability to incite desire. Still a Marxist, Baudrillard goes on to argue that the reproduction of the mode of production has become dependent upon the expansion of consumption, on the reproduction of the act of consumption, thus inaugurating a new epoch in the history of capitalism.

For a Critique of the Political Economy of the Sign (1972) was a unique attempt to develop a radical theory of language as a supplement to Marxism. The title essay is a brilliant "deconstruction" of structuralism. In Saussure's theory of the sign, the signifier or word is distinguished from both the sig-nified or mental image and the referent. Saussure then marvels at the arbitrariness of the relation between signifier and signified and shows how one *value* of the sign is constituted by structural relations with other signs. Baudrillard reverses this strategy: Saussure's problem only arises because he has *separated* the elements of the sign in the first place, using the signified and the referent as "alibis." Political economy has a similar strategy: it separates the commodity into exchange value (price) and use value only then to have use value as the alibi for exchange value. Just as Marx exposed the strategy behind the theory of the commodity in political economy, Baudrillard does the same for the theory of the sign by undermining the formalism of the theory of the sign. He has thus prepared the way for a historical analysis of the sign as the mode of signification within capitalism, a task accomplished in *The Mirror of Production. For a Critique* goes farther than Henri Lefebvre, Barthes, the *Tel Quel* group or Bakhtin in opening the path to a social critique of language because it historicizes both the structural and the social aspects of the sign.

The Mirror of Production (1973) marks Baudrillard's parting of the ways with Marxism. Henceforth the critique of the political economy of the sign is presented not as a supplement to the critique of political economy, but as its successor, as the new basis for critical social theory. The book was written with a force and systematicness that was not equalled again by Baudrillard. Each of Marx's major positions (the concept of labor, the dialectic, the theory of the mode of production, the critique of capital) are in turn revealed as mirror images of capitalist society. Marxism emerges in Baudrillard's pages not as a radical critique of capitalism but as its highest form of justification or ideology. (pp. 2-4)

Baudrillard does not rest with a critique of Marxism; he goes on to develop what is perhaps the pinnacle of his early writings; a historical theory of sign structures. The weakness of Saussure's structural linguistics and Barthes' semiology was their ahistoricity, the formalism of their categories. Baudrillard remedies this deficiency by outlining the structural stages of the formation of contemporary language usage. He argues, somewhat nostalgically, that pre-industrial societies maintained a "symbolic" structure to communications: signs included words that were attached to referents and were uttered in a context that held open their possible reversal by others. During the Renaissance language began to lose its reciprocity when an abstract code, analogous to money, slowly transformed them. Hence the era of the sign emerged. Baudrillard now theorizes capitalism as a reflection of this change at the level of the economy, a subordinate aspect of the history of modes of signification. In the late twentieth century, signs become completely separated from their referents, resulting in a structure that resembles the signal: signifiers act like traffic lights, emitting meanings to which there is no linguistic response. The composite organization of such signifiers is termed the code by Baudrillard, a concept which he never adequately defines. The code operates by extracting signifieds from the social, redeploying them in the media as "floating signifiers." Television ads especially but not exclusively constitute a new language form in which the code transmits signifiers to the population who are subject to this "terroristic" mode of signification.

Symbolic Exchange and Death (1976) draws out the pessimistic implications of the theory of the code, marking a change in Baudrillard's political stance. As the politics of the sixties receded so did Baudrillard's radicalism: from a position of firm leftism he gradually moved to one of bleak fatalism. In *Symbolic Exchange and Death* he searches desperately for a source of radicalism that challenges the absorptive capacities of a system with no fixed determinations, a world where anything can be anything else, where everything is both equivalent to and indifferent to everything else, a society, in short, dominated by the digital logic of the code. Baudrillard's pathetic conclusion is that only death escapes the code, only death is an act without an equivalent return, an exchange of values. Death signifies the reversibility of signs in the gift, a truly symbolic act that defies the world of simulacra, models and codes.

The book is flawed by the totalizing quality of Baudrillard's writing. Still, its value lies in the refinements it provides of many of the themes of Baudrillard's earlier works. In it Baudrillard grapples, as nowhere before, with the problem of characterizing the structure of communication in a world dominated by the media. This important issue, too much neglected by critical theory, becomes the mainstay of his writing after 1976. Although Baudrillard treats this theme with hyperbole and vague formulations, he has initiated a line of thought that is fundamental to a reconstitution of critical theory. (pp. 4-5)

In *On Seduction* (1979) Baudrillard makes a turn toward a post-structuralist critique of the hermeneutics of suspicion. Theories that deny the surface "appearance" of things in favor of a hidden structure or essence, theories like Marxism, psychoanalysis and structuralism, now come under attack. These interpretive strategies all privilege forms of rationality. Against them Baudrillard celebrates the Nietzschean critique of the "truth" and favors a model based on what he calls "seduction". Seduction plays on the surface thereby challenging theories that "go beyond" the manifest to the latent. The model of seduction prefigures Baudrillard's later term, the hyperreal, with all of its post-modernist implications. At the close of the book, Baudrillard tentatively suggests that seduction might be a model to replace the model of production.

In *Simulacra and Simulations* (1981) Baudrillard extends, some would say hyperbolizes, his theory of commodity culture. No longer does the code take priority over or even precede the consumer object. The distinctions between object and representation, thing and idea are no longer valid. In their place Baudrillard fathoms a strange new world constructed out of models or simulacra which have no referent or ground in any "reality" except their own. A simulation is different from a fiction or lie in that it not only presents an absence as a presence, the imaginary as the real, it also undermines any contrast to the real, absorbing the real within itself. Instead of a "real" economy of commodities that is somehow bypassed by an "unreal" myriad of advertising images, Baudrillard now discerns only a hyperreality, a world of self-referential signs. He has moved from the TV ad which, however, never completely erases the commodity it solicits, to the TV newscast which creates the news if only to be able to narrate it, or the soap opera whose daily events are both referent and reality for many viewers.

If Baudrillard's argument of hyperreality has a modicum of validity, the position of the New Critics and deconstructionists must be taken seriously. The self-referentiality of language, which they promote against materialists, phenomenologists, realists and historicists as the key to textual analysis, now in Baudrillard's hands becomes the first principle of social existence in the era of high-tech capitalism. Critical theory faces the formidable task of unveiling structures of domination when no one is dominating, nothing is being dominated and no ground exists for a principle of liberation from domination. If Auschwitz is the sign of total tyranny as the production of death, the world of "hyper-reality" bypasses the distinction between death and life.

The pessimistic implications of *Simulacra and Simulations* are brought home in *Fatal Strategies.* Here Baudrillard attempts to think the social world from the point of view of the object, a seeming oxymoron. Like the post-structuralists, Baudrillard assumes that the era of the representational subject is past. One can no longer comprehend the world as if the Kantian categories of time, space, causality, etc. are necessary, universal paths to truth. Baudrillard takes this to imply that the subject no longer provides a vantage point on reality. The privileged position has shifted to the object, specifically to the hyperreal object, the simulated object. In place of a logic of the subject, Baudrillard proposes a logic of the object, and this is his "fatal strategy." As the reader will discover, the world unveiled by Baudrillard, the world from within the object, looks remarkably like the world as seen from the position of postmodernists. (pp. 5-6)

The concurrent spread of the hyperreal through the media and the collapse of liberal and Marxist politics as master narratives, deprives the rational subject of its privileged access to truth. In an important sense individuals are no longer citizens, eager to maximize their civil rights; nor proletarians, anticipating the onset of communism. They are rather consumers, and hence the prey of objects as defined by the code. In this sense, only the "fatal strategy" of the point of view of the object provides any understanding of the present situation.

In the recent essay **"The masses: the implosion of the social in the media,"** Baudrillard recapitulates the theme of his work in the 1980s: the media generate a world of simulations which is immune to rationalist critique, whether Marxist or liberal. The media present an excess of information and they do so in a manner that precludes response by the recipient. This simulated reality has no referent, no ground, no source. It operates outside the logic of representation. But the masses have found a way of subverting it: the strategy of silence or passivity. Baudrillard thinks that by absorbing the simulations of the media, by failing to respond, the masses undermine the code. Whatever the value of this position it represents a new way of understanding the impact of the media. Instead of complaining about the alienation of the media or the terrorism of the code, Baudrillard proposes a way out: silence. (p. 7)

Baudrillard's writing is open to several criticisms. He fails to define his major terms, such as the code; his writing style is hyperbolic and declarative, often lacking sustained, systematic analysis when it is appropriate; he totalizes his insights, refusing to qualify or delimit his claims. He writes about particular experiences, television images, as if nothing else in society mattered, extrapolating a bleak view of the world from that limited base. He ignores contradictory evidence such as the many benefits afforded by the new media, for example, by providing vital information to the populace (the Vietnam War) and counteracting parochialism with humanizing images of foreigners. The instant, worldwide availability of information has changed the human society forever, probably for the good.

Nevertheless Baudrillard's work is invaluable in beginning to comprehend the impact of new communication forms on society. He has introduced a language-based analysis of new kinds of social experience, experience that is sure to become increasingly characteristic of advanced societies. His work shatters the existing foundations for critical social theory, showing how the privilege they give to labor and their rationalist epistemologies are inadequate for the analysis of the media and other new social activities. In these regards his critique belongs with Derrida's critique of logocentrism and Foucault's critique of the human sciences. Unlike these post-structuralist thinkers, Baudrillard fails to reflect on the epistemological novelties he introduces, rendering his work open to the charges outlined above. For the critical theorists, Baudrillard represents the beginning of a line of thought, one that is open to development and refinement by others. (pp. 7-8)

> *Mark Poster, in an introduction to* Selected Writings *by Jean Baudrillard, edited by Mark Poster, Stanford University Press, 1988, pp. 1-9.*

RICHARD VINE

In a world of rampant academic celebrity (as opposed to earned fame), there is no cachet equal to that of the mysterious French intellectual. Whatever else one may say of Foucault, Barthes, Derrida, Lacan, Bataille, Lévi-Strauss, and now Baudrillard, they have certainly perfected the oracular wiles necessary to win abject American admirers. (p. 40)

Born in Reims, France, in 1929, Jean Baudrillard spent two decades, 1966 through 1987, teaching at the satellite university in Nanterre, site of the student uprising that precipitated the May 1968 disruptions in Paris and beyond. Since that epochal spring, he has produced a score of (mostly short) books dealing in a quasi-structuralist, quasi-semiotic manner with the impact of the mass media on economic and social commerce. In this body of work, Baudrillard's thinking has passed through three phases—actually shifts of strategy, tenor, and emphasis rather than content—comprising an hysterical escalation from the post-Marxist (1968-71), to the socio-linguistic (1972-77), to the techno-prophetic. Even limiting our examples to the principal titles available in English (since our topic is Baudrillard's sway over certain American intellects), we can witness the author beginning with qualified statements and reasonable—sometimes almost testable—theoretic correctives, passing quickly to pure speculative assertion, and ending with sci-fi prophecy of a sort intended to induce the very effects it predicts.

The two books of Baudrillard's post-Marxist phase, *The System of Objects* and *Consumer Society*—published in France in 1968 and 1970—examine the psychological imperatives of consumption in an advanced capitalistic economy. The first argues that meaning, not use, is primarily transferred through consumer objects and that the individual in effect buys a group identity and a metaphysical order with each over-determined purchase. The second contends that the individual—to the extent that he matters at all—merely fulfills the needs of the productive system under the *illusion* that he is servicing his private wants.

Baudrillard's impatience with Marx (who, after all, foolishly believed that need and scarcity were genuine) bloomed into explicit dissociation in *For a Critique of the Political Economy of the Sign* (1972) and *The Mirror of Production* (1973).

Here Baudrillard announces not only that the sign prevails over social and economic activity, but that—in an improvement over Saussure—all alleged connections between referent (the real thing), signified (the concept of the real thing), and signifier (the marker for the concept of the real thing) have been definitively ruptured, if indeed they ever obtained. In this schema, signifiers "implode" to interrelate arbitrarily, in and of themselves, with no necessary correspondence to anything beyond their own chaotic but sovereign permutations. Of these we are observers at best, hypnotized slaves at worst.

If all of this sounds a bit like a Japanese monster movie entitled "Television: Master of the Universe," it should. From this point onward—through *Symbolic Exchange and Death* (1976), *The Beaubourg Effect* (1977), *Forget Foucault* (1977), *On Seduction* (1979), *Simulations* (1981), *Fatal Strategies* (1983), *The Ecstasy of Communication* (1987), and *The Evil Demon of Images* (1987)—Baudrillard's argument, though subject to a dizzying array of variations, remains essentially constant. Television, advertising, and cybernetic technology are making the world safe for solipsism. "Fatal"—i.e., inconsequential—events arise and die in "ecstasy" (pure, empty, self-parodying form) without changing the exploitive equilibrium in which we are held, except to make us helplessly aware of our state through their "catastrophes." We are "seduced" by the charm of appearances, only to realize that there is nothing beyond appearances and that our own best maneuver is to practice surface manipulation ourselves, to seduce in turn some portion of the system by becoming so much like it, so perfect a clone, that it is forced to change or to reveal some new facet in order to maintain its authority over us. Of this strategy, no better example could be cited than Baudrillard's recent *America* (1986), in which the United States is treated not, in the manner of Tocqueville, as a noble and thrilling (though necessarily imperfect) experiment in democratic rule but as an hallucinatory spectacle whose greatest virtue is its glorification of trash: "The latest fast-food outlet, the most banal suburb, the blandest of giant American cars or the most insignificant cartoon-strip majorette is more at the center of the world than any of the cultural manifestations of old Europe."

Even this compressed survey makes Baudrillard sound much more systematic than he actually is. In fact, his thought does not develop at all. He is simply an aphorist who seized upon half a dozen borrowed concepts twenty-odd years ago and has rung changes on them ever since. Thus it is both frustrating and deceptive to seek progressive modulations between one text and another. They are all basically one book, and any fifty consecutive pages of Baudrillard are essentially the *whole* of Baudrillard. (pp. 40-1)

Baudrillard is determined to dazzle his way out of the professorial ghetto. His longing, though not exactly that of the moth for the star, unceasingly draws him into ever more florid formulations. Thus his critique of society only *begins* with the academic orthodoxy of our day:

> In order to function, capitalism needs to dominate nature, to domesticate sexuality, to rationalize language as a means of communication, to relegate ethnic groups, women, children and youth to genocide, ethnocide and racial discrimination.

True, this litany contains, properly speaking, no ideas at all, only unexamined articles of faith. But no matter. This is a credo; these are the things one must *say first* in order to gain a hearing among our vanguard culturati. Students and young artists tend to find such "truths" self-evident, even comforting, since they comprise the lore most consistently heard from their "deepest" teachers and intellectually raciest friends. Real titillation begins only when the writer promises to go farther, to share forbidden pleasures even more lurid than these refurbished Marxist clichés.

We now live, Baudrillard claims, in a culture of the hyperreal. Our lives are shaped, indeed constituted, by symbols functioning without reference to tangible objects, individual identities, or biological needs, all of which have in every important sense ceased to exist. Only signifiers *are* in this essentially dematerialized universe. Mere simulacra—the distant imitations of, or pure signs for, a lost and often already phony reality (the "country breakfast" at a shopping mall, the off-the-shoulder blouses worn by every waitress in a franchised "Mexican" restaurant)—combine and recombine in an apparent "free play." Yet even the interactions of simulacra are dictated by an irresistible DNA-like social "code" that fosters "consummativity," the perpetual motion of a humanly pointless but systemically self-sustaining capitalism.

The recurrent metaphor here is Disneyland. Everything in this magic kingdom conspires to enrapture the unquestioning through the deployment of more-real-than-real simulations. Such a world, such a fantasyland, beguiles us while exercising a surreptitious repression. To be sure, it frees us from the tiresome myths of individuality, originality, and authenticity. "All the great humanist criteria of value," Baudrillard exults, "all the values of a civilization of moral, aesthetic, and practical judgment, vanish in our system of images and signs." But it also mires us in a homogeneous stasis controlled by and for the phantasm itself. The greater, more mysterious, more impetuous portion of our being, our non-pragmatic "ambivalence," goes unacknowledged and untapped. Ontologically, we count for nothing. The system, by means of its all-powerful code—expressed especially through advertising, television, and the news media—steadily generates the arbitrary and controlling "models" from which all that we experience and do is derived; we are defined and coerced by endless, falsely "unique" replications à la the relentless serial imagery of Andy Warhol. (pp. 41-2)

One cannot overcome such a system: one can only refuse its blandishments and desist—desire nothing, cease production, seek no rewards and steadfastly refuse them when offered, become a postmodern stoic. Only then can one possibly return to the primal reciprocity—the "reversibility" and "responsibility"—of true symbolic interaction. Not the univocal, unidirectional "discourse" of media to audience, of government to citizen, of manager to employee, of advertiser to hungering psyche; but the direct, immediate, whole person to whole person give-and-take of primitive gift exchange, of the May '68 message walls, of pure conversation, of sex. Only such a transformation is able to "rescue us from the demands of rationality and to plunge us once more into absolute childhood."

There you have it, the whole of Baudrillard's seductive philosophy and the common weakness at which it aims: absolute childhood—a craven exemption from thinking, responsibility, and physical effort. (pp. 42-3)

Those for whom signification is all and facture is nothing have made Baudrillard the fulfillment of his own prophecy. He has become an aesthetic commodity, one whose sign value bears no relationship to its alleged referent. "Baudrillard" no longer signifies a man or a body of work but a speech-act of tribal identification on the part of the speaker. It translates as: "I know what's happening on the art scene today. I have read—or at least heard about—hip deconstructionist theory and am eager to explain the former in terms of the latter (since, God knows, it doesn't make much sense to me otherwise). I know that trashing the system while living off its surplus the way Andy did is extremely cool." Certainly the Baudrillard corpus could itself serve as a veritable handbook on how to be an au courant intellectual. In it, all the major components fall dutifully into place. Indeed, thanks to Baudrillard, we can now spell out the seven commandments of contemporary social analysis.

1. *Dissociate yourself from conventional life, capitalism, and the vulgar bourgeoisie—preferably by discovering in the unlikeliest places half-hidden machinations of repressive control.*

Eager to be ever more *maudit* than thou, Baudrillard manages to surpass the imaginative fecundity of even the magisterial Foucault. First he weighs in with the now familiar claim that the definition of madness is but a ploy, that "every 'psychological dysfunction' *vis-à-vis* 'normality' (which is only the law of the capitalist milieu) is open to a *political* reading." He then proceeds, via a social interpretation of physical disease, to caution us against the pathological dangers of bourgeois hygiene. Conveniently, no mention is made of what science and attendant public health measures have accomplished against cholera, typhoid, smallpox, diphtheria, yellow fever, malaria, influenza, polio, leprosy, syphilis, etc. Instead, Baudrillard's argument, such as it is, resembles a bizarre crossbreeding of Christian Science with those lunatic 1950s Communist-conspiracy tirades against the fluoridation of city water supplies. . . . (p. 43)

2. *Purport to extend and correct the prevailing vanguard position. (Add ten points if you can do so through a "reflexive" argument that turns key doctrinal precepts back upon themselves.)*

A major preoccupation of radical thinkers, from the founding of the Frankfurt School onward, has been the search for an alchemic formula that would somehow rid critical theory of such real-life Marxist impurities as chronic low productivity, avant-garde condescension toward "the masses," brute censorship, and, most embarrassing of all, that nettlesome Gulag. Baudrillard's solution is the magic of "transparency," which renders all such difficulties instantly unreal. Had Marx only had the benefit of modern semiotics, he would have realized that commodification explains not simply one element of the capitalist system but the system in toto, along with its very presuppositions. There is no biological essence of man, according to Baudrillard, hence no constant and irreducible requirement for food, shelter, and safety: "the 'vital anthropological minimum' doesn't exist." It is an illusion conjured up after the fact to justify and perpetuate the productivist enterprise: "there are only needs because the system needs them." Everything essential to humankind transpires symbolically, as is evident when Baudrillard asks, rhetorically, "is loss of status—or social non-existence—less upsetting than hunger?"

The monstrosity of such a conception in light of, say, the recent famine in Ethiopia is best contemplated in purely humorous terms. Imagine, then, Monsieur Baudrillard in a restaurant. He peruses the menu fastidiously, selecting at last, with the waiter's recommendation, medaillons of veal accompanied by lightly buttered haricots verts, followed by a simple green salad, fruit and mixed cheeses, espresso, and a sliver of apricot tart—complemented by a delicate Chablis and, to finish, a noble but little known Armagnac. Then, without a quiver, and without so much as having *seen* any food, Baudrillard languidly calls for his check, says a gracious farewell to the maître d'hotel, and departs, having "consumed" the signs of a satisfying repast and fulfilled all the essential requirements of symbolic exchange.

3. *Disdain quantitative measures and hard evidence. Spin elaborate theories out of a few anecdotes.*

Baudrillard cannot afford to concede the validity of empirical standards of proof, for to do so would invite a great many unsettling questions. Exactly how, for example, is my grandmother's need to sleep *caused* by the manufacture of beds? Does her sleepiness increase with a rising rate of box spring production? Anyone can see that this kind of thinking might lead directly to science, which Baudrillard considers merely "a system of defense and imposed ignorance." For him, positivism, that hereditary curse of the Enlightenment, sets up criteria which, in their alleged objectivity, create a false "reality" by excluding whatever does not conform to a limiting, conventionalizing language: "the object of a (given) science is only the effect of its discourse."

Now you and I might take it for granted that science is nothing more or less than a way of talking about the world—the entire point being that this particular way of talking (in the second law of thermodynamics, for example) more accurately and consistently approximates the way things actually happen in the cosmos than do the winsome speculations of a three-year-old, of an Eskimo shaman, or, for that matter, of the Archbishop of Canterbury. But to Baudrillard this circumspection is precisely what invalidates science. If empiricism cannot give him everything, and at once, it is worse than useless: it is an impediment.

Perhaps this anti-positivism accounts for the proliferation of flat-footed errors throughout Baudrillard's oeuvre. The howlers include a belief that in an art auction "one cannot participate without being present," that "in the United States couples are encouraged to exchange wedding rings every year," that a credit card "frees us from checks, cash, and even from financial difficulties at the end of the month." Perhaps, too, it is why slipshod or cavalier are probably the kindest words that can be applied to Baudrillard's purported scholarship. Here, even his proponents express reservations, as in the anonymous "Notes on the Translation" prefacing **Selected Writings:** "Baudrillard rarely provides full citations in his own notes. . . . At other times [his] quotations have not been located anywhere in the text he cites."

4. *Find inventive new applications for some standard postulates from today's master disciplines, anthropology and structural linguistics.*

Baudrillard does not think about the world; he thinks about what current hit-parade intellectuals have thought about the world. And like the Pop serialists he occasionally mentions, he appropriates most readily from the tabloid celebrities, the academic equivalents of Liz and Marilyn, Jackie and Troy. Saussure, Lévi-Strauss, Bataille, McLuhan—simply to evoke their names is to account for four-fifths of Baudrillard's research, the rest apparently consisting of long, selfless hours in front of a television set.

Such a procedure almost understandably gives rise to a vision of society as an outsized suburban high school, where all are forced, willy-nilly, to consume and all are judged by the sophistication of their material dialect. ("Which designer label do you wear?" having become, apparently, the prevailing version of "What's your sign?") (pp. 44-5)

5. *Systematically invert—or "transvalue"—all major tenets comprising the dominant doctrine of the previous generation. (If you are writing in France after 1968, subvert existentialism.)*

They all want to kill Sartre. Kill him and step into his exalted, world-historical place. Baudrillard's oedipal blood lust is so strong that his entire theory is structured in reaction to the great father's ghost. Thus "existence precedes essence" becomes "the precession [*sic*] of simulacra"; "authenticity" becomes "the individual is non-existent"; "good faith" becomes *"truth does not exist"*; "man is freedom" becomes "the hegemony of the code"; choice, responsibility, and anguish become "ambivalence" and "free play"; "man is nothing else than his plan" becomes "there are no longer any projects"; "to choose . . . is to affirm at the same time the value of what we choose" becomes "value is totalitarian." Et cetera.

6. *Sensationalize your language. When in doubt, be murky. When stating the ludicrous, be melodramatic.*

Aristotle talks like this: "What is the highest of all practical goods? Well, so far as the name goes there is pretty general agreement. 'It is happiness,' say both ordinary and cultured people; and they identify happiness with living well or doing well." Jesus talks like this: "Beware of false prophets, which come to you in sheep's clothing, but inwardly they are ravening wolves." Freud talks like this: "Every man must find out for himself in what particular fashion he can be saved." Baudrillard, by contrast, talks like this: "Identity is untenable: it is death, since it fails to inscribe its own death. Such is the case with closed, or metastable, or functional, or cybernetic systems, which are all eventually waylaid by laughter, instantaneous subversion (and not by a long dialectical labor), because all the inertia of these systems works against them."

Shall we conclude from this that Jean Baudrillard has a more complex mind than Aristotle, Jesus, or Freud? An alternative—and more plausible—explanation is that Baudrillard is steeped in the politically useful aesthetics of gibberish. His obfuscation is a matter of taste, of training, and of expediency. (pp. 45-6)

This charged obscurity, when it is not the result of sheer incompetence, derives from a will to convert or to subjugate. It creates a false aura of profundity and at the same time enables the author to elude full responsibility. (p. 46)

Pharisaical writers count heavily upon our desire for psychic economy. If a reader must invest great effort to trick out the author's meaning, he will—particularly if he is academically insecure—be predisposed to accept it, rather than admit the utter waste of some portion of his intellectual energy and ever-diminishing life. Yet even this is a relatively healthy response. For there is often something infinitely crueler at work in truly execrable prose—a verbal sadism, a calculated terrorism of the word.

Baudrillard proceeds not by logic and evidence, but by a prophetic insistence appropriate to his role as the Kahlil Gibran of post-industrial France. Such writing imposes upon the reader rituals entirely of the author's devising, "purification" ceremonies addressed to the gullibility and self-loathing of the intellectually young. Normalcy, expressed in the consensual meaning of words and in the practice of language as a communicative (and hence communal) act, is derogated as naïve. The reader is cut out and cut off, immured like Justine/Juliette in a dark world of totalitarian rule where political "discipline" is applied to—and eventually welcomed by—those who are not as smart as they should be, nor as "good."

The special irony is that here we are dealing with an author who is himself obsessed with intimations of repression and control on every side. Those who most dread manipulation, it would seem, are those who know what *they* would do, given the chance. *"The discourse of truth is quite simply impossible,"* Baudrillard tells us. There is no "truth," no "reality" for language to convey; but there is, apparently, much for it to invent, and to inflict.

7. *Never face a problem when you can define a new problematic. Offer your disciples deliverance "beyond good and evil," once they agree to be ideologically devout.*

Clearly, we cannot decide what is right until we know what is true. But by setting up a mode of inquiry that precludes true and false judgments, Baudrillard makes moral choice and action unthinkable.

The gimmick-mongers of contemporary French thought are guilty of many logical and factual errors, but these are as nothing compared to their fundamental moral dereliction. For their infatuation with the indeterminacy of texts, the decentralization (and denaturing) of the authorial subject, the provisional quality of every explication, etc., yields a Vichy interpretation of literature—wishfully proposing a world in which no particular individual is responsible for any particular act, in which the capitalist *system* ruins lives day and night, while no upstanding leftist intellectual, whatever his views, could possibly be accused of complicity in the slaughters of the Khmer Rouge or the admissions policies of Soviet psychiatric hospitals. For twenty years now we have suffered the ascendancy of the congenitally evasive. They have taught us their fear of social virility, their horror of *virtù*.

What is it Baudrillard so ardently wants? Something simple and impossible—a revision of the basic terms of existence, "a revolution that aims at the totality of life and social relations." This philosophic pathology weaves its web between the myth of the Golden Past (primitivism) and the myth of the Utopian Future (unfettered symbolic exchange, ambivalence, worldwide youth liberation). "Take your desires for reality," Baudrillard quotes approvingly from the rhetoric of May 1968. Thus he condones the commission of *any* act, so long as it conduces to a privately defined state of Grace.

This overview cannot, in good conscience, be concluded without an apology. Baudrillard's most thorough, most sensitive readers will know that many important points have been passed over in silence, and that the whole of his work has been treated with indefensible kindness. . . . Is gentlemanly deference the proper response to a man who can speak of "the inconsequential violence that reigns throughout the world"—"inconsequential" because it merely tears bodies open without altering, to his satisfaction, "a system of planetary control"? Genteel diplomacy, perhaps, is unsuited to a man who, in a rapture over the telepathic and telemetric precociousness of the disabled, laments that the rest of us are "condemned by our lack of disabilities to conventional forms of work," and holds that the fortunate afflicted "can become wonderful instruments precisely because of their handicap. They may precede us on the path towards mutation and dehumanization."

Perhaps Nanterre is a world fundamentally different from the one the rest of us inhabit—i.e., the world where real beggars cadge real food on real New York subway cars. We are justified in suspecting, however, that the primary difference lies in the perceiver. Baudrillard, like every professional intellectual, is a creature of privilege. He has not had to sacrifice the most alert hours of his most active years to labor or commerce, to the sheer business of earning a living. He is not subjugated to the common life, commuting to office or factory and forced to do his human thinking on the fly. He is, rather, a prime beneficiary of the system he claims (perhaps ingenuously) to detest—one who enjoys luxuries of time and mental cultivation unmatched in all of history, except among the aristocratic and ecclesiastic estates. Baudrillard was paid by the nation of France—which is to say, largely through the taxes of working women and men—to spend his days and nights reading, thinking, writing, and talking to students and professional peers. Such dissipation may have been his undoing, and ours, to judge from the attitude he developed toward his fellow citizens:

> For a long time, I was very "cool" about producing theories. . . . I didn't think it had very much to do with anything. It was a kind of game. I could write about death without it having any influence whatsoever on my life. When someone asked me, "What can we do with this? What are you really analyzing?" I took it very lightly, with great calm. . . . I maintained a position of distrust and rejection. That's the only "radicalness" I can claim. It might have something to do with my old pataphysical training: I don't want culture; I spit on it.

And there, in contempt for everyday people leading everyday lives, the simulationist's smug autocracy begins.

Clearly, Baudrillard has disqualified himself from serious intellectual regard. (pp. 46-8)

It is time for Baudrillard and his American apologists to stop making themselves ridiculous, time for them to stop luring the impressionable into a fun house that we who have lived to re-emerge know to be a chamber of horrors. Their vaunted infantilism—based on the fatuous notion that man uncontaminated by law and civilization is a creature of sweet temperament, a generous if occasionally mischievous flower child—would be quaintly laughable were it not so dangerous. (p. 48)

Richard Vine, "The 'Ecstasy' of Jean Baudrillard," in The New Criterion, *Vol. VII, No. 9, May, 1989, pp. 39-48.*

STEVEN HELMLING

Jean Baudrillard has been a presence on the French scene since the mid-sixties, and a name it has become increasingly fashionable to drop in the United States since about 1980. The near-simultaneous publication here of **America** and **Selected Writings** offers American readers a chance to see why. **America** has been widely (and derisively) reviewed, while the **Selected Writings** has gone virtually unnoticed; yet it is the latter book that would better serve the American reader interested in checking Baudrillard out. (p. 204)

The central theme [of all of Baudrillard's writings] is that we live in a media-saturated "hyperreality," a "culture of the simulacrum" induced by the proliferation of signs, that amounts to a collective solipsism. This may sound like an old story: complaints about the power of the media and advertising have been a man-in-the-street concern for more than a generation; while highbrow anxieties about the tyranny of culture have been endemic in the West at least since the Enlightenment, and have sustained critical traditions, variously reformist or revolutionary, ever since. But the last great revolutionary spasm in the sixties has left a legacy of confusion and ambivalence. What to attack?—and on behalf of whom? Among intellectuals, especially in France, liberalisms and Marxisms alike are in retreat. The working class remains an object of piety, but not much more, while the autonomous "subject" or self, once the presumed hero and beneficiary of the revolt against culture, has now been cast as the enemy, inevitable point d'appui for all right-thinking counter-culture "critique."

But if the motives of cultural critique are no longer so easy to sort out, that circumstance makes all the more urgent, intensifies rather than abating, the general will-to-critique. If culture-bashing must go on, and now more than ever, then Baudrillard is as satisfying a culture-basher as we presently have. To read his impassioned denunciations of advertising, consumerism, "commodification," TV, and the conduct of politics in a media age, is to see everything you most despise about our culture trashed in the manner that it deserves. It's like reading a highbrow Hunter Thompson, and Baudrillard's Gallic Gonzo is often uncannily prescient: a passage that perfectly skewers the Age of Reagan, for example, might turn out to have been written in 1969. (pp. 204-05)

Baudrillard's great stroke has been in locating his object of attack: "the culture of the simulacrum." The Corporation has replaced the Church and the State as the institutional villain of revolutionary scenarios, but Baudrillard directs his animus not against its monopolistic trade and marketing practices, its manipulations of credit and money, or its coercion, co-optation, and corruption of governments. These abuses take place out of the public view, and attacking them would involve the paranoid histrionics of the "exposé." Baudrillard focuses instead on what is in plain sight: the media, themselves the property of large corporations, and avowedly designed to serve not merely corporate interests but the ideology of corporatism. In a milieu dominated by technologies of communication, the corporate cornucopia solicits the consumer in a context not of competing realities, but only of competing images. Hence what Baudrillard calls "hyperreality": a universe of signs referring only to other signs, where the consumer (whether of TV dinners or of "the news") consumes not a thing but, as Wallace Stevens might say, "ideas about the thing."

To charge that a consumer product is not a thing but an utterance might not seem very acute, since that has been precisely the message announced in advertising for years. "It's not a car/watch/toilet bowl/fill in the blank, it's a *statement*": thus does advertising advertise not so much an ostensible product as its own power to turn a thing into a sign. But Baudrillard puts the case with a moral ferocity that some, at least, will find a pleasure to read, in prose that is grittier, at once more cool and more heated than the stratospheric eloquence of

many of his compeers. Of course, Baudrillard has been at pains to confer on the commonsense appeal of his argument an aura of large "theoretical" rigor, which involved him, for many years, in an effort—complete with pages of quasi-mathematical formulae—to develop Marx's distinction between use value and exchange value along Saussurean lines, in a way that would erase use value altogether, leaving the commodity a "floating signifier" without a signified, bearing only exchange value manipulable by commercial interests without reference to any reality external to the economy of signs. (p. 205)

Baudrillard's emplotments of historical change are of the sort that require an unhappy ending; and his gloomy view of a media-dominated world is a conceit rather than an analysis, and therefore totalizing, as any conceit will be, especially when serving a moralizing or paranoid vision. His rhetoric, in short, would lose much of its bite if obvious solutions or escapes were ready to hand. But if anyone among his dramatis personae is spared the contemporary subjection to simulacra, it is the masses, not as a consequence of any heroic resistance on their part, but simply because the power of the media is still—but for how much longer?—too limited to impose its hegemony that far down. (Compare Winston Smith's vision of the proles in *1984*.) The obduracy of the masses is imaged as deafness, sleep, and finally even death, and thus hardly indicative of "strategies" you and I might pursue. And who exactly Baudrillard's "masses" are—workers? *lumpen?*—is left vague. What it all adds up to hardly deserves to be called an argument, but as an apocalypse it has its satisfactions.

Much counter-culture critique is apocalyptic, of course, and if Baudrillard's seems more forceful than most, it is because he has directed his fury at an easy target: the system of signs that constitutes the cultural surround. Among many of Baudrillard's peers, discussion directs its apocalyptic ambitions not outward on the culture, but instead at a much more problematic object: the autonomous "subject," alias the bourgeois self. As a fact of individual life, "the self" usually remains recalcitrant to grandiose projects of reform and change, and for most of us, this is about as close to "a lesson" as the sixties had to teach. But mere experience notwithstanding, as a token of thought, "the self" is endlessly plastic to utopian will. . . . (pp. 205-06)

Baudrillard bypasses this whole discussion, but his account of "the culture of the simulacrum" often seems to abut the new utopianism of the self in odd and oblique ways. The non-referential, polyvalent, arbitrary, endlessly circulating system of signs that Baudrillard indicts often sounds remarkably like the "decentered," multivocal, intersubjective semiosis that laborers elsewhere in the vineyard celebrate as offering deliverance from the categories of "subject" and "self"—the project recent "literary theory" encodes in terms of *écriture*, textuality, indeterminacy, the death of the author, and so on. These idealizations have often been modeled on popular culture—for Baudrillard, no conduit for subversive authenticity, but rather the epitome of "the simulacrum" commodified—and, in the late seventies, on a peculiarly French fantasy of American culture, to which Baudrillard's dyspeptic *America* is partly a retort.

The multivalent, "open" self that post-sixties counter-culture criticism proposes as a project and an ideal, in short, looks embarrassingly like the commodity-glutted, image-sotted "subject" that Baudrillard indicts as an effect of late media-capitalism. Baudrillard nowhere engages this disagreement frontally—he goes no further than the occasional aside dismissing Lacan, Deleuze and Guattari, and the like—but his example helps focus the peculiar chicken-and-egg dilemma in which post-sixties utopianisms of the remade self are entoiled. Injunctions to remake the self, from Isaiah to Sartre, have assumed that the autonomy of the self from culture was the goal. The contemporary effort has been to expose "the autonomy of the self" as a narcissistic fantasy, a crypto-totalitarian wet dream of personal power, and to deconstruct the rigidity and general uptightness—the repression of "openness"—that this fantasy has engendered. Baudrillard, in effect, raises the question, Open the self to *what?*—not, surely, to the very "culture" whose impositions prompted our revolt in the first place? But what else is there? And he helps focus the paradox that the contemporary assault on the self is in its way only another symptom of the dynamic of self-consciousness and self-concern that has characterized the West from the Old Testament to Saint Paul, Luther, Calvin, Pascal, Descartes, Freud, and beyond.

This point may sound paleo-Marxist—to dismiss fixation on the self as "bourgeois" has been a standard Marxist move since before Freud—but it's one that Marxists in our post-Marxist period seem shy of making. Baudrillard's motive in making it is not, I think, Marxist: despite his occasional sentimentalism about "the masses" on the one hand, and his carefully cultivated "postmodern" aura on the other, Baudrillard's disgust with the "culture of the simulacrum" damns precisely what "postmodernism" is usually celebrated for embracing, and thus encodes a nostalgia akin to that of early twentieth-century modernists (Bergson, Husserl; in English, Eliot, Pound, Williams, Stevens) for "immediated [unmediated] experience." His rejectionist *contemptus mundi* is very much that of an old-style intellectual, an "opposing self"; at no point does his afflatus steer itself into anything resembling an enthusiasm. No such style of intellectualism, no such style of "self"-hood, either, is presently fashionable in Baudrillard's French-academic milieu—which may help measure the achievement represented by that "carefully cultivated postmodern aura," and may explain, too, Baudrillard's caution about declaring his differences with his contemporaries more directly. But Baudrillard's twist on what is by now the orthodoxy of highbrow counter-culture thinking is interesting and

provocative—and should compel those who do not behold in, say, the Sex Pistols, an image of their desire. (pp. 206-07)

Steven Helmling, "A Postmodern Jeremiah," in The Kenyon Review, *n.s. Vol. 12, No. 1, Winter, 1990, pp. 204-07.*

FURTHER READING

Hays, Michael. "A Response to Mark Poster on Jean Baudrillard." In *The Question of Textuality: Strategies of Reading in Contemporary American Criticism,* edited by William V. Spanos, Paul A. Bové, and Daniel O'Hara, pp. 289-93. Bloomington: Indiana University Press, 1982.

    Traces the anthropological roots of Baudrillard's critique of Marxism, also assessing Baudrillard's presentation of Marxist theory, and Poster's explication of the subject.

Kellner, Douglas. *Jean Baudrillard: From Marxism to Postmodernism and Beyond.* Stanford: Stanford University Press, 1989, 246 p.

    The first book-length treatment of Baudrillard's theories in English, this work offers a lucid interpretation and evaluation of Baudrillard's ideas.

Mellancamp, Patricia. "Seeing Is Believing: Baudrillard and Blau." *Theatre Journal* 37, No. 2 (May 1985): 141-54.

    Compares Baudrillard's theory of simulation with Herbert Blau's writings about and for theater.

Valente, Joseph. "Hall of Mirrors: Baudrillard on Marx." *Diacritics* 5, No. 2 (Summer 1985): 54-65.

    Discusses Baudrillard's move from a Marxian to a semiological analysis of culture and economy, uncovering difficulties similar to those of Marxism in Baudrillard's discourse.

Watt, Stephen. "Beckett by Way of Baudrillard: Toward a Political Reading of Samuel Beckett's Drama." In *Myth and Ritual in the Plays of Samuel Beckett,* edited by Katherine H. Burkman, pp. 103-23. Rutherford, N.J.: Fairleigh Dickinson University Press, 1987.

    Utilizes Baudrillard's theories on the status of objects to analyze the political content of Beckett's works.

Erskine Caldwell

1903-1987

(Born Erskine Preston Caldwell) American novelist, short story writer, nonfiction writer, journalist, autobiographer, and scriptwriter.

Considered among the most popular and controversial American authors of the early twentieth century, Caldwell is best known for his works of fiction that depict the plight of impoverished southerners through graphic realism and comic pathos. A fervent opponent of social exploitation, Caldwell frequently portrayed grotesque rustics who are reduced to an animalistic state of ignorance, bigotry, and violence by arbitrary economic and political forces. Although several critics regarded Caldwell's fusion of humor and social commentary as inappropriate, others agreed with Sylvia Jenkins Cook that Caldwell skillfully "increases the burden of comic horror the reader has to bear until the episodes finally become intolerable and a recognition of their tragic implications is inevitable." Several of Caldwell's works, particularly the novels *Tobacco Road* and *God's Little Acre,* have been recurrently banned and censored due to explicit sexual content, yet have earned extensive praise for their vivid evocation of southern dialects and folkways. While critics generally considered his later works to be derivative of his earlier fiction, Caldwell is cited with such authors as John Steinbeck and Ernest Hemingway as a significant contributor to the development of social themes in contemporary American literature.

Caldwell's first two novels, *The Bastard,* the story of a man whose deprived childhood figures in his later criminality, and *Poor Fool,* which examines corruption in boxing, garnered little critical or popular attention. However, his subsequent novels, *Tobacco Road* and *God's Little Acre,* achieved widespread notoriety upon being named in a highly publicized obscenity trial. *Tobacco Road* centers on the Lesters, a family of Georgia sharecroppers who are so debased by poverty that they disregard the needs of others to fulfill their own immediate physical and sexual needs. The novel features, among other characters, the protagonist Jeeter Lester and his slow-witted son, Dude, who agrees to marry a physically repulsive woman in exchange for a new car. After a disastrous trip into town with his wife and father, Dude wrecks the car by running over Jeeter's mother as the family watches indifferently. At the novel's conclusion, Jeeter sets fire to his land to prepare it for planting, but the brush burns out of control and Jeeter and his wife are killed.

God's Little Acre chronicles the declining fortunes of the Waldons, another sharecropping family. At the bidding of their obstinate patriarch Ty Ty, the Waldens ruin their land by obsessively digging for gold. Consumed by complex sexual entanglements and betrayals, the family is ultimately destroyed when Ty Ty's son murders his brother in a jealous rage. This story is juxtaposed with that of Will Thompson, Ty Ty's son-in-law, who becomes the unofficial leader of his fellow cotton mill workers during a strike that is deliberately prolonged by company and union authorities. Will is killed, however, when he attempts to break into the mill and start the machines for the workers. Business, agricultural, and political groups from the South charged Caldwell with exaggerating the living con-

ditions in their region, and in several instances labeled his fiction as communist propaganda. Nevertheless, *Tobacco Road* and *God's Little Acre* eventually won international acclaim for their powerful depictions of social and economic conditions that dehumanize the poor and undermine such cherished American values as hard work and individualism.

Tobacco Road and *God's Little Acre* are the first of ten novels that Caldwell later termed his "cyclorama of Southern life." Although the series is not linked by characters or events into an overall historical framework, Caldwell's "cyclorama" provides a comprehensive portrait of the southern social milieu. Such novels as *Journeyman,* the story of a self-proclaimed preacher whose passionate revivals release the repressed sexuality of his congregation, and *Trouble in July,* which focuses upon a complacent sheriff's involvement in a lynching, garnered praise for their incisive treatment of compelling social issues. Later works in the cyclorama include *Tragic Ground, A House in the Uplands, The Sure Hand of God, This Very Earth, Place Called Estherville,* and *Episode in Palmetto.* While objecting to the sensational plots of these novels, critics have commended Caldwell's use of a direct, unsentimental prose style that skillfully conveys his characters' oppressive existence. Robert Hazel commented: "[We] can conclude that the nature of the action in Caldwell is precisely what its language makes it, and that the world is, among other things, one of plain speech, of local idiom, of vulgar rather than fine motivations and actions, of a uniform levelness, of a consistent and impressive monotony, a desicated world where the lifting of a hand or foot seems to be arduous and significant, a world lacking in poetry."

While most of Caldwell's novels have failed to achieve the renown of *Tobacco Road* and *God's Little Acre,* several are recognized for their effective rendering of his characteristic themes and concerns. Malcolm Cowley referred to *The Sacrilege of Alan Kent,* a fictional autobiography constructed around a series of epiphanic events, as a "prose poem that corresponds on a lesser scale to Whitman's 'Song of Myself'." *Georgia Boy,* considered one of Caldwell's best if most overlooked novels, portrays the complex relationships between the twelve-year-old narrator, his eccentric parents, and his best friend, a young black farmhand. Together with William Faulkner's *The Reivers,* this novel is regarded as among the most insightful treatments of adolescence in the American South. Caldwell's other novels to achieve critical recognition include *A Lamp for Nightfall,* the story of a small New England community whose tranquility is threatened by outsiders; *Miss Mama Aimee,* a darkly humorous narrative concerning an aging woman, her prostitute daughter, and a lecherous preacher; and *The Weather Shelter,* the story of a mulatto boy and his search for acceptance in a small southern town.

In addition to his novels, Caldwell gained notoriety for his short stories, many of which are gathered in such collections as *We Are the Living, Kneel to the Rising Sun, Southways,* and *The Complete Stories of Erskine Caldwell.* Caldwell's short fiction, like his novels, frequently features disenfranchised characters whose private conflicts expose widespread social inequities. "Candyman Beechum," one of Caldwell's most frequently anthologized stories, revolves around a spirited black mule skinner who dies rather than obey a racist white sheriff. Another piece, "Daughter," focuses upon a man who murders his beloved daughter rather than allow her to starve. Following his arrest, a mob of equally inpoverished individuals gathers around the jail, but rather than lynch him as expected, they overwhelm the authorities and release him. In "Kneel to the Rising Sun," a black sharecropper speaks out against his landlord on behalf of another tenant, a white man, who later betrays his comrade when forced to choose between their friendship and racial loyalties. Sylvia Jenkins Cook observed that "Caldwell demonstrates the capacity of the short story to deal powerfully with social themes by creating an intense emotional effect which need never be dissipated, as in the novels, by comic diversions, unduly complex philosophy, or explanatory sociology."

Caldwell is also the author of several works of nonfiction that reflect his concern for the plight of society's underprivileged. Along with his many controversial articles on this subject, Caldwell gained notice for *You Have Seen Their Faces,* a collaborative effort produced with his second wife, the renowned photographer Margaret Bourke-White. Originating from their desire to document the conditions described in Caldwell's fiction, *You Have Seen Their Faces* combines Bourke-White's photographs with essays and captions by Caldwell that illustrate the squalid living conditions of poor southerners. Caldwell and Bourke-White also won praise for *North of the Danube,* a text with photographs that records their tour through Czechoslovakia during the rise of fascism in the late

1930s. In addition to his collaborations with Bourke-White, Caldwell composed several well-received autobiographical works. These include *Call It Experience,* an informal recollection of his writing career; *Deep South,* a memoir of his father, an itinerate preacher; and *In Search of Bisco,* about Caldwell's attempt to find the black playmate whose childhood friendship influenced his racial attitudes.

(See also *CLC,* Vols. 1, 8, 14, 50; *Contemporary Authors,* Vols. 1-4, rev. ed., Vol. 121 [obituary]; *Contemporary Authors New Revision Series,* Vol. 2; *Contemporary Authors Autobiography Series,* Vol. 1; and *Dictionary of Literary Biography,* Vol. 9.)

PRINCIPAL WORKS

NOVELS

The Bastard   1929
Poor Fool   1930
Tobacco Road   1932
God's Little Acre   1933
Journeyman   1935
The Sacrilege of Alan Kent   1936
Trouble in July   1940
All Night Long   1942
Georgia Boy   1943
Tragic Ground   1944
A House in the Uplands   1946
The Sure Hand of God   1947
This Very Earth   1948
Place Called Estherville   1949
Episode in Palmetto   1950
A Lamp for Nightfall   1952
Love and Money   1954
Gretta   1955
Claudelle Inglish   1958
Jenny by Nature   1961
Close to Home   1962
The Last Night of Summer   1963
Miss Mama Aimee   1967
Summertime Island   1968
The Weather Shelter   1969
The Earnshaw Neighborhood   1971
Annette   1973

SHORT STORY COLLECTIONS

American Earth   19330
We Are the Living   1933
Kneel to the Rising Sun   1933
Southways   1938
Jackpot   1940
The Courting of Susie Brown   1952
The Complete Stories of Erskine Caldwell   1953
Gulf Coast Stories   1956
Certain Women   1957
What You Think of Me   1959
Men and Women   1961
Stories of Life, North and South: Selections from the Best Short Stories of Erskine Caldwell   1983

OTHER

Tenant Farmers   (nonfiction)   1935
Some American People   (nonfiction)   1935

You Have Seen Their Faces [with Margaret Bourke-White] (nonfiction) 1937
North of the Danube [with Margaret Bourke-White] (nonfiction) 1939
Say! Is This the U.S.A. [with Margaret Bourke-White] (nonfiction) 1941
Russia at War [with Margaret Bourke-White] (nonfiction) 1942
Moscow Under Fire (nonfiction) 1942
All-Out on the Road to Smolensk (nonfiction) 1942
Call It Experience (autobiography) 1951
Around about America (nonfiction) 1964
In Search of Bisco (autobiography) 1965
In the Shadow of the Steeple (nonfiction) 1967
Writing in America (nonfiction) 1967
Deep South (nonfiction) 1968
Afternoons in Mid-America: Observations and Impressions (nonfiction) 1976
With All My Might (autobiography) 1987

HORACE GREGORY

When Erskine Caldwell published **American Earth**, a book of short stories last year, it was evident that here was a young man who was ready to write an unusually good first novel. First of all he had the knack of telling a story in the intimate folk manner that reminds one of Mark Twain and Sherwood Anderson. In other words, he tells lies engagingly, exaggerating a point here and a point there, but never violating the essential truth of a character or a situation. The people that he chose to write about were of the American backwoods, of the far South or of Maine. He clothed the whole with a warm vibrant prose that permitted the release of a poetic imagination and a charmingly boyish personality which contained something of the anti-intellectual, inarticulate naiveté that we associate with Ernest Hemingway.

It is not too much to say that his novel, **Tobacco Road**, lives up to all expectations. The scene is laid in the deep South, Georgia, and again we have a portrait of Mr. Caldwell's American primitives. We are concerned here with the misadventures of the Lester family, once good, prosperous tobacco farmers, but now degenerated into poor white trash, who against reason and their own ability to farm anything at all attempt to raise cotton in impoverished soil. Principally, we have to deal with Jeeter, a man of forty-five or fifty, father of seventeen children. By the time the story opens, most of the children have left home, drifted to a mill town some miles away from the farm. Pearl, a yellow haired, blue eyed girl of twelve, has just married a neighbor who earns the miraculous sum of a dollar a day working a coal chute down in the railroad yard. Neither Pearl nor her husband is satisfied with the match, for Pearl doesn't understand what being a wife means. . . . There is Ellie May, older than Pearl but unmarried and afraid to leave home because she has a hair lip. Duke, the sixteen year old son, a trifle less than half witted, spends days, weeks and months throwing a ball against the house and catching it on the rebound. There is Grandma Lester, who is shoved away from the table at meal times because she eats too much of what little good Jeeter can steal. There is Jeeter's wife, battered and broken down with the raising of

too many children, and last of all, Jeeter himself, who hopes by miracle to raise credit for fertilizer and cotton seed.

The action of the story centers around Duke's marriage with Bessie, a widowed, lady preacher of thirty-eight who has $800 in the bank. By promising Duke an automobile with a horn that really honks, Bessie wins his reluctant consent to marry her. . . . The car, of course, is a great event in the Lester family who had once owned a dilapidated Ford, long since useless, even for junk iron. How Duke wrecks the car in the crazy fashion of a Joe Cook act at the Palace is Erskine Caldwell's symbol of the Lester family's decline. Anything falling into the hands of a Lester means destruction. The family is irrevocably doomed.

Consciously or unconsciously—one is never quite certain—Mr. Caldwell drives home the agricultural decay of the South. Mr. Caldwell does not pretend to be an economist; and I would say that more than half of his effects are produced by an artist's instinct for selecting significant detail. The result, however, is far more impressive than any statistical record that may be drawn up concerning the poverty, illiteracy, physical and mental degeneration of the Southern farmer. Here and there, throughout the course of the novel one finds an episode or the expression of a point of view that throws a searchlight upon existing conditions in the South. The poor whites are afraid of being laughed at by the Negroes, but the Negroes are always at some safe distance down the road, laughing aloud at the misfortunes of the Lesters. The bankers, vaguely outlined but secure beyond the reach of the farmer, control his destiny by the abuse of the credit system. There is no real co-operation between Jeeter and his neighbors, nor between Jeeter and the men in the small town who once held mortgages upon his farm, but have now discarded their holdings and have left him to starve. In a sense they are as prodigal, as irresponsible as Duke himself riding the widow's Ford, running down a Negro and finally killing his grandmother. The brutal, savage, fantastic humor of the automobile scenes in the novel seem to be related to the more significant episodes in the completer history of the Southern peasant.

It is possible to read a number of implications into Caldwell's novel, perhaps a great deal more than he himself intended; but the fact remains that Mr. Caldwell is dealing with important material. More than this alone, Mr. Caldwell's humor, like Mark Twain's, has at its source, an imagination that stirs the emotions of the reader. The adolescent, almost idiotic gravity of Mr. Caldwell's characters produces instantaneous laughter and their sexual adventures are treated with an irreverence that verges upon the robust ribaldry of a burlesque show.

Horace Gregory, "Our American Primitives," in New York Herald Tribune Books, *February 21, 1932, p. 4.*

LOUIS KRONENBERGER

It is always distinctly interesting to read a novel which has nothing in common with other novels, which has a sense of life all its own and a personality wholly its author's. **God's Little Acre** is surely such a book. Leaving all other questions momentarily aside, no more original novel has appeared in America for a long while. Perhaps nobody has tried to write one so original, perhaps nobody has dared. For Erskine Caldwell has roundly dropped the bottom out of realism, swung people around like a cat by its tail, and made a few acres of Georgia soil into something more productive than even the richest soil can be.

The Waldens live on those few acres: old Ty Ty, the father of the family; his daughter, Darling Jill; his son, Shaw; his son, Buck, and Buck's beautiful wife, Griselda. Within easy driving distance, across the border in Carolina, live Ty Ty's married daughter, Rosamond, and her husband, Will. Will is a mill worker, but the rest of the family—except for one son who has climbed up in the world and dropped his relations—are all employed on the farm helping Ty Ty find gold. For years and years the old man has been certain that if only he digs deep enough in the right spot, he will stumble onto gold; and when he and his sons have dug a hole pretty deep and found nothing, they shift ground and start digging again somewhere else. The farm is scarred with gaping holes, the farmhouse is tottering on its foundations, corn and cotton have long since ceased to grow, the Waldens are flat broke, and still, obsessed by his mad dream, Ty Ty feverishly whips them on. Only one other thing divides their interest in life, and that is sex. Most of the sex takes place right in the family. . . . For a long time the amorous merrymaking is treated with a shrugging of shoulders; Ty Ty himself regards it with patriarchal benevolence. . . .

Mr. Caldwell creates his world with a broad but pervasive humor. Although the comedy plays constantly on one string, it miraculously escapes monotony. Ty Ty himself is remarkably well sustained, more amusing for his nonchalance toward what goes on and his rich rolling speech than for his obsession—an obsession you can't quite convince yourself he believes in—for gold. The whole situation on the Waldens' farm reads like an elaborate off-color story skillfully combined with an enlarged comic strip. The hopeless search for gold, year after year, resembles the frustrated endeavors of Pa's Son-in-law or Jiggs or Caspar Milquetoast, week after week, to make the grade.

Were this all, one could acclaim Mr. Caldwell for putting simple materials under intense pressure and achieving a fine piece of comic writing at once realistic, naive and insane. But near the end of *God's Little Acre* Mr. Caldwell proceeds to tear down all he has built up by resorting to melodrama and tragedy. The cuckolded Buck goes berserk, only fails to murder his brother-in-law, Will, because Will is killed in a labor riot, and succeeds in murdering his brother, Jim Leslie, and in killing himself. We are prepared for no such dénouement and when it comes we are in no frame of mind to accept it. In comedy, as Strachey has pointed out, though human nature and human actions are revealed, their consequences are suspended. In comedy the logical results of human conduct must not be shown, or, if they are, it must be in a mood which harmonizes with the mood that preceded it. In *God's Little Acre* we are wrenched out of a fantastic world of mad searching and robust animality into a world of low greed and willful lust. At the end one is reminded of nothing so much as *Desire Under the Elms*. The whole business blows up: the plot goes awry, the mood is shattered, the characters change their spots.

In many respects this is an unusual book. It is original, vigorous, lusty. But no novelist of modern times ever made a more serious mistake than Caldwell did when he ceased to woo the comic muse and began paying stiff, self-conscious homage to the muse of tragedy.

Louis Kronenberger, " 'God's Little Acre' and Some Other Recent Works of Fiction," in The New York Times Book Review, *February 5, 1933, p. 6.*

THE SATURDAY REVIEW OF LITERATURE

A novel that will lift the noses of the sensitive, Erskine Caldwell's *God's Little Acre,* is nevertheless a beautifully integrated story of the barren Southern farm and the shut Southern mill, and one of the finest studies of the Southern poor white which has ever come into our literature. Writing in the brutal images of the life of his poor white people, Mr. Caldwell has caught in poetic quality the debased and futile aspiration of men and women restless in a world of long hungers which must be satisfied quickly, if at all.

This book is the full maturity of the promise Mr. Caldwell showed in his *Tobacco Road* of a year or so ago. There he dealt with the poorest poor whites, men and women too sodden for any feeling beyond the simplest hungers. Living like dirt, their tragedy was no more moving than the sweeping of dirt away. In *God's Little Acre* he writes of the Waldens, divided between farm and mill, who, still sordid, still lacking in anything above animal morality, are nevertheless moved by some vigor of desire. Their world is one in which women are beautiful until pellagra comes with quick ugliness. In Ty Ty Walden's restless digging for gold, in Will Thompson's determination to start the machines turning again in the padlocked mill, in the general masculine desire for the body of Griselda, he creates, in the vigorous terms of character and humor and lust, the struggle out of which the tragedy grows.

The story centers about the pitted Georgia farm where Ty Ty, contemptuous of cotton and food crops, digs great holes in persistent and foolish search. The acre which he set aside for God moves at Ty Ty's restless will all about the farm for as he tells his loose daughter's fat and lazy suitor, "I'd hate to have to see the lode struck on God's little acre the first time, and be compelled to turn it all over to the church". . . . In the end all the increase that comes to God's little acre is quarrelling and fornication and death.

As Ty Ty moves God's little acre about, so Mr. Caldwell carries his characters on automobile rides to Augusta, to Scotsville in the mill section of South Carolina, in such a way that the rides themselves seem symbolic of the aimless restlessness of his people. . . . Only Ty Ty in his digging, and his son-in-law, Will Thompson, in his direct action radicalism are moved by any definite aim, and in each of them that single-mindedness of concept and desire endows them with a quality of manhood even if it does not save them from futility and helplessness.

It would be a mistake to consider Mr. Caldwell a grim realist. Behind his grim, sometimes shocking, details he is a poet, occasionally almost lyric, and a poet whose sensitiveness to life is made strong and whole by a vigorous sense of humor. His comedy in *God's Little Acre* is full and rich as it grows out of his characters. Pluto Swint, who wants to be sheriff but is too fat and lazy to get around to his campaigning, waits in huge bashfulness until Darling Jill Walden becomes pregnant by someone else so she will marry him. Will Thompson, caught red-handed in adultery on his way to heroism, runs naked through the streets of Scotsville from his wife's pistol. Ty Ty Walden is sure his daughter, Darling Jill, knows too much about the moon to bring disgrace upon his family.

From such rough native comedy, Mr. Caldwell turns to his poetry in his description of the mill town. Remarkably his frank poetry fits easily into his more earthly story. He writes without arousing any sense of intrusion such passages as:

> The men who worked in the mill looked tired and worn, but the girls were in love with the looms and the spindles and the flying lint. The wild-eyed girls on the inside of the ivy-walled mill looked like potted plants in bloom. Up and down the Valley lay the company towns and the ivy-walled cotton mills and the firm-bodied girls with eyes like morning glories, and the men stood on the hot streets looking at each other while they spat their lungs into the deep yellow dust of Carolina. . . . In the mill streets of the Valley towns the breasts of girls were firm and erect. The cloth they wove under the blue lights clothed their bodies, but beneath the covering the motions of erect breasts were like quick movements of hands in unrest. In the Valley towns beauty was begging, and the hunger of strong men was like the whimpering of beaten women.

There are in American literature few descriptions of industrial conflict so simply, so directly, and so accurately done. Never once is Mr. Caldwell pointing a finger at injustice. He is drawing men and women. His story of industrial conflict grows in a room where a mill hand is committing adultery with his sister-in-law, and it grows there more clearly than in any detailed tractarian description that has ever been written. So also he draws the Southern farm in crude terms of human life and the red barren land emerges in reality. Not once does Mr. Caldwell cease to be the artist. To him the sharp imprecation of a whore on a back street in Augusta is as much a detail to be shaped into articulate beauty as any primrose that ever grew on any river's brim. It is an attitude safe from prurience in none but the ablest hands, but Mr. Caldwell has them. Those who see his ugliness and not his beauty are unable to see the forest for the trees.

"Farm and Mill," in The Saturday Review of Literature, *Vol. IX, No. 31, February 18, 1933, p. 437.*

GEORGE STEVENS

In the country of *Tobacco Road* and *God's Little Acre*—in that fabulous area, populated by monsters, which he calls Georgia—Erskine Caldwell lays the scene of [*Journeyman*]. It tells of a few days in the community of Rocky Comfort, during which the inhabitants fall under the spell of a lecherous, gun-toting, corn-drinking journeyman preacher named Semon Dye. Semon cheats the men out of their money, makes himself free with the women, winds up his proceedings with a burlesque revival meeting, and skips out before daybreak, leaving the populace with a well-brewed emotional hangover.

All this takes the reader even further south in the observation of humanity than Mr. Caldwell's previous novels; but readers of *God's Little Acre* will find nothing essentially surprising in the characters of *Journeyman.* Because of the author's apparent predilection for characters in the lowest stratum of human society, the impression has got about that he is a realist. . . . To apply this label to Erskine Caldwell suggests that his stories are drawn from observation rather than imagination. The evidence of *Journeyman* points to the opposite conclusion. The characters talk a strange language—peculiar literary expressions mixed with the native idiom. The details of community life are left somewhat vague, and the economic

status of the characters seems to vary inexplicably. One gets the impression that everybody for miles around has the hookworm. Characters fade in and out, with no definite origins or destinations. These are loose ends which a realist would not leave.

Above all, everything has the effect of exaggeration. Clay Horey has had five wives. His friend up the road makes incredible quantities of white mule, which they all drink by the gallon. *Journeyman* has reality, but it is the reality of a nightmare, not of observation. And the characters behave like characters in a nightmare. . . .

All this has perfect consistency as an imaginative work. Its value as such is another question. The effect of Erskine Caldwell's writing varies with different readers, depending on taste and previous experience in modern fiction. What seems disgusting to some seems funny to others, and those who find certain passages humorous have compared Mr. Caldwell to Mark Twain. To the present reviewer, this comparison seems far fetched. There may be humor, by some definitions, in *Journeyman,* but it is like laughing at a deformity. One may concede that Erskine Caldwell's writing is forcible, genuine, and interesting, and leave the rest of the burden of proof on the affirmative.

It is probably dangerous, at this stage of Erskine Caldwell's career, to try to "place" him. But one may hazard a guess. Our guess is that the products of Mr. Caldwell's imagination are not sufficiently significant in themselves to evoke a profound imaginative response generally; and that he has not the power of language to create such a response by purely literary means. But his books have, as we said, their own reality. Perhaps they present scenes and characters unlike any you have observed before; but after you have read his books, you may find scenes and characters that will remind you of them. This is entirely different from saying that Mr. Caldwell is a realist—it is, in fact, just the opposite.

George Stevens, "The Fabulous Land Along Tobacco Road," in The Saturday Review of Literature, *Vol. XI, No. 29, February 2, 1935, p. 457.*

KENNETH BURKE

Erskine Caldwell's most revealing work is a "sport." I refer to the last story in *American Earth,* **"The Sacrilege of Alan Kent."** It is divided into three sections, with wholly non-Caldwellian titles, "Tracing Life with a Finger," "Inspiration for Greatness," and "Hours Before Eternity." In these words we catch a tonality of brooding which, though so much a part of America as to have been pronounced by Poe, is more generally associated with the pious satanists who developed the ways of Poe in Europe: Baudelaire, Rimbaud, Lautréamont, and the early Gide. This work is as unique to Caldwell in manner as it is in mood. Whereas his other stories, long or short, are written with the continuity of the undulations along a moving caterpillar's back, **"The Sacrilege"** is a chain of brief numbered paragraphs, each bluntly set off from the rest. Done with the solemnity of a farewell or a testament, they contain a kind of aphoristic rhetoric, except that the aphorisms are less ideas than tiny plots. We note here a formal resonance, a stentorian quality, obtained by a swift recital of plagues, monstrosities, horrors, obsessions, disasters and gigantesque imaginings, set against a tender counter-theme: "I never heard a girl whose face and body and eyes were lovely say anything but lovely words." Here we have the symbol of the wanderer, driven by unnamed sins and called by vague visions of a homecoming in female sweetness. The swift segments shunt us back and forth between brutality and wistfulness. Perhaps the grandiose, the violent, and the gentle qualities of the piece are all fused in this bit of purest poetry: "Once the sun was so hot a bird came down and walked beside me in my shadow." A section in *Pagany* containing this item was the first thing by Caldwell I ever saw. For days I was noisy in my enthusiasm—but I could not understand how it went with some of his other work.

Now that we have five books to examine, the connections are more easily discernible. It seems to me that Caldwell has elsewhere retained the same balked religiosity as distinguishes **"The Sacrilege,"** but has merely poured it into less formidable molds. We may detect it, transformed, as the incentive leading him to blaspheme and profane for our enjoyment. We may glimpse this balked religiosity in the symbolic transgressions and death penalties that give shape to the plots of *Tobacco Road* and *God's Little Acre.* It is the explicit subject matter of much conversation in all his novels. It is revealed by an almost primitive concern with sexual taboos, and with fertility rites rising in opposition to the theme of castration. In its temperate, more social aspects, it shows as a tendency to deny humans their humaneness as though the author, secretly abased, wanted to "drag others down" with him. Entertainingly, it appears in still more attenuated form as caricature and humor, the mental state of "refusal" here inducing extravagant incongruities that sometimes can be received with laughter, but are frequently so closely connected with degradation and acute suffering that the effect is wholly grim. Towards the end of his longer works, the goad of balked religiosity provokes grandiloquent moralistic passages wherein his subnormal mannikins, strangely elated by the story's symbolism, transcend themselves and speak of vital purpose with almost evangelical fervor (plus a slight suggestion that they had read D. H. Lawrence). And in an unexpected episode of *Journeyman,* his latest book, Caldwell has even gone so far as to introduce a quality of other-worldliness into the very midst of his human rabbit hutch—for in no other way can I interpret the section . . . where three men take turns at peering out through a crack in the wall of the barn, while one sermonizes: "It's sitting there and looking through the crack at the trees all day long that sort of gets me. I don't know what it is, and it might not be nothing at all when you figure it out. But it's not the knowing about it, anyway—it's just sitting there and looking through it that sort of makes me feel like heaven can't be so doggone far away."

In taking balked religiosity as the underlying theme upon which his successive works are the variations, I do not want to imply that Caldwell, like Hemingway, is preparing himself for a return to Rome. His recent powerful story in *Kneel to the Rising Sun,* indicates that he can make the change from negativism to affirmation by choices usually called secular. In so far as he is moved by the need of salvation, he seems minded to find it in the alignments of political exhortation, by striving mainly to see that we and we take the right side on matters of social justice. But as partial vindication of my proposal that his cult of incongruity seems to stem from the same source as his social propaganda, I should note that, precisely in this story of a lynching, his emphasis upon the playful scrambling of the old proprieties abates: instead of the humorist's refusal, as shown in his earlier zest to garble the conventions, we get a sober assertion of positive values. He does

not merely act to outrage an old perspective by throwing its orders of right and wrong into disarray: he subscribes to an alternative perspective, with positive rights and wrongs of its own, and with definite indications as to what form he wants our sympathies and antagonisms to take. Incidentally, this development suggests the ways in which a motivation essentially non-political or non-economic can be harnessed in the service of political or economic criticism.

Whether one so apt at entertaining us by *muddling* our judgments will be equally fertile in *stabilizing* judgments remains to be seen. My guess would be that he won't, since he would have to master a whole new technique of expression. His very abilities tend to work against him. Recently I heard one man complain that Caldwell "has yet to learn that the revolution begins above the belt." And I incline to suspect that, in the learning, he may begin to find himself psychologically unemployed. A literary method is tyrannical—it is a writer's leopard-spots—it molds what a writer can say by determining what he can see; hence I should imagine that Caldwell would have to develop by satirizing more complex people rather than by pleading unmistakably for simple ones. But that is a guess about tomorrow's weather.

When I say that Caldwell's particular aptitude has been in scrambling or garbling proprieties, I refer to his deft way of putting the wrong things together. An unendowed writer, for instance, might strain to engross us by lurid description of the sexual act—and the result would be negligible. But such an uninventive writer would probably be quite "proper" in the sense that he accepted the usual conventions as to the privacy of this act. Caldwell can be much more stimulating by merely so altering the customary situation that people are looking on and commenting in the blandest fashion, as in the comically inappropriate episode of this nature in *God's Little Acre.* Or he may have Ty Ty say, without confusion, such things to his daughters and daughter-in-law as would "properly" be said only under the greatest of morbid intensity. By an astounding trick of oversimplification, Caldwell puts people into complex social situations while making them act with the scant, crude tropisms of an insect—and the result is cunning, where Lawrence, by a variant of the same pattern, is as unwieldy as an elephant in his use of vulgar words for romantic love-making. Probably only in the orgy at the end of *Journeyman* does Caldwell become so undiplomatic in his treatment. Here, with almost the literalness of an inventory, he has us observe in each member of the congregation that phenomenon which so mortified Saint John of the Cross, the fact that, since the body has less channels of expression than the mind, acute religious ecstasy may be paralleled neurologically by sexual orgasm.

In the psychology textbooks, we read accounts of experiments whereby the higher centers of an animal's brain are removed, with the result that the animal's responses to stimuli are greatly simplified. A frog, so decerebrated, may jump when prodded, eat when fed, and croak when caressed—but it is evident that with the operation the poor fellow's personality has vanished. . . . He has lost the part of himself that is sometimes called free will and which Bergson names the "center of indetermination." And his ways, as compared with the ways of a whole frog, are distinctly grotesque. Caldwell often seems to have performed such an operation upon the minds of his characters. As Ty Ty Walden complains in *God's Little Acre,* "There was a mean trick played on us somewhere. God put us in the body of animals and tried to make us act like people." It is a just complaint of Ty Ty's, as the creature of his own private creator. What the decerebrated frog is to the whole frog, Caldwell's characters are to real people. In view of which, it is positively incredible that his extravaganzas, imagined in a world essentially as fantastic as Swift's, should ever have passed for realism.

Pearl, the image of better things in *Tobacco Road,* does not even *speak.* Anderson's gropers stuttered, but in this book the golden-haired childs wife who is charged with the novelistic duty of upholding a little corner of glory in the midst of degradation, is totally inarticulate. For her there is no such verbal key as that with which the great sonneteer unlocked his heart. Though married, she sleeps alone; she will not look at her uncouth husband; she refuses to discuss his appetites with him . . . ; and in the end, still wordless, she vanishes, doubtless to become a prostitute in Augusta. Silk stockings in the city, we feel, is her noblest conceivable utopian negation of the physical and spiritual impoverishment all about her; but to her understanding of this little, she will bring a deep, innate delicacy, invisible to all but the novelist and his readers.

In this discussion of Pearl, I may seem to have involved myself in a contradiction. For I speak of Caldwell's subhuman characters, yet I credit them with great delicacy. Here we come to the subtlest feature of Caldwell's method. Where the author leaves out so much, the reader begins making up the difference for himself. Precisely by omitting humaneness where humaneness is most called for, he may stimulate the reader to supply it. When the starved grandmother in *Tobacco Road* lies dying, with her face ground into the soil, and no one shows even an onlooker's interest in her wretchedness, we are prodded to anguish. When these automata show some bare inkling of sociality, it may seem like a flash of ultimate wisdom. I suspect that, in putting the responsibility upon his readers, he is taking more out of the community pile than he puts in. Perhaps he is using up what we already had, rather than adding to our store. He has evoked in us a quality, but he has not materialized it with sufficient quantity. (pp. 232-33)

I have denied that Caldwell is a realist. In his tomfoolery he comes closer to the Dadaists; when his grotesqueness is serious, he is a Superrealist. We might compromise by calling him over all a Symbolist (if by a Symbolist we mean a writer whose work serves most readily as case history for the psychologist and whose plots are more intelligible when interpreted as dreams). (p.234)

In books of complex realistic texture, such as the great social novels of the nineteenth century, we may feel justified in considering the psychologist's comments as an intrusion when he would have us find there merely a sublimation of a few rudimentary impulses. The important thing is not the base, but the superstructure. With fantastic simplifications of the Caldwell sort, however, the symbolic approach has more relevance. Thus, the selection of extreme starvation as a theme for *Tobacco Road* is found to take on a significance besides that of realistic justification when we link it with passages in *God's Little Acre* where Ty Ty, admiring Griselda, declares that the sight of her "rising beauties" makes him feel inspired to "get down and lick something." How possibly explain as mere reporting the episode in *God's Little Acre* about the girls who have replaced the men in the factory, and of whom we read the dreamlike statement, "When they reached the street, they ran back to the ivy-colored wall and pressed their bodies against it and touched it with their lips. The men who

had been standing idly before it all day long came and dragged them home and beat them unmercifully for their infidelity"? A factory that could induce such surprising antics must have peculiar connotations not realistically there. And perhaps we come closer to them when recalling how, in this same factory, where the rebellion of the workers takes very unreal forms, Will finally fulfills his determination to "turn on the power," but only after his perverted rape of Griselda. When the old grandmother dies, the sight of her face in the dirt simply reminds her son Jeeter that the soil is right for planting. Immediately after, he is destroyed by fire.

The symbolic relations submerged here begin to suggest themselves when we recall the following facts: In both *Tobacco Road* and *God's Little Acre* we are told that there are two types of people, those who stay on the farm and those who go to the factory. Both Jeeter of *Tobacco Road* and Ty Ty of *God's Little Acre* are the kind that stay on the farm, the first hoping to plant again (a frustrated hope) and the second digging in the bowels of the earth for gold (an exceptional obsession to motivate an entire book about contemporary Georgia, though we may legitimately remember here the golden-haired Pearl of *Tobacco Road*). In one of the short stories, **"Crown Fire,"** we learn from the course of the plot that the fire symbol is linked with partial female acquiescence; and in **"The Sacrilege,"** where the "offense" is unnamed, we are told, "My mother saw from her bed the reflection in the sky of red wind-fanned flames. She carried me out into the street and we sat in the red mud shivering and crying"—sitting in this same soil with which Jeeter is so impotently preoccupied (since he cannot buy the seed for planting) and which Ty Ty turns into sterility by digging there for gold. After Will carries out in actuality the perverse inclination Ty Ty speaks of, Will can "turn on the power" in the factory. But though Will here seems to deputize for Ty Ty, Ty Ty's son commits a murder and must run away. Ty Ty moans that blood has been spilled upon his land, whereupon he is freed of his obsession to dig gold; and as the son is leaving, Ty Ty wills that God's little acre be always under him. Both books are thus permeated with symbolic sins, symbolic punishments, followed by symbolic purification. At the end of each, and following the orgy in *Journeyman,* there is the feeling that a cleansing had taken place, that the character who, at the last transformation, is the bearer of the author's identity, is free to "start anew." All this is magic, not reason; and I think that we are entitled to inspect it for the processes of magic. The balked religiosity of which we spoke is evidently linked with the devious manifestations of "incest-awe"; the plots are subtly guided by the logic of dreams.

I am not by any means satisfied by the psychoanalytic readings of such processes to date, though I do believe that in moralistic fantasies of the Caldwell type, where the dull characters become so strangely inspired at crucial moments, we are present at a poetic law court where judgments are passed upon kinds of transgression inaccessible to jurists, with such odd penalties as no Code Napoleon could ever schematize.

The short stories (republished in *American Earth* and *We Are the Living*) as a whole seem too frail. They are hardly more than jottings in a diary, mere *situations* that Caldwell, with his exceptional turn for narrative and his liquid style, manages to palm off as plots. I call them diary jottings because they often give the impression of having suggested themselves to him in this wise: If you were sitting alone in a strange room, you might think, "What if someone knocked at the door?" If Caldwell were similarly placed, such a thought might occur to him, and there he would have his story.

He has a sharper sense of beginnings than most writers, as witness in the long story, *Journeyman,* Semon Dye's formal entrance in the lavishly balky and noisy car. Here is a mock announcement of the hero's approach, done with such a blare and fanfare of brasses as Wagner summons to herald the approach of Siegfried. Thus, the author tends to begin with some oddity of situation, which as likely as not suggested itself without a resolution, so that the story merely fades away rather than closes. He shows a surprisingly naïve delight in all the possible ramifications of the thought that girls may be without panties, and he seems to have searched the length and breadth of the country for new situations whereby some significant part or parts can be exposed for us. The basic formula seems to be the use of two unrelated orders of events until they are felt to be related. He gets very appealing pictures of adolescent love—but his most successful venture in the shorter form is probably **"Country Full of Swedes,"** where a family returns to their house across the road after a couple of years' absence, and their sudden prevalence in the locality is amusingly magnified until, for all their obvious peacefulness, they take on the qualities of a vast invasion.

Caldwell's greatest vice is unquestionably repetitiousness. He seems as contented as a savage to say the same thing again and again. Repetition in his prose is so extreme as almost to perform the function of rhyme in verse. In analyzing the first four chapters of *Tobacco Road,* I found that it was simply a continual rearrangement of the same subjects in different sequences: Jeeter wants Lov's turnips, Lov wants Jeeter to make Pearl sleep with him, Jeeter's own turnips all have "damn-blasted green-gutted turnip-worms," hair-lipped Ellie May is sidling up to Lov, Dude won't stop "chunking" a ball against the loose clapboards, Jeeter hopes to sell a load of wood in Augusta—about ten more such details, regiven in changing order, make the content of forty pages. Sometimes when reading Caldwell I feel as though I were playing with my toes. (pp. 234-35)

Kenneth Burke, "Caldwell: Maker of Grotesques," in The New Republic, *Vol. LXXXII, No. 1062, April 10, 1935, pp. 232-35.*

WILLIAM DU BOIS

Erskine Caldwell has come back from the steppes at last. He returns with a heart-warming book about the South he understands so completely, a book in which the Caldwell trademarks of dry rot, degeneracy and despair are conspicuous by their absence. His admirers may rejoice now that his stint as a Russian correspondent has ended.

Georgia Boy might well have been subtitled "Life With Father on the Tobacco Road." The comparison between Clarence Day and the Morris Stroup of these light-hearted sketches is inevitable—and more apparent than real. Both characters are "universals" in the best sense of Plato's term. But the life story of Pa Stroup, as glimpsed through the mind of his 12-year-old son, William, is a magnificent tribute to the inertia that dwells so comfortably in the Southern soul. Morris Stroup is sly as a hound dog as he pursues his ease and the elusive half dollar; he is single-minded as a mule in his misconception of a citizen's duty in a democracy. In short,

he is Jeeter Lester with the psycopath burned clean away—as disarming a no-account as you will meet in a month of Sundays. . . .

Mr. Caldwell's readers need not be reminded that his Georgia is far removed from the ruined pillars of Margaret Mitchell's Tara or that his people are worlds apart from Berry Fleming's red-clay rogues. The Caldwell cosmos is a part of the pine barrens that sweep south across the Florida line to Okeechobee—a land of palmetto scrub and chinaberry trees and played-out sandy loam that manages to look bone-dry an hour after a downpour. Its people are the incredible residue of British migration, inbred and aloof; most of them, it would seem, were born to share-crop since the days of Oglethorpe—or, like Morris Stroup, to dream of easy riches in the shade.

It is unfair to complain if these people seem cunning or corrupt or fanatically unjust. Most of them are too amoral for such easy judgments, too hopelessly removed from the revolutions that rock the world today. Mr. Caldwell has dissected them before with searing bitterness. In *Georgia Boy* he writes of them with a tolerance that comes close to tenderness.

Perhaps this mellow mood is a by-product, after all. For it is evident from the first page, that young William Stroup loves his wily old scoundrel of a father with all his heart, that he would follow him in all his hare-brained plots to lick the world—providing the licking did not require too much effort. When Pa sets out to make his fortune collecting scrap-iron, it seems only natural to William that they should include the neighbors' washtubs and pump-handles. When the elder Stroup enters into a "swopping match" with a band of gypsies, William is not surprised to see his old man vanish into the haymow with the queen—and emerge, an hour later, with the queen's bankroll. For Pa considers himself the first Casanova of the county, as well as its most sapient philosopher: his come uppance with a perfumed traveling saleswoman (when Ma is away at the Ladies' Aid) is an hilarious case in point. You will also go a long way to find a funnier story than the Stroups' misadventures in the Universalist belfry, during the mailman's wedding. . . .

But no synopsis can do justice to the engaging quality of *Georgia Boy.* Take Handsome Brown, the soft-spoken, dimwitted Negro yardboy—a perfect case of arrested development in a race groping for its destiny. Take Ida the mule, and College Boy the fighting rooster, both of whom are as real as your Congressman, and much more amusing. Take the bitter moment when Pa realizes that Ma has served up College Boy in a pie. Or Handsome Brown's Iliad with five goats on the Stroup roof. . . .

Other Southern writers, such as William Faulkner, have refracted their social satire through a child's mind with greater brilliance and depth; Mr. Caldwell himself has used children before as pure biblical symbols of fate in the making. *Georgia Boy* can stand on its own special merits, for all that. This reviewer would have to go back to Huck Finn to find a more companionable story-teller than Pa Stroup's William.

The story that William tells is too slight to be called a novel, though Mr. Caldwell's publishers have given it that arbitrary label. It is rich with character for all its slightness; the social meaning is there, under its easy comedy. Probably the pundits will lose no time in blue-printing all its people, including Ida; probably they will find fixations without number, and abundant overtones of evil. But this is the plain duty of pundits, when dealing with a writer of Erskine Caldwell's stature.

This reader admits that he enjoyed *Georgia Boy* for its laughter, and let the overtones fall where they may. Taken in that spirit, it is an unalloyed delight.

William Du Bois, "Southern Laughter," in The New York Times Book Review, *April 25, 1943, p. 6.*

RAY B. WEST, JR.

It seems likely that the spirit of reform is at the bottom of most comedy, but it is a spirit which must rise from the body of the work, not exist outside and behind it, forcing it toward a preconceived end. Erskine Caldwell, whose finest works are predominantly comic in tone, often fails to encompass and enclose his material in the same way that [Sherwood] Anderson did. He succeeds best, however, as in *Tobacco Road* (1932) and *God's Little Acre* (1933), when he presents his rural Southerners with the characteristic vigor and lustiness of the traditional rustic. He fails most utterly when he attempts a novel of sociopolitical protest, such as *All Night Long* (1942), which he subtitled *A Novel of Guerrilla Warfare in Russia,* and which is obviously intended to depict his protest against Nazi brutality during the Russian invasion. Although few of his short stories succeed as well as the best of his novels, they illustrate the same extremes of success and failure. A native of Georgia where he was born in 1903, Erskine Caldwell has written of the life he knew as a boy among the poor whites and the Negroes, and his most persistent theme is the brutality of Southern agrarian society in its attempt to preserve a decayed social system.

Insofar as bulk is concerned, Caldwell is undoubtedly the most prolific writer among the moderns. He is what his most sympathetic critics persist in calling "a born story-teller." Henry Seidel Canby places him squarely in "the Mark Twain tradition": "Indeed in these tales, and others which throb with indignation against a maladjusted world in spite of the horse-play and mock innocence on top, Caldwell is Mark Twain's spiritual heir." But there is a significant difference between Mark Twain and Erskine Caldwell. In Twain's most bitterly ironic stories such as "The Mysterious Stranger," "Captain Stormfield's Visit to Heaven," and "The Man That Corrupted Hadleyburg" there is a well-defined and at least partly defensible skepticism always before the reader. Caldwell's stories of social protest come to depend too often upon an obscure, because badly defined, concept of some future corrective judgment. Thus, in what is perhaps his most respected short story **"Kneel to the Rising Sun,"** the author finally reaches outside the story for a sentimental conclusion, a view of "the round red sun," which somehow, by its warmth, gave Lonnie, the principal character in the story, strength to rise to his feet after a night of violent injustice. The sun is obviously symbolic, but its use as the climactic symbol (fortified by its use in the title) is not necessarily the result of the major events which have come before. The promise of life-giving warmth is not a promise of mere physical regeneration but a promise of something for which "the round red sun" stands in the author's mind, perhaps the rising sun of social revolution: the dispossessed kneel, like Lonnie, beaten to the earth, but facing the regenerative warmth of social reform. If this interpretation is correct, then the symbol serves to transform a skillfully told story of betrayal into a tract asserting faith in a particular solution to the problem of social justice. For the story is really concerned with the effects of injustice upon the natural instincts for friendship and loyalty between two men of different races. If this interpretation is incorrect, then the symbol is obscure and too much attention is focused upon it.

The relationship between Twain and Caldwell, despite Mr. Canby's statement, exists primarily in those stories in which the least throb of indignation against a maladjusted world is evident, for Erskine Caldwell's most common method is the technique of traditional American humor—the tall tale. The Handsome Brown stories, **"A Country Full of Swedes," "Candy-Man Beechum,"** and **"Hamrick's Polar Bear"** all depend upon grotesque distortions and exaggerations of character and incident told with a quiet understatement. This is the technique Twain raised to a high point in *Huckleberry Finn* but which in many of his minor works represents little more than an intensification of a typical frontier attitude toward nineteenth-century concepts of nature and society, at best a genuine reflection of his time, at worst merely an extended joke. Neither Caldwell nor Twain is as successful in his short stories as he is in his best novels. . . . Humor can be accomplished in a short space if it is planned and incisive—highly self-conscious. When it is not, when it is improvisatory or when it is allied to broad social concepts, either it tends to become mere pointless entertainment or it demands time to construct a believable background of setting, character, and social myth. *Huckleberry Finn* and *Tobacco Road* provide this more leisurely development, but the majority of Erskine Caldwell's short stories do not. (pp. 53-6)

Ray B. West, Jr., "Fiction and Reality: The Naturalists," in his The Short Story in America: 1900-1950, *Henry Regnery Company, 1952, pp. 28-58.*

ROBERT HAZEL

In books about [Southern] writers, whether in transition, mid-, or uneasy passage, we usually find an essay about Erskine Caldwell tacked on to the end like the little red caboose behind the train. A procession of our novelists would not be complete without that smudged and inherently funny little car, yet we seem embarrassed by its presence and the need for it.

This attitude toward the necessary but unwanted has always perplexed me. My experience with Caldwell was from the first one of almost constant delight. I am not embarrassed about, by, or with Caldwell. My reaction to him involves both exasperations and admirations, and this may explain certain excellences and defects, but not explain them away. Likewise, they may have to do with Caldwell's Southernness, or lack of it, but neither does Caldwell's Southern background explain them away.

Caldwell "can't write," in the sense that Dreiser couldn't write but James could. . . . Style seems to elude certain men. It is really an easy distinction to draw. It is meant simply that Caldwell's language as language does not possess a very interesting life. Language is no particular friend of his and he has to go it alone, the hard way of a writer who has not found within him the capacity to love language. This does not mean a lack of ear, for Caldwell has heard accurately and put down the living speech of his men and women. It means, in practice, that the world of men and women which Caldwell creates lacks that final rhetorical dimension which transfigures the worlds of writers such as Wolfe and Faulkner. Scottsville does not lie for us amid peaks of language as do

Altamont and Jefferson. This is not even to say that one wishes it did. Rather one is content that Caldwell, having a more immediate sociological concern than Wolfe or Faulkner, and further removed thereby from conditions which had nourished an heroic grammar, eschewed an English rhetoric of a sort which has lingered, which has even been caused to linger by the Agrarians, who had certainly no genuine concern with plain speaking. Caldwell could and did stake out his acre and work it. Any literature, and certainly Southern literature as a body, is a group effort. And without Caldwell's reportage this marvellous country of his would have been lost, another "country not heard from."

I am not saying that it is better to be given a world in whatever language than not to have been given it at all. An immediate sociological concern may have assigned to Caldwell a language true to his task. In this he diverges from a group of Southerners who remain suspicious not only of sociology as such but of a mode of operation based upon the semi-science. What occurs, at any rate, in the writer who has not addressed himself to the problem of language for its own sake, is that stresses are created which must be absorbed elsewhere and re-asserted within the particular mode. In Caldwell, the solution, reportage as mode, forces him into one of the excellences of journalism. Caldwell made a great virtue of dialogue as a carrier of action. His local speech advances his narrative cleanly. In Caldwell we have a functionalism of action rather than of diction, of mythos rather than melody. It would seem—and one says this with genuine amusement—as if the persons who buy millions of his books must have agreed with Aristotle that action is most important in a work. Such a statement, of course, requires modification. For in our understanding of language in relation to the world of action, we must insist upon the fact that the created world is a function of the language itself. Given this slightly different, but not invalidating, twist to our understanding, we can conclude that the nature of the action in Caldwell is precisely what its language makes it, and that the world is, among other things, one of plain speech, of local idiom, of vulgar rather than fine motivations and actions, of a uniform levelness, of a consistent and impressive monotony, a desiccated world where the lifting of a hand or foot seems to be arduous and significant, a world lacking in poetry. When poetry wants to steal into this world, it is not realized—as in the instance of the girls with eyes like morning-glories who work in the mill—it is impregnated with sentiment only. In the world created by the language of Caldwell, there is no valid occasion for poetry. There are only poetized attitudes about all the chimney-sweepers who come to dust. There is a difference. The most poetically resonant novelistic languages seem to be written by men who contain in themselves not enough poetry to be poets, but enough so that working assiduously they create good prose. Caldwell lacks this resonance. Stylistically, Caldwell is not a Southern writer.

This section might be called character as exaggeration, or caricature. The particular exaggeration is innocence, a peculiar and grotesque and malignant innocence which Caldwell alone has been able to fill his world with. . . . Caldwell seems to make a world culpable, not its particulars, to make large forces guilty, not persons. The social (I use the word loosely) attitudes of the 20's and 30's had developed strongly enough that Caldwell could produce, as others did, the guiltless man. Ty Ty is irrascible and indestructible, but above all innocent. Perhaps it is because he has no consciously realized, turned and weighed values. He has not even the rudi-

mentary and static love of land which is Jeeter's most nearly conscious value. He doesn't even stop to consider why he wants to strike gold on his farm. He is a mindless slave of processes, not ends. And from evidences of behavior in the body of Caldwell's work, we can infer safely that if Ty Ty had found gold he wouldn't have known what to do with it any more than a child would. Caldwell's people live that unexamined life which is not worth living, except of course to the tenacious egos themselves, if only because they subsist on animal faith, the final value in a world where all else is ruin. (pp. 316-18)

In force-feeding ideas of impersonal nature into his fiction, Caldwell has departed from the stream of Southern writing and taken to the brush, to a jungle of forces, not the intensely personal and dramatic area of guilt and expiation which has bounded a remnant and vestigial society, a society driven in upon itself and forced to look at motives, a process of intensification which has helped put Southern writing in its present position of leadership. Caldwell has laid his emphasis elsewhere. He has dealt with sub-men who are beyond good and evil as truly as are the super-men of the *Künstlerroman*. Caldwell's characters are certainly beyond tragedy. To show Caldwell's divergence more clearly, we can note an interesting instance in which Faulkner chose to make his persons innocent and a society guilty—*The Wild Palms*. He attempted a tragic action, but in choosing an antagonist named society, an impersonal, amorphous, faceless, characterless force, he failed. And he didn't try again in this vein. It has been said of another Faulkner novel, *As I Lay Dying*, that he singularly denied his persons tragedy, whereas in his other work he permits his characters tragic status. The inference was that in this novel the characters were *below* tragedy and, one might add, were too nearly like Caldwell's sub-men to achieve tragedy. At any rate, whether the persons of *As I Lay Dying* are tragic or not, we do note that in this work Faulkner came his closest to poaching on Caldwell's acre. There are other parallels and approximations, here significant in a picture of Southern literature, which Faulkner and Caldwell share. But the shared areas are largely reduced to particularity, not scheme. Both writers share the mules, the plowlines, and the red-necked men, but their unifying schema are as far apart, and as near, as tragedy and comedy, as terror and laughter. Given their different contexts and visionary designs, one cannot interchange particulars, cannot for example say *incest* and mean both writers at once.

The Snopes and Bundrens [of *As I Lay Dying*] are cousins to Ty Ty. A third generation Snopes might own a textile mill where Ty Ty's son-in-law would go on strike. This Snopes probably wouldn't let Ty Ty come to his house in town to visit. Jason Compson rides an old Ford, a camphor rag about his neck. Caldwell's people ride old cars (or crack up new cars, so they become old—he insists upon a junk-filled world where men bale newspapers without a market for the bales—the agrarian South is shown in passage between the mule and the Model A, unable to afford, but purchasing for a spree, a new car, meeting the jangling industrial South emerging in mills, urban and rural elements juxtaposed and productive of the crackling ironies which are germane to Caldwell's situation humor.)

The innocence of which I speak, is related in simplest terms to an attitude found generally in the world of Caldwell's people: a man ain't to blame: "If you've got a rooster, he's going to crow." It is an attitude which is pre-psychological and expressive of a certain large and bland tolerance and negligence and not much questioning. This attitude, in contrast with the more inquisitive and energetic attitudes held by most of us in the audience, provides an important lever for Caldwell's humor. The boy ain't to blame if he wants to chuck a ball against the side of the house, or drive a car without oil. Another boy ain't to blame because his sister-in-law is so beautiful that he just has to have her. . . . I say pre-psychological and this necessitates one refining explanation. The reason why these persons are pre-psychological is not that they are guiltless for being what they are. Psychologists do not hold any man guilty of his desires, his impulses, or even certain rather destructive acts. But Caldwell's characters are pre-psychological insofar as they do not, need not, and will not alter the patterns of their desires or the patterns of fulfillment. In their innocence, they do not know enough to wish to change or to seek means to divest their acts of destructive power. Again the unexamined life, pre-psychological. A candidate for the office of county sheriff ain't to blame if he instructs other men where to find an albino and how to rope him, as long as they don't get too rough. Here is one of the cruel paradoxes that give a sting, a poisonous and vivid inflammation to the humor of Caldwell. He lances social sores, boils, cancers. The laughter produced is as fire. It burns the throat. In examining this matter, we are touching tender skin on us and our time. . . . We do not feel it is appropriate to laugh sadistically at the evil in ourselves, projected, or at the expense of other persons. It is one of Caldwell's particular virtues as a humorist that he confronts us with symbols which start laughter only to smother it in the pain of sympathy or revulsion. His is a humor of the preposterous, often free enough of pain, involved merely with such attributes as sloth (Pluto's lazy vote-counting) or stupidity (Ty Ty's insistence that his gold digging is carried on scientifically) but when the preposterous becomes outrageous the humor adds another dimension, becoming doubly pathetic.

If Caldwell's world is without tragedy, it contains pathos—often of an irritating sort. The irritation may perhaps be an encompassing emotion within us, which does not often come to the surface to disturb our enjoyment, a feeling that there is no excuse, finally, for the life lived in that world. This may be our feeling. It has nothing to do with Caldwell's success or failure. Caldwell's problem was to create a world, not to prejudge it. (pp. 318-21)

A humor of situation, which is also a humor of the preposterous, is what Caldwell has given us with such overwhelming success that it bears further notation. There is little need to comment on its gusto, or the "Rabelesian" or "Chaucerian" labels which have adhered to it. Suffice it to say that these words contain quite precise meanings more than tag-words ordinarily do. Certainly the humor is gusty, uniquely gratifying, a largess, a bounty, for which one always thanks the giver. We cannot thank Caldwell too much or too often for giving us the robust and depraved and homely and vulgar tom-foolery as no one else has given in our time. His literalities, equivalents and approximations, particularly concerning the sex content in the lives of his people, come forth genuinely incorporated and derived from the traditional and popular mind-body of the rural South. Can anyone, especially those who know the region, ever forget or stop laughing at Ty Ty's praise for beautiful Griselda, remembering the thousand times he has heard it from a thousand obsequious adorers of a profaned virgin. The laughter is immense, but with just enough truth and sadness in it to keep it from being utterly

coarse. And when sadness falls on Caldwell's humor, the gusto, which we associate with health, diminishes—as in the scene involving Will Thompson, when he declares he has to take his sister-in-law because when he first saw her he promised himself some of that and he just can't break his own promise. Gusto plays on the surface but is engulfed finally in our deeper apprehension of Will's sickness, and an entire landscape caving under the sickness which has produced him. As far as the eye sees, there stretches the ultimately humorless inferno of Caldwell. That the animal fails to attain humanity is not finally laughable. Or is it? Take either point of view, and Caldwell has provided amply for you. Or admit no yes-or-no answer, and Caldwell has provided a world complex enough. I do not know, certainly, how Caldwell himself feels about that world of his creation. It doesn't matter. We can know, from his stated preoccupations with certain social problems, how he must have felt about the actual world to which his fictional world bears some relation. The relation may be put thus: satire is the name of the relation of the real world of fiction to the actual world of fact. But satire is a too easy name, too easily pronounced and let pass. We must, in observing the relation between those actual and real worlds, account for the sums and multiplications of particular elements and their alignments in given instants, otherwise how could we honestly say that Caldwell's world is funnier than ours *and* crueller *and* sadder?

Let us examine. The world Caldwell makes is a Southern world. It is not simply a world economically determined and which could be any place. Although various determinisms, compatible with and suitable to Caldwell's scene, are at work, they no more provide full explanations of that work than of any other work of stature. . . . Caldwell's contextual obligation to the Southern land and what grows and dies on it is incontestable. Here he is a Southern writer. I quote a friend's recollection of Georgia country after a trip across the state several years ago:

> . . . the retinal highway shimmering in the brain, the dustladen roosters, the laddered growth of corn southward, the claypowdered broad leaf tapering into pecan signs and turpentine pine, into the rutted swamp bridges, then the exotic verdure. The cold grease clotted grits, the thin etherized coffee. The 25c straw hat, the sullen, evasive eyes above beard stubble, the clay-red roadmapped neck. Hadacol, Mail Pouch peeling off the barns, J. C. Penney and Piggly-Wiggly, overalls—Lee and Headlight, brass studded. The sunset town: the all-nite Greek's in a sputter of neon, the leaner outside, the protuberant adam's-apple, the quid, the wen, the new baby-shit Florsheims . . .

What my friend wrote was a description of an actual world, but it is also obviously, and without conscious intent, a description of Caldwell's real world. The description leads us to believe, for the moment at least, that the relation between the worlds is nigh identity—until we reflect on the grotesque alignment of particulars from the actual world, which distinguishes the real. From this actual description, we could not even begin to predict the variants, the singular monads reflected by their fictional universe, that one stubbled face would belong to a Pluto Swint, another to a man who was tricked into paying money to copulate with his own wife. No, the real world is as different as it is superior. It permits combinations of elements in mixtures not actually possible. Caldwell permits us to be surprised. He also inures us to surprise by building consecutive layers of surprise. When we see Ty

Ty digging for gold, we are surprised. When Pluto suggests an albino to divine the lode, we are surprised. But by the time Darling Jill drives away in Pluto's car, we are prepared. (pp. 321-23)

To build a world demands an inclusion of vigorous terms, and to build an infernal world of instinctual human life, without the purity of the instinct of animals, requires Caldwell's terms, his special troupe of irrational puppets, his dusty stage hung with burlap. In his zeal to make ample provision, Caldwell runs the risk of over-stocking, of the needless multiplication of examples, of displaying the same set of objects in a too little varied action. But this is to err on the right side. Many "tests" of a novelist have been put forward. I suggest that among these tests, one which is of first importance is: How adequate, how complete is a writer's projection of a world? To apply this criterion we must disregard the nature of that world. . . . It is customary for the critic to hold up the fictional world to *the* actual world (as though he knew what *the* world is) and to judge by the mirror theory. But no writer can project *the* world. . . . We do not even re-create *the* world; we create worlds. A writer creates a world and populates it with a set of objects—forces, ideas, persons, etc., and signifies these things by an elaborate system of signs—or he fails to do so. From the drift of these notes, I hope it will be supposed that Caldwell created a world abundantly and successfully, a world sufficient unto itself, which bears significant relation to other fictional worlds (to the Southern worlds particularly) and, further, a world indispensable to the constellation we call Southern literature. (pp. 323-24)

> *Robert Hazel, "Notes on Erskine Caldwell," in* Southern Renascence: The Literature of the Modern South, *edited by Louis D. Rubin, Jr. and Robert D. Jacobs, The Johns Hopkins Press, 1953, pp. 316-24.*

LOUISE Y. GOSSETT

Social criticism—at least in the form of social unease—permeates much of Caldwell's work, particularly that written during the thirties. At this time, in addition to fiction, he published **Some American People** (1935) and **You Have Seen Their Faces** (1937), reports on the dispossessed worker in the United States. Having found a salable formula for his fiction, Caldwell has continued to publish novels and short stories with predictable characters and events. Later novels—*A House in the Uplands* (1946), **The Sure Hand of God** (1947), **Place Called Estherville** (1949), and **Episode in Palmetto** (1950)—continue the series which he calls a "cycloramic depiction of the South." These books are populated by decadent families, prostitutes with varying degrees of crude honor, murderers, and corrupted children, figures who lack the inner consistency and carefully reproduced Southern idiom which gives characters in his early novels a recognizable if a less than engaging individuality.

The accuracy with which Caldwell reported sociological conditions is verifiable. But when he translates into novels and short stories facts about land impoverished by cotton growing and people exploited by tenant farming, sharecropping, and mill work, the fiction is violent, flamboyant, and grotesque. About the violence Caldwell made no apology. In an interview he asserted that the South is a violent country:

> I've seen a man beat a mule to death because the
> sun was hot and he was tired and tense, sick of the
> endless sameness of his life. I've been in a barnyard
> at the end of a day in the cotton fields when the boss
> came over to ask why a mule was lame. A Negro
> explained that the mule had stepped in a rabbit
> hole. The boss beat the Negro unconscious—
> knowing the Negro couldn't fight back. I've been
> an unwilling witness at a number of lynchings.

He also indicated that he intended his work to teach as well as to entertain. He does not have to say that lynching and cruelty are wrong. He can activate consciences "by showing people oppressed to hopelessness and impoverished to hopelessness. . . . When in 1927 he left the Atlanta *Journal* to write fiction, he was determined "to write about Southern life as I knew it."

The comments do not mean that Caldwell made a transcript of Southern life, but they do indicate that his concern for problems in the South was in the beginning serious. "I wanted," he declares, "to tell the story of the people I knew in the manner in which they actually lived their lives from day to day and year to year, and to tell it without regard for fashions in writing and traditional plots." In fact, the very extremity of his concern may have betrayed him into exaggerations which defeated his purpose. The reduction of human complexities to economic or political exploitation increases the amount of violence but reduces its impact.

The plot in most of Caldwell's early novels is a social problem so far advanced that it either threatens to or actually does destroy the characters. No character, however, blames himself for his condition; the fault lies with the landlord, the loan company, the mill owner, the merchant who refuses credit, or the politician. And failing all these, there is God Himself. The problem is formulated in almost doctrinaire terms. The accompanying narrow view of human beings tends to squeeze out their humanity altogether.

In **Tobacco Road** (1932) Caldwell preaches that Captain John should have taught his tenants better methods of farming instead of abandoning them to starve without the equipment and the credit to make a crop. The condition of the poor white as well as the Negro has preoccupied Caldwell. Historically, both groups were subject to the apathy of malnutrition, disease, and fatigue brought on by inadequate food, improper sanitation, and long work hours. Unschooled, these people were suspicious and distrustful. The poor white, it is true, had status in his color. By this virtue he could subscribe to the code of white supremacy. Although the refinements of plantation life never filtered through to him, he could claim the myth. He might also possess the independence of the frontiersman jealous of his self-reliance and his belongings. In Caldwell's fiction, however, the poor white has become a physiological automation. (pp. 16-18)

The defeat, actual or threatened, of man by economic change is one of the most productive sources of violence for Southern writers. It is possible, of course, to read the whole history of sectionalism in the United States as a conflict between agricultural and industrial economies. This conflict engages writers who want to define the consequences of the kinds of answers given to the question whether the ultimate value is the profit or the person, the increase in capital, or the relation of the work to the worker. Following the economic collapse of the South after the Civil War, it seemed to men like Henry Grady that industry would solve Southern problems. The region needed to diversify its economy in order to minimize agricultural depressions and to secure funds for needed services like education, but whether a radical shift in the economic basis of the South would destroy more than it would construct has been a continuing argument. The fear is that industrialism will destroy the individuality, the rural virtues, the graciousness of the South; the hope is that it will make all prosperous.

Whatever the gain or loss, social and economic dislocations—the substance of violence—have been inevitable. The collision of inherited agrarianism and its peculiar social institutions and philosophy with industrialism challenges the Southerner either to defend or to attack the inheritance. By using violent people and acts, grotesque exaggerations of appearance and behavior, and contorted diction, the writer testifies to his own shock and goads the reader into paying attention to the implications of the changes.

In *God's Little Acre* (1933) and *Tragic Ground* (1944) Caldwell makes the factory and the lure of cash the enemy. The corruption of the farm and the town is embodied in Ty Ty Walden and his son-in-law Will Thompson. On the land, Ty Ty is not a devoted agrarian like Jeeter Lester. Instead of farming he digs for gold. Avarice toward the land is also avarice toward God, for the acre set aside as a tithe is so mobile that a gold strike would never have to be shared with the church. In town, Will Thompson leads the workers to oppose arbitration to end the strike at the textile mill. The threatened violence of the workers seems indecisive beside the power of the mill owners. Company police shoot Will in the back. The Douthits of rural Beaseley County occupy tragic ground when Spence is laid off at a wartime powder plant and the family is caught in Poor Boy, a slum of shacks where uprooted war workers live. The bumbling efforts of the Welfare Department to rehabilitate the Douthits caricature bureaucracy. Spence's son-in-law Jim Howard instructs the welfare worker: "If you want to do the right thing, you ought to put all the blame on Poor Boy. . . . The finest folks in the world would get mean and bad if they had to live in a place like this."

Such social determinism is implied throughout Caldwell's work. The degrading external pressures which Caldwell detects serve him twice. They are a simple and inclusive explanation of the nature of his ravaged characters, and they prescribe a violent mode of expression. Thus both motivation and style are inherent in the view which Caldwell takes.

In addition to portraying what happens when the poor Southern white denies the land and goes into the factory, Caldwell makes use of the chief cause of violence within the social organization of the South itself—the relation between Negro and white. Between the two, any action, whether the official course of state or local governments or the private move of a citizen, has been able to claim justification if it were advanced as a buttress to white domination. During and following Reconstruction, violence against a Negro was satisfying because it defied the Yankee intruder and it asserted the power of the Southern white. (pp. 18-20)

The focus of the Southerner's insecurity after the Civil War became not slave insurrection but what Wilbur J. Cash calls the rape complex. The high position of the woman set apart to preserve the purity of the Anglo-Saxon became a symbol of the superiority of the white Southerner. The taboo against sexual relations between white women and black men was absolute. To lynch a Negro for attacking a white woman was not lawless violence but chivalric protection of the future. No amount of rational discussion about the little likelihood of rape could allay this inflammable anxiety. Caldwell uses violence most trenchantly when he deals with rape and mob hysteria in *Trouble in July.* In the novel the sheriff clearly acts out the intent of public opinion: lynch law alone should apply when black rapes white. Political expediency is systemized to let violence win.

The fact that an innocent Negro jail prisoner is abducted by the mob as a substitute for the culprit involves Sheriff Jeff McCurtain personally in the case because "Sam Brinson is a sort of special friend of mine, even if he is a colored man. I just couldn't stand having something bad happen to him." McCurtain rescues Sam but fumbles until Sonny Clark is lynched. The shock of hearing Katy Barlow confess that she had lied about being raped and of seeing her stoned to death by the same men who earlier had eyed her lustfully, jolts the Sheriff into recalling his oath of public office to perform his duty "without fear or favor." "I reckon I had sort of forgotten it," he remarks in a burst of self-awareness given to few of Caldwell's characters.

McCurtain, who to himself and his friends seems an acceptable, likeable person, shows in the glare of violence as a bumbler whose ineptness threatens the political order of the state. Caldwell's incompetents are undeterred not only by law but also by religion. They reflect the intellectual conservatism and the radical emotionalism of the Bible Belt. In them the fervor which brought Protestant missionaries to the frontier to quicken and convert the sinners has degenerated into self-indulgence. Their background is the groups of unlettered, superstitious poor whites and Negroes who listened to hellfire-and-brimstone preachers. Luridly drawn pictures of sin and damnation have about them the glamor of the forbidden, and more than one congregation has been titillated by graphic references to human weakness. The juxtaposition of spiritual impulses and sexual satisfactions in orgiastic religious demonstrations has provided Caldwell and other Southern writers a fruitful source of commentary on the violent, erratic behavior of man.

In *Journeyman,* characters with travesties of names enact a religious experience in the mode of a tall tale. Caldwell, however, says that he had often observed counterparts of his chief character in Georgia, Florida, and the Carolinas, and the story he considers "one of the indigenous phases of life in the South. Semon Dye, an itinerant lay preacher, has a riverboat gambler's way with liquor, loaded dice, and women. After winning everything his host Clay Horey possesses, including his wife, he conducts a revival, a festival of sex. For people isolated on dreary, unproductive bits of farms, the violence is too welcome a change to be disapproved. Clay pities the next folk to fall victim to Semon, but he admits, "I reckon they'll be just as tickled to have him around as I was."

Clearly, Caldwell finds in rural Georgia and other parts of the South situations which indict the social order, but often he lets the violence which should sharpen the indictment become so exaggerated that it dulls the effect. Caldwell eases the reader into his material by comedy in the early tradition of broad oral folk humor, lustily biological in content. This method might be a clever presentation of violence in the idiom of the country people to convince the reader of the need for reform; the comedy goes astray, however, when entertaining incongruities become monstrous absurdities and caricatures which are horrible and repulsive rather than amusing. As the situations and characters approach these extremes, the social indictment falters. If the comedy alone is the point, then the social zeal is too prominent. The reader has to work harder to feel satisfied that he knows what the author's purpose is, and lacking this satisfaction he may dismiss the fiction as mere sensationalism.

The plight of the countryman in the city, for example, is a theme open to comic, satiric, or tragic development. In *Tobacco Road* the encounter is handled lightly. The marriage of Sister Bessie, widow and purveyor of her private religion called "Holy," and Dude, Jeeter's sixteen-year-old son, in Augusta is a comedy of errors. From the clerk's stumbling explanation, Bessie confuses venereal diseases with mites. She objects to paying a two-dollar fee for getting married, which is the Lord's doings anyway. But she and the clerk good-humoredly satisfy the official forms. Later, when Bessie, Jeeter, and Dude bring a load of wood to town to sell, they treat themselves to a dingy hotel room and innocently expose Bessie. She spends the night being shunted from room to room, enjoying this strange hotel life. "It ain't like it is out on the tobacco road," she tells Jeeter.

The sketches in *Georgia Boy* (1943) maintain this joking mood. The poor, lazy, illiterate Southern white in these stories is Pa Stroup, whose cunning is beguiling. He schemes, lies, and steals his way in and out of encounters with paper baling machines, silk tie salesladies, gypsies, lively grass widows, and cockfighting. In the background his wife bends over the wash-pot with which she earns a living for the improvident family. The life of their Negro handyman, Handsome Brown, who, like all the Negroes in Caldwell's fiction, does the unpleasant work—whether it be chasing goats from the ridgepole of the house or substituting as a feeding ground for woodpeckers to keep the night silent for Pa's sleep—is treated for humor rather than social criticism. Underneath this humor, however, is the misery of poverty and racial discrimination which Caldwell portrays directly in other works. . . . [Ignorance] and innocence are amusing and are not blown up into Gothic horrors, but the rollicking life can also be read as social criticism.

Violence operates best in Caldwell at this level. When the characters become involved in destructive acts of murder and arson, Caldwell overtaxes their single dimension. Spence Douthit trying to rescue his daughter from prostitution is the ageless country bumpkin unwittingly discovering the pleasures of sin in the city. The Spence Douthit who knows that his friend Floyd is guilty of murder and arson is wooden because, unlike great comic characters, he has not been created to respond to the tragic as well as the comic. At the end of *Tragic Ground*, Spence is extricated by his son-in-law from the desperate life which has ruined Floyd, but the machinery of the rescue does not obscure the fact that Spence now looks more like a monster than a clown. And the final question which he raises is not how to reform society, but how to transform human nature.

Caldwell's portrait of human nature, despite his insistence that he writes directly from observation, seems a caricature. The essential strokes are few: apathy, irresponsibility, amorality, defective intelligence, limited experience, and uninhibited sensuality. The life of people thus constituted is a brief thrashing about in a wasted country where violence relieves the dreariness. The mirror which Caldwell says that he holds up to human nature reflects not a representative selection of mankind but a private chamber of horrors. The serious intention is to convict landlords and factory owners of mutilating

human life by warping its economic base. With decent wages and adequate shelter, then, these people presumably would grow clean, energetic, and conventionally well-behaved. Some of them do go off to town and prosper, but even these retain their old patterns. Jim Leslie, who lives on Augusta's Nob Hill, is as lecherous as his father Ty Ty. It is difficult to imagine Caldwell's characters having a past or future against which to measure any rise or fall. The degradation of the moment fills the foreground and obliterates the perspective, and the texture of time which complicates the work of Faulkner and Wolfe is absent. Change in the form of psychological or spiritual growth is not possible in these characters. Instead, their monotony of personality is an extension of the deadly tedium which surrounds them.

The victims of malnutrition, disease, debilitating climate, and boredom, these people are embedded in apathy and lethargy which would seem to belie the possibility of violent action. . . . The whites candidly recognize that Negro labor is essential to them. When Semon Dye shoots the Negro Hardy who tried to recover his wife from the preacher, Clay Horey worries that it is planting time, and he will have to go to work if Hardy dies. The crowd of lynchers in *Trouble in July* defends its method of keeping Negroes in order by hanging one occasionally instead of sending them out of the country as Narcissa Calhoun proposes. One of the men comments, "Hell, if there wasn't no more niggers in the country, I'd feel lost without them. . . . Besides, who'd do all the work, if the niggers was sent away?"

A fatalistic acceptance of what is justifies sloth. "I was born poor," Spence Douthit informs the welfare worker, "and I'll die poor, and I won't be nothing but poor in between." Caldwell makes clear that Spence, who was resigned to a life dependent upon charity, considered rebellion against this condition futile. He therefore has no sympathy for Floyd's protest by killing Bubber. Jeeter hands the Lesters' economic problems over to God to solve. Having provided land and sun and rain, He ought also to furnish seeds and fertilizer.

Despite the prevailing apathy among these people, there is inexhaustible sexual energy. It is the chief cause of violence and the center of the most extreme situations. The possibility that Spence is running after the pretty young social worker brings his wife screeching from her invalid's pallet. Throughout the novels fights break out as the men defend the females they possess. (pp. 21-6)

The classic case of violence in the South involving race relations and sexual taboos is, of course, lynching. Caldwell and Faulkner compound the horror by lynching innocent men, the white Lee Goodwin in *Sanctuary* and the Negro Sonny Clark in *Trouble in July*. In Caldwell's novel the lynching is preceded by wanton attacks on innocent Negroes under the pretense of trying to locate the suspect Sonny. Men break into Luke Bottomly's cabin and beat the Negro and pour turpentine over his wife. They terrify Amos Green's wife, who is alone, by catechizing her about how Negro rapists should be treated. Someone fires a chickenhouse, and while the crowd pauses to watch the flames, a few men sneak back to Amos Green's cabin. When the lynchers finally meet Sonny, they first blast away at the rabbit he has been carrying in his shirt. Caldwell has to give only the briefest account of the actual lynching because he has fully exploited its mood and manner in building up tension before the event.

The most violent coloring in Caldwell's fiction is extracted from sexual exploits. These occur as public performances. Perhaps Caldwell is remembering the publicity given to "family feuds, secreted births, mysterious deaths, violent quarrels, desertions, infidelities, and scandalous love-makings" in discussions at the cottonseed oil mill where he worked briefly as a boy. By including one or more spectators in the story to comment on the activities or to converse amiably with the participants, Caldwell violates social convention in the direction of the grotesque. . . . [Public] displays make another point for Caldwell. Privacy is a luxury unknown to the poor. They lack the dignity of being able to withdraw and be aware of their own individuality. The presence of witnesses reduces the possibly romantic private relations to gross physical contacts. When the shocks and surprises of these accumulate, they seem the attributes of a subhuman species to which violence is native. Occasionally Caldwell relieves the monotony of exploitative sex by introducing a kind of tenderness. Lov Bensey, who married Jeeter's daughter Pearl when she was twelve, has never been spoken to by his wife, but he has a bewildered dependence on her beauty. She herself wants only to escape from the tobacco road where no one ever laughs. Ty Ty defines sexual energy as God in man, but his simple identification is thwarted by the preachers who set up inhibitory rules which keep man in trouble.

Ty Ty seems to have in mind narrow morality of the sort which deems the refusal to dance, drink, smoke, or apply cosmetics the mark of a godly life. Such negativism, labeled "puritanism," has been blamed by critics like H. L. Mencken for the backwardness of the South. This kind of repressive religion has existed alongside the tradition of easy sociability in a tension which at its best reminds the Southerner of the difference between the demands of this world and the next, and which at its worst, misconstrues legalism for faith. Religion as mere restriction and proscription invites the violent parody which many writers have made of it. That passion for the spirit and passion for the flesh may be easily confused provides an anomalous violence which is simple to exploit.

Because in Caldwell's fiction trouble springs from the single dimension of caricature, its violence is a momentary disturbance rather than a permanent revelation of human nature or of the South. The people are cartoons and the social propaganda an elongated comic strip. Both the characters and the incidents are portrayed vigorously, but their created world is too contingent upon special circumstances to be convincing. The grotesque enlargement of a few traits is a literary method which bypasses the tragic implications of the comic for the sake of horror that is never resolved into pity. (pp. 27-9)

> *Louise Y. Gossett, "The Climate of Violence: Wolfe, Caldwell, Faulkner," in her* Violence in Recent Southern Fiction, *Duke University Press, 1965, pp. 3-47.*

SYLVIA JENKINS COOK

The poor whites who appear in the fiction of Erskine Caldwell, though not so clearly differentiated in terms of private history and psychology as Faulkner's, represent a broader social spectrum—from starving squatters and wily, opportunistic farmers to urban mill workers and small-town politicians. Caldwell also draws heavily on the cruel comedy and pathos of tradition but in the service of a very different social and political vision. Like Faulkner, Caldwell protested against the dangers of deducing sociological categories from what he

called "the crafty dishonesty of fiction," but during the 1930s much of his major fiction and nonfiction demonstrates a clear adherence to the ideals of the literary left wing, if not to their methods.

The political ideology of Caldwell's writing has not attracted a great deal of attention, largely because interest has been diverted by either the grotesque comedy or highly publicized obscenity trials that attended his work's appearance. Nevertheless, the social history and economic victimization of poor whites play a significant role in his writing, even when they are not, as in true proletarian novels, the central issues. To mistake them for such is to be guilty of the kind of futile reductivism that led one critic to assert the literary superiority of Caldwell over Faulkner merely because he offered a practical remedy for a stagnating agriculture, while Faulkner seemed only to despair. In fact, much of the pessimism in Caldwell's novels comes from the recognition that the suffering and degeneracy of his characters is virtually irremediable; each generation that survives in *Tobacco Road* is more damaged than the previous one—scarcely an encouraging situation for revolutionary change.

Caldwell's locale, like Faulkner's, is restricted—in his case to Georgia and South Carolina—and his people share similar traits: they are stubborn and randomly violent, prone to obsessive loyalties and fervent evangelical piety, both of dubious integrity; they are susceptible to disease and hunger and easily lured into fantastic money-making schemes at the expense of tedious and small-yielding labor on their land. Yet, despite similarities of setting, incident, and character, the individual details are unified into a very different creative scheme. Where Faulkner's characters finally win compassion through the fullest exploration of their humanity, Caldwell's demand justice for a humanity that is so destroyed as to be scarcely recognizable.

Caldwell's *Tobacco Road,* published in 1932, offers a number of such superficial similarities to Faulkner's *As I Lay Dying* and a radical divergence in its vital concerns. It is also a family novel about rural poor whites in a state of crisis, though in *Tobacco Road* it is absolute starvation that prods the Lester family briefly into their tragicomic action. Thus poverty is a crucial motivating force in Caldwell's novel and is directly responsible for some of the moral decisions taken by his characters. . . . Jeeter, like Anse Bundren, is almost a caricature of idleness, but sound reasons for his apathy are provided by Caldwell's insistence on the discouraging effects of an economic system that prevents him from taking any initiative. *Tobacco Road* has an abundance of gruesome funereal humor too, which illustrates a clearly contrary use of this favorite folk idiom. One of Jeeter Lester's more macabre preoccupations is a tale of his father's burial which is told repeatedly, with apparent relish for its grisly climax:

> The following afternoon at the funeral, just as the casket was about to be lowered into the grave, the top was lifted off in order that the family and friends might take a last look at the deceased. The lid was turned back, and just as it was fully open, a large corn-crib rat jumped out and disappeared in the woods. . . . One by one the people filed past the casket, and each time it became the next person's turn to look at the body, a strange look came over his face. Some of the women giggled, and the men grinned at each other. Jeeter ran to the side of the box and saw what had happened. The rat had

eaten away nearly all of the left side of his father's face and neck.

Unlike the unfortunate efforts of the Bundren family and their neighbors to add dignity and ritual to death, there is no inner complexity of generous motivation in Caldwell's people; poverty, ignorance, and isolation set up a dehumanizing barrier between them and the reader so that we see them laughing rather than shuddering at a partially devoured corpse.

Both **Tobacco Road** and *As I Lay Dying* use the familiar comic episode of country bumpkins' exposure to the sophisticated ways of the city and their consequent economic and sexual exploitation. . . . Yet while Faulkner uses the incidents as a comment on the callousness of the supposedly refined urban sensibility, in Caldwell they merely emphasize the freakishness of the Lesters. Even in their interpretation of poor white stoicism, the ideological tendencies of the two authors are clear, for while Cash Bundren's suffering is heroic as well as foolish, the Lester family's endurance is closer to the steady and involuntary deadening of all emotional response. They turn for relief to the only available opiate that they have: " 'When I has a sharp pain in the belly, I can take a little snuff and not feel hungry all the rest of the day. Snuff is a powerful help to keep a man living'." Such examples demonstrate that the traditional image of the poor white had some considerable degree of adaptability to personal aesthetic design. However, a closer analysis of Caldwell's work shows that southern comic horror presented many more difficulties in the context of his crusading social material than in Faulkner's highly personalized universe.

From the critical reaction to Caldwell's novels, it is apparent that a vision of the poor that mixed macabre humor and social realism was liable to the worst types of misinterpretation. When he was praised it was for his "twisted comic sense," for the ability to provoke laughter at "the failure, the man left behind, the quaint person,"—in short for his direct appeal to a strain of humor which appreciates the exoticness of the freak and finds portraits of degenerate humanity amusing but which fails to connect them to any moral purpose. Finding Jeeter Lester's trip to town to sell blackjack "hilariously funny," such critics were disturbed by any serious elements Caldwell tried to introduce because they were incompatible with the comedy. They saw Caldwell's work as a twentieth century version of *Georgia Scenes* and would have preferred that he not adulterate the comedy with too profound a moral. Some were so disturbed by the candor of his treatment of the sexual diversions of the poor that, although appreciating his social purpose, they felt that he had "manured his ground too well for fibrous growth." Ironically, prurient shock was the main effect of Caldwell's work on the public. Even the *New Masses,* from which he might have expected some sympathy for his efforts to make revolutionary use of southern primitivism and traditional humor, warned that "bad sociology does not improve fiction" and read him a brief lesson in proletarian anatomy: "They are all dying of pellagra and starvation, yet other organs beside their stomachs seem to plague them the most." A closer examination of **Tobacco Road** may well show that the clash between techniques mars it irreconcilably, but it will also show that it has generally been found wanting in a category that was entirely inappropriate to it.

The novel is an account of the last starving days in the lives of the Lesters, dispossessed tenant farmers. Caldwell creates in them people who are so intellectually debased and emotionally brutalized that we scarcely recognize them as being of our own species. . . . In addition to their alienated sensibilities, Caldwell's people are often physically warped and hideous—Ella May Lester has a harelip which frightens off all suitors; Sister Bessie has two holes in the middle of her face, so that looking at her nose was "like looking down the end of a double-barrel shotgun." Nor are these people given any opportunity such as the Bundrens are to redeem themselves through any secret and sensitive consciousness normally hidden from the world. If their grotesque behavior and appearance are a mask for any core of nobility, Caldwell refuses to divulge it. There are no interior monologues, and external language is reduced to the most mechanical and formulaic utterances which scarcely constitute a means of communication. . . . No one is responsive or sympathetic to the predicament of anyone else. Indeed, though we wait hopefully for a single sign of humanity or kindness, Caldwell refuses to ease the burden of acceptance—the economic plight of these people has made irredeemable monsters of them. The origins of this degradation are revealed to us in interpolated passages of social history and rather uncharacteristically articulate speeches by Jeeter Lester. These heavy-handedly leave no doubt that a corrupt system of land tenure has been responsible.

The artificiality of this technique of interpolation stems from Caldwell's effort to view poverty simultaneously from two very different points of view—to comprehend the historic and economic reasons for it and secondly, to realize it in terms of the family that is suffering. Thus Caldwell must demonstrate the relationship of inertia, disease, and insensitivity to starvation, while the antics of his characters seem to belie any naturalistic explanation. His use of humor as a vehicle for the display of outrage, squalor, and injustice has much in common with the theater of the absurd, but it also has the major shortcoming attributed to that form by Martin Esslin: "it cannot provide the thoughtful attitude of detached social criticism." In a novel there can be some solutions to this problem, though Caldwell's—the inclusion of explanatory sociological passages—shows some awkwardness in integrating them into the main comic-grotesque narrative. They also tend to be rather overtly sermonizing in contrast to the style of the rest of the book. For example, the following is part of a long passage about the depletion of the soil, first by tobacco, then cotton; about the decline of the Lester family, the loss of their land, and their final abandonment by their landlord, Captain John:

> There was no longer any profit in raising cotton under the Captain's antiquated system, and he abandoned the farm and moved to Augusta. Rather than attempt to show his tenants how to conform to the newer and more economical methods of modern agriculture, which he thought would have been an impossible task from the start, he sold the stock and implements and moved away. An intelligent employment of his land, stocks, and implements would have enabled Jeeter, and scores of others who had become dependent upon Captain John, to raise crops for food, and crops to be sold at a profit. Co-operative and corporate farming would have saved them all.

Such passages might have been better removed from the narrative completely and placed in separate, nonfiction interchapters as both Dos Passos and Steinbeck were to do effectively.

Where Caldwell is most successful as a social critic is in demonstrating the difficulties of creating a consciousness of oppression in a distinctly subrevolutionary class. Religion is traditionally a powerful reactionary force in radical fiction against social innovation, particularly in the rural South, and Caldwell uses it initially as the poor whites' rationale for their submissiveness. " 'God is got it in good and heavy for the poor. But I ain't complaining, Lov. . . . Some of these days He'll bust loose with a heap of bounty and all us poor folks will have all we want to eat and plenty to clothe us with'." However, with the advent of Sister Bessie and a closer examination of this piousness, we discover that religion to the Lesters is a form of emotional excitement which has relatively little effect on their moral behavior, either in relation to their promiscuity or, more importantly, to their acceptance of any code of endurance. A much more powerful conservative force, particularly in the men, is an attitude of mystical love and reverence for the land which prevents them from abandoning an obviously hopeless situation and moving into the cotton mills of Augusta. Jeeter's evocation of the torment of the people in the mills from "spring sickness" is a moving image of the desperate loyalty of land-loving people. " 'You can't smell no sedge fire up there, and when it comes time to break the land for planting, you feel sick inside but you don't know what's ailing you'." . . . Ironically, it is this time-honored and completely pointless tradition of burning broomsedge in the spring that brings death to Jeeter and Ada when the flames envelop and destroy their house. Thus they are both literal and symbolic sacrifices to an antiquated agricultural system.

The extent to which the members of the Lester family are aware of the real economic reasons for their plight gives Caldwell a further excellent opportunity to illustrate the problem of expecting peasants to act like proletarians. When Jeeter is confronted with city merchants refusing to give him credit and warning him that his folly will drive the whole family to the county poor farm, he replies bitterly, " 'Then it will be the rich who put us there. . . . If we has to go to the poor-farm and live, it will be because the rich has got all the money that ought to be spread out among us all'." Such a speech might have pleased the *New Masses* critics who had been admonishing Caldwell to go left, but Jeeter has neither the physical nor moral stamina to keep his wrath simmering. A trip to Augusta in Bessie's new car and his first meal in weeks give him a rather different perspective: " 'Augusta is a fine place. All these people here is just like us. They is rich, but that don't make no difference to me. I like everybody now'." Hatred and class consciousness subside rapidly on his full stomach.

The humor in **Tobacco Road** develops from satire of the incongruous activities of country innocents into a bleak parody of man's most destructive and vicious tendencies. The relatively lighthearted humor of the sexual antics is a means of establishing a comic mode that will then have to take the strain of the more macabre, absurd, and violent comedy. Caldwell steadily increases the burden of comic horror the reader has to bear until the episodes finally become intolerable and a recognition of their tragic implications is inevitable. Thus a quarrel between the Lesters and Sister Bessie starts out as childish horseplay—the participants poke each other in the ribs and hurl abuse while the old grandmother scurries across the yard to get a better vantage point for the fight. When she is halfway there, the automobile reverses over her, an accident which is merely another piece of slapstick come-dy to the Lesters. . . . The tone is detached as the injuries of the old woman are catalogued, but such callousness now provokes a contrary emotional involvement on the part of the reader, who feels first horror and then guilt for his laughter.

The same process of steadily impinging horror through comic disaster is used in the account of the adventures of Dude and Bessie in their new $800 automobile. The succession of catastrophes that leads to its destruction is reminiscent of the progressive dismemberment of Nathanael West's hero, Lemuel Pitkin, in *A Cool Million,* which also uses black humor to illustrate political horrors; but its southern origin may be traced to similar tales of violent dissection from Sut Lovingood. . . . The ultimate extension of comedy for the reader is despair, though this is never the case with the Lesters themselves. They are incorrigibly optimistic. "Jeeter firmly believed that something would happen so he would be able to keep his body and soul alive. He still had hope left." " 'The ground sort of looks out after people who keeps their feet on it'." Such myths as these, of the survival of the land and the people, are consistently undermined. Even the advocation of collective farming scarcely seems a viable solution any longer, though Caldwell implies that in the past it might have saved the situation. Now the land is exhausted and the people drained of everything but a faith which can only further their own destruction. At the end we see the whole futile process beginning again in the hands of an even more incompetent generation. The unfittest have survived, and we are left with a sense, not of admiration at the endurance of humanity, but of shame at the perpetuation of such lives.

God's Little Acre, published in 1933, presents a much more appropriate and hopeful situation for the testing of Marxist ideas in literature than that of the subrevolutionary class of **Tobacco Road.** The setting is divided between the rural farm of Ty Ty Walden in Georgia and the cotton-mill town in South Carolina where his daughter and son-in-law live and work. Ty Ty is possessed by the notion that there is gold on his land (a theme also explored with tragicomic effects in *The Hamlet*) and neglects cultivating the earth in order to concentrate his energies and those of his family on this fruitless and obsessive search. In the urban sections of the novel, we see another world where productive work has ceased—in this case because of a strike in the mills. Here, the impetus to work is a powerful one on the side of the mill employees, who dream of turning on the power in the mill and running it themselves.

The major concern of the novel is the way in which deprived people search for satisfaction of their physical and spiritual hunger and the nature of the substitutes that they accept—a theme that led directly to an obscenity charge against it by the New York Society for the Suppression of Vice. Although it was cleared in court of pornography charges, critics continued to find fault with Caldwell for his frankness, frequently at the expense of an honest reading of the novel. W. M. Frohock says of it, "The fierce animal sexuality of some of the characters, not to mention the bloodshed, has less to do with the rest of the material than with our present novelistic conventions"; yet it is precisely in sexuality, the lust for gold, violence, and mystical religious faith that these people seek compensation for the hollowness of their lives, the result of generations of deprivation. Hunger becomes a basic metaphor that yokes together the various energies that supply and consume people's lives. It connects Ty Ty Walden's reverence for gold, the land, and the sexual power of women with Will Thompson's ritual worship of machinery, violence, and dynamic force. None of these elements could be detached from the book without destroying the complicated metaphor of interdependency and compensation.

Though it is much less gruesome than *Tobacco Road,* the method of the novel is again comic, relying almost completely for its humor on the innocence of the participants toward their own moral depravity and mental obliquity. Ty Ty, like Jeeter Lester, is a failed farmer, but he has abandoned the growing of cotton not through lassitude but because of his fascination with gold. He diverts the labor of his family to this end and neglects to feed his two black workers, who are the only people doing any productive cultivation of the land. He is prey to all manner of superstitions, which he endorses in the name of science. . . . Ty Ty's confidence in the secret and rich abundance of the earth is directly connected to his fascination with sex and female beauty. To his daughter-in-law Griselda he says, " 'The first time I saw you . . . I felt like getting right down there and then and licking something'," an obeisance which in its imagery suggests a strong connection between women and nature as literal sources of sustenance. This was emphasized in an early psychoanalytic study of the oral imagery—biting, sucking, licking—of the sexual acts of the book. Ty Ty thus views sexual activity as a token of faith in nature and a means of worship. . . . It is his delight in the beauty of Griselda that brings about the tragic conclusion of the novel, for by celebrating her beauty, he provokes a fight between his sons that results in the murder of one and the presumed suicide of the other. Ty Ty is left to pronounce a bitter elegy on the difficulties of fusing the godly, natural way of life, which is that of the animals, with the moral restraints imposed by man-made religions: "God put us in the bodies of animals and tried to make us act like people. . . . A man can't live feeling himself from the inside and listening to what the preachers say. . . . A man has got God in him from the start, and when he is made to live like a preacher says to live, there's going to be trouble. . . . When you try to take a woman or a man and hold him off all for yourself, there ain't going to be nothing but trouble and sorrow the rest of your days." The old man's reverence for the spirit of procreation is distorted in a sterile, hungry world into a desire for selfish possession which leads to bloodshed and fratricide on the acre of land devoted to God.

In the factory world of the novel, machinery replaces the earth as the dynamic and sustaining power equated with sexual energy, but here it is a male rather than a female force. Consequently, it exerts a strange power over the factory girls: it makes them seem subservient to the machines they work, so that they regard both the machines and the mill with a kind of passionate awe. They can scarcely bear to leave them to return to the men at night. "When they reached the street, they ran back to the ivy-covered walls and pressed their bodies against it and touched it with their lips. The men who had been standing idly before it all day long came and dragged them home and beat them unmercifully for their infidelity." This strange sexual jealousy is partially, but not wholly, explained by the economic relationships of the men and women: "the mill wished to employ girls, because girls never rebelled against the harder work, the stretching-out, the longer hours or the cutting of pay." The connection between women as scabs and men as cuckolds lies in their attitude to the machines themselves: "The men who worked in the mill looked tired and worn, but the girls were in love with the looms and the spindles and the flying lint." The mills in the town of Scotsville have lain idle for eighteen months during the strike, and the men dream of turning on the power again and taking control. The prospect of doing this becomes a kind of ritual chant in the conversation of the men, an end in itself, unrelated even to the production of cotton cloth: it is as though the mechanized power of the factory has come to symbolize for them all natural energy and initiative.

Will Thompson is the hero who unites both incredible sexual energy and the courage to break into the mill and turn on the power. He is the most interesting figure in the novel as a possible prototype for a visionary revolutionary leader—one of the generation of poor whites who have abandoned all hope of eking out a living from the land and have moved permanently into town to work in the mills. He is a skilled weaver who takes pride in his craft; having transferred his loyalties utterly to the town, he has no rural nostalgia. . . . The strike in Scotsville has turned into an effort by the owners to starve the workers into submission, a course that Will resents bitterly. His impassioned drunken speeches on the owners show a keen consciousness of class injustice, which Ty Ty and his sons, left behind on the farm, are more immune to. . . . For Will the break has been made with the land and all the traditions of the past—now he is constantly in the company of large numbers of people who share his plight and are united by their anger against the enemy. "The workers had reached an understanding among themselves that bound every man, woman, and child in the company town to a stand not to give in to the mill."

The general behavior of strikers and bosses in *God's Little Acre* parallels fairly closely that of the other more specifically propagandistic novels—the mill tries to evict people from their homes, the workers harden their resolution, and there is extreme disillusion with the AFL, who, under guise of arbitration, appear to the starving workers to be merely making easy money by prolonging their plight. The impetus is, according to radical theory, to violent and cooperative action, but the motives in *God's Little Acre* are as complex as those of the men who beat the factory girls for kissing the mill walls. The machinery has appropriated more than their economic assertiveness; so when Will finally assumes the leadership of the strike, it is because his long-smoldering anger needed the catalyst of his sexual encounter with Griselda to transform it into revolutionary action. . . . Afterwards, the population of the town surges anxiously around the mill; Will rips up his shirt and casts the pieces from one of the upper windows of the mill to where the women below fight for the fragments; then, as the roar of machinery begins, there is the sound of bullets exploding. Will Thompson has followed the revolutionary hero's path to glorious martyrdom.

However, the mill does not start; the other leaders are arrested and the people's plans thwarted. Like Ty Ty and his family on the land, the mill workers in the town lapse into despair. The crisis serves to unite and solidify the people of Scotsville as Will's body becomes their communal property, but Caldwell finally refuses to make any commitment to the future value of the sacrifice or to hint at any "great beginning." "The men with bloodstained lips who carried him down to his grave would someday go back to the mill to card and spin and weave and dye. Will Thompson would breathe no more lint into his lungs." Although Caldwell's economic sympathies are clearly apparent throughout the book, he refrains from any of the polemical interpolations which so disrupted the texture of *Tobacco Road.* Instead, he creates for the first time a classic bourgeois villain who embodies the antitheses of all Will's qualities. This is Ty Ty's oldest son, Jim Leslie, who has disowned his family, become rich in the city as a cotton broker, and married a woman who will have nothing to do with his "linthead" relatives. . . . Jim Leslie, in accepting dishonest and corrupt work, has also abjured the saving power and grace of sex: his wife is " 'as rich as a manure pile' " with awful looks and gonorrhea. It is his frustration and selfishness that provokes the eventual murder. Even the least class-conscious members of the rural Waldens are provoked to horror at Jim Leslie's evictions of poor people from his tenement property and his attachment of their furniture: " 'I'm sorry to hear that you're selling poor people's household goods, son. That would make me ashamed of myself if I was you. I don't reckon I could bring myself to be so hard on my fellow creatures'." These admirable sentiments from Ty Ty are less so in the light of his own neglect of his black sharecroppers, but the comic incongruity between his words and actions is not nearly so harmful in the context of his intimate rural community as the calculated, impersonal code of urban capitalism.

The *New Masses* was once again dissatisfied with what they now began to claim was an artificial cleavage between Caldwell's known political opinions—his support of the Communist candidate in the previous presidential election—and his aesthetic development. They found his approach to sex in *God's Little Acre* "healthy" but warned of latent "decadent possibilities." They thoroughly approved the inclusion of the mill-town strike episodes but found his treatment of them "fantastic, disconnected, unbound to any semblance of reality, artificially grafted to the rest of the book." Their demand for absolute proletarian realism, for a more "thorough investigation into the causes of the southern industrial struggle," was outside the scope of Caldwell's aesthetic vision. It is perhaps the strongest indictment of the *New Masses* and those who saw art as a class weapon that they failed to appreciate or encourage a writer whose faith in art and imagination led him to experiment with symbolist and surrealist techniques as effective means of presenting material of contemporary social concern. After *God's Little Acre* Caldwell made one more attempt at reconciling his comic-grotesque technique with the poor white's ever-worsening situation—in his collection of short stories, *Kneel to the Rising Sun,* 1935. Then his work tends to separate into two streams: serious social material becomes the powerful nonfiction journalism of *Some American People* and the picture-text genre of *You Have Seen Their Faces,* while the fiction tends increasingly to sensationalism.

In the volume of short stories, *Kneel to the Rising Sun,* Caldwell demonstrates the capacity of the short story to deal powerfully with social themes by creating an intense emotional effect which need never be dissipated, as in the novels, by comic diversions, unduly complex philosophy, or explanatory sociology. In the story **"Daughter,"** a sharecropper, Jim Carlisle, is arrested for having shot his eight-year-old child Clara. Jim sits bewilderedly in the town jail, and as a crowd begins to grow outside, he can only repeat ritualistically, " 'Daughter's been hungry, though—awful hungry. . . . I just couldn't stand it no longer.' " As the crowd builds, the background of the murder begins to emerge—Jim's landlord, Colonel Maxwell, has withheld his shares as payment for an old mule that died. Jim, too proud to borrow from his neighbors when he felt that he had honestly earned enough to support his family himself, was eventually driven to the desper-

ate act of killing his starving child to alleviate her misery. The crowd is steadily growing in size now around the jail. . . . The whole situation parallels the classic arousal of a lynch mob; the sheriff deliberately leaves the jail unguarded as the crowd's fury mounts. The climax of the story comes with the realization that their fury is directed not against Jim but against the Colonel and that they are breaking into the prison to free him with the sheriff's tacit cooperation. There are no polemical speeches on class exploitation or social revolution, but miraculously, the hostile mob has been transformed into the sympathetic masses. They are neither educated proletarians nor sophisticated rhetoricians, but they do not require a high level of articulation to make their point: " 'Pry that jail door open and let Jim out. It ain't right for him to be in there'."

In these stories, Caldwell still refuses to endow his poor whites with any of the qualities essential to heroism—they remain victims rather than leaders—but they are fumbling toward a sense of comradeship that is constantly exposed to destruction by their enforced peonage to another class for the basic means of subsistence. **"Slow Death"** is something of a classic salute to proletarian brotherhood. The story opens in a grim kind of Hooverville under a bridge by the Savannah River. . . . Out of this community of despair, two unemployed friends walk through the city, where "the traffic in the streets sounded like an angry mob fighting for their lives." They have no prospects of work nor any friends or organization to turn to, and when one of them is knocked down by a car, the driver insists he is faking injury in order to get money. All the hostile forces converge as the injured man dies a miserable death while his protesting friend is knocked unconscious by a policeman. However, this loss of consciousness is also a symbolic one, for on gaining his senses again, a turning point in submissiveness has been passed. Though the first friend is dead, he is now being dragged along the street by a nameless rescuer, from whose pocket the policeman's nightstick protrudes. The two are retreating as fugitives, but the fraternity of the poor, as well as the movement from passive resentment to active opposition, has been established between them. There is now a glimmer of hope that the words of the dead man may yet be fulfilled, " 'Somewhere there's people who know what to do about being down and out. If you could find out from them, and come back, we could do it'."

This rather sentimental triumph is not typical of Caldwell's short stories of the poor; for the most part they remain shockers where sex and violence are the chief bargaining agents. They produce revulsion and shame rather than the more desirable wrath of revolutionary action. The most typically horrifying is **"Masses of Men,"** which plays with some irony on the favorite proletarian collective noun, for the men here are seen as at best indifferent, at worst positively hostile, to the world of women and children, who are at the very bottom of the whole structure of oppression. The story pits moral debasement, in the form of the man Johnson, against the steady starvation of the woman Cora and her three children. Cora goes out to prostitute herself for a little money for food, but having been repeatedly rejected, proves more than ready to offer her nine-year-old daughter Pearl for a quarter. The center of the story plays cowardly lust against aggressive hunger: complaining petulantly about the unheated room, the man hangs back for fear of being caught in such a hideous crime; the woman urgently displays the attractions of the child and pleads for his money. It is clear that no moral alternative is available for Cora if she is to keep her children alive, and the ruthless transaction, eventually completed, enables her to buy a little food. The point is effectively made that no taboos are sacred in a world which permits the first atrocity of starvation, for that already constitutes a crucial debasement of any ethical system.

The longest story in the collection, **"Kneel to the Rising Sun,"** deals in greater complexity with another aspect of the question of ethical confusion in the loyalties of the poor and with the southern codes of behavior that obstruct a true identification of economic interests on the part of the poor white. The setting is rural again, among the black and white sharecroppers of Arch Gunnard; the method is close to allegory, since every character represents a recognizable social class or attitude, although the story is equally effective on the immediate literal level. Arch Gunnard's tyranny over his impotent workers is symbolically illustrated in his favorite hobby, docking their dogs' tails. His victim in this story is Nancy, the old hound of his white sharecropper Lonnie, a model of timid acquiescence. Lonnie's family is starving because of short rations; he is agonized by his dog's torture and shamed by the greater courageous resistance of the black sharecropper Clem; yet he makes no objection. The pattern of the whole story is established in this early tail-cutting incident—the greater Arch's atrocities, the greater Lonnie's acceptance and the greater Clem's opposition. When Clem questions Lonnie about his endurance of such a situation, his response summarizes the anachronistic folly of the loyalty of lingering serfdom when the lord has abdicated all his responsibilities: " 'I've been loyal to Arch Gunnard for a long time now. I'd hate to haul off and leave him like that'."

This horror is, of course, only a small foretaste of what is to come—Lonnie's inert loyalty will be tested much more stringently than by a suffering animal. His old father, wandering around at night in search of food, falls into Arch's pigpen and is hideously devoured by the snapping hogs—presumably the rich growing fat on the starving poor. Again, it is Clem rather than Lonnie who speaks up for justice by attacking Arch bitterly for his treatment of his tenants. The result is the formation of a lynch mob to get Clem and Lonnie's inevitable choice between black defender and white master. "He knew he could not take sides with a Negro, in the open, even if Clem had helped him, and especially after Clem had talked to Arch in the way he wished he could himself. He was a white man, and to save his life he could not stand to think of turning against Arch, no matter what happened." However, Clem manages to extract the promise that at least Lonnie will not divulge his hiding place. In the crisis, Lonnie fails him: the habit of obedience to white and hatred of black is too strong, and he betrays Clem to the death of a hunted animal. The final action of the story takes place against the flaming background of the red rising sun, a powerful symbol of future bloodshed, against which the oldest southern tragedy of racial betrayal is set. This story and many of the others in the collection are among the best to come out of the proletarian art movement of the thirties, for in them Caldwell demonstrates his ability for compassionate but controlled writing with few lapses into leftist formulas, manifestos, and facile solutions that take no notice of the particular problems of the South.

In the same year as **Kneel to the Rising Sun,** Caldwell published a work of nonfiction, **Some American People,** that dealt with the contemporary plight of the poor. One of the book's three sections is devoted to anecdotes culled from a west-to-east trip across the United States, another contains some violent, muckraking journalism on conditions in the auto industry in Detroit, and the final section is on southern tenant farmers. The broader political and economic perspective on the South's problems and the contrary tone in discussing poor whites in this factual reportage is a useful indicator of how Caldwell excluded, refined, exaggerated, and concentrated this material in his fiction. Most striking in the nonfiction is the complete absence of any comic or ironic vision of the poor, who are presented solely as victims with all ridicule stripped away. Without the earthy folk humor that acts in the novels and stories as something of a counterforce to any completely naturalistic understanding of poor whites, they become mere sociological specimens, acting in accordance with clear economic laws. . . . The horror of these tenant farmers' lives is stark when unadulterated with personal folly and eccentricity, but the omission of the complex responses their degenerate antics provoke in the fiction makes it simpler for Caldwell to propose solutions to their problems. He advocates here the abolition of the landlord-tenant system and the introduction of collective farming, despite his pessimistic rejection of such measures in **Tobacco Road** as already too late to serve such people as the Lesters.

Two years later Caldwell returned again to documentary writing on the poor of the South in the picture-text book he did with photographs by Margaret Bourke-White, **You Have Seen Their Faces,** 1937. Each photograph is captioned with a quotation in which Caldwell imagines what the sentiments of the subject might be. Thus, though the longer essays in the book attempt to place the poor in a historical, geographical, sociological perspective, the emotional and aesthetic weight is largely carried by the fictional method. Once again, the South is peopled by rogues, knaves, fools, layabouts, and fanatics as well as the noble, toiling victims of an unjust economic system. There is anger in these captions, as children tell of being forced to stay away from school to work in the fields, and families describe trundling all their possessions over back roads in constant search of jobs and food—but there is also humor and inertia. . . . **You Have Seen Their Faces** emphasizes most clearly the dichotomy between Caldwell's fiction and nonfiction in their social values and shows how closely those values are tied to the aesthetic method he is employing. When he makes the slightest imaginative move away from reportorial sociology, even in such a small way as writing fictional dialogue for actual people whom he has interviewed, his indignation rapidly becomes transmuted into fascination with personal eccentricities and tragedies that counterpoint his hopes for masses of poor whites acting in concert to improve their lot.

Caldwell's use of grotesque comedy to further a vision of the southern poor white that is both radical and pessimistic demonstrates a certain versatility in that tradition of humor and folklore. Though he and Faulkner were often bracketed together as primitivists, decadents, or naturalists, Faulkner used the same material in a conservative and finally quite optimistic vein. Faulkner established with it a sense of community with traditions of independence and personal generosity worthy of perpetuation, while Caldwell used the same material in recording the breakdown of rural community and family life and the enforced exodus of country people to the cotton mills. The myth of the land in Faulkner had made it an affirmative, stabilizing, life-giving force to the people who remained loyal guardians of it; in Caldwell the myth is empty and destructive, since the land itself is exhausted and barren—it brings only misfortune to those who reverence it. The absurd humor of the poor whites in Faulkner was a means for revealing their basic humanity, their follies, passions, and weaknesses, while in Caldwell it is a means of emphasizing the freakish and alien qualities of people whose physical and mental depravity has inevitably encroached on their spiritual integrity. Faulkner, like Caldwell, noted the incongruous mixture of stoicism and violence in the poor whites; but while the stoicism was for him noble and the violence disruptive, in Caldwell stoicism becomes the apathy induced by needless suffering, and violence is a first step toward revolution and relief. A major difference between the two writers in their relationship to the poor white literary tradition is in their use of history. Caldwell fills in only the historical background necessary to understanding the shape of the present predicament of the poor; he recreates for the reader the regional traditions and myths that provide "truths" for his characters to live by. However, such "truths" are constantly undermined in validity for the reader, who is not encouraged to share the characters' faith in them, and hence tends to rely on them more as tools of naturalistic speculation. In Faulkner's case, these "truths" held a lingering validity even when their purveyors proved corrupt; he expended as much care on the genesis of these myths as on their decadence. He discovered the best aspects of the old southern code still embodied in the yeomen farmers and plain folk and pitted their resistance against the ravages on all established society of those people (mostly poor whites) who had abjured all ties with family, community, and history and had become faceless agents of material progress. Caldwell's vision of social exploitation is much more conventionally left-wing in terms of class warfare, for his compassion rests almost exclusively on the poor white victims of wealthy landlords and industrialists. Nevertheless, Caldwell refuses to commit his fiction to any absolute explanation of poor white degeneracy in terms of economics or his readers to any clear-cut emotional response to their activities. The idiocy, violence, religious hysteria, and promiscuity that certainly appear to stem from their material deprivation nevertheless do not constitute the features of a very wholesome advancing proletariat. Caldwell showed that the literary treatment of the poor white might produce a shocking indictment of the society that had cultivated this grotesque figure for amusement, pity, and profit. He left unresolved the question of whether that literary tradition would support the metamorphosis of its protagonist into the kind of hero the *New Masses* was demanding. (pp. 64-84)

> *Sylvia Jenkins Cook, "Caldwell's Politics of the Grotesque," in her* From Tobacco Road to Route 66: The Southern Poor White in Fiction, *The University of North Carolina Press, 1976, pp. 64-84.*

ROBERT H. BRINKMEYER, JR.

Erskine Caldwell has written that the only purpose he had in mind when he wrote *Tobacco Road* was to describe as realistically as possible the lives of Southern poor whites. "I wanted," Caldwell writes in *Call It Experience,* "to tell the story of the people I knew in the manner in which they actually lived their lives from day to day and year to year without regard for fashions in writing and traditional plots." But one need not read far into the novel to realize that *Tobacco Road* is something quite other than a documentary. If indeed this is a mirror held up to the Georgia countryside, then it is one

of those trick mirrors one sees at amusement parks which distorts everything into grotesque sizes and shapes. The world of *Tobacco Road* is, as just about every critic who has written on this novel has asserted, a realm of grotesque exaggeration, where everything—characters, settings, and situations—is twisted into bizarre and horrible shapes.

Caldwell's use of exaggeration has caused a good deal of consternation amongst critics who have tried to explain what he was really up to in this novel. Everyone accepts that Caldwell wrote the novel with a social purpose in mind, namely to draw attention to the plight of the tenant farmers and to make some suggestions on how to improve their condition. But why, then, the critic must ask, did he distort things to such an extreme, thereby making them comically absurd? And why did he apparently write the novel in the tradition of the Southwest humorists, a form whose history and very nature embody aristocratic disdain for backwoods people? Social realism and comedy, two separate and apparently incompatible purposes, seem to be at work in the novel; and the prevailing critical trend finds the novel flawed as a result of this mix: too comical for social indictment, and too socially zealous for pure humor.

But what I want to suggest here is that Caldwell's use of the bizarre and grotesque does not work against his sociological purpose, but actually is a part of a coherent narrative strategy designed to electrify the sensibilities of his readers and to arouse sympathy in them for the oppressed tenant farmer. Using comic exaggeration to arouse compassion rather than contempt is a difficult line to walk, and many readers, not surprisingly, have regarded Caldwell's comic exaggeration *merely* as comic exaggeration. But this is not what Caldwell intended, and he constructs signposts along the way to guide the sensitive reader from this interpretation.

Essentially what Caldwell tries to do with *Tobacco Road,* I believe, is to lure the reader into believing he is reading a novel that is primarily comic, written in the vein of the Southwest humorists, only to pull the rug out from under him later in order to teach him a lesson. Caldwell's strategy is to establish first in the reader a stance of detachment from the material of the novel. He wants the reader—like the traditional audience of the Southwest humorists—to look at the characters with curiosity and detachment, and, most importantly, with condescension. (pp. 47-8)

The novel's opening scene works effectively to establish this posture with the reader. The seduction of Lov (rape is a better word), the fight for the turnips, the description of the wasted house, car, and countryside all point to a world far removed from and irrelevant to most modern Americans. Human actions are reduced to drives for animal necessities—sex and food—and the emotions of love, respect, and sympathy are nonexistent. The old grandmother, we learn, survives only by eating whatever grass and nuts she can scavenge from the woods, and is scorned by the others because she sometimes pilfers food scraps. The reader, working through this first scene, easily slides into the role of the enlightened being looking down on his inferiors.

The rest of the novel progresses with scenes as grotesque as this first one, continuously re-enforcing the reader's stance. But, at the same time, and this is what makes *Tobacco Road* so bold and innovative, Caldwell introduces information and situations which reveal the shortcomings of assuming such a position. He suggests with this strategy not only the snobbery and ugly emotions which form the base of such an attitude, but also the essential falsity of the stance itself: these folks whom you see only as grotesques, having nothing to do with you, he implicitly suggests to the reader, really have everything to do with you and your way of life.

One way Caldwell suggests this crosscurrent of meaning is through his characterization of Jeeter Lester. At first glance Jeeter appears to be totally lacking in any redeeming values: he is crude, selfish, violent, and his wretchedness seems to strike no corresponding chords in the reader. Rather than an instantaneous bond of identification, the basic impulse the reader feels is rejection. But as Caldwell suggests time and again in the novel, there is a lot in Jeeter which speaks directly to the reader. At the core of this superficially repulsive man lies a vital life-force which keeps him going against overwhelming odds. . . . Jeeter emerges, on one level, as an embodiment of that typically American wish for backwoods freedom. . . . [He] is part of our collective consciousness.

Jeeter's plight as a farmer also speaks tellingly to the reader, for it represents the destruction of a central figure in American ideology and mythology, the independent husbandman. Besides possessing an unquenchable life-force, Jeeter also has a profound love of the land. Each spring, when the smells of burning sedge and newly plowed earth fill the air, his blood quickens and he yearns to be working the dirt. In another time and place, in an environment where he had the opportunity to work and to be rewarded fairly for his efforts, Jeeter might represent the classic American husbandman, the ideal farmer who Jefferson saw as the backbone of American democracy. In the twentieth century of this novel, however, Jeeter represents the figure of the small farmer gone bad, not so much through his own faults, but rather through the oppressive mechanisms of a social system which places no value on the individual. The actions of Captain John, Jeeter's farmer boss, who gave up the land, leaving his sharecroppers without farm supplies or credit backing, epitomize the cruelty of the present-day system. . . . (pp. 48-9)

Jeeter's ill treatment at the hands of Captain John represents more than just bad luck; it calls into question the entire economic system which destroyed him, and of which the reader is a part. Indeed, his fall illustrates the destruction of a traditional lifestyle and values in the name of "progress," and it calls upon the reader to open his eyes and ask himself whether this sort of heartless technological and economic development is really the true fruition of the American dream.

But Jeeter's fall has an even more significant message for the reader. Jeeter's family, as Caldwell tells us, was once well-to-do, and has for several generations experienced a devastating decline. Taxes, soil depletion, and low agriculture prices have slowly stripped the Lesters of a thriving family farm. The nadir of the decline is Jeeter's present plight—no land and no credit to buy the supplies needed to plant. Lively prosperity, by the time Jeeter comes along, has been reduced to stasis and starvation. The significant point here is that the Lester family was once a part of the system, but has been destroyed by it. The family which we see is surely grotesque and dehumanized, not because of their inherent nature but because they were twisted into these shapes by poverty and oppression. And the implicit message, devastating in scope, is that what happened to the Lester's could happen, under the present economic system, to anybody—the reader included! The Jeeters are at the mercy of an uncaring system; and anybody who falls victim to the debt collector may end up in the same boat with Jeeter.

While the Lesters no longer have any hold on the American scheme of things—the system has spit them out and passed them by—Caldwell makes it clear that they still hanker for the same material successes that the typical American does. As they grovel for food and money, Jeeter and his family become grotesque parodies of the American drive for wealth and power. And even more American is their lust for Bessie's new car, the central prestige symbol of American culture. Distorted as the images are, Jeeter's and his family's actions mirror those of American society.

All of these qualities of Jeeter and his family indicate the relevance of their story to the reader, and demonstrate the mistake that one commits if he reads these characters as merely comic grotesques that have nothing to do with the real world. Caldwell's message is a disturbing conclusion for the reader to come to, for Caldwell has set him up early to see the Lesters merely as comic misfits. The reader first watches the Lesters with disdain, only to come to the shocking realization that the Lesters are disconcertingly recognizable images of "normal" Americans. Caldwell's strategy accomplishes several things. First, it educates the reader by making him more aware of himself and his role in American society. Second, by showing the essential similarities between the characters of *Tobacco Road* and all Americans, the strategy creates a bond of sympathy and identification between the reader and the Lesters.

To realize a bond of sympathy and identification with the Lesters is not a flattering experience for anyone. The typical reader will go to any length to resist such a move by holding fast to his detached and condescending stance. So Caldwell with another narrative technique reveals to the reader the ugliness of those who maintain such a posture. Throughout the novel the Lesters and their clan come into contact with the "civilized" people of the modern city, in this case Augusta, Georgia. Time and again—the encounters with the loan company representatives (seen in a flashback), with the car salesmen, and with the proprietors of the hotel-whorehouse, to name several important instances—these city dwellers scorn helpless country people and take from them whatever they can get. Their laughter at and abuse of the Lesters and Bessie is a grotesque manifestation of the attitudes of the unsympathetic reader who also laughs at the Lesters. The heartless city people, Caldwell suggests, are no different from the genteel reader who refuses to recognize himself in the Lesters.

All of these narrative strategies used by Caldwell ultimately lead back to the social purpose of the novel—to call attention to the plight of the Southern poor white farmer and to enlist the reader's aid in helping to change things. By educating the reader both in the injustices of the economic order and the essential falseness of looking down on people like the Lesters, Caldwell hopes the reader will better sympathize with the cause which undoubtedly was a major motivating force behind the work—the destruction of the system of tenant farming.

That so many people read *Tobacco Road* as humor . . . is, I think, not so much an indictment of Caldwell's art, but one of the American reading public. A comic interpretation is the easy way out, a way to disregard not only the plight of a segment of our population but also the injustices of the whole economic system, and the darker sides of ourselves which are mirrored in the people of **Tobacco Road.** Granted, Caldwell asks a lot of the reader. It's a bold challenge and not a glamorous one to take up. But Caldwell does his best to get us to rise to the occasion, and his effort is a powerful one. (pp. 49-50)

Robert H. Brinkmeyer, Jr., "Is That You in the Mirror, Jeeter?: The Reader and 'Tobacco Road'," in Pembroke Magazine, No. 11, 1979, pp. 47-50.

ELIZABETH PELL BROADWELL AND RONALD WESLEY HOAG (INTERVIEW WITH ERSKINE CALDWELL)

[Pell Broadwell and Hoag:] *Mr. Caldwell, your readers think of you as both a Southerner and a Southern writer. Do you?*

[Caldwell]: I consider myself an American who was born in the South. I say that because, although I recognize differences in dialect and styles of living among the various regions of the country, over all I've rejected the notion that I was some sort of regional character. When I was young, I had the good fortune to have parents who moved almost every year from one Southern state to another. But the fact is I've lived only about a third of my life in the South—twenty years to start with and then eight years more, in Florida, in the 1960's and '70's. For almost another third of my life, or close to it, I was in New England. The other third, so to speak, has been spent in the West. So I was never really a Georgian, a Floridian, or a North Carolinian. I was always an American in that sense. I have had no great allegiance to any one place, and that's true even today. I don't know how long I'll be here in Arizona. Where I'll go next, I don't know.

How would you characterize your attitude toward the South? Have you perhaps had a love-hate relationship with this region?

Well, that's something to ponder. As I was growing up, I did resent the South. I resented its economy and its sociology. I resented the lack of opportunity in general, and especially the fact that the black people there were not accorded the same opportunity as the white people. I happened to have grown up among black people in various places, and I was unhappy that—economically and socially—they were always second-, third-, and fourth-class citizens. On the other hand, I would also say that, just like anyone who has a homeplace, I have always had a deep regard for this region. I do not hate the South. I have always liked the South and liked its people, even though I had these qualifications because of some of the conditions there.

Why did you move to the Southwest?

I came here to the western part of the country for the same reason I went to New England when I left the South—to get a perspective on life. By "perspective" I mean that you can look at something from afar and find minute details you would not see if you were right on top of it. You can live too close to a region to write about it. Each move I've made, I made for that reason—purposely and, I think, successfully. Also, when experiences are the basis of your writing, you write about wherever you have been. So, if you live in different regions, you have different experiences to write about.

But most of your writing has been about the South.

That's true. I was and probably still am prejudiced about that to a great extent. I do prefer to write about the South. My reasoning—and I guess my excuse, if I have to make an ex-cuse for writing about the South—is that I'm better acquainted with it than other places. I know the territory, the people, the climate, the economics and sociology—lots of things that a writer needs to know about. (pp. 84-6)

*The years you spent in New England, especially Maine, produced many fine short stories but only one published novel, **A Lamp for Nightfall.** Why is this?*

I suppose because I didn't get to know the area well enough to do any more with it. The character of the people and of the state is very different from what I was used to in the South. So I was more or less forced to rely upon my Southern experience. I was too impatient to learn all I would have to know about New England in order to write novels about it. That one book, as you say, was the only novel I ever published about New England. I wrote another one, *Autumn Hill,* but it never appeared in print. (p. 86)

Your father was a minister in the Associated Reformed Presbyterian Church. Did his attitudes about religion influence you?

It could be that his attitude toward the profession of the ministry influenced me a great deal. You see, my father was interested in the whole field of religion more or less as a sociologist would be. He never relented from his idea that religion should involve a socialized, economic kind of life instead of just purely the worship of a God. He also thought that religion was being prostituted by money-making concerns, especially among some of the more evangelical ministers. . . . Before I stopped going to church at the age of fifteen or so, my father would take me to these various denominations, especially to the more violent sort of evangelistic camp meetings—the Holy Rollers and whatnot. And from observing these meetings, I got the idea that this violent type of Southern religion was not for me. It was a little bit too farfetched, so far as I was concerned.

*Farfetched religions play an important part in **God's Little Acre** and, of course, in **Journeyman.** Is there a fundamental similarity between the religion of Ty Ty Walden, in the former, and that of Semon Dye in **Journeyman?** Perhaps in a shared emphasis on sexuality?*

No, I don't think so. Ty Ty's religion was his own personal, private affair; he was not trying to push it onto everyone else. Dye, though, was a salesman, a high-powered salesman of his evangelical brand of religion. I think that this is an important difference between the two.

Is there anything of value in the evangelical, emotional experience that Semon Dye brings to the town of Rocky Comfort?

Well, he brings a relief from the monotony of living; that's for sure. The emotionalism generated by his actions and his talk was a physical release for the people there. Dye was very adept at his profession. He was a real pro at arousing emotions. He knew exactly which button to push and when to push it in order to set the people off in a blaze of glory. I guess maybe he had to have some feeling for what he was doing; but how sincere it was, I don't know.

Is Semon Dye genuinely disturbed by his failure to convert Lorene, the prostitute?

That depends on what you mean by "disturbed." Having this opposition, this one failure out of his whole congregation, probably does bother him. It hurts his ego. Lorene was not easily taken in by his soft talk. What happens is that two people come together there and each is determined to have his own way. But Dye doesn't succeed in converting her; and, on the other hand, she does not really succeed in showing up his inability to convert her. I think the fact that Lorene provides a contrast, though, shows that there is a possible resistance to religion if you want to confront it. You don't have to surrender yourself to this fraudulent type of activity.

Fate of some sort seems to function importantly in several of your novels. Do you consider yourself a fatalist or a determinist?

I think that my close association with the Presbyterian religion might have had some effect on me. As I understand it, the Presbyterians are predestinarians; they believe that what is going to happen is going to happen. I think that way myself to a degree. For example, I know I'm going to die, so I'm prepared for it. I'd say that I do have a slight prejudice in favor of fate being absolute, and maybe that belief influences me when I write. Of course, I know that a person has the ability to change his own life and to direct his own existence to some extent. But at the same time, I think, fundamentally, we are all people of nature and nature is going to get us one way or another. So I'm going along with nature.

In **God's Little Acre,** *was Will Thompson fated to die?*

I don't know whether he was or not. He was a headstrong young man who had a dream that he was going to get that mill started up again. I suppose if there hadn't been a strike, then something else would have come along that Will would have taken a definite stand for. He had a kind of determination that could be applied to any facet of life. It just happened in the book that he applied it to the mill.

But it seems that if the mill does not destroy him, then his brother-in-law Buck will. He can't win.

Well, that whole story got to be pretty complex. I had difficulty sorting it out myself as I went along because so many people were involved. Sometimes I regretted that I allowed so many characters to get into the act: [*laughing*] I couldn't control them all.

The men in **God's Little Acre** *are all more or less enamored of Griselda. Is she meant to be some sort of ideal woman?*

Not necessarily. I purposely created three or four different personalities among the women, from Darling Jill all the way through to Rosamond. You may have admiration for one; you may have pity for another. It depends on your own attitudes as a reader. But my purpose there was to display these distinct personalities that you can find in my town, your town, anywhere you go in life.

Do you foresee any problems with this generation or future generations of liberated women who read your books?

No. I don't at all. Many of the women I've been associated with, who have known me and my work, have been liberated for a long time.

In two of your other novels about the South, **Tobacco Road** *and* **Tragic Ground,** *the characters seem to be innately lazy and unwilling to help themselves. But at the same time they are presented as victims of economic oppression. Is this a contradiction?*

I don't think so. You see, the Lesters and the Douthits belonged to a class of people that had completely lost the ability to survive. Many years ago in several parts of the South, the poor whites simply lacked the necessary elements of nutrition. When you're in poverty and your sustenance consists of only one or two items—we'll say corn bread and greens—your body is just not getting all that it needs to function. . . . Often they contracted pellagra and hookworm, both of which were very prevalent in the South of that day. Now, pellagra and hookworm would not be apparent to the naked eye. So what happened was that even though nothing appeared to be wrong with these people, they had serious diseases which resulted in habitual laziness. They really were not able to help themselves.

In other words, they do act shiftless and lazy, but this behavior is the result of poverty and diet?

Yes, exactly. They would try to overcome their inertia, but since they had no money for medical treatment they were unable to do so. They couldn't get rid of the diseases that caused their misery. The most they could do was try to alleviate it. . . . (pp. 87-90)

That explains the laziness, but what about the apparent moral depravity of a character such as Jeeter Lester, a man who will deny crumbs of food to his own starving mother?

When a person is subjected to a very severe beating in life, he might get the feeling that he has to protect himself first. Therefore, he's not going to give his wife or his mother anything to eat; he's going to keep it for himself. That might be one of the attitudes a person in such a defeated position would assume.

Many of your poor whites are at times violent people. Is their violence, perhaps, also a response to their defeated position?

Oh, violence and cruelty have been part of Southern existence for a long time. I think personally that they're probably caused by the hardship of life itself. A person can feel that he is defeated and is unable to rise above his situation in life; he can feel at the mercy of fate. This would cause tremendous resentment. If a person has been shortchanged by his landlord, or if his landlord has taken something away from him, resentment builds up until he's got to find some kind of release for it. And just hitting the ground with a stick won't do it; he has to hit something animate. (p. 90)

Many critics, among them Donald Davidson, the Southern Agrarian, have said that you exposed the South at its worst. In retrospect, do you think that you have slandered or distorted the South in your books?

I had no intention at all to try to make the South look worse than it was. But I never considered myself a spokesman for the South either. I think everybody has a right to give his own version of life, and I was just giving mine.

Then you believe your fiction portrayed the South as it actually existed?

Well, all fiction is a distortion. You have to shape, to add and eliminate. You cannot simply photograph a story; a story must be given variations of depth and color, of light and shadows. Every piece of fiction is a distortion to some extent because something has been omitted and something has been added. But I do not think that I distorted anything beyond recognition. (pp. 90-1)

At one time you described ten novels that you had written

about the South as a "Southern cyclorama." What, specifically, did you mean by this term?

I saw those books as representative vistas, or visions, of the South. The thread I had in mind was not really a single theme but a process, you might say. I was just picking out various phases of Southern life to write about, of life as exemplified by the small-town politician, the schoolteacher, the boarding-house keeper, by a colored brother and sister in one of those little Southern towns. I would say it was an attempt to cover the South in many of its different phases, including its social life, its religious life, and so forth.

Do you become emotionally caught up in the lives of the characters you create? Do you suffer and triumph with them?

No, not to that extent. I do get very close to these people, of course; but I don't live their lives for them.

When you explored the South with Margaret Bourke-White in preparation for **You Have Seen Their Faces,** *did you have a specific goal in mind or were you seeking what you've just called "representative vistas"?*

Well, for **You Have Seen Their Faces** I set out particularly to learn what was causing all the trouble in the agricultural South. And I discovered almost immediately that the basis of the economic difficulties of the people there was the sharecropper system. It was very obvious to me that if this system continued, the people would suffer. But fortunately things soon changed.

Yet despite the evils of sharecropping, it seems that in **Tobacco Road** *Captain John seals the Lesters' fate when he sells the land and puts an end to their life as his sharecroppers.*

Well, there must have been something he could have done to alleviate their situation, but you can't blame the landlord for everything that goes wrong. You see, it was the sharecropping system itself that was the real wrongful use of human life. It made a person an economic slave. The sharecropper had no hope of ever being able to overcome his position in life. He ended up as an outcast, both physically and socially.

You Have Seen Their Faces, *through its photographs and its text, also portrays some problems in the South that seem more social than economic, at least on the surface.*

Bourke-White and I witnessed many injustices during our travels. For example, all over the South, every state had chain gangs. I've seen them all the way from Tennessee to the Carolinas, to Alabama and Georgia. I remember that the first time I saw one my reaction was total abhorrence. . . . Seeing these chain gangs was a turning point in my life. I feel sure that if this condition of human bondage had continued, it would have threatened American civilization. It's very fortunate that chain gangs became obsolete when they did.

In your first book of nonfiction, **Some American People,** *you say that "merely to see things is not enough," that "only the understanding of man's activities is satisfying." How did these beliefs affect your writing?*

When you're young, you're very curious about what goes on in the world. Really, you don't even have to go out looking for material to write about. The material is already there and it comes to you; it forces itself upon you. Then you have to try to understand it and form a judgment of it.

Did you hope that **Some American People** *would lead to the reform of those things that you judged to be wrong?*

Oh, I might have made a few suggestions in that book, but now I don't even remember what they were. I was mainly an observer there, recording the difficulties in American life during the early 1930's, the time of the great Depression. I was affected emotionally by my travels because what I saw taking place was not in keeping with what I believed to be the American standard of living. And I was afraid that the suffering I observed was probably only the initial stage of something—something that should not be allowed to continue. That book was written before the Depression had spread across the whole country. . . . (pp. 93-4)

You refer to yourself as an "observer," but in both of these non-fiction books the subject matter and the manner in which you present it clearly amount to a call for some sort of reform.

I'm a writer, not a reformer. I've always considered myself essentially an observer, a bystander. Besides, these two books you mention are in a different category from my other writing.

In the early 1930's Marxist critics embraced your books because of what they perceived as a reformist aim in them. Later these critics became disaffected with your work. What happened? How would you characterize your relationship with the Marxists?

Well, I never thought of myself as being in partnership with the Marxists at any time. I never, in all the years of my life, considered myself to be a Marxist, Communist, or fellow traveler. . . . I'm sure that especially in my early years I was willing to accept praise from critics of any stripe, and of course I did not like to get adverse criticism. But I never fell out with the Marxist critics because I was never in their camp to begin with. So whatever happened between us was their doing, not mine. (p. 95)

[In **Tragic Ground** *], Jim Howard comes home from the war in Europe a changed man. Apparently he has experienced something there that enables him to break away from Poor Boy, the Gulf Coast shantytown that drags Spence Douthit and others down. Just what did Jim Howard discover in Europe?*

Well [*smiling*], I wasn't there with him so I wouldn't know exactly. I would imagine that his experience in France showed him a type of civilization that he was not accustomed to back home but that he probably admired very much. Whatever he saw, it was a contrast to what he had known back in Arkansas or wherever, and certainly at Poor Boy. It made him want something better for himself, and so he got out. You see, the traditional French countryside is a very stable, solid environment in which to live. The work ethic there has something to do with this, I think. The peasant classes in Europe have a tradition of solid labor to rely on. They work hard, but they get something for it and they're proud of what they do. Their American counterpart has had none of that background and none of that training. I think the European peasant has been much better off economically and socially than his American cousins, at least until fairly recently.

You studied sociology and economics in college, did you not?

Yes, at the University of Virginia and at the Wharton School of the University of Pennsylvania. My interests as a student were not catholic at all; they were based primarily on those two subjects. (pp. 95-6)

To further your writing, you apparently chose to study potential subjects for your own work rather than the literature produced by other writers. Do you not see a value to literature courses or to courses on the craft of fiction?

I classify people in two different categories—writers and readers. If you're teaching literature so that people will know how to tell what's good and what's bad, how to select their reading, well, that sounds okay. But if you're trying to teach writing, which is something else entirely, I don't think you'll succeed. [*Shrugging*] I'm just a writer, though. I don't read. (pp. 96-7)

Many commentators have linked you to the tradition of Southwest Humor, as exemplified by Longstreet, Harris, Hooper, and others. Have you been an admirer of this group?

I hardly knew they existed. I can't recall his name, but there is one particular Georgia writer of maybe a hundred years ago who wrote little squibs of stories—one page, two pages, three pages long. I've seen them but I didn't read them; I don't even know what they're about. Now, several people have given me books of stories written in a vernacular or in dialect. They seem to think I should read these stories because that would inspire me to write similar ones. But why anyone would believe that I want to imitate a writer, any writer, is something I don't understand. I can't see it at all. So I just turn those books away—get rid of them. I only write like myself.

*Your celebrated short story **"Candy-Man Beechum"** differs stylistically from almost all of your other fiction. It has, in fact, been called a prose folk ballad. Was this a particularly difficult form to work with?*

Difficult? No, no trouble at all. I did it as an experiment, and I've found that experiments always have a certain ease to them—which is not to say that they're slight. In **"Candy-Man Beechum"** my experiment was to see if I could convey the sense of dialect, the feeling of dialect, by the rhythm of a sentence instead of by the sounds of speech. I wanted to prove to myself that rhythm is superior to dialect as a means of capturing Southern speech in fiction. You see, I have always had a dislike for dialect in stories. I think it's a very reprehensible kind of talk for a writer to use in his work.

Do you mean the graphic, phonetical representation of dialect on the page?

Yes. The reader should not have to decipher that sort of thing; it's too great an obligation to impose upon him. I've always felt that dialect should be outlawed for that reason.

*Another of your works with a distinctive style is **The Sacrilege of Alan Kent**, which has been described as a prose-poem. I wonder if this piece might have been a transition between your writing of poetry and your writing of fiction?*

It might have been, yes. Anyway, it was in that same era. What happened was that I was in the state of Maine then, trying to write fiction—or trying to learn how to write it. I would have written anything I thought might help me reach that goal because fiction was what I really wanted to do all along. **The Sacrilege of Alan Kent** was just one more experiment in that direction.

Did you give any thought to sticking with this particular form as something that you had pioneered?

No, I didn't view it in that light at all. I published the first part of **Alan Kent** in a little magazine in Boston called *Pagany*, and the editor there kept urging me to send him more and more of this same material. That was the only thing that encouraged me to write the next two parts. *Pagany* paid no money, though; and I was sure none of the bigger magazines would want this sort of thing. So in the end I had to do something different in order to make a little money.

You've obviously devoted your life to writing, but would you continue to write if you made no money at it?

[*Laughing*] That depends. Not now, I guess. Now I'd have to do something else to support myself. But in the days before I sold anything, I published probably fifty short stories in little magazines that paid no money at all. To me that was training, though; that was preliminary. I was willing to do anything to learn how to write because my expectation, or at least my aim, was that sooner or later a commercial magazine would pay me money for my stories—maybe *The Saturday Evening Post* or something. So I kept on sending out a short story every day, day after day, to these well-known magazines. It took a long time, but finally I got results.

Was there ever a time when you came close to giving up writing?

No, no. I would have been a failure if I had tried to go into any other profession, I'm sure, because I would not have been happy with anything else. (pp. 97-9)

*You have written that **Tobacco Road** began as a short story and eventually worked its way into a novel. How did this transformation take place?*

When I was living with my parents in Wrens, Georgia, there were perhaps fifteen or twenty tobacco roads throughout that whole region. I used to take trips with my father around the countryside, and we would see the kind of life the people there were living. Even then I was very interested in the fiction that could be written about this part of the country. Later, I started scribbling and ended up with a few characters in a setting. Then I think I probably had something that might have been a short story in itself; but it was inconclusive, and I was not satisfied with it. I could not tell everything I wanted to tell in a short story, so I decided to ditch that idea. I began writing at length about the subject later on when I lived in South Carolina. After that I wrote some more of the book in New York, then went to Maine and finished it. So in a total period of about a year, I suppose, I wrote the book in those three different locations. But I always stayed right with the region that I had started out with, which was a place in Richmond County, Georgia, near my parents' home in Wrens.

At what point do you usually know whether you're working on a novel or a short story?

Right from the beginning, as a rule. The novel and the short story are quite different. I don't think the **Tobacco Road** sort of thing ever happened to me again.

You've said that you do not write with a plot in mind. In more general terms, do you have any kind of a formula at all for writing a book or story?

Well, I would say that you build a story step by step up to a certain point. When you reach that point, you cannot go any further. It's important then to let the reader down right away, to jump off a cliff with him—to do something to end that story on a high note.

Is the process of writing a disagreeable effort for you or something you look forward to?

It all depends. If it's going well, I want to get right back at it again. But if I'm having trouble—which does happen sometimes—why, then I wake up with a headache. [*Laughing*] Yes, it can be a real troublesome thing if it's not going well. (pp. 99-100)

Malcolm Cowley, in And I Worked at the Writer's Trade, *describes his impression of your image as a writer. He says, in part: "Caldwell presents to the world, and to himself, the writing man as an ideal. . . . His only aim is to set down, in the simplest words, a true unplotted record of people without yesterdays. Past literature does not exist for him, and he is scarcely aware of having rivals in the present. As with Adam in the Garden, every statement he makes is new." Is this description—with its emphasis on experience, originality, and freedom from literary tradition—accurate, do you think? Do you recognize yourself, or perhaps your persona, in the words of this long-time admirer of your fiction?*

I have no personal image in my own mind, either about what I am or what I do. I don't even think of myself as a writer, by name. I would not try to create myself as a big man or a leader or anything of that sort. In my view I'm just a subsidiary character to the whole process of writing. The only thing that really interests me is what I'm trying to make—the story itself that I'm trying to get told. That's it. (p. 101)

> *Elizabeth Pell Broadwell, Ronald Wesley Hoag and Erskine Caldwell, in an interview in* The Georgia Review, *Vol. XXXVI, No. 1, Spring, 1982, pp. 83-101.*

FURTHER READING

Benedict, Stuart H. "Gallic Light on Erskine Caldwell." *The South Atlantic Quarterly* LX, No. 4 (Autumn 1961): 390-97.

> Compares and contrasts Caldwell's critical reception in the United States and France.

Frohock, W. M. "Erskine Caldwell—The Dangers of Ambiguity." In his *The Novel of Violence in America,* pp. 106-23. Dallas: Southern Methodist University Press, 1950.

> Delineates "the strongly powerful admixture of comedy and violence" that characterizes Caldwell's work. Excerpted in *CLC,* Vol. 1.

Korges, James. *Erskine Caldwell.* University of Minnesota Pamphlets on American Writers, No. 78. Edited by Leonard Unger and Ted Wright, No. 78. Minneapolis: University of Minnesota Press, 1969, 48 p.

> A biographical and critical survey of Caldwell's career. Excerpted in *CLC,* Vol. 1.

MacDonald, Scott. "Repetition as Technique in the Short Stories of Erskine Caldwell." *Studies in American Fiction* 5, No. 2 (Autumn 1977): 213-25.

> Examines how Caldwell's fiction achieves the lyricism of a folk ballad through the repetition of words, phrases, and sentences.

Rundus, R. J. "A 'World Indispensable'?—Caldwell, the Critics, and the Shaping of One Man's Literary History." *Pembrooke Magazine,* No. 11 (1979): 140-54.

> Cites specific critical references to survey the widely divergent response to Caldwell's work.

Thompson, James J., Jr. "Erskine Caldwell and Southern Religion." *Southern Humanities Review* 5, No. 1 (Winter 1971): 33-44.

> A favorable appraisal of Caldwell's portrait of Protestant evangelism in the South.

Annie Dillard

1945-

(Born Annie Doak) American nonfiction writer, essayist, autobiographer, poet, and short story writer.

Best known for *Pilgrim at Tinker Creek,* her Pulitzer Prize-winning meditation on nature, Dillard is esteemed as an inspirational author of fiction and nonfiction that explores religion, philosophy, natural phenomena, the role of the artist in society, and the creative process. Commended for her startling imagery and precise prose, Dillard characteristically focuses on minute details in art or wildlife, investing her observations with scientific facts and recondite allusions gathered from her broad reading in science and literature. From this scrutiny of minutiae, she investigates wider philosophical implications; for example, in one episode of *Pilgrim at Tinker Creek,* Dillard reflects on nature's intricacy as she describes the 228 muscles in the head of a caterpillar. In her subsequent works, Dillard examines theology, literary theory, and her own childhood, offering personal revelations on artistic pursuit and the meaning of existence. Michael Edens observed: "Dillard's books, whatever their nominal subjects, constitute her spiritual autobiography, and that's the riskiest kind of writing. . . . Dillard's best work honestly provides something that can only be called revelation, and that something cannot be faked."

The poems in *Tickets for a Prayer Wheel,* Dillard's first publication, express her longing to sense a hidden God through expositions on love and desire. Praised by the few critics who reviewed it, the collection was eclipsed by the remarkable reception of Dillard's next book, *Pilgrim at Tinker Creek,* which the author described as "what Thoreau called 'a meteorological journal of the mind.' " Following the progression of seasons from January to December in Virginia's Roanoke Valley, this work chronicles the evolution of the observer's consciousness through meditations on a wooded environment. In highly personal essays replete with scientific facts, Dillard recounts her expeditions into the forest, relating both her horror at scenes of predatory violence and her joy at glimpses of natural beauty. In dense poetic language, she probes the theological significance of this paradoxical relation between splendor and cruelty that "trains me to the wild and extravagant nature of the spirit I seek," as she states. Beauty and death, Dillard concludes, are balanced components of the mystery of creation. While some reviewers deemed the book overly self-involved or maintained reservations about Dillard's glorification of apparent chaos, most extolled her informative description and bold, unique style.

A plane crash that disfigured a neighborhood child prompted Dillard to reevaluate her religious beliefs, resulting in *Holy the Firm,* a dense study of divine intent—the ancient question of why a seemingly benevolent God allows innocents to suffer. Ostensibly a journal of autumn days spent on Washington's Puget Sound, this work illuminates the random violence in natural and human events. In compact, sonorous language,

Dillard contemplates the metaphysical significance of human pain and concludes that a Creator is not required to justify divine deeds to the created. While some reviewers considered *Holy the Firm* more obscure and self-conscious than *Pilgrim at Tinker Creek,* most praised its graceful, potent observations.

In *Living by Fiction,* Dillard concentrates on current literature, surveying the methods of several contemporary writers and analyzing recent literary theory. Directing her work to a educated but non-academic audience, she begins with an informative and sympathetic introduction to the postmodern fiction of such authors as Vladimir Nabokov, Italo Calvino, and Jorge Luis Borges. With vivid metaphors and an enthusiastic tone, Dillard defends postmodern "narrative collage" techniques, which supplant the traditional modes of sequential description and consistent viewpoint, displacing emotional elements for intellectual motifs. Dillard then implores readers "to loose the methods of literary criticism upon the raw world"; she argues that the metaphysical universe can best be discerned through the interpretive techniques of fiction and literary criticism. "Do art's complex and balanced relationships among all the parts, its purpose, significance, and harmony, exist in nature?" she asks. "Is nature whole, like a complicated thought?" Through art objects, Dillard asserts, humanity can often perceive relationships that reflect the order of the universe. Some reviewers castigated Dillard's various arguments in *Living by Fiction* as amateurish or inconclusive, but many regarded her explorations as inventive and challenging. Vance Bourjaily observed: "After Part One, the book is all fireworks. . . . [It] is almost as if Annie Dillard's pattern for her book of criticism has some of the same collage impulse as the fiction she admires. If this is so . . . it is by no means damaging, for there is no sense of disorder. Rather the book proceeds like wonderful conversation, moving here and there as the reader's pen continues to fill the margins with response."

Dillard returns to natural observation in several of the fourteen essays collected in *Teaching a Stone to Talk: Expeditions and Encounters*. In such pieces as "The Deer of Providencia," an account of an Ecuadoran deer that slowly chokes itself to death in an attempt to free itself from a noose, and "Life on the Rocks: The Galápagos," which relates Dillard's encounters with exotic species, she depicts the suffering and splendor prevalent in nature. The title essay, "Teaching a Stone to Talk," queries humanity's need to discover metaphysical truth in familiar objects, as exemplified by scientists and poets who try to discover universal laws by examining material evidence such as stones, trees, and creeks. Reviewers lauded "Total Eclipse" for its dramatic portrayal of human vulnerability under the threat of cosmic events.

An American Childhood, Dillard's next book, garnered praise as a singular work of autobiographical storytelling. Chronicling her childhood from ages five to fifteen, Dillard's self-portrait illustrates the adventures of a young mind discovering the physical universe. Formerly a precocious and inquisitive child, Dillard affectionately describes her original notions about aging, philosophy, snobbery, religion, ballroom dancing, and dating. While a few critics asserted that the book lacked a range of characters and a well-developed plot, most reviewers hailed *An American Childhood* as a delightful and spirited memoir. In *The Writing Life,* Dillard scrutinizes the creative process and elucidates the challenges of literary production. A study of a writer at work, the book explores the sources of inspiration and urges tenacity in the pursuit of expression. Dillard's personal essays address common artistic afflictions such as frustration and despair, which are occasionally overcome in moments of artistic revelation "when passages seemed to come easily, as though I were copying from a folio held open by smiling angels." Reviewers lauded several of the book's anecdotes, especially a metaphorical account of a stunt pilot as an artist of the sky. Some critics found *The Writing Life* overly fragmented and often self-indulgent, but many praised Dillard's incisive commentary and lyrical style. Stephen Chapman commented: "For non-writers, [*The Writing Life*] is a glimpse into the trials and satisfactions of a life spent with words. For writers, it is a warm, rambling conversation with a stimulating and extraordinarily talented colleague."

(See also *CLC,* Vol. 9; *Contemporary Authors,* Vols. 49-52; *Contemporary Authors New Revision Series,* Vol. 3; and *Dictionary of Literary Biography Yearbook: 1980.*)

PRINCIPAL WORKS

Tickets for a Prayer Wheel (poetry) 1974
Pilgrim at Tinker Creek (essays) 1976
Holy the Firm (essays) 1977
Living by Fiction (criticism) 1982
Teaching a Stone to Talk: Expeditions and Encounters (essays) 1982
Encounters with Chinese Writers (nonfiction) 1984
An American Childhood (autobiography) 1987
The Writing Life (essays) 1989

JOHN BRESLIN

Between her Pulitzer Prize-winning first book, ***Pilgrim at Tinker Creek,*** and her much slimmer and more overtly Christian meditation, ***Holy the Firm,*** Annie Dillard shifted her visionary focus from a small valley in Virginia to the vastness of Washington's Puget Sound. . . .

In ***Living by Fiction,*** Annie Dillard moves her books onto center stage, and we learn that fiction, which she had once, disparagingly, associated with the self-conscious sophistication of urban life, has long been one of her secret passions. Fiction of all kinds, not least the experimental, modernist and post-modernist novels and stories that have dominated literary discussion this century, from Joyce and Kafka to Pynchon and Borges. With the same combination of enthusiasm and empiricism that she brought to her meditations on muskrats and creek beds, Dillard sets out to explore our contemporary fictional terrain. But the big questions are still very much in the forefront, and unabashedly so in her very first sentences: "This is, ultimately, a book about the world. It inquires about the world's meaning. It attempts to do unlicensed metaphysics in a teacup. The teacup at hand, in this case, is contemporary fiction." Four pages later she makes plain her own metaphysical (or better epistemological) assumptions: "The book as a whole sees the mind and the world as inextricably fitted twin puzzles. The mind fits the world and shapes it as a river fits and shapes its own banks." . . .

After an initial taxonomy of the modernist phenomenon in literature, which for all its abstraction and brevity gives a clear and sympathetic account of this century's fictional innovations, Dillard takes up this question of populism as the first of her two major themes. Fiction, she argues, can never surrender its ties to the world beyond the page no matter how brilliantly certain modern writers (Joyce, Stein) have tried to make language the only hero and the only theme. Not words themselves but what they refer to constitute the novel's inevitable subject matter. The modernist movement has sharpened serious writers' awareness of art's infatuation with itself and of the artist's freedom to manipulate the pieces of his world (time and space, the real and the imaginary) as he sees fit. But it has not driven out naturalist fiction or reduced its practitioners to the status of dodos: witness, e.g., Graham Greene, Anthony Powell, John Updike, Saul Bellow.

Criticism has been important in this development, at once explaining and nurturing the self-referential qualities of modernist writing, but also fitting even the most radical experiments into a traditional canon that links our century to a still quite lively past. Indeed, literary criticism has itself become something of an art form, claiming since the days of Matthew Arnold to give us the rigor and the certainty we used to expect from metaphysics and religion. Is it possible, then, that the big questions, which have always been Annie Dillard's ultimate concern, may best be handled today by texts and their interpretation? A positive, if tentative, answer to that question is the burden of her book's third section and the real reason why the book itself was written.

Skepticism in its all-devouring, radically agonistic form is the dragon that must be slain if we are to reach the treasure of meaning. Dillard intrepidly wields her vorpal blade of common sense and snicker-snacks her way, with distinctions between madness and sanity, knowledge and understanding, fact and interpretation, to a bold and surprising analogy between the world of texts and the world itself. Can we read the world the way a critic reads a book? Are the tools of literary interpretation available—indeed, uniquely available—to the searcher after life's meaning? Dillard would have it so, but in making the claim she also reveals her own strong bias in favor of "deep" fiction where the surface sheen, however brilliant, invites us to search for ideas that speak about more than aesthetics. Purity is the enemy here: it would strip symbols of their "material energy" and thus destroy their role as probes from the world of sense into the world of ideas. Life is messy, and "pure" fiction represents it badly. In characteristically snappy phrases Dillard rejects the suborning of art to utilitarian purposes: "[The art object] does not 'help us to see' like an optometrist; it does not 'make us realize' like a therapist; it does not 'open doors of us' like a butler." It *does* nothing but it *is* something, a fresh creation that makes claims on our interest and even our affection. Does this art object by its very order and harmony and coherence also tell us about the way the world is, and even perhaps something about the world's maker? Dillard devoutly hopes so. And, to judge by her earlier books, believes so as well. But living by fiction here rather than by faith she offers instead a Socratic "I do not know."

Whether the field of investigation is nature or fiction, Annie Dillard digs for ultimate meanings as instinctively and as determinedly as hogs for truffles. The resulting upheaval can be disconcerting, as is her unbuttoned prose on occasion in this book ("But that's the breaks."); still, uncovered morsels are rich and tasty ("the rim of knowledge where language falters"; "fiction's materials are bits of world"; art is a "material mock-up of bright idea"). For them and for her common sense and for her unabashed love of fiction, many stylistic and even syllogistic lapses can be forgiven. *Living by Fiction* won't win a Pulitzer Prize, but it merits the attention of the rest of us amateur litterateurs and metaphysicians.

John Breslin, "The Feel and Fabric of Fiction," in Book World—The Washington Post, *April 4, 1982, p. 4.*

VANCE BOURJAILY

Living by Fiction is a stimulating book, one of those in which quality of thought and felicity of prose seem consequences of one another. It is also one to be read with pen in hand, ready to fill the margins with notations of consent and disagreement, additional instances and contrary considerations.

The book has nothing to do with how to earn a living by writing fiction. The title can be explained by inverting a quotation from Jorge Luis Borges, one of Annie Dillard's most cherished authors, who wrote of the philosophers on one of his mythical planets: "They judge that metaphysics is a branch of fantastic literature." Literature of the kind Miss Dillard calls "contemporary modernism," and which is most often fantastic fiction, she judges to be a branch of metaphysics. She feels that it is in such fiction, rather than in history, theology, the sciences or social sciences, that one may find ideas that give meaning to life in an apparently meaningless world.

The contemporary modernists—she apologizes for the term as being "a dreadful mouthful . . . I trust the clumsiness of the term will prevent its catching on"—include 25 or 30 writers. Those she discusses in some detail, in addition to Borges, are Vladimir Nabokov, Samuel Beckett, Robert Coover, John Barth, Donald Barthelme, Thomas Pynchon, Italo Calvino and Julio Cortázar. Considering that such writers have been called metafictionists, superfictionists, post-modernists, fabulators and other names by critics, Miss Dillard's phrase seems not such a dreadful mouthful.

In the first section of her book Miss Dillard describes their theories, innovations and techniques, though, as she says, there is no "thoroughgoing, cradle-to-grave contemporary modernist outside of France. . . . Each writer is a one-man camp, unallied and unarmed, a lone bivouac under heaven." She also says that most contemporary writers, no matter what they are called by the critics, use at least some of the techniques listed. But even with these graceful disclaimers, Part One of *Living by Fiction,* in which she analyzes the characteristics of contemporary modernism, provokes argument. (p. 10)

Here are the pure and perfect attributes (or some of them) of contemporary modernist fiction, according to Annie Dillard and the theorists she follows, most importantly Alain Robbe-Grillet: It is a fiction of the surface, analogous to much 20th-century painting in which elements that are traditionally rendered in perspective to give an illusion of depth and roundness appear on a single plane. Depth and roundness in traditional fiction come from sequential narration with realistic detail and a point of view—often that of one of the characters—which involves us as closely as possible with the story and its people. In place of this, Miss Dillard describes a method she calls "narrative collage." Using this method, the writer creates a surface we are invited to view distantly, either because the point-of-view character is a joke—a dinosaur, a breast, a cow, an idiot, an axolotl (whatever that may be) or because the author is willing to expose himself as the artificer of the pattern. The elements exposed on the surface of the collage, sometimes startlingly but always with control, are fragments of time, fragments of narrative line, bits of character, causes separated from their effects, paradoxes and a randomness in spatial handling that deprives the work of any familiar setting and the action of any familiar context. "So," she writes, "the contemporary modernist deliberately flattens the depth elements in his art. He replaces the emotional strengths with intellectual ones."

Now there are readers and writers whose minds can handle critical theory and esthetic abstractions. All honor to them. Annie Dillard is one. There are others who read pragmatically and write intuitively and ask nothing more sophisticated of a piece than "Does it work?" For such people it is sometimes hard to agree that things work because they fit theories. Even in the terms of Miss Dillard's definition of narrative collage, it is difficult to see what the theoretician finds in common between the arbitrarily contrived tedium of Beckett's novels and the fascinating playfulness and poetry of James Joyce's *Finnegans Wake*. Why is a protest book that is as lucid, iconoclastic and emotional as Coover's *Public Burning* an example of the same sort of fiction as the labyrinthine Pynchon tease *Gravity's Rainbow?* (pp. 10, 22)

The dissenting reader might say: Well, what's lucid is lucid, what's dense is dense; the inventions of geniuses like Nabokov and Joyce go on working at awesome lengths, but some of the other writers examined in this book would fit our attention span better if they'd keep their stuff shorter; it's nice to wade or leap a sparkling stream, but a bog is a bog. Finally, Miss Dillard has rested too much of her argument on Nabokov, who is, after all, everybody's Nobel laureate but Sweden's. We all claim him, and she herself eventually concedes that his characters are round, his work emotional, although whether she would grant that there is social criticism, too, in *Lolita* and *Pale Fire* isn't clear.

Enough. After Part One, the book is all fireworks. There is no way that a review can compress and outline the ideas. They do not, on first reading, appear to be linear; it is almost as if Annie Dillard's pattern for her book of criticism has some of the same collage impulse as the fiction she admires. If this is so—and the suggestion is made very tentatively—it is by no means damaging, for there is no sense of disorder. Rather the book proceeds like wonderful conversation, moving here and there as the reader's pen continues to fill the margins with response. (p. 22)

She approves the fact that fiction uses the world as its material. Purity may be desirable to the artist, but it can also be forbidding to an audience. Unlike fiction, Miss Dillard says, the other modern arts "have rid themselves of all impure elements including the audience." Hence, contemporary modernism in literature has not replaced the other kinds of fiction, nor does she feel it should. She relishes the fact that success in fiction isn't dictated by experts. She likes the way writers overlap critical categories and have not altogether discarded tradition; she finds the situation quite healthy.

In the final third of the book, she takes on the big question—"Does the World Have Meaning?"—and asks whether fiction can interpret the meaning, if there is one. She ends her book by saying: "I am sorry; I do not know." But before that she develops her own view with care: Now "Art is a terrible interpreter. . . . Art prizes originality more than fidelity." But through criticism we can examine the world the artist has made and we may "gain insight about the great world" morally and metaphysically. "Fiction . . . is a worldwide object for interpretation." But " . . . it does not 'help us to see' like an optometrist; it does not 'make us realize' like a therapist; it does not 'open doors for us' like a butler." Rather " . . . the art object is a cognitive instrument which presents to us, in a stilled and enduring context, a model of previously unarticulated or unavailable relationships among ideas and materials . . . a chip off the universal order, and partakes of its being." (p. 23)

Vance Bourjaily, "Contemporary Modernists—a Dreadful Mouthful," *in* The New York Times Book Review, *May 9, 1982, pp. 10, 22-3.*

KATHRYN KILGORE

Living by Fiction is Annie Dillard's loving and eloquent exploration of modernist and post-modernist literature. Her neat dissection of fiction is her cosmic key to that ancient, modernist subject: understanding what we are. She takes some fine risks and offers the reader many grounds for argument, especially if you happen to think a lot of post-modernist fiction is two-dimensional, boring, and decadent—or at least more interesting as a concept than a reality.

Comprehension of this book requires taking its three sections in their order and at their word; suspend disbelief for a while and argue at the end. The first section of the book, which is fairly traditional, is an explanation and defense of what Dillard calls the contemporary modernist style of, among others, Calvino, Davenport, Borges, and Sorrentino—writers usually classified as post-modern. (p. 40)

Then, in the second section, Dillard analyzes trends in contemporary writing, both in the modernist and the "plain prose" style. She discusses the nature of language, that "fabricated grid someone stuck in a river"; she examines our resistance to generalization, which itself is "the most general trend we know." She explores why writers still write traditional fiction, how far in the direction of abstraction post-modernist fiction might go, and discusses the roles of the critic and of the audience in judging and influencing writing. The contemporary modernist style is the result of a sophisticated "familiarity with the provisional nature of literary texts and the relative nature of historical value." Post-modernist fiction has been influenced, if not created, by critics, especially the New Critics' aesthetic of modernist poetry; and in fact "fiction in this century has been moving closer to poetry every decade." On the other hand, the wide audience for traditional fiction has the effect of preserving it. The audience does not keep fiction responsible, "it merely inhibits its development away from the traditional."

Next Dillard gives us "metaphysics in a teacup." The third section of the book takes flight, balanced on the information in the first two sections. It begins with Octavio Paz's thought that since the breakdown of religion and metaphysics, "we have criticism instead of ideas, methods instead of systems," and that "Criticism . . . *the only modern idea* . . . is a kind of focusing of the religious impulse." Dillard takes it as positive that criticism has reached this exalted position. "Science studies 'things as they are.' " The interpretive fields study "already edited selections and humanly meaningful arrangements": fiction creates a primary interpretation from all sorts of data, and literary criticism is an interpretation of interpretation. What Dillard wishes is that we could skip fiction altogether and "loose the methods of literary criticism upon the raw world"; but it makes no sense for critics to interpret the meaning of cracks in a sidewalk and other raw data, just as it makes no sense for scientists to seek human meaning in the nonhuman. To interpret the world critics would have to see it as an artifact; i.e., see the universe as having a creator.

After writing herself into this corner, Dillard backs out one step and claims, instead, that fiction writers, who can examine any and all of the world's data, both human and scientific, come closest of all to interpreting "the raw universe in terms of meaning." But, she then concedes, fiction is a terrible interpreter. The problem is we know that fiction "traffics in understanding," but does it also actually "traffic in knowledge"? By section three, Dillard as contemporary modernist critic is try-ing to practice her craft on "the raw world." (pp. 40-1)

On the question of whether the universe can be comprehend-ed and by whom, why pin our hopes on the post-modernist fiction writers? In its purest form (which it often isn't) con-temporary modernism is quite antithetical to life as we pre-sume to know it. Post-modernism leaves out references to the world, to experiences we still may hope we hold in common. It's true that plot, narrative, character, action in time and place are prerelativity, pre-Wittgensteinian, old-fashioned, artificial formulations. But without at least some shadowy forms of familiar references, without the ineluctable modality of the audible and the visible, we are left tangled in the tyran-ny of pure language, an ultimate power but an untrustworthy authority, an engine traveling alone, trafficking in dreams, untroubled by the gravity of moral vision.

"Do art's complex and balanced relationships among all the parts, its purpose, significance, and harmony, exist in nature? Is nature whole, like a complicated thought? Is history pur-poseful? Is the universe of matter significant?" Dillard finally wonders.

To ask these questions, to compare the idea of life with living, has never worked, never will. It both violates the concept of language and trespasses on the world in which we eat and sleep, trying with a net made of categories, to catch and pin us safely back in the box of our minds. "Whole," "purpose-ful," "significant" are suspiciously linked to "In the begin-ning was the Word . . . "

Living by Fiction is maddening but enchanting. Its carefully analyzed, beautifully written theories do hairpin turns and sometimes end up off the wall. The book is rarefied: Dillard, mirroring contemporary modernist fiction, has only slight in-terest in historical perspectives, references, the social context of her subject. Whole chunks of modern literature, many criteria for analyzing knowledge, are left out, and by omis-sion, seem dismissed. But so what; she's gutsy.

I'm not sure whether Dillard really believes that contempo-rary modernism will lead to discoveries or to our salvation. But I admire her exploration. Marshall Berman says, in *All That Is Solid Melts Into Air,* "The twentieth century may well be the most brilliantly creative in the history of the world. . . . And yet, it seems to me, we don't know how to use our modernism; we have missed or broken the connection between our culture and our lives." In some idiosyncratic way, Dillard is trying to reestablish the connection, and this seems crucial. (p. 41)

Kathryn Kilgore, "Metaphysics in a Teacup," in The Village Voice, Vol. XXVII, No. 28, July 13, 1982, pp. 40-1.

DAVID SUNDELSON

Annie Dillard has written a weak book in a noble cause. Her cause is literature and interpretation, which she defends as uniquely valuable guides to human experience and its mean-ing. Dillard aims at a literate but not scholarly audience—those who "read and reread the world's good books"—and *Living by Fiction* is almost entirely free of footnotes and criti-cal jargon. Reading it demands no special expertise, and such a book could perform a real service. In a time when more and more students abandon Shakespeare for public relations, we

need a strong, popular voice to tell us how culture keeps anar-chy at bay, to define once more the true function of criticism. Unfortunately, Dillard is no Matthew Arnold. Although she claims that her book is "about the world," she has nothing like Arnold's familiarity with society and politics—with churches and classrooms and street meetings—or his belief that a knowledge of literature can affect what takes place in them. *Living by Fiction* says nothing at all about living, and Dillard's discussion of fiction, sensible enough at the start, descends rapidly into platitudes and vagueness. . . .

Dillard provides a clear and sympathetic introduction. While her broad categories are useful—her notion of "texts which stress pattern over reference," for example—superficiality is a weakness here and throughout the book. Dillard can con-vey the charm of particular works, Calvino's *Invisible Cities,* for instance, but she rarely devotes more than a few sentences to any one of them, and her discussion of the intellectual background of modernist fiction is far too sketchy. (p. 535)

In the first section of *Living by Fiction,* this superficiality seems a small price to pay for lucid exposition and engaging style, for vivid metaphors that advance a coherent and plausi-ble argument. Dillard writes that the flattened characters in modernist fiction are "no more lonely than chessmen," and the image reminds us of the elaborate, gamelike structures she has already discussed. In the rest of the book, however, this balance disappears: the argument gets weaker and weaker until style is all that remains. Part Two consists of barely connected musings about popular fiction, critics, pub-lishers and prose style, and Part Three (grandly entitled "Does the World Have Meaning?") takes on metaphysics. Both are plagued by dubious generalizations, half-truths and outright contradictions.

"Formerly the novel was junk entertainment," Dillard de-clares, leaving us to wonder what period "formerly" refers to and whether Jane Austen and Flaubert wrote "junk enter-tainment." We are told on one page that "people still magi-cally regard novelists as helpless, fascinating neurotics," but learn four pages later that "the will to believe in the fiction writer as Paul Bunyan is shockingly strong; it is emotional, like the will to believe in Bigfoot, the hairy primate who stalks the Western hills, or in the Loch Ness Monster." Here Dillard is parading her associations instead of making a point. There is a similar aimlessness in the frequent feverish bursts of rhetorical questions: "What if another novelist, say a housewife in Illinois, contrived a novel about a fictional murderer who was executed to national fanfare? What if this fabrication matched Gary Gilmore's actual life? What if it matched Mailer's text? Would the meaning be the same? Would anyone give a blessed fig?" It is hard to say whether the last question is facetious or triumphant or something else entirely, and the point of the whole passage remains obscure.

A defender might claim that images are more important for Dillard than evidence, that she sacrifices logic and coherence for greater intensity and personal flair. Perhaps, but the ex-change is a poor one. In the absence of a sustained argument, the images have to do too much, and many of them are senti-mental or simply ludicrous. "Each writer is . . . a lone biv-ouac under heaven." The art object is "like an enthusiastic and ill-trained Labrador retriever which yanks you into traf-fic." Dillard's tone, a peculiar mixture of whimsy and ear-nestness, cannot hide the sloppiness of her thinking, which is at its worst in the section on metaphysics. . . .

The final chapters of *Living by Fiction* tempt one to declare that criticism should be left to the professionals, to scholars and professors. This would, of course, be a mistake. There is every reason why a thoughtful and popular writer should try to answer questions about the value and purpose of literature. But this book only shows how not to do it. (p. 536)

David Sundelson, "Matthew Arnold She's Not," in The Nation, New York, Vol. 235, No. 17, November 20, 1982, pp. 535-36.

CHRISTOPHER LEHMANN-HAUPT

I'll grant the effects are always powerful in Annie Dillard's *Teaching a Stone to Talk: Expeditions and Encounters,* a collection of 14 essays by the author of *Pilgrim at Tinker Creek* and *Living by Fiction,* among other books. I was amused by the icy wit of **"An Expedition to the Pole,"** in which Miss Dillard compares a contemporary Roman Catholic mass, conducted to the accompaniment of a guitar group called Wildflowers, with the extremes to which humankind has pushed itself to reach the poles of the globe.

She finds especially ridiculous the Wildflowers' singing of the Sanctus—"Heaven and earth (earth earth earth earth) / Are full (full full full)"—as well as the fact that when Robert E. Peary reached the North Pole in 1909, he planted there, according to L. P. Kirwan, "the colours of the Delta Kappa Epsilon Fraternity at Bowdoin College, of which Peary was an alumnus." To this Miss Dillard reacts wryly: "Wherever we go, there seems to be only one business at hand—that of finding workable compromises between the sublimity of our ideas and the absurdity of the fact of us." . . .

I got a sense of esthetic fulfillment from Miss Dillard's title essay, **"Teaching a Stone to Talk."** She does know a man who has undertaken such an exercise, she confesses. But what she is getting at is not so absurd. Once upon a time, the Hebrew people asked God to quiet down. "Let not God speak with us, lest we die," the people told Moses. Moses took the message, passed it along, and God agreed. But now that the Sacred Grove has been abandoned, we ask that the smallest stone may talk. That is figuratively what science and religion are up to. That is what Miss Dillard is doing in all her meditations on nature—asking God to speak to us through His stones.

Yet I wonder at times if Miss Dillard isn't too effective with her imagery, if she doesn't sometimes strain for her results. I think of the eagle she writes of that a man once found with the dry skull of a weasel fixed by the jaws to its throat (**"Living Like Weasels"**), or of "the lopped head of a boa, open-mouthed, on a pointed stick" "for decoration," (**"In the Jungle"**), or of a small deer in a village in Ecuador slowly choking itself to death in its struggle to remove a rope from around its neck. (**"The Deer of Providencia."**)

Sometimes I wonder if Miss Dillard isn't doing more—or is it less?—than proving she can stare unblinkingly at nature's indifference to suffering. At times I wonder if she isn't simply trying to spook us

Still, her final piece gives me pause about drawing any hard conclusions. In it she writes of standing by the bank of "a sunny backwater upon which dozens of water striders are water striding about. They seem to be rushing so they don't fall in. I soon discover that these insects are actually skidding along on the underside of a cloud. The water here is reflecting a patch of sky and a complete cumulus cloud. It is on the bottom of this cloud that the water striders are foraging."

Now, it could be that something about this image touches a universal nerve—something about the way that the earth and the sky are connected in it. But I know that it touches a chord in me, that it sprang a trapdoor into my past and dropped me sprawling into some dreamy childhood afternoon when there was nothing more pressing to do than watch water striders skittering along the undersides of clouds.

It opened me clean up. Thus sensitized, I was particularly alert to the sound of the bicycle in the woods behind Miss Dillard as she stands by that sunny backwater, the sound of the cards slapping against the spokes of the wheel as the child on the bike comes whirring down the hill. "I can see her through the woods downstream where the road evens out," writes Miss Dillard. "She is fine, still coasting, and leaning way back."

"We do love scaring ourselves silly," the next paragraph begins. Miss Dillard scared me, because, as she has earlier warned us, the cards that are slapping the spokes of the child's bike happen to be aces and eights, the "dead man's hand" in poker, and the phrase "leaning way back" comes from an article the author once read on how to jump off a speeding train if you ever have to. But nothing so very dreadful happens. The fall that ensues is not off a bike but out of timeless childhood afternoons of watching water striders skid along clouds. This is what the piece is about, what *Teaching a Stone to Talk* is about—the fall into nature and relentless time.

What I'm trying to get at is only this: If such an offhand image can do such things to me, then I can't really speak for what the other images in the book may do to you.

Christopher Lehmann-Haupt, in a review of "Teaching a Stone to Talk," in The New York Times, November 25, 1982, p. C18.

HELEN BEVINGTON

Not many people, it's safe to say, care to look a weasel in the eye. Or to sit in an Ecuadorean jungle on the banks of the Napo River idly studying a tarantula the size of one's hand as it seizes moths. Or to stroke a giant tortoise's neck in the Galápagos islands, with a friendly sea lion settling to sleep on one's arm. But it's fascinating to watch Annie Dillard doing so, especially if one is familiar with her through her Pulitzer Prize-winning book, *Pilgrim at Tinker Creek,* and knows her capacity for living, as she says, "in tranquility and trembling" among the wonders and splendors of the world.

Tinker Creek is in a valley of Virginia's Blue Ridge Mountains, where she lives, not only as a pilgrim but with a message. Her introductory note to [*Teaching a Stone to Talk*] warns that it is not to be considered a random collection of expeditions and encounters: "Instead this is my real work, such as it is." She preaches Thoreau's doctrine and her own—"Do what you love"—and like Thoreau she takes pains to clarify how that is done, how passionately she loves what she is about. A weasel lives as he's meant to, and the principle is the same for all, though it would take enormous energy and curiosity as well as clear thinking to live as Annie

Dillard does. She makes it sound like a profitable enterprise. (p. 13)

[Dillard went to the Galapágos islands twice], the second time to look more closely at the palo santo trees, holy trees—silent, mute, lifeless and covered with lichens. She also went to Barter Island inside the Arctic Circle, where all she could see was colorless sky and a mess of frozen ice. And she goes back in memory to a farm where she once lived alone, where the silence was heaped in the pastures, on the fields, where there was only silence, and it "gathered and struck me. It bashed me broadside from the heavens above." She has a taste for cosmic silence. She likes to look through binoculars at mirages, to confirm them for what they are, illusory, to sharpen the vision and mystery. Since we're on the planet only once, she says, we might as well get a feel for the place. "I alternate between thinking of the planet as home—dear and familiar stone hearth and garden—and as a hard land of exile in which we are all sojourners."

The taking of these extraordinary expeditions, which is Annie Dillard's lifework, occasionally has its perils. Once she was present at a total eclipse of the sun and lived to tell the tale. Early one February morning she and her husband drove to a hilltop in the state of Washington near Yakima to watch the miracle. Many people were about, bundled up in caps and parkas. "It looked as though we were scattered on hilltops at dawn to sacrifice virgins, make rain, set stone stelae in a ring." Then the light went out, and from the hills on all sides came screams. Fervently she prays that she, that you and I, may never see anything more awful in the sky. It was a near thing, as if the people had died on the hilltops of Yakima and were alone in eternity. Afterward, the two of them with a sigh of relief rushed down the hill and thankfully escaped to a breakfast of fried eggs. Enough of this sort of glory is enough. (pp. 13, 19)

[Dillard] is a fine wayfarer, one who travels light, reflective and alert to the shrines and holy places after first carefully selecting them for herself. She sets out again and again, seeking other landscapes, other encounters. Or she stays at home, thriving and surviving, no more scared than anybody. "I have not been lonely yet," she says, "but it could come at any time." (p. 19)

Helen Bevington, "Tranquil & Trembling," in The New York Times Book Review, *November 28, 1982, pp. 13, 19.*

DOUGLAS BAUER

One of the things that sets Annie Dillard apart from lesser nature writers is the extraordinary energy she gets from her experience. One often thinks of nature's appeal as the promise of some ultimate storm's eye where the mind can drift and eddy, but exactly the opposite occurs when she confronts a landscape, populated or not. A kind of meditative adrenalin is evident in the 14 essays that comprise *Teaching a Stone to Talk.* There's no sense of Dillard moving further and further toward a contemplative core, eyeing the coastline at sunset until the alpha waves reach the shore. Nature, for her, is a fuel and there's a clear sensation of mental and perceptual propulsion in the thought and movement of her writing. While it's true, as the title suggests, that she applies a Romantic democracy to all the pieces of the solar system, the effect of her eagerness is to turn Wordsworth inside out: Annie Dil-

lard's essays recollect tranquility with emotion, lyrically charged.

Perhaps it's inevitable that Dillard's nature gets her going, even agitated, for she senses in it not the slightest hint of repose. In fact she sees and imagines manic movement all around her. . . . Where others seek in nature the escape of rhythmic stillness, she advises that we'd best keep a deft and nimble pace or it will surely run us over, honking and cursing as it passes.

What she sees, too, uniquely, eccentrically, poetically, are the finite dimensions of what the rest of us think limitless. . . . "The Napo River . . . catching sunlight the way a cup catches poured water; it is a bowl of sweet air, a basin of greenness, and of grace, and, it would seem, of peace." And, of our zipping, hurtling solar system: "I have read . . . that [it] is careering through space toward a point east of Hercules . . . When we get 'there,' . . . will we slide down the universe's inside arc like mud slung at a wall?"

Equally and oppositely, she knows the infinite skills of tables and bowls and rocks, and here she's most allied with poetic tradition. She sees into the life of things. "Reports differ," she calmly writes of a neighbor's committed efforts to give his favorite stone the power of speech, "on precisely what he expects or wants the stone to say. I do not think he expects the stone to speak as we do . . . I think instead that he is trying to teach it to say a single word, such as 'cup' or 'uncle.' " In any case, it is, she says, altogether "noble work, and beats, from any angle, selling shoes."

As, most surely, she convinces us it does, although I believe Annie Dillard could also locate, carefully observe and persuasively explain the holy mysteries of retailing. And this is both the ultimate charm and intelligence of her work—that instinctive willingness to look a second time, more closely; to give all about her the benefit of her keen and unskeptical mind. She sees all the elements of the world as in a cooperative battle, a harmonious war, and for her *every*thing is a "thing"—"human life, tenderness, the glance of heaven," as just one of the many lists she likes to compose makes clear. . . .

Even in a collection almost uniformly splendid, I have favorites—**"Living Like Weasels," "The Deer at Providencia," "Sojourner."** Her art as an essayist is to move with the scrutinous eye through events and receptions that are random on their surfaces and to find, with grace and always-redeeming wit, the connections. Once in a great while she seems to me to strain—**"An Expedition to the Pole"** grew too abstract in its efforts to join the many elements she'd gathered up for it until it reached a gorgeous, thin level of pretentiousness. I like her work most when she keeps the parts of metaphor relatively few and simple—when she sees, in **"The Deer of Providencia,"** the obvious and wholly elusive commonness among the struggles of a rope-bound deer, a badly burned man in Miami, and the insistent endurance of us all.

Most of all, I liked **"Life on the Rocks: The Galápagos,"** which might have served as the concluding essay, for in it she describes the casual grouping of humans, sea lions, flies, finches, all of which commingle with apparent disregard for the notion of territorial imperative. She walks among them all. Sometimes they nuzzle her. Sometimes she lets them. Sometimes everybody moves aside for everybody else. It seems, finally, the essence of Annie Dillard's nature, as she measures with a yardstick the length of fleeting breezes and listens with respect for the stone's first word.

Douglas Bauer, "Annie Dillard at Play in the Fields of the Lord," in Book World—The Washington Post, January 2, 1983, p. 6.

GARY McILROY

Readers of Annie Dillard's *Pilgrim at Tinker Creek,* a work in many ways reminiscent of [Henry David Thoreau's] *Walden,* are usually disappointed by its virtual neglect of society. It is accomplished, says Hayden Carruth, [see *CLC,* Vol. 9] "with little reference to life on this planet at this moment, its hazards and misdirections, and to this extent it is a dangerous book, literally a subversive book, in spite of its attractions." This must be put into perspective. *Pilgrim at Tinker Creek* has been well received. . . . Many critics, nevertheless, wish it were more like *Walden,* exploring the history of the social world as well as the natural history of the woods. Before deciding on the merits of this criticism, we need to consider what this argument ignores.

In the early seventies, during the time Dillard wrote her "mystical excursion into the natural world," she was living with many close neighbors near Roanoke, Virginia, in the immediate vicinity of Hollins College. She lacked the perspective to engage in a social discussion in the manner of Thoreau: "This is, mind you, suburbia," she says in a later essay. "It is a five-minute walk in three directions to rows of houses. . . . There's a 55 mph highway at one end of [Hollins] pond, and a nesting pair of wood ducks at the other. Under every bush is a muskrat hole or a beer can." Her overriding concern is how to convey the idea of the wilderness, how to recover the aura of the frontier. Dillard's perception of the steers that graze on a nearby pasture illustrates the difficulty she has of even locating the boundary between nature and society. They are a constant reminder of the encroachment of the social order:

> They are all bred beef: beef heart, beef hide, beef hocks. They're a human product like rayon. They're like a field of shoes. They have cast-iron shanks and tongues like foam insoles. You can't see through to their brains as you can with other animals; they have beef fat behind their eyes, beef stew.

There are other emblems of society that turn up in the woods. On a high hill, where Dillard watches "an extended flock of starlings" each dusk, someone had unloaded a pile of burnt books, "cloth- and leather-bound novels, a complete, charred set of encyclopedias decades old, and old, watercolor-illustrated children's books." On the quarry path she finds a discarded aquarium. Why someone hauled it so far into the woods to throw away is a mystery to her. But taken together these cultural artifacts suggest a renouncement of society and a commitment to the exploration of nature: "I could plant a terrarium here. . . . I could transfer the two square feet of forest floor *under* the glass to *above* the glass, framing it . . . and saying to passers-by look! look! here is two square feet of the world." She cherishes the same dream as Thoreau: "If America was found and lost again once, as most of us believe, then why not twice?" [from Thoreau's *Cape Cod*]. Only by relinquishing her hold on society can she imaginatively revive the promise of the new world.

This is not to suggest that the criticism of *Tinker Creek* is unfounded. Dillard sometimes diverts our attention from society when a greater discussion seems warranted by her own narrative. "Sitting under a bankside sycamore" one day, Dillard contemplates what it means to live in the present. Before she can direct her attention to the natural world around her, she must first acknowledge the powerful undercurrents of the unconscious. She is daydreaming, fantasying: "I am in Persia, trying to order a watermelon in German." Continuing in this vein, she sees "the tennis courts on Fifth Avenue in Pittsburgh, an equestrian statue in a Washington park, a basement dress shop in New York city—scenes that I thought meant nothing to me." This may be. But isn't it incumbent upon a writer who claims that nature "is my city, my culture, and all the world I need" to explain the persistence of such images which inhibit her ability to concentrate on the natural phenomena at the creek?

Yet if the weakness of *Tinker Creek* "resides in what it fails to consider" [according to Eva Hoffman in *Commentary,* October, 1974], it is curious that the few passages which do deal with society are unsatisfying. Dillard is criticized for not doing more of what she does least convincingly. We need to consider what we are asking of her. . . . While it is true that Thoreau devotes a considerable amount of attention to society in *Walden,* he did not attempt to find a middle ground between it and his experiment in the woods. He was not anymore than Dillard a social engineer. "In one half-hour," Thoreau boasted, "I can walk off to some portion of the earth's surface where a man does not stand from one year's end to another, and there, consequently, politics are not, for they are but as the cigar-smoke of a man" [from Thoreau's "Walking"]. (pp. 111-13)

Dillard, in the midst of Watergate, wrote a book against the currents of the time: "The kind of art I write is shockingly uncommitted—appallingly isolated from political, social, and economic affairs. There are lots of us here. Everybody is writing about political and social concerns; I don't. I'm not doing any harm." The note of defensiveness is clear. She is up against a strong cultural trend. (p. 113)

The appearance of other people in *Walden* and *Pilgrim at Tinker Creek* is another measure of the writers' attitudes toward society. While Thoreau's friends and acquaintances make up a large part of his narrative, Dillard's do not, despite the fact that she mentions many of their names. . . . These are merely references, however. The social interchange is usually off-stage. . . . She moves so far away from society that she sees it only as a world of shadows and symbols. She is a displaced romantic, out of touch with the fashion of the time:

> I have often noticed that these things, which obsess me, neither bother nor impress other people even slightly. I am horribly apt to approach some innocent at a gathering and, like the ancient mariner, fix him with a wild, glitt'ring eye and say, "Do you know that in the head of the caterpillar of the ordinary goat moth there are two hundred twenty-eight separate muscles?" The poor wretch flees. I am not making chatter; I mean to change his life.

(pp. 114-15)

Dillard knows the danger, we may assume, of a too-close association with the legends surrounding Thoreau. She does not want to be perceived as a hermit, so she speaks of people in passing, assuring us she is part of the community. But by naming her goldfish Ellery Channing, a teasing reference to

[Thoreau's closest friend], she announces firmly that her personal life will remain private. At the same time she commits herself to a metaphorical rendering of her life in society through her relationships and encounters with the animal world. . . . "This Ellery" has "a coiled gut, a spine radiating fine bones, and a brain." He also has a heart. Dillard recalls how years ago she looked through a powerful microscope and saw the individual red blood cells of a goldfish pulsating through a section of its transparent tail. . . . This rosary of cells, a symbol of the sanctity of life, is a common bond between Dillard and the fish, between animal life and human life in general, and between Dillard and other people. The symbolic richness of the goldfish is expanded by Dillard's later discussion of the spiritual significance of the fish in Tinker Creek, and especially by the affinity between fish and the early Christian church.

Ellery Channing is Dillard's most powerful cultural symbol, representing her detachment from society as well as her acknowledgement of the common bond of all living things. It is the detachment, however, which carries the greatest weight. Her relationship to the social world in *Tinker Creek,* and what may be read as her underlying attitude toward it, is ambiguous and largely indifferent. She does not succeed in encompassing within her vision any but the most fragmentary consequences for society at large. The Pilgrims' errand into the wilderness was a community's joint venture; the Transcendentalists' return to nature was a limited fellowship of the spirit; Dillard's exploration of the Virginia woodlands is the solitary search of the soul.

Dillard's social isolation is seen most clearly in "Flood," where the overflowing creek and the coming together of the community to combat it paradoxically suggest even greater detachment than those chapters which do not mention society at all. The narrative is a flashback, brought to mind by the first pounding rain of summer. It signifies a switch in the emphasis of *Tinker Creek* from a celebration of nature to an accounting of its grimmer aspects. The intricacies of the year's new life are now caught up in a headlong rush toward destruction. . . . It is the incursion of nature into society that necessitates Dillard's sudden recognition of Tinker Creek as a part of a larger world. It is now "our creek," because "like a blacksnake caught in a kitchen drawer," it presents a social problem. But although the narrative suggests a meaningful coming together of neighbors to observe and combat the ravages of nature, the overall impression is one of mild coexistence. The people come together quickly and disperse even faster. They stand like spectators or so many vagrants poking at the remains of some ruin. (pp. 115-16)

The exacting limits of this social exchange set the narrator more apart than ever. The townspeople meet as strangers, cooperating out of a shared danger. Nature offers no bridge to human relationships, but merely accentuates the common struggle for survival. One metaphor, significant as free association, most clearly conveys Dillard's attitude toward the people of the town. Some of the women, she observes, "are carrying curious plastic umbrellas they don't put up, but on; they don't get under, but in. They can see out dimly, like goldfish in bowls." (p. 117)

Although Thoreau and Dillard characteristically turn away from society, they do not lose their social instinct. Both seek community in the woods. Thoreau makes a companion of a mouse, who comes out "regularly at lunch time" and picks up the crumbs at his feet. . . . (p. 118)

Unlike the animals that live with Thoreau or treat him as a neighbor, the animals in Dillard's woods tend to flee from her. She is as alien in the woods as she is in society: "The creatures I seek have several senses and free will; it becomes apparent that they do not want to be seen." She identifies instead with their wariness, their essential vulnerability. . . . [She] is not surprised when animals flee: they have learned the lesson of the jungle. When she walks through a field teeming with grasshoppers, not one of them senses her peaceful intent: "To them I was just so much trouble, a horde of commotion, like any rolling stone." A green heron, trying to feed along the creek, watches Dillard instead, "as if I might shoot it, or steal its minnows for my own supper." These animals are her "companions at life." She does not dismiss them, even at home:

> I allow the spiders the run of the house. I figure that any predator that hopes to make a living on whatever smaller creatures might blunder into a four-inch square bit of space in the corner of the bathroom where the tub meets the floor, needs every bit of my support.

These life and death entanglements in *Tinker Creek* function as a parallel to the sinister elements of society, illustrating the dimensions of the social world which have prompted her retreat. (pp. 119-20)

The spiritual-aesthetic experience which Thoreau and Dillard cultivate in the woods is by necessity a solitary one. The Puritans did not celebrate mass, but awaited the direct indwelling of God. There was not one religious experience, but many private ones. It is not surprising that John Field catches no fish when he finally joins Thoreau or that Dillard is unsuccessful in showing muskrats to other people. Whenever two or more gather in the woods, the likely outcome is a manifestation of society, not religion. Annie Dillard goes into the woods to claim her spiritual heritage. Like a prophet, she travels alone. (p. 122)

> *Gary McIlroy, "'Pilgrim at Tinker Creek' and the Social Legacy of 'Walden',"* in South Atlantic Quarterly, *Vol. 85, No. 2, Spring, 1986, pp. 111-22.*

CATHERINE PETROSKI

Think, for a moment, of writing about your own early years—say from age 5 to 15—and consider the problem of getting, first, a grip on all that material, and then organizing and writing about it coherently and in such a way that readers will hang on every word. . . .

[*An American Childhood* does] this so consumately with Annie Dillard's '50s childhood in Pittsburgh that it more than takes the reader's breath away. It consumes you as you consume it, so that, when you have put down this book, you're a different person, one who has virtually experienced another childhood. You have been with this child on her summer visits to her grandparents' river house and on the boat trip she took (as an adolescent of the opposite sex did on the Mississippi) down the Ohio River with her dad. You have been inside her head as she watches her younger sister materialize. You have gotten a microscope on Christmas and discovered moving protozoa in a drop of water. You have gone to dancing class to learn, not just the fox trot, but a certain social ease. You also have discarded the ridiculous notion of religion in a fit of adolescent agnosticism.

Autobiography by definition would seem to require a singular subject. In *An American Childhood,* we get both more and less: Those people who figure large in her early life assume almost mythic proportions, but the author wisely spares her reader the undifferentiated, and what could be trivial, aspects of her childhood. Somehow, we experience the sensation of a summer's droning tedium without being bored for a second. (p. 1)

Dillard follows a straightforward chronology in *An American Childhood.* This is not to say the writing is simple or unadorned. Like the river she uses as a unifying metaphor, each mile forward brings with it several more of meandering among serendipitous associations. In one, Dillard does the impossible: explaining the family private jokes without deadening their infectious good humor. There are meditations on the family's linguistics, on the portents of the nearby branch library, on the day of a huge snow, on the character of solid Presbyterianism, on an insect collection, on the dancing class's final exam.

In elaborations and playful, poetic digressions lie high stakes and heavy risks. Only a self-assured writer dare intentionally violate the commandment "Thou shalt not digress." Dillard does it, and manages to induce the reader not to get impatient. And to feel sad that it must come to an end.

An American Childhood is neither an adult's paean to romanticized memories nor the opposite sort of retributive memoir most readers would wish the writer never committed to paper. Dillard has not flinched at capturing the private fears alongside the rapturous joy, the humble alongside the grand, the comforting rituals alongside the bedeviling puzzlements, the intellectual alongside the sensual. For an autobiographer to comprehend such a wealth of memory with such balance and understanding shows remarkable maturity, and for a writer to share it is an act of singular generosity. (p. 12)

> Catherine Petroski, "Childhood Relived," in Chicago Tribune—Books, *September 13, 1987, pp. 1, 12.*

CYRA McFADDEN

Toward the end of this endearing account of growing up in Pittsburgh, Annie Dillard writes a sentence that sums up its astonishing richness of detail: "It all got noticed." . . . In *An American Childhood,* she demonstrates her gift of total recall and an eye that misses nothing, records everything.

The book begins when Dillard is 5 years old. With the shrewdness of a forensic scientist, and with her sense of humor already well formed, she hits upon the most important difference between children and adults. "Our parents and grandparents, and all their friends, seemed insensible to their own prominent defect, their limp, coarse skin.

"We children had, for instance, proper hands; our fluid, pliant fingers joined their skin. Adults had misshapen, knuckly hands loose in their skin like bones in bags; it was a wonder they could open jars. . . . " Obvious as this is to Dillard, who hides her revulsion out of tact, the decrepitude is lost on the ancient ones. "Adults were coming apart, but they neither noticed nor minded."

Her affectionate tone here is the tone of the book throughout. If there's such a thing as the perfect childhood, Dillard lived it—securely loved, given exactly the right amount of freedom, encouraged to indulge her limitless curiosity. In this sunny memoir, which reminds one of an Impressionist painting, her memories shimmer on the page. (p. 1)

[*An American Childhood*] explains why the poet in her keeps getting yanked offstage and supplanted by the comedian. At her parents' knees, too, she learned to deliver a punch line; play straight man, "an honorable calling . . . despised by the ignorant masses"; appreciate sight gags, running gags and "the top of the line, the running sight gag." When her parents manage to pull off the latter feat, she writes, their children heard tell of it just "as other children hear about their progenitors' war exploits."

With her two younger sisters, Dillard spends idyllic summers at her paternal grandparents' house on the shore of Lake Erie. There the lifelong close observer notes the rivalry between the grandmother she calls Oma and her own mother. Their "long, civilized antagonism," she comes to understand, is a form of class warfare.

Like her mother, the children look down on Oma for her terrible taste in household decor. The grandparents have lots of money, "an embarrassing Cadillac" and no aesthetic sense. Only later does Dillard reflect that "Matters of taste are not, it turns out, moral issues. . . . We thought that merely possessing a gaudy figurine was a worse offense than wholeheartedly embracing snobbery."

In her family's comfortable, sprawling house, with its "bright sunporch" and a glowing golden sandstone wall her mother designed, Dillard begins "a life of reading books, and drawing, and playing at the sciences." This life she pursues with passion, as caught up in a book called *The Natural Way to Draw* as she is by sandlot baseball, hunting for buried treasure in the alley next door and constantly expanding the boundaries of her known world. Looking back on the explorations she makes on foot and by bike, she feels again what she felt then, time having heightened memory instead of dulling it. What joy and relief she felt, she writes, when she came home at night "exultant, secretive" from her latest ramble. "From the very trackless waste, I had located home, family and the dinner table again."

The book describes her life through childhood and young womanhood, to the point where she leaves for college. In a Pittsburgh that seems the very essence of America, "a clean city whose center was new," she grows up absorbing the sense of infinite possibility, along with plenty of calcium, in her bones. How typically American, too, are her cheerful optimism, her enterprise and her confidence that she can learn anything and master any skill if only she puts her mind to it.

The world is Annie Dillard's oyster. The oyster is worth a course in marine biology, a series of drawings, a poem celebrating its place in God's scheme of things. The world enthralls in its mysterious and cunning intricacies.

Loving and lyrical, nostalgic without being wistful, this is a book about the capacity for joy. (p. 14)

> Cyra McFadden, "The Sweetness of a Pittsburgh Girlhood," in Los Angeles Times Book Review, *September 20, 1987, pp. 1, 14.*

NOEL PERRIN

Some mystics see an aura around things. Such a talent greatly increases the power, majesty, drama and interest of this humdrum world. One of William Blake's more famous passages describes his reaction to sunrise, as opposed to the response of ordinary Englishmen. " 'What,' it will be questioned, 'when the sun rises, do you not see a round disc of fire somewhat like a guinea?' 'O no, no, I see an innumerable company of the heavenly host crying, "Holy, Holy, Holy is the Lord God Almighty." ' "

Annie Dillard is one of Blake's company. She may or may not see auras—but she invariably sees *something* beyond what is just there. In the meditative book *Pilgrim at Tinker Creek,* she saw the coming of God in the attempt of three Canada geese to land on her frozen duck pond. She continues to see beyond the visible in her autobiography, *An American Childhood.* This woman is either unusually sensitive or prone to exaggeration, the reader thinks. Both things are true. . . .

The book is Ms. Dillard's equivalent of Wordsworth's *Prelude.* The full title of that work is *The Prelude; or, Growth of a Poet's Mind: An Autobiographical Poem.* Ms. Dillard has written an autobiography in semimystical prose about the growth of her own mind, and it's an exceptionally interesting account. She is one of those people who seem to be more fully alive than most of us, more nearly wide-awake than human beings generally get to be. (Thoreau once said he had never met a man who was fully awake—but he was forgetting about women, and he hadn't met Ms. Dillard.) She is a stunning observer. There is a passage in this book, a rather long one, in which she talks about adult skin as perceived by a child. She begins with an event: herself as a little girl, pinching up the skin over one of her mother's knuckles, and watching in fascination as it stays ridged up instead of instantly returning to smooth shapeliness as a child's hand does. The passage grows into a meditation on how parents (in her case, very young and very good-looking ones, though she didn't know it then) physically appear to a child. It seemed to me, reading it, that skin had never been adequately described before.

She thinks about time, about death, about Pittsburgh streetcars doomed to their tracks, about herself probably doomed to a future in the Junior League and a good Pittsburgh marriage. The year she was 13, she notes, "I was reading books on drawing, painting, rocks, criminology, birds, moths, beetles, stamps, ponds and streams, medicine." She's also looking through a microscope at her own urine, having complicated fantasies and night fears, being reckless in cars, idolizing aristocratic youths, telling jokes in the expert way her parents taught her. It makes lively reading, all these things with their auras.

And yet, *An American Childhood* is not quite as good as it at first promised to be. By choosing to make the book an account of the growth of her mind, an inner rather than an outer narrative, Ms. Dillard almost necessarily forfeited plot. Except at the end, the book does not build; there is no continuous narrative. And though scores of people appear, only two of them are real characters: Annie Dillard herself and, for one wonderful chapter, her mother.

Also, the mystic's heightened prose can become mere mannerism, and from time to time in this book it does. I believed easily, reading *Pilgrim,* that Ms. Dillard felt the presence of God in the flight of those three geese; she made me feel it too. Or at least she made me feel a great power and intensity in the occasion. But when in *An American Childhood* she describes her first encounter with formal philosophy at age 16,

and refers to "Platonism as it had come bumping and skidding down the centuries and across the ocean to Concord, Massachusetts" (it was on its way to meet Emerson), skepticism comes unbidden to the reader's mind. Plato's thought? Bumping and skidding? Fine, vivid language, certainly—but would it be either more or less true to say that his ideas tiptoed daintily down the centuries, or walked in galoshes through the Dark Ages, carrying an umbrella?

In short, isn't Ms. Dillard overwriting here? I think the answer is yes. It's the romantic's temptation, and she is an extreme romantic. Still, overwriting and all, *An American Childhood* remains a remarkable work. Blake overwrote too.

Noel Perrin, "Her Inexhaustible Mind," in The New York Times Book Review, *September 27, 1987, p. 7.*

STEPHEN CHAPMAN

Once, Annie Dillard recalls, she told a friend who is a crewman on a ferryboat that she hates to write. Her surprised friend replied, "That's like a guy who works in a factory all day, and hates it." That made her ask herself: "Why did I do it?. . . . Why wasn't I running a ferryboat, like sane people?"

This collection of essays [*The Writing Life*] might be read as an attempt to answer that question. For nonwriters, it is a glimpse into the trials and satisfactions of a life spent with words. For writers, it is a warm, rambling conversation with a stimulating and extraordinarily talented colleague. . . .

Dillard is one of our most gifted writers; her first book, *Pilgrim at Tinker Creek,* is one of the most memorable works of our time. This collection is far less ambitious than *Pilgrim* or her last book, *An American Childhood,* but it is filled with the sort of nuggets her admirers await—the illuminating anecdote, the deadpan aside, the odd historical reference, the masterly metaphor.

No one can accuse Dillard of romanticizing the writing life. "Much has been written about the life of the mind," she snorts.

> The mind of the writer does indeed do something before it dies, and so does its owner, but I would be hard put to call it living. . . . Many writers do little else but sit in small rooms recalling the real world. This explains why so many books describe the author's childhood. A writer's childhood may well have been the occasion of his only firsthand experience.

That insight also suggests the book's main weakness. Dillard is a lyrical, funny writer, with a sure grasp of words and a quirky, interesting mind. But this collection has a claustrophobic quality. Her gaze is bounded by the four walls of her office, and while she sees things there that no one else would notice, the reader, like the writer, longs for some fresh air and sunshine.

Good as she is at ruminating on various subjects at random, she is better at describing what she has seen and done. In *The Writing Life,* Dillard doesn't see or do much. The chief exception comes in the best piece, a story about a stunt pilot named Dave Rahm whom Dillard saw at an air show and later persuaded to take her for a ride.

"He slid down ramps of air, he vaulted and wheeled," she writes of his air show performance.

> He piled loops in heaps and praised height. He unrolled the scroll of the air, extended it, and bent it into Möbius strips; he furled the line in a thousand new ways, as if he were inventing a script and writing it in one infinitely recurving utterance until I thought the bounds of beauty must break.

After reading that description, the actual show would be superfluous.

Despite its flaws, there is enough to the rest of *The Writing Life* to make it worthwhile. This may not be Annie Dillard at the peak of her powers, but it's still Annie Dillard.

> Stephen Chapman, "Annie Dillard's Essays Weigh the Joys and Woes of Writing," in Book World— The Washington Post, August 27, 1989, p. 6.

SARA MAITLAND

This is a tricky review for me to write. Annie Dillard is one of my favorite contemporary authors. Over and over again, beyond the point of wonder, I have not only enjoyed reading her work, but have found that it nourishes—inspires—my imagination and my own work. . . .

So how am I to say that *The Writing Life* irritates me, that I find it overwritten, self-important and, therefore, unrevealing? This may of course say more about me than it does about the book. . . .

Ms. Dillard says of the writer: "He is careful of what he reads, for that is what he will write. He is careful of what he learns, because that is what he will know."

I cannot treat myself, as a writer, so preciously, and doubt that anyone else either should or does. . . .

Annie Dillard is a wonderful writer and *The Writing Life* is full of joys. These are clearest to me when she comes at her subject tangentially, talking not of herself at her desk but of other parallel cases—the last chapter, a story about a stunt pilot who was an artist of air, is, quite simply, breathtaking.

There are so many bits like this, Ms. Dillard at her best, taking the easily overlooked, the mundane, and revealing it as the beautiful, the important, the meaningful truth that is certainly is. She knows so many things—stories and histories and facts and scraps—and she probes them for meaning so surely. As admiration mounts, you really do have to ask yourself: Is she being honest when she tells us to take care about what we read? Because no one could know in advance that there is worthwhile material to be found in as many strange byways as she finds them.

Unfortunately, the bits do not add up to a book. Near the beginning of *The Writing Life,* Ms. Dillard states categorically:

> Writing a book, full time, takes between two and ten years. . . . Thomas Mann was a prodigy of production. Working full time, he wrote a page a day. That is 365 pages a year, for he did write every day—a good-sized book a year. At a page a day, he was one of the most prolific writers who ever lived. Flaubert wrote steadily, with only the usual, appalling, strains. For twenty-five years he finished a big book every five to seven years. My guess is that full-time writers average a book every five years:

> seventy-three usable pages a year, or a usable fifth of a page a day. . . . On plenty of days the writer can write three or four pages, and on plenty of other days he concludes he must throw them away.

I don't know if I can face these gloomy statistics. I don't know if they are true. But if Ms. Dillard believes them, then perhaps that explains the problem with *The Writing Life.* It has not been given its necessary time; it is not a full two years younger than *An American Childhood,* her wonderful autobiography. Are these the scraps that she concluded must be thrown out of that work, or are they notes toward a book that might have been?

To be fair, later she also writes:

> One of the few things I know about writing is this: spend it all, shoot it, play it, lose it, all, right away, every time. Do not hoard what seems good for a later place in the book, or for another book; give it, give it all, give it now. . . . Something more will arise for later, something better. These things fill from behind, from beneath, like well water. Similarly, the impulse to keep to yourself what you have learned is not only shameful, it is destructive. Anything you do not give freely and abundantly becomes lost to you. You open your safe and find ashes.

That flamboyant energy and generosity are at the heart of Ms. Dillard's craft. It is not her fault that I am not really interested in how writers write, but in what they write. In real books about real things.

> Sara Maitland, " 'Spend It All, Shoot It, Play It, Lose It'," in The New York Times Book Review, September 17, 1989, p. 15.

WENDY LAW-YONE

Can anyone who has heard Glenn Gould at the keyboard ignore what he has to say about piano playing? Can anyone who has ever read Annie Dillard resist hearing what she has to say about writing? Her authority has been clear since *Pilgrim at Tinker Creek*—a mystic's wonder at the physical world expressed in beautiful, near-biblical prose. . . . Since then her distinctive voice has taken on poetry, literary criticism, narrative essays and autobiography.

Now, in *The Writing Life,* Dillard reflects on the creative process. The result—part essay, part series of metaphors—is intriguing but not entirely satisfying. In the hands of a stylist as skilled as Dillard—a stylist with the ability to make the progress of an inchworm not only interesting but suspenseful—it's easy to be smitten by the brilliance of the parts and hard to determine why they somehow fail to make a whole. This elegant and ironic book is without doubt the work of a dedicated and inspired artist, but it's a sketch rather than a finished portrait.

The Writing Life is clearly not intended as a manual on craft; it is a study of the writer at work. I suspect the average reader interested in the business of writing will want to know not only what the job is like but how it's done. That the reader will have to go elsewhere to find out. This is not to say that *The Writing Life* is without important advice for those with a serious interest in writing; but the advice is moral, not practical—the directions oblique, not straightforward. A Zen-like analogy to chopping wood, for example, instructs the woodchopper/writer to "aim past the wood, aim through the wood; aim for the chopping block."

Write what you know has always been the accepted wisdom of creative writing programs. Not enough, says Dillard. Write what you alone know: "You were made and set here to give voice to this, your own astonishment." This may surprise—although it probably won't deter—the multitudes of writers sitting at their desks at this very moment in the belief that it's enough to have a good story to tell. For Dillard, the challenge of every book, is its "intrinsic impossibility . . . it is why no one can ever write this book." The writer's stunt is to write it in spite of that. . . .

Writers love to describe their work as ordeals involving blood and gore ("Writing is easy; all you have to do is sit in front of the typewriter until beads of blood form on your brow," etc.) In Dillard's case, "even when passages seemed to come easily, as though I were copying from a folio held open by smiling angels, the manuscript revealed the usual signs of struggle—bloodstains, teethmarks, gashes, and burns." Writing, it appears, requires the writer to be bloody but unbowed, ready to take on circus-like feats of animal-taming and acrobatics. A work in progress can become wild overnight, like a lion. "You must visit it every day and reassert your mastery over it. . . . You enter its room with bravura, holding a chair at the thing and shouting, 'Simba!' " Well, it's been a while since I tamed my last lion, but I do know this much: I used to think, much like Dillard, that getting a sentence right was a form of alligator wrestling—until I watched a fellow in Fort Lauderdale, Fla., who wrestled alligators for a living. Give me sentences any time. . . .

A lot of questions go unanswered in *The Writing Life.* Still I enjoyed every page. I especially enjoyed the privileged peek into the window of Annie Dillard's private study: the cigarettes and the coffee; the doodles on the legal pads; the clothespin clamped over a finger as a painful reminder that water has been left to boil on a stove; the pages laid out on a conference table ("You walk along the rows; you weed bits, move bits, and dig out bits. . . . After a couple of hours, you have taken an exceedingly dull nine-mile hike. You go home and soak your feet"). It's enough to be able to see that even Annie Dillard, when she is finishing a book, will let the houseplants die.

Mine, I regret, are doing just fine.

Wendy Law-Yone, "Annie Get Your Pen," in Book World—The Washington Post, *September 24, 1989, p. 4.*

MICHAEL EDENS

[In] *Pilgrim at Tinker Creek,* Annie Dillard wrote that she had "no intention of inflicting all my childhood memories on anyone"; in her last book, *An American Childhood,* she did exactly that. She wasn't wrong, really, to break that promise—*Childhood* was a very good book, almost a great one—but still, it indicated how attenuated and self-obsessed her work was becoming. Now, in *The Writing Life,* Dillard has gone one step farther down that path: She has moved from writing about herself to writing about writing about herself.

The Writing Life isn't a bad book, exactly—I don't think Dillard is capable of writing anything awful—but it's thin and fragmented, and self-pitying. Nothing comes more easily to a writer than moaning about the creative agony of the artist, but Dillard has always had such perfect, poetic taste and such a fine sense of the ridiculous that I would never have expected it of her. Though her work has probably never sold in proportion to its merit, she does have a Pulitzer Prize and at least one best seller under her belt. So it's just plain embarrassing when she whines that writing is "work . . . so meaningless, so fully for yourself alone, and so worthless to the world, that no one except you cares whether you do it well, or ever." Ten minutes at a job that really is meaningless might change her mind. (p. 435)

Even on a subject as barren as this one, though, Dillard's prose style remains amazing. Reviewers tend to use adjectives such as "luminous" and "radiant" in describing her writing. That usually means vague and sentimental and pseudopoetic—but she's not. Her prose is rich when it needs to be, but she never merely assembles conglomerations of syllables for their own sake. The nature writing in Dillard's *Pilgrim at Tinker Creek* can take the reader's breath away with its beauty, but she never yields to the temptation to be falsely pretty. . . . More important, everything in that book, and in most of her others, has a meaning beyond the literal. I sometimes believe that Dillard took Blake's "To see a world in a grain of sand/and a heaven in a wild flower" as her job description.

Most of Dillard's books have moments of immense beauty and power—that is why it is so jarring how silly some of the metaphors in *The Writing Life* are. Writing desks hover "thirty feet from the ground"; the writer, she says, must crank "the engine of belief that keeps you and your desk in midair." (Trust your feelings, Luke. The Force will be with you.) A two-page chapter is devoted to a typewriter that turns volcanic, "exploding with fire and ash." It shakes the walls and floor of her house in its fury; she grabs a bucket of water to douse it, but decides to leave it be, though the eruptions recur randomly through the night. A couple of days later, it works just fine. I know Dillard wants us to think deep mystical thoughts about creative fire, but the only deep thought I had was this: Could one of the most brilliant writers of our time be dumb enough to want to pour water in a burning electrical appliance?

One could be cynical and argue that there's a reason *The Writing Life* seems mostly self-obsessed: that Dillard has been navel-gazing so long that her chin has become permanently attached to her chest. But I don't really think that's the problem. Yes, most of her books are ultimately about herself, but they are really about how she transforms what she perceives. . . . Dillard's books, whatever their nominal subjects, constitute her spiritual autobiography, and that's the riskiest kind of writing—her books work only if every sentence is an epiphany. That's a word critics have debased beyond recognition, but Dillard's best work honestly provides something that can only be called revelation, and that something cannot be faked. So there may be a good reason that her last couple of books have been merely about the inside of her head: What else can you write when the epiphanies don't come? (pp. 435-36)

Michael Edens, "Mothballed," in The Nation, *New York, Vol. 249, No. 12, October 16, 1989, pp. 435-36.*

Autran Dourado

1926-

(Born Waldomiro Freitas Autran Dourado) Brazilian novelist, short story writer, and essayist.

One of the most prominent Brazilian novelists of the post-World War II era, Dourado is often compared to American novelist William Faulkner for his focus on the effect of the past on the present and for approaching regional and family history as fate and myth. Dourado's fiction is generally set in small towns in his native Minas Gerais, a state north of Rio, and often revolves around archetypal characters whose selfishness renders them unable to experience love or happiness. Malcolm Silverman asserted: "Dourado's is an endless, repetitive and cyclical drama, and for this reason he deliberately leaves protagonists and settings open-ended. . . . Laced with interior duplications, the novelist's stories do not stop, but rather turn to the timelessness so prevalent at their beginnings. . . . Timelessness is, in itself, universality; and it is precisely Autran Dourado's ability to project universal patterns of human behavior while focusing on introspective individuals that makes him one of Brazil's leading fictionists."

Dourado's first work, *Teia,* is a novella that introduces his concern with disturbed characters and unusual situations. This novella delineates the conflicts that arise following the confused narrator's arrival at a boardinghouse terrorized by a domineering woman. In Dourado's first novel, *Sombra e exílio,* a man struggles to overcome an innate inferiority complex and to break free of his depraved family, which consists of his unfaithful wife, his widowed mother, and his dissolute brother. Although these characters were generally faulted as unconvincing, those in Dourado's next novel, *Tempo de amar,* are regarded as more clearly defined. This work centers upon a lackadaisical protagonist who returns to his hometown of Cercado Velho upon graduating from boarding school. Unable to assimilate with bourgeois society, Dourado's hero procures sex from a young woman on the condition that he will leave town with her, but after she becomes pregnant, he finds himself emotionally incapable of leaving. *A barca dos homens,* Dourado's most highly acclaimed novel, traces the moral consequences that arise after a man provokes fate. The man falsely claims that a harmless simpleton has stolen his gun and poses a threat to his community.

Dourado's next book, *Uma vida em segrêdo* (*A Hidden Life*), recalls Gustave Flaubert's lyrical novel *Un coeur simple* in its simple story of a young country girl who travels to the city to live with her uncle after her father dies. Unable to adjust to her new surroundings, she seeks out other outcasts and briefly finds companionship by adopting a stray dog. *Ópera dos mortos* (*The Voices of the Dead*), a complex novel characterized by abrupt shifts in tense and narration, is set in a gothic manor house owned by Rosalina, a psychotic and isolated woman who lives with her housekeeper. Haunted by her ancestral history, Rosalina pursues a passionate sexual affair with a handyman by night and becomes cold and reserved by day, alternately reflecting the influence of her grandfather, an unethical, lustful landowner, and her father, a repressed neurotic. After bearing the handyman's child, Rosalina is taken

to a mental institution. John Naughton commented: "It isn't the tale that counts but the way Dourado circles its events, building up an absorbing picture of the private worlds inhabited by his three characters, and providing an exquisitely detailed case study of the tragic irreversibility of sexual commitment."

Dourado divided his next work, *O risco do bordado* (*Pattern for a Tapestry*), into sections he termed "blocks," which may be read as a novel or as a group of interrelated short stories. In these vignettes, João da Fonseca Nogueira returns to his forgotten hometown and attempts to preserve his past, including the Sao Mateus boarding school, as well as his family history. Harriet Gilbert commented: "[*Pattern for a Tapestry* demonstrates]—with dexterous sleights of imagery and phrase—that forgetfulness is just an ingredient of memory; that, if we are to recapture the past, it must either fit or be *made* to fit into a pattern." The novel *Os sinos da agonia* (*The Bells of Memory*) is set in the small town of Vila Rica de Ouro Preto, the center of the gold rush that transformed Brazil during its colonial period. This work focuses on the institution of slavery as the gold supply depletes in the late eighteenth century. Although Dourado initially denied political or historical intentions in writing the novel, his translator, John M. Parker, indicates that the book conveys his perceptions of the early 1970s in Brazil, when his country's military regime was active and fears of economic collapse were common.

In addition to his novels, Dourado has written many collections of short fiction, including *Três histórias na praia, Solidão solitude,* and *Armas y corações. As imaginações pecaminosas,* a volume revolving around the sexual indiscretions of the dignified residents of a small town, conveys Dourado's characteristic concern with fate and violence as well as a strong element of humor.

(See also *CLC,* Vol. 23 and *Contemporary Authors,* Vols. 25-28, rev. ed.)

PRINCIPAL WORKS

NOVELS

Sombra e exílio   1950
Tempo de amar   1952
A barca dos homens   1961
Uma vida em segrêdo   1964
   [*A Hidden Life,* 1969]
Ópera dos mortos   1967
   [*Voices of the Dead,* 1981]
O risco do bordado   1970
   [*Pattern for a Tapestry,* 1984]
Os sinos da agonia   1974
   [*The Bells of Agony,* 1988]
A serviço del-Rei   1984

SHORT FICTION

Teia   1947
Três histórias na praia   1955
Nove histórias em grupos de três   1957
Solidão solitude   1972
Três histórias no internato   1978
Armas y corações   1978
As imaginações pecaminosas   1981

OTHER

Uma poética de romance: matéria de carpinteria   (essays)
   1976

THE NEW YORKER

[In *A Hidden Life*], Biela, a peasant girl from the Brazilian backlands, is wrenched from the familiar world of her father's farm and sent to live with sophisticated urban cousins. The change is almost crushing, but after trying briefly and vainly to emulate their ways she finds her own method of adjusting to her new environment—by living as a servant. She thus sacrifices her tenuous claim to a place in society, and can attach her powerful affections only to painfully unsuitable objects. Unfair as a comparison to Flaubert's *Un Cœur Simple* may be, the tale of a simpleminded peasant woman living and loving in alien surroundings has already been perfected. Pathos demands more skillful treatment than this. (pp. 118-19)

   A review of "This Is the Castle," in The New Yorker, *Vol. 45, No. 3, March 1, 1969, pp. 118-19.*

LEO L. BARROW

A Hidden Life tells the story, simply and without literary sophistication, of a little country cousin who, after her father dies, comes to live with her uncle's family in the city. Biela's eighteen years on the farm with her eccentric old father leave her poorly prepared for her new life and too old to adapt. . . .

Although Biela makes a few efforts to fit in, her goodness and simplicity are revealed in her attempts to move in an opposite direction. While most people in Brazil and in the whole world for that matter, both in literature and life, flee from the low and mean, Biela seeks her place among the colored servants, the sick and the forgotten.

The novel begins and ends in straight narrative. Autran Dourado doesn't even bother to separate the dialogue, mostly of the "he-said-and-then-she-said" variety, from the narrative. In the original work, he lumps everything—narrative, description, dialogue—into rather loose, easygoing paragraphs. . . .

The almost childlike simplicity of *A Hidden Life,* both in its tone and in its lack of technical resources, may well indicate literary sophistication. Biela is above all a plain country girl and the simple narrative suits her as well as her unfashionable calico dresses.

Technical sophistication and experimentation seem to be the rule in contemporary novels, and Brazil is producing more than its fair share of these. Biela's story, though old-fashioned, should furnish a few hours of enjoyable reading for those who still like a good story well told. It may even stir a few minutes of reflection on man's indifference to his kin and kind.

   Leo L. Barrow, "Nice Niece," in Book World—The Washington Post, *April 13, 1969, p. 10.*

DAVID J. LEIGH, S. J.

Who's your favorite Brazilian novelist? Even devotees of Latin American literary giants such as Borges or Garcia Marquez will probably have trouble naming any major Brazilian writers, much less singling out Waldomiro Freitas Autran Dourado as their bedside favorite. Only one of his many works has even been translated into English (*A Hidden Life,* 1967); [*The Voices of the Dead*] has managed to live a hidden life of its own before [an English translator] found a publisher for this version of *Opera dos Mortos,* Dourado's masterpiece, which has survived six editions in Portuguese. It will be lucky to survive one printing in English.

Not that it starts all that badly. The opening chapters of baroque prose, mixing stream of consciousness with opinionated psychologizing by an anonymous voice of the town, build a mysterious portrait of the manor house in a small Brazilian town in Minas Gerais north of Rio. Within the manor lives the psychotic grandaughter of an unscrupulous landlord who terrorized the local population and then left his property to his neurotic son, at whose death all the clocks were stopped to freeze Rosalina in the past where she is victimized by the 'voices of the dead.' Into this gothic setting rides Jose Feliciano, alias Joey Bird, who is an illegitimate wandering mulatto fighting his own ghosts and godfather. He manages to get a job as Rosalina's handyman around the manor and eventually slithers past the deaf housekeeper and into Rosalina's bedroom. The result of this melodramatic middle portion is an endless series of maudlin inner monologues . . . and another bastard, soon buried by the deaf housekeeper. The novel ends with the police, the army, and her old rejected suitor leading the heroine away as the narrator appears out of the monologue to comment: "There went Rosalina, our thorn, our grief." (pp. 368-69)

Critics who have called Dourado's impressionistic style "Faulknerian" may be a bit hysterical, but the name of Faulkner does conjure up the latter's best short story as a contrasting example that reflects back the melodramatic meanderings of this novel—namely, "A Rose For Emily." If Dourado has truly gained his main reputation as a short story writer, he might have done well to recast the present tale of Rosalina in that more manageable genre. (p. 369)

David J. Leigh, S. J., in a review of "The Voices of the Dead," in Best Sellers, *Vol. 41, No. 10, January, 1982, pp. 368-69.*

KATHA POLLITT

On the central square of Duas Pontes, a hot, dusty village in the Brazilian interior, sits the dilapidated mansion of the Honório Cota family. Within lives the family's last representative, the beautiful recluse Dona Rosalina, still carrying on a feud that her father, one of those politician-landowners known historically as *colonels* in Brazil, had with the town over an election years ago. Surrounded by family portraits and stopped timepieces, her only human contact her mute old servant, Quiquina, Rosalina spends her days making cloth flowers and watching the town from her window. At night, she drinks. Rosalina is haunted by family ghosts—her father, the proud, honorable, finally embittered businessman-politician, and her grandfather, a landowner whose lusts and brutalities are local legend.

Into this house of dead men and silent women comes the mulatto Joey Bird, a wandering one-eyed jack-of-all-trades from distant parts, who becomes Rosalina's handyman and eventually her lover. . . . Haughty and cold to him by day, as befits her father's daughter, by night she proves herself her grandfather's true descendant. No good can come of this, thinks Quiquina, and she is right. Rosalina becomes pregnant and mad, in that order.

Let readers whose familiarity with Brazilian fiction is limited to the novels of Jorge Amado . . . be advised: Dourado's obsessive, doom-ridden vision [in *The Voices of the Dead*] is as far from Amado's humane, playful sensuality as Duas Pontes is from downtown Bahia. And there is no resemblance between Amado's limpid prose and Dourado's heavy, slow, rich poetic language, with its insistent working of a small cluster of symbols—cloth flowers and real ones, guns, blindness, stopped clocks, craters, graves, dead children. The writer Dourado most resembles is William Faulkner. He shares Faulkner's thematic concerns—the grip of the past on the present, regional history as fate and myth, inescapable family destinies—as well as some stylistic ones, including the use of a collective village voice, like that of a Greek chorus, as a narrative device. Dourado's plot in this book, with its orgiastic and secret liaison between bastard mulatto laborer and proud white virgin recluse, is reminiscent of a similar episode in *Light in August.*

The Voices of the Dead is the sort of novel that is often described as "powerful" and "intense" and "Aeschylean," to suggest that the characters are grand and passionate actors trapped by a grim family fate. The challenge of this kind of story is to persuade the reader that the characters really *are* fated—no easy task in the 20th century (**Voices,** written in 1967, seems to be set some decades earlier). Sometimes I believed Dourado. There is real pathos, for example, in Rosalina, alone in her drawing room, fashioning a huge white organdy rose and daydreaming about wearing it to a party with her husband; the happiness that is impossible for her, we realize, is no lofty and otherworldly ecstasy, but the ordinary, domestic kind—music, friends, an evening out. But much of the time my disbelief refused to suspend itself—when, for example, my attention was drawn, for the 20th time, to the "dark forces" propelling the lovers, and the family portraits, and the stopped clocks, and the mansion's architecture, which, we are constantly reminded, embodies a fusion of the savage grandfather (who built the first floor) and the repressed father (who built the second). So insistent is Dourado on these symbols, and so resolutely does he confine Rosalina's interior monologues to them, that I found myself wondering if the real reason the poor woman can't go outside is simply that Dourado won't let her.

The belabored symbolism, the concoctedness, of Rosalina's story explains, perhaps, the book's muted emotional appeal. The prose alone, while hardly crisp or swift, has its pleasures, like swimming in honey:

> But she couldn't handle the watches, she must never handle those watches. The watches worked a spell, though stopped they carried on ticking just like that lost soul in the house at night, with the windows open, the silent starry night outside, the wind whistling in the corners of the square, stirring the curtains, the doors banging, there was always a door banging in the depths of the night, when she was sleeping, immersed in sleep.

Indeed, there are set pieces of massive beauty that stand out like dreamy, densely textured arias (the novel's Portuguese title is, in fact, **Opera dos Mortes**): Rosalina's drunken reveries of girlhood sex play; her first erotic encounter with Joey, when she gives him an organdy rose and he fastens it in her hair; Quiquina's delivery of Rosalina's baby, which Quiquina plans to kill and probably does. The best scene is the last: Mad Rosalina, clad in white like a bride or a corpse, is escorted down the stairs by the local authorities, who have come to take her away, while the townspeople, admitted to the mansion after so many years, stand in silent awe.

Maybe certain ideas don't translate well—for example, that a young woman could be so emotionally dominated by a grandfather she had never seen. Then, too, it may be that certain characters make sense only in their national context. I had trouble placing Joey Bird. Is he one-eyed in order to glimpse hidden truths, a hunter of meaning as well as small game, a Brazilian version of Mellors from *Lady Chatterley's Lover?* Or is he just what he seems, a lazy, coarse, stupid and commonplace person, whose one-eyedness signals lack of imagination and on whom Rosalina's tragedy is largely wasted? (pp. 13, 23)

Katha Pollitt, "Dark Forces, Tainted Blood and a Grim Family Fate," in The New York Times Book Review, *January 24, 1982, pp. 13, 23.*

JOHN M. PARKER

A new book by Autran Dourado is always a literary event in Brazil, and this latest volume will not disappoint the author's devotees. *As imaginações pecaminosas* (*Sinful Minds*) is a collection of ten short pieces interlinked—with the exception of the last two—by encounters with or references to many of the same characters and by their communal presence in the author's fictional world, the small town in the state of Minas Gerais which he has named Duas Pontes.

There is a further, stronger connecting thread running through these stories, conveyed by the book's title (with its hinted echo of *Les liaisons dangereuses*) and brought home forcefully by the very short opening piece, **"Um ajuste de contas" (A Score Settled)** . . . : the sexual skeletons in the closets of the apparently respectable townsfolk and the violence visited on some of them as a result of their proclivities. **"Um ajuste de contas"** provides or proposes a clamorous, anticipated punishment for the list of sexual transgressions and social taboos which Dourado locates in the imaginary inhabitants of his invented community. In **"Queridinha da família"** (**"The Family Sweetheart"**) an elderly businessman's passion for the celluloid Shirley Temple overflows, with (at least) incestuous suggestions, onto a pubescent schoolgirl and results in his being killed by a hired gun; in **"Pedro imaginário"** (**"Pedro the Image Carver"**) the crime committed by two brothers, who murder their sister and her priest lover ostensibly to avenge the family honor, barely conceals an incestuous jealousy shared by both; horribly, even less acceptably violent is the death of Emílio Amorim, the flautist, found strangled and viciously knifed, at the climax of a scandalous homosexual relationship.

Yet humor is not absent from the pages of *As imaginações pecaminosas,* as when Dourado once more ironizes the macho myth of Brazilian society in **"Noite de cabala e paixão" ("Night of Cabala and Passion")** in which Dr. Viriato is driven to allege sexual inadequacy in an attempt to repel the advances of an unmarried female patient. The story climaxes in hilarious confusion when nature and the willing virgin provoke the elderly doctor into a display of passion which leaves that lady literally in a state of shock, needing his medical attention. A sense of the ridiculous is maintained until the closing lines of the story, where Viriato thinks of Luizinha as his inner demon. And perhaps this is the key to what may be symbolic relationships in these short tales: the Other represents the unconfessable in ourselves.

To whom, though, do the "sinful minds" of the book's title refer—the characters, the townsfolk or the readers? For Dourado, like the great Machado de Assis . . . is a specialist in the subtle art of suggestion, making of his leisurely narratives a minefield of half-truths and partial explanations, depending on a chorus-type narrator who derives his information essentially from the characters themselves and stands in some awe of the town's "intellectuals." Thus Dourado's microcosm gains some new characters, whose secrets permeate the atmosphere of Duas Pontes, broadening the author's Freudian vision: the id rearing its ugly head, so that the town's respectable inhabitants would find it difficult to boast of being morally superior to the denizens of the local whorehouse. (pp. 495-96)

John M. Parker, in a review of "As imaginações pecaminosas," in World Literature Today, *Vol. 56, No. 3, Summer, 1982, pp. 495-96.*

DAPHNE PATAI

In his novels Autran Dourado has repeatedly described the lives of human beings, withdrawn and relatively isolated, who exist on the margins of society. Biela in *Uma Vida em Segrêdo* (1964; in English: *A Hidden Life*), Rosalina in *Ópera dos Mortos* (1967), and Mariano in *O Risco do Bordado* (1970)—all are of this type. At the same time that he has focused on the singularity of these lives, the very titles of Dourado's novels indicate his penchant for allegory. These characteristics were already evident in his 1961 novel *A Barca dos Homens* [*The Ship of Men*], in which the simple-minded man/child Fortunato acts as a catalyst for an entire community.

One summer day, on the island of Boa Vista, Fortunato is accused of stealing a revolver. He flees and is pursued by soldiers and vigilantes who are convinced that Fortunato must be killed before he shoots someone. This situation sets in motion a complex series of actions involving the entire island; from the local prostitutes to the local priest, all are to varying degrees affected by, and implicated in, the hunt. During the day and night on which this hunt occurs, time is slowed down, intensified, and laden with possibilities. The novel, however, does not deal so much with the disruption of everyday life by unforeseen events as with the subjacent potentialities for violence and sudden change that are able to come to the surface by means of the pursuit and sacrifice of an innocent. Fortunato, as the object of this pursuit, thus becomes an agent of change.

The pattern is a familiar one. An exceptional being—in this case with limited intelligence but remarkable acuity regarding nature—is sacrificed "for the sake of " a community. One can discern, in this pattern, that the form of a belief has greater durability than the content. The pagan origin of the Christian concern with sacrifice and resurrection is the case in point. But whereas in ancient religions it was believed that human sacrifice was required for the sake of the continuation of things necessary to human physical survival, in Christianity the sacrifice appears as an event necessary for the spiritual salvation of humanity. In the Christian myth cycle, Christ's sacrifice ensures the rebirth of the soul, not of vegetation. This perhaps corresponds to an increasing mastery over nature. In *A Barca dos Homens,* however, Dourado evokes and then deviates from the pattern created by Christianity. While stressing the mystery of nature's cycles, he depicts an old pattern now utilized for entirely mundane purposes. (pp. 191-92)

By the very selection of focus and arrangement of words, the writer "brackets" or "reduces" reality, thus directing the reader to that part of it which he or she wishes to explore. . . . An island, as the scene of a novel, may well be a perfect metaphor for the bracketing and refocusing in which the novel necessarily engages. The artist, [Maurice] Merleau-Ponty, has written, "is one who arrests the spectacle in which most men take part without really seeing it and who makes it visible."

In the case of *A Barca dos Homens,* the title itself (*The Ship of Men*) invites the reader to view this island metaphorically, as a microcosm. Paradoxically, then, while limiting the horizons of his novel to the sea around the island, Dourado gives the reader to understand that not a mere fragment, but a representative human drama, will be enacted. (p. 192)

Although the novel is narrated by a third-person omniscient narrator who frequently slips into a kind of interior monologue, this posture is interrupted several times by a first-person narrator who thinks of himself as a chronicler. This is first hinted at early in the novel when a description of Luzia telling stories to the children is interrupted by the phrase "this story that I am putting together," which plays on the Portuguese word *história,* meaning both story and history. . . .

Dourado, in a brief commentary on the novel, explains that the diction of this narrator is a fusion of three voices, that of Fernão Lopes, that of Pero Vaz de Caminha, and that of the collective narrators of the *História Trágico-Marítima* (*Tragic History of the Sea*), whose ships are mentioned in the novel. This device is not maintained with any consistency throughout the novel since, as has been noted, the central narrative posture is that of an omniscient narrator, a technique unavailable to the historian or chronicler. What Dourado's use of this narrative voice suggests is an image (albeit ironic) of the novelist as the chronicler of the new land that is the world of his novel. At the same time, the reader becomes aware of the distance and events that, for example, separate Pero Vaz de Caminha's letter of 1500, describing the beauties of Brazil and the innocence of its Indians, from the modern class society described by Dourado. This distance and contrast cast an ironic retrospective glance toward the reigning colonialist fiction of the benefits accruing to the colonized land and its people in the service of "the Empire and the Faith": "a glory that never was," as the narrator says.

Is one to interpret these parodies of chronicles as an effort on the author's part to lend credence to his narrative? On the contrary, the appearance of these fragments—while giving a more concrete aspect to the ship metaphor in the novel's title—actually serves as a reminder of the distance between such historical accounts and the imaginative constructions of the novelist. And yet even Henry James, who would have been outraged at Dourado's narrative intrusion (which he would have considered as the betrayal of a sacred trust), recognized that the novelist and the historian have the same aim, that of describing the truth as they see it. (p. 193)

Although these narrative intrusions (which represent a fiction within a fiction, for Dourado is hardly a Renaissance chronicler and is certainly not speaking as himself in these segments) disturb what might be called the narrative unity of the novel, in other respects the novel presents a highly unified structure. In the manner of a somewhat expanded classical drama, unity of place is carefully preserved as the reader becomes acquainted with the limits of the island: its beaches and cemetery, its rich and poor sections, its town hall, factory, brothel, and church; all these basic elements of modern life appear, on a reduced scale, on this island surrounded by the sea. Temporally, the narrative displays an even tighter unity, for the events it describes occur primarily in the course of one day and night. (p. 194)

In *Point Counter Point* (1928), Aldous Huxley developed his contrapuntal theory of fiction (continuing André Gide's attempts in *The Counterfeiters* [1925]) in part through the diaries of Philip Quarles. Commenting on the multiple points of view he wished to bring to bear on the same event, Quarles writes, "Each sees . . . a different aspect of the event, a different layer of reality. What I want to do is to look with all those eyes at once." This contrapuntal technique, which constitutes an attempt to apprehend reality, is motivated by a perception of reality as dense and multidimensional, in need of viable approaches. It thus reflects a sense of the complex nature of re-

ality that a stable narrator, like a solitary individual, is unable to convey fully. . . .

The ability to circle around a particular moment in time, as it were, is one of the unique features of fiction, setting it apart from all other forms of discourse. The dimensions of a particular moment are thus revealed in a way that is simply not available to us in everyday life. . . .

Our own immediate involvement in life normally precludes the distance and perspective on events that the novel provides and exploits. In reading a novel a new perspective is made available through our distance as readers and through the writer's spatialization of time. The novel, in this way, can create a greater awareness of the real nature of time that we, in the immediacy of our sense impressions, cannot apprehend, and this is that our time is shared by the many living subjects experiencing it, each of whom has a separate (although interpenetrating) version of it to describe. This *gestalt* afforded us by literature should be kept in mind as another possible aspect of what Joseph Frank has termed "spatial form." Frank considers spatial form in modern literature to signal the abandonment of historical time for the "timeless world of myth," but clearly it need not always have this significance. As indicated by the contrapuntal novel—from Gide through Huxley, and now in Autran Dourado—the spatialization of time may be an attempt to convey a sense of the mystery of time in human life, and may therefore constitute an effort not to escape from time but to reveal something of its nature.

In *A Barca dos Homens,* the spatialization of time occurs primarily through the contrapuntal technique, which focuses on different characters as they pass through the same moments during one particular day. (p. 195)

At the center of the novel is the figure of Fortunato, but the two parts of the novel circle about him in different ways. In the first part, "The Harbor," eight chapters present all the figures of the novel who are brought together and set in motion through Fortunato's purported theft of Godofredo's revolver. The problem of how to move the characters about is resolved by the use of an essentially theatrical model: each chapter may be considered an act divided into different scenes. The various acts indicate geographic shifts while the scenes within an act display a relative geographic unity. Throughout the eight chapters of part one, there is an ever-increasing range of involvement. We begin with Luzia and the children; move on to Maria, Fortunato, and Godofredo; then to the peripheral elements that will be brought into play by Godofredo's accusation: Lieutenant Fonseca, the soldiers, Tônho, the prisoners, the prostitutes, and, finally, Brother Miguel. Part one thus circumscribes all the major elements in the life of the island: individuals and institutions.

The contrapuntal technique begins on the level of the individual chapters. Chapter two ("The Spiders"), for example, begins with Maria watching Fortunato through the window at 9 A.M. and then focuses on her thoughts, followed by Godofredo's, as they prepare to go to the beach. As in other chapters, a space between paragraphs indicates a change of scene and a corollary change of perspective. The narrative focus then shifts to Fortunato's morning; that is, the same time span just experienced through Maria's and Godofredo's perspectives is re-experienced through Fortunato's as he orchestrates a fight between two spiders. Again there is a change of scene as the narrative focus settles on Maria and Godofredo at the beach. They return to the house, where the scenes, as it were, join together: Godofredo sees Fortunato, who had entered the house looking for some bottles into which to put the remains of the spiders, jump out of the bedroom window, leaving open the dresser drawer. Thinking Fortunato has stolen his gun, Godofredo calls after him to return.

At the same time, this chapter as a whole repeats the time span (the morning hours) that has already been described from the point of view of Luzia and the children in the preceding chapter. Thus the individual scenes within a chapter, as well as the interrelationship of chapters, reveal a contrapuntal structure, with the specific relationships between scenes in each chapter being essentially spatial, based on groupings of individuals who are or have just been together in one place. (p. 196)

What becomes evident thematically in part one—that Fortunato is the focal point of the events of this day—is reaffirmed structurally in part two, entitled "Waves on the High Sea." The significance of the titles Dourado gives the two parts, as well as the title of the eight chapters in part one, should not be overlooked, for they too function as a kind of authorial direction to the reader. There are no chapter divisions as such in part two; rather, Fortunato's interior monologue is the one controlling element, and, in fourteen segments, it alternates with sections focusing on the thoughts and activities of the other characters. here, too, Fortunato is a center, a base from which all the rest radiates, and his narrative forms one sequential whole interrupted by the other characters' reflections, all of which duplicate one another in time.

The continuity of Fortunato's narrative in part two places him at the center of our awareness, which parallels his role at the center of events in the novel; now he does not move or act, but rather awaits his fate passively, hoping to be saved by Tônho. While he waits, others act around him. This is a significant contrast: the catalyst, having performed his role, is again a passive element.

As in part one, which focused on the day, this night time too is stretched out so that the reader experiences diachronically what, within the world of the novel, occurs synchronically. Again, specific references signal this duplication of time: the chiming of the church bell, heard by different characters, the sound of shots, the crossing of paths.

At the end of the novel, the narrative focuses on the remaining characters in quick succession as they awake to the new day. Here the contrapuntal technique, and the novel, is brought to a close with the words of one of the three escaped prisoners: "You mean to say that each of us will now go his own way?" (p. 197)

[In] *A Barca dos Homens* the reader's growing awareness of a possible prefiguration is an important element in the reading process. Perhaps this in part explains the . . . effectiveness of this novel: our understanding and insight are engaged by the slow unfolding of the drama and by our own developing sense of its correspondence to an old pattern. The author does not attempt to impose analogies on us with too sudden references to Christ. Instead, Fortunato is slowly revealed as an innocent about to be sacrificed, and the reader is thereby prepared for the other characters' dawning awareness of Fortunato as a Christ-figure. (p. 198)

Fortunato is first introduced to the reader through the perspective of Luzia, his mother:

> But it was useless talking to her son, he would never understand things right: his dull and suspended gaze, his moist mouth open. . . . Fortunato's eyes pursued a different vision, they were naive, turned inward, static when they didn't succeed in catching the meanings of words. He understood only when they spoke about things. . . . The aura that surrounded Fortunato, his eyes directed inward or beyond.

Only Tônho, "a ruin of a fisherman, a drunkard," understands him. With rare exceptions, the people of the island fear Fortunato. . . .

Almost thirty years old, Fortunato is a man/child, in touch with nature: " . . . Fortunato's eyes were as meek as fish. They calmed the clouds, they worked the waves that no one could understand." He spends his days wandering around the island; at times he suffers from a restlessness and when it occurs he walks so much that his feet bleed. He understands pain and asks his mother "why that thorn in his chest hurt so much." He understands things only "by their smell, their sound, their color and shape." (p. 199)

The figure of the fool has been described as a perennial one in life and literature. Barbara Swain analyzes this figure as follows:

> But whatever his special attributes, the creature behind the mask and the name when he is genuinely one species of the great genus fool has one inevitable characteristic: he appears from some point of view erring and irresponsible. He transgresses or ignores the code of reasoned self-restraint under which society attempts to exist, is unmeasured in his hilarity or in his melancholy, disregards the logic of cause and effect and conducts himself in ways which seem rash and shocking to normal mortals. But he is a fool because his extravagancies are supposed to be due not to intention but to some deficiency in his education, experience or innate capacity for understanding. He is not to blame for them, and society, amused at his freedom from the bonds of its conventions, laughs at him while it condemns him.

But the fool figure is not merely the object of ridicule: "The unconscious wisdom occasionally brought forth by the unreasonable mind of the 'innocent' and the belief in his association with the powers of nature added a portion of respect to the patronizing amusement with which the fool was regarded." Moreover, real fools were often "regarded with a mixture of disdain and superstitious awe as the privileged children of God, 'sacred beings having some mysterious connection with the unknown.'"

The combination of innocence and intelligence that deviates from the norm has occurred in many literary figures. Slochower refers to the "mythic tradition of the 'Fool' who disregards or is unaware of worldly demands and conditions. Such is the foolishness of Buddha, Parsifal, Emanuel Quint, Prince Myshkin and Alyosha Karamazov. These Fool-Figures act without 'reason,' ignoring practical considerations." Jesus has also been depicted as a fool, and the fool's cap, the grotesque cap worn by court jesters who, as the butts of ridicule at court, suffered wrongs daily, became "a widespread symbol of believers in Christ, who were determined to suffer wrongs gladly, to be fools for Christ's sake . . . " But in these last examples, an attitude of conscious self-sacrifice is apparent, totally lacking in a character such as Fortunato. Although this is an important element from the point of view of the subjective character attributed to the fool-cum-Jesus figure, it is less significant when viewed from the perspective of the persecuting public whose aim is to destroy, not to extract a self-immolation. (pp. 200-01)

[In many ways], Fortunato resembles Benjy in William Faulkner's *The Sound and the Fury.* Whereas the fool figure may originally have rested on innocence rather than on idiocy, in more recent literature, perhaps conforming to the need of a modern audience for a suitable scientific guise, the label of mental retardation has been added to the portrait. Benjy, in Faulkner's novel, is thirty-three (the same age as Christ at the time of his death), and he too has been "neutralized" by society, via his castration long before. But Benjy's level of intelligence is apparently lower than Fortunato's, for he can neither speak nor make logical connections between events. His narrative is thus largely that of a recorder capable of making sensorial associations. He is unable to reflect on his pain or fear, yet for the sake of the narrative he must be able to record, without comprehension, what he hears and sees. Fortunato operates at a level beyond this. In a most crucial sense, however, Benjy plays an essentially different role than does Fortunato. He is not a catalyst, as is Fortunato, but merely another aspect of the tragedy of the Compson family.

The narratives of both Benjy and Fortunato have a similar effect on the reader. The paradox of simplicity and depth is combined in such characters, and the image of unexpressed pain, inarticulate and of an unknown intensity, is very hard to bear. (p. 201)

Luzia, Fortunato's mother, bears a strong resemblance to the figure of Dilsey in Faulkner's novel: the black nanny who is a kind of earth mother. In still another literary allusion, this time to the episode of Inês de Castro in Camões' *Lusíadas,* the irony of Fortunato's name is touched on: Maria associates Fortunato's name with the word "fortune" (fate, destiny). . . .

Throughout much of **A Barca dos Homens,** we do not know if Fortunato is in fact innocent of the theft of the revolver, but even before it becomes clear that he is, we have seen how quickly the community mobilizes to eliminate the threat it perceives in him. Fortunato's strangeness, the people's view of him as crazy and abnormal, clearly plays an important role in the violence of the reaction against him. The recognition is not long in coming that the sacrifice of an innocent to the wrath of the community is a reenactment of an old pattern. As if to stress the obvious nature of this persecution, the first clear reference to the pattern is attributed to Helena, the oldest child of Maria and Godofredo. She witnesses Luzia's suffering and is reminded of a print she once saw called "Madonna and Child" (also the name of this chapter):

> Some day I'll tell the girls at school about the persecution and death, she thought. . . . Persecution and death. The word death shook her deeply, startled her. Death and resurrection. Again she felt the thud, like when she was growing. No, how it was that they caught Fortunato, how this happened in my house on Boa Vista, she began to relate.

Luzia also associates Fortunato with Jesus:

> No one believed that Fortunato was good, they

were all against him. Why do I have such a son? What did I do? He was good, she was certain. She saw him as the Child in the print of Our Lady of the Rosary, playing with the purple mantle, the gold of the brocade. But now he was like the Dead Lord—he was a man—after they unnailed him from the cross, in his mother's lap, his body pierced, his wounds still bleeding. She began to cry once again. . . .

(p. 202)

Brother Miguel, too, senses the parallel between Fortunato and Christ as he prepares his sermon for the following day and struggles with the best way to express the idea that "every day someone sacrifices someone." The seed of doubt already exists within him as he tries to relate these elements. . . . He imagines that if he can save Fortunato he will be brought out of the circle of doubts, yet when Luzia and Tônho ask him to help, he takes refuge behind a hierarchy of responsibility and says: "The order and security of the city are the lieutenant's concern, not mine."

Brother Miguel's initial words reflect his loss of orthodox faith, for he views Christ's crucifixion not as a sacrifice to redeem man but as the habitual action of brutal man; that is, he sees Christ as an object, not as the free subject of his sacrifice. This is why he can compare Fortunato to Christ: both are victims of man's brutality. Implicitly, then, Brother Miguel denies the importance of Christ's accepting gesture, and his final acknowledgment of apostasy is to be anticipated. By this token he must leave the nave of God to join that other nave, of men. (p. 203)

All these threads are brought together at the beginning of part two when the narrator describes the "dense vigil" affecting the city, from the town hall to the local brothel:

> A mystery was making itself felt, growing to fulfill its destiny and die only to be born again from the ashes, and once more live out its clamor and die. Life sprouted from invisible channels, there was death and resurrection, life went on.

To each person involved in the drama, however, the hunt for Fortunato appears in a slightly different light. For Brother Miguel, it provides the final confirmation of his loss of faith, the final result of his preoccupation with Judas, with whom he now identifies. He is helpless, unable to save Fortunato. Moreover, he sees Fortunato purely in terms of his own spiritual needs and plays with the possibility that Fortunato is his testing ground before coming to a mundane conclusion . . . : "Men kill and die, that is men's destiny. Each one can kill the other. Each man can destroy his fellow man. This is man's destiny, his freedom." This is then transformed into the exculpation: "No one can save anyone. We can only save ourselves, as we save our skin."

But it is Zuleica, one of the prostitutes, who makes explicit the connection between the child about to be born to Dorica and the life about to be taken. She wants to protect Fortunato: "Isn't Dorica going to have her child today? I'd have my child too, who they want to kill, that mob. They're going to kill him, she shouted." To Zuleica, awaiting the birth of Dorica's child, the pattern is clear. "One dies, another is born" and it is she who decides to name the new child Fortunato, thus bringing to a full circle the pattern of death and birth.

Two main aspects of the Christ prefiguration appear in **A Barca dos Homens.** The more obvious one, dealt with previously, emphasizes the continuity of life, with birth and death forming an endless cycle. In the Christian world view, the sacrifice of Christ means a spiritual regeneration for all people, symbolized by Christ's resurrection. This leads directly into the second aspect of the prefiguration, which does not deal specifically with Christ but rather with persecution and death as an instrument of change. Not the spiritual condition, but the actual lives of the residents of Boa Vista are changed by the hunt for Fortunato. In this second case, death and rebirth are metaphors evoking the changed condition of several characters within the novel. Although not the only one, the most clearly delineated instance of this metaphor relates to the entry into manhood of the young soldier Domício. (p. 204)

In *A Barca dos Homens,* although the lives of many of the characters undergo a change on the night of the hunt for Fortunato (for indeed it is the function of sacrifice to modify the condition of those who undertake it), it is the young soldier Domício's experience that most clearly reproduces the structure of an initiation rite. By the same token, his experience provides a clear image of the violent patriarchal values of the society into which he becomes integrated.

Domício, described as "very young, almost a boy," is taken under the wing of an older soldier, Gil. In order to keep the reader attuned to the father/son aspects of their relationship, rather than merely identifying them by their names Dourado repeatedly refers to them as "the younger soldier" and "the older soldier." Gil identifies with Domício, who reminds him of himself when he was young, and offers to arrange that Domício stay guarding the jail instead of going out on the hunt for Fortunato, but the young soldier is offended. Among the soldiers, a hierarchy of age and experience is established, with the oldest soldier of the detachment being the least belligerent:

> . . . Gualberto . . . who had a wife and four children, thought it was idiotic of them all to want to show what men they were. He was more careful, he knew how things stood. He looked carefully at the faces of those soldiers who were going into combat, some for the first time. He laughed inwardly. There was no combat at all, the men were all really crazy, they didn't know what else to do. The best thing was to defend oneself, not to play the hero, he had once learned. No one is a hero by a long shot. How could they think of someone they knew like Fortunato, and think of him as an enemy.
>
> (p. 205)

[Chapter three], in which the reader first encounters the soldiers, is entitled "The Town Hall"; the subsequent chapter (six) focusing on Gil and Domício is entitled "The Beginning of a Man," and, as the title indicates, the theme of initiation into manhood explicitly plays an important part.

Domício wants to think through what is happening to him: "It was an important day in his life as a soldier, in his life as a real man. . . . Perhaps he would die, perhaps he would kill for the first time." He remembers his fantasy, his anxiety, and both wants to be and fears being alone. "He wanted to think about how he was suddenly beginning to feel older." He becomes ever more aware of the potential for his own transformation—through a series of events that he does not question: "He had an intuition, even a deep fear, that after this battle . . . he would emerge a man, he would be another person." . . . Domício continues to think in this vein, view-

ing his situation as an ordeal from which he will emerge either a man or a coward. He is eighteen years old and anxious to join the world of men, and he feels he can do this only by passing through a series of trials. (pp. 205-06)

As Domício's preoccupation with proving himself continues, the reader perceives that despite the apparent modernity of the society described, the requirements for becoming a "man" are extremely rigid, like specific rites of passage, and so affect the individual that he too adopts these definitions of himself and his status as the only possible ones, while ignoring the smaller, more humane voice that tells him this is all nonsense—a voice that is unsupported by the society of which he is a part. Throughout this section of the novel, it is apparent that underlying these ordeals is the idea that to be a "man" is not a natural condition, but a status one must struggle to attain, a status that must be validated by one's group.

Feeling like "a father who teaches his son about life," Gil takes Domício to the brothel, where his sexual initiation occurs. Later, once again searching for Fortunato, Domício already feels that he has changed: "It's strange that after he left Maura, after his chest felt pure and empty, he began to understand better." Confident now of his masculinity, he thinks affectionately of his bond with the older soldier: "He was like a son going out with his father to hunt or fish for the first time. The *cachaça* in his canteen, the dare to see if he was really a man. I'm a man, he thought. He laughed, satisfied." (pp. 206-07)

But if in primitive societies an initiation rite constitutes an unequivocal change of status, in the world of this novel the accolade of manhood is never finally won, but is rather forever being challenged anew. Domício's concern with being a man, not showing cowardice, fighting for the respect of others, is echoed in virtually all the major male characters except Fortunato and Brother Miguel. Tônho, Godofredo, Fonseca—all fear the loss of manhood and are driven by that fear. For Domício, too, the initiation, through liquor and women, is only an approximation of manhood; the major ordeal is still before him. As he and Gil climb the rocks toward Fortunato's hiding place, Domício feels that "his ordeal was really beginning. Everything that had happened before seemed to be unimportant. His turn had come. He had to follow through." . . . When they see Fortunato, Gil shoots first—and misses. Then, in a perfect conclusion to his initiation into manhood, Domício aims and hits Fortunato. The final exchange between Gil and Domício concludes the rite by bestowing recognition upon Domício:

> You, said the older soldier turning toward him.
> I, thought Domício.

In an interesting parallel, these words occur at another point in the novel, involving Maria. This day also marks a break in her life, and, although her experience does not follow an initiatory pattern, she thinks in terms of a drastic change in her life. The previous night seems far away: "It seemed so old, so intensely had she lived that day"; and again: "Tomorrow I won't be the same, something in my life broke today, for good, inevitably. She would have to follow a new path." Her hatred for Godofredo, her husband, explodes on this day, matched in its intensity by her fascination with Fonseca. In a final quarrel, she shouts at Godofredo: "From today on I'm another person, one you don't know, one I've hidden for a long time"; and: "So many things happened today. . . . We're no longer the same."

The *you—I* exchange takes place between Fonseca and Maria when she arrives at his office, but whereas Domício's shooting of Fortunato is the culmination of his initiation rite, Maria's going to Fonseca constitutes a beginning, for both of them, of a new and still undefined situation; hence they address a question to one another:

> You? he said, his eyes open in amazement.
> I? she said, because she could not manage to articulate any other word.

At the end of the book Maria thinks: "Much has happened. It's as if I had been born again."

For the other characters, too, life is different on that day. Helena thinks: "Tomorrow everything would be different and clear, time would have passed, life would again be set aright . . .". While arranging for the hunting of Fortunato, Fonseca thinks: "This day would be different." Even the usual camaraderie between the prisoners and the soldiers breaks down: "But the day was different, there was some grief, some muted rancor in the prisoners' hearts; some distrust, dread, fear in the soldiers' eyes." (pp. 207-08)

In one of the novel's crowning ironies, Godofredo, who sets in motion the events of the novel by his accusation against Fortunato, is the only major character who explicitly seeks to avoid change. His one hope is to return to his previous life, before Maria's open revolt. The last line devoted to him at the novel's end describes the following morning: "In the living room, Godofredo said now it's all over, life will return to normal."

Although the break in the normal course of life affects virtually all the characters, a question remains concerning the extent to which the changes that occur are freely entered into by the characters. The stress on the uniqueness of this day suggests that something in the outside world is responsible for the changes that the characters undergo. Granted that one's actions are always in response to some perception, the use of the Christ prefiguration and hence the acceptance of the inevitability of Fortunato's death raise the problem of what possibilities for human initiative and intervention exist within the world of this novel. What is the significance of the frequent appearance in the novel of a mechanistic view of the world, and how does this view interact with the myth?

As is clear from the analogies drawn by the novel's characters between Fortunato and Christ, Fortunato's death is a foregone conclusion. Maria, for example, thinks: "For I'm certain that they're going to kill him." This is one of the aspects of resorting to myth that makes it vulnerable to the criticism that it is ahistorical and invariably ideological. The recognition of the pattern serves as a kind of explanation: things always were this way and are again this way. What could not be avoided before can certainly not be avoided now; indeed, it is all a part of the overall scheme of things. Such an explanation serves as a justification for a particular status quo, in this case for passivity in the face of the slaughter of an innocent.

Paralleling the Christ prefiguration throughout the novel is a repeated use of the metaphor of the world machine: once set in motion, the machine cannot be stopped. However, the myth and the metaphor constitute two different orders of explanations, which, in this particular case, are related and coincide. The myth, as invoked by different characters holding various degrees of religious belief, at least attributes a minimum of meaning to the pattern now being repeated; where death and even sacrificial murder are seen as a prelude to birth, as a part of the ongoing cycle of life, they can be accepted as "natural" phenomena. Fortified by religious belief, they are more than natural; they are divinely ordained. In both cases, however, there is a sense not only of order but also of meaning inherent in the acceptance of this pattern.

The metaphor of the world machine, on the contrary, suggests a juggernaut-like motion before which one can merely resign oneself but which offers no human meaning, no possible consolation. It is an anonymous and mechanistic view of the universe in which individuals are alienated from nature and helplessly subjected to its domination.

The problem of the order of the universe is first raised by Luzia in her meditations on the relationship between man and nature—nature in the form of the sea, the dominant force in the life of the island. (pp. 208-09)

For Luzia, "the sea was jumbled together with men. . . . Everything was so fused, everything like the wave-rolling-out and wave-rolling-in of the sea." In her mind " . . . it was hard to think about the men who kill the fish and the fish kill the men through the sea and the men. . . . " As Luzia leaves the Beach Cemetery (itself the symbol of the strange relationship between fishermen and the sea, with which the novel begins and ends), she continues to be preoccupied with this cycle: "But the thought sea, fish, men, fish, sea, men, men and sea and fish and fish and sea continued for a long time still stirring within her."

Maria too ponders the problem of the order of the universe as she watches Fortunato absorbed in some small animal. . . . (p. 210)

In the characters of Luzia and Maria there is a concern with the movements and order of nature; they are attuned to the world around them, even as they puzzle over it. Fortunato's reactions are simpler and his ideas therefore more rigid; hence his fascination with the spiders fighting and his strong sense of the order and justice that must be present in their motions and struggle. By contrast, Godofredo is described as a man who "had opinions about everything." This characteristic, which at first Maria had found amusing, she now sees as hateful and fraudulent, a protective covering that he uses to avoid confronting reality. With the sole exceptions of Brother Miguel and Fortunato, all the other male characters in the novel translate the problem of order into a concern, indeed an obsession, with their place in a world order narrowly defined by the rigorous demands of "manhood." But within the novel male and female characters alike have recourse to the machine metaphor, in some cases because they truly have no power to affect events (Luzia and Helena) and in others because they choose to remain unaware of alternatives, and perhaps exculpate themselves in this way.

The metaphor first occurs in a description of Luzia's anguish over the hunt for Fortunato: "She wanted to understand, to go to the heart of a nature that was invading her, to understand the laws that govern the world, the machine of which she was now an insignificant piece, the machine that no human force could stop, once it had been set in motion. Human life is worth nothing, anyone can kill, anyone can die. Every dog has his day. The machine of the world was too complicated for her. Understanding was becoming difficult." (pp. 210-11)

However, it is when Godofredo utilizes this same imagery that we see most clearly its potential as an excuse and exculpation. Godofredo's accusation had set off the hunt; he had actually thought Fortunato had stolen his revolver; yet, when he finds the revolver elsewhere and realizes his mistake, he does not inform the police. Instead, he hides his responsibility behind the machine metaphor: "I won't say anything, because everything, the world outside, the life set loose no longer depends on me. I will be overwhelmed, not even I will be able to face myself again." (p. 211)

[In *A Barca dos Homens*], the ultimate victim of the belief in the mechanistic metaphor is Fortunato. By acting as if what *may* happen *must* necessarily happen, that is, by literally believing in the mechanistic model of the functioning of the world, the characters become accomplices in the realization, the bringing about, of a mere potential or propensity.

It is important, in understanding the novel, to perceive that by describing the way various characters within the novel have recourse to this explanation, and by revealing their motives and states of mind, Autran Dourado is, as it were, laying bare the metaphor as a human creation. He is not making a statement about how life "is," but rather describing how people live it. . . . In Dourado's novel, the theme of using and being used is further developed through the mechanistic metaphor that reveals that man's use of other men is inherently different from the cycle of man/fish/sea over which Luzia broods.

As the title of the novel indicates, the main metaphor utilized by Dourado is that of the ship of the world. It was already an old and well-known symbol when Sebastian Brant published his *Das Narrenschiff* (*The Ship of Fools*) in 1494, in which the fools represent the world's sinners. . . . Katherine Anne Porter adopted Brant's title for her novel, *Ship of Fools,* in 1962, and stated at the beginning of the book that "the image of the ship of this world on its voyage to eternity" suited her purpose exactly. "I am a passenger on that ship," she wrote. Autran Dourado, by utilizing the posture of a chronicler, reinforces the idea that he too is such a passenger. This is a case of a metaphor that, although very old, is not yet a cliché, for it still has the power to illuminate. (pp. 212-13)

In Dourado's novel, however, the image of the ship has another and more immediate function as well: the island's economic survival is dependent upon fishing. Just as Luzia's thoughts about the cycle of nature take the specific form of meditations on the relations between men, fish, and the sea, so it is fitting that the characters of the novel, living as they do in close dependence upon the sea, should utilize metaphors relating to ships and to the sea in general. The ship metaphor is thus a multivalent one in the novel, utilized to illuminate both the collective and the individual, the mundane and the sacred.

The ship, Erich Neumann, writes, is an example of the "vessel symbolism of the Feminine." It is "an analogy of the womb," as C. G. Jung says,—but Neumann points out that it is also the ship of the dead, for "the ocean is experienced archetypally not only as a mother but also as the devouring primeval water who takes her children back into herself." (p. 213)

A number of these aspects of the ship metaphor occur explicitly in *A Barca dos Homens.* Aside from the title, the most generalized use of the metaphor occurs when the narrator adopts the tone of a chronicler and explains why he enters into details: "for everything is needed for deep understanding of the account that I am creating of the pitiful voyage of the ship of men." As if in sympathy with the forces unleashed on the island, the sea is violent on this day. Throughout the novel, numerous references are made to the sea, as well as to the fact that no ship would venture out in such waters. The ship as a protective shell (womb) is an image that frequently occurs in connection with Tônho, who no longer has the courage to put out to sea. . . . It is Amadeu's taunting remark, when the three escaped prisoners come across Tônho sleeping in the boat ("This isn't a boat, it's his bed", that induces Tônho to make a heroic and futile effort to reach Fortunato by sea. In the course of this effort Tônho dies, as he had himself predicted: "A fisherman dies in the sea."

If the boat Madalena is considered as a woman, sometimes mother, sometimes lover, conversely Luzia, attuned to the sea, is several times likened to a boat: "Luzia's walk was soft, her body swaying heavily, like a ship in the waves, soft and rhythmic like the waves themselves." . . . Here it is the stability of a ship, riding the waves, that is stressed.

By contrast, when Brother Miguel resorts to the ship metaphor, he refers to the vulnerability of a small boat on a rough sea: "Many times he had found himself on a difficult path, not knowing what direction to take. Everything dark and misty, no light, no voice was guiding his boat on the high sea." . . . Having failed in his effort to help Fortunato, Brother Miguel walks away from the town hall "like a ship that advances into the sea, while the land disappears in the distance."

If the ship provides the only protection afforded to the novel's characters, the sea without the ship is more threatening still. Jung considers the sea, or any large expanse of water, to signify the unconscious. Certainly in the novel's female characters—in Maria, Luzia, and Helena in particular—there is an abundance of imagery relating both to the sea and to a light/dark dichotomy, to an awareness of the dark side of life. (p. 214)

Although the dominant imagery in the novel (relating to the ship and the sea) is suggestive of what have traditionally been considered feminine forces in life, the action of the novel is determined by forces that, given this traditional polarity, may be considered masculine: the desire for self-assertion, the need to prove oneself a man among men. This is accomplished in two principal ways: by dominating women and by controlling other men. Domício and Fonseca are ultimately successful in both of these areas.

Throughout the novel there is an emphasis on the collapse of old structures as characters enter the night and grope their way toward light. Since, even more than the ship and sea imagery, this has a conventional nature, it suffices here to mention its appearance. It merely constitutes another aspect of the systematic use of imagery to set this day apart from other days—for it is the day of a sacrifice. The end of the book, describing the dawn of a new day, is thus a return to light after a night of agony. . . .

There are two main ways of imaginative looking in literature: we can either look at a character, as we do when that character is described, or we can look through the character's eyes at the world. Often we do both at once, as when we see one character from the perspective of another. (p. 215)

In *A Barca dos Homens*, with its extensive interior monologue, free indirect discourse, and traditional third-person narrative, both ways are utilized as the narrative moves in and out of the characters, eliminating and re-establishing distance. But throughout all these processes there occurs an explicit and repetitive reference to eyes, to how they look and what they see. (p. 216)

Seeing is the means by which people initially make contact, however tenuous, both with one another and with the world—but it is not the only means, or even a sufficient one. Don Ihde, in his phenomenological study of auditory perception, discusses the tendency, derived principally from Aristotle's *Metaphysics*, to consider perception primarily in terms of the visual. By contrast, Ihde wants to emphasize the auditory dimension of perception and argues that by overemphasizing the visual, other aspects of our experience of people may be hidden. (p. 217)

In *A Barca dos Homens*, the emphasis on eyes and seeing is paralleled by a lack of emphasis on speaking and hearing. The novel contains relatively little dialogue and we learn much more about what the characters are thinking than about what they say to one another. While this results in extensive auditory communication to the reader (who, through the interior monologues and free indirect discourse, hears the voice of the character, as it were), focusing on this aspect of the novel reveals that there is little communication between the characters. Such speech as occurs in the novel is frequently a display of a struggle for power, as in the conversations between Maria and Godofredo, Godofredo and Fonseca, Maria and Fonseca, and Fonseca and Brother Miguel. In addition, things that are *not* said acquire great importance in the novel: Godofredo's silence after he realizes that his accusation is false; the sexual hunger of Fonseca's look; and, most striking, the fact that nobody speaks to Fortunato in the course of the novel, nobody seeks an explanation from him—rather, he is immediately isolated and hunted. Only Tônho and Brother Miguel hope to talk to him; the other men desire merely to find him and kill him.

Throughout the novel, then, characters move toward and away from one another, enter into and withdraw from one another's field of vision, but communication does not usually occur. Thus, although we perceive the characters as united on an island and all implicated in the events of this day, a strong sense of their separateness and isolation is conveyed. They see one another but, for the most part, do not recognize one another.

The effect of this silent and individual "seeing" is reiterated by the contrapuntal technique that, in its spatialization of the hours of this day, suggests once again the lack of communication between the characters. This effect is perfectly illustrated in the final two pages of the novel. Here, in twelve successive short paragraphs, twelve characters (or groups of characters in the case of the children and the escaped prisoners) begin the new day. Although the narrator utilizes the word "said" in describing their thoughts, whatever "talking" is done is primarily to oneself. Communication is not toward the outside world but toward oneself, in that silent subconversation which people constantly conduct with themselves. (pp. 217-18)

Two interlocking systems exist in *A Barca dos Homens* that convey and define the novel's characters and their situation. One system utilizes imagery relating to nature and natural phenomena: the cycle of men, fish, and the sea; the dichotomy of light and dark; the act of seeing through which perception of nature and of others occurs. The second system involves the human need for patterning devices that serve as explanations; hence the turn to thoughts of Christ and man's recurrent cruelty, to the mechanistic metaphor, to the ship metaphor; all are ways toward the interior organization of perception, the location of meanings and reasons—whether accurate or not—in the face of events.

The combination of the two—imagery of a generalized type for the world of nature and patterns of an equally well-known type for the relations between human beings—seems to point to a kind of eternal recurrence, a sense of the inevitable rhythms of nature and life. There is the danger that this emphasis will ultimately destroy one's sense of the specific and individual by presenting an inherently fatalistic image of life.

On the other hand, within this overall continuity and cyclical quality there is change, and it is precisely through the communal pursuit of an individual that change is brought about. The change involves the sacrifice of an innocent who is resurrected not in a personal way, but rather in two divergent manners. The first is through the child born to the prostitute Dorica at the same time as Fortunato is killed, another fatherless child that will bear his name, thereby intertwining his death with the coming to life of a new creature; the second is through the fact that the hunt becomes the occasion for change in the lives of others, setting in motion a series of attempted self-realizations.

The image of the ship of men does not, then, deprive the characters of individual destinies (which, as the last two pages of the novel indicate, the survivors have still to work out), and the murder of Fortunato does not constitute a definitive fatalistic representation of human potential. Rather, . . . Fortunato's murder reflects the fact that men have the potential to use others as means to their own ends. That these ends are practical and social is abundantly shown by emphasizing most of the male characters' concern with proving themselves as men according to an obviously restricted and brutal definition.

In *A Barca dos Homens*, Autran Dourado has succeeded in introducing the known and patterned elements of myth without at the same time denying individuality and responsibility. While nature is cyclical, human life is finite and unique. The problem for human beings is precisely how to understand the interplay of their particular limited life within a continuous and impersonal nature. Unlike Adonias Filho, Autran Dourado resists merely appealing to inarticulate and ancient forces. Rather, by illuminating the personal elements that lead to Fortunato's death and the way events are brought about and then used by the people involved in them, he allows us to see men both creating their actions and also refusing responsibility for those actions once they are underway. Far from merely depicting man's ongoing brutality, Dourado focuses on the unrelenting pursuit of growth and change, actively, even ruthlessly, seeking its means. Man's freedom to kill is also freedom to create. (pp. 218-19)

Daphne Patai, "Autran Dourado: The Sacrifice of the Innocent," in her Myth and Ideology in Contemporary Brazilian Fiction, *Fairleigh Dickinson University Press, 1983, pp. 191-219.*

HARRIETT GILBERT

> . . . all these family stories. The events he had been involved in, those he had only witnessed, those he had heard told. Those he had invented himself and no longer knew if they had happened or not . . .

Such are the rich, thick, nubbly threads of Autran Dourado's *Pattern for a Tapestry,* published in Brazil in 1970. . . .

The 'he' referred to is Joao da Fonseca Nogueira, a man attempting to extract his boyhood from the past, to rescue the Sao Mateus boarding school; the small town to which he returned each vacation; his parents; his uncles; his aunt Marguarida; the whorehouse to which he delivered some shoes with Zito, his smart older friend. Also to be saved is the family folklore—which, as such things tend to be, is crusted with gothic suicides, secret passions and madness.

There is also the wider legend of Xambá the bandit, a man who vanished from Joao's home town leaving only a 'luminous trail of crimes, barbarities and acts of vengeance. Which we gradually forgot in the mists and quagmires of memories, of hearsay, of whispers'. While Joao is concerned with reversing such forgetting, his author is busy demonstrating—with dexterous sleights of imagery and phrase—that forgetfulness is just an ingredient of memory; that, if we are to recapture the past, it must either fit or be *made* to fit into a pattern. Each of the first six sections of his novel is an apparently disconnected, arbitrary act of remembrance—yet, in each, he has sewn some half-hidden stitches, all of which can later be tugged to the surface. Then, whatever colour emerges (unease at the mention of Uncle Zózimo; the warm smell of Milk of Roses in a prostitute's armpits) vibrates both backward and forward through the book, exposing the design of personal obsessions that Joao has created from his past.

The final section, in which the town's bandit is remembered by a series of witnesses, makes obvious Joao's fallibility. It is here, however, that Dourado plays his last trick: revealing with subtlety, humour and affection how memory's betrayal of past events is also its act of homage.

> *Harriet Gilbert, "Truth Games," in* New Statesman, *Vol. 107, No. 2768, April 6, 1984, p. 35.*

JONATHAN KEATES

The concentration staggers before yet another Latin-American novel about childhood fantasies by 'one of the most important post-war Brazilian writers.' Autran Dourado is, as it turns out, a good writer, which is more important than being important, and *Pattern For A Tapestry* . . . is a work whose alluring complexities of structure and imagery never clog the narrative's memorable simplicity. Everything tells here, and the control of symbols, echoes and cross-references among the work's seven sections is masterly.

Dourado's theme encompasses the loss of innocence as young Joao visits a brothel, watches his uncle die, indulges a crush on an Italian high-wire artiste and slowly explores for himself the essentially fulfilling nature of guilt. Finest of these episodes is 'Man As He Is Clothed,' embracing Joao's ultimate perception of limitless human frailty. Illusions of machismo crumble in the figure of the giant mulatto Xambá, stupendous at first in picaresque exploits and appetites, but reduced at the end to a blubbering wreck when threatened with a flogging by the cynical police who have pulled him in as a horse-thief.

> *Jonathan Keates, "Moorland Magic," in* The Observer, *May 6, 1984, p. 21.*

NICHOLAS RANKIN

[*Pattern For a Tapestry,* a] re-creation of adolescence in 1930s back-country Brazil, is both authentic and cunningly wrought; it also deals, in an interesting way, with a perennial obsession of South American writers: the nature of manhood.

On publication in 1970, the book puzzled some in Brazil who thought it not a proper novel; there wasn't a "story", nor consistent "characters", and who was this huge mulatto outlaw called Xambá, barely mentioned before, taking over all five sections of the last chapter?

The novel is about growing up as a male, and into the mystiques of manhood. "João was discovering, without being aware of it, that things and people were linked together in a never-ending round-dance." To achieve this effect, John M. Parker suggests in a useful introduction, Autran Dourado does not offer a "horizontal and linear" narrative. He mimics more closely the way memory works, processing in carefully detailed prose what de Quincey called "this tumult of images, illustrative and allusive". Dr. Alcebiades, a key informant of the last chapter, says "I'll never get to the point I'm aiming at. Old people are like that, we keep getting side-tracked." Unreliable narration or not, all the points join up in "the constellation of pain" Dourado skilfully depicts.

The author calls his chapters or narrative units "blocks", and suggests they can be read in different orders, like Julio Cortázar's *Rayuela.* Each chapter is a stage in the blossoming inner life of the fatherless adolescent João de Fonseca Nogueira, and they cover the principal rites of passage of human (male) experience.

Sex, being primal, makes "The Bridge House" of the initial chapter a brother. But by the sixth, also sexual, "Leaping Bull" chapter, the sensuous images absorbed in the first have become fused with incestuous memories of João's naked mother, and overlaid with a thwarted passion for an aunt, whose frustrations end in the fetters of the Church. Death, with Latin inevitability, comes next. When João is at boarding-school, his uncle Maximino begins his death throes next door. João feigns a grief he does not feel, and gets an afternoon off school. Love runs third. The boy is smitten with "Valiant Valentina", an acrobat from the travelling-circus; he lies to his pals about what they did together.

Family relationships and conflicts make up chapters four and five. "The Prodigal Son" is Uncle Zózimo who behaves strangely; nobody will talk about his funny-shaped ear. Finding that it is the result of a suicidal wound and apprehending the horrors of schizophrenia, João gains the knowledge that admits him to the adult key-holders of the family skeleton-cupboard. In the chapter called "A Family Affair" he finds out about Grandfather Zé Mariano, who left his bossy wife to live with his illegitimate son, and who died alone, feral and fetid.

Dourado writes of human universals in a precise locale. "A cold night, outside the wind rustled in the old mango trees in the garden, in the avocado tree, in the flat-topped cashew-tree." He contrives a particular adolescent sensibility strikingly well: swoons of passion, fears and ignorance, dissembling, doubt and wonder.

The last chapter throws the whole book into relief. When, "after many years away, now a grown man, João returned to Duas Pontes" he conceals his own self, and is only interested in an old-time desperado, scarcely mentioned to date, a gunman on horseback from the southern border of Minas Gerais with São Paulo. "The name that he bore—Xambá, with its strange vibrations that appealed to the imagination, conjuring up African, Arabian and Oriental tales"—designated a daring and heroic figure that the boy had once looked up to. . . .

Xambá is the unregenerate *macho* animus, old Adam, the dark Other. As João has now grown into a writer, he teases from different sources the story of Xambá's manhood. There is silent courage under the doctor's knife, painfully extracting a bullet; there is humiliation by a prostitue who rides and lashes him with a silver whip; then capture by the corrupt police. Mighty Xambá shows "disgraceful" cowardice before a Corporal's whip and confesses all. That night, he is shot "trying to escape."

This seventh chapter, "Man As He Is Clothed", demythologizes the Brazilian male ideal. Under the reified hero of male sexual aggression is just another man, whose weakness lies in his sexuality. Lead and cold steel he can take, but not the whip, because he had enjoyed it earlier at the hands of a woman he loved. Xambá's shadow casts doubts back over the book. The mythic hero whom João and the other boys admired and emulated embodied all the fantasies of freedom; the true history they all had to live, growing into "manhood", was dominated by repression and constraint. . . .

[Despite] its uninspired English title, **O risco do bordado** is a sensitive and truthful evocation of growing up male, by a writer worth noting.

Nicholas Rankin, "Growing into Manhood," in The Times Literary Supplement, *No. 4240, July 6, 1984, p. 761.*

JOHN GLEDSON

[**The Bells of Agony**] is set in the late eighteenth century, in Vila Rica de Ouro Preto (literally, Rich Town of Dark Gold), the centre of the great gold rush which transformed Brazil during the colonial period, but which by the time of the novel is showing clear signs of reaching exhaustion. Decadence is one of Dourado's favourite themes—strong, aggressive, creative existence always seems to be a thing of the past. He is one of several fine Latin-American writers to have felt and assimilated the influence of Faulkner, and he shares with him too a sharp, even cruel perception of the relationship between races in societies marked by slavery. The initial dialogue, between Januario, the outcast (murderer) son of a Portuguese merchant and his Indian concubine, and his black slave, is all the more sensitive for pulling no punches. Such complex and involved feelings all too rarely reach the surface in Brazilian writing, yet in Dourado they are at home, partly because *he* is at home in an atmosphere of tragedy, of characters irrevocably closed in on themselves and only able to affect others destructively: when Januario, the mestizo, proclaims that he is so "stuck close" to his slave Isidoro that he could be his relative, the slave knows better:

> His stink impregnated clothes, nose, memory. The smell that a thousand bars of soap . . . would not succeed in removing.

The atmosphere of the novel is genuinely akin to that of stage tragedy: Dourado calls his chapters acts, and has plainly acknowledged sources in Euripides, Seneca and Racine—above all, *Phèdre*. These sources matter less than Dourado's brilliantly controlled style, which has the mesmerising effect of well-played drama. It is slow, repetitive, often using short, verbless sentences, usually cast in the form of a monologue in which the narrator nevertheless has some corroborative, at times interpretative role. The three central characters, Malvina, the young wife of an older, wealthy man; Gaspar, her stepson, a brilliantly convincing recreation of Racine's Hippolyte; and the half-breed Januario, whom Malvina takes as a lover in order to use him—all find their memories of and aspirations to happiness gradually enmeshed in something much more sinister. Unable to act on their own behalf, they end up taking their cue from slaves, whom they use—and here Dourado gives a deft Brazilian touch to his classical French model—as confidantes, good listeners whose apparent passivity can become dangerous.

[John M. Parker] argues in his helpful introduction that the novel is in a sense political too—that its atmosphere of paranoia and economic collapse conveys something of Dourado's perceptions of the period (1972-74), when there was no hint of relaxation in the hard-line military regime. . . . The novel's original prefatory note, explaining that this is "not a historical novel, much less a realist one", which I confess always seemed unnecessary to me, is now revealed as a ploy, a cover by publishers fearful of the censors. Certainly, the fact that we are now permitted to take this more immediate content seriously does not detract from the novel's power; quite the reverse. We are lucky to have it in such a splendid version. . . .

John Gledson, "Taking Their Cue from the Slaves," in The Times Literary Supplement, *No. 4477, January 20-26, 1989, p. 58.*

Coleman Dowell

1925-1985

American novelist, short story writer, and dramatist.

Often linked with the American southern literary tradition, Dowell explored themes of fatalism and sexual obsession. While critics compare his works to those of Carson McCullers and William Faulkner, Dowell is credited with focusing on the melodramatic moments of ordinary life with a compassion and humor that often eluded both renowned authors. Lauded for his lyrical prose style, Dowell frequently employed a disjointed method of narration that has alternately confused and impressed critics. His novels and short stories often address the loneliness, desires, and falsehoods of human existence. Dowell explained: "[My] concern is psychology, the subterranean, the awareness that what's said is not what's meant, and that what we do is not what we would like to do."

Dowell's first novel, *One of the Children Is Crying*, is a psychological study of family life based on memories of his childhood in rural Kentucky. This work, which Dowell identified as a "fictional farewell" to his family, examines the psyches of the McChesneys, adult siblings who attempt to come to terms with their painful pasts and their father's brutality when they are reunited at his funeral. This work and *Mrs. October Was Here,* a satirical fantasy about revolution, did not attain the critical acclaim of Dowell's subsequent novel, *Island People.* This allegorical work revolves around an anonymous failed playwright who lives on a island with his dachshund and passes time by writing about Jeremiah and Beatrix Dresden, a fictitious poet and his ugly but erotic wife. The playwright's journal entries gradually reveal that Beatrix has taken over his mind. The work's complexity, shifting points of view, and sense of disembodiment prompted several critics to compare *Island People* to T. S. Eliot's *The Waste Land.* Edmund White asserted: "[Once] inside the book, the reader encounters teeming, charged emotions, dark and active with pain. Coleman Dowell . . . has evidenced courage and invention in creating a work of art so original and difficult as to be alive to baffling and baffled perceptions."

In the novel *Too Much Flesh and Jabez,* which Gilbert Sorrentino described as "a meticulously and subtly composed tour de force on the imagination," Dowell explores the consequences of sexual repression through the story of Miss Ethel, a retired schoolteacher who is still a virgin at the age of 70. She writes a book about Jim Cummins, a farmer she imagines as endowed with an enormous penis, who becomes physically involved with Jabez, a hermaphroditic boy. By recreating Jim Cummins, who was actually a prize pupil with whom she was infatuated, Miss Ethel attempts to deal with her loneliness but ultimately creates victims of her subjects. Dowell's last novel, *White on Black on White,* recalls *Island People* in its story of an unnamed narrator who escapes city pressures by moving to an island with his dachshund. However, this character is a homosexual who becomes obsessed with his housemate, Calvin, a black heterosexual assassin for the Mafia. Calvin abuses the narrator's affections by hinting about an affair he is having with Ivy Temple, a white woman who later confesses her lust for black men to the narrator at a party. The final section is devoted to Ivy's childhood friend Cayce

Scott, a black policeman who also attends a party where an articulate woman expounds on the subject of sexual obsession. While some critics found the work idiosyncratic, others praised Dowell's political and psychological insights.

Throughout his career, Dowell wrote numerous short stories for periodicals, many of which have remained uncollected. Some of his short fiction was published posthumously in the critically lauded volume *The Houses of Children: Collected Stories.* More surrealistic than his longer fiction, these pieces are narrated by children whose ingenuous visions of the world are shattered by the intrusion of adult reality. Several critics likened Dowell's narrators to Ernest Hemingway's adolescent protagonist Nick Adams, a troubled youth attempting to understand a savage world. The child narrator of "The Moon, the Owl, My Sister," one of two surviving sextuplets, explains that he is concerned about his sister, whom he believes will succumb to the forces of nature and leave home. As he describes his life, his identity as a field mouse becomes evident. The protagonist of "Writings on a Cave Wall," a youthful caveman, asserts that cannibalism is a part of his family's existence and realizes at the story's conclusion that he will probably become the group's next meal. Lorrie Moore commented: "[The selections in *The Houses of Children*] are odd tales, rhetorically rich and strange of subject, with an intense lyricism that is one moment lucid and elegant and the next recondite and bewildering. Dowell's are narratives for which the reader is never quite prepared."

In addition to novels and short stories, Dowell also wrote several plays, including *Gentle Laurel, The Indian Giver,* and *The Tattooed Countess.* These works, however, were largely critical and commercial failures. Although he consistently garnered critical praise for his novels and short stories, Dowell never attained the public approval he craved, and in 1985 committed suicide.

(See also *Contemporary Authors,* Vols. 25-28, Vol. 117 [obituary] and *Contemporary Authors New Revision Series,* Vol. 10.)

PRINCIPAL WORKS

PLAYS

Gentle Laurel   1957
The Indian Giver   1959
The Tattooed Countess   1961
Eve of the Green Grass   1963

NOVELS

One of the Children Is Crying   1968; also published as *The Grass Dies*
Mrs. October Was Here   1974
Island People   1976
Too Much Flesh and Jabez   1977
White on Black on White   1983

SHORT FICTION COLLECTIONS

The Houses of Children: Collected Stories   1987

THE TIMES LITERARY SUPPLEMENT

Coleman Dowell's publishers bravely compare him with Faulkner and Carson McCullers. There are times in the early chapters of [*The Grass Dies*] when the reader feels so bludgeoned by gross sexual description, by madness and alcoholism and humanity's decay that he suspects a parody. But soon Mr. Dowell's real ability to handle his characters, to draw each of them into the central predicament of the book—they are siblings, gathered to the old family farm for the funeral of their father—takes hold. The pace quickens, the tensions and revelations of the story, though occasionally too pat and literary, are interesting.

Father had been an old goat, letting the farm go to ruin while he went whoring, and seeking to undermine each of his sons and daughters in some way. The two eldest, Robin and Erin, had taken over the roles of father and mother and managed to protect the others at their own expense. Robin, taunted beyond endurance by his father, has abandoned the farm and submerged himself in drink in New York; Erin has become an old maid, propping up house and parents. We see into the marriages and careers of the younger ones who have adjusted tolerably well to their disabilities.

Thus the total impression of the funeral gathering is one of comedy with tragic asides. Mr. Dowell's Roseville is yet another Southern town that seems closer to sixteenth-century England than to the twentieth century, but he is a powerful enough writer to make us swallow the strong brew.

"Old Goat," in The Times Literary Supplement, *No. 3441, February 8, 1968, p. 141.*

JOHN KUEHL

Island People is the most recent work of a truly gifted American writer, Coleman Dowell. His first two books, *One of the Children Is Crying* (1968)—a realistic novel about family life—and *Mrs. October Was Here* (1974—a satirical fantasy about revolution—prepared the way for this brilliant contemporary allegory.

In *Island People* the notion that "EACH MAN IS AN ISLAND" is dramatized through geographical juxtapositions, just as the notion that "One need not be a Chamber / to be Haunted" is projected through architectural symbols.

Dowell's isolated and obsessed protagonist contends, "ALL THERE IS, IS FRAGMENTS, because a man, even the lowliest of the species, is divided among several persons, animals, worlds." This nameless figure finds bits and pieces of an elusive identity in characters from the nineteenth century past and the 20th century present. Passive and refined, middle-aged and bi-sexual, Protestant and southern, he periodically escapes the "prison of self " by loving or hating his alter ego, the aggressive and primitive, young and feminist, Jewish and northern Beatrix. She represents allegorical "bad," while the protagonist's dachshund, Miss Gold—"precious malleable strut of the earth"—represents allegorical "good." Their opposition poses "bitch" against bitch.

Having moved from 1968 realism through 1974 fantasy, Dowell has produced fiction that most nearly resembles a modern "poetic sequence" or "architectonic novel." This is apparent in his techniques, which, as in all skillful literary work, mirror the author's concerns.

For example, the narrative voice of *Island People* alternates between two dominant storytellers, creating what the protagonist calls "collaboration." . . . Metamorphoses of the narrative voice are accompanied by point of view shifts involving first, second and third person; but, even if we could pin the protean protagonist down, we would face an additional dilemma: "I have endowed the 'I' of this book with total recall—(though there will be a lot he will not want to recall, and will manage, sometimes, not to)."

It seems fitting that Dowell's dominant storytellers are a "failed playwright" (protagonist) and a "New Novelist" (Beatrix) because the inaccuracies both purvey characterize "the process of Art." In one instance, Chris admits "the facts given . . . by Victor over many a long afternoon had been distorted by . . . imagination," and, in another, the protagonist regrets "romanticizing" Low's "Psycopathy" and reducing "my complex Indian to a single-strand nobility." Since in *Island People* reality is mental rather than physical, verbal rather than actual, the protagonist may also proclaim: "When I write 'he ran,' I see neither him nor running. I see two words." As Life becomes Art, Art becomes Game, so, besides several allusions to literary personages like D. H. Lawrence, there are numerous references to literary procedures like "Some compulsive neatness or need, some awareness of the circularity of events, perhaps, insists that I end this composition before the coda, as it began." The Art-Game has both a positive and a negative side. On the one hand, through "the act of creation, we 'forgive' the objects of our imagination;" yet, on the other, we erect a "word-jail," in which even the "personal desire for continuity is . . . mainly literary."

Fragmentation, the principal motif of *Island People,* dictates structure as well as focus. The book juxtaposes various genres—journal entries, stories, essays, poems, etc.—and thus conveys the "erratic journeying" of the "Saint of Wanderers, Christopher, or plain Chris." Like the latter's stories, this "journeying" is "without endings;" like his play, *Coursing,* it is "static." (pp. 602-03)

The sectional headings of Dowell's—"THE GAME," "CAUGHT," "TRIALS," "THE SENTENCE"—indicate the protagonist's nightmare world has *moral* continuity. Indeed, he conducts "his own trial for the murder of a love—nameless, undefined; whether of person or pride, his own or other's or others', or of talent or judgment, he cannot tell."

Though *Island People* is a brilliant contemporary allegory incorporating themes and techniques associated with achievements like T. S. Eliot's *The Waste Land* and William Gaddis's *The Recognitions,* it also excels at the older literary attributes. We are given memorable individuals who participate in vivid scenes which range from the comic to the tragic. Furthermore, as Tennessee Williams has observed, the "level of prose writing" resembles "a long, marvelously sustained narrative poem." One brief passage will illustrate Coleman Dowell's finely-wrought style:

> I turned on the Christmas lights. In the glowing room, fire fallen to embers, the Dresdens looked like young dreamers in a ballet. Each sleeping profile thrust upward carving out the wine-jelly Christmas sheen of the room. They were perfectly strange to me, characterless as people sleeping on a stage when the curtain goes up. Dimly felt tendrils ran from my breast to summer and turned back and groped for the Dresdens but did not touch them, restrained by my desire.
>
> (p. 603)

John Kuehl, in a review of "Island People," in Commonweal, *Vol. CIII, No. 19, September 10, 1976, pp. 602-03.*

EDMUND WHITE

Someone once said that every novel is also a theory of the novel. If so, then the theory *Island People* seems to be propounding is that only through brief journal entries, many separate stories, a changing cast of characters and a phantasmagoria of musings, questions and revisions can a novelist assemble his own shadowy, insular feelings. . . .

[In the story, a] man living on an island with only his dachshund for company writes about the visit, possibly real but probably imaginary, of Jeremiah and Beatrix Dresden, a handsome poet and his hideous but sensual wife. In subsequent journal entries it becomes clear that Beatrix has completely taken over the imagination of her own creator and has begun to dictate his stories. We read several of these stories—and each time learn that the narrator has been insulted or infuriated by Beatrix's inventions. Beatrix appears in several guises: as a rich and powerful but insane "succubus" named Else; as Sabra, an Israeli pimping for her Brazilian husband; and as Miriam Webster, the wife of a successful Broadway playwright.

Similarly, the narrator is cast in several different roles. He appears as Claudo, the ringmaster of a smart Manhattan set; and as Chris, a wealthy homosexual who has affairs with two hustlers—the birthmarked Low and the Puerto Rican Victor. Interspersed among these tales of idle, backbiting characters are scenes in the life of a boy who lived on the island in the last century. He loses his beloved mother, murders his stepmother with a spade and runs off to sea.

This summary, of course, is only provisional, because no single character stays put and assumes a definite existence except Miss Gold, the dachshund. Everyone is someone else. Beatrix is modeled on a painter named Clytie Steuber. Chris is presumably a stand-in for the narrator, though towards the end of the book we learn that he may actually be a portrait of Clytie (now called Else) in drag. Although the story of Claudo is set in the past, he is actually meant to show us what may happen to Chris when he grows old in the future. Perhaps the strategy of this novel may be contained in a line from a letter that the narrator writes to one of his characters: "The point of verbal communication, as I see it, may be to expose the possibilities of insincerity in oneself and others."

These convolutions function as a formidable barrier between the reader and the text. But once inside the book, the reader encounters teeming, charged emotions, dark and active with pain. Coleman Dowell, who is also a playwright and composer-lyricist, has evidenced courage and invention in creating a work of art so original and difficult as to be alive to baffling and baffled perceptions. The writing style is often preposterous. ("The woman, a power on Wall Street, is an ennuyante of stature.") The melodramatic tone of scene after scene is reminiscent of Lawrence Durrell at his most excessive. Nevertheless, there is nothing else quite like *Island People.*

Edmund White, in a review of "Island People," in The New York Times Book Review, *September 19, 1976, p. 40.*

GILBERT SORRENTINO

This novel is a meticulously and subtly composed *tour de force* on the imagination, that of Miss Ethel, a 70-year-old spinster schoolteacher, now retired, and the author of *Too Much Flesh and Jabez.* She has written, as Mr. Dowell states in the "frame" within which her novel rests, a "perverse story"; what a delicate ambiguity suffuses that phrase! Mr. Dowell—like all writers whose intelligence rummages through the minutiae of life, turning and sifting them until he has isolated some few things that will not be reduced—writes prose in which meanings shift just as they appear to assume some clarity. Whatever is "perverse" in this story is so only because it is a symptom of a general emotional decay—its effluvium, so to speak.

Miss Ethel's private *roman à clef* is the tale of a dirt farmer, Jim Cummins, his bitter marriage, his first and only love affair, and his seduction of and by Jabez, a strange, near-hermaphroditic boy who comes to stay at a farm down the road during a summer drought in the first year of World War II. The fictional Jim is Miss Ethel's invention, made from the real Jim, who at one time had been her star pupil, a marvelously intelligent boy whose brain "she saw as abnormally large, an organ too large for his own good," in this town of stupid "good old boys." In her novel Miss Ethel transforms this brain into a monstrous phallus, a transformation precisely apt for the story that Mr. Dowell wishes to tell through her story. We have here, of course, the materials of a dirty joke, and, like all good dirty jokes, its heart is cold and empty.

Miss Ethel is ignorant of sexual love—ignorant, for that matter, of all the modes of love—and so her novel, quite beautifully, embodies an oddly chaste and off-center pornography. What we are permitted to see through her fantastic and crippled opus is her imagination's desperate attempt to come to terms with her own loneliness, her desolation of spirit—the plight she has survived all her life. Mr. Dowell's peculiar talent allows him to reveal this state in passages that are bloodlessly erotic or infused with a comic sense that is both sour and cruel.

A case might be made that in this novel Mr. Dowell is sketching out once again a treatise on sexual freedom as fulfillment, the sexual act as panacea for emotional ills. I cannot for a moment see it this way. It seems clear that had life granted Miss Ethel sexual release, it would have been the counterpart for the furiously cynical experience she imagines for her characters; and if we are tempted to view Jim's release with Jabez as the magic that will free him from his marriage, we face the reality of Jim's presence as an invention of Miss Ethel's thwarted desires. (p. 6)

The novel is "perverse"—to return to that word—in that it belies, as it displays, its subject. It is not a novel about Jim, or his wife, or Jabez. It certainly is not about homosexuality. It is not, finally, about sex—which is used as the base upon which its formal structure is built. By a deft sleight-of-hand the supposed theme of sexual fulfillment that Mr. Dowell makes his book turn on, almost as if he were giving the reader a comforting addendum to what he already believes, is perceived as the clear pane through which we may discern the terrible loneliness and waste of a human being. The characters Miss Ethel has spun out of her despair are absolute extensions of that despair—victims, as is their creator. (p. 29)

> *Gilbert Sorrentino, "Perverse Story," in* The New York Times Book Review, *January 1, 1978, pp. 6, 29.*

TERENCE WINCH

To call a work of art "interesting" is usually to say the worst thing possible about it. The word is sometimes a euphemism for "terrible." But this new novel [*Too Much Flesh and Jabez*] by Coleman Dowell is interesting without being terrible. Which is not to say that it is completely successful: the characters are given more mystery and signifiance than they earn during the narrative, but the narrative itself is often captivating.

The story takes place in the South during World War II and features a farmer who is, as the blurb puts it, "overly endowed." His wife, as fate would have it, has no openings for a man of her husband's qualifications. The farmer's condition is Dowell's literal metaphor for sexual and emotional incompatibility. The farmer and his wife, and the other characters as well, are people with dreary, guilt-ridden spiritual interiors. Everyone in the novel is obsessed with the farmer's plight.

The novel itself is a frame story, purporting to be the imaginative memories and fantasies of an old woman who was once the enamored teacher of the farmer. She invents an androgynous boy named Jabez who is able to accommodate the farmer. But the "perversity" of their encounter leads to further psychic and physical explosions.

Richard Chase defined the central tradition of American fiction as "romance," by which he meant the kind of fiction that explores the dark "underside of consciousness," focusing on the "complex truths unavailable to realism" rather than on "the spectacle of man in society." The South, having produced writers like Faulkner and Flannery O'Connor, has always been the most fertile source of American romance. Coleman Dowell is very comfortably a part of this tradition.

> *Terence Winch, "Too Big for His Britches," in* Book World—The Washington Post, *January 29, 1978, p. L4.*

COLEMAN DOWELL (INTERVIEW WITH JOHN KUEHL AND LINDA KANDEL KUEHL)

[Kuehl and Kandel Kuehl]: Your first novel, **One of the Children Is Crying,** *and your last,* **Too Much Flesh and Jabez,** *are set in the South. As a Kentuckian, do you regard yourself as a regional writer?*

[Dowell]: No, I discovered that the hillbillies in Vermont are precisely the same as the hillbillies in Kentucky. I can set a book anywhere. It doesn't make any difference since my concern is psychology, the subterranean, the awareness that what's said is not what's meant, and that what we do is not what we would like to do. (p. 274)

Children are central to so much of your fiction; they seem to be a preoccupation of yours.

I'm very protective toward children and would sooner die than hurt a child or an animal. I myself was corrupted when I was just a five-year-old, an incident I fictionalized in *Island People.* I was raped by a teen-aged American Indian who worked for my aunt. I never told anyone about it and this act went on, so I never had any innocence. Things that I was made to see were things that one shouldn't be made to see as a child. Children have sexuality; they play with each other. That's fine, but no adult should come anywhere near them. I'm a great avenger when it comes to kids and I hope that that shows in my books. I have a terror of somebody taking a kid's childhood—it's so brief. Children should believe in the Easter Bunny and Santa Claus. They should not have to come to terms with reality. (pp. 275-76)

It may be true that children shouldn't have to come to terms with reality, but in **One of the Children Is Crying** *Robin and Erin seem to do the other children a grave disservice by sheltering them from life's sordid details.*

The crime was not overprotection but fostering confusion about who their parents were. Robin and Erin never penetrated each other—if they had, I wouldn't have had a book—and their repression was what made them take over the role of parents. They usurped this role, took the parents away and didn't give them back. Had they just protected the other children from what the father was doing—the incest and all that—it would have been good. The child should not be exposed to life. Why should he be burdened with his father's misbehavior?

How autobiographical is **One of the Children***?*

Somewhat. I used our first initials for the six children [in my family], but we're not recognizable. However, my sister Pearl—the one who died of leukemia—is Priscilla in this novel. She was beautiful and depraved in an innocent kind of way. The book was a fictional farewell to both my family and to any religious belief or feeling. (p. 276)

Once a strong image establishes itself in your mind does all else stop until you've transformed it into a novel, or are you able to work on other projects at the same time?

Well, while I was writing **One of the Children Is Crying,** I started **Too Much Flesh and Jabez,** finished **One of the Children,** gave up **Jabez** and started **Island People,** stopped that and wrote all of **Mrs. October Was Here** in six months, went back to **Island People,** finished it, then back to **Jabez.** That's the only way I can work.

These four novels were written more or less simultaneously, then, and yet they are radically different in form.

I'll tell you what I think is responsible. I detest being typed. I'm sure an actor has this same fear of having to play the villain always or the juvenile when he's sixty-five. For instance, in a review of **Jabez,** *Publishers Weekly* said, "He has a reputation as a serious novelist, but he can't be categorized." The idea that one can be categorized is repellent to me.

Are there any works-in-progress now?

Two. One of them is a family saga, though nobody will recognize it as such. It's called **The Eve of the Green Grass,** the title of the play presented at the Chelsea which formed its basis. I've written two plays and five hundred pages on this family. They have haunted me for twenty-odd years. The other work is entitled **White on Black on White,** where a white is writing about black and white relations. It contains a black hit man and a white psychopath. It's hermetically sealed and this is why I'm dying to break out of it and why it's so difficult to write. I don't know what possesses me to write about murder and hatred. I'm a kind person myself and I like kind people. I have no reason to write about violence except that I feel it's valuable.

Your short fiction is quite different from your novels, including the two you have just described. It veers toward fantasy and even surrealism. . . . Do you enjoy writing short fiction?

Very much. I'm even breaking the plot of one of the new novels down into sections because writing a novel where you can only go forward is too claustrophobic.

Norman Mailer once said that the sedentary conditions of novel-writing led him to compose poems as a kind of relief.

I'm not a poet and feel a little bad when people say **Island People** is poetic because poetic prose is a failure. Poetry has to be compressed and my one published poem, printed in England this year, is a compression of a section of **White on Black on White** entitled "The Snake's House." I used to say that I wrote novels because I didn't have time to write poetry, but the truth is I don't have the talent. You take a novel and compress it into a few lines, with all the meanings, all the reverberations. (pp. 278-80)

The central portions of **Jabez** *seem to be poetic in the sense of a ballad.*

They are. **One of the Children** too. Vaughan Williams has done some very nice settings of some ballads and there was one, "Cold Blows the Wind Tonight, My Love, and One Small Drop of Rain," that I played over and over while I was writing it. All the snow and rain, depression and death in that book is in the ballad. As a matter of fact, I think everything I write grows out of Kentucky ballads—even **Island People.** I grew up on folk songs, which my father liked to collect. The Scotch influence, you know. Folk music is the best, purest musical influence anybody can have. I wrote a lot of people, including [James] Laughlin, and said, "I cannot write a symphony, so this book is mine." There are symphonies based on ballads. **Island People** is a conscious thing and I worked very hard on its musical structure. It is pure music as far as I'm concerned. The themes that recur are finally tied up, are codas. There are things in the first paragraph that set up the last sentence. (p. 280)

Hart Crane thought of The Bridge *in symphonic terms, which suggests that he needed a new organizational principle to express a new reality and that this and other musical forms helped him to eliminate the need for story or plot.*

Yet there's something marvelously dramatic about the progression of a symphony. And, as I said, **Island People** is symphonic. I'm a thematic writer and in symphonies you go back to a theme and reuse it. **Jabez** is about natural victims and **Island People** is about a man who is fragmented and who returns to the nineteenth century to find himself. (p. 281)

It's rather hard to imagine that the author of **One of the Children** *could write anything as formally complex as* **Mrs. October** *and* **Island People.** *Did something intervene?*

Neither in my reading nor in my life. You see, like Anthony Burgess, Graham Greene, and many others, I have the disease of boredom. I'll do almost anything to keep from being bored, which makes life dangerous for me because I take chances. Besides, **One of the Children** is not so straightforward; it goes back and forth. (pp. 281-82)

The Waste Land *has obviously influenced your fiction. For example, the drought in* **Jabez.**

The drought and the business about the land are absolutely literal. We suffered this in Kentucky and would have to haul water for the garden from the creek. As in India, the drought would be followed by a monsoon. Even in the city I'm terribly anxious when it doesn't rain.

Were you consciously aware of the poem?

In **Island People,** but not during the writing process. I started to use an epigraph from *The Waste Land,* then thought the connection should be plain enough. I used the soul-searching, the sense of the disembodied, the looking for grace, the foreign languages and civilizations. Incidentally, before I cut three hundred pages out of the book, I had a lot more about the nineteenth century.

In Eliot the narration is androgynous, epitomized by Tiresias, who represents all women and all men. Isn't the narration of **Island People** *androgynous, too?*

Well, the dust jacket shows the superimposition of the male and the female. Yes, I'm trying to make them merge in myself and in other people. It would be nice if we didn't have this split, if they could be friends. The ideal thing is a perfect balance between the two in a personality because both the male and the female have wonderful strengths as well as weaknesses. (pp. 282-83)

The narrative complexity of **Island People** *is well expressed by two sentences: "To deal with Clytie Steuber I invented an 'I' who invented a 'Beatrix.' Which is to say that Beatrix may as easily have invented Chris, whose name appeared not in the story but afterward!" Evidently, your reader, like the reader of* The Waste Land, *must be aware of how personae function here and elsewhere to untangle the sense.* **Island People** *employs first-, second-, and third-person voices.*

That was to help the reader as much as I could. I wanted the book to be understood and I think that it was, to a great extent.

The episodic structures of **Mrs. October** *and* **Island People** *might indicate that you have lost your faith in continuity.*

The loss is forced. Our information is given to us by spot announcements. Even old movies are interrupted by commercials and messages. This would drive anybody from the eighteenth or nineteenth century mad. We aren't allowed continuity; there is no time for it, no place for it.

Yet you treat history.

We can't stop history. In all of my books except the first one, people are writing about other people. This is quite modern. We get our information through somebody talking about somebody else, in the newspapers, on television. Gossip is our great thing. (pp. 283-84)

[Which] of your books do you like best?

Mrs. October because it's most completely mine. It's the most deliberate of the novels and it's full of delicious things that I did for myself. So much of the book is layered that I don't expect anybody to see all the puns and allusions.

Does the title echo "Kilroy was here"?

Yes, "Kilroy was here" and the October Revolution are precisely what the title comes from. (p. 285)

Here you use a first-person narrator we don't detect till the end, till the epilogue. Are we to assume Aurelie Angelique—AA—really tells the story?

She's one facet of the creative personality that I broke down into its components: Mrs. October, the revolutionary; Roman Chainey, the counter-revolutionary; and AA, the spy and freak with the long, long neck who can turn her head completely around. This is my autobiography, a very personal book. And I didn't know for quite a time which of these facets was myself, but I said, "I'll know who is writing the book eventually." At some point, way past the middle, I decided AA was closest to me because I have always felt like a freak and am a sort of spy. I made her a woman and a black, though at the end she's getting out of these roles. She says that there are people who claim she's not a woman or even a black and that they could be right. So finally I identified myself to the reader.

There are other important characters, Omerie Chad, for example.

I split Omerie and made Wanda part of the Omerie-Madame Alexis facet because I became fond of Wanda. One of the things I still dislike about the book is that I had to turn her into an automaton at the end, a sluttish, modern woman who just looks at television and has her hair done, whereas she was shaping up to be a damned good revolutionist. I really hate having had to sacrifice her.

The novel contains a crucifixion. Is Mrs. October a Christ figure?

I never had any religious sense about it at all. The writer tends to crucify himself and that book is about writing, just writing. Mrs. October wants them to crucify rather than hang her and so she draws the crucifix and names the parts. (pp. 285-86)

So the novel is about writing.

It is. For instance, her long sleep is the time you gather energy between books for another foray. I was interested, too, in seeing how close writing and revolution are, since revolution is also an art. In **Mrs. October** I was atoning for having caused death in the first book and the stories. This had to do with my central preoccupation: the responsibility of the creator to the created, a very, very moral thing with me. It may go back to being a child whose prayers were not answered, though I hate to think it's something as simple as that. But I do believe you have an enormous responsibility if you create a character and then kill him. One of the few times marijuana did anything for me I saw myself at fourteen and at fifty-three and I felt exactly the same because my concerns were pretty much the same. Under the influence of grass, I was able to remember being afraid of God, the Creator, at fourteen, and myself, the creator, the person writing the books, at fifty-three. To dispatch characters is a terrible thing. After the first novel, I suffered for letting Erin and Robin die. Perhaps I didn't work hard enough to save them. If somebody has to die, it's such a shocking thing that you had better have a strong reason. I detest people like Harold Robbins, not because they don't write very good English. Such writers are utterly immoral. They let the most awful things happen to their characters for no reason except the buck. Characters are much more than invention unless you are just a polemical writer.

So your anger was directed toward Mrs. October, who, as one facet of your own creative personality, killed a lot of revolutionaries?

That's right—punish, punish, punish. We set these worlds up, order and destroy them. I'm angered by the lack of order everywhere. I was writing **Mrs. October** when Nixon was pulling everything down and my loathing went right into **Island People,** where the White House is called the nation's "potty." I just despise politicians. (pp. 286-87)

Mrs. October *is a satire. Why do so many comic satirists tend to be scatological, to have an excremental vision?*

The impulse to write satire is the impulse to shit on people, the world, whatever.

And this impulse involves a horror of bodily functions?

I wouldn't deny it, but when you criticize the body you are also criticizing the body politic. Good satire must be hateful, as far as I'm concerned, or it won't succeed. Frequently, when I was writing **Mrs. October,** I was deeply depressed, especially about Mrs. Hackett, though I think it's funny now. I love Mrs. Hackett, who is a very important character. One of my most original things was to view parts of the revolution through her eyes. How else could I show you my extreme distaste for prurient children's books? This poor little old woman thinks she's a child again; let her see the filth children are exposed to! Mrs. Hackett can't abide the world, it's so ghastly. Senility is the only way back to childhood and I must allow one character to escape in life, the one I like best.

You didn't mind destroying her?

Well, she was an old woman and she had to die and I think I killed her to get her out of the world she had to face and couldn't face. (p. 288)

The people you save tend to be childlike. Effie in **Jabez,** *for example.*

I don't think Effie is childlike. She's an interesting, likeable woman I regretted getting rid of midway in the novel. This little birdlike thing is a realist who just doesn't happen to like sex with her husband, Jim, because he's so big he hurts her. Otherwise, she'd probably like it.

But not Miss Ethel?

That's right, the person writing the story. She's got to make the child an androgynous male because she can't allow herself to be penetrated even in her fantasies, though it's okay for a boy. As narrator, she doesn't allow Effie, or even sexy Ludie to be penetrated either. Miss Ethel is a virgin, very much like a nun. She hides her sexuality. Out of revenge, she invents Jabez. She withholds and withholds, then dies. It's Jim's narration at the end. He takes over and finishes her life and her book.

Can you explain why you feel this was your most difficult work?

I had to be restrained, to hold myself back. Unlike *Island People,* writing *Jabez* was like riding a team of horses while holding them reined in. It was very, very hard.

Is it accurate to say that form and content are inextricable here?

More so than in the other books. In *Jabez* the words themselves are the thing. (p. 289)

The theme of the "unlived life" is conveyed in **Jabez.** *Does Miss Ethel destroy herself and others through idealism and perfectionism?*

That's her central problem. She wanted to make Jim into a politician so he could effect the changes she wanted to bring about. Just being an idealist sets you down as a victim.

You speak of "natural" victims.

A "natural" victim is what you are by your very nature. In other words, Jim, by the nature of having such a large cock, is a "natural" victim. Miss Ethel, on the other hand, is a victim because she's made herself into one. She's continued to be a virgin, which drives her mad, and she makes men pay for her virginity by punishing the most masculine male she can find. She takes the real Jim, whom she doesn't know, and changes his big brain into a big cock.

Is what she does the result of a conflict between mind and body?

That's a terrible conflict, though sometimes it can be funny. When I was very young, I craved for release from sexual desire because it seemed to stand between me and accomplishment. I didn't start writing novels until I was forty and I

should have written much more. About the only other major concern in my life has been sex. I am obsessed as a writer and as a person with my own and other people's sexuality. I'm not prurient at all. I don't like pornography. What concerns me is the repression of the sexual impulse, which is one of the nastiest things ever given us by Christianity. Most crime is built on sexual repression. As far as I'm concerned, having sex is like smelling a daffodil—it's very simple. But there's always a hell of a conflict between the cerebral and the instinctive, a conflict I share. (p. 290)

John Kuehl, Linda Kandel Kuehl and Coleman Dowell, in an interview, in Contemporary Literature, *Vol. 22, No. 3, Summer, 1981, pp. 272-91.*

EDMUND WHITE

[Coleman Dowell's novel] *White on Black on White* is a transcript of America's unconscious, a translation out of the mumbling or shrieking patois of our collective nightmare about race. Structuralists have suggested that the unconscious conforms to paradigms, that it arranges experience into patterns, which in social terms would be male and female or old and young—and in the United States would also be Northern and Southern, straight and gay, rich and poor and, most particularly, Black and white.

(Even orthography reveals a reality by disguising it: Blacks, having no power, receive the empty honor of a capital letter whereas whites, owning and controlling everything, hide behind their lower-case façade, the not-so-charming discretion of the bourgeoisie.)

Good fiction, like all art, is useless, a realm so fully bodied forth that it cannot stand for another but must lead a separate existence, which parallels but never transects life. A named meaning is a dead meaning. Or so we say. Of course there's something too air-tight about such a definition, too philosophically absolute (wasn't Kant the origin of the idea?) to be adequate to an art that is at least half journalism and whose very medium is language, the code that has no function save symbolic. Coleman Dowell's book reminds us of the difficulties of any definition of the novel that's not piebald, for *White on Black on White* exemplifies Chekhov's remark that good fiction must be half fairy tale and half newspaper story.

The newspaper half deals with Blacks in prison, the early Civil Rights movement, the Vietnam War, the echoes of race riots. The fairy tale aspect of the book is frightening and progressive, in the sense that an illness progresses. The narrator, a white man of independent means, a writer, conceives a hungry physical passion for a Black man, Calvin, who's heterosexual, an ex-convict, now a hit man. The two spend a few weeks together season in a rented summer house on Long Island. Calvin alternately hates and befriends his companion and alternately cherishes the white man's old, blind dog Xan and threatens to beat in her brains. The white man alternately lusts after Calvin (his lust is never fully satisfied) and despises him. The mood is tense and grows tenser. Two men and a feeble dog circulate through Partridge House, a luxurious glass structure waiting to be broken. Both of them drink constantly and too much (Calvin gin, the narrator brandy)—and since we see things only through the narrator's eyes, the ellipses and distortions of his drunkenness occlude our vision.

This opening section is subtitled "The Snake's House," a name explained by this passage:

But I lay awake remembering a time on the farm when I had found a snake and a toad in primitive congress. The toad was partially swallowed, the snake too far gone in passion to try to move. I took a stick and forced their separation. The snake, hissing, went into its hole but the toad sat there covered with narcotic slime. With the stick I prodded it until it moved, but too sluggish for me and I picked it up in disgust and put it far from the hole. Sometime later, propelled by certainty, I went back to the spot and found the toad, recognizable by the undried slime, once again beside the snake's house waiting.

In the same way the narrator is terrified by the menacing Calvin and cannot leave him.

The section begins ritualistically with each of the two men shaving the other's head, as though imposing baldness on themselves were a way of achieving fraternity and defeating the distinctions of race. But race is everywhere around them. Serena Westlake, a post-deb neighbor, can't help drooling over Calvin and uttering jive talk to suggest how soulful she can be. The coolly scathing narrator paraphrases in satiric indirect discourse Serena's childhood recollections: "She thought that her constant state of feeling pissed off was because in those days she was surrounded by funky exciting Blacks with whom she was forbidden to get down."

The language of this single sentence comically captures the two cultures, oscillating between the white "constant state" and the Black "pissed off" or, more rapidly, the dialect "funky" and the bland "exciting," the Victorian "forbidden" and the contemporary "get down."

In this honky resort, Calvin begins to wonder "where the niggers live." As the two men drive through the attractive and only slightly faded "slums" of Greenport, they see another interracial couple, a Black policeman and a red-haired white woman. (These two people later turn out to be principal characters, Ivy and Cayce.) Calvin reacts by muttering obscenely about the "sickness" of whites obsessed by Blacks, while the white narrator thinks about queers fixated on "normal" men. In each case the forbidden heightens desire—*doubles* the narrator's desire for Calvin, who is both Black and heterosexual.

Early on in the book the narrator is grumbling about Calvin's playing the radio constantly and too loud. Almost parenthetically he recalls, "When I had visited Jamaica, Long Island, the Sunday before we left for the country, to meet Calvin's wife and daughters, I had heard to my amazement that WBLS was kept on full blast and that they somehow were able to talk around it . . ." What this passage reveals in its casual, everyday manner is that Calvin is not just an instrument of the narrator's passionate ambitions, not just a stray integer in the calculus of race but . . . a family man, that is, someone whom others have liens on. And this connectedness, this social integration, is characteristic of Dowell's entire novel, which presents a reality of imperious great aunts and sassy nieces, of tenderly devoted brothers and sisters, of stern, disapproving mothers and their outlaw children, of neighbors, childhood friends, couples of long standing. These are people who have a social existence, who are implicated into the thick stuff of humanity. They cannot be pornographic actors. Lust demands isolation (Partridge House) to work out its diabolic (because single-minded) designs; life avenges itself on lust by creeping back in, washing in like junk floating up on the tide and stranded high on the beach. The tension between the lonely exaltations of the pornographic imagination and the banal to-and-froing of daily life provides a subliminal dialectic to Dowell's novel. It's a book about people looking at each other: a public novel. (pp. 113-14)

In the second section Calvin has vanished and the narrator is back in New York, remembering him, longing for him, repeatedly "telling" (as one tells beads) the things Calvin has left behind—toiletries, a bit of marijuana. In this section, which might be called *Calvin disparu,* the beloved is "spiritualized," in that his essence is freed from the opaque materiality of his presence; his spirit, liberated from resistant actuality, can now be more fully assimilated to the thoughts of the lover, that is, the beloved can now become the perfect hero of the lover's story. . . . Absence permits readerly art to triumph over the illegibility of reality. The narrator constructs a tantalizing tale of Calvin's life on the basis of a single document: a telephone bill. While Calvin had been living with the narrator, he had secretly placed many long-distance calls. Now, by calling those numbers as listed on the bill, the narrator is able to speak to Calvin's young, illegitimate daughter, to an unidentified (and very surprised) woman, to Calvin's severe, disapproving mother, to an angry, cast-off Black gay man, then to one who is still enamored ("You lookin for him too? I sure wish he was here now, that sweet devil"), finally to a desperate Spanish woman.

The narrator's obsession with Calvin leads him to what we can only call racist thoughts. Were these thoughts expressed as the author's own or presented in an essay as the truth, we'd slam the book shut. But, given the dramatic context, these thoughts (for instance, "The 'cool' stance is essential to febrile Blacks, otherwise they would incinerate themselves") are valuable data about how race is perceived. The narrator, after all, is a middle-aged upper-class Southerner who freely if not always clearly recognizes how charged, how corrupt, how over-determined his feelings toward Blacks are. We might even be tempted to say that his sexual obsession with Blacks is nothing more than a condensation of those feelings, desire itself nothing but a simplification of emotional contradictions. The narrator's companion Berthold, a German immigrant, has none of these responses to Blacks—no anger, no guilt, no lust, little curiosity. For Berthold, Blacks are not the Other, simply others, unimportant people beyond his social horizon. The politics of **White on Black on White** are irreproachable because they are documentary not propagandistic, because the book renders rather than recommends.

Obsessives search out companions in anguish, just as the characters in any extended piece of narrative must be matched with doubles—the psychological principle of life paralleled by the constructive principle of fiction. The narrator finds Ivy, a chance acquaintance at a dinner party but one recognized quickly enough as a fellow traveler, if a "traveler" is a peripatetic salesman of small goods. The goods in this case are brief encounters with Blacks. The narrator is a Southern gay man drawn to a single Black, whereas Ivy is a Yankee heterosexual woman attracted to a whole host of Blacks. She first discovers this taste while participating down South in the early Civil Rights movement. One of the unwritten chapters of our history has been the true account of the sexual aspect of the Civil Rights movement; Dowell writes it now. He moves from the rhetoric of fraternity to the plain talk of sexual curiosity, the false ideal of universal humanity giving way to the spontaneous recognition of deep (and exciting) racial differences.

Nabokov once remarked that Freud got it all wrong. It's not that we come to love a woman's lustrous hair and smooth skin because we associate them with sexual pleasure. Rather the reverse: we want to sleep with a woman because we hope somehow to possess that hair and skin we've admired since childhood. The so-called secondary sexual characteristics are the primary focus of desire. Childhood is an absence because children cannot possess what they love; adulthood is a frustration because sexual possession is only momentary. What Ivy demonstrates is that the most extreme form of adult love focuses on what is purely Opposite, what is Black to one's white; for her, making love to countless Black men condenses more and more moments of possession until, charged with these bursts of energy, she performs a miracle: she becomes Black herself and kills a white man. In this sacred frenzy (insanity) she becomes Black *by* killing a white, so steeped in hatred and love are the two races, so totally do they depend on one another for both their identity and annihilation. (pp. 115-16)

When Ivy holds back information about her sexual encounters, the narrator hungers for those details: "It was not just prurience; I insist upon that. It was also a hunger for knowledge, knowledge of the way Blacks see us whites, see us differently as woman and as men, as we see them, male and female, differently, a historical weight pressing upon and distorting that vision as variously as cataracts and belladonna." A few pages later, Ivy visits a Black prisoner with whom she has been exchanging pornographic letters: "Ivy felt sure that he had specialized in white women and could imagine that such a man wore a special sign for the seekers or the initiate, just as women like herself must be marked in some way for Black men to see." (p. 116)

Ivy, as a white who loves Blacks, is an outcast deity. Her descent into degradation (physical dirtiness, poverty, drug addiction, venereal disease, prostitution) is a simultaneous ascent toward the ideal of fraternity she had once glibly espoused as a young Civil Rights fighter. She earns with suffering and ecstasy what she had once so lightly professed. The saint must endure, not merely proclaim. Clearly etched as all the action is, nevertheless an atmosphere of fantasy or, better, mythology clings to these pages, as though a photo-realist were to add unnatural, excruciating highlights to his literal renderings.

Ivy goes into Central Park and fraternizes with bums under a culvert all night long, passing the bottle and drunkenly submitting to sex some twenty times with five men. In her mind they are all "mer-creatures in the grotto." This episode of transformation, a regression in the service of enchantment, this intimacy-in-anonymity and life-in-death—this rich, disturbing metamorphosis bears all the marks of myth, not as recollected in tranquility but as improvised through experience. If the cave is the womb of rebirth, it is one fertilized by five nocturnal fathers—as though to compensate for the one father Ivy never had. (Freudians call Blacks "nocturnal fathers," tracing racism back to the primal scene.)

This mythic crisis releases a flood of other archetypal scenes and situations. The second half of the book occurs on an island that is poor, rural, definitely isolated from the mainstream of American culture. In this redneck outpost Ivy grew up in brother-sister intimacy with Cayce Scott, a Black boy (one of the few Blacks on the entire island). Now Ivy returns, worn, ill, disgraced, a tramp, to discover Cayce who's become quite literally the "soul of respectability," i.e. a policeman.

These two characters point the way to a Black and white utopia for if the title **White on Black on White** sometimes means the superimposition of Black and white bodies in sexual congress, here it simply locates a vision of sexless love, the only pure (that is, static) emotion in Dowell's fiction;

> She lay her head for a moment backward onto his white-linen clad shoulder, and one of his big hands with the preposterously phallic thumb lay upon her black-silk clad shoulder, and it was marvelously intricate, like looking inside them: white on black on white on black on white. But, lovers? And again there was the brother-sister impression, devoid of eroticism, full of some old sweetness like mutual memories of a playroom on a rainy day, and innocence of everything.

So suggestive is this vision that the narrator is inspired to write Cayce's memoirs for him. The impersonation of a Black by a white (a Black, moreover, who is meditating on whites) provides the final meaning of the title, the *on* signifying "about" as who should say *On Love.*

The final section of the novel . . . is a set of Chinese boxes. The containing box is the narrator, by nature a voyeur, by trade a writer. The document we're reading is his work, so long as we accept Dowell's fiction (Dowell's own consciousness, of course, is the shadowy outermost envelope, once we break through the fictive membrane). The next box in is Cayce, whose memoirs we're presumably reading, though in fact these pages are the narrator's attempt to become Cayce (an instance not only of a white becoming Black but also of a gay becoming straight). Cayce finally interrupts this narrative to give corrections and to provide his own version. Cayce, in turn, is trying to understand Ivy and to reconstruct her lost time in Harlem. Such a reconstruction, of course, we the readers have already read, based on the narrator's talks with Ivy (but with his distortions—and hers, since she displays both candor and canniness).

All of these boxes might seem to constitute only one more dull post-modernist "experiment." But since Dowell's entire effort is to define each race in terms of the other, to uncover their interdependence, to build up a palimpsest of white on black on white, the Chinese-box construction is syntactically parallel to the semantic content—indeed the form *is* the message, which turns out (surprisingly in such an angry book) to be optimistic: the races *can* understand each other, approximately if not perfectly. As Cayce himself says of the narrator's impersonation, "There's not a lot I'd object to or change . . ." Indeed, so convincing is Dowell's own performance that we keep wondering whether *he* is Black or white. Our speculations about him amount to a secret dialectic that accompanies any reading. I suggest the publisher might preserve this dimension by suppressing the author's portrait. To be sure, in this masterful novel we already have his true likeness, the portrait of his perverse and wise sensibility. (pp. 116-17)

Edmund White, "Thoughts on 'White on Black on White'," in The Review of Contemporary Fiction, *Vol. 2, No. 3, Fall, 1982, pp. 113-17.*

MERIAM FUCHS

It would be difficult to classify the short stories of Coleman Dowell. Their realism is often tempered by surrealism, and their irony is often diffused by a dreamlike lyricism. It would also be difficult to classify the characters of Dowell's short stories. Protagonists who at first seem comprehensible, even transparent, develop into complicated and unpredictable beings. Marriott, the abandoned husband in **"If Beggars Were Horses,"** seems familiar, almost mundane, in his numerous insecurities, but by the end of the story he reveals himself to be startlingly imaginative in venging himself on his former wife. The narrator of **"My Father Was A River"** presents himself as cold-hearted and diabolical. However, the more he expounds upon his malicious qualities, the gentler and more pitiable he becomes, yet he never realizes this himself. (p. 118)

[The readers of Dowell's short stories] learn to expect the unexpected, for the ever-changing nature of the protagonists, or their increasingly complex passions, are at the heart of Dowell's work. In the midst of this, however, there remains one constant, and that is the authorial stance. Wayne C. Booth calls the "implied author" the voice of the writer, as it governs both first- and third-person works of literature. In Dowell's short stories, the implied author is usually a strong and compassionate presence. The characters may wound, maim, take revenge or have incestuous desires; whatever their motives and whatever their courses of action, the implied author is sympathetic and compassionate. Humanity is fragile.

Erroneous character perceptions are evident in the first line of **"My Father Was A River"**: "They called me a good child. It made me feel even more set apart, a sort of social leper. . . ." The narrator, who is the son looking at his past, assumes that his parents never understood how very *bad* he was. To illustrate the degree of their ignorance, he presents two of his sadistic childhood fantasies. The first was the desire to "fly into an orgy of rage and kick tables, legs, faces [of his relatives], until all became splinters" and the second was to metamorphose into "grass and willow trees, hovering protectively over my mother's grave, watered by my father's dear tears." The narrator even succeeds for a time in convincing the reader that he was indeed a vindictive and malicious child, who cherished his father but tried to destroy his mother.

The narrator believes that his parents' oblivion of his basic nature was one reason for his plan to prove his malevolence. But more significant reasons begin to emerge. His parents were lenient and trusting, allowing him more freedom than other children his age. "I was free," he says, but the experience afforded no happiness, for he interpreted it as a form of his parents' neglect. He further observed his parents' slow, silent seductions and their shared secrets as he was conveniently left to roam the landscape by himself. It gradually becomes clear to the reader that it was the narrator's jealousy of his parents' intimacy—rather than any inherent evil in his nature—that led to his desire for revenge.

In his twelfth year the narrator decided to upset the balance of power in the household. By daylight he was the perfect son, well scrubbed and well behaved. By night he became "a dark child with dark secrets," pursuing nocturnal creatures he thought incarnated his father's spirit. Drawn to the river, he visited it each summer night and flirted with its rhythms. One night he entered the stream, convinced it was the arms of his father. The boy's courtship with the river echoes his parents' relationship. He purposely defers his pleasure, thinking he and his father are slowly seducing each other, as he observed his parents doing. Then he tries to stay away but is soon drawn to the rhythmic pleasures again.

The son is certain that an ordinary person is able to concentrate on a single object with such intensity that "eventually time will reveal to him each mystery, flaw, and virtue of that object." When he knows the river, he shifts his focus to a fox, and finally to a mountain lion. For instance, each night he waits for the fox that preys on his father's hens. Slowly, night after night, the fox grows to trust the young boy, to view him as a signal to proceed in his plundering. One night the boy seals the henhouse and offers himself to the fox. He feels both the control and the excitement he experienced with the river.

Despite what he believes, the narrator is not evil and does not know every mystery, flaw, and virtue. The more he insists that he is, and that he does, the more flawed his own perceptions become. In the concluding section, appropriately called "Chaconne," the irony becomes even more obvious. The narrator returns to the fictional present and compares himself to a swamp plant that sprouts nothing but wild branches. He is still trying to be understood by his mother, whom he has betrayed and whom he addresses now. He accuses her of innocence, but in fact only reveals his own. He does not realize that he has always wanted the opposite of the freedom that was his parents' gift to him. His mother, in a sense, belonged to his father, as he belonged to her; the river belonged to the earth; the fox to the nocturnal murders; the mountain lion to all of the landscape. Only the son has suffered the freedom of oneness.

It is up to the reader to balance the narrator's self-loathing with his overt desires to be loved by his father and his more subtle needs to be cared about by his mother. The balance is restored, to an extent, through the authorial voice that permeates even the first-person perspective. First, details are ordered so that the son's lack of self-knowledge colors all of what he says. Second, authorial control is made implicit by the vague context of the narrator. The reader knows only that these events occurred when the youth was twelve years old, but location remains a mystery, as do the whereabouts of both parents and the narrator's present age. It is important to realize that the narrator's voice blurs the sensibilities of both the child and the adult. The child somewhere in time and place becomes the adult somewhere in time and place, with the same preoccupations. The wounded child is the vulnerable adult, never forgiving himself and never understanding his own fragility. (pp. 118-19)

A character who never reaches confounding proportions but who . . . [reveals] rather surprising, and unexpected, traits is Marriott in **"If Beggars Were Horses."** He is now in middle age, ruminating on why Lisa, his wife of twenty-five years, left him. Her departure was the cause of his serious illness— he stopped speaking for a time and lost more than sixty-five pounds. Marriott thinks back to his wedding day. He "watches himself staggering under bride-weight" with the attempt to carry Lisa up the stairs to the bridal chamber in his mother's house. He focuses on his "inability" to do what he wanted and what he was expected to do. "Human weight, earth-mired wants, and expectations" frighten him because he worries that he is a "noman." He imagines: "A woman and a noman twisting in swathed distaste on the mother-made bed." The womb is far from a comfortable place to be; Marriott thinks of creatures hanging from its walls as bats hang from treetops. At this point, a reader will have no doubt about the protagonist's fears and personality. Marriott is plagued by self-doubt, fears of impotence, and dread of loneliness.

Soon he notices familiar furniture being moved into the house across the hedge, where Lisa grew up. Too timorous to watch directly, through a shaving mirror propped against the windowsill he awaits Lisa's arrival in her mother's home. He realizes how slender she is and how most middle-aged couples allow themselves the pleasure and security of mid-life bulges knowing that they will go through it together; it is, from Marriott's perspective, a sign of trust. Lisa, though, remained slim, in readiness for the time when she would be single. This reference to weight becomes important.

The third-person point of view begins to pun on words concerned with weight. "[Marriott] grew to fit the shape of the present and found strength to draw the outlines of a more robust future and to look forward to growing to fit that shape too." In other words, Marriott stops thinking about the past and starts planning for the future. The implied author is exercising control, subtly preparing the reader for the culmination of motifs dealing with weight. Marriott gains strength. He cooks rich foods and gains a good deal of weight. As if through psychic communication, he encourages his new neighbor (Lisa) to eat, to enjoy afternoon sherry, to settle in with a quart of ice cream at night. A reader makes the logical inference that Marriott is sadly trying to simulate the middle-aged marriage that he does not have. However, Lisa *has* been eating. Marriott sees her one night in her kitchen and his revenge for her abandonment seems gloriously achieved: "Despite the double chin and the large bust thrusting in profile, he could not mistake his wife for anyone else in the world." He wants to lean out his window to shout his love, but manages to control his glee.

The reader can enjoy Marriott's success while wondering whether it is fantasy or fact. Lisa now has the middle-aged fat without the security of a middle-aged husband. But there is more. The moment Marriott realizes that Lisa is no longer ready for a free and easy single life, he is relieved, but for a surprising reason; he can stop preparing all those rich dinners and begin to lose weight. After all, "Flatulence . . . was for ladies. . . ." The implication, naturally, is that he will make himself ready for just such a life!

The authorial control in **"If Beggars Were Horses"** is superb. The third-person point of view introduces Marriott as "sick" and presents him in the process of seeing himself twenty-five years earlier—fearful, weak, dominated by women. The implied author distances the protagonist from the reader until Marriott's characterization seems established beyond a doubt. Hence, the reader is completely unprepared for the triumph of the husband at the end. Marriott's imagined tableau of Lisa counterbalances his memories of his wedding day. He envisions moving-men dismantling the wall of Lisa's home, ostensibly to help remove her, since she is too heavy to maneuver herself. "He asked himself if he had perhaps gone too far, but the drowsy boy within him, to whom it was unthinkable that there could ever be too much billowy femininity, entered sleep smiling." Revenge is complete.

Dowell's characters change. They appear to do tricks, in a sense, to shift and become what is least expected of them. The weak ones reveal some strengths, the strong ones reveal some vulnerability, and the evil ones show their innocence. But no one should think of this as a formula by which Dowell works. The shifting instead should be taken as a sign that he enjoys complicated structures. It should also suggest Dowell's interest in unpredictable characters. Whatever their conflict, whatever their sin, the authorial voice forgives them all, should forgiveness ever be needed, and treats them lovingly and compassionately. (pp. 120-21)

Meriam Fuchs, "Coleman Dowell's Short Stories," in The Review of Contemporary Fiction, *Vol. 2, No. 3, Fall, 1982, pp. 118-21.*

GILBERT SORRENTINO

Island People is a rich and complicated work that employs a small complement of techniques for its effects, but employs these techniques with unsettling brilliance. It deals, I think, with the idea of salvation through the act of writing, although who is saved is a question that the book never answers. It is, in essence, a ghost story, or, more accurately, a book of exorcism. One of the many ghosts (who may all be one ghost) exorcised is the ghost of self. (p. 122)

We might fairly say then that *Island People* is a work in which the ghost(s) of self are banished through the act of writing, and banished so completely that this self no longer exists, as author, persona, or invented characters. The reader is left with no sure grip on the text since the text of *Island People* doesn't exist: we have a book that might be titled *"Island People."* Its creator invents a writer who invents a character; this character takes possession of him and forces him to create an alter ego for himself, and it is this alter ego who attempts to write a novel called *Island People,* but who never does.

Dowell so arranges it that we are never really certain exactly *who* is writing *what,* or if the *who* that we suppose to be the writer of any given *what* is the author, the narrator's narrator, or the character who has taken possession of the writer. What we hold in our hands as *Island People* is a book that has avoided being the *Island People* of the alter ego. Through this act of multiple evasion, this willed ambiguity (for instance, there are journal entries that purport to comment on the developing novel but that may very well be part of this novel's text), the ghosts, who could, perhaps, have emerged from the pages of a conventional narrative, i.e., one which "reflects life," are denied presence, are banished to the pages of an "unwritten" book, the house that they may haunt forever.

These ghosts are lured, so to speak, into the house of the text we have by means of curious, quasi-archaic passages that simply *appear,* that is, we have no evidence as to who might have written them: they are not documents, or pseudo-documents, but brief fictional episodes. These passages act as a literary ouija board and the personages they call up are a nineteenth-century family and its involvement in hatred, violence, and murder. They are called into the present so that they may be banished to the book's pages.

Tricked by a narrative that has as its author *not* its author (nor do we know who its author is); whose chapters turn out to be not chapters at all, but a series of short stories by or about the narrator (invented by an invented character who in turn has been invented); that marshals a population of characters who are really mirror images, distortions, inversions, perversions, and caricatures of each other, the ghosts have no purchase on the real world *outside* the novel. They are imprisoned forever in the text called *Island People.* This may also be viewed as Dowell's commentary on the novel as a closed system, i.e., real ghosts have been rendered powerless by trapping them in fiction, fiction deployed so that its artificial nature cannot be mistaken.

Island People functions as a medium whereby real ghosts are called up by a shifting and multiplex character whom they haunt; he rids himself of them by turning them and all the characters they have possessed (which characters also haunt him) into fiction, wherein they are trapped, so that he may be free. The techniques of the work are ways of foiling the ghosts: There is no discoverable narrator; the island is everywhere and takes many guises (the scenes are claustrophobic and, even when laid outdoors, are cut off from everything else, "isolate"); the characters are images of each other, masked by age and sex and name, all of them not only vaguely or overtly similar, but also curiously like the figures of the nineteenth-century family—so that they, in effect, are ghosts of ghosts.

None of the ghosts can cross over via the medium of the text, since it is, indeed, a "labyrinth sealed with lead," whose "threads" lead "nowhere." They may haunt its pages, but there is no *self* to haunt. The ghosts have been banished to the text, and the self to a myriad insubstantial selves that disintegrate and scatter. Only this work of pure invention remains, a work whose center cannot be found, as it exists somewhere between the artifact and its creator, and neither are "what they are." (pp. 122-23)

> *Gilbert Sorrentino, "Some Remarks on 'Island People',"* in The Review of Contemporary Fiction, *Vol. 2, No. 3, Fall, 1982, pp. 122-23.*

BOB HALLIDAY

Over the past decade or so, Coleman Dowell has amazed and puzzled his readers with a series of strikingly designed works unconventional enough to deserve a shelf to themselves. No two of the five novels he has published resemble each other, but all share a theme which binds them in sequence: the compulsive way we use our imaginations to re-create and distort those we wish to love, and the loneliness and estrangement which result.

In *Island People,* Dowell's dream-enigmatic 1976 novel, a writer in retreat on a small island off New England is transformed as he interacts with the island people of the title, obsessed presences generated by different strata of his own imagination. With *White on Black on White* Dowell returns to this setting, but this time the reader is set among people made inaccessible to each other by racial anxieties and the sexual obsession they engender.

"I began to write this as a sort of sixties comedy," Dowell says, "but somewhere in the middle of the attempt a remark was made that made me change my focus from a short story to a novel. The catalytic remark was that white men see black men as criminals and black men see white men as queers." . . .

The novel which resulted is made up of three concentric stories, each an autobiographical account by one of the characters, but all seemingly related and embellished by a single person, a novelist who remains anonymous throughout the book. Although each of the composite stories reflects and extends upon the others convincingly, when juxtaposed they reveal so many coincidences, symmetries and seemingly contrived correspondences that the reader becomes uncomfortably aware of his informant's inability to keep his own obsessions from refracting what has been related to him by others.

Like the writer in *Island People,* this novelist, whose story forms the book's first section, is setting up housekeeping together with a pet dachshund on an island to escape city tensions. This time, however, there is a third member to the party: Calvin Hartshorne, a disturbed young black Vietnam War veteran with whom the writer, who is homosexual, is infatuated. As narrated in the writer's journal their island existence is a Grand Guignol of sexual psychological warfare. Calvin torments the writer with hostile aloofness, constantly hinting at an affair he may be having with a white woman who lives on the island; the writer retaliates with jealous surveillance, and attempts to control Calvin by exploiting his simplicity and superstitiousness. Innumerable jabs are made at emotionally vulnerable spots. . . . (p. 3)

By now the reader is losing trust in the narrator. Calvin has been presented so selectively that he threatens to retreat into the racist caricature, sexy and dangerous, with which the writer titillates and torments himself. His sexual presence eclipses almost everything else, with hints of his confusion and volatility, his frustrated respect and affection for the writer revealed only inadvertently in the pages of the journal. And the writer, reacting to the Calvin he has created for himself, sneaks around like a thief, spying on the black man and placing fraudulent phone calls to check up on him. Physical violence is avoided, but both are already mutilated by the intense and destructive emotions they have inflicted on each other.

The same lethal mixture of interracial sexual obsession and contempt saturates the two accounts the writer presents following his own, but in each the grotesquerie is stepped up to the point where the reader's suspicion of his narrator is intensified. In the first Ivy Temple, a young woman he meets at a party, relates to the writer the story of her own obsession with black men. After an affair with a black coworker during a civil rights demonstration in Selma, Ivy is drawn into a downward spiral more horrifying than that which overtook her namesake, Faulkner's Temple Drake.

In the final and most striking story Cayce Scott, a black policeman who had been Ivy's childhood friend, attends a dinner party given by an imperious old woman who seems to straddle the two races, and who focuses the spirit of racial obsession into a long and potently written monologue.

In these two narratives misperception is pushed to the limit, with stories embedded in other stories, and everything at the mercy of a disturbed narrator. It remains for Cayce Scott to cut through all this in his long reflection on the book's action which forms a kind of coda to *White on Black on White.* As a black policeman who is feared by dishonest whites, Scott reverses Dowell's stereotype, and emerges as the only character in the novel not defeated by his obsessions. Through his revelations, presented as transcribed tapes untampered with by the writer-narrator, Dowell permits the other characters, shadowy and refracted until now, to be more completely revealed. Cayce's concluding demand for cleansed perceptions, for love based on sincerity and respect, is angrily passionate and has great emotional power. (pp. 3, 7)

[Race] really doesn't seem to be at the center of this book. It serves as a vehicle for the more disturbing insights Dowell offers on the power of obsession, particularly sexual obsession. His tortured island people must transcend their fantasies by learning to respect the ones they wish to love, if they are to achieve the love and respect which can redeem them. (p. 7)

Bob Halliday, "Triple Fugue: Race, Sex and Obsession," in Book World—The Washington Post, *July 17, 1983, pp. 3, 7.*

DAVID EVANIER

Coleman Dowell's fifth novel, **White on Black on White,** is a maddening apparition. It is a bold examination of black pain and anger and white guilt that crackles with insights but is hindered by its unnovelistic structure. Mr. Dowell's vibrant dialogue and characterization are constantly undercut by numbing forays into a language of excess used for long sermons and unlikely philosophical digressions.

In Mr. Dowell's novel, all interracial sex is seen as aggression and political anger, masochism and revenge. The book begins with a white male narrator's account of his homosexual obsession with a black hit man. The second section is the same narrator's story of a white civil rights worker, Ivy Temple, and her obsessive desire for black men, which takes her from Selma, Ala., to Harlem, where she becomes involved in heroin addiction, prostitution and murder. Ivy in turn tells the history of a bitter black woman whose father and five brothers were either murdered or psychologically destroyed by racist white society. Cayce Scott, a black high school classmate of Ivy's and a policeman and Vietnam vet, is the focus of the later part of the novel, his story narrated by the white male of the early chapters. The epilogue is spoken into a tape recorder by Cayce.

"The book is about misconceptions and masks hiding obsessions and masks being removed at some midnight signal revealing some other obsession entirely," Cayce writes in his diary. Throughout, this kind of convoluted language is interwoven with examples of superb dialogue. Mr. Dowell's difficult and idiosyncratic novel is devoid of plot and structure and at times is impenetrable. But its psychological acuity, political insight, ferocious energy and authenticity of place partly compensate for its narrative awkwardness.

David Evanier, in a review of "White on Black on White," in The New York Times Book Review, *November 13, 1983, p. 14.*

RENA S. KLEIMAN

The Houses of Children is the posthumous collection of short stories by Coleman Dowell, a Kentucky-born writer who committed suicide in 1985. It marks the first time any of his several dozen short stories have been presented in book form.

Dowell selected the stories himself in July, 1985, just a year after renouncing writing altogether. A month later, the 60-year-old novelist-playwright-composer-lyricist-free-lance model jumped to his death from his New York City apartment.

Dowell has always been considered a writer's writer. This collection makes that phrase his epitaph. His prose ranges from enigmatic metaphor to brilliant epiphany. As in his previous five novels, Dowell demonstrates a love of words for their own sake. The sheer density of his prose is at times beyond deciphering.

In *The Houses of Children,* Dowell sets his eyes on the violent and the lurid in modern life: the insane, the senile, the cannibal, the hunchback, the loner, the freaks. He looks at these not with the judgments and pronouncements of the adult world but with the empathy of a youthful compatriot.

His subjects are children of all kinds: the child of the apocalypse, the child of a field mouse, the child of a river; the childhood of the retarded, the childhood of the abandoned, second childhood.

Though Dowell is often compared to others in the Southern school—Flannery O'Connor, William Faulkner, even Tennessee Williams—this collection is more reminiscent of Hemingway's *In Our Time.* Like Nick in those stories, Dowell's boy narrators see and record, but do not yet have the power to understand what they see.

In **"Wool Tea"** the child narrator, known only as the Kid, finds himself captivated by the woman who has seduced him as a joke and who gave his brother the sexual disease that has sent him to a sanitarium. Similarly, the boy-observer in **"Writings on a Cave Wall"** records his cannibalistic world as placidly as he recalls eating his sister's baby. Later, when his mother brings him some meat and it appears he may be the next subject for his family's hearty appetites, he muses, "It will be fitting. As a babe I fed upon her."

Repeatedly, the child's idealized vision of the world is destroyed by adult reality. The boy in **"The Great Godalmighty Bird"** learns as an adult that the world sees the grandmother he loves as a disfigured hunchback, a freak. . . .

At times, the author's artifice is too clearly visible. We see the stitching, not the tapestry, as the characters take a back-seat to the writer. Thus, despite some powerfully evocative prose, **"My Father Was a River"** comes off as an author's exercise; **"Singing in the Clump"** seems an experiment in point of view; and **"Ham's Gift,"** in which an abandoned child awaits an imaginary kingdom come, fails through a nearly incomprehensible ending.

Dowell is successful when his gaze is fixed on character rather than form, as it is in **"Mrs. Hackett"** and **"In the Mood."** The first story charts a woman's descent into second childhood propelled by her wildly abusive lesbian daughter.

"In the Mood" is the author's answer to the apocalyptic vision: Johnny returns from the war and ends up, broken-nerved, in a mental hospital because he dare not reveal to his family his new identity: He is the singer Glenn Miller.

His aunt Mary is Johnny's civilian counterpart who faces the horrors of modern non-war: life, death, aging, time. Mary has also forged a new identity through a divorce, face lifts, a new life in California. But she is betrayed by her own hands, literally, and so she has taken to wearing gloves even to sleep, to somehow shut out the signs of aging.

Yet where Johnny finds peace is in his insanity, Mary is hounded by her unavailing quest to stop time. In the end, Mary faces her enemies and Johnny's in a hallucinatory dream that recalls Hemingway's "our nada who are in nada" dialogue in "A Clean, Well-Lighted Place."

"Enemies are as strong as God," he writes.

> We give them their strength because we cannot see them; the strength of the unknown, the unseen, the suspected. When we pray—when we pray in battle—we pray to our enemies as well as to God— 'Miss us this time, spare us this time.' Because we

pray to them, they become God to us. When we kill them . . . we know it is God we have killed.

Like Hemingway, Dowell is saying: If war doesn't get you, if a cannibal, sexual disease, or being a freak of nature doesn't get you, just wait, life itself will get you in the end. Both authors, it seems, said it not only with their work, but with their lives.

> *Rena S. Kleiman, in a review of "The Houses of Children: Collected Stories," in* Los Angeles Times Book Review, *May 24, 1987, p. 6.*

LORRIE MOORE

[The stories in *The Houses of Children*] are odd tales, rhetorically rich and strange of subject, with an intense lyricism that is one moment lucid and elegant and the next recondite and bewildering. Dowell's are narratives for which the reader is never quite prepared. In one story, **"Singing in the Clump,"** incidental birds are given dialogue. In **"Ham's Gift"** a man's journey into Canaan and Eden is revealed, finally, as a seizure of epilepsy. In yet another, **"The Moon, the Owl, My Sister,"** the narrator is a field mouse. These are discomfiting stories. They skip steps. They rearrange time. They often have aspects of greatness without first being good.

Certainly Coleman Dowell has a way with a sentence. Poetry abounds here, so much so that large sections of the collection read like prose poems, language gone both lovely and berserk. A girl swinging on a gate is said to be "not counting the *backs,* counting only the *forths; forth* and *forth* and *forth* she swung, imagining the gate was taking her to the moon." In **"My Father Was a River"** the narrator describes his mother as "a light woman, quick and evanescent. When she entered a room she had already left it. Her beauty was contained to the point that little of it showed." The narrator describes himself as "a dark child filled with heavy secrets, when the first in a chain of revelations presented itself to me. It was my favorite hour, midnight—that perfect hour when struggling day has been completely devoured, its tail disappearing down the throat of night."

Such sentences can serve to ground Dowell's work imagistically and keep it from floating off into what the writer and editor Bradford Morrow, in the book's postscript, calls a "prose of intense 'breakage.' " Dowell does conduct some less than successful dictional experiments, however. In **"The Silver Swanne,"** a multilayered metafiction, he attempts, quite earnestly it seems, an imitation of an 18th-century literary voice. The protagonist, looking for butter, "found the coolly sweating crock at last in an icy room, a subcellar through which water rapidly and deeply coursed, a monstrously individual springhouse with labyrinths radiating long fluvial veins of impenetrable murk beneath the house and away, whence came the sighing sounds. This chthonian temple, the pantry?" More engaging is **"Writings on a Cave Wall,"** whose narrator is a cannibal:

> I remind me how they divvied up the sticks among us five young ones that day . . . [when] the roots from which our bread was made were as afar and untouchable as stars, and the hunters came at nightfall with bone weariness and increased weakness their sole bag, we ate my sister's pet talking crow that could converse in long phrases like a man, and even parse a sentence. Although ate is

hardly fitting for the feather sucking we children did.

Some of the collection's most beautiful writing is in Dowell's lead story, **"Wool Tea,"** about a young boy in the 1920's who has his first exposure to, among other things, marijuana. It "made him drowsy but it also made him feel as if he was running a high temperature and was drunk on rock and rye, like the time he had whooping cough. Then, like now, his legs had seemed to be as big as houses. The things he looked at wavered like heat over asphalt. All the sounds of the day came to his ears twice."

Because Dowell's prose style is, for better or for worse, impossible to ignore, it is sometimes difficult to apprehend his subjects and themes. Certainly the collection is about houses—the stories are suffused with references to them—houses as embodiments of all personal construction and endeavor: families, love affairs, marriages, works of art. In **"The Silver Swanne,"** the narrator's own ghost story, the house is a rambling seaside "Toll House," a haunted mansion of a haunted soul. In **"Wool Tea"** the protagonist sees his own troubled house as "an endless world like eternity that turned in on itself and spiraled around and around, some parts of it freezing and some parts of it burning and in some parts the possibility of great joy." In **"Writings on a Cave Wall"** the house is quite literally a cave, a grotto of grotesque, into which "things [are] taken squirming and fighting in sacks."

This story is Dowell's most explicit and pessimistic allegory of the scrivener's life, but throughout the collection the literary vocation figures prominently, in dark and disquieting tropes. The creative process seems, for Dowell, a kind of personal Gothic: children pursued, maidens estranged, men left tongueless, limbless, sleepless. Literary work becomes a construction of hidden staircases, secret chambers, a dwelling of cannibals, a house in which persons must die in order simply to leave. These are no casual stories. They are jagged and engulfed in shadow. And they often speak in a slightly mad metafiction, a struggled-for spookiness and dislocation, like that of children playing ghost games—a light held under the chin in the dark, a voice cryptic and surreal—as if desiring to unnerve especially themselves.

> *Lorrie Moore, " 'Down the Throat of Night',"in* The New York Times Book Review, *May 24, 1987, p. 17.*

JOHN KUEHL AND LINDA KANDEL KUEHL

At the time of Coleman Dowell's death on 3 August 1985, his work was known to only a small audience. . . . Now, two years later, there are already signs of a Dowell revival, since . . . [the issue of] a new title, *The Houses of Children,* consisting of thirteen short pieces previously published in *New Directions in Prose and Poetry, AMBIT, Conjunctions* and the *Review of Contemporary Fiction.* The fourteenth, **"Mrs. Hackett,"** is an altered excerpt from *Mrs. October Was Here* (1974). (p. 258)

Except for **"Mrs. Hackett,"** the first eight stories are focused on and narrated through the eyes or in the voices of young males, one a cave dweller and one a mouse! Often we encounter such lonely figures during their awakening to heterosexual, homosexual, and even incestuous urges. These urges, which remain secretive within familial situations, become complex and vivid as a result of psychological insight and lyrical prose. Fittingly, Dowell transmits his primal dramas via rural landscapes. Several of the first eight stories should impress us (e.g., **"Singing in the Clump," "My Father Was a River," "The Moon, The Owl, My Sister"**) but none more so than **"The Great Godalmighty Bird,"** where love between grandson and grandmother is explored. Here, by juxtaposing third- and first-person accounts that view events forty years apart, a self-conscious narrator introduces two important themes: the unreliability of memory and the acceptability of freakishness.

The last six stories differ from the first eight in many ways. Predominantly omniscient tales, their protagonists tend to be paired adults at odds with each other. Cities and small towns replace farms, and symbiotic relationships replace erotic desires. Less lyrical, but more comical, the second group exploits surrealism. Thus, during **"I Envy You Your Great Adventure,"** an obsessed playwright helps dismember his worshipful companion, then deserts him. And, during **"If Beggars Were Horses,"** an abandoned husband, victimized by matriarchy, becomes well again while he wills his estranged wife to grow grotesquely fat. **"The Silver Swanne,"** which Morrow considers Dowell's "greatest work of short fiction," closes *The Houses of Children*. Certainly, this "ghost story" is its longest and most difficult selection, alternating November 1770/1840/1980 sections to show a process of reincarnation spanning three centuries. Preoccupied with death and evil, **"The Silver Swanne,"** like *Island People* (1976), treats house and mind as mirror structures.

Death also serves as a powerful force in the newly issued paperback edition of *One of the Children Is Crying* (1968). Though the first and most conventional of Dowell's novels, it nonetheless prefigures many thematic motifs and structural techniques that compose the rich tapestry of his later stories and novels. An old drafty farmhouse in a desolate winter landscape is the setting for the Christmas reunion of the six McChesney siblings accompanied by their spouses and offspring; however, instead of gathering to celebrate the birth of a savior in the seasonal spirit of love and joy, they have been summoned home to coordinate the funeral preparations for their father, a man who had inspired in his progeny shame, hatred, and awe.

The novel, composed of a tripartite structure respectively labeled "The Gathering," "The Clan," and "The Leavetakings," explores the lives of each of the McChesney children, juxtaposing their traumatic childhood experiences with their contemporary emotional crises. Insanity, incest, homosexual-

ity, alcoholism, adultery, and suicide mark this ill-fated family as it finally is forced to acknowledge both the destructive and redemptive powers of love while laying to rest along with their father the myth of consanguineous unity.

Coleman Dowell referred to *One of the Children Is Crying* as his "fictional farewell" to his own family, [see interview above]. Heralded as a masterpiece by its earliest reviewers, this novel can perhaps serve as a fictional greeting to a new family, those readers unfamiliar with the work of this brilliant and disturbing artist.

Exploring the underside of life with compassion, humor, and honesty, Dowell presents a world in which individual integrity can survive in the face of collective destruction, a world where even the dead help to resurrect the living. Though with his death a courageous and talented voice has been silenced, the increasingly enthusiastic interest in his work, evidenced by the posthumous publication of both stories and novels, is an encouraging sign that he will continue to reach those interested in reading a masterful chronicler of that "poor forked creature" man. (pp. 258-59)

> *John Kuehl and Linda Kandel Kuehl, in a review of " 'The Houses of Children: Collected Stories' and 'One of the Children Is Crying'," in* The Review of Contemporary Fiction, *Vol. 7, No. 3, Fall, 1987, pp. 258-59.*

FURTHER READING

Kuehl, John, and Kuehl, Linda Kandel. "The Achievement of Coleman Dowell: A Bibliographical Essay." *The Review of Contemporary Fiction* 7, No. 3 (Fall 1987): 227-32.

　　Descriptive list of Dowell's complete works, including an overview of notable criticism.

The Review of Contemporary Fiction: Paul Bowles/Coleman Dowell Number 2, No. 3 (Fall 1982): 85-148.

　　Special issue, half of which is devoted to discussion of Dowell's fiction. The magazine collects eleven essays, including an interview by John O'Brien and a character study by Thom Gunn.

Umberto Eco

1932-

Italian scholar, novelist, essayist, and editor.

Eco is a best-selling author of erudite mystery novels that are informed by his scholarly pursuits, which include philosophy, religion, medieval history, and semiotics. In his influential semiological treatises, Eco analyzes the signifying systems through which cultures perceive existence and communicate meaning symbolically. This study of linguistic, aethestic, and quotidian cultural symbols informs Eco's fiction, which often demonstrates the procedural affinity between cosmological inquiry and criminal investigation. Employing and often parodying the conceits of the detective genre, Eco portrays sleuths who decode or create cryptic physical and metaphysical signs, thereby dramatizing semiological theories concerning interpretive processes. His characters represent various religious and philosophical methodologies, through which Eco surveys such manifold disciplines as science, politics, mythology, occultism, and Christianity.

Set in a Benedictine abbey in northern Italy in the year 1327, Eco's first novel, *Il nome della rosa* (*The Name of the Rose*), is both an elaborately detailed medieval detective drama and a semiotic novel of ideas. When several monks are murdered in a sequence that echoes biblical prophecies of the Apocalypse, Brother William of Baskerville is summoned to apply his enlightened deductive powers to solve the mystery. From this central scenario, Eco creates an antinomy between the modern values of rationality and humor, represented by William, and the superstition and severity of the Middle Ages, as embodied by Jorge de Burgos, the blind and aged guardian of the abbey's labyrinthine library. A maze of literal and metaphoric possibilities and obstacles, the library conceals the key to the mystery—a collection of heretical texts considered so incendiary that their discovery prompts several murders. William's search for truth is confounded by dogmatic authorities, including officials of the Inquisition, and this conflict reflects differences between modern humanism and absolute submission to the Church. Critics lauded Eco's ingenious plot and challenging intellectual discourse. Franco Ferrucci observed: "The narrative impulse that commands the story is irresistible. That is no mean feat for a book in which many pages describe ecclesiastical councils or theological debates . . . Yet Mr. Eco's delight in his narrative does not fail to touch the reader." Despite its occasionally cerebral tone and frequent Latin quotations, *The Name of the Rose* achieved widespread international popularity and was adapted for film in 1983.

In *Il pendolo di Foucault* (*Foucault's Pendulum*), Eco extends the scope of his metaphysical study to include many of the historical and religious mysteries of the last two millenia. Although the novel revolves around a seedy publishing house in contemporary Milan, it examines mystical phenomena from Stonehenge to the Crusaders' Jerusalem to exotic rituals in modern Brazil. Three editors involved in publishing texts that deal with occultism and esoteric practices are supplied a spurious manuscript by a man they believe is a charlatan. The man disappears a few days later and is presumed to have been murdered for divulging cultic secrets. Pondering the

manuscript, which declares that the medieval Knights Templar discovered a mystical energy source of devastating power known only to initiates, the editors playfully construct an extravagant conspiracy theory. With the aid of a computer and some quixotic analogies, they create a 600-year long web of arcane correlations linking the Templars' secret to the motives of such historical figures as the Benedictines, Marx, Freud, and Hitler. As they reinterpret most of human history to fit their theoretical matrix, the three editors begin to believe their own fabrication and, as ardent occultists learn of the secret, esoteric extrapolation precipitates murder and human sacrifice. Reviewers offered widely divergent interpretations of the novel which, while it follows the myriad twists of the editors' ruminations, finally condemns their illogical folly. Some critics denounced Eco's allusive style as laborious, encyclopedic, and inappropriate for the novelistic form. Salman Rushdie remarked: "[*Foucault's Pendulum*] is humourless, devoid of character, entirely free of anything resembling a credible spoken word, and mind-numbingly full of gobbledygook of all sorts." Other reviewers, however, extolled Eco's metaphysical inquiry. Joseph Coates commented: "[Eco's] plot can be read as a metaphor for modern science or for the whole manipulative arrogance of Western thought (as opposed to the message of Eastern religions) according to which man must master and exploit nature—and ultimately destroy it. With this book, Eco puts himself in the grand and acerbic tradition of Petronius, Rabelais, Swift and Voltaire."

Eco is also a popular newspaper and magazine columnist, and several of his essays concerning American culture are collected in *Travels in Hyperreality*.

(See also *CLC*, Vol. 28; *Contemporary Authors*, Vols. 77-80; and *Contemporary Authors New Revision Series*, Vol. 12)

PRINCIPAL WORKS

NOVELS

Il nome della rosa   1980
   [*The Name of the Rose,* 1983]
Il pendolo di Foucault   1989
   [*Foucault's Pendulum,* 1989]

OTHER

Il problema estetico in san Tommaso   1956   (criticism)
   [also published as *Il problema estetico in Tommaso d'Aquino,* 1970]
Opera aperta: forma e indeterminazione nelle poetiche con-temporanee   (criticism)   1962
   [*The Open Work,* 1989]
Trattato di semiotica generale   1975
   [*A Theory of Semiotics,* 1976]
Lector in fabula: La cooperazione interpretative nei testi nar-rativa   1979
   [*The Role of the Reader: Explorations in the Semiotics of Texts,* 1979]
Semiotics and the Philosophy of Language   1984
Sign of the Three: Dupin, Holmes, Peirce [editor with T. Se-beok] (essays)   1984
Travels in Hyperreality   (essays)   1986

STUART KLAWANS

Publishers' notions of economic prudence guard our nation from foreign opinions more efficiently than even the McCar-ran-Walter Act. Were it not for the success of Umberto Eco's one novel, **The Name of the Rose** . . . , we could hardly ex-pect to see this collection of Eco's journalism in our bookstores. . . .

The pieces collected [in **Travels in Hyperreality**] are Eco's off-the-cuff public reflections, most of them from the 1970s, a continuation of his academic work rather than an exception to it. **"Travels in Hyperreality,"** the longest essay in the book and the one put up front presumably as most attractive to Americans, is an amused disquisition on certain tendencies in our mass culture. Another half-dozen articles report on the United States, or at least make extended reference to it. This, I think, is more than crafty editorial selection. Eco's scholarly career often draws him away from Bologna to New York, New Haven and Bloomington, Indiana; his semiotics has as its point of origin not so much Ferdinand de Saussure's Gene-va as the Harvard of C. S. Peirce. Indeed, Eco goes so far as to boast in one of his essays that he was the first on his block

to wear blue jeans. His opinions may not be so foreign after all—merely cosmopolitan.

That said, one must join Eco (who is writing explicitly for "cultivated," perhaps Americanized, Europeans and for "Europeanized Americans") and admit that the America he discovers is wondrous and strange indeed. Venturing out of the university towns, out of the big cities' islands of cosmo-politan culture, he finds that the real America is far from the land he once summarized as "the home of glass-and-steel sky-scrapers and of abstract expressionism." "You have only to go beyond the Museum of Modern Art and the art galleries," he writes, "and you enter another universe, the preserve of the average family, the tourist, the politician." Here is an America "obsessed with realism," and with more than real-ism. It is the America of the Lyndon B. Johnson Memorial in Austin, Texas, of the Movieland Wax Museum in Buena Park, California, of Forest Lawn Cemetery and Ripley's Be-lieve It or Not! museums, of William Randolph Hearst's San Simeon, of Santa Claus Village, Disneyland, Marine World and Oral Roberts's broadcasts.

Here America displays for itself its ideas of art, architecture, history, nature and religion in representations that "must be absolutely iconic, a perfect likeness, a 'real' copy of the reality being represented. . . . The American imagination demands the real thing and, to attain it, must fabricate the absolute fake." This is what Eco calls hyperreality—for example, the three-dimensional wax reproduction of Leonardo's *Last Sup-per.* (In his tireless researches, Eco visited no fewer than seven of these, and that was just on his way from San Francis-co to Los Angeles.)

With a botanist's exactitude, Eco distinguishes the species of the hyperreal. Some specimens, like the L. B. J. Memorial, remind him of Superman's Fortress of Solitude at the North Pole: "Everything that has happened in his adventurous life is recorded here in perfect copies or preserved in a miniatur-ized form of the original." And just so, the L. B. J. Memorial displays *everything,* from honeymoon snapshots and a chunk of moon rock to a full-scale (and hyperreally immaculate) replica of the Oval Office. Then there are the Enchanted Cas-tles, like San Simeon, where the visitor is distressed by "the fear of being caught up by this jungle of venerable beauties. . . . It is like making love in a confessional with a prostitute dressed in a prelate's liturgical robes reciting Bau-delaire while ten electronic organs reproduce the Well-Tempered Clavier played by Scriabin." (p. 666)

[Eco] refuses merely to sneer at American hyperreality. He laughs—it would make a cow laugh, as Huck Finn put it— but he also admits that "our journey into the Absolute Fake" goes beyond "irony and sophisticated repulsion," and raises some difficult questions. Chief among them is, How can a so-ciety regain contact with the past?

It is greatly to Eco's credit that he poses the question. His an-swer, though, disappoints. He wants to avoid "second-hand Frankfurt school moralism," he says, and yet that's precisely what he delivers, concluding that hyperreality serves to make us all docile consumers. Well, sure. Nor is **"Travels in Hyper-reality"** the only essay that proceeds from enticing observa-tions to a somewhat banal climax. For all his learning and acuity, Eco often performs better as an entertainer than as an analyst.

What's missing from **Travels in Hyperreality** is reality it-self—that is, ordinary, day-to-day reality. (In an era of semio-

ECO

CONTEMPORARY LITERARY CRITICISM, Vol. 60

tics and deconstruction, one uses the term with some shame, but how else to proceed?) Granted, any social critic working at a certain level of abstraction must gloss over mundane details, yet semiotics, I think, takes a special pleasure in making common reality disappear. The mundane shows up only for the sake of turning into the symbolic, and the symbolic soon goes up in a puff of smoke.

Eco is adept at such disappearing acts; in fact, they are one of his characteristic gestures. *The Name of the Rose* begins and ends with the disappearance of a manuscript. What's more (and I hope I'm not giving away too much of the plot) the solution of the tale's mystery comes about through the disappearance of the solution. This, as the old leftists said, is no accident. In the latest book, to take a trivial example, Eco argues that a sports-mad society, by piling commentary on top of reportage on top of obsessive viewing, arrives at the point where "sport as practice, as activity, no longer exists." And sport does vanish in Eco's term, yet I can assure the alarmed reader that Michael Jordan is out there all the same.

Similar dodges keep cropping up, most disturbingly in Eco's political essays. Many of them relate to the Red Brigades' actions, arguing quite skillfully and justly that the brigadiers behaved as if the political system were run by a top-hatted, pinkie-ringed man with a cigar in one hand and a bag of money in the other. There is, of course, a political system, Eco says, and it does operate according to a plan. But the plan "is no longer intentional, and therefore it cannot be criticized with the traditional criticism of intentions." Rather, one needs a model of power as a pervasive network of relationships, symbolic in character, living "thanks to thousands of forms of minute or 'molecular' consensus."

The image comes from Foucault. Eco develops it by distinguishing this internal, symbolic power from force, which is external and specific. But now comes the disappearing act. Once the idea of physical coercion has been spirited away from that of power, the relationship between them is left unexamined, so that it too might vanish by neglect. Might political activity itself—apart from the necessary and pleasant act of criticism—disappear as well? (pp. 666,668)

Whatever the strategy of each essay, common reality always seems a little slippery in Eco's writing. . . . Eco's visit to hyperreality follows various Houdini turns and is followed by still more. They're entertaining, granted; but that's a sign of Eco's complicity, his participation in designing his own wax museum Inferno. In his travels, Eco often came upon certificates by so-called European authorities attesting that the fakes on view were authentic copies. In his essay on hyperreality, Eco serves a similar function. The cosmopolitan reader feels free to laugh precisely because Eco's unimpeachable academic rigor guarantees that the laughter is sanctioned.

But who's the joke on? (p. 669)

Stuart Klawans, "The Disappearing Act," in The Nation, *New York, Vol. 242, No. 18, May 10, 1986, pp. 666, 668-69.*

GEORGE GARRETT

"Reports From the Global Village"—falling roughly halfway through the sequence of essays and articles which Umberto Eco has gathered together under the general title *Travels in Hyperreality*—the wily and witty Italian philosopher, histo-

rian, semiotician and author of the best-selling novel, *The Name of the Rose,* offers a surprising proposition: "All the professors of theory of communications, trained by the texts of twenty years ago (this includes me), should be pensioned off." Mr. Eco is only kidding, of course; and the reader who has followed him that far knows it instantly, being already experienced in the rhetorical stances, several kinds of ambiguity and stylistic fun and games Mr. Eco employs to consider almost everything under the sun—holography, wax museums, **"The Return of the Middle Ages,"** Superman and *Casablanca,* Federico Fellini and Michelangelo Antonioni, the survival of ancient African religious sects and cults in contemporary Brazil, Jim Jones and his murderous temple, the Red Brigades and terrorism in general, Marshall McLuhan and Charles Manson, Woody Allen and St. Thomas Aquinas, the social and personal implications of snug-fitting blue jeans and the secret meaning of spectator sports.

Nothing if not self-reflexive, Mr. Eco establishes early that he knows what he is up to and is sympathetic with what the reader has to put up with. Speaking of the experience of American wax museums, he says: "When you see Tom Sawyer immediately after Mozart or you enter the cave of *The Planet of the Apes* after having witnessed the Sermon on the Mount with Jesus and the Apostles, the logical distinction between Real World and Possible Worlds has been definitively undermined." Some readers might conceivably react by taking comfort or cover in the multiple styles—from podium academic to vernacular buck-and-wing, expertly and gracefully rendered, revised from other translations, into the living American lingo by the virtuoso William Weaver—Mr. Eco uses to play his games and at the same time to touch on some big and serious problems. But he poses a question which ought to warn us against taking any purely esthetic approach to this work: "Is stylistic evidence valid in establishing what is the 'right' meaning of the *Iliad* or whether Bo Derek is more desirable than Sigourney Weaver?" . . .

Because Mr. Eco is very adroit and civilized, and very Italian, he overcomes the considerable handicap of being (as he boldly and naïvely claims) a bona fide European intellectual. We are spared heaping servings of French ennui and the regimented dialectic of the Germans. Because he has great charm and a light heart (and knows about the American convention of the pie-in-the-face) we are likewise spared the heavyweight facticity of, say, Harold Bloom or the intricate songs and sorrows of Susan Sontag. There is indeed a lot of fun to be found in these explorations of appearance and reality, fact and fiction, sign and symbol.

There is one minor flaw, at least for this sympathetic reader. Like many another good European, Mr. Eco just can't resist taking a series of ritual and routine cheap shots at America and Americans. However, since most of these are firmly based on inaccuracy and stereotypical misapprehensions, they don't hurt much. Our own poet of signs and symbols, Robert Frost, made the American case once and for all in "Mowing," one of his earliest and most subtle poems—"The fact is the sweetest dream that labor knows." Mr. Eco isn't serious enough in his anti-Americanism to bother to get all his facts right and in a row. Meantime, he must know well enough that nobody was ever ignored or went broke by making fun of the Americans. Good luck to him.

George Garrett, "Semioticians Have More Fun," in The New York Times Book Review, *July 27, 1986, p. 7.*

JOHN UPDIKE

The general essays of *Travels in Hyperreality* verge, some of them, on the linguistically technical, and some on the fadingly topical, but the best of them recall the jeux d'esprit of the late Roland Barthes in his journalistic, foreward-writing mode. Eco does not quite convince us, however, as did Barthes, that he is in possession of a wholly new tool of perception, a cerebral instrument that by a quick process of reduction and reassembly gives familiar and commonplace matters a bright, freshly facetted aspect. Barthes had something of the puckish perverse, the smirk of the true provocateur, whereas Eco is relatively benign and earnest—he is the plump, cigarette-puffing tutor who sits across from us at his littered desk and gently conveys the rueful truth that our honors thesis would be much better if he could only write it himself. . . .

As an essayist, Eco has two strengths, two areas where he is unusually knowledgeable and therefore especially interesting: the Middle Ages, upon which *The Name of the Rose* was an animated disquisition, and the New World, where he is a well-acclimated tourist. The title essay, the longest in this collection, ranges across the United States in search of instances of the native appetite for "the real thing" (to quote the Coca-Cola commercial) and (to quote many another) "more." Realer than real are Disneyland, Forest Lawn, the Movieland Wax Museum, Old Bethpage Village on Long Island (where changes in sheep produced by breeders flaw the otherwise perfect reconstruction of an early-nineteenth-century farm), and three-dimensional wax versions of Leonardo's *Last Supper.* . . . In the Palace of Living Arts in Buena Park, for five dollars the dumbfounded tourist could (until 1982, when the Palace closed) view colored wax reproductions of famous marble statues like Michelangelo's *David* and the *Venus de Milo* (her arms considerably restored) and 3-D travesties of such celebrity paintings as the *Mona Lisa,* Ingres's *Grande Odalisque,* and Thomas Lawrence's *Pinkie,* complete with a concealed fan that stirred her silk dress. This bold, if not commercially successful, attempt to bring closer to the American citizenry the wonders of European culture—"the fetishization of art as a sequence of famous objects"—is brother, Eco suggests, to such massive conglomerate appropriations as Hearst's San Simeon and the Ringlings' Venetian palazzo Ca' d'Zan in Sarasota; thence to the Getty Museum, with its authentic masterworks in a re-created Roman villa, is a short, if tastefully trodden, step. Eco is not insensitive to the pathos of our vulgar homages, the "something disarming about this search for glory via an unrequited love for the European past," nor quite unmindful of Old World wax museums and reliquaries that also strive for what might be called hyperreality. He takes a dainty philosophical delight in the paradoxes of such marriages of the synthetic and the actual as ecologically-minded zoos and marine parks where "Nature has almost been regained, and yet it is erased by artifice precisely so that it can be presented as uncontaminated nature," and artificial Old West towns whose fake shops sell actual goods for real money. In the entertainment industry, he tells us, "when there is a sign it seems there isn't one, and when there isn't one we believe that there is. The condition of pleasure is that something be faked." He leaves few semiotic nuances of our recreational fakery unravelled. . . . (p. 70)

[An] American native, becoming the object of so lively and amused an anthropology, grows, like anthropologically considered natives the world over, rather restive with possible objections, such as that most of the hyperreal sites Eco surveyed are to a great extent aimed at the entertainment and edification of children. More than once, for light on our essence, he draws upon comic strips, with which he shows an encyclopedic acquaintance. . . . Eco's tour begins with an exhilarating prospectus—"There is. . . . an America of furious hyperreality, which is not that of Pop Art, of Mickey Mouse, or of Hollywood movies. There is another, more secret America (or rather, just as public, but snubbed by the European visitor and also by the American intellectual). . . . It has to be discovered"—but ends on a sour, somewhat Marxist note:

> The ideology of this America wants to establish reassurance through Imitation. But profit defeats ideology, because the consumers want to be thrilled not only by the guarantee of the Good but also by the shudder of the Bad. . . . Thus, on entering his cathedrals of iconic reassurance, the visitor will remain uncertain whether his final destiny is hell or heaven, and so will consume new promises.

Semiology, the study of signification born from the semantic theories of Ferdinand de Saussure, is limited, as a tool of cultural analysis, by its necessary focus on propaganda—that is, the loading of discourse, visual or auditory, with messages of salesmanship and social reassurance. . . . In **"Striking at the Heart of the System,"** Eco concludes that the terrorists' mythology, which he couches in rather recondite comic-strip terms—"their Disney-like mythology, in which on one side there was a wicked individual capitalist named Uncle Scrooge and on the other the Beagle Boys, a cheating rabble, true, but with a certain charge of crazy amiability because they stole, to the tunes of proletarian confiscation, from the stingy, egotistical capitalist"—has become obsolete, because Uncle Scrooge has gone multinational, and "the system" is now "headless and heartless." As such, it displays "an incredible capacity for healing and stabilizing," and "manages things in such a way that, except for the inevitable outsiders, everybody has something to lose in a situation of generalized terrorism." Eco, reading the signs, takes comfort in the conclusion that power has become unlocatably diffused. . . . In **"Language, Power, Force,"** citing Barthes, Georges Duby, and Michel Foucault, Eco proposes that power in today's world is, like language, subject to many small adjustments but never to revolution; change expresses itself as "progressive adjustment through slow, marginal shifts, in a centerless universe where all is margin and there is no longer any 'heart' of anything."

Our world, Eco believes, resembles the medieval world, with its intricate and shifting alliances between clergy and nobility, clergy and populace, national monarchies and monastic orders. The barons of multinational capitalism are observed "to medievalize their territory, with fortified castles and great residential complexes with private guards and photoelectric cells." Fantasy fiction and movies are riding a "neomedieval wave," and this nostalgia, the essay **"Living in the New Middle Ages"** explains, is really a search for self-understanding, as we traverse our post-imperial landscape of personal insecurity, wandering thieves and mystics, plagues and massacres, monastery-like university campuses, and a gaudy artistic culture pasted together from the flotsam of the past. . . . Eco's belief—easier to entertain, perhaps, in semi-anarchic, picturesque Italy than on the tame plains of the United States—that we are living in a new Middle Ages gave urgency and weight to his fourteenth-century novel, and a "coded" quality that added to its detective-story pleasures. These essays, too, take life from his historical passion. . . . But our neomedieval world is also the global village of mass communication, and Eco takes as topics pop songs, *Casablanca, 2001,* how to trick the phone company and how "the system" builds such technological thievery into its balance sheets, and the procedure whereby interest in sports becomes interest in media discourse upon sports: "Born as the raising to the nth power of that initial (and rational) waste that is sports recreation, sports chatter is the glorification of Waste, and therefore the maximum point of Consumption. On it and in it the consumer civilization man actually consumes himself."

In this self-consuming, heartless society of all margin, communication becomes an end in itself, a kind of floating brain without central content. The international exposition, as exemplified in Montreal's Expo '67, builds on communicatory style pure and simple. "A country no longer says, 'Look what I produce' but 'Look how smart I am in presenting what I produce.' . . . Each country shows itself by the way in which it is able to present the same thing other countries could also present. The prestige game is won by the country that best tells what it does, independently of what it actually does." . . . The show per se, rather than the thing shown, matters more and more, whether the topic is sports discourse replacing sports, guerrilla publicity-seeking, or "the levels of institutional cultural showmanship that have been reached in the United States." These essays, shaped by the semiotician's interest in secondary meanings, have an air of removal that consorts awkwardly with their occasional reflex of Marxist terminology—e.g., "He [a visitor to a trade fair] has only accepted his role as consumer of consumer goods since he cannot be a proprietor of means of production." The Marxism of Western European intellectuals must itself be taken as a sign, a bit of plumage whereby they recognize each other, since surely with the dismal example of Eastern Europe next door they can't want to turn Italy into Rumania, or France into China. Marx imagined that the world in its true workings, in the structure of its layered power, could be analyzed and then actually altered; Umberto Eco's reflections, generally amusing and often brilliant, glint off the surfaces of processes simultaneously elusive, inexorable, and feather-light. "Machines for communicating," as Eco says of clothes, make up the human world, a shell of sheer significations like a suit of armor with nothing in it. Such a suit, in the delightful fable *The Nonexistent Knight,* by Eco's fellow-countryman Italo Calvino, walks and fights and falls in love; but can there truly, we who are inside the world must ask, be nothing at all inside? (pp. 70-2)

John Updike, "Ecolalia," in The New Yorker, *Vol. LXII, No. 26, August 18, 1986, pp. 70-2.*

HERBERT MITGANG

The Name of the Rose, a murder mystery, was set in a medieval monastery in northern Italy and featured an English sleuth named William of Baskerville. *Foucault's Pendulum* is less of a detective story and more of a metaphysical study of the search for an answer to some of the religious and historical mysteries of mankind during the last two millennia. It is set in modern Milan, Paris and Brazil and reaches back to Stonehenge and Crusader Jerusalem. This time Mr. Eco's narrator, named Casaubon, keeps asking himself how Sam Spade would solve the mystery. An inside joke lurks behind every Eco bush; in George Eliot's *Middlemarch,* Casaubon is an elderly pedant writing a key to all the mythologies.

Foucault's Pendulum is a quest novel that is deeper and richer than *The Name of the Rose.* It's a brilliant piece of research and writing—experimental and funny, literary and philosophical—that bravely ignores the conventional expectations of the reader. Mr. Eco . . . seems to be having the best time of all. He throws in just about everything in his head and library—in Latin, French, Italian, German, Hebrew and computerese. In fact, a computer plays an important role in advancing the plot.

Since Mr. Eco is a semiotician—one who interprets the meaning of signs and symbols—he shouldn't mind too much if I call him an academic conjurer more than a novelist. His new novel reads as if it was written by the most popular lecturer on campus with the instincts of a Catskill Mountains tummler who keeps the one-liners coming so the guests won't check out on a rainy weekend. . . .

The truest and shortest sentence in the novel reads: "I digress."

And yet despite the many false alarms and diversions in *Foucault's Pendulum,* on almost every page Mr. Eco comes up with some fresh notion or turn of phrase that displays his original mind. He describes the Mona Lisa as "an androgynous Medusa only for esthetes." The Crusaders were adventurers who went to Jerusalem because it was "sort of the California of the day, the place you went to make your fortune." The wide boulevards of Paris were designed not for esthetic reasons but to trap anti-government rioters. The main activity of book publishers is "losing manuscripts."

Foucault's Pendulum, in case you were wondering, does have a plot. It centers on the effort by three editors in a Milan publishing house to discover the meaning of a coded message from the Knights Templar, who were once so rich and powerful in Europe that they posed a threat to kings and popes. Before they were forcibly disbanded after being accused of sorcery and homosexuality, the Templars went underground and passed along a secret document on harnessing magnetic currents. By placing the document under a pendulum invented by Jean Bernard Léon Foucault, the 19th-century French physicist, they could supposedly find the navel of the earth and thus rule men and nations. The novel begins in an old abbey church in Paris, part of a complex that actually holds Foucault's pendulum.

The coded message has been given to the editors in a manuscript by a certain retired colonel with an Adolphe Menjou mustache who wants to write a book. The colonel disappears, the victim of outside forces known as "They." But the editors press on, feeding information into their computer, which is named Abulafia, after the medieval Jewish cabalist. Among other discoveries, the Protocols of Zion are proved to be falsehoods. The printouts from Abulafia (Abu for short) provide information to interpret the manuscript. Does it contain real secrets—or is it only a Crusader laundry list?

Once the reader gets on the Eco carousel—going around in circles but never quite catching the brass ring because the author is too honest or too clever to have a cheap reward waiting at the end of the ride—it's hard to get off. Mr. Eco may be leaving a number of different impressions: about zealots, overambition, false prophets, the illusion of rationality, the cancer of the spirit, governmental deception and dictatorship, the bounties of the natural world—provide your own interpretation.

Whichever, after a ziggurat of ideas in 120 challenging chapters, in the spirit of **Foucault's Pendulum** I'm inclined to say:

Ecco Eco! Bravo Mickey! Bravo Eco!

Herbert Mitgang, "Inside Jokes from the Knights Templar to Snoopy," in The New York Times, October 11, 1989, p. C21.

SALMAN RUSHDIE

[In the 1960s] the bookshops seemed to be full of volumes with titles like *Illuminatus,* in which it was suggested that the world was run by this or that occult conspiracy. . . .

The only writer who ever managed to transmute the base metal of the illuminatus-novel into art was Thomas Pynchon, who succeeded in making the necessary connections between the occult and political worlds, and who constructed a rich metaphorical framework in which two opposed groups of ideas struggled for textual and global supremacy. . . .

Pynchon once wrote a short story called "Under the Rose," its title an Englishing of the Latin 'sub rosa'. **Foucault's Pendulum,** the obese new volume from Umberto Eco, . . . is an illuminatus-novel for the end of the Eighties, a post-modernist conspiracy fiction about, I suppose, the world under the name of the rose. It is, I regret to report, a very faint Eco indeed of those old Pynchonian high jinks. It is humourless, devoid of character, entirely free of anything resembling a credible spoken word, and mind-numbingly full of gobbledygook of all sorts. Reader: I hated it.

The plot of **Foucault's Pendulum** (which begins on page 367 of this 629-page book) is surprisingly uncomplicated. Three weird publishers, Belbo, Diotallevi and Casaubon ('wasn't he a character in *Middlemarch?*'), are employees of a two-faced publishing house, Garamond/Manutius, whose visible Garamond face is that of a straight, upmarket company, but whose true Manutius nature is that of a vanity press for self-financing authors ('SFAs'). Tired of the endless stream of cranky manuscripts about Templars and Rosicrucians and such-like twaddle, our three heroes decide to make up the ultimate conspiracy theory, their own private totalisation of occult knowledge. Their inventions, the bad fiction within this fiction, are fed into a computer named Abulafia after a medieval Jewish cabbalist. Then, in a ridiculously melodramatic finale involving the eponymous Pendulum (no relation, incidentally, to the philosopher) and massed hordes of crazed mystics, the fictional Plan starts to come true . . . Edgar Allan Poe is among the myriad references in this book, but it doesn't help. This Pendulum is the pits.

It's just possible that, inside this whale, there's an enjoyable smaller fish trying to get out. The unscrupulous world of the vanity press and the fleecing of its feeble authors is depicted with some verve, and there are moments when the ponderous narrative sparks into life. But the spark is instantly snuffed out, buried under page after page of Higher Bullshit. Here is a typical paragraph:

> So those are the Massalians, also known as Stratiotics and Phibionites, or Barbelites, who are made up of Nasseans and Phemionites. But for other fathers of the church, the Barbelites were latter-day

Gnostics . . . and their initiates in turn called the Borborites Hylics, or Children of Matter, as distinct from the Psychics, who were already a step up, and the Pneumatics, who were the truly elect . . . But maybe the Stratiotics were only the Hylics of the Mithraists. 'Sounds a bit confused,' Belbo said.

And this is what passes for dialogue: ' "Are you saying I'm superficial?" "No . . . what others call profundity is only a tesseract, a four-dimensional cube." '

Eco, the consummate postmodernist, is perfectly aware of all possible criticisms of his text, and lets us know that he knows. 'We're talking in stereotypes here,' one of the characters astutely obverves. And 'Maybe only cheap fiction gives us the measure of reality,' Belbo muses. That's Eco hinting that he intends to play deliberately with the form of the penny dreadful. And, because he is enough of an intellectual to know that hokum is hokum, he has not written an 'innocent' late-Sixties illuminatus novel but a 'knowing' version, a fiction about the creation of a piece of junk fiction that then turns knowingly into that piece of junk fiction. **Foucault's Pendulum** is not a novel. It is a computer game.

One way of playing it is to spot the references. Apart from Pynchon, *Middlemarch* and Poe, there are touches of *The Maltese Falcon, Raiders of the Lost Ark, Ghostbusters, The Lord of the Rings* (Belbo/Bilbo), *Gone With the Wind, The Magus,* 007, and a classic SF story called "The Nine Billion Names of God." There are also political references to the radical turmoil of Italy in the Seventies, but, unlike Pynchon, Eco fails to make the connections work. And at the very end, in Casaubon's conclusion ('I have understood. And the certainty that there is nothing to understand should be my peace, my triumph.'), there's more than a touch of the ancient Japanese poet Basho who travelled to the seat of wisdom, the Deep North, to learn that there was nothing to learn there.

Unfortunately, the journey to this truth is so turgid that it's impossible to care about reaching the goal. This is Spielbergery without action or bullwhips, and if, as Anthony Burgess threatens on the jacket, 'this is the way the European novel is going,' we should all catch a bus in the opposite direction as soon as possible.

Salman Rushdie, "Cabbalistic Babble and Gobbledygook," in The Observer, October 15, 1989, p. 49.

ROBERT IRWIN

I cannot remember which novelist it was who remarked, 'When in doubt what to write next, have some character come through the door quoting great chunks from some obscure hermetic text.' Whoever it was, Umberto Eco has obviously taken his advice to heart. The result is that his second novel, **Foucault's Pendulum,** reads like *Raiders of the Lost Ark* with all the action sequences taken out (leaving Indiana Jones peacefully sitting in his university office, sorting through his file cards and going through his lecture notes to prepare a lengthy and learned paper on the locations of the Ark of the Covenant and the Holy Grail).

The plot, which thinly trickles through the novel, begins with Jacopo Casaubon in the Paris Conservatoire des Arts et Métiers, a 13th-century church which has been turned into a museum of technology. After some rapt contemplation of Foucault's pendulum (an instrument designed to demonstrate the diurnal motion of the earth) 'the still point of a turning world' in this crazy book, Casaubon goes off to hide himself in one of the exhibits, a box with a convenient periscope.

Why is Casaubon spending the night in a box with a periscope in a museum of scientific instruments? A flashback explains all. The flashback runs for over 500 pages, taking in flashbacks within flashbacks on the way. (pp. 25-6)

There are, it is true, some inspired and amusing set pieces on, for instance, the cosmic significance of the proportions of a newspaper kiosk; on the Cabalistic Tree of Sephiroth considered as if it were a motor car made by Fiat; and on the decoding of a medieval laundry list. But more often Eco's humour seems forced, the joshing inserted to lighten the load of exposition. An earnest lecture on Rosicrucianism, in chapter 30, is not made less wearisome by punctuating it with a bit of bedroom slap and tickle, and Eco's ironies have given enough delight after a few hundred pages.

The novel is, as the phrase goes, richly allusive, but allusions to more exciting fiction like Poe's *The Gold Bug,* Meyrink's *The Golem,* Sue's *The Mysteries of Paris* and Dumas's *The Count of Monte Cristo* are only likely to remind the reader of what he or she is missing in *Foucault's Pendulum.*

Eco's novel is a *roman à thèse.* Considered as a romance it is pretty dismal. As a thesis, a new kind of thought experiment, however, it is much more interesting. In *Semiotics and the Philosophy of Language* (1984), Eco wrote about the Cabalistic way of interpretation as 'the very play of deconstruction' in which the 'ultimate truth is that the text is a mere play of differences and displacements'. Every reader can make his own.

Foucault's Pendulum presents history as an open book to be creatively reinterpreted. The ludicrous researches of Casaubon, Belbo and Diotallevi have been used to demonstrate how the world can be remapped, by ditching positivism and modern ideas of verifiability. 'The Three Musketeers' employ various forms of paralogic or pseudo-rationality. By reasoning in defective similes and making heavy use of analogy and appeals to dubious but mutually supportive authorities, they can make anything connect with anything, the Druids with nuclear energy, Count Cagliostro with Adolf Hitler and the ley lines with James Joyce. The paranoid model of reality they come up with is really a Fascist one.

All this should be of considerable interest to semioticians, sociologists and historians of ideas. *Foucault's Pendulum* shows an interesting thinker working on interesting material, but a novel is not the ideal vehicle for these strange and original meditations. (p. 26)

Robert Irwin, "Signs and Wonders," in The Listener, *Vol. 122, No. 3136, October 19, 1989, pp. 25-6.*

JOSEPH COATES

[In *Foucault's Pendulum,* Eco] looks at what happens to the residual need to believe that afflicts people who can no longer find anything to believe in. And he uses his findings to diagnose the madness that has led Western man to the point of killing himself because, like the victim in a spy thriller, he knows too much.

The name of the narrator is the first hint of this. Casaubon, studying philology in Milan during the revolutionary student unrest of the early 1970s, does indeed share his name with "a character in *Middlemarch,*" as a character in this novel notices. But his real ancestor, unmentioned in the text, is more likely the scholar Meric Casaubon, who in 1656 published a skeptical look at ecstatic religious belief in his "Treatise Concerning Enthusiasm; As it is an Effect of Nature: but is Mistaken by Many for either Divine Inspiration, or Diabolical Possession"—a book that helped Swift hone the satiric edge of "A Tale of a Tub" and that relates pointedly to Eco's farrago of religious and diabolical fanaticism.

Casaubon, though he is an unbeliever immune to "credulity," to being "borne away by a passion of the mind," is nevertheless "looking for an honorable faith" and is incurably curious about the '70s' epidemic of belief—in occultism, in revolution, in movements of all kinds. In the course of his search he meets Jacopo Belbo, editor of a small scholarly press who has a desperate "hunger for the absolute" while sharing Casaubon's inability to find a cause or belief worthy of credence.

Belbo admits to Casaubon that he's looking for something that corresponds to "the only fixed point of the universe"—the geometrical point from which, supposedly, Foucault's pendulum swings to prove the rotation of the Earth. Belbo, a fascinating characterization, is a man who lives at one remove from his life: a warrior born just too late for World War II and just too early for the revolution, an aspiring writer who instead edits, a lover platonically bound to a flagrantly unfaithful mistress.

His assistant, Diotallevi, represents a third variety of modern religious experience in his irrational belief, against all evidence, that he's Jewish. It's possible that Eco is playfully paralleling this trio with the three allegorical passengers in Swift's tub (who stood for the Catholic, Anglican and dissenting Protestant churches of 18th Century England): three honest attempts at faith in what critic Nicola Chiaramonte calls "an age of bad faith."

At any rate, Eco excels at showing how these stances implicate the three of them willy-nilly in lunacies that none of them takes seriously for a minute. Belbo calls in Casaubon to check out a tome asserting that a plot allegedly begun by the Knights Templar in 1307 is nearing fruition in the year 2000.

The apparent murder and disappearance of its author tends to confirm his loony belief that neo-Templars are out to silence him by any means; and soon details from his book materialize in all kinds of places. When Belbo's publisher, who also runs a posh vanity-press scam, decides to tap this market for madness, the deluge really begins. . . .

The editors' lethal danger begins not because they begin to believe in this stuff, but because it—and a few of its murderously sincere followers—begins to believe in them, and to imagine that Belbo and his computer have a real fix on what followers of the Plan seek: a pipeline to the knowledge that will make them Masters of the World.

And in a way these fanatics prove themselves right; as Casaubon notes, Belbo's "enthusiasm for the Plan came from his ambition to write a book," which his computer at last freed him to do. "No matter if the book were made entirely of errors, intentional, deadly errors. . . . [T]he moment you pick up the clay, electronic or otherwise, you become a demiurge, and he who embarks on the creation of worlds is already tainted with corruption and evil."

Foucault's Pendulum is Eco's magical mystery tour of the Western mind, or at least the paranoid part of it that "can't endure the thought that the world was born by chance, by mistake," as Casaubon's girlfriend Lia says, "just because four brainless atoms bumped into one another on a slippery highway. So a cosmic plot has to be found—Gods, angels, devils."

The book isolates man's mad tendency to look outside himself for revelation that can be found only in the kind of interior, mystical belief Casaubon achieves at the end, as he serenely awaits his executioners.

The Templar/Rosicrucian/Masters of the World plot can be read as a metaphor for modern science or for the whole manipulative arrogance of Western thought (as opposed to the message of the Eastern religions) according to which man must master and exploit nature—and ultimately destroy it.

With this book, Eco puts himself in the grand and acerbic tradition of Petronius, Rabelais, Swift and Voltaire, as does his conclusion:

"I have come to believe that the whole world is an enigma, a harmless enigma that is made terrible by our own mad attempt to interpret it as though it had an underlying truth."

Joseph Coates, "Believing in Belief," in Chicago Tribune—Books, October 22, 1989, p. 3.

JOHN BAYLEY

At one moment in *Foucault's Pendulum* someone snaps his fingers excitedly and says: 'It's obvious. Reich was definitely a Templar.' 'Everyone was, except us,' retorts his colleague. That is indeed the point. Hermetic investigation always reveals that every secret society and mystic body of lore, from the Masons and the Illuminati to the Elders of Zion and the Order of the Golden Dawn, turns out to have a higher or perhaps a subterranean unity. Freud of course was a Mason or a Templar too. The author and his reader, in a cheerful conspiracy of two, are the only people outside all this kind of thing.

And since outside it, all the more able to participate in it with readerly and writerly zest. Umberto Eco seems to be having it both ways, as he did in *The Name of the Rose,* offering mystery, quest and romance, while retaining, for himself, and for us, the privilege of the higher frivolity. It is in a sense an old trick, which his fellow-countryman Ariosto practised in epic verse with especial felicity. But it is also very up-to-date, conforming with contemporary critical specifications for all literary activity, and yet done with wit, learning, bravura and a sense of style worthy of the culture and society that produced the Renaissance. As Sterne's sentimental traveller might have said, they do these things better in Italy.

Like *The Name of the Rose, Foucault's Pendulum* shoots at every fictional goal in sight: satire, fantasy, sophisticated fun, cautionary tale for the times. By scoring each time it could still be said to lose the match, for novels that have something for everybody usually have no soul of their own. The story does not take itself seriously enough to be Science Fiction, nor does it possess that deep inward dottiness which gives an imaginative persona to *The Lord of the Rings, King Solomon's Mines, The Hound of the Baskervilles.* At the same time, it is supremely chic. Its deftness and scholarly style go with great good humour, more like Ariosto's than Voltaire's; and while its deadpan exposition of historic cults and mysteries is both hilarious and absorbing, its nuggets of generalising 'wisdom', most frequent in the book's final chapters, never lapse into pretentiousness. The narrator-hero Casaubon reflects at the end, as he awaits probable liquidation at the hands of the Masters of the Hollow World, that 'the certainty is that there is nothing to understand.' 'I understood the Kingdom and was one with it,' he continues, eating a peach and contemplating the vines where once the dinosaurs wandered about. 'The rest is only cleverness. Invent; invent the plan, Casaubon. That's what everyone has done, to explain the dinosaurs and the peaches.'

The rest is only cleverness. And the cleverness is what matters, at least to the masculine intellect, whether it is inventing atom bombs, spawning secret cults that all turn out to be the same, or writing novels. Women are rather different: they have children, and the hero's mistress Lia, who has been helping his research, has one in the course of the book, giving him a different attitude to the way things are. In Eco's sprightly narrative this is less banal than it sounds, but it does pin things down. Something is going on beyond the unbearable lightness of writing: procreation, and cultivating the garden. But the novel, as novel, is not going to give up as easily as that. The surprise it has in store is that beyond the male need to invent—history, science, metaphysics, mysticism— something really *is* going on, an Evil Principle, the Diabolicals, whom human ingenuity discovers almost by accident in the course of its asinine craze for diversion and self-deception.

The experienced reader will see at once what motif has been made use of here—one that used often to be encountered in ghost stories. Those on the quest, sleeping in the haunted house or whatever, are doing it for fun: but beyond all the pretences and ghostly properties something really *is* there. . . .

[Apart] from supplying a title, the pendulum's more important job is to hang the chief editor under the earth, in the final dénouement when fantasy discovers that it has created terrible fact, or at least helped to will it into being, and the players and devisers of the game are confronted with the real horror film, with one of their number the girl to be sacrificed, and another the victim of an almost literal cliff-hanging. A good touch here: the editor, whose name is Belbo, which can hardly help recalling Tolkien's Bilbo, is unable even at the last moment not to see his predicament in terms of a scenario. Moreover the sight of all these synoptic and synergistic Diabolicals at their fell work redeems and recovers for him 'his most genuine gift: his sense of the ridiculous'.

A sense of the ridiculous, and its consummation in terms of art, is some sort of antidote against that obsession with power embodied in secret rituals and inner rings and world-transforming formulae. Belbo's last words to the Diabolicals are uttered in Piedmontese dialect, *Ma gavte la nata,* a phrase he has uttered before and which means roughly, 'let the cork out'—a reference to persons so inflated with their own portentousness that they should be decorked from behind, like champagne bottles. Eco's chapters have epigraphs, one of which is from Karl Popper: 'the conspiracy theory of society comes from abandoning God and then asking: "Who is in his place?"' This goes with the heading of the final chapter, which comes from Giordano Bruno, who was burnt by the Inquisition in the Roman marketplace, and who wrote that although 'fate has ordained the viscissitude of shadows and light, the greatest evil comes from those who hold it certain that they are in the light.'

Eco's superb entertainment is a way of putting these ancient truths into an art form fashionable and acceptable today. Anthony Burgess is quoted as saying that it exemplifies 'what Post-Modernist fiction is about, with its learning—real and bogus—its concern with books talking to books . . . its semiological obsession': 'This,' Burgess says, 'is the way the European novel is going.' One sees what he means, but the book does not read like that somehow. The admirable translation by William Weaver conveys a wonderfully Ariostan easiness of style, a genuine gaiety far removed from the kind of modish fiction of today which suits Burgess's clinical and depressive prognosis on the modern novel. Bad modern novels do indeed sound and read as Burgess says, mingling the obligatory 'seriousness', clung to by reviewers, with jokes, obscenities, fantasies, pseudo-scholarship. *Foucault's Pendulum* may give the impression of being like that, but somehow triumphantly isn't. For one thing, Eco's scholarship (so far as I can guess) is real, however engagingly grotesque the uses he makes of it.

We need a more seductive explanation, says Belbo at one point, after creating an ingenious scenario in which Masonry is invented by the Jesuits from their esoteric knowledge of the Templars (remember that St Bernard initiated this cult by sucking three drops of milk from the Black Virgin of Isis) in order to justify their existence and have something to fight head-on. In one sense, Eco has produced his own version of *The Satanic Verses.* But he has less in common with Rushdie than with Kundera, the brilliant author of *The Unbearable Lightness of Being,* in that both are obsessed with social and novelistic kitsch, and have to find more and more seductive ways of overcoming it. (The most rewarding essay in his little collection **The Open Work** is on **"The Structure of Bad Taste."**) One pioneer of Modernist fiction, Robert Musil, remarked that the novel existed in order to destroy kitsch. But also, perhaps, to make the right, the new use of it? The 'heroism' of Belbo, like the parenthood of Lia and Casaubon, is not unlike the 'weight' of Tereza, heroine of Kundera's novel, in that both express something deep and true which kitsch has vulgarised and made use of. Belbo is finally a 'character' like Tereza, whom the *Reader's Digest* would kitschify into 'the most unforgettable character I have met'. Eco is sagely and sensibly aware of the novel's doomed quest to shake off the stereotypes of kitsch, and of how it can become more and more kitschily sophisticated in the process. In the Milan bar where the editorial games begin, his narrator has noticed how fanatic radicalism has gradually been undermined by the sophistication of consumer growth. 'I could write the political history of those years based on how Red Label gradually gave way to 12-year-old Ballantine and then to single malts.' The grail of the terrorist in fictional time becomes a beaker of Laphroaig.

> John Bayley, "Let the Cork Out," in London Review of Books, *Vol. 11, No. 20, October 26, 1989, p. 15.*

ALEXANDER STILLE

Since its publication in Italy last fall *Foucault's Pendulum* has provided several new twists to what has come to be known as the Eco phenomenon. The novel has sold more quickly than any book in Italian publishing history, while becoming the center of a fierce national controversy.

Rumors that Eco was working on the book were eagerly picked up by the Italian press as early as two years before the book appeared. Fearful that advance publicity would cheapen the book's image and dilute the impact of publication, Eco and his publisher tried to keep the book under tight wraps as long as possible, releasing its title and nothing more. If the strategy was intended to prevent prepublication publicity, it backfired. In a fever of curiosity, the Italian newspapers competed ferociously in acts of journalistic espionage, trying to obtain pirated copies of the novel and writing articles based on leaks, rumors, and thirdhand information. Anticipation built to such an extent that when the book finally appeared, 500,000 copies were sold before the first buyers had a chance to grapple with it and tell their friends what they thought.

But within several weeks the Eco phenomenon boomeranged. Readers who had bought the book for faddish reasons gave up when confronted with the labyrinthine complexities of a novel that explores the mysteries of the Jewish cabala, hermetic philosophy, and a thousand years of esoteric thought. Eco was accused of having shrewdly manipulated the press in a plot to push sales. "Eco is a genius of our culture," one critic wrote, "a genius of self-promotion." To his dismay, Eco has become a kind of literary Midas: everything he does makes news and sells copies. Even his decision not to appear on television was perceived as another clever maneuver to attract attention. But the attacks, predictably, only had the effect of selling more copies. The same papers that were busy creating the Eco phenomenon were often the ones denouncing it. . . . (pp. 125-26)

Lost amid all the hype and controversy is the book itself, a highly ambitious but not altogether successful novel that is far less well suited to the role of best seller than was **The Name of the Rose.** Underneath the scholarly dress of **The Name of the Rose** beats the heart of a standard detective novel—it is no accident that it was adapted into a Hollywood movie starring Sean Connery. *Foucault's Pendulum* is almost the opposite: a genuinely serious (and genuinely difficult) book masquerading as a detective novel. *Rose* has a conventional narrative structure, with a single story that unfolds over the course of a week; *Foucault's Pendulum* is a sprawling and structurally innovative novel that moves back and forth in time, and in and out of various literary genres, in emulation of James Joyce's *Ulysses* (about which Eco has written extensively).

It is difficult to make a single, overall assessment of *Foucault's Pendulum,* precisely because it is several books wrapped up in one, some more successful than others. It is, simultaneously, a realistic novel of the Second World War, a contemporary novel about the failures and disillusionment of Italy's revolutionary left, a comic satire of the Milan publishing world, a history of Western mysticism, and a detective story set in the lunatic fringe of occult sects. At the same time, it is a study of literary creation, which looks inside the computer of the book's main character and examines the process of writing *Foucault's Pendulum.* The novel's structure embodies its mystical subject matter: it is divided into ten parts—named for the ten *sephirot* (or "lights") of the Jewish cabala—and 120 chapters (120 being a number of special significance in mystical numerology).

The book begins at the end, as the narrator, Casaubon, hides inside the French museum where the Pendulum of Foucault hangs. . . . Casaubon's friend and colleague Jacopo Belbo has been kidnapped by an occult sect, and Casaubon believes that something terrible will happen under the Pendulum at midnight.

The rest of the book is an attempt to explain what has led the two characters to this desperate pass. . . .

Unlike Eco's first novel, *Foucault's Pendulum* contains a strong autobiographical element. The central character, Belbo, like Eco himself, is a skeptical intellectual from the northern region of Piedmont. Both were born in 1932, members of what Belbo calls the wrong generation: too young to have fought in the war or in the anti-Fascist resistance, but too old to have participated in the student movement of the late 1960s. One of the pleasant surprises of the novel is that Belbo's autobiographical writings (which Casaubon reads on Belbo's computer disks) reveal Eco to be a realistic novelist of genuine talent. The scenes of the final days of the Second World War, which draw on Eco's adolescent experiences, have an elegiac beauty and warmth that are a welcome contrast to the artificiality and cold cerebral tone of other sections.

Equally successful is Eco's comic portrait of the publishing world, which he knows well from his years as an editor at Milan's Bompiani. Belbo and his colleagues relieve the boredom and futility of their jobs by inventing courses for an imaginary School of Comparative Irrelevance specializing in useless or impossible subjects such as the history of agriculture in Antarctica, crowd psychology in the Sahara, contemporary Sumerian literature, Morse syntax, and urban planning for nomads. (p. 126)

In preparing *Foucault's Pendulum,* Eco assembled a library of some 1,500 volumes on black magic, astrology, alchemy, and mysticism. He has stuffed as much of his library of esoterica as would fit between the covers of *Foucault's Pendulum,* including a list of 720 variations in the Hebrew name of God, the mathematical dimensions of the Egyptian pyramids, the prophecies of Nostradamus, *The Protocols of the Elders of Zion,* and the rituals of the Brazilian macumba. Several characters are little more than talking encyclopedias of the occult, and their long monologues have all the narrative excitement of the average Ph.D. dissertation.

Although scholarship is supposed to be Eco's forte, the erudite sections of *Foucault's Pendulum* are perhaps the weakest elements of the book. His affection for medieval philosophy made some of the theological disputes in *The Name of the Rose* come alive, but Eco fails to do the same with esoteric thought. By linking every disparate occult movement and secret society into a single crackpot conspiracy, Eco makes all the groups he examines seem monotonously similar and equally absurd.

In order for the novel to work, Belbo and Casaubon's plan must seem compelling and at least partly plausible, both because Belbo is eventually seduced by it and because we are forced to read about it for roughly half of the book's 656 pages. Instead, it is about as convincing (and as interesting to read) as Lyndon LaRouche's conspiracy theories. Even Eco's publisher, Valentino Bompiani, admits that one of his first reactions to the book was that it needed rigorous cutting.

But just as one is about to throw up one's hands in exasperation over a long digression, Eco will return suddenly with one of the many flashes of brilliance that almost redeem the novel's tedious stretches. Interest invariably picks up when the novel returns to Belbo's personal experiences. Indeed, one often wishes that Eco had centered the book more on Belbo. But as a literary modernist, Eco is determined not to write simply a realistic novel. Instead, he has produced a postmodern novel, which combines various literary forms and is both a story and its own interpretive guide. As Eco explained in an interview last June, "It was important for me that Belbo was a blocked writer. This allowed me to make the story of the novel the story of how the novel was written."

Defending the obscurity of his novels and the scholarly quotations strewn through them, Eco insists that he is creating a participatory experience for the reader similar to that of his characters. Since the characters plow through piles of occult nonsense, so must the readers of *Foucault's Pendulum.* "Even in my scholarly work, I have always operated on the theory of the modern reader as a reader constructed by the work," Eco says. "The reader has to undergo a sort of ordeal in order to become what the book wants. . . . I am always a little discouraged by people who say 'But I don't understand Latin'. . . . if I wanted you to understand it I would have translated it. . . . Sometimes difficult ideas and passages are put there as magic spells."

The ideas that underlie *Foucault's Pendulum* are extremely interesting, but often they are more intriguing to contemplate in the abstract than to experience on the written page. The result is that *Foucault's Pendulum* is more a brilliant idea for a novel than a fully satisfying creation. (pp. 127-28)

> *Alexander Stille, "The Novel as Status Symbol," in* The Atlantic Monthly, *Vol. 264, No. 5, November, 1989, pp. 125-29.*

WALTER KENDRICK

The misleading title of *Foucault's Pendulum* is no doubt an arcane joke, one of many. In its opening pages, the novel lays out two ways of looking at the pendulum and the universe. Casaubon, the narrator (another joke, on *Middlemarch's* fusty scholar), observes that the pendulum's period is governed by "the square root of the length of the wire and by π, that number which, however irrational to sublunar minds, through a higher rationality binds the circumference and diameter of all possible circles." Halfway reasonable, but dangerous. Mathematicians call numbers like π irrational because they never come out even. But to suppose that the family π seems irrational only to "sublunar minds," to personify some "higher rationality" that perceives the brood as plainly as we see $2 + 2$, means to court death and welcome it.

Casaubon's next sentence takes the plunge:

> The time it took the sphere to swing from end to end was determined by an arcane conspiracy between the most timeless of measures: the singularity of the point of suspension, the duality of the plane's dimensions, the triadic beginning of π, the secret quadratic nature of the root, and the unnumbered perfection of the circle itself.

This is lunacy. Not only does it attribute guile to numbers, it also seeks to incriminate the innocent series 1-2-3-4 and to deify numberlessness. You could die from such ideas.

In *Foucault's Pendulum,* one major character dies from them literally; another succumbs to cancer, cellular innumeracy; a third, Casaubon, ends up waiting for the murderers who will kill him because he knows the truth about a lie. The lesson is simple: real knowledge comes from the patient, thorough application of logic and reason; false knowledge, the product of thinking by analogy, leads to madness, despair, and death. Swollen though it is to 641 pages, *Foucault's Pendulum* has nothing else to say.

It's a banal lesson. Medieval fallacies didn't die in the glare of Enlightenment; they only went underground, where they proliferated as Rosicrucianism, Freemasonry, cabalism, numerology, astrology, palmistry, satanism, and a stupefying array of other claimants to secret, forbidden knowledge. Especially in America, that paradise for cults and conspiracy theories, the last few years have yielded a bumper crop of balderdash, from ELVIS LIVES! to the piffle of crystals and harmonic convergences.

Evidently, similar manias have been flourishing in Italy, where they caught Eco's attention and inspired him to squelch them by the unlikely means of a novel. Readers of *The Name of the Rose* know, of course, that Eco writes fiction the way other people compile encyclopedias. Inside his fat first novel, a skinny little mystery struggled to get out through layer upon layer of medieval and semiotic flapdoodle. The effort failed, but the blubber was beguiling on its own. In *Foucault's Pendulum* Eco wantonly spews out the kind of outré erudition that captivated the estimated 1.5 million readers who bought *The Name of the Rose*. . . .

This time, Eco dishes up trencherloads of information on secret societies, from the medieval Knights Templars to today's moon and devil worshipers. It's amusing enough, particularly the million or so words about the Templars—who they really were and what legend made them. The trouble is, most of the facts merely trace the sadly tangled webs Western culture has spun out of wishes and faulty reasoning. They are, in a sense, false facts even when they're true.

The monstrously attenuated plot of *Foucault's Pendulum* concerns a plan by three up-to-date, computerized scholars—Casaubon, Belbo, and Diotallcvi—to weave all the secret societies of the past thousand years into one centuries-old, world-spanning cabal. At first, they treat the project as a sort of gigantic crossword puzzle. Furiously brainstorming, bending and stretching historical coincidences, they can make a millennium's disparate delusions look as if everything hung together in a single design. What fun! . . .

Suspicions multiply, and soon the men grow drunk on their home-brewed brand of unreason: "wanting connections, we found connections—always, everywhere, and between everything. The world exploded into a whirling network of kinships, where everything pointed to everything else, everything explained everything else . . ."

This is bad enough, but skulking behind the potted palms are fools who believe in the treasure of the Templars, the miracles of the Rosy Cross, the whole dizzy mess. Half in jest, half in innocence, Casaubon and his friends lure the believers into view, and Hell follows with them. (p. 29)

Along with the metaconspirators, most of the other fools are male. Unlike *The Name of the Rose* (an all-male entertainment, appropriately enough for a novel about monks), *Foucault's Pendulum* has a contemporary setting, so Eco introduces a few women. They're faceless and indistinguishable, but at least they're neither virgins nor whores. The trouble with Eco's women is that they're wise. Lia, Casaubon's lover, knows the truth—the true truth, not the simulacrum those ditzy men go scurrying after. . . .

Lia's interventions in *Foucault's Pendulum* are the novel's closest thing to the sign that lights up saying AUTHOR'S MESSAGE. The message isn't wrong, and if it must be delivered, a woman might as well do it. Even a happily fecund woman who spreads her legs like a neolithic Venus. Even a Venus with a brain. But there are other ancient errors than conspiracy theories. Some involve the myth of feminine gut wisdom, and Eco swallows them whole.

No one expected *The Name of the Rose* to hit the big time; *Foucault's Pendulum* may do the same. . . . But if Eco tops the charts again, momentum will be the sole culprit. Superficially, *Foucault's Pendulum* looks like another romp by everybody's favorite semiotician. Instead of celebrating intellectual pyrotechnics, however, this novel tries to douse them. It condemns as folly the very pleasure it pretends to offer. Back in 1983, when Eco's first novel took off, critics expressed amazement that the chowderheaded reading public had flocked to such a mercilessly cerebral performance, crammed with hard words and almost devoid of sex. But *The Name of the Rose* celebrated and conveyed the austere exhilaration of intellectual calisthenics. Like a censorious schoolmarm, the Eco of *Foucault's Pendulum* would rein joy in and sober it up.

It's a critical cliché that second novels fail, especially when they follow grand successes. Fifty-seven-year-old professors of semiotics seldom face such problems, but they've seldom wowed the world with first fictions at the age of 48. All bets are off when it comes to Umberto Eco. You can fault *Foucault's Pendulum* on every point that's usually invoked when novels are judged: characters (faceless), plot (thin), language (verbose and pompous). But *The Name of the Rose* had all these flaws, and it soared. *Foucault's Pendulum* fails for a more profound reason. At bottom it hates itself—and us for reading it. (p. 30)

Walter Kendrick, "Lesson Zero," in VLS, *No. 80, November, 1989, pp. 29-30.*

RICHARD EDER

[*Foucault's Pendulum*] is an artichoke with 641 leaves and not much heart. There is some real pleasure in artichoke leaves, but what with the work and the scratchiness you probably wouldn't undertake one unless you thought there would be a heart in it.

True, in *Foucault's Pendulum* the absence is part of the point. Its elaborately branched story about the search for an ancient secret whose possession will confer world mastery is both an illustration and a parody of the contemporary literary doctrines of semiology and structuralism. . . .

[Eco's] new book is a bravura series of variations and reverses on the structuralist view that the important reality in a text is the text itself. *Hamlet,* for example, is not "about" a melancholy prince and the difficulty of action. It is "about" Shakespeare's telling the story. He might have told it differently.

In one of many witty passages in *Pendulum,* in fact, Belbo, a nervous and suggestible book editor who is jealous of his authors, imagines himself coaching Shakespeare. Don't set it in France, he advises; set it in a less distinctive place, say, Denmark. How about having the ghost come in at the beginning instead of the end? And couldn't we improve on: "To act or not to act, that is the problem"?

Belbo, in other words, is "deconstructing," showing the inner flux and instability of monuments. Structuralism, like modern science—which it aims to be—divides the visible into subatomic particles. At that level, a chair and the thumbtack placed upon it are much the same. So are Superman and Keats. In physics, a lot of energy has been liberated. In literature, a lot of scholarly activity has been liberated, but perhaps less energy.

To tell what *Pendulum* is about, itself requires a certain deconstruction. The plot is the least of it, being, essentially, an invention of the characters. Only at the end does the invention appear to come true, although this "coming-true" also is an invention. Through it, Eco makes his point—satirical, serious and above all ambiguous.

Essentially, then; or rather, unessentially: Belbo, Diotallevi and the narrator, Casaubon, three Milan intellectuals of varying stripes and edginesses, work for Garamond, publisher of a few serious books and of a great number of vanity items, paid for by their authors. (p. 3)

Using scraps of history, and reams of mystical and cabalistic writing through the ages, the three construct [the genealogy of the Secret of the Knights Templar]. The Templar tradition, they decide, has been fragmented and passed in bits into the hands of any number of rival secret societies.

Such figures as Roger and Francis Bacon, Descartes, Voltaire, Frederick the Great of Prussia, and Adolf Hitler had connections with them. . . .

It is a double semiological joke. If reality is simply a text, then the Milan trio can, simply by writing it, proclaim the secret of the universe. But if, to reverse things, text is reality, it can materialize and gobble them up.

Eco hovers astride the joke, neutrally and with evident glee. At the end, the narrator reflects that the only reality is in such things as the taste of a peach and the sound of a trumpet. And, after all, Belbo has died rather than reveal the details of a map that is pure invention. Is it Eco's message that there is a reality worth dying for beneath the text? But it is text to say so.

Eco's jokes are splendid. There is Belbo's beloved computer. Casaubon struggles with elaborate numbers and combinations to get into it, but the machine keeps repeating: "Have you the password?" Finally, Casaubon gives up and writes: "No." That, of course, is it.

There is the imaginary college that the trio devise in their spare time, offering courses in Potiosection (slicing soup) and Mechanical Avunculogratulation (building machines to greet uncles). There is Lia, Casaubon's wonderfully sage girlfriend, who examines the Templar message—upon which the whole phantasmagoric structure rests—and concludes that it is simply a medieval merchant's list of things to do that day.

We could have used more Lia. There are any number of good things in *Pendulum,* but a novel is not a truffle-hunt. Its central paradox is neat and springy, but a novel is not a mousetrap either.

Eco's conceits are buried in a vast verbiage, a wearying thicket of occultist lore and scholarship. A whole leaden section is devoted to a visit to Brazilian voodoo ceremony; another to a tired occultists' orgy. There is a seeming infinity of false leads and circling suppositions.

Eco's game demands quite a few more reader candles than it is worth. *Name of the Rose* may have been the best-liked half-read novel of its day. *Pendulum,* I suspect, will be well-liked too; and only one-quarter read. (p. 15)

Richard Eder, "Umberto's Truffle-Hunt," in Los Angeles Times Book Review, *November 5, 1989,* pp. 3, 15.

ROBERT ADAMS

Obsession is the first premise of Umberto Eco's second novel, *Foucault's Pendulum.* It is an encyclopedist's black comedy, sprawling across close to a millennium, from the first crusade to [1988], and wandering around at least three continents. In mere physical dimensions, it's surely close to a world's record shaggy-dog story. Like his Renaissance forebear, Rabelais, Eco never uses one word where fifty will do, never hesitates to provide all the circumstantial preliminaries of a basically simple process. When the pace slows or the scenery turns drab, he resorts to extended periods to Steven Spielberg special effects, to pastiche, parody, and Grand Guignol. Best of all, he doesn't take himself too seriously; in the midst of his most macabre scenes, there's a continual flow of high spirits that raises this second novel well above (as it seems to me) the first one, *The Name of the Rose.* Not that both books don't have their longueurs. Professor Eco is a word man, and when his always incipient logorrhea takes over, there's nothing to do but step aside and let the spate run its course.

Without giving away too much of the story (which in any case has to be straightened out if a summary of it is to make any sense), it can be taken as a premise that three jocose young fellows—Belbo, Diotallevi, and Casaubon—are working for a seedy vanity publisher in present-day Milan, Signor Garamond(!). Provoked by the number of occult and esoteric manuscripts that have to be read, the junior editors persuade the semiliterate Garamond to set up a division of the press that will specialize in hermetic books. . . .

[Casaubon tells the story of the medieval Knights Templar] to his two fellow editors (or, as they soon take to calling themselves, his co-conspirators); and they proceed to build themselves a structure of correspondences and coincidences on the assumption that the old Templars not only survived into the twentieth century as an organized conspiracy but retained dreams of their ancient power. Only, over the centuries, some parts of their invaluable wisdom had been misplaced. It must now be recovered and reassembled, but by whom? The three conspirators, drawing on lavish contributions from manuscripts submitted for publication, but also rummaging through archives and covert cross-references in printed texts, pursue the evidences of this shadowy, transsecular wisdom. In conversation among themselves, they never abandon the formula that this is only a game, a fantastic imaginative invention—but in their heart of hearts they gradually come to believe their own absurdities.

For it all fits; on one level or another every bit of absurdity they can dream up fits with the previously established parts of their structure, confirming it as it confirms them. The law of obsession takes over; a random speculative fact fitted into their established speculative structure suddenly takes on a new luminous meaning. If there's a gap in the structure, they look for the missing piece, and inevitably, miraculously, they discover it—all the while reassuring one another that they are proceeding by the strictest laws of scholarship. "Grant just one absurdity," say the severe logicians, "and anything you want can be made to follow (*sequitur quodlibet*)."

The merry mythplaiters of Milan have an unlimited appetite for absurdities; they accumulate them wholesale. The philosopher's stone and the gift of immortality are only the beginning; they are easily woven into the Baconian theory of Shakespeare, the tomfooleries of Cagliostro or Madame Blavatsky, and the Protocols of the Elders of Zion. All are façades or fronts for the machinations of the mysterious crypto-Templars. Metaphors, in service to the structure, are briskly converted to facts; because some surviving Templars perhaps went underground after 1314, modern descendants of the order are to be sought in cellars, catacombs, sewer lines, and subway systems. (p. 3)

So far the three accomplices have been nothing but a trio of amateur fantasists meeting occasionally in a back room to play a private game. But their hobby does not go long unnoticed. Under the guise of helping in their investigations, apparently commonplace but pertinacious personages start to infiltrate their councils, instruct them in secret proceedings, bring them into illuminate circles. They attend occult gatherings and are queried by an interested policeman. First one of their informants drops out of sight for entirely imaginable but not very explicit reasons, then another. Gradually it becomes clear to the unfortunate conspirators that they are becoming victims of their own cabal. (pp. 3-4)

What does any of this have to do with the pendulum set up in Paris by the highly respected physicist J. B. L. Foucault? . . . The connection is diaphanous, atmospheric—fictional, in a word. For Eco a museum of outdated technology is a *louche* and spooky place to set a story of Gothic intrigue, and the pendulum, as an object uniquely free of the earth's motion, makes of St. Martin one of the world's mysterious strong spots. Bonus points come from an unspoken association with the pit and the pendulum of Poe's short story. But structurally it's not a very tight joint.

No artist in miniature, Umberto Eco has provided in his new book an overflowing macédoine enriched with hallucinations, excursions, allusions, retrospectives, and parodies from other periods, places, and stylistic traditions. One price of this verbal richness is that the book doesn't have much space to create characters: most of them are mere stencils. Another consequence of all the verbal richness is that the best way to read the book is fast. One of the major effects at which it aims is kaleidoscope; one doesn't get, and shouldn't try to grasp, a moment to assemble the pieces, run down a reverberation, or take in the richness of an overtone.

At a given moment, even a careful reader may not be able to tell whose consciousness he is following; and there are too many verbal byways and offshoots to explore them all. Okay, so Belbo's computer, which is summoned up to recite sections of the narrative or just to play games, is named Abulafia after a Spanish cabalist of the Middle Ages, and the A of Abulafia is required to give the Milan conspirators initials representing the first four letters of the alphabet. But this is squeezing the juice out of a dried fig. Eco is a joker, a constant joker, but

his jokes, like most good ones, have something childish and rowdy about them; they're open, not cryptic. So far as I can make out, there's very little in *Foucault's Pendulum* akin to the semiotic overtones that provoked a good deal of portentous analysis of *The Name of the Rose.* Like the movies of Ingmar Bergman, which also suggest many "profound" speculations but which fade overnight into a memory of impressive commonplaces, the novel of Umberto Eco is a structure of impressionistic illusions. Or would be, if it weren't for the blessed injection of a blunt, tough sense of humor. . . .

[Note] the boldness and intimacy with which Eco flings himself into a hallucinatory fantasy dictated by the disintegrating Belbo to his machine. Starting from the ironic assumption that he is Shakespeare's editor rewriting a first draft of *Hamlet,* he plunges through Conrad's adventure story into the maelstrom of history lashed to a foam by the character's overwrought brain.

> Why not set it in Denmark, Mr. William S.? Seven Seas Jim Johann Valentin Andreä Luke-Matthew roams the archipelago of the Sunda between Patmos and Avalon, from the White Mountain to Mindanao, from Atlantis to Thessalonica to the Council of Nicaea. Origen cuts off his testicles and shows them, bleeding, to the fathers of the City of the Sun, and Hiram sneers filioque filioque while Constantine digs his greedy nails into the hollow eye sockets of Robert Fludd, death death to the Jews of the ghetto of Antioch, Dieu et mon droit, wave the Beauceant, lay on, down with the Ophites and the Borborites, the snakes. Trumpets blare, and here come the Chevaliers Bienfaisants de la Cité Sainte with the Moor's head bristling on their pike. The Rebis, the Rebis! Magnetic hurricane, the Tower collapses, Rachkovsky grins over the roasted corpse of Jacques de Molay.

Some of these allusions are common knowledge, some can be supplied from other parts of the novel, some are altogether private. The associative connections are mostly arcane. No matter. Discursive expository prose is the common mode of plain sense, but not here. The scene is high tension. Because Eco knows something about the flickering pace of the electronic media, the suggestive powers of swift juxtaposition, he is not bound to statement.

The Name of the Rose was complained of because the exposition got in the way of the narration, and of other fictional values as well; readers were even heard of who failed to stay the distance. Eco's best friend would hardly deny that in *Foucault's Pendulum* he got all the mileage there is out of a single wiredrawn jape. Knowing all there is to know about the occult is knowing a lot that's not worth knowing in the first place. But most entertainments in our blasé world depend on a precarious suspension of disbelief. Umberto Eco, if not a mage, is a juggler with lots of moves and an almost hypnotic line of patter. It's a good show, which from time to time almost persuades you to forget the sorcerer's warning against taking it seriously. (p. 4)

Robert Adams, "Juggler," *in* The New York Review of Books, *Vol. XXXVI, No. 17, November 9, 1989, pp. 3 4.*

GEOFFREY STOKES

On a working visit to America to promote his new novel,

Foucault's Pendulum, Eco has endured readings, book-signings, lectures, and, of course, interviews. This interview, over lunch at Zinno, is the last obstacle standing between him and the plane that will, later this evening, carry him and his wife back to Italy.

Even tired, however, Eco remains a formidable intellect. It's a pretty good bet, no matter *how* much you know, that he knows more than you do. . . .

Among the ideas he is both worrying at and playing with at the moment is the problem of (over)interpretation. *Foucault's Pendulum* is, to the extent it can be said to be "about" *anything,* about the interpretation of texts, and his forthcoming scholarly book is called *The Limits of Interpretation.* Also, of course, he is going through the often astonishing process of having his novel interpreted by book reviewers (admirers mostly, but also Walter Kendrick of this newspaper, who—in a review Eco half-grudgingly respects—gave *Foucault* a sound thrashing [see excerpt above]). And yet, he insists, the risk of being badly interpreted is one the novella—and the novelist—*must* take: "When writing, what you want your reader to do is to make connections between points of your text—even points you have yourself not foreseen.

"Even so, there should be a limit to that. My novel is against *over*interpretation, but interpretation is the great problem of human science. We are interpreting animals, and the fact that in *Foucault's Pendulum* I parodize overinterpretation doesn't mean that I am against interpretation. *The Open Work* [Eco's much revised 1962 collection of literary and aesthetic essays in praise of complexity's demands and opportunities] is there; I can't deny it. But there must be a threshold beyond which the interpretation is farfetched.

"Is there a rule? No. There is no rule. But there is, once again, a balance criterion, an economy criterion: Does this interpretation add something to this text? This way of interpreting the first chapter, can it be useful also in interpreting the last chapter? Or do you need two different frameworks? This is an economic principle spelled out for the first time by Saint Augustine: If your key for interpreting, let us say, page 10 can hold also for page 250, it could be, conjecturally, a good key. If it holds only for page 10 and then collapses at page 12, maybe you are wrong.

"That is so *even* if you believe that you are not bound by something called the intention of the author. *That* is a very ghostly category, because I discover sometime in my readers that they discover in the text something I did not know was there—but when they discover it, I say, 'Okay, is possible. The text can provoke also this connection.'

"Sometimes you find, though, crazy connection. You say, 'Okay, this explains maybe this page, but it doesn't explain all the rest.' "

But we are always, particularly with classic texts, reinventing them from generation to generation, even reader to reader. Are you saying that unlike Gertrude Stein's Oakland, there is a there there, a level beyond which a text will not yield?

"Yes. I will give you an example, even though I am the author and I believe an author should never say whether an interpretation is good or bad—because he's the least entitled person to do that. *But,* there are certain cases in which you say, even though I were not the author, I could not say that. For example, a Spanish newspaper wrote of the *Pendulum* that it is a blasphemous book because the author says that Jesus married Maria Magdelena. But I think that if you look at the book, you see that this was an idea of one of the characters, but you cannot say that the *author* said so." (p. 39)

If overinterpretation is such a danger, why do you court it by writing first-person narratives?

"For a young novelist, as I am—as a novelist—the first person is easier. Also, for me, is a reaction against the omniscience of the 19th century narrator. The first person is more problematic; you don't *know* what is happening to you, while the omniscient novelist who knows what is in your head is too dogmatic. So this is my way to escape a certain trap of knowing too much. And it is a way to set the reader free.

"Suppose I set up the final Sabbath of the *Pendulum* in the church in third person. I would have bet on the reality of what happened. Putting it in the mouth of Casaubon, you can still believe that it was a *cauchemar,* a nightmare due to the exhilaration of something, so it is a little more ambiguous, you don't know whether it is true. With the third person, is too much."

Why?

"Because is the voice of God. Who is the only one who knows what passes in your mind, in his mind, in my mind. Third person is really a romantic attitude—though it can be used ironically, I suppose—but first person is more tolerant, more open to the possibility of a wrong conjecture."

But the novelist is God, within the novel—if not in the first draft, then surely by the time proofs are being corrected.

"It can be a neo-Platonic God, a Christian God, it can be a Buddhist God, it can be a Jerk, a God who is unable to cope with his own creation. It can be a God at the first day of creation who doesn't know, as yet, what His job is."

Eco explains that a God-in-training is the theme of a novel, as yet unpublished in English, by Rutgers professor Franco Fiorucci, but finally returns to the notion of first person as liberating for the reader. "When you write," he says, "is a strange cocktail of humility and arrogance, but you can at least *try* to be a little humble to your reader, by leaving him/her free to interact. But," he cautions, "the first person can be a very unloyal tree. In third person, the reader is ready to identify him or herself with all the characters; with first person, the reader is trapped, is obliged to identify with the narrator."

There are ways out of this (in *Foucault's Pendulum,* Eco in essence uses two first-person narrators), but these often seem contrived. Perhaps it is better merely to live with the apparent paradox of entrapment *in order to* liberate. In either case, however, the impulse toward liberating the reader—which Eco celebrates in *The Open Work* and practices in his novels—is much at odds with his practice in the bulk of his writing. *In your scholarly and critical works (and, for that matter, in much of your journalism), you want to march your readers, syllogism by syllogism, toward a fixed conclusion; is this sort of writing, then, by definition inferior?*

"Some months ago, I was in a symposium in which the theme was the difference between 'creative' writing and 'noncreative' writing. A silly distinction—why should you think Sophocles is creative and Plato isn't?—but never mind, because there *are* two different ways of being creative, of being original. What is the *real* difference?

"I think writing scholarly, as an essayist—'noncreatively,' as they but not I would say—you make an inquiry, and you try to reach *a* single conclusion—or at least the definition of a plurality of conclusions, but a *single* definition. Then you want to convince your reader that *this* is the good conclusion, and if the reader doesn't accept it, you say, 'You're stupid!' And you spend your life defending that conclusion, so the rule of the game is, 'Am I right or not?'

"In writing creatively, a novel, you're not bound to a definite conclusion. On the contrary, you want to set up the contradictoriness of life. You show two characters, but you are not deciding at the end, who is right, who is wrong. They can be both right.

"But as an essayist, even the most impressionist essayist in a way wants to impose his conclusion, while even the most dogmatic—let's say Stalinist—novelist in a way leaves the final conclusion open because no matter what moral he *tries* to put on it, he has—if he is a good novelist—created characters who *force* him to leave the reader free to make his own ethical or aesthetic conclusions. This is the difference between a business talk—be there Thursday, bring a thousand dollars, and sign the contract—and a love talk."

But even love talks can end in a contract of sorts—and business talk is notoriously ambiguous. Isn't everything open to interpretation?

"There is an old essay, by Walter Benjamin, suggesting that in a technological age, messages are received in an 'unattentional' way. That is, I work while I'm listening to the radio; it is irrelevant whether the radio broadcasts rock or Doris Day. I make a sort of patchwork of them. So I transform something that was meant to be very dogmatic—to make you laugh, to make you cry—into a free collage, in the same way that with a remote control, I can make the television into a Picasso. But there is a difference between this and works that were *meant* to be open.

"Look at this ceiling," he says, gesturing toward the square, padded baffles that hang below the structural ceiling. "This ceiling can remain a ceiling as it remained until one second ago. But at a certain point, you look at it and you transform it into a sort of Mondrian, or you start musing about certain concepts in modern architecture. Before your interpretative act, it was a piece of engineering, but we are transforming it. Yet if we do it with Mies van der Rohe, it is more fun, it brings us more excitement."

So the aesthetic satisfaction in a creative work is to some extent a function of its openness to a variety of interpretations?

"Yes."

And the simpler satisfactions of a Doris Day song or a detective novel are in the directness of their message, the clarity of their conclusion.

"That's right."

Umberto Eco, eating oysters and sipping a gin martini underneath what is either a Mondrian or a ceiling, has invented the "open" detective story. Which is of course impossible.

On the other hand, neither does the ceiling fall down. (p. 40)

Geoffrey Stokes, "Eco Eco Eco Eco," in The Village Voice, *Vol. XXXV, No. 2, January 9, 1990, pp. 39-40.*

JOHN UPDIKE

Borges inspired a character, the blind Jorge of Burgos, in **The Name of the Rose,** and also the book's central image of a labyrinthine library, an essentially infinite library, as a universal metaphor. Another Borgesian notion, that of a Cabalistic conspiracy running beneath things, putting men in touch with diabolical deities and staining and twisting history, informs Eco's second novel, **Foucault's Pendulum,** which, like his first, is bulky, recondite, intricate, and best-selling. . . . In attempting to expand one of [the] Borgesian *frissons,* with their union of curious fact and macabre fancy, their solemn conspiratorial tone, their expert trafficking along that shadowy borderline where knowledge becomes arcane and thought becomes madness, into a six-hundred-and-forty-page, hundred-and-twenty-chapter saga of research and rumor in modern Italy, Paris, and Brazil, Eco has not reckoned with the possibility that *frissons* are not infinitely expandable. Borges was always brief; he wrote with a poet's ear; his own blindness and reclusive habits gave his mental explorations a peculiar and inimitable resonance, an earnest sorrow and uncanny repose. He had the voice of a sphinx. Eco, contrariwise, appears to be a postmodern intellectual as animated as he is intelligent, a mental extrovert whose cerebrations spill over into a number of disciplines beyond his two special fields, semiotics and the Middle Ages, and who can write engagingly (as was demonstrated in his 1986 collection **Travels in Hyperreality**) about most matters and who gives excellent interviews. **Foucault's Pendulum** is a monumental performance, erudite beyond measure and, insofar as Eco's brainy presence on the page is enjoyable, enjoyable. But as a tale of human adventure, erected upon the not quite interchangeable characters of three Milanese editors who prankishly cook up a secret sect called Tres (Templi Resurgentes Equites Synarchici) and are consumed by their creation, it totters and sags, and seems spun-out and thin.

The medieval characters of **The Name of the Rose** had at the least the solidity and color of their richly evoked fourteenth-century milieu. Those of **Foucault's Pendulum** belong to our era, and they seem, rather than creations of the author's erudition, victims of it. They are disposable plastic holders that pour out ribbons of information, of facts and quotations all tied around the central notion that the Templars . . . in truth survived and, by means of a relay system of hidden initiates who are supposed to meet six times, in six different countries, at intervals of a hundred and twenty years, are invisibly progressing toward a secret concerning the earth's "telluric currents" that will enable its holders to rule the world. . . . This great plot involves everyone from the Rosicrucians to the Jesuits, Francis Bacon to Cagliostro, the Freemasons (of course) to the Jews (perhaps), and was the real reason, it would seem, that Napoleon invaded Russia and Hitler perpetrated the Holocaust. If this last joke seems in dubious taste, a better joke is that the three editors reason from a cryptic document, entrusted to them by a prospective author who then vanishes, which is finally demonstrated to have been simply a merchant's delivery list. Better yet is the underlying jest that our human lust for conspiracy theories and secret organizations is so keen that a donnish parody of a cult becomes a murderously real one. There can't be too many hermetic stones left unturned in this ransacking of texts, this orgy of citation and paraphrase. . . . The enterprising Italians have already published a dictionary of Eco's strange words and quotations—*Dizionario del Pendolo di Foucault. . . . Foucault's Pendulum* is a dense and inventorial novel that lacks, and needs, an index.

It also needs more blood, more human juice. It has some. Casaubon, the narrator and the Templar expert who provides most of the scholarly ingredients of the three editors' witches' brew, fathers a baby in the course of the novel, and the birth inspires a few sentences striking in their unlayered simplicity, their humble celebration of the *Ding an sich.* . . . In general, even in bed, [Casaubon] is too busy reading to give his women enough attention to make them real to any reader but himself. But Eco, who was born in 1932, has had experience of being a child, university student, and intellectual in these last, stormy years of Italian history, and whenever he drops his occult texts and describes a village war between the resistance and the Fascists, or a student riot of the sixties, or the bar where the idle wits of Milan gather, an unforced authenticity breaks through, a breezy sense of witness, suggesting what he might write a novel about if he could ever forgo his ingenious schemes of signification and self-deconstruction, of encyclopedic foolery.

The most bloodless of the three heroes is Diotallevi, a Piedmontese who thinks he is a Jew, and who exists only to waste away, infected by the terrible sacrilege of the plot he has joined in concocting. He sees in the cancer that afflicts him the product of intellectual tampering, a transposition in the DNA alphabet generated by the mock conspiracy's devilishly clever transpositions of fact. . . . Diotallevi at his liveliest has little vital presence, and Belbo, the most active of the pseudo occultists, has a fitful and strained one. He is a generation older than Casaubon but draws what fictional life he has from the same roots: Milanese bohemia and an obsession with texts. . . . His character is spelled out but doesn't quite read convincingly. His lady love, the flighty, promiscuous, pinball-playing Lorenza, exists only to symbolize the Gnostic goddess Sophia, and his word-processed effusions, brilliant jumble though they are, just add to this novel's crushing burden of textuality. . . . Though Belbo is shown as rising to a certain heroism before his demise, and his rustic boyhood is intently scanned for an epiphany, he becomes in the end just a toy on a string, and our patience with the novel's plethora of symbols snaps at the point where we are told, of his eccentrically twitching body, that "Belbo hanged from the Pendulum would have drawn, in space, the tree of the Sefirot, summing up in his final moment the vicissitude of all universes, fixing forever in his motion the ten stages of the mortal exhalation and defecation of the divine in the world."

Some rather sweet morals are extracted from this papery honeycomb. The "real secret," in terms of bodily health, is "to let the cells proceed according to their own instinctive wisdom." "It's wrong," Lia tells the inventive Casaubon, "to add to the inventings that already exist." "Truth is brief," Casaubon tells us, near the conclusion of more than two hundred thousand words supposedly confided to paper in the space of two days. He remembers the childhood bliss of biting into a peach, and says, "Like Belbo when he played the trumpet, when I bit into the peach I understood the Kingdom and was one with it. The rest is only cleverness."

Eco's tower of cleverness, which melts in the mind as it is climbed, is a remarkable intellectual phenomenon, however

flimsy and lopsided as an imitation of human actions. One has to think back to the Brothers Grimm and Henry Wadsworth Longfellow to find an academic turning from scholarship to achieve such popular success. Eco is an initiate and an adept in the critical mysteries, whose magus is Jacques Derrida, that have supposedly rendered literature obsolete. *Semiotics and the Philosophy of Language* (1984) and *The Aesthetics of Chaosmos* (1989) are the titles of two of his books that will not make the best-seller list and a million-dollar-plus paperback advance. Derrida-ism, however liberating its effect upon university English faculties, does not offer much encouragement to creative writing. Indeed, insofar as it has revealed the once-revered canon of English-language literary classics to be largely a bag of dirty tricks played by imperialist white males upon minorities and women, it might be supposed to exert a depressive effect. For who wants to add to a bag of dirty tricks? And Eco's novel does come burdened by a complicated, if not downright guilty, conscience. His practical answer to the difficulties of making literature is to appropriate what he calls "dime novel" plots and pump them full to bursting of professional learning. Belbo and Casaubon, those two faces of one post-structuralist coin, argue the case for "cheap fiction": "Maybe only cheap fiction gives us the true measure of reality. . . . Proust was right: life is represented better by bad music than by a Missa solemnis. . . . The dime novel . . . pretends to joke, but then it shows us the world as it actually is—or at least the world as it will become. . . . History is closer to what Sue narrates than to what Hegel projects. Shakespeare, Melville, Balzac, and Dostoyevski all wrote sensational fiction. What has taken place in the real world was predicted in penny dreadfuls." The inclusion of the canonical names muddles what I take to be the basic point: popular romantic narration, by seizing upon our dreams and manipulating our passions, presents the forces that shape the world—"the world as it will become"—as opposed to relatively inert and backward-looking highbrow realism. In this, Eco echoes Borges' distrust of the modernist mandarins, his reiterated preference of Wells and Chesterton over Henry James and James Joyce. But, of course, mandarins distrust themselves, as heroes: Joyce's triumph was to move from the mind of Stephen Dedalus into that of Leopold Bloom—to put a dime-novel mentality in a narrative frame of Thomistic rigor and Homeric grandeur. Eco's strategy in *Foucault's Pendulum* is the reverse: to put his three Milanese bibliophilic polymaths in a dime-novel plot. The novel gothically begins with Casaubon hiding for hours in a kind of periscope within a darkened museum, and ends with a scene of ritual revelry and sacrifice like something out of *Salammbô*. That cumbersome and punishing novel, indeed, is the nearest analogy I can think of for this de-luxe monstrosity, this million-dollar penny dreadful. (pp. 117-20)

John Updike, "In Borges' Wake," in The New Yorker, *Vol. LXV, No. 51, February 5, 1990, pp. 116-20.*

FURTHER READING

Bruss, Elizabeth, and Waller, Marguerite. "An Interview with Um-

berto Eco." *The Massachussetts Review* XIX, No. 2 (Summer 1978): 409-20.
> Discussion of semiotic theory and Structuralist, Marxist, and Anglo-American critics.

De Lauretis, Teresa. "Gaudy Rose: Eco and Narcissism." *SubStance* XIX, No. 2 (1985): 13-29.
> Examines *The Name of the Rose* as a practical demonstration of semiotic theories.

Eco, Umberto. "Reflections on *The Name of the Rose.*" *Encounter* (April, 1985): 7-19.
> Eco discusses the impetus, structure, and title of his novel.

Friedrich, Otto. "Return of Ecomania: A Successor to *The Name of the Rose* Sweeps Italy." *Time* (March 6, 1989): 71.

Mackey, Louis. "The Name of the Book." *SubStance* XIV, No. 2 (1985): 30-9.
> Contrasts the use of humor in *The Name of the Rose* to the novel's description of Aristotelian comedy.

Richter, David H. "Eco's Echoes: Semiotic Theory and Detective Practice in *The Name of the Rose.*" *Studies in Twentieth Century Literature* (Spring 1986): 213-36.
> Postulates that Eco's work is a critique of various detective fictions and historical novels.

Stephens, Walter E. "Ec[h]o in Fabula." *Diacritics* (Summer 1983): 51-64.
> Dense, scholarly study of the influence of semiosis in Eco's narrative strategies.

Sullivan, Scott. "Superstar Professor: Umberto Eco Bridges the Worlds of High Academe and Popular Culture." *Newsweek* (September 29, 1986): 62-3.

John Fante

1909-1983

American novelist, short story writer, and scriptwriter.

Fante is best known for autobiographical novels that center upon the adventures of Arturo Bandini, a struggling young writer who seeks literary success and romance in Los Angeles during the Depression of the 1930s. Critics praise Fante's lyrical, dynamic prose, vivid evocations of place and character, and ability to create ironic yet sympathetically humorous fiction. Although his books originally received little critical or popular attention, many of them have enjoyed an enthusiastic reevaluation following their republication in the 1980s. Bob Shacochis observed: "[Fante's] work deserves to be preserved among the voices of his day—for the singular flavor of the lives it speaks for, his vision of a bygone world, and that vision's influence on the here and now."

Fante was born in Colorado to working-class Italian immigrant parents. His father, a stonemason who suffered from alcoholism, and his mother, a devoutly religious woman, served as models for characters in several of Fante's stories and novels. Fante left for Los Angeles in the early 1930s intent on becoming a successful writer. He lived in poor conditions while working numerous odd jobs and writing short stories. In 1932, Fante's first published story, "Altar Boy," appeared in H. L. Mencken's celebrated magazine, *American Mercury.* Over the next decade Mencken acted as Fante's mentor, printing many of his stories, suggesting that he write screenplays for the cinema, and helping him to find a publisher for his first novel, *Wait Until Spring, Bandini.* Set in a small Colorado town, this work begins the saga of Arturo Bandini, a character whose life closely resembles that of Fante's. Dissatisfied with his poverty, his heritage, and his father's infidelities, the adolescent Arturo dreams of transcending his past through a career in baseball. *Ask the Dust,* which many critics consider Fante's best work, continues the story of Arturo Bandini, now in his early twenties and living in penury in Los Angeles. This novel focuses on Arturo's fluctuating fortunes with writing and his tumultuous relationship with Camilla, an emotionally unstable Mexican waitress who is in love with a man who abuses her.

Fante's third work, *Full of Life,* humorously recounts events surrounding his wife's first pregnancy and her conversion to Catholicism. Although generally considered a novel, this book was originally marketed as an autobiography, for characters share the real names of Fante and his wife. Fante also wrote a screen adaptation of the novel for which he received an Academy Award nomination. From 1940 onward, poor sales of his first three books forced Fante to devote much of his time to writing screenplays for Hollywood studios. Despite his dislike for screenwriting, Fante was successful and his work was well respected in the film industry. He did not publish again until *The Brotherhood of the Grape* appeared in 1977. This novel focuses on the final days of seventy-six-year-old Nick Molise, an Italian-American patriarch whose alcoholism and womanizing result in familial discord despite his son's attempts to reason with him.

Dreams from Bunker Hill is a fragmentary novel that centers on Bandini's frustrations as a Hollywood screenwriter and his affair with his elderly landlady. In *1933 Was a Bad Year,* Fante chronicles the adventures of an adolescent Italian-American baseball player whose aspirations of playing in the major leagues clash with his father's desire that his son follow him into the bricklaying trade. *The Road to Los Angeles,* which was finished in 1933 but remained unpublished until 1985, contrasts Bandini's outrageous delusions of being a great writer with the reality of having to work demeaning jobs to support his mother and sister.

(See also *Contemporary Authors,* Vols. 69-72, 109 [obituary]; *Contemporary Authors New Revision Series,* Vol. 23; and *Dictionary of Literary Biography Yearbook: 1983.*)

PRINCIPAL WORKS

NOVELS

Wait Until Spring, Bandini   1938
Ask the Dust   1939
Full of Life   1952
The Brotherhood of the Grape   1977
Dreams from Bunker Hill   1982

1933 Was a Bad Year   1985
The Road to Los Angeles   1985

SHORT FICTION COLLECTIONS

Dago Red   1940
The Wine of Youth: Selected Stories   1985

SCREENPLAYS

Full of Life   1957
Jeanne Eagles   [with Daniel Fuchs and Sonya Levien]   1957
Walk on the Wild Side   [with Edmund Morris]   1962
The Reluctant Saint   [with Joseph Petracca]   1962

DRAKE DE KAY

Readers of John Fante's short stories in *The Atlantic Monthly, Scribner's* and *The American Mercury* know that he has already demonstrated a mature grasp of character and that he has an instinct for narrative values. It remains to determine whether the accomplished short story writer can produce a creditable novel.

Svevo Bandini, [protagonist of *Wait Until Spring, Bandini*] an Italian stonecutter, lives with his wife and three sons in a 10,000-population town thirty miles from Denver. A typical peasant of the hot-blooded Abruzzi breed, Svevo is madly in love with his beautiful young wife, proud of his American-born boys (Arturo, the eldest, is 14), and proud of his profession. But work is hard to find and the family has for years been desperately poor. They are constantly in debt to the grocer; the bank harries them for the interest of the mortgage on their little house; the boys suffer the humiliation of knowing that they are the only pupils of the parochial school whose parents pay nothing for their education. Not being a stoic, Svevo expresses his bitterness with infantile abandon. Colorado Winters, the banker, the grocer and his mother-in-law call forth a wild torrent of blasphemies and obscenities in two languages.

Maria, on the other hand, is portrayed as a woman of Madonna-like serenity, never complaining of her lot as the wife of Svevo, and this despite her mother's loudly expressed pity for her. After fifteen years Maria still loves her husband passionately. What if he occasionally gets drunk? What if the children sometimes go hungry because their father has lost his last dollar at cards? Her man's rough, masculine passion and her own deep religious faith make life eminently worth living. Moreover, whatever his faults, she knows Svevo will never prefer another woman.

The crisis occurs when Svevo's brawny good looks attract the town's richest widow—a beautiful and cultured American who regards the mason merely as an instrument to satisfy her physical desires. And now an amazing change takes place in Maria. The docile, saintly wife is transformed into that most dangerous of her sex—a woman scorned. Without giving away the dénouement it may be said that the author achieves an ending true to the psychology of his characters and humanly satisfying to one's sense of justice.

Not the least interesting of the story's minor aspects is Arturo's attitude toward his parents and his social environment.

The boy hates his name, because it marks him as of Italian extraction. For his mother he feels a curious mixture of love, hatred and contempt. Her suffering over Svevo's escapade rouses fierce anger against his father; but when the boy glimpses his errant parent in the siren's house, evidently living in the lap of luxury, his rage turns to admiration. What a man! Some day he, Arturo, will be loved by a great lady. The boy's calf-love for a pretty schoolmate, his mental tortures over problems of religion and sex, his childish ambitions—these and other thoughts and experiences of adolescence are handled with the acuteness of a writer who has made a serious study of boy nature.

Drake De Kay, in a review of "Wait Until Spring, Bandini," in The New York Times Book Review, *October 23, 1938, p.6.*

JAMES T. FARRELL

Fante has written short stories of Italian-American-Catholic childhood which have appeared in various magazines, and his first novel, *Wait Until Spring, Bandini,* concerns itself with the same material. One of the most moving of recent first novels, it deals with an Italian workman's family in a small Colorado town. The characterizations are excellent, except for that of an American woman who has an affair with the father.

The description of the family's home life is tender and poignant; in it Fante perceptively establishes the contrast between parents and children, and that among the children themselves. For instance, the notable difference of meaning of the Catholic religion to the devout mother and the conscience-perplexed older son is illustratively revealed: it is a difference defined by the contrast of peasant Italy and contemporary America. Also, Fante's treatment of parochial-school education is both balanced and understanding. He is clever, witty, perceptive. Unfortunately he struggled too much to give his story a plot, and herein he brought in his conventional characterization of the American woman. His material furnishes a better plot in itself. However, despite this criticism, *Wait Until Spring, Bandini* is a work rich in its humanness, a novel by a man of genuine talent.

James T. Farrell, "Two Second-Generation Americans," in The Atlantic Monthly, *Vol. 163, No. 1, January, 1939.*

EDA LOU WALTON

[*Wait Until Spring, Bandini*] tells the story of an Italian-American family in Colorado. The son, an Italian of the second generation in this country, is the chief interpreter of the little drama that takes place between a lusty father and a religious mother.

The characters are real; the style is excellently adapted to the presentation of a simple, untrained mind attempting to articulate and arrange ideas growing out of the contact of the Italian with an alien culture; the whole story is fully imagined and convincing. Actually the plot is very simple, being a quarrel between a husband who suddenly begins to feel important in a new situation and a wife who clings to God until her husband deserts her and then, with precise fury, has her vengeance. But it is not the plot that makes the interest of the book; it is rather the innumerable correct details of life in such a family, together with the quality of the writing. . . .

Mr. Fante's quick images of people and his abrupt but rhythmical sentences bespeak more than the usual skilful novelist. *Wait Until Spring, Bandini,* although it has no such powerful theme, reminds one of Silone's *Fontamara* in its use of a pruned yet at times rich prose to convey the speech of a somewhat inarticulate people. Mr. Fante clearly has deep knowledge of a folk.

> *Eda Lou Walton, "Italy in Colorado," in* The Nation, *New York, Vol. 148, No. 3, January 14, 1939, p. 72.*

PETER MONRO JACK

[*Ask the Dust*] is a clever little story by a second virtuoso Saroyan being the first and better who dramatizes the life of a young writer in all of its brash young egotism. There is a migration of sorts, since Mr. Fante's alter egotist, Arturo Bandini, leaves a settled home in Colorado for the transient and curious life of Los Angeles. But his journey is not of any public interest. It is the private romanticism of a young boy in love with fame. Mr. Fante . . . does manage to turn this ordinarily embarrassing ambition and exhibitionism into a good and readable story.

How much of it is personal history can easily be left to the reader to decide. Mr. Fante's first story was bought in 1932 by H. L. Mencken for *The American Mercury.* Bandini's first story is bought by a J. C. Hackmuth for his magazine. It is called "The Little Dog Laughed," and Bandini arrives in a Los Angeles boarding-house hotel with dozens of copies in his cardboard suitcase ready to autograph all of the dozens for people who have not the slightest interest in it. . . . On every other page "The Little Dog Laughed" is quoted and discussed, to remind us that Arturo is a great writer, neglected for the moment like Poe, Whitman, Dreiser, et al., but destined to take his place on the bookshelf with the B's, alongside Arnold Bennett, who is not quite as good as Bandini. All of this is surely a wry sort of autobiography, a rather touching and amusing burlesque of a young writer smothered in his own conceit, but with an alarm clock to remind him on occasion that he will have to write more and other stories, and that experience is urgently needed.

The experience that Bandini meets with is the story of the novel. It is not particularly new or important, but it is at least very well told. There are two ways of telling it: through the character of this boastful Bandini himself, and through the realistic setting in Los Angeles. Both are equally well done, but the California locale, so carefully particularized in every detail of street, beach and outlying desert, is very effective. . . .

[Bandini] is absurd in everything he does. When he makes some money through selling a story he tips his landlady (who had come from New England) to her ineffable disgust. Down and out, he steals milk from a wagon, only to find that it is buttermilk which he cannot drink. His first sexual experience comes from a crazy old woman who is killed the same night in an earthquake. At last he falls in love with a Mexican "Greaser" who uses and despises him, preferring a tubercular bartender, who in turn despises her. It is all very tragic and very comical, with Bandini, the great writer, romanticizing

all his failures into great adventures and marvelous short stories that his fabulous editor will publish and send checks for.

Mr. Fante deliberately mixes his seriousness with his satire. At one time we have the young writer proclaiming his amazing talents to the stars: and the next moment he is apologizing for his inability even to carry out the slightest part of his romantic schedule. It is at once a warning and a warming-up party for young writers. What is interesting is the style; what is more interesting is that style can't effect miracles; that one may be a young writer with talent but that in the end one's experience counts for everything. It is a novel both for the reader and the writer of a young novelist gaining the experience to write a novel. It is a novel experience. But on the whole, novels about novelists, particularly young novelists, make a tour de force rather than a naturally interesting story.

> *Peter Monro Jack, "A Brash Young Man in Love with Fame," in* The New York Times Book Review, *September 19, 1939, p. 7.*

E. B. GARSIDE

John Fante's writing is a kind of poetry. It is no use arguing that his endings do not rhyme, or that the words do not at all resemble splinters of glass stuck in half-column rows. Fante's poetry breathes in life from a whirligig American existence, far greater than its aggregate members, far wider in scope than any church door. This life is not savored with myrrh, but with hamburger and onions, or perhaps with marijuana smoke. It is brightened only with the sight of a spick waitress, whose proud legs flash in a beer joint where damp sawdust and never a rose strews the floor. It is not much of a life. But it is all some people have, mute legions of them, all the way from leaky-nosed Boston to Long Beach, where nature is a slut in sandals.

Bandini, dark of hair and eye and longing to be called Jones, first popped on the literary scene in *Wait Until Spring, Bandini.* [In *Ask the Dust*] he has removed to the polo-shirted wraiths and papier-mâché of Los Angeles, which he attempts to subdue in the grand manner by the odd method of writing stories. Whether it is the fault of a faultless climate, or because of the oranges snarling liquidly in his stomach,—for Bandini exists almost exclusively on oranges,—his inspiration is for a long time undependable. It is mostly his forty-page letters of tribulation to Hackmuth, editor nonpareil, which get into print—that is, after ending and salutation have been trimmed.

Such a lonely soul, Arturo Bandini, destined like all of us to learn the hard way. It does not matter the smallest tittle that Bandini is bursting with love, eagerness, and passionate understanding. He is alone, and the darlings on the billboards thumb their noses at him.

Ask the Dust realizes to the full the quizzical wonder inherent in Saroyan's fragmentary writings, and recognizes the cruelty of man's lot besides. Fante strikes home as surely as Halper in *The Foundry,* or Swinnerton in *Nocturne,* to use two divergent analogues. The love of Camilla for Sammy and her disintegration when it is not accepted would start tears from a stone. Fante must have lived this out at some time. And now that he has written his *Werther,* let us hope fervently he can go on to another *Faust.*

E. B. Garside, "John Fante vs. John Selby," in The Atlantic Monthly, *Vol. 164, No. 6, December, 1939.*

HARRY LORIN BINSSE

[*Ask the Dust* is] a strange novel, one which is most emphatically *not* recommended for reading by the young, or even by the old who dislike sordid pictures of immorality. . . . Yet in many ways it is quite an extraordinary piece of work, and a very Catholic piece of work at that. We recognize in all the activities of the hero the normal weaknesses, the occasional normal strength by which man is distinguished from both beast and angel. Particularly human is the hero's revulsion to sin, his realization that when he fulfils—or sets about to fulfil—a normal human desire forbidden in the moral code, the fulfilment turns to ashes. Not that this realization acts as a deterrent. In real life it never does, nor does it in this novel.

There is one very beautiful passage in the book which must particularly appeal to a Catholic reader—the passage in which the hero ruminates on what it is to "lose" the Faith, and realizes that the Faith really is not lost, but merely hidden for a time, like the reality of the ocean to a man whose childhood was passed on its shores but who has not for many years seen sea or shore. Here is one of the most profound analyses I have ever read of that peculiar Latin trait, whereby men are baptized, married, buried in Church, but don't otherwise practice their religion. (pp. 140-41)

Harry Lorin Binsse, in a review of "Ask the Dust," in The Commonweal, *Vol. XXXI, No. 6, December 1, 1939, pp. 140-41.*

IRIS BARRY

The best tale [in *Dago Red*] is **"One of Us,"** which most delicately and movingly describes the funeral of a small child from the point of view of another child about the same age. This boy is fascinated by the fact that the father of his dead comrade does not weep, as every other one of the large Italian-American family does with abandon. The effect that his curiosity has on the bereaved father is beautifully indicated.

But Mr. Fante has a special faculty for making clear, with considerable economy and sincere feeling, the strong but transitory moods and conflicts engendered by family life, or between growing children. He does not romanticize childhood and his little boys are demons; but one begins by admiring their toughness and ends by liking their defencelessness, courage and plain badness. . . .

The content of this new volume is perhaps somewhat repetitious, the situations seem almost as familiar as the characters. Father roars and thrashes his sons; mother cooks and lovingly watches the others eat her savoury dishes. The boys play baseball, pilfer things from stores, go to first Communion, commit sins of varying degrees, suffer disappointments and apparent injustice, torment little girls and bring dogs home with them. Still, the material is wonderfully well observed and understood and ably communicated. Poor Father's complex operation with the siren, Coletta Drigo, is really extremely funny even when Mother throws the kitchen soap at him, even when he comes home hopelessly drunk with lipstick smears on his collar. The story which explains why the boy-hero of these tales did not like to be called a Wop is effec-

tive. Perhaps it is because Mr. Fante writes so well that one half wishes he would vary his theme now just the least bit.

Iris Barry, "The Raw Justice of Life," in New York Herald Tribune Books, *September 29, 1940, p. 2.*

MARIANNE HAUSER

[*Dago Red*] is a book where the author's talent lies over each page bright as sunlight on a fresh green lawn. It is neither a novel nor a collection of short stories, but a freely constructed family portrait, seen impressionistically through the eyes of a small boy, and the mind of young manhood. Fante's style is clear and simple, so simple that it could easily grow mannered under the hands of a lesser artist. . . .

The people in *Dago Red* are all at once good Catholics, good Americans and typical Italians who live in a small town out West, not far from Denver. Compared to great happenings, their family events are not spectacular, but for Jimmy they spell thrill, excitement, drama. . . . Each episode stands off clear, brightly colored like the scenes on old under-glass paintings to which Fante's writing seems akin in its naive simplicity and strong expressiveness.

Jimmy's father, a bricklayer by profession and a crazy artist at heart, is a far more than temperamental character. Strong arms and an undisciplined mind, an unpredictable display of cruelty or warmth, and a constant need to boast make him an inconvenient yet lovable comedian. Nobody fears him much as long as he works; but in Winter, when the mortar freezes and the cold wind makes his hands grow stiff, he has to go home and wait for Spring. This is the time when his craziness becomes a menace to all, a source of continuous excitement for his children, and of continuous worries for his wife Maria. All her life Maria has known little else but hard work. Poverty and worries have made her old before her time, and silent rather than hard. Patiently she endures her husband's fantastic temperament, and it is only when she finds him unfaithful to her that a sudden torrent of wild passion breaks loose. She then cries out aloud and throws pots and pans, proving that she is as hotblooded as her husband and as Italian.

The chapters are well rounded, like Valenti Angelo's expressive woodcuts which introduce each episode. Yet despite its loose construction, the book does not fall apart. It is held together organically by the tales of Jimmy's development. Out of early childhood impressions grow the problems of his later life. Nationality and religion color the boy's background and decide his growth. To the child religion is something so natural that it has a physical rather than mystical effect. His feelings after the confession are described beautifully in the story of his first communion. "I never felt so clean. I was a bar of soap. I was fresh water. I was bright tinfoil. I was a new suit of clothes. I was a haircut. I was Christmas Eve and a box of candy. I floated. I whistled. Some day I would be a priest."

Marianne Hauser, "The Portrait of an Italian Family," in The New York Times Book Review, *September 29, 1940, p. 7.*

HARRY SYLVESTER

[Fante] began to write at a time when there was a cult of the naïve prevalent in American letters, and while he has never been consciously naïve like Mr. Saroyan, he perhaps used the child's point of view in his stories a bit too much. This is noticeable in most of the early stories. It was a difficult task Mr. Fante set for himself, to use a child's psychology and phraseology, even, and yet to give his stories the subtlety of distinguished fiction. He failed more often than he succeeded, and his self-appointed task has not made for a good style.

One tires somewhat of the same Italians, rendered in considerable detail; and despite his accuracy and frequent sharp observation, Mr. Fante's work can be pretty dull. Eleven of the thirteen stories in [**Dago Red**] concern the same family, and while Mr. Fante has written little that is untrue, he has managed to include much that is trivial. The twelfth story, **"The Wrath of God,"** seems definitely to mark a change for the better and is the best story in the book.

Whereas the frequent references to the Church in the early stories lead one to believe that for Mr. Fante the intellectual content of Catholicism is delineated by the Baltimore Catechism, **"The Wrath of God"** shows that Mr. Fante, unlike almost all other American writers, is aware of the subtleties, scope and general ramifications of Catholicism. It is a fine story, almost perfect, and one that not even Graham Greene would be ashamed to own. (p. 533)

Mr. Fante appears to be one of those people who is in the Church one day and out the next. But he is a good writer and it is not too much to hope that he will be one of the few Americans we can look to . . . for truthful and subtle interpretations of Catholicism in fiction, as distinguished from the horrible drivel, written in a mixture of holy water and honey, which has come down to us under the name of "Catholic Fiction." (pp. 533-34)

Harry Sylvester, in a review of "Dago Red," in The Commonweal, Vol. XXXII, No. 26, October 18, 1940, pp. 533-34.

P. M. PASINETTI

[**Full of Life**] is presented by the dust-jacket as "extravagant domestic comedy," like certain Cary Grant pictures. Even from the cover drawings you guess it has to do with the Young Married Couple: there are going to be the domestic and psychological difficulties connected with the first pregnancy, the Young Husband's confusion, and, since the narrator is of Italian origin, you know that there is going to be the Loving Mother with Ancient Superstitions and the Rustic Father who promises to be Quite a Character. You begin to worry.

But as soon as you start going through the book you forget your worries entirely. I even felt that Mr. Fante must have been so sure of his serious artistic purposes that he daringly liked to work in cliché-ridden territory to prove the freshness of his view. He is very successful in doing so.

The central theme is indeed the heroine's approaching motherhood. She is, to put it vaguely, the attractive American girl who also "reads," while her husband, John Fante, the narrator, the son of an immigrant from Ignazio Silone's region of Italy, is an American writer; in fact, one settled with an office and a secretary in the Los Angeles area—a script-writer. And they expect their first child. (p. 17)

The more you read, even if occasionally you laugh out loud, you realize this short novel is quite a serious book. For instance, you read: "A woman's confinement was a bad time for a man. Creation gave her terrible strength . . ." By then you are used to taking such simple and deep words at their full value. Part of the woman's strength is used in a religious conversion—she embraces the faith of *his* parents. The relation between her motherhood and her renewed religiosity presented certain dangers, especially now that religion is, so to speak, a literary fad. Mr. Fante, as he avoids the horrors of cuteness in dealing with his comic effects, avoids pretentiousness in handling his serious theme; nor does he let himself be tempted by the images of his Italian background (the parents' archaic and picturesque beliefs) into building some pompous myth of motherhood. He is restrained and persuasive. . . . (pp. 17-18)

[Also] the main supporting character, the Italian father, is very acceptable, in fact unforgettably interesting, and not the usual "pastoral" creation we feared he might be. The balance of attachment and opposition in the American son's feelings is beautifully worked out. In this particular sense the novel shows a conjunction of Old World and New World which cuts quite deep into the level of sentiments, atavisms, and "culture" in general. For doing so while remaining a concrete and lively story, the book, in its intentional limits, is extraordinarily successful. (p. 18)

P. M. Pasinetti, "Immigrants' Children," in The Saturday Review, New York, Vol. XXXV, No. 17, April 26, 1952, pp. 17-18, 33.

JOANNA SPENCER

[**Full of Life,** by John Fante], starts out to be a witty and charming account of a man's adjustment to his wife's pregnancy. Tender and extremely funny, the book follows the prenatal growth of the Fante's baby, with its attendant effects on the mother. . . . Joyce Fante goes through work obsessions, too. The first is housekeeping of unprecedented violence. Then comes planting outside the house, moving the shrubbery around. The Fante in-laws also become involved, when the kitchen floor of the young couple's Los Angeles house is eaten away by termites, and John coaxes his father, an Italian immigrant bricklayer, to come repair the damage. The elder Mr. Fante comes, not much interested in the repair job, but determined to have a grandson. . . .

Another desire of Joyce's is to join the Catholic Church. At first the reader is led to think this belongs in the same category as reading Gesell and taking showers in the middle of the night, but it soon becomes clear that this is an extremely serious and moving experience, culminating just before the birth of the child in the formal ceremony of entering the Church. John, a Catholic who has many years ago drifted away from his religion, tries to share her experience and finds he cannot, but retains his attitude of sympathetic wonder at what is happening to his wife. The book ends with the birth of the child, leaving the reader touched, and, at the same time, somewhat surprised that the significant religious experience should have been coupled with such a lighthearted, charming account of pregnancy.

Joanna Spencer, "Pre-Natal," in New York Herald Tribune Book Review, April 27, 1952, p. 9.

JOE DEVER

[John Fante] really should be better known as a serious writer able to evoke the human comedy wisely and pungently out of an earthy Italian-American background which was centered largely in Denver and San Juan, California. (p. 155)

In *Full Of Life* he tells the rollicking and heart-warming story of his wife's first pregnancy. He calls Fante, Fante, and so on; it is all very candid to a fetching degree.

Yet, autobiographical writing is dangerous, over the long run, because there are only so many veins to a mine. This will be Mr. Fante's problem in the future, as is now manifest in the desperate retrogression of Mr. Saroyan. Good autobiographical writing is worth the risk of ultimate dryness, however; time cannot mellow reprintable material, and when the literary coffin is opened, there is the smell of good earth and fresh air.

For when an autobiographical writer is good, he is very, very good, as in this work. Herein, a successful screen writer finds himself, through the hilarious yet ennobling experience of fathering a child and "mothering" a mother whose bibles are Dr. Spock and the Bible.

Hitherto, Fante was all for birth control and had apparently read and suffered his way out of the Church. His loss of faith had a remarkable sweetness about it when you consider his intellectual honesty, subdued bitterness and lack of animosity toward the clergy.

Anyway, Fante journeys to San Juan from Los Angeles and fetches papa Nick, an engaging paisano who has very strong ideas on the subject of grandsons and more grandsons. Wife Joyce is reading and suffering her way *into* the church. Papa Nick, who hasn't been to Confession in many years, thinks her conversion is a fine thing. In fact, he thinks anything this zany, pregnant woman does is a fine thing, because she is bringing his indirect blood and bone into the world. (pp. 155-56)

There are many delicious and moving vignettes in the work: Joyce Fante reading Canon Law and needling her husband: "If I die, you can't marry my sister." Father Gandolfo, her mentor, answering Fante's complicated objections to the Church with verbatim statements from the penny catechism. The false-alarm rush to the maternity ward. The power and solemnity of birth, binding husband, wife and baby together with hoops of steel. (p. 156)

Joe Dever, "Laughter Mixed with Woe," in The Commonweal, Vol. LVI, No. 6, May 16, 1952, pp. 155-56.

JOE DAVID BELLAMY

[*The Brotherhood of the Grape*] revolves around Henry Molise, a civilized and sedentary man who has flown in from L.A. hoping to act as a peacemaker when he learns that his aged parents in San Elmo, Calif., are considering a divorce. In a swell of filial piety, Henry is euchred into a futile expedition into the Sierras with his implacable old stonemason of a father, Nick, and his drinking cronies—the brotherhood of the grape—for the ostensible purpose of constructing a stone smokehouse. The project, meant to be a culminating act of some sort for the old man, turns out to be a drunken fiasco that both aggravates and unites father and son in unexpected ways, and leads to old Nick's eventual collapse and death. Though this may not seem a likely scenario for comedy, and it isn't entirely, Fante's instinct for farce tempers the agony and travail.

A sample of the desperate conceit Henry has to deal with in his father: the old man has squashed his youngest son Mario's chances to play professional baseball because of his wish that the boy remain under his thumb as an apprentice stonemason. In a fit of cheek, Mario quits. As punishment his father refuses to speak to him for years afterwards, in fact, crosses to the other side of the street when he sees Mario approaching. On Sunday afternoons Nick goes out to the ballpark (where Mario is still trying to pick up the pieces of his ruined career) to root vehemently for the opposing team. One boozy day when Mario hits a home run to win the game, his enraged father leaps from the stands, tackles him as he rounds third base, and has to be dragged off by the police. . . .

John Fante has an economical style, a measured confident gait, and a feel for one-liners and the unanticipated quintessential gesture. *The Brotherhood of the Grape* is alternately full of cleansing laughter and as comical as a toothache. (p. 31)

Joe David Bellamy, in a review of "The Brotherhood of the Grape," in The New York Times Book Review, March 6, 1977, pp. 30-1.

GERALD VOLPE

Ask the Dust is most probably autobiographical in the following themes: the hero's struggle to become a successful writer: the schizophrenic-like tension between the pull of his parents' comforting life, which he has abandoned for Los Angeles, and the searing existence in the urban environment; the sexual and romantic needs of a healthy young man of twenty (concretized in his love-hate relationship with Camilla the Mexican), and his more general feelings of existential angst (which surely find a main source in the second generation problems of adaptation). In Fante's work generally, existentialism (individual man struggling against nature and other humans) and Freudian psychology (the search for the mother) fuse with earlier preoccupations of the Italian-American novel (the struggle of the urban immigrant, the fight for a piece of the action in mainstream America, the sense of being out of joint).

The novel is set in Los Angeles during the Great Depression, and the action moves from a seedy residential hotel on Bunker Hill to the Mojave Desert. The author immediately establishes his "persona" as a penniless writer, alienated from his Yankee-dominated surroundings, tenaciously hanging onto the American dream. As the novel progresses, Bandini reveals other elements of his personality. He contributes to racial antagonisms as a result of prejudices experienced in his childhood. He is anti-clerical but tends to religiosity; he rails at God for permitting evil and suffering in the world; he is unable to separate sex from commitment and love for he has a deep moral nature. He fears death, the common end of humankind, but he vaunts his faith in himself, in his own talent, and in his manhood. A kind of black-humored pessimism pervades much of the novel.

The style depends on ironic juxtaposition, a kind of Charlie Chaplin kaleidoscope, jumping from one scene to another, via flashback, present-tense narration and reveries of success at the typewriter and with all the "princesses" he will meet in his travels. Declarative sentences, parataxis, colloquialisms, apostrophe, lush lyricism—these are the main building blocks of a style that Bukowski characterizes in the preface as a "flow". Every so often, a personal use of language shocks the reader: "son of miseried parents", "the tremblers were ceasing".

In chapter four Bandini meets the Mexican bar waitress Camilla, whom he turns through sheer fantasy into his "Mayan princess." Their love-hate relationship is symbolic of ethnic hostilities as well as the larger male-female antagonism. The tormenting affair, which takes up the greater part of the novel, is essentially stillborn and ends in tragedy. It is the motherly and physically ravaged Vera Rivken ("a slice out of life") who surprisingly inspires Bandini to write a successful novel when he believes that an earth quake is visited upon Southern California by an avenging God to punish the young man for his mortal sin against Vera. It is Vera's self-sacrifice that regenerates Bandini, while Camilla disappears into the dust of the Mojave desert. The novelist is born in the pain of despair and the hope of universal love. (pp. 93-5)

> *Gerald Volpe, in a review of "Ask the Dust," in* MELUS, *Vol. 7, No. 2, Summer, 1980, pp. 93-5.*

GERALD LOCKLIN

[*The Wine of Youth: Selected Stories*] consists of two sets of John Fante stories: those from his 1940 collection *Dago Red,* and seven later tales. . . . He was rediscovered in the 1970's through the surfacing of his, in retrospect, obvious influence upon Charles Bukowski. . . . (p. 482)

Dago Red is a masterpiece of second-generation immigrant literature. The titles of some of these related stories (or chapters of a disjunctive bildungsroman) are self-explanatory: **"First Communion," "Altar Boy," "Big Leaguer," "The Odyssey of a Wop," "Hail Mary."** The young protagonist's Denver world is epitomized in his baseball games against schools named Emerson, Thoreau, Whitman. It is a beautifully goofy world of ethnic and sexual contradictions in which a boy can make a pin-up of a nun, and a nun can tell a student, "You are a dirty boy, and I have a notion to beat you to death." Here real boys don't ever say they're sorry, and their poor but proud mothers send the nuns pots of macaroni. Aspiration, acculturation, sublimation, and hyphenation—Italian-American, Penseroso-Allegro, Catholic-Pagan—these are the counter-forces that drive John Fante in search of artistic fusion.

The later stories are certainly not superior to the earlier, but they are interesting in light of the contention of Bukowski and others that Hollywood took its toll on Fante's literary talent. **"One-Play Oscar"** is strictly Bad News Bears: A fifty-year-old cop in one play as fullback unifies the ethnically diverse **"All-Americans"** against the Japanese Settlement Team, which features the unstoppable plunges of the manchild Irish Hagarono. The story has heart-warming plastered all over its marquee. Still, Fante is a craftsman even at sentimentality and it's easy to see why he was a success at the Dream Factory. None of the other stories is that patently commercial. For some reason Fante burdens the young protagonist of **"Scoundrel"** with an Irish surname, but the story does convey the power and compassion of the Church in the American neighborhood. **"The Dreamer"** and **"Helen, Thy**

Beauty Is to Me—" provide unusual views of Filipino laborers for whom the money to be made in the West Coast fields and canneries is good pay indeed, even if the life is hard, seasonal, and peripatetic. The problem is that there are no potential wives.

It is, however, in **"A Nun No More," "In the Spring,"** and **"My Father's God"** that Fante is at his happiest amidst the passions of that functioning family life that he left behind in coming to L.A. (where at the center of the fictional worlds of West, Chandler and others, as shown by Paul Skenazy, reigns the dysfunctional or perverted family). A girl refuses loveless betrothal; a father welcomes back a prodigal son (who's hopped a train with the dream of a baseball tryout); a patriarch leaves the religion of the priests to his wife and children, preferring for himself the pre-Christian deity of his bootleg wine. (pp. 482-83)

> *Gerald Locklin, in a review of "The Wine of Youth," in* Studies in Short Fiction, *Vol. 22, No. 4, Fall, 1985, p. 482-83.*

GERALD MANGAN

> I decided to eat at Jim's Place, because I still had some money. I ordered ham and eggs. While I ate, Jim talked.
>
> He said "You read a lot. Did you ever try writing a book?"
>
> That did it. From then on, I wanted to be a writer.
>
> "I'm writing a book right now", I said.
>
> He wanted to know what kind of a book.
>
> I said "My prose is not for sale. I write for posterity."

John Fante was twenty-two when he gave this dry account of budding aspirations, in an early chapter of *The Road to Los Angeles* (1933), a first novel that remained unpublished until after his death in 1983. The narrator is Arturo Bandini, the endearingly vainglorious hero of the trilogy now reprinted as the Bandini Saga, *Wait Until Spring, Bandini* (1938), *Ask the Dust* (1939) and *Dreams from Bunker Hill* (1982). Reappearing under various names in the stories in *The Wine of Youth* (originally published in 1940 as *Dago Red*) and the early, undated novel *1933 Was a Bad Year,* this ubiquitous persona shares most of the given facts of Fante's own early life. The son of poor Italian-Catholic parents in small-town Colorado, whose burning ambitions lead him to the bright lights of Los Angeles, Bandini is clearly the *alter ego* in what amounts to a serial autobiography.

Fante seems to have sold most of his prose, after all, but posterity has been lamentably slow to evaluate it. This may be partly explained by the twenty-five years of silence that followed *Full of Life* (1952), when he was occupied with screenwriting and increasingly disabled by illness, but there is something mysterious in his complete absence from the roll-call of 1930s novelists. Like Steinbeck and Dos Passos, his roots lie very much in the working-class naturalism evolved by Sinclair Lewis's generation; but his boldly egocentric approach helps to set him apart from the more earnest sagas of the Depression, and invites closer comparison with William Saroyan and the early Henry Miller. As a conspicuous living exponent of the genre, Charles Bukowski contributes a reverent preface to *Ask the Dust* invoking him as a lifetime influence . . . , and hinting at a story of "terrible luck, and a terrible fate" that still remains to be told.

As a young man in downtown Los Angeles, "starving and drinking and trying to be a writer", Bukowski was well placed to identify with Bandini, in the same circumstances; but Fante was evidently not encouraged to be quite as raw as Bukowski in his portrayal of them. *The Road to Los Angeles* seems to have been rejected as too "provocative" for the period, although its nearest approach to indecency is a relatively tactful treatment of the adolescent hero's sexual fantasies, and his rather more shameless confessions as a thief and liar. A shiftless casual worker, sharing a cramped flat with his mother and sister, poring over "art-model" magazines and metaphysics, and dreaming of love and fame, Bandini is an archetype of the proletarian autodidact, who has fallen under the spell of Nietzsche. Ashamed of his background and enraged by his poverty, he is bitterly scornful of all the Catholic virtues, and painfully torn between desire and contempt for women.

The story is episodic and largely unresolved, except for his eventual departure, but fortunately Fante had by then distanced himself just enough to exploit its comic potential. The delusions of grandeur lead to broad farce on his first day at a fish-cannery, when he proclaims his superiority in typically lofty style ("I'm not here permanently: I'm a writer"), and proceeds to humiliate himself by vomiting convulsively in front of the entire Filipino work-force. . . . The comedy is Quixotic in the truest sense, but it alternates subtly with the darker side of his megalomania—notably in the incestuous tensions that arise from his frustration, and an unforgettable scene where he wreaks gory vengeance on a colony of crabs.

His next novel—actually his début—looked further back for a more mature view of his origins, and proved to be his masterpiece. Set in the snowbound foothills of the Rockies in Colorado, which form a permanent white backdrop to the action, *Wait Until Spring, Bandini* is a lucid and strikingly unsentimental account of a close-knit family struggling, against the odds, to survive hard times with dignity; and its most impressive achievement is the central portrait of his parents. Svevo Bandini, the peasant bricklayer from Abruzzi who can't lay bricks for the snow, dominates the landscape like a wounded bear—clearing the yard to assuage his fury, and snapping at his three unruly sons. While he gambles away his pittance in the local pool-hall, his pious wife Maria prays for his soul; and the crisis develops when her censorious mother announces an impending visit. Svevo goes on a drunk in dread of her arrival, succumbs to the allure of a rich widow, and leaves Maria to endure the mystery of his absence. . . .

A lesser novelist might have made a monster of this figure; but Fante's skilful rendering of Svevo's viewpoint, in the third person, enables us to sympathize with the volatile pride that makes his poverty all the more insufferable. His eldest son Arturo, who comes into focus only gradually, has obviously inherited enough to identify with his father's shame; and this growing mutual reflection gives the novel much of its force. In his dreams of baseball stardom, his worship of the movies, and his obstinate passion for a pretty Italian classmate, Arturo displays the same impulsive hubris that drives his father to infidelity; and when it threatens Maria's health, there is a rare poignancy in the role he assumes to reconcile them. From a wintry atmosphere of sin, instilled at

school by a strong cast of nuns, the narrative moves unobtrusively towards a sense of redemption.

Fante may have been exaggerating slightly when he wrote, in the prefatory note to the new edition, that "all of the people of my writing life, all of my characters are to be found in this early work", but it is certainly true that he re-worked the material in many different forms; several books soon merge together, as parts of a single vivid picture. The short stories give the most complete version of his Italian-Catholic roots and boyhood traumas: the terrors of hell and the joys of absolution, the stigma of "dago" blood, and the sheer claustrophobia of the one-horse town. *1933 Was a Bad Year* is a slight but sharply-drawn account of his dogged efforts to escape a future in brick-laying, as mapped out by his father, and sign up as a pitcher for the Chicago Cubs. Poverty lends a hand in his defeat, as it does when he courts a local rich girl, but both of these escape bids are characteristically clumsy.

By the time he does light out for the territory on the Coast, literature has replaced baseball as the dream-route to riches. His eye is on the Nobel Prize more than on Hollywood, and the second and third novels of the trilogy—*Ask the Dust* and *Dreams from Bunker Hill*—complete the chronicle of his struggle in that direction. There is a large element of introspection in this adoption of the artist as hero, and it may be that writers will read the books with a more acute sense of recognition than other readers; but it is hard to think of many more entertaining versions of the familiar story. Bandini is aflame with the conviction of his genius, once again; but Fante leaves no corner of his vanity unexposed; and his quixotic quest remains grounded in the fallen world of Sancho Panzas—the bartenders, waitresses, landladies and whores who cast a cold eye on his self-esteem.

Sprawled between the ocean and the desert, Los Angeles makes the perfect setting for the extremes of his own nature; and it is painted in detail, with a rare intensity of colour—the saloons and drugstores, the flea-pits and flop-houses, the jails and hop-joints, the dance-halls and burlesque-shows. In a cheap hotel with flimsy walls, Bandini lives on credit and oranges, labours for weeks to describe a palm-tree, and pours out his soul in letters to the only editor who buys his fiction. In both novels the plots are subordinate to the self-portrait; but in *Ask the Dust* his main fixation is Camilla, a neurotic Mexican waitress who inspires a lurid kaleidoscope of emotions—from worship to contempt, from impotence to frantic lust, from pity to a touchingly sublime resignation. When he narrowly survives an earthquake, in one of the most haunting episodes, it appears as one of the lesser upheavals of his life.

In following the pattern of his own experience so closely, Fante seems not to have displayed any great faculty for pure invention; but it is also easy to assume that little of imaginative significance occured to him after the year of Pearl Harbor. Although *Dreams from Bunker Hill* was dictated during his final years, after he had lost his sight, it takes the same story forward only a year or so, to his first spell on a Hollywood payroll. Bandini shares a bed with an elderly landlady, and a house with a world-weary English colleague, but he is still the same callow youth at the end of it—going home on a Greyhound to his mother's pasta, and making an ass of himself at a gathering of his former social superiors.

Bandini's tireless braggadocio to the folks back home . . . is comically at odds with the anguish he actually feels as an overpaid eunuch. When not lusting vainly after his secretary, or twiddling his thumbs in the studio office, he is frittering away his energies on a worthless western, so mutilated by his co-writer that he has to withdraw his credit. It's a compelling account of a common disillusionment, shared by many real writers; and its surface wryness does not distract us from the sense that it crystallizes a few decades of frustration.

Gerald Mangan, "Artist of the Fallen World," in The Times Literary Supplement, No. 4381, March 20, 1987, p. 303.

JACK BYRNE

[*The Road to Los Angeles*] about a young man breaking away from his family and roots in San Pedro and the Los Angeles Harbor to become a writer is valuable not only as evidence of the writer's promise as a novelist, but also as a document about the kind of contemporary writing that was rejected in the years just prior to World War II. . . . Fante's alter ego, Arturo Gabriel Bandini, is the central figure in a domestic tragedy of the 1930s not unlike thousands of others. Bandini, a recent high school graduate whose father is dead, is required to take menial jobs in order to support his mother and teenage sister—ditch digger, dishwasher, flunkie on a truck, grocery clerk, worker in the Soyo Fish Company. So what? Tom in *The Glass Menagerie* works in a shoe factory (like Williams). Like Bandini, he, too, has a mother and sister. And like Bandini, in the end he runs away—he to the Coast Guard, Arturo to Los Angeles. What makes Fante's *Road* worth reading is that he has, in Bandini, created a memorable character who is the victim of immature fantasies—especially about women and the profession of writing—which will force him out of San Pedro and the demoralizing and demeaning jobs available at that time. Unlike Joyce's Stephen Dedalus, who at the end of *The Portrait* welcomes the life of a writer, Bandini has yet to produce anything worth reading. His sister Mona, responding to his manuscript, "Love Everlasting or The Woman a Man Loves or Omnia Vincit Amor," 69,009 words, says it all: "It's silly. Plain silly. It doesn't grip me. It gripes me. . . . It's the worst book I ever read. . . . You fool. You can't write. You can't write at all." True. Bandini can't write as he runs away from his family, though he may later, but John Fante can, and did. (pp. 206-07)

Jack Byrne, in a review of "The Road to Los Angeles," in The Review of Contemporary Fiction, Vol. 8, No. 1, Spring, 1988, pp. 206-07.

BROOKE K. HORVATH

Published originally in 1952, *Full of Life* was John Fante's most commercially successful novel. . . . Having much in common with his other work—particularly the novels chronicling the adventures of Arturo Bandino, an aspiring Italian-American writer—*Full of Life* reveals the autobiographical sources of Fante's inspiration by presenting Fante, his wife, and father stripped of fictional camouflage: "I walked out into my front yard and stood among roses and gloated over my house. The rewards of authorship. Me, author, John Fante." Indeed, as Mullen notes, the novel was so manifestly autobiographical, it was marketed initially as nonfiction.

The story, a small masterpiece of quiet comedy, follows Fante through the months of his wife's first pregnancy, during which time she suffers a conversion to Catholicism and begins to dote on her father-in-law, a stereotypical yet warmly drawn Italian immigrant fetched from his Sacramento Valley home to repair his son's new but termite-infested house beautiful. Papa Fante, who likewise dotes on his daughter-in-law (always referring to her as Miss Joyce), finds little to applaud in the city-slick ways of his son, who makes his living, good Lord, writing stories! Papa's presence in the house off Wilshire at this tense and trying time makes for much comedy—and for much touching sentiment, as in this scene after Joyce has given birth to the grandson papa has been awaiting for so long:

> Papa was standing at the window in the waiting room. I put my hand on his shoulder and he turned. I didn't have to say anything. He began to cry. He laid his head on my shoulder and his weeping was very painful. I felt the bones of his shoulders, the old softening muscles, and I smelled the smell of my father, the sweat of my father, the origin of my life. I felt his hot tears and the loneliness of man and the sweetness of all men and the aching haunting beauty of the living.

It is this warm humanness, this sorrow-laced love—pushing on but never breaking through the boundary between sentiment and sentimentality—that makes Fante more than an American P. G. Wodehouse. Given the qualities of the fiction we often value today, *Full of Life* will seem to many a terribly unfashionable novel, which is too bad for us. It is a novel, in short, full of life. . . .

Brooke K. Horvath, in a review of "Full of Life," in The Review of Contemporary Fiction, Vol. 8, No. 3, Fall, 1988, p. 169.

LEM COLEY

It is a truth universally acknowledged that a young man in possession of a pregnant wife must be a comic figure, and *Full of Life* (1952) is a series of anecdotes on that theme. Fante uses his own name, and apparently the episodes are true. A 30-year-old screenwriter and his wife move into their first house—four bedrooms, rose bushes, peaked roof, picket fence, just off Wilshire Boulevard—to start a family. Soon she's lying in bed propping up Arnold Gesell's *Infant and Child in the Culture of Today* on the visible evidence of her pregnancy. She has whims, takes up gardening. He's admiring her belly one night, thinks he feels two heads, and sneaks down to the hospital at 3:30 a.m. to pester the doctor.

The book is saved when she falls through the kitchen floor—termites—and Fante heads for the Sacramento Valley to visit Momma and Poppa and bring the old man back to L.A. to fix the kitchen.

The best joke is that Pop never repairs the kitchen floor. He tears out the living room wall and builds a ten-by-six foot stone fireplace, fit for the hall of the mountain kings, to keep his grandson warm during the long L.A. winters. . . .

There's a nice period irony when the wife, a small town WASP, decides she wants to be taken into the church and starts reading Newman and canon law. Fante is appalled. For him Catholicism is the ghetto, women in black shawls, Momma asking him if he goes to mass. Leaving the church is personal liberation, moving into modern American life. But she's an intellectual too, moving towards the early fifties Christian chic of Eliot, Greene, Lowell, O'Connor, Tate, and Waugh.

The upshot is that a baby boy arrives. Everybody's happy. Pop goes home. *Full of Life* was made into a movie with, I should guess, very little rewriting necessary to render it suitable for the screen.

Pop is also the main energy source in *The Brotherhood of the Grape* (1977), although this is a darker work with some of the raw-onion bite of Fante's first novel. He published *Brotherhood* when he was 69, a year before diabetes blinded him. Here he kills off his father, the irascible, priapic, alter ego and scene stealer Fante had fought with, put down, and showed off so often in his fiction.

At 76, Pop—this time named Nick Molise, "Old Nick"—still fights for his right to party. As the book opens, his wife of 51 years finds lipstick on his drawers and a fight ensues.

When Henry, the screenwriter son, comes up from Redondo Beach to help out, he finds himself conned into serving as his father's hod carrier. Pop wants to build a smokehouse for a crony who has a motel above the Donner Pass. The day after it's finished, the smokehouse collapses, and the day after that, Old Nick collapses into a diabetic coma. Back home in the hospital, recuperating, he sneaks out and heads for Angelo Musso's winery, where Henry finds him seated at a picnic table under a grape arbor drinking Chianti and eating prosciutto with his buddies from the Cafe Roma (the "brotherhood of the grape"). He dies there.

This book grows on you. When Fante is going right he can find the seam between slapstick and something harshly passionate—a little like Fellini at times. In the thirties reviewers compared him to Saroyan, and you can see what they meant, but Edmund Wilson in "The Boys in the Back Room" (1940)—an essay about the West Coast writers like Horace McCoy and Steinbeck who were Fante's contemporaries—spoke of Saroyan's instinct to "exploit this theme of loving-kindness and of the goodness and rightness of things; and there is perhaps a just perceptible philistinism." Not so Fante. The scenes in *Brotherhood,* for example, where father and son build the stone smokehouse are not milked for a phony, redemptive reconciliation. And yet so much of the enormous field of emotional activity generated by the father-son dyad is put into play. As far back as the first novel, *Wait until Spring Bandini,* Fante focused on the father's adulteries.

Black Sparrow Press has done a good deed by reissuing this work, which is vivid and open, in contrast to today's attenuated fiction. Still, I don't quite see Fante as a writer who had to be resurrected. I suppose there is a certain regional appeal, and the friendship of Charles Bukowski, who wrote an admiring preface to another Black Sparrow Fante, may have influenced this prestigious press to bring out these books. There's a telling moment in *Full of Life* when Fante cannot follow his wife back into the church. "How could I confess that for which I had no remorse." This is admirable and healthy by contemporary standards, but it may bar a novelist from the top rank. In both of these books, Fante pauses for a detour past one of his favorite stories—his days as a starving young writer in L.A. Now, this is a theme of many classic novels, but in them the poor boy from the provinces must not only make it in the city but keep his soul intact. In Fante, the soul never seems at risk.

Lem Coley, "California: No Remorse," in The American Book Review, Vol. 11, No. 1, March-April, 1989, p. 8.

FURTHER READING

Bukowski, Charles. Preface to *Ask the Dust,* by John Fante, pp. 5-7. Santa Barbara: Black Sparrow, 1980.
Brief tribute to Fante, whom Bukowski identifies as "a lifetime influence on my writing."

Clark, Tom. "The Luck of John Fante." *Los Angeles Times Book Review* (9 April 1989): 4.
Biographical and critical overview.

Manguel, Alberto. "Chic Bums." *Saturday Night* 104, No. 3710 (May 1989): 63-5.
Profiles the recent popularity Fante's books have enjoyed among French readers.

Shacochis, Bob. "Forgotten Son of the Lost Generation." *Vogue* 177, No. 3269 (December 1987): 190, 192, 202, 210.
Appreciative evaluation of Fante's works spurred by the resurgence of interest in his writing.

Spotnitz, Frank. "The Hottest Dead Man in Hollywood." *American Film* XIV, No. 9 (July/August 1989): 40-4, 54.
Article on the spate of Fante's novels that are being adapted for film. Offers a positive assessment of Fante's career.

Marilyn French

1929-

(Born Marilyn Edwards; has also written under the pseudonym Mara Solwoska.) American novelist, critic, and short story writer.

Best known for her first novel, the highly popular feminist polemic *The Women's Room,* French is an author of controversial, emotional works that provoke both enthusiastic and antagonistic responses from reviewers. A former homemaker whose academic aspirations led her to Harvard during the politically turbulent 1960s, French draws upon her experiences of motherhood, divorce, academia, and political activism to describe the concerns of women who eventually rebel against domesticity, sexual submission, and occupational discrimination. While some critics denounce French's ideological fiction and nonfiction as belligerent and declamatory, her works are widely read and often examined in women's studies courses.

Generally considered one of the most influential novels of the modern feminist movement, *The Women's Room* follows the evolution of Mira, a repressed and submissive woman trapped in an unsatisfying marriage who eventually divorces, returns to academia, and adopts feminist values. From the stultifying suburban milieu of the 1950s to the male-dominated counter-culture of the 1960s, French depicts sexism in America as a pervasive and pernicious social force that acts to advance the oppression and exploitation of women. Through various characters, French illustrates the psychological and physical abuses frequently inflicted on women, and, by depicting meetings involving these characters, French recreates consciousness-raising dialogues that often inspired women to political activism. Augmenting French's discussion of moderate feminism is a more radical orientation represented by Val, an eloquent member of the group who becomes militant after her daughter is sexually assaulted. When the rape trial becomes more an indictment of the young woman than of the rapist, Val joins a women's separatist colony that advocates the violent overthrow of patriarchal American society. Some reviewers were offended by French's sympathetic treatment of Val's position and variously castigated the novel as ideologically clumsy, virulently anti-male, or artless and grim. Many critics, however, suggested that the novel's popularity confirmed its integrity. Anne Tyler concluded: "Marilyn French has written a collective biography of a large group of American citizens. Expectant in the 40's, submissive in the 50's, enraged in the 60's, they have arrived in the 70's independent but somehow unstrung, not yet fully composed after all they've been through."

French extends her commentary on gender relations in her second novel, *The Bleeding Heart,* a chronicle of a love affair between Dolores, a divorced feminist writer seeking an egalitarian relationship, and Victor, a married executive with traditional values. To cultivate a healthy alliance, each confronts past tradegies and failures in marriage and parenthood, and Dolores persuades Victor to reassess his assumptions about gender roles. While some reviewers declared the novel overly rhetorical and unconvincing, others admired

French's candid illustration of midlife anxiety and her revealing inquiry into sexual stereotypes.

French combines her interest in political doctrine and her scholarly pursuits in *Beyond Power: On Women, Men, and Morals,* a broad theoretical work that reinterprets world history from a feminist perspective. Often compared to the comprehensive metahistorical essays of Jean-Jacques Rousseau and Michel Foucault, French's treatise surveys such diverse disciplines as anthropology, medicine, political science, philosophy, astronomy, zoology, and law in its argument against patriarchal domination. According to French's thesis, humanity's original egalitarian, mother-centered societies were overthrown by a conspiracy of men obsessed with a desire for control over women and nature. With the pursuit of power as its impetus, patriarchal culture enslaved women, supplanted peaceful communities, and devised social structures emphasizing male-centered religion, property rights, and the division of labor. French argues that as a result, females have suffered in every human society from ancient Greece to modern China. Critical reaction to *Beyond Power* was diverse and emphatic; while some reviewers berated French's postulate as fallacious and inane, others defended the book as innovative and erudite. Benjamin Barber observed: "French has boldly crashed disciplinary boundaries on her way to writing a genuine sythesis and critique of our civilization, past and present. . . . [Though] the argument is broad and controversial—and intentionally polemical—it is offered with judiciousness as well as passion, and rings with noble conviction."

French's next novel, *Her Mother's Daughter,* examines emotional and familial bonds between four generations of American women, beginning in the early 1900s. Frances, a widowed Polish immigrant who is forced by poverty to send three of her four children to orphanages, consigns her bitterness to her daughter Isabelle. In turn, Isabelle's overprotective nurturing prompts her rebellious daughter Anastasia to achieve success in a competitive male world but also to neglect her own children. French invests her narrative with myriad domestic details to demonstrate the sobering effects of unwanted pregnancies, abusive husbands, and tedious household responsibilities. While some reviewers deemed *Her Mother's Daughter* laborious and dismal, others praised it as a validation of maternal travail. Alice Hoffman concluded: "There is no one good mother in this novel and no easy answers, but Marilyn French does offer us hope of reconciliation between mothers and daughters. . . . Ms. French continues to write about the inner lives of women with insight and intimacy. What she's given us this time is a page-turner with a heart."

(See also *CLC,* Vols. 10, 18; *Contemporary Authors,* Vols. 69-72; and *Contemporary Authors New Revision Series,* Vol. 3.)

PRINCIPAL WORKS

NOVELS

The Women's Room   1977
The Bleeding Heart   1980
Her Mother's Daughter   1987

OTHER

The Book as World: James Joyce's "Ulysses" (criticism) 1976
Shakespeare's Division of Experience (criticism) 1981
Beyond Power: On Women, Men, and Morals (feminist theory) 1985

PAUL ROBINSON

Marilyn French is known primarily for her best-selling novel *The Women's Room,* which describes the emerging feminist consciousness of a group of middle-class women in the 1960s. She has also written studies of Shakespeare and Joyce. Nothing in her previous books, however, prepares one for the intellectual range and scholarly energy of *Beyond Power,* which is nothing less than a history of the world (from the cavewomen to the Sandinistas) seen through the critical prism of contemporary feminism. Indeed, "a history of the world" is too modest, since it is also a work of prescription and speculation. In reading it I was reminded of the grand metahistorical essays of Rousseau, Hegel, Freud, and, more recently, Michel Foucault. Such undertakings can't be judged by the usual empirical criteria. They demand a more latitudinarian standard, one that measures their ability to reshape our assumptions and suggest a new vision.

In the time-honored tradition of metahistory, French's book begins with a foray into speculative anthropology, which aims to reconstruct our cultural origins. The central drama in this story is the transition from "matricentry" to patriarchy. Matricentry was characterized by close ties between mother and child, a nonhierarchical social order, and harmonious relations between human beings and their environment. French's account of it sounds remarkably similar to the state of nature described by Jean-Jacques Rousseau in his *Discourse on the Origin of Inequality.* Patriarchy, by way of contrast, disrupted the tie between mother and child, placed men in authority over women, established hierarchical institutions, and, most important, subjected nature to domination. (pp. 1, 14)

What explains this fateful transformation? French answers that it was caused by a change in values. Matricentry gave way to patriarchy, she argues, because one set of ideals—one sensibility—was ousted by another. To be precise, a "masculinist" ideology of control displaced the matricentric values of pleasure and mutuality. "Humans came to see themselves in a new light . . . Their self-definition changed. And the new definition was the foundation stone and the *raison d'etre* of patriarchy."

Most modern historians, even those who aren't Marxists, will find this insistence on the primacy of ideas naive. They are almost constitutionally averse to the notion that ideas might exercise a decisive role in history. Rather, they prefer to trace changes in the intellectual realm to structural changes in the economy and society. French will thus have to look for support to the metahistorians of an earlier era—to thinkers like Hegel and Nietzsche—who also were unashamed to attribute great historical transformations to developments in the realm of thought. . . .

One of the difficulties of her argument is that after the patriarchal regime has been established, the rest of history seems like little more than a footnote. The course of Western civilization involves only a replaying in ever intensified form of the original revolution. Her account is nonetheless startling in so far as it reverses our familiar assumptions about the accomplishments and failures of Western culture. What we have traditionally regarded as the high points of our history turn out, when passed through this critical feminist grid, to mark unhappy reassertions of the patriarchal ideal, while some of the darker moments get rehabilitated, because during them patriarchy was temporarily in disarray. . . .

Although the history of the world has been largely a story of unremitting sameness, French recognizes certain moments of protest when feminine values were able to find expression. Such protests occurred, for example, in the origins of Christianity, Protestantism, and socialism. Voices of opposition can also be heard in the poetry of courtly love during the Middle Ages, the salon culture of *ancien régime* France, and the 19th-century cult of domesticity. But the feminizing Jesus quickly gave way to misogynistic St. Paul, just as Protestantism prepared the ground for modern science and capitalism. Likewise, socialism, though often hostile to patriarchy, was compromised from the beginning by its exploitive attitude toward nature and its commitment to revolutionary violence, the very essence of the masculinist ethos.

Only in modern feminism does French detect a sensibility that might finally overthrow the patriarchal order. Her optimism is guarded, however, because she recognizes that feminism is hardly of one mind, and there is no guarantee that it will succeed where earlier oppositional movements have failed. Still, she remains persuaded that the way out, like the original revolt, must lie in a transformation of values. "Only a fundamental moral revolution," she writes, "can provide what is needed for real change in human institutions and behavior."

The most interesting aspect of her book is its evaluation of the different strains within contemporary feminism. One of these—the mainstream, in fact—is committed to the ideal of equality, and it measures success in terms of women's ability to win entry into the male power structure, whether in the economy, intellectual life, or politics. Not surprisingly, French takes a dim view of this egalitarian project. "Assimilation is death," she asserts, and she identifies her own work with the anti-assimilationist tendency that has become increasingly prominent in feminist theory (Carol Gilligan's *In a Different Voice,* on which French draws extensively, is a representative document of this school). The anti-assimilationists take as their goal the "revalorization" of feminine qualities, arguing that only when patriarchal ideals have been rejected will we transcend the antagonisms that set us apart from one another and from nature as well. Moreover, French has the intelligence to recognize the similarity between her own position and that of certain female opponents of feminism, such as the adepts of the right-to-life movement, who seek to purchase a realm of security for themselves and their children—an enclave of feminine values within a patriarchal universe—by abdicating all claims to power. Of such women she writes: "In the distant future, they may be seen more as part of the feminist struggle for a more felicitous world than as antagonists to it."

French would probably resist the idea that her vision is reminiscent of St. Augustine's in *The City of God,* but I am nonetheless struck by their affinity. Between an Edenic past and an eschatalogical future stretch for both the unchanging millennia of the "city of man," an era of sustained alienation during which all hopes of release must be satisfied with a furtive, underground existence. Like Augustine's, her history is exhilarating in its boldness, but ultimately numbing in its relentless catalogue of atrocities. I, at least, found it hard to sustain the prospect of redemption through 600 pages of closely argued and richly documented misery. And while I appreciate her corrective to the standard version of Western civilization, I can't shed the prejudice that humanity has been served (as well as abused) by those intellectual and cultural movements—such as Greek rationalism and modern science—that have sought to place us in control of our destiny. Put another way, I prefer the ambivalent judgment rendered by Freud in *Civilization and Its Discontents,* where the achievements of our heritage are carefully weighed against its psychic costs. (p. 14)

Paul Robinson, *"History and Her Story,"* in Book World—The Washington Post, *June 2, 1985, pp. 1, 14.*

LAWRENCE STONE

The message of [**Beyond Power: On Women, Men, and Morals**] is delivered early. It "rests on the assumptions that . . . it is possible for humans to create and live by a different morality; and . . . to create a more felicitous society." Today "virtue is equated with manliness; one proves one's manhood by demonstrating control over women, children, property, and other men." But "the philosophy that can offer us a new way of seeing is feminism."

Beyond Power is a passionate polemic about the way men have treated women over the past several millenniums. First Marilyn French . . . wanders through the anthropological zoo, pointing out the rare matriarchal societies that have been described in myth, those that may have existed and those that still exist among hunter-gatherers today. Here was a Golden Age indeed:

> Yes, there was a garden, and in it we gathered fruit and vegetables and sang to the moon and played and worked together and watched the children grow. For the most part life was good. . . . We were bound to the goddess who was immanent in nature.

But this Golden Age could not survive the growth of material wealth and the division of labor necessary for human beings to exert their control over nature. So the Golden Age gave way to the somber epoch of patriarchy in which we are still living. To demonstrate how bad it has been, Mrs. French takes off on a breathless run through Western civilization exclusively from the point of view of patriarchal sexism. The ancient Greeks come out badly ("relations between spouses were poor"), as do the Romans ("women had few legal rights and could not directly affect the course of the state"). . . .

Although Jesus personally was fair to women, according to Mrs. French, Christianity during the Middle Ages was oppressive. Then came the period of the witch trials and the Reformation, when the Virgin Mary, whose cult was "rooted in the old rich memory of the Mother Goddess," was demoted—"the 'epitome' of Protestantism is the word *Father*." The Enlightenment brought no help, since "the *philosophes* spoke of human rights: but women were not included in the term *human*." . . . Things only began to look up a little with the emergence of fully fledged feminist movements in the late 19th century.

Mrs. French then examines the lot of women under Nazism and Soviet and Chinese Communism and concludes that in Communist societies, "the degree of abuse of women permitted is lessened but the pecking order remains the same." As for the Islamic world, millions of women are forcibly subjected to clitoridectomy and infibulation (the mutilation and sewing up of the vagina), and millions of others are "maintained in seclusion." . . .

After this irretrievably gloomy appraisal of the human condition, the clouds lift as we turn to the future potentialities of feminism to do away with power in its present forms through a demand for sexual equality in all areas of life. . . .

It has to be emphasized that nearly everything Mrs. French says is true. The history of the treatment of women by men in the last 2,500 years of Western civilization is truly awful. One therefore has to sympathize with her passionate indignation and admire the single-minded zeal with which she has pursued her theory through the millenniums, through more than 500 pages of text based on sources ranging from Virginia Abernathy on female hierarchy to Heinrich Zimmer's *Philosophies of India* and including nearly 100 articles from *The New York Times.* But hers is nonetheless a deeply flawed book. In the first place, her former Golden Age is a myth. The lives of most, admittedly not all, primitive peoples discovered by anthropologists have turned out to be far from Mrs. French's vision of a loving utopia. Some, like the present-day Ik of Uganda as described by Colin Turnbull, are almost unbelievable in their relentless cruelty and selfishness. Mrs. French's attempt to resuscitate the noble savage in feminist drag is not convincing. Moreover, worship of a female does not do much to affect the lot of women one way or the other, to judge by the example of the cult of the Virgin Mary in the Middle Ages.

Furthermore, Mrs. French's blanket denunciation of patriarchy in all times and places since the Bronze Age obscures crucial differences in the treatment of women. It also has the paradoxical effect of virtually removing women from her story, although it is evident that at all times many women have been far from merely passive victims of a crushing patriarchal ideology. In some societies men have treated women like slaves, forcing the latter to do the backbreaking work in the fields while the men lazed around in the village. They have also locked women up indoors and not allowed them out unless heavily veiled. But in other societies, for example in most of northwestern Europe over the last millennium, men have done their share of the hard physical work and women have circulated at will. There is something fundamentally wrong with a book that cannot distinguish the lot of a woman in fifth-century B.C. Athens from that of one in 18th-century London. Mrs. French also largely ignores the critical variable of status. A rich, elite woman has often lived a life of pampered luxury, freedom and even power, a slave one of total submission to the arbitrary whims (sexual and occupational) of a master, and a poor woman one of crushing toil in the service of her husband.

Mrs. French fails to appreciate that what is extraordinary is not the long dominance of patriarchal power but the degree to which that elite male power has been eroded in our society over the past 200 years, first by the moral rejection and abolition of slavery and more recently by moves toward greater equality between the sexes in opportunity for education, jobs, choice of spouses, property rights and even political power.

Finally, if Mrs. French's vision of the past is unrealistic in its pessimism, her vision of a morally revolutionized future is equally unrealistic in its optimism. Human nature does not change much in its passions and appetites, and the record of successful women in the world suggests that given the chance, they are likely to be as power-hungry, aggressive and warlike as men—few psychologists would predict anything else. In the unlikely event that women were to direct what goes on in the bedroom and the board room, the future would almost certainly not be a utopia "beyond power" but merely the same old adversary system of dominance and submission run by bosses of a different sex. Mrs. French admits her dreams "may seem utopian, idealistic, or just simpleminded." I wish it were not so, but I think that is what they are.

Lawrence Stone, "Man's Inhumanity to Woman," in The New York Times Book Review, *June 23, 1985, p. 3.*

SUSAN DWORKIN

[French] has written a new book called **Beyond Power: On Women, Men, and Morals,** a huge scholarly work that challenges every single application of the vertical/hierarchical intellectual tradition. Finds all of it bankrupt. Rethinks science, history, and culture in a nonlinear way. And comes up with a proposal for the moral regeneration of individuals that will lead to nothing less than the rescue of the world.

How does French do this?

At length, first of all; don't think you can get away with skimming **Beyond Power;** you will have to read it all (nearly 700 pages), and it will take time.

Also with nerve. She has the colossal nerve to give her passions to a scholarly argument, to call the lust for power out-and-out evil and the pursuit of happiness an unmitigated good. She evaluates a vast range of sources with frank subjectivity: Aristotle as a bad anatomist, Christine de Pisan as a great writer who couldn't change a thing, the Code of Hammurabi as legal misogyny, the French Revolution as liberalizing laws for one good decade—too bad it didn't last—and a chilling description of Harold S. Geneen, former chair of ITT.

In case you had not realized that most history is distorted by self-delusive, male supremacist myopia, French shines the light of "re-vision." For example, you thought that in the 12th century nuns were cloistered and that cloistered meant silenced? French describes the great flowering of women in 12th-century Europe; women who sought the nunnery because it allowed them freedom to *think*. Essentially, French in **Beyond Power** gives us Western civilization from the Sumerians to Nixon. She doesn't give us much of Eastern civilization. I asked her why. She said, "If the world is destroyed, it will be because of Western values, not Eastern."

Her argument rests on the following portrait of human society: originally the *natural* human social organization developed along lines that were matricentric (focusing on the mother and her young) and matrilocal (revolving around the dwelling of the mother, home base also for her daughters and their children, while mature men lived separately). Roughly around the time of the development of agriculture, the state, and the warrior class, matricentric society was systematically destroyed by the rising tide of patriarchy.

"Patriarchy was not an attempt to revise matricentry," she writes,

> but to overthrow it. . . . From a loose grouping of people who lived democratically, even anarchically, patriarchy created a tight stratified society held in place by coercion; from a society dedicated primarily to love and bonding, fertility and continuation, patriarchy moved to dedication to power above all.

Why did patriarchy win over matricentry?

Because of several tactical advantages, French says.

The first, she says, is that power-madness, the cornerstone of patriarchy, is catching.

"Patriarchy is a militant ideology," French writes.

> To revere power above everything else is to be willing to sacrifice everything else to power. Many cultures accepted such a morality only with reluctance, but power worship is contagious. If a worshiper of power decides to extend his power over your society, your choices are between surrendering and mounting an equal and opposite power. In

either case, the power worshiper wins—he has converted your society into a people who understand that power is the highest good.

(p. 20)

This reads like the werewolf theory of history; the infecting bite spreading the contagion around the world. Yet is it really a contagion? Doesn't power ascend because people want it, because it makes them happy?

Sure, they want it, French says. Because they have been *taught* to want it. But no, it does not make them happy. (Now ensues the kind of conversation that captures the particular genius of Marilyn French. Scholar, schmollar, she always tests every insight—as she did in *The Women's Room*—by beating it against the mundane perceptions of everywoman's-everyday-life, especially hers.)

"Power brings the opposite of pleasure," declared French in a recent conversation.

> It brings enormous pain. All you have to do is look at the faces of people in power, you will see the pain. . . . [Power] is a very great strain. Because you lose the ability to trust. . . . Now there is only one reason to stay alive. And that is to have *pleasure*. And the true grounds of pleasure are communal. . . .

So French's thesis continues that when patriarchal values took over the world, an era of mind-boggling joylessness ensued. People were taught to separate the human from the animal, to exchange nature's pleasures for the ascetic satisfactions of so-called rational life. (p. 21)

Pragmatically, women and their values—as well as the goddesses that represented them—were laid in the dust by patriarchy. Femaleness was soon thought to be akin to animalness, messy and concrete, and maleness was soon thought to be the only kind of humanness, holy and abstract. Men were given pleasure substitutes to replace the female pleasures they now despised; such things as the acquisition of excess wealth, the domination of women and children, the testing of "strength" through combat against other, not particularly hated, men.

But if we don't naturally like power, why do we seek it?

Because we are taught, says French, that power will make us happy. But we are taught lies. This is the second great tactic of patriarchy, indeed of all totalitarianism: to make the big lie stick. " 'Civilization,' indeed," she writes,

> is largely a symbolic system, a carefully erected artificial world for which is claimed all sanity, courtesy, art and knowledge, while the real world is called *animal,* inconsequential, or evil. Civilization is founded on the Word, and the Word is a lie.

Is *all* history lies? I ask.

"Yes," she answers.

> The actual events that occurred in the past were probably different from the way we get them. For example, Miriam may well have been Moses; we know that later commentators went through the Bible and scratched out women's names and put in men's. But more important is that *the assumptions on which we have acted for the last four or five thousand years are false to nature!*

So we have a double whammy. We have people acting on false assumptions—for example, the assumption that man is very different from the animals; that the nature of man is to be in control; that obedience to a superior male is good; and that rightness, legitimacy, are identical with power; all of that is false. We have written history in a false and distorted manner in order to make that falsehood appear true.

(pp. 21-22)

"Patriarchy taught us to obey," French says,

> taught us that some people are humanly superior to others, and that is an absurdity. The whole notion of hierarchy is an absurdity. The only morality that's worth having must be firmly established in a single principle—*that we are all equally subject to the human condition.*
>
> Power in itself is not evil. It only becomes evil when it is its own end, when you can't use it to enjoy yourself. We still believe that power and control are the ways to get felicity. But if you put felicity *first* and then think about ways to get it, you would be astonished at how your life would change. Because to me, if you're enjoying yourself, you're going to do good for others. That's just inevitable. . . .

(p. 22)

It is to the feminist movement that French looks for a pragmatic return to the felicities of the matricentric past. "Feminism *is* a political movement demanding access to the rewards and responsibilities of the 'male' world," she writes. "But it is more: It is a revolutionary moral movement, intending to use political power to transform society. For such a movement, assimilation is death."

So now we are left with our mandate: transform society without resorting to power-lust. Seek "power to," but not "power over."

You have given us a difficult task, I say to Marilyn French. You say we must change what our culture values without becoming what our culture values, or else we shall all die.

"No transcendence except that of death is around the corner for any patriarchal institution," she writes.

> The millennium keeps arriving, empty-handed. The only transcendence possible for humans occurs through continuity, through the procession of generations . . . and continuity is a feminist ideal.

(pp. 22, 25)

For Marilyn French, the question of where we go from here is only asked of civilization because she asked it of herself. "I don't say that a moral revolution has to end with yourself," she said, "but it has to start there." . . .

"People go after what their culture values," she says.

> None of us is immune to that. I am very concerned with control, control over my work, controlling how people react to my work. . . . We go after power because we want respect; we want a certain status. But if our culture learned little by little to value something other than power, we would inevitably follow in *that.* . . .

Then *that* would get us respect; that would give us status; that's *our* millennium. "Life carries sorrows for all creatures," Marilyn French says in her wonderful book. "But it is possible to live with an eye to delight rather than to domination. And this is the feminist morality." (p. 25)

Marilyn French and Susan Dworkin, in an interview in Ms., *Vol. XIV, No. 1, July, 1985, pp. 20-2, 25.*

BENJAMIN BARBER

[*Beyond Power* is] a veritable one-woman feminist encyclopedia. It has the feel and heft of a book written to encompass not simply the entire field of feminist scholarship since Betty Friedan's *The Feminine Mystique,* but the entirety of scholarship on which the field draws. With nearly 60 pages of footnotes and a bibliography of perhaps 1,000 items, this 700-page book pretends to be a history of patriarchalism, but it is in fact a history of just about everything from the perspective of patriarchalism. French surveys a wealth of materials that would leave most scholars gasping: Astronomy, anthropology, education, paleontology, medicine, political science, zoology, law, psychology, literature, penology, philosophy, sociology, ethics and biology all come under her extraordinary scrutiny. A book on this scale is really several books and as such defies review. It has powerful virtues that invite extended discussion and awful defects that call for extended criticism. Neither can be more than hinted at here.

The great virtue of *Beyond Power* is that in our age of narrow specialization, French has boldly crashed disciplinary boundaries on her way to writing a genuine synthesis and critique of our civilization, past and present—a critique that offers us a powerful argument about patriarchy and nature, control and accommodation, power and love, men and women. By placing this impassioned argument in a universal context that takes in morals as well as history, French endows it with a Toynbeean sweep. Yet, though the argument is broad and controversial—and intentionally polemical—it is offered with judiciousness as well as passion, and rings with noble conviction.

The argument, egregiously abbreviated, runs something like this: We live in a patriarchal world defined by permanent rebellion against nature and things natural. Men have declared war on their bodies, their feelings and the natural condition that is their home, in an attempt to transcend mortality and become like the gods who are their finest invention. And because of their kinship with nature, women have been enslaved as part of the male quest for power and control. There is scarcely a single ill of modern society that cannot be laid at the door of this radical preoccupation with control—which French calls patriarchy.

Things were not always this way. In the beginning, . . . humans and animals alike dwelled together in matricentric harmony, governed solely by a simple, emotional egalitarianism. In French's own resonant counterbiblical imagery: "In the beginning was the mother. The word began a new era, one we have come to call patriarchy." The history of civilization since the coming of patriarchy has thus been nothing other than the history of our fall from natural, or feminine, grace. What we choose to call society is a vast network of power relations rooted in the word and its offspring science. Every improvement in economy, each reconstitution of the state, the division of labor, the coming of agriculture, the evolution of property are so many stages in the growth of dominion. Every step in the progress of the arts and sciences is a step toward the corruption of the species. Medicine, law, education and all of the other "helping professions" (French's teachers here are Foucault and Illich) are so many manifestations of the controlling structures by which patriarchy rules its world.

Now as readers may note, French's argument here bears an astonishing resemblance to that of Jean-Jacques Rousseau, who in his two *Discourses* attributed humankind's moral decline to the progress of the arts and sciences, demonstrating that each improvement in our ability to control nature is in fact an advance toward the decrepitude of the species. Like Rousseau, French celebrates nature, sentiment, feeling, eros and natural equality. Like Rousseau, she sees in civilization only corruption and injustice. And like Rousseau, she treats philosophy and enlightenment, with their vicious abstractionism and their reduction of human qualities to categories, as instruments of domination. The arts and sciences can at best, in Rousseau's brilliant metaphor, fling garlands of flowers over our chains.

What French adds to Rousseau's naturalist argument is the claim that civilization and its sins are essentially masculine in character, and that women carry vestiges of our original state of natural grace within their natures. To reclaim nature and this virtue is to overcome patriarchy, and it requires nothing less than a feminization of the world. . . . Such a world would become capable again of pleasure, the happiness that we have lost but that for French remains the key to the restoration of our morals.

Aristotle was the first to propose that happiness defined human nature; French concurs. Happiness is ours by nature if we are willing to abide by its principles. Power philosophies make us miserable by treating means as ends and by aiming at a transcendence that is beyond us. To get beyond power is to return to the world before patriarchy. If we do not manage this, French argues, the irony of history will see to it that we are destroyed by the very nature we aspire to master. That prospect looms before us: We have discovered and learned to manipulate the very essence of nature, the atom, and it seems increasingly unlikely that we will survive our knowledge of it. The bomb is dominion's final irony.

In this far-reaching argument, French confronts our society with a powerful critique. But its virtues bring in their train vices—deficiencies of evidence and of argument. It is hard to imagine anyone fully mastering the elephantine literature French has used. Although she tries hard to cite the relevant experts and is more than conscientious in discussing counterevidence (she looks long and hard at the role of women in the Nazi movement, for example, and she gives the women's antiabortion lobby respectful attention), the ambitiousness of her project often tempts her into hyperbole, oversimplification and generalization. As a consequence, her convictions sometimes are compromised by her errors, and her case is advanced only at the cost of distortion.

Several small items point to the larger problem: A Rousseauian source is misidentified and a quotation mistranslated, simply because French has depended on a clumsy secondary source; Augustine is presented as an enemy of free will, when in truth his doctrine of free will is the device by which he gets God off the hook for the evil men do; Hegel is simplified to a degree that costs French his historical succor in her case; for all his misogyny, Nietzsche is cast as a hero because he shares French's pejorative views of Christianity and science.

If evidence in a book this size can get out of hand, so can the argument. The most important question French must confront concerns the status of her anthropological, or "naturalist," argument. That the whole world was once matricentric, even if empirically sustained, is a proposition without moral force. Popular writers like Robert Ardrey and Lionel Tiger have argued that the world was once territorial, and a new crop of sociobiologists now contend that it was actually a theater of permanent aggression, but so what? Morals drawn from nature are dangerous inferences, whether they prove that we are by nature killers, aggressors, lovers or egalitarians. How humans ought to live cannot be inferred from how they do live by nature. After all, nature gives us both women and men, both love and aggression. Indeed, as Burke once wrote, artifice is our nature, and if French wants to justify matricentrism as good by nature, she must also justify patriarchy and its artifices as equally legitimate products of nature. Medicine may be power-science in defiance of nature, but natural illness kills, and artificial medicine saves. Law may be rationalized power and as such a weapon of patriarchy, but rationalized power is better than irrational power, and democratic patriarchy resting on a bill of rights is to be preferred to totalitarian patriarchy (toward which, French fears, we are moving). Rousseau finally recognized this and gave up his romanticism in favor of a more realistic view of what was possible within history.

Underlying these weaknesses in French's argument is the absence of any dialectical argument, with which she might have systematically exposed logical contradictions of patriarchy. She's in an intellectual bind here because, having dismissed reason as a tool of patriarchy, she cannot honestly enlist dialectical reason as a tool. A more dialectical perspective might have permitted French to see patriarchy as to some degree embedded in the world of matricentrism—a response to it that is as inevitable as matricentrism itself. And as matricentrism produced patriarchy, so patriarchy produces forces that erode it from within (this book included!). Unfortunately, *Beyond Power* is beyond dialectic. It relies on simplistic historical explanation, attributing to patriarchy every evil our world has seen.

Other problems are raised by French's espousal of the pleasure principle. Happiness understood in earthly, bodily terms is a limited and ambiguous moral standard. Pleasure may be variously defined (French acknowledges that men might find power itself pleasurable), and the pleasure principle is vulnerable to Socrates' question of whether it is better to be an unhappy man or a happy pig. At times, French's focus on the body suggests that pleasure lies in sexual liberation; at other times she clearly has something more in mind. Either way, she might want to consider John Stuart Mill's claim that happiness as an end defeats itself and that it can be achieved only as a byproduct of other ends.

Finally, French must face the question of whether the dark and terrifying portrait of the modern world she has drawn allows of amelioration, let alone cure. If patriarchy is so deeply embedded, if it has so long and decisive a history, if it is inextricable from the very structures of modern civilization and civilization's apparent vices as well as its putative virtues, then how can we ever liberate ourselves from it? French prudently disavows the use of male means (power, violence, revolution) to achieve the restoration of nature. But if these male means include education, reason and science—the word in all its forms—how can her beneficent vision be advanced? If patriarchy is as firmly entrenched as she argues, we are lost. If

it can be overcome, it cannot be so virulent as she argues and must be more ambivalent than she allows.

That there is so much to argue with in *Beyond Power* is of course one of the book's most attractive virtues. If it fails to achieve dialectical thinking, it certainly elicits dialectical thinking. For French's achievement is that she has succeeded in encompassing our precarious world with an intelligence that is animated by a deep concern for human survival. Her book is a moral treatise for women and men alike, a *Discourse on the Arts and Sciences* as poignant for us as Rousseau's was for the Enlightenment. Indeed, in ironic tribute to dialectical reasoning, it is a perfect example of what a civilized, progressive imagination can do to challenge the bleak hopelessness of modern society. *Beyond Power* honors the word it accuses, and proves in spite of itself that ideas may still be capable of undoing what—as power and patriarchy—ideas once did. (pp. 70-3)

Benjamin Barber, "O Pleasurable New World," in Psychology Today, *Vol. 19, No. 8, August, 1985, pp. 70-3.*

LORNA SAGE

The new feminism comes of age around now, and Marilyn French is taking stock. Her title [*Beyond Power: On Women, Men, and Morals*] might sound as though she was heralding that 'post-feminist' era lots of people (including some weary, guilty feminists) would like to believe in; but no. Nearly everything is still to do: most of the women who've penetrated the public world have been, are being, ritually assimilated. What the feminists turn out to want, says Ms French, is a moral revolution: 'Although they want access for women to decision-making posts . . . *they do not want women to assimilate to society as it presently exists, but to change it.*'

There's an obvious catch here, and the sheer size of this book (640 pages) is, among other things, a kind of advance warning sign of the amount of slog and hard labour even thinking about that eventuality entails. 'Boulder-pushing' Doris Lessing called it at the end of *The Golden Notebook*, boulder-pushing Sisyphus-style up the hill. The hill here consists in Patriarchy, traced back to its early origins and exhaustively documented in its current institutionalised forms. And the boulder is Sisterhood.

One part of Marilyn French's dilemma is that the boulder itself has to be continuously redefined too: feminism plus Greens plus Greenham women plus women in the Third World . . . and, of course, closer to home, women whose lives and interests circle back into the 'private' sphere always, having never really left it. . . . [Whether] 'working' officially or not, most women are still close to their traditional roles, and Ms French wants to recruit them too.

The result is a good deal of (deliberate) fudging about 'feminine' values we can all agree on—the importance of nurturing, fostering, community feeling, continuity, care for the environment, the survival of the species. Like Germaine Greer, she has come round to the view that motherhood is the political point, and the basis for a renewed polemic. 'Feminine' values, on this view, aren't so much the product of repression, stereotyping, or 'castration' (as in *The Female Eunuch*) as survivals from the period of human origins, and the recipe for future survival. . . .

It's an argument that proceeds by accretion, trailing hundreds of footnotes, and Ms French is obviously aware of the danger that if she convinces her readers too thoroughly, 'the projection of a matricentric world based on fragmentary evidence' will hardly be enough to persuade them that the present sickness isn't indeed terminal, that change is possible. She's engaged in a very difficult balancing act—all the more so because she's convinced that power-worship is so contagious that women can't infiltrate the inner sanctums without becoming denatured. There's a lot of miserable material on the way revolutionary governments have chewed women up and spat them out: in fact, one of the side-effects of all the work that's been done on women's history is to undermine the cause, by documenting the obstacles.

Which is where 'Morals' come in. Only by what used to be called a 'change of heart' can the book envisage a future. What Ms French has in mind is a kind of 'privatisation' of public life. She quotes (more than once) Simone Weil—'the common run of moralists complain that man is moved by his private interests: would to heaven it were so!' Except of course that heaven is part of the problem. We must realise our own transience, be more modest, think small:

> The end of life is the continuation of life . . . We are like soldier ants . . . We have encountered a river that separates us from sight of the future; we have a choice only to die where we stand, or to enter it.

With an incongruous echo of the heady days of the 1960s Ms French calls this the pursuit of the pleasure principle, but it sounds a lot more like pain. And in general a book less dedicated to the pleasure principle would be hard to envisage. The hunting-and-gathering society it looks back to has taken over in the writing too: ant-like, patient, laborious, in a word, boulder-pushing.

Lorna Sage, "Sisters of Sisyphus," in The Observer, *January 26, 1986, p. 50.*

SARA MAITLAND

Angela Carter once described **The Women's Room,** Marilyn French's international best-selling novel, as an etiquette book; 'really an instruction manual for the older woman postgraduate student' whose purpose is 'to teach people how to behave in social circles to which they think they might be able to aspire'. In **Beyond Power** French has extended this role to embrace the whole of history and under her firm and nanny-ish wing we can all learn better manners and move towards more gracious living, especially the boys who are always 'naturally' too rough.

Well I was taught my manners by a nanny and I don't altogether knock the process: good manners are indeed an aid to gracious living (called 'felicity' by French, and her great ideal) and God knows there is little enough of that around at the moment. . . .

But, like most good nannies, French sees things simply. We're all in the mess we are because men want power and have it while women don't and haven't. (I should say that I tend to agree with quite a lot of this incidentally.) So she falls back, rather derivatively, on the feminist version of patriarchal history, and takes the reader through a long and immaculate tour of the Great Feminist Moments—once upon a time

there was a wonderful society that was matricentral (loved mummy), matrifocal and matrilineal; then nasty old fathers messed things up and everything has been horrid ever since (if this reminds you of the morality of Barrie's *Peter Pan* it isn't my fault). In fairness to French she brings her basic good sense to the subject and manages to solve a problem that this particular version of history has always been dogged by—if matricentred power is so, so wonderful and unoppressive why should men wish to overthrow it? French suggests rather cleverly that it was precisely the leisure that the system gave them that allowed men the chance to abstract, to think 'transcendently', to distance themselves from the daily present tense and to create the concept of 'spirituality' over against 'nature' out of their own sense of marginality.

I can't help feeling that this is an attempt to make history conform to the discipline of depth psychology, a discipline which grows out of the Enlightenment and which French attacks on precisely that ground. The connection remains dubious, at least to me. I don't even want to say that she is descriptively wrong: the broad sweep of radical feminist pre-history is at least as satisfactory as other speculative models—in fact it is better, more pleasing aesthetically and more reasonable intellectually—but it is equally irrelevant.

This pre-historical model is not pleasure seeking, it is not the present-tense delight-in-itself which French argues that all knowledge should be, it is rather designed to authorise the conviction that if women were in charge again everything would be all right. Because underneath all the historical description French is idealist—I don't mean idealistic, I mean platonic: although she gives a proper nod in the direction of 'social conditioning' she really believes that this conditioning is like a blanket wrapped around a pure nugget of truth called 'femininity'—strip off the blanket and there She is, Eternal Woman waiting to be discovered. In the old version (Aquinas's) She is illogical, sensual, natural, pliable and therefore inferior; in French's version she is illogical, sensual, natural, pliable and therefore superior; but both believe the same thing, the Essential Woman. But I don't believe a word of it; I can't actually afford to believe a word of it because it is a political dead end: of course I believe in biological difference, but I don't believe in gender in any ontological sense. It is only if we believe that gender is socially constructed within history that we can believe that it is possible to deconstruct and—more importantly—reconstruct it within history.

On these shaky foundations French builds a marvellous edifice; it is detailed, self-assured, committed and complex; she has worked hard and her sources are impressively wide-ranging and far-reaching; every corner of contemporary society is examined and, although I think she is generous towards liberal individualism and ungenerous towards socialism, I do not question her good will and her thoroughness. But like the false prophets of the bible I feel that she 'cries "Peace, Peace" and there is no peace', because her faith is without foundation. Her analysis cannot really address, that is change, actual realities, as she herself admits: after 484 pages she comes clean—'The major problem facing feminists can easily be summed up: there is no clear right way to move.' . . .

And finally her book reminded me of my Nanny in yet one more way; she also went on and on saying things with great detail and great conviction and was in the end extremely boring.

Sara Maitland, "Nanny Knows Best," in New

Statesman, *Vol. 111, No. 2865, February 21, 1986,* p. 25.

JANE LILIENFELD

Important books which ask radical questions arouse fury, denial, fear and dismissal. Important feminist books, moreover, are those we are usually advised not to read. *Beyond Power* has produced extreme reactions in several reviewers, men and women, in the mainstream press, reactions reminiscent of the contempt and fear that met Kate Millett's *Sexual Politics* and Adrienne Rich's *Of Woman Born*. The similarity of responses to all three books is no accident; like its predecessors, *Beyond Power* crosses disciplines to argue for a sweeping reevaluation of the feminist debate as it is carried on by (primarily) white middle-class American academics.

Her earlier book on Shakespeare shows that Marilyn French can write standard academic criticism if she wants to. The contrast in style between that book and *Beyond Power* shows that she has deliberately chosen to address an audience wider than white American academics: here she speaks to a mass market of serious readers who fear that our planet is endangered by "male" values and "male" militarism, greed and ruthlessly shortsighted global helplessness. Like Elizabeth Gould Davis' *The First Sex, Beyond Power* starts with the dawn of our species and uses anthropology, mythology, economics, sociology and history to explain how malfunctions in gender relations arose. French goes some steps further than Davis to offer suggestions for change.

This program may delight the generally-educated, open-minded reader, but would (and has) appal(led) the academic one. Academic arguments follow highly ritualized etiquette, cover narrow ground and assume that the truth is established only by painstaking accretion of detail upon detail. New theses explain why and how former ideas were slightly incorrect and how the new ones more clearly explain the data. Academic argument is generally persuasive rather than assertive. Old ideas fade out slowly. Grand theories, of whatever kind, are advanced at great peril.

The risk is even greater within feminist theory, which has to do two things where traditional theory has to do only one: for feminism has to invent its discipline even as it works within it. Works ranging from Susan Griffin's *Woman and Nature* to Evelyn Fox Keller's *Gender and Science* show that the very bases of what were assumed to be impartial truths are skewed and gender-biased interpretations of experience which arise in part from self-serving, unconscious motives. Feminist theory is more than an assault on received opinion; it is an epistemological search for a true way to know and represent the human (male and female) condition.

Of course no feminist scholar has known enough to challenge the complete edifice of knowledge in all fields with the detailed scrupulosity that traditional scholarship demands. If the detail is sometimes simple-minded, then is the argument inadequate? For traditional scholars, yes. Can any grand theory be true if some of its details are deemed inaccurate by the specialist?

In a review entitled "Man's Inhumanity to Woman" in the *New York Times Book Review* [see excerpt above], Lawrence Stone trivializes the content and argument of *Beyond Power* beyond recognition. But after several paragraphs of urbane contempt he admits that "It has to be emphasized that nearly everything Mrs. [sic] French says is true." If so, then why does Stone go on to discount the book's arguments as personal neurosis and anger? Stone indicates that the book's scope includes prehistory and recorded time planet-wide; why then does he conclude his summary by asking "Are things all that bad for women in America in 1985?"—as if that question were the primary topic of the book? *Beyond Power* is a study of the effects of institutionalized gender dominance across time; Stone displays his own parochialism by complaining that "Mrs. [sic] French fails to appreciate that what is extraordinary is not the long dominance of Patriarchal power but the degree to which elite male power has been eroded in our society over the past 200 years." The global maladies which are French's subject pale before the spectre of the collapse of white male power in North America.

Few readers will be surprised to hear that joining the chorus of contempt were a number of women critics. Jane O'Reilly, writing in *Vogue* in August 1985, describes *Beyond Power* as "a relentless catalogue of every single nasty thing men have thought about [and] done to women since the beginning of recorded history," and complains that French "does not adequately explain everything." . . . Sara Maitland [see excerpt above] takes a similar line. Marilyn French, she says, reminds her of her nanny, who "went on and on saying things with great detail and great conviction and was in the end extremely boring." And Maitland reduces the book's argument to a nursery tale:

> once upon a time there was a wonderful society that was matricentral (loved mummy), matrifocal and matrilineal; then nasty old fathers messed things up and everything has been horrid ever since (if this reminds you of the morality of Barrie's *Peter Pan* it isn't my fault).

Not all the reviews were so blatantly out of sympathy with the book's intent and arguments as these; but they illustrate the pattern of mishearings, misrepresentations and denial that has greeted other major (typically white and middle-class) heterosexual and lesbian feminist critiques of the culture. Arguments are reduced to simple platitudes to be wittily dismissed by the reviewer, with an occasional tincture of pity for the feminist who had once been first-rate. Women critics in particular make a point of indicating that they themselves are feminist but definitely heterosexual, usually with children—and in any case not "one of them," no relation to the ostracized sister who has so embarrassed the rest of us good girls by allowing her illness—that is, her intelligent rage—to show. (p. 20)

[What do French's *Beyond Power,* Adrienne Rich's *Of Woman Born* and Kate Millett's *Sexual Politics*] have in common? They are ambitious; they aspire to explain a cultural system; they propose change. They do not advocate the demise of men as a sex or call for worldwide Amazon revolution; *but* they do not praise male achievement; they do not uphold the Holy Family; and they argue that our culture is in trouble because it lives by denial of the body, of feelings, and because it lies about power, force and mastery.

Marilyn French defines Patriarchy as a mode of life which completely denies the body and its needs, and which denies that any spiritual life must be body-centered, based on the real and the multifarious moment. Patriarchal thinking, she argues, hates the mess and stink of life. It hates that sex is not rational. It hates that excrement and putrefaction are inseparable from the frailty of the body and its bodily pleasures.

French's concept of a healthy materialism resembles that developed by Fernand Braudel in his introduction to *Capitalism and Materialism:* the physical structures of daily life are perpetuated for centuries because their residues are our collective human existence. . . .

Almost all of the qualities associated with what French calls pleasure, Braudel calls the material, and American academic feminists label domestic feminism, are qualities or cultural constructs labeled "women." "Women" smell. "Women" menstruate. "Women" have noticeable secondary sexual characteristics. "Women" are not assumed to be rational, but to be animal, to be bodily. "Women" are assumed to be weak, stupid, helpless. And "women" are assumed to be the carriers of sexuality, to be tempters of "men" who would not otherwise desire sex. "Women" are assumed to be less fully human than "men" because "women" are imprisoned in a certain kind of body which, it is assumed, has led to a deformed mental capacity. When "men," from St. Jerome to Herzog, look at "women," "men" see mess, stink, horror and their own vulnerability. To live a life excluding "women" is to live a Patriarchal life.

How did these ideas about "women" come to be central to our culture? The growth of early technologies buttressed, as French painstakingly shows, early Christian-institutional insistence on a virgin birth, the horrors of women's sexuality, the denial of death. Feminists in recent years have tacitly ignored the earlier arguments of Rosemary Radford Ruether, Mary Daly, Mary Chamberlain, Carol Christ and others, that the teachings of institutionalized Christianity are integral to Patriarchy. I am pleased to see French reminding us of what we already know. To claim that Christian morality underpins the economics of greed, the exploitation of women, of nature and of other cultures, is potentially so threatening and alienating for many readers as to be ungraspable. French proceeds with care to develop an irrefutable connection between male-dominated, institutionalized Christianity and the exploitation of the Other, denial of death and nature. A large and luminous synthesis of feminist thinking on religion is here brought to bear on the Renaissance, the rise of the nation-state and the economics of imperialist capitalism.

To explain the origins of culture is traditionally supposed to be a great thinker's right and duty. That Patriarchy exists worldwide, few feminist theorists would deny. How it originated from a woman-centered world or whether it did so is an unanswerable question. French offers state-of-the-art speculation about the origins of Patriarchy, postulating a prehistoric matrilocal, female-centered tribal and primate culture where men were peripheral and the children's bond to the mother and other females was the most important. To create a direct link from humans back to primate (or non-primate) group behavior is a leap that few can take with assurance; evidence from primatology is itself controversial. This section of the book is beautifully written, extensively researched and a solid synthesis of current controversial arguments in the field, but nevertheless it reads like wishful thinking. Who would willingly leave such a world and take up the power-mongering, slave-driving, body-denying life of the Patriarchy?

French claims that when we as a species began to kill other animals we made the first step to our present world. When we began to kill animals and eat them for food, we separated from our knowledge of ourselves as animals, from our bodies and from our vulnerability to death and accidents of nature.

But why is power addictive? She suggests that the mother world collapsed because Patriarchal cultures began to separate their victims from feeling, creating a compartmentalized personality structure in which feeling is warded off or deflected into anger and aggression. If one is deracinated, deprived of access to the body and to its pleasures and limitations, one will be more likely to crave power than simple physical sustenance and its peace.

Beyond Power is grittily specific about the social costs of Patriarchy. The most important chapters show how Patriarchy functions today in the form of corporate international cartels, government bureaucracies, medicine and the law. What percentage of corporate profits depends on the selling worldwide of violent pornography? French can tell us. In what specific ways and for what amount of profit does American corporate medicine sustain our government's priorities about militarism rather than a more equitable distribution of goods, services, health care and food? French can tell us. How many American businesses have moved plants overseas and use cheap female labor abroad, thus depriving male and female workers here of jobs and exploiting non-union laborers in other countries? French can tell us.

In the recent spate of mass-market feminist books about men, this is one of the very few that gives us the information we need to make a more humane world for women and men alike. French does this by showing how those intellectual values and unexamined assumptions she has defined as Patriarchal enable men to oppress other men, and to encourage men to abuse women and those groups labeled "non-human" rather than organize to achieve a more equitable system. The effects of oppression on men are crucial to her theoretical conceptions of Patriarchy and how to change it. French follows other social theorists in arguing that all oppressed peoples introject the oppressor as the truly human and learn to devalue that which is their non-oppressor self and side with the oppressor against their own group. That men, too, suffer, gives hope that men are potentially available to arguments about how we might eradicate that suffering.

French is excellent in discussing how the mechanics of being raised under oppression encourage the oppressed to collude with the oppressor. But when will this collusion cease?

One answer is to be found in economics; but this is a topic that is oddly placed within the text. In a book so realistic about the crucial realities of a material world, its pleasures and torments, there seems to be little accounting of the actual costs to women and children of poverty, limited opportunity, the hopelessness bred of despair, and the contributions of these circumstances to women's and men's being cowed and bullied by a degradation our culture tells us does not exist and anyway cannot be changed. French tells us that one in five people on our planet never have had nor ever will have enough to eat for one day in their lives. A book which argues that the material bases of pleasure are one way out of oppression, spiritually and physically, needs to have a very real accounting of the brutality of hunger.

French leaves us asking, is material pleasure the highest political good, the highest moral good? and, if it is, how can it be made into a force for political, worldwide, internal and external change? But how many people today, desperately hungry, trapped by racism or ill-health or illiteracy or exhaustion, have access to pleasure as she defines pleasure? If one is so constantly worried about food, shelter and children, the moment is stolen and desiccated. Oppression kills the spirit and the body; adequate resources create the possibility for the best in human beings. What realistic and non-insulting way is there for a white, middle-class person to talk about the privileges of this kind of pleasure for the desperate?

The major problem in this book is a problem common to academic feminist theory in America—the inability to reconcile the existence of class warfare with the belief that women are a class linked worldwide. When one compares Nancy Hartsock's *Money, Sex and Power* (1984) to French's brief discussion of women and socialism, one understands better French's limitations. Hartsock, like French, sees that power means a life that denies the body, feelings and death, and that insists on competition and aggressive acquisition. Both agree that pleasure comes from a human power to accept the body, death, sensuality. But Hartsock's definition of feminist materialism is fully grounded in philosophical opposition to "Athenian" definitions of the citizen's daily life, and in a Marxist tradition of working-class consciousness. Hartsock's awareness of racial and class differences within women's daily experiences contrasts sharply with French's race- and class-neutral definition; she is able, unlike French, to specify how and in what ways women's commitment to the bodily, the emotional, the diurnal, the reproduction of other human beings, can lead to real alternatives, to a life Beyond Power.

But this criticism cannot outweigh *Beyond Power*'s massive contribution to feminist theory. A synthesis of feminism and socialism within the context that French has created is yet to come. Perhaps in her next book French can solidify her blueprint for Utopia; I look forward to it. (p. 21)

Jane Lilienfeld, "The Dangers of Theory," in The
Women's Review of Books, *Vol. IV, No. 1, October,*
1986, pp. 20-1.

BEVERLY FIELDS

[In 1977], Marilyn French published her first novel, *The Women's Room,* a polemical fiction that burned its way across the pages and read as fast as fire. . . .

What was in question then, however, and remains so now, is the degree to which French is able to accommodate her ideology to the aesthetic demands of fiction.

The truth is that French's fancy has grown increasingly restrained with each successive novel. Her second, *The Bleeding Heart,* lacked the intensity of *The Women's Room,* while carrying that novel's techniques of sexual melodrama perilously close to pornographic fantasy.

This new novel, *Her Mother's Daughter,* elaborates a theme that runs more or less quietly through her first two books: the ways in which female submission to male society, with its accompanying suppression of rage, is passed like contagion from mother to daughter.

Perhaps the quiet assertion of the theme was enough, or perhaps the pause between fictions, during which French produced *Beyond Power,* her ambitious essay on patriarchy, cost her some storytelling momentum. Whatever the reason, *Her Mother's Daughter* seems not to have been shot from the same bow of burning gold that sent forth *The Women's Room.*

The narrative chronicles the lives of three generations of mothers in chain-step with their daughters. Frances, a Polish immigrant, is driven by early widowhood and poverty to deliver three of her four children to public care. Bella, the daughter Frances chooses to remain with her, absorbs her mother's angry memories of her improvident and drunkenly violent husband as well as her conflicting feelings of love and resentment toward her children. Anastasia, Bella's daughter, is the third carrier of the germ of female suffering, which she in turn transmits to her daughter, Arden.

As in her first two novels, French presents all the male figures as bearers of the patriarchal standard, at best indifferent to their children and at worst ready to beat them. Toni, the gentle lover Anastasia turns to after her divorce, paragon of sensitivity and nurturing care who tends her children while she pursues, under her new name of Stacey Stevens, an international career as star photographer, proves to be no exception.

The polemics are not the only difficulty with this book. For one thing, the heavy-handed technique of flashing backward and forward in the course of narrative events slows down the reading.

What French presents in the figure of Bella is her daughter's effort to understand her through an imaginative reliving of Bella's experience. Early in the book, Anastasia expresses this effort in terms resonant with the wish to do for the mother what the father could not: "Listening, putting myself into her, becoming her, becoming my grandmother, and in the process give her the strength and hope she needs. Return the liquids I drained from her."

There may be an underlying connection between this expression of longing to restore health and pleasure to the mother and the presence in all of French's novels of the chance to escape from the patriarchal male to the arms of another woman. . . .

All this is not to say that the novel is without its fine moments. The recurrent image of a female insect, the midge, for example, which reproduces asexually and at the cost of her own destruction, is a splendid metaphor.

"Midge mothers," French tells us, "may sacrifice themselves entirely for their young, but the young never have to hear about it." One could wish, however, for more metaphor with less comment.

But for that kind of writing, this long novel could be traded for the 10-line poem, called "Housewife," by Anne Sexton, which concludes: "A woman is her mother./ That's the main thing."

Beverly Fields, "The Flame Flickers," in Chicago
Tribune—Books, *October 11, 1987, pp. 6-7.*

ANNE SUMMERS

In this long and presumably autobiographical novel [*Her Mother's Daughter*], Marilyn French has written what some American feminists would call Herstory. The tale is that of four generations of an immigrant family, and the voices we hear are those of its female members, principally the narrator, her mother and grandmother. The narrator's serial marriages and affairs and her commercial and artistic successes are juxtaposed and contrasted with the poverty, hardships, restrictions and marital cruelties endured by her foremothers. As the narrative unfolds, the emancipation of Stacy Stevens née Anastasia Dabrowski is shown to be more illusory than real; despite every conceivable change in outward forms, it is the older women's experience which imprints itself on her inner life. "The truth is it is not the sins of the fathers that descend unto the third generation, but the sorrows of the mothers."

Sins are active, and sorrows are passive. The grandmother and mother in this story do not so much act as accept, survive, grieve and—above all—deny all sense of deserving. Theirs is the duty of giving without receiving, of mothering without hope of being mothered in return: bitterness, anger, confusion and depression are their portion, following as inexorably as the physical consequences of a deficient diet. Their lives take place in their heads, and in such dreams as they permit themselves. These are, indeed, anti-heroines in the truest sense of the word; and French could, by holding them continuously in focus, have produced an extraordinarily powerful anti-novel, a wholly dissident account of non-action and non-achievement on the part of those not permitted to be agents.

But she does, of course, have a heroine, and her story even has a moderately happy ending. Stacy Stevens works through and rises above the feelings of emptiness, worthlessness and bereavement which are her female heritage; she restores relations with the children she thought her failed marriages and successful career had lost her; and when she finds a lover who is a woman, they are able to mother each other.

Psychotherapeutic homily becomes increasingly obtrusive as, learning to forgive herself, the author/protagonist moves towards her conclusion. The last third of the novel is the least satisfying, uneasy in its shifts of tone and register, conventional in its what-happened-next underpinning. Like the conscientious Polish-American housewives from whom she is descended, French is unwilling to let anything go to waste. Diary jottings, travelogue, the gleanings of the counselling session, have all been added to the soup.

It is a pity that the profound and remarkable qualities in French's writing are so often swamped by the commonplace. In the earlier part of the narrative, the urban immigrant community is observed with painful clarity; tragedy and despair are allowed to speak for themselves; and the human talent for misery is superbly portrayed, constantly at war with and colonizing the desire to choose and to act freely. By the end, everything has to be spelled out, explained, talked over—with the lover, with the children, through the diary. The defect is one of substance as well as style. The narrator's need to justify her own life to herself has become the overriding justification of the novel; too vast a battleground has been staked out for too small a cause.

Anne Summers, "Dissidents and Discontents," in The Times Literary Supplement, No. 4412, October 23, 1987, p. 1158.

ALICE HOFFMAN

[In 1977], Marilyn French published *The Women's Room,* a raw and explosive examination of women's lives so timely it was as much a cultural phenomenon as a literary one. In her third novel, *Her Mother's Daughter,* Ms. French continues to imbue what used to be dismissed as "women's issues" with the significance they deserve. Partly because of her, it is no longer the insult it once was to have a novel dubbed a "woman's book"—meaning, one assumes, that its concerns include relationships and family ties, small items such as birth, death, passion.

While it's probably true that women will appreciate *Her Mother's Daughter* more than men will, it is not because men won't be—or shouldn't be—interested in the issues Ms. French ably addresses, but because women will be far more familiar with the territory. The rocky terrain explored in this multigenerational chronicle is the complex, mysterious realm of mothers and daughters. The questions raised are no less fascinating for their familiarity: How much can one expect from one's mother, one's daughter, oneself? What constitutes being a good mother? Is a daughter doomed to repeat the mistakes of her mother and grandmothers?

The author charts the histories of four generations of women, beginning with Frances, a Polish immigrant living in Brooklyn early in the century, whose life is marked by loss. The widow of an abusive alcoholic, Frances is forced to give up three children she cannot support, keeping one daughter, Bella, with her. To be a chosen child is a mixed blessing, and Bella and her mother are tied together less by love than by sorrow. . . .

The vision in *Her Mother's Daughter* centers on an inevitable link in the behavior of mothers and daughters, so it is not surprising that although Bella pledges to be a better mother than the cold, distant Frances, Bella's own daughter, Anastasia, is repelled by Bella's bitter self-denial. Nor is it surprising when the rebellious Anastasia, who wears purple lipstick and black eye-pencil, repeats family history and, like her mother before her, is forced into an early, loveless marriage by an unplanned pregnancy. Anastasia's need to understand and come to terms with her mother is at the core of the novel. Their estrangement is continually scrutinized as we follow Anastasia's progress first as a young mother on Long Island in the 1950's and later, after her divorce, as a professional photographer (renamed Stacey Stevens) who raises two children alone before marrying and supporting a much younger man. (In this novel, being supported is the kiss of death for a relationship, and Ms. French forcefully demonstrates the intrinsic tyranny in a financially one-sided marriage.)

Unlike Frances and Bella, whose thwarted personal desires are twisted into despair, Anastasia attempts to have it all—children, career, unrestrained sexuality—despite her growing realization that her own daughter, Arden, views her as selfish. . . .

Ms. French is a deft storyteller, and in *Her Mother's Daughter* she has quite a good story to tell, which makes it all the more maddening when the narrative is broken up into bits and pieces. Shifts in time and narrator that are intended to emphasize the characters' common experiences often disrupt the flow of the novel. But the novel's most serious flaw is that several of the characters are stereotypes: the hardworking immigrant unable to show affection, the pretty, mindless little sister named Joy, husbands and fathers who are either weak and ineffectual or abusive bullies. Even Anastasia in her two incarnations seems less a fictional character than a familiar case history. Interestingly, the use of stereotypes may bring *Her Mother's Daughter* a wider readership; with a few altered details many people may feel as if they were reading a page from their own family history.

There is no one good mother in this novel and no easy answers, but Marilyn French does offer us hope of reconciliation between mothers and daughters. Though *Her Mother's*

Daughter suffers from problems that are often found in sprawling page-turners—too little attention to structure, characters manipulated to work out an author's idea, an over-abundance of dramatic incident—Ms. French continues to write about the inner lives of women with insight and intimacy. What she's given us this time is a page-turner with a heart.

Alice Hoffman, "Momma Never Said Good Night," in The New York Times Book Review, October 25, 1987, p. 7.

ANDREA FREUD LOEWENSTEIN

Could it be, I wondered, as I set aside Marilyn French's new novel [*Her Mother's Daughter*] with a sigh of relief, that I've read too many of these mother-daughter books lately? Because the happy news is that after years of being an unrespectable topic, mothers and daughters are suddenly in. You could teach a course on the subject and have a hard time choosing the books; you could hold special sessions of the M.L.A.; you could write several doctoral theses. (p. 134)

[This] new rash of novels and autobiographical accounts confirm what has been evident to women all along: For many of us, our mothers are one of the ruling passions of our lives. Why, then, did I feel so fed up with *Her Mother's Daughter*, which is brimming with mothers and daughters and with what, at first glance, looks like passion?

Anastasia, the third of the three generations of mothers in the book, recalls: "My mother cried. It must be my first memory." As the pain begins "to creep around from her heart into her limbs," her mother, Belle, wonders "how anyone could cry so much, how it was physically possible to have that many tears inside you." Anastasia pictures the dinner table of her childhood and thinks, "All I want to do is cry. Cry for them all, Cry, cry, cry: I could die crying and still not cry enough to let out all my grief, their grief." After 686 similarly sodden pages, I found myself feeling quite sympathetic to the sometimes kind, sometimes dastardly but always wooden men who populate the book along with the weeping women.

Perhaps I am merely defending myself against the force of all that pain? French would probably think so. Prepared for such reactions, she takes time out for the occasional word to unfeeling (presumably male) readers like me: "Go ahead, blame her. . . . Yes, blame her if you dare, you son of a prick!" And, when Ed and Belle, Anastasia's parents, stay (miserably, of course) together: "But, lover of happy endings, they stayed together. . . . Isn't that what you want to hear?" In fact, I didn't care what happened to Ed and Belle, or to anyone else in the book. Anastasia tells us, "I stopped [trying to rescue my mother] from sheer hopelessness. I came to understand that it was useless to urge her to do anything because she was suffering from sickness of the heart, an incurable disease." And, "I try not to feel. I try to think. . . . But I am overwhelmed with feeling—with hopelessness. It doesn't matter what you do or how you try: the same things happen, over and over and over and over. There is no escape."

This depression, with its accompanying exhaustion and hopelessness, passed down from mother to daughter, is the theme of French's novel. It also unfortunately permeates the language and tone of the entire book. Grief or obsession can lend a writer precision of tone and a knife-edged awareness; the loved (or mourned or hated) object is scrutinized closely, often with a great deal of projection but almost always with tremendous energy. Depression is, on the other hand, merely deadening and narcissistic. My encounter with *Her Mother's Daughter* reminded me of an endless visit with a friend who talks about herself for hours, with no sparkle to her language or love for her subject. She gets through many handkerchiefs, but I can weep no sympathetic tears. My strongest feeling, easier to admit in the case of a book, is boredom and irritation, followed by guilt.

In depression, it is hard to notice the other. And the women in *Her Mother's Daughter* are difficult to distinguish. Belle is the most memorable, if only in her unpleasantness: Always cold, critical and dissatisfied, she seems enough to drive any daughter mad. (pp. 134-35)

Belle's mother, Frances, is even more vaguely drawn. She is loving, passive and almost always miserable. French (through Anastasia) goes so far as to compare her to the Jews from her Polish village who were "shot, thrown in a pit, and covered with lime." . . . French's need to resort to this unfortunate shortcut says something about the inability of the writing here to show, not tell us about, the quality of Frances's life. In fact, this very long book seems full of shortcuts: the cliché, the sudden, inexplicable change of tense and/or point of view, the repetition of catch phrases—used to avoid real feeling and the real writing that goes with it. The listing of menus or household tasks may be a device meant to remind us of the droning repetitiveness of women's lives, but here, it only succeeds in boring the reader.

Anastasia, the third mother and daughter in the book, is easily recognizable as the precocious child in *The Women's Room.* Gifted and outwardly independent, anxious not to repeat her mother's and grandmother's misery, but nevertheless always miserable, she passes through the stages of marriage, young motherhood, disillusionment, divorce, remarriage and feminism—complete with a woman lover. . . .

The section on Anastasia's travels, presented retrospectively through old journal entries about the excitement of sex and airplane food, is as embarrassing as if the depressed friend, after four hours of moaning, had suddenly got up with a bright smile plastered on her face and begun to tell adventure stories. One particularly false tale, involving Stacy's coverage of a failed and amateurish effort to invade Cuba led by someone named Woody Hedgecock, may be French's way of relating to the wider world and inserting some (very mild) politics: "In my heart I didn't support what the men I was covering were doing." On the whole, political reference is absent from the book. The women at its center are Polish in heritage but have lost their names and identity; they are totally uninterested in anything but themselves. One thing *Her Mother's Daughter* does achieve is a claustrophobic sense of the kind of sealed-off existence that cannot be touched by the outside world. (p. 135)

[The mothers in several other current mother-daughter books] are portrayed with a passion and energy which is also a form of respect—and which is conspicuously lacking in *Her Mother's Daughter*. Still, even that is not quite enough to explain why I should feel so uncharitable toward French's novel. It's a depressed and depressing book but not a destructive one; and Marilyn French, even at her lowest ebb, is a good enough storyteller to make most people want to read to the end.

My answer, finally, is that I am a daughter. My mother writes me long letters but finds it hard to spend time with me unless I am happy. I want her love and approval with a longing that can never be fully met; at the same time, I have nightmares about becoming her. . . . We need books about mothers and daughters, but if they are to help us understand and heal the wounds, they must speak of our mothers with respect, with passion and with insight. Such books are being written and published by small presses in small editions that go rapidly out of print. Meanwhile, we are served *Her Mother's Daughter.* (p. 136)

Andrea Freud Loewenstein, "Bound Together," in The Nation, *New York, Vol. 246, No. 4, January 30, 1988, pp. 134-36.*

BARBARA LEVY

Her Mother's Daughter can be read as an extension of *The Women's Room;* Anastasia is clearly the spiritual sister of Mira from the earlier book. This time French has written a four-generation novel that follows the maternal line: Arden, daughter of Anastasia, daughter of Bella, daughter of Frances, the immigrant from Poland. French identifies with Anastasia, and based the characters of Bella and Frances on her own mother and grandmother.

There is much to admire in this novel. French is a superb story-teller, with a sense of detail even Salinger could envy. The most interesting sections cover Bella's childhood. Born in New York in 1904, her father died when she was nine, leaving her mother so destitute that Bella's two brothers and baby sister were taken to an orphanage; for the time being, Frances was allowed to keep one baby. Even though her tyrannical husband had built up a lucrative tailor shop, he didn't believe in life insurance: "He wasn't going to leave behind a rich widow who would turn over his hard-earned money to some new man."

Bella began school with many strikes against her—she didn't speak English, her vision was poor and she was deaf in one ear from a neglected childhood illness. But the childhood affliction hardest to bear was her mother's inability to show her any love.

According to her daughter Anastasia, Bella inflicted the same cold behavior on her own two daughters. Anastasia is determined not to repeat the pattern, and is careful to cuddle her son, trying to compensate for her husband's refusal to kiss his boy-child as well as for her own mother's neglect. But later her daughter, Arden, claims she felt the same neglect, compounded by jealousy of her brother.

The novel emphasizes the similarities between mother and daughter by alternating between Bella's life with Ed (whom she had to marry because she was pregnant), and Anastasia's life with Brad (whom she had to marry because she was preg-

nant). But Anastasia, unlike her mother, gets a divorce, becomes a successful photographer and enters the sixties with a wonderful lover eight years her junior. Yet, despite her exciting career, financial independence and active sex life, her suspicious nature and bitterness make her very much her mother's daughter.

Anastasia's bitterness is directed not only at men but also at the fate in store for all women who have children:

> For generations—for centuries—for millennia . . . women gave up their lives, any hope of a life, to raise the kids, to make things better for the kids, to preserve the children, And the children, in their turn, *turn:* the mother was a martyr, screamer, a calculating bitch. She was not what was wanted. There is no end to the bitterness in their hearts against the mother, no end in mine, no end in yours, no end in theirs.

Although I don't endorse this peroration, my objection is not to Anastasia's bitterness but to French's pat causality: because Bella's teacher once reprimanded her for not combing her hair, she combs Anastasia's so fiercely her scalp grows calloused. Because Bella cared for middle-class trappings, Anastasia lives a Bohemian existence. Because Bella sacrifices herself for her children, Anastasia puts her career first. At work, she dare not admit to having children, lest she lose out on the choice travel assignments.

The novel ends on a note of acceptance: Anastasia declares she will accept the limited affection her mother can give. And she finally accepts Clara as her lover, making this yet another novel where a woman turns to another woman for sexual and emotional sustenance. But I find Anastasia's sudden interest in women unconvincing. Until the age of 50, she never has a close woman friend and is quite smug about being the only woman in a man's world. It is rather too convenient that she suddenly discovers her admiration for women and women's issues when the only job she can get is for a women-run magazine, after her male-run outfit folds.

Despite my reservations, I find French a thoughtful and skilled writer. Her insights can be profound. Whatever you do, as a mother, is wrong. However much you love your children, it will not be enough. The worst move is to sacrifice yourself for them. As Anastasia notes, "the absence of self is a punishment of others." But if you move in Anastasia's direction, and develop your own life, your children will feel neglected. In the long run, it does not matter. They will love you (and hate you) whatever you do. (p. 18)

Barbara Levy, "Their Daughters' Mothers," in The Women's Review of Books, *Vol. V, No. 7, April, 1988, pp. 17-18.*

Carlos Fuentes

1928-

Mexican novelist, dramatist, short story writer, scriptwriter, essayist, and critic.

Fuentes is widely regarded as Mexico's foremost contemporary novelist. His overriding literary concern is to establish a viable Mexican identity, both as an autonomous entity and in relation to the outside world. In his work, Fuentes often intertwines myth, legend, and history to examine his country's roots and discover the essence of modern Mexican society. Fuentes commented: "Our political life is fragmented, our history shot through with failure, but our cultural tradition is rich, and I think the time is coming when we will have to look at our faces, our own past." This tradition incorporates elements of Aztec culture, the Christian faith imparted by the Spanish conquistadors, and the failed hopes of the Mexican Revolution. Fuentes uses the past thematically and symbolically to comment on contemporary concerns and to project his own vision of Mexico's future.

During the late 1950s and 1960s, Fuentes gained international attention as an important writer associated with the "boom" in Latin American literature. Along with such authors as Gabriel García Márquez and Julio Cortázar, Fuentes published works that received widespread acclaim and drew international interest to the important contributions of Latin American authors to contemporary literature. Fuentes's work, like that of several writers associated with the "boom," is technically experimental, featuring disjointed chronology, varying narrative perspectives, and rapid cuts between scenes, through which he creates a surreal atmosphere. For example, in his first novel, *La región más transparente* (*Where the Air Is Clear*), Fuentes uses a series of montage-like sequences to investigate the vast range of personal histories and lifestyles in Mexico City. This work, which provoked controversy due to its candid portrayal of social inequity and its socialist overtones, expresses Fuentes's perception of how the Mexican Revolution failed to realize its ideals. The frustration of the revolution, a recurring theme in his writing, forms the basis for one of his most respected novels, *La muerte de Artemio Cruz* (*The Death of Artemio Cruz*). The title character of this work is a millionaire who earned his fortune by ruthless means. Using flashbacks, the novel shifts between depicting Cruz on his deathbed, his participation in the Revolution, and his eventual rise in business. Through this device, Fuentes contrasts the exalted aims that fostered the Revolution with present-day corruption. *The Death of Artemio Cruz* is generally considered a complex work that demands the reader's active participation.

In the novella *Aura,* Fuentes displays less concern with social criticism than previously and makes greater use of bizarre images and the fantastic. The plot of this novel involves a man whose lover mysteriously begins to resemble her aged aunt. Fuentes employs a disordered narrative in *Cambio de piel* (*A Change of Skin*) to present a group of people who relive significant moments from their past as they travel together through Mexico. Fuentes's concern with the role of the past in determining the present is further demonstrated in *Terra nostra,* one of his most ambitious and successful works. Many critics believe that this novel exceeds the scope of his earlier fiction, extending the idea of history as a circular force by incorporating scenes from the future into the text. *Terra nostra* is divided into three sections: "The Old World," which concerns Spain during the reign of Philip II; "The New World," about the Spanish conquest of Mexico; and "The Next World," which ends as the twenty-first century begins. By tracing the evolution of Mexico beginning with the Spanish conquest, Fuentes depicts the violence and cruelty that originated in the Mediterranean area and was perpetuated in Mexico through Spanish colonialism.

In *La cabeza de la hidra* (*The Hydra Head*), Fuentes explores the genre of the spy novel. Set in Mexico City, this work revolves around the oil industry and includes speculations on the future of Mexico as an oil-rich nation. Fuentes's later fiction investigates Mexico's relationship with the rest of the world. *Una familia lejana* (*Distant Relations*), for example, involves a Mexican archaeologist and his son who meet relatives in France; on another level, however, this work is about the interaction between Mexican and European cultures. In this novel, an old man relates a tale to a man named Carlos Fuentes, who in turn relates the tale to the reader. Through the inclusion of ghosts and mysterious characters, Fuentes also introduces fantastic events into otherwise realistic settings, a technique prevalent in Latin American literature that is often termed magic realism. In *Gringo viejo* (*The Old Gringo*), a study of Mexican-American relations, Fuentes creates an imaginative scenario of the fate that befell American journalist Ambrose Bierce after he disappeared into Mexico in 1913. Michiko Kakutani commented: "[Fuentes] has succeeded in welding history and fiction, the personal and the collective, into a dazzling novel that possesses the weight and resonance of myth."

Cristóbal nonato (*Christopher Unborn*), a verbally extravagant novel, continues Fuentes's interest in Mexican history. This work is narrated by Christopher Palomar, an omniscient fetus conceived by his parents in hopes of winning a contest to commemorate the quincentenary of Christopher Columbus's arrival in the Americas. According to contest rules, the male baby born closest to midnight on October 12, 1992 whose family name most closely resembles Columbus will assume leadership of Mexico at the age of twenty-one. The novel's nine chapters approximate Christopher's gestation and allude to Columbus's voyage, which Fuentes views as a symbol of hope for Mexico's rediscovery and rebirth. Narrating from his mother's womb, Christopher uses wordplay, literary allusions, and grotesque humor, combining family history with caustic observations on the economic and environmental crises afflicting contemporary Mexico. *Christopher Unborn* satirizes Mexico's government as inept and its citizenry as complacent, warning that the country's collapse is imminent without change.

(See also *CLC,* Vols. 3, 8, 10, 13, 22, 41; *Contemporary Authors,* Vols. 69-72; and *Contemporary Authors New Revision Series,* Vol. 10.)

PRINCIPAL WORKS

NOVELS

La región más transparente   1958
   [*Where the Air Is Clear,*   1960]
Las buenas consciencias   1959
   [*The Good Conscience,*   1961]
La muerte de Artemio Cruz   1962
   [*The Death of Artemio Cruz,*   1964]
Zona sagrada   1967
   [*Holy Place,*   1972]
Cambio de piel   1967
   [*A Change of Skin,*   1968]
Cumpleaños   1969
Terra nostra   1975
   [*Terra Nostra,*   1976]
La cabeza de la hidra   1978
   [*The Hydra Head,*   1978]
Una familia lejana   1980
   [*Distant Relations,*   1982]
Gringo viejo   1985
   [*The Old Gringo,*   1985]
Cristóbal nonato   1987
   [*Christopher Unborn,*   1989]

SHORT FICTION COLLECTIONS

Los días enmascarados   1954
Aura   1962
   [*Aura,*   1965]
Cantar de ciegos   1964

Chac Mool y otros cuentos   1973
Burnt Water   1980

ESSAYS

Paris: La revolución de mayo   1968
Tiempo mexicano   1971
Cervantes: o la crítica de la lectura   1976
   [*Cervantes: Or the Critique of Reading,*   1976]
Myself with Others: Selected Essays   1988

DRAMAS

Orquídeas a la luz de la luna: comedia mexicana   1982
   [*Orchids in the Moonlight: A Mexican Comedy,*   1982]

MALVA E. FILER

Octavio Paz writes in *The Labyrinth of Solitude* that Mexicans are, for the first time in their history, "contemporaries of all mankind." This claim to full membership in a world of expanding and diversified culture is also at the core of Carlos Fuentes' fiction and essays. The collected articles of **Tiempo mexicano** are a result of his concern with this subject, while the novel *A Change of Skin* attempts to recapture his Mexican experience as part of the universal historical drama. "We are contemporaries through the word," he says, echoing Paz's idea. "In order to name ourselves, we have to name the world; and the world, to name itself, has to name us." The effort to encompass an infinite reality makes of Fuentes' novel a labyrinth of time, such as the infinite novel left by Ts'ui Pên in "The Garden of Forking Paths." Its goal is unattainable, as acknowledged by a narrator who bears the family name and shares the madness of Balzac's character Louis Lambert. We are told, indeed, in Fuentes' novel, that "madness may be the mask too much knowledge wears." Freddy Lambert will leave us on "the morrow of an impossible feast," but his "personal happening" is, for him and for his readers, a forceful and transforming experience. The text, while discrediting itself as an adequate means of representing reality, claims none the less to be truthful to it. . . . *A Change of Skin* is Fuentes' most ambitiously designed work before **Terra Nostra.** The following pages analyze some aspects of this novel as they relate to the author's view of Mexico and that country's possible role in a culturally pluralistic world.

Fuentes' choice of time and setting points to the deeper meaning of his book. The day is Palm Sunday, April 11, 1965, on the eve of Holy Week; the place is Cholula, where Mexican history has deep roots and where voices of the past still break into the present. This is a unique stage on which to represent the drama of a Mexican history that has been made, says Fuentes, by the coexistence of diverse, even conflicting cultures: the mythic and cosmic conceptions of the Indians; the Spanish version of Christianity; the individualistic values of the European bourgeoisie; and the faith in science, reason, and progress borrowed from the industrially developed countries. . . . The novel's description of Cholula's church stresses the overlapping of traditions: Christ, as conceived by the natives, has his wounds covered with blood and feathers; the baptismal fonts are the ancient pagan urns where the hearts of the sacrificed were cast; the Arabic arches stand on the tezontle-stone floor; the sixteenth-century chapel combines an austere simplicity with the rich Renaissance-style ornamentation that was imposed by the Romantic spirit of the last century.

Religious syncretism also is evident at Cholula. In *Tiempo mexicano,* for instance, Fuentes refers to the Indians' concept of cyclical time and to their belief in a founding God, a belief which caused them to understand Christ not as the Savior but as the God of the Origins. According to Fernando Benítez, whose expertise in Mexican Indian culture Fuentes greatly admires, the ceremonies of the "coras" during Holy Week attribute the Creation to Christ. In the Indians' understanding of the Passion, Christ's sacrifice does not redeem humanity, but his blood assures that the sun will not die and Quetzalcoatl's maize will continue to grow on this earth. The ancient Mexican gods, says Fuentes, were conceived as protectors against change, for the Indians thought that the future could bring only destruction. In fact, memory of their origins and fear of the future dominated the society of the Aztecs. Religion, politics, and art were each a form of exorcism, a way to postpone the catastrophe. The Aztecs accepted the inevitability of change, but not without first building elaborate safeguards. Every fifty-two years, a cycle was closed, and the past had to be "cancelled, denied, destroyed or covered like the seven successive pyramids at the ceremonial center of Cholula." Human blood was required to win another reprieve, so that new life could grow.

A Change of Skin is clearly centered around this theme of a cyclical time (represented by the seven pyramids), the idea that "the end of a cycle required, as homage to the arrival of the new, that the old should disappear." Fuentes believes that Mexico has kept the original conception of sacrifice as necessary to maintain the order of the cosmos. This, he holds, is Moctezuma's real revenge, and the "final victory of the Indian world in Mexico." The novel summons the whole world to participate in the sacrificial exorcism of Cholula, for guilt is universal and the apocalypse can be averted only by cancelling the past. Western civilization is tried and convicted, as man seeks to free himself from "the old schizophrenias of the Greco-Christian-Judaeo-Protestant-Marxist-industrial dualism." The ceremony involves, as in the ancient ritual, the offering of human blood, here represented by the execution of one of the characters. An introduction to the last part of the book carries the announcement that the narrator, now identified as Xipe Totec, Our Lord of the Flayed Hide, is changing his skin. Finally, at the close of the novel, he indicates that he is an inmate of Cholula's asylum for the insane, a place symbolically named Our Lord Lazarus, "he of the resurrections."

In order to build up to its climax at the Gran Cu of Cholula, the text strives to produce a kaleidoscopic view of our own times. Frequent incursions into past centuries show that progress is mere illusion, that past and future exist here and now. Violence is presented as being the same, no matter who the perpetrators are or who their victims, in evocations that switch from the cruelties of both Spaniards and Indians to the atrocities of the Inquisition, the concentration camps, Hiroshima, and Vietnam. The open-ended, inexhaustible list also includes the Molotov-Ribbentrop pact, the Moscow trials under Stalin, and Trotsky's murder. Everybody is implicated, even the beatniks who judge and condemn the preceding generation. "There is no historical progress, . . . only a repetition of a series of ceremonial acts." This is part of Fuentes' intended message in the novel. (pp. 121-23)

Fuentes believes that Mexico, aware of its own overlapping

of cultures, should avoid an illusion of progress that has proven self-destructive to those societies where it has succeeded most. In both *Tiempo mexicano* and *A Change of Skin,* he compares the United States' "mechanical ruins" of progress with the "natural ruins" of Mexican underdevelopment: "If Mexico is nature in ruin," says Javier in the novel, "the United States is machines in ruin. In Mexico everything is a ruin because everything is promised and no promise is kept. In the United States all promises have been kept. Yet it is a ruin just the same." The author clearly feels that his country still has time to avoid the mistakes of its more prosperous neighbor. Since their independence, Latin American nations have followed the "triumphant model" of progress, empiricism and pragmatism. By so doing, says Fuentes, they have adopted the ideologies of their exploiters, the "antiutopian time of progress, of being" as against the "moral time" of that which should be, and can only be desired or imagined. (pp. 123-24)

The narrator of *A Change of Skin* assembles memories that run through centuries of human experience and failure. He needs to take possession of the past before he can cancel it. His evocation of the characters' voices is an attempt to reenact and render meaningful his own Mexican experience made of Greek and Judeo-Christian tradition, of Indian myths and Spanish Catholicism, of European culture and the American manufactured world. Before the start of a new cycle, he tries to mold that experience into a totality. This is the novel's "impossible feast." In fact, the writer's immediate problem is, according to Fuentes: "How to employ a fragmented, sequential discrete medium—language—yet achieve the impression of totality of wholeness, and above all, of presence." Javier, mirroring the narrator, pursues his own elusive totality in *Pandora's Box,* only to discover that "words could not conquer the fragmentation of reality."

Although to recapture total reality is admittedly impossible, the novel does succeed in reviving the time of "being" and "progress," even though it falls short of imagining the new, utopian, Mexican time. The cyclical concept of life would seem not to allow for anything but the repetition of the past. In fact, Fuentes' narrative is consistent in presenting a pessimistic view of the world, according to which the new is always condemned to acquire the negative features of the old. From his first novel, *Where the Air Is Clear,* to *A Change of Skin,* he critically examines his country's past and present, decrying its inability to break away from old and self-destructive patterns. In *Terra Nostra* and *The Hydra Head,* his more recent novels, he imagines Mexico's future, but only as a fatalistic recurrence of the past. Yet, it would be incorrect to identify the author's own position with this pessimistic outlook. In essays and lectures Fuentes has expressed his belief in Mexico's ability to build "a generous and revolutionary utopia," based on the cultural realities resulting from its coexisting histories. To that effect, a "screening effort" must be made, to "effectively separate the oppressive, dead weight from the living and liberating realities." The aim should be a "creative recreation," as represented by two great poems of Mexican literature: *Death without End* by José Gorostiza and *Sun Stone* by Octavio Paz, where Western linear discourse struggles with the spirit of Indian cyclical time in order to reestablish reality on a new foundation. (pp. 124-25)

A Change of Skin may be read as an exploration of the possibilities of prose fiction to create its own synthesis of language and time. More specifically, the text can be interpreted as an effort to rescue the reality of Mexican experience by creating its fiction. "We are resolved to invent our own reality," says Octavio Paz. "Spanish American literature . . . is both a return and a search for tradition. In searching for it, it invents it. But invention and discovery are not terms that best describe its purest creations. A desire for incarnation, a literature of foundations." That desire, we believe, is Fuentes' main motivation in writing his novel. On the other hand, the "revolutionary utopia" must await its fiction; his characters are still going through the pains of their self-criticism.

The narrative is built on the recreated experiences of the protagonists: Javier, a Mexican intellectual who failed as a writer and became a United Nations bureaucrat; Elizabeth, his Jewish wife, who may be a Mexican but remembers herself growing up in the New York of the Depression; Franz, a Czech Nazi refugee, who designed the buildings of Terezin's concentration camp, and did not try to save his Jewish girl friend; Isabel, an uninhibited but somewhat faceless young Mexican woman. The ambiguity concerning Elizabeth's origin makes it possible for her to represent a feminine image of an American or Americanized view of reality, mingled with the complexities of her Jewish background. She is a product of mass education, increased intellectual and sexual awareness, and cosmopolitan life. Her frustration and neurosis are the price that she pays for these privileges. Isabel, the young and definitely Mexican woman, is presented as the least conflictive of the characters and, at the same time, as an unfinished product. She already lives in the sexually liberated world built by the older generation and takes it for granted. Not sharing and not understanding Javier's interpretation of Mexican life, she finds his writing laughable and his concern pointless. . . . She is a blasé, uprooted pursuer of her own pleasure. Her behavior typifies the imported and superficial sophistication that Fuentes considers a hindrance to the creation of Mexico's own future. Is she condemned to repeat Elizabeth's life, as Javier fears? In order to prevent this, he kills her, in one of the possible outcomes of the novel. Symbolically, Javier strangles Isabel with the shawl that Elizabeth had given to her. (pp. 125-26)

A Change of Skin has been compared to Cortázar's *Hopscotch,* an earlier attempt by a Latin American writer to convey his experience of contemporary life. Indeed, Javier shares with Oliveira a demolishing intellect and a total paralysis of will. While *Hopscotch* recaptures its author's Argentinian experience, *A Change of Skin* is, not surprisingly, a Mexican version of our time. Fuentes' intimate knowledge of his country's history and concern with its present realities emerge from within the book's universal framework. We find in these crowded pages numerous descriptions and critical comments dealing with Mexico City, the Mexican people and the unresolved conflicts of their way of life. The text, as much as the characters, repeatedly returns to modern Mexico from far away places and distant times. On one of these occasions, we are told: "Javier decided that the time had come to return to Mexico City, that he needed Mexico again, that if he did not face and overcome its terrible negations he would always believe that he had taken the easy road and his writing could have no value." Javier would go out and "roam all over the city," looking for contrasts, images, words, profiles, masks. He was trying to find his words in that world that belonged to him. However, despite a declared interest in Mexico's Indian past, he feels that his country's uneducated and mostly Indian citizens are like creatures of another species. To them, "we are Martians," Javier says. "We don't speak as they do or think as they do. . . . If we do see them, it's like the

zoo. . . . We are their enemies and they know it." He tries to break the barrier by provoking a fight in which they beat him up. The humiliating experience, sought with masochistic determination, momentarily dissolves the social and intellectual distance that separates him from that group. He was now "on their side of the cage." Javier's attempt at sharing the experience of the oppressed is rather unconvincing, but sufficiently indicative of the guilt that is typical of socially concerned intellectuals. Most of the time, though, he is satisfied with his role of interpreter and critic of Mexican society. His remarks generally echo the author's views. They are also close to the ideas of Octavio Paz, whose friendship and works have been credited by the novelist with being an "original and permanent inspiration" for his own books.

Fuentes thinks of Mexico as a country wearing a series of masks in the course of its history: At its origin, "a skin of stone, mosaic and gold," then "the baroque and frozen order of liberalism and modernity," and the mask of "peace and progress" under Porfirio Díaz. They were the masks of slavery and hunger that were broken by the revolution. He says that the exceptional, unmasking moments of Mexican history force the country to see itself in its own "depth of latent myths, palaces in ruins, tragic miseries, grotesque coups, painful betrayals," and "useless deaths." . . . One wonders what our social critic can offer to that mass of people, marked by "centuries of humiliation and frustrated revenge."

"We cannot return to Quetzalcóatl," states Fuentes, "nor will Quetzalcóatl return to us." Mexico should not settle, however, for "Our Lady the Pepsicóatl," which is the time being forced upon it by the "modern world": "a technocracy without cultural values, without political liberties, without moral aspirations and without esthetic imagination." Javier knows, also, that the clock cannot and should not be turned back. "Or do you really think," he pointedly asks, "it would have been better if the Spaniards had been defeated and we had gone on living under the Aztec fascism?" His frustration and guilt feelings are evident, however, when he faces his own experience. Javier illustrates the limitations and agony of an intellectual whose social ideas have not made a dent in the fabric of reality. He is paralyzed by an excess of knowledge and destructive skepticism. This type of personality and behavior recurs in Fuentes' novels. He portrayed it for the first time in *Where the Air Is Clear* through his characterization of Rodrigo Pola, also an ineffectual writer. *A Change of Skin,* while exposing the selfishness and parasitism of Javier, suggests on the other hand the opposite model of Vasco Montero, a successful poet who is actively committed to the social and political struggles of his time. In the last pages of the novel, Javier admits his failure and condemns himself: "The world didn't change. It denied me and refused to notice me. . . ." He declares his passive, irrelevant life to be as guilty as Franz's Nazi past, and more cowardly: "What was action in him in me was only possibility, latency. In me it lacked all greatness, all courage. I have been a kind of larva Franz." "A soul of jelly, like Javier's, is far more guilty than mine," says Franz. This is also the opinion of the narrator who, unhappy with the turn of events leading to Franz's execution, would like to change his story.

The novel's verdict is clear: Javier should not survive, the possibilities of his experience have been exhausted. It is safe to assume also the author's agreement with a negative evaluation of this character. Lonely intellectual exercises, such as those engaged in by Javier, are not what culture is all about, according to Fuentes. He understands culture to be a collective and disciplined effort to address all the needs of human life, from economic satisfaction to the fullest development of each human being. Javier represents the type of "innocuous" intellectual that the author criticizes and rejects. Obviously, he is not the kind of human material with which to achieve a creative synthesis of the past and invent, as Fuentes envisions, Mexico's own model of development. Freddy Lambert knows it, as he knows it all, in his own mad wisdom.

Fuentes' novel, both through its narrator and through Javier himself, aims at a reality that is different from the one which Javier represents. As pointed out by Julio Ortega, *A Change of Skin* "pursues another world, another time: the new space where reality is invented." This was also Javier's ambition, stated at the beginning of his aborted book: "A novel discloses what the world has within itself but has not yet discovered and may never discover." However, Fuentes' narrator and characters are trapped by a text that, like the life it recaptures, devours its own creatures as well as their hopes. The future, symbolized by a bundle of rags (or a child), is swallowed and digested by the present, a yellow dog whose "hunger is far from being sated." Time is, in this novel, the eternal consumer that must, like the god Kronos, devour its children in order to exist. Freddy's narration remains, challenging death with the power of its own creation. Writing a story is, like the ceremony at Cholula, a way to postpone the final destruction. "The 'lies' we spinners of tales tell," says Lambert, "betray the 'true' . . . in order to hold away . . . that day of judgment when the beginning and the end shall be one." In Fuentes' novel, we may conclude, not only are Mexicans the contemporaries of all mankind, but all mankind has been made to participate in the exorcism, and the shaping, of a Mexican time. (pp. 127-30)

> *Malva E. Filer, " 'A Change of Skin' and the Shaping of a Mexican Time," in* Carlos Fuentes: A Critical View, *edited by Robert Brody and Charles Rossman, University of Texas Press, 1982, pp. 121-31.*

RONALD CHRIST

If [José] Donoso's macabre masque doubles decor with denunciation while pretending to do neither—the gold-tipped fence around the Ventura house is made from the subdued natives' lances—Fuentes's leaner chamber work [*Distant Relations*] takes the double as pretext, and in the manner of theme and variations, intensively develops its extensive implications in hushed tones. Essentially a *pas de quatre,* with two pairs of fathers and sons named Heredia, framed in the *pas de deux* of a storyteller named Branly on a Proustian quest as narrated by a Jamesian narrator, named Fuentes, *Distant Relations* posits the "correspondence among all things," a Borgesian/Baudelairian universe of wonderful-to-think-so symmetries.

For example, the Latin American son and father are named, respectively, *Victor, Hugo*—that multiple madperson who reportedly believed he was himself. Not surprisingly, then, the Mexican Heredias arbitrarily—that is, fatalistically—seek out their French counterparts who merge the boys into a single creature, the one, perhaps, looming over the fictional storyteller and fictionalized author at the novel's end. . . . The rigorous geometry of Fuentes's super-nature is elaborate, witty, and ponderous; for, if some will dismiss the book as a sociohistoric horror story, gussied up with precious correspondences—ranging from famous French writers who hail from Latin America, like Jules Supervielle, to characters in *Strangers on a Train,* Hitchcock's tennis thriller of murderous doubles—others must see *Distant Relations* as a coolly reflective book on the eternal Latin American question of identity.

Fuentes suggests that humans and their cultures become themselves by dying into their preterite ghosts, who then haunt their present existence. In this novel the New World Heredias are both inheritors and legacy of the Old World Heredias, as their self-same names suggest, and the old French teller of the tale to the Mexican author, who is Fuentes, virtually disincarnates the literary tradition vivified by the younger novelist, both former ambassador to France and Mexican cosmopolite. Transferred to history, as so often done by means of surrealist jump-cuts in this narrative dedicated to Buñuel, the personal narrative looms in vaster images: "The Creole revolutions weren't fought for *liberté, égalité, fraternité,* but to acquire a Napoleon. That was and still is the secret desire of the ruling class of Latin America."

Whether read for such paradoxical acuities or for comparable politics among characters, *Distant Relations* is a fleeting snowflake of unique arrangements, constantly, in its own words, establishing "analogy without sacrificing differentiation." Both Donoso's and Fuentes's books, in fact, are on the cool side, one as if behind the glass of a decorative arts museum, the other under the yellowed lens of a leather-cased magnifier. Both signal their critical signs from afar, challenging their translators . . . as well as their readers to see more where there is apparently less, affect where there is evidently only effect. (pp. 307-08)

> *Ronald Christ, "Fictional Diets," in* Partisan Review, *Vol. LIII, No. 2, 1986, pp. 305-08.*

GEORGE KEARNS

In one sense, Carlos Fuentes' *The Old Gringo* takes place in the revolutionary Mexico of Pancho Villa; in another, in some symbolic contemporary state just south of the border, for it's loaded with obscure, heavy mutterings from which, I think, both Mexican and North American readers are supposed to take home some message about the relationship of their countries. My best guess about what that message is, would be that our nations are locked in an agonistic Oedipal struggle. One version of the message comes along with the improbable thoughts of Tomás Arroyo, a young, illiterate revolutionary general:

> When the two gringos left Mexico, he wanted them
> to say: "I have been here. This land will always be
> a part of me now." That's what I ask of them. I
> swear: it's the only thing I ask. Don't forget us. But,
> more than anything, be us and still be yourself . . .
> and fuck it all.

In yet another way, *The Old Gringo* is only superficially set in Mexico: too often it sounds as if it's taking place in Faulkner country. The three main characters are doom–ridden very much in old Bill's way, their consciousness weighed down by the pasts of their races and families (all three have heavy, *heavy* problems with their fathers). Sometimes the prose gets embarrassingly close to the Mississippi master's:

> he saw in the passing Chihuahua landscape, in its
> tragic gesture of loss, less than Arroyo could tell

him but more than he himself knew. . . . As if the story kept flowing without interrupting the rhythm of the train, or the rhythm of Arroyo's memory (the gringo knew that Arroyo was remembering, but he only knew: the Mexican stroked the papers as he would stroke his mother's cheek, or the curve of his lover's hip), each watched . . . etc. etc.

The sentence piles up clauses for another 122 words. People are always "thinking" or "feeling" things forced upon their minds by Fuentes' rhetoric. . . . And then, of course, the obligatory touch of post-modern self-reflexivity: "Was he here to die or to write a novel about a Mexican general and an old gringo and a Washington schoolteacher lost in the deserts of northern Mexico?" The *very novel that Fuentes has written!* Finally, we have a good swatch of Lawrentian sex, which I won't quote out of sheer embarrassment for it. I really hate sex scenes where every little movement carries dark symbolic freight.

Actually, Fuentes had a clever idea here, for the old gringo turns out to be Ambrose Bierce, who in his old age, as my Columbia Encyclopedia says, "disappeared into Mexico, where all trace of him was lost." Fuentes imagines Bierce's last days, and borrows freely from the old wit's cynical aphorisms. Bierce doesn't want to fade away, as old soldiers are supposed to do, but to join up with Pancho Villa and go out in style. "To be a gringo in Mexico . . . ah, that is euthanasia." Being shot to rags against a Mexican wall "beats falling down the cellar stairs." Inside all the cotton-wadding *The Old Gringo* is a colorful historical novel, filled with vivid, often moving scenes of the peasants' revolt against their masters, and with Pancho himself riding in for a strong appearance. I think that historical novel is what Fuentes wanted to write, but didn't think he could without losing his world-class standing. It's good enough reading if you can ignore the portentous symbolism and rhetoric. (pp. 129-30)

George Kearns, "Revolutionary Women and Others," in The Hudson Review, *Vol. XXXIX, No. 1, Spring, 1986, pp. 121-34.*

JONAH RASKIN

The Old Gringo is set 71 years ago along the border between Mexico and the United States. On Main Street in El Paso there are "soda fountains and hiccupping Fords"; in the desert, Pancho Villa leads guerrillas against the Federales. In Washington, D.C., Woodrow Wilson speaks about the "New Freedom," and in the San Francisco *Chronicle,* William Randolph Hearst demands invasion and war. All this sounds familiar: guerrillas in Latin America, jingoistic press lords, a president who dangles the carrot of democracy. Carlos Fuentes's characters step across the frontier of the past and into the present. Ambrose Bierce, the old gringo, is a muckraking journalist who has lost his radical ideals; Bierce could pass for an aging '60s reporter marooned in the '80s. "We are caught in the business of forever killing people whose skin is of a different color," he says.

Fuentes raises consciousness about genocide and revolution in his new novel, but he's after a bigger story, as old as Cain and Abel. He casts the old gringo as the father; Tomás Arroyo, a peasant turned general, as the son; and a young gringa schoolteacher named Harriet Winslow as mother/daughter/sister. Their tragedy is staged in the hot, dry, dusty desert of Chihuahua, a land of "rebellion and suppression, plague and famine." It's a mythic place as well as a real one, a kingdom where nothing seems likely to grow but everything thrives and everything is possible. It is a place close to home and far away: a boundless world between God and the Devil.

At the age of 71, Ambrose Bierce comes to Mexico with the aim of dying in battle, preferably at the hands of Mexicans. That feat proves more difficult than he imagines, though in the end he gets to die twice—killed in hot blood, executed in cold. He's also buried twice, first in Mexican soil, and then in Arlington National Cemetery, in a grave marked by another man's name. Midway through the novel Bierce wonders, "Was he here to die or to write a novel about a Mexican general and an old gringo and a Washington schoolteacher lost in the deserts of northern Mexico?" *The Old Gringo* might be Bierce's sardonic last book.

The Ambrose Bierce part of *The Old Gringo* is delightful, but the rest of the book is disappointing. The novel moves in too many directions at once, dispensing an inadequate sort of justice to the characters. At times, the material seemed better suited to a movie than a novel. . . .

Fuentes has long been a master dialectician, and though he still does the old dialectical dance with finesse, his moves are more obvious in *The Old Gringo,* his steps slower. He allows the book to drift between history and myth, political parable and love story, murder mystery and psychological tour de force. In *The Death of Artemio Cruz* and *Terra Nostra,* Fuentes combined genres, collapsed categories, and created bold works that made up their own rules as they went along; these were frontier fictions that bridged consciousness and unconsciousness, history and legend, the exotic and the grotesque.

In *The Old Gringo* Fuentes works with the same material, but I had the feeling that for the first time he was relying on formulas. Part of the problem is the length of the book. At 199 pages, *The Old Gringo* is half as long as *The Death of Artemio Cruz,* and an eighth the length of *Terra Nostra.* Fuentes doesn't have the space to do what he does best: plunge readers into the hidden recesses of his characters' minds and at the same time allow language to pile up around their heads in thick drifts, until they feel lost in a blizzard of words that enables them to see, to feel, in a revolutionary way.

In *The Death of Artemio Cruz* and *Terra Nostra* the prose screams, shouts, bawls, wails. Carlos Fuentes flies high, turns somersaults, defies the laws of gravity. *The Old Gringo* is more conventional, more clichéd. Reading earlier Fuentes occasionally made me feel that I was present at the birth of language itself; in his new novel, the language shows signs of age.

Jonah Raskin, "Borderline Case," in The Village Voice, *Vol. XXXI, No. 13, April 1, 1986, pp. 57-8.*

FERNANDA EBERSTADT

Fuentes's first two novels, *Where the Air Is Clear* (1958) and *The Good Conscience* (1959), together form a crossroads, each marking his indebtedness to a different literary tradition. Though published later, *The Good Conscience* is clearly the author's first novel. It is set in the heavy, almost dyspeptically ornate colonial silver-mine town of Guanajuato, and tells of a family of Spanish merchants who came to Mexico in the 19th century to make good. Written in a deliberately archaic, period-piece manner, the novel opens with a leisurely history of the Ceballos family, nicely entwined with the history of their provincial capital as it is buffeted and scourged by Mexico's bloody uprisings and its unhappy brushes with empire.

The Good Conscience, however, is not the novel it starts out to be. From a tale of the provincial grand bourgeoisie, a class and generation which the historian Frank Tannenbaum has described as "locally bred colonists who for all purposes felt themselves to be living in a foreign country," *The Good Conscience* abruptly changes course when it reaches the 20th century and becomes instead a steamy coming-of-age story, charting the autoerotic and religious fervors of its hero, Jaime Ceballos. Now we are in a world of adolescent alienation and rebellion, as Jaime bucks his family's conformism by sheltering a union organizer on the lam, befriending an Indian scholarship student who dreams of class warfare, working on the railroad (where he encounters his estranged mother operating as an alcoholic evangelist-hooker, but is too prissy to approach her), flagellating himself in the desert, and masturbating in church before the image of Christ.

The novel concludes with a discomfitingly abrupt reversal. On being told by the parish priest that his religious and (implicitly) political yearnings are not true imitations of Christ but rather manifestations of an overweening pride, Jaime embraces conformism with a vengeance, kissing off his Indian friend and cynically embarking on the moneygrubbing legal career for which his family has prepared him. In later Fuentes novels, Jaime Ceballos will reappear as a Mexico City sophisticate, a faceless figure at high-society soirées.

For all its headlong shiftings of gear, for all the glib cynicism of its denunciation of bourgeois values, and for all its crude lashings of self-pity, *The Good Conscience* is quite a gripping and colorful book. Anyone reading this youthful novel will feel himself in the hands of a confident and powerful if somewhat sensational writer, one gifted with abundant natural talents and not too much brain. The book is interesting, too, in that it suggests a course Fuentes's work might have taken: of fast-paced adventure writing in the 19th-century manner with a strong undercurrent of social criticism. Instead, as we shall see, Fuentes's desire to be not just a novelist but an intellectual heavyweight led him to work in fancy literary forms which make mincemeat out of his native gifts.

If *The Good Conscience* is a truncated revamping of the French tale of the provinces, *Where the Air Is Clear* . . . could be described as a flawed gem of high modernism. On the level of manifest content, *Where the Air Is Clear* sets out to portray post-revolutionary Mexican society in its full array of luxury, tyranny, and wretched inequality, and to herald its imminent collapse. On another level—for *Where the Air Is Clear* is also an unrelentingly mystical piece of work—the novel depicts the survival, beneath Mexico's overlay of internationalism and modernity, of its secret pagan gods with their insatiable demands for bloodshed and betrayal.

The "hero" of this novel, in unabashed homage to James Joyce's personification of Dublin in *Ulysses,* is Mexico City itself; the title refers, sardonically, to the capital's perennial smog. . . . Fuentes, in the person of Ixta Cienfuegos, a mysterious stranger who is simultaneously man-about-town and the reincarnation of the Aztec god of war, takes us through many layers of Mexico City by eliciting confessions from bankers, cabdrivers, cooks, kept girls, beggars, revolutionary heroes, accountants' wives, and dispossessed aristocrats.

Of these, by far the most compelling is the life story of Federico Robles, a ruthless and sentimental tycoon whose rise and fall form a cautionary symbolic tale of modern Mexico. Born on a dirt floor, the son of an Indian peasant whose wife was raped by the local landowner, Robles becomes, successively, a protégé of the local priest; a cavalry officer under the governor-turned-revolutionary-leader Venustiano Carranza, fighting first the dictator Victoriano Huerta (who in 1913 had wrested the presidency of Mexico from the freely-elected Francisco Madero) and then the brigand Pancho Villa; a provincial lawyer holding much credit with the new government; and, finally, one of the richest and most powerful men in Mexico. In the novel's obligatory reversal of fortune, Robles's financial empire collapses because of unsound speculations, his brittle wife dies in a fire, he marries his blind mistress, and, absolved of the sin of capitalism, becomes a humble cotton farmer up north.

Where the Air Is Clear is full of pungent evocations of the sights, sounds, smells, tastes, and textures of the city, exciting action, and freshly captured battle scenes. . . . But the novel is marred by authorial self-indulgence and pretentiousness. Fuentes here mimics the more exaggerated mannerisms of the modernist style, transposing to a Mexican setting that stylized clatter of sounds and traditions which one critic has aptly described as the juxtaposition of Bartók with bar-talk. Much of *Where the Air Is Clear* is a highly self-conscious mélange of advertising slogans, refrains from popular songs, and overheard fragments of cocktail-party chitchat. The pastiche is made more local but no more palatable by being interspersed with lyrical streams of consciousness about Aztec sacrifice, plumed serpents, and darkness—incantations which run on for ten pages at a clip without hope of a comma, let alone a full stop. That, despite these efforts to smother it in affectation, *Where the Air Is Clear* remains an energetic and engrossing book is a tribute to Fuentes's gifts as a storyteller.

Those gifts are most effectively displayed in *The Death of Artemio Cruz* (1962), a slighter but stronger brother to *Where the Air Is Clear,* being the story of a powerful financier's deathbed journey into his own past. Cruz is a man who was made by the Revolution and whose cynical cooptation of its ideals makes him in turn symbolic of the failures of modern Mexico. As a character he is also the most developed and the most stylized example of a type that recurs in Fuentes's fiction.

The resentful, barefoot bastard of a Veracruz landowner and a mulatto servant girl, the youthful Cruz runs away to join the Revolution after he accidentally murders his uncle. We follow his rise in the ranks of Venustiano Carranza's army by means of disguised acts of cowardice; his crazy, unmanning love for a young camp follower who is strung up by Huerta's Federalists; his capture by Pancho Villa's army, notorious for its slaughter of prisoners and of innocents; and his escape from death when he betrays to his captors his own army's whereabouts. After the Revolution, Cruz marries the aristocratic Catalina Bernal and takes over her father's heavily mortgaged estate. At the time of his deathbed reminiscences, in 1959, Artemio Cruz's Mexican empire encompasses chains of newspapers and hotels, mines, timber concessions, pipe foundries, and (in a piece of characteristic Fuentes symbolism) the fish business. More importantly for Fuentes's purposes, Cruz is a front man for numerous American corporations seeking to evade Mexican restrictions on foreign holdings.

Artemio Cruz is elaborately constructed (thanks, this time, to the influence of the French *nouveau roman*) in three separate persons and tenses. The first-person present catalogues Cruz's silent sickroom excoriations of his spineless family . . . ; the rather strained second-person future, likewise in interior monologue, traces Cruz's physiological functionings and malfunctionings . . . ; the mercifully conventional third-person past retails Cruz's historical recollections. These last, constituting the most interesting portions of the book, move backward in time to 1903, when we are introduced to Cruz's natural grandmother, a lunatic harridan living in an abandoned Veracruz hacienda, who herself recollects the palmy days when she and her husband, a military man, had "glittered in the makebelieve court of His Most Serene Highness, General Santa Anna" (deposed by the Liberals in 1855). In this way is the history of the republic comprehended within the clotted brain of a rich mulatto bastard on his deathbed.

For Fuentes's final verdict on men like Artemio Cruz, and on the republic they helped to found, we turn to the end of the novel:

> You will bequeath this country: your newspaper, the hints and adulation, the conscience drugged by lying articles written by men of no ability; . . . You will bequeath them their crooked labor leaders and captive unions, their new landlords, their American investments, their jailed workers, their monopolies and their great press, their wet-backs, hoods, secret agents, their foreign deposits, fawning ministers, elegant tract homes, . . . their fleas and wormy tortillas, their illiterate Indians, unemployed laborers, rapacious pawnshops, fat men armed with aqualungs and stock portfolios, thin men armed with their fingernails: they have their Mexico, they have their inheritance. . . .

According to Fuentes, the failure of Mexico to translate the Revolution's original idealism into an honest, just, and equitable polity is to be blamed on this new class of military-men-turned-tycoons-and-politicians who have shielded themselves "behind glory to justify rapine in the name of the Revolution, self-aggrandizement in the name of working for the good of the Revolution," and who have perpetuated ancient cycles of exploitation and inequalities of wealth by selling out to North American imperialism. (That the Revolution might have been a corrupt or self-serving proposition from the start is a prospect he does not entertain.) Yet it must also be said that for the early Fuentes, these men also retain something irresistibly heroic about them. Complex, witty, divided, Artemio Cruz and Federico Robles possess a depth of feeling that outmatches everyone around them, including the insipid counter-heroes whom Fuentes introduces to remind us of the unmet spiritual needs of the masses.

The Death of Artemio Cruz is in many ways Fuentes's best work, and certainly his most disciplined and concentrated, notable for the richness of its prose and the subtlety of its insights into human relations, especially in their more devious modes. Yet it too suffers, like its predecessors, from its self-imposed formal constraints. Fuentes's mannered veerings from first person to second to third, his tricky allusiveness and ellipses, his unpunctuated prose poems (which some-

times seem to mimic a crafty old bully's determination to be boring on purpose) all serve to wreak in the name of art an unnecessary and finally debilitating havoc. That all this fragmentariness is intended to duplicate the movements of human consciousness itself is no consolation to the reader who comes to literature to see how true artists overcome fragmentation by a unifying effort of the imagination.

In the two decades following the publication of *The Death of Artemio Cruz,* Fuentes embarked on a succession of experiments with different voguish literary forms. In novellas like *Aura* (1962) and *Birthday* (1969), he adopted the southern offshoot of surrealism known as "magic realism". . . .

Fuentes's world outlook can be readily extrapolated from his views on Mexico. Taking into account the shifts and modifications of this outlook over the years, it can best be described as left-wing utopian with an overlay of sentimental anarchism. Primarily, his role in this hemisphere has been as a cultivated and (all things considered) rather patrician denouncer of American imperialism, colonialism, and big business. In addition to his role as nay-sayer to imperialist exploitation, Fuentes has served as a devout and ardent defender of revolution, making no distinction (at least for polemical purposes) in either aims or results between the American Revolution of 1776 and the Cuban Revolution of 1959—or, for that matter, the Paris student riots of May 1968, on which he published a slim volume, accompanied by photographs, declaring that "This revolution is ours, too."

Fuentes's habit of blurring distinctions is abetted by another habit, which is to deny the role that ideology plays in revolution. For example, he insists that Marxism-Leninism is simply a "label" for Latin American revolutionaries like the Sandinistas and the Salvadoran FMLN, a label covering the sorts of services formerly provided in the region by the Roman Catholic Church. That the Soviet Union might be involved in affixing this particular label is regarded by Fuentes as a canard, or a pretext for an American invasion.

In Fuentes's mind, it comes as no surprise to learn, the Soviet Union and the United States are "spectral siblings." The one has its Brezhnev Doctrine, the other its Monroe Doctrine; the one has Eastern Europe, the other its "Caribbean Warsaw Pact"; the one invaded Afghanistan, the other Grenada. The only difference is that while Russia is a stagnant gerontocracy unable and unwilling to lift a finger in the international arena, the United States is an active global slave-master.

The toll all this attitudinizing has taken on Fuentes's talents is painfully evident in his most recent novel, *The Old Gringo,* in which relations between the United States and Latin America, long an implicit theme of his fiction, become the main event.

The Old Gringo's point of departure is the disappearance into revolutionary Mexico of the American satirist, journalist, and short-story writer, Ambrose Bierce. The action unfolds in 1914 at a Chihuahuan hacienda occupied by Pancho Villa's rebel army, which is gathering strength for its march south to occupy Mexico City.

A brief and sparsely written novel, *The Old Gringo* describes the triangle formed among Ambrose Bierce—a lean, bitter, quixotic old man who, we are told repeatedly, has "come to Mexico to die"; Tomas Arroyo, a young general in Villa's army, out to avenge centuries of exploitation and oppression; and Miss Harriet Winslow, a headstrong young schoolmarm from Washington, D.C. who has been hired as a governess by the now-fled owners of the hacienda and whose determination to give her money's worth obliges her to stay on to teach Villa's Indian followers how to read and write.

For a Fuentes novel, the action is both fairly listless and elliptical. Much of it occurs offstage or in dreams while other characters sit in Arroyo's luxurious Pullman car, delivering soliloquies about Mexican destiny and North American wickedness. As in one of those reverse Westerns that are low on action and high on moralizing about the just grievances of the red man, *The Old Gringo* falls into the stock division of good guys vs. bad guys. "Haven't you ever thought, you gringos, that all this land was once ours? Ah, our resentments and our memories go hand in hand," sighs one *comandante,* gazing north at El Paso.

Pop psychologizing takes the place of character delineation in this novel, in which each protagonist is merely a type standing in for a particular political or cultural viewpoint. Arroyo, a stud whose private parts are described often and in lingering detail, is a spokesman for the Revolution's new order; Harriet, rather a figure of fun, develops from a knee-jerk American patriot with a missionary zeal into a confused and guilty liberal who denounces U.S. policy in Cuba and Mexico—"the backyards of my country, occupied by my country because our destiny is to be strong with the weak"; Bierce, who most speaks for the author, is a rebel and cynic, embittered by North American crookedness, hypocrisy, and ignorance and yearning after the dark, primitive soul of the Mexican Revolution. "Open your eyes, Miss Harriet, and remember how we have killed our Redskins and never had the courage to fornicate with the squaws and at least create a half-breed nation. We are caught in the business of forever killing people whose skin is of a different color. Mexico is the proof of what we could have been, so keep your eyes wide open."

The Old Gringo is almost deliberately indifferent to preserving historical propriety or avoiding anachronisms. Fuentes collapses chronology, misrepresents Ambrose Bierce's personal life, and confuses much of his career. The novel's historical liberties are most egregiously apparent when it comes to the sexual front—for although all Fuentes's books are dirty, *The Old Gringo* is the most implausibly so.

But Fuentes has played fast and loose with historical context for a reason. *The Old Gringo* is not really a novel about 1914, about Mexico, or even about Ambrose Bierce, but a weak and thinly disguised allegory of contemporary United States policy toward Central America, with Pancho Villa's charismatic rebellion a stand-in for the Nicaragua of men like Omar Cabezas, and Miss Winslow a little drummer girl in search of good sex and a revolutionary cause. "Ask yourself how many like me have taken up arms to support the Revolution," says a middle-class colonel in Villa's army. "We can govern ourselves, I assure you, *senorita.* . . . You don't think we're capable, then? Or do you fear the violence that has to precede freedom?" Thus *The Old Gringo,* little more than a wan storefront excuse for stilted polemics and gratuitous pornography.

Carlos Fuentes's is altogether a sorry case. He is a born novelist, endowed with boundless energy, sharp senses, an appetite for life, and a heady instinct for suspense, adventure, heroism, melodrama. These strengths are displayed to best advantage in one particular kind of writing at which Fuentes excels:

the battle scene. Perhaps no other contemporary fiction writer has evoked with such gusto and such precision a charge of the cavalry.

Yet Fuentes's artistic gifts have been increasingly eroded over the years by what can only be described as an irresistible tendency toward derivativeness. Even Fuentes's best work has been pressed by him into a succession of aesthetic molds which have obscured his virtues and inflamed his faults— those faults being self-indulgence and a certain cheapness of mind.

Similarly, the encroachment of politics upon Fuentes's novels has led increasingly to the recession of character and thought. In a true novel of ideas—and whether or not the reader finds the ideas themselves persuasive—there always remains an inner sanctum of human life and character upon which theory-mongering cannot intrude. . . . Fuentes's earliest novels maintain such a place, in which social condemnation and social prescription do not yet smother the irrepressibly natural longings of his characters to be rude to a dressmaker, to kiss a girl's neck, to lie in bed an extra hour, to chisel a cabdriver out of his fare, to own five acres of land. In his later work, however, and increasingly so as his career has progressed, human life with all its confusions and delights has receded, and the novel of ideas has instead turned into a kind of political demonstration, carefully marshaled by a very small and very loud party, with characters serving as banners and the sloganeering author as the only scheduled speaker.

Fernanda Eberstadt, "Montezuma's Literary Revenge," in Commentary, *Vol. 81, No. 5, May, 1986, pp. 35-40.*

SEAN FRENCH

Ambrose Bierce was a misanthrope, a nihilist, and America's most celebrated journalist. At the end of his career he decided not to fade away. In 1913, a bitter and beaten seventy-one-year-old, he lit out for Mexico and disappeared. Rumour has it that he joined Pancho Villa's revolutionary army and died in action the following year. Where history stops, the novel can begin: Carlos Fuentes's *The Old Gringo* takes up Bierce's story from the moment he crosses the Rio Grande with a suitcase containing two of his own books, a copy of *Don Quixote* and a Colt .44.

Fuentes clearly has only the most perfunctory interest in creating a plausible version of what might have happened. The "old gringo" (Bierce is never named: it is only through hints, allusions or reading the dustjacket that we find out the truth) rides across the desert and stumbles on a revolutionary detachment in Chihuahua commanded by the self-styled General Tomás Arroyo. He has led a rising on the estate where he was born and brought up as a virtual slave. The landowners have fled, but Harriet Winslow, the prim American schoolteacher they had hired, remains stubbornly behind. The general refuses to accept Bierce as a recruit until the old gringo demonstrates improbable skill with his revolver.

This novel is crammed with incident, much of it of the most melodramatic kind. We are told frequently that the old gringo has come to Mexico to die. He rides into battle with Arroyo's troops and performs acts of astonishing bravery, but he is not killed. Meanwhile Harriet Winslow is cured of her inhibitions in the course of a love affair with the virile General Arroyo. The tale reaches a predictably violent conclusion, and as in many a western only the woman survives to return to civilization.

But what is the book really about? Bierce wonders himself: "Was he here to die or to write a novel about a Mexican general and an old gringo and a Washington schoolteacher lost in the deserts of northern Mexico?" *The Old Gringo* is about Ambrose Bierce the man, but it also makes sophisticated use of his literary and political career. The form of the novel alludes to Bierce's celebrated short story, "An Occurrence at Owl Creek Bridge"; about a Confederate soldier being hanged from a bridge during the American Civil War. He feels the rope break and the story details his escape and journey across country. Finally he reaches home, but as he runs towards his wife everything goes black and he dies, swinging from the bridge. The whole story has taken place in his mind at the moment of his death.

Fuentes hints that this novel may be taking place in similar fashion in Bierce's mind as he dies. To complicate matters, the story is also unfolding in the confused memory of Harriet Winslow, reliving the events many years later in her Washington, DC, walk-up apartment. He is in her dream, but she is in his dream as well.

For the Mexicans, their country is all too real, and there are vivid evocations in this book of desert, heat and smells. But Mexico is also present as a state of mind, a subject of fantasy. Harriet Winslow and Bierce both enter Mexico as carefully delineated representatives of imperialism, with disdain for this primitive, chaotic country in the United States' back yard. Much in *The Old Gringo* is muddy, even on a second reading, but the anti-Americanism is clear enough. As Bierce puts it to Harriet, with the author's obvious approval,

> remember how we killed our Redskins and never had the courage to fornicate with the squaws and at least create a half-breed nation. We are caught in the business of forever killing people whose skin is of a different color. Mexico is the proof of what we could have been, so keep your eyes wide open.

This is a curious novel, alternately whimsical and immensely impressive. The vitality and virtuosity of Fuentes's narrative—in this superb translation, something like Jack London rewritten by Borges—are breathtaking. This is a story composed of fragments: moments of violence, passion or revelation, captured in memories and dreams. In other hands the effect could have been diffuse and boring, but Fuentes gives it the strange solidity of a fable. Yet much of the characterization—the demure schoolteacher, the macho rebel leader with "his uneasy sex, never restful"—is crude caricature. And the real subject of the novel, Mexico itself, which, we are told, redeems Bierce (compensating him "with a life: the life of his senses, awakened from lethargy by his proximity to death"), remains in the background.

> Sean French, "Shouting from the Backyard," in The Times Literary Supplement, No. 4344, July 4, 1986, p. 733.

ISABEL FONSECA

"To forget your past is to die", says Carlos Fuentes, quoting Pablo Neruda in an interview. *The Good Conscience,* a *Bildungsroman* describing the education and eventual corruption of Jaime Ceballos, may not secure Fuentes's immortality, but, written almost thirty years ago, it is an interesting reminder of the author as a young writer.

The Good Conscience begins in 1850 with the immigrant success of Ceballos's Spanish great-grandfather (in almost every Fuentes work we must relive the Revolution in order to grasp anything that follows). This huge sweep through time gives the book an epic quality, and implicates Mexico, not just Jaime, as the developing protagonist of the story. Jaime is a sensitive, profoundly religious boy who is punished for breaking the family rule that "life's real and important dramas should be concealed". He cannot comprehend that religion, for the stern relatives who raise him, means "fearing vice more than loving virtue". The surrounding characters—pinched, and pious in a solemn but not serious way—are well-drawn, if a bit extreme (women especially seem to fall into the nun category of his aunt Asunción, or lower, into the Dolores del Rio, coal-eyed, castanets-carrying school).

Jaime tries to salvage the spiritual note from the gaudy fanfare that passes for religion. As he grows, Catholicism goes from being a childhood game ("in the afternoon I played Mass") to the context for his first sexual experience (an orgasm at the altar) and finally to the safe social event that it is for the grown-ups (for whom Catholicism is synonymous with "Upper Class"). One of the most winning scenes is of Jaime and his unsuitable (Indian) friend, walking down the twisting yellow streets of their town in the hour when "the sun closest to man, the dying sun, shone on them". The two boys, addressing each other by surname only, discuss Nietzsche, Dostoevsky, Calderón, Vasconcelos, Stendhal and the purpose of life.

> 'So for you the most valuable action is not an individual one?'
> 'No. What is important is to be part of a general action, a movement.'

But what for the boys, equal for a time in their common enthusiasm, starts as "a movement" romantically symbolized by the Revolution, turns out to be two different and opposing movements. For the friend, togetherness will be that of peasants huddling in defence against the landowning likes of the Cebelloses, and for Jaime, caught in the ineluctable tumbling towards oligarchy, class obligations also prevail. Like Artemio Cruz in [*The Death of Artemio Cruz*], he abandons early ideals and becomes a hearty exploiter, he becomes a man.

Mirrors occur frequently in the novel. Jaimie is constantly checking his puffy adolescent face for spots, a suggestion of a whisker. Fuentes also writes as a mirror for his country. Mexico is defined in the Legend of Quetzalcoatl, the Plumed Serpent, the God who creates man and is destroyed by a devil who offers him a mirror. The devil shows him he has a face when he thought he had none. And so for Jaime: seeing who he really is means that forever after he will wear a mask.

Fuentes, who for all his grandiloquent erudition falls short in plot and character development, and can also fall for clichés, is well placed to reflect. He grew up and has lived much of his life outside Mexico. It is more real for him because it exists, first, in the mind. He evokes a pungent, aromatic Mexico—its religious rituals of blood and incense, hot crowded streets of palms, "perfumed quinces, and opened pomegranates"; a country of brightly coloured clothes in fiestas, of oranges "like tiny suns" rolling in the gutter. He also knows the other Mexico (and that there are two is the point), the arid, ancient "land original—obstinate, beyond salvation" . . . of "stone, dust and flapping black wings", the land of the pyramid.

Isabel Fonseca, "From Mirror to Mask," in The Times Literary Supplement, *No. 4369, December 26, 1986, p. 1456.*

ALFONSO GONZÁLEZ

[*Cristóbal nonato*] is a commentary on what Mexico might be like in [1992] if its leaders do not change their present policies. The main narrator of the novel is Cristóbal, an unborn fetus who, like Christopher Columbus five hundred years earlier, is discovering a new world, the world outside of his mother's womb. Through satire and clever linguistic play, an image of Mexico in 1992 begins to unfold: grotesquely deformed in its culture, language, and religion, mutilated in its territory, and buried in its own pollution.

Though there is frequent use of Mexican slang, the novel's sociolinguistic referent is that of the educated Mexican who also knows English. Its allusions to Mexican and World literature and history are recurrent. Its punctuation and some of its vocabulary are akin to blasphemy since they conform to English practices. The reader, who is shocked at first, and repelled throughout by the punctuation and some of its language, soon realizes that the erosion of Mexican Spanish parallels the disappearance of Mexican society, culture, and institutions as we have come to know them. The use of language in the novel is also comical. In a Joycean manner, the narrator is constantly playing with language. Mexico City has grown so fast that it is necessary to hire the well-known Irish "novelist" Leopold Bloom so that he can name the new streets, neighborhoods, and places that appear daily. This novelist-narrator cleverly anglicizes Mexican place names and hispanizes English words creating a comical, though grotesquely sad, new reality.

Each section of the novel is titled with fragments of Ramón López Velarde's "La suave patria" (The loving Fatherland), a political ode which exudes the optimism of some Mexicans soon after the Revolution at the beginning of this century. The content of each section contrasts sharply with the ideals expressed in its title and satirizes a leadership which has managed to lead Mexico to the point of no return in less than a hundred years. The author also satirizes the inaction and complacency of Mexicans who would rather believe that a loving, divine protector is going to help them change their situation, than do something in order to improve it.

In Fuentes's future world, economic interests will prevail over cultural and national values. The Americans, with the blessing of the ruling party who profits from this venture, are waging a limited "Vietnam-like" war in the jungles of Veracruz. The states of Campeche, Chiapas, and Yucatán have been leased to Club Med so that the government can pay the interest on an ever-growing foreign debt. Ixtapa is the southernmost city of a new country, Pacifica, which includes the Pacific coast of the United States, Canada, and Alaska, as well as Oceania, China, and Japan. Mexico's fragmentation is completed when we read that Mexican and American states adjacent to the border have declared themselves independent of both Mexico City and Washington. Mexamerica, as the new country is called, serves as a buffer zone, facilitating illegal immigration and providing cheap labor.

Though other Spanish-American writers have experimented with language in a Joycean manner (e.g., Guillermo Cabrera Infante and Fernando del Paso), and with the self-conscious narrative found in *Don Quijote* and in *Tristram Shandy* (e.g., Julio Cortázar and Vicente Leñero), few come close to the linguistic play between English and Mexican Spanish, and in the manipulation of the interplay between reader, narrator, and story which we find in *Cristóbal Nonato.* As for the apocalyptic vision of the novel, some readers will probably dismiss it since it comes from a man who, after all, lives abroad most of the year and therefore cannot possibly experience first hand the present Mexican situation. Such readers will be surprised to learn that Fuentes's vision is the fictionalized account of what sociologists, economists, historians, and poets are also saying to Mexico's leaders: change your course or face disaster!

Alfonso González, "Mexico in 1992 or 'Cristóbal Nonato', Carlos Fuentes's Latest Novel," in The International Fiction Review, *Vol. 14, No. 2, Summer, 1987, pp. 91-2.*

GEORGE R. McMURRAY

The setting of [*Cristóbal nonato*] is Mexico from 6 January to 12 October 1992, the gestation period of its protagonist. The latter, as the title suggests, is a fetus destined to be named for Columbus on the five-hundredth anniversary of the discovery of the New World. The unborn Cristóbal not only describes his own formation—one of many elements of fantasy—but also observes events surrounding the lives of his father, Angel Palomar y Fagoaza, and his mother, Angeles, of whose background we are told almost nothing. Orphaned as a child, Angel lived first with two eccentric aunts and then in the home of his paternal grandfather, formerly a general of the Mexican Revolution. His Uncle Homero, a corrupt millionaire and would-be politician residing in Acapulco, emerges as one of several villains, although his pompous speeches before illiterate Indians provide a source of humor. A more sympathetic uncle, Fernando Benítez, is an expert on Indian affairs and, as such, has perhaps been modeled after the well-known novelist and essayist of the same name.

Whereas in his previous fiction Fuentes . . . has focused on Mexico's present and past, *Cristóbal nonato* presents a horrifying vision of the future. The nation's crime-ridden, *caca*-inundated capital, referred to as Makesicko City, is populated by thirty million people and 128 million rats. The peso plummets to the incredible level of twenty-five thousand to the dollar, giving rise to *la economia del trueque* and the wholesale burning of paper currency. The bitter conflicts between classes find expression in an uprising of the poor in Acapulco, resulting in the leveling of the resort. Mexico's political chaos intensifies when President Ronald Ranger sends twenty thousand gringo soldiers and a fanatical fundamentalist preacher, Royall Payne, to Veracruz to protect the oil deposits from the *amenaza roja.* The novel ends with the birth of Cristóbal, whose parents are urged to abandon Mexico, with all its baggage of Occidental culture, and set sail for the Orient, the Utopia of the future.

Laced with satire, parody, and grotesque humor, *Cristóbal nonato* is a classic example of metafiction. It is replete with allusions, often ironically distorted, to other literary works, contributing to its own creative process; it exemplifies self-conscious literature in its preoccupation with language and affirmation of its deliberately fictive nature; and it suggests the self-begetting genre in the parallels between its own development and that of its embryonic narrator-protagonist. The novel looms as Fuentes's most ambitious since **Terra Nostra** . . . and, in many respects, as his most compelling and provocative to date.

> George R. McMurray, in a review of "Cristóbal nonato," in World Literature Today, Vol. 62, No. 1, Winter, 1988, pp. 96-7.

MICHAEL GORRA

[The prose in **Myself with Others**] moves easily between a discussion of Thomas Mann and an evocation of the "exuberant and dangerous" Mexico City nightlife of "whores, mariachis, magicians" that Fuentes enjoyed as a young man, with an urbanity that makes all questions of decorum irrelevant; with a combination of gravity and levity matched in English only by Philip Roth, to whom (with Claire Bloom) this book is dedicated.

A hundred years from now some of the essays in **Myself With Others** may have the importance for the history of late 20th-century literature that one like Hazlitt's "My First Acquaintance with Poets" does for students of the Romantic Movement. In **"The Other K"** for example, Fuentes describes how he, Julio Cortazar and Gabriel Garcia Márquez traveled across Europe by train to meet Milan Kundera in Prague—"There is no city more beautiful in Europe. Between the High Gothic and the Baroque, its opulence and sadness consume themselves in a wedding of stone and river." It was December 1968, the Russians had invaded that summer and the Latin American writers met the Czech novelist "in a sauna . . . one of the few places without ears in the walls." And Fuentes offers not just a memorable sketch of Kundera the man, "a mixture of prizefighter and ascetic" but of his fiction as well, a self-conscious fusion of the playfulness of Sterne and Cervantes with the dark laughter of Prague's original K, Franz Kafka.

Fuentes includes the commencement address he gave at Harvard in 1983 in which he criticizes U.S. policy in Central America: "We, your true friends, because we are your friends, will not permit you to conduct yourself in Latin American affairs as the Soviet Union conducts itself in East European affairs . . ." He writes on the films of Luis Bunuel and **"Gabriel Garcia Márquez and the Invention of America"**; on Cervantes and Diderot. And an essay on Gogol confirms what I've long felt, that the fantasies the Russian writer drew from the bureaucracy of Tzarist Russia have some connection not only to contemporary fiction in the Soviet bloc, but to the magical realism of the Latin American novel as well.

But the most exciting essays in the book are the autobiographical pieces with which it opens, and in particular **"How I Wrote One of My Books."** There he traces the inspiration for his third novel, **Aura** (1962), back to 1951, when he went to see "Maria Callas sing *La Traviata* in Mexico City when she and I were more or less the same age, twenty years old perhaps," and heard her young voice transformed "into that of an old woman . . . [fusing] youth as well as old age, life along along with death, inseparable." Yet Fuentes only understood that "I was looking at a woman I had known before, but she saw in me a man she had just met that evening." As

so often in Latin American literature, time seems liberated from chronology. Past, present and future collapse into one another—and not only in Fuentes' evocation of Callas, but in this essay itself.

Fuentes writes that La Callas "gave back to bel canto a life torn from the dead embrace of the museum." Much the same has been said about what Latin American writers have done for the novel in the last quarter century. The more modest form of the essay has never been in such trouble. But still one bows to the sense of freedom and daring that Carlos Fuentes has attempted—and succeeded—to bring to it here.

> Michael Gorra, "The Art of the Essay," in Book World—The Washington Post, May 1, 1988, p. 10.

ENRIQUE KRAUZE

In the family album of exiled writers (Conrad, Nabokov, Zamyatin, Kundera), a close-up of Carlos Fuentes reveals something odd about his image. Is he a willing exile from Mexico in the United States, or a reluctant exile from the United States in Mexico? He has become something of a star in North America, where he lived until the age of 12, to the extent that even an American congressman observed that "Fuentes is a great man. He knows so much about his country." The congressman had not read a single book by Fuentes; his opinion, like the opinion of so many others, had been formed by the omnipresence of the writer in the media.

In Mexico, Fuentes has an altogether different image. No one doubts his exemplary passion for literature and his professional attachment to it. He has published novels, stories, essays, drama, and countless articles. And yet for some time now his writings have been arousing irritation and bewilderment. Mexico is a country whose complexity has exhausted several generations of intellectuals, but Fuentes seems unaware of that complexity. His work simplifies the country; his view is frivolous, unrealistic, and, all too often, false. . . .

For Fuentes, Mexico is a script committed to memory, not an enigma or a problem, not anything really living, not a personal experience.

There is the suspicion in Mexico that Fuentes merely uses Mexico as a theme, distorting it for a North American public, claiming credentials that he does not have. The appearance of **Myself with Others,** then, is timely. Its autobiographical pages finally reveal the origins of his intellectual sleight of hand. The book shows Fuentes's lack of identity and personal history. From the very start, it's clear that he filled in this void with films and literature. His real world was his fictional world: a cinematic sequence of authors and works. Lacking a personal point of view and an internal compass, Fuentes lost his way through the history of literature and found himself condemned to the historic reproduction of its texts, theories, and personages. The key to Fuentes is not in Mexico; it is in Hollywood. The United States produces actors for movies, for television, for radio, for politics. Now and then it produces actors for literature, too. Carlos Fuentes is one of them. (p. 28)

Fuentes's was not exactly a life in exile, but an uprooting whose abrupt reversal in adolescence would leave a scar of ambiguity: "Mexico became a fact of violent approaches and separations in the face of which affection was no less strong than rejection."

The autobiographical pages make it clear that the only early links between Fuentes and his "paternal country" were a nationalism forged less by pride in the Mexican tradition than by resentment of the North American world, and by the determined effort he made throughout his childhood to preserve Spanish as his language. It is no exaggeration to see these links, respectively, as the origin of Fuentes's political and literary attitudes. When Fuentes finally approached "the gold and mud" of Mexico at the age of 16, language had already become "the center of his being and the possibility of joining his own destiny and that of his country into one." Mexico, the "imaginary, imagined country," was not a tangible, historical nation. It was only a victim of imperialism, an instrumental reality, a language.

Fuentes's struggle in Mexico to preserve the Spanish language led to the obsession with conquering it. The story of **Myself with Others** ends in 1950; to reconstruct fully the story of his struggle, one must turn to the testimony of friends, and to other incidental writings by Fuentes. Someone remembers that he became a mimetic being, all tongue and ears, a "brawler" with words. No wonder, because in Mexico the weapons of colloquial language are as sharp as, or even sharper than, real weapons. During those years he had already given up the idea of writing in English ("After all, the English language didn't need another writer"), but his use of Spanish indicated that he was tone-deaf to certain nuances, expressions, themes. He moved from reticence to excess: unexpected "damns," out of place "fucks." In sum, to a linguistic machismo. (p. 29)

In 1958 he published his first novel, **Where the Air Is Clear.** Closely following the visual methods of the *U.S.A.* trilogy ("Dos Passos was my literary bible"), Fuentes took an important step in Mexican narrative: he acclimatized the genre of the urban novel that had been introduced two years before, with fewer literary resources but tellingly and honestly, by Luis Spota in *Casi el paraíso* (*Almost Paradise*). His main formal inspiration was Balzac. "I am very Balzacian. . . . In *The Human Comedy* (or, if you prefer, *The Mexican Comedy*) there is room for many storys." The image is exact. Fuentes envisioned Mexican society as a vertical social and historical stage set. In the basement were the masked, unseen Aztec gods, embodied as faceless beings who carry out their designs. And above ground were the various social classes: the nostalgic aristocracy, the "Croesohedonic" bourgeoisie, the arriviste middle class, and at the bottom, the common people.

Fuentes's first book presaged the character of his entire work. The intellectual itinerary that he had chosen in order to learn about the country was transfigured into a strange confusion of genres. The characters had no life of their own: they simply acted out fashionable philosophical theses. A philosophical poet clearly inspired by [Octavio] Paz appears throughout the novel and dies in a manner that recalls the chapter on death in [Paz's] *The Labyrinth of Solitude;* the ruined banker does not consult a lawyer but discusses the essence of the Mexican spirit with Paz's alter ego; and so on. The most successful parody is not of the bourgeois class (Fuentes scorned it without knowing it), but of the aristocracy, to which he belonged without really belonging to it: its parties, its snobbery, its dandyism, its uprootedness. But finally Fuentes lacked the practical knowledge of social life that may be found in Balzac, for whom a bankruptcy, the work of a printing house, or the fall of the stock market were concrete realities, not symptoms of the life of a class. And he lacked something even

more important. "There, where your shoe pinches, is the touch of Balzac," wrote Harry Levin. In **Where the Air Is Clear** the common people do not suffer or work; they reflect philosophically on poverty in the setting of an endless and tragic binge.

Fuentes's first novel does not recall Balzac so much as that great actor of painting, Diego Rivera: immense texts and murals that proceed more by accumulation and schematic juxtaposition than by imaginative connection. Both are painfully rigid in suggesting the inner lives of their themes and characters, both treat them as theses or burden them with a didacticism that grows tedious, both have recourse to allegory. Texts that are murals, murals that are texts. The best of Rivera is the flowering of his forms and colors. The best of Fuentes is in the verbal avalanche of his prose.

The great Cuban poet Lezama Lima wrote that "I have found his novel strong, urgent, abundant, throbbing with symbols and masks." This verbal eroticism was the real substance of the novel, and it limned the central paradox of Fuentes's future work: there was something chimerical in his attempt to write the social novel of a reality he had not lived, something false that was supposed to be disguised by intellectual mimesis and lyrical expansion. But it was not disguised. Language was still the center of Fuentes's being, and Mexico remained an "imaginary, imagined country." His vast reading, diligent but independent of any experience that wasn't academic or folkloric, was never enough to correct his limitation. He never came to know the country that would be the central theme of his work. He thought he could resolve the deafness of his origins by turning it inside out: history, society, the life of the city, would be assimilated to the raging tumult of its voices. Balzac's characters still survive in the literary and popular memory of Europe. Nobody in Mexico remembers the characters of Fuentes. (pp. 29-30)

In **The Death of Artemio Cruz,** Fuentes attempted to expose the prototype of the Mexican revolutionary, caught up in lies, corruption, and murder. Pursued by the phantoms of his victims—the idealists, the collaborators, the friends—and gnawed by the memory of true love and its abrupt demise, General Cruz, a sort of Mexican Citizen Kane, dies a slow, vengeful death. Outside, on the painted walls and in the empty speeches of the Institutionalized Revolutionary Party (PRI), the revolution was dying with him. The novel was an immediate and unanimous success. It is generally believed to be the best novel that Fuentes has written. It is certainly the most sincere. At a distance of 25 years, one is still struck by the verbal fury of an implacable narrator who, out of the ideological optimism of the early 1960s, censures the impurity of a revolutionary undeserving of the name. The explosion of indignation worked marvelously well in the novel's language, but it made the character of Cruz unbelievable. His villainy was too perfect: he had committed each of the Seven Deadly Sins and violated all of the Ten Commandments.

In the revolutionary narratives of Mariano Azuela, Martín Luis Guzmán, and José Vasconcelos, you can almost smell the gunpowder in the pages: death is real, made up of terror, hatred, blood, and stench. The characters are buffeted by contradictory and unpredictable wind storms, and their reactions are ambiguous. Almost a half century later, **The Death of Artemio Cruz** did away with all this ambiguity. The historical revolution lost its real contours. It had become corrupt. There arose before it its own idealized image: Revolution with a capital R. Now the pages smacked of ink, not gunpowder. Fuentes's novel functioned as an indictment by the younger generation of intellectuals who, from the vantage point of a revolution that shone for them, wished to prosecute a revolution that they considered betrayed. (pp. 30-1)

Fuentes never speaks about the content of his words. In interview after interview, he insists that literary exploration is an exploration of language, inside language. Fuentes has very little intellectual curiosity. He looks for the script in an author or an ideology, and with that as a starting point, without reworking or conceptualizing it, he invokes the demons of language. In his hands, though, those demons often amount to no more than a cunning catalog of names. Thus, in the Aleph of *A Change of Skin,* which appeared in 1967, there are intersections of unconnected beaches and bullfights, crematoria and Aztec sacrifices, Theresienstadt and Cholula, Nazis and Jews, gringos and Mexicans who just want to get even; all things are the same thing, an optical illusion of "pulverized identities," as one critic put it. Thirty, forty names per page. (Hals, Klee, Capri, Dietrich, Lorre, Garbo, Cuauhtémoc, Milan, Singapore, and Cole Porter are all on page 150.) An abundant inventory of streets, magazines, cities, book titles, song lyrics, and above all films ("Not Greece, not Mexico, the world is called Paramount Pictures Presents"). Never has a novelist been so possessed by the noun.

The reader of *Myself with Others* can verify not only Fuentes's propensity for making catalogs, but also that his essays are as theatrical and derivative as his novels. His procedure may simply be an imitation of a popular writer (Kundera rediscovers Diderot, Fuentes rediscovers Diderot rediscovered by Kundera); a presentation of a popular theory (the odd avant-garde reading of *Don Quixote*); or an awkward attempt at a fiction based on other people's fictions ("Borges in action"). When the devices disappear, and Fuentes views the "others" from an independent "myself," the result may be a faithful and moving portrait, as in "Buñuel and the Cinema of Freedom." But this almost never happens. In the name of his right to experiment, Fuentes writes works without a center: vast, confused, formless, and oppressive literary happenings, parodies of novels that he or others have written, or parodies of themselves.

In 1968 Fuentes went a step further. He saw reality literally impersonating fiction. With novelistic opportuneness, the Revolution—the show of shows—returned to Paris. Fuentes saw words by Breton, Marx, Rimbaud, etc., on the walls, he recalled *Alexander Nevsky,* he listened to the young people talking about a European Moncada, he heard Sartre compare students to workers and praise the "admirable" pragmatism of Castro. On the basis of these images and sounds, Fuentes wrote **"Paris: The May Revolution."** This time the Aleph (in an illumination that made him feel like Borges, and Whitman) showed Fuentes the end of the Affluent Society. He saw a tide of change that would reach as far as Moscow and Washington, he saw the general will expressed with rocks and not with ballots, he saw strikes at Anaconda Copper, barricades in Arequipa, corrupt leaders in Mexico, he saw "the death of God and his privileged Western creation: white, bourgeois, Christian man."

A year later, when Fuentes returned to Mexico, he hung a huge photograph of Zapata in his study, he let his own mustache grow longer, and he paraphrased Daniel Cohn Bendit, one of the leaders of *les événements*: "We are all Zapatists." And he had more visions. He saw that Latin America had lived four centuries of "sequestered, unknown language," he

saw that our works should be works of disorder, that is, of an order contrary to the present one, he saw that the Latin American intellectual sees only with the perspective of the revolution: "To write about Latin America, to be a witness to Latin America in action or in language, means more and more a revolutionary act." In sum, he saw the novel in power, and power in the novel.

For the Guerrilla Dandy, there is no frontier between reality and fiction. Many years later, Fuentes revealed in an interview that he has always wanted to be a poet: "Richard III gave his kingdom for a horse. I would give all my books for a line by Eliot, Yeats, or Pound." It is only natural that in the optical illusion of his identities he has not seen himself for what he really is: a lyric poet lost in the novel and the essay, a spirited and abundant poet, though a little deaf to the beauty of the language. A macho, a stud, an Artemio Cruz who treats words like whores. His cherished need to impregnate everything with the sentimentality and the rhetoric of a lyric poet is the source of his problems as a novelist. In fact, Fuentes's old obsession with language ties him to a time, and to a rhetoric, that will pass very quickly. This novelist has run against the current of the novel's development. The author has not disappeared behind the text (as he was supposed to, after Flaubert, the Russians, Musil, Broch, Kafka, Nabokov, Faulkner); the text, instead, has disappeared behind the author. (pp. 32-4)

A word haunted Fuentes during [the late 1960s and early 1970s]: totality. He had been a "Joycean before reading Joyce." In *A Change of Skin,* one of his characters is possessed by a frustrated longing for the absolute: "to fix the past forever, to devour the present immediately, and to take charge of all imminence of the future." The fragmentation of reality seems vulgar to him. Years later, in an orgy of Joycification, his real self fulfilled his experimental dream: he wrote *Terra nostra.*

Obsessed by the mechanisms of power in Latin America, he had proposed to capture in a single vision the collective time of the founding of Ibero-America. In an essay written in 1973, **"Cervantes o la Critica de la lectura" ("Cervantes, or The Criticism of Reading"),** he had explained in detail the historical dimension of his project. He wanted to capture the Spain of the Counter-Reformation: monolithic, vertical, dogmatic, severe. Its perfect representation was the Escorial, Philip II's living tomb. Opposed to this fortress, and corroding it from within, was the *other* Spain, full of Arab sensuality, Jewish industry, Renaissance utopias, the Spain dreamed of in 1520 by the rebellious communards of Castile: democratic, pluralistic, tolerant, respectful of individual existence and local autonomy, watchful of the king—the Spain of Erasmus. The idea could not have been more ambitious. The novel's theme is the phantom, the dream, the desire for liberty in the walled cloister of the Counter-Reformation.

Fuentes could deal with the torments of the flesh in the Escorial, but the torments of faith escaped him: the novel recounts them ad nauseam, but it does not re-create them. The reason is clear. In *Terra nostra* he avoided throwing himself into the ring with his characters. He narrated the bullfight from an intellectual box. Or even less: he narrated a narration about the bullfight in the opacity of 800 pages, expressly accumulated in order to impose his majestic self on the reader: "I never think about the reader. Not at all. *Terra nostra* is not made for readers. . . . When I wrote it I was absolutely certain that nobody would read it, and in fact I wrote it with that in mind. . . . I gave myself the luxury of writing a book without readers." Joyce condemned the reader of *Finnegan's Wake* to spend as much time in reading the book as he had spent in writing it. Fuentes surpassed Joyce in *Terra nostra,* with its facile paraphrases and pastiches, and its transcriptions of encyclopedias and catalogs. The novel's real theme is its author's fascination with absolute power, not with the other Spain, the one that invented the word "liberal." The democratic values of the communards seem more alien to Fuentes than a Miuran bull. Ultimately, the book gives the feeling of a pathetically closed space: of totality that leads to asphyxiation.

In fragmentary passages, *Terra nostra* reads marvelously well, but its essay-characters do not really live their desires and their ambitions. In Fuentes, there is no existential exploration. His novels (*Terra nostra* most completely) are intra-literary—sometimes only intraverbal—exercises more akin to French structuralism than to anything Joycean. This lack of existential anchoring is the decisive difference between the actor and his model, but not the only one. Joyce worked at an extremely slow and steady pace, in careful and complex reflection. Fuentes proceeds by inspiration. . . . (p. 36)

Then, suddenly, briefly, Fuentes removed the makeup, came down from the stage, turned out the lights, and walked out incognito to wander through Mexico City. A line by Paz concerning the mythic destruction of the Aztec city came to mind: burnt water. In *Burnt Water,* which appeared in 1980, Fuentes plays no one but himself. It is not written by himself as a personage, but by himself as person. These four perfect stories show, again, that his calling as a writer is the authentic investigation into the tragic fate of the city he loved. Suddenly, in a kind of parenthesis in his career, Fuentes is not afraid to create "psychologizing subjectivity," characters who dare to feel tenderness, filial love, pity, and the most bestial hatred.

A poor old woman, surrounded by street mongrels, remembers the ancient palaces in ruins, and an invalid child listens to her. A native aristocrat clings to the decorative world of his house now situated amid decay and drug violence, a nest of rats that do not conquer him: they devour him instead. And in **"The Son of Andrés Aparicio,"** there is the life story of a lumpen turned bodyguard. Here the city is not unreal or purely visual. It is a visceral city, a city in pain. Here the extraordinary recreation of language is not the end, but the means. There are no useless names, no social or political didacticism, no reflections on the nature of the Mexican spirit, no sentimental lyricism. There are only four fragments that touch the Mexican soul of Carlos Fuentes.

This parenthesis of real feeling was closed, however, in the 1980s, when Fuentes definitively established himself in the country of his childhood and allowed himself the luxury of writing a nationalistic Western for American readers. *The Old Gringo* is a minor work. The book's explicit subject—Ambrose Bierce—is its least striking thing; Fuentes gives the basic facts, but he fails to penetrate Bierce's hallucinatory life. *The Old Gringo* is important, rather, because it reveals Fuentes's methods of appropriation and distortion with devastating clarity. The beginning of the novel is derived, for example, from *Memorias de Pancho Villa* (*The Memoirs of Pancho Villa*) where its author, Martín Luis Guzmán, narrates the twofold death of the English rancher Benton at the hands of a Villista. Who would notice? Nobody in the United States knows Guzmán. Then, along with Bierce, the novel presents an opaque, enigmatic Mexican general named Ar-

royo, and a God-fearing Methodist school teacher who eventually succumbs to the transfiguration, to the sexual, telluric strength of the general; and the similarity to Cipriano and Kate in D. H. Lawrence's *The Plumed Serpent* is certainly remarkable. As Fuentes has written, "Is there any book without a father?"

After liberating himself from the imaginary need to imagine, Fuentes goes on to rearrange completely the history of the Mexican Revolution. In *The Old Gringo,* briefly, Zapatism becomes Villism. Fuentes transports the peasant revolution of indigenous southern Mexico to the northern border. He situates his story in Chihuahua, where there were *no* problems concerning land, *no* conflicts between haciendas and communities, *no* peasants in ponchos, *no* people drinking mezcal. It was easier that way, because he could imitate Jesus Sotelo Inclán's book about Zapata, which no one in the United States (except John Womack's readers) would know. In 1971 Fuentes wrote that "literature says what history covers up, it forgets or mutilates." Many Mexican readers of *The Old Gringo,* however, found themselves convinced of precisely the opposite. (pp. 36-7)

Enrique Krauze, "The Guerrilla Dandy," translated by Edith Grossman, in The New Republic, *Vol. 198, No. 26, June 27, 1988, pp. 28-34, 36-8.*

CARL GUTIÉRREZ

Terra Nostra seems to exist in an atmosphere typified as much by the controversy it elicits as by the enigmas it raises. Reactions to the text range from outright attacks on the author's "dissimulated" stance and his attempts to manipulate, to less blatant condemnations of the author's failure to project "something to win." In reviewing the reactions the text has provoked, González Echevarría has called for readings which explore its seemingly threatening complexity. In his essay on the novel, "*Terra Nostra*: Theory and Practice," he addresses one initial problem readers of Fuentes face: the failure of Fuentes's own critical writings to account for the principles set in motion in *Terra Nostra.* Ultimately, González leaves open the search for an appropriate critical approach; yet one point remains clear: Fuentes is actively engaged in rethinking alternatives to linear models of history. González does not come to a favorable opinion of the project, arguing instead that Fuentes resembles the novel's patriarch, El Señor, who hoards knowledge and cultural codes.

The question of history, in *Terra Nostra* an issue of repetition and difference, is reduced, according to González, to a search for a cryptic lost origin, a search which sets the ground for the author's manipulation of the reader. In his discussion of the novel, González suggests that the title is emblematic of a contradiction between the attempt to create a common language between author and reader, and an attempt to shackle the exchange between the two by locating the common ground in a dead and "timeless" language. Rather than viewing this contradiction as an ironic strategem, pointing up the difficulty of finding a common ground, González chooses to ignore Fuentes's systematic critique of origins and the role of doubt in the novel. In doing so, González reinscribes a linear model of history by raising the search for an origin as the principle by which to judge the novel. In examining the text, we shall try to highlight the subversive aspects of the novel, particularly those relevant to the issue of origins, and to rethink the approach to origins typified by González. Then we will read, through *Terra Nostra,* theories which may prove helpful in elucidating the critical notions at work in Fuentes's experiments with history.

Terra Nostra attempts to discover a "common ground" for history, between Old World Spain and Latin America, between the masters and the servants. In carrying out this project, the novel enacts various strategies to subvert the traditional sense of history, understood as an objective interpretation of a distinct individual's linear progress toward a utopian goal. The crux of Fuentes's strategy involves setting conventional voices of time (paternity, progress, and linearity) into dialogue with heretical voices, so that the monologic power of traditional history may be dispersed. It may at first seem odd to talk about "voices of time," and yet, as Margaret Sayers Peden points out in her essay "A Reader's Guide to *Terra Nostra,*" in the attempt "to isolate the basic elements in *Terra Nostra*—time and place, character, symbol, theme, plot and structure, authorial voice—one quickly becomes aware of the difficulties, for time is place (as space), structure is voice, voice is time." Fuentes plays out a dialogue between rival voices of time in the novel by creating characters which double as desiring individuals and as mouthpieces for particular dogmas of temporality. These two aspects, of course, are not mutually exclusive, although combining the two goes against expectations of character development. The presumed spilling over of character into arcane dogma (often arcane rhetorics of temporality) creates highly stylized caricatures, which, like the title, open the question once again as to whether Fuentes is merely indulging in intellectual pyrotechnics.

To answer this question, we must first situate the ideological import of the "spilling over" (from character to ideology, from the pragmatic to the arcane). As one of a group of novels by Latin American authors intended to take up the subject of despotism, *Terra Nostra* actively seeks political alternatives. Inasmuch as the ideology of history has played a principal role in the despotic control of colonial and post-colonial populations, the structure of traditional history is itself caught up in providing a ground that would maintain existing forms of power. To imply that there are alternatives to the structure of history challenges on a formal level the skeleton which holds up the body of despotism. The "spilling over" that Peden describes, and that González will not abide, is fundamental to Fuentes's rebellion, which attacks the primacy of linear progress.

For the characters of *Terra Nostra,* the creation of a traditional history is often synonymous with the creation of an heir, and in this sense Fuentes draws on the strategic importance of the trope of childbearing when discussing history. El Señor, the despot of old world Spain, literally refuses to "spill over," to consummate his marriage, a refusal which goes hand-in-hand with his desire to halt history by controlling its progress and making himself its "end." The principle of exclusion El Señor must adopt to sustain his control infects everything in his ken; anything perceived as Other represents something to be dominated. What refuses to be dominated must be excluded and forgotten, an act which essentially relegates the unwanted to oblivion.

El Señor's attitude toward the written word exemplifies this attempt to exclude by forgetting. El Señor's dictum, that "only what is written exists," is perhaps the foremost statement of this principle. By appealing to the legitimacy of the written, El Señor attempts to exclude events which would threaten his familial claim to power. Writing history in this form becomes a way of ridding oneself of the past.

Because the past for El Señor is a wildly proliferating family spawned in a chaotic series of rapes by the seemingly tireless El Señor Sr., it poses a direct threat to any claim to legitimacy based on patriarchy. Inasmuch as El Señor wishes to encompass all that he knows with his word, the greatest threat to his control is that which he cannot know, and that which he cannot predict. Heirs outside his knowledge exist outside his word. Upon arrival, their dubious pasts must first be erased so they may be given an identity and incorporated into the paternal system. (pp. 257-59)

From the outset of the novel, the fear of being lost in time and the quest for redemption motivate responses to history. In the first chapter of the novel, Celestina, in a passage adapted from T. S. Eliot's *Four Quartets,* announces that "A people without a history is not redeemed from time." To the extent that the fear embedded in Eliot's lines reveals a nostalgia, it establishes the motivation for the creation of an origin. Inasmuch as this fear fuels the drive to dominate, it motivates the writing of history in its despotic, traditional sense, a history by which El Señor would colonize heretical discourses. Even as Eliot's lines are being recited, the prospect of a traditional history is being challenged; women are begetting children at a rate beyond comprehension, destroying the logic of a parental structure by giving birth to children who have no fathers. Emphasizing El Señor's failure to arrest the play of time and history, Fuentes suggests the inadequacy of the parental structure as it would be used to establish a traditional history.

The desire to construct a paternal lineage is representative of an all-encompassing desire to place time in a progressive frame which assumes distinct individuals move toward a definable end. Time, as a generative force, is perhaps so fundamental to Western thinking as to be virtually invisible. M. H. Abrahm's work, *Naturalism/Supernaturalism,* as well as Peter Brooks's *Reading for the Plot,* expose the generative notion of time *as* a recurrent plot. This plot, as examined by Abrahams from the advent of Christianity through the Victorian period, repeatedly invokes a three-phase scheme. First a Golden age is posited, one much like the world evoked by Blake's "Songs of Innocence," where strife is unknown. This stage is then disrupted by a fall into disharmony (most often the author's present state), and finally a third stage is projected, a stage which would unify contradiction and disharmony in some form of revelation. The plot projects the pilgrim migrating toward one purpose, one goal. It is in this sense that time itself is projected as generative.

The third stage is, however, thwarted in *Terra Nostra* by various heretical uses of the traditional model of time described by Abrahms. Nowhere is this more evident than at the "close" of the text. In an image of romantic unity, bringing both sexes together in one act of narcissistic love, the text simulates an androgynous conclusion. The stability this image of unity implies depends upon its suspension of time; but, betrayed by the passing hours, the final words of the novel interrupt what would be the smooth surface of two lovers embraced as one: "Twelve o'clock did not toll in the church towers of Paris: but the snow ceased, and the following day a cold sun shone." The projection of a highly ambivalent future deflates any "sense of an ending," subverting the traditional expectations demonstrated by Frank Kermode, expectations which, I would argue, would be satisfied by the ending which presented "something to win," some key which would unlock the text and at the same time work to exclude ongoing conflict.

The final lines of the novel introduce a question which permeates the whole of the text: What happens next? This question does not present itself in a "whodunit" style where the options have been fashioned to suggest a key, if only we could distinguish the "true" line of cause and effect. Varying representations of time subvert simple cause and effect in *Terra Nostra.* Events do not occur in a sequence leading to a conclusion. Instead, as in Borges's "Garden of Forking Paths," events appear to follow various orders. Cause and effect is not excluded, but it exists within a framework which emphasizes indeterminacy.

Conventional generative time is disrupted through various strategies. Sequences of narration often jar progression, as episodes appear seemingly without regard for their temporal setting. Repetitions of events—young men with strange markings washing ashore, for instance—challenge notions of progress. . . . All of these strategies subvert the trope of temporal progress toward completion.

El Señor complicates the notion of completion inasmuch as he is aware of his own failure to achieve perfection. In terms of the ideology he professes, this complication takes the form of domesticating doubt. During a penetrating critique of El Señor's system, Brother Toribio, El Señor's astrologer, explains how doubt is inscribed to create the illusion of openness. As Brother Toribio tells the heretical painter, Julian, "The only reason El Señor examines his doubts is to conserve an order; he places his trust in the fact that the truth revealed can withstand all assaults upon it." Interestingly, the despot's creation of an order which would make him all powerful ultimately makes him a prisoner as well. Again Brother Toribio explains: "El Señor is the prisoner of the idea of a world designed by a deity in a single act of immutable, irrepeatable intransformable revelation; you and I are the tributaries of the idea of a divine emanation which is perpetual flux, realized by continual transformation." It is significant that Brother Toribio's belief in flux does not represent itself as the Truth in an absolute sense and that it emphasizes the danger of incorporating doubt only to inscribe it in a larger order. . . . Concluding his critique of El Señor's beliefs, Brother Toribio announces the project of subverting despotic order and, implicitly, the model of time and history which frames the events within the despot's storyline, offering an alternative to the imminent destruction destined to accompany endless repetition. In the politics the text enacts, repetition takes the form of the repeated incarnation of despots, a result of the continual attempt to exclude alternatives to absolute, immutable truth. The undercurrent of heresy in the novel, always associated with a belief in flux and transformation, subverts the absolute constructs of Truth and Falsity necessary to maintain legitimacy because the change inherent in the heretical view undermines the static dichotomy.

The glimmer of hope embodied in Brother Toribio's statement, however, is quickly overshadowed as we are thrust back into the logic of despotism. One subsequent repetition of the despotic paradigm takes the form of Tiberius Caesar, who, like El Señor, caught in the throes of despair, determines to exercise complete control by ending history with his own death. His scribe, Theodorus, who is left to record the chronicle of Tiberius, understands the principle of unmitigated unity on which despotism is founded, yet he also understands his necessity as a witness. As Theodorus states, "Tiberius requires a witness of his character. . . . My death is deferred by Caesar's need for a witness." The scribe thus acts as a supplement which becomes a necessity, the outside which must exist for Caesar's boundaries to have meaning. Theodorus's function as a chronicler is to create a history which would likewise exclude all but the desires of Tiberius, a history which, in Tiberius's words, "should be at the service of legitimacy and continuity," and not at the service of "a natural world where chance prevails over action, a world which consequently is defined by dispersion." All that threatens Tiberius's attempt to create absolute unity must be expurgated. Christ, like El Señor's anonymous heir, must be destroyed, but this is not a simple act; in both cases these individuals transcend the control of their would-be masters. Christ poses the threat of a supernatural being, one which may be "a phantom of flesh or the flesh of a phantom." Like the Prince, circulating in a realm of words, Christ may overflow the boundaries of reality and illusion, and this problematic nature raises the question which ultimately destroys the foundation of the Roman Empire: "was it all illusion, deception, a comedy of roving, disembodied larvae and mischievous, ghostly lemures?"

The question leads the scribe to conclude that a "true history" may only be an illusion. "The true history," he finally asserts, "is not the story of events, or investigation of principles, but simply a farce of specters, an illusion procreating illusions, a mirage believing in its own substance." The scribe criticizes despotic history, but fails to open the question of possible alternatives, of the play of time which might offer something other than a "policy of despair." Having remained in the dichotomy of Truth and Falsity, he can conceive of no position other than one of passive deferral; he announces: "I, like Pilate, shall wash my hands and wait for time to decide." His attempt to stand outside of history is shortlived, as the scene ends with the "dead" Tiberius beckoning Theodorus to enter his chamber and once again fulfill the role of servant. Fuentes subverts any conclusions we might draw about the purely illusory nature of history; the decision not to act in this case is still a decision to participate.

By ignoring the prospect of temporal dialogue which Brother Toribio envisions and which Fuentes translates into narrative form, readers like González neglect the strategies subverting what would otherwise be a totalizing and manipulative project. The attempt to reduce *Terra Nostra's* project to the control of a despotic author may in fact reveal a nostalgia for the seeming comfort of absolute distinctions which only despotic forgetfulness may purchase. The repeating scenarios of despotism, however, do suffer breaks again and again. They fail because the interaction of various models of time, inscribed thematically as flux and transformation and inscribed stylistically in the various subversions of Abrahms's "plot," will not support the despotic narratives of history. Through the breaks in despotic time that these variations represent, *Terra Nostra* offers at least a chance for the creation of "alternatives to a policy of despair."

Returning to the accusation that Fuentes is perhaps a monger of formal and erudite intricacies, we may now respond that the desire for a more "explicit" politics in his works may in fact cloud a more pressing issue, in this case the question of how models of history have been used to dominate and how alternative, provisional histories might be envisioned. One mistake which seems all too inviting, as we have seen, is to look to theoretical structures for answers which would arrest dialogue. The colonizing manner in which works are often subjected to theory leaves many skeptical, and with good reason, since recent application often seems to enact the European conquest all over again. Yet it would be a grave mistake to ignore altogether those issues being raised in a theoretical context which may suggest, along with literary texts, alternative ways of reading and writing history. For this reason, it will be useful to situate the various debates surrounding the contemporary call for a "return to history" within our reading of *Terra Nostra.* (pp. 259-63)

For one of the most prominent post-structuralists, Jacques Derrida, the writing of history is inextricably bound up with the narrative's systematic exclusion or incorporation of contestatory voices, and with its strategic reinforcement of a particular voice within the text. Derrida's project, at this point at least, seems wholly consonant with *Terra Nostra*'s strategic use of voices in its rethinking of models of time. At the close of one of Derrida's essays, "Structure, Sign and Play," the question arises: can a common ground be developed to alter the metaphoric economy (of history) in such a way as to minimize the exclusion of contestatory voices? Derrida makes the move toward this "common ground," this *Terra Nostra,* at the close of his essay as he discusses the "irreconcilability" of the two dominant voices he locates in the Social Sciences: Nietzsche's affirmation of the past, and Lévi-Strauss's debilitating nostalgia. Derrida concludes, "For my part, although these two interpretations must acknowledge and accentuate their difference and define their irreducibility, I do not believe that today there is any question of *choosing* . . . we must first try to conceive of the common ground, and the *difference* of this irreducible difference." Choosing remains trivial, I would argue, because of Derrida's provisional insertion in a historicity which acknowledges the rhetorical status and structural economy of *the choice.* Thus, Derrida at least implicitly recognizes a larger structure of historically located power. Derrida's conclusion raises a provisional temporality in which whatever ahistorical qualities his discussion has taken are subverted by his own ambivalence toward that which is to come. He concludes the essay with "a kind of question, let us call it historical, whose *conception, formation, gestation,* and *labor* we are only catching a glimpse of today. I employ these words . . . with a glance toward those who . . . turn their eyes away when faced by the as yet unnamable which is proclaiming itself and which can do so, as is necessary, whenever a birth is in the offing, only under the species of the nonspecies, in the formless, mute, infant, and terrifying form of monstrosity."

That Derrida's meditation on history should turn to the monstrous echoes an emphasis throughout *Terra Nostra.* Beyond the very breadth of the novel, which has more than once received that epithet, monstrosity is explicitly thematized, usually with an intimate association between procreation and childbearing. This consonance between Fuentes's and Derrida's experiments with history may seem a bit surprising given the reception of Derrida who has been heralded as a proponent of an ahistorical, endless deferral of meaning. On the basis of the essay at hand, which clearly opens the door for some form of provisional historicity, we might examine the seeming contradiction and ask to what extent the readings of Derrida in the United States have been tailored to fit the ideological necessities of a community which has a great deal to gain by obfuscating the historical element in experiments like *Terra Nostra,* historical elements which bear a great deal on the United States' position in relation to Third World countries, and to Latin America specifically. (pp. 263-64)

Terra Nostra, in addition to seeking alternatives [to established structures of power], carries a warning which remains particularly applicable to those working with the literature of Latin America; any attempt to apply First World theoretical structures to Third World literatures must begin with a questioning of the particular ideological functions, either explicitly announced or unconsciously transmitted, in such structures. Such an interrogation will in turn alter the questions we bring to *Terra Nostra* and complicate ideologically forceful assumptions about author, text, reader, and the linear attainment of "something to win," or conquer, implicit in theoretical structures which seemingly liberate. (pp. 264-65)

Carl Gutiérrez, "Provisional Historicity: Reading through 'Terra Nostra'," in The Review of Contemporary Fiction, *Vol. 8, No. 2, Summer, 1988, pp. 257-65.*

JULIO ORTEGA

The fifth centennial of the discovery of America will result in more than one book, but Carlos Fuentes's [*Christopher Unborn*] anticipates it as a parody of the apocalypse. In *Christopher Unborn,* 1992 is the year in which every kind of crisis makes Mexico the capital of underdevelopment. Fuentes confronts us with a genuine Latin American nightmare, where all of our present miseries combine in a country that is dismembered, invaded, and plundered. The fifth centennial could not have a better visionary narrator. Out of a pretext, upon the landscape of a library of promises and frustrations, he has produced a post-text; because between Christopher Columbus and Christopher Unborn, between the discoverer and the colonized, America has lost its future.

Everything in *Christopher Unborn* is extraordinary, and by that standard it is a homage to the imagination of discovery; but it is at the same time a contradiction of the celebratory ritual: in place of the invention of America, here we see its miscarriage. In place of the utopia of Vasco de Quiroga, the future is occupied by the anti-utopia of Ronald Ranger.

History is the setting upon which the novel raises itself. The notion of an origin to commemorate is converted into an extravagant contest: the parents of the first child born on October 12, 1992, will be awarded a prize. From his mother's womb, preparing himself for the contest, Christopher assumes the narrative voice. In nine chapters (the months of the novel being born in our reading), Christopher records all the information about his parents, his relatives, his city, and his country. He listens to everything and inscribes it in his cells, in his prenatal memory, acting thus as a kind of Mexican computer "chip." The memory of Christopher (Columbus navigating in language) is, certainly, the act of writing itself. In this way, language (brilliant, overwhelming, circulatory) is really an amniotic (and semiotic) fluid; the novel, a maternal womb; and the reader (called Electurer—"Elector"), a witness who attends with humor the gestation of a profoundly humorous and impudent narration. The novel is joyfully born, from its historic placenta, with the fluidity and loquacity of a comic myth. History (linear time, nightmare of the future) and myth (circular time, comedy of the world turned upside down) merge in the discourse of a novel that, with the imaginative license of utopia (a genuine *tour de force* and Mexican tour), produces an extraordinary satire of the socio-political condition of Latin America. Not in vain does the patriarchal figure of Quevedo rise above the ruins; moral and stoic indignation blaze here behind the caricatural and grotesque spectacle. (pp. 285-86)

In his novels Fuentes is most incisive when he demonstrates, in the hidden recesses of a character, the optical illusions of the myth of identity, of the myth of the self, of the myth of the author as the center of the narrative. That is why Fuentes is our best postmodern author; his work is based not on repetition but on difference, not on the authorial monument but on relativistic fluidity, not on the modernist ideal of the total work but on the pure residue of change.

Christopher Unborn is something more. Here Fuentes has gone beyond his own work and his radicalism is complete. This is a less referential novel (the future he presents is a probabilistic calculation in the same sense of Posada's representations of everyday life from the grave), but at the same time it is his most political novel (the critique of power, that liberal virtue, gives way to lampooning and ferocious satire, that libertarian virtue). It is also, in spite of its hyperboles, highly specific; it is full of lively, pugnacious material. And it comes out of an apellative, comic, and digressive present. But, more than anything else, its language has ceased to be literary, and its characters do not pretend to complexity. The language is street language, irreverent and piquant, and the characters are obsessed, uncertain, and extravagant. This novel is like an implacable satire by Evelyn Waugh written with the flippancy of Carlo Emilio Gadda.

The energetically displayed freedom is stimulating. The narrator is possessed by his creative fury to such a degree that, even when he seems to become repetitive or excessive, he always recaptures the vivacity of the story thanks to the naturalness of his spoken language. In this sense, Fuentes makes no concessions to the audience; he is confident that the casual reader will soon lay down the book, and he summons the Electurer, the accomplice no longer active in the making of the text (the modernist ideal) but in the unrestricted verbalization of the world (because this novel is an inexhaustible conversation, at times a pleasant chat, at times manic, imprecatory, or witty). To the disaster of history and the failure of politics, then, we oppose the power of mockery. Fuentes imagines a Mexico measured by desperate indignation, and passes, by means of it, from criticism to condemnation and sarcasm. One could say that the novel is a stone aimed at the cyclopean eye of the PRI; yet man does not live by the PRI alone, but by PAN/"bread"—translator's note/as well, its underside, and also by other Mexican perpetuations, lashed one by one by laughter. There is no pity in this inhuman comedy of underdevelopment; Latin America appears as the ridiculous construct of ideological discourses, where a wretched reality denies the word. In this novel each character expresses his/her predestined corruption. Each struggles within his/her own discourse, no longer for self-justification but for self-exhibition in the spectacle of his/her own immoderacy. As in the best satiric tradition, the taboos have fallen.

This freedom to express is also the freedom to remake language. Everything said is here resaid; it passes through plays on words, through the pun, in a systematic way. (pp. 286-87)

The act of narrating is the main plot. The fact that the narrator is the chronicler of the world into which he will be born

makes possible the flow of the most diverse information, filtered by the very act that produces it and so controls it. This plurality is accumulative and circular, but also systematic and fluid. It expresses itself, furthermore, as a chronicle about the story: the reader is the permanent referent, and his presence splits the monologue into a dialogue. The story is also about the writings—scriptures—that prop up the given world, and is full of writers who rewrite history in order to lie by accumulation. In the setting of political catastrophe, the State reinvents manipulation, creating symbols both living and archaic. The creation of Mamadoc, essence of Mexican motherhood, is one memorable chapter, a tremendous Rabelaisian and baroque satire. Apart from that, nationality has been converted into a puppet theater. And the future is, inevitably and unfortunately, a byproduct of the present.

It is in this way that the narration posits a representation of the Crisis—and not just the Mexican crisis. Paying homage to the most desperate of our historical presents, this novel assumes that the crisis has become endemic and replaces reality with a veritable world turned upside down. Crisis is the only possible world: the dark lens of reality gone astray. To preserve lucidity, all that is left to us is words: not natural language, which is entirely insufficient, but subverted language. Thus, this carnivalization of Crisis (like a celebration in the cemetery) makes the grotesque its model and satire its meaning. The enthusiasm with which Fuentes traverses the Mexican pantheon reveals, once again, his cultivation of apocalyptic metaphor as a historical paradigm, his exploration of catastrophe as a regenerative setting. From this enthusiasm stems the creative force that unfolds the spectacle. The satire implies another model: that of passion communicating a common truth, no less urgent for its improbability. *Christopher Unborn* is a living fresco of disasters.

In effect, its characters seem to step out of a mural by Diego Rivera, another man impassioned by the festival-like spectacle of history. The characters are earthly, omnipresent, extravagantly animated. Above all, Uncle Homer: a leading figure in the PRI, a worshipper of creole Hispanism, a politician and rhetorician for every season. Opposed to him is Christopher's other uncle, Fernando Benítez, eponym of the writer Fernando Benítez, an anthropologist by trade, a democrat by vocation, and a permanent contradictor of the Crisis. The Ayatollah Matamoros is the leader of Mexican fundamentalism, that is, "guadalupismo" up in arms. And Mamadoc is the goddess of intimate populism. Uncle Homer, the father of the national discourse, expresses it well:

> You still need to learn, permit me to say, the virtues of the native dialectic by virtue of which, duly adapted, we are Mexicans because we are progressives because we are revolutionaries because we are reactionaries because we are liberals because we are reformists because we are positivists because we are insurgents because we are "guadalupanos" because we are Catholics because we are Spaniards because we are Indians because we are mestizos.

And, later, on the PRI:

> I can be a revolutionary because I believe in their most ancient slogans and legitimations; I can be a conservative because without the PRI we will fall to communism, I can be a liberal because without the PRI we will go to fascism, and I can be a Catholic millionaire and a progressive and reactionary revolutionary at the same time: the PRI authorizes

me all of this. . . . Without the PRI I would be an orphan of history!

Christopher's father is also a child of his time:

> I'm just a poor bastard, you realize that I've spent my entire life, from when I was born in 1968 until today in 1992, driven to despair by rage and impotence, I never even had a chance to feel a bit of optimism about this beginning or that vogue or this other restoration; a man of my times only got to feel corralled, desperate, furious: but at least furious is something, right?

The father has discovered the premodern world in Oaxaca, and asks himself, "Was only Mexico's past serious?" while, for his part, Uncle Fernando resists the assaults of the State in the name of the surviving natives, that other culture without a national destiny. And, nevertheless, history is not concluded, in spite of the nightmare:

> The observer introduces insecurity into the system because he cannot separate himself from a point of view and therefore the observer and his point of view are a part of the system and therefore there are no ideal systems because there are as many points of view as there are observers and each one sees something different: truth is partial because consciousness is partial: there is no universality other than relativity, the world is unfinished because the men and women who observe it are as yet unfinished and the truth, inexhaustible, fugitive, in perpetual movement, is only the truth that takes into account every arbitrary position and every relative movement of every individual in this world into which I make my way.

This radical relativism is what makes the novel a representation of subjectivity, and language its transitive material.

The discourse sharpens in its response to the malaise, with characteristic humor: "Mexico exists to screw us over," "He who pays, plays," "Mexico has always survived because it has known how to institutionalize everything—unfortunately, even its vices;" "an earthquake Mexican-style: classist, racist, xenophobic," "nothing works but everything survives," "they shared the creole vice: they needed someone to humiliate every day," "with a little palm-greasing"; and other popular turns of speech, especially in the chapter dedicated to Mexico City, "Mug Sicko Sity," a veritable verbal apotheosis. Out of this language Christopher is born, on the beach, along with his twin sister, in a ritual recommencement/rebirth. Between Oaxaca and Acapulco, between the true past and the prostituted present, between the political crises and the social cataclysms, this novel is born as a festive and corrosive metaphor that entails reading as the radical proposition of remaking the future with language—with rage and laughter. (pp. 288-90)

> *Julio Ortega, " 'Christopher Unborn': Rage and Laughter," translated by Carl Mentley, in* The Review of Contemporary Fiction, *Vol. 8, No. 2, Summer, 1988, pp. 285-91.*

WENDY LESSER

One might have guessed from such novels as *The Hydra Head, Distant Relations* and *The Old Gringo* that Carlos Fuentes is imaginative, intelligent, well read and politically thoughtful. One might even have guessed that he is witty. But what we could not know, until reading the essays in *Myself With Others,* is how absolutely charming he is.

This is not the charm of a writer who abjectly wishes to please at any cost. On the contrary, Mr. Fuentes's great charm consists in part of his high standards. He has enormous respect for both his readers and his subjects—subjects that range from Cervantes, Diderot, Gogol and Luis Buñuel to Jorge Luis Borges, Milan Kundera, Gabriel García Márquez and 20th-century politics.

About himself, Mr. Fuentes is both witty and ironic, both deeply convinced of his individuality and intensely aware of his place in a larger culture. (p. 22)

Mr. Fuentes spent much of his childhood in Washington, and from his insider-outsider position he is able to generate perceptions about the United States that are astute, sensitive and affectionately critical. Recalling his youth in this country in the 1930's, he comments on "the North American capacity for mixing fluffy illusion and hardbitten truth, self-celebration and self-criticism: the madcap heiresses played by Carole Lombard coexisted with the Walker Evans photographs of hungry, old-at-thirty migrant mothers, and the nimble tread of the feet of Fred Astaire did not silence the heavy stomp of the boots of Tom Joad."

He has a similarly removed perspective when speaking about Mexico ("the imaginary, imagined country, finally real but only real if I saw it from a distance") and, above all, about himself. Of his first novel, he remarks, "I myself feel about it like Marlowe's Barabbas about fornication: that was in another country, and, besides, the wench is dead."

The frequent literary allusions in Mr. Fuentes's work are part of what I mean by his respect for readers: he assumes we've read the books he has and confirms our shared culture in throwaway remarks like the ones I've quoted. This tactic is welcoming rather than exclusionary, intended to reach across cultures rather than build fences around them. And indeed, if one had to think of a single word that represented Mr. Fuentes's moral and esthetic position, it would probably be "open."

The value he places on openness—in literature as well as in politics—can be felt in all these essays. . . . In the one on Gogol, he defines "the literary and moral identity of the novel as the form of an unfinished speech, as work which is perpetually open." And film too can have this virtue, as he points out in regard to Buñuel: "The true mode of this filmmaker is the open ending, the unfinished story, the devolution of responsibility to its purest and most original site: the conscience and the imagination of each filmgoer."

Such attitudes may sound vaguely like deconstructionist literary theory, in which every text boils down to reader response. But they could not be more different. Whereas literary theorists tend to deny the existence of any firm foundations, preferring instead to be buoyed up only by their own hot air, Mr. Fuentes manifests a profound belief in the permanent value of certain artworks. (pp. 22-3)

I find his faith in great artworks of the past enormously convincing, and moving—and heartening, because it doesn't prevent Mr. Fuentes from discovering much to admire in his contemporaries. The artists he examines in this book form part of a set of literary touchstones, among which he numbers Rabelais, Shakespeare, Sterne, Poe, Dickens, Balzac, Lewis

Carroll, Kafka and Proust. Over and over, he returns to these writers and their literary virtues, which include the capacity to break down linear time and create multiple time schemes, the corresponding ability to bridge the gap between the characters' fictional world and the readers' real one and, through both these techniques, the power to preserve that openness that Mr. Fuentes so values in great art.

Openness is a virtue we ought to value in him as well, for it enables him to cross the barriers our own age has erected— not only the obvious ones between Old and New World writing, literature and politics or the masterpieces of the past and the writing of our contemporaries, but also such impediments as the one separating general readers from academic critics. Like George Orwell's essay on Dickens, or Walter Benjamin's on Kafka, Mr. Fuentes's learned but fluent pieces on Cervantes, Diderot and Gogol speak to both the nonacademic and the academic camps. (p. 23)

> *Wendy Lesser, "Nervy on the Greats," in* The New York Times Book Review, *July 17, 1988, pp. 22-3.*

JOHN CALVIN BATCHELOR

Christopher Unborn is a pell-mell magazine of his talent. Fuentes writes as a statesman and an imp, a literary traveler and a vulgarian. You don't have to favor a sentence to recognize that he speaks from authority, you don't have to agree with a notion to know this is a man who can get a crazy job done. In truth, at 61 he's demonstration of the novelist as tyrannical crybaby and if that sounds like a slap it's because Fuentes's sense of the ridiculous demands it. He's in the same sort of playpen where brats like Dostoevski, Hugo, Wells and Sinclair Lewis misbehaved. Whatever else can be said of this gang, they made folk mad and they meant to.

Christopher Unborn is a cunning turn of crybabyhood. At 200,000 translated, kaleidoscopic words it's entirely narrated by a fetus who names himself Christopher and who is ranting mad about his dear country-to-be, Mexico. The time is the first nine months of 1992 in and around Mexico City. Christopher is hastily conceived on a beach because his mom and dad hope to win a loony national contest that will make the male child born at midnight October 12, 1992, the divine heir apparent to Mexico. Out with democracy, in with regency based upon the 500th anniversary of Christopher Columbus's famous accident.

And so Christopher glances around and can't shut up about what he sees, especially since for the first few months he doesn't have eyelids so there's no way to shut out chaos. Mexico in 1992 is a Hollywood disaster. It's partitioned by cuckolded bankers and poetic rebels, ruled by a government of clever idiots called the PRI, so deep in trouble that the last 92 incorruptible Indians worship a pile of feces they are raising like a ziggurat. No one's truly upset by all this of course, except Christopher, whose task it will be to take over as king of all the ziggurats. (pp. 1, 6)

Christopher's ranting has a plot but not too much of one because he's a well-read fetus and the author he most resembles is Tristram Shandy—"Digressions are the sunshine of reading." His mom and dad are Angeles and Angel, 22-year-old idiot savants who dress retro and roam around reading Plato and hustling the rich for favors. Fortunately for mom and dad Christopher's paternal uncles, the Fagogas, are wealthy maniacs with ambitions. Uncle Homero wants to be a PRI

senator from the state of Guerrero: "Fagoga, he's okay/Hit a homer with Homero." Uncle Fernando wants to be the last ironic Mexican: "Elections come every six years, but misfortune is always with us."

Meanwhile, back in Mexico ("Makesicko") City, a Dantonesque finance minister has established a cult of national virginity by creating a pornographic puppet named Mamadoc, a former voluptuous typist whose vagina is lined with gems and sewn shut. It will be Mamadoc's job to suckle the king-to-be, Christopher. The cynical theory behind the contest is that "The only thing this country is interested in is the symbolic legitimization of power."

Fuentes' conceit is boundless and tireless. Christopher must be born however so the novel has a truly beginning ending. It seems that a rule of birth is that you forget what you know and so before he becomes another empty cabinet Christopher pleads with his "Reader" eloquently:

"We are all of us Columbuses, those of us who bet on the truth of our imagination and win; we are all Quijotes who believe in what we imagine; but, ultimately, we are all Don Juans who desire as soon as we imagine and who quickly find out there is no innocent desire . . ." (p. 6)

> *John Calvin Batchelor, "The Rage of Generations Yet Unborn," in* Book World—The Washington Post, *August 20, 1989, pp. 1, 6.*

SUZANNE RUTA

In *Christopher Unborn,* Carlos Fuentes has imagined the worst for his country's near future, but he's done it with so much humor, verve, invention, erudition and baroque whirligig plotting that the result is a vital, hopeful book, a great salvage operation in the trash heaps of Western culture, Spanish literature and Mexican history.

It's also an epic of disaster and survival. In 1985, Mexico City suffered one of the worst earthquakes in its history. While the Government hesitated, volunteer squads at once took over the rescue effort. It was an empowering experience when the country, cowed by 60 years of one-party rule, discovered that it could do "without instructions from a government, a party or a leader." A sense of that liberating discovery informs this otherwise pessimistic work. Inspired perhaps by the earthquake babies who survived for days in the ruins of a fallen maternity hospital, Mr. Fuentes has made the narrator of his apocalyptic novel an unborn child, a fetus gifted from before conception with fluent speech and total recall. He has also chosen to set the novel in 1992, the 500th anniversary of Columbus's arrival in the Americas. The voyage of the sperm up through the cervix and the baby down the birth canal replay Columbus's voyage, giving the new world a much needed fresh start.

For nine months and nine chapters, this omniscient shutaway chatterbox, Christopher Palomar (Spanish for Christopher Columbus), follows his parents' picaresque quest to save their skins and their sanity in a chaotic world. Mr. Fuentes, Mexico's leading novelist, has always been vastly ambitious, trying to get it all into one book—the whole generation that grew up with the Mexican Revolution in *Where the Air Is Clear*; the Holocaust and the Spanish conquest of Mexico in *A Change of Skin*; the Spanish legacy in *Terra Nostra.* But where these earlier works were somber and solidly constructed, like the Spanish-American churches Mr. Fuentes admires, *Christopher Unborn,* in keeping with the observation that "History is faster than Fiction (here, in Mexico, in the New World!)," steps up the pace, modernizes frantically and cuts loose with all kinds of post-modern tricks. It's frenetic, farcical, Rabelaisian and scatological, appropriating plot lines and characters from other writers and from Mr. Fuentes's own earlier work, mixing fact and fiction at will. Mr. Fuentes ransacks Conrad, Cortázar, the satirical poet Quevedo, Kafka, the Bible, Don Quixote, Don Juan, the novelist Juan Rulfo and the Mexican boy-wonder writers of the late 1960's who made rock lyrics, street slang and slum life part of their country's literary tradition.

The plot unfolds as, among about 50 other things, a contest between good and evil influences for the soul of Angel. The demon is Uncle Homero Fagoaga, corrupt, patrician, bigoted, self-indulgent, ready to defraud or even murder his nephew to enhance his own comfort. The angel is a real-life character named Fernando Benítez. Mr. Benítez, now in his 80's, is a kind of Mexican I. F. Stone, known for his books on the country's indigenous groups and for his humorous rectitude. In *Christopher Unborn,* he's another of Angel Palomar's uncles, a modern Don Quixote steeped in the language not of chivalric romance but of democratic progressivism. It's a language no one else in the country seems to speak any more. Like Quixote, Uncle Fernando is always in hot water.

Pulling the strings, like a sinister God the Father, is a fictional politico whose parents figured prominently in *Where the Air Is Clear.* Federico Robles Chacón is a technocrat who manipulates others into committing the mayhem that will consolidate his rule. There is no protest, of the right or the left, that he can't co-opt or coerce to meet his own ends. He represents all that is hateful and ridiculous in Mexico's entrenched one-party system. What looks, for example, like a peasant uprising that drowns Acapulco in its own solid waste turns out to be a P.R.I. move, engineered by Chacón, to clear a prime piece of real estate in order to rebuild from scratch with fresh opportunities for graft.

This slaughter of the innocents in Acapulco sends the vacationing Angel and his wife Angeles (who has a halo) fleeing inland. After many harrowing adventures they reach their Jerusalem, Mexico City, where Angel deserts his Angeles, an embodiment of authentic Mexican values, for the totally Americanized Anáhuac Valley-girl daughter of a corrupt financier.

This bare outline of the plot of *Christopher Unborn* can't begin to suggest the laughs Mr. Fuentes wrings from his pregnant material. And if the satire sometimes strains for effect, the straight-on social observation is always devastating.

It doesn't matter that most of the characters are only the sum of their literary sources, because the real dramatic hero of the book is language. The puns are what count: Makesicko Seedy, Opepsicoatl. The Simon Bully Bar is a Mexico City nightspot. The resort is either Acapulcalypse or Kafkapulco. What's in a name? Plenty. The onslaught of English debases the Spanish and Nahuatl names of gods and cities, just as gringo meddling and gringo models—Mr. Fuentes is explicit about this—have destroyed the country. But from this trashed language the author, like an inspired ragpicker, fashions new insights. Mock the Summa (for Moctezuma) is a concise formulation of one of Mr. Fuentes's main theses: that knowledge can never be static or complete. Heisenberg, not

Aquinas or Hegel, is his epistemological model. In Mr. Fuentes's view, ideology and dogma, whether Roman Catholic or Marxist, destroy life. But the richest pun runs the other way, with Spanish overpowering English—with T. S. Elote (*elote* is Mexican for corn on the cob) replacing T. S. Eliot. In fact, the entire book could be read as a cheerful, profligate rewriting of *The Waste Land,* as Europe's dour modernism jazzed up into something as nourishing and down to earth as the new-world staff of life, corn.

Because Mexico's ruling elite is so eager to imitate our country at its worst, this satire on Mexico as it is now fits our case as well. Mr. Fuentes has given an unborn babe the power of speech in order to bring the "odious eighties" to account. The decade's legacy to the next generation of Mexicans is as follows: colossal debt, appalling scandal, environmental pollution and a huge gap between rich and poor. Sound familiar? Until American novelists take it upon themselves to muckrake the Reagan years with equal vigor, Carlos Fuentes, with this book, must rank as our leading North American political satirist.

Suzanne Ruta, "Nine Months That Shook the World," in The New York Times Book Review, *August 20, 1989, pp. 1, 30.*

MAARTEN VAN DELDEN

Carlos Fuentes' concern has always been with first and last things. From *The Death of Artemio Cruz* to *Terra Nostra,* he has worked to uncover the origins of the Mexican civilization that makes up his fictional territory, and to project the possibility of its passing.

Fuentes' latest novel [*Christopher Unborn*] is once again about birth and death. The narrator recalls the remarkable fate of Mexico's "earthquake babies": Born just before the quake that struck Mexico City in September 1985, scores were pulled from the rubble, safe and sound, days after the disaster. This image of life's persistence under the most adverse conditions lies at the heart of the book.

But Fuentes imagines in *Christopher Unborn* a cataclysm far more destructive than an earthquake. Peering into the near future of his country, he fashions a tale of the most extreme form of social disintegration. The year is 1991, and the economic, demographic and environmental crises of the 1980s have reached overwhelming proportions. The population of Mexico City is now 30 million. The air pollution has grown so bad, a dome is being built that will "dole out to each and every inhabitant of the city a ration of pure air." When the story begins the national debt stands at $1,492 billion, and by the end has grown to an equally symbolic $1,992 billion.

The nation itself has virtually ceased to exist. Northern Mexico has seceded to become a new entity named Mexamerica, and the United-States Marines have occupied Veracruz. A U.S. oil consortium has absorbed the southern states. Club Med controls the Yucatan.

Although the satire here seems finally predictable, Fuentes' depiction of the new social forms that have developed in such hostile circumstances is richly inventive. At one point, for instance, a group of characters goes in search of the "Bulevar" in what is now known as "Makesicko City." Bulevar is "the place to meet in the capital, the place to see and be seen . . . but now with this scandalously wonderful singularity: where that meeting place was no one knew, as secret as language (the new languages) it mutated every day, every hour, in order to remain ungraspable, uncorrupted by writers, orators, politicians, or any other manipulators."

The fluid nature of this mysterious public space is partly a response to the individual's desire for community, partly a reflection of the fear that any arrangement of this kind will immediately become prey to some form of external control. On another level Fuentes' fantastic notion represents a skillful allusion to his own literary project: the creation of a work that will be a meeting place for readers, without losing its freshness and surprise once introduced into the public realm.

At the opposite extreme from the Bulevar loom the politicians. The faltering government has constructed a clangorous—and inevitably corrupt—world of symbols and contests to assert its authority while distracting the population. The principal symbol has been created by the smoothly sinister Federico Robles Chacon (son of the ill-fated banker in **Where the Air is Clear**), who is the youngest and most calculating minister in the present regime. Taking a rather unremarkable-looking woman from the secretarial pool in his ministry, he transforms her into the bizarre creature of the country's dreams: "Mamadoc," Mother and Doctor of all Mexicans, emblem of national unity and continuity.

The government's next move is to declare the Discovery of America contest: The baby born closest to midnight on October 12, 1992, and whose family name most resembles Columbus, will be installed the new ruler of Mexico at age 21 and given nearly unlimited powers. The weird competition provides the novel with its basic framework. Fuentes' narrator is a fetus, conceived by his parents in hopes of winning the contest. Speaking from his mother's womb and blessed with prodigious verbal gifts, the omniscient Christopher weaves together a history of his forebears and a description of the crumbling world that will soon receive him. The novel's nine chapters roughly parallel the nine months of Christopher's gestation. More important, they allude to Columbus' voyage, signifying the hope for a rediscovery and rebirth of this part of the Western Hemisphere in the midst of its coming apart.

The structure of **Christopher Unborn** gives ample scope for imaginative elaboration. Unfortunately, Fuentes has not realized its full potential. The formal rigor suggested by the division into nine chapters is never achieved. The narrator's development as a fetus is very loosely treated. Consequently, the ingenious device becomes little more than a superficial wink in the direction of the reader.

Another problem is Fuentes' tendency to preach at the reader. The stories the narrator tells about the world outside the womb are unfailingly comical, making this Fuentes' funniest novel to date. But as you read on you start wishing the narrator would stop interrupting himself. **Christopher Unborn,** like so much of Fuentes' work, celebrates openness, dialogue, pluralism. Yet here, as elsewhere, the author succumbs too frequently to the urge to spell it all out. Thus, a tale meant to be liberating becomes, in places, oppressive.

The book is more powerful and engaging when questioning some of its own assumptions. An apocalyptic novel, it manages wonderfully to be also a critique of the apocalyptic mentality. Fuentes exposes the unsavory element in fantasies of finality that are merely the expression of a buried desire to escape from the complexities of the here and now.

It is through the figure of Christopher's father . . . that Fuentes provides his most amusing and penetrating picture of some of the political and personal perplexities of our time. Angel Palomar was conceived "as a response against death" on October 2, 1968, the night of the Tlatelolco Massacre—the Mexican government's ruthless suppression of demonstrating students—and born on July 14, 1969. But having grown up in the years when the radical spirit of the '60s was waning, he becomes a measure of our distance from the past. Feeling the need to discover a new and more flexible political identity, he arrives at the definition of himself as a "rebellious conservative."

Angel's cultural and political confusions find expression in his personal life, too. One of the many subplots involves his abandonment of his wife in the middle of her pregnancy for the vain and shallow daughter of one of Mexico's richest families (they own a swimming pool in the shape of the United States). He convinces himself that his escapade is keeping alive his iconoclastic spirit. Still, he continues to be bewildered by the conflicting sides of his personality, and is unable to make his sexual life correspond to his politics. "His renascent sexuality, was it progressive or reactionary? Should his political activity lead him to monogamy or to the harem?" In its enactment of the comedy of desire, the novel is at its most provocative and worldly-wise.

Maarten van Delden, "The View from the Womb," in The New Leader, *Vol. LXXII, No. 18, November 27, 1989, pp. 17-18.*

FURTHER READING

Brody, Robert, and Rossman, Charles, eds. *Carlos Fuentes: A Critical View.* Austin, Texas: University of Texas Press, 1982, 221 p.
    Fourteen interpretative essays on various aspects of Fuentes's writing, focusing particularly on his novels.

De Aguilar, Helene J. F. "Secret Sharers: Memory in Proust and Fuentes." *Southwest Review* 70, No. 4 (Autumn 1985): 500-12.
    Highlights similarities between Fuentes's novel *Where the Air Is Clear* and Marcel Proust's *À la recherche du temps perdu.*

Durán, Gloria. "Carlos Fuentes as Philosopher of Tragedy." *The Modern Language Review* 81, No. 2 (April 1986): 349-56.
    Examines the influence of Marxism and existentialism on Fuentes's fiction.

Faris, Wendy B. " 'Without Sin, and with Pleasure': The Erotic Dimensions of Fuentes's Fiction." *Novel* 20, No. 1 (Fall 1986): 62-77.
    Discusses the importance of eroticism in Fuentes's writing.

González, Alfonso. "Krauze's Carlos Fuentes: Toward the Creation of a Myth." *The International Fiction Review* 16, No. 2 (Summer 1989): 99-102.
    Refutes Enrique Krauze's scathingly negative essay, "Guerrilla Dandy" (see current entry), which González views as a gross distortion of Fuentes's fiction and character.

Olsen, Lance. "Metamorphosis and Fuentes's *Aura.*" In his *Ellipse of Uncertainty: An Introduction to Postmodern Fantasy,* pp. 51-68. Westport, Connecticut: Greenwood Press, 1987.
    An analysis of fantastical elements and the theme of change in Fuentes's novella.

Ortega, Julio. *"A Change of Skin."* In his *Poetics of Change: The New Spanish-American Narrative,* pp. 147-59. Translated by Galen D. Greaser and the author. Austin, Texas: University of Texas Press, 1984.

> Exegesis of *A Change of Skin.*

Pérez, Janet. "Aspects of the Triple Lunar Goddess in Fuentes' Short Fiction." *Studies in Short Fiction* 24, No. 2 (Spring 1987): 139-47.

> Analyzes the role of the mythic White Goddess in several of Fuentes's stories.

The Review of Contemporary Fiction 8, No. 2 (Summer 1988): 147-291.

> Special issue devoted to Fuentes and Claude Ollier with essays by Gabriel García Márquez, Octavio Paz, Milan Kundera, and others. This collection also features a new short story by Fuentes and an interview with the author.

Swietlicki, Catherine. *"Terra Nostra*: Carlos Fuentes' Kabbalistic World." *Symposium* XXXV, No. 2 (Summer 1981): 155-67.

> Surveys some of the major elements of Kabbalism in Fuentes's novel.

Tittler, Jonathan. *"The Death of Artemio Cruz*: Anatomy of a Self." In his *Narrative Irony in the Contemporary Spanish-American Novel,* pp. 31-57. Ithaca and London: Cornell University Press, 1984.

> Examines how irony informs the meaning of *The Death of Artemio Cruz.*

World Literature Today 57, No. 4 (Autumn 1983): 529-98.

> Special issue devoted to Fuentes with essays by Gloria Durán, Margaret Sayers Peden, Wendy B. Faris, and others. Includes a selected bibliography.

Martha Gellhorn
1908-

(Born Martha Ellis Gellhorn) American journalist, nonfiction writer, novelist, short story writer, and dramatist.

An acclaimed war correspondent who reported on virtually every major world conflict during a sixty-year career, Gellhorn writes fiction and nonfiction works that illustrate the horrors of combat, scrutinize diverse political systems, and decry social injustice. As one of the first female foreign correspondents, Gellhorn defied social convention and military regulations to witness World War II from the front lines; among other exploits, she stowed away on a hospital ship to observe the Normandy invasion and accompanied British pilots on night bombing missions over Germany. Commended for economical language and potent imagery, Gellhorn's journalism focuses on the suffering of ordinary people rather than on the machinations of world leaders. In her fiction, Gellhorn addresses many of the same issues and events she covered as a reporter but often utilizes the fictionalist's freedom with plot and character to convey opinions considered inappropriate in conventional objective journalism. Set in Europe, Mexico, America, Africa, and the Caribbean, Gellhorn's short stories and novels examine political and personal conflicts ranging from fascism to marital discontent.

Gellhorn's first novel, *What Mad Pursuit,* derives from her three years at Bryn Mawr College and her subsequent experiences in the pacifist youth movement in Europe. With a conspicuous version of Gellhorn herself as its protagonist, the novel depicts the misfortunes of three women who leave college to pursue adventure in Europe. Published when Gellhorn was twenty-six, the book received little notice. In her second work, *The Trouble I've Seen,* Gellhorn fictionalizes her experiences as an investigator for the Federal Emergency Relief Administration during the American Depression of the 1930s. The book's four novellas characterize the destitute as formerly respectable, assiduous individuals debased by hunger and despair. In uncluttered journalistic prose, Gellhorn portrays such tragic figures as Ruby, an eleven-year-old girl who prostitutes herself to buy canned peaches and roller skates. Reviewers, including newspaper columnist and diplomat Eleanor Roosevelt, applauded the work as an accurate and affecting chronicle. A commentator for the *Times Literary Supplement* observed: "It is no diminution—in the circumstances rather an enhancement—of Miss Gellhorn's value and accomplishment to declare her more reporter than artist; she is photographing, not weaving personal patterns. She does it, however, with distinctive clarity and force."

With just a knapsack and fifty dollars, Gellhorn travelled to Madrid in 1937 at the height of the Spanish Civil War. There she encountered veteran war correspondents Ernest Hemingway and Robert Capa and submitted an article to the American periodical *Collier's,* thereby initiating a long and distinguished journalistic affiliation with the popular magazine. With some instruction from Hemingway, Gellhorn learned the basic techniques of her profession: how to discern varieties of gunfire, how to dive out of cars and into trenches, and how to crawl through ditches. Gellhorn then traversed Europe, covering the rise of Adolf Hitler in Germany, the ad-

vancement of fascism in Italy, and the 1939 Russo-Finnish war. While reporting on the plight of Germans and Austrians seeking refuge from Nazism in Czechoslovakia, Gellhorn composed *A Stricken Field,* a novel set in Prague just before Czechoslovakia fell to German forces. The protagonist, American journalist Mary Douglas, explores the city's clandestine network of resistance fighters and refugees through the aid of her friends Peter and Rita, German Communists who escaped Nazi persecution in the Sudetenland only to be tortured later by German military police. Many reviewers praised Gellhorn's lucid expositions on Nazi oppression, but some reproached her novel as a transparently autobiographical attempt to transform journalism into fiction.

The Heart of Another, a collection of nine short stories, was warmly received by critics who remarked favorably on the apparent influence of Gellhorn's husband, Ernest Hemingway, whom she married in 1940 and divorced in 1945. Many reviewers hailed the volume as a more mature, proficient work, particularly commending Gellhorn's lean and affecting narrative "Portrait of a Lady," which describes the odious seduction of an indifferent Finnish pilot by an emotionally starved American journalist. "Goodwill to Men," an account of an American's effort to free a German antifascist from a French concentration camp, was lauded for its sharp depiction of beleaguered Paris just prior to the city's German occupation.

Often extolled as her most dramatic works of fiction, Gellhorn's next two novels, *Liana* and *The Wine of Astonishment,* reflect her diverse experiences in the 1940s. *Liana,* composed while she was living with Hemingway in Cuba, examines the tragic life of a Caribbean mulatto woman whose destitute family forces her into servitude as the wife of a wealthy white islander. After Liana's despotic husband coerces her to behave like a European, she is ostracized by both racial groups. Following a brief affair with a schoolteacher, Liana commits suicide. Critics complimented the novel for its absorbing narrative and disturbing commentary on racial and sexual inequality. *The Wine of Astonishment* treats parallel themes from the perspective of two American soldiers involved in the Battle of the Bulge. Between unnerving combat scenes in the frozen Belgian forest, bigoted Lieutenant Colonel Smithers and his Jewish driver, Jacob Levy, confront their terror, sorrow, and preconceptions on the battlefield and in the city. At the novel's controversial climax, Levy happens upon Dachau, where he beholds emaciated survivors of the Holocaust, and his consequent fury against the Nazis compels him to deliberately drive his jeep into a crowd of German civilians. While a few critics considered the novel's plot improbable or unbalanced, most agreed with Myles Green: "[Gellhorn knows] how to dramatize the insignificance and splendor of the individual in the vast insanity of a world at war. . . . [Many readers] will find her artistic transformation of this material even more absorbing than the tale she spins against and within it."

Gellhorn's next two volumes of short fiction, *The Honeyed Peace* and *Two by Two,* are also highly regarded. Several of the stories in *The Honeyed Peace* examine the anxious, fragile character of shattered European communities following World War II. The title piece recounts the public harassment and private anguish of a French woman whose husband, accused of wartime collaboration with German authorities, commits suicide in prison. In "Exile," an insensitive German intellectual, having previously fled Hitler's regime, shuns his relatives in Kansas City after grasping the extent of his cultural alienation. Reviewers lauded Gellhorn's spare but powerful prose in *Two by Two,* a collection of four long stories that focus on the pleasures and travails of marriage. The book's last work, "Till Death Us Do Part," garnered admiration for its affectionate tribute to a famous war photographer clearly modeled on Gellhorn's friend Robert Capa, who had recently been killed by sniper fire in Vietnam.

Although Gellhorn's later works received less critical attention than those published during the peak of her celebrity, her mature fiction is regarded by some critics as her most artistic and complex. These works employ unconventional forms to illustrate the psychological traumas inherent in modern life. Ben Eckhardt, the protagonist of Gellhorn's novel *His Own Man,* is an American student in Paris torn between his education and a fashionable materialism that sanctions his affairs with wealthy, vacuous European women. The stories in Gellhorn's next collection, *Pretty Tales for Tired People,* illuminate the delicate balance between personal freedom and moral responsibility. In "The Fall and Rise of Mrs. Habgood," for example, the eponymous devoted wife discovers her husband's adultery and leaves him, but then rejects a new lover's marriage proposal after realizing that she finds loneliness preferable to a marriage of inequality.

Gellhorn's blithe novel *The Lowest Trees Have Tops* has been praised as an engaging comic study of a utopian Mexican community founded by Americans who fled McCarthyism. *Travels with Myself and Another* contains Gellhorn's often humorous recollections of her most troublesome excursions in Asia, the Caribbean, and Russia, including some trips through China with a person that she consistently calls her "Unwilling Companion," who is widely identified as a fictional representation of Ernest Hemingway. Wider critical notice attended *The Weather in Africa,* a collection of three novellas with various African settings, in which Westerners are admonished for their careless intrusions into a foreign milieu. Victoria Glendinning concluded: "This is a stunningly good book. . . . [These stories] are fiction, but they are so drenched in inside knowledge that information, attitudes, atmosphere and landscape—the outer and inner weather of Africa—are conveyed in the narrative itself."

Throughout the 1950s and 1960s, Gellhorn continued to travel and report on major conflicts, publishing accounts that maintained her reputation for lucid exposition and arresting imagery. In 1959, several of her war articles were published as *The Face of War,* a highly acclaimed collection that has since been updated with excerpts from Gellhorn's observations on the wars in Vietnam and Central America. The collection was later reissued and supplemented by a second volume, *The View from the Ground,* an assortment of Gellhorn's peacetime reports that depict inhuman conditions around the world and expound upon the specter of nuclear conflict. Although some commentators objected to Gellhorn's unsympathetic characterization of Palestinians in Israel, most hailed her striking portrayal of Adolph Eichmann's trial for war atrocities in Jerusalem and lauded her perceptive essays on McCarthyism and Vietnam. David Honigmann remarked: "If anyone is able to rescue us from Santayana's over-quoted warning that 'those who do not remember the past are condemned to relive it,' it is Martha Gellhorn [who asks]: 'If the agony of the Second World War did not teach them, whatever would?' "

(See also *CLC,* Vol. 14; *Contemporary Authors,* Vols. 77-80; and *Dictionary of Literary Biography Yearbook: 1982.*)

PRINCIPAL WORKS

NOVELS

What Mad Pursuit   1934
A Stricken Field   1940
Liana   1944
The Wine of Astonishment   1948
His Own Man   1961
The Lowest Trees Have Tops   1967

SHORT FICTION COLLECTIONS

The Trouble I've Seen   1936
The Heart of Another   1941
The Honeyed Peace   1953
Two by Two   1958
Pretty Tales for Tired People   1965
The Weather in Africa   1978

NONFICTION COLLECTIONS

The Face of War   1959; revised and enlarged, 1967, 1986
Vietnam: A New Kind of War   1966
Travels with Myself and Another   1978

The View from the Ground   1988

PLAYS

Love Goes to Press [with Virginia Cowles]   1946

LISLE BELL

Because of a whisper of scandal, Sue was expelled from college. On general principles and by way of protest against academic and narrow minded authority, Charis walked off the campus forever. Because she admired everything that Charis did, Judith did likewise. Martha Gellhorn's novel [*What Mad Pursuit*] follows these three little maids from school out into the world of men.

What Mad Pursuit studies the attitudes and agonies of the modern young female who exercises more freedom than sense in "living her own life." In one way or another, the leading figures in this story come to grief, and the reader is supposed to applaud the way in which they meet it and ignore the fact that it could have been avoided. One's admiration for heroines who can take it on the chin is dampened by a realization that no one invited them to stick their chins out in the first place.

> *Lisle Bell, in a review of "What Mad Pursuit," in* New York Herald Tribune Books, *November 4, 1934, p. 18.*

THE NEW YORK TIMES BOOK REVIEW

That insidious quotation, "Nothing ever happens to the brave," prefaces Miss Gellhorn's novel [*What Mad Pursuit*] and serves as its theme. Hemingway still has much to answer for. *What Mad Pursuit* is a brash, incredibly youthful story of three girls who leave college precipitately and hurl themselves headlong upon the pricklier thorns of life. Considering that they are rich, carefully bred, and only about 19, the range of their experience is startling.

Sue, killed by a former lover after a month of marriage, and Judith, who consoles Sue's husband to her own cost, are merely minor characters. The real heroine is Charis, eager for life and recklessly generous. Her hatred of injustice causes her departure from college, her loss of a newspaper job, and her quixotic dash to California for the purpose of aiding Mooney. (Pretty thick, this episode is.) Finally, in Paris, she has a single, disillusioning experience of sex which she later discovers has left her diseased. At once she renounces the man she loves, hands him over to Judith, and faces the future with that gallantry possible to "the brave."

Crude as it is, there is something fresh and appealing about this book. It would be more likable if Miss Gellhorn were not so enamored of her own heroine, and if she did not dabble so ineffectually with questions of social justice, but nevertheless it is not nearly so shoddy as it may sound. Miss Gellhorn is clever, and has both sensitiveness and vitality. If she does not go Hollywood, as she easily might, she may do good work. Her present effort is palpably juvenilia. (pp. 7, 20)

> *"Three Modern Girls," in* The New York Times Book Review, *November 18, 1934, pp. 7, 20.*

THE TIMES LITERARY SUPPLEMENT

The general title Miss Gellhorn gives to her sketches [in *The Trouble I've Seen*] is no mere phrase. These pieces are presented as fiction, and doubtless are intended as such with all the usual "no reference to any living person" implication; but [as H. G. Wells states in a preface, she] . . . has been actually a Federal Emergency Relief Administration worker, and knows beyond a doubt what she is writing about.

One could wish it otherwise, could wish it possible to believe her stories merely the unbalanced products of a morbid imagination. But that, unhappily, is clearly just what they are not. It is no diminution—in the circumstances rather an enhancement—of Miss Gellhorn's value and accomplishment to declare her more reporter than artist; she is photographing, not weaving personal patterns. She does it, however, with distinctive clarity and force. She has met these people, one can hardly question, again and again—Mrs. Maddison trying to hold her pride and her family together, even on relief; Joe and Pete, victimized strikers seeking vainly to keep their footing in a dissolving world. . . .

There is not much, and that wholly natural—if occasionally violent—drama, no forcing of events into abnormal rhythms. Life goes on, wavering to and fro across the poverty line, the stress of unemployment, underfeeding and unbroken hopelessness bringing irritations, stresses, the sense of shame and degradation which gnaws at family unity. . . . Miss Gellhorn does not idealize or otherwise sentimentalize her characters. She sees them as human beings, some resilient, some easily broken, some vocally angry, some dumbly enduring, some bitter against this order of things which denies men the opportunity to work for their livings, some accepting and making the bad best of it all, some, like Mrs. Maddison, soothing and strengthening themselves with dreams of "the future, which never came, but was at least always there to dream about."

Mr. Wells makes no extravagant claims for the book in his appreciative preface, but points succinctly and directly to its importance in suggesting that though these particular cases are American their parallels are to be found in almost every country in the world to-day, and that it is scarcely possible to read these pages through without feeling

> a new strength of resolve, to learn, to work, to persist in learning and working for such a wilful reorganization of human life as will make these stories at last seem like an incredible nightmare of misery in the history of mankind.

> *"American Tragedies," in* The Times Literary Supplement, *No. 1792, June 6, 1936, p. 477.*

MABEL S. ULRICH

When a book seems woven not out of words but out of the very tissues of human beings, on first reading its evaluation as literature is almost impossible even to a hardened reviewer. [*The Trouble I've Seen*] is such a book. Its four stories ring as true as a report from a relief worker's notebook and it is not until you have closed its covers on little Ruby's mother "dragging down the street" the wrong way to her house, and have emerged a little from the ravaging pity the characters have evoked, that you begin to think of the art inherent in their telling.

Miss Gellhorn, we are told, was sent by Harry Hopkins [federal administrator for emergency relief programs] to travel over our country and study the lives of the unemployed. From all that she met and felt she has chosen four groups from four regions and through them she has shown us the physical and spiritual tragedy of millions who in the past few years have seen the collapse of their faith in life. And she has told their stories with so profound and sympathetic an understanding that she has not once been tempted into exaggeration or sentimentality.

All four have to do with Americans once confident in their ability to win a secure future for themselves and their families, now on the relief rolls. With the exception of Joe the labor-leader, they scarcely attempt to understand their situation. They belong to the multitudes who have asked only for the simple things—a home, friends, enough to eat, and the job which makes these possible. When through no fault of their own they see their security gone, their lives stripped finally of dignity and independence, they are left desperate, bewildered, or hopelessly passive. Their pain is the intolerable one of mortally hurt children made only the more poignant by that saddest and most heartening of all human qualities, the courage of the defeated. . . .

This is a tragic book, but in no sense a morbid one, not even a "depressing" one in the usual meaning of that word. Miss Gellhorn has seen not only physical hunger and spiritual despair on the relief lines. Existing side by side with these she has seen love and courage. Her vivid clarity spares us nothing. We are often moved to an almost intolerable pitch, but she leaves us with a renewed faith in the worthiness of the human struggle and eager to clear the decks for action.

There are still thousands of people in the United States who think of the relief problem in terms of taxes only; thousands more who dismiss it from their consciousness with the vague belief that if a man is willing to work he can surely get *something,* or by oft-repeated stories of shovel-leaners and chiselers. All of these should read Miss Gellhorn's book. Those who have had first hand experience with the complexities of relief work will rejoice that through this clear-eyed young woman hundreds of their own "cases" have found a voice.

> *Mabel S. Ulrich, "The Courage of the Defeated," in* The Saturday Review of Literature, *Vol. XIV, No. 22, September 26, 1936, p. 7.*

EDITH H. WALTON

Martha Gellhorn's first novel, **What Mad Pursuit,** was a brash, giddy, theatrical little tale—written, however, with a certain freshness and spirit. It was very bad and very youthful, but at least it had life in it. . . . [Though **The Trouble I've Seen**] does not entirely deserve the praise which H. G. Wells accords it in his preface, Miss Gellhorn's second book is startlingly superior to her first.

Properly speaking, **The Trouble I've Seen** is not a novel. Rather, it is a collection of four long short stories, or novelettes, unified by a basic theme Writing out of warm sympathy, pity, indignation, Miss Gellhorn has dramatized the unfortunate millions living on relief and struggling so hard to retain some poor, desperate remnants of pride. Her scene shifts widely—South, East, Middle West and West—but in each case the predicament, the misery are the same. Through the medium of tiny individual dramas she shows one what it

is like to live on relief, what stratagems it necessitates, what sacrifices of hope and integrity it entails.

Few of Miss Gellhorn's characters belong among the naturally idle and supine. Most of them have been, all their lives, self-respecting and hard-working; they are bewildered by what has happened to them; they look back, pathetically and nostalgically, to the days when they were "real folks." On the whole it is the men who take dependence hardest. Humiliated and lost, shorn of their masculine prestige, they are apt to sink all too quickly into a kind of sullen lethargy. The women, being realists, adapt themselves more easily. They have families to care for and food orders to stretch out; unlike their husbands, they still have a task to do.

It is because they are so typically true that these tales are so tragic. . . . Being a good reporter with an eye for the small, significant, heartbreaking detail, Miss Gellhorn makes one feel these people's plight and wince.

With the exception of **"Joe and Pete"**—a rather routine and second-hand account of the effects of a lost strike—all the stories in this book are sharply real.

"It's not our fault," young Lou says fiercely to her lover. "We *can't* be ashamed. We may as well go ahead and die if we're ashamed." This, as much as anything, is the keynote of Miss Gellhorn's book—and it is what saves it from being a sentimental glorification of mere passive endurance and courage. Miss Gellhorn is rarely sentimental. She knows what she is talking about. She sees these people as human beings, reacting to the same circumstances in definitely different ways.

The Trouble I've Seen, then, is more than a collection of case histories decked up in the trappings of fiction. These are real stories—warm, moving, dramatic—with a certain appealing quality which makes them no less devastating. It is merely Miss Gellhorn's misfortune that her book comes a little late, that the material which she handles so vividly is already sadly familiar. To a surprising extent, considering the background which her first novel indicated, Miss Gellhorn has been able to identify herself with these victims of depression. She writes well; she is not patronizing; her insight, for an outsider, is compassionate and shrewd. There is room in her book for a stronger note of protest, but if one takes it on its own terms, it is effective, veracious and obviously sincere.

> *Edith H. Walton, "Four Panels Illustrate Martha Gellhorn's Theme," in* The New York Times Book Review, *September 27, 1936, p. 3.*

MARIANNE HAUSER

Suffering as a result of political or economic pressure has become a standard theme in current literature. . . . A long line of twentieth-century martyrs files through our novels, united by their helplessness against the invincible "monster," be it a war, the management of a bank, or a governmental decree. . . .

The theme of undeserved, inescapable suffering carries Miss Gellhorn's story [in **A Stricken Field**]. Men and women, clean-minded, brave, enduring, struggle for their course and against their fate, defeated at the end by the "monster" which, in their case, is Hitler's Germany. They are refugees from the Sudeten territory, from Austria and German cities. They hide in Prague, a dead city after the Munich peace, but know they must leave; they must return to Germany and face prisons and concentration camps. We watch their misery and their defeat, side by side with Mary Douglas, an American journalist who has come to Prague during the crisis. Mary Douglas represents the very spirit of the book; she is human, full of sympathy and pity; she is observant; she is good-hearted, and intelligent enough to be realistic. Yet she is a type rather than a human being, and at times we wish, for the novel's sake, that she were less noble and more real.

This holds true for most of Miss Gellhorn's characters. They seem too perfect, too much moulded on the plot. Her heroes wear their labels too obviously. Not that we doubt the possibility of their heroism. There have been many Peters in Germany or Czechoslovakia who would rather be beaten to death than give away vital secrets. The Peter in *A Stricken Field* is one of them. We know many things about him and Rita, the brave girl he loves. Yet they both fail to come truly to life. They appear like a device, invented to add more human interest to a good and truthful newspaper story.

The tone of compassion underlying each of the chapters is convincingly sincere; it comes close to sentimentality only when woven novelistically into the plot. At times the love between Rita and Peter appears painfully sweet, growing dubiously melodramatic when Rita listens in the cellar to the voices and noises of the Nazis who torture her lover to death.

It is no accident that Miss Gellhorn, a journalist by profession, is at her best when describing general events or sketching the political background. If her individual characterizations lack vitality, she knows how to describe a crowd; how to paint the despair of people. . . .

It is regrettable that her leading characters and her plot are so close to the heroic pattern. *A Stricken Field* is told with sensitivity. Mary Douglas's pity is the author's own pity for the misery that she has watched. It is hard for the reviewer to point out the weakness of a novel which in spirit is so much on the right side, and which reveals so clearly the author's strength of feeling.

> Marianne Hauser, "Orphans of the Twentieth Century," in The Saturday Review of Literature, *Vol. XXI, No. 20, March 9, 1940, p. 10.*

EDITH H. WALTON

In 1936 Martha Gellhorn published a moving and excellent book, *The Trouble I've Seen.* Based on her experiences as an investigator for the Federal Emergency Relief Administration, it proved not only that she was an exceptionally good reporter but also that she had real qualities of imagination and insight. Fiction though they were, her tales of the stubborn, self-respecting unemployed had an accent of truth that was almost unbearable. Since then Miss Gellhorn has branched out more widely. She has been in Spain, she has been in Czecho-Slovakia; currently, she has been writing a series of articles on Finland, which rank among the best commentaries from that scarred and snowbound front. (p. 6)

Knowing this background, one cannot very well miss the flavor of autobiography in Martha Gellhorn's new novel. *A Stricken Field* has as its scene Czecho-Slovakia—more specifically, Prague—just after the Munich pact. The story is told, moreover, from the viewpoint of an American, Mary Douglas, who so obviously stands for the author that a disguise seems superfluous. A journalist—young, sleek, beautiful, precociously experienced, but with an impulsive and pitying heart—Mary descends upon Prague from the Paris plane with hardly any conception of what she is going to find there. Simply, she has been told to get a story—as have the other ambulance-chasers of disaster, her fellow-correspondents, whom she meets and drinks with presently in Prague's hotels. She has no idea that within the space of a week she is to be so torn, so shaken, so terribly disturbed.

The Prague which Mary finds is a city tense, nervous, desolate, bitter with regret because its battle is unfought. Wistfully, it feeds on memories of how fine its army was, wonders if war itself could have outmatched the shameful present. (pp. 6-7)

As for the plot of *A Stricken Field,* it is almost nonexistent. What there is of it concerns a German Communist, Rita, whom Mary tries futilely to save and befriend. It is through Rita—who has found, in exile, a brief security and love—that Mary is introduced to the underground movement and to the heartbreaking efforts of the Sudeten refugees to establish some kind of a shelter, however perilous. Because she sees, thanks to Rita, so much that is both ghastly and gallant, it is impossible for Mary to be as detached as the other journalists from the suffering all about her. . . .

Largely because it wavers so on the borderline of fiction and non-fiction, *A Stricken Field* is a hard book to appraise. Considered as a novel it is something of a failure—lacking as it does most of the elements that give a novel pith and point—yet its material is so poignant and so well handled that one cannot dismiss it lightly. Miss Gellhorn, as she has previously proved, is an admirable reporter. She has intelligence, feeling, a seeing eye, and she writes a clean, contemporary prose which depends for its effect upon understatement. Why she did not tell this story in the first person, and as a record of her own experience, I really cannot imagine. All that is weak and theatrical in it springs from her effort to go beyond good journalism into a field as yet alien to her. *A Stricken Field* is at its best a compelling book and a moving one, but as a novel it is weak. Miss Gellhorn has done better in her articles. (p. 7)

> Edith H. Walton, "In Prague," in The New York Times Book Review, *March 10, 1940, pp. 6-7.*

ROSE FELD

In her experiences as roving war correspondent Martha Gellhorn, who is Mrs. Ernest Hemingway, has found the inspiration and the material for the nine short stories published under the title, *The Heart of Another.* . . . This collection of tales and sketches shows a marked difference in her writing, a maturity and direction which owe not a little to the Hemingway influence. There is nothing derogatory in this statement; it would be strange indeed if two writing people emotionally and intellectually drawn to each other did not consciously and subconsciously influence each other's work. It is because of this undoubtedly, that one is caught at times in sudden recognition of a situation a point of view, a method of expression. These are pure Hemingway, which is to say they are romantic under a surface of hardness, they are bitter with disenchantment, they are frank with physical and functional details.

This is especially true in two of the stories, the longest and the best in the book, **"Portrait of a Lady"** and **"Good Will** to Men." In the first Miss Gellhorn is concerned with the selfish love of a woman correspondent for a Finnish aviator; in the second with the sacrifice of men by a Communist leader. Both end on a note of frustration and defeat, but this conclusion is reached only as a result of contrasting the good and the heroic against the base and the brutal. The bitterness, in other words, which underlies much of Miss Gellhorn's writing lies not in disavowal of nobility of human action but in its destruction by the momentarily powerful.

A Mrs. Maynard, a rich but none the less able war correspondent, is the "lady" who is portrayed in the story of that title. She has a rich and indifferent husband in New York whose prestige she enhances by the dispatches which carry her name. In Lappeenranta, Finland, she meets Lieutenant Lahti, an officer in the aviation service who has made a brilliant record shooting down Russian planes. . . .

The ill-fated pursuit of Lahti by the enamored Mrs. Maynard makes the meat of this story. As Miss Gellhorn writes it, it is more than a tale of physical desire and unwilling capitulation. The woman, despicable as she seems in the eyes of the young aviator, is moved by something besides physical need; she is possessed by an urgency made up of the conviction that in him and with him lies the cure for the emotional emptiness of her life.

Against his will, the young officer takes her and in spite of his distaste finds himself caught in a moment of exaltation and ecstasy. The scene of his seduction—it is hardly less—is strongly reminiscent of the sleeping-bag episodes in *For Whom The Bell Tolls*. It has the same quality of whirling in space, of isolation in union. "What is it you love?" the woman asks the young man when it is over, anxious for some word of personal feeling and he replies, simply, "I love Finland." And then his words made him hate her for they were dear and sacred and she was only a "high-class whore who made you do what you did not need and left you worn out and useless and then took your secrets and threw them around as if they were without value."

In **"Good Will To Men"** it is again a woman correspondent who takes the leading part, but this time as an observer rather than an actor. Returned to Paris after service, first in Spain and later in Finland, Elizabeth Dalton has one more assignment to cover before she can go back to America. This is a personal one and concerns a prisoner in a concentration camp in France. Max Ohlau, a German Communist writer who had fought with the Loyalists in Spain, had been horribly wounded and had later escaped to France. Knowing what will happen to him under a Fascist regime, whether it be German or French. Elizabeth feels she must do everything in her power to obtain his release.

In her description of Elizabeth's efforts to interest her friends in the fate of this man, Miss Gellhorn gives a brilliant picture of France before its downfall. It is not so much that the people she talked to were powerless to do anything, but that they were unconcerned and indifferent. The climax of the story lies in Elizabeth's interview with Karl Jensen, leader of the German Communists in France who had been instrumental in sending Max and others like him to fight for the cause in Spain. Here Miss Gellhorn gives caustic expression to her disillusion with the Communist regime and its leadership. For in Karl the girl discovered not a man with a feeling for humanity but a creature concerned with a machine. . . .

The portrait of Karl is excellent, Miss Gellhorn getting her effects in a mounting tension of understatement that builds up to a shattering indictment of the man and his program.

"Luigi's House" and **"A Sense of Direction,"** the two other full-length short stories in this volume, are equally notable for their psychological penetration of a human being in conflict with himself and the world. In the first, Luigi, a Corsican farmhand, fearing to lose the land which is his only security, forever makes it his by death: in the second, an Italian officer fighting with the Loyalists in Spain futilely seeks a moment of release from the life of the battlefields. Here, as in her other tales, Miss Gellhorn writes with a mature understanding that goes beyond conventional lines.

The five additional tales that make up the volume are sketches rather than short stories. Each of them has a place in this book by virtue of the title, its analytical glimpse into the hearts of men. They are slight as compared with the other stories, serving as examples of stylized journalism rather than creative effort. The book's distinction is not these sketches but the excellence of the two principal stories and Miss Gellhorn's very real talent for evoking a scene and an emotion.

Rose Feld, "Men at War, Women at 'Peace'," in New York Herald Tribune Books, *November 2, 1941, p. 2.*

MARIANNE HAUSER

"Between wars, and home from wars," Martha Gellhorn has written [*The Heart of Another,* a volume of] short stories about troubled Europe. It is a rather uneven collection, not so satisfactory as a whole, but with two very fine pieces in it. The stories, nine altogether, take us to Cuba and Finland, Paris, Madrid and Corsica, the noise of guns rumbling directly or indirectly in the background. Miss Gellhorn, who is a keen observer and a good reporter, rarely fails in putting over whatever she wants to say. Her writing is honest, convincing, and in **"Luigi's House"** and **"Portrait of a Lady"** it is even inspired. However, except for these two stories, one can't get rid of that uncomfortable and somewhat embarrassing feeling to be shown across the war on a sightseeing bus.

Perhaps it is the mixture of journalism and art which makes most of these stories appear a bit flat or even empty. Miss Gellhorn describes rather than creates. This would be no disadvantage did she not present her observations, feelings and plot in a fictional manner which calls for deeper imagination.

In **"Good Will to Men,"** for instance, she gives an authentic picture of Paris at war. Madame Fleury's preposterous apartment, the atmosphere of futility, selfishness and defeat, Elizabeth's hopeless efforts to get a German anti-Fascist out of a French concentration camp—all this is pictured effectively and in the right spirit. Yet there is nothing to hold the scenes and characters together, no driving force or emotional center that lifts the story above the level of general information. We do not mean at all that a short story must necessarily have a climax or a thoroughly balanced construction. But it must show inspiration.

This is why **"Good Will to Men,"** one of the longer stories, seems the least successful, and why we like **"Luigi's House"** and **"Portrait of a Lady"** so much. In both these stories the author has something to tell that goes beyond newspaper reporting or vaguely compassionate sensitivity.

"Luigi's House" is an intense study of fear and unrelenting stubbornness. This tale about a Corsican farmer, who would not give up his land on which he had worked and lived for eleven years, is a remarkable piece of writing, sparing in its dramatic accents and deeply moving. It has all the vibrations of **"Summer Resort,"** another story about Corsica, yet while the tragic element in **"Summer Resort"** impresses us as too thin and somewhat glassy, **"Luigi's House"** shows a more profound psychological insight and fine poetic feeling. (pp. 20, 22)

"Portrait of a Lady" is an equally intense and even more mature story. It tells of Mrs. Maynard, a beautiful, self-centered, shallow creature who travels through Finland to watch the war and write a book about it. . . . The contrast between her eccentric personality and the white, war-torn country comes off superbly. We think that, as in **"Luigi's House,"** the end does not quite live up to the rest. None the less it is a strong, unusual story, gripping and painfully true. (p. 22)

> *Marianne Hauser, "Noise of Guns," in* The New York Times Book Review, *November 2, 1941, pp. 20, 22.*

NYM WALES

Aren't Americans who go abroad ever going to tell us about anything but themselves? I picked up [*The Heart of Another*] by an intelligent American journalist expecting to get a fresh interpretation of the European scene today. Instead, I found myself half-consciously thinking back more than a decade ago, when we used to read about much the same type of incident in *The Sun Also Rises, Farewell to Arms, The Green Hat,* and a flood of similar books. The same bright, sophisticated conversations. The same fundamentally provincial, and thoroughly charming, American point of view. . . .

Yet Martha Gellhorn is not a throwback to the twenties. It must be that neither her Europe nor its American observers have changed, in spite of the cataclysm. Or it may be that the deeper and more dramatic strata of events have not claimed her attention. In any case, it is of interest to note that almost nowhere in these stories is there acknowledgment of the basic issues involved in this war. For this reason, the stories have a certain sterility, a certain lack of warm aliveness—much as the American lady journalist, in **"Portrait of a Lady,"** who could not unfreeze in Finland except by seducing a recalcitrant Finnish aviator. Miss Gellhorn does not intentionally evade the dark ugly waters underneath. She merely skates over them, with a bantering scarf in the wind, hoping to avoid a dunking. Taking her own words, from the story **"A Sense of Direction"**:

> Maybe you could not survive a war if you really thought about it, thought about what it meant and who suffered and the dead. Maybe you could only last out a war if you just bumbled through every day, wondering and worrying about small personal things. I slept long before I could follow that idea through and besides I would not have reached any important or useful conclusions.

There is nothing amateur about Miss Gellhorn's short-story method. . . . All these nine stories are finished products, by a competent writer. Most of them are so factual that they seem to describe real incidents, instead of demonstrating a fiction talent, and this feeling is intensified by the author's use of the first-person narrative in all but one or two cases. Miss

Gellhorn certainly out-Hemingways the master in her treatment of women. She is an extremely keen observer of manner and custom, and the detail in her stories is extraordinarily well-handled. Her style is witty and amusing; brilliant at odd times. And she is not afraid to use the mid-west phrases— "that was all the further he had ever gotten."

Technically, the best short story in the book is **"Luigi's House."** The subject is slight and not a memorable one, but it is original, and the plot is managed with much skill. As in Somerset Maugham, the story moves with apparent leisurely pointlessness through maddeningly endless detail, until the undercurrent of suspense brings you shock up against a wall. This tale rather spoils the reader for the rest of the book, for you keep expecting a similar carefully-built-up climax. But the others are mostly a series of plotless incidents and anticlimaxes, though always gracefully handled.

"Good Will to Men" has the ingredients of a vital and first-rate story, but it is too superficial and does not quite come off. It is the most interesting subject in the book and shows a good deal of perception. Laid in Paris before its fall, the narrative deals with the fruitless and half-hearted attempt of the inevitable American lady-journalist to secure the release of an anti-Nazi German writer from a concentration camp. It approaches a certain degree of philosophy, and also explains why there is no fire and enthusiasm in Miss Gellhorn's studies of the European scene. . . .

[The nine stories in *The Heart of Another*] take place in the midst of dramatic happenings and the materials were gathered from personal experience and travel; but they are all minor affairs that never reach the heart of any situation, they are surface designs thinly traced, lines without mass or movement, as in the flat unemotional school of modernistic painting and thinking.

> *Nym Wales, "Gellhorn . . . ," in* The Saturday Review of Literature, *Vol. XXIV, No. 30, November 15, 1941, p. 11.*

WOLCOTT GIBBS

[In the play *Love Goes to Press*], Martha Gellhorn and Virginia Cowles wrote what I'm sure they liked to think of as a satire, dealing with the adventures of two female correspondents on the Italian front. To the best of my knowledge, this was the first work to treat the late war on such frivolous terms and presumably it indicated that the time has come when we can properly consider the humorous aspects of Armageddon. This may well be a healthy sign, demonstrating the extraordinary resiliency of the human spirit, and it seems a pity that the play itself couldn't have been a little better, especially since both authors are experienced military reporters and ought to have known what they were talking about.

With so much material at their disposal, however, the ladies mysteriously decided to focus on love. One of their heroines, an intrepid blonde, entangled herself with a British Public Relations officer, who, though strongly prejudiced against women messing around battlefields, presently succumbed to her noisy, journalistic charm; the other—fortunately dark, since otherwise they were almost indistinguishable—was still helplessly attracted to her ex-husband, an unscrupulous writer who not only stole her stories but also managed to get himself engaged to a camp-show entertainer. . . . These romances were by no means uncomplicated, since both girls were almost as preoccupied with scoops as they were with sex and spent a good deal of their time thinking up ingenious ways of smuggling themselves up to the front and getting shot. Much of *Love Goes to Press* was said to be autobiographical, and it is quite possible that Miss Gellhorn and Miss Cowles were indeed able to commandeer ambulances and even airplanes to take them behind the enemy lines practically at will. I can only say that it seemed a little silly to me, almost as if somebody had been tinkering around with an idea for a moving picture.

In spite of this generally discouraging report and the play's abrupt failure . . . , there were some rewarding moments in the course of the evening. The camp-show girl was a fine, stylish caricature; the heroines' cheerful habit of calling up a general, conceivably the hero of El Alamein, whenever childish Army regulations threatened to cramp their activities was rather engaging; and there was a really hilarious scene toward the end, when the Public Relations man explained to his fiancée the delights of her future life in his native Yorkshire. . . . All this was very satisfactory entertainment, and I wish I could say that the rest of the play measured up to it. The reason it didn't, I guess, was that while the authors were occasionally able to see their characters as a couple of good, hearty comics, they were unable to get away from the contrary notion that the girls were also talented, sensitive, and pretty damn picturesque figures, of some serious dramatic consequence. The result was a blend of the glamorous and absurd that may, I suppose, easily have been the truth but was moderately confusing on the stage just the same. (p. 47)

> *Wolcott Gibbs, "Oddments and Remainders," in* The New Yorker, *Vol. XXII, No. 48, January 11, 1947, pp. 47-8, 50.*

ROSAMOND GILDER

Love Goes to Press, [a play] written by two war correspondents, is, one hopes, a libel on the profession. If this is the way Martha Gellhorn and Virginia Cowles themselves behaved in the pursuit of their newspaper assignments, it would seem wise for the high command to banish all women journalists from the next war. Presumably the whole affair was supposed to be funny but since their writing lacks wit and their plotting any elements of conviction one is driven back to a criticism of the content of the play and the strange ethics as well as the incredible human callousness exhibited by the characters portrayed. (p. 18)

> *Rosamond Gilder, "Rainbow over Broadway," in* Theatre Arts, *Vol. XXXI, No. 3, March, 1947, pp. 12-18.*

BENNELL BRAUNSTEIN

Because women have the greater penchant for grace, compassion and tenderness in their living and writing, they are at an initial handicap in approaching the subject of war. Martha Gellhorn has come closer to that subject [in *The Wine of Astonishment*] than any other American woman writer. Her war is a *Farewell to Arms* kind of intimate drama in which nothing is sacred but an individual's integrity and where courage and honor really have no meaning except in a very personal and a social way. Between people, only love has any effectiveness and it is too often over-energized and too violent for its own good.

In that kind of drama the important consideration is always personal experience and the writer's deepest concern is with the plain facts of experience. Miss Gellhorn has here given it that treatment. She has overdone a simple story and manipulated it for effect, but the effect is unmistakable. War, to her, is a very human affair. She never lets us forget it.

The Wine of Astonishment is a small canvas painted principally in cigarette smoke gray, decorated sparsely with girlish chatter and soldier talk and given a protective coating of cognac. Its central locale is Luxembourg City; 1944 is the time. Its significant characters are four in number: Lieutenant Colonel John Dawson Smithers . . . ; Jacob Levy, an engaging, handsome and self-conscious GI who has lived a shadowy and pointless life that has left him waiting always for something bad to happen; Dorothy Brock, a Red Cross girl who knows that men must find women to stop thinking about them; and Kathe Limpert, a waitress with the gentleness and innocence of a new-born kitten.

For the most part, these people act and react to the rhythm of the war. . . . [The] four pass over the winter stalemate on the borders of the Rhineland, see the frenzied German effort of the Battle of the Bulge withstood, and drift apart as the American forces roll on into Munich. There, Levy suddenly meets up with the sick, dead eyes in the yellow bony faces, the black teeth and the emaciated bodies covered with gray striped rags creeping with lice. Dachau is too much for him and he cracks in a fit of violence. . . . [Despite the novel's] numerous flaws, Martha Gellhorn has succeeded in coming amazingly close to the war.

> *Bennell Braunstein, "Smoke of War and Cigarettes," in* New York Herald Tribune Weekly Book Review, *October 3, 1948, p. 10.*

MYLES GREEN

One of the briefest and best of the current crop of war novels is [*The Wine of Astonishment*] by the author of *Liana.* Miss Gellhorn writes in a vigorous style, suggestive at many points of an ex-husband called Ernest Hemingway. She is both witty and warm. She knows how to create character, how to keep a story rolling, how to dramatize the insignificance and splendor of the individual in the vast insanity of a world at war. Ten years of first-hand observation of the fighting fronts in Europe and Asia have gone into this taut, tender, tough book; and many a reader will find her artistic transformation of this material even more absorbing than the tale she spins against and within it.

The Wine of Astonishment treats centrally of four characters divided into two pairs of lovers. There are, first of all, Lieut. Col. John Dawson Smithers and Red Cross girl Dorothy Brock, who are involved in an affair that is simultaneously inflammable, tragic and charmless. Theirs is a struggle against loneliness and the sure knowledge of disillusion; that they cannot attain peace of spirit makes them all the more solicitous of the chances of Smithers' jeep driver, Pfc. Jacob Levy, and his Luxembourg sweetheart Kathe. Dorothy is lost on the merry-go-round of sex. Smithers, a finely turned characterization, recognizes in his battalion the deepest passion of his life. At the same time, in the midst of the fatigue and strain of command, he understands with a fierce, disillusioning prescience how humiliatingly trivial his future is likely to be once he gets home. . . .

Jacob and Kathe, on the other hand, have a dream of the future. . . . Kathe, the little Luxembourg waitress, waits on destiny as well as soldiers, dreading the inevitable day when Smithers' battalion, rested and re-equipped, will again be ordered to the front. Jacob struggles with all manner of hard things, his Jewishness, his inability to communicate with Kathe except by gesture and dictionary, his fear of death (twice wounded, he thinks the third hit will end his luck), and his overwhelming sense of outrage as he takes an impromptu tour of Dachau.

This last, however, leaves this reader unconvinced. It seems unlikely in the extreme, and at any rate it is artistically unpersuading, that a man as sensitive as Jacob could for so long have been so naive about concentration camp atrocities. But if this attitude is unreal, Miss Gellhorn's picture of Dachau is memorable.

Memorable, too, are her pictures of men at the front, on leave, at parties, in the rubbled towns of Germany and amid its fat, prosperous looking farms. In her scenes of action she achieves those two contradictory parts of the military whole: she pins down the irreducible incident with perfect lucidity at the same time that she conveys an impression of battle-blurring confusion.

Miss Gellhorn's talents were never better exhibited than in this humanly penetrating novel of war.

> Myles Green, "Taut, Tender, Tough," in The New York Times Book Review, October 17, 1948, p. 44.

JAMES HILTON

Perhaps from necessity a modern writer's perceptions are excellently adapted to portray change and decay, the dissolution and disruption of society. Martha Gellhorn is such a writer, with the modern journalist's advantage of having been sent everywhere to report the progress of the disease and with the modern American's sheer advantage of being an American. This last has enabled her to have the right passport and visas, money enough to sample the best bars and hotels and an entree into all the heartbreak houses of Europe.

The result, in a collection of stories called *The Honeyed Peace,* is a survey to which the title supplies an ironic keynote. For the peace described lacks tranquility and its honey is always bittersweet. Wit and a half-desperate gaiety have survived, however, and in their phosphorescence Miss Gellhorn puts her power of observation to work and animates it with a certain wise compassion.

["The Honeyed Peace"] explores the tragedy of a French collaborationist who had collaborated only a little more than many who condemned him when the war ended. . . . With a background of immediately post-war Paris, free from bomb-damage yet spiritually shattered by the German occupation, this vignette of "victory" is both moving and memorable.

Other stories deal with such themes as the Spanish war, a chance encounter between two passengers sharing a seat on the plane from Miami to New York, . . . and an American novelist trying to write amidst the distractions of his life and family in Paris. The longest story, **"Venus Ascendant,"** analyzes the sexual awakening of an upper-class Englishwoman by a Continental sophisticate; both these types are such old

fictional favorites that there cannot be much new to say, though Miss Gellhorn gives them a hard, bright gloss and neatly packages her findings.

Perhaps the best story of all is one of the shortest—**"Exile."** In this we encounter a fifty-five year old refugee from a university town in Württemberg—a worshipper of Heine, cultured, bookish, and liberal enough to have left Hitler's Reich voluntarily to seek a new home in a free country, yet so arrogant and insensitive that his cousin in Kansas City could not long endure him as a guest, nor a local bookseller keep him as an employee. So he set out for points unknown and it was never discovered what happened to him. . . . In probing this maddening yet not contemptible intransigence, Miss Gellhorn confesses by implication a good deal of the bafflement that the German character has often occasioned.

The Honeyed Peace bridges the gulf between journalism and interpretive fiction, a difficult thing to do and here done very well indeed.

> James Hilton, "Bittersweet Honey from Post-War Hives," in New York Herald Tribune Book Review, August 30, 1953, p. 6.

PATRICIA BLAKE

[*The Honeyed Peace*] suggests what is already on record— that Martha Gellhorn is a first-rate war correspondent. They show, for example, her journalistic gift of isolating the pertinent and pathetic detail that illuminates the virtually indescribable totality of a wartime situation. More, Miss Gellhorn's prose is competent, compact, and facile. Reading *The Honeyed Peace,* one has a vision of its author striding with confident step from fighting front to teletype and back again. Her fiction is an interesting extension of this activity.

The stories in *The Honeyed Peace* are almost all about extreme situations, the stock in trade of any good correspondent. [**"The Honeyed Peace"**] is about the trials of the wife of a French collaborator in hostile, hysterical, post-liberation Paris: the wife is refused purchase of a negligee in a fashionable shop because she is "an enemy of France"; the husband commits suicide in prison. Another story, **"Shorty,"** has to do with a devoted German couple during the Spanish Civil War, who, in Hemingwayesque fashion, are busy fighting Franco. Suddenly the wife, Shorty, takes to cheating on her husband on all Republican fronts, thereby earning everybody's justified contempt, especially after the broken-hearted husband is killed. Fortunately, Shorty redeems herself later on, during the German occupation of France, by saving her new husband and baby from the Gestapo. . . .

Almost all the stories have as a general theme the sense of futility, loss, and let-down, which accompanies peace. Curiously enough, the best story of the lot has nothing to do with war, suicide, etc. **"Venus Ascendant"** is a witty, rather leisurely account of how a middle-aged, middle-class Italian Don Giovanni seduces an English girl on a holiday in Rome—and transforms a lumpish cut of British tweed into a full-fledged *appassionata.* This is a happy choice for the final story of the book. Amusing and unimportant, it gives the reader some relief from Miss Gellhorn's cataclysmic view of human existence.

> Patricia Blake, "In Extreme Cases," in The New York Times Book Review, August 30, 1953, p. 4.

WILLIAM PEDEN

The characters of Martha Gellhorn's short stories, collected in a volume called *The Honeyed Peace,* seek contentment in various ways. Uprooted by war and its aftermath, some of them pursue the honeyed peace of a reason-for-being as a professional hunter stalks his quarry. Others approach it circuitously. Still others flee from it. The end result, however, is the same. Discontent ebbs and floods like tidewater through the lives of these expatriates whose stories constitute no additional page to the literature of the decay of moral values in an increasingly materialistic society. Because Miss Gellhorn is an expert reporter . . . , and a better than tolerable storyteller, the reader is temporarily interested in her characters' cannibalistic efforts to obtain some sort of happiness. He is seldom, however, moved or edified. Most of Miss Gellhorn's people, to quote from one of her stories, are "simply of no value" whatever.

The protagonist of **"Exile"**—all of Miss Gellhorn's characters are exiles of one kind or another—is typical. Heinrich, a middle-aged intellectual who has studied aimlessly for years, leaves his native Germany because the Nazis have been "disgusting about Heine." He attaches himself like a barnacle to relatives in Kansas City. After sapping what little energy this unlovable and unloving ménage possesses, he wanders back into the dark from which he had emerged. . . . Heinrich, it is obvious, possesses some admirable qualities. But he is also a physical and moral weakling, and a refugee from duty as well as from tyranny. His plight would be tragic if Heinrich were not such a parasite; it would be comic if he were not also a man—or a half-man—of good will.

Such an individual is the protagonist of almost all of Miss Gellhorn's stories. He is the best-selling novelist, his life centered around his own worthless novels, whose collapse is depicted in **"A Psychiatrist of One's Own."** He is the charming woman of **"The Honeyed Peace"** who wore silks and furs while others struggled and endured. . . . All of these characters are moral cannibals. Yet they are at times admirable as well as revolting and detestable. . . . It is difficult to remain concerned for any length of time with their melancholy wanderings between a past which was better, a now which is not good, and a future which is unthinkable.

William Peden, "Postwar Flotsam and Jetsam," in The Saturday Review, *New York, Vol. XXXVI, No. 37, September 12, 1953, p. 38.*

CLAUD COCKBURN

Miss Gellhorn's title [*Two by Two*] implies that these four admirable stories—I would call them 'novelettes' were the term not absurdly debased—are about marriage. So they are. There is no deception. But the spy from Outer Space who hooks the book from the stall on the point of a cosmic ray with the idea of finding out how the earthmen are operating this institution nowadays, will be happy to discover that although each of these tales is concerned with a profoundly and vividly particularised relationship, each offers more than his spy ring perhaps hoped for: an authentic smell, that is, of mid-century earth-life in general. The aroma is bitter but astringent. For Miss Gellhorn is entertaining without being relaxing. She can communicate the eerie sadness or horror of a situation, the claustrophobia of an apparently blind alley, and still despise despair; her writing draws a sharp and necessary line between melancholy and melancholia.

How strange and stupid it is that the term 'competent', applied to craftsmanship, should have become one of very chilly praise, even of mild contempt. Competent to do what, may one just inquire? In Miss Gellhorn's case, competent, for instance, to turn a potential cliché . . . into a story twisted taut with emotional suspense, in which 'stock' characters jump into life and movement, and engage our sympathy with a sentence, a gesture, a sudden flare of comprehension or dismay. Competent, too, to paint into a tragi-satirical satire on English high-politicking, an exquisitely moving picture of small children; or, in the third of these stories, to flash a torch into a New York mantrap of disease, money and love.

The last story ["**Till Death Us Do Part**"], and the finest, has for its central character the scarcely disguised figure of Capa, the world-famous photographer who was killed a few years ago in a Far Eastern jungle. To evoke and make credible, as it were, that strange portent of our time, must seem, to those who knew him, an immense achievement. Miss Gellhorn does more than that, for here the figure of 'Bara' becomes, like his own camera, an instrument for evoking a world in which the dominating characters are not single human beings but rather Madrid under siege, bombed London, Belsen, and the troubled mob of the survivors. (p. 353)

Claud Cockburn, in a review of "Two by Two," in New Statesman, *Vol. LV, No. 1409, March 15, 1958, pp. 353-54.*

COLEMAN ROSENBERGER

In *Two by Two* Martha Gellhorn chooses marriage as the window by which to look into the lives of her characters. The words of the wedding service provide the titles for the four long stories which make up the volume: **"For Better for Worse," "For Richer for Poorer," "In Sickness and in Health"** and **"Till Death Us Do Part."** The men and women in the four stories move in four widely disparate environments, but in each they move two by two. The fact of marriage, cherished or found hateful, yielding strength or torment, is a central fact in the lives of each of them.

One of the characters here, who has witnessed man's inhumanity from Barcelona and Helsinki to Buchenwald, values the reading of Trollope in London above going off to new fighting in Java. This is a character in whom the author may or may not see aspects of herself, but one suspects that Trollope is an author whom Miss Gellhorn holds in very high regard.

Like Trollope's, Miss Gellhorn's men and women are minutely observed, shown with revealing detail upon detail, and the scenes in which they move are each, for the duration of the story, real and immediate.

The range of Miss Gellhorn's scenes is extraordinary. . . .

In each, the author creates the scene with sureness and with verisimilitude.

If Miss Gellhorn has, as it seems to me, some of the virtues which have attracted readers to Trollope for a century, it is fair to say that she exhibits also some of Trollope's weaknesses. With all the impact of her stories, she still seems at times to remain too detached, too uninvolved, too much, perhaps, the reporter of surfaces.

But the virtues may be quite enough for the long haul. One of her characters muses of a volume: "Whatever happened to the book now, it would be saved in libraries, and in time the right people would find it." Miss Gellhorn's *Two by Two* is worth finding.

Coleman Rosenberger, "With This Ring I Thee Wed," in New York Herald Tribune Books, *March 16, 1958, p. 10.*

WILLIAM PEDEN

The four long stories in Martha Gellhorn's new book [*Two by Two*] take their titles and their basic themes from the four vows of the marriage service. . . . With a writer less skillful, such framework devices might be inhibiting and restricting. Such is not the case here.

Miss Gellhorn has written an admirable book in which each impressive story, though complete in itself, adds something to the effect of every other story. Thus the final impression created by *Two by Two* is more like that of a novel than the customary collection of short stories.

A seasoned foreign correspondent as well as a fiction writer, Miss Gellhorn is a perceptive observer of events and people alike. Set against the background of World War II and the years immediately following, her stories contain some memorable individuals. There is Prince Andrea Ferentino, who . . . faces the conflict between his hopes for a future in America and the demands of the past at Torrenova, "the only land on earth." Or Tim Bara, celebrated Hungarian war photographer, who is perhaps the most fortunate of all of Miss Gellhorn's protagonists; he is killed by a sniper's bullet in Java without ever having been forced to compromise or retreat as does Andrea, or the likable young English statesman of **"For Richer for Poorer,"** or the bedeviled American of **"In Sickness and in Health."**

These are good men, responsible and intelligent and in their own ways brave. They believe in themselves. But, at the same time, they are harassed by an awareness of their duties to their women—and to a world that is increasingly more demanding, more bewildering, more destructive.

Miss Gellhorn's women are something else again. . . . [They] tend to be either predatory or pitiable. . . . Villainess or victim, the end result is the same—most of these women create weakness rather than impart strength. They are more likely to destroy than to save.

What, then, remains? Are there no alternatives suggested, no ways out? "If you lived in a desert," one of the characters comments,

> you had various choices; you could kill yourself or go mad or plant flowers. It was only planting flowers in a desert, and the flowers neither changed the desert nor had much chance to survive, but the act of planting was good, because bravery was good.

The same thought is expressed, in less symbolic language, by the same character: "The only thing to do, as long as you are alive, is live." And live Miss Gellhorn's people and her stories do. *Two by Two* is fiction by an adult for adults. It makes some much-publicized recent novels about fundamental

man-woman relationship appear, if only by contrast, rather silly.

William Peden, "The Thing to Do Is Live," in The New York Times Book Review, *March 23, 1958, p. 4.*

HERBERT MITGANG

Derived from her articles over the years in *Collier's* magazine, Martha Gellhorn's *The Face of War* is a brilliant anti-war book that is as fresh as if written for this morning. Seldom can a correspondent assemble past writings from various locations and watch a clear pattern emerge, yet her pieces fall into place in a grand design. Her opinions, because they are rooted in these finely drawn scenes from four wars, deserve to be read by many people.

Her point is this:

> The world's leaders seem strangely engaged in private feuds. . . . Their talk sounds as if they believed nuclear war to be a thing that can be won or lost, and probable. . . . I believe that memory and imagination, not nuclear weapons, are the great deterrents.

The author's memories of war are vivid. . . . Her first report is from Madrid in 1937, her last from Dachau in 1945. The names and datelines tell their own story.

Battles are ephemeral, but the people about whom Miss Gellhorn reports survive. There are the bomb-wounded children of Barcelona ("In Barcelona, it was perfect bombing weather"), the firemen dousing the flames in Helsinki ("War started at 9 o'clock promptly"). She was in an airplane over Chungking ("From the air you would not know how these smashed houses looked or sounded as they collapsed"); with the Frenchmen on the Italian front on the way back to Paris ("They are fighting for the honor of France, which is not just a phrase but the personal, undying pride of every one of them"); with the Americans in the Battle of the Bulge ("The bodies of Germans were piled on the trailer like so much ghastly firewood").

Her reporting and writing have the novelist's emotional skill. In Dachau, the meaning of these events of the Thirties and Forties all seemed to coincide in horror. The face of war was and is ugly—and this is a stirring editorial.

Herbert Mitgang, "A Message for Today," in The New York Times Book Review, *March 22, 1959, p. 10.*

THE TIMES LITERARY SUPPLEMENT

[*The Face of War*] is another despairing cry from one who has seen many of the facets of war at close quarters. Mrs. Gellhorn acted as a war correspondent for *Collier's* and wrote her descriptive pieces from Spain in 1938 and from most of the fronts except the Russian during Hitler's war. Much of what she wrote she has now resurrected and bound together into a book by means of explanatory introductions and protesting comments. She justifies it all with the remark that what is wanted to-day is "memory and imagination, not nuclear weapons or the deterrents."

Hers was good reporting to begin with. Its pictures of the

beastliness and tragedy of war are honestly matched with balancing experiences of what soldiers and airmen and Red Cross workers endured. . . .

"War," she says in one of her comments, "was always worse than I knew how to say." That, of course, is the feeling of all sensitive people who have had to come close to it. It oppressed many a one who had had to endure the filth and futility of sodden trenches in the Kaiser's war. It so oppressed them that they came back fully persuaded that mankind would never condemn itself to a repetition, and some of them wrote all the misery into their books. Yet a generation was enough to bring something like a repeat performance.

Now Mrs. Gellhorn begins her attempt to keep memory green and to stimulate imagination by confessing that "wars are to be expected." But her point to-day is that then it was the "same nameless tragedy" of the present whether it was in Madrid or Helsinki or Chungking, whereas men now have the means to destroy the future as well and contemplate doing it "for the sake of freedom." She asks: whose freedom?

A pacifist from her youth, she does not deny or try to exclude hate. Her articles confess her hate of those German legions that forced their terror into France, of the torturers that made beastly the underground tunnels of Ivry and made sacred for the French the nearby cemetery. . . . All this revived evidence of what war entails does at least enable her to declaim: "Let us not think anyone can use frightfulness in a good cause." And for her the zenith of modern frightfulness would consist in the use of nuclear weapons.

Her arguments, thus backed by the tales she told all those years ago, are powerful. Only her belief that men must by now have learnt the lesson of self-interest vitiates her thesis. She admits that mankind in the lump, however prudent, however humanitarian, has found no way to do the leading and to make sure it shall not lead to war. We who remember the horrors and can imagine worse, she says, are the led, the governed, the nameless victims. And there the case against the right of any leader to condemn the future rests.

"The War to End War," in The Times Literary Supplement, *No. 3002, September 11, 1959, p. 515.*

NIGEL NICOLSON

[*The Face of War*] is a collection of dispatches from four recent wars—Spain, Finland, China and the European end of the Second World war. They were first published in *Collier's.* . . . [Gellhorn's] business was to get herself to the war, and to say what war felt like, how it affected the attackers, the defenders and the innocent. She could have made a new book about her experiences, lifting the better phrases from her past articles. She spurned the idea. She has courageously reprinted the articles themselves, tidying the hurried syntax a bit, but damaging none of their immediacy. Undoubtedly she was one of the best correspondents whom the War produced, and today her articles are as fresh as striped shirts returned from the wash.

War-reports like Miss Gellhorn's appear to write themselves. You have only to go to a front-line position, on board a hospital ship, to a prison camp, or on patrol in a fighter-bomber, and make a mental note of the details observed and the remarks made, to become, as Miss Gellhorn describes herself, 'a walking tape-recorder with eyes'. . . . How can you go

wrong? You can go wrong by indiscretion, by overwriting, by attributing false motives, by the misuse of the dangerous literary device of understatement, by making your word-pictures unbelievably neat or heroic. She made none of these mistakes. She only erred when she came to point morals.

Her moral is, 'War is a crime against the living and always has been'. It is a dangerous platitude, and one which Miss Gellhorn herself contradicts. War is not always a crime. For if a people are living under a tyranny, or are threatened by one, it can be noble to overthrow it by force. She was in no doubt whatever that the Spanish Republicans were right to fight. So were the Finns, the Chinese. The Second World War, she writes in a concluding passage, was waged to abolish Dachau and everything that Dachau stood for: her only qualification of the rightness of that war is that we should have started it three years earlier, in Spain. So in her view war can be a legitimate means of defending the living, as well as a crime against them. (pp. 517-18)

Her book is not a No against all war. It is one of the loudest Yesses yet pronounced. She does not see her soldiers and airmen as unwilling instruments of politicians, but as thinking human beings making a splendid personal choice. She willed them on by her pen. But the other side, whether they were Spanish fascists, Japs, Russians (when fighting in Finland), or Germans, particularly Germans, were almost without exception mean, brutal and despicable. 'Cologne,' she could write, 'is a startling sight. We are not shocked by it'; and then, as if a little ashamed of herself, she adds, 'which only goes to prove that if you see enough of anything you stop noticing it'. She does herself discredit: she never stopped noticing misery. The reason why she did not grieve over Cologne was because it was German. Similarly she admires patriotism, but not German patriotism: 'They were simply not people like us; there was no common place where we could meet'. But there was: the battlefield, and the beastly emotions induced on it. When the GIs during the Battle of the Bulge told her that the Ardennes was 'wonderful Kraut-killing country', she did not flicker an eyelid. The Germans were simply obstacles to be removed, like road-blocks, and the process was not horrible because it demanded great courage on the part of her friends.

This is all very well, and was perhaps necessary at the time. But does it become a great No against war when reprinted fifteen years later? I do not think it does. (p. 518)

Nigel Nicolson, "A Woman at the Wars," in New Statesman, *Vol. LVIII, No. 1492, October 17, 1959, pp. 517-18.*

W. G. ROGERS

The terrace of that popular American drinking spot, the *Café des Deux Magots,* is crowded because, as [*His Own Man*] opens, the warm April sun is inviting the people of Paris outdoors. A Frenchwoman, jumping up to go to her office, jogs an American and spills coffee on his pants. Since the *Deux Magots* serves painfully hot coffee, since the man has no trousers to spare, and since he is due almost immediately at a class at the Sorbonne, he is triply annoyed. They exchange earnest apologies and wry, ungracious acknowledgments.

Jessica de Camberges, rich but distressingly frustrated, works at a bureau that looks after refugees. Ben Eckhardt of Milwaukee, distressingly poor but self-sufficient, is a student of Chinese. He has a fellowship, and he is a model pupil, indeed a model Left-Banker. He lives by plan—modest room as base of operations, so many hours' study, visits to museums where admission is inexpensive, and occasional affairs with obliging girls of the neighborhood. If it isn't exactly a racket, at least he has things all sewed up neatly. But women will unsew for him, and Jessica pulls the first thread.

An independent fellow, and proud of it, he is reluctant to accept favors from the wealthy de Camberges family. But eager for a husband for their unsexy problem daughter, they wear down his resistance. . . . The cagey American boasts of never playing for keeps, and Jessica seems to like it that way, too. Thus, while still reserving weekends for her, he finds himself, a presentable bachelor, taken up by a still flashier, richer crowd led by Liz Langham, an English girl.

[Despite] his steadfastness in being unsteadfast, in flitting from love to love to classroom, in going his own way with no strings attached, they develop possessive feminine notions, they insist on strings. [Ben] stays "His Own Man" to a degree he couldn't have imagined, thanks to Miss Gellhorn's ingenious ending.

For all the sobering note at the climax, this is less a morality than an entertainment. The talk is always amusing, the story turns this way and that with a credible and delightful unpredictability, and it's all as nice and naughty as Paris. You're sure to have fun.

> W. G. Rogers, "As Nice and Naughty as Paris," in New York Herald Tribune Books, *August 6, 1961,* p. 4.

GENEVIEVE CASEY

With an admirably light touch, Martha Gellhorn delivers in *His Own Man* a sermon as witty as it is telling against the sin of selfishness.

Three characters, each of them using the other, spell out her little morality play, laid in Paris, all the way from the Left Bank to the Avenue Foch and the Place Vendome.

Ben Eckhardt is a foundation bum, a relatively recent version of the perennial student.

Ben meets his nemesis when he leaves the simple pleasures of the Left Bank for the Haut Monde on the other side of the river. Having become addicted to the finer things of life . . . , Ben becomes involved with a strange, not-so-young but very rich French woman, who has her own brand of selfishness.

His life is further complicated by his liaison with a terribly rich English woman. . . .

In the farce that follows, he eventually loses the woman he might have loved, and both women lose the man they thought they wanted. Martha Gellhorn could not have stated more cleverly and succinctly that the "wages of sin are death."

> Genevieve Casey, "Witty Sermonizing," in Chicago Sunday Tribune Magazine of Books, *September 10, 1961,* p. 3.

HONOR TRACY

The three long stories in [*Pretty Tales for Tired People*] are not pretty and, except that they make no demands on the reader, are anything but suitable for the tired. Each is a morality, concerned therefore with types rather than individuals: the man of overweening ambition, the soft mindless woman who loves and ruins him, the man building a career on falsehood, the woman who realizes her true nature too late—all of them, through vanity or egoism or blindness, more or less coming to grief. They are so lightly written as to slip down like oysters, and if afterwards they prickle and burn it is due to matter rather than manner: honest productions of a journalist, they are told plainly and without any pretense of art.

For a journalist, it must be said, Miss Gellhorn shows a fine disregard for the factually probable. Indeed, she carries her enviable hardihood to the pitch of laying two of her stories in England, with the result that occasionally they leave the ground altogether. Ouida herself could hardly have produced a more memorable picture of English academic life than that in **"A Promising Career."** Here, a man becomes the youngest headmaster ever of a leading public school on the strength of a good degree, a creditable war service and "a stylishly written, scholarly book" on the taxation system of the Hapsburgs. In the intervals of instructing the young, this fortunate man, Claud, dallies with a succession of ladies. . . . The world knows nothing of Claud's activities—as difficult to hide in England, alas, as anywhere in this vale of tears—at 43 he is offered the headmastership of Rotherham, one of the Big Four of English schools. But even this is to be a stepping-stone to his real goal, for after a few years there, and another stylish and scholarly book, he means to become head of a Cambridge College.

The world of grey reality, where pigheaded School Boards insist on qualifications and prefer headmasters to be married . . . , is firmly swept away; and if the rest of the story were on this level it might be hard to take Miss Gellhorn seriously. Yet when the absurdities are forgotten, we see that an accurate eye and a sharp understanding have been at work, that the fairytale has its own peculiar truth and that those involved have been moving to their downfall as surely as the characters in a Greek play. . . . The outcome is never in doubt, yet our interest is held to the end: none of the characters is at all sympathetic, yet we can feel for them every one.

The second story ["**The Clever One**"] deals with a careerist again, but one driven by racial terror as well as ambition. Hitler is rising to power: Théodore Ascher is a Viennese Jew. He moves to Paris, then, noting the shakiness of France, to London and finally, after Munich, to New York where he will surely be safe and rich at last. . . . But he has fled across the world from something only to find it lying in wait for him on the other side, non-violent, true, but implacable as ever: he has toiled, schemed, betrayed to no purpose, and the eventual realization breaks him.

This is a big theme and should have resulted in a fine work, but Miss Gellhorn has thrown it away. Virtue overdone is apt to look like vice, and her habitual economy of expression suggests here a poverty of the imagination. We are never once shown Théodore doing anything, we are merely told that he did it, and the bald recital moves us about as much as would the obituary of a stranger.

Summary plays too large a part again in **"The Fall and Rise of Mrs. Habgood."** . . . [When Faith Habgood discovers her husband's adultery] she tears raging off to France, to find a new self on which to build a new life. . . . [Philip, her new lover] treats her like the *femme fatale,* not to say tart, she has always unconsciously yearned to be and wishes to marry her into the bargain. But

> the truth was that she had been married enough for one lifetime. Being a wife was a condition of soul, a state of mind, irrespective of the man you married . . . like Frederick the Great's mule, which attended all the wars and remained a mule.

The writer excels in such astringencies and we pleasurably mark up the bull's-eyes as we read. Her mistake was to try and establish husband and lover as independent figures rather than imply them through the central character of Faith: it just could not be done in the space and we are back to that old obituary column.

I fear, moreover, that Ouida herself might have boggled at the ending where Señora Habgood runs (without previous experience of the trade) a luxury hotel on the Spanish coast at fifteen guineas a day: bless her, El Rif in Tangier is only five. (pp. 21-2)

> Honor Tracy, "Not for the Weary," in The New Republic, *Vol. 152, No. 13, March 27, 1965, pp. 21-2.*

MARTIN LEVIN

The three short stories in Martha Gellhorn's *Pretty Tales for Tired People* might really be the synopses of three novels. Jampacked with detail, they lack totality, the aiming at a single effect that is the earmark of the wellmade short story. Neither are they in the fashionably disheveled format that characterizes introspective fiction. Taken as case histories of love among the upper crust, their particulars—for which Miss Gellhorn has a loving eye—are interesting, but they leave the reader feeling let down for want of a narrative focus.

"A Promising Career" is the dossier of a proper British headmaster who derails his life for a woman who is palpably not worth it. In "The Clever One," a protean Viennese lawyer succeeds at the bar in three different countries, and sheds three wives, none of whom he truly understands and one of whom crumples his self esteem. "The Fall And Rise Of Mrs. Hapgood" depicts the emergence of a British matron from a chrysalis of sexless respectability into a new identity as a Fun Person. All three stories are unified by a gently cynical view of cuckoldry, adultery and universal myopia, and by Miss Gellhorn's well tempered realism. But all could use a third act. (pp. 22-3)

> Martin Levin, in a review of "Pretty Tales for Tired People," in The New York Times Book Review, *April 18, 1965, pp. 22-3.*

THE TIMES LITERARY SUPPLEMENT

The slick infidelities covered by the three stories in [*Pretty Tales for Tired People*] take place internationally but well within the cool climes of the Atlantic community—London, Paris, New York, Valais, Touraine. [Gellhorn offers] a very Anglo-Saxon approach—deadpan, realistic, moral, but keeping the squalor within the limits of charm, wit and entertainment.

"The Clever One" is the best of the three because it takes place largely in America and, however cosmopolitan she may be, the author seems to have a deeper knowledge of the American way of life and creates more plausible characters. The rise of the able, complacent German-Jewish refugee and his crack-up in the hands of a personalized America is harsh and excellent. The England of the other two stories is rather starry-eyed in the fashion of an early story by Evelyn Waugh—in fact "A Promising Career", which is about an ambitious schoolmaster, reads just like that. . . . [Though] it is all about sex, the story never dips into the sort of detail which might embarrass the reader yet gives excellent asides: those who ought to know, know just what is meant.

The London of her stories may be as dated as London itself, but it is some consolation that according to the author there is nothing to beat the English woman, "their toughness, their interest in men's talk" and above all "the coolness of the woman in public and the violence of the woman in bed". "American women" (who are so scornful of their English equivalents) are "fantastically garrulous about their own concerns and [demand] every attention from a man including frequent declarations of love" . . . which does not make for the Great Society.

Martha Gellhorn may take a moral line, create characters who are basically nasty and come to a bad end: but she cannot help making it all seem good fun for lucky (rich) people. Consequently it could be said that she fails to measure up as a serious, dutiful artist. In fact she is true enough to a realistic idiom, if only because the sort of people she portrays (with the knowledge of an insider, not the yearning of an outsider) see their lives in terms of racy, romantic novels and try to live them out that way.

> "High Infidelity," in The Times Literary Supplement, *No. 3321, October 21, 1965, p. 933.*

D. A. N. JONES

Martha Gellhorn's three stories about East Africa [collected in *The Weather in Africa*] suggest that British expatriates, settlers or visitors, bring their own "weather" with them, their own climate of opinion and feeling. She certainly brings her own. Like other Americans writing about Anglophone Africa she obscures the dark continent with clouds of smoke from the melting-pot. British people make her think of American class prejudice. African people make her think of American race prejudice.

In the first story, "On the Mountain", she introduces Jane, a snobbish English girl, brought up in her parents' hotel on the slopes of Mount Kilimanjaro. She goes to England, as an entertainer, hoping to make the big time. A spiteful lover tells her: "You'll never be Lena Horne, never, get it? You'll never never never make the Savoy." Eventually, Jane appears at the Savoy in Harrogate—and the horrid fellow turns up, to jeer: "Congratulations, Goldilocks. You made it after all. The Savoy!" There is something so American about this—in the tone of the dialogue, the distinction between the sticks and the Great White Way—that one cannot take it seriously as an account of English behaviour.

Jane returns to the hotel where, in spite of the nation's independence, she bosses the African servants in an imperial way and even attempts to boss the wealthy and powerful African guests—until she perversely falls for a caddish African civil servant. This man, we are told, "hated Jane's white skin for he knew he longed to be white like her. . . . Insanely, he was revenging all his people by scourging one white woman." The relationship is possible, of course, but not interestingly plausible: it is more like an American cliché than an observation about African-British love affairs.

Martha Gellhorn makes guesses about what males think, what British people think, what Africans think. The second story, **"In the Highlands"**, is about an English farmer who is very fond of African children. The African adults on his farm are presented as a Greek chorus of nitwits. . . . It sounds too much like "Hiawatha" to be credible. . . . Similarly, when the farmer stops to look at the view, we are told that the Africans, the Watu, "agreed that Soft Voice was praying. His God commanded him to stop anywhere, any time, and stare at Africa, praying". There seems no reason to suppose that the Watu would have thought anything of the sort. It is merely romantic guesswork.

The third story, **"By the Sea"**, avoids the guesswork problem, for the most part. It is told in the first person, by an American woman visiting Africa to help her recover from the death of her child. She wishes she could have one child a year, as (she believes) African women do. Then, she runs over and kills an African child. She herself goes to hospital and is told by English people that she has nothing to blame herself for: the child and his family were to blame for the death. She is indignant, thinking these English people heartless. So far, it is a credible monologue. But then the story switches into the third person and goes wrong. A villainous African enters her hospital ward, demanding money for the family of the dead child. The American woman commits suicide. The story suddenly becomes very artificial.

Martha Gellhorn has a great deal of valuable experience and a lively imagination, when her creativity is not distracted by generalizations about class and race. But she seems to be essentially a subjective writer, who should stick to the first person singular and not attempt the God's-eye view.

D. A. N. Jones, "Melting-Pot Shots," in The Times Literary Supplement, *No. 3982, July 28, 1978, p. 838.*

VICTORIA GLENDINNING

[*The Weather in Africa*] is a stunningly good book. The novelist and onetime foreign correspondent Martha Gellhorn has the storyteller's gift, which is also the good journalist's gift, and her writing makes one think again about the generally uneasy relationship between reportage and fiction. In her case it seems a uniquely happy one. The three stories in this book are fiction, but they are so drenched in inside knowledge that information, attitudes, atmosphere and landscape—the outer and inner weather of Africa—are conveyed in the narrative itself. She is never didactic. For example, in the first story, **"On the Mountain,"** she writes not about the concept of paternalism but about one particular aging, sympathetic couple who run the Travellers' Rest Hotel on Mount Kilimanjaro:

> They were incurably old colonialists, not the wicked ogres of propaganda either, kinder and more responsible employers than Africans were, ready to expend time and thought and money to help any Africans in their neighborhood. . . . Like good of-

ficers, they cared for and liked their troops. But there it was: Africans were Other Ranks.

The couple has two daughters. The depiction of besotted parents blinkered to the shortcomings and defects of a favorite child (which has nothing specifically to do with Africa) is most cunningly done. Arrogant Jane, the spoiled pet, has a frenetic and secret love-life with a black man whom she despises and who despises her. Meanwhile, her sister Mary Ann quietly runs the hotel and builds up a solid, loving relationship with a gawky, reliable botanist. This is a very moral tale—as they all are.

The other two stories are set in postwar Kenya. The true heroine of **"In the Highlands"** is Africa itself, in particular the beautiful and derelict farm with which Ian, a lonely, war-scarred English bachelor, falls in love. . . . He at first treats his black workers as friends and equals, but they do not respond. So "no more jolly chat, no more stripping off his shirt to give a hand and an example." Immediately they like him better, and work harder. The Bwana must be the Bwana. It is only with a mixed-race little girl whom he adopts that Ian can make any personal contact at all.

Ian's frightful wife in **"In the Highlands"** talks of staying at the Travellers' Rest, and the hotelier's daughter Mary Ann, with her husband and family, have walk-on parts in the last story, **"By the Sea."** Mrs. Jamieson, the central figure in this story, has glimpsed "a sturdy sunbaked woman and a tall thin man," notices that their baby was "wonderful, serene and confident" and that the family "looked as if they were always happy." It is a tribute to Martha Gellhorn's skill that the reader recognizes this "sunbaked woman" at once as Mary Ann, a few years on—with a complacent pleasure in knowing much more about her than Mrs. Jamieson does.

Mrs. Jamieson is a complete outsider. She is in tourists' Africa—a luxury hotel on the coast of Kenya, where she is on vacation to forget a broken marriage and the death of her young son. On a car-drive to see some beautiful little red birds in their habitat she runs over and kills a black child. Shattered by what she has done, she lies in her hotel room physically and mentally deranged. The European housekeeper comforts her. "These people," she is told, "they have so many children, one a year. . . . They don't feel about life the way we do." (p. 9)

The sexual passion between resentful black man and prejudiced white woman in the first story, revoltingly abused by both, led to the destruction of both. The well-meaning white farmer in the second story could get along with his black farm hands only if he adopted an authoritarian manner. In this last story even Mrs. Jamieson's emotional identification with a black mother, bereaved like herself, is disallowed. A black waiter in the hotel is instructed to extort money from her: "I am cousin of father of that boy. You kill that boy. You give one thousand shillings for father."

There is only qualified hope to be got from Martha Gellhorn about the likelihood of whites living in equality and understanding with blacks in Africa. The tragedy of those for whom there is now no place is that, perpetually wrong-footed by history like the bewildered white people in these stories, they love the land of Africa—for the way of life it affords, and for its beauty, its flowers and birds and animals. Mrs. Jamieson, threatened by the waiter, in her delirium throws herself off the balcony. The housekeeper says, "Poor woman. She should never have come to Africa." And poor Europeans, all those that remain; they should never have taken Africa. It did not belong to them. (p. 18)

Victoria Glendinning, "Colonials," in The New York Times Book Review, *March 30, 1980, pp. 9, 18.*

ALAN BRIEN

About Martha Gellhorn's *The Face of War* [expanded and reissued in 1986] I find it difficult to write with any restraint. This anthology contains the best prose on its subject written by anybody, from Madrid in 1936 to Managua in 1985. You could simply take all the articles and books written by male war correspondents and flush them down the plug hole. And, so long as you had this, you would have 90 per cent of everything worthwhile. Tele-portation proved! This familiar SF device actually exists when you have a writer like Martha Gellhorn who can lift you out of your seat, transmit you through space and time to all the dreadful crossroads of 50 years on the path to universal disaster, so you smell, feel and taste everything. Her introductions, dated '59, '67, and '86, make fascinating polemics in themselves as she doubts whether anything written, or read, changes the future. I feel she is too pessimistic, even if she is right. As Pascal advised a bet on God, so we must bet on survival. Then we have a tiny chance, otherwise nothing.

Alan Brien, "Lifelines," in New Statesman, *Vol. 111, No. 2879, May 30, 1986, p. 28.*

ELENA BRUNET

Liana, first published in 1944 [and reissued in 1987], is the powerful story of a young mulatto native from the fictional French Caribbean island of Saint Boniface, whose marriage to an island white leaves her captive and friendless, ostracized from the community into which she marries and from her own people as well. Marc Royer takes Liana as his mistress when she is 16; he is a relatively wealthy, though vulgar, man with good business sense. Four years later, when he decides to marry her, the decision does not grow out of love: "Marc took her because he could not have Marie; (Liana) was something he had bought for use when he could not have what he loved."

Liana tries as best she can to adopt the manners, speech and attire of a white woman, but, rather than accept her into their fold, the island whites entirely cut the two of them out of white society. For Liana, known on the island as a "careless and laughing and lovely" girl, has inherited a dead life.

Pierre Vauclain, [the local schoolteacher] who had recently arrived on the island from the fighting in Paris (it's World War II), opens new worlds to Liana. They read books together, take picnics on Saturdays and eventually become lovers. As they hear from radio broadcasts that the United States has joined World War II, Pierre decides to return to France and the army he had deserted. Having lost a love who was her only ally and friend in this isolated world, Liana, this "shy and gay and . . . soft and loving" woman takes her own life. Gellhorn has written a novel about race, prejudice, love and betrayal that is engrossing, but very, very disturbing.

Elena Brunet, in a review of "Liana," in Los Angeles Times Book Review, *August 2, 1987, p. 14.*

BRETT HARVEY

When I tell people I'm working on a piece about Martha Gellhorn, flickers of recognition war with bewilderment on their faces. "Martha Gellhorn . . . Martha Gellhorn . . ." they murmur vaguely. "Sounds familiar, but . . ." I prompt: "War correspondent? Novelist? Short-story writer?" They shake their heads. I prod: "Married to Hemingway?" Their eyes focus. "Ah! Martha *Gellhorn!* Right!" Gellhorn deserves better than this eclipse by her marriage to a Great Man. In her 55-year career, she has covered nearly every major conflict on the planet as a war correspondent, written six novels, six collections of short stories and novellas, and two books of nonfiction, and contributed reams of articles to magazines and journals. The only one of Hemingway's four wives who refused to make *him* her career, Gellhorn fought hard for her independent life as a self-supporting journalist. As if all this weren't enough, she was a stunning, sexy blond (still is for all I know) with charm, wit, and awe-inspiring physical courage.

Now Gellhorn seems to be on the verge of getting some long-overdue attention. [Her 1940 novel, *A Stricken Field* was reissued in 1986] as well as an updated version of her collection of essays *The Face of War.* [Recent reissues also include] a new nonfiction collection called *The View from the Ground* and an even more up-to-date version of *The Face of War.* (p. 10)

The Face of War and *The View from the Ground,* are an amazing record of Gellhorn's travels and concerns over the past four decades. She has lived in Italy, Mexico, Africa, and England, and covered the Army-McCarthy hearings, the Eichmann Trial, the Six Day War, Spain after Franco, and Vietnam. In 1966, she went to Vietnam for the *Guardian* and within two months her reports had so infuriated the South Vietnamese Government that she was barred from the country. For six years afterwards she had "a writer's block made of solid concrete," which she attributed to being "cut off from the only useful work I could have done to discredit the war . . . the only work that had any value for me." Gellhorn doesn't seem to have slowed down perceptibly in the '80s, a decade rendered "infuriating and shabby" by Margaret Thatcher and Ronald Reagan. These days she's writing about the British miners' strike, torture in El Salvador, the U.S. presence in Nicaragua, and nuclear disarmament.

Discovering Martha Gellhorn was like finding a new thorny, passionate, funny friend. We come from the same prosperous middle-western background and share the mixture of guilt, self-deprecation, and *noblesse oblige* that often come with that territory. "I have a wonderful and privileged life," she wrote Eleanor Roosevelt. ". . . the only way I can pay back for what fate and society have handed me is to try in minor totally useless ways to make an angry sound against injustice."

Gellhorn is also of my mother's generation and class, and reminds me of my mother and her friends. . . . My mother had some of Gellhorn's longings but channeled her literary ambition into writing sophisticated cookbooks—a kind of writing she thought of as "not important." I suspect that Gellhorn felt similarly about her journalism—a pity, because she's a better journalist than a fiction writer. Gellhorn saw journalism as a means to get places and gather material for the fiction she evidently considered her "real" writing. Her second book, *The Trouble I've Seen,* set the pattern she would follow, more or less, throughout her career. Convinced that her reports on the Depression would have greater impact as fiction, she distilled them into a deliberately schematic book of four novellas about victims of the Depression— children, young people, the middle-aged, and the elderly. Many of the characters in *The Trouble I've Seen* are sanitized, made saintly by their poverty. Gellhorn's original letters to Harry Hopkins [federal administrator for emergency relief programs], some of which are reprinted in *The View from the Ground,* are starker and more powerful. She writes from Massachussetts:

> Now about the unemployed themselves: this picture is so grim that whatever words I use will seem hysterical and exaggerated. I have been doing more case visiting here; about five families a day. And I find them all in the same shape—fear, fear driving them into a state of semi-collapse; cracking the nerves; and an overpowering terror of the future. . . . I haven't been in one home that hasn't offered me the spectacle of a human being driven beyond his or her powers of endurance and sanity.

In her reports to *Collier's* from the Spanish front, her eye for detail is superb, her style spare and wry. Hotel concierges apologize for the regrettable inconvenience of a lobby dusted with powdered cobblestone. Children play in the rubble of a gutted apartment building with a bathtub dangling by its pipes far above them. In a munitions factory, women sit at tables and sew explosives—glittering little beads, like sequins—into sacks made of pink linen and white silk for mortars. Gellhorn and her fellow journalists stroll a few blocks to the trenches in a local city park. "No matter how often you do it, it is surprising just to walk to war, easily, from your own bedroom where you have been reading a detective story or a life of Byron or listening to the phonograph, or chatting with your friends."

My favorite recent piece of Gellhorniana is an article in *Granta* called **"Cuba Revisited."** Returning to Havana for the first time in 41 years, she enthusiastically reports safe streets, cheap plentiful books in bookstores (she remembers no bookstores in the old days), lively street life, a notable absence of police. Gellhorn the sybarite observes that Cuba has managed to have a revolution that didn't destroy pleasure. She's very taken with the abundance of delicious beer, rum, and cigars, as well as the fact that Cubans get two two-week paid vacations a year. Gellhorn the feminist spots that

> the main cause of a different, open, pleasurable lifestyle is the change in women. The old Hispanic and Catholic custom of the women at home—isolated, the daughter guarded, the stiffness of that relation between men and women—is truly gone. Women are on their own at work, feeling equal to men, and showing this with new confidence. Girls are educated equally with boys and chaperonage is dead. There is a feeling that men and women, girls and boys are having a good time together, in a way unknown before.

Gellhorn the maverick remarks as she's leaving that though "Cuba now is immeasurably better than the mindless feudal Cuba I knew. . . . [it is] no place for a self-willed, opinionated loner, which is what I suppose I am. Never a team player—though I wish this team, this people, well."

Even as a journalist, Gellhorn's stubborn integrity, her nose for bullshit, and her clean, ironic style are often undermined by a vein of sentimentality. You always know who the "good" people are because they're the ones who are strong and quiet and gentle. Sometimes Gellhorn just saves time by calling them "wonderful." Her fiction, while rich in language, is nearly always deformed by her strong opinions. Gellhorn was never satisfied with simply recording what she saw, and trusting that it was powerful enough to move people.

A Stricken Field is a noble dud of a novel based on Gellhorn's real-life attempt to help a group of German communists who were being forced to return home to face torture and probable death. One of Gellhorn's many lovable qualities is her inability to stay on the sidelines. When journalism wasn't working fast enough, or at all, she took action herself. Unfortunately, her outrage distorts *A Stricken Field* and muddies its effect. She jumps in and out of her characters' heads, introduces new characters to make her point, and then abandons them. A torture scene, probably based on fact, which would have been bloodcurdling if simply reported straight, seems melodramatic and contrived. What remains powerful about *A Stricken Field* is the vivid description: a dark road at night suddenly swarming with the Czech army, retreating without ever having fought; refugees streaming back into Germany "like people escaping a flood, with the water rising and spreading behind them."

A Stricken Field is unusual because the heroine, Mary Douglas, is a fairly straight-forward portrait of a strong-willed, compassionate reporter acting on her beliefs. In many of Gellhorn's novels and stories, the female characters are warped by her ambivalence. There's a character that haunts her fiction, a glamorous, brittle, world-weary blond, slightly dilettantish and sexually promiscuous. This was perhaps Gellhorn's idea of how others saw her. In **"Portrait of a Lady"** [collected in *The Heart of Another*], this character turns up as an American war correspondent who, while covering a crack Finnish bomber squadron, falls in love with the arrogant, taciturn squadron commander.

On the face of it, this is a fairly heavy-breathing magazine romance. The heroine, Mrs. Maynard (Gellhorn never bothers to give her a first name!) has green cat-eyes and wears a perfectly cut black ski suit with a beaver greatcoat over her shoulders. In spite of the clichés, Mrs. Maynard emerges as a highly competent journalist trying to do her job while distracted by passion. Gellhorn is not without flashes of feminist insight that are very modern indeed. Mrs. Maynard asks herself: "Why can't I look at him the way he looks at me? I want to see how he is made, too." At dinner with the fliers, she asks questions about bomb weights and anti-aircraft guns, while intensely aware that Lahti, a misogynist boor, is waiting for her, as a woman, to sound ignorant. Then the brisk reporter takes over. "She was eager for the meal to end now. She had learned all she needed to know and she wanted to write it down before she confused the figures."

Later (presumably after writing her story) she goes to Lahti's room and seduces him. "I love you," she murmurs, to which he barks, "If you talk, I will take you back to your room. It is all right, but not with talking." After they have sex, Mrs. Maynard tries to get Lahti to talk about love and, just like a woman, doesn't comprehend when he says he loves his country, his planes, flying. Lahti's plane crashes at the end, and Mrs. Maynard goes into a frenzy of grief so self-centered it repels her driver as well as the reader. Although Gellhorn paints Lahti as a bit of a brute, her sympathy is clearly with him, the man-with-a-mission.

Even when the protagonist is a woman, Gellhorn's heart is usually with the men in her stories. Her novel *Liana* is skewed by this curious failure to empathize with her female characters. Set on a lush French island, *Liana* is the story of a love affair between a beautiful young mulatto woman and the man her husband, Marc, has hired to tutor her in English. Marc has virtually bought Liana; in return for the comfort of his home, she has turned herself into a kind of white wife. He's even given her a new name, Julie. Liana dresses up in European clothes and tries, pathetically, to act and sound European. Pierre Vauclain, the young French schoolmaster, encourages Liana to shed her European ways and revert to a more sensual and natural self. When Marc discovers their affair he befriends Pierre, playing on the young man's obsessive guilt at being a safe distance away from the war in France, and then offers him the means to get home. Liana, abandoned by Pierre and unable to return either to Marc or to her family, kills herself.

The compelling relationship is not between Liana and Pierre, but between Pierre and Marc. At the beginning of the novel, Marc is the coarse materialistic brute, Pierre the sensitive natural man. But Marc woos Pierre almost like a lover, and eventually the two men begin to resemble each other. Pierre justifies leaving Liana by telling himself that she is a child: "You could be friends with a child on its own terms but to be truly friends with a woman she had to be your equal." Marc begins to identify with Pierre's patriotism and resolves to do what he can to help his island survive the war. They become, in a sense, one man—or *man.* They have purpose, ideals. Liana has only love to give her life meaning. Gellhorn herself said the novel is "the story of two men who finally go home, in their various ways, and a woman who has no home." She understands the cruel sexual and racial politics of Liana's position, and depicts them with deadly accuracy. But she views her heroine with distant tenderness. This novel came out of Gellhorn's sojourn in the Caribbean and is shadowed by the author's guilt about being so far from the war. Pierre speaks for her when he says, "*I want to go back . . . I want to go back because I am revolted to be safe.*"

In *The Weather in Africa,* her last piece of fiction, the women represent what Gellhorn despises. The book consists of three novellas set in a newly independent Africa, where the balance of power has shifted and the presence of whites is always conditional. **"On the Mountain"** concerns two sisters who have come home to Mount Kilimanjaro to help their parents run the family hotel. Gellhorn draws the sisters with such bold strokes they could be characters in a fairy tale. Mary Ann, "small, cosy and dark," is the good sister who works hard and acts right. Jane is the golden-haired beauty—a vain, arrogant snob who detests Africa and the Africans. She is almost too bad to be true, and Gellhorn metes out a terrible punishment.

Jane becomes infatuated with Paul Nbaigu, a "new African": educated, Christian, a low-level bureaucrat. They embark on a loveless, compulsive affair that rapidly spirals down into degradation for both of them. As Jane finds herself more and more dependent on him sexually, her contempt for both of them grows. Paul uses his power over her to play out his own hatred of whites by humiliating her sexually. Inevitably the relationship destroys them—and you can't help feeling they get what they deserve. Mary Ann also gets what she deserves:

a kindly, rumpled botanist who worships her. Despite Gellhorn's heavy didactic hand, **"On the Mountain"** exerts fascination as a psychologically convincing portrait of a relationship poisoned by racism and self-hatred.

"In the Highlands" pits a good man, Ian, who loves and respects the land and the African people, against his wife, a termagant named, with heavy irony, Grace. The least of Grace's sins is her attempt to "civilize" Ian's rough and masculine domain by covering it with English chintz. She adopts a white baby, names her Joy, and turns her into a monstrous replica of herself. Eventually, Ian drives Grace out of his house and out of Africa. All Gellhorn's narrative skill cannot make up for the lack of nuance in this ugly portrait.

The last novella, **"By the Sea,"** is the most successful of the three. It's a harrowing story of a woman whose car accidentally hits and kills an African child. Mrs. Jamieson—again Gellhorn distances us from her character by not giving her a first name—has come to Africa "for a change" in the aftermath of a mental breakdown. As the story progresses, we learn that her breakdown was precipitated by the death first of her mother, then of her eight-year-old son. Mrs. Jamieson's grief and guilt make her vulnerable to the violence of the African landscape. The accident merges in her mind with the death of her son, and in the end a clumsy blackmail attempt sends her over the edge. "She should never have come to Africa," Gellhorn has someone say at the end of the story, rapping us smartly over the head with her theme—that Africa is essentially unknowable and that even the most well-meaning whites have no place there. Though **"By the Sea,"** like the book as a whole, is wildly overdetermined, Mrs. Jamieson is as close as Gellhorn comes to empathy for a female character.

Gellhorn, if I read her right, was a classic "man's woman." She always preferred the company of men and had a real romance going about soldiers of every kind. She adored and idealized their careless bravery, their camaraderie, their black humor. *The Wine of Astonishment* is the novel in which she boldly attempted to get inside the skin of a soldier in combat. You can almost feel her gathering everything she's got—empathy, imagination, and her own real experience—to dive into the terror and filth and blood and dismemberment of war—as if she wanted to prove she could write it as good as any man.

The novel concerns two soldiers in the Battle of the Bulge—Smithers, a dedicated redneck lieutenant-colonel from Georgia, and his young driver, Jacob, an assimilated Jew from St. Louis. Reading her surrealistic scenes of combat in the blue-white winter forests of Belgium made me realize how accustomed we are to battle scenes set in the tropical terrain of Southeast Asia:

> The German artillery rolled over them in furious cracking waves, and his head felt as big as a balloon, growing high and naked above his shoulders. Then the artillery would stop and the silence was unnatural and threatening. The strange mists of the forest floated in rags through the trees or crept upwards from the ground; the smoke of a phosphorus shell stood fixed in a white plume; branches split and fell; mud-covered figures moved in the shadows; and the silence became as cold as the cold colorless sky.

Near the end, the novel swerves onto quite a different track when Jacob Levy almost by accident wanders into the newly liberated Dachau. The experience forces him into a terrible consciousness of his own identity. Leaving the village of Dachau, he drives his jeep at speed, deliberately mowing down a group of laughing German civilians. . . . Although the last section of the book seems clumsily glued on, there's no denying its impact. Again Gellhorn writes directly out of her feelings—anguish, rage, shame—heedless of how she was warping her novel's symmetry.

You'd think that a writer as intensely subjective as Gellhorn would be incapable of writing humor, which requires a certain amount of distance. Not so. She can be extremely funny. Nearly all her books are veined with dark humor, and she did write two comic novels, one of which, **His Own Man,** I haven't been able to track down. The other, a 1969 novel called **The Lowest Trees Have Tops,** is a breezy and charming satire about a colony of dotty American expatriates living in a Mexican village.

In 1978, Gellhorn published a book called **Travels with Myself and Another** that has to be one of the funniest travel books ever written. Its conceit is "horror journeys" and it includes trips to Africa, Moscow, the Caribbean, and Israel, as well as the trek she and Hemingway made into China in 1941. This piece is a glowering, Perelmanesque chronicle of heart-stopping flights over mountains in tiny, rickety planes, bone-jolting jeep rides through jungles, terrifying journeys on ancient Chriscrafts, and rooms which feature planks for beds, overflowing toilets, and clouds of malarial mosquitoes. "I wish," says the author in one such room, "to die." Hemingway, although referred to throughout as U. C., or "Unwilling Companion," emerges as a splendid fellow traveler—patient, unflappable, able to see comic possibilities in the most appalling conditions. This is the only thing I've ever read that made me think it might have been *fun* to be married to Hemingway.

Travels with Myself and Another is such a hoot it's really a shame she didn't do more of this kind of writing. But then Gellhorn wouldn't be Gellhorn if she weren't contrary. Her contradictions endear her to me. She's a pacifist who could never stay away from war, indeed seemed driven to push in as close as she could get to every battlefront. She's a feminist with a blind spot about women. She fought hard to subdue her ambition and hunger for excitement, and squash herself into the role of helpmeet to the most celebrated writer of her day. She tried to be a wife, but she simply couldn't stay home. And finally she had the sense and the guts to buck the prevailing stand-by-your-man-no-matter-what-especially-if-he's-a-Genius ideology, and carve out an independent life for herself. For a woman with an appetite for fun and booze and comfort and good conversation, Gellhorn has spent a hell of a lot of time in terrible places, with wretched accommodations, recording people's misery and suffering. She may not be a *great* writer, but she never bores, especially if you read her work in the context of her singular life. I like knowing there's a Martha Gellhorn in the world. I like her style. (pp. 12-14)

Brett Harvey, "Being There," in VLS, No. 61, December, 1987, pp. 10, 12-14.

GRACE HALSELL

Martha Gellhorn says her life began in 1930. Then 21, she set off with a suitcase and $75 for Paris to become a foreign correspondent. She's been traveling, and writing, ever since.

The Face of War, originally published in 1959 [and reissued in 1988], contains a selection of her stories that were printed at the time she wrote them for American and English journals. The updated book includes her reports on Vietnam and the civil war in El Salvador.

Gellhorn begins her career in Spain, during the Civil War. In that open, intimate conflict, she writes, it was always surprising "just to walk to war." . . .

At an RAF station in England, she watches English, Canadian and American pilots take off on a raid, to be gone most of the night. She awaits their return, joins them in their breakfast and identifies with these young men. . . .

After World War II she goes to Java, and describes the Netherlands' East Indies war as an armed revolt against colonialism. . . .

Her most compelling reports are from Vietnam. She visits hospitals filled with our allies, innocent men, women and children mutilated by bombs dropped from U.S. planes. In 1966, she makes plain that Americans are killing and wounding three or four times more people than are the Viet Cong.

Unlike previous wars in which the primary object was to win territory, the U.S. mission in Vietnam was to destroy enemy bodies. And it was the first war on record where one side—the United States—used "body count" and "kill ratio" to define a victory. While tens of thousands of small farmers and their families had survived the Viet Cong, they would be killed by our bombs. "We are uprooting the people from the lovely land where they have lived for generations. . . . Is this an honorable way for a great nation to fight a war 10,000 miles from its safe homeland?" As for the suffering of the mutilated people, she wrote, "We big overfed white people will never know what they feel."

Gellhorn terms articles in **The View From the Ground** peacetime reporting, but here also one finds a persistent theme: We all are diminished by war. In one article, written from Rome in 1944, she begins by saying that the countryside is beautiful and that one would hardly know that Italy had been at war. But then she takes her readers to an orphanage crowded with children whose parents were killed in war, and she takes us to hospitals, with beds filled by children hit by bombs or bullets. War, she writes, is "an idiocy, a prison, and the pain it causes is beyond telling or imagining."

She warns especially against our arsenals of nuclear weapons. Even if we do not make war, by our "playing" with these weapons, "we poison the air, the water, the soil of our planet, damage the health of the living and weaken the chances of the unborn."

In her travels, she comes to know H. G. Wells and gets invited by F. D. R. and Eleanor Roosevelt to live a while at the White House, and along the way she also finds the time to become the third wife of Ernest Hemingway. . . .

[Gellhorn says very little] in these books about Hemingway. Rather, she stays very much on course as to what is meaningful to her: her research, her articles and her books. All of her essays are well-written and timeless and I find her evaluation of war—as our primary evil—most significant.

Grace Halsell, "Martha Gellhorn: War Correspondent," in Los Angeles Times Book Review, June 19, 1988, p. 9.

LORRAINE E. McCORMACK

With work as her only opium and with her insatiable curiosity about the human condition, Gellhorn has spent a lifetime covering conflict, from the Spanish Civil War to Vietnam to Central America. [In three works republished in 1987 and 1988—*The Face of War, The View from the Ground,* and *Liana*—Gellhorn's] focus is on the moral aberrations that cause wars, the valiant people who fight them, and the innocents whose lives and homelands are forever altered because of them. . . .

Racism, oppression, and the moral exigencies of war, recurrent themes in Gellhorn's nonfiction, are the constant stars in *Liana*'s Caribbean sky. The story is a deceptively simple one of a wealthy, white landowner who attempts to change everything about his Black wife, Liana, to make her acceptable to his white community. Liana accepts the arrangement to escape her dismal living conditions and to help support her family. Desired but despised by her husband, Liana leads an empty, hopeless life until her tutor, Pierre, kindles within her a dream of love. . . .

Although set in a lush tropical isalnd, *Liana* has no pictures of flowers in riotous colors, or of a sun-sparkled sea. The atmosphere under the tropical sun is gloomy and hopeless. Only a fall night that Liana enjoys alone seems peaceful. . . . For Liana, wrapped in a lie, there was no room to breathe or to live and, worst of all, there was no one to care. Considering when this book was written, it is easy to understand the source of its cynical tone, but Liana's tale lacks even the grim humor and the hope that Gellhorn manages to find in most of the real occurrences she reports.

[*The Face of War* contains thirty-five republished articles] Gellhorn wrote on wars in Europe, China, Java, the Middle East, Vietnam, and Central America. These articles, which originally appeared in *Collier's, The Guardian,* and other popular publications on both sides of the Atlantic, were written in the midst of the fray. As portraits of war, they are genuinely hair-raising, heart-stopping testimonies to the valor of those who survived the carnage day by day and those who succumbed.

In her introduction, Gellhorn speaks of journalism as her personal passport "to the spectacle of history in the making." Her images of that spectacle are haunting in their beauty and their horror, like Finnish soldiers, camouflaged in white, gliding silently into battle on skis. Some of the images go beyond horror, such as Dachau, napalm, and Italian orphanages full of tiny, silent amputees. Gellhorn does not spare us the pain of revisiting these atrocities, because if we look closely enough at what war really is, we will choose peace. Won't we? . . .

The View from the Ground is an excellent follow-up to *The Face of War.* Gellhorn rounds out themes from her wartime writings by reexamining the human conditions in Germany, England, Poland, Spain, Israel, Palestine, Cuba (where she lived during her marriage to Ernest Hemingway), and, most provocatively, the United States. The wartime writings are sharp and spare, and they pique our curiosity about this remarkable writer. The peacetime writings give us a satisfying ration of feelings along with the facts. Her artful dealings with government officials and her penchant for living room interviews with citizens show her skills as a canny information gatherer and a tireless debunker of government propaganda. Her personal experiences with racism in Haiti, protest against nuclear weapons by the women of Greenham Common, and other issues that affect our lives are colorfully but thoughtfully narrated, often so candidly that we cannot predict which view she will espouse until the story has been told. She explains, "Journalism is education for me; . . . writing is payment for the chance to look and learn."

It does not matter if you accept her cynical assessment of refugee life in the Middle East or her invective on greed-driven governments. Gellhorn's purpose is to stimulate your appetite for enough information to form an opinion of your own, and she succeeds brilliantly. She requires collaboration of her readers. "The act of keeping the record straight . . . is a form of honorable behavior, involving the reporter and the reader." Her work is a reminder to those of us who learn our history from television miniseries that we have a responsibility for the world we live in, and an imperative to keep ourselves informed about its workings.

Lorraine E. McCormack, "Travail, Opium Unique," in Belles Lettres: A Review of Books by Women, *Vol. 4, No. 1, Fall, 1988, p. 21.*

KIRSTY MILNE

This collection of Martha Gellhorn's peacetime journalism [*The View from the Ground*] spans six decades, complementing the fine and harrowing reports [previously reissued in] *The Face of War.* In these pages she watches Adolf Eichmann being tried in Jerusalem for the murder of European Jewry; joins peaceful protests in Washington against the Vietnam war; puzzles over communist economics in Poland; and holds her breath with Spain after the death of Franco.

That one person in a lifetime could bear witness to all this gives *The View from the Ground* the burnished status of a historical document. But there's nothing here of the fossil; Martha Gellhorn's writing is spiked with intelligence, individualism and moral indignation.

She celebrates private heroism in the torture rooms of El Salvador and the muddy tents of Greenham Common. Subjects where melodrama or sentiment might lurk get direct and fearless treatment. Visiting Italian orphanages after the war, Gellhorn does not avoid the obvious poignancy of children left homeless, injured and sometimes deranged by the bombing of Italian cities. But she digs beneath the pathos to pinpoint a buried social problem: how to heal the terrible scars left by the war on the coming generation.

Very occasionally, her genuinely felt anger congeals into a righteous sarcasm and her powers of perception are directed to proving a point—nowhere more obtrusively than on a tour of Palestinian refugee camps in Jordan and the Gaza strip before the 1967 war. In championing Israel she, who elsewhere deals so forcefully in the uniqueness of suffering, seems determined to deny the Palestinians theirs. Because the Poles are cultured and rueful, they command her admiration and her sympathy; but when Palestinians complain loudly about their statelessness, Gellhorn hears only self-pity and invention—a rare blindspot in the vision of a humane and independent-minded woman.

Kirsty Milne, "An American Cassandra," in New Statesman & Society, *Vol. 2, No. 67, September 15, 1989, p. 36.*

DAVID HONIGMANN

The View From the Ground collects the highlights from [Gellhorn's] career as a peacetime journalist, starting at a lynching in the Deep South in 1936 and ending with her return to Cuba half a century later.

In one sense, it is a companion piece to *The Face of War;* in another, all of Gellhorn's writing is war reporting, only in this volume it is either the run-up to conflict or else the bitterness and morals of its aftermath that concern her, rather than the actual fighting. As *The Face of War* puts it, 'When a war ends, it is not over. Unfinished business remains . . . The greatest war of the world, to date, spawned almost ceaseless little wars.' A report here which at first seems to be a celebration of Italy's postwar recovery soon finds Gellhorn visiting the orphanages packed with war victims, meticulously documenting that unfinished business. . . .

Gellhorn always turns her age to good account, whatever it is at the time she writes. At the start of her career, after leaving Bryn Mawr 'in a hurry to get started', she plays the naïve *ingénue,* asking unfashionably frank questions about the Depression and the administration of the National Recovery Act. She brings the uncomfortable news that the unemployed are not, in the main, work-shy and unemployable, and that much of the education they are being given is so impractical as to be worse than useless to them.

Later, by contrast, her startling range of experience (she has seen all of war's 'horrible repetition', from Finland and Canton to Java, Vietnam and Central America) gives her authority when she needs it. After an encounter with hedonistic hippies ('for sheer one-track dullness these kids took the cookie') in Israel at the start of the Seventies, in *Travels With Myself and Another,* she mused on the equal boredom of cruise ships and noted, offhandedly, that the longest time she ever 'passed on the waves' was '18 days in 1944, crossing the Atlantic on a dynamite ship'. . . .

The curse of collected journalism is hindsight, unless the journalist silently discards his or her mistakes. But Gellhorn's record is largely sound. When the Czechs are optimistic about their chances under Hitler, she disillusions them; when in 1947 Hanns Eisler is put through the wringer by the House of Un-American Activities Committee, she denounces McCarthyism's 'flawless travesty of justice' as an 'American reign of terror; no concentration camps, no gulags, no executions, just cowardly ostracism and unemployment, and it was enough'. Her wide knowledge of totalitarianism in Europe (both concentration camps and gulags, notice) is rebuke enough to its pale American imitation.

Her hatred of McCarthyism is on display again when she reports on the House of Commons in 1956, when a Labour Member who has fingered Kim Philby as the Third Man under the cover of parliamentary privilege is forced to withdraw his accusation. To this day, her belief that Macmillan and the others who protested were 'factually wrong . . . but morally right' does not waver. The logical end of a disregard for what the Americans call 'due process' is, after all, summed up in the testimony of a torture victim from El Salvador which she reproduces, without superfluous comment, towards the end of this excellent collection.

Her view of England, her adopted home to the extent that she is able to live in any one place for long without getting fidgety, changes radically. In *The Face of War,* she notes that in wartime all the British failings become strengths: 'Slowness, understatement, complacency change into endurance, a refusal to panic, and pride, the begetter of self-discipline.' Her view of the Fifties in Britain is coloured by this enthusiasm of the convert; her affection for a low-key election campaign and a good-humoured House of Commons makes it all seem very long ago now.

Maybe it all seems long ago to Gellhorn as well: the Eighties she finds 'infuriating and shabby', at least in Britain and the US. She is reluctant to draw morals—the final chapter of *Travels With Myself and Another* was stubbornly titled 'Non-Conclusion'—but finally she allies herself with a 'global fellowship [of] men and women concerned with the welfare of the planet and its least protected inhabitants'.

If anyone is able to rescue us from Santayana's over-quoted warning that 'those who do not remember the past are condemned to relive it', it is Martha Gellhorn: 'If the agony of the Second World War did not teach them, whatever would?'

David Honigmann, "Wars and Rumours of Wars," in The Listener, *Vol. 122, No. 3137, October 26, 1989, p. 31.*

JEREMY HARDING

As a young girl growing up in St Louis, Missouri, Martha Gellhorn had a habit of poring over maps; riding on the city's tramcars, she would imagine she was bound for distant places with exotic names. Seventy years later, her war dispatches, fiction, travel writing and the peacetime journalism—collected [in *The View from the Ground*]—bear witness to a lifetime of wanderlust. From the clattering cars of the St. Louis Transit Authority, the dreamy child has disembarked as a grown woman in Europe, Asia, the Middle East, Latin America, the Caribbean and Africa. In all these places she has set down what she saw in her journalism and worked what was less readily apparent into her fiction: five novels, two collections of stories and four groups of novellas.

Gellhorn's reputation rests largely on her work as a war correspondent who cut her teeth in Spain during the Thirties, going on to cover most of the major European fronts in World War Two and never quite retiring from the game. In her seventies she was in Nicaragua and El Salvador, fulminating against the Reagan Administration's Central American policy. Her fiction is less well-known, although the first collection of novellas, *The trouble I've seen* (1936), received generous praise from Graham Greene and H. G. Wells. For years, her literary standing was compromised by her ties to Ernest Hemingway in the Thirties and Forties. This has long since ceased to be the case. *The Face of War,* her collected war reporting, is one of the most readable accounts of conflict in the 20th century, unspoiled by convictions which would have been disastrous in a less able writer. Two new editions have appeared since it was first published in 1959. There is one group of novellas currently in print, a book of travel writing and two novels. *The View from the Ground,* which spans half a century of peacetime journalism, is a welcome addition to the list of Martha Gellhorn's available work.

Even in her peacetime reporting, Gellhorn has stuck to her guns: those of the convinced anti-Fascist, champion of labour and critic of American foreign policy who has witnessed one catastrophe after another with a growing sense that governments are on the whole pernicious things, and that poor people must remain in their place if they wish to remain in their skins. Hers is an unambiguous view of the world, which has many villains and countless victims: refugees, orphans, conscripts, persecuted minorities, the unemployed and the disenfranchised. Yet her beliefs are expressed with a grace and good humour largely absent from the two hegemonies—those of Reaganism and Thatcherism—which she takes to characterise the Eighties ('an infuriating decade'). In her career as a reporter, Gellhorn has rarely let her anger slide into self-righteousness and, in the end, amused self-deprecation is never far away.

Gellhorn left the United States for Europe in 1930, at the age of 21. By her own account, she cut a rather comic figure. 'I intended to become a foreign correspondent within a few weeks,' she writes, 'and Paris was the obvious place to launch my career.' She took a cheap room with a mirror on the ceiling—curious, she thought, 'but perhaps that was a French custom.' She showed up at the *New York Times* offices and announced that she was available for work. Little came of it beyond a lunch invitation—'my enthusiasm for free meals was unbounded'—and a tip from the bureau chief that she was staying in a brothel.

By 1934, she was back in the United States looking for work. Harry Hopkins, the director of the Federal Emergency Relief Administration, agreed to see her. 'I painted my face like Parisian ladies, lots of eye shadow, mascara and lipstick, which was not at all the style for American ladies then and certainly not for social workers in Federal employment.' She told him she knew 'a lot about unemployment and was a seasoned reporter; the first was true enough, the second not.' Hopkins hired her to report on the successes and failures of the Roosevelt Administration's welfare policies. For a year, she travelled up and down America filing reports to her boss on the state of the nation's poor. Three of these are 'cut and stuck together' in the first section of *The View from the Ground* under the title, 'My Dear Mr Hopkins'. They are interesting only in so far as they show off her powers as an 'advocacy journalist'—she used the reports to press for more comprehensive and generous relief—and because they prefigure *The trouble I've seen,* her first literary success, which drew directly on the same material to produce a more dramatic study, this time in fiction, of American poverty.

The book appeared in 1936, introduced by H. G. Wells, with whom she was staying in London. The dust of favourable notices had scarcely settled before she set off for Madrid, moved by the Loyalist predicament but with no idea of how or for whom to write in support of *la causa.* The first unsolicited dispatch she sent to *Collier's* in New York earned her a job with the magazine. Her career as a war correspondent was under way. In 1938 she arrived in Prague, her disillusion with the role of the major powers in Spain fired to anger—against the British, above all—by Munich and the annexation of Sudetenland. Salvation, however, might still come from across the Atlantic, where her readership lay. In Prague she embarked on another attempt to alert the American public to the dangers of Fascism, just as she had hoped to do in Spain.

"Obituary of a Democracy", her report on Czechoslovakia, appeared in *Collier's* in December. It contains much of the background material she would use a few years later in *A Stricken Field,* a full-length novel set in Czechoslovakia. It is one of the finest reports in this collection, depicting a country in turmoil, with large numbers of refugees on the move

like insects seething over a tree stump. Yet the scale of the disaster is relentlessly human. 'In the north,' she writes,

> you got a feeling that the whole country was moving, lost, fleeing. On the road you passed a peasant's cart with a blue enamel pail hanging from it, with a funeral wreath of dead flowers sitting up on top of the mattresses. Four people walked beside it. The women were eating dry bread; they had two slices apiece in their pocketbooks. They did not speak to each other and they walked with great weariness.

This is Gellhorn at her best, the eyes wide and the mouth set, invoking the lowest common denominator of political upheaval: the displaced person.

There are only four reports from the Forties, since Gellhorn spent the first half of the decade covering the war and, in the time she had left, fighting a rearguard action against the subversive resentments of Hemingway, whom she met shortly before her departure for Spain in 1937 and married in 1940. They parted in December 1944. In the interim, Hemingway had jeopardised her career, and arguably her life, by signing on as a *Collier's* correspondent to cover the war in Europe. One front-line reporter per paper was the rule laid down by the American Forces. Hemingway's reputation was the bigger of the two and Gellhorn had to wing it through Europe, reporting for the magazine with no official accreditation. Within weeks of the break-up, she was covering the Battle of the Bulge and by May 1945 she had written one of her finest reports—on Dachau. She would mull over the question of Nazi atrocities in two more reports, one from Nuremberg in 1946 and another, published here, on the trial of Adolf Eichmann, 16 years later.

Spare and matter-of-fact, Gellhorn's thumbnail portraits of Nazi dignitaries raise the familiar but disturbing issue of the individual whose atrocities seem all the more puzzling because he does not look like an ogre. Speer had 'a face you could see anywhere, in any subway, in any drugstore', while Frank 'looked patient and composed, like a waiter when the restaurant is not busy'. At the trial of Adolf Eichmann in Jerusalem, she paints a more sinister, Baconesque portrait of the defendant caged in bullet-proof glass, occasionally producing a large white handkerchief and blowing his nose.

Although they languish in a rather different cage—one of delinquence and resentment—Gellhorn's Palestinians are almost as grotesque. A staunch supporter of the Jewish state, she has clearly decided that her friends' enemies, must, in the nature of things, be hers as well. **"The Arabs of Palestine"** was written three years before the PLO came into existence and another five before it became a significant force. The Palestinians whom she interviews are thus Nasserites, *faute de mieux.* Many of them appear to have had no political education and most tend, in her view, to exaggerate the catastrophe which has befallen them. She finds them eaten up with hatred: they 'gorge on hate, they roll in it, they breathe it.' They are Nietzschean slaves with one crucial shortcoming: their resentment is inauthentic and so they cannot win. They have no serious wish to return to their homes and within one generation they will 'merge into the Arab nations'.

Israel at any price was the understandable priority and one senses that at this point in her career Martha Gellhorn has cut a number of losses. The Palestinian question is too complex, too tiring to consider after the epic struggle against Fascism, the shock of Dachau, and the eerie business of the Nazi trials in which justice is, in the end, as unsatisfactory as the crimes in question are absolute. This is not to say that Gellhorn steps down. That would be out of character. But there is a hint that her terms are being redefined. It is to be found, alongside the anger and dismay, in her report on the Eichmann trial. In the conclusion to her own summing-up, she casts the figure in the cage not merely as an uncommon criminal but as a 'warning that the private conscience is the last and only protection of the civilised world.'

Gellhorn's pact with conscience seems to adjourn some lengthy trial of her own, in which the writer who has practised journalism, as a form of political intervention for 25 years acknowledges defeat—defeat in Spain, in Czechoslovakia, at Dachau, none of them quite redeemed by the Allied victory—and accepts that her case against oppression and injustice, having failed to change the world, will now have to rest largely on personal conviction. In fact, the court never convenes for a full session again, for Gellhorn is quickly bored by questions of personal motivation. Instead, she makes a run for it, returning to the fray with all her former anger and energy. On handguns in America, the war in Vietnam, the miners' strike, El Salvador, the approach is more or less unaltered. Similar conclusions about the ills of American imperialism, the follies of government and the evils of poverty are drawn. Regimes commit the same crimes, the powerful

are still cowards and abusers, the poor are still pushed around. From pasture to pasture in Martha Gellhorn's extensive grazing, there is no such thing as greener grass.

What emerges instead is a set of archetypes for 20th-century politics, disposed like figures on a ground: from Spain, Czechoslovakia, Vietnam and Central America comes the stooping refugee; from the Depression, the 'basement' of the Great Society and the dole queues of London at the end of the Seventies comes the poor man in the developed capitalist state; from a bestiary of bad or indifferent leaders—Franco, Hitler, Ronald Reagan, Margaret Thatcher—comes the bully. Finally there is the figure of technology, the only abstract on display, which has haunted Gellhorn ever since she saw the effects of German armaments in Spain and which remains for her an instrument used by the powerful to punish the poor. In her writings from the Seventies and Eighties, these archetypes have solidified in the collieries of South Wales, the prisons of El Salvador and the homes of the unemployed in London, but seldom does the work feel like a rehearsal of old preoccupations. It is wholly attentive to the matter in hand.

Jeremy Harding, "Her Guns," in London Review of Books, *Vol. 12, No. 5, March 8, 1990, p. 14.*

Albert Innaurato

1948?-

American dramatist and scriptwriter.

In his plays, Innaurato blends naturalism and surrealism to center on the need of individuals to be loved and understood. Many of his protagonists are grotesques, eccentrics, and misfits caught up in comic situations that often border on farce, and Innaurato addresses the ways in which people are judged by appearance and sexual preference. Focusing on characters forced into absurd or impossibly competitive situations, Innaurato stresses the intrinsic strength and dignity that enable individuals to transcend background and environment. He blends pathos and wit to explore the effects of society on personal life through such topics as sexual dilemmas, prejudice, and the search for love. Identifying all of his protagonists as extensions of himself, Innaurato acknowledged: "I write about things that obsess me, there's no question about it. Naturally there are reflections of my life in my plays." He added: "I'm also very concerned with understanding and acceptance, of oneself and of the world, and of trying to make a balance between the infantile need to transform the world into one's own object and the adult's realization that you can't ever do that, that you have to find a way to live in this world. That's a crucial thing in all my plays."

Born into an Italian Catholic family in South Philadelphia, where many of his works are set, Innaurato was a sensitive, precocious child interested in the problems of those rejected by society. He began composing opera librettos at the age of eight, and several critics have noted similarities between his mature writing style and operatic forms. Frank Rich commented: "As a writer, Mr. Innaurato has an intense operatic voice, by turns comic and sentimental, that lingers in the ear." His first major play, the black comedy *The Transfiguration of Benno Blimpie,* is based on a nightmare he had in which he recalled the brutality of parochial school and the Catholic fixation with suffering. Benno, a grossly overweight adolescent who literally eats himself to death, functions as a Christlike symbol of the innocent victim of society. Innaurato's next work, *Gemini,* concerns Francis, a Harvard student who is unsure of his sexual preferences. His confusion is intensified when two wealthy, attractive classmates—a brother and sister—travel to Francis' home in South Philadelphia to celebrate his twenty-first birthday.

While Innaurato's first two works were generally praised, his ensuing plays were dismissed by some critics as disorganized. *Ulysses in Traction* concerns a group of theater students trapped in a school rehearsal hall during a race riot, while *Passione* revolves around a Philadelphia man whose wife returns to him after a ten-year absence. The familiar setting and clownish, eccentric characters of *Passione* prompted several reviewers to regard the play as a redundant version of *Gemini.* Infuriated, Innaurato retaliated against critics in his next play, *Coming of Age in SoHo.* The protagonist of this work, a bisexual named Bartholomew "Beatrice" Dante, is a thirty-six-year-old author suffering from writer's block since the phenomenal success of his book *Little Boy Bound.* Desperate for new material, he soon encounters a fifteen-year-old prep school runaway on his doorstep who promptly becomes the

object of Beatrice's benign affection. A young German boy also appears, however, claiming that he is Beatrice's son by Henrietta Schlussnuss, a German anarchist whom Beatrice describes as a "terrorist with artistic ambitions—like a critic." Meanwhile, Beatrice's ex-wife, a Mafia princess, is running for Congress, and the Mafia wants the couple to remarry to ensure the Catholic vote. The play ends as Beatrice furiously types up a new manuscript. Reviewers applauded the playful humor and farcical action of *Coming of Age in SoHo,* but Innaurato viewed their reactions as negative, incorporating this judgment into his next play.

The title characters in *Gus and Al* are Austrian composer Gustav Mahler and Innaurato himself, portrayed as a neurotic homosexual playwright despondent over the reviews of his latest work. While trying to commit suicide in a time machine built by his pet gorilla, Al ends up in Vienna, Austria at the turn of the century, hurled through the window of Gustav Mahler's house. Mahler is also wallowing in self-pity, following the poor critical reception of his *Fourth Symphony,* and the two become kindred spirits. Their platonic friendship is threatened, however, by Mahler's amorous relationship with the acerbic Alma Schindler, who treats Al as a perpetual outsider. Al finally realizes that he must reject Gus's world and try to reconcile the difficulties in his own life. While critics faulted the ending as stilted, *Gus and Al* was lauded for its colorful characterizations and is generally regarded as Innaurato's most celebrated play since *Gemini*.

(See also *CLC,* Vol. 21 and *Contemporary Authors,* Vols. 115, 122.)

PRINCIPAL WORKS

PLAYS

I Don't Generally Like Poetry, But Have You Read "Trees"?
   [with Christopher Durang]   1972
The Life Story of Mitzi Gaynor, or Gyp   1973
The Transfiguration of Benno Blimpie   1973
Earth Worms   1974
The Idiots Karamazov [with Christopher Durang]   1974
Urlicht   1974
Gemini   1976
Ulysses in Traction   1977
Passione   1980
Coming of Age in SoHo   1984
Gus and Al   1989

OTHER

Verna: USO Girl   (television script)   1978

ELIZABETH STONE

"I have very ambivalent feelings about being called 'The Playwright of Little Italy,'" says Albert Innaurato, the author of several plays, including the long-running Broadway comedy *Gemini*, about a Philadelphia Italian-American who attends Harvard, and is paid a surprise summer visit at home by two WASP classmates. "I'm so aware of how individual a vision I have.

> Growing up, I felt American and I felt Italian, but I didn't often feel Italian-American. When I was growing up in Philadelphia, the closest friend I had was my grandfather, who was Italian, and, by extension, his friends, who all talked Italian around me. With them I felt Italian.

"But the rest of the time I was off by myself, reading, or playing the piano, or listening to opera—I've been an opera fanatic from the time I was a very young child. By the time I was 9, I was totally unlike any other kid in the neighborhood. I was acquainted with names and ideas and concepts that no one else had ever heard of. I was reading Freud and Nietzsche when I was 12."

As a "gifted child," Albert left the neighborhood Catholic school and entered a special high school.

> At first, the freedom was terrifying, but by leaving at an early age and going to Central, I broke the ties and forced myself—or was forced, or both—to adjust to a different world view. I became an honorary WASP. At Temple, when I met some of the neighborhood boys again, they were still talking as they had talked in high school. To them I sounded affected, which I probably was, and to me, they

sounded like gangsters in a B movie, which they weren't.

Did growing beyond what he had been involve any ethnic self-contempt? "I think at that time it did," says Albert. . . . "I didn't mention my background or my parents. I didn't mention that I was working class. I cut off visiting my family, and when they wanted to visit me, I kept putting them off."

Albert Innaurato did not have an easy time as a WASP pretender. "The first adjustment I had to make to WASP middle-class life was leaving the table hungry. The portions are always so tiny and bland, especially to me, coming from a family where they put so much on the table." (p. 90)

> I was not only attracted to WASP's, but I wanted to act like a WASP and achieve like a WASP. The American culture is one that emphasizes external achievement over internal achievement, a society that emphasizes financial standing. I had never felt when I was growing up that personal worth was determined exclusively by achievement.

Part of Albert's problem at Yale, though, was that the WASP's were not accepting of his plays. "I was a real abrasive eccentric to them, and though they were the ones who should have seen the talent in the work, they didn't."

At about this point, says Albert, his repudiation of his family began to dissolve.

> My father and his family—the working-class Italians—they were the first ones to really support me as an artist. I don't mean that they read my plays—I didn't offer them, and they didn't ask. But that's when I began to see them as people not to be ashamed of or to avoid. That's also when I began to see what it had cost them to live in the society— that some of the 'vulgarity' and 'crassness' was a defense that I would adopt. Our defenses were different—I had a wider reference range, and I talked faster—but our feelings weren't.

Albert believes that both stages of his experience are reflected in the main characters in *Gemini.* "It shows them unsympathetically and yet sympathetically because I disliked these people for a while and judged them as stupid, limited and narrow, but among them was a readiness to accept people and to include them." (pp. 90, 93)

What about the references in *Gemini* to "nigger Italian"? Where did that come from? "I made that up," says Albert, "though subsequently I've had Italians come up to me and tell me that it's true—that they feel we're the blacks and the WASP's are white. I didn't feel black, although I did feel a certain ethnic difference, but not to the point of being excluded." (p. 93)

> *Elizabeth Stone, "It's Still Hard to Grow Up Italian," in* The New York Times Magazine, *December 17, 1978, pp. 90, 93.*

ROBERT BERKVIST

Nobody has ever accused Albert Innaurato of a penchant for understatement. The world he depicts in his early plays is peopled by an assortment of grotesques that would not seem out of place in the nightmarish visions of Hieronymus Bosch. They are bizarre characters, often driven by murderous appetites and anxieties. In *The Transfiguration of Benno Blimpie,* the first of his plays to be commercially produced and to attract critical acclaim, Benno is a grossly obese young man whose physical needs drive him to a hideous act of self-destruction.

In some of his other works (six Innaurato plays have just been published . . . [and are collectively] titled, appropriately, *Bizarre Behavior*), the characters include a band of homicidal nuns, a blind woman who crawls around swatting at cockroaches, a gaudy transvestite and a Mother Superior who happens to be a bisexual hunchback.

Mr. Innaurato finally embraced the more or less workaday world in his 1977 play *Gemini,* a broadly humorous look at the Italian-American residents of a South Philadelphia neighborhood. Significantly, *Gemini,* is now in its third year on Broadway and is Mr. Innaurato's only commercial success to date. The comedy's most eccentric character is an overweight teen-ager whose passion for all forms of public transportation borders on the kinky.

Where do they come from, those outsize creations who bleed and bellow in Mr. Innaurato's work? The playwright says that certain aspects of his own life and character are part of the mix—his angry recollections of parochial-school violence, for example—but he insists that he himself is surprised by some of the characters who come spilling out of his imagination. "Sometimes I think I'm a medium," he said the other day, staring at the ceiling of his Chelsea apartment. "I hear these voices—they come out through me—and I love them. I really *feel* for them. They're not grotesques or clowns, they're real people." . . .

A couple of years ago, with *Benno Blimpie* a *succès d'estime* and *Gemini* digging in on Broadway, he was being hailed as one of the most promising of the new crop of playwrights that included Christopher Durang, David Mamet and Michael Cristofer. Then Mr. Innaurato came up with *Ulysses in Traction,* a play about a group of theater students trapped in a drama school rehearsal hall during a race riot. *Ulysses,* produced Off Broadway, was drubbed by the critics, and Mr. Innaurato, who does not take kindly to criticism, went seething back to his typewriter.

Now he has a new play, *Passione,* and he is feeling a shade defensive. The comedy centers on a Philadelphia man whose Southern-born wife returns to the family fold after a 10-year absence. It had its first exposure last spring at Playwrights Horizons, and Mr. Innaurato is still fuming at some of the critical comments it drew at that time. He is especially sensitive to the accusation that *Passione* is simply an echo of *Gemini.*

"This play simply can't be called *Son of Gemini,* or anything like that," he said heatedly.

> O.K., so it takes place in South Philadelphia, like *Gemini,* and it's also about an Italian-American family, but that doesn't mean it's *Gemini 2*. It's funny—either I'm accused of writing 'spaghetti plays' all the time or, when I write about something else, as I did in *Ulysses in Traction,* I'm told that I should stick to spaghetti. So you get into this insane double bind.

> I write about things that obsess me, there's no question about it. . . . Naturally there are reflections of my life in my plays. But nothing that happens in *Gemini* is the least like anything in my own life.

Sure, I know something of the situation in *Passione,* but I can't say these are literally my parents or that I am the son in the play or that the neighbor down the street was real. . . .

> I'm . . . very concerned with understanding and acceptance, of oneself and of the world, and of trying to make a balance between the infantile need to transform the world into one's own object and the adult's realization that you can't ever do that, that you have to find a way to live in this world. That's a crucial thing in all my plays. *Passione,* especially, is about a clash of cultures, and about people who desperately don't want to get together, don't want to accept and acknowledge each other, but who finally realize that it's one of the only pleasures you can really have.

> (p. 1271)

Looking back at his youth, Mr. Innaurato thinks he was probably the kind of adolescent who made grownups uncomfortable.

> I was very verbal and I wrote things that seemed a little weird at the time—this was in the early 60's, remember. I've always loved people who are sort of odd, overtly eccentric or offputting. I love to imagine what they're like inside, what it would be like to be that person, or to reach out to that person. I'm interested in emotional needs—how people deal with lovelessness.

> My really bizarre early plays came from inexperience, both in life and in art. But what I treasure in those plays is the imagination involved. I was making up life. I was very much alone as a child, not miserable but alone. I didn't know anything about relating to people. So I was creating a world in my plays. I guess I was drawn to the bizarre. There are some pretty naked concerns in my work. Sexual concerns, for example, and reflections of the physical violence and brutality I encountered in the lower-class Catholic schools I went to, along with an excessive concern for the more bizarre aspects of Christianity, a fixation on suffering. Those nuns worshiped pain and loved to inflict pain. It was very crazy. But there are no nuns in *Passione.* I don't think I'm ever going to write about nuns again.

His passions are theater and music, especially opera. . . . "When you have a great piece of music, and you have a fine artist interact with that music and profoundly connect with it, it becomes a mystical experience," he said fervently.

> When I feel contact with that kind of genius, with a Maria Callas or a Janet Baker, for instance, it makes my life better.

> I feel the same way about theater. When there's no trickery, but simply fine writing intersecting with powerful performances, it's thrilling to me. I have a very physical reaction to the theater; I get very excited.

> I think you have to love the theater, beyond having a career. Sure, I want a career, want the acclaim, but even when there was nobody interested in me and my work, I wrote plays. When no one would read them, when I didn't have anyone to show them to, I wrote plays. I've written through the most terrible days. I don't want a badge for that, it's just my life."

> (p. 1272)

Robert Berkvist, "Innaurato's Characters Even Surprise Himself," in The New York Times Biographical Service, Vol. 11, No. 9, September, 1980, pp. 1271-72.

FRANK RICH

Although **Coming of Age in SoHo** does fail, it does so after a lively first act in which we hear the author's special voice in all its operatic vigor. Mr. Innaurato remains one of the few writers around who would dare to float running gags about *Tristan and Isolde,* Sara Lee pound cake and *Soldier of Fortune* magazine in the same play.

Coming of Age is a seemingly autobiographical account of a 36-year-old writer, an Italian-American from South Philadelphia, who is traumatized by his inability to live up to an early success. Mr. Innaurato's early hit was **Gemini,** a comedy about growing up Roman Catholic and sexually ambivalent in South Philadelphia. In **Coming of Age,** the hero is Bartholomew Dante—who goes by the Dantean nickname of Beatrice. His early triumph was a fabulist novel titled *Little Boy Bound,* and he is not sexually ambivalent. "I'm a homosexual who suffers temporary amnesia in the presence of strong-willed ladies," Beatrice explains.

When we meet him at his new SoHo loft, Beatrice has just jettisoned a strong-willed lady who's been his wife for 14 years: Patricia, a bright Mafia lawyer now running for Congress. Patricia still desires her husband—whatever his sexual calling—but Beatrice refuses to return, even when threatened with gangland retribution. Eager to refuel his lapsed career, he believes that a new, ascetic life will once more allow him to be that "impossible thing," an artist.

As befits the literary styles of both Beatrice and his creator, **Coming of Age** is itself a mixture of the fabulist and the real: A standard writer's-block play is laced with wild conceits reminiscent of such past Innaurato endeavors as **The Transfiguration of Benno Blimpie** and **Passione.** Along with the Mafiosi, the playwright's most woolly inventions include two intellectually precocious boys who fortuitously arrive at the loft to spur Beatrice's regeneration: Dy a 15-year-old Wasp runaway from St. Paul's preparatory school, and Puer, a 14-year-old, German-accented computer genius. Dy soon becomes Beatrice's surrogate son. Puer, we discover, is the hero's actual, long-lost son—fathered during a fling with a German terrorist back in the drug-sated 1960's.

Mr. Innaurato sets this all up with characteristic brio in Act I, using dialogue that rarely aspires to the naturalistic. Not unlike the players in a Preston Sturges movie, those in **Coming of Age** speak in opulent paragraphs whatever their age or social station. You never know when a Mafia hood will sound off about literary invective, or when a kid will deliver a discourse on narrative in the modern novel. Some of the ensuing jokes are contrived or cute, but many more are funny. Leave it to Mr. Innaurato to imagine a video game inspired by *Death in Venice,* or a putative CBS-television series about a gun-toting, club-footed nun named Mother Trigger.

More important, the author makes us care about his sensitive on-stage alter ego. While Beatrice is capable of self-pitying diatribes against such nemeses as critics, agents and the Church, he is also engaged in a genuine struggle to define and preserve a literary mission in an increasingly illiterate American culture. His attempts to grapple with sex and love are

equally searching. Though one expects Beatrice to make camp sport of women (as he does while singing "Walk On By"), he is equally persuasive delivering a tender reminiscence of a joyous heterosexual attachment. Nor does the protagonist shy away from the conflicts attending his chaste relationship with the young Dy: Intentionally or not, Mr. Innaurato seems to be re-examining the similar father-son pairing in *Torch Song Trilogy.*

When **Coming of Age** collapses in Act II, it's because the author replaces tough self-questioning with sentimentality and loses stylistic control. After a frantic and flat attempt to resolve the play farcically with his Mafia subplot, he transforms previously absurdist characters (notably the German son) into stock figures so that Beatrice can predictably come of age as both a father and an artist. Meanwhile, the comic speeches are succeeded by pretentious, mawkish sermons that spell out the evening's thematic preoccupations with *Peter Pan,* resurrection and the various meanings of bondage. . . .

For all its failings, **Coming of Age in SoHo** is an honest rite of passage from which Mr. Innaurato can honorably move on.

Frank Rich, "Albert Innaurato's 'Coming of Age in SoHo'," in The New York Times, February 4, 1985, p. C14.

MEL GUSSOW

Albert Innaurato made his New York playwriting debut in 1976 with **The Transfiguration of Benno Blimpie,** a tragicomic nightmare about a young man who was literally eating himself to death. Later that year he followed it with **Gemini,** domestic comedy variations on the subject of sexual and familial identity. In tandem, the two plays established Mr. Innaurato as one of the most original playwrights of his generation.

Actually his talent was first evident several seasons earlier when the Yale Repertory Theater presented **The Idiot's Karamazov,** a delirious literary travesty co-authored by Mr. Innaurato and his Yale Drama School classmate, Christopher Durang. **The Idiot's Karamazov** represented a triple breakthrough—of the authors and of their leading lady, Meryl Streep, playing an impossibly decrepit version of the translator Constance Garnett. Each of the three went on to deserved, individual accolades. It is Mr. Innaurato, however, who, after his initial success, has had the most difficult time of adjustment.

His subsequent plays have suffered from various artistic ailments, either in the writing or in the staging. These included **Earthworms** (a Pygmalion relationship between an aged homosexual and a hillbilly), **Ulysses in Traction** (revolution on campus) and, most promisingly, **Passione,** a return to the South Philadelphia of the author's youth for a brawling comedy about prodigal parents and clownish offspring.

In the introduction to his collection of plays, published under the apt title, **Bizarre Behavior,** Mr. Innaurato expressed the feeling that he was haunted by "a fear that some of the freedom and spontaneity of the earlier plays" had "swum away from me, recoiling from its imprisonment in a naturalistic framework." As an admirer of the author's work, one began to share his trepidation. At least in **Ulysses in Traction,** there was a tenseness that seemed to contradict the essential Innaurato.

As it turns out, that fear is baseless. **Coming of Age in SoHo**—his first play in four years—is bustling with the frenzy of imaginative life. This is not to indicate that the work is in any sense well-made. The author's intellect leads him into moments of self-indulgence. Too many of the characters speak in an intellectual manner, and some of his epigrams and epithets are excisable. The playwright is acting as his own director, and he is not his own best editor. But the play has a heartiness and a fullness of vision that is all too rare in the contemporary theater. No matter how strange or unsympathetic his characters may seem, they are created with affection, and that is exactly how we receive them.

The hero is an American semblance of Dante, a South Philadelphian novelist and poet named Bartholomew Dante, wandering in the hell of his own failure—a path that is strewn with literary references to sources running from *Peter Pan* to Unamuno. Though the play is resident in SoHo, the contemporary artist's Bohemia, the author has not strayed from the natural habitat he knows so well. It is always a risky business to identify plays (or novels) as autobiographical, but more than most of his peers, Mr. Innaurato seems to stir the ashes of his past in search of art and identity. South Philadelphia was his birthplace and that of his various alter egos—in **Coming of Age** and other plays. The playwright once wrote about the "synchronicity" of **Benno Blimpie,** how the play carried around with it the past, present and future. A similar statement might be made about the hero of **Coming of Age.**

In the play we find such favorite Innaurato obsessions as the repressive effects of a Catholic education (especially emasculating nuns, a subject that also obsesses his former collaborator, Christopher Durang), the Italian-American heritage, grand opera, divergent strands of sexuality and fattening food. Though this may sound like a self-serving dict, Mr. Innaurato refreshingly retains his love-hate ambivalence and his comic *passione.*

Sitting in his unfurnished loft, hands on typewriter keys, Bartholomew Dante, the author of the novel, *Little Boy Bound,* contemplates the blankness before him. Feverishly he searches his mind for a new story to tell. "Scandal, ostracism—is that a plot?" he quizzes himself, and then dismisses the idea. Cherishing his privacy while craving distraction, he suddenly finds himself the object of an invasion. The loft is occupied by his almost-ex wife, who is a lawyer as well as the daughter of a Mafia don; a teen-aged middle-American runaway who chronicles his adventures in the manner of Margaret Mead, and the hero's long-absent son, the child of a brief fling with a character referred to as "Henrietta the terrorist," who is herself imprisoned forever in Germany. There is more, much more, and in at least one regard there is too much. Even by Innaurato standards, the runaway is a manufactured character.

The story, as it develops, deals with the Mafia family's insistence that the wayward Dante return to his wife for the duration of her campaign for Congress, as if her husband's presence would be just the ticket to reassure Catholic voters. Considering his exotic life style, that notion is more farfetched than any Hitchcock Maguffin—and it serves the same purpose. It is a contrivance to get the plot rolling. The maneuver does, however, have relevance on a symbolic level. It is an attempt to force the novelist to come to terms with his past. The title of his novel, *Little Boy Bound,* frequently evoked, refers not only to physical bondage but to a man who has been stunted in childhood. He wants to free himself from his bonds and to rediscover his muse. But, wherever he turns, someone is staking a familiar claim on him—his wife and her family, his own son who is trying to convince him to accept the meaning, if not the reality, of his paternity.

Dante is a richly textured artist-in-crisis. Next to him, the most interesting character is his son, Puer (Latin for boy). A stowaway from Germany, he is a computer whiz and a penetrating analyst of his father's work. His conversation is filled with calculated references to such matters as the novelist's "acute if unsteady sense of reality." Sometimes it sounds as if Puer is recycling the playwright's own reviews. It should be stressed that for Mr. Innaurato the attitude is one of self-criticism rather than self-pity. (p. B3)

The novelist cannot believe that Puer is his descendant. The boy is too much a child of his age whereas Dante is trapped in a Wagnerian time warp. Life for him is an attenuated aria, instead of a bleep-bleep of computer programming. Repeatedly, his classic world is impinged by modern times—prickly punk hairdos, adolescents who learn about life from *Soldier of Fortune* magazine. All of this has a semblance of reality but as we know from past journeys with Mr. Innaurato there is something rarefied about the bizarre behavior of his characters, in this instance, immersed in a SoHo never-never land.

Along with Sam Shepard, David Mamet and Christopher Durang, Mr. Innaurato is a playwright with a sharply personalized contemporary style. His writing crosses an effusive wit with the heightened quality of opera. (pp. B3, B14)

In **Coming of Age,** Mr. Innaurato has his moments as a moralist, making a full share of socially responsive points about responsibility. But he does not neglect his playful sense of humor. Thinking about the great authors of the past, his hero questions how they managed to continue to write in the face of adversity. "Did they actually think their writing mattered?" he asks, silently answers in the affirmative and, with a look of amazement, wonders how many more novels Balzac would have produced if he had a typewriter and central heating. One can also imagine the increased productivity of Bartholomew Dante if he followed his son's direction and learned to love the word processor. (p. B14)

Mel Gussow, "Innaurato Survives a Period of Adjustment," in The New York Times, February 10, 1985, pp. B3, B14.

JOHN SIMON

Albert Innaurato's **Coming of Age in SoHo** is a likable mess, but a mess all the same. Seemingly more rewritten than written, it started out with a middle-aged female protagonist; withdrawn and revised, it came back and out of the closet with a male one. This is Bartholomew Dante, known as Beatrice, who wards off his not-quite-ex-wife's efforts to repossess him with "I'm not bisexual, I am a homosexual who suffers temporary amnesia in the presence of strong-willed ladies." A promising situation: Beatrice has moved out of the conjugal abode after fourteen years and set up sparse housekeeping in a loft furnished with a typewriter, a *Death in Venice* computer game he has invented, some tentative sticks of furniture, and the Sara Lee pound cake, Häagen-Dazs ice cream, and unspecified coffee on which he subsists. And here is Patricia Gianbatista Dante, daughter of a Philadelphia Mafia don, trying to reclaim him. But already we can sense shaky construction: Fourteen years of marriage can by no stretch, or shrinking, of the imagination constitute a "temporary amnesia." Why and how were these two married so long?

Well, there is something about her having been the prettiest girl in class, hit on by all the jocks, and preferring someone gentler, brighter, more caring. There is a play in that. There is also a play in the hero's not having lived up to an early literary success (corresponding to Innaurato's early dramatic smash, **Gemini**). The widely read children's novel about bondage and implied pedophilia, *Little Boy Bound,* was followed by failures; now 36, Beatrice wants to find himself and overcome his writer's block. There is a play in that too.

So far, the tone has been that of serious comedy. Now, in rapid succession, there enter into Beatrice's life *(a)* Dy, actually Odysseus McDowell, a hectic fifteen-year-old Wasp on the lam from St. Paul's, where, as an example of how not to write, they read B. Dante, whom Dy admires, wants to stay with, and write about; and *(b)* a precocious, brilliant, highly motivated fourteen-year-old, Puer, the child he had by another temporary amnesia, Henrietta Schlussnuss, a German "terrorist with artistic ambitions—like a critic." Puer, upon his mother's getting life, has come to find his "fahzer." . . . Why the woman's name? Because Beatrice, who here keeps listening to Mascagni and Mahler, is, like Innaurato, a buff, enamored of the great lieder singer Heinrich Schlussnuss. Here we are getting into in-jokes and absurdism, what with Henrietta's having tried to abduct an entire Wagnerian cast for artistic as well as political reasons, and Puer, who is a wizard at languages, computers, and existential psychology, juxtaposed with Dy, the rebellious Wasp and writer in the making. Level II.

Level III: Patricia has a big mafioso brother, Pasquale, and a little mafioso henchman and handyman, Danny, and there is a whole subplot about kidnapping Beatrice and threatening him with the deaths of the tied-up boys—Puer, Dy, and his stiff of a Harvard brother, Trajan—unless he returns to Patricia. This is a slightly updated Kaufman-and-Hart farce that clashes with both the serious and the absurdist comedy. What **Coming of Age** suffers from most is disunity of tone. Much is made of Beatrice and Patricia's having read Unamuno together; well, Unamuno said it in *How to Make a Novel:* "But is there any language without a story, or any fineness of language without a story finely told?" The play tries to make it on wit, resourcefulness, clever language; but where is the fineness of story to support the superstructure? And is there any framework sturdy yet elastic enough to prop up such a mixture of pathos and whimsy, esoteric wise-cracks and simple *cris de coeur?*

There are snazzy bits of invention, satisfying gags, and moments of bittersweet insight, but the disjointed, piecemeal plotting makes one wonder whether it isn't all a strategy of evasion: Instead of hard, comic-sad nourishment, Innaurato scatters painless junk food at us. Can he not find the right plot, is he scared of lapsing into sentimentality, or is he afraid of the full truth? At one point, Beatrice tells Dy, whom he'll put up, "I have an old rollaway bed for when my mother visits. I also have a rollaway life—but that is another story." I was wishing for that other story instead of the one that kept being rolled out. (pp. 102-03)

John Simon, "Odd Couples, Bizarre Trios," in New York *Magazine, Vol. 18, No. 7, February 18, 1985, pp. 101-03.*

EDITH OLIVER

Albert Innaurato is one of the boldest and most original dramatists at work today. He is also—rare indeed—a true humorist. The hero of his **Coming of Age in SoHo** is an Italian-American writer named Bartholomew Dante, but called Beatrice, who has left his wife of fourteen years (and her Mafia connections) for a loft in SoHo. He is homosexual—something his wife has always accepted quite cheerfully—and a lapsed Catholic. He has been unable to write; now he plans to get a divorce and start fresh, sexually and professionally. But his wife, who has decided to run for Congress, wants him back for the Catholic vote, and her brother and her father, Mafia don, intend to see that she gets him. As the play begins, Beatrice is seated alone at his typewriter, producing nothing (to the sound of opera recordings) and trying out plot ideas aloud: "This sensitive Italian-American has landed on this planet of blond people; they think he's a sissy." There is a knock on the door, and in comes young, blond Dy. He is a boy of fifteen, on the run from his family and his prep school. He begs to be allowed to stay, producing on demand what was once called "a racking cough." Beatrice tells him to go home but is ignored. Another knock, and in comes a fourteen-year-old boy, with a thick German accent and a non-stop spiel, who claims to be Beatrice's son by a German terrorist after a brief, intense fling. His name is Puer (what else?). He, too, wants to stay, and does. There is much plot and much activity, in which, by the way, the emotions run as deep and ring as true as do the marvellous jokes. Beatrice very gently falls in love with Dy, who soon gets a job at a local McDonald's, and he listens in affectionate bewilderment to Puer, a computer wizard. But the wife and her Mafia retinue keep intruding on the SoHo loft, and so does Dy's older brother, a student at Harvard, who has been searching for Dy to bring him home. All is resolved, of course, in a way that is touched with nobility (and melodrama, too—those opera records do not go for nothing). By curtain time, Beatrice's wife has relinquished him, Dy goes home—as chaste, to use Beatrice's word, as when he arrived—a father and son have claimed each other, and the typewriter keys begin to tap.

The action is so bountiful, brimming over with comic and dramatic ingenuity—wonderful surprises (sight and sound)—that I can't even think about it now without laughing, and I'm damned if I'll describe it further and spoil the fun.

Edith Oliver, in a review of "Coming of Age in SoHo," in The New Yorker, *Vol. LX, No. 53, February 18, 1985, p. 110.*

ALBERT INNAURATO [INTERVIEW WITH **JOHN LOUIS DiGAETANI**]

[*The interview excerpted below originally took place on August 2, 1986.*]

[DiGaetani]: *Mr. Innaurato, one of the things I like about your plays is the Italian theme you sometimes use. Italian culture has not had much of an effect on serious theatre in America.*

[Innaurato]: Well, the basic thing they always say in creative writing courses is "Write about what you know," though I don't think that all my writing is autobiographical or based solely on my own experiences. Nonetheless, I have written my plays especially about what I know, which is basically Italian-American customs in a very Italian-affiliated neighborhood in Philadelphia, and then dealing with a different world. This world is not really inimical all the time, but it is alien to some degree to the culture that both you and I knew growing up. And I especially, because I went to prep schools and an Ivy League college, experienced a very different kind of culture from what I'd known. Sometimes it was funny, and sometimes it was embarrassing, and then from that tension theatrical situations can arise, and it's a handy way to get a drama or a comedy going.

You also dramatize the problems of being overweight. . . . You present overweight in some of your plays as a form of suicide. For example, in **The Transfiguration of Benno Blimpie** *the main character is eating himself to death, a kind of suicide.*

Well, he is literally eating himself. He's chewing on his bones, his flesh. I mean, he's consuming himself. Blimpie is meant to be a vision or a version of a certain kind of artist who burns out and dies into his art. Blimpie is a failed artist who is unable to make any of the connections that you need to make in order to survive in a career. And what happens when your art meets a dead end? You either give up entirely or you start becoming your art, you start consuming, you start becoming your art to the point that your art is consuming you, and that's really what he does. His death becomes his final work of art, and I think it's a vision of an artist in a dying art form, in a society that has contempt for art as we understand it, or whose use for art is a commercial use—that is, to make money and buy prestige. With that there will be many more artists who fall through the cracks, who aren't socially useful, in the way that Shakespeare was socially useful, in the way that Mozart and Beethoven were, however much their misery and poverty have been glamorized and distorted, because neither was as badly off as our playwrights would have us believe. But nonetheless they were socially useful artists. Their art filled a social purpose—for entertainment, for intellectual pursuits—and they have a large audience. But I think Benno Blimpie is in a way a version of our twentieth-century art form, with no audience and no support and no civilization supporting him, who had no option but to die, and the weight becomes a symbol of the outside or the person who is instantly recognizable—somehow a failure in our society. In a society as obsessed with cosmetic appearance as ours is, anyone who does not adhere to the norm is immediately seen as a freak. (pp. 87-9)

[In] southern Italian culture the worst thing you can call someone is a "fruit," and in **Gemini** *Francis begins to dread that homosexuality may be part of him. Am I reading the play properly?*

Oh yes, I think so. I also think that there are many strands in Italian culture, and most cultures really. I mean Italians in my experience, real Italians, are very tolerant so long as they don't know about it, and even if they know about it, as long as you don't confront them with it, they don't care. And I think that's true of most cultures about sexual secrets of all kinds. So long as you're not out in the open about it, it's fine. There is, however, an American need to be totally honest—gay lib is an American phenomenon and an American need. It's part of American culture; maybe it's a curious inversion

of the Puritan ethic—to admit, to live openly, not to pretend. It's a very European trait for the homosexual to marry and have children but then carry on a very open sexual life with other men, but that seems uncomfortable for Americans. And I think that in **Gemini** that's reflected in Francis; he goes to Harvard, and the play takes place at the end of the sixties, which was a big decade of turmoil for gay lib, for all kinds of liberationist politics. For Francis there's this need not to hide, not to want to hide. And he doesn't want to have a girl friend just to comfort his father because he feels that's not ethical for the girl. He doesn't want to use the girl in that way, and at the same time he has some attraction to the girl, so that's the clash. I mean an Italian would want to hide it, to be macho. The American middle-class drive is to be open and call a spade a spade. Meanwhile there's the person. In all my plays I deal with the person who doesn't really fit into any kind of prefabricated identity, either a gay identity or a straight identity. Francis is genuinely attracted to this woman and is bisexual.

He's genuinely attracted to her brother Randy as well.

At the same time because he's probably bisexual, you see. And there's very little tolerance in our society for that. Gay people are often hostile to bisexuality and refuse to believe it exists, but in fact it does.

What makes your plays distinctive? What do you think you've contributed to the American theatre?

I don't think I've contributed anything to the American theatre. But I can tell you what people don't like about my plays, and that may be what I've contributed. In **Coming of Age in SoHo,** for example, people were really shocked that parts of the play were almost burlesque in their humor, and then there was a demand made on the audience to take the characters, despite the humor, very seriously and to try to get people to see a life-or-death seriousness beating under them and their eccentric behavior. You see, television has made it impossible for some Americans to understand that you can be flamboyant, peculiar, or very eccentric and be human. That underside of reality is rarely presented in our popular art form, and even our most intellectual critics watch much more television than they go to the theatre or even read, so that almost subconsciously they've adopted a TV aesthetic, which has to be very straightforward. In my plays, there's a lot of grotesquerie, a lot of eccentricity, and a lot of flamboyant behavior, but I never see the people as cardboard, or as zanies.

Yes, I think one of the things you contributed most is your form of humor; you do use comedy to make very serious points, which is nothing new, but you do it in a new way. Also, I like your use of language. The combinations of the American English and southern Italian dialects are interesting. One of the things I don't like much about television is that the use of language there is generally so tedious.

Well, it's often very ordinary. It's a deliberate shutting down. You see, as in sexual experience, I don't believe in limits. I don't believe experiences are black or white. I don't believe in the small screen in life since I think life is not a small screen. I don't believe there is *one* sexual feeling. I think that in the course of a lifetime we all have many sexual feelings, though we may or may not choose to act on them.

That's like Thomas Mann's Death in Venice, *when an apparently heterosexual artist all of a sudden falls in love with a fourteen-year-old boy, much to his woe. Is life full of these ugly surprises?*

I don't think they're ugly, they're just life! Life isn't a twenty-four-minute TV drama interrupted by commercials every six minutes. Or maybe a change is more typical now, or at least in America people are more willing to pursue these things and not immediately reject them. And I also think that some people have much more decided and rigid notions of what is acceptable and what isn't. For example, one of the critics who reviewed my play *Passione* said, "Oh, Innaurato is an Italian and can't really write about American southern women." Well, I spent fourteen years of my life, every summer, in the South because my mother had friends down there, and her best friend had a farm about forty miles out of Knoxville in the Great Smoky Mountains. It was really very rural and countrified, and I heard that speech every summer for fourteen years, day in, and day out. And I have very good ears. So the speech those two Southern women speak is absolutely accurate, not exaggerated, not false. Yet this man assumed it had to be false; and many more people read and believe reviewers than ever see a play, and that has become a reality of our times, especially if it's in the *New York Times*. What amazes me is that it is so corrupt, and this is why I sometimes think art is dead in our times, why I think the theatre is dead. (pp. 90-2)

One of the things you imply in **Ulysses in Traction** *is that if theatre is dying, the university theatre has destroyed it.*

Oh, I don't think you can say that! I think the pathos is that the institutional theatres in this country are basically run by intrigue and terror, and there's constant money trauma. Undeniably university theatre provides many people with a hands-on experience they can't have in the professional theatre. And obviously of all the people who work in the university theatre there are some very talented, very sophisticated people. Also, talent is talent! There are people who are perfectly content teaching college and who are very talented, who are better directors than some of the people who make a lot of money directing extravaganzas like *Cats,* but the point is I believe in audience. When you don't have an audience, when you have some kind of protection in the form of a subsidy, whether it's the university paying your bills or the state, then you're in a less real world.

To get back to your plays, I really like their allusions to music, especially to opera—for example, **Urlicht,** *with the references to the Mahler song and the Mahler Second Symphony, and all the operatic allusions in* **Gemini.**

Well, I'm a passionate opera-lover.

Which of your plays do you like the best?

I often don't like them, and I'm often disappointed in them. I rarely feel that I've achieved very much or as much as I wish I had or wanted to when I started. At the same time, when time has elapsed and I go back and read them, I'm often surprised at what I did. There are moments in *Gemini,* and even in a relatively weak play like *Ulysses in Traction,* that have a kind of spontaneity. I'm a very intuitive writer, and that's bad in a way. I think my writing has a kind of stream to it and it's very spontaneous and very intuitive, and I think there's an unevenness when that's the case. (p. 93)

In the introduction to your collected plays, you state that you feel your plays lack action. Could you elaborate on that?

Yes. I think you need an action in plays. I mean plays shouldn't be static, shouldn't just sit there. You need something to be happening, You need a motor, and I have trouble finding a motor.

There is a lot of action in **Gemini.** *I kept wondering what would happen at that birthday party.*

Well, a more successful example of that occurs in several of my other plays. I'm also speaking in terms of the continuum, and I just think that I tend to operate in terms of character and in terms of emotion, not really in terms of an underlying action or underlying story.

One of the recurrent tensions I see in your work is the conflict between the happy, comic, jolly versus the sad, depressed, suicidal, and of course this is a conflict in most people. I think part of the source for this conflict may be that Italian culture is very negative about the homosexual element in people, and Catholicism exacerbates that. I think this engenders in some creative people a kind of self-hatred or a suspicion that they are really frauds, that success is not really theirs.

Well, I think that's accurate. I think that in many artists, or many people who try to be artists, there is a suspicion that it's all a joke or a fraud. That's why I keep talking about audiences. You need some kind of external check, some way to say, "Well, I've achieved that," or "I've achieved this," and if you don't have that, it's hard, after a time, to believe the talent is real. No one that I know can lock himself in a garret and say rejection doesn't matter. It does matter enormously if one is very sensitive to being dismissed, to being mocked, to being shrugged off, to being ignored. I don't know how anyone, anyone, can ignore that, and I don't know that anyone has. (p. 94)

Albert Innaurato and John Louis DiGaetani, in an interview in Studies in American Drama, *Vol. 2, 1987, pp. 86-95.*

CLIVE BARNES

Shakespeare is dead! Beethoven is dead! And Albert Innaurato isn't feeling so well lately, either.

That old vaudeville joke seems to provide the drift—the subtext, as it were—of Innaurato's free-wheeling and sporadically amusing autobiographical fantasy, *Gus and Al.*

Innaurato at 40 depicts himself as suicidally inclined following what he considered the derisive reviews of his recent play. . . .

At home, it appears, he has an ape called Kafka that he has saved from vivisection, who is so far in advance of normal simian intelligence that he has invented a time machine, whose travel patterns are linked to music.

The desperate Innaurato, still clutching the literally critical notices, decides to do away with himself by short-circuiting both the machine and his wretched existence.

Fortunately for posterity, the plan ends with Innaurato—who had been listening to Mahler—being catapulted into 16 Ringstrasse, Vienna, in 1901, Gustav Mahler's home, where he lived with his sister, Justine, and his devoted amanuensis, Natalie Bauer Lechner.

The composer, also 40 years old, and the playwright immediately find common ground in the attacks of critics and other vermin, and are soon buddyboyishly calling each other Gus and Al.

Al—with his pre-knowledge of Mahler's posthumous fame—takes comfort that Gus, in his time, was also the whipping boy of critics.

Well, who can tell? Innaurato may perhaps prove to be as grossly underestimated in his day as Mahler was in his—it's a pretty and, for Innaurato, doubtless comforting thought—but this peg for the play apart, what the playwright has hung on it is modestly entertaining.

For we see the eruption into the Mahler household of Mahler's future wife, Alma Maria Schindler—the sometime composition pupil of Alexander von Zemlinsky—tearing into the complaisant composer like Ibsen's Hilde Wangel spearing Solness in *The Master Builder.*

The formidable Alma—who was eventually to find fame in sequential matrimony!—is a most amusing portrait, and the way she forces Mahler to consult Sigmund Freud (yes—historically—Mahler did go to Freud, although I'm not sure it was for treatment of sexual malfunctioning as here) proves engaging.

Innaurato also has fun—as well as finding a poetic resonance—in a time-warped meeting between himself and his future grandfather as a young man, a scene none the worse for being reminiscent of the movie *Back to the Future.*

The trouble with all this Walter Mittyish wish-fulfillment—which is given a weak ending, by the way—is that it has more than a touch of self-indulgence to it.

Gus and Al seems more of a *jeu d'esprit* than a play. Perhaps Innaurato, having got it out of his system, will be able to return to the more realistic genre of *Gemini* or the symbolic fantasy of *Benno Blimpie* which first made his name.

I hope that Innaurato, unlike Shakespeare, Beethoven and Mahler, is at least feeling a little better now.

> *Clive Barnes, "Walter Mitty in Vienna," in* New York Post, *February 28, 1989.*

FRANK RICH

It's hard to believe that four years have passed since Albert Innaurato, the author of *Gemini* and *The Transfiguration of Benno Blimpie,* last had a new play in New York. As a writer, Mr. Innaurato has an intense operatic voice, by turns comic and sentimental, that lingers in the ear. Even *Coming of Age in SoHo,* his jumbled comedy of 1985, retains a vivid afterlife. Among other distinctive traits, it may be the only play ever to have changed the gender of its protagonist (from female to male) during previews.

Gus and Al, Mr. Innaurato's pleasant new work, is in part a response to the poor reception that greeted *Coming of Age* (a play that was itself, in part, a response to the disappointing Broadway fate of *Passione*). He is hardly the only New York playwright obsessed with his critics. . . . [And Mr. Innaurato] isn't really bitter. The protagonist of his play, a South Philadelphia-bred playwright named Al Innaurato, takes consolation in shopping sprees at Tower Records and a solitary mixed review, from *The New York Times.*

The Gus of *Gus and Al* is another victim of critical disfavor, Gustav Mahler. Through circumstances that shouldn't be examined too seriously, Al travels from Manhattan, 1989, to Vienna, 1901, where he becomes the composer's friend and temporary housemate. Gus is glad to meet Al because he is blocked on his Fifth Symphony and is "surrounded by silly women," including his ambitious sister Justine and his friend and chronicler Natalie Bauer Lechner. Both men's lives are soon complicated further by the intrustions of Alma Schindler, Gus's bride-to-be, and the consultations of Sigmund Freud.

Next to Mr. Innaurato's usual theatrical eruptions, *Gus and Al* is decidedly a chamber piece. The jokes are mild (while sometimes very amusing), the emotions are muted, and the tone is often ruminative. Having just turned 40, Al worries that he is "a preposterous homosexual fat man who has nothing to offer." Mr. Innaurato's play is the story of Al's redemption. The writer finds solace in the past both by taking Gus's inspirational advice and by surviving a *Death in Venice*-like infatuation with a young Italian man whose family name sparks the evening's funniest double-whammy gag.

Though *Gus and Al* lacks dramatic glue and periodically falls into discursive doldrums, it is flecked with sweetly written passages. . . . Al's self-pity isn't self-martyrdom so much as a rueful hypersensitivity to the modern world with which he is perpetually at odds. It's tough for Al to be a playwright in an age in which, as he tells a baffled Gus, "we do Shakespeare with TV actors and break-dancing and rock-and-roll." Mahler has his own problems, not the least of which is his pivotal position in a farcical love triangle whose collisions give the evening its sporadic theatrical shape.

Mr. Innaurato is far less pungent when he moves from his specific characters to general observations about the 20th-century charnel-house horrors that evolved from *fin-de-siècle* Vienna. As usual, his happy ending, in which Al abruptly learns to rise above his own cynicism and "hug life," seems forced and treacly. The platitudes disperse, however briefly, when Al returns home to confront his abusive landlady and his roommate, a runaway laboratory ape known as Kafka. . . .

[The landlady tells] Al upon his return home that "anyone who can put up with an ape and travel through time can't be all bad." Roughly the same tentative sentiments apply to the erratic Mr. Innaurato, who, for a playwright struggling through a mid-career crisis of confidence, is looking pretty good.

> *Frank Rich, "Innaurato Befriends Mahler in 'Gus and Al',"* in *The New York Times, February 28, 1989, p. C17.*

JOHN SIMON

Albert Innaurato's *Gus and Al* is so engaging, so heart-tickling a comedy that you heartily wish it were funnier and more disciplined than it is. The blend of mocking autobiography and freewheeling fantasy makes for a bubbly brew, the truly funny lines (though few) are enchanting, and the comic castigation of a mad world combined with disarming self-deflation makes you want to hug this play even while rapping its knuckles for going slack, self-indulgent, and muzzy too often, and most particularly in its sappy ending.

Al is, of course, the thinly disguised fat author, driven to suicidal despair by the poor reviews for his last play, and further tormented by a shrewish landlady demanding back rent. His two consolations are classical records, notably Mahler—the Gus of the play, a slender composer of opulently thick music—and Kafka, an escaped laboratory ape who believes in Al's talent and has invented a time machine that, instead of helping Al out of this 1989 world forever, temporarily projects him into the somewhat better and certainly more operatic Vienna of 1901, smack into the house of Gustav Mahler, who is trying to recover from the bad reviews of his Fourth while struggling with his Fifth. The household into which the overweight Al bursts like a "fat genie" also includes Gus's sis, Justine, who wants to marry and get away from having to take care of her brother; Natalie Bauer Lechner, Gus's Boswell, who wants to marry the unloving Gus and take care of him; and, eventually, the tempestuous Alma Schindler, who interrupts to woo Gus and wow Al.

Later, at Mahler's summer villa, there is also Dr. Freud to dispense dubious wisdom, and Camillo, a handsome young *Gastarbeiter* from Italy who turns out to have special significance for Al, and (unseen but discussed) Viennese composers of the turn of the century and New York drama critics from after the century, like last week's milk, has turned. The debates on art past and present, the interactions of passions requited and frustrated, have their undeniable charm, if only the wit were less erratic and the construction less wobbly. And if—while I'm wishing—the play weren't so parochial despite its cosmopolitan trappings: Few people not involved in the insanities of New York theater will apprehend, let alone appreciate, Innaurato's finer points.

Yet there is indisputable though intermittent fun here. . . . Not a well-rounded play, this, by any means, despite its rotund hero, but author and audience could do a lot worse in a lean season. (p. 75)

> *John Simon, "Whose Broadway is It, Anyway?" in* New York *Magazine, Vol. 22, No. 11, March 13, 1989, pp. 72, 74-5.*

EDITH OLIVER

Gus, of Albert Innaurato's comedy *Gus and Al* is Gustav Mahler; Al is the dramatist himself, here portrayed as overweight, homosexual, invariably humorous, even when depressed, and still smarting from what he considers the unfavorable critical reception of his recent *Coming of Age in SoHo.* (I remember the reviews as being pretty favorable on that one.) We first meet Al in New York, where he lives with an ape named Kafka, who operates a time machine. The time machine sends Al from the present back to Vienna in 1901, where he meets Mahler, another artist unappreciated in his time, whose music he loves, and with whom he is prepared to share the glooms. He shares more than that. He moves into the Mahler household—with the composer, now stuck on the last movement of his Fifth Symphony, his doting sister Justine, and a doting spinster named Natalie Bauer Lechner, who is writing his biography. Al is happy and comfortable until the dramatic entrance of—well, of course, Alma Schindler, that eminent disturber of peace and comfort, who marries Mahler, making him the first of her clutch of celebrated husbands. The action moves every which way, and the glooms disperse among funny scenes and witty lines, and touching ones, too. There is nothing smart or superficial

about this dramatist; everything is heartfelt. Al meets Dr. Freud, a neighbor, who briefly considers treating him ("Do you have a private income?"), and he also meets Mahler's young gardener, who he realizes is his future grandfather—the affectionate grandfather of his early play *The Transfiguration of Benno Blimpie,* another very personal work. The ending (New York, 1989) is happy.

Gus and Al is loose-limbed and at times is not as dramatic as it might be, but it finds Mr. Innaurato as audacious as ever, his temperament—the bleak lows, the funny highs—still rampant.

> *Edith Oliver, "Zaks Rides Again," in* The New Yorker, *Vol. LXV, No. 4, March 13, 1989, p. 74.*

LAURIE WINER

The critics have not always been kind to Albert Innaurato.

But he is not a playwright temperamentally inclined to let a discussion of his work remain one-sided. In his pseudoautobiographical new play, *Gus and Al,* Mr. Innaurato manages to drag his bad reviews right onto the tiny stage. . . . He is far from crippled by rejection. *Gus and Al* shows him to be in top comic form, writing with a sweetness and an audacity that is unmistakably liberating.

Mr. Innaurato begins by dispensing with the most basic theatrical conventions, such as inventing a new identity for an autobiographical protagonist. The hero in *Gus and Al* is called, oddly enough, Albert Innaurato. He is, even more coincidentally, an overweight, blocked playwright who has trouble reconciling the ambivalent reception to a play called *Coming of Age in SoHo.* And while the real Mr. Innaurato might soothe his woes in the music of Mahler's second symphony (he wrote a play named *Urlicht,* after a song from that symphony), the fictional Al travels back in time to the Vienna of 1901 via a ludicrously low-tech time machine invented by a talking gorilla. There he is hurled through a window into the study of Gustav Mahler, who is composing his fifth symphony and who is—wouldn't you know it—also in a bit of a funk.

Gus and Al, as an eager-to-be-hip Mahler soon dubs them, are roughly the same age (40) and have elicited the same degree of critical scorn from their peers. Once Mahler accepts that the large man who has flown in through his window clutching a bunch of newspapers is in fact a visitor from the future, the two misunderstood artists engage in a duet of dueling bad reviews ('a preposterous fat man with nothing to offer,' goes one nightmare critique for Al) and general commiseration.

If this premise sounds like fun, and it is, Mr. Innaurato uses it to construct a wide-ranging conversation between 19th- and 20th-century (or is it 20th- and 21st-century?) man. The tone remains light, reinforced by the playwright's flow of good jokes. . . . But, as befits the author of *The Transfiguration of Benno Blimpie,* harsh realities are never far beneath the surface.

As it happens, Al arrives in Vienna at a pivotal moment in Gus's love life. Mahler's hard-nosed sister Justine is eager to leave the nest and marry, but not until Gustav, as she calls him, is in the care of a suitable mate. The prime candidate is Natalie Bauer Lechner, the worshipful biographer who is so in love with "the master" that she caresses his discarded towels.

Natalie resents Al's arrival, because he easily wins the master's affections by injecting a little 1989 irreverence into Mahler's slightly stuffy, barely modern universe. But another Mahler fan soon usurps Al's place in Gus's heart—the acid-tongued Alma Schindler. . . . ("Her rudeness is like an aphrodisiac," rhapsodizes Mahler.)

Al becomes a much-abused confidant for just about everyone, including a Mahler neighbor, Dr. Freud, and the assistant to Dr. Freud's gardener.

Alliances shift quickly once the frighteningly aggressive Miss Schindler arrives. Entering Gus and Al's platonic bedchamber late at night, she seduces Gus in the time it takes a cat to blink. Gus is dazzled by her ruthlessness; in their union, Gus and Alma begin to resemble a mini-master race. Those who are not up to snuff—Natalie the spinster and Al the homosexual—will be expelled from the household in the most heartless way.

Alma's verbal assaults transform Natalie from a doormat into a fighter (albeit a losing one), and she and Al join together as perpetual outsiders who have crossed time and space to find communion. Gus, alas, must also come to reject Al and the post-nuclear despair that he ultimately reveals: The composer, after all, is a man of his time and must have his own kind of despair and euphoria.

Such period *Weltschmerz*, such old-fashioned passions require their own special antique diction. So Mr. Innaurato invents a mock decorous language for his Viennese characters. They express the most brazen sentiments in polite sentence constructions. Obviously, Al knows that this is a culture whose niceties soon will come crashing down on its head, but he relishes the chance to speak in genteel circumlocutions. Warming up to the challenge early on, he tells Mahler: "I am not a man [pregnant pause] for the women."

Unfortunately, the playwright does not sail all the way through the evening on such gusts of slyness and invention. Toward the end of his Viennese visit he sinks in the whipped cream of a glib uplift. This conclusion feels forced.

Al and, presumably, the audience are supposed to come away from their visit somehow healed and uplifted. The brush with Mahler puts one in mind of another and truly solacing encounter with a great, long-dead artist—in Stephen Sondheim's *Sunday in the Park With George*. But that musical interlude with a contemporary sculptor spoke from the heart, as it were, to modern malaise, when the blocked artist sang "Move On." *Gus and Al* on the other hand, makes one wonder how deeply Mr. Innaurato believes in the balm he is bringing us from the past. Instead of Mr. Sondheim's moving renunciation of spiritual stasis, Mr. Innaurato lets his hero off the hook with an inexplicable attack of euphoria. . . .

Still, when Natalie urges Al to "walk through the forest blessing life," although she may not have hit on the most cogent way out of *fin de siecle* despair, her blithe spirit is in keeping with the lyricality of Mr. Innaurato's voice at this point in his varied career.

Laurie Winer, "Albert's Excellent Time Trip," in The Wall Street Journal, *March 13, 1989.*

FURTHER READING

McDaniel, Linda E. "Albert Innaurato." *American Playwrights Since 1945: A Guide to Scholarship, Criticism, and Performance,* edited by Philip C. Kolin, Greenwood Press, 1989: 209-16.

Extensive bibliography of Innaurato's works as well as secondary sources.

Merriam, Eve. "Short Plays, Small Musicals." *Broadway Song and Story: Playwrights/Lyricists/Composers Discuss their Hits,* edited by Otis L. Guernsey, Jr., 1985. New York: Dodd, Mead & Co., 1985: 405-13.

Discussion with Terrence McNally, David Mamet, and Innaurato in which the playwrights comment upon their works and the history of theater.

Shirley Jackson

1919-1965

American novelist, short story writer, and nonfiction writer.

Jackson wrote several best-selling novels, but she is usually identified with "The Lottery," a classic short story that established her literary reputation as an author of gothic horror fiction. This frequently anthologized tale of victimization exemplifies the central themes of Jackson's fiction, which include such ordinary yet grotesque realities as prejudice, psychological malaise, loneliness, and cruelty. In works that often contain elements of conventional gothic horror, Jackson chronicles the universal evil underlying human nature. Jackson wrote in a deft, unadorned prose style that contrasts with the veracity of her nihilistic vision; similarly, the charming hamlets which serve as her settings ironically underscore the true malevolence of their inhabitants. Mary Kittredge asserted: "[Jackson's fiction] was the result of an exquisitely sensitive double vision that would have seemed an affliction to a less determined or talented writer. She saw the magic in the mundane, and the evil behind the ordinary. She saw that the line between the cruel and the comedic is sometimes vanishingly narrow."

Born into an affluent family in San Francisco, California, Jackson rebelled against her parents' superficial lifestyles and the restrictions that were placed upon women of her social class, and chose to spend much of her time alone writing in journals. Beginning in early childhood, Jackson claimed to possess psychic abilities and to be acutely aware of the clandestine thoughts and thinly-concealed viciousness of her upper-class community. In her first novel, *The Road through the Wall,* she wrote of a snobbish neighborhood in suburban San Francisco and sketched its moral collapse as a result of prejudice and murder. This work affirmed Jackson's loathing of intolerance and bigotry. A plain, overweight woman, Jackson continually embarrassed her socially conscious mother, and further disgraced her Protestant family by marrying Stanley Edgar Hyman, a left-wing Jew and fellow student from Syracuse University who later became an eminent literary critic.

Following their marriage, the couple moved to the quaint village of North Bennington, Vermont, where Hyman taught English at the town's prestigious college and Jackson began publishing stories in various magazines. The diversity of her popular stories in such periodicals as *The New Yorker, Good Housekeeping, The Hudson Review, Woman's Day,* and *The Yale Review* thwarted the efforts of most critics to neatly categorize her work. After her death, Hyman explained his wife's eclectic work: "Shirley Jackson wrote in a variety of forms and styles because she was, like everyone else, a complex human being, confronting the world in many different roles and moods. She tried to express as much of herself as possible in her work, and to express each aspect as fully and purely as possible." Despite general critical indifference, reviewers cite several enduring characteristics in Jackson's works. By omitting specific mention of such technical aspects as time and place, for example, Jackson shifted her thematic focus to universal human problems. Her style is compared to that of nineteenth-century author Nathaniel Hawthorne, who, like

Jackson, disguised actual motives in rudimentary plotlines and sketched deceptively simple characters who reveal their true natures through gestures and mannerisms. Also as in Hawthorne's fiction, Jackson's works reveal the pressures exerted upon individuals by society. Carol Cleveland maintained: "In Jackson's world, the guilty are not greedy or crazy individuals, but society itself acting collectively and purposely, like a slightly preoccupied lynch mob." This belief is manifested in the short story, "The Lottery," originally published in 1948 in *The New Yorker.*

Invariably regarded as Jackson's most notorious work, "The Lottery" was described by Mary Kittredge as "beautifully imagined, sparely and gracefully written, a one-two punch of a story." On a lovely June morning, the citizens of a tranquil village gather in the town square for an annual drawing. Amidst laughter and gossip, families draw slips of paper from a ballot box until housewife Tessie Hutchinson receives the paper with a black mark on it, and the villagers stone her to death as a ritual sacrifice. The shocking impact of this unanticipated ending is intensified by Jackson's casual, detached narrative and serene setting. After publishing the story, *The New Yorker* received hundreds of letters and telephone calls expressing disgust, consternation, and curiosity, and Jackson herself received letters concerning "The Lottery" up to the time of her death. Many readers asked that Jackson interpret the theme, while some macabre individuals requested directions to the fictional town to observe the event. The latter people, Jackson later noted, embodied the human depravity depicted in her story.

Following "The Lottery," Jackson wrote dozens of stories, refining her emphasis on the need for individual identity in a repressive society. Many of her works have never been collected, but *The Lottery; or, The Adventures of James Harris* compiles several early short stories. Jackson twice received the Edgar Allan Poe Award, first for "Louisa, Please Come Home" in 1961 and again for "The Possibility of Evil" in 1965. The first story revolves around Louisa, a young woman who leaves home on her sister's wedding day, ignoring her family's pleas that she return. After four years, she relents, but has changed so drastically that the family cannot recognize her. Her very identity seems to have disappeared. "The Possibility of Evil" centers upon Adela Strangeworth, an elderly woman who enjoys sending slanderous and erroneous notes to people in her small town, anonymously informing them of their "wickedness."

Jackson was perpetually intrigued with the powers of the mind, and her fiction is replete with psychological insights. Her protagonists are frequently forlorn, socially misfit young women who undergo turbulent passages into adulthood. In Jackson's second novel, *Hangsaman,* seventeen-year-old Natalie Waite mercifully escapes her father's oppression by leaving home to attend college. She does not have the social skills to adjust to the uninhibited environment, however, and so she invents Tony, an imaginary female friend. Tony soon becomes more frightening than friendly, and in a climactic scene, Natalie is forced to choose between reality and her imaginary friend. Many critics viewed Tony as Natalie's *doppelgänger,* regarding Natalie's rejection of her as an imperative step toward maturity and sanity. Jackson's next novel, *The Bird's Nest,* is a psychological study based on a true case of multiple personality. Jackson's protagonist, Elizabeth Richmond, a somber, bland woman who is convinced she is responsible for her mother's death, invents alternate personas as a result of being unable to deal with guilt. With the help of a psychiatrist and an eccentric aunt, Elizabeth gradually regains control of her psyche. Generally regarded as Jackson's wittiest novel, *The Bird's Nest* was lauded for its comic yet compassionate treatment of mental disorder.

Jackson's next work, an apocalyptic, satirical novel titled *The Sundial,* centers upon eleven boorish people who believe that the end of the world is near. Seeking sanctuary in a sprawling gothic estate, they burn the books in the library, irrationally stock the shelves with canned olives and galoshes, play cards, and bicker endlessly. At the novel's conclusion, the group is still waiting for Armageddon. Although Jackson presents the ironic possibility that these narcissists will spawn a new generation, critics generally felt that the repugnance of the characters overwhelmed the book's thematic content. A gothic manor again plays a crucial role in *The Haunting of Hill House.* This work concerns an experimental psychic study held at Hill House, an eerie edifice that is presumed to be haunted. Research participants include Eleanor Vance, a timid, repressed woman with astonishing psychic powers. The other people brought to Hill House are confident and self-centered and soon alienate Eleanor from the only environment in which she was ever comfortable.

Jackson's last novel, *We Have Always Lived in the Castle,*

combines many of her most vital concerns—psychology, isolation, and evil—with a curiosity in black magic. Jackson possessed more than 200 books on the subject and seriously considered herself a witch, as did her friends and family. The resulting ostracism she endured from her community in North Bennington informs *We Have Always Lived in the Castle,* the story of two sisters victimized by their small New England village because of the unsolved mass murder of their family. Although neighbors believe the murder was committed by Constance, the older sister, Constance knows that her psychopathic younger sister Merricat poisoned the family by putting arsenic in the sugar bowl. In return for her sister's protection, Merricat shrouds Constance from the villagers' hostility and from the outside world. When their cousin Charles arrives hoping to collect the family fortune, the sisters' close alliance begins to crumble and Merricat burns down the house in a desperate attempt to kill Charles. After the fire, the neighbors stone the house and its inhabitants, and Charles departs, leaving Merricat and Constance to seek refuge in their burned-out mansion. Here Jackson questions the traditional definition of normality, suggesting that the villagers' violence is deviant behavior, while Merricat's actions are prompted by a psychological disturbance that should evoke sympathy and understanding. *We Have Always Lived in the Castle* was nominated for a National Book Award, and remains Jackson's most critically acclaimed novel.

Following the publication of *We Have Always Lived in the Castle,* Jackson began to suffer from severe mental and health problems. She sensed stronger animosity from the Bennington villagers, a justifiable fear since she had publicly admitted that they were the archetypes for the characters in "The Lottery." Her acute anxiety was aggravated by colitis, asthma, and agoraphobia, and she died of heart failure in 1965. After her death, Hyman published two omnibus volumes of her works, *The Magic of Shirley Jackson* and *Come along With Me.* Both are notable for amassing previously uncollected stories, but *Come along With Me* is especially significant for its title work, a comic novel that remained unfinished at the time of Jackson's death. The protagonist, a recently-widowed woman with a penchant for sorcery, embarks on a new life in the city. Carol Cleveland asserted: "This fragment has humor, verve, an undercurrent of eeriness, an appreciative echo of Flannery O'Connor, and is quite unlike any novel Jackson had yet published. *Come Along with Me* demonstrates that from the beginning to the end of her writing career, Shirley Jackson was at work mixing genres, confounding the expectations of the self-righteous and the placid."

(See also *CLC,* Vol. 11; *Contemporary Authors,* Vols. 1-4, rev. ed.; *Contemporary Authors,* Vols. 25-28 [obituary]; *Contemporary Authors New Revision Series,* Vol. 4; *Dictionary of Literary Biography,* Vol. 6; and *Concise Dictionary of American Literary Biography: The New Consciousness,* 1941-1968.)

PRINCIPAL WORKS

NOVELS

The Road through the Wall   1948
Hangsaman   1951
The Bird's Nest   1954
The Sundial   1958
The Haunting of Hill House   1959
We Have Always Lived in the Castle   1962

SHORT FICTION COLLECTIONS

The Lottery; or, The Adventures of James Harris   1949

NONFICTION

Life among the Savages   1953
Witchcraft of Salem Village   (juvenile)   1956
Raising Demons   1957

OTHER WORKS

The Magic of Shirley Jackson   (short stories and novels)
     1966
Come Along with Me   (short stories, novels, and lectures)
     1968

GRANVILLE HICKS

Shirley Jackson, who died a year ago at the age of forty-five, has never received the appreciation she deserves. I cannot boast that I was one of the few who recognized from the first the power and excellence of her work. I was impressed, as were many other people, by "The Lottery" when it appeared in *The New Yorker* in 1948, and there were other early things that I liked; but then I was thrown off by the many pieces she wrote about her children. . . . Then, pretty much by accident, I read *We Have Always Lived in the Castle* when it was published in 1962, became aware of what I had been missing, and read everything else of hers I could find.

Now there is an omnibus volume, *The Magic of Shirley Jackson,* which has a brief, frank, and poignant preface by her husband, Stanley Edgar Hyman. The book contains a novel, *The Bird's Nest;* both of the volumes made out of the family sketches, *Life Among the Savages* and *Raising Demons,* and eleven short stories, including of course "The Lottery."

I must admit that, although I have revised upward my opinion of the kid stuff, I could do with less of it than we have here. Some of the pieces are extraordinarily funny, hilarious in a classic American way; but in others the humor is labored, some are written to a formula, and two or three are sentimental. At the same time I can only admire the skill with which Miss Jackson managed to convince hundreds of thousands of women that she and her husband, a brilliant literary critic, and their four outrageously precocious children were a typical American family. She was able to make her problems sound like their problems, and appear both funny and soluble. She walked her tightrope with tremendous savoir faire, but I am not sure that she was comfortable on it.

Hyman says that people have been surprised that "the author of her grim and disturbing fiction" should have written "two light-hearted volumes about the spirited doings of our children." "Shirley Jackson," he goes on,

> wrote in a variety of forms and styles because she was, like everyone else, a complex human being, confronting the world in many different roles and moods. She tried to express as much of herself as possible in her work, and to express each aspect as fully and purely as possible.

This is all very well, and I am not going to suggest that Miss Jackson's complexity at times seems schizoid; but I do think that some of the sketches are merely talented potboilers and needn't have been included in this collection.

Among the short stories are two or three funny sketches, such as **"My Life with R. H. Macy,"** but most of them are dominated by Miss Jackson's sharp sense that despair, cruelty, and madness lie just below the surface of life. **"Pillar of Salt," "Renegade,"** and **"Elizabeth"** are all stories of that sort, and in three pages **"Colloquy"** makes a pointed comment on American life. One of the finest is **"Flower Garden,"** in which a better than average small-town housewife abandons her good intentions to follow the racist prejudices of her neighbors. The best is the most famous, **"The Lottery."** By whom is Mrs. Hutchinson stoned to death? By the ordinary people of the town, pleasant people, often good people, who nevertheless turn joyfully to violence and cruelty when the release of the blacker elements of their natures is sanctioned by tradition. (p. 31)

Although it is not my favorite among Miss Jackson's novels, *The Bird's Nest* is a remarkable book, in terms both of insight and technique. It is the story of a girl with four personalities, and what is miraculous is that it never once sounds like a case history. Chapters of objective narrative and description alternate with the observations of Dr. Wright, who is trying to reassemble the fragments of Elizabeth Richmond's character. Wright, not an orthodox psychiatrist, is a mildly pompous eccentric who insists on talking about Elizabeth, Beth, Betsy, and Bess in human terms. The only other character of importance is the girl's—I nearly wrote "girls' "—aunt, Morgen Jones, who contributes much of the humor and the drama of the book. It is she who makes Miss Jackson's point, by saying, after she has accepted Dr. Wright's diagnosis, that she isn't sure but what she has two or three personalities herself.

Well-informed about the views of the Freudians and of other schools of psychology, Miss Jackson was never interested in psychological theories for their own sake but only for the literary use she could make of them. Hyman states the case exactly: "If the source of her images was personal or neurotic, she transformed these images into meaningful general symbols; if she used the resources of supernatural terror, it was to provide metaphors for the all-too-real terrors of the natural." In *The Sundial* a group of people become convinced that the world is coming to an end and that only they are to be saved; what Miss Jackson reveals about these people before she is through with them is a dreadful commentary on humanity in an age of imminent disaster. In *The Haunting of Hill House,* which makes more direct use of conceivably supernatural phenomena than any of the other novels, the first sentence indicates the true character of the book's theme: "No live organism can continue for long to exist sanely under conditions of absolute reality; even larks and katydids are supposed, by some, to dream." Her last novel, *We Have Always Lived in the Castle,* which ought to have been in this collection, shows her at her most skillful, making the not quite credible as real as this typewriter of mine. It also suggests, perhaps a little more ruefully than was customary with Miss Jackson, some desperate truths about mankind.

Miss Jackson was certainly not the first writer to assert that there is evil in everybody, but what might be merely a platitude becomes a great truth because of the depth and consistency of her own feeling about life and because she was so extraordinarily successful in making her readers feel what she felt. She plunges the reader into a world of her creating and leaves him wondering about what he has always believed to be the real world. (pp. 31-2)

Granville Hicks, "The Nightmare in Reality," in Saturday Review, *Vol. XLIX, No. 38, September 17, 1966, pp. 31-2.*

ELIZABETH JANEWAY

> [In] collective killing, the condemned man is taken out to a field and stoned. Everyone has a share in his death; everyone throws a stone. . . . No one has been appointed executioner; the community as a whole does the killing. The stones stand for the community; they are the monument both to its decision and its deed.

> [For] the threat of death hangs over all men and, however disguised it may be, even if it is sometimes forgotten, it affects them all the time and creates in them a need to deflect death on others.

These paragraphs are taken from pages 49 and 50 of *Crowds and Power,* by Elias Canetti. I am willing to bet that the number of people who associate them with Canetti's interesting socio-anthropological study are less than a dozen; and that the number of people who think instead of another piece of writing by another author would run up into the hundreds, if not into the thousands. That piece of writing, of course, is **"The Lottery"** by Shirley Jackson. It was first published, incidentally, in 1948, 12 years before Mr. Canetti's book appeared in the German original, 14 years before it was translated.

A spontaneous dual insight of this sort is becoming less rare than it once was. Fiction and sociology have always tended to range over the same subject matter, but both had for years been largely occupied with realistic minutiae. . . .

[Though] Canetti's paragraphs are thought-provoking and even haunting, Shirley Jackson's story marks its readers like a scar. All that Canetti put into *his* discussion is contained in **"The Lottery"**; and note that it ends as the first stone flies. It makes its effect without having to state a moral about humanity's need to deflect the knowledge of its own death by inflicting death on a victim. That uneasy consciousness is waked in the reader himself by the impact of the story.

"The Lottery" is included in this collection of Miss Jackson's work [*The Magic of Shirley Jackson*], which has been put together by her husband, Stanley Edgar Hyman. Fourteen years and a great deal of fame have not abated its chill one whit. But there are 10 more stories in the first section here to remind us that neither the chill nor the skill of **"The Lottery"** is due to freakish chance. Some, like **"The Tooth"** and **"The Daemon Lover,"** are familiar; some, like **"Renegade"** and **"The Pillar of Salt,"** are less so. But again and again the cold knowledge of what humanity can be, of its old bloody roots, moves behind the casual patterns of modern living. In the midst of life, say these stories, we are in—barbarism.

Three full-length works make up this generous collection, *The Bird's Nest* (which has always been my favorite of Miss Jackson's novels), and two books which could hardly seem more different from it—at first glance. *Life Among the Savages* and *Raising Demons* are both about family life in a small New England town, which is where Shirley Jackson lived with her husband and children until her death last year. They

are discernibly the sort of thing that runs in women's magazines to amuse the readership, but they are still by Shirley Jackson: that irrepressible imagination has got into the familiar genre.

Here is daily life with a professor-husband who bears the faintest castemark of absent-mindedness, with four children, two dogs and a varying number of cats, plus a cast of thousands, as the movies used to say—neighbors, teachers, P.T.A. members, plumbers, movers, repairmen. But this everyday housewifery reads as if one had taken the slightest possible dose of LSD. Everything is a little larger, a little brighter, a little more so. Family conversations are more madly and creatively confused than the average family can achieve.

After a hundred pages it becomes quite plausible that among the family problems, to be dealt with gently but firmly, was a younger daughter's gift for witchcraft. Miss Jackson's ability to enlarge experience is used to heighten it into hilarity; but her comedy walks the knife-edge of farce without tipping over into impossible exaggeration. Her household is not different in kind from millions of others. It's just that the usual processes of inadvertence, complication and improvisation have been carried a bit further than usual.

There are two kinds of fantasists. One sort enlarges the world, the other depletes it. It depends, I think, on where and with what the writer begins: with an idea, or with reality. The process of depletion starts with a rigid metaphor—that the world can profitably be compared to a college campus, for instance—and then cuts its coat to fit its cloth. Since the world by definition is larger than any metaphor, such exercises seem (to me, at any rate) to vitiate its color and variety.

Shirley Jackson's fantasy is of the other sort. She begins with reality and her metaphors and analogies always reach out from a living center. They extend the reader's emotions and insights as well as his logical grasp. In her stories and novels the boundary between the world and the dream shifts and varies; the dreaming leaks through and colors reality. The strange thing about fantasy, we find, is that it is so familiar and so powerful. . . .

The Bird's Nest is a novel based on an actual, and famous, case of multiple personality, but what Miss Jackson makes of it is far from a case history. It's the story of Elizabeth Richmond, which is the name given to the outer appearance of a body that houses four warring spirits, Lizzie, Betsy, Beth and Bess. Their struggle is so agonizing that Lizzie-Elizabeth, who is the public personality, has become little more than a shell for the raging battle inside. Her energy is exhausted. Her fellow workers at the Owensville Museum find her colorless and uninteresting. And then one day she receives a letter—

> 'dear lizzie,' the letter read, 'your fools paradise is over now for good watch out for me lizzie watch out for me and dont do anything bad because i am going to catch you and you will be sorry and dont think i wont know lizzie because i do—dirty thoughts lizzie dirty lizzie.

It is a letter from Betsy, the first overt sign that this second personality has sucked enough strength from her host to be ready to break through. With Betsy's appearance—she shouts obscenities at a neighbor whose only offense is to sing "Mandalay" too often—the whirlwind descends. Poor Elizabeth is tossed like a straw-filled dummy from attitude to attitude.

Her face, her voice, her way of speaking and acting change as the interior contenders for life pull the body back and forth among them. Betsy seizes control and runs away to New York. But Betsy, a powerful, mischievous child who has delighted in teasing Lizzie and tormenting overly sweet Beth, is suddenly confronted with a new peril—Bess emerges from the depths, as hostile to Betsy as the latter has been to her weaker "sisters." Now it is Betsy's turn to fall into the terror of oblivion and the void.

Miss Jackson's great gift is not to create a world of fantasy and terror, but rather to discover the existence of the grotesque in the ordinary world. Dr. Wright, trying to wrestle with Elizabeth's transformations, as Hercules wrestled with the Old Man of the Sea, is a very "ordinary" man. Elizabeth's aunt, Morgen, with whom she lives, is certainly a "character," but a thoroughly down-to-earth one. Betsy's tricks are as funny as they are frightening, and funny in a satisfying and familiar way. Who hasn't wanted to shout obscenities at the friend who is over-ready to entertain? The grotesque is so powerful here just because it takes off from everyday life and constantly returns there until we do not know ourselves quite where we are; until we feel that every day has a little Halloween in it.

Sadness and pleasure join for the reader of this collection, pleasure in the work and sadness at the thought that there will be no more. Let us be thankful that Miss Jackson's energy and fertile talent produced so much in her 46 years. *The Magic of Shirley Jackson* was real and powerful, and its spell abides.

> Elizabeth Janeway, "The Grotesque Around Us," in The New York Times Book Review, *October 9, 1966, p. 58.*

GEOFFREY WOLFF

"It has always been a comfort to me to make stories out of things that happen, things like moving, and kittens, and Christmas concerts at the grade school, and broken bicycles. . . . " This is the chattily domestic assurance of a lady whose most celebrated novel is narrated by an 18-year-old girl who poisoned to death her brother, her aunt, her mummy and her daddy at the age of 12. And whose best-known story is about a harmonious, happy village that each year chooses by lot a townsman to murder with stones.

Yet, *We Have Always Lived in the Castle* and **"The Lottery"** notwithstanding, Shirley Jackson was not being ghoulishly macabre, or even ironic, when she spoke of her comfort in making stories out of things that happen. The occasion for her remark was a lecture called **"Experience and Fiction"** (1958), during which she also said ". . . nothing is ever wasted; all experience is good for something; you tend to see everything as a potential structure of words."

Shirley Jackson's particular genius was to discover the commonplace details that co-exist with poisonous events, and the deadly, supernatural possibilities that agitate the commonplace. Her characteristic manner was to compose a tale of rather ordinary occurences so that it gradually began to radiate menace and corruption. She did this not by writing on several levels—hiding, as Hawthorne often did, her "real" intention—but by permitting a character's psychic life to reveal itself through representative gestures. Her stories seem ingenuous, yet they are impacted, implacably *written*. "Magic" is

a word so commonly abused to modify "style" that it has lost its minted look. But if there is still any excuse to couple the two words, Shirley Jackson's effects provide it. The reader is moved beyond his expectations by some manipulation of his understandings that is complex and artful.

Now, three years after Shirley Jackson's death, her husband, the critic Stanley Edgar Hyman, has edited a collection of her writing [*Come Along With Me*]. Besides the title piece, a lamentably short first section of an unfinished novel, the collection includes 16 stories and three lectures.

Come Along With Me presents samples of Miss Jackson's work from 1938 to 1965. They are invariably about women, and usually about women trying to escape: from their parents or their husbands or the memory of their dead husbands. Typically, the heroine is described after she has run away; her motives for fleeing are lightly sketched or left entirely unrevealed. The story usually concerns itself with how she is affected by the liberation she sought.

In **"A Day in the Jungle"** (1952) a wife has fled her (presumably) ordinary husband to hole up in a hotel, which he locates without difficulty. When he telephones to reason with her, she agrees to meet him for dinner, but insists that for her it shall be no more than one way among many to pass the evening, that she will not return to him. Starting out for the restaurant, she is ". . . very much aware of the fact that for the first time she moved knowingly and of choice through a free world, that of all her life this alone was the day when she had followed a path she made alone . . ."

One paragraph later, as she walks along the street, fear begins to tug at her sleeve:

> The loving concern with which she put her feet down one after another on the sidewalk became without perceptible change, terror—was the cement secure? Down below, perhaps no more than two or three feet below, was the devouring earth, unpredictable and shifty. The sidewalk was set only upon earth, might move under her feet and sink, carrying her down and alone into the wet choking ground, and no one to catch her arm or a corner of her coat and hold her back.
>
> (p. 18)

Although very short, this story does many things. The plot describes a separation and a reconciliation. The underlying "meaning" concerns the danger of freedom from the known. Yet without at all straining for effect or implication, the story manages to substantiate paranoia, to invest objects with supernatural energy.

In **"The Lottery"** (1948) the environment is comforting and fruitful. The village is imagined as the apotheosis of the concept of community. Friendship and trust and good will are everywhere evident. There is solace in the gentle weather, the green trees, the ordered town—a town that must be the ideal of all in this country who would maintain law and order, who would resurrect the old values. Just one thing (often with Miss Jackson it is *just one thing*): to cultivate this paradise the good citizens must ritually sacrifice one of their number every year. This barbarism, too, is carried out in both a democratic and civilized manner. A family, and within that family one person, is chosen by lot.

To be told of **"The Lottery"** is doubtless to suspect it of the worst kind of sham and artifice. To read it is to know that it does not unappropriately join a brutal action to a pastoral setting. The story seems perfectly true. A sense of community is won at a price, and communal guilt and fear are seen as more binding than communal love.

We Have Always Lived in the Castle (1962—not in this volume) is Miss Jackson's most justly famed exploration of the nature of *communitas,* family unity, guilt and inheritance. It is, without qualification, the darkest, most sinister novel I have read. Mary Katherine Blackwood is mad, a murderer, a witch, and a child. Her sister, Constance, is a beautiful girl, 10 years older than "Merricat," teetering between madness and self-understanding. The girl's uncle, Julian, an urbane old man who is the only survivor of Merricat's remarkable crime besides Constance, similarly rocks back and forth from lunacy to wholesome good sense. The three live in a beleaguered old mansion. The townspeople suspect gentle Constance of the crime and are unnaturally cruel to the Blackwoods. A series of quite unbelievable crises end in the death of Uncle Julian, the grotesque mob insanity of the villagers, the partial burning of the house, and the complete self-isolation of the sisters in crazed retreat from a hostile world outside their boarded-up windows.

We Have Always Lived in the Castle forever verges toward Gothic Romance but never surrenders to it. The murder six years before, centerpiece of Merricat's narrative, is understood as at once a parable of supernatural power and a real event, heavy with expected consequence. Magic and witchcraft exist wholly in the mind: The tale does not indulge that impossible mix of the physical and the surreal characteristic of James' *The Turn of the Screw.* Miss Jackson's way, open and straightforward, is much more chilling.

The secret of her art in this novel is her "comfort" in describing "those things that happen." Food is important to the Blackwoods, and gardening, and household neatness and hospitality and good manners and straight talk. It is the perversion of these qualities (poison in the family's sugar) that so unnerves us. The madness is so tangled with the ordinary that we cannot shrug it away or hide from it. The blatant symbols—poison, the garden, the collective will of the community, the inherited house cleaned by fire—are not things and ideas that stand for something other than themselves. Rather they are the life of the novel.

In Freud's lexicon, the dream, or nightmare, is an allegory of hidden motives. In Miss Jackson's great novel, the nightmare lives on the surface, so terrifying because it seems so ordinary.

In none of Miss Jackson's tales that I have read is there an overt suggestion of sexuality. A very early story, **"A Cauliflower in Her Hair"** (1943), hints, in a kind of premonition of *Lolita,* at a father's desire for his young daughter's casual school acquaintance and at the child's sophistication. It is impossible for me to tell whether Miss Jackson's repression of explicit sexuality was a function of personal nicety or aesthetic intention, but it is a strange omission. It is also, intentionally or not, very sexy. One wonders what the 18-year-old murderer looks like, feels like. Physical touch is all Miss Jackson leaves unnamed and unexplored; we are made very alive to its absence. (pp. 18-19)

Come Along With Me would, I presume, have been a very funny novel. It is about a widow who buries her artist husband and moves to a rooming house in a strange city. (Miss Jackson sets many of her stories in rooming houses of strange cities.) Aside from *We Have Always Lived in the Castle,* the unfinished book exhibits Shirley Jackson's best prose. By 1965 she had mastered the kind of nutty-serious dialogue that she had tended toward for a long while. The heroine meets her landlady for the first time and is asked:

> "And what do you do, Mrs. Motorman?"
>
> "I dabble in the supernatural. Traffic with spirits. Seances, messages, psychiatric advice, that kind of thing."

There it is: the casual voice describing, comfortably, as though it were commonplace, the incredible. We hear the voice again in my favorite of Mrs. Motorman's many marvelous lines. "Once an old man followed me, but he turned out to be real." That "but" is astonishing—wonderful—but of course . . . (p. 19)

Geoffrey Wolff, "Shirley Jackson's 'Magic Style'," in The New Leader, *Vol. LI, No. 17, September 9, 1968, pp. 18-19.*

GUY DAVENPORT

It was in plain old clapboard and potted geranium reality that Shirley Jackson recognized the strange discontinuousness of things which she elucidated with such unnerving insight. That the familiar can become alien, that the level flow of existence can warp in the batting of an eye, was the theme to which she most often returned. She liked characters whose minds seemed to be untidy and a touch hysterical, but whose fanatic grasp of reality is in some inexplicable way deeper than we can understand. The motivations she preferred to study were never those of reason nor yet of circumstances nor of passion—but of some dark quality in a psychological weather when the glass is falling and the wind beginning to wrinkle.

Like all splendidly accomplished artists, especially those highly sensitive to human suffering, she began to move her choice theme toward the comic, finding in her peculiar subjects, as with Mozart and Mann, a gaiety born of sharpness of understanding. Thus her last novel [*Come Along With Me*], only 25 pages of which she lived to write, is still about the nonconsecutive universe but is written with abandoned and frivolous hilarity. It is about a widow who suddenly moves to another town, changes her name while mounting a pair of steps, and proceeds to reactivate the extrasensory knack she had as a child and which marriage had shifted. Shirley Jackson's comic sense had always been a rare one; in this unfinished novel she was clearly going to let it have its day.

Stanley Edgar Hyman, the historian of ideas and Shirley Jackson's husband, has gathered [in *Come Along With Me*] sixteen stories, five of them unpublished, and three "lectures" (a word too dull for these lively talks), one of which is an appalling record of the public's response to her famous story, **"The Lottery."**

Of the unpublished stories, the surprise is in **"The Rock,"** a tale so emblematic that the setting (as settings tend to do in Shirley Jackson) carries the meaning, and the characters wander around like ghosts. Mr. Hyman wisely demonstrates the range of Shirley Jackson's imagination in his choice of stories. There are domestic comedies on the one hand and pure fantasies on the other. There are clinical penetrations into madness and senility, and allegories of fairly portentous philosophical weight. Yet everything this author wrote, no matter how innocent the surface, had in it the dignity and plausibility of myth.

Everyone has felt the anthropological echo in **"The Lottery,"** and if we look carefully at her characters and plots we can see how subtly they suggest rites and mysteries. . . . [With Eudora Welty and Flannery O'Connor, Jackson] shared the ability to construct narratives of strictest contemporary reality that nevertheless prove to be transparent of surface, allowing motifs and fables as ancient as our civilization itself to show through.

This last novel, for instance, was clearly to have been about the escape of a captured spirit into a different life that would turn out, as so often before in Shirley Jackson's tales, to be a deeper loneliness but one more tolerable because it is at least in one's own terms and by one's own choice. Only things haunted by our own touch are worth having; our hell is to live with things haunted by another's hands. Shirley Jackson knew better than any writer since Hawthorne the value of haunted things.

> Guy Davenport, "Dark Psychological Weather," in The New York Times Book Review, September 15, 1968, p. 4.

JOHN G. PARKS

"The Possibility of Evil," one of Shirley Jackson's superb stories, provides a key to much of her fiction. It contains many of the elements basic to her work, including a sensitive but narrow female protagonist, a gothic house, economy of language, intimations of something "other" or "more," a free-floating sense of depravity, experiences of dissociation, and a final turn about in events or a judgment.

At seventy-one, Miss Adela Strangeworth, the protagonist of **"The Possibility of Evil,"** lives alone in the house on Pleasant Street built two generations earlier by her family. She is proud of her house—"with its slimness and its washed white look"—and especially proud and protective of the beautiful roses that lined the front of the house. She knows everyone in town, and she loves her town so much that she has never spent more than a day away from it her entire life. In fact, "she sometimes found herself thinking that the town belonged to her." As she goes about her life she wonders about the behavior of her fellow townsmen, and sometimes comments, if not to them, then to herself.

For a year now Miss Strangeworth has been sending little notes to various townspeople, using common colored writing paper and writing with a dull stub pencil in a childish block print. She did not sign her name. "She was fond of doing things exactly right." The notes were cruel, gossipy, and vicious, based on half-truths or on none at all. . . . She was always after the "possible evil lurking nearby," because "as long as evil existed unchecked in the world, it was Miss Strangeworth's duty to keep her town alert to it. . . . There were so many wicked people in the world and only one Strangeworth left in the town. Besides, Miss Strangeworth liked writing her letters." This is her secret contribution to keeping her town sweet and clean, her private war with the forces of evil. After her nap and dinner she takes her evening walk in order to mail the notes she had written that day. She thinks: "There was so much evil in people. Even in a charm-

ing little town like this one, there was still so much evil in people." Preoccupied, she did not notice when one of her letters fell onto the ground. But two teenagers saw it and picked it up; since Miss Strangeworth did not hear them when they called her, they decided to deliver the letter to the address; they thought: "Maybe it's good news for them." Miss Strangeworth awakes the next morning happy that three more people will receive her notes: "Harsh, perhaps, at first, but wickedness was never easily banished, and a clean heart was a scoured heart." But when she opens her own mail that morning she finds a little letter very much like the ones she sends. "She began to cry silently for the wickedness of the world when she read the words: Look Out at What Used to Be Your Roses."

Like many Jackson stories this one has a parable-like quality about it—we do not know where or when the story takes place; we are given just enough information to see the universality of the human problem involved. Even with the undercurrent of comic irony the story is reminiscent of many of Hawthorne's tales, his characters haunted by the idea of a knowledge beyond knowledge and so utterly committed to achieving it that they become perverted in the process, such as Goodman Brown and Ethan Brand. Here, Shirley Jackson summons up one more fierce Puritan who personally takes on the forces of evil. . . . Miss Strangeworth is not aware that her own humanity is corroded by making the struggle against evil her sole reason for living. She is corrupted by her own narcissism. As Lionel Rubinoff observes [in *The Pornography of Power*]: " . . . by pretending to be angels we shall surely become devils. . . . [Because] the possibility of real virtue exists only for a man who has the freedom to choose evil." This freedom Miss Strangeworth cannot and will not give, because she herself holds an evil belief: "a belief that one *cannot do wrong*," to use D. H. Lawrence's remarks about one of Hawthorne's characters. Lawrence concludes: "No men are so evil to-day as the idealists, and no women half so evil as your earnest woman, who feels herself a power for good." Paradoxically, Miss Strangeworth is doing evil in order to further good. Miss Strangeworth reveals the unscrupulosity of the devout, and the only people more unscrupulous than the devout are the frightened, and they are often the same people.

Shirley Jackson reveals a fundamental problem here, one especially crucial in American culture: the revelation of the imagination that sees evil only *out there,* and which thus must be smashed at any cost. Miss Strangeworth does not see that evil is a component within us all that can be transcended only through its recognition and acceptance. . . . Lionel Rubinoff observes: "It is the excessive rationalistic and abstract apocalyptic imagination that defines evil as an object of scorn, or as an incurable disease. The apocalyptic imagination is sober, passive, and detached. It seeks to reduce mystery to rational order. It sits in judgment, protected by certainty, and condemns." This is Miss Strangeworth before she opens her own letter of judgment which may have torn the veil of innocence from her imagination and open her to a reconsideration of "the possibility of evil."

Though she is northern and urban Shirley Jackson is here reminiscent of Flannery O'Connor, who frequently brought a "moment of truth" to her characters, though it usually arrived too late, as in her story "Greenleaf." Writing about her own work Flannery O'Connor said: "St. Cyril of Jerusalem . . . wrote: 'The dragon sits by the side of the road, watching those who pass. Beware lest he devour you. We go to the Father of Souls, but it is necessary to pass by the dragon.' No matter what form the dragon may take, it is of this mysterious passage past him, or into his jaws, that stories of any depth will always be concerned to tell." This aptly describes what Shirley Jackson is doing in her fiction. She brings many of her characters by or into the dragon, or, to change the image, she brings them to the edge of the abyss: some fall, some cling desperately to the edge, and only a few find their way to safety, but such are evil's possibilities. (pp. 320-23)

John G. Parks, " 'The Possibility of Evil': A Key to Shirley Jackson's Fiction," in Studies in Short Fiction, *Vol. 15, No. 3, Summer, 1978, pp. 320-23.*

LYNETTE CARPENTER

[This excerpt was originally presented as a paper at Hofstra University in November, 1982.]

Shirley Jackson's short story, **"The Lottery,"** published in 1948, was responsible for the greatest amount of mail ever received by *The New Yorker* up to that time in response to a piece of fiction. Jackson herself once said, "It was not my first published story, nor my last, but I have been assured over and over that if it had been the only story I ever wrote or published, there would be people who would not forget my name." Now, seventeen years after her death in 1965, an informal survey will indicate that most people remember neither Jackson's name nor the name of her famous story, although most people can, with a little prodding, reconstruct a fairly accurate plot summary out of their memories of high school or college English. Jackson's story has become a part of our educational, and therefore cultural, heritage; her name has been forgotten. And despite her remarkable achievement of both critical acclaim and popular success during her lifetime, she has been virtually ignored by critics and written out of literary history since her death. I would like to suggest that the reasons for this neglect are also reasons for the reevaluation of Shirley Jackson by feminist critics. I will argue that traditional male critics could not, in the end, reconcile genre with gender in Jackson's case; unable to understand how a serious writer of gothic fiction could also be, to all outward appearances, a typical housewife, much less how she could publish housewife humor in *Good Housekeeping,* they dismissed her. Feminist critics, on the other hand, should be able to appreciate the variety of Jackson's writings and the range of her experiences as wife, mother, and Great American Novelist.

To the extent that she is remembered at all, Jackson is remembered for her gothic fiction or psychological thrillers, and one might well contend that writers of gothic fiction have rarely held a secure place in literary history. Worse for Jackson, she was a humorist as well; one of the distinguishing features of her work is a delicate balancing of humor and horror that is bound to make the reader uneasy. In *The Road Through the Wall* (1948), for example, when the comically portrayed thirteen-year-old neighborhood outcast hangs himself, our shock is compounded by our previous guilty participation in laughter at his expense. We may even feel betrayed because the author induced us to laugh at a character she knew to be tragically doomed. A similar situation occurs in *The Haunting of Hill House* (1959), in which the narrative's gentle mockery of the main character does not prepare

us for her suicide at the end. Jackson's habit of mocking the doomed must have seemed to many traditional readers decidedly unfeminine.

Still, perhaps the literary historians would have accepted Jackson had she led the ill-fated life of an Edgar Allan Poe. But she did not conform to stereotype. Married to distinguished critic Stanley Edgar Hyman, she was, by published accounts, a model mother, hostess, PTA activist, cookie baker, and faculty wife. And if, in the end, she fell victim to severe nervous depression, no one considered it madness, since model wives and mothers did not, in those days, go mad. How could such a woman write stories about thirteen-year-old suicides, human sacrifice rituals, twelve-year-old girls who dispatched their families with arsenic? To make matters worse, she called herself a witch.

Historians might know less about Jackson's life had she not published numerous domestic sketches throughout her career, collected in *Life Among the Savages* (1953) and *Raising Demons* (1957). Although Jackson herself never called these sketches autobiographical, most readers take them to be slightly modified accounts of actual events. . . . They are humorous tales in the vein of Jean Kerr and Erma Bombeck about the everyday trials of managing a household and raising children. Stanley Edgar Hyman once wrote that critics did not understand Jackson because they could not reconcile these stories, published in such magazines as *Good Housekeeping, Woman's Day,* and *Woman's Home Companion* with what they considered her more serious work, published in such journals as the *Hudson Review,* the *Yale Review,* and *The New Yorker.* In fact, the sketches display some of the same preoccupations as Jackson's fiction—her interest in the psychology of women and children, her fascination with fantasy worlds and characters, as well as with split or multiple personalities, and her appreciation of irony—but the tone is clearly different. Hyman's comment suggests that since critics were at a loss to explain how one writer could produce both gothic horror and cheerful housewife humor, they gave her up. We might also ask whether writers of domestic sketches have ever been taken seriously as writers. Is it not possible that Jackson's publication of housewife humor in the *Woman's Home Companion* hurt her literary reputation, caused critics, in the last analysis, to reconsider their estimation of her other work? If so, Jackson is overdue for a feminist reevaluation. (pp. 143-44)

In fiction, she writes most often about women. The typical Jackson protagonist is a lonely young woman struggling toward maturity. She is a social misfit, not beautiful enough, charming enough, or articulate enough to get along well with other people, too introverted and awkward. In short, she does not fit any of the feminine stereotypes available to her. She is Harriet Merriam in *The Road Through the Wall* (1948), an overweight teenager who thinks to herself, "You'll always be fat, . . . never pretty, never charming, never dainty," and who may have been the one to murder pink and white, doll-like Caroline Desmond because the little girl was everything Harriet was not. She is Natalie Waite in *Hangsaman* (1951), whose feelings of isolation and alienation during her first few months away at college generate a fantasy other, an imaginary friend. She is Elizabeth Richmond in *The Bird's Nest* (1954), whose adolescent confusion about her mother and her mother's lover splits her at last into a tangle of discrete personalities. She is Eleanor Vance in *The Haunting of Hill House* (1959), whose feelings of rejection and social displacement ultimately lead her to suicide. She is Mary Katherine Blackwood in *We Have Always Lived in the Castle* (1962), who lives with her sister in a state of siege, barricaded against a town's hostility. She is Mrs. Angela Motorman in *Come Along With Me* (unfinished, 1965), whose world has always been peopled by creatures no one else can see. She is even Aunt Fanny in *The Sundial* (1958), whose life of uselessness as a maiden aunt is vindicated by a vision of doomsday.

These women are all victims, and several are clearly victimized by men. Elizabeth Richmond's split personality in *The Bird's Nest* is a result of her mother's neglect, but also of sexual exploitation by her mother's lover. Patriarchs, however, are often the villains. Natalie Waite's father in *Hangsaman* attempts to continue his proprietary control of her intellectual development even after she has gone off to college, just as Aunt Fanny's father presides over her life from beyond the grave by sending her visions of Armageddon. Mary Katherine Blackwood of *We Have Always Lived in the Castle* is the strongest of Jackson's heroines: she retaliates against her tyrannical father by poisoning him, along with most of the rest of her family. Patriarchy is not beside the point in this novel; Mary Katherine's brother, heir to Blackwood male power, gets the most arsenic. The climax of the novel occurs when a male cousin, supported by the men of the town, attempts to assume her father's role as family head and dictator.

Equally interesting to the feminist critic should be Jackson's portrayal of women's relationships to other women, beginning with her portrayal of adolescent friendships in *The Road Through the Wall.* For most of the girls on Pepper Street, allegiances are drawn by intimidation; the most outspoken and audacious girls attract followers, until a tacitly understood hierarchy exists. Overweight Harriet Merriam, however, manages to develop a close friendship with the Jewish outcast Marilyn Perlman, until Mrs. Merriam intervenes. Without someone to share her ostracism, Harriet falls victim to despair. In *The Haunting of Hill House,* the lonely Eleanor Vance becomes infatuated with the beautiful Theodora when both are invited to a haunted house by a psychic investigator. The appearance of a young man introduces rivalry, tension, and cruelty into the relationship, as Eleanor struggles to maintain her favored status with Theodora. Eleanor kills herself when she is sent away and perceives that she is again to be excluded.

But the closest female friendship is that between the sisters, Mary Katherine and Constance Blackwood, in *We Have Always Lived in the Castle.* With all of the family dead from arsenic poisoning except Uncle Julian, who has been left a feeble-minded invalid by the attack, the Blackwood patriarchy has evolved into a matriarchy, and Constance Blackwood is its benign ruler. Mary Katherine, or Merricat, the narrator, says of her older sister, "She was the most precious person in my world, always," and the narrative is punctuated by their declarations of love for each other. Although Constance mothers Merricat, Merricat tries to protect Constance from the townspeople, who believe that Constance was the murderer despite her acquittal. The visit from a male Blackwood cousin signifies more than an attempt to reinstate the Blackwood patriarchy; it is also an attempt to undermine the love between the sisters upon which their matriarchal harmony depends. Cousin Charles tempts Constance with a romantic illusion of heterosexual happiness, a life more natural, in his eyes and in the eyes of the townspeople, than the life she is living with her sister. Merricat fights back and wins. After a cataclysmic confrontation which exposes Cousin Charles' greed and the murderous hostility of the townspeople, and which leaves Uncle Julian dead of a heart attack, the two women resolve to spend the rest of their lives together in isolation, and barricade themselves against intrusion from the outside world. In the final pages of the book, Constance tells her sister, "I am so happy."

The story about the persecution of two women who choose female companionship over heterosexual romance will sound familiar to many readers familiar with feminist writings on witchhunts and witchhunters. The connection is made explicit in the novel: Merricat aspires to be a witch, constantly devising spells and charms, but it is Constance who possesses the wise woman's knowledge of plants and their properties. Jackson herself owned a large collection of works on demonology. In the mid-fifties, she wrote *The Witchcraft of Salem Village* (1956). Yet even earlier, Jackson had established herself as a champion of the persecuted and the oppressed. At Syracuse University in the late thirties, she and Hyman had waged a bitter campaign against racial discrimination in campus housing. Her first novel, *The Road Through the Wall,* portrays discrimination against Jews and Orientals. (pp. 145-47)

Finally, a feminist critic should be better able to piece together Jackson's life and art than a traditional critic. . . . After Betty Friedan's analysis of the pathology of the feminine mystique, or even Erma Bombeck's witty commentary on Supermoms, how can we read a catalogue of Jackson's virtues as wife, mother, and great American writer without wondering how she kept her sanity? She was chauffeur to a family of six (her husband did not drive), PTA mother, Little League supporter, a wonderful cook, an energetic hostess, and a one-time president of the faculty wives' club at Bennington College. But she was also a prolific writer, and wrote every day, taking time out to serve refreshments at regular Thursday night poker games. *We Have Always Lived in the Castle* was written during the early years of Jackson's illness, when she found the company of others increasingly difficult to bear and began to withdraw into seclusion. She created Mary Katherine Blackwood, a narrator all contemporary reviewers labeled mad, shortly before beginning psychiatric treatment for her own anxieties. (p. 147)

When she died of heart failure in 1965, she was working on a new novel, *Come Along with Me*—apparently a "happy book." It was the first Jackson novel to feature a female protagonist close to Jackson's own age. The narrator is a recent widow who buries her husband, sells her house, picks a city at random, and gleefully starts off for a new life under a new name. The book can be seen as a celebration of new beginnings. Ironically for Jackson, however, who had once been assured that her name would not be forgotten, the book marks the end of a distinguished career and the beginning of critical forgetfulness. Writing is the way out. (pp. 147-48)

Lynette Carpenter, "Domestic Comedy, Black Comedy, and Real Life: Shirley Jackson, a Woman Writer," in Faith of a (Woman) Writer, *edited by Alice Kessler-Harris and William McBrien, Greenwood Press, 1988, pp. 143-48.*

JOHN G. PARKS

Mrs. Arnold of Shirley Jackson's story **"Colloquy"** (1944) feels driven to see a psychiatrist because of her confusion and bewilderment over her loss of " 'a world where a lot of people lived too and they all lived together and things went along like that with no fuss.' " The psychiatrist tries to get her to accept "reality," which to him means to accept and adapt to a world with "cultural patterns rapidly disintegrating." Mrs. Arnold refuses to adapt to the doctor's "disoriented world" and leaves his office. But the reader senses that the price for her refusal to accept the doctor's, and the rest of society's, definition of reality will be loneliness and madness. This story is in many ways representative of the concern of most of Jackson's fiction, which is to reveal and chronicle the outrage, at times tempered with laughter, stemming from the violation of the self by a broken world. Through the effective use of gothic conventions Jackson reveals the contours of human madness and loneliness in a disintegrating world generally bereft of the meliorating power of love and forgiveness. (p. 15)

[Very] few of her protagonists achieve much of a victory over oppression. Indeed most of Jackson's protagonists are emotionally violated and must struggle desperately to overcome their estrangement and dislocation, and most of them fail.

Appearing in the same year as her famous story **"The Lottery,"** Jackson's first novel, *The Road Through the Wall* (1948), chronicles the collapse of a small community due to its own inner demonic contradictions. By focusing upon a whole neighborhood, rather than upon a single violated protagonist as in her other novels, the novel creates an effective metaphor or microcosm for the tensions inherent in the culture in the postwar period. Moreover, whether the protagonist is individual or collective, the novel adumbrates and begins exploration of one of Jackson's primary concerns throughout her career: the dark incomprehensible spot or stain upon the human soul and our continuing blindness and, hence, vulnerability to it. Jackson's fiction refuses to compromise with the glib psychologies of our therapeutic age.

The story takes place in Cabrillo, a fictitious suburb of San Francisco, in 1936. It concerns a group of families and single individuals who live side by side in relative privacy and in apparent harmony, a kind of cross section of middle-class and upper-class aspiring families. Their children attend school together and share the street in play. Some of the parents gather weekly for sewing, and less frequently for parties. The apparent security and equilibrium of this community are broken and destroyed by a series of events. The first important event is the tearing down of the wall in order to extend and join Pepper Street with the one beyond the wall. This serves as a kind of catalyst for the rest of the action and the climax of the story. A three-year-old girl is discovered missing from a party at one of the homes, necessitating an all-out search. Missing also is a thirteen-year-old boy who "acted funny." Panic and wild imaginings spread. The little girl is soon found dead, her head smashed in by a rock. The boy is accused of murder, but before anything is found out he hangs himself. The important thing about the novel is not the plot, but, rather, as in most of Shirley Jackson's stories, the gradual unfolding of the layers of human personality, sometimes in response to, other times causative of, events.

The novel operates on two complementary levels. On one level the novel presents an exposure and examination of the social morals and manners of a community. The presence of a Jewish family and the incipient and, at times, outright anti-Semitism of the community, and the hidden envies due to economic differences are instances of this. These are symptomatic of what is going on at a deeper level—the level of the inner workings of the personality, and this is ultimately what the novel is seeking to delineate. The real world of the novel is not the world of social realism. There are enough features about it to indicate otherwise. The way the novel begins gives it the quality of the fairy tale or fable: "The weather falls more gently on some places than on others, the world looks down more paternally on some people. Some spots are proverbially warm, and keep, through falling snow, their untarnished reputations as summer resorts; some people are automatically above suspicion." And the use of the old gothic convention of the old woman making prophecies is further evidence that the novel is not just concerned with social conflicts. Its concern is with the inner demonic cancer of the community and how it eats away and destroys not only individuals, but families and the social unit as a whole. In short, beneath the mask of the ordinary lies unrecognized terror.

The Road through the Wall exemplifies what Irving Malin calls the "new American gothic" [in his book of the same title], in which the psyche is given priority over society, or, in Malin's words, "the disorder of the buried life must be chartered." The new American gothic employs a microcosm, with love as a primary concern. The weakling characters struggle with narcissism which often destroys others as well as themselves. Their narcissism leads them to make reality into a reflecting mirror of their own compulsions. The chief microcosm is the family, which "dramatizes the conflict between private and social worlds, ego and super-ego." In new American gothic, as in old gothic, there is often a confused chronology and dream quality about the narrative. The old conventions of the gothic—the haunted castle or house, the voyage or flight, and the reflection—function now as images of narcissistic love and antagonism. Nearly all journeys end in failure or disaster. The narcissism of the characters intensifies their isolation and loneliness, creating a kind of vicious, self-destructive cycle.

Using the neighborhood as her microcosm, Jackson presents a series of short glimpses into the households on the street—the tangled relationships, the lovelessness which produces its own poison that strangles and chokes off spontaneous life. The youngster accused of murdering the three-year-old girl is a victim of familial lovelessness. The evidence against him is circumstantial at best, but, with few exceptions, the street accepts his guilt. The crime or accident raises the larger issue of human responsibility. The novel depicts a community so fragile and sick that the ultimate responsibility is diffuse and all are implicated, no one is innocent. That few even glimpse this possibility betokens a community bereft of imagination and morally bankrupt.

Against this background of communal failure, Jackson moves in her second novel, *Hangsaman* (1951), into an initiation story tracing the descent into madness of an individual protagonist and her apparent return to a tenuous grasp upon reality. Natalie Waite, a college freshman, spends half her time in an imaginary world where she is being questioned by a detective regarding a murder, leaves family and home for college, and faces loneliness, hostility, and rejection by most of her peers, encounters the duplicity of institutions and adult life, falls into a relationship with a strange girl named Tony, who may herself be wholly imaginary, and comes near to a loss of self through absorption or suicide before finally emerging from the woods, literally as well as figuratively, to a new self-understanding and a new approach to tangible reality.

Natalie does, however, make the frightful transition from innocence of a sort, to experience, to the beginning of adult life. (pp. 16-19)

Natalie needs to escape from the heavy dominance of an egotistical and narcissistic father who seeks to create Natalie in his own image. Her mother has escaped from her dominating husband by fleeing into drink so that she offers no solace to Natalie in her time of need. (p. 19)

Out of desperation and loneliness, Natalie retreats deep into herself and her rich fantasy life. Writing fervently in her secret journal, she dreams of a time when people will fear her and she will be revered and respected. She lives with the feeling that something momentous is about to happen to her. She develops a close relationship with Tony, another despised girl on campus. To Natalie, Tony is exotic, clever, intelligent, and self-possessed. However, it is not clear throughout the novel whether Tony is real or an imagined creation that fulfills Natalie's need. In any case, Tony functions as Natalie's *Doppelgänger,* and as such represents Natalie's own growing fragmentation and self-alienation. Together they read the Tarot cards, and walk about the town like two Alices in a Wonderland of their own making. From the significantly named "Paradise Park," the winter-abandoned recreation area, Tony leads Natalie into the woods for a decisive encounter. If Tony is real, the scene may suggest a homosexual seduction or a kind of vampirism by her dark double, as in some of Poe's stories, or possibly even suicide. As a fantasy projection, the threat is psychic destruction through narcissistic nihilism. In either case, Natalie loses self and retreats from reality. But at the last moment, Natalie repels the dark other's embrace and returns to the school and to a renewed sense of reality. Out of her own inner resources, Natalie is able to repel the threat of her "dark lady" and make a successful, though perilous, passage to the world of experience and the knowledge of good-and-evil.

Shirley Jackson's fiction is filled with lonely, desperate women who reflect the disintegrations of modern life. This is seen quite clearly in Elizabeth Richmond, the disintegrating protagonist of *The Bird's Nest* (1954), Jackson's third novel. She is twenty-three years old when we first meet her in the novel, and lives with her eccentric maiden aunt, Morgen Jones, in an ugly, almost gothic, house. Her mother died when Elizabeth was nineteen, and since that time she has not spoken intimately with anyone; her life has become a virtual blank. She works in the upstairs office of the local museum because her aunt felt the job would give Elizabeth a more definite identity. But when the museum begins to undergo renovation, Elizabeth's precarious hold on reality slips, and she falls prey to a form of "possession" all too common in the modern world. As Rollo May describes it [in *Love and Will*]: "Loneliness and its stepchild, alienation, can become forms of demon possession. Surrendering ourselves to the impersonal daimonic pushes us into an anonymity which is also impersonal; we serve nature's gross purposes on the lowest common denominator, which often means with violence." The violence in which Elizabeth indulges, as her demons come to the surface to haunt her, is a convoluted kind turned against her own fragile self.

While Shirley Jackson was a lifelong student of mental illness, and all of her novels explore some aspect of the inner life, *The Bird's Nest* is doubtless her most overtly psychological novel. She got the idea for the novel in part from reading Morton Prince's 1905 study entitled *The Dissociation of a Personality,* which records the case of a person with several successive personalities. Besides the complex psychic struggles of the patient, Jackson was also struck by the role of the psychiatrist, and how oblivious he appeared to the possibility that the various personalities of his patient might be creations of his own imagination. This same obtuseness is made a part of the character of the novel's Dr. Victor Wright, the rather oddball meta-psychiatrist who patterns himself after Thackeray. This purblind but essentially benevolent doctor treats Elizabeth for two years with the use of hypnosis. When he discovers four competing personalities in Elizabeth, he gives each one a name and sets out to fulfill the godlike role of creating a new person. He definitely likes some of the personalities better than others; indeed, he recoils instinctively from the demonic aspects of Elizabeth's psyche and seeks to destroy them in the name of his self-declared superior judgment and goodness. Despite his benevolence, it is quite clear that the pretentious good doctor is not aware of the implications of his treatment. (pp. 19-21)

Unlike Natalie of *Hangsaman,* who had no adult guides to turn to in her journey, Elizabeth is aided by the eccentric Aunt Morgen, whose quick, but masculine and coarse, wit makes her a perfect foil for the pompous Dr. Wright. It is from Aunt Morgen that Elizabeth learns the truth about her mother's death—Elizabeth was not to blame for it as she had believed. With the release from guilt, Elizabeth is able to make the journey back to wholeness—her four personalities disappear and a new one emerges. At the end the doctor and Morgen assign her a new name, Victoria Morgen, thus making her a product of both their imaginations, an ending not without irony and ambiguity.

The novel, as the first two, employs several features of the gothic. While the gothic mansion is not given much prominence, it is described as an ugly monstrosity well suited to an eccentric maiden aunt. There is the journey or flight from imprisonment when Elizabeth escapes to New York in search of her mother. And there is the reflection when the disintegrating Elizabeth sees her image in all the shiny surfaces of a room, symbolizing her growing schizophrenia and loss of control, and there are the split personalities which were always cropping up in Poe and the vampire novels.

The gothic house is a prominent feature of Jackson's last three novels. It serves not just as the focus of action or as atmosphere, but as a force or influence upon character or a reflection of character. . . . The house not only reflects the insanities of its occupants, but serves as a fitting microcosm of the madnesses of the world.

One is used prominently in *The Sundial* (1958), which employs all the gothic conventions for comic and satiric purposes. (pp. 21-2)

Showing her ability to find pity and terror in the ludicrous and the ludicrous in terror, Jackson created a fantasy of the end of the world which parodies the apocalyptic imagination, while at the same time portraying it. The novel is a full exposition of the poem by William Empson entitled "Just A Smack at Auden," especially this verse:

> Shall we go all wild, boys, waste and make them lend,
> Playing at the child, boys, waiting for the end?
> It has all been filed, boys, history has a trend,
> Each of us enisled, boys, waiting for the end.

At the end of the novel eleven self-elected survivors of the imminent end of the world are all there waiting, with Mrs. Halloran dead and propped up against the sundial on the lawn of the great Halloran estate, the windows and doors battened down from the inside as protection against the growing winds of doom. Some play bridge. Others talk of the realism of a recent movie. A few drink scotch and yawn in anticipation. " 'My,' Mrs. Willow stretched, and sighed. 'It's going to be a long wait,' she said." Indeed it is, for we leave them feeling that they will still be waiting to enter their hoped-for brave new world when the supplies they have stored in the library have been used up. The disconfirmation of apocalypse will doubtless lead only to new "revelations" and to new calculations for their waiting game. No matter, for they have already sealed their doom, which this grisly tale of comic horror and fantasy reveals.

The novel is concerned with the nature of belief, with the way desperate people grasp a belief and make it their truth, with how belief and madness combine, in turn, and lead to more desperate behavior, with how belief can be a form of madness itself, making people into grotesques. Jackson portrays twelve people who become grotesques because they need, and desperately want, to believe in the apocalyptic revelations of the mad spinster Aunt Fanny, who herself is in a desperate contest, a power struggle for control of the massive Halloran estate with the matriarch Mrs. Halloran. Before Mrs. Halloran can gain total control of the estate and carry out her threatened banishments, Aunt Fanny has a "revelation" from her dead father of the impending end of the world. The only survivors, he reveals, will be the residents of the Halloran mansion, who will enter a new and better world. Because everyone else longs to accept the revelations as fact, Mrs. Halloran is forced to concede to their belief and attempts to control a household of people who now regard themselves as a new chosen race.

In preparation for the new day, the Halloran clan burn all the books in the library and stock it with tons of food and supplies, and, remembering Robinson Crusoe, a grindstone, several shotguns, and hunting knives. Mrs. Halloran draws up a list of rules for conduct in the new era, setting herself as the sole monarch. But Mrs. Halloran fails in her attempt to control both present and future, for on the night before the expected new day, she falls or is pushed down the stairs, and her corpse is propped up against the sundial on the lawn.

The insane revelations of Aunt Fanny speak to a sense of loss and of the possibility of recovery that each within the house feels. Each is filled with what one of the characters calls "a kind of unholy, unspeakable longing." It takes over the self: "It is a longing so intense that it creates what it desires, it cannot endure any touch of correction. . . . This longing feeds the need to believe, no matter how bizarre the belief. And yet, at one point in their preparations, Mrs. Halloran remarks: "I wonder what nonsense we would be engaged in, if we were not doing this," to which her courtier, Essex, replies: " 'It is probably just as well that we have some nonsense to occupy us; just think of the harm we could do if we were bored.' " Mrs. Halloran and Essex, on one level at least, still realize that what they are engaged in is a fiction, a masquerade, a game, and can indulge in irony about it. But as they continue to play, the game becomes reality, each player acts in deadly earnest, and they become trapped in their own fiction and lose the capacity to change it. What begins as "harmless nonsense" evolves into a game involving unimagined consequences. The novel satirizes a human condition in which gull-

ibility, cupidity, and culpability reign virtually unrestrained by moral principle, and create a community of the survival of the worst.

In *The Sundial* Shirley Jackson portrays the elitism of the apocalyptic mind that sees only itself as being worthy of survival and salvation. It is an imagination which accepts powerlessness and surrenders human responsibility to what it regards as an overpowering destiny, in the name of which any crime is possible. To the Halloran household the world will end and begin again with itself as the inheritor. (pp. 22-4)

While a setting for what begins as a mad masquerade party in *The Sundial,* the gothic house in a real sense is the chief character of *The Haunting of Hill House* (1959), Jackson's fifth and probably most popular novel. Its presence is felt on nearly every page. The house is over eighty years old and carries the unsavory reputation of death, madness, revenge, and suicide. It is marked by "clashing disharmony," everything off center, made entirely at "wrong angles," all the small aberrations adding up to a rather large distortion. Its basic structure is laid out in concentric circles, with rooms surrounded by other rooms—a "mother house." It is a fitting metaphor for madness, for the irrational, for an illogic that perversely coheres. . . . It is this house which welcomes home the utterly guilt-ridden, lonely, and loveless protagonist, Eleanor Vance, who surrenders willingly to its dark embraces, her own fragile self dissolving and fusing with the substance of Hill House.

Eleanor Vance, another of Jackson's violated women, is brought to Hill House as part of a scientific experiment into psychic phenomena. She is so fragile and vulnerable that her survival is questionable from the beginning. Her chief foil, reminiscent of Dr. Wright of *The Bird's Nest,* is Dr. Montague, a pompous academic representing scientific rationalism and logic. He is little more than an intellectual voyeur, knowing very much, but really understanding very little, especially when it comes to the mysteries of the human personality and the human heart. Terror and fear, the fatuous doctor believes, can be explained and controlled in terms of logic and will: " 'Fear . . . is the relinquishment of logic, the *willing* relinquishment of reasonable patterns. We yield to it or we fight it, but we cannot meet it half way.' " This militant rationalist shows little compassion for Eleanor's loss of sanity and banishes her from the house to protect his so-called experiment.

The character Theodora is another of Jackson's "dark ladies," recalling the figure of Tony in *Hangsaman.* She is the opposite of Eleanor. She is secular and much experienced, exotic and exciting, representing, in part, what Eleanor might have been if her life had not been so restricted and inhibited. At times Theodora's ministrations to Eleanor verge on the lesbian. At other times she ridicules Eleanor, and when Eleanor desperately reaches out for help, Theodora turns away abandoning her to her lonely dissolution. (pp. 24-5)

There is no place in the world for Eleanor. Unlike the Apollonian Dr. Montague, the Dionysian and cynical Theodora, Eleanor has no resources to call upon for survival. Her loneliness and schizophrenia find a welcome in the chaos of Hill House. If Eleanor is abandoned to suicide, the house remains unconquerable, eluding the vain assaults of rationality and pointing to the mysterious and incomprehensible.

The gothic mode serves well Jackson's purpose to explore the depths and contours of female violation in the modern world. Alfred Kazin writes [in his *Bright Book of Life*] that

" 'woman's fiction' exists not as writing by women but as inordinate defensiveness against a society conceived as the special enemy of the sensitive." In Jackson, he says, the stories reveal a pattern of "assault, deception, betrayal," where a woman as victim is the protagonist and her defenselessness is the story. While we may disagree with his assessment of "woman's fiction," his suggested pattern applies well to most of the protagonists of Jackson's novels.

Violation, in the sense of assault, deception, and betrayal, is the concern of Jackson's sixth and last complete novel *We Have Always Lived in the Castle* (1962). Here also, as in so much of Jackson's work, there is a sense of primal sin and darkness pervading a world where forgiveness is lacking, where love is ambiguous, where hatred and hostility are all too ready to surface into action. (pp. 25-6)

For the first time in Jackson's novels, the tale of violation and defenselessness is told by a first-person narrator, the mad eighteen-year-old Merricat Blackwood, who murdered four members of her family with arsenic six years before the story starts. Merricat's older sister, Constance, was accused but acquitted for lack of evidence. For six years they have lived in constant tension with the villagers, who resent the Blackwoods for their wealth and for the fact that a mass murder went unpunished. To Merricat the village is a wasteland filled with gray, drab, and hateful people, while her "castle" is a place of peace, light, and harmony. Constance is a virtual handmaiden of nature, raising and canning fruits and vegetables, and tending flowers all over the estate.

The volatile tension between the lovely pastoral Blackwood home and the hostile, resentful village wasteland breaks into violence soon after cousin Charles Blackwood comes to visit. Ostensibly coming to help Constance, it is clear that he is really after the Blackwood fortune. Merricat senses his threat to their idyllic existence and seeks to purge the estate of his presence. When a fire breaks out, cousin Charles brings in the villagers to help. In a scene of terror reminiscent of Hawthorne's witches' Sabbath in "Young Goodman Brown," the villagers go on a rampage through the house and Merricat and Constance flee to the woods. When they return the next morning their proud mansion is a gutted ruin, but the two women close themselves in to create a new life in the remaining rooms. Some people come to help but are not received. Many of the villagers return at night and leave baskets of food with notes of apology.

The novel closes with the image of a ruin nearly completely covered with vines with two sisters huddled in fragile happiness within it. . . . In a very real sense, the Blackwood sisters are children of nature, though not in perfect harmony with it because of the lingering guilt-burden of the murders. The ruin symbolizes not only their crime, but also the crime of dark retribution perpetrated against them in anarchic passion by the maddened villagers. The real horror of the novel comes not so much from the unpunished murders by a twelve-year-old child, but largely from the inexplicable madness and violence of the so-called normal and ordinary people of the world outside the Blackwood home.

Like her story **"The Lottery,"** *We Have Always Lived in the Castle* has to do with a kind of primordial sense of sin and defilement, which casts an ambiguous character upon love and forgiveness. The novel explores the dark dynamics of a virtually pre-ethical level of human experience—defilement, dread, retribution, revenge. This is the level where evil and

personal suffering are still connected. Fault gives rise to the anticipation of punishment, which strengthens the bond between doing evil and suffering ill. This pre-ethical sense of defilement and vengeance is opposed in the novel by an ethical order of innocent sacrificial love and forgiveness, as seen in the figure of Constance and the world she creates. The villagers, representative of the world, cannot or will not forgive without an act of vengeance or retribution—hence, the mindless outbreak of violence and rage against the helpless Blackwood sisters. Perhaps this violence is somehow necessary; it has its role, its part to play in the mysterious dynamics of forgiveness and atonement. It did lead to a new order of love, though fragile and precarious because the world about it is still uncomprehending and unable to accept a world where forgiveness obviates retribution. Love seeks to bring order out of chaos and strength out of weakness, and perhaps the ruin of the castle will symbolize that, as well as the shame of lovelessness.

Shirley Jackson's gothic fiction is an effective mode for her exploration of the violations of the human self—the aching loneliness, the unendurable guilt, the dissolution and disintegrations, the sinking into madness, the violence and lovelessness. Her fiction fits well the description John Hawkes gives of several modern authors. There is

> a quality of coldness, detachment, ruthless determination to face up to the enormity of ugliness and potential failure with ourselves and in the world about us, and to bring to this exposure a savage or saving comic spirit and the saving beauties of language. The need is to maintain the truth of the fractured picture; to expose, ridicule, attack, but always to create and to throw into new light our potential for violence and absurdity as well as for graceful action.

This applies well to many of Jackson's fictions, especially to *We Have Always Lived in the Castle,* where disorderly or mad love summoned up evil darkness, setting in relief the bright light of forgiveness. . . . In the tales of Shirley Jackson, poetic justice and moral virtue do not win out as in many popular gothics and fairy tales, for she is true to her vision of the evil of our time. And she places her trust in the fact that if a tale is good and powerful, one need not explain or defend it, one need only tell it. (pp. 26-8)

John G. Parks, "Chambers of Yearning: Shirley Jackson's Use of the Gothic," in Twentieth Century Literature, *Vol. 30, No. 1, Spring, 1984, pp. 15-29.*

LYNETTE CARPENTER

When Mary Katherine Blackwood, at the age of twelve, poisoned her family by putting arsenic in the sugar, she was careful not to endanger her sister Constance, whom she calls "the most precious person in my world, always." Now, six years later, with everyone dead but the invalid and feeble-minded Uncle Julian, Constance has become head of the Blackwood family, which consists of Constance, Mary Katherine (affectionately called Merricat by her sister), Uncle Julian, and Jonas the cat. When the events at the beginning of Mary Katherine's narrative take place, they live in seclusion in the Blackwood house, surrounded by extensive Blackwood property, barricaded against the intrusion of the outside world. They might have continued to live contentedly enough, had their neighbors allowed it. But female self-sufficiency, Jackson suggests, specifically women's forceful establishment of power over their own lives, threatens a society in which men hold primary power and leads inevitably to confrontation. (p. 32)

Jackson's last completed novel and a best seller, *We Have Always Lived in the Castle* is her most radical statement on the causes and consequences of female victimization and alienation, a theme that runs throughout her work. The novel may represent a personal culmination for Jackson, who suffered a nervous breakdown shortly after its publication in 1962; her journal from that period records longings for "freedom and security," "self-control," and "refuge" that echo the novel's central concern with the self-determination of women in a safe environment.

When the book opens, masculine authority has already suffered a decisive defeat at the hands of Mary Katherine Blackwood, its narrator (although the identity of the poisoner is not revealed or confirmed until the climactic scene much later): the poisoning has resulted in a transfer of power from Blackwood men to Blackwood women. The motive for the poisoning is not clear at first, but we are given clues in the characterizations of the victims throughout the narrative. Of the men, the most clearly drawn figure is John Blackwood, father of Merricat and Constance and head of the Blackwood family. A redoubtable patriarch, he was a man of property who, as Uncle Julian relates, "took pride in his table, his family, his position in the world." . . . John Blackwood's power in his family and his community derived not only from his gender but also from his material wealth. Six years after his death, Merricat says of the villagers, "I knew they talked about the money hidden in our house, as though it were great heaps of golden coins."

A financial failure, John's brother Julian was dependent on his brother's charity and subject to his authority. In a society that values masculine authority and the accumulation of private wealth and defines that accumulation as a male responsibility and prerogative, Uncle Julian was twice victimized by expectations he could not fulfill. He is perhaps the Blackwood man who most deserved to survive the assault, yet his continuing denial of Merricat's existence serves as a reminder of her former status in the Blackwood family and of her especial invisibility to the Blackwood men. Both legally and symbolically he must be rendered powerless (in/valid) in order to ensure the empowerment of Constance and Merricat. His invalid state no doubt confirms the general belief that financial failure for men leads to powerlessness, dependency, emasculation. The heir to the Blackwood money and property was ten-year-old Thomas, Constance and Merricat's younger brother, who, according to Uncle Julian, "possessed many of his father's more forceful traits of character." It was no accident that Thomas used the most sugar. (pp. 32-3)

[Constance and Merricat's mother] emerges as the primary keeper of the Blackwood possessions, a woman obsessively tidy and aloof. Her snobbery, inherited by her daughters, later ensures their seclusion: "Our mother disliked the sight of anyone who wanted to, walking past our front door, and when our father brought her to live in the Blackwood house, one of the first things he had to do was close off the path and fence in the entire Blackwood property." Like Blackwood wives before her, she added her share of material goods to the Blackwood family wealth. But in one important respect she broke with the tradition of the Blackwood women: she was a bad cook. . . . To the visiting Mrs. Wright's question about Mrs. Blackwood's cooking, Uncle Julian replies with a shudder, "I personally preferred to chance the arsenic." Mrs. Blackwood's indifference to the kitchen and garden not only sets her apart from her daughters but violates the creative tradition of the Blackwood women, whose accumulated preserves Merricat calls "a poem."

Functioning as the family preservers, the Blackwood women, cleaners and dusters of Blackwood property, lavished attention on a different kind of preserves, burying the fruits of their creative labor beneath the accumulated wealth of their dowries and other Blackwood acquisitions. What property they brought to the Blackwood house became Blackwood property, by law or tradition passed from father to son rather than from mother to daughter, as Merricat suggests by her comment on the Rochester house: "Our mother had been born there and by rights it should have belonged to Constance." While her daughters appear to value objects as artifacts from the domestic history of the Blackwood women (a respect they do not afford masculine possessions), Mrs. Blackwood deviated from her female predecessors and from her daughters in valuing the objects over the foodstuffs, the teacups over the tea itself. This attitude aligns her with the Blackwood men, whose highest regard is reserved for money, a thing of no intrinsic value. Obsessed with the preservation of order in her drawing room, she had not allowed her daughters to enjoy its beauty, making it a monument to Blackwood physical wealth and spiritual dessication.

The Blackwood family exploited its women if they were docile and dismissed them if they were not. Mary Katherine, the middle child who was neither a useful daughter nor a male heir, had no appropriate function in the family and was frequently dismissed from its presence for her rebellion against its laws. On the day of the poisoning she had been sent to her room without supper, as Constance reports with a smile: "Merricat was always in disgrace. I used to go up the back stairs with a tray of dinner for her after my father had left the dining room. She was a wicked, disobedient child." Constance's reminiscence suggests whom Merricat disobeyed, whose will she opposed. Six years after the fall of the Blackwood patriarch, she is still being dismissed by the surviving male member of her family, Uncle Julian, who insists that she is dead.

Merricat's raging rebellion, culminating in her overthrow of the Blackwood patriarchy, established Constance as the head of the Blackwood family and the sisters' mutual affection as its binding force. At first glance, theirs may appear to be a relationship between opposites—Constance, the domestic, traditional, even unimaginative one, and Merricat, the unrestrained, creative, imaginative one. Yet Merricat's self-imposed rules and her insistence on routine reveal an obsession with order, just as Constance's skill at growing and preparing food reveals her creativity. Although Merricat's rules do not allow her to prepare food, she helps Constance in the kitchen and garden. Merricat's knowledge of poisonous plants, upon which she bases much of her claim to magical power, comes from Constance.

This shared knowledge, passed from sister to sister, is only one manifestation of a deeper bond between the two women, a bond that has ultimately united them against the Blackwood patriarchal power structure. Constance herself had been a victim of that structure; as elder daughter, she was the unpaid, unrecognized family servant. The smile with which she reports her sister's disobedience suggests her sympathy.

In revealing deadly secrets to Merricat, Constance empowered her sister to use them and therefore shares responsibility for the deaths that followed. Yet her complicity was more direct, according to the account Uncle Julian gives Mrs. Wright: "It was Constance who saw them dying around her like flies—I do beg your pardon—and never called a doctor until it was too late. She washed the sugar bowl." Constance herself purchased the arsenic—"to kill rats," she explains, with another smile for Merricat. The general belief that Constance was the poisoner both underscores Merricat's invisibility to a society that has no place for her and points to Constance's actual guilt. She not only protected her sister by destroying evidence; she aided her by waiting to call the doctor. (pp. 33-4)

Having vanquished one patriarchy, the women are confronted with another in the form of a village controlled by men, by other fathers. Although Constance has been acquitted of murder, the two women must remain vigilant against the encroachment of hostile villagers. Merricat explains, "The people of the village have always hated us," but the sisters are more vulnerable now that they no longer have the protection of the Blackwood men; the town's hostility has become overt, expressed, active. The original source of that hostility was the Blackwood economic and social self-sufficiency, a self-sufficiency underscored by the Blackwood sisters' survival. Villager Jim Donell complains of "the way they live up in their fine old private estate, with their fences and their private path and their stylish way of living." That this conflict can now be viewed in terms of sexual politics is suggested by Merricat's description of the village power structure: "In this village the men stayed young and did the gossiping and the women aged with grey evil weariness and stood silently waiting for the men to get up and come home." In such a society, the Blackwood wealth might be an affront, but Blackwood wealth in the hands of women is a travesty. Initially, the village women in general are silent, weary noncombatants in the struggle between the male villagers and the Blackwood sisters. . . .

The parallel between a witchhunt and the attempt to purge the village of the Blackwood sisters is suggested first by Merricat's own experiments with magic. When she tells us in the third sentence of her narrative, "I have often thought that with any luck at all I could have been born a werewolf," she expresses a longing for power that is one of her chief characteristics. Her magic words and charms constitute attempts to gain power over a world in which, first as the second girl child in a patriarchal family and then as a grown woman in a patriarchal society, she is essentially powerless. . . . With any luck at all, Merricat could have been a "real" witch, but her magic is largely ineffectual. What power she has derives from the knowledge she has gained from Constance about plants and their properties. This knowledge links Constance with the countless women healers of the past who were persecuted and executed as witches. (p. 34)

Jackson, whose works include *The Witchcraft of Salem Village* (1956), owned an extensive collection on witchcraft and demonology. She would certainly have known the major sources, including the now infamous *Malleus Maleficarum* (1486), or Hammer of Witches, used for over 200 years as a guide to the identification and punishment of witches. Its authors' fear of female power is particularly evident in their attention to the threat of actual or perceived castration. These anxieties about male sexual impotence suggest anxieties about male political impotence as well. The Church fathers were threatened by female indomitability and by the followers attracted by women who lived outside the regime of the Church and the familial social unit it controlled.

Thus, significantly, Merricat and Constance are seen as witches because they choose to live outside the boundaries of patriarchal society, because they choose to live with women rather than with men, and because they have challenged masculine power directly by the poisoning. The invalid Uncle Julian survives as a reminder to the patriarchal village of the two women's choice and of their ability to act on that choice. Their only other male companion, the black cat Jonas, completes the popular image of two witch sisters with their feline consort, the Devil in disguise.

If the primary source of the village's hostility is not simply Blackwood self-sufficiency but female self-sufficiency, then the most logical attack would be an undermining of the relationship between the two women. In fact, the beginning of the final assault on the Blackwood women is marked by a visit from Helen Clarke, who, as self-proclaimed friend of Constance, bears a revealing message to her, "It's spring, you're young, you're lovely, you have a right to be happy. Come back into the world." Several unspoken premises lie behind this piece of advice, not the least ludicrous of which is the assumption that the world, or in this case the village, could make Constance happy. Of course, Helen Clarke also assumes that Constance is not happy living with her sister, indeed could not be happy living with a woman when she is young and lovely enough to attract a man. Ultimately, she tempts Constance with the illusion of romantic happiness upon which the continuation of masculine dominance so heavily depends, and Constance is tempted because she forgets or discounts her own past experience. Her choice and Merricat's of celibacy or homosexuality (the latter an option made less explicit here than in other Jackson novels), their replacement of heterosexual romance with sisterhood as their central emotional bond, makes them less vulnerable to sexual coercion by men and keeps their fortunes out of men's hands. Constance's marriage would not only disrupt the relationship between the sisters but would also bring them and their wealth back into the realm of masculine control and restore patrilineal inheritance. That a woman initiates the assault suggests the degree to which village women have come to collude with men in the perpetuation of women's oppression.

Helen Clarke's visit prepares the way for the arrival of Cousin Charles Blackwood, Merricat's archrival, who aspires to be the new Blackwood patriarch, a pretender both to family position and to the family fortune. Appropriately, as Constance tells Merricat, "he looks like Father"; his face exposes him to Merricat as "one of the bad ones." Charles is the son of Arthur, the only Blackwood to be more acquisitive and less generous than Constance and Merricat's father. And he immediately begins to acquire things: Father's room, Father's place at the table, Father's gold watch chain, Father's clothes. If, as Merricat tells Constance, "Charles is a ghost," she recognizes immediately whose ghost he is. His presence causes a series of confrontations between the values of the Blackwood women and the values of the Blackwood men. . . . Having dismissed Uncle Julian as inconsequential, he attempts to enlist the sympathies of the only other male member of the household, Jonas.

The village men, who have always hated Blackwoods before, form an alliance with Charles because he embodies their means of destroying the Blackwood women. . . . The men's acceptance of Charles is a recognition that his family name is not as important as his gender. Their friendship signals approval of his plan to restore Blackwood wealth to masculine control.

To Merricat's horror, Charles' campaign begins to succeed, and the relationship between the two sisters changes:

> She [Constance] was increasingly cross with me when I wanted Charles to leave; always before Constance had listened and smiled and only been angry when Jonas and I had been wicked but now she frowned at me often, as though I somehow looked different to her.

To masculine eyes, Merricat does look different—not imaginative, independent, and interesting, but eccentric, rebellious, and dangerous. Under Charles' influence, Constance experiences shifts in vision and begins to talk and act strangely:

> "We should have been living like other people. You should . . . " She stopped and waved her hands helplessly. "You should have boy friends," she said finally, and then began to laugh because she sounded funny even to herself.

Besieged by Charles, Constance takes on maternal guilt for depriving her sister of a "normal" life, while recognizing that her sister would find, indeed has found, a "normal" life intolerable. (pp. 34-5)

Merricat's stubborn resistance to Charles leads to a cataclysmic confrontation between the forces of the male power structure and the forces of female self-sufficiency. The scene is richly symbolic. Still seething because of Charles' attempt to assert a fatherly authority over her, Merricat discovers a family heirloom, a saucer from her great-grandmother's dowry, being used as an ashtray in her father's bedroom, now Charles' room. She says, "I brushed the saucer and the pipe off the table into the wastebasket and they fell softly onto the newspapers he had brought into the house." Her act literally sparks a conflagration as two symbols of masculinity, the pipe and the newspaper, begin to burn.

That Merricat herself starts the fire complicates the symbolic reading of this scene as a witch burning. It is the only point in Jackson's novel when the reader is asked to believe that Merricat's perceptions are limited, inadequate. She does not seem to be aware of what she has done. From her perspective, she has disposed of Charles' pipe and newspapers, which in turn have started a fire; they are to blame, not she. The sentence following her description of her actions reads, "I was wondering about my eyes; one of my eyes—the left—saw everything golden and yellow and orange, and the other saw shades of blue and grey and green." Although the reader might suspect that Merricat is intelligent enough to know a fire when she sees one, she does not clarify the passage by identifying what she saw. When Charles and Constance later smell smoke and Constance remembers Charles' pipe, Merricat responds, "Would it start a fire?", suggesting that she is not aware of the situation, unless her true motive is to disrupt Charles' relationship with Constance by blaming him. Yet, although she might wish to destroy Charles' (and her father's) room, she could hardly wish to destroy the house that she and Constance love so dearly, again unless she believes the sacrifice necessary to repudiate the material heritage of the Blackwood men and to exorcise her father's ghost.

The fire brings the villagers and the fire fighters; Jim Donell, the village spokesman and Merricat's greatest enemy next to Charles, is their chief. The firemen put out the fire, despite one woman's exhortations to "let it burn." His duty done, however, Jim Donell carefully removes his fire hat and leads an assault on the house. . . . The mob stones the house as an extension of the two women who live in it and strongly identify with it. The scene recalls other stonings, including the ancient practice of stoning witches and the fictional stoning in Jackson's own fable about a sacrifice ritual, **"The Lottery."** The villagers attempt to destroy the women by destroying the house, focusing their energies on the drawing room and the kitchen, special domains of the Blackwood women; they leave Charles to struggle with the family safe, protector of the monetary legacy of the Blackwood men. Their rage is directed at those objects most precious to Constance and Merricat, the dishes and silverware contributed by Blackwood grandmothers, great-grandmothers, aunts, and great-aunts, and at the foodstuffs that Constance holds sacred. Adding insult to injury, they leave the house a mess when it has only just been tidied, a severe blow to Constance. They verbally abuse and physically threaten the two sisters, who are saved, ironically, by Uncle Julian's death. The crowd leaves not out of respect for the sisters but out of respect for Uncle Julian, whom they perceive to have been the sisters' last surviving victim. Defeated, Charles leaves as well.

The confrontation of the fire scene is necessary to prove to Constance what Merricat has always believed—that heterosexual romance is a dangerous illusion, that patriarchy is an inherently destructive institution, and that no compromise is possible. Just as Constance has always felt a responsibility to take care of Merricat, to be a kind of mother to her, so Merricat has always felt a responsibility to protect Constance from an outside world her sister has not clearly understood, a world of hatred and violence. To Merricat, the overthrow of the Blackwood patriarchy six years before had been an act not merely of vengeance but of self-preservation; banished from the family's presence one too many times, she was in very real danger of disappearing altogether. Now, with renewed conviction, Constance and Merricat turn their backs on the outside world, barricading themselves inside the ruined house. There are no more compromises: they do not answer the voices that call to them; they do not allow Helen Clarke in for tea. Dishes and silverware have been broken or bent in the onslaught, sugar has been spilt, but the preserves of the Blackwood women stand undisturbed in the cellar, emblems of the sisters' survival. Ironically, they also retain possession of the safe, a bitter reminder to Charles and the villagers that their survival constitutes a victory not only in their own terms but also in those of the village men.

When the offerings of food begin to arrive from the villagers, the accompanying notes express regret and shame for individual acts of destruction, but the scene evokes other scenes of ritualistic food offerings to ancient deities. Fear seems a more likely motive than genuine regret, especially as tales about the house and its two invisible occupants spread throughout the village. Women speak in hushed voices on the front lawn and frighten their children with stories of the sisters' penchant for eating little girls and boys. The sisters' perceived power has grown since the fire: after all, they are two witches who have survived a burning and a stoning.

At the same time, the food offerings establish a new relationship between the Blackwood women and the women of the village, perhaps recalling that deities can be simultaneously loved and feared. In this matter, the village women seem able to assert themselves, as the sisters imagine: "We thought that the men came home from work and the women had the baskets ready for them to carry over." . . . The sisters come to know the village women by their distinctive culinary traits, and the food becomes a means of communication, its careful preparation a sign that the women feel more than fear toward the rebellious Blackwood sisters.

Readers and critics have struggled to explain the effect that *We Have Always Lived in the Castle* has on them. . . . [Many] express discomfort at being made to identify with a madwoman, but is Merricat mad? If paranoia depends upon delusion, Merricat is not paranoid because the hostility she perceives in the villagers is real. Like most of Jackson's protagonists, she seems young for her age, but immaturity is not madness.

Perhaps the aspect of Merricat's character that is most difficult to accept, however, is the violence. Early in the book, the violence of Merricat's fantasies is horrifying; while confronting hostile villagers in the grocery store, she says, "I would have liked to come into the grocery some morning and see them all, even the Elberts and the children, lying there crying with the pain and dying." The villagers' hostility, although misdirected if they believe the poisoner to be Constance and not Merricat, might at first seem a justifiable response to a daughter's particularly cruel murder of four members of her family. Readers' sympathy with Merricat remains uneasy, even though they may feel, as Stuart Woodruff has suggested, that "parricide on such a scale is certainly regrettable, but the real horror in Miss Jackson's novel originates elsewhere" [see Jackson's entry in *CLC*, Vol. 11]. Yet the villagers' own violence invalidates once and for all their moral judgment of the sisters and indicates that the poisoning is only one violent action in a world where violence threatens to erupt at any moment, a world familiar to readers of Jackson's fiction. Thus Merricat's belief that she is literally embattled is confirmed, and her rage against the villagers is justified. Within the context of feminist psychology, rage is the most appropriate response to oppression. In Jackson's time as now, it was also the most dangerous, the most likely to be labeled madness and treated by institutionalization.

Merricat's rage against her family and the murders that resulted from it are less justifiable on the basis of the scant information her narrative provides; apart from sketchy descriptions of the victims and their treatment of Merricat, the reader has only Constance's word that "those people deserved to die." Because the danger to Merricat in this case seems to be one of psychological or emotional violence rather than physical violence, many readers feel uncomfortable with her response. Ihab Hassan has written that the novel addresses "the human ambivalences of guilt and atonement, love and hate, health and psychosis." By identifying Charles with Father and with the villagers, Jackson relates physical and psychological violence; both can destroy human beings. (pp. 35-7)

Lynette Carpenter, "The Establishment and Preservation of Female Power in Shirley Jackson's 'We Have Always Lived in the Castle'," in Frontiers: A Journal of Women Studies, *Vol. VIII, No. 1, 1984, pp. 32-8.*

PETER KOSENKO

In her critical biography of Shirley Jackson, Lenemaja Friedman notes that when Jackson's story **"The Lottery"** was published in the June 26, 1948 issue of the *New Yorker* it received a response that "no *New Yorker* story had ever received": hundreds of letters poured in that were characterized by "bewilderment, speculation, and old-fashioned abuse." It is not hard to account for this response: Jackson's story portrays an "average" New England village with "average" citizens engaged in a deadly rite, the annual selection of a sacrificial victim by means of a public lottery, and does so quite deviously: not until well along in the story do we suspect that the "winner" will be stoned to death by the rest of the villagers. One can imagine the average reader of Jackson's story protesting: but we engage in no such inhuman practices. Why are you accusing us of *this*?

Admittedly, this response was not exactly the one that Jackson had hoped for. In the July 22, 1948 issue of the *San Francisco Chronicle* she broke down and said the following in response to persistent queries from her readers about her intentions: "Explaining just what I had hoped the story to say is very difficult. I suppose, I hoped, by setting a particularly brutal ancient rite in the present and in my own village to shock the story's readers with a graphic dramatization of the pointless violence and general inhumanity in their own lives." Shock them she did, but probably owing to the symbolic complexity of her tale, they responded defensively and were not enlightened. (p. 27)

A survey of what little has been written about **"The Lottery"** reveals two general critical attitudes: first, that it is about man's ineradicable primitive aggressivity, . . . ; second, that it describes man's victimization by, in Helen Nebeker's words, "unexamined and unchanging traditions which he could easily change if he only realized their implications" [See Jackson's entry in *CLC*, Vol. 11]. Missing from both of these approaches, however, is a careful analysis of the abundance of social detail that links the lottery to the ordinary social practices of the village. No mere "irrational" tradition, the lottery is an *ideological mechanism*. It serves to reinforce the village's hierarchical social order by instilling the villagers with an unconscious fear that if they resist this order they might be selected in the next lottery. In the process of creating this fear, it also reproduces the ideology necessary for the smooth functioning of that social order, despite its inherent inequities. What is surprising in the work of an author who has never been identified as a Marxist is that this social order and ideology are essentially capitalist.

I think we need to take seriously Shirley Jackson's suggestion that the world of the lottery is her reader's world, however reduced in scale for the sake of economy. The village in which the lottery takes place has a bank, a post office, a grocery store, a coal business, a school system; its women are housewives rather than field workers or writers; and its men talk of "tractors and taxes." More importantly, however, the village exhibits the same socio-economic stratification that most people take for granted in a modern, capitalist society.

Let me begin by describing the top of the social ladder and save the lower rungs for later. The village's most powerful man, Mr. Summers, owns the village's largest business (a coal concern) and is also its mayor, since he has, Jackson writes, more "time and energy [read money and leisure] to devote to civic activities" than others. (Summers' very name suggests that he has become a man of leisure through his wealth.) Next in line in the social hierarchy is Mr. Graves, the village's second most powerful government official—its postmaster. (His name may suggest the gravity of officialism.) And beneath Mr. Graves is Mr. Martin, who has the economically advantageous position of being the grocer in a village of three hundred.

These three most powerful men who control the town, economically as well as politically, also happen to administer the lottery. Mr. Summers is its official, sworn in yearly by Mr. Graves. Mr. Graves helps Mr. Summers make up the lottery slips. And Mr. Martin steadies the lottery box as the slips are stirred. (pp. 27-8)

However important Mr. Graves and Mr. Martin may be, Mr. Summers is still the most powerful man in town. Here we have to ask a Marxist question: what relationship is there between his interests as the town's wealthiest businessman and his officiating the lottery? That such a relationship does exist is suggested by one of the most revealing lines of the text. When Bill Hutchinson forces his wife, Tessie, to open her lottery slip to the crowd, Jackson writes, "It had a black spot on it, the black spot Mr. Summers had made the night before with [a] heavy pencil in [his] coal-company office." At the very moment when the lottery's victim is revealed, Jackson appends a subordinate clause in which we see the blackness (evil) of Mr. Summers' (coal) business being transferred to the black dot on the lottery slip. At one level at least, evil in Jackson's text is linked to a disorder, promoted by capitalism, in the material organization of modern society. But it still remains to be explained *how* the evil of the lottery is tied to this disorder of capitalist social organization.

Let me sketch the five major points of my answer to this question. First, the lottery's rules of participation reflect and *codify* a rigid social hierarchy based upon an inequitable social division of labor. Second, the fact that everyone participates in the lottery and understands *consciously* that its outcome is pure chance gives it a certain "democratic" aura that obscures its first codifying function. Third, the villagers believe *unconsciously* that their commitment to a work ethic will grant them some magical immunity from selection. Fourth, this work ethic prevents them from understanding that the lottery's actual function is not to encourage work *per se* but to reinforce an inequitable social *division* of labor. Finally, after working through these points, it will be easier to explain how Jackson's choice of Tessie Hutchinson as the lottery's victim/scapegoat reveals the lottery to be an ideological mechanism which serves to defuse the average villager's deep, inarticulate dissatisfaction with the social order in which he lives by channeling it into anger directed at the *victims* of that social order. It is reenacted year after year, then, not because it is a mere "tradition," as Helen Nebeker argues, but because it serves the repressive ideological function of purging the social body of all resistance so that business (capitalism) can go on as usual and the Summers, the Graves and the Martins can remain in power.

Implicit in the first and second points above is a distinction between universal participation in the lottery and what I have called its *rules* of participation. The first of these rules I have already explained, of course: those who control the village economically and politically also administer the lottery. The remaining rules also tell us much about who has and who doesn't have power in the village's social hierarchy. These remaining rules determine who gets to choose slips in the lot-

tery's first, second and third rounds. Before the lottery, lists are "[made] up of heads of families [who choose in the first round], heads of households [who choose in the second round], [and] members of each household in each family [who choose in the last round]." The second round is missing from the story because the family patriarch who selects the dot in the first round—Bill Huchinson—has no married male offspring. When her family is chosen in the first round, Tessie Hutchinson objects that her daughter and son-in-law didn't "take their chance." Mr. Summers has to remind her, "Daughters draw with their husbands' families." Power in the village, then, is exclusively consolidated into the hands of male heads of families and households. Women are disenfranchised.

Although patriarchy is not a product of capitalism *per se,* patriarchy in the village does have its capitalist dimension. (New social formations adapt old traditions to their own needs.) Women in the village seem to be disenfranchised because male heads of households, as men in the work force, provide the link between the broader economy of the village and the economy of the household. (pp. 28-9)

[Women] have a distinctly subordinate position in the socioeconomic hierarchy of the village. They make their first appearance "wearing faded house dresses . . . [and walking] shortly after their menfolk." Their dresses indicate that they do in fact work, but because they work in the home and not within a larger economy in which work is regulated by finance (money), they are treated by men and treat themselves as inferior. When Tessie Hutchinson appears late to the lottery, other men address her husband Bill, "Here comes your Missus, Hutchinson." None of the men, that is to say, thinks of addressing Tessie first, since she "belongs" to Bill. Most women in the village take this patriarchal definition of their role for granted, as Mrs. Dunbar's and Mrs. Delacroix's references to their husbands as their "old [men]" suggest. Tessie, as we shall see later, is the only one who rebels against male domination, although only unconsciously. (p. 29)

On its surface, the idea of a lottery in which everyone, as Mrs. Graves says, "[takes] the same chance" seems eminently democratic, even if its effect, the singling out of one person for privilege or attack, is not.

One critic, noting an ambiguity at the story's beginning, has remarked that "the lottery . . . suggests 'election' rather than selection," since "the [villagers] assemble in the center of the place, in the village square." I would like to push the analogy further. In capitalist dominated elections, business supports and promotes candidates who will be more or less atuned to its interests, multiplying its vote through campaign financing, while each individual businessman can continue to claim that he has but one vote. In the lottery, analogously, the village ruling class participates in order to convince others (and perhaps even themselves) that they are not in fact *above* everyone else during the remainder of the year, even though their exclusive control of the lottery suggests that they are. Yet just as the lottery's black (ballot?) box has grown shabby and reveals in places its "original wood color," moments in their official "democratic" conduct of the lottery—especially Mr. Summers' conduct as their representative—reveal the class interest that lies behind it. If Summers wears jeans, in order to convince the villagers that he is just another one of the common people, he also wears a "clean white shirt," a garment more appropriate to *his* class. If he leans casually on the black box before the lottery selection begins, as a President, say, might put his feet up on the White House desk, while leaning he "talk[s] interminably to Mr. Graves and the Martins," the other members of his class, and "seem[s] very proper and important." (Jackson has placed these last details in emphatic position at the end of a paragraph.) Finally, however democratic his early appeal for help in conducting the lottery might appear—"some of you fellows want to give me a hand?"—Mr. Martin, who responds, is the third most powerful man in the village. Summers' question is essentially empty and formal, since the villagers seem to understand, probably unconsciously, the unspoken law of class that governs who administers the lottery; it is not just *anyone* who can help Summers.

The lottery's democratic illusion, then, is an ideological effect that prevents the villagers from criticizing the class structure of their society. But this illusion alone does not account for the full force of the lottery over the village. The lottery also reinforces a village work ethic which distracts the villagers' attention from the division of labor that keeps women powerless in their homes and Mr. Summers powerful in his coal company office.

In the story's middle, Old Man Warner emerges as an apologist for this work ethic when he recalls an old village adage, "Lottery in June, corn be heavy soon." At one level, the lottery seems to be a modern version of a planting ritual that might once have prepared the villagers for the collective work necessary to produce a harvest. (Such rituals do not necessarily involve human sacrifice.) As magical as Warner's proverb may seem, it establishes an unconscious (unspoken) connection between the lottery and work that is revealed by the entirety of his response when told that other villages are considering doing away with the lottery:

> Pack of crazy fools . . . listening to the young folks, nothing's good enough for *them*. Next thing you know, they'll be wanting to go back to living in caves, nobody work any more, live *that* way for a while. Used to be a saying about 'Lottery in June, corn be heavy soon.' First thing you know, we'd all be eating stewed chickweed and acorns. There's *always* been a lottery.

But Warner does not explain *how* the lottery functions to motivate work. In order to do so, it would have to inspire the villagers with a magical fear that their lack of productivity would make them vulnerable to selection in the next lottery. The village women reveal such an unconscious fear in their ejaculatory questions after the last slip has been drawn in the first round: "Who is it?" "Who's got it?" "Is it the Dunbars?" "Is it the Watsons?" The Dunbars and the Watsons, it so happens, are the least "productive" families in the village: Mr. Dunbar has broken his leg, Mr. Watson is dead. Given this unconscious village fear that lack of productivity determines the lottery's victim, we might guess that Old Man Warner's pride that he is participating in the lottery for the "seventy-seventh time" stems from a magical belief—seventy-seven is a magical number—that his commitment to work and the village work ethic accounts for his survival. Wherever we find "magic," we are in the realm of the unconscious: the realm in which the unspoken of ideology resides.

Old Man Warner's commitment to a work ethic, however appropriate it might be in an egalitarian community trying collectively to carve an economy out of a wilderness, is not entirely innocent in the modern village, since it encourages villagers to work without pointing out to them that part of their labor goes to the support of the leisure and power of a business class. Warner, that is to say, is Summers' ideologist. At the end of his remarks about the lottery, Warner laments Summers' democratic conduct: "Bad enough to see young Joe Summers up there joking with everybody." Yet this criticism obscures the fact that Summers is not about to undermine the lottery, even if he does "modernize" it, since by running the lottery he also encourages a work ethic which serves his interest. Just before the first round drawing, Summers remarks casually, "Well, now . . . guess we better get started, get this over with, so's we can go back to work." The "we" in his remark is deceptive; what he means to say is "so that you can go back to work for me."

The final major point of my reading has to do with Jackson's selection of Tessie Hutchinson as the lottery's victim/ scapegoat. She could have chosen Mr. Dunbar, of course, in order to show us the unconscious connection that the villagers draw between the lottery and their work ethic. But to do so would not have revealed that the lottery actually reinforces a *division* of labor. Tessie, after all, is a woman whose role as a housewife deprives her radically of her freedom by forcing her to submit to a husband who gains his power over her by virtue of his place in the work force. Tessie, however, rebels against her role, and such rebellion is just what the orderly functioning of her society cannot stand. Unfortunately, her rebellion is entirely unconscious.

Tessie's rebellion begins with her late arrival at the lottery, a *faux pas* that reveals her unconscious resistance to everything the lottery stands for. She explains to Mr. Summers that she was doing her dishes and forgot what day it was. The way in which she says this, however, involves her in another *faux pas:* the suggestion that she might have violated the village's work ethic and neglected her specific job within the village's social division of labor: "Wouldn't have me leave m'dishes in the sink, now, would you Joe?" . . . When Mr. Summers calls her family's name, Tessie goads her husband, "Get up there, Bill." In doing so, she inverts the power relation that holds in the village between husbands and wives. . . . Her final *faux pas* is to question the rules of the lottery which relegate women to inferior status as the property of their husbands. When Mr. Summers asks Bill Hutchinson whether his family has any other households, Tessie yells, "There's Don and Eva. . . . Make them take their change." Tessie's daughter Eva, however, *belongs* to Don and is consequently barred from participating with her parents' family.

All of these *faux pas* set Tessie up as the lottery's likeliest victim, even if they do not explicitly challenge the lottery. That Tessie's rebellion is entirely unconscious is revealed by her cry while being stoned, "It isn't fair." Tessie does not object to the lottery *per se,* only to her own selection as its scapegoat. It would have been fine with her if someone else had been selected.

In stoning Tessie, the villagers treat her as a scapegoat onto which they can project and through which they can "purge"—actually, the term *repress*" is better, since the impulse is conserved rather than eliminated—their own temptations to rebel. . . . But ultimately these rebellious impulses are channeled by the lottery and its attendant ideology away from their proper objects—capitalism and capitalist patriarchs—into anger at the rebellious victims of capitalist social organization. Like Tessie, the villagers cannot articulate their rebellion because the massive force of ideology stands in the way.

The lottery functions, then, to terrorize the village into accepting, in the *name* of work and democracy, the inequitable social division of labor and power on which its social order depends. When Tessie is selected, and before she is stoned, Mr. Summers asks her husband to "show [people] her paper." By holding up the slip, Bill Hutchinson reasserts his dominance over his wayward wife and simultaneously transforms her into a symbol to others of the perils of disobedience.

Here I would like to point out a curious crux in Jackson's treatment of the theme of scapegoating in **"The Lottery"**: the conflict between the lottery's literal arbitrariness and the utter appropriateness of its victim. Admittedly, Tessie is a curious kind of scapegoat, since the village does not literally choose her, single her out. An act of scapegoating that is *unmotivated* is difficult to conceive. This crux disappears, however, once we realize that the lottery is a metaphor for the unconscious ideological mechanisms of scapegoating. In choosing Tessie through the lottery, Jackson has attempted to show us whom the village might have chosen if the lottery had been in fact an election. But by presenting this election as an arbitrary lottery, she gives us an image of the village's blindness to its own motives.

Possibly the most depressing thing about **"The Lottery"** is how early Jackson represents this blindness as beginning. Even the village children have been socialized into the ideology that victimizes Tessie. When they are introduced in the second paragraph of the story, they are anxious that summer has let them out of school: "The feeling of liberty sat uneasily on most of them." Like their parents, they have learned that leisure and play are suspect. As if to quell this anxiety, the village boys engage in the play/labor of collecting stones for the lottery. Moreover, they follow the lead of Bobby Martin, the one boy in the story whose father is a member of the village ruling class (Mr. Summers and Mr. Graves have no boys), in hoarding and fighting over these stones as if they were money. While the boys do this, the village girls stand off to the side and watch, just as they will be expected to remain outside of the work force and dependent on their working husbands when they grow up.

As dismal as this picture seems, the one thing we ought not do is make it into proof of the innate depravity of man. The first line of the second paragraph—"The children assembled first, of course"—does not imply that children take a "natural" and primitive joy in stoning people to death. The closer we look at their behavior, the more we realize that they learned it from their parents, whom they imitate in their play. In order to facilitate her reader's grasp of this point, Jackson has included at least one genuinely innocent child in the story—Davy Hutchinson. When he has to choose his lottery ticket, the adults help him while he looks at them "wonderingly." And when Tessie is finally to be stoned, "someone" has to "[give] Davy Hutchinson a few pebbles." The village makes sure that Davy learns what he is supposed to do before he understands why he does it or the consequences. But this does not mean that he could not learn otherwise.

Even the village adults are not entirely hopeless. Before Old Man Warner cuts them off, Mr. and Mrs. Adams, whose last name suggests a humanity that has not been entirely effaced, briefly mention other villages that are either talking of giving up the lottery or have already done so. Probably out of deep-seated fear, they do not suggest that *their* village give it up; but that they hint at the possibility, however furtively, indicates a reservation—a vague, unconscious sense of guilt—about what they are about to do. The Adamses represent the village's best, humane impulses, impulses, however, which the lottery represses.

How do we take such a pessimistic vision of the possibility of social transformation? If anything can be said against **"The Lottery,"** it is probably that it exaggerates the monolithic character of capitalist ideological hegemony. No doubt, capitalism has subtle ways of redirecting the frustrations it engenders away from a critique of capitalism itself. Yet if in order to promote itself it has to make promises of freedom, prosperity and fulfillment on which it cannot deliver, pockets of resistance grow up among the disillusioned. Perhaps it is not Jackson's intention to deny this, but to shock her complacent readers with an exaggerated image of the ideological *modus operandi* of capitalism: accusing those whom it cannot or will not employ of being lazy, promoting "the family" as the essential social unit in order to discourage broader associations and identifications, offering men power over their wives as a consolation for their powerlessness in the labor market, and pitting workers against each other and against the unemployed. It is our fault as readers if our own complacent pessimism makes us *read* Jackson's story pessimistically as a parable of man's innate depravity. (pp. 29-32)

Peter Kosenko, "A Marxist/Feminist Reading of Shirley Jackson's 'The Lottery'," in The New Orleans Review, *Vol. 12, No. 1, Spring, 1985, pp. 27-32.*

CAROL CLEVELAND

Shirley Jackson is one of the most haunting, and haunted, figures in American literature. In the spring of 1948, a young housewife was pushing her baby up a hill in a stroller. She conceived the idea for a story, went home and wrote it and in twenty-four hours mailed it in all but published form. The story was **"The Lottery."** Outwardly her life was one of energetic normality, involving the production of four children, numerous birthday parties and thousands of brownies. Inwardly she constructed and executed a scathing moral analysis of American society.

Stanley Edgar Hyman has described his wife's warmth and motherliness and readers of her two family chronicles, *Life Among the Savages,* and *Raising Demons,* realize that they are dealing with a dedicated and talented comedian. But the same mind that was driven to domestic frenzy by **"The Birthday Party"** was also meditating on horrors, both familial and universal. When the first of her six novels appeared in 1948, she had been publishing stories in national magazines for seven years. In all the novels and many of the more than ninety stories she wrote, she deals with serious, not to say grim, themes. She explores psychological horror and literal murder. She delineates the iron laws of society untempered by morality and her best work mixes these sources of terror inextricable and inimitably. The family chronicles are notable for their non-corrosive irony, for the funny surprises and awful revelations that life has in store for the unwary mother. But the only form of derangement that appears in these books is the mental fatigue that a mother of four is subject to. These memoirs are early and admirable examples of an American literary subgenre: the diary of the mad housewife. Jackson was among the first to admit publicly that, while motherhood might be a useful institution for children, it was not conducive to serenity in the mother.

Jackson's serious work, while shot through with comic episodes, is suffused with a sense of individual peril and cultural catastrophe. The irony in her fiction is dramatic, and bleak. The surprises her characters face are not funny, and the revelations are liable to be pure hell. **"The Lottery,"** for its economy of means and dramatic impact, is a classic American short story. Set in the present day, it shows us a perfectly ordinary town full of good citizens preparing for their annual lottery. Not until the final moments of the action does it become clear that the "winner" of the lottery will be stoned by the rest of the village. The story can serve as an important focal point for an analysis of Jackson's vision of the modern world and its terrors because sociological horror, including murder, is one of the two mainsprings of Jackson's serious work. **"The Lottery"** is the quintessence of this part of her vision. In **"The Lottery,"** society murders literally. In her longer fiction, society takes more indirect means to the same end. (pp. 199-200)

In Jackson's world, the guilty are not greedy or crazy individuals, but society itself acting collectively and purposely, like a slightly preoccupied lynch mob. In Jackson's fiction, there are no ties of trust or dependence to be weakened. Like the villagers in **"The Lottery,"** her characters speak of trivia while someone collects a pile of stones. Crime, even murder, is constantly being committed in her world, but there is usually no one innocent enough to bring the guilty to justice. The crimes being committed here are not illegal, and therein lies their terror. (pp. 200-01)

In **"The Lottery,"** Tessie Hutchinson's last words are "It isn't fair, it isn't right." What is about to happen to her is, of course, perfectly fair and right by the logic that has guided her life up to that moment. Victims are always chosen "fairly," by blind chance, and it is eminently "right" not to risk crop failure, possibly the rationale for the Lottery. Tessie has, like the rest of the town, steadfastly refused to imagine the lottery from the victim's point of view until forced to. Tessie pays a heavy penalty for her share in her society's lack of vision, of sympathetic imagination. The penalities inflicted on the victims of prejudice, another symptom of lack of imagination, are often subtler than stoning, but they can be just as effective. These subtle stonings, or brutal blindnesses, are significant themes of the five novels that will be treated here.

Jackson was concerned with prejudice in college, long before the publication of her first *New Yorker* story, **"After You, My Dear Alphonse"** (1943), which speaks lightly but tellingly of racial prejudice. **"Flower Garden"** (1949), cogently discusses prejudice as part of a long emotional suicide, and **"A Fine Old Firm"** (1944), delicately points out the anti-Semitism on the American home front. In these stories, the victims of prejudice are either black or Jewish or tolerant. And the bigots are busy inflicting their prejudice on their own children. In four of the five books I will discuss, the children of the morally blind are particularly susceptible to psychological damage.

In *Raising Demons* and *Life Among the Savages,* Jackson gives the reader portraits of four egregiously healthy, imaginative children. The oldest, Laurie, creates an imaginary classmate for his first months at school, a child who conveniently absorbs all the punishment Laurie's own misbehavior calls down. The second child, Jannie, creates an extended family more to the liking of her romantic nature than the boring people she lives with. The last two children, Sally and Barry, frankly practice magic and actually disappear physically into an imaginary kingdom for several hours. All of Jackson's children return to the fold of reality when imagination has served their temporary needs. The youngest brilliantly captures the healthy child's sense of security and identity when he responds to his father's question "Where did you go?" by explaining "You are the daddy . . . and I am the Barry, and Sally is the Sally, and Jannie is the Jannie and Laurie is the Laurie and Mommy is the Mommy." A healthy child can wander into imaginary kingdoms and come back in time for dinner because he knows he is standing safely within the circle of his family's love and attention.

In *The Haunting of Hill House, The Bird's Nest* and *Hangsaman,* Jackson gives the reader portraits of three young women in various degrees of mental and emotional disarray, which has been caused or exacerbated by their families. Eleanor Vance, Natalie Waite and Elizabeth Richmond are all entering on the same crucial phase of their growth—the last step into the adult world as independent people. All find themselves coming seriously apart when confronted with this task.

Jackson had a strong penchant for mixing genres and reversing conventional expectations. In *The Haunting Of Hill House,* she takes a tired formula from the gothic romance and turns it inside out to tell a genuine ghost story with strong roots in psychological realism. The classic gothic formula brings a vulnerable young girl to an isolated mansion with a reputation for ghosts, exposes her to a few weird happenings to heighten the suspense, then explains the "supernatural" away by a perfectly human, if evil, plot and leaves the heroine in the strong arms of the hero. In *House,* the heroine is exceedingly vulnerable, the weird happenings quite real, the house really haunted.

Eleanor Vance, as unmarried daughters have been expected to do, has spent her youth taking care of a bedridden mother. This has "left her with some proficiency as a nurse and an inability to face strong sunlight without blinking." Eleanor's sister and brother-in-law have rewarded her for this long and faithful service with a cot in their daughter's bedroom and half interest in a car. The "strong sunlight" that Eleanor blinks at is normal life; she is incapable of relaxed adult conversation; she is desperate for an independent, satisfying life, and she is almost completely without the means of achieving it. She has so little experience that she will take anything offered.

What fate offers is Hill House, which is mad. She is summoned by Dr. John Montague to be part of a ghost-hunting house party. She has been chosen because of a poltergeist incident dating from her adolescence. Jackson assumes that poltergeist phenomena happen, that they are the result of repressed emotion and that Eleanor is author and victim of the increasingly frightening events that follow the installation of the party of four at Hill House. Jackson also assumes that houses and other locales can be the centers of evil associations—wells of misery and agony waiting for suitably tenuous human beings to drink from them. What Eleanor needs in order to have any hope of survival is a place to belong, where she is welcome for herself, not suffered as a duty. Hill House welcomes her. She is exactly the personality it has been waiting for.

It is the house, with its doors that shut by themselves, rendering the casual guest simultaneously trapped and lost, that drives Eleanor past her ability to understand or cope with her own emotions. Her fellow ghost-hunters are very ordinary people, ill equipped to understand the despairing love affair that develops between Eleanor and the perverse house. What they can understand is her need for human relationship and they reject it. Their responses, individually and as a group, to Eleanor's deterioration constitute another social sacrifice, less violent than the conclusion of **"The Lottery"** but just as effective. (pp. 201-03)

Eleanor passes by stages from her first terrified revulsion at the house to basking in what she feels to be its warmth and acceptance of her. From horror at the scrawled message that appears in the hall one morning, "Help Eleanor Come Home," she progresses to a state of intimate awareness of the life and breath of the house, including its older ghosts. She has almost reached this stage when Mrs. John Montague arrives for the weekend, a stock comic treatment of the insensitive battle-ax. Mrs. Montague's system of belief in planchette messages is so perfect that she is impervious to the real manifestations of Eleanor's progress from a living, if fragile, human being, to genuine ghostliness. To Mrs. Montague is given the task of summing up, with detailed dramatic irony, the process of Eleanor's dematerialization. She addresses her husband:

> Perhaps you do not feel the urgency which I do, the terrible compulsion to aid whatever poor souls wander restlessly here; perhaps you find me foolish in my sympathy for them, perhaps I am even ludicrous in your eyes because I can spare a tear for a lost abandoned soul, left without any helping hand; pure love—.

A few hours later, when Eleanor has been rescued from probable suicide at the invitation of the house, Mrs. Montague asks, "with great delicacy," "Does anybody agree with me . . . in thinking that this young woman has given us quite enough trouble tonight?" A few hours later, Eleanor is dead. She crashes her car into the tree at the bottom of the drive, happy that she has found a way to stay at Hill House—happy except for a few questions that flick through her mind at the end: "*Why* am I doing this? Why am I doing this? Why don't they stop me?"

One of Jackson's favorite devices is to give her characters tags from nursery rhymes or ballads that run like refrains through their minds and may also comment upon plot or theme. Eleanor's refrain is "journeys end in lovers meeting." This is the last reversal of gothic convention, but not the final irony. Eleanor has met her lover; the house has desired her far more than her family or society as represented by her fellow ghost-hunters. As elsewhere in Jackson's world, those whose death society finds convenient do in fact die, having been sentenced to it long before by lethal inattention. As long as Eleanor had some slight use as nurse or psychic sensitive, she was tolerated. As soon as she began to demand full attention, to disturb the peace, it became necessary to dispense with her completely.

The most poignant treatment of this theme occurs in an uncollected story titled **"The Missing Girl"** (1957). Young Martha Alexander goes missing from the Phillips Educational Camp for Girls Twelve to Sixteen on a Monday, but her disappearance is not reported until the Thursday because it is so very hard to tell that she is gone. After a thorough search of camp records and an interrogation of its teachers, it is found to be impossible to prove that she was ever there. Indications there certainly are, but no *proof*. Seen only as a face in a crowd, peripherally and glancingly, Martha has made

dangerously little impression on her world. If she ran away (if she was ever there at all), she was never found and if found, not recognized.

Martha was missing before she disappeared. Eleanor lived for over thirty years as a convenience to someone else and ended as a ghost. Identity is extremely fragile in Jackson's world and it can be as dangerous to have too much of it as to have too little. Those whose gifts and energy make them stand out from the crowd may be criminally mishandled because of their visibility.

The ordeal of Natalie Waite in **Hangsaman,** a novel of psychological detection, stems from having too much of the wrong kind of attention. Like Eleanor Vance, she is vulnerable, and for reasons that are only superficially differnt. Eleanor's family used her as a nurse, or unpaid personal servant, while totally neglecting her emotional and social development. Natalie, at seventeen, is the daughter of an overpowering, overbearing father, a professional critic, and a mother who has been bullied into submission by him. (pp. 203-05)

Leaving the hothouse environment of her home for her first year at college, [Natalie] finds herself trapped in the claustrophobia of the sensitive. . . . Her room is her only retreat from the demands for a secure personality, or a seamless facade, either of which would come in handy and neither of which she has.

Increasingly depressed and isolated in her room, she begins to find herself haunted by an imaginary "friend." Like any adolescent, she has a deep need to be loved for her singular, irreplaceable self. All the real people in her world fail miserably to give her any attention that is not a reflection of their own needs. . . . Natalie does not know precisely who she is, but she is sure she is tired of being a perfect student with no friends. So she creates an imaginary friend named Tony. One critic, [John O. Lyons], took Tony to be a real person and a Lesbian. Tony is something much more dangerous, a creation of Natalie's hyperactive imagination, an imagination fed by loneliness and disappointment that life on her own is even more emotionally unrewarding than life at home.

The conclusion of **Hangsaman** is, by contrast with Eleanor Vance's fate, a happy one. But to emerge victorious from her struggle with the forces of darkness, Natalie must first identify her enemy and then defeat her. . . . Like Eleanor, Natalie falls in love with her enemy. Her soul mate Tony embodies Natalie's vigorous imagination, her growing but unfocussed sense of mastery and her total rejection of the common herd. (pp. 205-06)

The climax of the novel follows Natalie's and Tony's attempt to escape from the dull, maddening, threatening world of the ordinary. In it, Natalie imagines that every person she sees is part of a conspiracy to entrap her: the whole world has become a stage, and all the automata on it merely actors in a play whose purpose is to destroy her. This fantasy is a more elaborate version of an earlier series of interrogations by an imaginary detective who has tried to make her admit guilt for some unspecified crime, probably murder. Both fantasies reflect the extreme pressure of her father's attention: in his love and his demand for perfection, he scrutinizes every letter, every sentence. (p. 206)

Near the end of their journey, Natalie reflects on the state of her universe, which is also the progress of her illness:

If *I* were inventing this world, . . . I would gauge my opponent more accurately. That is, suppose I wanted to destroy the people who saw it clearly, and refused to join up with all my dull ordinary folk, the ones who plod blindly along. What I would do is not set them against numbers of dull people, but I would invent for each a single antagonist, who was calculated to be strong in exactly the right points. You see what I mean?

Tony, as usual ahead of Natalie, replies grinning:

The trouble is . . . that you've got this world, see? And you've got enemies in it, and they're enemies because they're smarter. So you invent someone smart enough to destroy your enemies, you invent them so smart you've got a new enemy.

Natalie recognizes here what will soon be dramatized: that Tony is such a masterful creation, such a perfect complement for Natalie, that she is dangerous. Tony is socially assured where Natalie is not; forthright where Natalie is paralyzed by indecision; she is a natural leader and a powerful storyteller, and she faintly resembles. . .[Natalie's father]. After she has led Natalie to an isolated wood, she begins to paint with words the worlds she and Natalie can dominate and soon puts an imaginary foot down on the sands of the tropical island that is sometimes a sign of danger in Jackson's world. The warm sands of that island tempt the visitor to stay forever, casting off all ties to the real world. But that world, though ugly and depressing, is necessary to sanity.

The real world reasserts its importance in Natalie's consciousness by the most unromantic of means: cold feet. The more conscious she becomes that she is cold, damp, far from home and frightened, the greater her awareness that Tony demands absolute trust, absolute allegiance and the most intimate love. And Tony is finally brought to admit the truth of Natalie's realization that there is "Only one antagonist . . . only one enemy." Tony admits that she herself is the enemy, the queen of Natalie's personal world of madness.

Tired, bereft, but self-possessed, Natalie hitches a ride back to town with a couple who warn her of the dangers awaiting young girls alone in the woods, another example of the multiple levels of dramatic irony that Jackson likes to assemble. Natalie *has* had a nasty sexual encounter, but it was not in these woods. It was with a guest at a party given by her father. The metaphorical woods she has been lost in, her own distorted imaginative world, she is carrying back to town with her. But Natalie has found her way out of those woods. The last sentence of the book summarizes Natalie's personal victory and perhaps Jackson's only vision of salvation: "As she had never been before, she was now alone, and grown-up, and powerful, and not at all afraid."

Natalie has solved the mystery of her enemy's identity, a feat that very few people in Jackson's world accomplish. . . . [By] recognizing her own evil, she has at least a hope of minimizing its impact on others. Since the vast majority of Jackson's characters assume themselves to be innocent, they can quite easily project their own fears and hostilities onto their less powerful neighbors.

For Elizabeth Richmond in **The Bird's Nest,** Natalie's ordeal would have seemed simple. There are six major characters in **Nest** and Elizabeth is four of them. Here too, the heroine's family bears major responsibility for her failure to grow up whole. From an emotionally difficult childhood, culminating in the traumatic death of her mother, Elizabeth has emerged in literal fragments. There is *Elizabeth,* sober, repressed and dutiful; *Beth,* who is sweet, affectionate, and dumb; *Betsy,* gleefully unrepressed and malicious; and finally *Bess,* cold, calculating, and defensive. (pp. 206-08)

Elizabeth's four selves are the expression of a logical campaign for survival among the peculiarly difficult conditions of her life. The daughter of a beautiful, very careless woman, Elizabeth grew up alternately smothered by her mother's attention and desolated by her emotional vagrancy. At the beginning of her own sexual maturity, an encounter with the last of her mother's lovers left her hopelessly confused about betrayal and adulthood. Her mother's death seemed to follow immediately upon a fit of anger at her and at that point Elizabeth buried her confused emotions and turned them into discrete selves. Each of her four selves knows part of the truth about herself and her mother, and none of them can bear to know the whole truth.

Jackson's mixture of forms in this book is original and daring. She mixes medical mystery with social comedy. The drama of the battle between the heroine's four selves for control of her life is perfectly serious and includes a convincing attempt at murder. But Jackson uses the book to remind us that mental health, if it can be achieved, must function in a world of very imperfect people. Dr. Victor Wright is ostensibly the detective in the mystery of the origin of Elizabeth's multiple selves. Actually, with his passion for Thackeray and his distaste for evidence of evil and sexuality in young girls, he is a figure of fun. Nor is Elizabeth's slow groping toward full consciousness noticeably hastened by her Aunt Morgen, a figure of fine comic dimensions. (pp. 208-09)

An unconscious conspiracy develops between Morgen and Dr. Wright. Neither Morgen nor Victor Wright is really prepared to meet a whole, integrated Elizabeth Richmond, because that woman has a mind of her own. She also has normal sexuality, about which Morgen is ambiguous, fearing it may turn out to be her mother's promiscuity. And finally, Elizabeth has a sense of the ridiculous which, as *Betsy,* she exercises on Dr. Wright, contributing to his dislike of her. . . . The crisis is finally brought on when Elizabeth's four selves are alternating so rapidly that Morgen concludes she must be institutionalized. *Betsy* helps bring on this decisive threat, with nice irony, by making her aunt a mud sandwich, served shortly afterward by the dutiful *Elizabeth.* Jackson is not afraid to milk multiple personalities for laughs: another episode has Elizabeth's four selves taking four successive baths under her aunt's weary eyes.

But Morgen and Victor Wright are dogged and brave, if sometimes misguided, and they are rewarded by the beginning of Elizabeth's healing, the coalescing of her four selves. She and Dr. Wright agree on the proper way to describe this event when he reminds her that "you have just eaten your four sisters." That this metaphor is an important clue to Jackson's understanding of human society and psychology is confirmed by a reflection of Dr. Wright's at the comic soiree that closes the book: "Each life, I think, . . . asks the devouring of other lives for its continuance; the radical aspect of ritual sacrifice, the performance of a group, its great step ahead, was in organization; *sharing* the victim was so eminently practical."

There must be a victim, Jackson suggests. It is not whether one eats people that makes the difference between health and illness, but whom one eats and the degree of recognition the victim is accorded. The villagers of **"The Lottery"** simply sacrifice one another without recognizing an intimate relationship. They take life without even tasting it imaginatively. . . . Natalie's father has consumed her mother whole, but not Natalie. His demands on her are the product of his love as well as of his perfectionism. Aunt Morgen has digested her sister's life as a means of maintaining her own strength and identity. Dr. Wright's vanity has been nourished by the *Beth* in his patient, and he must learn painfully that if he wants any *Beth* at all, he will have to swallow some *Betsy* too.

But those who achieve the soundest health are the ones who learn to eat themselves. Natalie Waite, in the course of her illness, eats her world and its inhabitants. Later she devours herself to gain the necessary strength to keep from being eaten by others. Elizabeth Richmond and Natalie first personify the evil, the anti-social, in themselves as other people. Then, having come to know their enemies from a (relatively) safe distance, they painfully recognize their own complex and frightening identities, and assimilate them.

In Jackson's world, a healthy and complex moral growth is possible for individuals, but almost never for large groups of people. In *The Road Through the Wall,* Jackson worked out her strong feelings on the subjects of class insularity and racial prejudice. *Road* surveys the life of the twelve families who live on Pepper St., which runs through a moderately affluent suburb in California. The wall which runs along intersecting Cortez Road is the major symbol of their isolation, not just from the ugliness of the world, but from the consequences of their own lives. On one short block of Pepper St., a microcosm of WASP society, there is an aristocratic enclave, an upper and lower middle class, a Jewish ghetto, a lower class and a couple of isolated old women. When the wall is torn down at the beginning of the summer that is the book's time span, things begin to fall apart, at first subtly. The destruction of the wall is the beginning of a process that will render the neighborhood less protected from the poverty, and the appearance of poverty, that these people fear. Jackson tells the reader in the Prologue that the WASP men of Pepper St. "thought of their invulnerability as justice." Then she demonstrates just how invulnerable they really are and how much justice they have in them.

The Desmonds are the aristocracy, upwardly mobile, conscious of it, gracious and well-mannered, completely vacuous. They are the parents of an adopted son, chosen for his physical perfection, and of a long-awaited, cherished daughter of their own. The Roberts, the Donalds, the Ransom-Joneses and the Merriams represent the upper middle class. The lower middle class is composed of the Catholic Byrnes and the first-generation immigrant Martins. The Perlmans live in an invisible ghetto that only their daughter Marilyn seems conscious of at the beginning of the summer.

At school, lower-class Helen Williams has made it clear to Marilyn Perlman that she is different and had better remember it. Helen is precociously forward with boys, malicious and a bit vicious with her younger sister. She's not a nice child and the mothers of Pepper St. know it, but none of them makes Helen off-limits to her own children. This sanction is reserved for Marilyn, after she and Harriet Merriam strike up an acquaintance and become "best friends" in the middle of the summer. Harriet's feverishly proper, ludicrously "cultivated" mother explains Harriet's transgression to her and

one of the few human contacts in the book is broken. Some of the children on the street have picked up their parents' prejudices easily, but some have to learn the hard way.

The Williamses . . . move out in the middle of the summer. Their replacements in the rented house are, on the level of realism, both pathetic and admirable. On the level of symbol, they complete the scathing analysis of American society that Jackson makes in this book. Into the rented house moves Frederika Helena Terrel, a child of great awkwardness and little beauty, who is apparently the major caretaker for her retarded and unruly younger sister Beverly. This job she performs faithfully and imaginatively. She is one of the best mothers on the block.

Among the children, the adult social hierarchy is being reproduced as faithfully as they copy their elders' prejudices. The aristocrats are those boys who are athletic and attractive to women (even if the women are twelve-year-old girls and Helen Williams). (pp. 209-11)

[A] serious case of ostracism within the family is young Tod Donald, whose fate it is to be the inept younger brother of a member of the football team and victim to the pernicious Virginia Donald, who has nearly ignored her brother out of existence. Virginia is precociously mean, more than ready to assume the mantle of the departing Helen Williams.

Like their parents, these children have no sense of morality, only a loosely fitting set of manners. Besides Frederika Terrel's faithfulness, the one solidly moral act in the book belongs to Marilyn Perlman. When she finds herself part of a group of children baiting Frederika, she turns to Virginia, the ringleader, and says "You shut your fat mouth."

The climax emerges in a series of disjointed, telling vignettes. Three-year-old Caroline Desmond is found to be missing after a party which most of the block attends. (It is one of Jackson's eerie parties at which some people seem to have a good time, but not with each other, and other people have a terrible time.) Hasty inquiries are made and a search organized. (p. 212)

When the search for Caroline Desmond comes up empty, the adults congregate and Pat Byrne mentions Tod's strange behavior and his absence. It is immediately assumed that the two children are together and that Tod must know something. While the mob of public opinion stands on the village green letting a stray remark from Pat Byrne coalesce the guilty verdict around Tod, Mr. Donald stands at the door of his house, with a finger in his book. He moves toward the group and then retreats, awash in the tide of his own estrangement. Tod has delayed returning home for fear of being laughed at for thinking anyone was looking for him. When he does return, he finds that *everyone* is looking for him and that all the authority in the world (in the figure of a policeman) is asking, then demanding, that he confess. After a lifetime in the shadows, Tod is unable to bear this spotlight. He hangs himself. And "Hanging, his body was straighter than it had ever been in life."

Caroline Desmond's death is not so much solved as it is swept under the rug. She is found in a creekbed, her head crushed by a rock, clad in her yellow party dress. Mr. Merriam and Mr. Perlman, both ineffectual but kind, discuss the matter and doubt that Tod had the strength to pick up the rock. Mrs. Merriam feels that Tod got off too easily and is sure that he was up to no good with Caroline (rape of a three-year-old by a thirteen-year-old is what she has in mind). The truth is stranger than even Mrs. Merriam can imagine. Early in the book, Tod, who "rarely did anything voluntarily, or with planning, or even with intent acknowledged to himself," had wandered into the Desmond house after watching Mrs. Desmond and Caroline leave. Inside, he finds his way to the closet that holds their clothes, sits down at the back and repeats all the obscenities he knows. Leaving the house and lying on the lawn, he crushes the delicate yellow blossom from a shrub.

An earlier incident suggests that Tod's subconscious mind is as active as his conscious one is passive. One evening when he has been pushed out of a group of girls and rejected by a group of boys, Tod is "possessed of as strong a desire for punishment as he had ever achieved," and throws a handful of rocks at the girls. This gesture fails of its object when no one is seriously hurt and Virginia inquires whether he was aiming at a window. Clearly Tod envies Caroline, the most cherished child on the street. Clearly he has had at least one impulse to destruction in order to be repaid in the commodity he is starving for—attention.

It is possible that Tod did kill Caroline in a sort of moral accident. If he did, on impulse or by accident, crush her in her yellow dress as he had crushed the blossom, he apparently goes to his death unaware of what he is being punished for. His thoughts that night, as Jackson reports them, show a total ignorance of what has happened to Caroline.

Road is a sociological horror story wrapped around a mystery. The book is full of lost children: Caroline Desmond is the object of an instant, massive search which cannot change the fate that has already overtaken her. Beverly Terrel, although often lost (and invisible to most of Pepper St. because of her extreme neediness), is always found because her sister is always looking. But Tod has been lost for his entire thirteen years and has been starving slowly. Caroline's death may have been an accident, a murder by a vagrant, or the act of a person of diminished capacity.

Jackson leaves the question both unanswered and unanswerable on the evidence she gives us. Because no one in the Pepper St. community has cared enough to find out what happened, with unerring mob instinct, they have picked the weakest among them as the scapegoat. Caroline's death might or might not have been preventable. But Tod Donald's suicide could have been prevented by any number of people—by someone saying, at the right time, "You shut your fat mouth." (pp. 213-14)

Jackson was not on record as a feminist, but she undoubtedly noticed that girls are more easily imposed upon, if not murdered, than boys. From the family chronicles, we know that she found life as a wife and mother entertaining, exhausting, and well worth doing. From her treatment of certain dessicated "career girls" in her short stories, we know that she envisioned one of the alternatives to conventional family life as fearful. All the more unexpected, then, is the fragment of a novel Jackson was at work on when she died. In it she gives us as narrator a woman in the process of liberating herself totally from duty and convention. She has paid her dues to society in marriage to one Hughie, a nice man and a bad painter, and at his death, which she feels as a relief, she sets out for a suitably anonymous city to discover a new identity more or less by feel. She decides to call herself Mrs. Angela Motorman, reports that she "dabbles in the supernatural," and tries out her skill at shoplifting in the last chapter. This fragment has humor, verve, an undercurrent of eeriness, an appreciative echo of Flannery O'Connor, and is quite unlike any novel Jackson had yet published. *Come Along With Me* demonstrates that from the beginning to the end of her writing career, Shirley Jackson was at work mixing genres, confounding the expectations of the self-righteous and the placid, examining the lot of women, and exploring the differences between crime and evil. (pp. 217-18)

> Carol Cleveland, "Shirley Jackson," in And Then There Were Nine . . . More Women of Mystery, edited by Jane S. Bakerman, Bowling Green State University Popular Press, 1985, pp. 199-219.

MARY KITTREDGE

No one, I think, was better than. . .[Shirley Jackson] at skewering an emotion, a setting, or a small event on a sharply-honed turn of phrase, then holding it up to the clearest light where it could be seen wriggling, humorously or horribly as the occasion required.

In addition to imagination, industry, and acute insight, she developed, by the "simple" method of daily practice, a pyrotechnical command of ordinary language, which she used economically but to spectacular effect. Whether in her domestic comedies or her stories and novels of psychological horror, she combined acute observation with absolute mastery of tone and clarity of expression. (pp. 3-4)

Her two "fictionalized" accounts of . . . domestic life convey a happiness that could not have been entirely invented; family love fairly shines through the pages of *Raising Demons* and *Life Among the Savages.* (p. 5)

Raising Demons, at first glance, could not have sprung from the same consciousness as the doomed-dog story, **"Renegade."** But on closer inspection all Jackson's work shows a single theme, and that theme is magic.

Here is the small town of the 1950s, where the soda-fountain owner will hand you a blank check to pay for your childrens' lunches.

Here is that same town again, getting ready to murder your family's pet with a nail-studded choker.

The visions seem equally clear and true. There is some evidence that Shirley Jackson regarded her humorous books as "potboilers," but from this distance it is not so easy to dismiss them. They are the other side of horror; they show us what life is like when the magic works, when the good spells hold. The domestic rituals described in them are the routines that keep life from disintegration.

In *Raising Demons* and *Life Among the Savages,* the horror is not absent; it is merely held at bay, as the titles themselves forcefully hint. If we pour in energy enough, these books suggest, we can hold off entropy for a while. With casseroles and shopping trips, coin collections and Little League, we may ring ourselves with the common charms that keep madness away. One thinks of the praying maiden in the Thurber cartoon: "Lord, please let me be just an ordinary girl."

But she was not. She was a writer of skill and vision, who saw that without constant and energetic applications of magic, things come apart, we shatter and fall. In her tales of haunting, madness, and murder, she described the disorder that may result when magic is ignored, or badly used, or mistaken through carelessness, lack of imagination, laziness, or simple bad luck.

In most of the novels, disorder is characterized by mental instability, a difficulty with which Shirley Jackson was familiar, and in all of them the main character retreats or is driven from the real world, into a life of the imagination. The heroine's perceptions, however mad, are presented as reasonable and her actions as well-justified.

The continuing conflict, Real World vs. Imaginary life, surfaces in each of Jackson's horror novels, and in each it is more completely developed. In each, the grasping tentacles of madness and the anatomy of magic—white, black, and the shades between—are drawn in more delicate detail.

Her first novel, *The Road Through the Wall,* contains no supernatural elements but does contain at least one precursor of the oddness that will be developed in her later books; the story that ends with the murder of a child and the suicide of another takes place in a California suburb where many of the streets have no names, and the houses are unnumbered.

In *Hangsaman,* a college student suffers a mental breakdown and creates an imaginary friend to help her cope. But the friend's unreality makes her dangerous and as she becomes more uncontrollable and malicious, the heroine realizes that in order to regain sanity she must resist the lure of the unreal. To regain health, she must find and use the force of her own personality, integrate her own magic with the pleasures and obligations of real life.

In *The Bird's Nest,* the conflict is heightened; the "imaginary friends" are not imaginary. They are real personalities, not creations of the character's mind but truly existing facets of it, and they do not want to die. They want to do mischief, and they are vociferous about their "rights." Through them, mental disorder takes on dimension and pathos, and demonstrates willful malevolence against a haplessly passive victim-heroine.

In this novel, too, the heroine (with the help of a suggestively witch-doctorish psychiatrist) must cast off her passive victim's status, find her own "powers" (of will) and stand up to the real world, partly symbolized here by a wellmeaning but dragonish aunt. As she did in *Hangsaman,* Shirley Jackson demonstrated in *The Bird's Nest* that magical thinking and magical fantasies by themselves are not only useless but dangerous; to bring happiness, the real magic of the human personality must be purposefully grasped and wielded with determination.

Jackson's next novel was *The Sundial,* a story of magic in the hands of fools. The supernatural events and odd occurrences in it are interpreted by the novel's characters as messages from the late Mr. Halloran, whom they believe is warning them of the end of the world. Once again, Jackson seems to be saying that magic is as magic does, for the characters and especially Mrs. Halloran take the coming "end of the world" as an opportunity to demonstrate small-mindedness, antiintellectualism, ambition, and simple greed. Luckily, the book was written in a comic style and many of its episodes are quite funny; otherwise the characters would be difficult to endure.

The Sundial offers no psychological explanations of the numerous supernatural events that occur in it, and in this re-

spect represents a shift in Shirley Jackson's treatment of the subject. In previous books, weird happenings grew out of weird psyches; here, however, they occur independently and are apparently meant to be taken at face value; the snake that appears in the house, for example, is no ordinary snake, but it is quite real and not a figment of madness or imagination.

In *The Haunting of Hill House,* Jackson takes this shift a step further, giving the evil force not just reality, but personality and purpose. As in *The Sundial,* the supernatural in *Haunting* is neither product nor facet of the main character's mind; it is outside her, and independently real. It does not occupy her; rather, it lures and seduces her away from the pains and problems of the real world into a ghostly existence as another haunting spirit. In *Haunting,* the evil is developed to the point of winning the conflict; there is no happy ending for the heroine, because her character is too weak for the battle. She does not choose madness, but is overwhelmed by it.

In *Haunting,* the most "supernatural" of her full-length works, Shirley Jackson for the first time gives the devil his due. She puts her damsel into mortal distress and leaves her there, completely unrescued. The potential for disaster is fully explored; the evil force is developed into a completely independent and alien entity, and is shown to be a power that can triumph.

In this bleak and chilling twist on the house-with-the-terrible-secret gothic, the heroine dies. While she is the most psychically sensitive of the guests at Hill House, she is also the most susceptible to the forces there. Her personality is weak and poorly integrated; her "magic," the magic of life, is not sufficiently developed to survive a confrontation with the magic of death. With few satisfactions of her own, she has throughout her peril been wishing to merge herself with someone else, so that she will not have to make a life for herself. She harbors also the expectant fantasy that she will be rescued.

But the rescuing prince never appears. Unable to rescue herself, she succumbs to the power of the house, which chillingly grants her desire and makes her life part of its own.

Shirley Jackson's last completed novel was *We Have Always Lived in the Castle,* a book which embodies a twist of another kind. In it, the magic is unaligned, chaotic; the setting combines the comfortable domestic rituals of Jackson's comedies with the desperate strategies of an unrepentant arsenic-murderer. Within a rigidly constructed routine designed to ensure the antiheroine's security, a scenario of the most chillingly amoral madness is played.

Like the mother in *Demons* and *Savages,* the mad girl in *Castle* is a strong and determined user of domestic magic; in *Castle,* however, the forms and rituals of daily life are not allowed their own organic development. They are as rigid—and as brittle—as old grave markers. In Jackson's comedies, growth and change are regarded as necessary if inconvenient elements of life; in *Castle,* the antiheroine's main objective is to keep everything just as it is, for only in an unchanging static world can she protect her bizarre and fragile persona.

The attack of reason on madness is personified in *Castle* by a young man who arrives unexpectedly to challenge the status quo, and his underestimation of the antiheroine's mad magic is the second tragedy of the book. His practical sanity is a pitifully poor weapon against the murderer's elaborate, ritualistic system of defense. Like the heroine in *Haunting,* he just doesn't understand what he's up against, until it is too late.

In *We Have Always Lived in the Castle,* strong magic is not enough to fend off chaos, for magic has no moral alignment of its own. In the domestic comedies, Shirley Jackson's magic is a force in the service of love; in *Castle,* magic takes on the chaotic nature of the book's mad anti-heroine, losing its beauty but retaining its power.

Finally, among the novels there remains a fragment entitled *Come Along with Me,* about a woman who has cast off the obligations and guilts of the past, but who receives intermittent communications from the dead. Unfortunately, Shirley Jackson was unable to complete the book before her own death. (pp. 6-9)

Shirley Jackson's short stories differ from her novels mainly in that their thematic conflict is generally resolved when the story opens. Many of them are vignettes demonstrating the barrenness of lives devoid of magic, or in which it has been misperceived; in "Elizabeth," for example, the main character fantasizes that her life will be transformed as if by magic. Under her armor of cynicism, she is as childish as the victim in *Haunting,* dreaming of rescue while failing to understand that she must break the spell of passivity for herself.

Some of the stories demonstrate the arbitrariness of luck; in "The Tooth," a sane and sensible woman takes a painkiller, loses her mental equilibrium, and through no fault of her own is unable to find her way back to sanity.

In "The Demon Lover" a lonely woman is seduced into madness by the man of her dreams, her rescue fantasy smashed just as it seemed realized. Whether or not he ever existed outside her dreams is a question left for the reader to decide.

A few of the stories feature blithe survivors, like the unfinished heroine of *Come Along with Me.* "My Life With R. H. Macy" is a short romp with a girl who refuses to be reduced to a number. "One Ordinary Day, With Peanuts," features a suitably nutty married couple, one of whom dispenses serendipity while the other doles out irritations to the world.

In the Edgar Allan Poe Award-winning story, "Louisa, Please Come Home," a young woman deliberately transforms herself into a survivor, then discovers that she has done the job too well, changing herself so thoroughly that her family no longer recognizes her when at last she does respond to their plea.

"The Lottery," by which Shirley Jackson's work was introduced to a wide readership, has been subjected to so much interpretation and amateur psychologizing that it would be too bad to subject the poor battered object to any more comment. Suffice it to say that something about that story really got to people; in the first weeks after it appeared in the *New Yorker,* upwards of three hundred readers of the story wrote to the magazine, mostly in protest or to cancel their subscriptions.

It was, and is, a shocking story. It is also beautifully imagined, sparely and gracefully written, a one-two punch of a story. . . . (pp. 9-10)

The story has been anthologized so thoroughly that anyone who recognizes Shirley Jackson's name at all says, "The Lottery," in an almost Pavlovian response. It was dramatized for the stage, and for television, and in one particularly unlikely

adaptation was transformed into a ballet. It has been read in English textbooks by generations of high-school students, and if my informal survey has any validity, it is the only thing many people remember of what they read in that period. It made her fame, and surely assisted in making what was to be her fortune. Despite the anger and suspicion with which it was originally met, it has jolted hundreds of thousands, perhaps millions, of readers.

In its history, in its subject and theme, in its manner of production, and in its effect on Shirley Jackson's life and career, "The Lottery" at once demonstrates and validates the major theme of the author's life and work:

If you practice the ritual, you'll get the magic. (pp. 10-11)

In all the aspects of her life, . . . [Jackson] fought whatever obstacles she encountered at least to a draw. Her success in the horror genre, like her successful domestic comedy, was the result of an exquisitely sensitive double vision that would have seemed an affliction to a less determined or talented writer. She saw the magic in the mundane, and the evil behind the ordinary. She saw that the line between the cruel and the comedic is sometimes vanishingly narrow.

She wrote it all down, day after day, on good days and bad, creating enormous pleasure for her contemporary audience and contributing at least one story to the ranks of the best horror that has been written. Perhaps the worst that can now be said about Shirley Jackson's work is that there simply was not enough of it.

But then, there is never enough of that brand of magic. (p. 12)

> Mary Kittredge, "The Other Side of Magic: A Few Remarks About Shirley Jackson," in Discovering Modern Horror Fiction, *edited by Darrell Schweitzer, Starmont House, 1985, pp. 3-12.*

FRITZ OEHLSCHLAEGER

[In "A Critique of the Sampling Plan Used in Shirley Jackson's 'The Lottery' "] John H. Williams notes what he takes to be a "flaw" in the two-stage process by which the victim is selected. . . . Readers of the story will recall that the first round of the drawing determines a household from which the victim is to be drawn; the second round, the single victim from within that household. Williams points out that under such a system "individuals who are members of smaller families are more likely to be chosen as the sacrificial victim," and he then proposes a new plan that would keep the two-stage process but have the same effect as simply "selecting one individual at random from the village." But perhaps instead of correcting the story's "flaws," we should look at the lottery as Jackson designs it for a key to its meaning. The nature of the process by which the victim is selected gives each woman a very clear incentive to produce the largest possible family. Each child she has gives her a better chance of surviving if the marked paper falls to her household in the first round. What I am suggesting, then, is that one way the story can be seen is as the depiction of a patriarchal society's way of controlling female sexuality. (p. 259)

A conflict between male authority and female resistance is subtly evident throughout "The Lottery." Early in the story, the boys make a "great pile of stones in one corner of the square," while the girls stand aside "talking among themselves, looking over their shoulders at the boys." Later, as the Hutchinsons file up to draw their papers from the box, it is a girl who whispers, "I hope it's not Nancy." This girl's expression of a purely personal feeling is perceived by Old Man Warner as a threat to the social order, as is indicated by his bitterly exclaiming, "It's not the way it used to be," when presumably everyone subordinated personal feelings to the social demands of the ritual. It is also a woman, Mrs. Adams, who presents the story's most significant challenge to the lottery. When at one point her husband Mr. Adams remarks that "over in the North village they're talking of giving up the lottery," Old Man Warner gives vent to a tirade on the folly of departing from what has always served its purpose. Mr. Adams makes no response, but his wife does, pointing out to the Old Man that "some places have already quit lotteries," an oblique but nevertheless real gesture of resistance. That Jackson wants us to read Mrs. Adams's statement as a gesture of resistance is reinforced by what she does with the Adamses at the end of the story. Mr. Adams is at the front of the crowd of villagers as they set upon Tessie Hutchinson. No mention, however, is made of Mrs. Adams's being involved in the stoning.

There is a strong pattern of detail in the story, then, suggesting that those who are most discomfited by, or resistant to, the lottery are women. On the other hand, men control the lottery. Mr. Summers and Mr. Graves are its official priestly administrators, and when they need help, they inquire whether any of the "fellows" might want to give a hand. The lottery is arranged by families and households, women being assigned to the households of their husbands, who draw for them in the initial round. That the society is a heavily patriarchal one is suggested in many other ways as well. As the people gather at the outset of the story, the women stand "by their husbands," and Jackson sharply distinguishes female from male authority. . . . [When] Mrs. Hutchinson complains that the draw has been unfair, her husband tersely and authoritatively commands her, "Shut up, Tessie." And when it becomes clear that Tessie has drawn the marked paper, Bill "forced the slip of paper out of her hand" and "held it up" for the crowd to see. The details Jackson chooses to describe the administrator of the lottery, Mr. Summers, and his wife further clarify the nature of male power and female submission in the lottery's community. Mr. Summers is given his position because people feel "sorry for him" as one who "had no children" and whose "wife was a scold." The woman who is without children is dismissed as a "scold," a challenge to male authority. The childless man, on the other hand, is elevated to a place of special responsibility and even sanctity.

The reading of **"The Lottery"** I am developing is reinforced, too, by looking at the story within the contexts established by its most important allusions. Certainly the whole motif of a woman's being stoned to death recalls the eighth chapter of the Gospel of St. John, in which Jesus frees the woman taken in adultery by directing that man who is without sin among the scribes and Pharisees to cast the first stone. . . . Unfortunately there is no one in **"The Lottery"** to rebuke the powers so forthrightly as Jesus does in 8 *John*. The powers get their scapegoat; the woman pays. Only perhaps in 8 *John* does the woman escape paying, and that is, of course, because another scapegoat stands in her place.

The name of Jackson's victim, Tessie Hutchinson, links her to two women who do pay. [In her essay, " 'The Lottery': Symbolic Tour de Force," (see Jackson's entry in *CLC*, Vol.

11)], Helen Nebeker relates "Tessie" to "Theresa" and "Anastasia," but this seems to me to overlook a much more obvious allusion to Tess of the D'Urbervilles. Hardy's novel is about the way "the woman pays" for crimes committed by men who hold sexual and spiritual power. . . . Certainly Jackson's ending is especially reminiscent of Tess's last moments at Stonehenge as the men close in upon her from behind the encircling stones and the "whole country is reared" to prevent her escape.

The name of Jackson's victim also links her to Anne Hutchinson, whose Antinomian beliefs, found to be heretical by the Puritan hierarchy, resulted in her banishment from Massachusetts in 1638. While Tessie Hutchinson is no spiritual rebel, to be sure, Jackson's allusion to Anne Hutchinson reinforces her suggestions of rebellion lurking within the women of her imaginary village. It indicates too that what the men of Jackson's village seek to kill is a principle of rebellion that is specifically female and, I would argue, based in sexuality. We should remember that Hawthorne associates Anne Hutchinson with another woman taken in adultery and accused by Pharisees, her partner among them. As Hester is led out of prison, she passes the wild rose bush that may have "sprung up under the footsteps of the sainted Ann Hutchinson." (pp. 259-61)

One may well ask whether Shirley Jackson understood the connection between Hester Prynne and Anne Hutchinson in the way that I am suggesting. Is there reason to believe that Tessie Hutchinson stands in some relation to the Anne/Hester figure of history and Hawthornean romance? In answering these questions, a look at Shirley Jackson's little-known first novel, **The Road through the Wall,** can be of great help. Published in 1948, the same year as **"The Lottery,"** **The Road through the Wall** displays several remarkable similarities to Jackson's famous story. It is about the people on a single street of a small, isolated community, in this case situated in California. Its theme is scapegoating, directed by the ordinary middle class people of Pepper Street at a whole series of victims: a Chinaman, a young Jewish girl, a somewhat slow-witted boy, a poor girl, a girl whose mother is suspected of prostitution, and a high-school girl who has run away to get married. The name of this last girl, Hester Lucas, quite obviously recalls Hawthorne's great heroine. Jackson's Hester, proud of her sexuality, comes to work as a maid for the Robertses, but loses her job after Mr. Roberts makes unsuccessful advances toward her. Hester's last scene in the novel clearly points up the book's links to **"The Lottery."** In it she plays a game, "Tin-Tin," with the Pepper Street children, a game whose "elaborate ritual" was "determined by the children and their fathers and their grandfathers operating individually on an immutable theme." This game of the "fathers" has a "victim," although when it falls to her Hester is able to turn this status into an opportunity to embarrass Mr. Roberts. Her victimization remains relatively comic, involving no more than the loss of her job. The most serious scapegoating in the novel is reserved for the slow-witted boy, Tod, who also happens to be remarkably attracted to Hester. When a young girl from the community is killed—her head smashed by a rock—Tod is accused on the slimmest evidence. Before it is even clear whether the girl's death was the result of accident or murder, the utterly confused Tod hangs himself. He dies because of the community's need to ascribe guilt.

Clearly **The Road through the Wall** exhibits many remarkable affinities with **"The Lottery."** What is most pertinent here is the understanding of sexuality it reveals; Hester is a threat because she accepts her sexuality proudly and arouses the potentially adulterous male. Moreover, in the Tin-Tin game, she occupies a victim's role analogous to that of Tessie Hutchinson in **"The Lottery."** This close analogy of Hester and Tessie Hutchinson—grounded perhaps in Hawthorne's association of Hester Prynne and Anne Hutchinson— underscores what is evident from the lottery's selection process: that one goal of the ritual is to contain the potentially disruptive force of an awakened female sexuality.

Jackson's choice of her victim's name strongly reinforces her suggestion about how the lottery is designed primarily to control women, but it ought not to be read as an indication that Tessie is a heroine with the stature of an Anne Hutchinson or Hester Prynne. Tessie fails to be a heroine, and the way that she does so testifies to the success with which the male-dominated order has imposed itself upon her. It is crucial to note that her most grievous failure lies in betraying another woman, her married daughter, by suggesting that she be considered a member of the Hutchinson household for the second stage of the lottery. Jackson emphasizes women's turning against one another, too, through her pointed depiction of the brutality of Mrs. Delacroix and Mrs. Graves in setting upon Tessie. At the beginning of the story, the girls stand together watching the boys gather the stones, but as those girls become women, the involvement in marriage and childbearing that the lottery encourages pits them against one another, blinding them to the fact that all power in their community is male.

Jackson had a clear precedent in New England history of ritual, collective murder in which women responded to the pressures of male authority by betraying one another: the trial and execution of the Salem witches. Some years after she wrote **"The Lottery,"** Jackson wrote about the witchcraft hysteria in a book for adolescents called *The Witchcraft of Salem Village.* Some of the similarities between that book and the story are so close as to suggest that the witch trials may have been in Jackson's mind when she was writing **"The Lottery."** The description of people gathering for the first day's examination of the witches, for instance, closely parallels the opening of **"The Lottery"**: "By early morning, almost the entire population of the village was assembled, the grown-ups talking anxiously and quietly together, the children running off down the road and back again, with wild excited shouts." As the lottery is conducted by a pair of men, so the witch examinations are presided over by a pair of magistrates, one of whom, Hathorne, is clearly, like Mr. Summers, in control. In addition, Jackson's explanation of how the delusion began could apply equally well to the reasons behind the lottery's continuing hold on its people. Discussing the role of Mr. Paris, minister in Salem village and father of one of the children believed to be afflicted by the witches, Jackson remarks: "No one dared to leave the only protection offered the people—the protection of Mr. Paris and their church. Eventually they came to believe that if they worked together wholeheartedly and without mercy they could root out the evil already growing among them." These lines reiterate the central, terrifying import of **"The Lottery"**: that people can be brought to work together wholeheartedly and without mercy if they believe that their protection depends upon it.

A very important similarity between Massachusetts at the time of the witchcraft hysteria and the village of Jackson's

story lies in the relations of power between men and women. As in Jackson's village, all power in the witchcraft trials lay with men: Mr. Paris; Magistrates Hathorne and Corwin; Deputy Governor Thomas Danforth; Judges James Russell, Isaac Addington, Major Samuel Appleton, and Captain Samuel Sewall. The "afflicted" in the trial were girls, who, like Tessie Hutchinson, responded to the pressure of male authority by betraying others of their own sex. Although Jackson does not include specific demographic information about the witches in her book on Salem, it is worth adding that Tessie Hutchinson conforms rather well to the profile of women found to be witches. Carol Karlsen has shown [in her dissertation "The Devil in the Shape of a Woman: The Witch in Seventeenth Century Massachusetts"] that the group most vulnerable to accusations of witchcraft included women between the ages of forty and sixty, or past the prime childbearing years. Accused women in this age group were also more likely to be executed than younger women suspected of witchcraft. The ages of Tessie's four children indicate that she is past the years of her peak fertility. Jackson does not give us all these ages specifically, but we do know that Tessie has a daughter old enough to be married, a son whose "over-large" feet and order in the lottery mark him as an adolescent, a twelve-year-old daughter Nancy, and a boy so young that he must be helped to draw his piece of paper. Tessie is, then, both a woman approaching middle age and one who has had recent difficulty in conceiving children, as the age gap between Nancy and little Dave indicates. I am not arguing that there is collusion between the men who administer the lottery and Bill Hutchinson to eliminate Tessie because she has passed the peak years of childbearing. What I am suggesting, however, is this: that given the purpose of fertility within marriage that the design of the lottery unquestionably fosters, Tessie is an extremely appropriate victim.

It might be objected to my line of argument that the lottery also apparently has male victims. But such is obviously a necessary part of the process by which it retains its hold over the people who participate in it. A lottery that killed only women over forty could hardly expect to retain popular support for long, at least in part because it would lose its mystery. The lottery must appear to be fair, and it must give the villagers the sense of being narrowly spared by a mysterious power and thus justified. Still I would insist that we cannot discount Tessie's charge that the lottery is not fair. On one level, as John H. Williams has pointed out, the lottery is indeed unfair; its two-stage design means that the selection of a victim is not a purely random process. Moreover, we cannot deny Tessie's charge by saying that all the operations of the lottery appear to be fairly handled, for an obviously flawed lottery would neither mystify the villagers nor interest the reader. Neither can we argue for its fairness by saying that no one, other than Tessie, comments on any unfairness, for obviously everyone has a very strong stake in believing it was conducted fairly. In short, if the lottery is unfair, it is reasonable to assume that its lack of fairness would be evident only to the victim.

A reading of the story in the several contexts I have supplied here dramatically underscores what is evident from the design of the lottery itself: that its primary social consequence involves women's turning over the control of their fertility to men. Jackson depicts a society in which authority is male, potential resistance female. . . . The young girl's simple hope that the victim not be her friend Nancy is the force that would destroy the lottery, as Old Man Warner recognizes. Suppression of the personal is the function of the lottery, which it accomplishes primarily by causing women to submit control of their sexuality to men of secular and priestly authority. The design of the lottery is without flaw; it serves perfectly the patriarchal purpose of denying women consciousness by insisting that they remain part of nature, part of the fertile earth itself. (pp. 261-64)

> *Fritz Oehlschlaeger, "The Stoning of Mistress Hutchinson: Meaning and Context in 'The Lottery'," in* Essays in Literature, *Vol. XV, No. 2, Fall, 1988, pp. 259-65.*

FURTHER READING

Breit, Harvey. "Talk with Miss Jackson." *The New York Times Book Review* (26 June 1949): 15.

Interview conducted following the publication of "The Lottery" in which Jackson discusses her writing techniques and favorite authors.

Friedman, Lenemaja. *Shirley Jackson.* Boston: G. K. Hall & Co., 1975, 182 p.

Biographical and critical study in which Friedman scrutinizes Jackson's short stories and novels. Includes extensive bibliography.

Hyman, Stanley Edgar. "Shirley Jackson: 1919-1965." *Saturday Evening Post* 238, No. 25 (18 December 1965): 63.

Posthumous tribute by Jackson's husband.

Lainoff, Seymour. "Jackson's 'The Lottery.'" *The Explicator* XII (March 1954): Item 34.

Discusses the influence of Sir James G. Frazer's *The Golden Bough* on Jackson's story.

LeCroy, Anne. "The Different Humor of Shirley Jackson: *Life among the Savages* and *Raising Demons.*" *Studies in American Humor* 4, Nos. 1 & 2 (Spring-Summer 1985): 62-73.

Analyzes Jackson's nonfiction works and charts her success within the genre of domestic humor.

Nebeker, Helen C. "'The Lottery': Symbolic Tour de Force." *American Literature* 46 (March 1974): 100-07.

Highly regarded essay in which Nebeker examines the symbolism of "The Lottery" at various levels. See excerpt in *CLC,* Vol. 11.

Oppenheimer, Judy. *Private Demons: The Life of Shirley Jackson.* New York: G. P. Putnam's Sons, 1988, 304 p.

Excellent, detailed biography. Contains many photographs.

Woodruff, Stuart C. "The Real Horror Elsewhere: Shirley Jackson's Last Novel." *Southwest Review* 52 (September 1967): 152-62.

Maintains that the true madness of *We Have Always Lived in the Castle* exists in the supposedly "normal" facade of the outside world. See excerpt in *CLC,* Vol. 11.

Harper Lee
1926-

(Born Nelle Harper Lee) American novelist.

The following entry augments criticism on Lee's novel *To Kill a Mockingbird* (1960) excerpted in *CLC*, Vol. 12.

In her first and only novel, *To Kill a Mockingbird*, Lee draws upon her childhood experiences as the daughter of a southern lawyer to portray the moral awakening of two children in Maycomb, Alabama, during the 1930s. Recalling her experiences as a six-year-old from an adult perspective, Jean Louise Finch, nicknamed "Scout," describes the circumstances that involve her widowed father, Atticus, and his legal defense of Tom Robinson, a local black man falsely accused of raping a white woman. In the three years surrounding the trial, Scout and her older brother, Jem, witness the unjust consequences of prejudice and hate while experiencing the value of courage and integrity through the example of their father. The winner of the Pulitzer Prize in 1960, *To Kill a Mockingbird* achieved immediate popular acclaim and in 1962 was adapted by Horton Foote into an Academy Award-winning film. Although occasionally faulted as melodramatic, *To Kill a Mockingbird* is widely regarded as among the most sensitive and revealing portraits of the American South in contemporary literature. R. A. Dave contended: "[The novel's] small world assumes a macrocosmic dimension and expands into immensity, holding an epic canvas against which is enacted a movingly human drama of the jostling worlds—of children and adults, of innocence and experience, of kindness and cruelty, of love and hatred, of humour and pathos, and above all of appearance and reality—all taking the reader to the root of human behaviour."

To Kill a Mockingbird opens with the mature voice of Scout recalling her upbringing in Maycomb, "a tired old town" reluctant to surrender its past traditions to progressive change. Cared for by Calpurnia, a black housekeeper, Scout and her brother are rarely allowed to leave their street, except to meet their father on his way home from the courthouse. Although Atticus belongs to one of the area's oldest families, he is portrayed as an individualist whose struggle to raise his children as tolerant members of society forms the central conflict of *To Kill a Mockingbird*. However, the journey of Scout and Jem toward understanding begins in their own world when they meet seven-year-old Dill Harris, a diminutive, mischievous summertime visitor to Maycomb whom Lee later stated she had based upon author Truman Capote, a childhood companion. Dill suggests to Scout and Jem that they make Arthur "Boo" Radley, the town recluse, leave his family house, where he has remained unseen since his arrest and subsequent release from jail for an adolescent prank fifteen years earlier. Believing rumors that Boo dines on raw squirrels and roams their street by night, the children dare one another to approach the Radley porch or to peer inside Boo's window. Critics observe that the behavior of the children toward Boo subtly reflects the dynamics of racial prejudice in which fear and misconception, rather than knowledge, dictate behavior.

In the fall, Dill departs and school begins, forcing Scout and

Jem to abandon their pursuit of Boo. As a first grade student, Scout starts "off on the wrong foot" with her teacher, Miss Caroline, after attempting to explain why the son of a proud local sharecropper refuses Miss Caroline's offer of a quarter to buy his lunch. Scout resolves never to return to school after Miss Caroline decrees that she may no longer read with her father, as it will interfere with her education. When Atticus later divines the reason for her unhappiness, he asks Scout to first consider the viewpoint of Miss Caroline, a novice teacher, before judging her actions, hoping that Scout will apply this stratagem to future conflicts. Critics often interpret the contrast between Miss Caroline and Atticus as the first of Lee's many ironic comments upon the ineffectiveness of institutional education as compared to the lessons gained through contact with others.

Later in the school year, Scout and Jem discover chewing gum hidden in a tree on the Radley property, the first of many objects to appear there, including polished pennies, a pocket knife, a broken watch, and two carved dolls resembling Scout and Jem. Other mysterious events transpire; for instance, when Jem abandons his entangled pants on the Radley fence after attempting to spy on Boo, he returns to find them crudely sewn and neatly folded. Yet the mystery of Boo is soon overshadowed by Atticus's involvement in Tom Robinson's case. In the months preceding the trial, Scout and Jem endure the taunts of classmates whose parents object to their father's defense of blacks. Although Atticus instructs his children to ignore their insults, Scout overhears him expressing concern during a Christmas visit with her uncle. Atticus senses in Scout and Jem an innate sense of truth that may be nurtured or corrupted by the example of adults, a conviction that several commentators perceived as Lee's personal belief. Atticus hopes that by observing his defense of Tom, his children will not succumb to the prevailing prejudices of the community.

For Christmas, Atticus gives Jem and Scout their first air rifles but cautions that "it's a sin to kill a mockingbird" because the birds "don't do one thing but sing their hearts out for us." The children view their father's own disinterest in guns as proof of his often frustrating staidness, but their opinions change when they learn that Atticus once earned a reputation as "the deadest shot in Maycomb County" after killing a rabid dog on their street. Their concept of heroism formed by this incident is subsequently tempered when Atticus asks Jem to read to their neighbor, Mrs. Dubose, a recovering morphine addict. When Mrs. Dubose dies, Atticus tells his son that in witnessing her struggle Jem saw "what real courage is, instead of getting the idea that courage is a man with a gun in his hand. It's when you know you're licked before you begin but you begin anyway and you see it through no matter what." According to commentators, Atticus fulfills this ideal in his defense of Tom.

The next spring, Calpurnia takes Scout and Jem to her church while their father is away on business. Like Atticus, Calpurnia is perceived as a link between the races by virtue of her humanistic compassion and moral courage. Through her example and that of the other members of the church, the Finch children gain a new understanding of black people— particularly Tom Robinson—as human beings. Following the service, Scout asks if she may visit Calpurnia at her house, but abandons the idea when Atticus's sister, Alexandria, arrives unexpectedly. Alexandria endeavors to counteract what she perceives as the negative effect of her brother's liberal views on his children. Primarily concerned with such superficial issues as class, family breeding, and, in Scout's case, ladylike manners, Alexandria embodies traditional southern mores as embraced by Maycomb society.

Dill returns shortly after Alexandria's appearance, but the joy of his arrival is overshadowed by tensions surrounding the transferal of Tom from the state penitentiary to the county jail for his trial. On the eve of the hearing, a threatened lynching is narrowly averted when Scout, having followed Atticus to the jail along with Jem and Dill, recognizes a schoolmate's father in the crowd and politely inquires about her friend. Made self-conscious by her innocent questions, the group disperses. On the morning of the trial, townsfolk crowd the courtroom to hear the testimony of Mayella Ewell, the alleged rape victim, who lives in abject poverty with her shiftless father, Bob. Both she and Bob claim that Tom attacked her after being asked inside their fence to break up an old chifforobe for firewood. During cross-examination, however, Atticus proves their accusations false before reconstructing the actual incident with Tom on the witness stand. According to his testimony, Mayella, after misinterpreting his previous acts of kindness, had attempted to seduce him. Ewell then discovered them together and forced Mayella to charge Tom with rape. At the climax of the trial, Atticus delivers his closing argument, in which he charges the jury to

put aside prejudices and fulfill their duty as participants in a democratic system of justice. After a two-hour deliberation, the jury finds Tom guilty.

Critics generally agree that the narrative falters at this point, as Scout and Jem attempt to comprehend the verdict amid what has been characterized as contrived speeches against racism by adults. After the trial, the disbelief of the children gives way to shock when Tom is killed during a prison escape attempt. Few whites express outrage at his death, apart from Atticus and the publisher of the local newspaper, who compares the incident to "the senseless slaughter of songbirds by hunters and children." Although the controversy subsides in the fall, Bob Ewell, discredited in court by Atticus, begins to threaten the Finches and finally attacks Scout and Jem as they walk home from the school Halloween pageant. Trapped inside her wire costume, Scout sees a stranger carry off her brother but soon realizes that it was Boo, whom she instinctively recognizes standing in Jem's room. The monster of neighborhood legend is revealed to be a shy, childish man who saved Scout and Jem by killing Bob Ewell. When Atticus and the sheriff decide not to expose Boo's deed to the town, Scout agrees, reasoning that it would be "like shootin' a mockingbird." Commentators maintain that this image of the songbird unites the characters of Tom and Boo, who both emerge as innocent victims of a prejudiced community. After walking Boo home, Scout stands on the Radley porch and, seeing the tree where their unseen friend once deposited gifts, believes that now she has nothing more to learn "except possibly algebra."

Following the publication of *To Kill a Mockingbird,* some reviewers dismissed the narrative voice of Scout as unconvincing for a girl not yet ten years of age. However, subsequent critics have recognized Lee's rendering of a child's perspective through an adult's evaluation as among the most technically expert in contemporary literature. According to commentators, Lee adroitly exposes the turbulence underlying southern society and psychology while presenting the possibility of its elimination through the understanding of individuals. Edgar H. Shuster asserted: "The achievement of Harper Lee is not that she has written another novel about race prejudice, but rather that she has placed race prejudice in a perspective which allows us to see it as an aspect of a larger thing; as something that arises from phantom contacts, from fear and lack of knowledge; and finally as something that disappears with the kind of knowledge or 'education' that one gains through learning what people are really like when you 'finally see them.'"

(See also *Contemporary Authors,* Vols. 13-16, rev. ed.; *Something about the Author,* Vol. 11; *Dictionary of Literary Biography,* Vol. 6; and *Concise Dictionary of American Literary Biography: 1941-1968.*)

HARDING LeMAY

In her first novel, *To Kill a Mockingbird,* Harper Lee makes a valiant attempt to combine two dominant themes of contemporary Southern fiction—the recollection of childhood among village eccentrics and the spirit-corroding shame of the civilized white Southerner in the treatment of the Negro. If her attempt fails to produce a novel of stature, or even of original insight, it does provide an exercise in easy, graceful writing and some genuinely moving and mildly humorous excursions into the transient world of childhood.

Set during the depression, the story is recalled from the distance of maturity by Jean Louise ("Scout") Finch, whose widowed father, Atticus, was a civilized, tolerant lawyer in a backward Alabama town. An older brother, Jem, and a summer visitor from Mississippi, Dill, share Scout's adventures and speculations among figures not totally unfamiliar to readers of Carson McCullers, Eudora Welty, and Truman Capote. . . . [The children] play their games of test and dare with ill-tempered old ladies, buzzing village gossips, and, most especially, with the mysterious occupant of the house next door who has never been seen outside since his father locked him up over fifteen years earlier. It is through Boo Radley whose invisible presence tantalizes the children, that Miss Lee builds the most effective part of her novel: an exploration of the caution and curiosity between which active children expend their energies and imaginations.

In the second half of the novel, Atticus defends a Negro accused of raping a white girl. The children add to their more innocent games that of watching a Southern court in action. They bring to the complexities of legal argument the same luminous faith in justice that sweeps through their games, and they watch, with dismay and pain, as the adult world betrays them. And here, perhaps because we have not been sufficiently prepared for the darkness and the shadows, the book loses strength and seems contrived. For everything happens as we might expect. The children are stained with terror and the knowledge of unreasoning hatreds but gain in insight and in compassion, and the author, deliberately using Atticus and an elderly widow as mouthpieces, makes her points about the place of civilized man in the modern South.

The two themes Miss Lee interweaves throughout the novel emerge as enemies of each other. The charm and wistful humor of the childhood recollections do not foreshadow the deeper, harsher note which pervades the later pages of the book. The Negro, the poor white girl who victimizes him, and the wretched community spirit that defeats him, never rise in definition to match the eccentric, vagrant, and appealing characters with which the story opens. The two worlds remain solitary in spite of Miss Lee's grace of writing and honorable decency of intent.

> *Harding LeMay, "Children Play; Adults Betray," in* New York Herald Tribune Book Review, *July 10, 1960, p. 5.*

GRANVILLE HICKS

Harper Lee's *To Kill a Mockingbird* gives a friendly but for the most part unsentimental account of life in an Alabama town in the 1930s. The narrator, Jean Louise (commonly called Scout) Finch, is writing of a time when she was seven or eight years old, and the book is in part the record of a childhood. Their mother being dead, Scout and her brother Jem have been brought up by their father, a lawyer and legislator, and by a Negro servant, Calpurnia. The father, Atticus Finch, is an unusual man, and their childhood is in many ways a unique one.

Miss Lee, however, is not primarily concerned with childhood experience; she has, in her own way, written a novel about the perennial Southern problem. Atticus is assigned to defend a Negro charged with raping a white woman, and, to the dismay of his neighbors, he really tries to defend him. Through Scout's eyes we watch the growth of resentment in the community, and then we see the trial itself, in which Atticus is inevitably defeated. After that there is a melodramatic conclusion.

Miss Lee's problem has been to tell the story she wants to tell and yet to stay within the consciousness of a child, and she hasn't consistently solved it. Some episodes in the trial and the melodramatic conclusion seem contrived. But her insight into Southern mores is impressive, and in Atticus she has done a notable portrait of a Southern liberal. (p. 15)

> *Granville Hicks, "Three at the Outset," in* Saturday Review, *Vol. XLIII, No. 30, July 23, 1960, pp. 15-16.*

FRED ERISMAN

When Mark Twain stranded the steamboat *Walter Scott* on a rocky point in Chapter 13 of *Huckleberry Finn,* he rounded out an attack on Southern romanticism begun in *Life on the Mississippi.* There, as every reader knows, he asserted that Sir Walter Scott's novels of knighthood and chivalry had done "measureless harm" by infecting the American South with "the jejune romanticism of an absurd past that is dead." This premise does not stop with Twain. W. J. Cash, writing almost sixty years later, continues the assertion, observing that the South, already nostalgic in the early nineteenth century, "found perhaps the most perfect expression for this part of its spirit in the cardboard medievalism of the Scotch novels." As recently as 1961, W. R. Taylor, in *Cavalier and Yankee,* several times alludes to Scott as he traces the development of the myth of the planter aristocracy.

For these three men, and for many like them, Southern romanticism has been a pernicious, backward-looking belief. It has, they imply, mired the South in a stagnant morass of outdated ideas, from which there is little chance of escape. A more hopeful view, however, appears in Harper Lee's novel of Alabama life, *To Kill a Mockingbird* (1960). Miss Lee is well aware of traditional Southern romanticism and, indeed, agrees that it was and is a pervasive influence in the South; one of the subtlest allusions in the entire novel comes in Chapter 11, as the Finch children read *Ivanhoe* to the dying but indomitable Southern lady, Mrs. Henry Lafayette Dubose. At the same time, she sees in the New South—the South of 1930-1935—the dawning of a newer and more vital form of romanticism. She does not see this newer romanticism as widespread, nor does she venture any sweeping predictions as to its future. Nevertheless, in *To Kill a Mockingbird,* Miss Lee presents an Emersonian view of Southern romanticism, suggesting that the South can move from the archaic, imported romanticism of its past toward the more reasonable, pragmatic, and native romanticism of a Ralph Waldo Emerson. If the movement can come to maturity, she implies, the South will have made a major step toward becoming truly regional in its vision.

As Miss Lee unfolds her account of three years in the lives of Atticus, Jem, and Scout Finch, and in the history of Maycomb, Alabama, she makes clear the persistence of the old beliefs. Maycomb, she says, is "an old town, . . . a tired old town," even "an ancient town." A part of southern Alabama from the time of the first settlements, and isolated and largely untouched by the Civil War, it was, like the South, turned inward upon itself by Reconstruction. Indeed, its history parallels that of the South in so many ways that it emerges as a microcosm of the South. This quality is graphically suggested by the Maycomb County courthouse, which dominates the town square:

> The Maycomb County courthouse was faintly reminiscent of Arlington in one respect: the concrete pillars supporting its south roof were too heavy for their light burden. The pillars were all that remained standing when the original courthouse burned in 1856. Another courthouse was built around them. It is better to say, built in spite of them. But for the south porch, the Maycomb County courthouse was early Victorian, presenting an unoffensive vista when seen from the north. From the other side, however, Greek revival columns clashed with a big nineteenth-century clock tower housing a rusty unreliable instrument, a view indicating a people determined to preserve every physical scrap of the past.

Miss Lee's courthouse, inoffensive from the north but architecturally appalling from the south, neatly summarizes Maycomb's reluctance to shed the past. It is, like the South, still largely subject to the traditions of the past.

The microcosmic quality of Maycomb suggested by its courthouse appears in other ways, as well. The town's social structure, for example, is characteristically Southern. Beneath its deceptively placid exterior, Maycomb has a taut, well-developed caste system designed to separate whites from blacks. If Maycomb's caste system is not so openly oppressive as that of John Dollard's "Southerntown" (where "caste has replaced slavery as a means of maintaining the essence of the old status order in the South"), it still serves the same end—to keep the blacks in their place. The operations of this system are obvious. First Purchase African M. E. Church, for example, "the only church in Maycomb with a steeple and bell," is subjected to minor but consistent desecration: "Negroes worshiped in it on Sundays and white men gambled in it on weekdays." The whites, moreover, clearly expect deferential behavior of the blacks. . . . The Finch children, attending church with Calpurnia, their black housekeeper, are confronted with doffed hats and "weekday gestures of respectful attention." And, in the most telling commentary of all upon the pervasive pressures of the caste system, when Calpurnia accompanies Atticus Finch to convey the news of Tom Robinson's death, she must ride in the back seat of the automobile.

Even more indicative of Maycomb's characteristically Southern caste system is the power of the sexual taboo, which has been called "the strongest taboo of the system." This is dramatized by the maneuverings during Tom Robinson's trial of allegedly raping Mayella Ewell, a central episode in the novel. Although Tom's infraction of the black man-white woman code is demonstrated to have been false, he is nonetheless condemned. The caste taboo outweighs empirical evidence. As Atticus says later of the jury, "Those are twelve reasonable men in everyday life, Tom's jury, but you saw something come between them and reason. . . . There's something in our world that makes men lose their heads—they couldn't be fair if they tried." Despite the presence of a more than reasonable doubt as to his guilt, despite the discrediting of the Ewells, the chief witnesses for the prosecution, Tom Robinson is condemned. As Atticus points out, the entire prosecution is based upon "the assumption—the evil assumption—that *all* Negroes lie, that *all* Negroes are basically immoral beings, that *all* Negro men are not to be trusted around our women." Tom's conviction is mute testimony to the strength of that caste-oriented assumption.

Another illustration of Maycomb's archetypal Southernness that is as typical as its caste system is the ubiquitous system of class distinctions among the whites. Miss Lee's characters fall readily into four classes, ranging from the "old aristocracy" represented by Atticus Finch's class-conscious sister, Alexandra, to the poor white trash represented by Bob Ewell and his brood, who have been "the disgrace of Maycomb for three generations." In presenting the interaction of these classes, she gives a textbook demonstration of the traditional social stratification of the American South.

The upper-class-consciousness so manifest in Aunt Alexandra appears most strongly in her regard for "family", a concern that permeates Part II of *To Kill a Mockingbird.* Like the small-town aristocrats described in Allison Davis's *Deep South,* she has a keen appreciation of the "laterally extended kin group." Although the complex interrelationships of Maycomb society are generally known to the Finch children, it is Aunt Alexandra who drives home their social significance. . . . In her insistence that family status be preserved, Aunt Alexandra typifies the family-oriented aristocrat of the Old South.

No less well developed is Miss Lee's emphasis upon the subtleties of class distinction. In this, too, she defines Maycomb as a characteristically Southern community. It has its upper class, in Aunt Alexandra, in the members of the Missionary Society, and in the town's professional men—Atticus, Dr. Reynolds, Judge Taylor, and so on. It has its middle class, in the numerous faceless and often nameless individuals who flesh out Miss Lee's story—Braxton Underwood, the owner-editor of *The Maycomb Tribune,* or Mr. Sam Levy, who shamed the Ku Klux Klan in 1920 by proclaiming that "he'd sold 'em the very sheets on their backs." It has its lower class, generically condemned by Aunt Alexandra as "trash", but sympathetically presented in characters like Walter Cunningham, one of the Cunninghams of Old Sarum, a breed of men who "hadn't taken anything from or off of anybody since they migrated to the New World." Finally, it has its dregs, the Ewells, who, though more slovenly than the supposedly slovenliest of the blacks, still possess the redeeming grace of a white skin. These distinctions Aunt Alexandra reveres and protects, as when she remarks, "You can scrub Walter Cunningham till he shines, you can put him in shoes and a new suit, but he'll never be like Jem. . . . Because—he—is—trash." For Aunt Alexandra, the class gap between the Finches and the Cunninghams is one that can never be bridged.

The existence of a caste system separating black from white, or of a well-developed regard for kin-group relations, or of a system of class stratification is, of course, not unique. But, from the simultaneous existence of these three systems, and from the way in which they dominate Maycomb attitudes, emerges the significance of Maycomb's antiquity. It is a representation of the Old South, still clinging, as in its courthouse, to every scrap of the past. Left alone, it would remain static, moldering away as surely as John Brown's body. So too, Miss Lee suggests, may the South. This decay, however, can be prevented. In her picture of the New South and the New Southerner, Miss Lee suggests how a decadently romantic tradition can be transformed into a functional romanticism, and how, from this change, can come a revitalizing of the South.

The "New South" that Harper Lee advocates is new only by courtesy. In one respect—the degree to which it draws upon the romantic idealism of an Emerson—it is almost as old as the Scottish novels so lacerated by Mark Twain; in another, it is even older, as it at times harks back to the Puritan ideals of the seventeenth century. By the standards of the American South of the first third of the twentieth century, however, it is new, for it flies in the face of much that traditionally characterizes the South. With Emerson, it spurns the past, looking instead to the reality of the present. With him, it places principled action above self-interest, willingly accepting the difficult consequences of a right decision. It recognizes, like both Emerson and the Puritans, the diversity of mankind, yet recognizes also that this diversity is unified by a set of "higher laws" that cannot be ignored. In short, in the several Maycomb townspeople who see through the fog of the past, and who act not from tradition but from principle, Miss Lee presents the possible salvation of the South.

Foremost among these people is Atticus Finch, attorney, the central character of Miss Lee's novel. Though himself a native of Maycomb, a member of one of the oldest families in the area, and "related by blood or marriage to nearly every family in the town," Atticus is not the archetypal Southerner that his sister has become. Instead, he is presented as a Southern version of Emersonian man, the individual who vibrates to his own iron string, the one man in the town that the community trusts "to do right," even as they deplore his peculiarities. Through him, and through Jem and Scout, the children he is rearing according to his lights, Miss Lee presents her view of the New South.

That Atticus Finch is meant to be an atypical Southerner is plain; Miss Lee establishes this from the beginning, as she reports that Atticus and his brother are the first Finches to leave the family lands and study elsewhere. This atypical quality, however, is developed even further. Like Emerson, Atticus recognizes that his culture is retrospective, groping "among the dry bones of the past . . . [and putting] the living generation into masquerade out of its faded wardrobe." He had no hostility toward his past; he is not one of the alienated souls so beloved of Southern Gothicists. He does, though, approach his past and its traditions with a tolerant skepticism. His attitude toward "old family" and "gentle breeding" has already been suggested. A similar skepticism is implied by his repeated observation that "you never really understand a person until you consider things from his point of view . . . until you climb into his skin and walk around in it." He understands the difficulties of Tom Robinson, although Tom Robinson is black; he understands the difficulties of a Walter Cunningham, though Cunningham is—to Aunt Alexandra—"trash"; he understands the pressures being brought to bear upon his children because of his own considered actions. In each instance he acts according to his estimate of the merits of the situation, striving to see that each receives justice. He is, in short, as Edwin Bruell has suggested, "no heroic type but any graceful, restrained, simple person like one from Attica." Unfettered by the corpse of the past, he is free to live and work as an individual.

This freedom to act he does not gain easily. Indeed, he, like Emerson's nonconformist, frequently finds himself whipped by the world's displeasure. And yet, like Emerson's ideal man, when faced by this harassment and displeasure, he has

"the habit of magnanimity and religion to treat it godlike as a trifle of no concernment." In the development of this habit he is aided by a strong regard for personal principle, even as he recognizes the difficulty that it brings to his life and the lives of his children. This is established early in the novel, with the introduction of the Tom Robinson trial. When the case is brought up by Scout, following a fight at school, Atticus responds, " 'If I didn't [defend Tom Robinson] I couldn't hold up my head in town, I couldn't represent this county in the legislature, I couldn't even tell you or Jem not to do something again. . . . Scout, simply by the nature of the work, every lawyer gets at least one case in his lifetime that affects him personally. This one's mine, I guess'." He returns to this theme later, observing that " 'This case . . . is something that goes to the essence of a man's conscience—Scout, I couldn't go to church and worship God if I didn't try to help that man'." Scout points out that opinion among the townspeople runs counter to this, whereupon Atticus replies, " 'They're certainly entitled to think that, and they're entitled to full respect for their opinions . . . but before I can live with other folks I've got to live with myself. The one thing that doesn't abide by majority rule is a person's conscience'." No careful ear is needed to hear the echoes of Emerson's "Nothing can bring you peace but yourself. Nothing can bring you peace but the triumph of principles." In his heeding both principle and conscience, whatever the cost to himself, Atticus is singularly Emersonian.

The Emersonian quality of Atticus's individualism is emphasized in two additional ways—through his awareness of the clarity of the childhood vision . . . , and through his belief in the higher laws of life. The first of these appears at least three times throughout the novel. Early in the Tom Robinson sequence, an attempted lynching is thwarted by the sudden appearance of the Finch children, leading Atticus to observe, " 'So it took an eight-year-old child to bring 'em to their senses, didn't it? . . . Hmp, maybe we need a police force of children . . . you children last night made Walter Cunningham stand in my shoes for a minute. That was enough'." The view is reinforced by the comments of Dolphus Raymond, the town drunk, who sees in the children's reaction to the trial the unsullied operations of instinct. And, thus suggested, it is made explicit by Atticus himself, as, following Tom Robinson's conviction, he tells Jem: " 'If you had been on that jury, son, and eleven other boys like you, Tom would be a free man. . . . So far nothing in your life has interfered with your reasoning process'." The point could not be more obvious; in the unsophisticated vision of the child is a perception of truth that most older, tradition-bound people have lost. Atticus, like Emerson's lover of nature, has retained it, and can understand it; it only remains for that vision to be instilled in others.

Linked to this belief is Atticus's recognition of the diversity of man and his faith in the higher laws—although, significantly, his higher laws are not the abstruse, cosmic laws of Emerson, but the practical laws of the courts. Atticus, by his own confession, is no idealist, believing in the absolute goodness of mankind. In his courtroom argument he acknowledges his belief that " 'there is not a person . . . who has never told a lie, who has never done an immoral thing, and there is no man living who has never looked upon a woman without desire'." To this he adds his recognition of the randomness of life: " 'Some people are smarter than others, some people have more opportunity because they're born with it, some men make more money than others, some ladies make better cakes than others—some people are born gifted beyond the normal scope of most men'." At the same time, he also believes that these flawed, diverse people are united by one thing—the law. There is, he says, " 'one way in this country in which all men are created equal—there is one human institution that makes a pauper the equal of a Rockefeller, the stupid man the equal of an Einstein, and the ignorant man the equal of any college president. That institution, gentlemen, is a court'." In this, his climactic speech to the jury, Atticus makes clear his commitment. Like the Puritans, he assumes the flawed nature of man, but, like Emerson, he looks to the higher laws—those of the court and of the nation—that enable man to transcend his base diversity and give him the only form of equality possible in a diverse society. Like the Emerson of the "Ode to Channing," he argues:

> Let man serve law for man;
> Live for friendship, live for love;
> For truth's and harmony's behoof;
> The state may follow how it can.

Atticus will, indeed, serve law for man, leaving the state—his contemporaries—to follow how it can. He, at least, has absolved him to himself.

Throughout *To Kill a Mockingbird,* Harper Lee presents a dual view of the American South. On the one hand, she sees the South as still in the grip of the traditions and habits so amply documented by Davis, Dollard, and others—caste division along strictly color lines, hierarchical class stratification within castes, and exaggerated regard for kin-group relations within particular classes, especially the upper and middle classes of the white caste. On the other hand, she argues that the South has within itself the potential for progressive change, stimulated by the incorporation of the New England romanticism of an Emerson, and characterized by the pragmatism, principles, and wisdom of Atticus Finch. If, as she suggests, the South can exchange its old romanticism for the new, it can modify its life to bring justice and humanity to all of its inhabitants, black and white alike.

In suggesting the possibility of a shift from the old romanticism to the new, however, Miss Lee goes even further. If her argument is carried to its logical extension, it becomes apparent that she is suggesting that the South, by assimilating native (though extra-regional) ideals, can transcend the confining sectionalism that has dominated it in the past, and develop the breadth of vision characteristic of the truly regional outlook. (pp. 122-33)

Miss Lee sees such a development as a distinct possibility. Maycomb, in the past isolated and insulated, untouched by even the Civil War, is no longer detached from the outside world. It is, as Miss Lee suggests through the Finch brothers' going elsewhere to study, beginning to seek for what it does not possess. (This quest, however, is no panacea, as Miss Less implies with the character of the pathetically inept Miss Caroline Fisher, the first-grade teacher from North Alabama, who introduces the "Dewey Decimal System" to revolutionize the Maycomb County School System.) Moreover, Maycomb is being forced to respond to events touching the nation and the world. The Depression is a real thing, affecting the lives of white and black alike; the merchants of Maycomb are touched by the fall of the National Recovery Act; and Hitler's rise to power and his persecution of the Jews make the power of Nazism apparent even to the comfortable Christians of the town. Maycomb, in short, like the South it represents, is becoming at last a part of the United States; what affects the nation affects it, and the influence of external events can no longer be ignored.

The organic links of Maycomb with the world at large extend even further, as Miss Lee goes on to point out the relationship between what happens in Maycomb and the entirety of human experience. The novel opens and closes on a significant note—that life in Maycomb, despite its Southern particularity, is an integral part of human history. This broadly regional vision appears in the first paragraphs of the novel, as the narrator, the mature Scout, reflects upon the events leading up to the death of Bob Ewell:

> I maintain that the Ewells started it all, but Jem, who was four years my senior, said it started long before that. He said it began the summer Dill came to us, when Dill first gave us the idea of making Boo Radley come out.
>
> I said if he wanted to take a broad view of the thing, it really began with Andrew Jackson. If General Jackson hadn't run the Creeks up the creek, Simon Finch would never have paddled up the Alabama, and where would we be if he hadn't? We were far too old to settle an argument with a fist-fight, so we consulted Atticus. Our father said we were both right.

The theme of this passage—that events of long ago and far away can have consequences in the present—is echoed at the novel's end. Tom Robinson is dead, Bob Ewell is dead, Boo Radley has emerged and submerged, and Scout, aged nine, is returning home. The view from the Radley porch evokes a flood of memories, which, for the first time, fall into a coherent pattern for her: the complex interaction of three years of children's play and adult tragedy is revealed in a single, spontaneous moment of intuitive perception. "Just standing on the Radley porch was enough," she says. "As I made my way home, I felt very old. . . . As I made my way home, I thought what a thing to tell Jem tomorrow. . . . As I made my way home, I thought Jem and I would get grown but there wasn't much else left for us to learn, except possibly algebra." She has learned, with Emerson, that "to the young mind every thing is individual. . . . By and by, it finds how to join two things and see in them one nature; then three, then three thousand; and so, tyrannized over by its own unifying instinct, it goes on tying things together . . . [discovering] that these objects are not chaotic, and are not foreign, but have a law which is also a law of the human mind." When the oneness of the world dawns upon a person, truly all that remains is algebra.

Miss Lee's convictions could not be more explicit. The South, embodied here in Maycomb and its residents, can no longer stand alone and apart. It must recognize and accept its place in national and international life, and it must accept the consequences for doing so. It must recognize and accept that adjustments must come, that other ways of looking at things are perhaps better than the traditional ones. Like Emerson's individual, it must be no longer hindered by the name of goodness, but must explore if it is goodness. If, to a perceptive and thoughtful observer, the old ways have lost their value, new ones must be found to supplant them; if, on the other hand, the old ways stand up to the skeptical eye, they should by all means by preserved. This Atticus Finch has done, and this he is teaching his children to do. By extension, the South must do the same, cultivating the good that it possesses, but looking elsewhere for the good that it lacks. . . . If the South can learn this fundamental lesson, seeking its unique place in relation to human experience, national experience, and world experience, all that will remain for it, too, will be algebra. (pp. 134-36)

Fred Erisman, "The Romantic Regionalism of Harper Lee," in The Alabama Review, Vol. XXVI, No. 2, April, 1973, pp. 122-36.

R. A. DAVE

To Kill a Mockingbird is quite an ambiguous title, the infinitive leaving a wide scope for a number of adverbial queries— how, when, where, and, of course, *why*—all leading to intriguing speculation and suspense. One is left guessing whether it is a crime-thriller or a book on bird-hunting. Look at it any way, the title hurts the reader's sensibility and creates an impression that something beautiful is being bruised and broken. It is only after he plunges into the narrative and is swept off into its current that he starts gathering the significance of the title. After buying the gift of an air gun for his little son, Atticus says: 'I would rather you shot at tin cans in the backyard, but I know you will go after birds . . . but remember, it's a sin to kill a mockingbird.' And when Scout asks Miss Maudie about it, for that is the only time when she ever heard her father say it is a sin to do something, she replies saying:

> 'Your father is right. Mockingbirds don't do one thing but make music for us to enjoy. They don't eat up people's gardens, don't nest in corncribs, they don't do one thing but sing their hearts out for us. That's why it is a sin to kill a mockingbird.'

And as the words 'it's a sin to kill a mockingbird' keep on echoing into our ears, we are apt to see on their wings the mockingbirds that will sing all day and even at night without seeming to take time to hunt for worms or insects. At once the moral undertones of the story acquire symbolical expression and the myth of the mockingbird is seen right at the thematic centre of the story. The streets of Maycomb were deserted, the doors and windows were instantaneously shut the moment Calpurnia sent round the word about the dog, gone mad in February not in August. . . . There was hush all over. 'Nothing is more deadly than a deserted waiting street. The trees were silent, the mockingbirds were silent.' During moments of peril, such as these, even the mockingbirds do not sing! That the little girl should see in the dog's march to death some motivation of 'an invisible force' is as significant as her being struck by the silence of the mockingbirds. We have several such moments of eloquent silence in the novel. But what is more disturbing is the behaviour of the neighbours, who open their 'windows one by one' only after the danger was over. Atticus could protect them against a mad dog: he could not protect the innocent victim against their madness! As the Finch children along with their friend Dill waver at the portals of the Radley House on their way to solve the Boo mystery, we again hear the solitary singer:

> High above us in the darkness a solitary mocker poured out his repertoire in blissful unawareness of whose tree he sat in, plunging from the shrill kee, kee of the sunflower bird to the irascible qua-ack of a bluejay, to the sad lament of Poor Will, Poor Will, Poor Will.

And when they shoot Tom Robinson, while lost in his unavailing effort to scale the wall in quest of freedom, Mr Underwood, the editor of *The Montgomery Advertiser,* 'likened Tom's death to the senseless slaughter of songbirds by hunters and children.' As we find the mockingbird fluttering and singing time and again, the whole of Maycomb seems to be turning before our eyes into a wilderness full of senseless slaughter. The mockingbird motif, as effective as it is ubiquitous, and a continual reminder of the thematic crux, comes alive in the novel with all its associations of innocence, joy, and beauty.

The mockingbird myth is there in American literature and folklore. In Walt Whitman's "Out of the Cradle Endlessly Rocking", we have a tender tale of mockingbirds, the tale of love and longing and loss. . . . The mockingbird myth is most powerfully used by Whitman, who travels back and forth on the waves of childhood memories with a mist of tears through which 'a man, yet by these tears a little boy again', sings a reminiscence. The mockingbird symbol in the novel acquires a profound moral significance. For, unlike the world of tender love and longing of Walt Whitman's Alabama birds, Harper Lee's Alabama presents a bleak picture of a narrow world torn by hatred, injustice, violence and cruelty, and we lament to see 'what man has made of man'. It brings out forcefully the condition of Negro subculture in the white world where a Negro, as dark as a mockingbird, is accepted largely as a servant or at best as an entertainer. But apart from the symbolical identity, *To Kill a Mockingbird* has an astonishing technical kinship with Whitman's "Out of the Cradle Endlessly Rocking". Both, Whitman and Harper Lee, recollect childhood memories after many years have gone by. In both, the poem and the novel, we see a parabolic pattern. After years, the narrator goes back into the past, swimming across a flood of memories, and then comes back floating onwards towards the present moment and beyond. The way childhood memories impinge on adult consciousness, turning 'a man, yet by these tears a little boy again', gives a new dimension to the autobiographical mode, and heightens dramatically the reported impressions by the fact that what happens to the artist's consciousness is more important than the actual happening itself. In the novel, Harper Lee instals herself avowedly as the narrator and depicts not only the external world of action, but the internal world of character also. (pp. 311-13)

Harper Lee has a remarkable gift of story-telling. Her art is visual, and with cinematographic fluidity and subtlety we see a scene melting into another scene without jolts of transition. Like Browning's poet, Harper Lee is a 'maker-see'. She unfolds the wide panorama of Maycomb life in such a way that we, the readers, too, get transported in that world within world and watch helplessly, though not quite hopelessly, the bleak shadows of the adult world darkening the children's dream world.

To Kill a Mockingbird is autobiographical not merely in its mode of expression but also in quite a personal sense. If David Copperfield is Charles Dickens and Stephen Dedalus in *A Portrait of the Artist as a Young Man* is James Joyce, Jean Louise Finch (Scout) is unmistakably Harper Lee. If we examine the internal evidence, we can easily infer that in 1935, while Hitler was persecuting the Jews in Germany and Tom Robinson was being tried in Maycomb, Jean Finch Scout, the narrator, was 'not yet nine'; perhaps she was born, like her creator, in 1926. The identification between the narrator and the novelist is apparent. The novel with its autobiographical mode strikes a psychological balance between the past, the present, and the future. The writer projects herself into the story as Scout in the present. What she narrates is the past. And as the past is being unfolded the reader wonders how the writer's retrospect will lead her on to the future, which is a continual mystery. This evokes in the novel considerable suspense. We follow the trial of Tom Robinson and the ostracising of the Finch family, holding our breath. But unlike David Copperfield who casts a backward glance over a long-travelled road or Stephen Dedalus who grows from childhood to youth and to manhood seeking aesthetic vision and development in exile, Scout Finch concentrates on a single phase, a moment of crisis in which childhood innocence was shattered by the terrifying experiences of the adult world.

It is a memory tale told by a little girl, Jean Louise Finch, called Scout in the novel. She becomes a mirror of experience and we see reflected in her the Maycomb world. Her memories recollected in imaginative tranquillity become a dramatised action and the fiction gets an extraordinary gloss of veracity. A white girl's accusation of her rape by a Negro causes a huge upheaval that rocks 'the very old and tired town of Maycomb'. It all began the summer when Scout was six and her brother Jem ten. We find the Finch family caught in the storm of the white, popular reaction, but braving it all with remarkable steadfastness, courage and fortitude. The two motherless children and their father face the ordeal so heroically that it lifts the story from the probable melodramatic and sentimental doldrums and makes *To Kill a Mockingbird,* which is a winter's tale, a heroic one told in a lyric way. Apart from the mockingbird symbol which is pervasive, we have several other symbols. When it snows in Maycomb, after years and years, the county school declares a holiday, and we see the Finch children trying to make a snow-man. But there is more mud than snow:

> 'Jem, I ain't ever heard of a nigger snowman,' I
> said.
> 'He won't be black long,' he grunted.

And he tries to cover it with some snow-flakes, making it white. But at night Miss Maudie's house is on fire, and Scout watches 'our absolute Morphodite go black and crumble'. The snow-man turning alternately white and black suggests how frail and skin-deep is the colour. Besides, Miss Maudie's flowers, too, caught in the flames, symbolise innocence in the grip of fire. And as we see the yellow flames leaping up in a snowy, dark night we have the symbols of the white snow and the coloured flames standing for cold hatred and fiery wrath that might lead to the crack of the world as visualised by Robert Frost in his poem "Fire and Ice." Symbolism lends poetic touch to the novel that depicts not only the external world of action but also the internal world of character. For, here the novelist registers the impact of the central action not so much on the protagonist as on the others. Both Boo Radley locked in his own home for fifteen long years for some trifling adolescent pranks so that his father could find the vanity fair of the society congenial, and Tom Robinson sentenced to death for a rape he never committed, are kept as invisible as the crimes they never committed. Two such innocent victimisations paralleled with each other intensify the tragic view of the world and recall the terrifying prognosis: 'So shall the world go on: to good men malignant, to bad men benign.' What happens to the innocent victims, who are largely shut out from us like beasts in a cage, is really not as important as the way it stirs the world around. The novel that opens with the theme of persecution taking us back to the ancestor, Simon Finch, who sailed across the Atlantic to escape reli-

gious persecution in England, keeps the victims generally off the stage, invisible while the prolonged tensions between the protagonist minority and the antagonist majority shake the small world of Maycomb with an ever increasing emotional and moral disturbance. In this oblique handling of the central theme we have, what Virginia Woolf describes as 'a luminous halo, a semi-transparent envelope'. It is an effective artistic device. All this is presented through the fascinating, though disturbing, flash-backs, and the continual backthrust intensifies the unforgettableness of the narrator's experience.

Maycomb is a microcosm, and the novelist's creative fecundity has peopled it well. We have a cross-section of humanity: men and women, young and old, good and bad, white and black. *To Kill a Mockingbird* presents a memorable portrait gallery. Generally it is the evil characters that are better portrayed than the good, Satan rather than God. But Harper Lee's emotional and moral bias seems to put her more at ease with good people than bad. The wicked characters tend to be hazy whereas the good characters stand out prominently throbbing with life. Bob Ewell and his allies are just paper-figures. Again, the women in the novel are better delineated than the men with the probable exception of Atticus. But her highest achievement in characterisation is manifest in children who at once spring to life. If the successful delineation of children characters is a mark of creative genius, Harper Lee has attained a notable success. Unlike her grown-up characters who easily tend to be caricatures seen in concave and convex mirrors, these children are wonderfully true to life. We have some most unforgettable vignettes. . . . [Think] of Dill getting sick of the trial and breaking down. It is Mr Raymond, the man 'who perpetrated fraud against himself by drinking Coca Cola in a whiskey bag' who says:

> 'Let him get a little older and he won't get sick and
> cry. Maybe things will strike him as being—not
> quite right, say, but he won't cry, not when he gets
> a few years on him.'

And we have the sad juxtaposition of the two worlds. We have children—Jem, Scout, Dill and the whole lot of them with an insatiable sense of wonder and curiosity. It is they who are bewildered by the ways of the grown-up world and confronted with the most disturbing problems like 'What exactly is a Nigger-lover Atticus?' 'What is rape, Cal?' When Tom Robinson is adjudged to be guilty, it is their young hearts that we see bleeding:

> I shut my eyes. Judge Taylor was polling the jury:
> 'Guilty . . . guilty . . . guilty . . . guilty . . .' I
> pecked at Jem: his hands were white from gripping
> the balcony rail, and his shoulders jerked as if each
> 'guilty' was a separate stab between them.

And here is Atticus, the defence counsel, the hero of the trial scene, but for whom the trial would have seemed as if out of Kafka's world. At least the phantasmal jury and the accusers all seem to have been people who should not have surprised even Joseph K. The trial was over, but not so the heartquakes of the young, although they knew, as Scout points out, 'in the secret courts of men's hearts Atticus had no case'.

> 'Atticus—' said Jem bleakly.
> He turned the door way. 'What, son?'
> 'How could they do it, how could they?'
> 'I don't know, but they did it. They've done it before and they did it tonight and they'll do it again,
> and when they do, it seems that only children will
> weep. Goodnight.'

Atticus is the protagonist, reticent, dignified and distant. When the entire white world seems to have lost its head, it is he who remains sane and firm. He is a wonderful combination of strength and tenderness. He is a stoic and can withstand the ostracism and persecution with almost superhuman courage and fortitude. He is a widower but treats his motherless children with so much affection and understanding that they call him 'Atticus'. They are about his only friends in a world in which he is lonely. It is in the trial scene that we see Atticus at his best, exposing the falsehood and meanness of the white world intent on destroying an innocent Negro. If Jean Scout, the daughter, keeps the wheel of the story turning, Atticus is the axle. He is a man who seems to have been made to approximate to Newman's idea of a gentleman. He never inflicts pain on others, but strives to relieve them of it even at the cost of his own and his children's suffering. It is a highly idealised character. He stands up like a lighthouse, firm, noble, and magnanimous.

But the children and Atticus, with a few other probable exceptions like Calpurnia and Sheriff Tate, and the victims are about the only normal fold in the novel. These Maycomb women are quite funny. They are the comic characters in a tragic world; they play the chorus in the novel. Here is Aunt Alexandra, 'analogous to Mount Everest . . . she was cold and there', betraying the novelist's eye for the ridiculous:

> She was not fat, but solid, and she chose protective garments that drew up her bosom to giddy heights, inched in her waist, flared out her rear, and managed to suggest that Aunt Alexandra's was once an hour-glass figure. From any angle it was formidable.

We have 'Miss Stephanie Crawford, that English channel of gossip', and Miss Dubose who was horrible: 'Her face was horrible. Her face was the color of a dirty pillow-case, and the corners of her mouth glistened.' But Calpurnia, the nurse, who reminds us of Dilsey in Faulkner's *The Sound and the Fury*, and Miss Maudie are the only two women who have beneath their tough exteriors abundant humanity. Calpurnia, who leads a double-life, takes Jem and Scout to the Negro church the way Dilsey takes Benjy to the Easter service in Faulkner. Here we are in the church; the novelist has almost actually taken us in:

> The warm bitter sweet smell of clean Negro welcomed us as we entered the churchyard—Hearts of Love hair-dressing mingled with asafoetida, snuff, Hoyt's Cologne, Brown's Mule, peppermint, and lilac talcum.

But there is a counterpoint. Lula, a Negro, protests against the visit of the white children; and Calpurnia retorts: 'It's the same God, ain't it?' Calpurnia has brought up these motherless children. It is the persons like Atticus and Calpurnia who try to bridge the chasm dividing the whites from the blacks. But it is in Miss Maudie that we have a most remarkable woman. When her house is burnt up, she replies to Jem with robust optimism: 'Always wanted a smaller house, Jem Finch . . . Just think, I'll have more room for my azaleas now.' When the whole of Maycomb is madly excited over Tom's trial, without ever realising that it was not so much Tom as the white world on trial, Miss Maudie does not lose her head: 'I am not. 'Tis morbid watching a poor devil on trial for his life. Look at all those folks, it's like a Roman carnival.' When children put all sorts of queer questions about Arthur Radley, she replies pat:

> 'Stephanie Crawford even told me, once she woke up in the middle of the night and found him looking in the window at her. I said what did you do, Stephanie, move over in the bed and make room for him? That shut her up awhile.'

She tells the Finch children:

> 'You are too young to understand it . . . but sometimes the Bible in the hand of one man is worse than a whiskey bottle in the hand—oh, of your father.'

And here is the heart of the matter—the dichotomy between appearance and reality. Things are not what they seem. Both Arthur Radley and Tom Robinson, who are punished for no crimes they ever committed, are the representatives of all innocent victims. In fact, Radley stitching Jem's pants torn during the children's pranks against himself, leaving gifts for the children in the tree hole, throwing a blanket round Scout while she stood shivering in a dark, cold night watching the house on fire, and finally saving children's lives from the fatal attack of Bob Ewell, is more human than most of the Maycomb fold. He is not the blood-thirsty devil as pictured in the popular fantasy. And so is Tom, who was driven only by compassion to respond to Mayella's request for help. She had assaulted him. There was no rape. But in the court Bob Ewell shamelessly 'stood up and pointed his finger at Tom Robinson: "I see that black nigger yonder ruttin' on my Mayella."' Ewell and evil are almost homophones. They are filthy parasites, a blot on society. This shows how culture has nothing to do with colour. The novelist's moral and emotional identification with the whole problem is so great that the verdict of the trial upsets her, too. For a moment she seems to be losing her grip on the story. The characters are on the brink of losing their identity, and the novelist, in her righteous anger, is on the point of reducing them to mere mouthpieces. For even the children stunned by the judgment fumble for words, and for a while the narrative is in danger of getting lost in the doldrums of discussion—dull, heavy, futile. This can be understood in the context of her having patterned the story after the model of a morality play with a distinct line of demarcation between good and evil, right and wrong, beautiful and ugly. Like Ewell, Cunnigham, too, betrays his character through connotation. The finch, the family name of Atticus, means a songbird like the mockingbird. It is the Finch family that pits itself against evil in defence of good. Jem Calways (sounds like Gem) and Scout are names that do not fail to evoke a sense of value and selfless service, whereas Jean, which is a variation of Joan, distantly clicks into our memory that angelical girl, Joan of Arc, battling for a great cause.

To Kill a Mockingbird is a regional novel. Like Jane Austen, who does not care to go beyond the district of Bath, or Thomas Hardy who hardly, if ever, takes his story out of the confines of Wessex, Harper Lee sticks to Maycomb in Alabama. The small world assumes a macrocosmic dimension and expands into immensity, holding an epic canvas against which is enacted a movingly human drama of the jostling worlds—of children and adults, of innocence and experience, of kindness and cruelty, of love and hatred, of humour and pathos, and above all of appearance and reality—all taking the reader to the root of human behaviour. Time does not have a stop in Harper Lee's world, but it moves on lazily. The cycle of seasons keeps on turning with the ever-returning summer, and life in Maycomb, 'a tired old town', flows on in all its splendour and ugliness, joys and sorrows. Harper Lee, in her firm determination to keep away from the contemporary trend of experimentation without ever succumbing to the lure of following the footsteps of novelists like Hemingway and Faulkner, returns to the nineteenth century tradition of the well-made novel with immense facility. If she at all betrays any influence, it is from the past rather than the present— Jane Austen's morality and regionalism, Mark Twain's blending of humour and pathos in the jostling worlds, Dickens's humanitarianism and characterisation, Harriet Stowe's sentimental concern for the coloured folk. If by modernism we mean whatever that is anti-traditional, Harper Lee is not a modern, though a contemporary novelist. The contemporaneity of *To Kill a Mockingbird* is incidental, its universality essential. She tells the story with astonishing zest and yet a leisureliness characteristic of the past age. For instance, about a century divides *To Kill a Mockingbird* from Harriet Stowe's *Uncle Tom's Cabin* but there is no fundamental difference either about the content or the technique of the novels. In both we see an astonishing streak of sentimentality, an irresistible love of melodrama and the same age-old pity for the underdog. But Harper Lee has an unusual intensity of imagination which creates a world more living than the one in which we live, so very solid, so easily recognisable. It all looks so effortless, so very uncontrived. But it is painful to see the way the harsh realities impinge mercilessly on the juvenile world of innocence. Harper Lee has an intense ethical bias and there is about the novel a definite moral fervour.

The novelist, in an unmistakable way, has viewed one of the most fundamental human problems with the essentially Christian terms of reference, and we see emerging from the novel a definite moral pattern embodying a scale of values. As we notice the instinctive humanising of the world of things we are also impressed by the way Harper Lee can reconcile art and morality. For *To Kill a Mockingbird* is not a work of propaganda, it is a work of art, not without a tragic view of life. The novelist has been able to combine humour and pathos in an astonishing way. But comedy and tragedy are, in the final analysis, two sides of the same coin. The novel bubbling with life and overflowing with human emotions is not without a tragic pattern involving a contest between good and evil. Atticus in his failure to defend the Negro victim, eventually hunted down while scaling the wall in quest of freedom, the innocent victim, and Arthur Boo, who is endowed with tender human emotions and compassion, but is nearly buried alive in the Radley House, which is a veritable sepulchre, simply because his father loved to wallow in the vanity fair, and the suffering Finch children, they all intensify the sense of waste involved in the eternal conflict. 'The hero of a tragedy,' observes Freud in *Totem and Taboo,* 'had to suffer; this is today still the essential content of a tragedy.' By that norm, *To Kill a Mockingbird* could be seen to hover on the frontier of a near-tragedy. The tragic mode is no longer a monopoly of the theatre. Like the epic that precedes it, the novel that succeeds it, too, can easily order itself into a comic or a tragic pattern. . . . *To Kill a Mockingbird* has the unity of place and action that should satisfy an Aristotle although there is no authority of the invisible here as in a Greek tragedy. With Atticus and his family at the narrative centre standing like a rock in a troubled sea of cruelty, hatred and injustice, we have an imitation of an action which is noble and of a certain magnitude. And the story, that is closed off on the melancholy note of the failure of good, also is not without its poetic justice through the nemesis that destroys the villain out to kill the Finch children. In fact, twice before the final catastrophe the story seems to be verging on its end. The first probable terminal is chapter twenty-one, when Tom is con-

victed and sentenced; the second is chapter twenty-six, when Tom is shot dead—not killed but set free from the coils of life, as it were—and there is nothing really left. But the novelist wants to bring the story to a rounded-off moral end. Like a symphony it starts off on a new movement after touching the lowest, almost inaudible key, and we have the crescendo of its finale. Here is exploration, or at least an honest attempt at exploration, of the whole truth which is lost in the polarities of life. But Harper Lee who lets us hear in the novel the 'still, sad music of humanity' is immensely sentimental. Her love for melodrama is inexhaustible. Hence, although her view of human life is tragic, the treatment is sentimental, even melodramatic. However, though not a tragedy, it is since *Uncle Tom's Cabin* one of the most effective expressions of the voice of protest against the injustice to the Negro in the white world. Without militant championship of 'native sons' writing in a spirit of commitment, here is a woman novelist transmuting the raw material of the Negro predicament aesthetically. . . . As we read *To Kill a Mockingbird,* a thesis novel, we notice an unfailing moral order arising out of the flux of experience which is the evolution of human consciousness elaborated through the structure of events, without ever raising the age-old problem of art and morality. There is a complete cohesion of art and morality. And therein lies the novelist's success. She is a remarkable story-teller. The reader just glides through the novel abounding in humour and pathos, hopes and fears, love and hatred, humanity and brutality—all affording him a memorable human experience of journeying through sunshine and rain at once. *To Kill a Mockingbird* is indeed a criticism of life and that, too, a most disturbing criticism, but we hardly feel any tension between the novelist's creativity and social criticism and the tale of heroic struggle lingers in our memory as an unforgettable experience while its locale, Maycomb County—'*Ad Astra per Aspera:* from mud to the stars'—stretches itself beyond our everyday horizon as an old familiar world. (pp. 314-23)

R. A. Dave, " 'To Kill a Mockingbird': Harper Lee's Tragic Vision," in Indian Studies in American Fiction, *M. K. Naik, S. K. Desai, S. Mokashi-Punekar, eds., The Macmillan Company of India Limited, 1974, pp. 311-23.*

WILLIAM T. GOING

One of the things about [T. S.] Stribling that disturbed Robert Penn Warren in 1934 when he was writing about the new Pulitzer Prize winner was that the author "has never been interested in the dramatic possibilities of a superior white man brought into conflict with his native environment," a matter that has challenged many serious Southern novelists like William Faulkner and Caroline Gordon. A quarter of a century later Miss Lee has done precisely that for the Alabama scene [in *To Kill a Mockingbird*]. Even though it is usually easier to write about the spectacular, wicked man, Miss Lee has chosen the more difficult task of writing about the quiet, good man. Other novelists have been concerned with this type of man—the thoughtful, well-educated Southerner at quiet odds with his environment like the minor character Gavin Stevens in Faulkner's *Intruder in the Dust.* But Miss Lee has made him the central figure and hero of her novel and succeeded at the same time in writing an exciting and significant story.

The epigraph from Charles Lamb—"Lawyers, I suppose,

were once children"—indicates the two aspects of *Mockingbird,* childhood and the law. The plot can be simply stated: Atticus Finch, one of Maycomb's leading attorneys, is the court-appointed defender of Tom Robinson, accused of raping Mayella Ewell, a daughter of the town's notorious poor white-trash family. In this struggle he is unsuccessful—at least the all-white jury finds Tom guilty, and he is killed escaping from prison before Atticus can gain a hearing on the appeal. But to a certain extent the case is not altogether lost; certain precedents have been set. Instead of a young lawyer who defends only for the record's sake Judge Taylor appoints a distinguished lawyer who chooses to fight obvious lies and racial hatred so that he and his children—and ultimately Maycomb itself—can remain honest and honorable people. No one except Atticus Finch ever kept a jury out so long on a case involving a Negro. And in the process of the trial Atticus's children have matured in the right way—at least in his eyes.

The struggle of the children toward maturity, however, occupies more space than Atticus's struggle to free Tom, the central episode. Through their escapades and subsequent entanglements with their father and neighbors like Miss Maudie Atkinson, Mrs. Henry Lafayette Dubose, and particularly the legends about Boo Radley, the town's boogie man, Jem and Scout learn what it means to come to man's estate. In Part I, an evocation of the happy days of summer play, the process is begun. With their friend Dill Harris from Meridian they enact the weird stories about Boo Radley—how he sits in his shuttered house all day and wanders about in the shadows of night looking in people's windows, how he once drove the scissors into his father's leg, how as a not-too-bright adolescent he had terrorized the county with a "gang" from Old Sarum. Might he even be dead in that solemn, silent house, the children wonder. Miss Maudie gives, as always, a forthright answer to that question: "I know he's alive, Jean Louise, because I haven't seen him carried out yet." Although Atticus forbids these "Boo Radley" games, the children go on playing. . . . (pp. 23-4)

In the midst of these juvenile Gothic masques the children begin to learn something about the difference between gossip and truth. When Jem tears his pants and is forced to leave them behind on the wire fence during their night expedition to peek through the Radleys' shutters, he later finds them crudely mended, pressed, and hanging over the fence. When Miss Maudie's house burns during a cold night, all the neighborhood turns out to help and to watch. Scout, who is told to come no closer than the Radleys' gate, discovers that during the confusion a blanket has been thrown round her shoulders. Jem realizes that this thoughtful act was not performed by Mr. or Mrs. Radley, who have long been dead, and he saw Mr. Nathan, Boo's brother and "jailer," helping haul out Miss Maudie's mattress. It could have been only Boo.

One of the most interesting features of *Mockingbird* is the skill with which Miss Lee weaves these two struggles about childhood and the law together into one thematic idea. . . . [She] does a neat workmanlike job of dovetailing her plots. When Scout attends her first day at school, the morning session is devoted to explaining the Cunningham family to Miss Caroline so that she will understand she must not lend Walter any lunch money. The Cunninghams are poor but proud. When the Sunday night lynching party arrives at the jail, it is Jem and Scout, who, having slipped off from home, see their father calmly reading a newspaper by the light at the

jail door, sitting in one of his office chairs. Hiding in the doorway of the Jitney Jungle, Scout rushes forward in time to disconcert the Cunningham mob by asking innocent questions about Walter, her classmate—her father had always taught her to talk to folks about the things that would interest them.

The afternoon session of Scout's first day at school had been taken up with Burris Ewell and his dirt and defiance of Miss Caroline. It is Burris's father who brings the charge of rape against Tom Robinson.

This neatness that makes for economy of character portrayal is successful when it avoids the appearance of too convenient coincidental circumstances—a fault that *Mockingbird* does not entirely escape. But in the more important aspect of thematic development the novel is successful. Carson McCullers and Truman Capote have written with insight about Southern childhood, and William Faulkner has traced the legal and moral injustices done the Negro just as Eudora Welty has underlined the quiet patience of the Negro's acceptance of his bleak world. Harper Lee has united these two concepts into the image of a little child—schooled in basic decencies by her father even though "ladylike" manners of the superficial sort that Aunt Alexandra admires are sometimes lacking—who turns the tide to stop the Sunday night lynching. After the trial when Jem cannot comprehend the injustice done Tom Robinson by the jury, he asks his father, "How could they do it, how could they?" Atticus replies, "I don't know, but they did it. They've done it before and they did it tonight and they'll do it again and when they do it—seems that only the children weep."

Almost all readers will agree that the first two-thirds of *Mockingbird* is excellent fiction; the difference of opinion will probably turn upon the events after the trial. The major incident here is the school pageant about the history of Maycomb County as written by Mrs. Merriweather; the performance is the town's attempt at "organized activity" on Halloween. On their way home from the pageant, Ewell attacks the Finch children to get even with Atticus for making him appear a complete and guilty fool at Tom's trial. Scout is saved from the knife by her wire costume representing a Maycomb County ham; Jem receives a painful broken arm. And Ewell is killed with his own knife by Boo Radley, who again lurks opportunely in the shadows. Later that night after visits from the doctor and the sheriff when Scout is allowed to walk home with Mr. Arthur, she stands for a moment on the Radley porch seeing the knothole in the tree where Boo had once left them pitiful little presents of chewing gum and Indianhead pennies. She half realizes as a child of nine, and now as an adult she more fully realizes, what their childish antics must have meant to a lonely, "imprisoned," mentally limited man like Mr. Arthur, and she recalls her father's word to Jem that "you never really know a man until you *stand* in his shoes and walk around in them. Just standing on the Radley porch was enough."

Thematically the aftermath of the injustice done Tom and the growing up of a boy and girl are brought together in the Halloween episode. The structural problem of joining Boo Radley and Tom Robinson into some sort of juxtaposition is solved, but the slapstick comedy of the school pageant and the grotesque coincidental tragedy and subsequent salvation are perilously close to the verge of melodrama. . . . To keep this section of *Mockingbird* from seeming altogether an anticlimax to the trial of Tom, it should at least have been denominated Part III. Then the story would have been set off into its three components of School and Summer Play, Tom Robinson's Trial, and Halloween Masquerade. Such a device would distribute the thirty-one chapters into the equal grouping of Miss Lee's apparent planning, and at the same time it would not force the Halloween tragi-comedy to seem quite so close to the climactic trial.

It is strange that the structural *forte* of **Mockingbird,** the point of view of the telling, is either misunderstood or misinterpreted by most of the initial reviewers of the novel. Phoebe Adams in the *Atlantic Monthly* calls it "frankly and completely impossible, being told in the first person by a six-year-old girl with the prose and style of a well-educated adult." Richard Sullivan in the *Chicago Tribune* is puzzled and only half understands: "The unaffected young narrator uses adult language to render the matter she deals with, but the point of view is cunningly restricted to that of a perceptive, independent child, who doesn't always understand fully what's happening, but who conveys completely, by implication, the weight and burden of the story." [These reviews are excerpted in *CLC,* Vol. 12.] More careful reviewers like Granville Hicks in the *Saturday Review* [see excerpt above] and F. H. Lyell in the *New York Times* [see also *CLC,* Vol. 12] are more perceptive. The latter states the matter neatly: "Scout is the narrator, reflecting in maturity on childhood events of the mid-Thirties."

Maycomb and the South, then, are all seen through the eyes of Jean Louise, who speaks from the mature and witty vantage of an older woman recalling her father as well as her brother and their childhood days. This method is managed with so little ado that the average reader slips well into the story before he realizes that the best evidence that Atticus has reared an intellectually sophisticated daughter is that she remembers her formative years in significant detail and then narrates them with charm and wisdom. She has become the good daughter of a good man, who never let his children know what an expert marksman he was until he was forced to kill a mad dog on their street. Atticus did not like to shoot for the mere sport of it lest he kill a mockingbird like Tom Robinson or Boo Radley; and mockingbirds must be protected for their songs' sake.

This modification of a Jamesian technique of allowing the story to be seen only through the eyes of a main character but to be understood by the omniscient intelligence of Henry James is here exploited to bold advantage. The reader comes to learn the true meaning of Maycomb through the eyes of a child who now recollects with the wisdom of maturity. Along with Scout and Jem we may at first be puzzled why Atticus insists that Jem read every afternoon to old Mrs. Henry Lafayette Dubose in atonement for his cutting the tops off her camellia bushes after she taunted him about his father's being "no better than the niggers and trash he works for." But we soon learn with Scout that Atticus believed Jem would become aware of the real meaning of courage when he was forced to aid a dying old woman in breaking the narcotic habit she abhorred.

Jean Louise's evolving perception of the social milieu in her home town as she grows up in it and as she recalls her own growing up involves the reader in an understanding of the various strata of Maycomb society and its Southern significance. After Jem has brooded about the trial, he explains to Scout that

> "There's four kinds of folks in the world. There's the ordinary kind like us and the neighbors, there's the kind like the Cunninghams out in the woods, the kind like the Ewells down at the dump, and the Negroes."
> "What about the Chinese, and the Cajuns down yonder in Baldwin County?"
> "I mean in Maycomb County. The thing about it is, our kind of folks don't like the Cunninghams, and the Cunninghams don't like the Ewells, and the Ewells hate and despise the colored folks."
> I told Jem if that was so, then why didn't Tom's jury, made up of folks like the Cunninghams, acquit Tom to spite the Ewells?

After considerable debate Scout concludes, "Naw, Jem, I think there's just one kind of folks. Folks."

This naively sophisticated sociological rationalization is far more valid and persuasive in its two-pronged approach. As mature readers we realize its mature validity; as observers of children we delight in their alert reactions to the unfolding events. The convolutions of the "mind of Henry James" have given way to the immediacy and pithy wisdom of Jean Louise's first-person narration.

Though Miss Lee may not have solved all her problems of style in the dual approach of child eyes and mature heart, **Mockingbird** demonstrates the powerful effect and economy of a well-conceived point of view. . . . (pp. 25-9)

Miss Lee, in a sense, has actually revealed more of Alabama history from the Simon Finches of old Saint Stephens to distrusted Republicans like the Misses Barber from Clanton than does Stribling in [*The Store*], his much longer historical novel. The spirit of history is as important as the events of history, and Miss Lee presents Miss Caroline as an outsider from Winston County because she represents to this Maycomb community what every South Alabama child knew about north Alabama: a place "full of Liquor Interests, Big Mules, steel companies, Republicans, professors, and other persons of no background." Miss Lee has mastered an eclectic technique of a meaningful point of view along with validity of idea and freshness of material. She echoes Faulkner in her deep concern for the inchoate tragedy of the South, and like him she is not afraid to pursue the Gothic shadows of Edgar Allan Poe. But her eclecticism is her own: she has told a story of racial injustice from the point of view of thoughtful children with "open, unprejudiced, well-furnished minds of their own," as the *New York Times* has phrased it. And in Atticus Finch she has created the most memorable portrait in recent fiction of the just and equitable Southern liberal. (pp. 30-1)

William T. Going, "Store and Mockingbird: Two Pulitzer Novels about Alabama," in his Essays on Alabama Literature, *The University of Alabama Press, 1975, pp. 9-31.*

Ken Ludwig

19??-

American dramatist.

A lawyer from Washington, D. C., Ludwig came to popular and critical attention on Broadway with *Lend Me a Tenor,* a farce originally produced in London. Set amidst an opera company in Cleveland, Ohio, the play involves a famous, womanizing tenor who is scheduled to perform the lead role in Giuseppe Verdi's opera *Otello.* When the company's distraught manager and his inept assistant discover that the tenor will be unable to perform, the manager replaces the tenor with his assistant. The audience is duped, and mistaken identities and comic situations abound as two identical Otellos compete for the affections of various women following the opera. Clive Barnes commented: "Ludwig is a writer who will descend to any depths for a good laugh . . . , but his real skill is a gift for farcical situations."

PRINCIPAL WORKS

PLAYS

Lend Me a Tenor 1988?
Sullivan and Gilbert 1988

JOHN BEMROSE

Sir Arthur Sullivan and Sir William S. Gilbert gave the world some immortal musicals, but to each other they offered mostly insults. The authors of *The Mikado, The Gondoliers* and a dozen other classics of the popular stage quarrelled frequently and bitterly, sometimes over matters as trivial as the price of a carpet in one of their theatres. Now the two men are portrayed at their argumentative best (or worst) in *Sullivan and Gilbert. . . .* The dramatic parts by American playwright Ken Ludwig are capable of provoking everything from loud guffaws to sentimental tears. But what gives the show its horn-piping exuberance is the songs, written by the battling masters themselves.

When the curtain goes up it is 1890, and the actors and management of London's Savoy Theatre are preparing a revue of Gilbert and Sullivan songs to be presented to Queen Victoria. The occasion has brought together Gilbert and Sullivan after a 10-month cooling-off period following one of their many squabbles. They make up, but not for long. Gilbert discovers that Sullivan is engaged to a singer half his age—and he loudly disapproves. Meanwhile, the rehearsal swirls on around them, with the production's chorus pumping out such favorite Gilbert and Sullivan tunes as "Three Little Maids" and "Never Mind the Why and Wherefore". . . .

[Gilbert finally emerges as] a domineering buffoon who redeems himself with self-deprecating humor. "After all these years, I can only recognize two songs," he says at one point. "One is *God Save the Queen* and the other isn't." That tacit admission of how much he needed Sullivan's musical abilities points to *Sullivan and Gilbert's* premise that respect and affection were at the bottom of their stormy relationship. That may be true or it may be a sentimental manipulation of the facts. In either case, it makes for some excellent theatre.

John Bemrose, "Operetta's Odd Couple," in Maclean's Magazine, *Vol. 101, No. 30, July 18, 1988,* p. 55.

HOWARD KISSEL

As soon as the curtain went up on *Lend Me A Tenor,* unleashing the almost blinding white resplendence of Tony Walton's Art Deco set, I knew I would enjoy the play. This hunch was confirmed moments later when I heard a sound calculated to bring joy to any genuine theater lover's ears: the thud of a well-slammed door.

Now door slamming is an art that has languished in the American theater in recent years. Actors have been more concerned with making political statements or developing their "sense memory" than learning to slam a door with the gusto necessary for farce. In Ken Ludwig's play, the dazzling cast not only slams with élan, but they coordinate their slammings with a precision rare this far from Paris.

Walton's set has six finely sculpted, deeply resonant doors. Need I say more? Need I actually describe the silly plot, which is peopled by an egocentric Italian tenor (yes, I know I'm being redundant); his histrionic wife; three other women who adore him; a crafty, aspiring American tenor; a pompous Cleveland impresario, and a resourceful bellhop?

As you might imagine, the plot would not withstand intense scrutiny. But, unlike another recent comedy that falsely calls itself a farce, *Tenor* does obey the peculiar logic of the genre.

It begins in the believable world and then snowballs into mirthful absurdity. It also follows another law of farce, depicting sex as mechanical and thus *un*-vulgar.

Ludwig's taste is also clear from his musical choices: He has two men sing the great duet from *Don Carlo*, which left me so happy I could excuse puns like someone ordering champagne, asking "Is Mumm all right?" and being told, "She's fine."

Howard Kissel, " 'Tenor' Opens with a Bang," in Daily News, New York, *March 3, 1989.*

CLIVE BARNES

The nuttiness of a farce can be very sweet, and if you are feeling under the weather—or even over the weather, for that matter—and you believe that manic laughter is the best medicine, let me prescribe for you [*Lend Me a Tenor,* a] lovely dose of pure, operatic idiocy.

The scene of Ken Ludwig's prime rib-tickling comedy is Cleveland, Ohio, in 1934. The Cleveland Grand Opera Company—did Cleveland have a Grand Opera Company in 1934? No matter!—is putting on Verdi's *Otello*, with a world-famous tenor, Tito Merelli.

As we open, Saunders, the exquisitely harassed and magnificently unscrupulous manager, is waiting with impatience and his gofer-flunky, Max, for the tardy arrival of the soft-womanizing, hard-drinking tenor, who eventually turns up unexpectedly with his long-suffering but tempestuous wife.

It would be unfair to give away Ludwig's plot—which is logical enough, even obvious, when it happens, but has a happy touch of outrageous surprise to it.

Suffice to say it hinges on doors being opened and shut, honors lost in disguise—the ladies in question are Maggie, who is Saunders' daughter and Max's girlfriend, and Diana, a prima donna with secondary motives—plus monumental misunderstandings and mishaps, with identities so mistaken that they are almost totally lost.

Ludwig is a writer who will descend to any depths for a good laugh . . . but his real skill is a gift for farcical situations.

At the play's critical juncture, the plot calls for two lookalikes (the selection of the opera *Otello* was not quite fortuitous) to whiz in and out of the scenery like two cuckoos in the same clock with fairly similar ideas on time.

The play originated in London a few seasons back—but there its general reputation did not tempt me to rush to see it. However, I suspect that from London to here it has undergone quite a sea change.

Clive Barnes, "It's Something to Sing About," in New York Post, *March 3, 1989.*

FRANK RICH

A farce should be cleverly built, energetically directed and buoyantly acted, but there is one thing it absolutely must be: consistently funny. . . . [*Lend Me a Tenor*] is an impeccable example of how to construct and mount a farce—up to a point. *Lend Me a Tenor* is all things farcical except hilarious.

There are some scattered big laughs, certainly, though one must wait through most of Act I for the first of them to arrive. The prime buffoon is Mr. [Saunders], attired in the white tie, top hat and tails of a Cleveland opera impresario in 1934. [He] has just learned that his imported star for the night's sold-out performance of Verdi's *Otello*, the legendary Italian tenor Tito Merelli, is too ill to go on. The news that $50,000 worth of tickets may have to be refunded does not sit well. Mr. [Saunders] turns comatose from the shock, then reddens with apoplexy, then flies into a shrieking, violent rage, and finally subsides into an open-mouthed stupor, looking like a bloated marlin just after the fisherman has removed the hook. . . .

[Merelli's antithesis is] Max, the nerdy, bespectacled Cleveland Grand Opera Company gofer who harbors Walter Mitty fantasies of being a great tenor himself. When he is drafted by Mr. [Saunders] to impersonate the ailing star in *Otello*, [Max] carries out the hoax in high style, mimicking [Merelli's] personality (and singing voice) as effortlessly as Clark Kent turns into Superman.

Such is Mr. Ludwig's unabashedly silly, highly workable premise. In *Lend Me a Tenor,* two Otellos (in identical costumes and chocolate makeup) pop in and out of six slamming doors in a two-room hotel suite, all the while pursued by a bevy of understandably confused Desdemonas that includes Tito's long-suffering Italian wife . . . , Max's would-be fiancée and an ambitious soprano determined to sleep her way to the Met. What's more, Mr. Ludwig, who is a lawyer as well as a playwright, has done the hard work of crafting the machinery of farce. Unlike the lackadaisical Neil Simon of *Rumors,* he carefully maps out his mistaken identities and close shaves, even to the extent of making certain that each Otello clocks the same time at lovemaking (15 minutes, if you must know).

So why does *Lend Me a Tenor* fail to rise into comic pandemonium? . . . [One should not] look too critically at the credibility of Mr. Ludwig's plot or characters. As is demonstrated in the evening's breathless coda—a silent-movie frenzy—farcical clowning has little to do with reality and a lot to do with the illogical lunacy of wind-up toys.

The play's real comic shortfall is in its details rather than in its master plan. The lines are almost never witty, settling instead for the hoary double-entendres that so titillate the West End (where *Tenor* was a hit in another production). Worse, too many of the farcical situations seem like pale echoes of those in similar works from the play's period (notably Broadway's *Room Service* and Hollywood's *Night at the Opera*, both of 1935). While farces always trade in stock elements, and while the author's homage to a Marx Brothers past is intentional, the old tricks must be augmented by new inventions if the audience is to be ambushed into riotous laughter. A final scene—or third act—that might have topped the traditional set-ups with fresh, hysterical surprises never arrives. . . .

With its speedy gait, . . . the play looks so much like a prime example of its genre that one is all the more frustrated by the shortage of belly laughs. But the evening provides professional, painless fluff even so. If, as *Lend Me a Tenor* would have us believe, a Cleveland audience of 1934 can mistake a rank impostor for the world's most celebrated opera star, it would be foolish to underestimate the prospects of a simulated farce on Broadway in 1989.

> *Frank Rich, "When One Tenor Is Much Like Another," in* The New York Times, *March 3, 1989, p. C3.*

EDWIN WILSON

[In *Lend Me a Tenor*], Maggie, the daughter of an opera impresario and the girlfriend of his assistant, is hiding in a closet in a hotel bedroom. If she is discovered, there will be disaster for all concerned. A famous singer staying at the hotel goes to the door to deposit a coat and suitcase, but when he opens it, Maggie has successfully hidden and is nowhere in sight. Suddenly the singer opens the door again and the audience waits expectantly for the ill-timed discovery, but again, no Maggie. Then he opens the closet door a third time, and the audience, this time expecting an empty space, sees Maggie standing there like a hatcheck girl in a restaurant ready to receive the coat and bag. The sudden twist, the rightness of the image of the hatcheck girl—these are drawn from the essence of farce, and in *Lend Me a Tenor,* . . . Ken Ludwig has created that rare thing—an American farce.

> *Edwin Wilson, "Farce and Tour de Force," in* The Wall Street Journal, *March 8, 1989.*

JOHN SIMON

The good news about Ken Ludwig's farce *Lend Me a Tenor* is that—unlike, say, Neil Simon's *Rumors*—it is free-flowing, honest-to-goodness, unforced farce; the not so good news is that it is a lot less funny than it ought to be. Mistaken identities, cross-purposes, double entendres of which each party understands only one non-meshing half, doors flying open on mayhem and banging shut on people's noses—all the ingredients are here, knowingly deployed.

Will the world-famous tenor Tito Merelli make it in time to appear as Otello for the Cleveland Grand Opera Company? Or will Saunders, the general manager, go nuts? And will Max, Saunders's assistant, conquer his girlfriend, Maggie, Saunders's daughter (it's 1934, and such affairs can still be platonic), or must she first have a fling with someone more romantic—such as Merelli, known as Il Stupendo? And as for Tito and his temperamental wife, Maria—will their marriage survive his harmless flirtations or will she, this time, leave him conclusively? And what happens when Tito accidentally takes too many sleeping pills? (Uh-uh, you won't wring a single answer out of me.)

And that's not all. Everybody either wants to be a tenor (this includes Max and a pest of a bellhop) or to bed the tenor. . . . But not Saunders, who wants neither to be nor to bed Merelli and who doesn't want to refund $50,000 or waste the expensive shrimp bought for the post-opera party. With Il Stupendo stupefied by pills into catatonia—or is it death?—could opera-buff Max, in Otello costume, fool Cleveland into taking him for both the Moor and Merelli? Less may be more, except in Moors, where more is fun, and two Moors unleashed on it can cut all Cleveland from its moorings. I can tell you no moor—sorry, no more.

Ludwig handles farce-writing well enough but not quite with that Roman-candle fulguration that whirls into ever brighter, higher hilarity. Yet he does have his good, sturdy, crowd-pleasing yocks, as well as the occasional, more precious, touch of true lunacy, as when someone reading an ostensible suicide note stops nonplussed: "The fur is gone?" He is promptly corrected: "The fun is gone." (p. 74)

> *John Simon, "Whose Broadway Is It, Anyway?" in* New York *Magazine, Vol. 22, No. 11, March 13, 1989, pp. 72, 74-5.*

James A. Michener

1907-

(Born James Albert Michener) American novelist, short story writer, nonfiction writer, essayist, and art historian.

Among the most popular and prolific of American novelists, Michener is known primarily for historical epics that chronicle events of various regions and their people from prehistoric times to the present. He first gained attention with his 1947 novel, *Tales of the South Pacific,* for which he received a Pulitzer Prize, and has enjoyed continued success with such panoramic works as *Hawaii, The Source, Centennial,* and *Chesapeake.* By employing an abundance of well-researched information on the social, cultural, and historical background of his subjects, Michener invests his novels with an encyclopedic quality and combines entertaining narratives with historical erudition. Despite their diverse topics, Michener's books share a theme: the defeat of common prejudices and the promotion of harmonious human relations.

Although commercially successful, Michener's fiction has garnered an uneven critical response. Such early works as *The Bridges at Toko-Ri* and *Sayonara* were commended for their steady pace and unified structure. Michener's later, longer novels, however, have been faulted for lacking these same qualities. The frequent time shifts, large casts, and vast scope of events in these works are regarded by some as impediments to serious reader involvement. While some reviewers consider Michener's characters often flat and unrealistic, others laud his entertaining and informative narration of regional histories. Despite mixed critical reviews, Michener remains one of America's most commercially successful authors.

Michener's later works of historical fiction have enjoyed widespread popularity. These include *The Covenant,* a saga of the development of South Africa; *Space,* the story of the United States space program; and *Poland,* which follows that country's progress from early centuries to the present. *Texas,* a novel commissioned to celebrate the state's sesquicentennial, recounts factual events from 450 years of the region's recorded past. This work introduces five fictional Texans whose antecedents were involved in pivotal episodes, from Spanish explorations and Civil War battles to oil drilling and recent immigration disputes. While some reviewers considered the novel's characters mere symbols of virtue or two-dimensional witnesses to historical events, others praised Michener's accurate detail and riveting narration. In homage to the United States Constitution on its bicentennial, Michener published *Legacy,* an uncharacteristically concise novel that contains both the text of the Constitution and the related story of the fictive Starr family, an exemplary American clan whose most current member is called to testify before a Senate committee that is investigating the Iran-Contra scandal. As Major Norman Starr recalls the accomplishments of his forbears, who have variously signed the Constitution, served on the Supreme Court, and commanded Confederate troops, he deliberates over whether to refuse self-incrimination by invoking the Fifth Amendment.

Michener returned to his signature format with the regional epic *Alaska,* which begins with the formation of North Amer-

ica's land mass and follows the state's progress from its early settlement by Russia up to the oil boom that began during the 1970s. Some reviewers remarked that the novel fails to capture the state's immensity or to delineate frontier temperaments, but several commended Michener's compassionate examination of native Alaskan concerns. *Journey,* an excised chapter from *Alaska* published separately as a shorter novel, describes the 2,043-mile trek of four explorers across the Canadian Yukon. *Caribbean,* another of Michener's best-selling novels, is a fictionalized history of the scattered islands between North and South America. While some critics deemed Michener's plot improbable and his characters stereotypical, others defended the work as informative and entertaining. John Hearne commented: "Given the scope of the task which Michener has set himself, he has done his chosen region proud. *Caribbean* is a work which anybody strange to the islands and wanting to know something about them could read with confidence. All the essentials are there; and a skilled and studious novelist has embedded these essentials in a deeply felt, highly responsible tale."

(See also *CLC,* Vols. 1, 5, 11, 29; *Contemporary Authors,* Vols. 5-8, rev. ed.; *Contemporary Authors New Revision Series,* Vol. 21; and *Dictionary of Literary Biography,* Vol. 6.)

254

PRINCIPAL WORKS

NOVELS

Tales of the South Pacific   1947
The Fires of Spring   1949
The Bridges at Toko-Ri   1953
Sayonara   1954
Hawaii   1959
Caravans   1963
The Source   1965
The Drifters   1971
Centennial   1974
Chesapeake   1978
The Covenant   1980
Space   1982
Poland   1983
Texas   1985
Legacy   1987
Alaska   1988
Journey   1989
Caribbean   1989

OTHER

Return to Paradise   (short fiction and travel sketches)
   1951
The Voice of Asia   (nonfiction)   1951; also published as
   Voices of Asia,   1952
The Floating World   (art history)   1954
Selected Writings   1957
Rascals in Paradise [with A. Grove Day]   (biographical
   studies)   1957
The Bridge at Andau   (nonfiction)   1957
Japanese Prints: From the Early Masters to the Modern
   1959
Report of the County Chairman   (nonfiction)   1961
The Modern Japanese Print   1962
Iberia: Spanish Travels and Reflections   (nonfiction)   1968
America vs. America: The Revolution in Middle-Class Values
   (nonfiction)   1969
The Quality of Life   (essays)   1969
Facing East: A Study of the Art of Jack Levine   1970
Kent State: What Happened and Why   (nonfiction)   1971
A Michener Miscellany, 1950-1970   1973
About "Centennial": Some Notes on the Novel   1974
Sports in America   (nonfiction)   1976

NICHOLAS LEMANN

[*Texas*] is, like most of Michener's work, a sweeping panorama of regional history done in the form of a novel. Michener came up with his formula before the word "novelization" had been invented, but it fits his work quite well: this is a novelization of Texas history. In his words, it "strives for an honest blend of fiction and historical fact." When it's time to recount the story of the battle of the Alamo, for instance, he invents a handful of characters on both sides and has them engaging in dialogue with Jim Bowie, Davy Crockett, and General Santa Anna. In the grand design of the book, the governor convenes a five-member task force to study Texas history for the sesquicentennial, and its talky meetings are interspersed in a narrative that traces all its members' family histories.

Texas history is in some ways an ideal Michener subject. Because it is largely separate from the mainstream of American history—its roots are in the Spanish empire, not English colonization—it's still an unfamiliar subject for most people. And the mythic quotient is probably higher than New England's. . . . Michener, who has good news sense, gives only a light once-over to the most familiar Texas subjects—there's very little on cowboys—and gets a lot of mileage out of the underpublicized Spanish-Mexican side of Texas history, and out of the non-western part of the frontier.

As light history, it's pretty good. Everyone is entitled to a theory as to why of all American writers Michener is the most popular, and mine is that he appeals not only to our desire for melodrama but also to our practical side—he crams his books with facts, so that one may feel that the long hours spent reading one qualify as self-improvement. As a novel, though, its only real virtue is some degree of yarn-spinning power. The many characters aren't one-dimensional, but they're two-dimensional: brave yet headstrong, kind yet lazy, etc. (though all members of minority groups tend to be just plain good). None of them stays in mind as embodying the complexity of real life.

The reason is not exactly a lack of art on Michener's part; it's more that the form dictates that everything novelistic must be in the service of delivering history. . . . While it's hard to argue with success, it seems Michener's natural gift would be at a kind of informal narrative history, and forget translating every thought into a worked-up line of dialogue.

That's a problem generic to Michener; there's one other problem for this book in particular. Michener is one of the last of the good liberals, a gentle Quaker-educated man. Texas in its dominant strain is not liberal at all—it's tough, practical, prone to violence, worshipful of money. To Michener's great credit, he grapples earnestly with the Texas character in a way that Texas' own writers often don't, and convincingly roots it in the experience of the early white settlers from the mid-South. He correctly points out how poor and uncivilized Texas was for so much of its history. But he just doesn't seem to be able to work up much genuine feeling about Texas as it is now. The romantic past captivates him; the year 1900 doesn't arrive until page 825. He pretty much skips the '30s, '40s, '50s and '60s, and in the '80s he tends to be suitably awed by his businessman-characters' big deals but to grant them redemption only by giving them sneaking liberal sentiments. He has enough gumption to chide, but he's too nice to use anger or outrage as the center of a book. So inside the impeccably constructed big-book edifice is a hollow spot. I wonder if anyone will notice. (pp. 1, 13)

Nicholas Lemann, "James Michener's Ten-Gallon Epic," in Book World—The Washington Post, September 29, 1985, pp. 1, 13.

MICHIKO KAKUTANI

Unlike most novels, **Texas** comes equipped with six pages of acknowledgments, thanking experts for their advice on everything from "exotic-game Ranching" to "Honky-tonks," and a two-page reader's guide showing which characters are historical and which are fictional. The book is also full of the kind of information that one expects to find in an encyclopedia. . . .

No doubt such bits of knowledge, served up in the author's

utilitarian prose, are part of Mr. Michener's wide popular appeal: readers feel they're learning something, even while they're being entertained, and they're also able to absorb all these facts within a pleasant moral context: a liberal and a humanitarian, Mr. Michener argues for religious and racial tolerance, celebrates the old pioneer ethic of hard work and self-reliance, and offers such incontestable, if obvious, observations as "war forces men to make moral choices."

Still, one wonders why Mr. Michener did not simply write a narrative history of Texas—along the lines, say, of *Iberia,* his absorbing nonfiction study of Spain—instead of trying to package everything within the confines of a novel. . . .

Indeed it is in the attempt to "fictionalize" history—to connect several centuries of events through interrelated families and made-up anecdotes—that Mr. Michener's narrative begins to falter. In an effort to touch upon every important aspect of Texas life, Mr. Michener conjures up dozens and dozens of characters, rushing them on stage and off, before we have time to get to know them or care. As a result, most of these creations are either one-dimensional symbols of various virtues, or stick-figures whose main purpose is to witness an important historical event—the fall of the Alamo, say, or the quest for the Seven Cities of Cibola. To make matters worse, many of their sketch-like stories have a pasty, melodramatic tinge: a teen-age girl, who has been raped, tortured and mutilated by the Comanche, is rehabilitated through love; another young girl contemplates becoming a nun after her lover is killed by the Apache. Men fight duels over women and honor; and assorted murders, lies, and con jobs are perpetrated for the sake of money and land.

Though considerably less bloody and histrionic, the frame story—reminiscent of the one employed in *Centennial*—also seems overly contrived. It is Mr. Michener's conceit that a committee of prominent Texans . . . has been asked, by the Governor of Texas, to deliver a report on "two important questions": "How should our schoolchildren and college students learn about Texas history?" and "What should they learn?" Apparently their research into this matter—combined with their reminiscences about the roles their assorted relatives have played in local history—is supposed to provide the occasion for the historical chapters of *Texas.*

Perhaps Mr. Michener wanted the petty squabbling between the committee's members to form a sort of ironic contrast to the mythic dramas of Texas's past. As it is, though, the narrative never becomes more than an awkward pastiche of time present and time past—a hodgepodge of present-day arguments between liberals and conservatives, and ancient arguments between different religious and racial groups. Even more distracting is the tendency, on the part of the committee members, to engage in didactic exchanges that bear only the faintest resemblance to real conversations. . . .

Though such passages may have their place in a social-studies primer, they hardly make for compelling fiction; and in this case, they make *Texas* seem even longer than it is.

> *Michiko Kakutani, in a review of "Texas," in* The New York Times, *October 9, 1985, p. C20.*

HUGHES RUDD

Well, by heaven, you knew it had to happen sooner or later. James Michener, the fellow who writes the biggest books, has tackled the biggest state—Texas. Boy, has he cut a fat hog, as they say down home. Mr. Michener's *Texas,* at almost 1,100 pages, contains enough paper to cover several New England counties. The novel is so heavy you could probably leave it on a Lubbock, Tex., coffee table in a tornado and find it there when everything else was still in the air over Kansas City, Kan.

Texas is not literature in the classical sense, it is "trotting" journalism, history in a hurry. Admittedly, the history of the Lone Star State cries out for condensation—for all except true-blue Texans who can't get enough of it—but Mr. Michener has bitten off too much. People of various cultures and colors have been running around down there brawling and killing each other under one pretext or another since at least the 16th century, when our recorded knowledge of what is now known as Texas begins. . . . That's an awful lot of colorful characters to cram into one book, even a book as thick as this one. . . .

As a framework for all this, Mr. Michener has a fictional, modern-day governor of Texas create a task force, which he charges with figuring out how and what students should be taught about the history of their state. . . .

Mr. Michener moves the task force around the state to give the reader a geographical and social sampler. En route, he gets so carried away by locale that he refers to Abilene as the intellectual and cultural capital of west Texas. The fact is there *is* no intellectual capital of west Texas.

Right away this task force idea is in trouble. Though the fictional governor tells his appointees that modern-day Texans have no sense of their history, the fact is that students in the Texas school system probably get a bigger dose of their state's history than students in just about any other state. In my hometown of Waco, the state's history is still taught in the fourth grade. Throughout Texas, state history is obligatory in the seventh grade, and the textbook is almost as thick as Mr. Michener's novel. Why does the author think that a governor of Texas would believe Texas kiddies are undernourished on the battle of Goliad . . . and a host of other arcane matters? Well, to this reader, it's not clear why the author thinks that. True, standard Texas history schoolbooks go pretty light on such subjects as lynchings, massacres of those other than white Anglo-Saxon Protestants and the tendency of early Texas Rangers to shoot first and ask questions later—all topics that Mr. Michener touches on. And, of course, those subjects should be covered in the classroom if young Texans are to know the truth about their state. . . . [One problem with *Texas* is that] the temptation to nitpick is enormous. I missed, for instance, a detailed treatment of Texas in the 1930's, during the Great Depression and the Dust Bowl years when the skies to the north of town turned black at three in the afternoon. My father used to say after one of those dust storms, "Well, I've got Texas in my heart, but Oklahoma in my lungs." Mr. Michener tries to get Texas in his heart, and one has to like him for that, but he doesn't quite succeed. The subject is too large and the author's language too pawky. We get page after page of clichés hurriedly piled on each other as though Mr. Michener were scribbling notes he intended to flesh out with some "serious" writing later. Of course some readers may think Mr. Michener has been writing this way for years, but it sells like Lone Star longnecks on Saturday night. Texans like success, and the odds are they'll like most of this book. As for you in the rest of the country, read it. You'll get smatterings of knowledge about one of the most remarkable places on earth, and that's no Texas brag.

Hughes Rudd, "Four Centuries of Tex Arcana," in The New York Times Book Review, October 13, 1985, p. 9.

PETER APPLEBOME

There is one wonderful chapter in James A. Michener's latest epic, *Texas.* It's called "Loyalties," and in it Mr. Michener writes with great sensitivity and power about slavery, the Civil War and, most particularly, the siege of Vicksburg.

On the surface there seems to be a perverse sort of logic in a wedding of the encyclopedic wordiness of Mr. Michener and the sprawling excess of Texas. But although the author dutifully slogs through 450 years of history, the marriage never comes off, perhaps for a simple reason. Mr. Michener may be intrigued by Texas, but he doesn't seem to like it, and the result is a dreary, schizophrenic, utterly passionless book. . . .

Texas is not without value for those who can make their way through it. The research that went into it is exhaustive, and though there are factual nits to be picked, Mr. Michener does provide a comprehensive historical overview of the state. . . . More importantly, the book is marked by a sharp, critical intelligence that's quite a bit different from the stock John Wayne epic. Mr. Michener very acutely homes in on the tensions between Hispanics and Anglos and whites and blacks that have been at the heart of Texas history.

But he does not give those insights any sort of narrative force. This book takes the form of a series of generational sagas in which fictional characters and a few historical ones live out Texas history from the days of the Spanish explorers to the present. Each chapter ends with the deliberations of a committee of caricatured modern-day Texans charged with defining the essentials of Texas history for the coming sesquicentennial. The committee meetings function as bulky briefings on what the narrative alone should have been able to convey. A clunkier structure would be hard to imagine.

Moreover, while the committee meetings and much of the text presuppose the kind of chauvinism appropriate to an authorized sesquicentennial epic, the rest of the book tells a story peopled largely by fools and con men and swindlers and racists. . . .

There are other problems as well. There are so many diverse strands to Texas history that it's almost impossible to tie them together into a coherent narrative. Mr. Michener begins in 1535 with a Mexican muleteer in the time of Cabeza de Vaca, Coronado and the first Spanish explorers in what became Texas. He ends in modern times, with a Dallas Cowboy linebacker, a descendant of legendary Texas Rangers, being named director of the world's greatest museum of international sports art. (Could I make this up?) He tries to show the intervening events through the continuing stories of a handful of black, white and Hispanic families, but the historical scope is too broad for the narrative to work effectively. . . .

There are many interesting moments in the book's account of Texas life on the frontier and under Mexican rule, such as the stories of the Alamo and the warfare with the Comanche Indians, or the depiction of Sam Houston. But the last 200 pages on modern Texas, in which Mr. Michener mostly rehashes recent news stories, are a literary desert of dry prose inhabited by lifeless characters.

A good friend who has spent his whole life in Texas has long felt the state should change its name to Texasland, become a theme park and cater full time to the outdated Wild West fantasies its history provides. That's the final failing of Mr. Michener's book. *Texas* tells a lot about Texasland, but it's totally lost in dealing with Texas. There's probably a boffo miniseries here, but not much of a book.

Peter Applebome, "Wait for the Miniseries," in The Wall Street Journal, November 12, 1985, p. 26.

JUDITH MARTIN

There is only one sensible explanation for the startlingly uncharacteristic faults of James A. Michener's new historical novel, *Legacy.* Without that, it would be hard to understand why Mr. Michener . . . has written a flimsy and careless book. True, he has occasionally produced normal-sized works. But here he has taken on the mighty subject of the United States Constitution, as seen through the lives and idealistic struggles of a dynasty of American patriots and their contemporary descendant, who is called to testify at the Iran-contra hearings.

Yet the book is a mere 176 pages, and then only because the full text of the Constitution is appended. The novel itself, spanning more than two centuries of major American history, from the Declaration of Independence to the momentous Irangate Summer of '87 (the contemporary hero, a military officer involved in covert operations on the National Security Council staff in the White House, protests too much that he hardly knows Lieut. Col. Oliver North), is only 149 pages.

It contains trivial factual mistakes of the kind that could be an embarrassment to Mr. Michener:

The Chief Justice is given the incorrect title of Chief Justice of the Supreme Court; the correct title is Chief Justice of the United States. . . .

In addition, the behavior and language of the historical characters are anachronistic. Founding Fathers keep impetuously hugging one another, as if they were culturally demonstrative, rather than being Anglo-Saxons of a period of formal manners. They speak and write in modern clichés, jarring stylistically with period quotations in the book.

Sloppiness is evident, also, in character delineation, such as this internally inconsistent summation of James Madison: "a small unimpressive fellow in his late thirties, with a penetrating eye and a manner which indicated that he did not suffer fools easily."

Subtlety of character may not be Mr. Michener's strength, but the fictional family of secondary figures (nevertheless named Starr) who appear on the significant scenes of the American historical drama is particularly lifeless. They have few personal attributes, and are given to considering modern mainstream views, no matter what period they inhabit or idea they embody. . . .

The central ethical question of the book turns out to be whether it is quite nice for Maj. Norman Starr to take the Fifth Amendment before Congress. This crisis of conscience, with which he struggles on a Georgetown tennis court, is not even about whether to protect other people's lives or political careers, but about how, considering his lineage, he can most gracefully protect himself. . . .

All these shortcomings would be alarming in a work from someone with Mr. Michener's record and reputation if an explanation did not present itself: This is obviously not the actual book. Mr. Michener of course intended to produce a weighty tome to deal with a subject of the scope of two centuries of the United States Constitution.

What we have here, instead, is the book proposal. True, it is somewhat long for a proposal, but Mr. Michener usually writes long. Considering his reputation for historical research and breadth, it would have been an insult for his editor to remind him to flesh out the characters and story, check facts and period style and broaden the theme.

One can imagine that the intent was to return the proposal with some such comment as, "Great—you've done it again! Can you bring it in under 1,000 pages? Constitution will probably have to go—let them look it up."

Mr. Michener, after all, should certainly be trusted to deliver a completed work that would do justice to such a subject. One cannot, however, extend such trust to whoever accidentally allowed the book proposal to be printed and sold.

> *Judith Martin, "From Constitutionland to Iranorama," in* The New York Times Book Review, *September 6, 1987, p. 6.*

JOHN EHRLICHMAN

[*Legacy*] is the contemporary story of an Army major who works for the President's National Security Council. In fact, he works for Adm. John Poindexter. . . .

Evidently in early 1987, [Michener] was inspired and even upset by the refusal of Poindexter and Lt. Col. Oliver North to testify before the Intelligence Committee of the Senate. Beyond those motives, which apparently gave rise to *Legacy,* there is the obvious exploitation of the Constitution's Bicentennial. The almost gratuitous appendage of the full text of the Constitution (the final 24 pages) allows the publisher to peddle any unsold remainders as high school texts. (p. 1)

Michener's account of how a Senate witness and his lawyer prepare for the ordeal of a televised hearing in 1987 is both superficial and inaccurate. Nowadays (unlike, but thanks to, the nation's Watergate experience), witness preparation is a sophisticated Washington art form, best exemplified by the skilled team that worked with North for many weeks. . . . In *Legacy,* Zack McMaster, the Norman Starrs' lawyer, can't be much of a Washington lawyer; he doesn't even put Maj. Starr's wife into that chair where the cameras will show her supportively gazing at her husband.

The story is not unfamiliar: Maj. Norman Starr, U.S. Army, is in deep trouble because of his involvement with "the *contra* affair." . . .

Starr's old West Point "bunkmate," Washington superlawyer Zack McMaster, phones Starr one morning with the news that the Senate Committee wants to interrogate the major. Zack says: "Starr, old buddy, you're in serious trouble. . . . The angle isn't Iran. It's the *contras.*" And the improbably bad news is that the Senate plans to haul Starr to the Hill the very next day. . . .

But Zack sees a way out. Maj. Starr has an unbroken chain of distinguished ancestors; Zack will invoke Starr's heritage in mitigation of contra wrongs. . . .

While Zack arranges a short postponement of Starr's Senate appearance and holds lengthy meetings with the best legal minds in Washington, Starr and his wife remind each other of the Starr ancestors. Their reminiscence is a novelistic device that limps.

This little book is only seven short chapters about seven of Norman Starr's forbears and two chapters about Starr and his inner conflict over what to do when he goes to testify. Will he travel the Oliver North path—uniform, ribbons and Fifth Amendment—or will his heritage take him a different way?

Simon Starr (1759-1804), a friend of Alexander Hamilton, is said to have been an influential if silent member of the Constitutional Convention. His chapter is a 34-page gloss on the convention's debates, compromises and personalities, written for people who haven't read much about the Constitutional Convention and who liked *Space, Poland* and *Tales of the South Pacific.* Most of the other ancestors' chapters exemplify some familiar constitutional issue. One Starr was a Supreme Court justice who voted against slaves' rights in the Dred Scott case. Another was a suffragette. Grandfather Richard Starr hated Franklin D. Roosevelt and fought his attempt to pack the Supreme Court.

In the crisis, however, Starr (1951-) does not turn to his ancestors but to his immigrant father-in-law, who convinces him at breakfast one day that a man in uniform must follow a "higher law"—("the rule of common sense")—above and beyond written constitutions and statutes. In the father-in-law's opinion (as in mine), one who has served on the White House staff ought not to avail himself of the Fifth Amendment concerning his performance of his duties.

Maj. Starr has an epiphany there at the breakfast table, all dressed up in his fancy uniform with the fruit salad of ribbons on his chest, ready to go to the hearing chamber. In a book ostensibly about the Constitution, his decision may seem a *non sequitur,* based as it is only on the father-in-law's estimate of the societal demands of the times. But perhaps at that juncture, Michener was having a little trouble with the Fifth Amendment and North's right to invoke it. Starr is given to understand what he must do ("the sense of propriety on which society must rely") and marches off to the Senate. North invoked the Fifth Amendment. Starr will not.

A dramatic ending, but the brevity, research lapses and forced timeliness of this book tarnish Starr's dramatic nobility and in some measure defeat the author's original, worthy objectives. (p. 21)

> *John Ehrlichman, "Patriots Don't Take the Fifth," in* Los Angeles Times Book Review, *September 13, 1987, pp. 1, 21.*

CHRISTOPHER LEHMANN-HAUPT

[The transcendent message in *Alaska*]—if anything in Mr. Michener's relentlessly earthbound fictional world can be called transcendent—is that Alaska is a potentially turbulent spot in the world and that we Americans had better watch out, because if we don't start taking better care of it, the place is going to be snatched from us one way or another.

This message sums up the major theme of Mr. Michener's latest work, which is that if nature and Russia have been magnificently cruel to Alaska, it is as nothing compared to the way America, in its club-footed innocence, has kicked the place and its people around. And that, as far as this reader can see, is pretty much the long and short of this immense semi-fictional history.

Now, a few concessions ought to be granted. One is that Mr. Michener is still, sentence for sentence, writing's fastest attention grabber. It takes him, on the average, about half a paragraph to get you involved in what's happening next, whether it's the development of an ice age, a fight between a mammoth and a saber-toothed tiger or the construction of the Alcan Highway.

Another is that Mr. Michener is adept at manipulating our sympathies. No one in the book is entirely good or evil. . . .

Moreover, there is, as always with Mr. Michener's fiction, much of interest to be gleaned—for instance, that "since it is moving slowly northward as the San Andreas fault slides irresistibly along," the city of Los Angeles "is destined eventually to become part of Alaska." Or that men have navigated the frozen Yukon River all the way from Dawson to Nome riding *bicycles,* no less.

Or, as Mr. Michener explains: "The Aleutian word for Great Land was Alaxsxaq, and when Europeans reached the Aleutian Islands, their first stopping point in this portion of the Arctic, and asked the people what name the lands hereabouts had, they replied 'Alaxsxaq,' and in the European tongues this became Alaska."

The difficulty is, a reader tends to catch on to what Mr. Michener is up to long before he gets around to doing it. Reading *Alaska* is a little like being backstage with a magician, watching him prepare his show. You see him there with his enormous array of stage props: crustal plates, glaciers, volcanoes, mastadons, kayaks, harpoons, walruses. . . .

Next to them stand some 300 assistants, among them both fictional characters and real historical figures like Czar Peter the Great, Vitus Bering, Georg Steller, Capt. James Cook, Baron Edouard de Stoeckl. . . .

On a blackboard nearby is a list of the tricks the magician will perform: among them, the arrival of the first human beings in North America, the killing of a whale by a boatload of Aleut women, the Russian settlement of what would become Baranol Island, the sale of Alaska to the United States. . . .

There's a certain amount of entertainment in watching how the performer will fit these myriad pieces together. But somehow when you get in front of the stage, the show has lost its illusion. And you never experience anything resembling magic.

> Christopher Lehmann-Haupt, "Michener's Cautionary Tale of the 49th State," in The New York Times, *June 23, 1988, p. C21.*

GARY JENNINGS

Alaska has all the vivacity, drama, passion and humor of a National Geographic article without any pictures. It begins,

"About a billion years ago," and surely only a national monument could unblushingly describe in sitcom lingo the eons-long movement of this planet's tectonic plates: "Anything could happen . . . and did." . . .

By page 99, we're up to the 18th century, the explorer Vitus Bering and the Russians who first claimed Alaska. Now, since there are still 769 pages to go, but only a couple of centuries, the pace slows to a plod. The reader may begin to yearn for those good old days of creeping continents and shambling mastodons; their doings were a lot more frisky than any recounted from here on.

Alaska's history, according to this version, has mainly been a series of endings-with-a-whimper. The native peoples make tiresomely repetitious tries at wiping out the white men, but flub the job every time. The United States Government buys Alaska from Russia, and then doesn't want it. The gold rush peters out dismally. The oil boom goes bust. None of this is much enlivened by the most wretchedly cumbrous writing since those Aleuts came up with "Alaxsxaq":

> Caught in this vise formed by Chinese in one jaw,
> illiterate white and Indian fishermen in the other,
> he felt himself so miserably squeezed that he spent
> one whole week fuming.

In the cast of stock frontier-novel characters noble natives, noble maidens, noble Mounties, a couple of noble dogs and even salmon—only one is actually *described* as being a mummy. This mummy, the mouthpiece of a shaman-ventriloquist, talks mummy wisdom: "In my long years I've found that many problems are solved by waiting." It is left for the reader to notice that every other character—whether a historical Captain Cook or a fictional Ravenheart—is likewise a mummy. Not one has a breath of life, only a label: "a man of resolute courage," "an imperious woman," "a manly young fellow" and my favorite, "a master waitress."

But those could sure use a better ventriloquist. Pity poor Agulaak, for instance: "Agulaak was left to stew in his own twisted imaginings." And the man who "would not gorge himself, just carefully ate all those things which would send energy through his body and antiscurvy fluids down his legs." And this chap of wondrously Leacockian behavior: "With a wild dive over the side he abandoned his cohorts and ignored the fact that he couldn't swim."

If every Alaskan of today is expected to procure a copy of *Alaska* out of state loyalty, this monumental slab of a narrative ought to help considerably to damp down the earthquakes up yonder.

> Gary Jennings, "A Nice Place for Mastodons," in The New York Times Book Review, *June 26, 1988, p. 7.*

CHIP BROWN

In his new historical novel, *Alaska,* James A. Michener has solved the problem of not having a thousand years to cover the whole state by employing an army of researchers. If nothing else, *Alaska* does justice to the scale of the "Great Land." At 868 pages, crowded with dates, historical and fictive figures, the book ranges catholically from the billion-year-old bumpercar stuff of plate tectonics to the political upheavals of the present day. There's really nothing important that Michener doesn't include, and that's the problem.

The kitchen-sink esthetic says nothing is extraneous. *Alaska* doesn't lack for explanations of the Richter scale, advice on how to drive a Caterpillar tractor, caulk a river boat and equip yourself for a climb on Denali. Even Dashiell Hammett makes a cameo; the bush scout Nate Coop spots him on Adak: " 'Is he an actor,' he asked some airmen as they finished talking with Hammett. 'No,' they said. 'Even worse. He's a writer.' "

A gratuitous slur, but it raises the question: Are the authors of historical novels free from the obligation to provide characters with emotional lives? Ought the publishing genius behind *Hawaii, Texas* and *Chesapeake* and numerous other books to tamper with his formula and give characters real personalities, idiosyncratic dreams, original thoughts? Michener chews away at history like the giant man-sized beavers that used to gnaw on the boreal forest. His strength is the sheer forward drive of his narrative. Every once in a while, he builds up the reader's affection for his people. But because they are constituted as totems, you never have the sense of having known them. To spend time with them is like reading the obituaries of journalists—the men are all context; they're the stories they covered.

In *Alaska* there isn't all that much to distinguish the likes of Vitus Bering, whose name lives on in the Bering Strait and the Bering Glacier, and a fictional character like Matriarch, a 44-year-old wooly mammoth. To his credit, Michener makes the bold move of penetrating the mammoth's mind. And to her credit Matriarch has the good sense not to talk like the two-legged characters. The two-legged ones are right out of a mini-series, saying things like "Flatch, I've been watching you. They don't come any better. I want you to trade back your four-seater Waco." (pp. 1-2)

Michener is rightfully sympathetic to the native inhabitants of Alaska—Aleuts, Athapascans, Eskimos—exploring at length their customs, their shamans, their rituals and trials. Again the reports are long on sociology; the "poetry" of inner lives is mostly received, not imagined.

His vision of the state's future is bleak: the advocate of preservation—a man who believes in helping the natives retain their subsistence hunting culture—is washed away in a tsunami, and the big game hunter who wants, in the popular Alaska phrase to "Californicate" the country, survives. This is ground that has been covered more tellingly in Joe McGuinness' *Going to Extremes,* and John McPhee's *Coming Into the Country.*

Alaska is a place where the personal response to land is part of what the land is: in wildness, we are braced by a sense of our own frontiers; we know a border between worlds; we enter into some relation with the infinite the better to see our mysteries reflected back. Writers who do not take adequate account of this may get the details right but will miss the spirit of the place entirely. (p. 2)

> Chip Brown, "James Michener's Alaska: Gold, Glaciers and Grandeur," in Book World—The Washington Post, *July 3, 1988, pp. 1-2.*

TOM BODETT

[*Alaska* is Michener's] newest and most ambitious study. I say "study" rather than novel because in patented Michener style, *Alaska* reads more like a history of the United States'

largest member than it does an epic novel. There's more subject than predicate, if you will.

But that's not to say that the subject is not a fascinating one. For nearly 900 pages, a size befitting of its topic, *Alaska* takes the reader on a journey through one of the bleakest, richest, most foreboding and highly inviting territories in our Republic, if not the world.

In true Michener form, *Alaska* covers a time span of about a billion years. Using an effective blend of fact and fiction, Michener brings the subject from its days as a fledgling body of land all the way forward to existing legal and moral ramifications of Alaska's land distribution.

The social implications of continental drift are a pet subject of the author's, but even the most cynical reader must admit to the credibility of the perception that our cultures are a product of their terrains. With Alaska being among the newest and most volatile of the planet's topographies, it is even more credible that this novel should feature the terrain as a major player. (p. 1)

Michener reveals a great respect and compassion for the Alaska Native very early in this novel and continues to wave their flag at every opportunity throughout. From the early Russian traders' abuse of the natives and near genocide of some segments of their population, to the present-day social and judicial inequities suffered by them, Alaska Native issues almost become the *raison d'être* of *Alaska.* (pp. 1, 7)

The characters that Michener creates are bigger than life and one-dimensional at the same time. Michener's human studies are void of passion but full of intent and industry. They tend toward spawning ingeniously intertwined clans without actually making love; children grow up without being reared, and they die nobly without pain or suffering. . . .

Michener has done a fine job of chronicling the long and confusing history of a perpetually ignored part of America. The author's intent, if there was any, is to point out the myriad abuses that Alaska has suffered at the hands of the federal government, unscrupulous confidence men, and self-serving corporate giants from Seattle.

Michener's attention in the latter part of the book to ANCSA (Alaska Native Claims Settlement Act), which is an ongoing and unresolved predicament faced by all Alaska Natives, is what gives *Alaska* its real purpose.

Whether crafted or by coincidence, Michener has verified the long struggle Alaska has had with garnering control over itself and its land and demonstrates mightily to those not concerned that this battle still rages today.

Avid Michener fans will find nothing surprising in *Alaska.* It is colorful, informative, and historically accurate. Although he at times attempts to wedge in sub-plots that later fizzle, overall it is a good long story well connected with somewhat contrived but believable family associations.

Michener critics will also find nothing refreshing in *Alaska.* It is a boiler-plated Michener near-plot at its finest. A method of the author's of introducing his readers to areas of the world he finds personally intriguing. Whatever one's opinions are of the Michener style, his subjects are absorbing, and at least with *Alaska,* few will escape the allure of the land and people he describes. (p. 7)

Tom Bodett, "Texas Was Too Small," in Los Angeles Times Book Review, *July 3, 1988, pp. 1, 7.*

Tom Vines, "Michener on the Northern Frontier," in The Wall Street Journal, *August 5, 1988, p. 15.*

TOM VINES

In his latest work, **Alaska** America's chronicler, James Michener, gives the 49th state the same Panavision treatment he previously lavished on Hawaii, Texas and the Chesapeake Bay. He begins with the migration of primitive humans across from Siberia and brings his tale up through the present moment.

He approached the project with his characteristic research methods, living in the region for a while and supposedly learning its history. Only somewhere, somehow, he lost his way. He fails to properly grasp the nature of the frontier culture, and only superficially understands the dilemma of the native people.

The individuals in this novel might just as well be from **Hawaii** or **Texas,** now dressed in sealskin and fur. Mr. Michener shows no comprehension of the basis of the frontier character, such as its tolerance of individualism and its emphasis on loyalty and other personal values. . . .

One example of Mr. Michener's insensitivity toward the frontier culture is his anthropomorphic portrayal of wild animals. On the frontier, animals by necessity serve as a source of food or work (and sometimes, danger). To be Disneyland-cute about them is a luxury that comes only with urbanization, when one's source of protein is obtained conveniently and hazard-free at the Safeway. . . .

Mr. Michener's handicap may be that he brings to Alaska an Eastern liberal theology about how all people, including those of the Alaskan frontier, should think and be. Thus, he becomes yet another missionary, albeit one in a literary cassock. While sympathetic to the population of the Alaskan frontier, particularly the native peoples, he consistently ascribes to those people what he may see as ideal thoughts and behavior, but ones that are in reality artificial and pretentious in this setting. . . .

The Michener Alaska is peopled primarily by two types: those doing bad, usually through greed and acquisition, and those doing good because they are, well, good people. Mr. Michener's villains of choice for **Alaska** are businessmen or entrepreneurs. In different stages of the book, these include: the Russian fur trader cruelly exploiting the natives; the cynical ship captain trading guns and whiskey for pelts; the Seattle corporation selling overpriced goods to the Alaskans; and lawyers from the Lower 48 bullying native corporations.

In a concluding and somewhat unbelievable scene, Mr. Michener hints that ultimately the greedy ones will win out and conquer Alaska. Mr. Michener is at times tolerant of their human failings, but he makes certain that the reader does not miss the point, such as in his characterization of a manager in a Seattle trading corporation: "It simply did not occur to Tom to question the morality of Seattle's intention to keep Alaska in a kind of serfdom, without political power or the right of any self-determination."

No doubt there are some dark examples of entrepreneurship in Alaska, but Mr. Michener's simplistic view of human society and his questionable use of history makes this aspect of **Alaska,** like so many other elements of the book, unworthy.

PETER C. NEWMAN

If Michener's writing possesses any cadence at all, it's about as subtle as a Sousa march; his stories are repetitive and sometimes silly; his characters so wooden that, as the Canadian critic Ken Adachi once noted, you could build a boat out of them.

Journey, Michener's latest, is a breakthrough for the prodigious author; it's only 246 pages long. But that's an illusion since it was originally conceived as part of his 1,136-page epic, **Alaska.** . . .

The plot is ponderously moved along by such arcane devices as rhetorical questions and stage directions, as in this typical paragraph about the Klondike gold rush:

> If the news of the strike could have such electric effect upon so many, why had it taken almost a full year to travel the relatively short distance from the Klondike to Seattle, less than thirteen hundred miles, as an eagle would fly? The explanation must be carefully noted, for it explains the tragic events that were about to destroy so many lives.

The style is a melange of old-fashioned bodice-ripper ("When she heard these words she actually sucked in her breath and drew back: 'You're not thinking of trying that route are you?' ") and stagey bravado ("Fellows! It's still ten degrees below freezing! But it feels like summer.") The plot revolves around 23 months in the lives of Lord Evelyn Luton, "the younger son of the redoubtable Lord Deal," and his four companions: Harry Carpenter (a veteran of the Afghan wars), Philip Henslow (Luton's nephew), Trevor Blythe (a "budding poet") and Tim Fogarty, an Irish manservant. They travel 2,043 miles trying to find an all-British route into the Klondike, which is in Canadian territory but much more accessible through Alaska.

Three of the explorers die along the way. This allows Luton—at all times a certified twit—to proclaim sentiments such as this, when his nephew is dying of frostbite because he has insisted on walking through Arctic storms wearing rubber boots: "I have a very queasy stomach when it comes to cutting off a man's leg, especially a young man's, but I shall do it if it needs being done!"

Michener gets his geography right, and his historic research is flawless. The party drifts down the Mackenzie River aboard their tiny Sweet Afton, but instead of wintering at a fur trading post, they're caught in the wilderness and spend the dark season inside a tiny cabin. . . . At home they employ servants for such a menial task, and Fogarty, "the unlettered man who had been brought along to serve his betters," admits he still finds "pleasure in heating Lord Luton's shaving water and in honing and stropping the razor." The Irishman is the best-drawn character in the book—not that he emerges as particularly multi-dimensional, but at least he is allowed a touch of ambiguity. His "betters" roundly condemn him for having poached their salmon streams back in the old sod yet depend on him to shoot caribou, their only fresh food supply.

Instead of ascending the Gravel and Stewart Rivers, which would have meant an easy trek to Dawson, Luton insists on fighting his way up the rapids of the Peel. That means another wilderness winter and its accompanying agonies. The books' only feminine interest is Irina Kozlok who is, to use a Michenerism, the "blond-haired temptress" rescued by Luton from Great Slave Lake. ("What could she be doing in Dawson? And how in God's name had she got here?")

You'll have to finish **Journey** to find out. And maybe that's the real point of Michener's books. They are truly awful, but you can't stop reading them.

> *Peter C. Newman, "A Stagey, Readable Leftover from Michener's 'Alaska'," in* Chicago Tribune—Books, *July 2, 1989, p. 4.*

THOMAS FLEMING

Journey is not absolute junk. But I suspect no one but James Michener could get it published. Mr. Michener says he was attracted to the idea because he wanted to show readers that the Klondike gold rush of 1897 had a "Canadian dimension." This book is an odd way to achieve that goal. The characters are four Englishmen and their Irish servant, whose interest in Canada is nil. Their leader, Lord Luton, despises Canadians almost as much as he hates Americans, both of whom frequently get his best known facial expression, a silent sneer. His motive for the trip from London to the Klondike is a witless, pointless determination to remind the world that Dawson City, the impromptu capital of the gold fields, was in Canada and could be reached from Edmonton, Alberta, without setting foot on American territory.

Mr. Michener gives us a fairly interesting glimpse of Edmonton, full of hustlers sending gold seekers into the wilderness with bad maps and worse equipment. But before and after this interlude, his characters are on their own. Deprived of the penumbra of facts in which he usually operates, Mr. Michener's limitations as a novelist are starkly revealed. His dialogue is wooden, his psychology naïve and heavy-handed, his choice of detail almost invariably wrong and sometimes tasteless. There is, for instance, an extensive discussion of the importance of emptying the bowels during an Arctic winter. Pompous, birdbrained Lord Luton, who leads three of the five characters to their dooms, cries out for an Evelyn Waugh, for comedic irony. Mr. Michener takes him seriously.

Then there is the padding. Michener worshippers probably won't mind his exhaustive description of the steamer that Luton and company take across the Atlantic and the trains on which they ride to Edmonton, although they have nothing to do with the story. But the most ardent worshipper may draw the line at reprinting no fewer than 12 poems from Palgrave's *Golden Treasury* as a tribute to the young would-be poet who died on the expedition. For a while I thought someone had accidentally bound my freshman English textbook into the manuscript.

For those with severe Michenermania, **Journey** intersects with **Alaska** on page 459 of the latter, where a half-starved Irishman and an equally cadaverous Englishman stagger into Dawson City some two years after they left Edmonton. There is no attempt to describe their ordeal. Even information addicts should be grateful to the editors who persuaded Mr. Michener to excise this side trip from his centuries-long trek through **Alaska.**

> *Thomas Fleming, " 'Alaska' or Bust," in* The New York Times Book Review, *July 9, 1989, p. 15.*

HERBERT MITGANG

In **Caribbean,** Mr. Michener is following the method he used so successfully in **Tales of the South Pacific,** his magical first novel: island-hopping, inventing fictional characters who interact with colorful real-life personalities and placing historic events within a changing landscape. It's a formula he has perfected in novels set in Spain, Israel, South Africa, Texas, Poland, Alaska and elsewhere. . . .

In **Caribbean,** Michener fans will notice that this time he permits himself a little more editorializing, based on his personal observations and recent political developments. His novel begins in the year 1310 on an island that would later be called Dominica and leaps the centuries to Fidel Castro's Cuba. Even American tourists familiar with some of the serene islands will find themselves enlightened by the information the novel delivers about the brutality, slavery and colonialism that once flourished in the Caribbean. . . .

Sailing through the pages of **Caribbean,** the reader encounters Columbus, Sir Francis Drake, Henry Morgan and other buccaneers, Adm. Horatio Nelson, Gen. Toussaint L'Ouverture and the cricket star Sir Benny Castain. In the background are European monarchs, sending out their captains to exploit the islands and people.

Toward the end of the novel, Mr. Michener invents an encounter between a Cuban physician, who has fled his homeland and become an important political figure in Miami, and Fidel Castro. They talk through the night about the differences between the United States and Cuba, the Hispanic communities in Florida, Texas and New York, and what might happen if diplomatic relations were restored. The doctor tells the dictator that his bond is now to the United States. In **Caribbean,** there appears to be a strong aura of truth behind the storytelling.

> *Herbert Mitgang, "The Caribbean as Lead Character in a Michener Novel," in* The New York Times, *November 2, 1989, p. C23.*

ROBERT HOUSTON

The novel [**Caribbean**] is at its best when the historical material it treats is at its most intrinsically dramatic; only with difficulty could an experienced writer fail to engage a reader with stories of England and Spain slugging it out on the Spanish Main, or of the Haitian revolution, or of buccaneers sailing off into unknown waters toward Cape Horn. And Mr. Michener, to his credit, does not flinch from detailing the horrors of slavery, or from facing the terrible racism that mars the romantic idealism of such Victorian sacred bulls as Carlyle and Tennyson. He and his researchers have done their homework well, as always.

Homework, however, cannot compensate for a novelist's lack of real respect for her or his material. What does one do, for example, with a writer whose description of a Mayan high priestess ("This little bundle of energy was no ordinary woman") would make even the editor of a retirement-colony newsletter blanch? Or a stylist who can bring himself to describe children as an "adorable lot of wide-eyed youngsters"?

In part because Mr. Michener's language is such a blunt instrument, and in part because he is such an insistent puppet master, the characters in *Caribbean* become, almost without exception, approximations of people, sentimentalized and flat, tools for the author's plot-related or didactic purposes. And if the characters aren't fresh and true, then neither the history nor the fiction can be emotionally true and affecting, regardless of the material's dramatic potential.

In fact, the key to Mr. Michener's problems in *Caribbean* is his seeming expectation that his readers will accept any sort of laziness of craft as long as they feel they are learning something, or at least being preached at comfortably. Clichés, stereotypes, wildly improbable plot manipulation and character motivations, clunky and exposition-heavy dialogue, simplistic politics, mawkishness, unjustified intrusion of the narrator into the action—what are such things as long as the cause of popular history is being served?

The answer, of course, is that to a conscientious novelist they are everything. Good historical fiction asks no less of a writer than does good fiction of any kind. *Caribbean,* unfortunately, is neither of the above.

> Robert Houston, "Paradise Tales," in The New York Times Book Review, *November 5, 1989, p. 22.*

JOHN HEARNE

The latest in Michener's series of historical fictions or fictionalized histories is *Caribbean,* an overview of the middle sea of the Americas, from the indigenous Indians who greeted Columbus to a contemporary marriage across the races between a black Haitian woman and the Trinidadian descendant of Indians from India. In between these two chronological points, Michener highlights a number of the more significant events in the histories—Mayan, Spanish, English, French and African—of those who have tried to seize or exploit the small islands scattered across a million-plus square miles of water that are what we mean when we talk of the Caribbean.

As we have come to expect of Michener, the broad outline of his chronicle is accurate. If many of the figures, historical and imagined, with which he peoples his story emerge as stiff and wooden and speak a dialogue we doubt ever got spoken, then that is a penalty attendant on this sort of book. What cannot be faulted, and what shines from the pages, is a great sympathy on Michener's part for the events he capsules and for the people who made the events happen. The Caribbean in these pages is never merely an exotic locale in which to set a superficial cloak-and-dagger romance. He treats his chosen region with immense respect, with a palpable decency that is utterly engaging and which deserves our close attention. If the tale sometimes loses conviction, it is because Caribbean history is fragmented, each island having had until very recently a separate development with little reference to its neighbor. The relative homogeneity of, say, Alaska or Hawaii is not to be found in the Caribbean. Despite the fact that the islands share a common, often brutal and monotonous experience, the water between them has created highly individualistic subcultures.

This geopolitical fact of life is reflected in the form Michener perforce adopts. Five hundred years of history and some 25 entities have to be covered by 16 carefully selected episodes widely spaced in time. What is remarkable and praiseworthy is Michener's accuracy in dealing with such a historical span. His essentials are correct, conscientiously so. It is only in small details that one native to the region can, occasionally, find him stumbling.

Those occasional uncertainties of interpretation and errors of fact are most noticeable, perhaps, as Michener approaches our own time. This may well arise from the fact that much of modern Caribbean history has yet to be written, and, lacking the perspective given by history and documentation, Michener the historian is less sure of his grasp on events. The chapter on the Rastafarian movement, for example, is not only fictionally slight but historically improbable in several particulars.

But these are cavils rather than serious objections. Given the scope of the task which Michener has set himself, he has done his chosen region proud. *Caribbean* is a work which anybody strange to the islands and wanting to know something about them could read with confidence. All the essentials are there; and a skilled and studious novelist has embedded these essentials in a deeply felt, highly responsible tale.

Given the limitations of the form for which Michener is now famous, it is difficult to see how he could have done better.

> John Hearne, "The Middle Sea of the Americas," in Book World—The Washington Post, *November 12, 1989, p. 4.*

Anaïs Nin

1903-1977

French-born American novelist, diarist, short story writer, and critic.

Nin is best known for her erotica and for her seven volumes of diaries published from 1966 to the end of her life. Her other works, which include novels and short stories, are greatly influenced by Surrealism, a movement initiated in the 1920s by artists dedicated to exploring irrationality and the subconscious, and by the formal experiments of such Modernists as D. H. Lawrence and Virginia Woolf, who employed expressionistic and stream-of-consciousness narration. Rather than relying on a chronological ordering of events as in conventional narratives, Nin wrote in a poetic style featuring repetition, omission, and pastiche as organizing principles. Critics favorably note her attention to physical details and the influence of sensory information on the moods, thoughts, and interactions of her characters. Nin's predominant subject is psychological, and her insights into the behavioral and thought patterns of women have been particularly praised as both astute and free of misanthropy.

Nin began her diary as an ongoing letter to her father, Spanish musician and composer Joaquin Nin, who abandoned his family when she was eleven years old. Nin kept a journal throughout her life, recording such experiences as friendships with famous artists and writers, her years in psychotherapy, and, eventually, her worldwide travels on speaking engagements. Because she edited and excerpted her original diaries for publication in seven volumes as *The Diary of Anaïs Nin,* many commentators assess them for insights they shed upon Nin's literary technique. Nin's diaries relate incidents in the present tense and feature real people who appear as carefully delineated characters in fully-realized settings. The diaries are divided according to theme and share many of the concerns expressed in Nin's fiction, including the life of the creative individual, psychoanalysis, the relation between the inner and the outer world, and the nature of sexuality. The volumes include photographs, conversations presented in dialogue form, and letters from Nin's personal correspondence, completing the impression of a thoughtfully orchestrated work of art rather than a spontaneous outpouring of emotions. Susan Stanford Friedman determined: "The *Diary* records Nin's attempt to create a whole identity in a culture that defines WOMAN in terms of her fragmented roles as mother, daughter, wife, and sister."

Nin's first published work, *The House of Incest,* is often considered a prose poem due to its intensely resonant narrative. This book achieves a dream-like quality through its emphasis on psychological states rather than on surface reality. Nin's next publication, *The Winter of Artifice,* contains three long short stories. The first, "Djuna," concerns a *ménage à trois* that closely resembles the relationship Nin depicted in her diary as existing between herself, novelist Henry Miller, and Miller's second wife, June. In "Lilith," Nin portrays the disappointing reunion of a woman with her father, who abandoned her in her childhood, while "The Voice" features an unnamed psychoanalyst and his four female patients who must learn to incorporate the emotions experienced in their

dreams into their conscious lives. *Under a Glass Bell,* another collection of Nin's short fiction, contains "Birth," one of her most celebrated pieces. In this story, a woman undergoes excruciating labor only to bear a stillborn child and discover that through this process she has been symbolically freed of her past. *This Hunger . . . ,* Nin's next collection of short fiction, extends her exploration of the female unconscious in psychoanalytic terms.

Cities of the Interior, which Nin described as a "continuous novel," is often considered her most ambitious and critically successful project. Between 1946 and 1961, Nin published the work in five parts; these installments were published as *Ladders to Fire, Children of the Albatross, The Four-Chambered Heart, A Spy in the House of Love,* and *Seduction of the Minotaur. Ladders to Fire* concerns Lillian, a character known for her violent temper, who is as dissatisfied with her extramarital affair as she is with her marriage. Lillian seeks the perfect lover as an antidote to the problems of her life. In *Children of the Albatross,* Djuna, a minor character in *Ladders to Fire,* is emotionally stunted due to her father's abandonment. Djuna prefers playing mother to a series of adolescent lovers rather than becoming involved in a mature relationship with a man. In *The Four-Chambered Heart,* Djuna gains a measure of self-awareness through her relationship with Rango, a Guatemalan musician and political activist. *A Spy in the House of Love,* Nin's most popular novel, features Sabina, a minor character in the earlier volumes. A woman looking for affection through sexual gratification, Sabina discovers she has never experienced love. *Seduction of the Minotaur* reintroduces Lillian, who realizes the preciousness of human life while travelling in Mexico and returns to her husband a more mature woman. *Collages* (1964), an experimental novel that relies upon pastiche unified by a single character, reworks themes from Nin's earlier novels.

Much of Nin's fame is attributable to the short erotic pieces she wrote for a patron while living in Paris during the early 1940s. Collected in *Delta of Venus* and *Little Birds,* these works have garnered much commentary regarding their status as literature. Although many feminist critics object in principle to sexually explicit literature, some have championed Nin's erotica, declaring that these stories advocate mutual respect and consent between the participants in a sexual relationship. Some critics defend Nin's graphic depiction of sexual situations as an exploration of psychological truths, while others emphasize that her artistry removes these pieces from the category of pornography.

(See also *CLC,* Vols. 1, 4, 8, 11, 14; *Contemporary Authors,* Vols. 13-16, rev. ed., Vols. 69-72 [obituary]; *Contemporary Authors New Revision Series,* Vol. 22; and *Dictionary of Literary Biography,* Vols. 2, 4.)

PRINCIPAL WORKS

NOVELS

The House of Incest   1936; republished in *Winter of Artifice. House of Incest,*   1974
Ladders to Fire   1946
Children of the Albatross   1947
The Four-Chambered Heart   1950
A Spy in the House of Love   1954
Solar Barque   1958; enlarged as *Seduction of the Minotaur,* 1961
Cities of the Interior   1959; consists of *Ladders to Fire, Children of the Albatross, The Four-Chambered Heart, A Spy in the House of Love,* and *Solar Barque;* republished under the same title with *Seduction of the Minotaur* replacing *Solar Barque,*   1961

SHORT FICTION

The Winter of Artifice   1936; enlarged as *Winter of Artifice: Three Novelettes,*   1974
Under a Glass Bell   1944; enlarged as *Under a Glass Bell and Other Stories,*   1947
This Hunger . . .   1945
Delta of Venus   1977
Little Birds   1979

DIARIES

The Diary of Anaïs Nin
  Volume I: 1931-1934   1966
  Volume II: 1934-1939   1967
  Volume III: 1939-1944   1969
  Volume IV: 1944-1947   1971
  Volume V: 1947-1955   1974
  Volume VI: 1955-1966   1977
  Volume VII: 1966-1974   1981

WILLIAM CARLOS WILLIAMS

When women as writers finally get over the tendency to cut their meat so fine, really "give" out of the abundance of their unique opportunity, as women, to exploit the female in the arts, Anais Nin may well be considered to have been one of the pioneers. I speak of her new book, **The Winter of Artifice,** hand printed by herself.

It's hard to praise a book of this sort. Either you say too much and overdo it or you say too little and seem to condemn. And I want to praise. To face an accusation of artiness would be its danger and nothing in a writer is more damnable. But if there is that that seems superlative, in the use of the words, in the writing, spotted like a toad though it may be or a lily's throat—then go ahead. Make the blunder. This is a woman in her own right.

In **"The Winter of Artifice,"** the first of these stories, from which the general title is taken, a man is carefully, lovingly placed in his living grave by a devoted daughter. In the second, **"The Voice,"** a woman destroys a psycho-analyst who is rather a baby—or perhaps shrewd enough, professionally, never to fall in love with a woman he knows he can get.

This doesn't sound so good: the familiar pattern common among female writers in recent years. The mantis that takes her mate in her arms, bites an eye out then consumes him to the last whisker. Transformed to a varnished packet of eggs he will be fastened anon to the thorn of some nearby rose bush. Women enjoy this sort of thing. With Anais Nin it is a means and not an end. (p. 429)

In these two stories of Anais Nin a titanic struggle is taking place below the surface not to succumb to just that maelstrom of hidden embitterment which engulfs so many other women as writers. I feel the struggle and find myself deeply moved by it. It's the writing itself which effects this sense of doomed love striving for emergence against great odds. It is in the words, a determination toward the most complete truth of expression, clean observation, accurately drawn edges and contours—at the best. But the characters of the story, do what they may, are drawn down. Something in the writing is not drawn down, survives.

To me the leading character of Anais Nin's first story and Lilith of the second are the same person though not spoken of as though they were, in the telling. They, as a matter of fact, complement each other: if the outcome of the first story had not been what it is the second would have missed its occasion for being. The young woman of **"The Winter of Artifice"** not having achieved what she set out to do, repossess her father, the development found in the second story becomes all but inevitable.

It is woman trying to emerge into a desired world, a woman trying to lift herself from a minor key of tenderness and affection to a major love in which all her potentials will find employment, qualities she senses but cannot bring into play. The age and times are against her. But if I speak of discovery here I mean that the strain, the very failures of the characters in both these stories tell of something beyond ordinary desiring. Whether Anais Nin is correct in her final analysis of what that is is something else again.

It is hard to say: the effect is, from my viewpoint, of a full vigor striving to emerge through a minor perversity. Another might read it the other way. Let it not be forgot that the girl's father of **"The Winter of Artifice,"** on whom she lavishes her love (not forgetting that without a quiver she abandons a resourceful mother who had made a home for her during her infant years) is not destroyed willingly. The girl who has lived for him, who has welcomed him a visitor in her dreams and flies to his side at the first opportunity, puts up a real fight to rescue him from his self-destroying lies. But he will not have it. He either won't or can't come clean with her until, after a tremendous effort, she gives him up and goes her way. (pp. 430-31)

The second story grows out of this failure. This time it is another person but the character is about the same. Lilith releases herself to her fate and who shall say whether she or The Voice is at fault in the end. She has been conditioned in the first story, or we have, and this second is the result of it. These might easily be the two first chapters of a longer novel of great promise.

Maximum vigor lies in two strong poles between which a spark shall leap to produce an equilibrium in the end. When we get a piling up at one pole without relief the feeling is transitional. A passage from the second story, **"The Voice,"** will show this piling up at the negative pole:

> Lilith entered Djuna's room tumultuously, throwing her little serpent skin bag on the desk, her undulating scarf on the bed, her gloves on the bookshelf, and talking with fever and excitement: . . . What softness between women. The marvellous silences of twinship. To turn and watch the rivulets of shadows between the breasts, . . . the marvellous silence of woman's thoughts, the secret and the mystery of night and woman become air, sun, water, plant . . . When you press against the body of the other you feel this joy of the roots compressed, sustained, enwrapped in its brownness with only the seeds of joy stirring . . . The back of Lilith, this soft, musical wall of flesh, the being floating in the waves of silence, enclosed by the presence of what can be touched.

This is the mood and the background, a stasis, an absolute arrest. Proust is one of its triumphs. But were that all, frankly, I shouldn't bother with the book though good writing will be good writing to the end of time. To me Anais Nin carries the impetus a little further; from that undertone a new melody tries to lift itself, tries and fails in what constitutes, I believe, an upturn in the writing.

For much of the confusion and all the "mysteries" concerned in a certain pseudo-psychologic profundity of style well known among women comes from a failure to recognize that there is an authentic female approach to the arts. It has been submerged, true enough; men have been far too prone to point out that all the greatest masterpieces are the work of males as well as of the male viewpoint or nearly so. Women swallow this glibly, they are the worst offenders. But the fact is, without "mystery" of any sort, that an elementary opportunity to approach the arts from a female viewpoint has been badly neglected by women. More important, without a fully developed female approach neither male nor female can properly offset each other. Am I right in presuming that Anais Nin cares a fig about that or even agrees with me in my main premise?

The male scatters his element recklessly as if there were to

be no end to it. Balzac is a case in point. That profusion you do not find in the female but the equal infinity of the single cell. This at her best she harbors, warms and implants that it may proliferate. . . . This female approach has only recently been recognized in its full dignity by women of distinction, in the past by them signally neglected. The term "female" has been too tied up with weakness, with effeminacy, suggestive of sickness to bear the close scrutiny necessary to get to the elemental worth out of the thing.

It begets a style beset with dangers which Anais Nin has far from escaped but from which I think she shows she is escaping or might escape to perform a completely outstanding work. It is a style whose faults made Virginia Wolff at times all but unreadable. Our own Kay Boyle stood on the brink many years ago: a careful arrangement of polished pebbles to simulate the shore of a sea, a fine-combing for effects, and words, words, words dusted and dressed—an inability, in short, to give the theme its head in a major (female) key and let the writing rest on that.

But where is there such a theme for a woman? Certainly not sand which cannot possibly be made to stand as a tower without a cement of understanding to hold it together. In a woman, something that links up her womanhood with abilities as a writer will allow her to draw abundantly upon that for her material. (pp. 431-33)

It's the *female* of the thing that still goes against the grain. To follow the prevailing myth: no one wants to be female but a few discerning men. Men, it is said, make the best modistes, the best cooks, the best little whores, the best, the best, etc. Women eat it up. Or fight against it. None wants it unless I am correct in believing that Anais Nin, much to her credit, begins to show the change in a positive attitude toward her opportunities and not a defeatist, reactionary one.

Anais Nin is in nothing that I detect a man. From this courage and it seems to require courage in a woman to be a woman in the arts consciously, basically and . . . tenderly! without rancour! I say, from this courage Anais Nin is developing her newness, her security.

It must be something of this to account for the confidence and vigor of the woman. Her style, when she doesn't start off into wordy symphonies which are after all derivative and which I do not like in her, has assurance, a unique assurance. It breaks down at times as I have asserted, runs off into "subtleties," attenuations, sound effects—the old difficulty. But when it speaks direct it transmits a feeling of depth. Reading, I feel free to enjoy. Nobody is slashing at my legs under the table, maliciously, as with so many women who imitate men. Anais Nin gives the impression of a woman for once sailing free in her own element, undisturbed.

Anais Nin hasn't written very much but I think everyone has read what she has written. We all remember the house-boat on the Seine, the shrieks and blinding pain of that childbirth with its gargantuan shadows and lightnings—that were not false. It has become an established image.

The thing is that though such writing is full of violence we do not find or seldom, in this case, a straining after effects. Or if we do it is *that* which must be discounted. The only way anyone, male or female, can ever get away from that is by having something momentous to say and saying it to the full exclusion of all else. The style may be florid or it may be lean, that isn't the point, but it must never slide off irrelevantly into unnecessary matter. (pp. 433-34)

If I say Anais Nin is a good writer I mean that at her best she writes devotedly, without lie or excess baggage, from some such secret source of power which I have been trying to disclose, like a pig buried under a rosebush, a secret having to do profoundly with her sex. No doubt I am more than half wrong in defining it, if I have done so.

But Anais Nin herself indicates in one passage, I think, that she is almost fully conscious in herself of what I have been saying. Look at this:

> The telephone rang and there was someone downstairs to see The Voice. It is urgent. This someone came up, shaking an umbrella dripping with melted snow. She entered the room walking sidewise like a crab, and bundled in her coat as if she were a package, not a body. Between each word there was a hesitancy. In each gesture a swing intended to be masculine, but as soon as she sat on the couch, looking up at The Voice, flushed with timidity, saying: Shall I take off my shoes and lie down, he knew already that she was not masculine. She was deluding herself and others about it, etc., etc. . . .

The entire passage is worth studying carefully.

In the first place it's good writing. No hesitancy here. No posturing. No over-elaboration. The sentences are well formed, the observation is accurate, the sensitivity unstrained. Absolutely not a touch of neurosis *in the writing*. Something the writer has observed and understood, something important, important enough to write about it truthfully. The subject matter itself is also interesting.

I have hazarded what I have had to say here on what is perhaps a somewhat unsupported opinion. Be that as it may this is the sort of thing, the sort of writing I have just quoted, that interests me, in detail, gives me the feeling that what I have been guessing about Anais Nin is right, permits me to take her most seriously. It is the sort of writing you do not find everywhere. It is the sort of writing makes me think that Anais Nin knows what she has hold of. Something that steadies her hand, keeps her from slipping into detached adjectives for effects; says, finishes and quits saying. That it is woman, surmounting her own history and turning to the arts for justification and relief, that is at stake. (pp. 434-36)

> *William Carlos Williams, " 'Men . . . Have No Tenderness': Anais Nin's 'Winter of Artifice,' " in* New Directions in Prose and Poetry, *No. 7, 1942, pp. 429-36.*

EDMUND WILSON

The unpublished diary of Anaïs Nin has long been a legend of the literary world, but a project to have it published by subscription seems never to have come to anything, and the books that she has brought out, rather fragmentary examples of a kind of autobiographical fantasy, have been a little disappointing. She has now, however, published a small volume called *Under a Glass Bell,* which gives a better impression of her talent.

The pieces in this collection belong to a peculiar genre sometimes cultivated by the late Virginia Woolf. They are half short stories, half dreams, and they mix a sometimes exqui-site poetry with a homely realistic observation. They take place in a special world, a world of feminine perception and fancy, which is all the more curious and charming for being innocently international. Miss Nin is the daughter of a Spanish musician, but has spent much of her life in France and in the United States. She writes English, but mostly about Paris, though you occasionally find yourself in other countries. There are passages in her prose which may perhaps suffer a little from an hallucinatory vein of writing which the Surrealists have overdone: a mere reeling-out of images, each of which is designed to be surprising but which, strung together, simply fatigue. In Miss Nin's case, however, the imagery does convey something and is always appropriate. The spun glass is also alive: it is the abode of a secret creature. Half woman, half childlike spirit, she shops, employs servants, wears dresses, suffers the pains of childbirth, yet is likely at any moment to be volatilized into a superterrestrial being who feels things that we cannot feel.

But perhaps the main thing to say is that Miss Nin is a very good artist, as perhaps none of the literary Surrealists is. **"The Mouse," "Under a Glass Bell," "Rag Time,"** and **"Birth"** are really beautiful little pieces. "These stories," says Miss Nin in a foreword,

> represent the moment when many like myself had found only one answer to the suffering of the world: to dream, to tell fairy tales, to elaborate and to follow the labyrinth of fantasy. All this I see now was the passive poet's only answer to the torments he witnessed. . . . I am in the difficult position of presenting stories which are dreams and of having to say: but now, although I give you these, I am awake!

Yet this poet has no need to apologize: her dreams reflect the torment, too. (pp. 71, 74)

> *Edmund Wilson, in a review of "Under a Glass Bell," in* The New Yorker, *Vol. XX, April 1, 1944, pp. 71, 74.*

DIANA TRILLING

[While] Miss Nin's narratives [in *This Hunger . . .*] borrow the manner of fiction, they are much more like case histories than like short fiction of any usual sort. Miss Nin's characters have many of the conventional appurtenances of fictional life: they have been born, presumably they live and will die; they look a certain way; they have friends, money, sexual relationships, even children. But they exist for their author only as the sum of their clinically significant emotional responses; we are made aware only of such activities, physical surroundings, and encounters with other people as Miss Nin conceives to be relevant to their psychic health. Every writer establishes a role for herself in her books, and Miss Nin's role is psychoanalyst to her group of typical women. Her sole concern with her characters—I had almost said patients—is with the formation and expression of their symptoms, and what goes on in the rest of their lives she rigorously ignores. For instance, we are told of Hejda that, having been born in the Orient, her face was veiled through her early years, but we are not told the name of the country of her birth; or, in connection with Lillian, Miss Nin suddenly mentions a husband and children, but because neither husband nor children influence Lillian's emotional development Miss Nin doesn't consider it pertinent to tell us anything about them.

So much abstraction of her characters from the context of their real lives, together with so much specific detail when it suits Miss Nin's purposes to be specific, gives a certain surrealist quality to her stories. But her approach is not properly described as surrealist, since, in the instance of each of her women, Miss Nin is primarily concerned to lay out a case. The method of *This Hunger . . .* is, as I say, the method of clinical history, but with two important differences—one, that Miss Nin relies, for effect, not only on her clinical observations and conclusions but also on her literary skill; and two, that whereas it is the intention of the writer of a case history only to add to our clinical knowledge, and if any wider comment is present it is present only by happy accident, it is the first intention of Miss Nin to make a full-sized literary comment upon life.

And yet I find *This Hunger . . .* both less good reading and less enlightening about life in general than many simon-pure case studies. Nor is this because I object—though I do—to the dominant poetical tone of Miss Nin's prose. Nor is it because I reject—though I do—the major implication of Miss Nin's stories: that women are done in more than men are, and largely *by* men, and that since the sufferings of men occasion suffering in women, they should be the objects of our bitter resentment, whereas the sufferings of women must rouse our deepest sympathies. The reason I think *This Hunger . . .* inferior to a good psychoanalytical case record is that its pschoanalysis is not science but pretension.

Now obviously, and all present-day tendencies to the contrary notwithstanding, I do not think that writers of fiction need a technical knowledge of the psychiatric professions. Quite the contrary, a comparison of the novelistic insights into human motivation before Freud and after Freud seems to me to indicate a persistent deterioration in psychological understanding as the post-Freudian novelists have tried to incorporate the findings of psychiatry in their art. But inasmuch as Miss Nin's whole aesthetic is based on the value of her clinical insights, one naturally looks for them to be at least as sound and revealing as those that make up the common stock in trade of the analytical practitioner. If Miss Nin were writing traditional short stories she would employ conventional fictional means—dramatic conflict, evolution of circumstances, etc.—to heighten our experience of life. Having discarded these means, Miss Nin must depend instead on the poetry of literalness and science. Her science must therefore be of a kind to set up good poetic vibrations: it must be good science.

What I mean by saying that good science makes for good poetic overtones can perhaps be illustrated by a sentence recently quoted to me from *The Development of Modern Physics,* by Einstein and Infeld. Expounding the rudiments of relativity, these authors write, "A straight line is the simplest and most trivial example of a curve." It is a simple scientific statement. But in the perfection of its simplicity and its scientific accuracy it is also a very beautiful poetic statement. Similarly, a good case history, by staying with simple scientific truth, can be a poetic statement about life. But Miss Nin's case histories, by substituting a conscious poeticizing of their material for the poetry inherent in the literal material itself and by making their observations on a very low, or drawing-room, level of the psychoanalytical science, are neither good clinical practice nor good poetic suggestion.

I have space to give only a single example of Miss Nin's insufficiency—her treatment of Hejda's youthful sadism. On the first page of her first case Miss Nin reports: "Hejda was then a little primitive, whose greatest pleasure consisted in inserting her finger inside pregnant hens and breaking the eggs, or filling frogs with gasoline and setting a lighted match to them." This rather sensational activity is never traced to its psychic causes, nor is it connected with later manifestations of Hejda's character. A certain carnivorousness is remarked upon; also, another cruelty she perpetrates upon a school friend. Then, on the last page of Hejda's history, when she has reached the stage where "when everything fails she resorts to lifting her dress and arranging her garters," Miss Nin adds: "She is back . . . to the native original Hejda . . . The frogs leap away in fear of her again."

Such analytical inadequacy may be the result, of course, only of ignorance. But I am tempted to borrow Miss Nin's own deterministic bias, and diagnose this kind and degree of ignorance as wilful; after all, more information was available to Miss Nin if she desired it. But it would seem that Miss Nin has looked to psychoanalysis only for what would serve the sexual chauvinism and self-pity of the modern female writer of sensibility.

Every so often Miss Nin's writing descends from the delicate feminine heights and indulges in straight commonsense observation of human beings as well as in undecorated prose. Then it indicates that, somewhere in her, Miss Nin has the powers that have always produced good science, good fiction, good poetry. But such deviations are only occasional; so I keep wondering why a book like *This Hunger . . .* could not receive commercial publication in these days when nothing sells like the sick psyche. (pp. 105-07)

*Diana Trilling, in a review of "This Hunger . . . ,"
in* The Nation, *New York, Vol. 162, No. 4, January 26, 1946, pp. 105-07.*

JAMES WOLCOTT

Art teaches us how to levitate, Anaïs Nin was fond of saying, and in [*The Diary of Anaïs Nin, Volume Seven (1966-1974)*] her toes seldom touch earth. It isn't art that's keeping her aloft, however, it's fame, favorable reviews, rapt adoration. *Volume Seven* covers the final years of Nin's life, as she emerges from the whispering shadows of cultdom to glide from lectern to lectern in her new role as the counterculture's Lady Oracle. (Nin died in 1977, after a long bout with cancer.) In the closing pages of *Volume Six,* Nin celebrates the cloudburst of approval which greets the publication of the Diary's first volume in the spring of 1966. Lawrence Ferlinghetti showers her with rose petals in a Berkeley bookshop, love letters crowd her mailbox, and reviewer Robert Kirsch swoons at length about her "poetic and supple" prose in *The Los Angeles Times.* As *Volume Seven* opens, Nin is still soaking happily in the ironies of success: "The same publishers who turned down my work beg for my comments on new works they are publishing," she notes with rueful pride. Even media personalities lower their knees in homage. "Television interview with Arlene Francis very deep. She knew my work. She is enormously intelligent and wise." Once you've tasted the wisdom of Arlene Francis, lesser fizz won't do.

Her genius vindicated, Nin finds herself constantly on the wing. She travels to Morocco, Japan, Germany, Bali, Cambodia; she descends upon hundreds of campuses, giving sixty lectures in a stretch from autumn 1972 to spring 1973; she stars and tours with a documentary by Robert Snyder titled *Anaïs Nin Observed;* and everywhere she goes she's bombarded with love. In Paris, Nin and Jeanne Moreau discuss a film adaptation of Nin's novel *A Spy in the House of Love.* Though *Spy* was never made, Moreau later directed and starred in *Lumière,* a film that (unwittingly, one assumes) captures the haughty narcissistic glamour of life among the Ninnies. Surrounded by women who adore her and men who worship her unblemished soul, Moreau's Sarah Didieux also seems to be exaltedly aloft. "At the end of the week," writes Pauline Kael in her review of *Lumière,* "she wins something like the Academy Award, except it's at a ceremony where she is the only one being honored, and her girlfriends and boyfriends are all there, gathered around, to be happy for her." Like *Lumière,* **Volume Seven** of the Diary is a cozy get-together. Sandlewood incense wafts through the air, windchimes tinkle, and into Nin's hands tremulous coeds press flowers, cookies, rice cakes, unfinished novels. The self-trumpeting climax of this celebration begins on page 200, where Nin lists tributes from readers whose lives have been transformed by the Diary. . . .

[In] the Diary every voice throbs with the same fruity lyricism. Nearly all of Nin's correspondents sound like Nin herself, something she's proudly aware of. "There was no ego in the Diary, there was only a voice which spoke for thousands, made links, bonds, friendships. . . . There was no *one* self. We were all *one.*" As Nin and her admirers trade confidences on astrology and self-realization, scattering showy adjectives like "luminous" and "labyrinthine" through their letters, the book becomes a choral hymn to hazy-mindedness.

Occasionally a few rude notes ruin the harmony. Nin is unnerved when "aggressive" feminists give her the raspberry during her talks. She complains to artist Judy Chicago, "At Harvard, three hostile, aggressive women prevented me from finishing my talk. Really psychotic! I was ashamed of them." One woman, described by Nin as "fat and gross and aggressive," corners her after a lecture and says she works fifty hours a week and doesn't have time for a fancy-schmancy, inner journey. Nin never seems to realize that feminists resented her influence not because they were envious but because they considered her Aquarian Age go-with-the-glow dreaminess "feminine" in the most softheadedly reactionary way. With their love of the ineffable sublime, the Nin cultists aren't much different from the P. G. Wodehouse heroine who believed that bunny rabbits were gnomes in attendance on the Fairy Queen. "Perfect rot, of course," grumbled Bertie Wooster in *The Code of the Woosters.* "They're nothing of the sort."

Even more troublesome to Nin than feminists are treacherous reviewers and fellow novelists. To Nin, critics are little more than fiends pitch-forking innocent babes into the furnace. ("Gore Vidal is now a critic, which means he is cremating people," she observes sourly in **Volume Six.** Vidal, whose memorable pan of Nin appears in *Homage to Daniel Shays,* is also the villain of **Volume Seven.**) In the winter of 1970-1971, Nin meets Edmund Wilson at the Princeton Club to receive his permission to print portions from his "portrait" in one of the Diaries. To her surprise, Wilson not only chuckles at the passages she assumed would anger him, but later sends a letter saying how charming he found her company. Sniffs Nin: "Of course I never asked him why, after praising **Under**

a Glass Bell, [see excerpt above], he never mentioned me again."

What makes the Diary such a comedy is that though Nin comes on as an ethereal yenta, gathering coeds like chicks beneath her silky wings, she's so relentlessly, *spitefully* competitive. After saying a few kind words about Marguerite Duras in **Volume Six,** for example, Nin can't resist quoting someone who praises her for being "more genuine, more human" than Duras. Even old friends like Lawrence Durrell get their knuckles rapped. . . .

Decades before the Diary was published, Henry Miller claimed that Nin's confessions would someday be ranked with those of Augustine, Petronius, and Rousseau. Yet as chronicle and gossip, the Diary is little more than a long tease, a fluttering of veils. In the diaries of Dorothy Wordsworth and Virginia Woolf, small moments inch across the page—visitors sip tea, frost forms on the windowpane—and yet one is always aware of an acute intelligence reaching beyond the day-to-day. Not so in Nin. When she travels to Bali and Fez, she revels in the exotic sensations of new aromas, new fabrics; but otherwise the details of her life are obscured by a perfumey mist. She doesn't seem to *see*—a Dorothy Wordsworth snowfall is worth a dozen descents into the labyrinth—and she uses clusters of adjectives where a single metaphor might do. And except for the large-scale portrait of Henry Miller and a few vivid glimpses of Artaud, Wilson, and Tennessee Williams, Nin seldom writes about people with novelistic exactness—she shrouds them in language too pretty to be anything but platitudinous.

Of Marguerite Young *(Miss MacIntosh, My Darling),* she enthuses, "Her hair weeps, her eyelids weep, but when her voice takes up the rhythmic spirals of her writing it is the female soul of Joyce, Joyce without the male ego, the intellectual juggler with language, it is the waves, the ocean of myths . . . ," and upward Nin spins in her own rhythmic spiral. Famous Names serve to confirm or deny her genius; unfamous admirers, like the mostly homosexual clique of "transparent children" in **Volume Four,** circle Nin, then ungratefully scatter. Flattery and betrayal form the Diary's alternating currents.

Now that this final Diary has joined Nin's novels, essays, and prose poems on the shelf, it's clear that her great gift was not for literature but for friendship and persuasion. For letters, lunches, blurbs, and lectures. Her surrealism is tame, a grazing of lazy centaurs. Even more embarrassing are her attempts at moist, hot sensuousness, not only in erotic entertainments like **Delta of Venus** and **Little Birds** but in a more ambitious effort like **A Spy in the House of Love** (only a writer beyond shame and taste could describe sexual intercourse as "a joyous, joyous, joyous, joyous impaling of woman on man's sensual mast"). But her career—her *life*—was a masterpiece of self-promotion.

The Nin industry will undoubtedly continue the promotion through tributes, analyses, reminiscences, photograph albums, and collections of letters; friendly critics will persist in trying to persuade us that she was a Proustian enchantress; but I suspect the hilariously vain *apercus* of **Volume Seven** will do more damage to her reputation than the cruelest slice from villainous Vidal. "So I shall die in music, into music, with music," she writes near the end of her struggle with cancer. Foolish sibyl that she was, Anaïs Nin gives herself a graceful send-off in the book's final pages, and her admirers will probably cling to their affection for her long after they've outgrown these preposterous Diaries.

James Wolcott, "Life among the Ninnies," in The New York Review of Books, *Vol. XXVII, No. 11, June 26, 1980, p. 21.*

MAXINE MOLYNEUX AND JULIA CASTERTON

Introduction: Julia Casterton

In 1970 Maxine Molyneux interviewed Anais Nin; they talked about her third volume of Journals, which had just been published in England. The transcript of the discussion went the way of all print that is not quickly presented to a reading public: it disappeared into a drawer and lay, often considered but never finally used, for ten years. Last summer Maxine and I began to talk about Nin's work. I had just read the erotica and also taught some of her fiction in a women's writing class. We remarked on how uneasily her work sits in the history of women's writing in this century, and the problems she presents to feminist analysis because of this. Although she died in 1977, her work presented itself to us as prodigious spread: a temporal spread in that her writing began early this century and continued until her death, and a cultural spread also, spanning and uneasily moving back and forth between Europe and America. The very history of her writing, then, assailed us as formidable, a perhaps undigestible chunk. So many other women writers had made their marks during that time and subsequently disappeared, perhaps to be rediscovered by our generation. Nin had, on the other hand, quite simply but quite unaccountably (in the light of the tragedies in store for others, notably Woolf and Plath, who made writing their choice) *carried on writing.* The persistence of Anais Nin was a question in itself.

We did not want to reject or ignore her work because it doesn't fit into any predictable pattern, because it cannot be cited in the same breath as that of contemporaries as diverse as Jean Rhys, Simone de Beauvoir, and Virginia Woolf, who can be far more unproblematically "claimed" as the literary grandmothers of present day feminist writers. On the contrary, her writing presented itself to us as perhaps more engaging and challenging because of the questions it raises about writing and femininity. She seemed to be a living exception to the notion of "the totality of women" that has bugged feminist theory for so long. While her highly-regarded contemporaries are involved in writing which indicates a general oppression of women, and are amenable to a theory of patriarchy that is now (perhaps wrongly) widely accepted, the importance of the father and the celebration of sexual difference that we find in Nin's work sets her apart; she stands as *another* voice, making different meanings and representations of women. She is a dissonant element that asks to be heard in a long line of women writers who can sometimes, perhaps mistakenly, be registered as a fully-constituted orchestra playing in harmony. She seems to be one of those stereotypes (mother/witch/child/whore) we thought we had cast off, and as such, she is a clanging cymbal to us.

Nin was always aware of the unacceptability and heterogeneity of her writing, but for quite different reasons from the ones we were thinking about. An emigree, an American in spite of herself, she recognized and acknowledged the problems of a writer trying to use forms (familiar and acceptable in Europe) in a country whose literary traditions were quite alien

to her own history as a writer. She was a problem in her lifetime, and accepted herself as such; and now, when the importance of surrealist writing is fully recognised in America, she presents problems of a different nature for feminists. We wanted to examine her *as* a problem, not dismissively or condemningly, but in a way which would perhaps reveal to us the inefficacy and unhelpfulness of blanket statements that feminists often make about women writers. (pp. 86-7)

Anais Nin interviewed by Maxine Molyneux

[Molyneux]: *You are, of course, best known for your fictional work, yet from reading the Journals/Diaries one can see that these are extremely important for you, and are by no means just an adjunct to the fictional writings. Are your Journals/Diaries in fact more important to you than your other writings?*

[Nin]: Yes. I think they are because they are fuller. Yet that feeling was not there at the beginning. I used to think that my novels were my best writing but the novels were the formal work and I find that people like the spontaneous, natural work better. Also, I think that probably in the Journals I unknowingly and unconsciously produced more complete portraits of people and went deeper than in the novels, and gave more. That may have been due to a natural shyness in the formal work, but the formal work, you know is fiction and I wasn't satisfied with that, I am more satisfied with the Journals.

[Volume One] *of the Journals/Diaries was published in 1931.* [Volume Two] *in 1934. The present volume carries the account of your life up to 1944. Are you planning to publish further volumes?*

Yes I am working on **Volume 4** and I think it will go as far as a **Volume 5.** I have to keep a few months ahead of what is being published to keep my feeling of honesty. The only way I can get this feeling of honesty is to convince myself that I was able to keep a secret, and since I was able to keep a secret for so long I suppose I believe that I will continue to keep it and that no-one will see what I wrote last month. Otherwise I would lose that thing that the diary has, which is that it is being written without the feeling that anyone is going to read it. (p. 87)

Does your style and approach change from one Journal to another?

Yes, my style changes as I change. It's living and changing with me. At first it's tentative and not so sure when you are in your twenties, and then you become a little more firm when you are in your thirties, and as you mature the style of course changes again. You become more incisive. You have a better knowledge of what is important. When you are twenty you think everything is important. In editing now, I try to take out repetitions and minor subjects, minor themes. When a person isn't described in full it's not very interesting and becomes name dropping, something people tend to do in diaries—you know—there's the joke about the person who writes "Andre Gide came to dinner" and doesn't say anything more about him. So where I have done that I take that out. When I just mention a name and don't give the person, I take it out.

Do you see the Journals as being primarily about yourself or about the people and society you know?

I think it's both. By exploring yourself you begin to understand others better, by knowing yourself you also make a better friend to others. I think that my portraits of other people are more important than my self portrait. And they are full length portraits. It's the relationship between people that really wins out in the Diary. The way the friendships developed and the relationships to people. That's why I never understood some of the reviews talking about the self portrait because the important thing in the Diary is the relationships between people. And I have a thousand characters in the diaries, so I wouldn't call it exactly a self portrait. (pp. 87-8)

What about the influences on your early work? You discuss your involvement with the surrealist movement in your journals. How important was this to you and also how did its sudden collapse affect you?

You know, surrealism really didn't die. Dogma always dies. The very severe laws of a movement die, but the influence of surrealism seeped in and came out in American pop art. It just becomes a little more denuded. Some of the writers that I wrote about in a book called the ***Novel of the Future,*** are still using surrealistic methods but they are not as dogmatic. There's John Hawkes (they are very little known in England I think), there is William Gowen published by Owen, and Daniel Stern. In other words we have some writers who at a certain moment in the novel, I don't mean all the way through, use a surrealistic way of taking flights, just as Miller did when he went off the ground in some surrealist passages. So it really hasn't died, it can't die, we need that.

But you did yourself identify with the literary surrealists?

I wasn't identified with the *dogma* and I don't think they would have accepted me, because I didn't obey all the rules. But I did use surrealism when it was suitable in a novel. When you are trying to deal with many layers of life simultaneously there is no other way to deal with it. If you are telling a very simple thing of external reality you can be very naturalistic and realistic but a moment comes when as the surrealists said our lives become past, present and future on three lines, as it were, musically, and you need the surrealist way of writing. Symbolic. And in a way a lot of the symbolism that the young use came out of that acting out, like burning their draft cards, covering themselves with blood. They did a lot of theatrical things that could have been inspired by Artaud. They try to present you with history.

What about the earlier generation? Were people like Gertrude Stein important to you?

We had a very strange attitude in the thirties. Everything that happened in the 20s was very, very ancient. We were beginning everything anew. A feeling everybody has. Gertrude Stein, Hemingway and Scott Fitzgerald are three people I never met. They belong to the 20s. We thought of them as the 20s. Of course surrealism was born in the 20s, but it became really full blown in the 30s. So those things we were not interested in. I wasn't really very attracted to Gertrude Stein. (pp. 88-9)

[What do] you think the role of the artist and the writer is today?

The role of the writer is not always a very conscious one. Some people say he reflects his period. Sometimes he's against it. Sometimes you seem to be against the trend as I was in the 40s, I seem to be not in the trend of American thinking. Sometimes you represent the future. So it's very dif-

ficult to know where a writer is going to be, how useful he is going to be. In the 40s I was thought to be outside American culture but this was a useful thing, and now I'm inside it, a vital part of it. In fact I lecture and my books are taught in American universities. So we can't predict very much what is the role of the writer. If he has any integrity he either represents his period or the conflict against it which represents the future. I think I represented the conflict and therefore became prophetic of the future. I didn't accept America as it was in the 40s.

Although you are now accepted into American literary culture do you still see yourself as playing a critical and even prophetic role?

Now I'm in my time. But you can't tell. I couldn't tell even at this time. I was treated as a foreigner then; and now, as you know, the American young have taken up Eastern religions and they read Hesse and read me and they have become terribly interested in the 30s. In other words, they are making all the connecting links which give them strength to make a new world. I have accepted the world that is to come, that I hope is to come. I have accepted the world of the young, and that means anywhere between twenty and thirty years old. You see, the people who are now, for example, professors at college were students ten years ago and they were reading me. Now they're teaching me. So I have a lot of hope that a lot of other people don't have about the future. And the young lawyers who are graduating, the very young ones in their thirties are the ones who are trying to work within the system, discovering laws by which they could stop war—and I'm in sympathy with all that.

Do you feel you have contributed to helping this cause?

I'm sure I have. (p. 90)

Perhaps you are a romantic.

Yes, but so many of them are, so many of the young are. They're trying to make much tenderer relationships between men and women, much less belligerent. I am not speaking of course of the radical students, the violent radical students. I am speaking of the hippies who want peace. Their motto is peace and love (laughs).

And you go along with that.

Yes. I don't even go along with women's emancipation movement because they are declaring war on men (laugh). I don't think men are responsible for our not growing or our liberation, because so many men have helped me to become liberated. I think that's something women have to do from within, and within their own frame. I consider myself liberated, but I was helped by men; so I'm not going to declare war on men. (pp. 90-1)

One of your observations in the diary is that to ignore the individual is destructive, and by knowing yourself as an individual you are helping "this cause" along.

Yes. Especially in America. You see I can't speak for Europe because really I haven't lived here for the last few years. But in America they had a period when all the writers were writing about alienation, the strange, being alienated from everybody, not caring, not being able to make a relationship. And all the time, women and I, not only I but women writers are writing about relationships. But they didn't want to read that, you know this was romantic, this was love. But today the young are fully aware of that and the reason they felt the alienation was that they wouldn't have any relation to themselves. So that is why I always deny when people say that the diary is self-concerned and self-engrossed; I say you have to begin with the self, you have to exist. Because otherwise you don't reflect others, you don't understand, you don't relate to others if you are selfish and if you are nothing. The young understand precisely that it begins by having your own integrity; then you are like a mirror or recorded. You are able to see others, understand them and relate to them.

Is it not difficult to launch this particular battle in America?

Yes, it is difficult for the students and for the young today; they are in great danger, but they are courageous. My battle was different. It was a subterranean battle, and for many years I was considered what is called an underground writer, which meant that I never came to the establishment surface publicity thing, but today it's all harder. They have to endure greater physical dangers but at least they're heard; they have the press and they are being listened to. But what they did for me was to give me the silent treatment, that is for twenty years the work was ignored, my existence was ignored—except in colleges. You see that was a different way of dealing with me. That was . . . Today, different things are brought to the surface and there is a bigger battle going on but they are at least heard. Their poetry is published, Negro poetry is published, the Negro is heard. There is much what they call "visibility." (p. 91)

Which way do you think things are going to go now? We seem to have got to a certain stage of "liberation," we are much freer from a lot of things, and if we are not free we are at least aware of what is wrong. How will the 70's and 80's develop?

Freedom is a dangerous thing. In America they had a great deal of freedom, for example, because they didn't have much tradition, and they didn't have the power of the parent. If you have a great deal of freedom given to you from the outside and you have no inner discipline or inner integrity, then you just go to pieces. A lot of Americans had done that, young Americans, because they didn't have anything to fight even against, because the parents were not there at all. They left them to do whatever they wanted. We didn't have tradition without throwing it all overboard. For example, they [Americans] don't learn how to write, they won't learn how to paint, they won't learn how to make films. They won't read the classics. In one way it made them more courageous about the future because they had nothing to respect in the past. Everything was to be destroyed, as they say. But on the other hand it's more important to know yourself, to have some kind of structure already, so that you can withstand experience. They can't withstand experience. They take drugs and they break down and they end up in asylums. They haven't anything. This is the point about my struggle for the inner life. I see the image—it's like going to the bottom of the sea to have oxygen; you have to withstand the pressure of the outside by having an equal inner life, clam up enough to withstand the outside and the freedom so that you can know yourself. You see, I feel free but I am directing myself, that's freedom. But I'm not free to destroy myself or to destroy other people's experiences. I think freedom means getting rid of dogma—dogmatic religion, dogmatic education, dogmatic parenthood, dogmatic everything—and [finding] the genuinely religious feeling. This is not particularly a dogma or a humanistic feeling, and is not particularly a system of politics. To find

political attitudes, wisdom and understanding of what is happening is not necessarily belonging to a group.

How do you find this genuine religious feeling?

Well you have to have your own, your own world, the thing that was condemned in the Diaries. This is the very thing from which, because I was uprooted and because I lost a father, I had to create an inner world to sustain me. If the young had that, they could cope with the whole world. I think that what it is, is that I accepted need for a personal world, and that this personal world was going to help me not get desperate about the world situation but to act in it, and to survive in it. I carried on a revolt against conventional publishers in the U.S. Finally they had to accept me. (pp. 92-3)

Commentary: Julia Casterton

To write about the "work" of Anais Nin would seem perverse. It is surely rather her life that shines out, not eclipsing but apparently transcending the delicately-built scriptural artifice through which she presents herself to us. Like others who have made the confession their mode, we imagine it is she we are reaching through her narratives (as though the narratives themselves were webs, enticing yet distorting vision), she who presents herself to us finally, wordlessly, the whole woman. And she encourages this fond delusion, for she is so very silent in the Journals. It is she who writes, yes, but rarely she who speaks in them ("I think that my portraits of other people are more important than my self-portrait"). Henry Miller, Antonin Artaud, Otto Rank, and what they say of her, "give" us this woman of seemingly endless tenderness, generosity, altruism, whose only self-affirming activity appears to be the writing of the diary, the diary that asserts her self-abnegation. (p. 93)

There is a subtle treachery about a diary: even after it has rendered a particular *milieu* articulate, its inhabitants have little power of appeal or redress: they have been written; the diary has fleshed them with words already. Anais Nin would protest that one writes a diary to preserve the things one loves, but it is as well to remember also that in the recreation of one's world through writing, there resides the need to master that world, to exert power over it. While the diary may seem to be, and be claimed by Nin to be, an accurate representation of a particular reality, it also contains a desire to control that reality.

In asserting the difference between the diary and the fiction, Anais Nin claims: "The Journals supply the key to the mythical figures and assert the reality of what once may have seemed to be purely fantasy. Such a marriage of illusion and reality—or illusion as the key to reality—is a contemporary theme." Are the Journals, then, the truth behind the fictions, the clue which facilitates one's escape from the fictional labyrinth? Or do the fictions represent realities lying behind the "truthful" observances of the Journals, realities which the veils of control and discretion have shrouded? I think both questions can be adduced, and that in the tensions between the two lie both the problems and potencies of Anais Nin's work. the fictionality of fiction and the truthfulness of "an honest record" are both placed under interrogation.

Such observations would seem to bear a totally disjunctive relation to the reflections on femininity made by Julia Kristeva in *About Chinese Women,* in whose opening sections she discourses on the marginality of the feminine under patriarchy:

. . .witch, child, underdeveloped, not even a poet, at best a poet's accomplice . . . woman is a specialist in the unconscious, a witch, a bacchanalian, taking her *jouissance* in anti-Apollonian, Dionysian orgy . . . A marginal speech . . . a pregnancy: escape from the bonds of daily social temporality . . . woman deserts the surfaces—skin, eyes—so that she may descend to the depths of the body, to hear, taste, smell the infinitesimal life of the cells.

And yet the disjunction would seem to be an actual one: Anais Nin appears as all the creatures on Kristeva's list at different moments in her diary, even while she is refusing the part of *simply* the poet's accomplice, simply the witch, simply the specialist in the unconscious, by her activity of writing herself as all these things, controlling her representations, naming others so she will not be wholly enthralled by their naming of her. Furthermore, she questions the whole notion of the marginality of the feminine by centralizing the marginal. She asserts that the artist must go *under,* below the surface of the narrative sequence (where events are told one after the other, in measured time), and so reach the heart of an experience. Such an experience is often, for Nin, marginal or outside the city: a barge rocking below the pavements, a tent in an astrologer's studio, the half-lights of the *demi-monde.* Anais Nin seems to define herself as Kristeva claims femininity is defined under patriarchy: witch-enchantress, perfumed, with kohl on her eyes; tiny, bird-like woman, too small to bear children; all-giving mother who buys spectacles for Henry Miller and so cannot afford stockings for herself; martyr, writing erotica against her will, for money, to keep her "children." She presents herself as a problem because she *uses* these labels, rather than refuses them, to assemble herself as an artist. What is so difficult about her is that although most women writers have struggled painfully against such debilitating labels, she seems to rejoice in them, to turn them to her own advantage in a way we have come to regard perhaps as manipulative, wheedling, underhand—just like a woman. In the Journals these definitions of femininity, which we now reject as constricting, are the means by which she writes about herself, the means by which she effaces herself. It is as though she were posing before them, playing with them, seeing if they fit. (pp. 94-5)

[Perhaps] one should think in terms of the complex archeology of the self, rather than self-effacement, when considering Nin's work. In the Journals she does not, indeed, present herself as a consistent, logical personality holding certain formed, firm opinions which can be expressed in a similar form to any interlocutor. Quite the reverse: she writes herself as a sort of conspirator in the self-revelation of others. With Caresse Crosby she is a fellow-adventurer, a sympathetic intriguer who encourages her flights, wild projects and fantasies; with Kenneth Patchen she is a force of discipline, refusing his continual demands of money as a strong mother would refuse the regressive demands of a child. This complex multiplicity of selves, layers of contradictory formations which do not immediately suggest any kind of unity, presents huge problems for the interviewer whose task must be to reach her subject and render her in a fashion accessible to her readers. Moreover, there is an incongruity between the exposition of a self composed of many traces and fragments which hang together in a questionable integrity and the self Nin presents in the interview, remarkable, in the light of her writings, for its consistency, homogeneity, the sureness of her response and the rationality of her arguments. Perhaps this clash could be explained by saying that in the interview Nin is looking back on her past life from the vantage point of the wisdom of age, but somehow one suspects this not to be the full explanation. Could it be that the interview is yet another conspiracy, this time with Maxine, and that far from offering an explanation, a key to the self of Anais Nin which reveals the unity behind the contradictions, it stands on the contrary as yet another contradiction, yet another facet of the self to be taken into consideration along with all the others?

I have selected several short passages from *A Spy in the House of Love* which seem to indicate the problem of selfhood as it presents itself in Nin's writing. At one point I interject a quotation from the interview which I feel illustrates the closeness of the Journals to the fictions, their common preoccupation with similar questions and problems. The pointed drawing-attention to this similarity is also partly by way of explaining my desire to speak of both the Journals and the fictions in the same breath.

> It was a woman's voice; but it could have been an adolescent imitating a woman, or a woman imitating an adolescent.

> One half of the self wants to atone, to be freed of torments of guilt. The other half of man wants to continue to be free.

> . . . the only way I can get this feeling of honesty is to convince myself that no one will see the one I wrote last month. (the interview)
> She was compelled by a confessional fever which forced her into lifting a corner of the veil, and then frightened when anyone listened too attentively. She repeatedly took a giant sponge and erased all she had said by absolute denial, as if this confusion were in itself a mantle of protection.

> Also the cape held within its folds something of what she imagined was a quality possessed exclusively by man: some dash, some audacity, some swagger of freedom denied to woman.

The compulsive desire to confess, to display one's guilts, and the simultaneous need to cover up the confession, to confuse the confessor: these fragments from *A Spy in the House of Love* seem to suggest the dilemma posed by the Journals, and also the delusive transparency of the self presented to Maxine in the interview, the self which claims to be all "there," available for the interviewer and the reader, and yet somehow seems to dodge and evade, to elude the questioner.

The act of confession implies a confessor, an eye that sees, an intelligence that approves or condemns—and the "art" of the Journals involves a series of flights towards and away from such a figure. The diary describes a struggle, away from the father, away from the analyst who seeks to force her to cease keeping a diary, away from the consuming demands of close male artist friends. But within this struggle resides a series of appeals to these men (all constellated round the image of "father") to shrive, to forgive, to direct. And perhaps it is in the imitation of the father (the cape swung cavalierly round the shoulders, the pursuit of sexual adventure, the determined taking-up of the pen to "produce" a world) that these guilts are worked through, explored, and on occasion escaped from: " . . . because I had lost a father I had to create an inner world to sustain me . . . " (interview).

But the father returns in many guises, and the writing forms perhaps an index of the permanent necessity of coming to terms with him. In *A Spy in the House of Love* he appears as the lie-detector, who corners Sabina and explains her to herself:

> Some shock shattered you and made you distrustful of a single love. You divided them as a measure of safety . . . There is nothing shameful in seeking safety measures. Your fear was very great.

The good father (the lie-detector/confessor) enables Sabina to confront the source of her divided loves, which is a fear of a repetition of the trauma that occurred in her past. Analogously, Anaïs Nin works through the divisions in her self throughout the diary, and perhaps by reference to the fictions one can adduce that the source of these divisions lies in her early separation from her father. One could go further and suggest that the fictional transformations of the father (into, for example, the lie-detector) prevent her ever totally rejecting him. Making him fictionally into a good father, or at least exploring the possibility of a good father, protects him and discreetly overlays his original betrayal. Could it be that this desire to protect the father (who also connotes the past, familial law, and some kind of regulated relation to the outside world) lies at the root of Nin's refusal to participate in or sympathize with political acts of dismantlement, political strategies that involve a head-on collision with state apparatuses? ("Freedom is a dangerous thing. In America they had a great deal of freedom because they didn't have the tradition, and they didn't have the power of the parent.") This is an interesting utterance in the context of an America riven with the conflicts and contradictions thrown up by the Vietnam war, and one would have wished Nin to be a little more specific. Is Vietnam the destructive game of an undisciplined child who needs the power of the parent to protect and prevent it from its own worst excesses? A piece of Mailer-like mass psychology which leads to the conclusion that the unspent aggressive tendencies of "mankind" should be channelled into harmless war games in some isolated corner of the Pacific? If this is indeed the import, then Nin's reasoning betrays a rather alarming facility for sliding from individual to social or political analysis, and perhaps an ultimate refusal to engage with the specific complexities of the public realm. In *Volume 3* of her Journals Nin repeatedly berates her friends who stick simply to political analysis, accusing them of disregarding the individual human aspect; her own comments indicate a massive swing in the opposite direction.

What is clear is that Nin reserves her approbation for those who are prepared to work for change from within pre-existent institutions, within a given body of law to discover the statutes which will secure the end of the war. According to her own analysis then, the powers of the father (political and legal apparatuses) are not wrong in themselves, and if one looks hard enough one will find an aspect of state/parental authority which necessitates a cessation of conflict in Southeast Asia. The other view, that Vietnam arose out of the distortions and deformations within the American legal/political system, Nin seems to reject altogether, and she has little time for those she dismisses as "the violent radical students" (interview). It appears from the interview that Nin's approach to political understanding takes her through an individualistic moralism, and that she finally remains in that thoroughfare. It is through transformations in the individual that she understands social and political change to be engendered: "Do you think you have contributed to helping this cause?" "I'm sure I have" (interview). And one does not wish to look askance at such an assertion, partic-

ularly in view of the demand for the integration of public and private change that has been made so potently by the women's movement. Nin goes further, however, and opposes the feminism that could have been marshalled in her favour: "I don't even go along with the women's emancipation movement because they are declaring war on men." She asserts that the origins of our oppression lie elsewhere, not in the collective desire of men to subject women. . . .

Do we find in Anaïs Nin's work, then, a striving towards an understanding of patriarchy, of her own location within a patriarchal social order? I think that would be too large a claim, and one should perhaps attenuate it by drawing attention to Nin's own consenting implication in the production and consumption of what on the surface appears as a quite conventional brand of erotica. (pp. 95-8)

The erotica are fascinating reading because of the way they manage to inhabit two worlds: the tantalizing, enclosed world of conventional pornographic fiction, an onanistic delight to the male (and perhaps also female) reader, and the world of women's desires, at odds with purely specular pleasure, a world which seeks its own gratification and gently, subtly subverts the demands made by the anonymous publisher who commissions the writing. Perhaps the most interesting fact about the erotica in connection with Maxine's interview is that Anaïs Nin does not mention them; they consumed a considerable part of her working life while she was writing the third volume of the Journals, and yet they are missing from her account of these years in the interview.

What can we make of this absence? Perhaps it has something to do with the possibility that the erotica stand as some kind of threat, an invasion of the inner world she has created in the Journals to sustain herself through the loss of her father. The security of the private sphere is threatened by the erotica, for in writing them she is forced to bend to the publisher's desires and pleasure; she is still writing, but within an alien mode, one where she is unable to create and sustain her own private world. During the years described in *Volume 3,* the writing of the erotica constitutes her only—forced and reluctant—engagement with the public world, until the time when she abandons all hope of being published by anyone other than herself, and gets to work on her own press. At a time when she could not obtain a readership, the publisher who consumes her amorous couplings is the only person with whom she enters into a professional relationship, the only person who gives her money for her writings.

The arrangement with the publisher involves a threat both to Nin's writing and to her closely private and preserved sexuality. And yet I believe the threat proves fruitful, for if she does not mention the erotica in her interview, neither does she mention her desires, her sexuality, in the published Journals. Only in the erotica do we catch glimpses of her understanding of her own and other women's desires and gratifications—and though these desires are represented in the framework of and under the pressure of the demands of a single, rich male reader, they are nevertheless glimpses we would otherwise have been denied. In her preface to *Delta of Venus* she delivers her apologia and attempts to justify offering them finally for open publication:

> Here in the erotica I was writing to entertain, under pressure from a client who wanted me to "leave out the poetry." I believed that my style was derived from reading of men's works. For this reason I long felt that I had compromised my feminine self. I put

the erotica aside. Rereading it these many years later, I see that my own voice was not completely suppressed. In numerous passages I was intuitively using a woman's language, seeing sexual experience from a woman's point of view. I finally decided to release the erotica for publication because it shows the beginning efforts of a woman in a world that had been the domain of men.

She goes on to say that until the unexpurgated edition of the diary is published the erotica are the only examples in her work of these "beginning efforts." There is a large irony here: we have moved from Nin's early assertion that the diaries are the key to the fictions to the admission that the erotica—written under conditions that would seem entirely inappropriate to the representation of female desire—provide a clue that, because the diary remains as yet in an expurgated form, is absolutely essential to an understanding of Anais Nin's particular literary strategies.

The erotica stand, I believe, as a salutory warning against the unified self that looms at the reader in the interview. They form a hole, snag, an imperfection, in the external uniform of goodness which the benign public self of Anais Nin presents to our disappointed and disbelieving eyes. (pp. 99-100)

> *Maxine Molyneux and Julia Casterton, "Looking Again at Anais Nin," in* The Minnesota Review, *n.s. No. 18, Spring, 1982, pp. 86-101.*

ROSALIND THOMAS

Although she felt that the inclusion of eroticism in literature was "like life itself," Anaïs Nin personally was opposed to focusing one's whole literary attention on the sexual life. Her main work, *Cities of the Interior,* embraces the sexual experiences of her central characters, but only as such experiences, like all other vital experiences, afford some understanding of the deeper, interior self. Most of all, Nin was concerned with the psychic development and full integration of her characters. Inasmuch as most of them were women and Nin's poetic language was particularly adept at revealing the feminine psyche, her fiction, though written primarily in the thirties, offers a female perspective toward sexual experience.

Had she lived, Nin probably would not have been surprised that her explicitly erotic work, which she valued less than her other writing, would finally make her a best-selling author. *Delta of Venus* (1977) and *Little Birds* (1979), her two collections of erotic work, though written long before, met the sexually-liberated tastes of the 1970s and gained attention, too, because these erotic stories were written from a woman's point of view. Although they were written at a dollar a page for a male patron and can, therefore, be set apart from Nin's more serious fiction, they are not really that divorced from her other work. Principally, that is because of a wholeness in Nin, as both a writer and a person. Though she called the deliberate writing of erotica "unnatural," she could not altogether deny to her own erotic writings the qualities of style and perception that distinguished her other work. As a person, she believed that the sensual and the spiritual were inseparable. She embraced sexual expression as a means of transcendence. Critic Wayne McEvilly, in his introduction to *Seduction of the Minotaur,* states that Nin's work belongs to the "literature of bread," that is, those works that affirm and sustain life. In this respect, her erotic work is at one with her life-affirming aims. She was personally opposed to focusing one's whole literary attention on the sexual life. "It becomes something like the life of a prostitute," she wrote in her *Diary.* The total concentration of either prostitute or literature on the sexual act denies the fullness and richness of sexual experience. Concerned, however, that sexual experience as described from a woman's point of view had been little represented in American literature, she decided to publish her own erotica at whatever risk it might entail to her being taken seriously as a writer. (pp. 57-8)

Nin wrote erotica while living in Paris in the early forties. Without her friendship with Henry Miller, she might never have considered doing such a thing. A book collector first offered Miller a hundred dollars a month to write erotic stories for a wealthy patron. Miller found after a brief period, however, that his interest in writing with "a voyeur at the keyhole [took] all the spontaneity and pleasure out of his fanciful adventures." He suggested that Nin write the stories instead. Like other of her artist friends who needed money, she accepted the offer. She became what she called the "Madame" of an unusual house of literary prostitution. She was the person who negotiated the sale of other hungry artists' erotic writings, as well as her own, protecting their identity and collaborating on the work in progress.

Nin never considered her erotic writing her "real work," which she temporarily put aside for what she referred to as "that world of prostitution." She recognized that, although she wrote only for the money and felt that her own natural style of expression was stifled by her "client," her own feminine point of view was still detectable, and for this reason she valued her erotic work to a certain extent. Like Miller, however, who did not want to use any of the material he was planning to use in his fictional work, Nin did not want to give the collector "anything genuine, and decided to create a mixture of stories [she had] heard, inventions, pretending they were from the diary of a woman." (p. 59)

Despite Nin's own personal denigration of her erotic work for its limited focus, it has been at least as successful as her other fiction. For one thing, her writing style lends itself rather naturally to this form of writing. In fact, while many might regard it as only vaguely related to her more general subject of the feminine spiritual and emotional life, the erotica contains many overlapping elements with her other fiction. The events in her erotic stories, for example, are simple, as they are in her other writings. She gives little background about characters' lives, and she suggests environments more than describes them. In both kinds of fiction, she emphasizes feeling, desire, and personal freedom. Most important in Nin's fiction is her characters' regard for dreams, fantasy, and the marvelous. As she defined it, dreams meant "ideas and images in the mind *not under the command of reason.*" Dreams, Nin felt, could help one transcend ordinary life. Like the nineteenth-century transcendentalists, she believed that the self had deeper rich layers of being which, with effort, could be perceived and assimilated into life as a whole. Where the earlier writers had turned to nature for their model, Nin turned to the creative life and to dreams. The relationship between dreams and reality is present in the erotica, although developed primarily in sexual rather than in the psychological terms of the rest of her fiction.

Despite prodigious efforts, Nin always had difficulty communicating her literary intentions. In part, because of its novelty and because it functions on a simpler plane, the erotica did not suffer the same abounding critical abuse as her other fiction. The criticism leveled at her for her other writing—that it was too narrow, emotional, and feminine—is the point of her erotic writing. The nature of the genre requires that it be accessible and focused. That it was written from a woman's perspective has simply enhanced its interest. For the first time, Nin's fictional style was not criticized for being "unconventional." In fact, critics and the reading public alike were more receptive to her writing than they had ever been before. With the publication of **Delta of Venus,** Nin made the *New York Times* list of best-selling fiction for the first and only time in her writing career.

No one has suggested that Nin's erotica is great art. Its interest resides primarily in its feminine perspective and in its unmistakable poetical quality. When she reviewed the erotica many years after writing it, Nin recognized that, in spite of the collector's demands, her feminine voice was not altogether stopped. "I was intuitively using a woman's language, seeing sexual experience from a woman's point of view."

In *Cities of the Interior,* Nin's women characters struggle for satisfying relationships with men and usually fail, while in the erotic writings their need for mutual desire and fulfillment, at least on one level, is reciprocated. The female characters in both genres search for the unknown, are exceptionally curious, artistic and feminine, and seek sexual fulfillment—but with particular men. Present in all of Nin's fiction is the unwavering conviction that individual initiative and creativity are positive solutions to life's ills. By living expansively one can change external circumstances to fit personal needs. "Transformation" is a term Nin uses frequently to describe the turning of a negative situation into a positive experience. In her work she points out some of the psychological obstacles which must be overcome in order to achieve harmony in one's personal life. In *Cities of the Interior* she is concerned with the dichotomy between the trained impulse to please, serve and nurture others, and the simultaneous need to fulfill oneself. This conflict is present in the erotica as well, but where, in *Cities of the Interior* Nin's women characters are paralyzed by this situation, in the erotica they frequently move ahead to take their pleasure. The immediate resolution, the gratification or fulfillment of one's desire explains, in part, the success of Nin's erotica.

Nin's erotic stories are quite obviously told by a woman. Her intention, despite orders from the collector, is not simply to titilate, but to describe the nuances, curiosity and passion which surround sexual experience. She writes of the impact of a man's perfume, of the sound of his belt being unbuckled, or particular clothes and certain gestures which arouse a woman's interest. She also delves into the emotional complexity of sexual relationships by writing of sensitive issues that could cause discomfort and alarm to the reader, but which accurately reflect the full range of sexual expression. Included in this discussion are such topics as impotence, violence and exhibitionism in men, and frigidity and manipulation in women. Still, one would not accuse Nin of writing in a "realistic" manner in her erotic stories. Although she deals with problems of sexual involvement, they are secondary to the experience itself, and often, the means of overcoming them is the real point of interest in the stories.

According to Nin, men and women are attracted to one another often for specific reasons which have little or nothing to do with the things we have been trained to believe. In one story, for example, a man convinces a prostitute to wear the clothes of a woman he has always desired, but loses interest when he discovers that she does not have a little mole on the inside of her thigh as the other woman had. Another story, about the death of passion, tells about a woman's lover coming to her without his customary exotic perfume and of her resulting indifference to him.

Throughout the erotica, personal desire and fulfillment are often very closely aligned with another's pleasure. Sometimes, in fact, much effort is made solely in the giving of pleasure to another person, and in this way the giver is simultaneously gratified. (pp. 61-3)

The only sadistic or violent moments in all of Nin's writing occur in the erotica, and they happen when one character takes pleasure at the expense of another. The characters in Nin's work who sexually abuse each other are doomed to separate, predictably with bitterness on both sides. Nin makes it clear that she does not object to domination *per se* in sexual activity, and even depicts ways in which it briefly can contribute to sexual fulfillment, primarily when it occurs with mutual consent. But in a story entitled **"The Basque and Bijou,"** she shows the inevitable frustration and resentment which comes from prolonged emotional and sexual domination. In the story, the Basque takes Bijou from a whorehouse to live with him as his model and sexual companion. Although Bijou is anxious to distinguish between her former life and her present circumstances as the model and companion of a respected painter, the Basque takes pleasure only in subjugating, humiliating, and exposing her in the presence of his friends. . . . The impact of Bijou's relationship with the Basque is that she has become "so accustomed to his fantasies and cruel games, particularly the way he always managed to have her bound and helpless while all kinds of things were done to her, that for months she could not enjoy her newfound liberty or have a relationship with any other man."

The relationship between the Basque and Bijou is exceptional in Nin's erotic work because elsewhere she stresses male tenderness and reciprocity in sexual relationships. Although the story cannot be ignored, it might best be perceived as an example of those aspects of sexual experience which Nin regards as powerful in a purely destructive way. It is also typical of her work that no sudden event or illumination changes the behaviour of a character for the purpose of a tidy conclusion. Only after much reflection, and usually emotional pain, too, does a character in Nin's fiction become aware in significant ways. In the erotica such character development does not take place.

Nin's erotic stories do go beyond the obvious depiction of two people simply getting together for the purpose of lovemaking. In particular, she focuses on women who have the faculty of arousing passion through illusion and curiosity, as well as through desire, which she frequently terms as "hunger." By creating a poetic veil around sex, Nin believes, one can orchestrate the senses while maintaining or heightening the mystery and power of the sexual experience. Much of what gives her erotic writing its feminine flavour is the examination of the "minor senses," as Nin refers to the fuel which "ignites" sexual interest. (pp. 64-5)

The imaginative role is not always shared by both lovers in Nin's work. Sometimes the male is forced to create a sexually vital experience without his partner. For example, in the story **"The Maja,"** the painter Novalis marries Maria, a Spanish woman, who is Catholic and bourgeois in her attitude about sex. To his regret, she refuses to pose for his paintings or even to let him see her naked body. When she becomes ill and the doctor prescribes pills which cause her to fall asleep, Novalis takes advantage of her drugged state by drawing back the covers and sketching her naked body for his paintings. After a time he loses all interest in Maria while she is awake, and waits to respond to her when she is abandoned and soft in sleep. Upon returning from a brief vacation, Maria fears she has lost Novalis when she discovers him on the floor of his studio making love to a painting of her. "He lay against it as he never had against her. He seemed driven into a frenzy, and all around him were the other paintings of her, nude, voluptuous, beautiful. He threw a passionate glance at them and continued his imaginary embrace." Maria responds to this scene by removing her clothes and, for the first time, offering herself "without hesitation to all his embraces."

Nin explores other forms of sexual fantasy in her stories, such as when one person allows or encourages a partner to project his or her own personal fantasies onto their sexual experience. Mutual enjoyment results from shared imaginative experimentation in Nin's world. Perhaps the most obviously autobiographical story, entitled **"The Model,"** describes the sexual awakening of a young woman who has become an artist's model. When an artist invites the model to go to the country where many artists are working for the summer, she accepts, thinking she can make some money there. But after she arrives, the artist insists on her having sex with him, and, when she refuses, he successfully prevents her from getting work with the other artists in the small town. She leaves the town and goes for a walk in the woods. There she comes upon a painter who agrees to hire her as his model. Draping her in a white sheet, he props her against a wooden box and tells her to go to sleep while he paints her. When she awakes, he is leaning over her, touching her very lightly. He tells her he once saw a woman in Fez asleep as she was, and that he had dreamed many times of awakening that woman just as he has awakened her. Then he asks her permission to live out the rest of his sexual fantasy from the past, which she allows him to do.

Regardless of the form the imagination takes in love-making, Nin consistently asserts the conjunction of sex and feeling. She explains, for example, how sex can generate maternal feelings towards a man: "She felt herself as a mother receiving a child into herself, drawing him in to lull him, to protect him." She also writes about a woman who wants to lose her virginity in order "to be made a woman." In order to be a "woman," she suggests, one must first feel like one. In most of the erotic stories, Nin hints that these feminine urges which make a woman more specifically aware of herself as a female derive from the combined effects of sex and feeling for a man. The character who wants to become a "woman" is seeking someone with whom to fall in love in order to fulfill her dream of womanhood. The woman who has maternal feelings for her lover also cares deeply for him in other ways. At one point her lover tells her that he knows: "you are capable of many loves, that I will be the first one, that from now on nothing will stop you from expanding. You're sensual, so sensual." She makes it clear to him, however, that she distinguishes between capacity and real desire stemming from feeling. " 'You can't love so many times,' she answered. 'I want my eroticism mixed with love. And deep love one does not often experience.' " In a different story Nin reminds the reader that this need for emotion in sexual relationships is not exclusive to women. In contemplating the enthusiastic response of her lover, the female narrator of the story muses: "Women

very often pursue him, but he is like a woman and needs to believe himself in love. Although a beautiful woman can excite him, if he does not feel some kind of love, he is impotent."

Along with the emotional ties that accompany sex, Nin is interested in the specific form and impact of women's desire for men. Although she is capable of exaggeration at times, she acknowledges in the "Preface" to **Delta of Venus** that her occasional caricatures of sexuality are deliberate and are prompted by anger toward her clinical patron. A noteworthy example is: "There was a picture of a tortured woman, impaled on a thin stick which ran into her sex and out of her mouth. It had the appearance of ultimate sexual possession and aroused in Elena a feeling of pleasure." On the other hand, Nin can use overstatement in a positive way and with humour to describe a woman's passion. At these times she is at her best; her short staccato sentences combine with her rather formal use of the languages to produce a comic effect. An example concerns the "Madam" of a house of prostitution who takes seriously her job of appraising men:

> All day Maman had nourished herself with the expeditions of her eyes, which never traveled above or below the middle of a man's body. They were always on a level with the trouser opening. . . . At times, in great crowds, she had the courage to reach out and touch. Her hand moved like a thief's, with an incredible agility. She never fumbled or touched the wrong place, but went straight to the place below the belt where soft rolling prominences lay, and sometimes, unexpectedly, an insolent baton.

Nin describes a feminine interest in men in more serious terms when she attaches a psychological dimension. Ironically, her psychological probing could surprise the reader who has followed traditional sexual myths about women. The reader learns, for example, that a female character's prolific sex life is due to numbness, that the reason for all her activity is based not on desire, but on her need to feel anything at all:

> She is always smiling, gay, but underneath she feels unreal, remote, detached from experience. She acts as if she were asleep. She is trying to awaken by falling into bed with anyone who invites her. . . . . I have never once heard of her resisting—this, coupled with frigidity! She deceives everybody, including herself. She looks so wet and open that men think she is continuously in a state of near orgasm. But it is not true. The actress in her appears cheerful and calm, and inside she is going to pieces.

The outcome of this story is that the narrator manages to awaken the frigid woman. In this particular case, the psychological dimension contributes to the interest and drama of the story. Often it is more of an aside or diversion from the events than central to them; sometimes it is even an intrusion. (pp. 66-9)

Nin's repeated psychological journeys into her characters in a genre which essentially, as she acknowledges, is one-dimensional, perhaps testifies to the struggle she had confining herself to this level. One gathers that she was a sensual woman, as she suggests herself in the "Preface" to **Delta of Venus**: "If the unexpurgated version of the **Diary** is ever published, this [erotic] feminine point of view will be established more clearly," thus hinting that her own personal sex life was important enough to her to record in her daily journal, and perhaps, one day, even publish.

Sexuality to her was a positive experience in its ability to affirm, nourish and inspire. It was an authentic human expression which, when combined with caring, could be as transcendent and creative a form of expression as any other. Through the wisdom and fulfillment gained from personal experience, including sensual expression, she argues throughout her writing, one learns about the true nature of the self. (p. 69)

Rosalind Thomas, "Anaïs Nin's Erotica: A Feminine Perspective," in Room of One's Own, *Vol. 7, No. 4, 1982, pp. 57-69.*

SUSAN STANFORD FRIEDMAN

Anaïs Nin began her diary as a child overwhelmed by her sense of abandonment when her artist-father left the family. From its beginnings, her diary functioned as a safe word-shop for self-creation, a place where she could attempt to integrate the multiplicity of selves she lived out into a meaningful whole. Certainly the selections Nin published as the eight volumes of the *Diary* testify to her sense of her own uniqueness. But uniqueness for Nin bears little relation to the concept of individualism as isolate being. Instead, Nin explores and defines her identity through relationship. When a male friend advises her "to become more egotistic . . . to live for myself, write for myself, work for myself," she responds: "But I feel alive only when I am living for or with others! And I'll be a great artist in spite of that. . . . It's right for a woman to be, above all, human. I am a woman first of all." Much of the *Diary* circles around this central conflict of how to be an artist and a woman when men repeatedly tell her they are mutually exclusive kinds of being. To integrate the two, Nin uses her diary to explore the connections between herself as an artist, the category WOMAN, and other women. She observes at one point: "And what I have to say is really distinct from the artist and art. *It is the woman who has to speak.* And it is not only the woman Anaïs who has to speak, but I who have to speak for many women. As I discover myself, I feel I am merely one of many, a symbol." (pp. 44-5)

The *Diary* records Nin's attempt to create a whole identity in a culture that defines WOMAN in terms of her fragmented roles as mother, daughter, wife, and sister.

Nin's constant search for wholeness, however, is not a quest for a sharply defined identity, outside all others. She reports that Henry Miller complained, "I feel no limit in you," and "an absence of boundary" is "perverse." She thinks, in turn: "How can I accept a limited definable self when I feel, in me, all possibilities? [Dr.] Allendy may have said: 'This is the core,' but I never feel the four walls around the substance of the self, the core. I feel only space. . . . What interests me is not the core but the potentialities of this core to multiply and expand infinitely. The diffusion of the core, its suppleness and elasticity." Nin's formulation of a fluid self anticipates [feminist theorist Nancy] Chodorow's concept of women's "more flexible or permeable ego boundaries," as does her insistence on finding an identity through empathy and relation rather than detachment and separation. The various men in the *Diary* who are disturbed by Nin's fluid, relational self (even as they benefit from it) operate from an individualistic concept of the ego which is at odds with feminine socialization.

Chodorow's theory of feminine selfhood is not prescriptive, but rather attempts to describe women's psychological development in a patriarchal society in which mothers (or women) perform the nurturing roles. While Chodorow stresses simply the differences in male and female gender identity, Nin embodies the dangers of fluidity and relationship for women in patriarchy—the destructiveness of autonomy denied. The feminine capacity for empathy and identification can lead into a kind of selfless abnegation, a self-less-ness epitomized by Nin's gift of her only typewriter to Henry Miller. To justify this act of self-negation and other, less tangible "gifts" to the male artists and analysts who feed hungrily from her empathy, Nin appeals to her identity as WOMAN. Even if she fails herself as an artist, she writes at one point, she will have been "the mother and muse and servant and inspiration" to the artist. In the second volume of the *Diary,* Nin prescriptively defines this mothering of the male artist as the basis for all women's creativity:

> The woman was born mother, wife, sister. She was born to represent union, communion, communication, she was born to give birth to life and not to insanity. . . . Woman was born to *be* the connecting link between man and his human self. . . . Woman has this life-role, but the woman artist has to fuse creation and life in her own way, or in her own womb if you prefer. . . . I do not delude myself as man does, that I create in proud isolation. I say we are bound, interdependent. . . . Woman's role in creation should be parallel to her role in life.

Nin's conflation of creativity and the relational feminine self leads her into troubling cycles of giving, breakdown, and recovery, each stage of which feeds into her writing. The self she records and constructs in the *Diary* is comprehensible only within a paradigm of the self that incorporates the significance of collective consciousness and gender difference for women's individuation. (pp. 45-6)

Nin tends to celebrate the very qualities of femininity that entrap her. . . . (p. 46)

Susan Stanford Friedman, "Women's Autobiographical Selves: Theory and Practice," in The Private Self: Theory and Practice of Women's Autobiographical Writings, *edited by Shari Benstock, The University of North Carolina Press, 1988, pp. 34-62.*

SHARON SPENCER

> The woman artist has to fuse creation and life in her own way, or in her own womb if you prefer. She has to create something different from man. Man created a world cut off from nature. Woman has to create within the mystery, storms, terrors, the infernos of sex, the battle against abstractions and art. She has to sever herself from the myth man creates, from being created by him, she has to struggle with her own cycles, storms, terrors which man does not understand. Woman wants to destroy aloneness, recover the original paradise. The art of woman must be born in the womb-cells of the mind. She must be the link between the synthetic products of man's mind and the elements.

(*Diary, 1934-1939*)

This passage was written by Nin in 1937 when she was deeply involved in the process of articulating a philosophy of writing that would serve her specific needs as a woman writer. She described her unique approach to writing fiction in various ways: as "symphonic writing," as "the language of emotions," and as "the language of the womb." The phrase "music of the womb" unites the two most original—and most basic—characteristics of Anaïs Nin's body of fiction. Her writing is "musical" because it achieves its experiential impact through carefully constructed lyrical passages built up of textured, interrelated images; it is a "music of the womb" because it became (in the late 1930s) a consciously articulated expression of woman's experience, aspirations, and values. Nin wanted to endow words with flesh and blood, so to speak, to instill an inner dynamism, or *élan vital,* to demonstrate the value of sensitivity, empathy, compassion, eroticism, sensual pleasure and love of all kinds, as well as an appreciation of the arts. She believed that these qualities had been killed by many male writers' "cerebral" approach to fiction, their tendency to dissect and analyze (to "kill" their materials), and their puritanical judgmental attitudes, defensive postures arising—she believed—from a fear of yielding to feeling. When Nin set out to create an authentically "feminine" fiction, she conceived and initiated an ambitious project, the "continuous novel" *Cities of the Interior.* The five individual titles are *Ladders to Fire* (1946), *Children of the Albatross* (1947), *The Four-Chambered Heart* (1950), *A Spy in the House of Love* (1954), and *Seduction of the Minotaur* (1959).

The "music of the womb" is radical in three distinct ways. First and most obvious, in the 1930s, 1940s, and 1950s Nin was unveiling and exploring themes that few women writers except Colette had taken on, tabooed subjects: love affairs between older women and younger men; single women's entanglements with married men; women's friendships with homosexual men; white women's attraction to black men; a woman's attempt to attain erotic self-expression in the absence of love or emotional attachment; father-daughter and brother-sister incest; motivations causing lesbianism. Technically as well, Nin's earliest published works were boldly experimental. Both *House of Incest* and *Winter of Artifice* were written while Nin was working out her ideas for the "music of the womb." For a time, beginning in 1933, she was working on both manuscripts simultaneously, but *Winter of Artifice* was not completed until 1939. In both books she abandoned realistic conventions of style, structure, plot, and characterization, choosing instead to create free, autonomous, and organic forms. Each book is unique; each has a distinctive conception and form. What unites these works, making them cohere as a unified *oeuvre* is the "music of the womb": their musicality (the lyrical and rhythmical organization of all literary units, ranging from the phrase to the chapter or episode) and their devoted excavation and articulation of woman's experience. Although Nin has often been labeled a Surrealist, she is closer to the fundamental impulse of Expressionism; she did not want to portray appearances but *essences,* and her literary forms were dictated not by tradition, but by the special individuality of each work, by "inner necessity" (to borrow a phrase from Vassily Kandinsky). (pp. 161-62)

[In *House of Incest*] the idea of incest is a controlling metaphor for all doomed, impossible loves, or for narcissistic self-love. The isolated and emotionally paralyzed narrator is split into parts, body separated from spirit, feeling from intelligence, love from desire. Jeanne is the narrator's guide on the perilous journey into the house of incest, a ghastly place of infertility and death. Powerful images piled on one another betray the energy of the frantic plunge:

> The rooms were chained together by steps. . . . The windows gave out on a static sea, where immobile fishes had been glued to painted backgrounds. Everything had been made to stand still in the house of incest, because they all had such a fear of movement and warmth, such a fear that all love and all life should flow out of reach and be lost.

Typical of the many images of infertility is a white plaster forest, a "forest of decapitated trees, women carved out of bamboo, flesh slatted like that of slaves in joyless slavery, faces cut in two by the sculptor's knife, showing two sides forever separate, eternally two-faced. . . . " The book has a nightmarish intensity and a quality of suffocation. It is a nocturne: dark, foreboding, and also cruel.

Winter of Artifice is among Nin's finest novellas, both because of its unique mode of lyrical exposition—its technical distinction—and its sensitive, profound treatment of a perilous subject: incest between adults. Published in 1939, *Winter of Artifice* may well be the first work by a woman to probe deeply the nature of this attraction and its emotionally crippling bondage. (p. 163)

An extremely sophisticated piece, *Winter of Artifice* resembles a musical composition more closely than Nin's other works. Its 64 pages are woven into 13 movements of unequal length whose theme is "Musique Ancienne," one woman's experience with the Electra complex. In the sixth—central—section, the novella rises to an emotional climax and crisis. The daughter allows herself to imagine total union with her father:

> Inside both their heads, as they sat there, he leaning against a pillow and she against the foot of the bed, there was a concert going on. . . . Two long spools of flutethreads interweaving between his past and hers, the strings of the violin constantly trembling like the strings inside their bodies, the nerves never still, the heavy poundings on the drum like the heavy pounding of sex, the throb of blood, the beat of desire which drowned all the vibrations, louder than any instrument. . . .

This rhapsody is extended and buoyantly sustained, subsiding into a slower rhythm and more muted tone. The dangerous dance of father and daughter now becomes a solo performance for the daughter, who begins to glide away. In the seventh section she recalls having given a dance performance when she was sixteen during which she imagined that she saw her father in the audience, approving her performance. When she asks him to verify this, "He answered that not only was he not there but that if he had had the power he would have prevented her from dancing because he did not want his daughter on the stage." Assured that her father wants to bind her with limitations, she tastes the foreknowledge of freedom. Regarding his "feminine-looking" foot, she fantasizes that it is really *her* foot, which he has stolen. This enables her to glimpse the truth that he wants to steal her mobility and freedom for himself. Literally, "tired of his ballet dancing" (a traditional, formally patterned dance contrasted to her more modern, freer way of moving), she demands the return of her own foot, and with it she reclaims the capacity to run from him.

While working simultaneously on *House of Incest* and *Winter of Artifice,* Nin wrote:

> *It is the woman who has to speak.* And it is not only the Woman Anaïs who has to speak, but I who

have to speak for many women. As I discover myself, I feel I am merely one of many, a symbol. I begin to understand June, Jeanne, and many others. George Sand, Georgette Leblanc, Eleonora Duse, women of yesterday and today. The mute ones of the past, the inarticulate, who took refuge behind wordless intuitions . . .

(*Diary, 1931-1934*)

In 1937 she articulated the characteristics of "womb oriented writing," thereby becoming the third woman writing in English (as far as I am aware) to have committed to paper the need for a feminine theory and practice of literature. Dorothy Richardson, of course, was the first, and Virginia Woolf the second. (pp. 164-65)

The writing of the womb must be alive: that is, natural, spontaneous, flowing (to use one of Nin's favorite words). It must have warmth, color, vibrancy, and it must convey a sense of movement (often Nin's characters are stuck, immobile, or paralyzed), the momentum of growth. Woman's literature (a literature of flesh and blood) must create syntheses; it must reconnect what has been fragmented by excessive intellectual analysis. Woman's creative works must be deep; they must trace expeditions into dangerous terrain. They must explore tabooed topics and forbidden relationships. Woman's art must be honest, even if the search for truth causes pain:

> Woman's role in creation should be parallel to her role in life. I don't mean the good earth. I mean the bad earth too, the demon, the instincts, the storms of nature. . . . Woman must not fabricate. She must descend into the real womb and expose its secrets and its labyrinths. . . . My work must be the closest to the life flow. I must install myself inside of the seed, growth, mysteries. I must prove the possibility of instantaneous, immediate, spontaneous art. My art must be like a miracle. Before it goes through the conduits of the brain and becomes an abstraction, a fiction, a lie. It must be for woman, more like a personified ancient ritual, where every spiritual thought was made visible, enacted, represented.

Nin now conceived the multivolume "continuous novel," *Cities of the Interior,* a project that involved transforming the diary, or parts of it, into fiction. Characterized by a richly inventive feminine imagery (drawn from women's preoccupations and occupations like work, cooking, decorating a home, feelings about pregnancy, clothing and makeup) and an organic spontaneous (thus unpredictable) structure, *Cities* takes as its theme the psychology of woman:

> Theme of the development of woman in her own terms, not as an imitation of man. This will become in the end the predominant theme of the novel: the effort of woman to find her own psychology, and her own significance, in contradiction to man-made psychology and interpretation. Woman, finding her own language, and articulating her own feelings, discovering her own perceptions. Woman's role in the reconstruction of the world.

(*Diary, 1944-1947*)

The originality of *Cities of the Interior* lies partly in its use of lyricism to convey character, situation, and action but even more definitively, in its radical concept of structure. It is a group of distinctly discreet but related volumes with individual titles, in Nin's words, "a continuous novel." The various women artist protagonists appear and reappear, now one and now another occupying the central position as "main character." The individual volumes can stand alone wholly without reference to the others, or they can be read as parts of an unfinished whole. The order of the component parts of the continuous novel does not affect the reader's comprehension of the whole. The volumes can be considered interchangeable. Nin achieved this by avoiding specific chronological references, which would have established a sequence, and by writing fluid open endings that provide links moving simultaneously forward and backward in time. (pp. 165-66)

Of the five novels, *Seduction of the Minotaur* (1959) is the most fully developed, the deepest in emotional range as well as the most technically accomplished. This novel derives its leisurely organic structure from the archetype of the journey; the several parts of the novel are journeys within the larger journey. *Seduction* begins with Lillian's arrival in Golconda where the people, whose "religion was timelessness" "exuded a more ardent life," and it ends with her "journey homeward." Golconda is Lillian's "territory of pleasure." Escaping from her "incompletely drowned marriage" with Larry, she is "maintained in a net of music, suspended in a realm of festivities." Between her arrival and her "journey homeward," she reluctantly undertakes a perilous inner journey. (Now we are in the "labyrinth" Nin mentioned when she expressed the need for women to confront dangers.) (p. 167)

The novel's major discovery (the goal of the dangerous journey) is the minotaur in Lillian's own personal labyrinth (unconscious), and this monster is none other than herself: "a reflection upon a mirror, a masked woman, Lillian herself, the hidden masked part of herself unknown to her, who had ruled her acts. She extended her hand toward this tyrant who could no longer harm her." (In contrast, Theseus murdered the minotaur, and exploited and abandoned Ariadne.) Lillian discovers that her belief in her own freedom is an illusion; still bound, she must rediscover vital aspects of the "primitive." She must learn to dance to "the music of the body" before summoning the emotional and spiritual power to reignite her love of Larry through enlightened understanding. Before she can be reconciled with Larry, she must seek and submit to the rite, to a *participation mystique.* (pp. 167-68)

At its most exalted, music was for Nin, as for many European writers, a way of entering the transcendent, even the sublime realm of experience. While "music of the body" may represent a parallel to the élan vital described by Henri Bergson (the basic dynamism of life), more sophisticated musical expressions represent parallels to more complex and intricate modes of experience: The "rhythm of life" (breathing, walking, the heart beat, dancing) has its counterpoint, or counterpart, in a more spiritual music. This more intricate, more subtle music provides "the continuity . . . which prevents thoughts from arresting the flow of life" as well as "a higher organization of experience."

This "higher organization of experience" (transcendence, the forgiveness, the revitalized and renewed love Lillian feels for Larry at the novel's end) becomes accessible to her only after the ritual *participation mystique* has been consummated. Only then is it possible for her to leave the labyrinth, not by retracing Ariadne's thread, but by simply rising above the maze. Several transformations occur, enabling Lillian to soar at last. One such transformation (and it is crucial) is her temporary change of relationship to Larry. Becoming his mother instead of his wife, she re-*imagines* Larry, thus giving birth to him in a new, more complex form.

Finally, then, the most richly embroidered theme of "music of the womb" is the need for love, not only the power of maternal love, with its transformative powers, but also agape, the love of friends, which is the essence of Nin's fraternal vision of marriage, viewed more as lifelong friendship than as erotic coupling. All the themes that appear and reappear in Nin's writings are related to the principle of Eros, or relatedness, as well as to the need for human beings to nurture and, when necessary, to heal one another. (pp. 168-69)

The tenderness, solicitude, and acceptance of the human need to nurture and to be nurtured characterize Nin's last "novel" as strongly as *Seduction of the Minotaur.* If *Seduction* is the most mature, the most fully developed and richly detailed example of the "music of the womb," *Collages* (1964) may be her most original book. Less musical than visual, as its title indicates, *Collages* is a composition of 19 juxtaposed vignettes. There are no narrative passages, no transitions between vignettes, no plot. Unity and overall coherence are provided by the dominant presence of Renate, a painter, and by the recurrence of related themes in the vignettes. There are many settings and many "characters"; all are swiftly sketched in Nin's vibrant imagistic prose. Among them are Leontine, a buoyant black singer; Henri, a master chef; the deliriously mad actress Nina Gitana de la Primavera; Nobuko, who every day selected her kimono to harmonize with the weather; Varda, creator of exquisite airy collages of women; the betrayed wife of a French consul, who invents a new love for herself. Although all have been wounded in some way (Renate by her selfish lover Bruce), all are resourceful and imaginative; they have woven self-sustaining worlds of fantasy around themselves.

The situations depicted in the 19 vignettes are varied, but each demonstrates transformation achieved through imagination. All celebrate the vital role of creativity, whether it is the charm of playing "make-believe," the power of fantasy to invent new personalities and lives for oneself when reality becomes unbearable, or specific artistic creativity such as that represented by the book's artists: Renate, Leontine, Varda, and a writer named Judith Sands.

In a typical nurturing act, Renate rescues the neglected and bitter Judith Sands (easily recognizable as a portrait of Djuna Barnes) from her lonely garret-like hideout. In the book's witty final vignette, the name of Judith Sands is saved from the jaws of a self-destructing apparatus that "eats" the names of artists and writers before exploding and burning. Symbolically, Nin alludes to the continuity of a tradition of women writers and restores Djuna Barnes to her place in that tradition.

To look back at *House of Incest*—an expression of entrapment, isolation, fragmentation, and suffering—and then to look at *Collages*—with its light, airy, confident tone and frequent examples of mobility—is to see the trajectory of Nin's

growth as woman and artist. Renate is assured and confident, entirely comfortable with her role as woman artist and with her many friendships; she is not at all dependent on her lover for her sense of value. When someone suggests that Varda make a portrait of Renate, he declines, explaining that she is *"femme toute faite."* He adds: "A woman artist makes her own patterns." Indeed, a definitively female narrative was Nin's ideal. It preceded by 40 years the theories of contemporary French writers, such as Annie Leclerc and Hélène Cixous, who argue the need for "writing the body," as Nin argued the need for writing the womb. (pp. 170-71)

Sharon Spencer, "The Music of the Womb: Anaïs Nin's 'Feminine' Writing," in Breaking the Sequence: Women's Experimental Fiction, edited by Ellen G. Friedman and Miriam Fuchs, Princeton University Press, 1989, pp. 161-73.

FURTHER READING

Anais: An International Journal. Anais Nin Foundation. 1983-
    An annual publication of critical essays pertaining to Nin's works.

Balakian, Anna. "' . . . and the pursuit of happiness': *The Scarlet Letter* and *A Spy in the House of Love."* Mosaic XI, No. 2 (Winter 1978): 163-70.
    Compares Nathaniel Hawthorne's with Nin's moral revisionism regarding sexual relationships.

Cutting, Rose Marie. *Anais Nin: A Reference Guide.* Boston: G. K. Hall and Co., 1978, 218 p.
    Offers an exhaustive annotated bibliography of Nin's works from 1937 through 1977.

Franklin, Benjamin V. *Anais Nin: A Bibliography.* Kent, Ohio: The Kent State University Press, 1973, 115 p.
    Provides a complete record of Nin's publications in English, exclusive of Canadian editions, with detailed descriptions of individual differences between editions.

Schwichtenberg, Cathy. "Erotica: The Semey Side of Semiotics." *Substance* X, No. 32 (#3 1981): 26-37.
    Utilizes Umberto Eco's definitions of substition, lie, and social convention to investigate the process of signification in Nin's short story "Lilith."

Under the Sign of Pisces: Anais Nin and Her Circle. Columbus: Ohio State University Libraries. 1970-
    A quarterly publication dedicated to exploring the influence of Nin and her contemporaries.

Milorad Pavić

1929-

Yugoslavian novelist, poet, and short story writer.

Pavić has garnered international acclaim for his best-selling narrative *Hazarski recnik (Dictionary of the Khazars: A Lexicon Novel in 100,000 Words),* an intricate, surrealistic work that combines elements of the historical novel, detective story, folk tale, and romance. Written in the form of a three-part encyclopedia about the Khazars, a once-dominant Turkish people who thrived in the Balkan region during the Middle Ages, *Dictionary of the Khazars* centers on a debate held in the ninth century between Christian, Jewish, and Moslem religious figures to determine the meaning of a dream experienced by the Khazarian leader, known as the kaghan. In the kaghan's dream, an angel tells him: "The Creator is pleased with your intentions but not your deeds." Each clergyman analyzes this statement from his own religious perspective, after which the kaghan converts to one of their faiths. To which religion the kaghan converts remains unclear, however, and each religious group believes it has won the debate. Pavić examines how the kaghan's decision resulted in the annihilation of the Khazars by Russian invaders two centuries later. Although set predominantly in medieval times, Pavić's novel has been interpreted as being politically relevant to the situation in modern Eastern Europe. Michael Dirda commented: "In [*Dictionary of the Khazars*] the reader is compelled to forge the connections for these fragments of Time and History, and by so doing to reflect upon the way we read and interpret the world." Pavić also published volumes of short fiction and poetry in his native country prior to attaining international renown with *Dictionary of the Khazars.*

PRINCIPAL WORKS

NOVELS

Hazarski recnik   1985
　　[*Dictionary of the Khazars: A Lexicon Novel in 100,000 Words,* 1988]
Predeo slikan čajem   1989

DOUGLAS SEIBOLD

Dictionary of the Khazars is a book so complex and idiosyncratic that it defies easy summary. Its author, Milorad Pavić, born in 1929, is a Yugoslavian poet and professor as well as a novelist; and if Serbo-Croation writing hasn't enjoyed the vogue in the West that other Eastern European literatures have, perhaps Pavić's novel will change that. *Dictionary of the Khazars* rivals Umberto Eco's *The Name of the Rose* in wit, invention and intellect and exceeds it in sheer whodunit intricacy.

The novel is written in the form of a three-part dictionary or encyclopedia devoted to the history and culture of the Khazars—a once-powerful people who flourished during the Middle Ages between the Black and Caspian Seas, in what is now the Soviet Union. According to historical record, the Khazars converted to Judaism from their original faith in the late 9th Century; by the end of the 11th Century, they mostly had been wiped from the face of the earth by Russian invaders.

As Pavić has it, the Khazars did not necessarily convert to Judaism. At the center of his story is a debate held in the late 9th Century between a Christian monk, Jewish rabbi and Moslem dervish at the court of the kaghan, the Khazar ruler. Their subject was a vision experienced by the kaghan, wherein an angel told him that "the lord is happy with your intentions, but not with your deeds."

Who won the debate, to which faith the Khazars actually converted and why and how that decision led to their extermination are the books' ostensible subjects. It is divided into three sections, one each composed of Christian, Jewish and Islamic sources concerning this "Khazar Polemic." But each faith's account of the debate and its outcome does not entirely correspond to those of the other two.

According to Pavić's introduction, the book can be read by selecting entries at random or by reading in sequence the entries for corresponding subjects in the three different sections. But if it is read straight through, a narrative gradually coalesces, one that leaps back and forth between the 9th Century court of the kaghan, a battlefield on a bank of the Danube near Constantinople in the late 1600s and a scholarly convocation that is being held in present-day Istanbul.

The book features a cast of characters who themselves travel back and forth through time and space. Most have at least one counterpart, either from one of the other faiths or on one of the other plateaus in time where the story takes place.

The effect is thoroughly, and deliberately, disorienting. But that's where the book's greatest pleasures lie—in unraveling its very tangled web in an attempt to resolve the mysteries surrounding the Khazars and their disappearance.

Even in translation the vitality of Pavić's style is remarkable. *Dictionary of the Khazars* is rich with pungent aphorisms and similes that emphasize the folk-tale-like character of the work. And out of this material, Pavić has drawn an impressively resonant inquisition into the natures of language, time, history and faith.

> Douglas Seibold, "A Novel of Intricate, Disorienting Pleasures," in Chicago Tribune—Books, November 6, 1988, p. 6.

MICHAEL DIRDA

In the best magical realist fashion, *Dictionary of the Khazars* appears not as a book but as the reconstruction of one particular copy of the lost 17th-century Daubmannus edition of an accursed handbook devoted to a people—at times reminiscent of Scythians, Bedouins or Cossacks—who lived near the Black Sea and suddenly vanished during the 10th century. Even their language has been forgotten, except by certain parrots.

At the climax of what little is known of Khazar history occurred the once famous "Khazar Polemic." Having dreamed the sentence "The Lord is pleased by your intentions, but not by your deeds," the khagan (or Khazar chief) demanded that representatives of three great religions explain this portentous variant of "actions speak louder than words." A Christian saint, a Jewish scholar and a Moslem teacher debated the dream's meaning. One of these sages so impressed the khagan that the Khazars converted to his religion. But since the Khazars were swallowed up by history—actually by the Russians, an act with plenty of modern East European vibrato—no one is sure who really won the polemic.

As often happens, all sides claimed victory, with the result that *Dictionary of the Khazars* is divided into three smaller lexicons: The Red Book (Christian sources on the Khazar question), the Green Book (Islamic sources) and The Yellow Book (Hebrew sources). Within each section the entries are arranged alphabetically; a few major figures appear in all three registries, but the accounts of their actions can vary greatly "like looking glasses that give a different reflection of the world."

By now, the astute will realize that we are entering the somewhat creaky funhouse of post-modernist fiction: Tongue-incheek scholarship, branching timelines, multiple Rashomonlike perspectives, footnotes and appendices, mirrors, dreams, symbolic murders, unreliable narrators, textual uncertain-

ties—all of it as old hat as the New Criticism. Nevertheless Milorad Pavić manages to pull out some new rabbits.

As with Borges or Garcia-Márquez, Perec or Calvino, this Yugoslav professor and first-time novelist knows how to support his textual legerdemain with superb portrait miniatures and entrancing anecdotes. And these, I think, rather than such subtleties as a Male and Female edition of the book, are what will keep most readers turning the pages. . . .

One reason to compose a "lexicon novel" is to subvert the chronological, to abolish the awful tyranny of Time: A novel, like a life, typically implies a succession of events, but a dictionary follows no master but the alphabet. In Pavić's book the reader is compelled to forge the connections for these fragments of Time and History, and by so doing to reflect upon the way we read and interpret the world. "Not individual lives, but all future and past times, all the branches of eternity are already here, broken up into tiny morsels and divided among people and their dreams." These words are actually applied to Adam Ruhani—a god-like being who encloses the cosmos in an eternal simultaneity—but they also offer a precise picture of *Dictionary of the Khazars.* Just as certain Khazar wise men spend their lives hoping to reassemble the fragmented body of Adam Ruhani, so the reader must take the hodgepodge of Pavić's novel and find its unifying elements. But since Pavić keeps yanking the narrative from beneath one's feet, it can be hard for a reader to keep his balance, let alone find his way.

From Pavić's three lexicons gradually unfold three interrelated histories. The earliest in time relates the Khazar polemic itself; the most recent reports a 1982 double-murder involving three Khazar scholars at the Kingston Hotel in Istanbul. Linking these two is the encounter on a 17th century battlefield of three dreamy adventurers with an unusual psychological quirk: When the Christian Avram Brankovich is asleep, he dreams that he is the Jew Samuel Cohen, and vice versa. Each is obsessed with finding his other self. The third in this trio, a Moslem named Yasuf Masudi, is specially trained in dream hunting—by which the adept can enter the dreams of others—and needs to locate the other two men to complete his own life. The common fate of this trio is observed by a lutist named Yabir Ibn Akshany, actually a demon, whose own destiny takes him into the 20th century and a fateful encounter at the Kingston Hotel.

For all its ingenuity and considerable fascination, *Dictionary of the Khazars* occasionally forgets that the secret of narrative is not so much to challenge the reader as to enchant him. Pavic's book has been compared to *The Name of the Rose,* but Eco's global best seller offered a lot of exciting Gothic hugger-mugger as well as extended arias on language, politics and theology: The reader wanted to know who was murdering those monks and why. Pavić's book—which, by the way, is strikingly beautiful, even by Knopf design standards—contains plenty of Zen-like parables and Arabian Night extravagances but needs a bit more human interest.

> Michael Dirda, "The Secrets of the Alphabet," in Book World—The Washington Post, November 13, 1988, p. 6.

ROBERT COOVER

Most written narratives express in some manner [a] tension between the unfolding narrative and its closed and inflexible text, but there are some, often thought of (in our time at least) as "innovative," which put it in the foreground. Such a book is the Yugoslav poet and scholar Milorad Pavic's witty and playful *Dictionary of the Khazars,* which, with its chronologically disturbed alphabetized entries and its cross-referencing symbols, allows each reader to "put together the book for himself, as in a game of dominoes or cards." The reader may pursue a topic as with a dictionary, read the book from beginning to end, from left to right or right to left, or even "diagonally," working "in threes." . . .

In truth, this is a book that is best read just about any way *except* cover to cover. For all its seeming complexity, it surrenders easily—even gratefully—to a reconstructed reading, and there are probably fewer choices for doing that than the author would have us believe. The dictionary is divided into three separately alphabetized books or "sources" (Christian, Islamic and Hebrew), prefaced by a set of "preliminary notes" and followed by appendixes (which in fact contain much of the meat of the narrative), and the story is divided into three periods in time, each of which has its three different central characters according to the sources. Thus: a 3-by-3 character matrix with subsets. The paths between the entries are plainly marked, and there are, after all, only 45 of these entries (and one of those a mere one-line reference), many fewer than one might expect in a "dictionary" of such presumed scope. Even getting lost, which is perhaps easier inside entries than between them, could be rewarding. Since this book responds in a sense to Jorge Luis Borges's appeal for a "history of dreams" (Borges lovers will find here many echoes and whisperings of the master librarian of Babel and discoverer of the "Encyclopedia of Tlön"), the pleasures it contains might best be absorbed in a free-associative dream-like passage.

The Khazars are said to be a lost people who flourished somewhere in the Balkans ("beyond the mountains," as it were) late in the first millennium. Though we are provided with a feast of entertaining folkloric anecdotes and "legends" applicable to any such fairy-tale kingdom, the only "historical" event chronicled is the "Khazar polemic," a fanciful ninth-century debate among three divines—Jewish, Christian and Muslim—for the souls of the Khazars, a debate from which the Khazars apparently never recovered. The present *Dictionary of the Khazars* announces itself as a 1980's reconstruction and updating of a destroyed 1691 book of the same name, which in turn was an amended reconstruction of the lost "dictionary" of the Khazar "dream hunters" of some eight centuries before, the sect that preceded and was absorbed by (or perhaps absorbed) the three religions. This ur-dictionary was a collection of dream observations, "along with biographies of the most prominent hunters and the captured prey," including the participants in the Khazar polemic.

This nesting of books within books, epochs within epochs, "inside one another like a set of hollow dolls," together with an alphabetical sorting of entries rather than a chronological one and the ability of many of the characters to pass in one embodiment or another from age to age, further "spatializes" time, convincing some of the company here that increments of time might be objects of a sort or that their lives might have been dreamed by others or inscribed in books "patterned according to a story told long, long ago." This is like Borges's celebrated metaphysicians of Tlön, who held that "*all time has already transpired and that our life is only the crepuscular and no doubt falsified and mutilated memory or reflection*

of an irrecoverable process," and "that while we sleep here, we are awake elsewhere and that in this way every man is two men." The Khazars too dream one another's waking days and "imagine the future in terms of space, never time." . . . (p. 15)

The first entry of the first (Christian) book (a similar entry appears at or near the beginning of the other two books as well) is Ateh, the Khazar princess and protectress of the cult of dream hunters. It is her immortal, shape-shifting and surreal spirit that presides over what is said to be, at least in its origins, her dictionary. She is a poet, a teacher, a counselor, a magician, a succubus of sorts, a seditionist and a kind of Zen master for whom all truths of this world are self-canceling, that cancellation being the closest one gets to universal truth.

The original dictionary, said to have been put together by Princess Ateh and her lover, the legendary Mokaddasa Al-Safer, greatest of the dream hunters (he was able "to tame fish in people's dreams, to open doors in people's visions, to dive deeper into dreams than anyone before him"), was supposedly a compilation of the experiences of the dream hunters, who, drawing on old folk motifs for their whimsical methodology, were (and are) essentially mystical seekers after poetic truth, the only kind of truth that survives Mr. Pavic's gentle mockery. History, scholarship, philosophy, religion, virtually all forms of learning and remembering (all "dictionaries") are ridiculed, dissolved into the dream of the sleeping, primordial giant Adam-before-Adam (Adam Cadmon, Adam Ruhani), whose body contains the universe and who "thought the way we dream."

The goal of the dream hunters is to "plunge into other people's dreams and sleep and from them extract little pieces of Adam-the-precursor's being, composing them into a whole, into so-called Khazar dictionaries, with the aim of having all these assembled books incarnate on earth the enormous body of Adam Ruhani"—an unlikely achievement, since Mokaddasa Al-Safer himself only managed to shape a single strand of his hair. Besides, as the devil himself warns, it is a mortally dangerous vocation, and the reconstructed Adam may turn out, alas, to be a monster.

The religious disputants at the Khazar polemic are also called dream hunters and dream readers, and so are credited with good intentions even while their arguments are reduced to the vaporous substance of dreams (the dream they have been called upon to interpret in the Khazar polemic centers on an angel's declaration to the dreaming ruler: "The Creator is pleased with your intentions but not with your deeds"). And, like the other "students of the Khazar question" chronicled here, the readers of this book become, ipso facto, initiates into Princess Ateh's dream-hunting cult, invited "to leave your reports and additions to the Khazar dictionary where all successful dream hunters leave theirs." "It is an open book," Mr. Pavic tells us in the preliminary notes, "and when it is shut it can be added to: just as it has its own former and present lexicographer, so it can acquire new writers, compilers, and continuers."

Which may well happen. This spatializing of the narrative time line, offering the reader a multitude of branching paths in place of the inalterable paginated sequence, with its tantalizing life-after-death illusion of an inexhaustible unending text, has a great appeal right now among computer-bewitched humanists. (pp. 16, 18)

For all its delights, for all the structural novelty and the comic inventiveness of the imagery, it must be said there is something rather light and airy about this book. It is fun to chase down all the linkages between entries; but as they are conjoined more by the bubbling repetition of motifs and the requirements of the formal devices than by real narrative event or development, it is, as Mr. Pavic himself suggests, a bit like working a crossword puzzle. Or, as though Princess Ateh were setting us exercises, like deciphering dreams, which are also known less for sustained story lines and substance than for their signifying structure and vivid surface.

When we first meet Ateh, she is preparing for bed by decorating her eyelids with letters that kill as soon as they are read, and so protect her in her sleep. Thus we enter the book as though going to sleep, our lids sealed with letters, and, though Ateh's own dreams, except for a brief dream-hunting adventure or two, are not recorded, it is as if this entire dictionary might be no more than a collage of her dreams, provoked by associations generated in part by this opening passage. The motif of letters with magical properties, for example, is threaded throughout the book, as are many other themes and motifs that appear in this short entry—salt, mirrors, metamorphosis, dream hunters, eyes, the Khazar polemic and dictionary, indeterminacy, doubles, translation, alternate stories, the varieties of time—any one of which could have an entry, or entries, of its own.

"Eyes," for example: Ateh's eyes here are silver, but others are "like two shallow dishes of onion soup," "as hairy as testicles," "like yellow grapes whose seeds showed through," "the color of damp sand," "the shape of eggs," "like two small blue fish," "like two trampled puddles," "like the wasps that transmit the holy fire: one eye masculine, one eye feminine, and each with a sting." There are eyes that drip colors into paints, others that can spell a name in the air and light a candle or swallow a soaring bird. Yet another character has breasts with eyelashes and eyebrows that "dripped a dark milk like a threatening glance."

These images are not developed or repeated, and some of them may apply, contradictorily, to the same person or be shared by different persons. They exist of and for themselves, for their moment on the page, and often the most stunning ones are oneliners applied to characters who seem to have no other purpose for being in the text than to exhibit the image. (pp. 18, 20)

If all of this is, as Mr. Pavic suggests, "something like a feast eaten in a dream," it is a feast for all that, and, faithful to his notion that all books are dreams and readers are dream hunters, an ebullient and generous celebration of the reading experience. His characters imitate those metaphysicians of Borges's Tlön, who "do not seek for the truth or even for verisimilitude, but rather for the astounding." I cannot read the Serbo-Croatian original and so am not the best judge, but, as all the above irresistible quotations should attest, Christina Pribicevic-Zoric's translation seems quite stunningly brilliant. It has a freshness, a sparkle, a delicacy and economy of phrasing reminiscent of that given to Gabriel García Márquez's *One Hundred Years of Solitude* by Gregory Rabassa, or William Weaver's splendid translations of Italo Calvino. (p. 20)

> Robert Coover, "*He Thinks the Way We Dream,*"
> in The New York Times Book Review, *November 20, 1988, pp. 15-16, 18, 20.*

JOHN LEONARD

Dictionary of the Khazars is easier to read than to describe. If Nabokov comes to mind, so do Pynchon (*Gravity's Rainbow*), Svevo (*Confessions of Zeno*), Borges (*A Universal History of Infamy,* "The Approach to al-Mu'tasim"), Cortazar (*Hopscotch*), Lem (*Solaris*), Eco (*The Name of the Rose*), Chandler (*The Long Goodbye*), Barthes (on magazine ads for Panzani pasta) and the Marx Brothers (Karl and Groucho). I'm not kidding. Without a list, there's no post-modernism. Pavić . . . is also a wag. If—just to pick on the French, although I'm sure he's making fun as well of lots of Balkan heavyweights I never heard of—he is sending up linguists like Saussure, anthropologists like Levi-Strauss, historians like Febvre and Le Roy Ladurie, and deconstructionists like Barthes and Foucault, he's also sending up his own Serbs. The Serbs, he suggests, have a Khazar-like identity crisis. They hunt one another in their dreams, quite like the priests of Princess Ateh, who gave her poems to a parrot.

But there I go already, making difficulties. According to Pavić:

Once upon a time in the eighth century, the Khazar kaghan, a sort of prime minister, had a moonlit dream in which an angel told him: "The Creator is pleased with your intentions but not your deeds." To read this dream the kaghan summoned to his capital Greek, Saracen and Jewish scholars for a great "Polemic." . . . These worthies interpreted the kaghan's dream through their separate sets of goggles and kaleidoscopes, after which he converted to their faith. (*Which* faith is not established; each religion thinks it won.) It was downhill from then on until the tenth century, when the Russian Prince Svyatoslav "gobbled up the Khazar Empire like an apple, without even dismounting from his horse."

Moving right along, as Pavić refuses to do, we find ourselves on the banks of the Danube in 1689, where the Serbian warlord Kyr Avram Brankovich is about to trifle with murderous Turks. Kyr Avram has been secretly compiling a dictionary of the long-lost Khazars, a catalogue of the biographies of the principals in the Polemic. It's hard work. He's had to learn the lingo from a Black Sea parrot who was taught it by the Princess Ateh, from the court of the converted kaghan, before the devil made her mute. He must also rely on what's left of the Great Parchment, a history of Khazaria tattooed on the body of an envoy to the Byzantine Emperor Theophilus, who itched himself to death. Kyr Avram goes to all this trouble because he's pursued in a dream by a redhaired Jew named Cohen, his double, who is also after Khazar secrets.

I must pause here to explain, as Pavić doesn't, that the Dream Hunters are a cult of Khazar priests under the protection of Princess Ateh, who project themselves back and forth in time. They pursue one another but they also pursue, in the "knots" of dreams, the broken body of the original Adam (Cadmon or Ruhani), whose angel-making reassembly, by glossaries and alphabeticons, will solve the universe. This first Adam was originally made of two times, masculine and feminine, "but later the particles of time enclosed in the human form steadily multiplied, and Adam's body multiplied, until it became an enormous state, like the state of nature." . . . (pp. 610-11)

To complicate matters, the Khazars believed "that to every person belongs one letter of the alphabet, that each of these letters constitutes part of Adam Cadmon's body on earth, and that these letters converge in people's dreams and come to life in Adam's body." The borderline between God's word and the human word runs between verbs and nouns; God's secret name is a verb. The red-haired Cohen, on awakening from a dream-death in which "all the names of the things around him began dropping off like hats," learns that "the numbers of the Ten Commandments are also verbs, that they are the last to be forgotten when one is forgetting a language and remain as an echo even when the Commandments themselves vanish from memory." Halevi was of the opinion that "vowels are the soul in the body of consonants." Rabbi Isaac Sangari, the Hebrew representative in the Khazar Polemic, felt that "all languages except God's are the languages of suffering, the dictionaries of pain." And so on.

If this isn't deconstruction, I'll eat my discourse.

Anyway, on the banks of the Danube, instead of the Turks, Kyr Avram meets his dream-double, Cohen ("priest" in Hebrew; "kaghan" in Khazar). And you know what happens when doubles meet in modernist literature: The novel dies. Again.

But Kyr Avram's dictionary, consisting of a red, a green and a yellow notebook, one each for the three religions, with a cross, a crescent or a Star of David to identify the source of every entry, doesn't die with him. It's removed from his library in Constantinople, fiddled with by an odd Prussian monk I won't bother to explain, and then published in 1691 by Johannes Daubmannus, in an edition of 500 copies, 498 of which will be burned by the Inquisition. Of the two remaining copies, one has poisoned ink on page nine and the other has a silver lock.

Between the Inquisition and 1982, the pages of the Daubmannus dictionary are dispersed, like the parts of Adam Cadmon's body. They are pursued by three scholars—modernist dream-hunters. Dr. Dorothy Schultz, a Slavist with a split personality; Dr. Abu Muawia, a Hebrew philologist with a hidden agenda, and Dr. Isailo Suk, an Arabist archeologist "with eyes . . . as hairy as testicles," meet to compare notes in Istanbul, the former Constantinople, where two of them are murdered. Who murders whom, and why, depends at least in part on which of Knopf's two editions, one "male" and the other "female," you choose to believe. Except for fifteen italicized lines, on pages 293 and 294, the editions are identical. The difference—having to do with history versus romance, religion versus love—is whimsical rather than profound.

And, of course, whatever edition we hold in our hands proposes itself as an encyclopedia and concordance, containing Kyr Avram's red, green and yellow notebooks, individually alphabetized; fragments, translated from the Latin, of the Daubmannus introduction; prefaces, appendices, footnotes, bibliography, "the sundry material . . . amassed and lost through the centuries by those who, with quills in their earrings, use their mouths as ink bottles," and illustrations that are themselves a kind of cryptogram. You can, and should, open Pavić anywhere you choose and read whatever you want to, backwards, sideways or upside-down. It doesn't matter, because each entry is independent, self-contained and cross-referenced—a chore to write, but pleasingly easy to read. Then all you must do is decide which sort of novel you want to fashion out of these enchantments and mystifications, these brilliant shards of vandalized cultures. (pp. 611, 613)

Think of *Dictionary* as a counteranthropology at least as interesting as any Levi-Strauss field trip to the Bororo or the Nambikwara.

The Khazars, for instance, worship salt, and in their musical language there are seven genders, one of them for lepers only. They can "read colors like musical notes, letters or numbers. When they enter a mosque or a Christian place of worship and see the wall paintings, they immediately spell, read or sing whatever is depicted in the painting, icon or other picture, showing that the old painters knew of this secret and unacknowledged skill."

They "carve all the outstanding events in their lives on a stick, and these signs are in the form of animals that represent situations and moods, not events. The owner's grave is built in the shape of the animal that appears most frequently on his stick. Hence, Khazar graves are divided into groups, depending on whether they are shaped like tigers, birds, camels, lynx, fish, eggs, or goats."

They use fishing nets for sails on some of the ships in their flotilla, and these ships sail like any other. When a Greek asks a Khazar priest how this is done, a nearby Jew replies, "It's simple. They catch in those nets something other than the wind." . . .

And finally, "The Khazars pray by weeping, for tears are a part of God, by virtue of always having a bit of salt at the bottom, just as shells hold pearls."

I suppose after all this I ought to tell you that *Dictionary,* besides being a spoof of structuralism and deconstruction and organized religion and the Serbian identity crisis, not to mention psychoanalysis (Lacan) and Marxism (Althusser), is also in its sinew antipolitical—except to say that big nations ought not to oppress little ones; and anti-ideological—except in behalf of "love as a compass"; a dreambook advancing the claims of art and the imagination against splitters of hairs and breakers of bones and bloodsucking systems of human engineering; an escape from history; a romance of ghosts. . . .

And it is, grand and grinning. But I read another novel, upside-down and backwards, and it seems to me that we are all Serbs. (p. 613)

John Leonard, "Alphabeticon," in The Nation, *New York, Vol. 247, No. 17, December 5, 1988, pp. 610-11, 613.*

ROZ KAVENEY

[Part] of Pavic's purpose in this short, seemingly chaotic, but nonetheless monumental work, [*Dictionary of the Khazars*], is to write a tribute to that part of the Balkans where Eastern Christianity, Islam and Judaism have stewed, feuded and fermented for so many centuries. It purports to be the lexicographical epic of a lost nation, but it is also a massive celebration of an actual but recent one, of the Yugoslavia around the future borders of which so many generations of saints and scholars quest, in this book, in search of lost knowledge.

This is a novel, but it takes the form of a dictionary, a dictionary in which we can read of fate of the Serbian warrior scholar Brankovich and of the very different, but equally doomed, faces that the Khazar princess Ateh wears in the legends of Judaism, Christianity and Islam. *Dictionary of the Khazars,* or rather the three dictionaries which compose it, one for each of the rival religions, mingle fantasy and fact, the poetic, the mythic and the deeply prosaic in one of the more unconventional versions of fictional form of even recent years. . . .

In the interstices of the text, we learn what little is known of the dream hunters, the Khazarian priesthood who traced items of dream from one sleeping mind to another. We also learn of a warrior whose catalogue of death blows stunned their contemporaries, and of a multiplicity of Kabbalic myths of Adam. We momentarily encounter a variety of the stock tropes of post-Borgesian fiction, down to the poisoned book we find in originally in Borges' *Universal History of Infamy,* but met again in Eco's *Name of the Rose.* We also learn of things that are not scholarly, of sudden memories of sensual brushings of fingers and of smelled blossom. Amid the mock scholarship, there are constant reminders that scholarship and religion and language and dreams refer to a world, a world of sensory impressions which Pavic excellently evokes. The readers prepared to do without the conventional consolations of plot will find their reward in a kaleidoscope of wit, knowledge, sudden bright images and momentary flashes of story.

> Roz Kaveney, "The Novel as Dictionary," in Books, London, No. 23, February, 1989, p. 18.

FRED MILLER ROBINSON

[*Dictionary of the Khazars* is] at once playful and serious (and sometimes beautiful), but its inventiveness shades into gimmickry, its visionary quality hardens into linguistic puzzles and games. Intended as serio-comic, it is neither as serious nor as comic as it could have been. It is in danger of becoming its own event, an imitation of itself.

The subject matter of *Dictionary* is so difficult to summarize that the reviewer is in danger of crowding out evaluation with detail. So I will be mercilessly brief. The Khazars are said to be a warrior tribe from the East who settled in the Caucasus between the seventh and tenth centuries A.D. According to ancient chronicles, their downfall began when their ruler invited a Christian, an Islamic, and a Jewish philosopher to engage in a debate in the form of a dream interpretation, from which he would decide to which faith the Khazars would convert. This "polemic," recorded in various manuscripts, including a dream dictionary composed by a Khazar princess, outlasted the Khazars.

In 1691 a Polish printer published a second dictionary, itself a compilation of three dictionaries: Christian, Islamic, and Hebrew. The printer's source was a Christian monk who dictated the entire book from memory, *his* sources a Serbian military commander, an Anatolian lute player versed in Islamic legend, and a Dubrovnik Jew, all of whom lived in each other's dreams and died together on the battlefield. The present, and third, dictionary, is a supposed reconstruction of the seventeenth-century one, based on surviving fragments and unreliable reconstructions of legends and dreams. It includes entries on three professors—a Serbian Arabist, an Arab Hebraist, and a Polish-Jewish Slavist—who meet in a conference in 1982. After comparing information on the Khazars, two of them are murdered and the third imprisoned. Such are the urgencies of comparatist scholarship today.

So a sort of murder mystery is built into Pavic's novel, the three professors acting out, as in a Borgesian dream, the con-troversies of the seventeenth- and nineteenth-century character triads, embodied in the three dictionaries, the three faiths. . . .

This is the barest bones, but enough to indicate Pavic's recasting of some familiar modernist obsessions, most prominently the inability of linguistic constructs to describe the nature of things. *Dictionary* is not really a dictionary (or dictionaries), but, in its own terms, an alphabetical "chain of biographies" of people who compose: music, poetry, polemics, stories, entries, editions, dreams—any material that comes to hand. The reader in turn is invited to compose this novel any way he chooses, reading entries at random, or following a system of signs, and so on (there is a helpful section called "How to Use this Dictionary"). In this way, the reader is turned into a protagonist-composer, a searcher for the whole among the fragments of other people's biographies, dreams and stories, a hero in search of a narrative.

Pavic wants his novel to be "a holy book or a crossword puzzle." But so conceived, it can only make its meditations seem playful, and its games ponderous. There are fine, surreal passages in this book, almost all of them occurring when a story is being told, and I can't help thinking that if Pavic had more faith in narrative, and in descriptive evocation, his novel would be closer to Nabokov, or to the Calvino of *Invisible Cities,* than to John Barth. It gives the odd impression, like its cover, of imitating something; in the quality of its exotica, legends and folk wisdom, it too often sounds like "Dungeons and Dragons."

To me, the most interesting aspect of this novel is its political/historical dimension. The Khazars are conceived as a sort of Ur-people of Eastern Europe and Western Russia, warlike and poetic: they have dream cults, they believe that an eyeless fish in the Caspian "marks the only correct time in the universe," and so on. Theirs is a culture of legend, apprehended through dream and fantasy, like any imagination of homogeneity.

But Pavic fortunately complicates this vision of a *Volk* by describing the Khazars as *functioning,* even at their height, as a minority culture. The Greeks, Jews, Saracens, and Slavs who have "come from all over" were put, by the more numerous Khazars themselves, administratively in charge. The Khazars subordinated their interests to those of the heterogeneous immigrants, because Khazars "share[d] their bread with everybody," an aspect of their nature that led to their downfall and dispersal. In this way, Pavic avoids imagining them as merely a pure but victim race, a Fascist fantasia. Instead, he sees their better natures as yielding to a multiplicity of cultures and faiths. He imagines them representing what people with differences have in common; they become not so much a lost race as a lost common humanity.

I wish such a vision, if I have read it correctly, were not almost buried in all this by-now-conventional modernist and linguistic abstraction, all these narrative masks, so that anything we might grasp can be localized and undercut as only the partial truth of a particular viewpoint. It might be time for us to realize that the best modernist works (*Ulysses, Berlin Alexanderplatz, Absalom, Absalom!, Paterson, To the Lighthouse, et al.*) are rooted in their respective cultures. Complex as they are, they do not aspire to be crossword puzzles or halls of mirrors of cosmicomics. The curse of an internationalist modernism has always been that it took language too seriously and not seriously enough, either masking or avoiding or rejecting a politics in game-playing—multiplicity become an abstraction rather than an informing vision of culture. One wishes *Dictionary of the Khazars* were less the international event it is advertised as being. One wishes it were more Yugoslavian.

Fred Miller Robinson, in a review of "Dictionary of the Khazars," in Boston Review, Vol. XIV, No. 1, February, 1989, p. 22.

VASA D. MIHAILOVICH

[*Predeo slikan čajem* (*Landscape Painted with Tea*)] is subtitled "A Novel for the Lovers of Crossword Puzzles." Like the *Dictionary* (with which it is comparable in many ways), the latest novel suggests a new way of reading rather than a new way of writing. It can be read the way a crossword puzzle is solved: horizontally or vertically. The horizontal reading reveals the plot, the vertical the characters. The novel follows the path and fortunes of Atanasije Svilar (alias Razin), a Serb of Serbian-Russian parentage: first his career as an insignificant architect in postwar Yugoslavia, then as a highly successful businessman in pharmaceuticals in the United States. The Serbian-Russian-American connection is one of the many puzzles that must be solved if the novel is to be understood properly. In fact, Pavić even includes instructions on "how to solve this book," paralleling the instructions for a crossword. (As is so much in Pavić's scheme of things, this is not to be taken literally.)

In the final analysis, the reader gets out of the novel as much as he puts in, just as the female protagonist, Svilar's tempestuous lover, at the end falls in love with the reader, asking him to solve their misery. Similarly, Svilar, at odds with his life, love, and career, settles down by building replicas of Josip Broz Tito's villas, thus trying to recapture some of the ties with his native country. Unfortunately, this activity too fails to bring him the happiness for which he yearns.

To go along with the novel's rather complex, playful, and certainly fascinating plot, Pavić uses his rich stylistic repertory: striking metaphors, similes, paradoxes, hyperboles, maxims, and other tropes, along with the technique known as "defamiliarization" or "making it strange" as defined by the Russian formalist critics of the twenties. By such means, Pavić has joined the elite of the international literary scene. . . .

Vasa D. Mihailovich, in a review of "Predeo slikan čajem," in World Literature Today, Vol. 63, No. 2, Spring, 1989, p. 335.

ANGELA CARTER

Milorad Pavic's *Dictionary of the Khazars* is an exercise in a certain kind of erudite frivolity that does not do you good *as such,* but offers the cerebral pleasure of the recognition of patterning afforded by formalism, a profusion of language games, some rude mirth. . . .

The whole of *Dictionary of the Khazars* is a kind of legendary history, and some of the individual entries have considerable affinities to the folk-tale ('The Tale of Petkutin and Kalina' in the section called 'The Red Book', for example): but I suspect, not so much the influence of an oral tradition—though that's still possible in Yugoslavia—as the influence of an aesthetic owing a good deal to Vladimir Propp's *Morphology of the Folk Tale,* first published in Russia in 1928.

Propp's thesis is that the traditional fairytale is not composed, but built up out of discrete narrative blocks that can be pulled down again and reassembled in different ways to make any number of other stories, or can be used for any number of other stories in combination with other narrative blocks. That is partly why there is no place for, nor possibility of, inwardness in the traditional tale, nor of characterisation in any three-dimensional way. If the European novel of the 19th and 20th centuries is closely related to gossip, to narrative arising out of conflicted character, then the folk-tale survives, in our advanced, industrialised, society, in the anecdote. . . .

A traditional storyteller does not make things up afresh, except now and then, if the need arises. Instead, he or she selects, according to mood, whim and cultural background, the narrative segments that feel right at the time from a store acquired from a career of listening, and reassembles them in attractive, and sometimes new, ways. And that's how formalism was born. . . .

Pavic advises the reader to behave exactly like a traditional storyteller and construct his or her own story out of the ample material he has made available. The main difference is, Pavic has made all this material up by himself. 'No chronology is observed here, nor is one necessary. Hence, each reader will put together the book for himself, as in a game of dominoes or cards.' The book is an exercise, not in creative writing, but in creative reading. The reader can, says Pavic, rearrange the book 'in an infinite number of ways, like a Rubic cube'. . . .

But who are, or were, the Khazars? 'An autonomous and powerful tribe, a warlike and nomadic people who appeared from the East at an unknown date, driven by a scorching silence, and who, from the seventh to the tenth century, settled in the land between two seas, the Caspian and the Black'. As a nation, the Khazars no longer exist, and ceased to do so during the tenth century after 'their conversion from their original faith, unknown to us today, to one (again, it is not known which) of three known religions of the past and present—Judaism, Islam or Christianity'.

The *Dictionary* purports to be, with some additions, the reprint of an edition of a book published by the Pole Joannes Daubmannus in 1691, which was 'divided into three dictionaries: a separate glossary of Moslem sources on the Khazar question, an alephbetised list of materials drawn from Hebrew writings and tales, and a third dictionary compiled on the basis of Christian accounts of the Khazar question'. So the same characters and events are usually seen three times, each from the perspective of a different history and set of cultural traditions, and may be followed through the three books *cross-wise,* if you wish. The 'ancient' texts are organised according to the antiquarian interests of the 17th century. As in *The Arabian Nights,* an exiguous narrative set in the present day is interwoven throughout the three volumes of the dictionary and provides some sort of climax.

The most obvious immediate inspiration for this 'plot' is surely a certain Volume XLVI of the *Anglo-American Cyclopaedia* (1917), itself a 'literal but delinquent reprint of the *Encyclopaedia Britannica* of 1902', in which Bioy Cesares and Jorge Luis Borges discovered the first recorded reference to the land of Uqbar. But instead of, like Borges, writing a story about a fake reference book that invades the real world, Pavic has set to and compiled the book itself, a book that contains a whole lost world, with its heroes, its rituals, its deaths, its mysteries, and especially its theological disputations, providing a plausible-enough-sounding apparatus of scholarly references that involve a series of implicit jokes about theories of authenticity just as the skewed versions of characters such as Princess Ateh, recurring three times, involve implicit jokes about cultural relativity. . . .

There is a blatant quality of fakery about the *Dictionary.* One imagines Pavic gleefully setting to with a Black and Decker drill, inserting artificial worm-holes into his synthetic oak beams. This fakery, this purposely antiqued and distressed surface, is what makes Pavic's book look so Post-Modern as to be almost parodically fashionable, the perfect type of those Euro-best-sellers such as Patrick Susskind's *Perfume* and Umberto Eco's *Name of the Rose* that seem, to some British critics, to spring from an EEC conspiracy to thwart exports of genuine, wholesome, straightforward British fiction the same way French farmers block the entry of English lamb. However, Yugoslavia is not a member of the Common Market and the British have developed a nervous tendency to label anything 'Post-Modern' that doesn't have a beginning, a middle and an end in that order.

Dictionary of the Khazars fulfils, almost too richly, all Wallace Stevens's prescriptions in 'Notes towards a Supreme Fiction':

   it must be abstract
   it must change
   it must give pleasure.

Most of the time, Pavic speaks in the language of romantic Modernism—that is, Surrealism. Al Bakri, the Spaniard, dies 'dreaming of salty female breasts in a gravy of saliva and toothache'. The Princess Ateh composes a prayer: 'On our ship, my father, the crew swarms like ants: I cleaned it this morning with my hair and they crawl up the clean mast and strip the green sails like sweet vine leaves into their anthills.' A man, a certain Dr Ismail Suk, waking, blinks 'with eyes hairy as testicles'. This is the characteristic speech of high Surrealism, with its clash of imagery and deformation of meaning.

Dr Suk is the hero of a section called 'The Story of the Egg and the Violin Bow' that boasts all the inscrutability of Surrealist narrative plus a quality of what one can only call the 'mercantile fantastic' reminiscent of the short stories of Bruno Schulz, with their bizarre and ominous shops and shopkeepers. . . .

In fact, there is a strong sense of pastiche everywhere, most engagingly in the collection of Islamic sources on the Khazar question, although the poem in question purports to have been written by the Khazar princess Ateh. It is a piece of spoof Kafka. A woman travelling to a distant school to take a test is subjected to bureaucratic misinformation and then told: 'you can't reach the school today. And that means not ever. Because the school will no longer exist as of tomorrow. You have missed your life's destination . . . .'

But this is a revisionist version of Kafka. Once her destination is withheld from her, the traveller searches for the significance of her journey in the journey itself—and finds it in one luminous memory, of a table with food and wine. 'On the table by the food a candle with a drop of flame on the top;

next to it the Holy Book and the month of Jemaz-ul-Aker flowing through it.' A happy ending!

There is the casual acceptance of the marvellous common to both Surrealism and the folk-tale. . . . (p. 8)

But the sense of the marvellous is most often created simply by the manipulation of language: 'Avram Brankovich cuts a striking figure. He has a broad chest the size of a cage for large birds or a small beast.' One way and another, the task of Pavic's translator, Christina Pribicevic-Zoric, must have been awesome, for among the Khazars we are living in a world of words *as such.* The vanished world of the Khazars is constructed solely out of words. A dictionary itself is a book in which words provide the plot. The Khazars are nothing if not people of the Book, dithering as they did between the three great faiths, the sacred texts of Christianity, Islam and Judaism. One of the copies of the 1691 edition of the *Dictionary,* we are told, was printed with a poisoned ink: 'The reader would die on the ninth page at the words *Verbum caro factum est.* ("The Word became Flesh.")' Almost certainly, something metaphysical is going on

The Khazars indefatigably enter that most metaphysical of states, dreaming. 'A woman was sitting by the fire, her kettle of broth babbling like bursting boils. Children were standing in line with their plates and dogs, waiting. She ladled out the broth to the children and animals and immediately Masudi knew that she was portioning out dreams from the kettle.'

The Dream Hunters are a sect of Khazar priests. 'They could read other people's dreams, live and make themselves at home in them . . . ' That is the Christian version. The Moslem Dictionary is more forthcoming: 'If all human dreams could be assembled together, they would form a huge man, a human being the size of a continent. This would not be just any man, it would be Adam Ruhani, the heavenly Adam, man's angel ancestor, of whom the imams speak.'

The book of Hebrew sources is most explicit. 'The Khazars saw letters in people's dreams, and in them they looked for primordial man, for Adam Cadmon, who was both man and woman and born before eternity. They believed that to every person belongs one letter of the alphabet, that each of these letters constitutes part of Adam Cadmon's body on earth, and that these letters converge in people's dreams and come to life in Adam's body.' (I am not sure that Pavic thinks of Freud when he thinks of dreams.)

So we can construct our primal ancestor out of the elements of our dreams, out of the elements of the *Dictionary,* just as Propp thought that if one found sufficient narrative elements and combined them in the right order, one would be able to retell the very first story of all—'it would be possible to construct the archetype of the fairy tale not only schematically . . . but concretely as well.' (pp. 8, 10)

[*Dictionary of the Khazars*] is a book to play with, to open up and take things out of, a box of delights and a box of tricks. It is a novel without any sense of closure, the product of a vast generosity of the imagination—user-friendly, you could say, and an invitation to invent for yourself. (p. 10)

Angela Carter, "Ludic Cube," in London Review of Books, *Vol. 11, No. 11, June 1, 1989, pp. 8, 10.*

GEORGE KEARNS

Flaubert devised the ideal of writing a book about nothing. In *Dictionary of the Khazars,* Milovad Pavić approaches one limit of that ideal: yet it's not *quite* about nothing. Or it's about such an excess of things, so many clues and branching paths, that each fragment of narrative places under erasure or cancels out another. In this maze, this game of Dungeons and Dragons for the sophisticated, Pavić keeps one reading at first for the moment to moment amusement of his richly embroidered surface, and then for the perverse obsession to discover if there is any foundation whatsoever to the history of the Khazars, any authority, even fictional authority, to certify the tales, legends, manuscripts, shards of anthropology, folklore, linguistics and polyglot scholarship gathered in the dictionary. To read is to observe the book one reads, the very concept "book," dissolve before one's eyes.

> "I work with something like a dictionary of colors," Nikon added [he is a figure of Satan], "and from it the observer composes sentences and books, in other words, images. You could do the same with writing. Why shouldn't someone make up a dictionary of words that make up one book and let the reader himself assemble the words into a whole?"
>
> Nikon Sevast then turned to the window, pointed with his brush to the field outside, and said:
>
> "Do you see that furrow? It is not a plow that made it. That furrow was made by the barking of a dog."

In Khazar-land you come to accept that possibility. . . . (pp. 339-40)

The *Dictionary* is a palimpsest of scholarship complete with battery of preliminary notes, appendices, bibliographies, illustrations and photo reproductions of Renaissance title pages and double-columned Hebrew-Latin text. In fact, there are three dictionaries, three sets of alphabetically-arranged encyclopedia articles, one each from Christian, Islamic and Jewish sources. As with any encyclopedia, the reader is free to browse through the entries *ad libitum:* one is no wiser for privileging any sequence. The convenience of alphabetical order allows us to begin, if we choose, with the (irreconcilable) Jewish, Islamic and Christian interpretations of the role played in Khazar history by the beautiful Princess Ateh. The Khazars, we gather, were a highly elaborated civilization in a world coded utterly differently from ours. They flourished in Eastern Europe from c. the third to the ninth centuries. At some time their leader, the Khagan, staged the great Khazar Polemic at which representatives of Islam, Judaism and Christianity each made the case for his religion. (The Christian spokespersons were those industrious proselytizers, SS. Cyril and Methodius. The Jewish chronicler of the polemic was the great poet-philosopher Judah Halevi [twelfth century].) The Khazars adopted one of those religions, and vanished into it—which one depends upon which historian-interpreters you trust, and they are far from disinterested. No substantial trace remains, beyond an infinite regress of traces, and it is possible that the Khazar language has been preserved only by having been taught to parrots, who teach it from age to age to other parrots.

Interest in the Khazars revived in the seventeenth century, and again in the early 1980s. At each stage Jewish, Christian and Islamic scholars compete for the soul of Khazardom through industry, (mis)interpretation, fabulation, skulduggery and necromancy. The *Dictionary* records the Byzantine accidents of textual transmission and the comic pathos of hermeneutical endeavors to arrive at truths of vanished pasts. All this is complicated by the transmigration of souls, or the power of some souls to dream their way into others. The Khazars and their seventeenth-century barbarous pursuers may still be among us. (pp. 340-41)

This *Dictionary* will seem to many the last word in decadence and triviality. My Paterian defense is to say that it produced for me a music not quite like anything I'd heard before. (p. 341)

George Kearns, in a review of "Dictionary of the Khazars," in The Hudson Review, *Vol. XLII, No. 2, Summer, 1989, pp. 339-41.*

Molly Peacock

1947-

American poet.

Peacock has stated that her strict, formal poetry reflects the sense of order she has craved since her chaotic childhood as the daughter of a depressive mother and an alcoholic father. Peacock's exploration of themes relating to fate, family, and the many different facets of love, are enhanced through strong rhyme schemes, skillful use of alliteration, and biting humor. David Lehman commented: "Peacock has a luxuriantly sensual imagination—and an equally sensual feel for the language. In mood her poems range from high-spirited whimsy . . . to bemused reflection. . . . Whatever the subject, rich music follows the tap of her baton."

Peacock's first collection, *And Live Apart,* introduces her preoccupation with the past. Instead of employing a bitter or hostile approach, Peacock views her personal history from the enlightened perspective of one who has reconciled herself to its shortcomings. The sonnets in Peacock's second volume, *Raw Heaven,* stress the manipulative aspects of desire and the ineffable quality of sex and sensuality. In "Desire," for example, Peacock compares sexual yearning to a pet's constant demands for affection. Several critics expressed admiration for her vivid, illuminating imagery, elegant rhymes, and bold consideration of such taboo topics as menstruation and masturbation. David Lehman observed: "Rhyme in *Raw Heaven . . .* reins in an exuberant imagination, imposing limits, order, form. The result is a sense of liberation rather than confinement. Often unusual, usually enjambed, Peacock's rhymes do more than glide us smoothly from line to line; they're the very agents of invention."

In her recent collection, *Take Heart,* Peacock continues to address inviolable topics, including the horrors and repercussions of physical and mental child abuse. Many of the volume's opening poems deal with the death of Peacock's father and her childhood memories of his alcoholism. Several critics praised her ability to illuminate universal concerns through intimate memories. In "Say You Love Me," for instance, her drunken father's aggressive demand for her unconditional love evolves into a study of humanity's need for acceptance and reassurance. Similarly, "Buffalo"—in which Peacock harshly recollects waiting in bars while her father drank—becomes a condolence for the bartenders who "shrink / from any conversation to endure / the serving, serving, serving of disease."

(See also *Contemporary Authors,* Vol. 103.)

PRINCIPAL WORKS

POETRY

And Live Apart   1980
Raw Heaven   1984
Take Heart   1989

ROBERT PHILLIPS

Molly Peacock's first book [*And Live Apart*] is devoted to recapturing the past, but for her the past is a point of reference, not an escape or a preferred world. Any reference to what has been is lashed to what now is:

> What was and a vision of what is
> walk down a long pew and meet
> on a day when nothing broken can be fixed,
> and everything is noticeably much more worn.
>
> Layer after layer of gauze has fallen over
> or layer on layer of color weathered off—
> if only the mind were a barn,
> if only a body waiting to be dressed.

Ms. Peacock uses the past for instruction, and as a gloss on her own behavior. When she finds herself planting a bed of petunias, even though she dislikes them ("Petunias smell like Vicks Vapo Rub" and are "sticky, like annually half-licked candy"), she acknowledges that her dislike is a disliking for her own origins ("People often hate the flowers / Grown by their aunts and mothers . . ."). This good-natured poem, then, on the nature of one's roots as well as on rooting nature, concludes with musings on growth and death, and kinds of knowing—logical, biological, hereditary and heretical.

Such ambition is evidenced throughout. Her concerns are big ones: the separations we make between one another, the reversals of love, the inescapability of fate, inevitabilities of inheritence, a concern for the language of emotion in conversation. All these come together in a notable sequence, **"Alibis and Lullabies,"** and, to a lesser extent, in a likeable poem about what I take to be her parents' store, **"Peacock's Superette."** The book is notable for plumbing the past without sentimentality, and for finding new solutions to old dilemmas. Anyone named Molly Peacock *should* be a poet, and Molly Peacock is. (pp. 427-28)

> Robert Phillips, "Poetry Chronicle: Some Versions of the Pastoral," in The Hudson Review, *Vol. XXXIV, No. 3, Autumn, 1981, pp. 420-34.*

DAVID LEHMAN

American Poetry since the end of World War II has been marked by the periodic need to break with prevalent fashions. In the rebellion against academic verse, perhaps the first thing to go was rhyme—with the inevitable result that a strictly rhymeless succession of assertions has become today's academic orthodoxy. A true departure from a stale convention is always a welcome development, and in *Raw Heaven,* Molly Peacock's superb new collection, rhyme returns triumphant. If you're under the impression that rhymed poetry tends to resemble nothing so much as a car in need of a lube job, you're in for an exceptionally agreeable surprise.

Molly Peacock has a luxuriantly sensual imagination—and an equally sensual feel for the language. In mood her poems range from high-spirited whimsy (a poem addressed to "Dogs, lambs, chicken, women—pets of all nations!") to bemused reflection (on "the sadness that prevails among families"). Whatever the subject, rich music follows the tap of her baton. "The largest bud in creation travels / up the swollen stem of the amaryllis / like a ship in a womb up a river," Peacock writes in **"Sweet Time,"** one of many poems that celebrate what D. H. Lawrence called "the hot blood's blindfold art"—the sexuality at the heart of nature. An insistence on the pleasure principle animates these poems; Peacock operates on the conviction that even "a chartreuse hell in the mountains" can yield "the wet smell / of possibility in everything." Heaven is a matter of raw sensations finely recorded: "A tangerine wrenched open, each section / fluttering on the rind like butterfly / wings on a bruised flower, or the erection / of the heads of raspberries."

Rhyme in *Raw Heaven* does what John Dryden said it should do: it reins in an exuberant imagination, imposing limits, order, form. The result is a sense of liberation rather than confinement. Often unusual, usually enjambed, Peacock's rhymes do more than glide us smoothly from line to line; they're the very agents of invention. "Transparency of desire," for example, tricks forth the "camisole of sweat on fruit on a spire / of a limb or a vine. The web ripeness spins."

"She Lays" shows Peacock at her most daring. About an auto erotic experience, the poem is intimate without being exhibitionistic, candid without any confessional stickiness. Peacock works up to—and earns—these grand concluding chords:

> This is self-love, assured, and this is lost time.
> This is knowing, knowing, known
> since growing, growing, grown;

revelation without astonishment,
understanding what is meant.
This is world-love. This is lost I'm.

We'll want to hear a lot more from this accomplished and original poet in the years ahead.

> David Lehman, in a review of "Raw Heaven," in Book World—The Washington Post, *September 2, 1984, p. 6.*

PETER STITT

In her second book, *Raw Heaven,* Molly Peacock writes about emotionally important subjects—family and love. . . . Her way of handling these charged topics is . . . rigorously and traditionally formal, however; nearly all of the poems rhyme, the meters are strong, and there is a lot of word play. In general, this attention to technique distances the subject matter from both writer and reader, and the result is a refreshing degree of objectivity. Of course there are exceptions to this rule, cases in which technique is overwhelmed by a powerfully affective subject matter. What comes through in such poems is a straight dose of unmeliorated truth—as is the case in **"Our Room,"** which begins: "I tell the children in school sometimes / why I hate alcoholics: my father was one," and ends: "The classroom becomes / oddly lonely when we talk about our homes." And Peacock inclines toward didacticism at times, concluding her poems with aphoristic lessons that are all too neat: "There's this in being out of love: / I own every blue day I'm not part of."

Yet this book is filled with little formal miracles, the sort of verbal dazzlement we grew up on but have starved for through the barren days of the plain style, the sort of thing James Merrill means when he praises Richard Kenney for scoring "A hole-in-one at word golf." For example, the beginning and the ending of another poem, **"Just About Asleep Together"**:

> Just about asleep together, tenderness
> of monkey-like swells of grooming ourselves
> just about stilled, the duet nonetheless
> whispers on, unshelving everything shelved
> by the day.
>
> • • • • • • • • •
>
>   . . . two bodies lie frankly
> foetal, knees drawn, crook into crook, wing by tit
> in the orbit of sleeping. And blankly
> shifting and waking without waking
> is that much touch that is our sleep making.

The lines exhibit end rhyme and internal rhyme, assonance and alliteration, word repetition and near repetition, and more. Indeed, the reader can gaze a long time at poems like these and still find them technically surprising.

In larger terms—speaking, that is, of technique that communicates meaning rather than technique that bears the pleasure of interlocking sound—Peacock shows herself master of something we might call the illustrative image. In her best poems, she develops an event or describes an object from the outside world, using it to reveal an emotional state taken from the inside world. The method is objectifying, and much of the reader's aesthetic pleasure derives from the sheer aptness (or, oddly, sometimes the inaptness) of the connection. For example, the sonnet **"Squirrel Disappears"**:

From the fence to the fire escape to this
tiny unexpected yard, his manic
tail quick as the fin of a maple seed is,
flip, flip, a squirrel stops for the scenic
view of sky, wires, restaurant rear, and dog.
Then off again. The air's brief clarity,
like an empty open hand before the fog
of belief disperses the disparity
of "here" and "gone," takes a chip out of time,
like a chipped minute out of love when a word,
a hard word, twitches and is off, its crime
the dissolution of where we'd been lured,
the tiny unexpected yard, love. Empty,
then brief bottomless disbelief in plenty.

In terms of content, this poem hinges on the word "like" in the tenth line; the point about love is nicely understated but poignant nonetheless. Peacock's method reminds us of Eliot's objective correlative, certainly, but it is also much like the extended metaphor or conceit of the metaphysical poets. As with the lines quoted earlier, this poem also performs through interlocking sounds and verbal play; I especially like the use of undoing words in the last few lines: "dissolution," "unexpected," "disbelief." It is truly an impressive performance, and nearly typical of the book as a whole. That all the poems in the volume are roughly the same length is a drawback, as is the occasional tendency toward literal statement mentioned above, but *Raw Heaven* is on the whole an excellent collection. (pp. 630-32)

> *Peter Stitt, "Objective Subjectivities," in* The Georgia Review, *Vol. XXXVIII, No. 3, Fall, 1984, pp. 628-38.*

MATTHEW GILBERT

One danger of formal poetry is artificiality. In unskilled hands, rhythm and sound repetition can turn a potentially powerful poem into a monotonous complex of sounds. Not so in Molly Peacock's second collection, *Raw Heaven.* Each poem is paced and rhymed, yet safe from seeming labored. Peacock knows how to use her instruments naturally; the reader may not give her scheme of repetition a second thought until Peacock wishes a desired emphasis. Her form gently complements her meaning. (p. 30)

Although Peacock structures her poems carefully, she nonetheless uses simple, familiar words. Her poems are in the rhythms of speech, even casual, much like the plain-speaking excursions made by most contemporary poets. But Peacock's overt use of form gives her poems a drive, a backbone. The impact of this combination is clear, for example, in her portrait of **"Desire"**:

> Like a paw,
> it is blunt; like a pet who knows you
> and nudges your knee with its
>   snout—but more raw
> and blinder and younger and more
>   divine, too,
> than the tamed wild—it's the drive for
>   what is real,
> deeper than the brain's detail: the drive
>   to feel.

The proximity of "real," "detail," and "feel" creates a resonance—a high-frequency vowel reverberation not unlike a child's whining—from three rather ordinary words. Most of these poems close similarly, with a striking couplet rhyme.

The substance of *Raw Heaven* in large part revolves around human drive. Peacock's quest is to experience, and characterize, unmitigated desire, "the worlds inside you" beyond **"The Land of Veils."** She listens to children, hoping to recall her own naked needs, "where the will / becomes visible." She constantly discovers the scent of the unadulterated. In fact, a number of her poems focus on smells that conjure up something essential. In **"And You Were a Baby Girl,"** Peacock's beach companion's "light but deep sweet smell of fleece / that was your infant skin thirty years ago," arouses her:

> I catch the tender
> spark of the faint comet of your infant
> smell, still, and am shocked and won't
>   surrender
> and then do—it is all the years have
>   meant,
> the damp baby smoke of rivalry
>   unfurled
> beyond the salt and oil of the
>   practicing world.

She is spellbound by uncivilized purity. The **"Cut Flower"**

>   in the vase, alone,
> alone and in command of its unrooted
> isolated state, was beautiful, for grown
> full nakedness right where I could
>   witness it
> was beautiful, huge and proximate.

But what makes this book a "drive for what is real," even more than her forceful longings, is Peacock's devotion to the strength of vision. She reveres the power of uninhibited perception, imagining herself as one daring to witness the world. . . . She no longer dreads the shorter days of winter, as she once did: "A grown woman loves any light or dark hour." We are shown existence through a pair of undaunted eyes. Peacock's poems avoid dissemblance, and are perhaps too explicit for some readers. There are no restrictive dedications tagged on to the poems, no tiring autobiographical quirks so many poets use in order to distinguish themselves; only a few details, a few easily inhabited essentials. In **"Novembers,"** she writes:

>   I'm telling you now I feel I
> Exist for the first time! Neither the
>   bareness nor
> Roughness demoralize—I realize I
> See much clearer what leafless branches
>   show.

The poems in *Raw Heaven* are not broken up into sections. Instead, they are presented as a succession of pieces which, with the benefit of astute ordering, become one far-reaching body of work. The book has an organic, deviceless quality. Peacock has chosen the perfect adjective herself; these poems are raw. And yet, in the best of ironies, they are also elegant. (pp. 30-1)

> *Matthew Gilbert, in a review of "Raw Heaven," in* Boston Review, *Vol. IX, No. 6, December, 1984, pp. 30-1.*

J. D. McCLATCHY

If many of the poems in Molly Peacock's new collection, *Raw Heaven*, seem slight or repetitive, it is because they are versions of one another. No matter the occasion of a poem, she returns to two basic themes: the idea of home, and the fact of the body. In one poem she even describes herself as a house. She is looking back on her childhood, as if into a glass paperweight, and enumerating its sorrows. Then she concludes:

> Not to carry
> all this in the body's frame is not to see
> how the heart and arms were formed on its behalf.
> I can't put the burden down. It's what formed
> the house I became as the glass ball stormed.

We come to embody our past, the poet claims, and its place in our lives is what we call our loneliness.

She writes too of the body's raw sensations and heavenly desires that console us for that loneliness: "Life's cache / is flesh, flesh, and flesh." We begin with the bodies of our parents:

> we tie about
> our bodies their lovely or ugly trappings.
> These are our parents' unwrappings,
> still warm and still smelling of another's body.

The bodies of others—of parents, lovers, children—fascinate this poet, and her own body she observes with some estrangement.

Raw Heaven is appealing and annoying in about equal parts. I like the sweet-and-sour tone of her descriptions, the darting or relaxed point of view. Twenty years ago a poet like Miss Peacock would have chosen Sylvia Plath as her model and written in a blood-hot, dissociated manner. Nowadays it is more likely that Elizabeth Bishop can show a young poem the way toward a more composed and thereby more dramatic poem. The poems in this volume work from detail toward definition, from image toward idea. This gives them their bite, but I am not everywhere convinced she has thought things through. When she says "Sin is something / pried out before its time, unresolved unreadiness," she is just tossing off a phrase. When she asserts "whoever loves a garden fears seasons," she is simply wrong. Her poems move quickly, but because of slapdash detours, they don't get as far as they might. And her wordplay, so high-spirited, is often aimless. Many young poets are turning again to the resources of form, a turn I applaud. But Molly Peacock's relentless rhyming is as automatic as another poet's jagged free verse; it merely chimes instead of doing the deep work of connecting. (p. 55)

> *J. D. McClatchy, "Cafe Chat and Body Language,"
> in* The New York Times Book Review, *December
> 2, 1984, pp. 54-5.*

CHRISTOPHER BENFEY

A second book of poems will often distill the windfalls of the first, and such is the case with . . . Molly Peacock. What was tentative in the early poems is now sure-footed; diffidence has given way to insouciance—what . . . Peacock calls "my bargain, the Pax/Peacock, with the world." (p. 500)

Yeats could imagine a "cold and rook-delighting heaven," and Emily Dickinson's heaven was "brittle," but what kind of transcendence would a raw heaven offer? Raw as opposed to what? Surely not cooked. In one of Dickinson's favorite genres, the definition-poem (but, like all the poems in *Raw Heaven*, in the form of a sonnet), Molly Peacock writes of **"Desire"**:

> Like a paw
> it is blunt; like a pet who knows you
> and nudges your knee with its snout—but more raw
> and blinder and younger and more divine, too,
> than the tamed wild—it's the drive for what is real.

Raw as opposed to tame, then: like a pet but a little (not too much) wilder. These lines seem to put odd restrictions on the "real," as though it can only be found just beyond the confines of domestication. Reality for Peacock is a wild animal—a squirrel, say, or a possum—that hangs around the house but doesn't come in. Domestication is in fact one of the major themes in *Raw Heaven;* zoos and pets fascinate this poet.

Peacock's taste for the raw makes taboos especially attractive to her. The Latin word *sacer,* as Freud liked to point out, partakes of the meanings of both sacred ("more divine, too") and unclean. Peacock likes to construct poems, like little shrines, around the traditionally unclean: dead animals, newborn babies, menstrual blood, "dirty" words. Taboos mark the fault lines of civilization, keeping separate what must remain separate, and Western poetry's obsession with purity—"pure poetry," "purity of diction," "to purify the language of the tribe"—makes it often a poetry of exclusion. Peacock aspires to an inclusive poetry, a poetry of the impure.

> The possum lay on the tracks fully dead.
> I'm the kind of person who stops to look.
> It was big and white with flies on its head,
> a thick healthy hairless tail . . .

> **("The Lull")**

She accepts the dead possum—"healthy" is the key word in the description—while her companion "[takes] the time to insult / the corpse." "That's disgusting," he says, but she finds this remark itself disgusting, a refusal to accept the raw. She calls her acceptance, in **"The Lull,"** her "Pax Peacock" with the world, as though the spectacular animal caught in her name had granted her the central insight that we are animals: "Dreams, brains, fur / and guts: what we are." (With this premise established, the following poem in the book begins: "Just about asleep together, the tenderness / of monkey-like swells of grooming ourselves / just about stilled . . .").

Since desire is "an eyes-shut, ears-shut medicine of the heart / that smells and touches endings and beginnings," Peacock relies on the darker senses of touch and smell to locate her subjects. To her sister she writes: "I loved your smell when you were a baby . . . a uriney whiff . . . the damp baby smoke of rivalry," or, still smokier:

> The smoky smell of menses—Ma always
> left the bathroom door open—smote the hall

> **("Smell")**

Peacock reminds us that the taboo against menstrual blood is, after all, a male one. Freud's unlikely explanation for the taboo is that menstruating women need protection because they are *helpless:* "Dead men, new-born babies and women menstruating or in labour stimulate desires by their special helplessness," he writes in *Totem and Taboo.* Another psychoanalytic explanation for the taboo against menstruation, castration anxiety, is also from the male point of view. Peacock's poem pursues one analogy. The smell smote the hall

> the way the elephant-house smell dazed
> the crowd in the vestibule at the zoo, all
> holding their noses yet pushing toward it.

The last line catches the ambivalence Freud found at the heart of taboo. But Peacock surrenders to the analogy, and lets it be the conclusion of the poem. Her theory of the repellent attraction of menstrual blood is simple:

> Years
> of months roll away what each month tells:
> God, what animals we are, huge of haunch,
> bloody and wise in the stench of bosk.

It seems to me—and it is perhaps an inherent danger of sonnets—that the door closes too soon here. A promising linguistic space has been mapped out in "the smokey smell of menses . . . Ma . . . smote . . ."—where ms's and esses and ems brew their own questions about the feminine—then allowed to disappear in a rather perfunctory development of an analogy ("The oxblood napkin landed / in the wastecan"). Some of the verbal energy is retrieved in the last couplet, with haunch and stench and bosk, but it is too late.

The tendency to close the door too soon is evident in many of Peacock's poems. She chooses the raw conclusion, but in such a way that it is tamed from the start. The Pax Peacock, then, seems to follow not much of a war. The violence in these poems is mainly in the past. It is the "violence of childhood," and many of Peacock's poems rehearse what she calls—using again the vocabulary of impurity—"the junk of childhood," and how it persists into adulthood:

> Dad pushed my mother down the cellar stairs.
> Gram had me name each plant in her garden.
> My father got drunk. Ma went to the country fairs.
> The pet chameleon we had was warden
> of the living-room curtains where us kids
> stood waiting for their headlights to turn in.

("Those Paperweights with Snow Inside")

"Not to carry / all this in the body's frame is not to see," Peacock concludes, "how the heart and arms were formed on its behalf." But what is characteristic of Peacock in this poem is the odd rhythm of raw and tame. She uses a kind of counterpoint: violence of parents played off against the garden; drunken father and avoiding / abandoning mother against the reassuring figure of the pet chameleon—a fairy-tale character of sorts—guarding the children. Scenes of domestic violence and alcoholism recur in Peacock's poetry; the house is no guarantee of domestication.

The diction of the poem is uneasy—"Dad . . . my mother . . . Gram . . . My father . . . Ma"—as though Peacock doesn't really know what to call these people, whether to keep them safely in the past, distanced from her, or to retrieve them by evoking the child's names for them. "Us kids" is simply awkward, especially paired with the relative sophistication of words like "warden." The rhymes seem reached for: lacking the playfulness of children's verse or the assurance of adult verse, they hover awkwardly in between. The rhyme for "kids" is, alas, "ids": "My mother took me to the library where ids / entered the Land of Faery . . ." Randall Jarrell found ways to hold this territory in rhyme, and more recently Gjertrud Schnackenberg has done so. Peacock isn't as deft as these poets, though, and her choice of subject often exposes her awkwardness.

Peacock's poems, while aspiring to the "raw" and "impure," finally rest, it seems to me, in the reassurance of pets and gardens. She devotes a full poem to each.

> Dogs, lambs, chickens, women—pets of all nations!

("Petting and Being a Pet")

That line is a poem in itself, but Peacock doesn't develop the polemic. It is, again, the animal similarity that attracts her. She doesn't address the domestication of women, their taming—as in *Penthouse* "pets" or **"The Taming of the Shrew"**—and concludes instead with our longing for "animal affection."

> Look how an animal is passed
> from lap to lap in a room, so many wishing
> to hold it. We wish to be in the vast
> caress, both animal and hand.

The "we" here is no longer the we of women; it is the we of human beings. Again the poem closes too quickly, with an epigrammatic couplet—"Like eyes make sense / of seeing, touch makes being make sense"—that doesn't open the poem so much as lock it up.

The garden is Peacock's other stay against the raw and wild. She states dogmatically, though she's probably only speaking for herself, "Whoever loves a garden fears seasons." This fear, she says, is a "fear of dirt nature, its crouch, the lesioned / back of earth."

> The swamp's spilled stomach is stared
> down by eyes in a garden. Seasons terrify,
> they terrify with their strict endurance
> and strict abandonment, like parents. Why?
> To garden is to love the instance, the dance
> of one's reason and the season, a time
> seized to be eased: a garden is a rhyme.

("A Garden")

That final assertion, "A garden is a rhyme," seems a curious retreat for a poet who set out to embrace the raw. Whatever terror might lurk in seasons seems thoroughly tamed here. And Peacock's chosen form is, of all things, the sonnet-sequence, itself something of a taboo form in twentieth-century English poetry. In her sonnets she rarely seems to be transgressing a sacred form, however, as Lowell or Berryman, with their more anguished sense of the weight of the sonnet's history, often seem to do. She seems rather to be seeking refuge in the sonnet's narrow rooms. Except for a certain tendency toward epigram, Peacock's sonnets show little sign of summoning the past energies of the form. Her rhymes—and these sonnets are relentlessly rhyming—are rarely part of the sense of the poem, nor are they particularly adept. Her sonnets are Shakespearean, but instead of finding ways of renovating the closing couplet she treats it like a trap to step into. The poems snap shut, mangling the catch. The effect can be unintentionally comic. . . .

> The paths are blind
> with wet new grass behind the rusty gate
> where my low blurry child home lies in state.

("Where Is Home?")

Molly Peacock's first book, **And Live Apart,** displayed experiments with many different stanzas and meters; there was even a villanelle. But she seemed to be not so much relishing the variety of English prosody as looking for a form in which she could feel at home. She seems too much at home in the confines of her new book. She is a poet of intelligence and energy. It may take looser forms to sharpen her vision. (pp. 500-05)

Christopher Benfey, "A Venusian Sends a Postcard Home," in Parnassus: Poetry in Review, *Vol. 12, No. 2 & Vol. 13, No. 1, 1985, pp. 500-12.*

CHRISTOPHER BENFEY

[In *Take Heart*], the very unreliability of Peacock's surrounding has drawn her to the regularities of meter and rhyme; form for her is less a graduated lens with which to view a patterned world than a fence to mark off expanses of chaos. In a recent symposium on the New Formalism, published in the journal *Crosscurrents,* Peacock has written that for many poets sonnets and villanelles seem too restrictive and "game-like" to be taken seriously, "destroying passion by regularizing it." "For me," she writes, "no order, no regularity, will ever be enough because I grew up in a situation where what was promised was rarely delivered." The household of alcoholic father and depressive mother that haunts all Peacock's poetry has given her a rage for order in which nothing is casually taken for granted, nothing safely under glass.

Peacock's last book, **Raw Heaven,** was remarkable for its bold exploration of terrain traditionally considered taboo— female masturbation; menstruation; the muck of the newborn and the stench of the newly dead ("I'm the kind of person who stops to look")—all fenced within the sonnet's elegant enclosure. Peacock's strength in her use of form is an awkwardness sufficiently authoritative that it reads as discomfort rather than ineptness; form in her poetry does not seem casually come upon but wrenched. In her new book, *Take Heart,* the taboo explored is child abuse and molestation. The best poems are bunched like a fist at the book's beginning, and deal with the death of Peacock's father. The poet is surprised that her emotion is more relief than grief, the "unexpected freedom" she commemorates in one sonnet, whose ending, however, is deftly qualified:

> . . . The release
> is the fact that the dead stay dead, thank
>   God, and
> you are free now to live until you die,
> nourished just by the fact that you're alive
> in the aftermath and now you rest in peace.

The ambiguous "now" makes one wonder whether the *requiescat in pace* applies to the living, as though we already have our epitaph.

Peacock's sonnets make no effort to conceal their rhymes and wrenched syntax. On the contrary, the elements of order are insistent, as when she describes what it felt like to wait for her father to leave a bar:

> . . . Outside, the wide
> endlessly horizontal vista raged
> with sun and snow: it was Buffalo,
>   gleaming
> below Great Lakes. Behind bar blinds we
>   were caged,
> some motes of sunlight cathedrally
>   beaming.

Some readers will wince at rhymes as jangling as these, but Peacock knows what she's doing. She's willing to risk artificiality to achieve the impression of a forced imposition of form.

Peacock writes with harrowing specificity about what can happen when paternal love (as in *King Lear*) demands proof:

> What happened earlier I'm not sure of.
> Of course he was drunk, but often he was.
> His face looked like a ham on a hook above
>
> me—I was pinned to the chair because
> he'd hunkered over me with arms like jaws
> pried open by the chair arms. "Do you love
>
> me?" he began to sob. "Say you love me!"

The scene continues in implacable terza rima, this vision out of a domestic Hell as immediate as Dante's. Only a sister's invention of a phone call interrupts the scene: "No, the phone / was not ringing. There was no world out there, / so there we remained, completely alone." This is Peacock's strength, to suggest by the artifices of form a way of negotiating the chaos around her. (pp. 32-3)

Christopher Benfey, "Dickinson's Children," in The New Republic, *Vol. 201, Nos. 3 & 4, July 17 & July 24, 1989, pp. 31-4.*

WILLIAM LOGAN

The last 30 years of American poetry have been a long love affair with the committed sins of confession. The mass of poets now reaching mid-career may often be distinguished only by their technical variations on a common theme, though technique is rare when poets prefer force of personality. . . . [Molly Peacock has] the virtue of having character, and of responding divergently to the impulse to provide a formal psychology of the middle class.

Molly Peacock's poetry is fraught with anxiety, frazzled with artifice. *Take Heart,* her third book, continues the wounded reflections that marked her last, where she discovered the perverse technique she has raised to formal consideration, the use of rhyme without meter.

She turns to her themes like an injured animal: to abortion, the loneliness of sexual relation and the emotional deadness of childhood with an alcoholic father. . . .

"Angry / dense and mulish" in her own estimation, Peacock seeks out the unlovely ways of her character. Rhyme is her idiosyncrasy, a private restraint that permits a public order. Though she employs rhyme only when convenient, and rarely precisely, she finds it a stimulus to imaginative display, and in its small adherences a permission for the release of repressed feeling: in this, rhyme is a Rorschach.

She is not immune to the brutality, the desire to shock or sicken, that confession easily succumbs to; but such shock gives her writing an electric vividness and control it otherwise lacks:

> A curette has the shape of a grapefruit spoon.
> They dilate the cervix, then clean out the womb
> with the jagged prow, just like separating the
> grapefruit from its skin, although the softening
> yellow rind won't bear another fruit. . . .

Peacock's strength is the stateliness of her self-hatred; she loathes her wish to be the perfect patient. Her poetry is most honest not in its submersion in carnality but in the minor betrayals of character. When she buys a fake fur she cannot afford, she is alive to all the implications of being false and buying false.

Peacock's narratives are nervier than her mediations: she

does not have the verbal gifts to make striking or memorable observations, and her notions near the fatuous ("What we don't forget is what we don't say," "The ocean's great to look at / because there's enough of it"). Even so, she is sometimes able to capture the complications and clumsiness, the fine moral messiness, of a life anxious to its edges.

William Logan, "Living between the Lines," in Chicago Tribune—Books, August 6, 1989, p. 5.

IAN GREGSON

From the start of her career as a poet [Molly Peacock's] been interested in the attempt to speak intimately—to speak about love in particular.

"A Kind of Parlance," in her first book *And Live Apart,* jokingly establishes an analogy between the calls of penguins and those of human lovers:

> In the rookery they find
> their partners by pitch.
>
> This is somewhere between you
> pressing against the screen yelling
>
> Mol-llleee! and the sound of it
> whispered in low registers.

She then describes a zoo-keeper talking to a sick penguin named Rocko. This calls into question the nature of speech itself since it's being used where, in the usual human way, it's useless. Or where it's reduced to mere sound:

> Rocko came slowly under her arm
> at four o'clock in the winter.
>
> She smoothed his head and asked
> the questions, "What's
>   the matter?"
>
> "Are you sick?" What's
>   the matter?"
> Just those questions, many times.

The lover/penguin analogy is then resumed to show that speech between lovers is a problem of an equally radical kind. Partly the problem is that human desire can't express itself properly in words—as she says in **"Desire"** (in her second book *Raw Heaven*):

> It doesn't speak and it isn't
>   schooled,
> like a small fetal animal with
>   wettened fur

Its proper language is touch—both Peacock and her lover envy Rocko, both feel "the desire . . . . . to move / slowly under the arm of that woman." So she speaks in **"Petting and Being a Pet"** (in *Raw Heaven*) of the desire to be fondled like a small animal, of "needing met by kneading of bone which is found / through flesh" and continues:

> Like eyes make sense
>   of seeing, touch makes
> being
>
>   make sense.

Here there's the old pun, very useful to Peacock, on "sense" in its intellectual and physical meanings. This is the crucial

conflict underlying her poems—the difficulty of speaking about the latter in terms of the former.

And the breakthrough Peacock made in *Raw Heaven* and which is consolidated in *Take Heart*, was to evolve a style that constantly, if implicitly, alludes to this expressive difficulty and makes it a part of her expressive means.

This is to some extent a matter of rhythm. Her lines, like Robert Creeley's, tend to move nervously, circumspectly; her line-endings cause abrupt halts and awkward pauses.

Unlike Creeley, though, she doesn't believe that form is an extension of content. At times her form and content seem deliberately at odds—as though the form is trying to contain something that won't be contained. There are sonnets in *Raw Heaven* where the pressure from within is so intense that their rhythms buckle and their rhymes distort; somewhere it is so great that they burst and overflow into 15 or 16 lines.

This style is especially good at negotiating risky subjects and so is crucial to Peacock in *Take Heart* when she's writing about her abortion and the death of her father. (p. 3)

"The Ghost," for instance, expresses her ambivalent memories of her pregnancy: The "ghost" of that pregnancy is a source of both comfort and alarm. Peacock makes a strange return in this poem to her theme of the need to be held and touched, here by this fetal ghost: "When I let it surround me, the embrace is / more mother than baby."

In other words, she wants her dead baby to embrace her, as though it were her mother. This is grotesque but it illuminates the complex of associations connected with this theme in her work—Freudian associations that link infantile and adult sexuality. For example the comfort that the lovers seek in **"A Kind of Parlance"**—of being tucked, like a sick penguin, under a caring arm—suggests this by placing parental and sexual love together. Sylvia Plath makes a similar Freudian reference in "Daddy" when she links her dead father and her husband.

Now Peacock's style is quite unlike Plath's. It's a curious mix of the cerebral—especially in her complex similes—and the direct, even the raw, in her references to biographical and physiological fact (for instance, to masturbation and the smell of her mother's menses).

But there's a link in the way both poets explore an obsession with their dead fathers and the effect they've had—and continue to have, even when dead—on their lives.

So *Take Heart* begins with poems related to the death of Peacock's father and thereby implies that the other poems in the book should be seen in the light of the poet's relationship with this overbearing and alcoholic parent.

Certainly **"The Ghost,"** with its bizarre reference to the parental embrace of an absence, suggests the wish to be embraced by an absent dream-parent:

> It's not a dead little thing without a spinal cord yet,
> but a spirit of the parent we all sought to have had,
> of possibility.

However, instead of this ideal parent, Peacock had a father who, when she was a small child, made her loiter outside the bars that his addiction drove him to, and who, when she was an adolescent, made her declare her love for him.

In **"Say You Love Me,"** the style that Peacock has evolved for dealing with risky subjects is used with great effectiveness. Pinned to a chair, she's cowering under her father who, although he's "hunkered over [her]" seems to be transformed by his need for love:

> Rage
> shut me up, yet "DO YOU?" was
>   beginning
>
> to peel, as of live layers of skin, age
> from age from age from him until
>   he gazed
> through hysteria as a wet baby
>   thing
>
> repeating, "Do you love me? Say
>   you do,"
> in baby chokes, only loud, for they
>   came
> from a man.

These lines are characteristic of Peacock in their telling awkwardness—in the halting quality that comes from treating "DO YOU?" like a noun, and separating "beginning" and "to peel" by a stanza break. This is appropriate because it insists on the tangle of emotions here.

Obviously, this is monstrous behavior on her father's part and it's not surprising that the poems following this one celebrate his death:

> The aftermath of death is a release
> from drunken midnight calls and
>   the unceasing
> responsibility without control
> of the one who stunted you.

But the stylistic awkwardness of **"Say You Love Me"** stresses that these feelings aren't simple. And given the context of this poem in Peacock's work—which often speaks of the need to be loved, as it were, like a baby—her father's becoming like a baby seems more understandable, if still unforgivable.

After all, Peacock's own response in **"The Ghost"** is similar to her father's—she wants to reverse the roles between herself and her child.

Peacock is conspicuously courageous in the subjects she is willing to tackle. That she's mostly successful in doing so in *Take Heart,* as in *Raw Heaven,* is because she's discovered a technique that meticulously follows the labyrinthine twists and turns of these emotional tangles. (pp. 3, 14)

Ian Gregson, "Baby Love," in Los Angeles Times Book Review, *August 20, 1989, pp. 3, 14.*

JAY PARINI

Take Heart is Molly Peacock's third book of poems. Her early work displayed a spiky wit, intelligence and a more than passing commitment to the conventions of formal poetry.

The same qualities are apparent here, as in **"How I Come to You"**:

> Even a rock
> has insides.
> Smash one and see
> how the shock
>
> reveals the rough
> dismantled gut
> of a thing once dense.

Here, as elsewhere, Ms. Peacock uses rhyme and meter as a way to cut reality into sizable chunks, the sense of the poem spilling from line to line, breathlessly, as the content slithers snakelike through its rough skin.

The best poems in *Take Heart* cluster around poignant autobiographical scenes, as in **"Buffalo,"** where Ms. Peacock calls up the image of a girl sitting in a bar with her alcoholic father, thinking of

> the horrible discipline of bartenders,
> and how they must feel to serve, how some shrink
> from any conversation to endure
> the serving, serving, serving of disease.

The poem widens into a vista of Buffalo in winter, "raged / with sun and snow," a season of bitterness reflecting the icy weather of the young girl's heart.

While I found a great deal to admire in this book, a fair number of the poems stumble into a curious, often deadly abstractness. **"Commands of Love,"** for instance, begins:

> The tragedy of a face in pain
> is how little you can do for it
> because it is so closed.

"Unexpected Freedom" opens:

> The aftermath of death is a release
> to finally grow away from the one
> who stunted you.

"Feeling Sorry for Yourself" starts:

> Feeling sorry for yourself is the right
> thing to do, the moral and human thing,
> for it takes you beyond contempt.

Such prosaic reflections seem true enough in their way; in a proper dramatic context, they could be revelatory. As it is, they seem flat, and the poems that grow out of them never attain the quick reality of Ms. Peacock's more successful work.

Jay Parini, "Bright Shards and Solid Pottery," in The New York Times Book Review, *October 22, 1989, p. 16.*

Ishmael Reed

1938-

(Born Ishmael Scott Reed; has also written under pseudonym Emmett Coleman) American novelist, poet, essayist, editor, and critic.

An original satirist and practitioner of experimental fiction, Reed is best known for novels in which he assails repressive aspects of Western religion, politics, and technology. Reed's fiction is distinguished by dynamic, playful language that encompasses a variety of dialects, from African-American slang to academic critical terminology. Although preoccupied with the myriad injustices engendered by Western civilization, Reed is primarily concerned with establishing an alternative black aesthetic, which he terms Neo-HooDoo. This concept focuses on such ancient rites as conjuring, magic, and voodoo, which Reed maintains will purge African-Americans and Third World peoples of Western conditioning and ultimately help them to regain their freedom and mystic vision. Many critics view Reed's novels as a reaction against or break from the naturalistic conventions of such black authors as Richard Wright, Zora Neale Hurston, and James Baldwin. Jerry H. Bryant observed: "[If Reed's] satires sound alike, they seldom fail to disclose a new dimension to America or to provoke us with a reading of history that reverses everything we have accepted as true. . . . With a virtually unlimited reservoir of revealing metaphors, he seeks to shame us out of our complacency and hypocrisy."

In his fiction, Reed often parodies literary genres to produce a combination of the ridiculous and the didactic. His first novel, *The Free-Lance Pallbearers,* burlesques the confessional style that has characterized much black fiction since the slave narratives of the eighteenth century. The novel's young hero undergoes a chaotic search for self-awareness in a power-obsessed, white-ruled society called HARRY SAM. In his attempt to assimilate into HARRY SAM, he learns that one must be one's own master, yet he is powerless to apply this knowledge and is ultimately crucified. Reed's next work, *Yellow Back Radio Broke-Down,* introduces his Neo-HooDoo concept. A spoof of Western pulp fiction, this novel concerns racial conflict in a small town in the Old West in which the forces of intuition and irrationality, as represented by the Loop Garoo Kid, are pitted against those of rationalism and science, as embodied in Drag Gibson.

Reed extends his Neo-HooDoo philosophy in *Mumbo Jumbo* and *The Last Days of Louisiana Red.* Both novels are parodies of the mystery genre in which a detective, Papa LaBas, attempts through voodoo to combat spells cast by the white establishment, which seeks to anesthetize the artistic and political black communities. LaBas also wishes to rebuild an aesthetic from the remains of black literary and cultural history. *Mumbo Jumbo,* set in Harlem and New Orleans during the 1920s, depicts the battle between two ideologies—Jes Grew, the instinctive black cultural impulse, and Atonism, the repressive, rationalist Judeo-Christian tradition. At the novel's conclusion, Jes Grew wanes after its sacred text is burned. Houston A. Baker contended: "[*Mumbo Jumbo* offers] a conspiracy view of history, a critical handbook for the student of the black arts, and a guide for the contemporary

black consciousness on the discovery of its origins and meaning." *The Last Days of Louisiana Red,* set in Berkeley, California, during the 1970s, revolves around Louisiana Red, a destructive mental state that afflicts certain black militants. The novel largely concerns LaBas's investigation into the murder of Ed Yellings, the black discoverer of a cancer cure and the creator of the Solid Gumbo Works, a business that uses voodoo to fight Louisiana Red. A subplot involves a black radical feminist group called the Moochers, whom Reed identifies as conspiring with white males to subdue black men. This theme is prevalent throughout Reed's work.

In *Flight to Canada,* Reed abandons Neo-HooDoo and combines satire, allegory, and farce to lampoon the slave narrative and, particularly, Harriet Beecher Stowe's novel *Uncle Tom's Cabin.* Set during the Civil War but mixing contemporary characters and artifacts with those from the 1860s to stress the similarity between the periods, *Flight to Canada* recounts a slave's escape from his master's plantation, his perilous freedom in Canada, and his return as a free man to the plantation in order to liberate other slaves. Roger Rosenblatt commented: "Reed's central literary joke is also his most sober point: the impossibility of escape (flight) from bondage except by way of oneself; and the attendant conception of North (Canada) as heaven." In *The Terrible Twos,* Reed distorts Charles Dickens's *A Christmas Carol* into a dark satire on racism and greed during the 1980s, equating the selfishness and destructive tendencies of the United States with those traditionally displayed by two-year-old children. The sequel to this novel, *The Terrible Threes,* projects these maladies into the near future, presenting a nation that descends into chaos after the neo-Nazi president of the United States discloses a White House plot to expel all minorities as well as poor and homeless people and to institute a fundamentalist Christian state. In *Reckless Eyeballing,* a caustic satire of literary politics, Reed castigates what he perceives as a conspiracy between white male publishers and black female writers to subjugate black men by incorporating negative depictions of them into their work.

Reed's poetry, which is collected in such volumes as *Conjure: Selected Poems, 1963-1970* and *New and Collected Poems,* typically explores themes found in his fiction. Combining black street argot with elements of mythology, voodoo, and pop culture, Reed affirms the liberating power of his Neo-HooDoo aesthetic while attacking what he views as the stultifying nature of Western cultural heritage.

(See also *CLC,* Vols. 2, 3, 5, 6, 13, 32; *Contemporary Authors,* Vols. 21-24, rev. ed.; *Contemporary Authors New Revision Series,* Vol. 25; and *Dictionary of Literary Biography,* Vols. 2, 5, 33.)

PRINCIPAL WORKS

NOVELS

The Free-Lance Pallbearers   1967
Yellow Back Radio Broke-Down   1969
Mumbo Jumbo   1972
The Last Days of Louisiana Red   1974
Flight to Canada   1976
The Terrible Twos   1982
Reckless Eyeballing   1986
The Terrible Threes   1989

POETRY

catechism of d neoamerican hoodoo church   1970
Conjure: Selected Poems, 1963-1970   1972
Chattanooga   1973
New and Collected Poems   1988

ESSAY COLLECTIONS

Shrovetide in Old New Orleans   1978
God Made Alaska for the Indians: Selected Essays   1982
Writin' Is Fightin': 37 Years of Boxing on Paper   1988

EARL ROVIT

I'm more impressed by [*Mumbo Jumbo*] than by Reed's earlier works (*The Free-Lance Pall-Bearers* and *Yellow-Back Radio Broke-Down*). Reed's considerable talents were never in question, but his seriousness was. Now in *Mumbo Jumbo,* particularly in the careful synchronization of the structure to the theme, the artistic form attests to the novel's sense of responsibility. *Mumbo Jumbo* is a highly playful—and all the more serious for that—examination of the relationship of the

Harlem Renaissance of the 1920s to the rest of American culture. The novel focuses on the figure of Papa LaBas who is seeking to understand and to stimulate the expression of authentic black consciousness as it flourishes in American jazz, dancing, drinking, etc., and as repressive (white) Protestantism struggles to stifle this flourishing. Reed deliberately entertains himself and his reader with a playful (but still serious) history of the whitewashing of black civilization. He begins with the capture of the deep Nile Valley culture by the followers of Aton and the seizure and distortion of ancient African wisdom by the Greeks; and he continues with the further repressions by Christianity and the final degradation at the hands of the Marxists and Freudians. Much of this reminds me of the similar didacticism in John A. Williams' *Captain Blackman,* but Reed writes as though it were a delight to write novels, and that delight is communicated to his reader. There is also an interesting use of different typefaces, photographs, charts, etc., which contributes to the sprightliness of the book. Reed is still tempted into plain silliness from time to time, but he has his poetic line to fall back on when he gets into trouble.

         Earl Rovit, in a review of "Mumbo Jumbo," in Contemporary Literature, *Vol. 15, No. 4, Autumn, 1974, p. 554.*

DAVID REMNICK

Reckless Eyeballing is not so much a jab as a bludgeon aimed at a corner of the cultural establishment. Feminist playwrights, Jewish producers, black militants—they all come in for a little damage. And why not? . . .

So yeah, why not have a black southern playwright named Ian Ball try to get his name off the "sex list" drawn up by tyrannical feminist theater moguls, Tremonisha Smarts and Becky French? And why not have Ball write a play called *Reckless Eyeballing* about a black man who was lynched because he stared at a white woman a bit too lasciviously? And why not have Smarts write a play about the virtues of Eva Braun?

Why not? Most prominent black writers have avoided, or have not found the time or inclination or luxury for, high comedy in their work. . . .

But a joke—and *Reckless Eyeballing* is really an extended joke with a series of set pieces on feminism, anti-Semitism, militancy, etc.—a joke either works or it doesn't. For the most part, *Reckless Eyeballing* doesn't.

Jokes are a concoction of image, timing and language. One missing piece, a dull stretch, an error of diction, and the whole contraption falls apart to the silence of the crowd. Richard Pryor is a brilliant satirist because of the sharpness of his images and mimicry, the timing of his spiels.

Reed has been as funny as Pryor at times but he seems off his game here. His oneliners are lame—"His figure show[ed] him to be losing a private Battle of the Bulge"—and the episodes are mainly long, spoken riffs on the particular idiocies of the theater and its attendant politicians.

What is so peculiar here is that Reed's cartoon characters are dated. The feminists, the "academic black Marxists," are all figures who seem more appropriate to a work of a decade ago. For example, the feminist play (which might be re-titled

Springtime for Eva), is not the sort of thing you'd see on Off (or even Off-Off) Broadway these days.

But what's most disappointing here is Reed's haphazard prose. In some of his earlier work, he had a voice that could be at once giddy and razor-sharp. He had a real voice, distinctive, insulting, wild, a voice that answered to no political or aesthetic dogma, only to Ishmael Reed.

Reckless Eyeballing, however, is recklessly casual. The prose is dull. . . .

The worst has happened. Ishmael Reed doesn't sound special. The ethnic jokes are so dull that they read—unintentionally—like the diatribes they are supposed to satirize.

> David Remnick, "Ishmael Reed, for the Fun of It," in Book World—The Washington Post, *March 16, 1986, p. 5.*

BRENT STAPLES

Mr. Reed's fiction has always bristled with parables, asides, voodoo rituals, razor blades and spikes enough to vex even the most competent plot summarizer. [*Reckless Eyeballing*] displays the familiar malice and discursiveness. And though it bludgeons several ideologies and individuals—Clint Eastwood's Dirty Harry, feminists, lesbians, New York intellectuals, anti-Semites, neoliberals and the new right among them—its central animus is clear. Mr. Reed is angry about what he perceives to be negative characterizations of black men in fiction and drama. He is livid about Alice Walker's novel *The Color Purple,* which shows up here thinly disguised as Tremonisha Smarts *Wrong-Headed Man.*

The principal male character in *Reckless Eyeballing* is Ian Ball, a black playwright who has suffered several flops because of Becky French's sex list. Like Mr. Reed himself, Ian finds his chief critics are women who view his works as muddled and sexist, though he thinks of himself as misunderstood, even persecuted. Ian also functions as Mr. Reed's attempt to blow a kind of raspberry at certain readers. Ian's fixation on breasts and buttocks is brought to the reader's attention again and again, as is his suspicion that, given the chance, he could seduce his way out of any difference of opinion with a woman. He is the novel's least damaged black male character only because his contemporaries have been driven to artistic impotence and near madness by feminists' "bad-mouthing" and "media head-whipping."

Through considerable interruption from parallel plots we try to watch the goings-on surrounding *Reckless Eyeballing,* the first of Ian's plays in which women keep their clothes on and have strong roles. The only male character is to be the skeleton of a black man who was lynched for raping a white woman with his eyes—that is, for eyeballing recklessly. Wanting to remove all doubt of the dead man's guilt, the offended woman has him exhumed and retried. When Ian's Jewish male director is beaten to death by the audience at an anti-Semitic play, "Reckless Eyeballing" falls under Becky's control. She delegates the directing chores to Tremonisha and diverts funds from the play to a production she hopes will rehabilitate the reputation of Hitler's mistress Eva Braun.

Thrown together, Ian and Tremonisha effect a rather lopsided rapprochement. Tremonisha denounces *Wrong-Headed Man* as a pandering piece of "finishing school lumpen" forced out of her by Becky French. She moves to a sleepy town in California, where she takes good care of her man and promises to get fat, have babies and write plays in which the husband and wife live happily ever after. As if we had not got the message, a second black feminist playwright, the author of *No Good Man,* suffers a bout with cocaine addiction and recants too, pledging to lay off black men, to write only plays that she can read in church on Sunday morning and by all means to keep her distance from those horrid white feminists.

Ian, meanwhile, forgives those who have transgressed against him—by forbidding their students to write dissertations on his *oeuvre,* for example—and decides, after working with Tremonisha, that the girls ain't so bad after all; they can change. If this resolution seems forced—and it does—keep in mind that Mr. Reed sometimes views his fiction as a form of voodoo ritual, a literary gris-gris doll that focuses a psychic "fix" on anyone he perceives to be an enemy of his tribe. Given this, certain writers might do well to drape the appropriate talismans around their word processors lest they share the fate of their sisters in this novel.

In *Reckless Eyeballing* as elsewhere, Mr. Reed occasionally produces genuine terror within farce—not at all an easy thing to accomplish. The novel, however, may serve well as incantation or rage or as a literary gauntlet hurled down, but its symbolism is heavy-handed and the spell suspending disbelief is often broken. Many of the characters are mere effigies tortured on the author's rack and made to issue the requisite confessions. Moreover, Mr. Reed seems to want his novels to be hard work. A devilishly funny plot line is obscured by arcane asides and sorties on ideological camps he wishes to demolish. Does he really think all will be well with black folks when black women quit the feminist plantation and come on back down home to church? And does he really think that books and plays, not more fundamental social relations, provoke lynchings symbolic and literal? And with yet another novel less written than punched out—and that sinister Flower Phantom set loose among us—we might ask Mr. Reed a question a knowledgeable interviewer put to him several years ago. Ishmael Reed, "why you so mean and hard?"

> Brent Staples, "Media-Lashes and Sex-Listed," in The New York Times Book Review, *March 23, 1986, p. 11.*

LARRY McCAFFERY

Early on in *Reckless Eyeballing,* one of the book's many beleaguered black men observes that "throughout history when the brothers feel that they're being pushed against the wall, they strike back and when they do strike back it's like a tornado, uprooting, flinging about, and dashing to pieces everything in its path." This passage provides a perfect entryway into Ishmael Reed's latest novel, for like many other black men, Reed obviously feels that "the brothers" are catching it from all sides—and not just from the usual sources of racial bigotry, but from '60s liberals now turned neo-conservatives, from white feminists who propagate the specter of the black men as phallic oppressor, from other racial minorities anxious to wrest various monkeys off their own backs.

But the central betrayers in Reed's new novel are blacks themselves, especially black feminists and artists whom he presents as having sold out and joined the white conspiracy to keep black men in slavery. So in *Reckless Eyeballing,* we see Reed striking back by creating a literary tornado, a book so irreverent and sweeping in its condemnations that it's certain to offend just about everyone. It's also an extraordinarily timely novel that depicts—in Reed's usual complex of penetrating satire, surrealism, allegory and farce—the central sources of confusion and pain confronting black men in contemporary society.

From the outset of his career, . . . Reed has insisted that black experience can't be "contained" in traditional white symbols and forms. *Reckless Eyeballing,* like Reed's other novels, self-consciously appropriates aspects of familiar forms—in this case, the detective formula and the search-for-selfhood motif (the latter virtually synonymous with "serious" black writing)—but then demolishes these structures by introducing his own distinctive blend of discontinuity, verbal play and jive talk, and outrageous (often offensive) humor.

The book's plot revolves around Ian Ball, a naive Southern playwright who has been "sex-listed" by feminists for his first play but who has now arrived in New York City with high hopes for a new play (*Reckless Eyeballing*) in which, as Ball puts it, "the women get all the good parts and best speeches." Ball initially has the support of several powerful allies—notably Jewish director Jim Minsk and feminist producer Barbara Sedgwick—but soon after the novel opens, things begin to unravel for him: Minsk is ceremonially murdered by a group of Southern racists (a scene showing Reed at his macabre, bitterly humorous best) and Sedgwick decides she wants to shuffle Ball's play off to a minor theater and devote her energies to a play that "reclaims" Eva Braun's reputation ("She may be a Nazi whore to sexists like you," she tells Minsk, "but to many of us, she epitomizes woman's universal suffering"). Soon Minsk has been replaced by Tremonisha Smarts, a black feminist playwright who gained fame for writing *Wrong-headed Man,* a lurid melodrama about a black man going on a spree of woman bashing, rape and incest; this spree, not coincidentally, recalls what occurs in Alice Walker's *The Color Purple,* as does the fact that a film version of Smarts' play is written, produced and directed by white males.

Smarts is also the first victim of a mysterious series of crimes in which well-known feminists are tied up and have their heads shaved by a black man who models his actions after the French Resistance, which used to shave the heads of women collaborating with the Nazi's. Detective Lawrence O'Reedy, a geriatric version of Dirty Harry, who is haunted by the ghosts of his racist past, eventually ties most of the novel's main characters to the case of the headshaver. As the hunt progresses, so does Ball's search for self-understanding and aesthetic guidance.

Reckless Eyeballing suggests that the forces currently oppressing black men have become increasingly complex. It's no accident that references to the recent rightward drift of the United States has ominous implications for all black men.

Reed is also aware that naked racial oppression has, for the most part, been replaced by more subtle but ultimately no-less-destructive influences on black people. By focusing on the dilemma of the contemporary black artist, Reed shows that black culture today is threatened just as much by co-opting and the myriad temptations of self-serving expediency as by violence. Thus his new novel angrily denounces the hypocritical attitude of many whites toward black society: While whites voyeuristically devour black culture for its pas-

sion, exoticism and flair, they also obsessively worry about any "reckless eyeballing" (note the puns in Ball's name) that blacks may perpetrate against their own domain.

Finally, it is Reed who is the real "reckless eyeballer" here; and he is certain to be cursed for having "the evil eye" by blacks as well as whites, as he probes into areas which most of us would prefer to keep concealed. Like several other notable black authors—Chester Himes, Charles Wright and Clarence Major—Reed presents a vision "reckless" in the extreme: raw, abrasive, sexist, irritating. But it's a vision that needs to be confronted (and perhaps challenged) by a public all too accepting of the deodorized banalities of "The Bill Cosby Show" and Steven Spielberg's *The Color Purple.*

Larry McCaffery, in a review of "Reckless Eyeballing," in Los Angeles Times Book Review, *April 20, 1986, p. 15.*

LIZABETH PARAVISINI

The reader familiar with Ishmael Reed's fiction will recognize his novels as parodies of popular narrative forms: *The Last Days of Louisiana Red* follows the structure of the whodunit; *Yellow Back Radio Broke-Down* shatters the conventions of the western; *Flight to Canada* is a revision of the fugitive slave narrative. In these works, parody, which is usually restricted to the imitation and distortion of literary texts, becomes a medium for social and literary satire. One consistent element in Reed's fiction to date has been his use of parody—which is directed inward, toward the text—to examine the extra-literary systems that are the province of satire. Nowhere does Reed blend his parodic and satiric intentions better than in *Mumbo Jumbo,* where he parodies a narrative form (the detective novel) whose identifying quality (the rational search for knowledge) is identical to the social, religious and philosophical principles he finds objectionable in Western culture. *Mumbo Jumbo* is both a satire of Western culture's concern with rationality and an example of the reorientation of older traditions possible under Reed's aesthetics of Neo-Hoodooism. (p. 113)

Because of the formulaic nature of the genre, a successful detective novel must adhere carefully to the expected pattern in order to fulfill the reader's expectations. Deviating from the pattern means transcending the genre [as Tzvetan Todorov observes]:

> As a rule, the literary masterpiece does not enter any genre except perhaps its own; but the masterpiece of popular literature is precisely the book that best fits its genre. Detective fiction has its norms; to develop them is to disappoint them: to "improve upon" detective fiction is to write "literature," not detective fiction.

Mumbo Jumbo "improves upon" detective fiction by following its structure while undermining its rationalistic suppositions. In this work, Reed's readers are challenged to the task of interpretation by the evocation of their expectations for a detective story before these expectations are disappointed. They are disappointed primarily by *Mumbo Jumbo* not being a tale of "methodical discoveries by rational means" of the circumstances of a mystery. There are "discoveries" and "means" in the text, but they are hardly "methodical" or "rational" in the way expected of detective fiction.

Structurally, however, the novel follows the pattern expected of the genre being parodied. The model of detective fiction chosen by Reed is that of the thriller, the type of narrative usually associated with the hard-boiled American tradition. Thrillers differ from whodunits—the most common type of detective fiction—in that they de-emphasize the discovery of the identity of the criminal as the chief aim of the plot, and focus instead on the unraveling of complex webs of conspiracy and murder. Thrillers are characterized by "rapid action, colloquial language, emotional impact, and the violence that pervades American fiction," leaving aside the "static calm, the intricate puzzle and ingenious deductions" of the whodunit, [according to George Grella].

In **Mumbo Jumbo** Reed has written a story that, at least structurally, reads like a thriller. The plot is a fairly elaborate one that begins with an outbreak of the Jes Grew epidemic, a psychic condition which embodies the freedom and vitality of the Afro-American heritage. The epidemic is in search of its text, which it must find if it is not to evaporate. The text is in the hands of Hinckle Von Vampton, the librarian of the ancient order of the Knights Templar, who is himself being sought by the Wallflower Order. They, in turn, want to find and destroy the text and "sterilize Jes Grew forever." To avoid detection, Hinckle has selected fourteen people and paid them a monthly salary to send the text around to each other in a chain. (pp. 114-15)

Although structurally Reed follows the basic narrative pattern expected of a thriller, his use of the elements of the genre within this structure systematically undermines the reader's acceptance of **Mumbo Jumbo** as a typical detective story. This systematic undermining takes three forms: the first is the use of the dialectical pattern of detective fiction as the framework for the presentation of the author's views on Western culture; the second is the breaking of the internal rational logic of the process of detection; the third is the consistent use of humor to underscore those aspects of Western culture (and detective fiction) Reed finds amusingly objectionable.

The dialectical structure of the thriller is the ideal vehicle for Reed's argument that throughout history, Western culture (which he identifies with Christianity) has used its power to suppress non-Christian cultural manifestations because their sensuality and irrationality were incompatible with Western thought. The novel's main plot offers Reed's evaluation of the fate of Black culture in White America, taking as its basis what Reed calls "the major aesthetic tragedy of Afro-American life in the 20th century—the disappearance of New Orleans Old Music." In **Mumbo Jumbo,** the ultimate "crime" that PaPa LaBas and Black Herman must prevent is the destruction of Black aesthetic roots (roots which link Afro-American culture to ancient African religion) which are threatened by the representatives of Western culture: the Knights Templar, "the discredited order which once held the fate of Western civilization in its hands," and the aptly named Wallflower Order. Both stand for what Reed calls elsewhere the "worst facet of Christianity, its attempt to negate all other modes of thought and to insist upon a singularity of moral and ethical vision." The dialectics are those of logic, squareness, lethargy and lack of feeling on the one hand; and emotion, mystery, intuition, and movement on the other. To counter the Christian-Western view of the world, Reed offers Black American folklore and language, African religion and myth. In **Mumbo Jumbo,** they are embodied in the Jes Grew epidemic, a psychic condition which causes the host to do "stupid sensual things," to go into a state of "un-

controllable frenzy." . . . The efforts to destroy the Text needed for the epidemic to fulfill itself are thus charged with symbolic significance, as are Hinckle's efforts to create a Talking Android who

> . . . will tell the J. G. C.'s that Jes Grew is not ready and owes a large debt to Irish Theater. This Talking Android will Wipe That Grin Off Its Face. He will tell it that it is derivative. . . . He will describe it as a massive hemorrhage of malaprops; illiterate and given to rhetoric.

These efforts support PaPa LaBas' "conspiratorial hypothesis" about a secret society molding the consciousness of the West.

This hypothesis is sustained by the novel's best-developed sub-plot, which is built around the same concept of cultural dialectics. The Mu'tafikah are "artnappers" bent on plundering museums (here called centers of art detention) and returning "detained" art to the countries of origin. The "conspiracy" (headed by Berbelang and bringing together a multiethnic group of art students) is Reed's comment on the diverging Western and non-Western views of the role of art in society. For the Mu'tafikah, the holding of collections of African, Egyptian, and Amerindian art in American museums has broken the links of these objects with nature, ritual, and mystery. This break is seen as the result of a concerted effort to destroy the fabric of non-Western cultures.

PaPa LaBas and Black Herman's "rational sober" account of Hinckle's crime provides the historical framework in which the Western/non-Western confrontation has developed. The elaborate explanation is offered through a sweeping account of Western culture's on again/off again struggle against non-Western cultures, a struggle which begins with Aton's displacement of Osiris and does not end with the destruction of the Jes Grew text. The conspiracy is unveiled in **Mumbo Jumbo** through the use of historical and pseudohistorical documentation: the background information on the Knights Templar, the murder of Osiris and the defeat of Aton, the villainy of Moses, Warren Harding's involvement in the plot against Jes Grew, the news blackout on the attack on Port-au-Prince by the U. S. Marines, the theory of the orchestration of the 1930's depression as the means of curtailing the progress of Black aesthetics in this country.

Historical and pseduo-historical elements are interwoven in the text in the manner usually found in spy thrillers. Here, their role is that of unveiling a confrontation that is cultural rather than criminal but which (since it is presented within the dialectical structure of the detective story) emerges as an ethical confrontation of good (non-Western) versus evil (Western culture).

Throughout the novel, Reed points to the West's concern with rationality as the most salient characteristic separating Western and non-Western cultures. Detective fiction, depending as it does on the rational search for truth, epitomizes the culture Reed satirizes in the text. In **Mumbo Jumbo,** Reed sets out to undermine the role of rationality both thematically (by revealing the folly of those characters who act rationally) and structurally (by making his search for truth not dependent on logic or reason). Unlike the traditional detective, whose identifying feature is his ability to connect bits of information in logical patterns through his powers of deduction, Reed's detectives rely on intuition, "knockings" and ritual to arrive at the truth. PaPa LaBas is an "astro-detective" practicing his Neo-Hoodoo therapy in his Mumbo Jumbo Kathedral; Black Herman is a noted occultist. Both are detectives of the metaphysical. (pp. 116-19)

Through these "detectives of the metaphysical" Reed systematically undermines the rational search for knowledge that characterizes detective fiction. The systematic undermining of the process of detection is accomplished primarily by making the process dependent on chance and intuition. (p. 119)

The dependence on chance and intuition constitutes an important structural break since the rationalistic exercise that is detective fiction does not allow for the intervention of either. Chance and intuition have no legitimacy within the rules of the genre since they break the internal logic of the narrative pattern to which the reader of this type of fiction is accustomed.

The critique of Western culture's concern with rationality implicit in the rejection of the rational process of detection also motivates Reed's attack on Freudian psychology as defender of the rational as opposed to the natural forces in the human psyche. Reed contends that Freud's lack of harmony with the natural world made him unable to see the validity of irrational manifestations. (p. 120)

The rejection of the prototypes of detective fiction, as well as the rejection of the rational process of detection, are underscored in the novel through the consistent use of humor. Humor is, in fact, one of the basic elements of Reed's Neo-Hoodoo aesthetic, as well as one of the basic elements of Black culture threatened by Western culture. . . . (p. 122)

In *Mumbo Jumbo*, the chief source of humor is the parody of the conventions of detective fiction and film. The examples of such parodic exercises abound: there is the gang war in Harlem between Buddy Jackson and "the Sarge of Yorktown" over a numbers and speak operation which ends with Jackson marching the Sarge to the subway, exhorting him to leave Harlem and "never darken the portals of our abode again": or the Cagney-movie atmosphere of the scenes between the Sarge and Biff Musclewhite, former police commissioner on the take, in one of which the Sarge is gunned down, half of his head scattered in the neighboring dinner plates. The genre is satirized in the parodic portrayal of the Knights Templar as ineffectual gangsters, and of Hinckle and Safecracker as bumbling musclemen. The assembly of suspects which leads to the identification of the culprit, a "must" in the classic detective story, is elaborately parodied in a scene which finds PaPa LaBas and Herman gate-crashing a high society party to arrest Hinckle and Safecracker, only to have the guests refuse to hand them over until they "explain rationally and soberly what they are guilty of."

The humorous themes and techniques Reed uses in these parodic scenes are linked to those of Black comedians such as Dick Gregory, Moms Mabley, Flip Wilson, Godfrey Cambridge, and Richard Pryor, who use their ethnicity as a source of humorous material. (pp. 122-23)

Thematically, perhaps more important models for Reed are Negro militants like Rap Brown and Jennifer Lawson, whose brand of humor "lays bare the artificiality of the adherence to the Judeo-Christian ethics in America"—the central theme of Reed's fiction. The following example from one of Lawson's comic routines parallels Reed's theme and comic rhythm in *Mumbo Jumbo:*

> Yeah, Christianize me and colonize me.
> Make me your slave and bring me your Jesus . . .
> The constitution said I was three-fifths of a person.

In Reed's novel, as in the work of these comedians, humor is an integral part of the critique of society and fiction implicit in the "dialogic" nature of parody. . . . (p. 123)

In *Mumbo Jumbo,* this critique of fiction and reality through humor is systematically dialectical (as is to be expected in a parody of a genre whose basic structure is dialectical) and thematically consistent. Humor, both technically and thematically, stems from the basic contention behind the plot of detection—the critique of the disconnection of Western culture from nature (itself an irrational force) and its insistence on rationality as its foremost principle.

This critique extends to the concept of time in the novel:

> Time is a pendulum [LaBas explains]. Not a river.
> More akin to what goes around comes around;

a view which moves the work away from the linear concept of time detective fiction shares with the Christian concept of history. Both the plotting of the typical detective novel and the Judeo-Christian apocalyptic view of history "presuppose and require that an end will bestow upon the whole duration and meaning, [according to Frank Kermode]. The end of *Mumbo Jumbo* both negates the final restoring of order and justice of detective fiction and reaffirms the aesthetic break away from the Western aesthetic code. The pyrrhic victory of PaPa LaBas and Black Herman—pyrrhic because they unveil the conspiracy but fail to save the epidemic and its text—is met with hope for the rebirth of Jes Grew in a more receptive aesthetic environment; an environment which is being created by texts like *Mumbo Jumbo* which embody the creating and liberating aesthetics of Neo-Hoodooism.

Mumbo Jumbo thus becomes one of Reed's most important contributions to the reinterpretation of Afro-American experience and culture evident in current historiography and sociology. Among Black American writers, this reinterpretation has often taken the form of parodies of detective fiction. (p. 124)

The parody of detective fiction has allowed these writers to move away from the logocentrism of Western models that has characterized interpretations of Afro-American culture and literature and towards an affirmation of that experience in texts that are not submissive to Western models. The "carnivalization" of these models (to use the term coined by Mikhail Bakhtin) has allowed these writers "to concentrate inventive freedom, to permit the combination of a variety of different elements and their rapprochement, to liberate from that prevailing point of view of the world, from all that is humdrum and universally accepted." As *Mumbo Jumbo* shows, the transformation of literary texts through parody leads to alternative structures which allow writers to supersede and reorient older traditions. (pp. 124-25)

Lizabeth Paravisini, " 'Mumbo Jumbo' and the Uses of Parody," in Obsidian II: Black Literature in Review, *Vol. 1, Nos. 1 & 2, Spring-Summer, 1986, pp. 113-27.*

DARRYL PINCKNEY

Reckless Eyeballing is in part a comic rebuttal to [several works] by black women since the Seventies, like Ntozake Shange's *For Colored Girls Who Considered Suicide When the Rainbow is Enuf* (1977), as well as Alice Walker's novels. These feminist works shared a mood in which black women began to question "myths," like whether freedom was to come first for the black man, or whether black women felt guilty because of the "emasculation" of the black male. *Reckless Eyeballing* is a satirical narrative that mocks racial and American sexual taboos in the manner of George Schuyler's *Black No More* (1931) or Chester Himes's *Pinktoes* (1961). It is the story of Ian Ball, a black playwright who has been "sex-listed," and who is trying to get back into favor with theatrical power brokers by writing a militant play for women. Ball may also be the "Flower Phantom," an intruder who shaves the heads of black women who, in his opinion, have collaborated with the enemies of black men.

The premise is a little nasty, even for Reed, but his gift is for the outrageous, for giving vivid expression to cultural controversies very much in the air. When one young black detective complains of a black woman playwright, "She makes out like we're all wife beaters and child molesters," an older black (male) playwright says:

> It's these white women who are carrying on the attack against black men today, because they struck a deal with white men who run the country. *You give us women the jobs, the opportunities, and we'll take the heat off you and put it on Mose,* is the deal they struck. They have maneuvered these white boys who run the country, but they have to keep the persecution thing up in order to win new followers, and so they jump on po' Mose.

The question is whether Reed has uncovered a rift or a rivalry between black men and black women. His characters compete to have their plays produced. In one scene Ian Ball is in a meeting with the white feminist producer Becky French and her protégé, the black feminist playwright Treemonisha Smarts. They are discussing his play *No Good Man,* which he has written according to the feminist line. It should be remembered that "reckless eyeballing" was an expression used in the South to describe a black man's glance—which a white woman could accuse him of and get him lynched. Treemonisha Smarts says:

> "Tell him what you want to do with his play. She wants to change your play so that the mob victim is just as guilty as the mob. She wants to drop Cora Mae's line about their being in the same boat. That's the collective guilt bullshit that's part of this jive New York intellectual scene. She wants you to change the whole meaning of the play. She's saying that the man who reckless eyeballed Cora Mae was just as guilty as the men who murdered him. . . . " Treemonisha and Becky were exchanging stares that were so dense he felt that they were probably looking right through each other.

> He thought of them in the same households all over the Americas while the men were away on long trips to the international centers of the cotton or sugar markets. The secrets they exchanged in the night when there were no men around, during the Civil War in America when the men were in the battlefield and the women were in the house. Black and white, sisters and half-sisters. Mistresses and wives. There was something going on here that made him, a man, an outsider, a spectator, like someone who'd stumbled into a country where people talked in sign language and he didn't know the signs.

This is, among other things, a paranoid update on the theme of the conspiratorial intimacy between Simon Legree and Cassie.

Reed's novels, among them *The Free-Lance Pallbearers* (1967), *Yellow Back Radio Broke-Down* (1969), *Mumbo Jumbo* (1972), and *The Last Days of Louisiana Red* (1974), are meant to provoke. Though variously described as a writer in whose work the black picaresque tradition has been extended, as a misogynist or an heir to both Hurston's folk lyricism and Ellison's irony, he is, perhaps because of this, one of the most underrated writers in America. Certainly no other contemporary black writer, male or female, has used the language and beliefs of folk culture so imaginatively, and few have been so stinging about the absurdity of American racism.

Interestingly, *Reckless Eyeballing* is one of Reed's most accessible, even realistic, works. Perhaps this has something to do with the constraints imposed by the subject matter. But it is also very different from other fictions that approach the subject of sexuality and black life, works in the naturalistic tradition like Richard Wright's *Uncle Tom's Children* (1938), Chester Himes's *If He Hollers Let Him Go* (1945), or James Baldwin's *Another Country* (1962). In these books every psychological brutality could be described so long as it conformed to the sense that even as a fiction, it was part of a documentary truth that reached back to the slave narratives. It is this high ground that Alice Walker herself attempts to claim. But it must be said that she is playing a safe hand, given the acceptability of feminism and the historical conditioning that has the country afraid of black men. Reed's subtext might be that the rape of black women and the lynching of black men are part of the same historical tragedy. (pp. 18-20)

> *Darryl Pinckney, "Black Victims, Black Villains,"*
> in The New York Review of Books, *Vol. XXXIV, No. 1, January 29, 1987, pp. 17-20.*

DAVID L. SMITH

Reed's views regarding feminism have often earned him the label of "sexist." . . . *Reckless Eyeballing,* an explicitly anti-feminist work, will likely reinforce that reputation. This view is unfortunate, although Reed invites it, because it misperceives the real character of his broadly libertarian vision. Ironically, one of our strongest spokesmen for personal freedom is commonly perceived as a crass misogynist.

In Reed's plot, *Reckless Eyeballing* is the title of a play by Ian Ball, a young black writer. Ball's first play, *Suzanna,* had won critical acclaim but earned Ball a place on the notorious "sex list" maintained by the feminists, who have seized control of the literary journals, publishing houses and theaters.

Much of the novel recounts Ball's struggle to restore his literary career by appeasing the feminists. Hence, *Reckless Eyeballing,* resembling the Emmett Till case, recounts the lynching of a black "sexual molester," whose corpse is exhumed, tried and judged guilty by his "victim" and a group of feminists.

Getting the play staged, however, is not so simple. When Ball's director, Jim Minsk, is murdered by a gang of anti-

Semites in a perverse ritual supposedly re-enacting the Leo Frank case, Ball is left at the mercy of Becky French. French wants to give precedence to a play exonerating Eva Braun, who "epitomizes women's universal suffering."

Becky moves Ian's play from The Lord Mountbatten, the main stage, to The Queen Mother, a small annex. (With these names, Reed takes a swipe at the Anglophilia of U.S. artists. The name "Ian Ball," invoking John Bull, indicates that Reed's protagonist is hardly exempt.) Though *Reckless Eyeballing* ultimately receives a successful opening, we never learn whether Ian's career is restored.

The novel's main subplot involves The Flower Phantom, a mysterious figure who punishes certain black women writers for their disparagements of black men by tying them up and shaving their heads, as the French did to women who collaborated with the Nazis. He does not harm them otherwise, and he always leaves behind his calling card, a chrysanthemum.

One of the novel's central issues is whether the Phantom is a misogynistic psychopath or an underground hero. The reader is encouraged to infer the latter.

The Phantom's first victim is Tremonisha Smarts, the author of *Wrongheaded Man,* a play which climaxes when an ape-like black man beats a woman and hurls her down the stairs. The plot of *Wrongheaded Man* brings to mind Ntozake Shange's *For Colored Girls,* but its movie version by the director and producer of "Little Green Men" links it to Alice Walker and *The Color Purple.* Reed denied in an interview that Tremonisha refers to any contemporary writer. Instead, he points to Scott Joplin's opera "Tremonisha" as his source. (p. 37)

Is *Reckless Eyeballing* a misogynist novel? Is Reed a misogynist author? Are anti-feminism and misogyny equivalent notions?

Clearly, Reed presents some bluntly sexist comments in the novel. Yet significantly, he presents such statements as opinions, not as truths, and often as laughable opinions. While Reed satirizes feminist characters and their hidden agendas in this novel, he does not attack the general principles of feminism.

Indeed, his characters all ultimately emerge as idiosyncratic and distinctive individuals, not merely as representatives of some "type." His hostility seems to be directed at the ideology of feminism which, in his view, creates victims, distorts history, and denies or thwarts individual desire, enterprise and aspiration. The ideas of female equality, independence, and professional achievement are taken for granted in the novel.

Reed's thoroughly comic vision sets him apart from most other contemporary writers who address serious political questions. Since Reed sees all people as flawed and quirky, he pokes fun at everyone to varying degrees. Though he clearly has preferences, he does not claim superiority for any particular group over any other.

The main point of his satire is to deflate such pretensions. He seems willing to forgive people's foibles but not other exploitative designs.

Ian Ball, the hero, is clearly an opportunist whose main concern is just to make it as a writer. By the end of the novel, we see Tremonisha Smarts as a troubled and rather confused but well-meaning writer who has been exploited by white feminists to advance their own designs. . . .

Obviously, Reed's caricature of feminism grossly oversimplifies a broad and diverse social movement, equating the whole with one of its minor and meanest elements. In this respect, his comments seem no different functionally from those of a bigot.

His distorted caricature of feminism will outrage many readers, causing them to overlook his valid and unobjectionable point that all individuals deserve to be respected and allowed the opportunity to succeed or fail on their own merits. This formulation lays bare the conservative libertarian underpinning of Reed's social philosophy. . . .

Unfortunately, Reed also makes the error which characterizes most of contemporary conservative thought: In extolling individual liberty, he forgets that society itself is the organization of individuals, whose interests both converge and conflict. Society does not exist without organization, and any form of organization necessarily privileges some interests at the expense of others. Merely to lament or decry the frustration of personal fulfillment is to miss the crucial issue, why and how existing social arrangements have been made and how they might be altered to serve a broader range of interests.

To focus exclusively on individual concerns leads merely to favoring one selfishness over another. In *Reckless Eyeballing* this philosophical error causes Reed to neglect an essential distinction. The wrong is for Becky French to abuse her position of power, not for her to occupy that position.

This fault notwithstanding, *Reckless Eyeballing* is a fascinating book to read because of its pointed comments on literary politics and its thoroughgoing good humor. Furthermore, despite his strong views and polemical manner, Reed displays far more generosity of spirit than has generally been recognized. As we wince at his caustic remarks on U.S. culture, we should also note his profound affection for the vitality and diversity of the culture. (p. 38)

David L. Smith, in a review of "Reckless Eyeballing," in The Black Scholar, *Vol. 18, No. 3, May-June, 1987, pp. 37-8.*

MICHAEL BOCCIA

The most obvious critical question to ask about *Cab Calloway Stands In For the Moon* is if the work is poetry or prose. It is neither, yet it is both. It is, as its subtitle explains, "D Hexorcism of Noxon D Awful (D Man Who Was Spelled Backwards)," that is a hex, a spell, a conjure. One foot in poetry, one foot in prose, this piece is in the netherworld of genre. Reed's creations are usually curses against convention, spells upon spelling, sins against syntax, libels on language. This work is no different. In this "hexorcism," Papa La Bas uses his spectral powers, his mojo, to drive off an enemy of the people, the evil Noxon, who pollutes the planet and destroys democracy.

Reed is most innovative through the imitation and synthesis of diverse art forms into writing. He fractures forms as we know them, and then fuses new shapes from the wreckage. Reed parodies form as much as he parodies ideologies by distorting familiar and traditional art forms to his own ends. *Cab Calloway Stands In For the Moon* is surrealistic, made of history and poetry, lists and musings, nightmares and dramas, all rolled into a crystal ball wherein Reed sees the foibles of Western culture.

Reed is the Jazzman of poetry, the Collage Artiste of fiction, the Shaman of Soul, and as such he transforms language as well as form. Language is hoodooed into submission: Reed transmutes "The" into "D," capital letters are forced to bow down, and quotation marks vanish. Even Reed's symbols, which include but transcend traditional interpretations, reflect the eclectic nature of his art. Symbols from ancient Egypt blend with lyrics of popular songs, astrology with baseball. The New York Yankees and Ammon Ra, Cab Calloway and the Moon, Minnie the Moocher and Richard Nixon, all share the stage.

Like most of Reed's work, this piece is a satire, with humor and politics forming a sweet and sour mix. Controversial on race, sex, politics, freedom, religion and everything else, his satiric barbs intentionally provoke his audiences yet are wonderfully ironic, witty, and humorous. The allegorical object of ridicule in *Cab Calloway Stands In For the Moon* is the Presidency as personified in Richard Nixon. Even the password for entry into Papa La Bas's coven is "Nix on Noxon." Attacking establishment positions on capitalism, materialism, and imperialism, Reed leaves few sacred cows ungored by his sharp pen. (pp. 250-51)

> Michael Boccia, in a review of "Cab Calloway Stands in for the Moon," in The Review of Contemporary Fiction, Vol. 7, No. 3, Fall, 1987, pp. 250-51.

THEODORE O. MASON, JR.

Reed's project has two distinct, though related parts. He wishes to loosen the stranglehold of the Judeo-Christian tradition on the cultural patterns of black people everywhere (not simply Afro-Americans). Further, he wishes to reestablish the virtue of fiction as performance on the part of the artist, wresting it from the domination of the West, which to his mind has emphasized contemplation and tranquility over performance and activity.

Two aspects of Reed's fiction make it problematic to place his work within the context of historical fiction. His emphasis on the fantastic and the surreal, if not the unreal, would seem to sever the relationship between the work of art and the world outside the work. The more fantastic the work, the more it demands to stand on its own terms without validation by comparison with the outside world. In other words, the more heavily presentational a work, the more likely it will subordinate propositional concerns such as historical faithfulness or accuracy. In a similar fashion, Reed's imperative toward performance would seem to emphasize the moment of the work itself and militate against an historical motive. Nevertheless, it is possible to recognize in Ishmael Reed's fiction a central place for the interweaving of history and fiction. He most nearly plays the role of an historical fabulist who seeks to revise fiction—to "rehistorify" it—by taking liberties with the established historical "facts" of Judeo-Christian culture. By doing so, Reed hopes to revise our historical understanding and create a new myth for black history. The tension between the requirements of history and the requirements of myth leads both to the richness and to the poverty of his fiction.

Reed's sense of history devolves from an understanding that the historical "facts" as we understand them are wholly fictions propagated by the masters of high Western culture. As such, this conventional account downplays (if it does not completely ignore) the significance of people of color throughout the world. In America, the influential role of Afro-American culture has been denied its proper historical place; it has, instead, been trivialized and marginalized. The writer, argues Reed, "rehistorifies" black fiction and black culture by firmly emphasizing the capacity of the text to record a revised history. But this recording of history requires a "rewriting" of the larger context of the past, both historically and mythically. Following this imperative, Reed's work must emphasize simultaneously both the historicity of the present and its mythic dimension relative to a revised cultural hegemony. It is simultaneously presentational and propositional. (pp. 97-8)

Although Reed does not share the Marxist preoccupation with the past "as the concrete precondition of the present," [as described by Georg Lukács], he nevertheless insists on the reality of recognizable patterns in history, which, according to his mythic schema, condition current events and are perpetuated by those same events. This emphasis on pattern, coupled with Reed's penchant for postmodernist formal practice, makes him more a contemporary version of the historical romancer than anything else. Reed's vision of history is cyclical, yet simultaneously linear, because it insists on the capacity of human agency to amend previous patterns.

These patterns derive from Reed's mythic view of the centrality of black consciousness in the world and the marginality of white consciousness in the world. The centrality of black consciousness has been hidden because of the appropriation of the sources of political and cultural power by European and American Whites. Reed's task as an historical writer is to reveal the hidden centrality of people of color everywhere, while depicting the mythic patterns controlling that history. This interest in history conditions Reed's undertaking in his most important work, *Mumbo Jumbo*. There he continues the same antirealist formal inclinations he displays in *Free-Lance Pallbearers* and *Yellow Back Radio*, but he simultaneously borrows from time-honored practice (insofar as historical fiction is concerned) by setting his story in a part of the past he takes to resemble the present. By using the 1920s as a background for his story about the "Jes Grew" epidemic, Reed establishes the connections between past and present that provide the groundwork for a mythic representation of black history and its relation to Judeo-Christian culture.

Concerning his use of history in *Mumbo Jumbo,* Reed says: "I wanted to write about a time like the present, or to use the past to prophesy about the future—a process our ancestors called 'Necromancy.' I chose the '20s because [that period was] very similar to what's happening now. This is a valid method and has been used by writers from time immemorial. Using a past event of one's country or culture to comment on the present. As some of the similarities between the Twenties and the Seventies Reed includes: government scandal, economic crisis, "negro-mania," a black aesthetic Renaissance, and the rediscovery of Egypt. At one level, Reed's strategy is as traditional as he claims, for certainly one can see the echoes of the later period in his representation of the earlier one.

But the connection between the Twenties and the Seventies is not the only historically fictive strategy Reed employs. He also rewrites the Egyptian myths of Osiris and Set in order to establish a mythic transhistorical opposition between two kinds of consciousness—the psychologically liberated and the mechanically inhibited. Osiris is the creator, the Human Seed who represents the possibilities of regeneration and aesthetic growth. Significantly, his polytheism gives rise to joyous creation and self-expression and, further, to a recognition of the intersection of the real and the spiritual, one of the hallmarks of Reed's Neo-HooDooism. Set, on the other hand, "went down as the last man to shut nature out of himself. He called it discipline. He is deity of the modern clerk, always tabulating, and perhaps invented taxes." In Reed's version of the myth, Set overthrows Osiris by trickery and tries to assume his place. His first act is the displacement of polytheistic spirituality by a monotheistic religion, Atonism—the precursor of Western faith. In fact, Reed constructs his myth so that the Moses of the Old Testament becomes a disciple of Set and continues his destructive practices. The influence of Set leads to Christianity's fundamentally repressive theology, which desiccates the spirit.

This conflict between Osiris and Set is reduplicated by the conflict between Papa Labas and the Wallflower Order in the fictive present of *Mumbo Jumbo.* Labas represents the Hoo-Doo tradition (Reed's term for the African and Afro-American tradition that stands in opposition to Judeo-Christian culture). He signifies the triumph of the spirit over Atonist singlemindedness. "Whoever his progenitor, whatever his lineage, his grandfather, it is known, was brought to America on a slave ship mixed in with other workers who were responsible for bringing African religion to the Americas where it survives to this day." This emphasis on spirit implies a concomitant respect for mystery and wonderment, in contrast to a scientific rationalism that seeks to explain and, by explaining, thereby control.

The agents of control and the metaphorical descendants of Set are the members of the Wallflower Order, whose dream is a world transformed into plastic:

> Everything is polyurethane, Polystyrene, Lucite, Plexiglas, acrylate, Mylar, Teflon, phenolic, polycarbonate. A gallimaufry of synthetic materials. Wood you hate. Nothing to remind you of the Human Seed. The aesthetic is thin flat turgid dull grey bland, like a yawn. Neat. Clean, accurate and precise but 1 big Yawn they got up here. Everything as the law laid down in Heliopolis 1000s of years ago. (Heliopolis, the Greek name for the ancient city of Atu or Aton.) . . . The Atonists got rid of their spirit 1000s of years ago with Him [Set]. The flesh is next. Plastic will soon prevail over flesh and bones. Death will have taken over.

Throughout the novel Labas and the Wallflower Order compete to find the seminal Osirian text, The Book of Thoth, which holds the secret of Jes Grew, the anti-plague that "threatens" the American populace in the novel. Jes Grew is an anti-plague because "it enlivened the host. Jes Grew is electric as life and is characterized by ebullience and ecstasy." Labas searches for The Book of Thoth to facilitate this anti-plague; the Order searches for the Book to wipe the plague out.

In *Mumbo Jumbo* the myth of Osiris and Set prefigures the action in the fictive present of the novel. In turn the fictive present of the novel is intended to prefigure the cultural history of America in the 1970s. The success of the novel depends upon the charged interrelationship between three levels of the text—the fictive present, the mythic background, and the historical reality outside the text. The mythic background helps us "historically" interpret the action in the fictive present of *Mumbo Jumbo.* Together the narrative present and the mythic background in turn offer the reader a way of interpreting a particular decade in American cultural history and the reader's present as well. The process of interpretation works backward, too, because the reader is clearly supposed to use an understanding of the present to reflect back upon and illuminate the myth that has determined that present.

The success of a novel such as *Mumbo Jumbo* depends upon more than simply the interaction of levels of the text itself. Its effectiveness also depends upon the reader's capacity to sustain the connection between the world outside the text and the world inside the novel. Although facilitating the connection between text and world generally is a problem for just about any text, in *Mumbo Jumbo* this problem becomes more acute and is even complicated by the very techniques Reed uses to create his novel.

In the traditional historical novel, the reader's capacity to maintain some connection between the world of the text and the historical reality outside the text is facilitated by the concreteness that Lukács saw as the hallmark of [Walter] Scott's work. This concreteness, which is really a species of historical verisimilitude, allows the work to masquerade more readily as a possible representation of history. The illusion of life implies the illusion of historicity. No historical fiction ever bridges the gap between itself and historical narrative or analysis, but this gap is lessened by the insistence on concreteness and by the admission on the part of the reader that the fictive drama he or she reads is a possibly accurate simulacrum of a real historical drama.

Reed's fiction works generally on principles that run counter to any impulse toward verisimilitude. In his second novel, *Yellow Back Radio,* he makes his aesthetic position clear. The near photographic precision of social realism (embodied by Bo Shmo and the Neo-Social Realist Gang) is rejected for a far more expressionistic form emphasizing performance. (pp. 100-03)

The most accurate analogy for Reed's fiction is neither the photograph nor the historical narrative, but the circus, which emphasizes performance and its distance from what we call reality . . . Undoubtedly this characterization of Reed's fiction is apt because so much of his work depends precisely on significant departures from reality for its effect. Reed feels free to do anything—from making his protagonist a black cowboy who knows Voodoo to rewriting Egyptian myth. The use of this absolute freedom accompanied by his penchant for humorous incongruity and elaborate language play makes for the power of his work. The imaginative expansiveness of his novels and the alternative vision of black culture they offer constitute significant values that cannot be ignored.

Yet the techniques that give rise to this expansiveness finally frustrate Reed's historical and mythic motives. Like the circus, which is most effective (perhaps only effective) while it is being performed, Reed's *Mumbo Jumbo* (and almost all Reed's fiction) works best while it is being read. During the experience of the text, the reader is nearly wholly controlled by Reed's manipulation of the elements of his fiction. The Wallflower Order, Jes Grew, Labas, Set, Osiris, and the others are given life and depth by the text and not by any pattern of correspondences with anything outside the text. In fact,

Reed clearly wishes to control the field of information in the novel in order to render irrelevant issues revolving around direct correspondence. Had Ishmael Reed's intentions been merely to create an exclusively expressionistic fiction in the hopes of being expansive or seriously diverting (like the circus), then his work would be far more successful.

Mumbo Jumbo, however, has explicitly more ambitious intentions extending beyond the effect of the text on a reader in the act of reading. Reed's design is to offer in the novel an explanation of black culture, a new myth, by revealing as false certain accepted fictions about black history—that it is "primitive" and insignificant, or merely a catalogue of suffering. But this intention to represent a myth of black history runs afoul of his ethic of performance and his expressionistic technique. The myth he creates and the culture he wishes to illuminate end up being exclusively a function of the text itself, rather than being relatively "independent" of and illuminated by the text. The historical motive is rendered artificial by Reed's inclination toward the wholly fanciful. By entirely forsaking historical verisimilitude, Reed removes his text even further than most from the realm of the historical. Rather than presenting us with a myth that illuminates history, he manages to substitute myth for history, emphasizing the fictionality of history more than the historicity of fiction. Quite clearly, the mythic and the historical need not be so opposed. For Reed, however, "history" has so often been appropriated by the racist dominant culture that "history" and the "historical" have become suspect, if not corrupt. The accuracy of the historical, with its emphasis on determinateness, gives way to the fanciful.

It would be a mistake to forget that this great tension in Reed's work between its fancifulness (his vision of literary art as a circus) and the persistent claims of his art to seriousness and truth makes for his considerable success. In his strongest moments, Reed succeeds in the mix and enlivens our understanding of history and culture, if only temporarily. Not infrequently, however, the synthesis of fancy and seriousness becomes brittle and breaks down, expressing less the historicity of Reed's fiction and more the patent artificiality of his vision of history.

In "The Blackness of Blackness: A Critique of the Sign and the Signifying Monkey," Henry Louis Gates, Jr. tries to defend Reed's novelistic practice in *Mumbo Jumbo* by pointing to its emphasis on "indeterminacy" as a significant value, over and against notions of closure, which dominated earlier forms of Afro-American literature and which also govern the writing of most kinds of history, either fictional or "factual."

> Reed's most subtle achievement in *Mumbo Jumbo* is to parody, to signify upon, the notions of closure implicit in the key texts of the Afro-American canon. *Mumbo Jumbo,* in contrast to that canon, is a novel that figures and glorifies *indeterminacy.* In this sense, *Mumbo Jumbo* stands as a profound critique and elaboration upon the convention of closure, and its metaphysical implications, in the black novel. In its stead, Reed posits the notion of aesthetic *play:* the play of the tradition, the play on the tradition, the sheer play of indeterminacy itself.

Gates arrives at this position by characterizing the "naturalistic" fiction of Richard Wright as the most famous domain of closure, a type of fictional practice criticized and revised by Ralph Ellison in *Shadow and Act.* Both Wright and Ellison are criticized and revised by Reed in *Mumbo Jumbo.* The revolt against closure not only affects fiction but interpretation and criticism as well.

> *Mumbo Jumbo* is a novel about indeterminacy in interpretation itself. The text repeats this theme again and again. . . . It is indeterminacy, the sheer plurality of meaning, the very play of the signifier itself, which *Mumbo Jumbo* celebrates. *Mumbo Jumbo* addresses the *play* of the black literary tradition and as a parody, is a *play* upon that same tradition.

The fundamental weakness of Gates's position is the "elevation" of indeterminacy. This is a surprising weakness, too, because I find it hard to imagine how anyone could advance indeterminacy as a signal value in the wake of Graff's *Literature Against Itself,* Lentricchia's *After the New Criticism,* or any of the recent revisions of poststructuralist criticism such as the New Pragmatism. Although indeterminacy assuredly has a kind of limited value (given a natural and appropriate suspicion of hard and fast inflexible positions), Gates pushes beyond this temperate position by elevating indeterminacy as *the* value in the pantheon of literary values.

"The Signifying Monkey" achieves this end by identifying narrative closure (and presumably hermeneutic "closure") with a racist hegemony. Actually, "The Signifying Monkey" makes Ellison the literary critical hit-man who "takes out" Richard Wright and his penchant for narrative closure, thus making way for narrative indeterminacy and the assumptions of Afro-American postmodernism as the cardinal values in the Afro-American literary discourse. "By explicitly repeating and reversing key figures of Wright's fictions, and by implicitly defining in the process of narration a sophisticated form more akin to Hurston's *Their Eyes Were Watching God,* Ellison exposed naturalism as merely a hardened conventional representation of 'the Negro problem,' and perhaps part of 'the Negro problem' itself. Gates achieves two ends in this passage. Hurston becomes elevated at the expense of Wright, whose narrative technique then becomes identified with a racist hegemony. Reed's revision of Wright, which jumps off from Ellison's revision, then becomes an act of political liberation because Reed rejects literary naturalism and the coercive values it implies. *Mumbo Jumbo,* by emphasizing play and decentralizing such concerns as narrative correspondence and closure, deconstructs an important part of the Afro-American literary canon while erecting, presumably, a new version of the canon—although the position that depends on such persistent fluidity constructs canons only with great difficulty.

Missing from this analysis, lost in the ecstasy of indeterminacy, is any recognition that the elevation of indeterminacy actually signals a fundamental political impotence (and completely undervalues, if it does not ignore, Reed's own commitment to some kinds of closure concerning the relationship between black culture and white). The emphasis on indeterminacy requires the admission that affairs in the realm of the determinate are fundamentally intractable, unsusceptible to liberating strategies that might make that realm less fixed, less hard and fast, less conventional, less oppressive. "Play" becomes cast as a useful opposing strategy but requires for the full exercise of its powers the creation of another "realm," somehow different from the real and insulated from the real (in Reed's *oeuvre* signaled by the metaphor of the circus and his emphasis on the presentational).

Gates's analysis errs on at least two counts. It exaggerates the values of indeterminacy and play by masking the degree to which a commitment to those values requires giving up any claim on the "real" (a realm Gates views as awfully susceptible to political and linguistic corruption). Further, he misreads *Mumbo Jumbo* by overstating the success of Reed's use of indeterminacy. Reed's novel actually provides a perfect example of the self-limiting nature of indeterminacy and play. The "liberation" offered by *Mumbo Jumbo* is only partial and temporary. The more aggressively asserted any aspect of this indeterminacy becomes, the less it looks like play and the more it becomes determinate and propositional (and readily identified with the concept of hegemony, which purportedly has only racist and oppressive connotations). Reed's novel actually breaks down because of the conflict between his interest in history and his emphasis on indeterminacy (between the determinate and play)—no concept of history that makes any claims on authenticity and determinateness can be anything other than oppressive. And the more complete and overarching the advocacy of indeterminacy as a value, the more it subverts the claims of history and the more it resembles ideas of closure and determinacy. (pp. 103-07)

In *Mumbo Jumbo,* Reed takes up more than he is able to handle and invites a degree of scrutiny that the novel simply cannot withstand. It breaks apart under the vastness of its own intentions. (p. 108)

> *Theodore O. Mason, Jr., "Performance, History and Myth: The Problem of Ishmael Reed's 'Mumbo-Jumbo',"* in Modern Fiction Studies, *Vol. 34, No. 1, Spring, 1988, pp. 97-109.*

GEORGE MYERS, JR.

According to Reed—in numberless essays, reviews, letters-to-editors, interviews and, now, in *Writin' Is Fightin'*—feminists hate him, the white man fears him, and he must dodge punches thrown at him from the Left and Right. He's sort of a good guy Morton Downey, Jr. There's been too much copy on Reed the fighter and too little on Reed the writer. Apparently he's been snared by the same traps of macho stereotype that befell Hemingway, Mailer, and other hard-boiled types: it's more lucrative for a fighter in the United States to go eight rounds, and be paid for it, than a writer—and the headlines come bigger.

Collecting 18 essays, reviews, and newspaper articles, *Writin' Is Fightin'* documents the best jabs of a novelist who still can be a contender in satiric fiction. One by one, Reed steps into the ring with idiot savants and new-wave racists, with the drug war in Oakland, "killer illiteracy," and our curriculum's "monocultural literature." The latter group, as you might guess, excludes books by Hispanics, Asian Americans, blacks, and others (and won't ever take the time to read Reed).

In **"America's Color Blind: The Modeling of Minorities,"** Reed beats up on one particular newspaper column written by Pete Hamill, which appeared in *The Village Voice* in 1987. In Reed's view, Hamill typified welfare recipients as "a lazy good-for-nothing dope-smoking black person." Reed dispatches Hamill's and other racist or weirdly skewed articles in this piece with facts and élan.

Reed's premium pieces here are a consideration of John Edgar Wideman's *Brothers and Keepers;* a feature on August Wilson; a skunk-shoot in which Reed slyly says he backs

Bernhard Goetz for president and Lt. Col. Oliver North for vice president. Reed also mulls **"Serious Comedy in Afro-American Literature"**; takes a revisionist look at George Orwell's most famous polemic; and offers a thirty-page California revery, **"My Oakland, There Is a There There."** To a piece, they are punchy if thoughtfully written, bolstered by a facile use of facts and figures, and at least tangentially about "learning to tolerate cultures that are different than our own."

Reed's most indulgent and mean-spirited piece carries his best title: **"Steven Spielberg Plays Howard Beach."** In this bit of bumptiousness, Reed defends himself against feminists who thrashed him for thrashing the film of *The Color Purple.* Why doesn't he just ignore the criticism and get on with it, with the writing of satiric fiction? (p. 23)

> *George Myers, Jr., "Tissue of Interpretations," in* The American Book Review, *Vol. 10, No. 6, January-February, 1989, pp. 13, 23.*

JACOB EPSTEIN

[In *The Terrible Twos*], which chronicled a fictitious conspiracy between big business, the White House and an impostor, Saint Nicholas, to take over the Christmas industry, and now in *The Terrible Threes,* Reed hypothesizes an American government of the 1990s, waging war against the Third World and "surps"—surplus people: the homeless, the poor, women, blacks and Jews. Reed's futuristic America is led by President Jesse Hatch, a neo-Nazi who denounces Ronald Reagan as a left-winger who presided over the biggest sell-out to the Soviets since Roosevelt at Yalta. The White House spiritual adviser, the evil Reverend Jones, encourages the Marines to round up the population and send them all to Sunday School. He urges passage of the Conversion Bill to "drive infidels out of the country." Americans will have to convert to Christianity or go into exile. The Republic is saved when Nola Payne, first woman chief justice of the Supreme Court, suffers a nighttime visitation from the ghost of the Supreme Court justice who decided against Dred Scott in 1837, now "condemned to wander around the American hell . . . (his) name spoken in disgust." The next morning, she rules against the Conversion Bill and topples the government of Jesse Hatch. Meanwhile, Reverend Jones encounters Satan himself (who wears a beeper) who assures the Reverend of his place in hell. Along the way, Reed targets: feminists, writers of minimalist fiction, neo-conservatives, a Social Darwinist newspaper columnist who affects a bow-tie and quotes heavily from the classics in order to bolster his shameless kow-towing to the ruling elite; daytime talk-show hosts and assorted ideologues who try to keep blacks and Jews (all "surps" in the government's eyes) from common cause.

Fans of Reed's earlier work will recognize the frenzied inventiveness of this work. Reed is our best literary example of what Claude Lévi-Strauss described in "The Savage Mind" as "the *bricoleur,*" drawing material and inspiration from anything and everything around him: popular culture, Yoruba cosmology, TV, the Bible and of course, the daily headlines. But fans may also be disappointed. In the depth of his rage, Reed perhaps spreads himself too thin. The early chapters jumble together in a melee of situations and characters. We track one character for three pages, then another for five, then another. Then another. The strands of Reed's narrative web together in the end, but the early going is disjointed and confusing. (*The Threes* will be almost impossible to understand without first having read *The Twos,* even though Reed provides a précis of the earlier book.) And of course there will be those who will take political issue with Reed's Brave New World, and who will dismiss it. But there will be others who won't.

Reed's vision of the future (and our present and past) is original and subversive. Subversion is out of style these days, but unfashionable or not, Reed is an always interesting writer and this book deserves to be read.

Jacob Epstein, "The Devil Wears a Beeper," in Los Angeles Times Book Review, *June 4, 1989, p. 2.*

JOHN O'BRIEN

[*The Terrible Threes*] begins where *The Terrible Twos* left off: now in the late 1990s, the country is in a state of chaos, having chased its president into a sanatorium after he revealed on national television a White House conspiracy to purge America of its poor and homeless, as well as to destroy Nigeria. The president was informed of the conspiracy by St. Nicholas, who, while greatly loved by Americans at Christmas time, is not believed in the rest of the year. The new president fears his impending indictment for his part in the conspiracy, while his chief adviser, the born-again Rev. Clement Jones (the first white man to truly learn and steal the way of black preaching), is hatching a plot to blame it all on another White House adviser whose name sounds Jewish (Americans won't have any trouble swallowing a Jewish conspiracy).

Also at work in this deliberately episodic novel are a host of other characters from *The Terrible Twos,* including Nance Saturday, Reed's failed detective who now drives a limo between La Guardia and Manhattan hotels while doubling as a social activist; the Pope; Black Peter and Black Peter's imposter. This novel, beginning on Thanksgiving and ending on Christmas (what could be more wholesomely American?), concludes with the return of President Dean Cliff from the sanatorium, only to see him kidnapped on the way to the White House. Always bordering on tragedy, Reed seems to be saying, America falls just short and ends in farce.

As satirist, Reed makes almost everyone uncomfortable at times: blacks, whites, liberals, conservatives, feminists, antifeminists, Christians and all shades of politicians. (p. 4)

Fortunately, Reed has never been greatly concerned with winning friends with his fiction, and besides, the true villainy in the novel is saved for males.

In much of his fiction, Reed could be charged with confusing fiction with essay and with overexplaining (need we be told that "Dickens" created "Scrooge"?). But Reed's fiction from the start has been an attempt to invent a "map" of Western ideas, politics, literature and history. Just as one is about to groan at his explanation of Scrooge, one sees his mapping at work, which consists of creating a kind of American and Western catalogue of names. Within only two paragraphs, the catalogue of proper names looks like this: Boston, Celtics, Marvin Hagler, Scrooge, Dickens, St. Nicholas, Rome, Rastafarians, Nance Saturday's Limousine Service, the Netherlands, Ralph Lauren, Tom Sawyer, Saint Peter and Dali.

The list goes halfway around the world, includes several centuries, and moves up and down the scale from low to high cul-

ture. Expand it, and you wind up with Reed's novel; you also wind up with a very strange inventory of the Western world, each item impinging upon the others, as though Ralph Lauren or Boston can be explained only by way of Dali. Which is precisely Reed's view. As topical as his satire is, Reed keeps an eye on the on-going struggles in the Western mind. At heart, he is a cultural anthropologist who is as much obsessed with the origins of our myths as he is with their present-day reenactments.

Above all, Reed is a political novelist, but with a twist. He is both bored by and suspicious of the conventional political novel with a realistic story and flesh-and-blood characters (his characters usually emerge from the world of cartoons and stereotypes, and lean in the direction of myth). For Reed, American politics in the present can be understood only in relation to the last 3,000 years. Though Reed appears to believe that every political gesture in this country has greed as its motive, politics is not possible without a constant recourse to American theology and mythology, both of which we see in the Rev. Jones's plan to use Bob Krantz as the scapegoat:

> So even though he converted—I baptized him personally—he's still a Jew at heart. We can say that he did it for Israel or something. You know, convince the Arabs that we're evenhanded, satisfy the Christian majority at the same time. We'll get public opinion on our side. Blame it on communism. That always works. Say that Krantz was part of some kind of worldwide communist conspiracy aligned with Satanists and Antichrists.

Reed's eerie, weird, implausible world has a way of sounding all too real, too much like what we hear on the evening news. And Reed has an unnerving sense of what will show up next on our televisions. He is without doubt our finest satirist since Twain. (pp. 4, 6)

John O'Brien, "American Funhouse," in Book World—The Washington Post, *June 25, 1989, pp. 4, 6.*

DARRYL PINCKNEY

The slave narratives tell of spirits riding people at night, of elixirs dearly bought from conjure men, chicken bones rubbed on those from whom love was wanted, and of drams taken as omens. Harriet Tubman heeded visions which she described in the wildest poetry. VooDoo, magic, spirit worship as the concealed religious heritage of the black masses, and literacy, control of the word as a powerful talisman, are among the folk sources of what Ishmael Reed calls the "Neo-HooDoo aesthetic" of his polemical essays, contentious poems, and pugnacious, elliptical fictions.

Reed's "Neo-HooDooism" is so esoteric that it is difficult to say what he intends by it, whether it is meant to be taken as a system of belief, a revival of HooDoo, the Afro-American form of Haitian VooDoo, or, as he has also suggested, as a device, a method of composition. Mostly Neo-HooDooism seems to be a literary version of black cultural nationalism determined to find its origins in history, just as black militants of the 1960s invoked Marcus Garvey or the slave rebellions. Neo-HooDooism, then, is a school of revisionism in which Reed passes control to the otherwise powerless, and black history becomes one big saga of revenge.

Black writers, Leslie Fiedler once pointed out, have been attempting to "remythologize" themselves and black people since the time of Jean Toomer, but in Neo-HooDooism writing itself becomes an act of retribution. Reed puts a hex or a curse on white society, or on any group in black life that he doesn't like simply by exposing them to ridicule: the whammy hits Rutherford B. Hayes, Millard Fillmore, Lincoln, Woodrow Wilson, black nationalists, black Maoists reading "Chinese Ping-Pong manuals," black feminists, white feminists, white radicals, television, what he conceives of as secret societies of Anglos, the master caste, and those who control the canon, the dreaded C word, and ignore Asian-American, Native American, and Hispanic literature, and get Afro-American literature all wrong. There is also much beating up of Christianity and the Catholic Church.

Fantastic in plot, satirical in tone, colloquial in style, and always revolving around what Zora Neale Hurston identified as the "wish-fulfillment hero of the race" in folklore, Reed's novels, with one smooth black after another blowing the whistle on covert forces that rule the world, are latter-day trickster tales with enough historical foundation to tease. . . .

Many black intellectuals in the 1960s sought to rehabilitate their identity through Islam, Black Power, or the principles of Ron Karenga, who held that black art must show up the enemy, praise the people, and support the revolution. Words were seen as weapons and whites were accused of "the intellectual rape of a race of people," but Reed was too quirky to become merely a black separatist. At his most rhetorical he claims to have a multinational, multi-ethnic view of the United States. He concocted his personal brand of chauvinism, one designed to dispense with the black writer's burden of interpreting the black experience.

The ground under the naturalistic problem novel of the 1940s, which depended on oppression for its themes, was eroded by the possibilities of the integration movement, and it led black writers in the 1950s to turn inward. But the black revolt of the 1960s brought a resurgence of protest literature. Though Reed shared its anti-assimilationist urges, maybe he didn't want to sound like everyone else who was hurling invective against the injustices in American society. Reed's work aims to dissolve or transcend the dilemma of the double consciousness of the black writer as an American and as a black that has characterized black writing since the slave narratives. Chester Himes, half of whose ten novels are hard-boiled detective stories from which Reed got a great deal, complained in his autobiography, *The Quality of Hurt* (1973), that white readers only wanted books in which black characters suffer. "Fuck pain," Reed said. "The crying towel doesn't show up in my writing."

To disarm racism and make room for his comic sense of the irrational, to free himself from the tradition of the black writer's double consciousness, Reed got rid of the confessional voice, the autobiographical atmosphere of Afro-American literature, "those suffering books" about the old neighborhood in which "every gum drop machine is in place." His first novel, *The Free-Lance Pallbearers* (1967), is a fitful, irreverent parody of the literature of self-discovery. The narrator, Bukka Doopeyduk, a luckless believer in "the Nazarene Creed," lives in a place called HARRY SAM, which is ruled by SAM, who is rumored to eat children, has been enthroned on a commode in a motel for thirty years, and rants about "all the rest what ain't like us."

The novel is madly scatological, waste overruns everything. Doopeyduk, "a brainwashed Negro" of the projects who listens to Mahler, becomes, by accident, a media star until he witnesses the "sheer evil" of SAM—performing backroom anal sex. He then tries to grab power, fails, and is crucified on meat hooks.

Along the way to doom Doopeyduk meets opportunistic black leaders, voyeuristic white radicals, academics, slumlords, television talk show hosts, all of whom Reed lampoons. Given the climate of the late 1960s, with antipoverty programs like HARYOU and best sellers about the inner city in which self-exploration often had an element of self exploitation, Reed's baiting of almost everyone has the calculated exhibitionism of funky stand-up comedy. For outrageousness, Reed's only peer is Richard Pryor.

There isn't much in this novel that Reed won't try to take the piss out of, including the legacy of *Black Boy* and *Invisible Man;* reports about the Vietnam War; the Book of Revelations; and militant rhetoric, which comes off as sell-out entertainment for masochistic white audiences. (p. 20)

Reed makes fun of VooDoo in *The Free-Lance Pallbearers.* Doopeyduk's wife's grandmother takes conjure lessons through the mail under the "Mojo Retraining Act," and while studying for her "sorcery exams" tries to shove her granddaughter in the oven to practice an exercise from the "witchcraft syllabus." VooDoo is part of the pervasive corruption in HARRY SAM, one more ridiculous thing about life.

But in his second novel, *Yellow Back Radio Broke-Down* (1969), Reed is serious about possession and spells, at least as a pose, though he is capable of saying anything to be sensational. Here in order to get away from white fiction as a model, and to return to a "dark heathenism," Reed puts Neo-HooDooism to the forefront in place of the crying towel of his experience as a black man in America. Anything that Reed approves of historically he says comes from HooDoo. "HooDoo is the strange and beautiful 'fits' the Black slave Tituba gave the children of Salem." Ragtime and jazz were manifestations of HooDoo, messages from the underground, and in his own day Neo-HooDoo signs are everywhere, like charges in an electric field.

Reed's Neo-HooDooism shares the syncretism of its model. Just as VooDoo absorbs Catholic saints to represent its spirits, Neo-HooDooism is comfortable enough with a California out-of-it-ness to become "a beautiful art form of tapestry, desire, song, good food, healthful herbs." Tall tales of how the weak overcome the strong through wit, toasts of the urban tradition, "positive" humor, and other "neo-African" literary forms—the entire folk tradition is, to Reed, a vast reservoir of HooDoo ideas to which he, its conservator, hopes in Neo-HooDooism to add "fresh interpretations" by "modernizing its styles."

Yellow Back Radio Broke-Down is a full-blown "horse opera" (spirits ride human hosts), a surrealistic spoof of the Western with Indian chiefs aboard helicopters, stagecoaches and closed-circuit TVs, cavalry charges of taxis. The wish-fulfillment hero in this novel is the Loop Garoo Kid, a HooDoo cowboy, not only "a desperado so ornery he made the Pope cry and the most powerful of cattlemen shed his head to the Executioner's swine," but also a trickster Satan. Loop Garoo conducts "micro HooDoo masses" to end "2000 years of bad news." He fights ranchers, the US government, and then Pope Innocent on behalf of the youth of Yellow Back

Radio, an intersection of historical and psychic worlds, a beleaguered town where the rule of the elders has been temporarily overthrown by an anarchist revolt that resembles the counterculture of the late Sixties. The Pope wants Loop to "come home," to make peace with the Big Guy.

Like Reed's subsequent novels, *Yellow Back Radio Broke-Down* is about many things and all at once. Pages flash with allusions to great issues of the moment, the novel seems to unravel, to carelessly shed its best layers, in order to get to an impatient message: the hero must not suffer, must win out over the whites in power, or at least dazzle them to a draw. Black magic, and black culture, must be recognized as a force as powerful as any other. (pp. 20, 22)

But curiously, while Reed approaches historical black culture with the enthusiasm of one who has just come across an offbeat work that supports his anti-establishment convictions on current matters, like whether the police have a hard job or whether black militants are anti-achievement in their vilification of the black middle class, he does not hesitate to go against received black opinion, to deplore the lack of skepticism among his black critics, as if each side of his mouth were aimed at a different audience and his purpose were to discomfort both.

He can find the good fight anywhere, often with other black writers. "Even the malice and vengeance side of HooDoo finds a place in contemporary Afro-American fiction," Reed says, a fish in its own water. Already in his second novel Reed is defending himself against the Black Aesthetic critics, the followers of the Black Arts movement, the "field niggers" who got "all the play" in the 1960s, denounced individualism, and endorsed the line that there was a uniform black experience, that blacks have only one language, that of their liberation. Reed has the Loop Garoo Kid meet up with Bo Shmo, a "neo-socialist" who tells Loop that he's too abstract, "a crazy dada nigger" whose work is just "a blur and a doodle." Loop says:

> What's your beef with me, Bo Shmo, what if I write circuses? No one says a novel has to be one thing. It can be anything it wants to be, a vaudeville show, the six o'clock news, the mumblings of a wild man saddled by demons.

Bo Shmo says:

> All art must be for the end of liberating the masses. A landscape is only good when it shows the oppressor hanging from a tree.

Reed says he uses "the techniques and forms painters, dancers, film makers, musicians in the West have taken for granted for at least fifty years, and artists of many other cultures for thousands of years," but this seems a device to protect the structural weaknesses of his madcap novels. Reed does not create characters, he employs types to represent categories, points of view. Plot, however, he has in overabundance, ever since his most ambitious novel, *Mumbo Jumbo* (1972), in which he began to use the detective story as the vehicle for his history of the Western world according to Neo-HooDooism.

What Reed probably finds most congenial about the suspense genre, in addition to its law of cause and effect, is the recognition scene in the library where the hero makes arrests and explains how he solved the case, which in *Mumbo Jumbo* means a lengthy deposition on the mysteries of black culture.

The exposition comes as a relief because of the complexity of the narrative, the noisy feeling of several voices going on at the same time. *Mumbo Jumbo* is dense with subplots, digressions, hidden meanings, lectures ("The Book of Mormon is a fraud. If we Blacks came up with something as corny as the Angel of Moroni . . ."). It is packed with epigrams, quotations, newsclips. The written text is interpolated with reproductions of drawings and photographs, illustrations that function as a kind of speech. Reed even appends a long bibliography about VooDoo, dance, Freud, art, music, ancient history, presidents, as if to say, "If you don't believe me look it up."

Mumbo Jumbo is set in the 1920s because of the parallels between the "negromania" that swept America during the Jazz Age and that of the late 1960s. A HooDoo detective, PaPa LaBas, tries to track down the source of the phenomenon Jes Grew, as the nationwide outbreak of dancing and bizarre behavior—"stupid sensual things," "lusting after relevance," and "uncontrollable frenzy"—is called. Jes Grew knows "no class no race no consciousness," and causes people to speak in tongues, hear shank bones, bagpipes, kazoos. It is "an antiplague" that enlivens the host, fills the air with the aroma of roses. This creeping thing, like Topsy, "jes grew," as James Weldon Johnson said of ragtime, and in *Mumbo Jumbo* it could mean many things in black culture. "Slang is Jes Grew."

In trying to give black feeling an ancient history, Reed reaches back to unexpected allies like Julian the Apostate who foresaw the "Bad News" of a Christian Europe, and eventually into Egyptian myth, to Set's murderous jealousy of his brother, Osiris. Reed believes that the past can be used to prophesy about the future, "a process our ancestors called necromancy," and in *Mumbo Jumbo* the earthiness of black culture and the repressiveness of white societies are a legacy of Set's uptightness.

The message of *Mumbo Jumbo* is difficult to grasp because of an abstraction on which the action of the novel hinges. "Jes Grew is seeking its text. Its words. For what good is a liturgy without a text?" An elite military group that defends the "cherished traditions of the West" successfully conspires to contain Jes Grew, to keep it from uniting with its text, its key of truth, which Reed calls the Book of Thoth, "the 1st anthology by the 1st choreographer." Jes Grew withers away without this text, but LaBas goes on with his obeah stick into the 1960s to tell college audiences about the good times that almost were and might be.

That the nature of the lost text is left for us to conjecture makes it hard to guess what Reed has in mind here as the written tradition for what he sees as the Neo-HooDoo aesthetic. The novel is anticlimactic, though Reed may mean that the mysteries of black culture can't be written down, that Jes Grew must remain in the air, always possible, but beyond the page. In fact, the suggestiveness of *Mumbo Jumbo* has made it a rich mine among poststructuralists who see it as a handbook of signs, a textbook of signifiers on prejudices about the quality of blackness since Plato, and an example of black literary autonomy. It has also been read as a critique of the Harlem Renaissance for its failure to come up with a distinct Afro-American voice.

Reed's novels after *Mumbo Jumbo* are variations on the theme of a total license that is not as liberating as it would seem. In them the hold of Neo-HooDooism begins to fade, or sinks into their soil. The later novels resort more to riddles, and reduce the detective novel to a hasty cycle of situation and exposition. The targets narrow. *The Last Days of Louisiana Red* (1974) puts PaPa LaBas in Berkeley. He rescues a HooDoo business, the Solid Gumbo Works, which performs good deeds, offers its clients a cure for cancer, and almost finds a cure for heroin addiction. This time HooDoo doesn't do battle with white theocrats, but with bad HooDoo, Louisiana Red, as practiced by the Moochers.

This is a satire on the hustlers of Black Power politics, with rallies and veiled references to posters of Huey Newton in his chair. . . . The plot involves opportunists in North African exile, a preacher who because he can't preach uses $100,000 of audiovisual equipment, and Minnie the Moocher, a heroine oppressed by the exaltation of her followers. (pp. 22-3)

Reed also draws on *Antigone* for this novel, offering a timid sister, brothers who slay each other, and a chorus, or Chorus, an "uncharacterized character," a vaudevillian in white tails, like Cab Calloway, who complains that his role declined because Antigone talked too much. Instead of being one who would not yield to earthly authority, a woman who did not believe that a man's death belonged to the state, Antigone, to Reed, is a selfish girl who wanted to have things her way. "You wrong girl," Reed says in a poem, **"Antigone, This Is It,"** "you would gut a nursery to make the papers," which makes her sound more like Medea. Nevertheless, she represents to Reed implacable hostility toward men and misuse of a woman's powers. Minnie the Moocher, Antigone's comic reincarnation, and her followers, dupes of the handed-down, hammered-in philosophy of the inferiority of slaves, are accused of not being able to "stand negro men attempting to build something: if we were on the corner sipping Ripple, then you would love us." (p. 23)

In *Flight to Canada* (1976), Reed's takeoff on the antebellum South, black women are also prominent among the boogey persons who get theirs. A black mammy in velvet, loyal to the incestuous, necrophiliac master, claims that Jesus got tired of Harriet Beecher Stowe, who ripped off *Uncle Tom's Cabin* from the narrative of Josiah Henson, and therefore caused one of her sons to be wounded in the war and the other to get "drownded." The light-skinned overseer tells the master, "I armed the women slaves. They'll keep order. They'll dismember them niggers with horrifying detail." The fugitive hero, Raven Quickskill, has a beautiful Indian lover and when they enter a tavern two of the female slaves help begin to "let out their slave cackle, giving them signifying looks." No black matriarchy for Reed.

In a **"Self-Interview"** in *Shrovetide in Old New Orleans* (1978) Reed asks himself, "Why you so mean and hard?"

> A. Because I am an Afro-American male, the most exploited and feared class in this country. All of the gentlemen, all of the ones who tried to be nice, are in the cemetery or sitting on a stoop humiliated and degraded and waiting for someone to hand them a bar of soap or waiting for the law some woman has called on them.

This is as much a flashback to the Sixties when the black male was an envied species as it is a reminder of current statistics about the low life-expectancy of black men.

Reed can't resist excess, overstating his case even when he has a valid one, as in *Reckless Eyeballing* (1986), another whodunit busy with plot, about the historical distortions of

feminism. Whereas his quarrel in the books of the Seventies was with the Stalinesque rigidity of black aesthetic writers, he now takes on black women writers who have received attention, as if Alice Walker's finding the goddess within her were a distraction from his story of black men versus white men. . . .

The Terrible Twos (1982) and its sequel, his most recent novel, *The Terrible Threes,* are set in the not-so-distant future mostly to undress the Reagan years. The detective in both books, Nance Saturday, who gets lost in the thick plots, remains aloof from the madness of trying to make it in the new white world, and becomes celibate out of a fear of infection. Neo-HooDooism itself has been pushed offstage entirely by a sort of Gnostic sect of questionable sincerity.

Reed is aware of the shift in the country's attention during the Eighties. *The Terrible Twos* opens with the "Scrooge Christmas of 1980," when it feels good to be a white man again and whites aren't afraid to tell blacks they aren't interesting anymore. There are more pressing problems. Reed's campaign to mention everything that has gone wrong in America results in a narrative that is all over the place, as if he were trying to work in everything from crime against the environment to offenses against the homeless. Instead of suspense or satire one is confronted with an extended editorial rebuttal.

The Terrible Twos is a souped-up version of *A Christmas Carol.* The northern hemisphere isn't "as much fun as it used to be." Hitler's birthday has become a national holiday, but the White House is alarmed by the number of "surplus people," worries that the world will turn "brown and muddy and resound with bongo drums" and the "vital people" will be squeezed out. A conspiracy unfolds to nuke New York and Miami and blame the destruction on Nigeria. Meanwhile, oil companies control Christmas, the Supreme Court grants one store exclusive rights to Santa Claus, and the economy depends on every day being Christmas for the "vitals." The conspiracy is threatened by the followers of Saint Nicholas and his servant or rival in legend, Black Peter. Saint Nicholas converts the President, a former model, by taking him to hell where Truman is the most tormented. The President is declared incapacitated when he reveals the conspiracy.

America has worsened in the new novel, *The Terrible Threes.* The temperature has dropped, larceny fills every heart, mobs roam the cities in search of food, evangelists who believe Jews and blacks are the children of the devil control the government and hope to establish a Christian fundamentalist state. "Who needs the yellows, the browns, the reds, the blacks?" These people are "the wastes of history." Saint Nicholas and Black Peter, a figure similar to Reed's earlier renegade heroes, compete to enlighten and to help people, and nearly bring back an age of liberalism until Lucifer himself interferes. To top it off, extraterrestrials, contemptuous of human beings, have their own plans for earth.

In this latest novel Reed writes of a country that has lost its soul, but he, too, seems uncertain of direction. His picture of "Scroogelike" America, "kissing cousin" of South Africa, of yuppies for whom the buck is the bottom line, of black people marooned in drug neighborhoods, is extremely bleak. Even Black Peter is chastised, ambivalent, exhausted. The extraterrestrials come like an afterthought, as if Reed were making a last-ditch effort to deny power over the future to Neo-HooDoo's opponents. His work has always had a certain bitterness, but that was part of its fuel. Compared to his reconstruction of recent American history as a sequence of Terribles (the first one, Reed says, began on November 22, 1963), of genocidal policies and cover-ups, his previous novels seem almost utopian.

But the problem with his parodies of the obvious and the obscure, his allegorical burlesques, pastiches of the fantastic—the problem with this gumbo (his analogy) is that he can't move beyond their negations. Neo-HooDooism needs what Reed would call Anglo unfreedom the way Christianity needs Judas's lips or, as the movie says, the way the ax needs the turkey. Similarly, Reed may have declined to take on the old-fashioned subject of the Afro-American's double consciousness, but his fictions are as dualistic in their representations of the egalitarian versus the hierarchical, HooDoo versus the Cop Religion. They buzz with conspiracy theories that pretend to explain the world, with the determination to set the world straight about the hypocrisy of "patriotic history." "Jefferson Davis died with a smile on his face." Paranoia, Burroughs said, is just having the facts, but a few facts are not as dangerous as Reed would have us think.

Reed's subjects involve large cultural questions, but often the transplant from the headlines is the quickest of operations. His novels are entirely of their day, nostalgic in their defiance of "the Judeo-Christian domination of our affairs," and vividly recall the era when the lightness of blackness was a revelation, when blacks were the catalysts of social change. Neo-HooDooism gave Reed a way to work with this, to reimagine it. Back then, in the **"Neo-HooDoo Manifesto,"** Reed could describe it as the "Now Locomotive swinging up the Tracks of the American Soul."

The shift in the cultural climate, the loss of that moment, may help to explain why in the Terribles Reed's remarkable fluency has dried up. The supporting atmosphere is missing, without which his books are suddenly vulnerable. This fluency, this back talk, is what animates Reed's work, for Neo-HooDooism is not the sort of mysticism or system that provides a language of symbols or infuses imagery, it has no widening gyres, no junkie codes. It is Reed's language that carries his mission of exasperation—the old black faith in the power of the word. . . .

Whether Reed's fictions are arguments for the reenchantment of Afro-American literature, are unmaskings of Western culture by written formulation, or are self-congratulatory texts about HooDoo as an untainted supply of material does not change the fact that his literary separatism is doomed to obsolescence because Afro-American writing only comes to life as a junction of traditions. Reed questions not only the social reality presented in Afro-American literature, but also the narrative tradition itself. To do so, he takes shelter in the black oral tradition without realizing that it makes him no more free than contemporary white novelists. Reed often speaks of his hero as "scatting," or uses Charlie Parker as an example of the Neo-HooDoo artist, free of the rules, blowing, improvising, and this wish-fulfillment hero becomes a stand-

in for Reed himself, the black writer floating far above an alien tradition in which he doesn't feel at home. But perhaps there's no way back, for black writers, to an innocent folk state. The writers of the Harlem Renaissance inadvertently discovered that there is no literary equivalent to dance or music, and no reconciliation either.

Once it's written down, the oral tradition becomes literature, as Neil Schmitz pointed out, and the experience of the black man in the library intervenes with the experience of the black man in the street, in Reed as much as it does in any other black writers. Reed's Neo-HooDoo tales are not as tall as the ones blacks used to tell. Still there's much to say for his own tales: after all, not to make fun of racist absurdities is to be still afraid of them. (p. 24)

> *Darryl Pinckney, "Trickster Tales," in* The New York Review of Books, *Vol. XXXVI, No. 15, October 12, 1989, pp. 20, 22-4.*

FURTHER READING

Fox, Robert Elliot. "Ishmael Reed: Gathering the Limbs of Osiris." In his *Conscientious Sorcerers: The Black Postmodernist Fiction of Leroi Jones/Amiri Baraka, Ishmael Reed, and Samuel R. Delany,* pp. 39-92. Westport, Connecticut: Greenwood Press, 1987.

   Detailed analysis of Reed's novels within the context of African-American literature.

Harris, Norman. "The Gods Must Be Angry: *Flight to Canada* as Political History." *Modern Fiction Studies* 34, No. 1 (Spring 1988): 111-23.

   Examines the impact of narrative viewpoint and time on character development in Reed's novel, explaining how these factors underscore aspects of African-American political history.

Klinkowitz, Jerome. "Ishmael Reed's Multicultural Aesthetic." In his *Literary Subversions: New American Fiction and the Practice of Criticism,* pp. 18-33. Carbondale, Illinois: Southern Illinois University Press, 1985.

   Explicates Reed's literary aesthetic in his novel *The Terrible Twos* and his essay collection *God Made Alaska for the Indians.*

Martin, Reginald. *Ishmael Reed and the New Black Aesthetic Critics.* London: MacMillan Press, 1988, 120 p.

   Discusses Reed's role as a catalyst of the new black aesthetic movement that revolutionized African-American literature in the 1960s.

McConnell, Frank. "Ishmael Reed's Fiction: Da Hoodoo Is Put On America." In *Black Fiction: New Studies in the Afro-American Novel Since 1945,* edited by A. Robert Lee, pp. 136-48. New York: Barnes & Noble, 1980.

   Traces the influence of Reed's Neo-HooDoo aesthetic on his novels.

Willy Russell

1947-

English dramatist and scriptwriter.

Best known for his play *Educating Rita,* Russell often bases his works in Liverpool, a city in northern England commonly associated with rigid working-class attitudes, poverty, and unemployment. Russell's characters are often individualists who seek self-realization despite the opposition of both their fellow Liverpudlians and British society in general toward ambitious members of the working class. Although his comedies appeal to audiences of diverse occupations, Russell's emphasis on universal themes allows him to transcend strictly regional concerns and to address broad economic conflicts. Edward Pearce commented: "Russell, charting the liberalising enlightenment of books and places, while staying in touch with the upper end of popular entertainment . . . , is using a popular medium for a grave end. It is his genius to straddle two cultures and talk brilliant sense to both."

Born in the city of Whiston, near Liverpool, Russell completed an undistinguished secondary school education prior to becoming a hairdresser and holding several industrial jobs. After returning to full-time study at St. Catherine's College of Education, Russell became a teacher and began writing dramas. His first play, *Keep Your Eyes Down,* was produced at the Edinburgh Fringe Festival in 1972. There Russell met director John McGrath, who introduced him to members of Liverpool's Everyman Theatre. His first professional production for the group, *When the Reds . . . ,* attracted modest critical attention, while the commercial success of Russell's next drama, *John, Paul, George, Ringo, and Bert,* enabled him to quit teaching and to pursue a career as a dramatist. Drawing upon his memories as an adolescent fan of the Beatles in Liverpool, Russell chronicles the group's rise to international stardom and their accompanying achievements and failures.

Breezeblock Park, a domestic tragicomedy, concerns two couples who compete for material success and respectability. Conflicts ensue when the adolescent daughter of one family becomes pregnant and decides to live with her boyfriend. Although Russell was faulted for a presumed lack of empathy for his characters, Anthony Curtis commented: "Mr. Russell's knowledge of the atrocities committed in the name of family solidarity is as complete as his understanding of how to keep a comedy on the move." *One for the Road,* which is frequently compared to the light, farcical works of English dramatist Alan Ayckbourn, relates the story of a man who decides on the eve of his fortieth birthday to trade his harmonious but tedious marriage for a life on the road. *Stags and Hens,* set in a Liverpool dance hall, centers upon a wedding disrupted by the arrival of the bride-to-be's ex-boyfriend, a successful popular music singer who prompts her to choose between domesticity and personal freedom.

Russell achieved international success with his next play, *Educating Rita.* Featuring only two characters, this work is set in the office of an alcoholic professor and failed poet who is forced to face his own limitations after being confronted with the unorthodox but invigorating insights of a naive twenty-

six-year-old Liverpool hairdresser. Despite pressure from her husband to quit school and conceive a child, Rita pursues her education and asks the professor to tutor her in English. Rita is ultimately forced to divorce her husband and sacrifice her originality in favor of academic conformity. Compared by critics to George Bernard Shaw's *Pygmalion, Educating Rita* garnered wide acclaim for its complex, realistic, and intelligent insights into universal conflicts. According to Diana Devlin, *Educating Rita* "provides a satisfying contemporary debate on several ideas—youth and maturity, teaching and learning, aspiration and cynicism."

Blood Brothers, a popular musical for which Russell wrote both the book and music, offers a variation on the theme of twins separated at birth. In this work, one twin remains with his impoverished working-class mother while the other attains a comfortable middle-class existence. According to Russell, the play emerges as "an indictment, not of people, but of the class system that divides them." Russell's interest in feminist concerns is evidenced in *Shirley Valentine,* a domestic comedy written in the form of a monologue. This play concerns a middle-aged Liverpool housewife trapped in an unsatisfying marriage who decides to travel with a friend to Greece, where she has a brief affair and decides to remain. Stella Flint commented: "The unlikely, unexpected success of the one woman show [*Shirley Valentine*] lies in Russell's easy craftsmanship. Where *Educating Rita* follows a format, playing each character against its foil, now through a solo performance Russell stealthily catches Shirley's private musings and subjects them to her own caustic judgement."

PRINCIPAL WORKS

PLAYS

Keep Your Eyes Down   1972
When the Reds . . .   1973
Sam O'Shanker   1973
John, Paul, George, Ringo, and Bert   1974
Death of a Young, Young Man   1975
Breezeblock Park   1975
One for the Road   1976
Stags and Hens   1977
Educating Rita   1980
Blood Brothers   1983
Shirley Valentine   1986

OTHER

King of the Castle   1973   (television script)
Our Day Out   1977   (television script)
Educating Rita   1983   (screenplay)
Shirley Valentine   1989   (screenplay)

W. STEPHEN GILBERT

[Russell's play *Breezeblock Park*] aspires, I think, to be a tragi-comedy. But the terms of the comedy prevent the achievement of tragedy, leaving the comedy looking distinctly tawdry and churlish.

The play is set in two council houses on a Waite's-type estate, the second act house being the mirror image of the first act one. The families therein mirror each other too: the wives, Betty and Reeny, are sisters who vie for supremacy in matters of material success, taste and respectability. Significantly, the locations are described in the programme as 'Betty's House' and 'Reeny's House'. Reeny's husband Ted is much more of a player in this game than is Betty's husband Syd. Ted agonises over his car, imposes home jury duty on his Christmas guests when 'New Faces' is on the box. Syd is more careless—carless too—and rather an endearing slob. Each couple has a teenaged child: Reeny and Ted's son John is (almost) swallowed whole in the battle to create a patina of some received idea of an ideal family life. But Betty and Syd's daughter Sandra is girding up to shatter the mould—and the mirror—by breaking out and going to live with the student by whom she is pregnant.

The putative tragic figure in this scheme is Betty, torn between the mores of her sister and the rejection of those mores, covertly by Syd, overtly and more dramatically by Sandra. As a scheme, this could well have worked. Obviously, the crushing of the spirit by the gruesome values instilled in the lower middle class is a sorry and a potentially inflammatory spectacle. The point at which Betty sees that Sandra is making the escape that she, Betty, was never brave enough to attempt could be a really heart-rending moment.

It's not [the actress's] fault that it isn't like that. . . . Russell helps not at all. When he has Betty's wiseacre brother present her with a vibrator and then pass it off as a drinks-mixer, he's indulging a destructive gag at the expense of the character—there's no way Betty's ignorance can be made to look anything but foolish.

Indeed, this clear contempt for the characters ruins Russell's chances of moving us. It's a dangerous ploy to have Ted wax pompous on theatre on the strength of a visit to *Waiting for Godot*. By definition, Russell's audience is alienated from Ted—*he* doesn't go to the theatre; *we* do and we know (or at least Russell assumes we do) about Beckett. The author relies on these put-downs to flatter the audience but in so doing he makes it impossible to be involved in the characters' lives.

Structurally, the play could do with some re-thinking. Betty's initial humiliation comes all in a rush at the end of a first act which has taken a great deal of time to become even mildly diverting. The second act follows the pattern of the first, taking us once more over the battlefield of keeping up with the relatives before again humiliating Betty in a rapid and climactic series of events. Part of the humiliation is the revelation that Betty and Syd 'had to' get married, something which Reeny, with her highly developed taste for *schadenfreude*, would surely have figured out at the time.

W. Stephen Gilbert, in a review of "Breezeblock Park," in Plays and Players, *Vol. 25, No. 2, November, 1977, p. 27.*

ANTHONY CURTIS

There is quite a lot of belly-laughter generated . . . in Willy Russell's *Breezeblock Park,* . . . but the author is also clearly making some social observations about the way working people live. . . . Mr. Russell places the new rich of the council estate under his microscope and he observes them threshing about trying to keep up with their inlaws and wrecking their children's lives in the process. It is a situation as old as the hills that had to be bull-dozed before this particular housing-estate could be built but none the worse theatrically for that. Mr. Russell's knowledge of the atrocities committed in the name of family solidarity is as complete as his understanding of how to keep a comedy on the move, though I could have done without the jokes about the vibrator. His best invention is his double setting; the interior of one sister's livingroom subtly mirroring the other's in which everything is the same but more expensive. (pp. 55-6)

Anthony Curtis, in a review of "Breezeblock Park," in Drama, London, *Winter, 1977-78, pp. 55-6.*

SIMON HOWARD

[The protagonist of *Educating Rita* is a woman] who learnt nothing at school and claims to remember only 'broken glass, torn books, knives and fights. And that was just in the staff room.'

Now a 26-year-old hairdresser, Willy Russell's heroine is determined to give it another try—to break away from a world where people don't want you to change, where every night is spent, drearily, in the pub. The middle classes would be heartbroken to hear her dismiss local working class culture as people being 'pissed or on valium'.

Rita has enlisted on an Open University Literature course and the first of the play's several short scenes brings her before her tutor, Frank. Not a promising start, since he's only doing it to pay for his drinking and anyway complains that the course interferes with pub hours.

In his office, where an empty, fallen bottle lurks behind every book, starts the education of Rita, whose name has been taken from Rita Mae Brown, author of her number one literary enjoyment, *Ruby Fruit Jungle*.

'There's less to me than meets the eye,' insists Frank. Which isn't entirely true, because he fails to promise much in the first place. But more of that later. He is a one-time author of poems devoted exclusively to his wife who rather obligingly left him so that he might stretch his literary range. Needless to say, he has since abandoned writing.

However, Frank is quite able to appreciate Rita's freshness of approach and realises it will be useless for exam purposes, so he tries to dissuade her from doing the course. But she insists, and is soon bracketing E M Forster with Harold Robbins. (In the post-Blunt era, she's probably not the only one.) An essay question on how to stage *Peer Gynt* is sensibly dealt with: 'Do it on the radio.'

Of course, the more she attends, the more furious her husband becomes and he takes to burning her Chekhov. He wants her to abandon the course and come off the pill. But the course has come to represent life itself, so she abandons him.

Frank becomes increasingly affected by her visits, cuts down on the drink and precipitates a sort of crisis when he asks her to a dinner party which she fails to attend. Rita is not going to be a court jester to his friends, she tells him. . . .

Her first visit to the theatre produces a wonderfully emotional essay that would be quite worthless in an exam. She realises that to go on she will have to be changed.

Time and a summer school in London produce from her trendy essays on Blake and an understanding of the classical allusions in Frank's old poems. At last she speaks to the full-time students. Frank, however, has returned to the bottle and has even delivered in lecture form the views on literature that Rita had brought on the first day: 'Assonance means getting the rhyme wrong', for example.

She has transformed, but Frank likens her story to *Frankenstein*, not *Pygmalion*. She responds by accusing him of wanting to 'keep the natives thick'. The whole scheme may be worthless in the end, but she has at least made the choice about her education, and that is the crux of the thing. To her husband, choice meant picking one of eight kinds of lager or deciding between Everton and Liverpool. (p. 19)

As with all of Willy Russell's work, there is an extraordinary imbalance in the quality of the writing. Character often makes way for an idea but, more dangerously, an idea sometimes makes way for an unnecessary quip. One often feels he fails to pay as much attention to his actual writing as to his thinking.

Nevertheless, the thought is important, as are his anger, sense of outrage and compassion. *Educating Rita* is undeniably flawed, but one certainly welcomes its having been written. (p. 20)

Simon Howard, in a review of "Educating Rita," in Plays and Players, *Vol. 27, No. 9, June, 1980, pp. 19-20.*

ROWENA GOLDMAN

[*Educating Rita*] centres upon the passionate desire of a young Northern girl to attain a proper education in order to equip her for the higher echelons of a life to which she so longingly aspires. Her transformation from a culturally naive modern girl to a successful student is at once subtle and striking in Willy Russell's sharp and witty dialogue. . . . From her first entrance into the study of her prospective tutor, who is to treat her to the delights of an Open University course, she rings true. She wanders wide-eyed around the study, touching the books and announcing that she wants an education, "a better culture". For Frank, the well-worn, quotation-battered intellectual, she is a refreshing change from the pretentious and take-it-or-leave-it attitude of the students he has been used to.

Rita works as a hairdresser and, in her mid-twenties, figures that there is more to life than 'creme' rinses and perms that go wrong. She wants to digest Chekhov and Shakespeare, Forster and Ibsen and she wants to pass exams. Frank's prime objective is to draw her away from the trashy paperbacks on which she has been reared and to teach her to appreciate and dissect the qualities of great literature. . . . Besides coming to grips with the slow learning process, Rita has problems with her husband, whom she tries to convince that an individual has a right to choose. "He thinks we've got choice because he can go into a pub and choose between eight different lagers", and she ends up with, inevitably, a broken marriage but, eventually, an education. Frank, however, does not see this new-found knowledge as a change for the better and in the end there exists between them a relationship not dissimilar to the psychiatrist/patient relationship in *Equus*. He has cured Rita of her so-called ignorance but her passionate innocence has gone. He is left wondering where he will ever find such honesty again and we are left wondering whether Rita, now fully equipped for a better life crammed with opportunities, will find greater happiness. (pp. 54-5)

Rowena Goldman, in a review of "Educating Rita," in Drama, *London, October, 1980, pp. 54-5.*

CLARE COLVIN

"As the leading characters are shot dead by the end of the evening, you could say this is very serious stuff for a musical—one down from "Springtime for Hitler." But it has been a popular event in Liverpool—there was quite a black market for final-night tickets." . . .

[Russell's *Blood Brothers*] continues the two-nations theme explored in *Educating Rita,* but its plot could have come from a folk ballad. It is the old classic of twin brothers separated through circumstances. One remains with his natural mother in an impoverished working-class family. The other is taken as a baby into a well-off, middle-class home and the secret of his birth is kept from him. The tragedy springs from their being unaware of each other's existence.

"The musical is very much in ballad form, and it is rife with superstition, which is crucial to the plot", says Russell. "It is an indictment, not of people, but of the class system that divides them."

He has written the music as well and considers it is easier to describe what it is not—"It is not pop music, it is not opera, it is not what I call American theatre music. I call it melodic, hopefully." He is now 35; his first major success, in 1974, was on a musical theme—*John, Paul, George, Ringo and Bert*—which drew on his experience as a 14-year-old fan of the Beatles in their heyday in the Cavern. . . .

Russell's early hit enabled him to give up his job as a teacher, partly, he says because it became embarrassing to receive his school salary when he considered what he was earning in the West End. Since then he has devoted himself to writing plays, but remains firmly rooted in Liverpool. He has just given up his post as Associate Director at the Liverpool Playhouse. . . .

To most outsiders, Liverpool means unemployment and riots, and it angers Russell that such a vital city should be left to decay. How has unemployment affected theatre, which, after all, relies on people having surplus cash for a night out? It made the auditorium emptier, Russell says, and people are reluctant to try anything that they do not know in advance they will like. . . .

Had Russell been born 15 years or so later, he might have been one of today's unemployment statistics. He grew up in a working-class family on a housing estate outside Liverpool—"a strange little island of Scouses in the middle of beautiful countryside"—and later moved to Kirby, then back to Liverpool. He left school at 15 with no O-levels and an unformed desire to be a writer, but no idea how someone with his background did so. After drifting through a succession of unskilled jobs, he decided, at the age of 20, to become a teacher and finally took his O-levels and A-levels. . . .

His entry into playwriting was relatively effortless. A half-hour play he had written for the drama department of his teachers' training college was teamed with two others he wrote to make up a triple bill which went to the Edinburgh Festival, where it was spotted by John McGrath. Russell was asked to write a play for the Liverpool Everyman. So came *John, Paul, George, Ringo and Bert,* which transferred from there to open in the West End a week before his twenty-seventh birthday. There followed other plays, *Breezeblock Park, One for the Road, Stags and Hens,* and then a modest two-hander, [*Educating Rita*]. . . .

"It just seems to have struck a chord. It connects with something people are interested in at the present time, especially women trying to find themselves, although it does not take a feminist line. It is much more about a teacher and learner relationship. Open University tutors tell me it is absolutely accurate—in a marriage, taking on the educative process is almost as threatening as having an affair. The human being changes for a while until she can synthesize what she is becoming with what she was."

When Columbia bought the film rights, Russell was "tempted to take the money and run", rather than get involved in the filming. But Columbia dithered, then Lewis Gilbert, the producer and director, came on to the scene and eventually they got the rights back and raised the money in Britain. Russell is glad now that they kept it British. The play, as was proved in the United States stage version, cannot be Americanized. Even if you give Rita a Bronx accent, there is no equivalent class system.

Clare Colvin, "Merseyside Comes to London Again," in The Times, *London, April 9, 1983, p. 10.*

TIMOTHY CHARLES

[Russell], along with a handful of other writers including Alan Bleasdale, has ensured that Liverpool has become known for its playwrights in the same way that the city was associated with music and its famous beat groups in the sixties.

Russell's plays are full of the 'Language of Liverpool'. His sharp ear for demotic speech can be seen in the rich humour that permeates his work. But he would probably shudder at being dubbed 'a Liverpool playwright', in the sense that his plays belong to that environment. Geographically he is associated with the city, because his roots are there, and because it is where his plays are first presented. But this doesn't restrict the validity of his plays when they are performed outside the city.

His plays have scrutinized the social structure and the living conditions of society. With two exceptions he has concentrated on the working class experience, his treatment of which is too universal to be considered parochial. The family in *Breezeblock Park* were economically superior working class; and in *One For The Road* he focused upon the first generation middle classes, trying to erase their former status. Significantly, though they may have moved up the social scale, they weren't appreciably content with their newfound situation.

Liverpool still has an inspirational hold on him. Despite dreaming of escape, like Dennis in *One For The Road,* he never quite succeeds. He explained the tight grip that the city had on him in an article which appeared in the *Times Literary Supplement* in 1978. "Liverpool is filthy dirty, depressed; there is the most uncomfortable pain about the place, but it is important to me. I feel secure here."

The thought of living in London makes him nervous. A fear of being absorbed into the middle classes, and that he wouldn't be able to function in a classless way (as he does in Liverpool), makes him keep his distance.

Stylistically *Blood Brothers* couldn't be more different from Russell's last play, *Educating Rita.* He has written the music for the new play. His only previous experience of songwriting was when he wrote and performed songs on the thriving folk circuit in the sixties. Reverting to that talent has meant that his career has come full circle.

Willy Russell was born in 1947 at Whiston near Liverpool. There was a strong tradition of storytelling in his family, who were 'thinking' working class. His school career in the 'D Stream' was undistinguished. At fifteen he left with one 'O' Level, in English Language, with little idea of what he wanted to do beyond a vague notion of wanting to become a writer. (p. 20)

It was whilst at St. Catherine's College of Education that he decided to become a dramatist. His first play, *Keep Your Eyes Down,* was taken by the college drama group to the Edinburgh Fringe in 1972. There it was seen by John McGrath who put Russell in touch with the Everyman [Theatre]. The following year, [Russell's adaptation of Alan Pater's novel *When the Tigers Are Coming O. K.,* titled] *When The Reds . . .* led to his writing a play for the Everyman's Touring Company, *Sam O'Shanker.* 1973 also saw his first play for BBC TV, *King of the Castle,* set in a factory.

His 'major break' came with his next play, *John, Paul, George, Ringo & Bert.* It was an accurate and honest account of the group's rise and fall, culminating in an abortive attempt to stage a reunion concert, and its success enabled him to give up teaching and concentrate on writing full-time. The show was notable for the ironic juxtaposition of songs against dialogue, and the sparkling Liverpool humour that has since become his trademark. The use of a narrator was a technique that was to reappear in his next stage play, *Death of a Young, Young Man* (1975), and again in *Blood Brothers.*

That same year, *Breezeblock Park* was produced. . . . A tragi-comedy, it dealt with the intense rivalry of two sisters, Betty and Reeny, and their barely concealed jealousies. Betty is at the centre of the play, torn between the consumer pride of her sister, and the rejection of those values by Sandra, her daughter.

There's a poignant moment when Betty sees that Sandra is making the escape that she was never brave enough to attempt. Sandra is the only person who attempts to break out of the social conditioning of her family. She announces she is pregnant by a student, Tim, with whom she intends to live. She strives to sample the cultural lifestyle that he embodies, yearning for the self-improvement that the family unit has denied her. Sandra can be seen as an embryonic 'Rita' in Russell's development.

Our Day Out (1977), his most successful television play, was drawn from his own experiences as a remedial teacher. The play follows a progress class on a day's outing to Wales. There is conflict between the contrasting attitudes of two teachers, Briggs and Mrs Kay, towards children for whom education in the academic sense of the word has become pointless. Mrs Kay treats the children with compassion, but Briggs, used to disciplining the academic streams, forgets the misery of the children's backgrounds, and denies them any enjoyment. His attitude is changed momentarily by Carol, who is so depressed by the thought of returning to Liverpool that she threatens suicide.

The play exposes the kind of middle-class hypocrisy that tries to impose dominant culture on unwilling kids, in the knowledge that if they don't fill the factories of England, no-one else will. It debunks the myth that working-class kids would still choose to stand on an assembly line, even if they had the freedom to choose not to. There is a bitter sense of injustice closely related to a concept of self-improvement running through this, and his next three stage plays.

Stags & Hens (1978) concerns a group of working-class people now grown up. Dave's mates meet at the same nightclub as Linda's, his bride-to-be. They are shown a better lifestyle in the person of Pete, the band's guitarist who is regarded as a hero having left the neighbourhood to seek fame and fortune. Carol attempts to escape to a better kind of life when she decides to run off with him. But she is thwarted by gang unity, which proves as inflexible as family unity. Thus she is prevented from escaping a culture that 'Rita' describes as being 'either pissed or on valium.'

The theme was developed in *Educating Rita* (1980), Russell's finest and most autobiographical play. Rita has escaped from the culture depicted in *Stags & Hens,* having endured the same type of schooling as the kids in *Our Day Out.* She

thirsts for knowledge and a 'better culture' that it will bring, in search of the freedom to choose how to live her life. Her transformation into an intelligent, mature student, is parallelled by Frank's decline into alcoholism. He represents the decadent middle-classes, and Rita is an example of the thriving working-classes and what they are capable of achieving, given the self-will to break away from their environment.

In this respect Russell has strong views on the working-classes' attempts to gain access to middle-class culture.

> Whilst the working-classes are accused of being philistines, there is a general attempt in this country to withhold culture from them . . . Literature is an invention by the middle-classes for their own benefit. The working-classes haven't accepted literacy yet, which is why it is so difficult teaching working-class kids whose traditions are in the spoken word. That's why I write for the theatre, because it's concerned with the spoken rather than the written word.

Blood Brothers encapsulates the themes running through the three previous plays, and it sums up the author's feelings on the subject. It examines the contrasting fortunes of boys separated at birth. One twin is given away by his working-class mother to a middle-class woman for whom she cleans. The middle-class twin, every opportunity bestowed upon him, goes from success to success. His working-class brother drifts from local comprehensive to depressing job, to the dole queue, and finally to a life of crime.

This is Willy Russell's most overtly political play. But politics never overshadow the theatricality of the modern fable. When I interviewed him, last November, he explained why he avoided making a propagandist stagement in his plays.

> I feel that lecturing an audience isolates them . . . Overstated politics and theatre do not mix. I try to achieve a synthesis of the two. But I would write a play devoid of politics if it were pungent theatre, in which case it would be implicitly political. My ideas are socialist in the broadest sense of the word.

There is a compassionate core in Russell's work that can best be seen in his endearing and sympathetic presentation of life's losers, all of who have an epic sense of their own importance. Through his writing it is possible to feel a sense of his characters' aspirations and their failed and foiled dreams. However, unlike the characters he creates, Willy Russell doesn't have an epic sense of his own importance. What sustains and characterises his best work is a raging, bitter sense of injustice. (pp. 20-1)

Timothy Charles, "Willy Russell—The First Ten Years," in Drama, *London, No. 148, Summer, 1983, pp. 20-1.*

TOM LUBBOCK

Stags and Hens is not a new play—1977 originally—but it's now receiving its London premiere, which I think it's safe to say, implying nothing, it would not have received, had it not been for the irrepressible subsequent success of *Educating Rita.*

The scene is laid in the toilets of a down market Liverpool dance hall. . . . On the eve of the wedding, complementary stag and hen parties arrive, by chance, at the same venue, 'with predictably hilarious consequences', and others. The device of the loos is quite a nice one, and neatly used. First act—mores observation: the ladies, regular little wives of Bath; the gents, cocksure/unsure peer-groupies; (they're 'characterised' of course, but that needn't detain us), and with enough illusions between them to promise pathos or enlightenment before bedtime. But to complicate matters: local boy—and bride-to-be's ex—made good, ie pop singer, turns up to play a gig, and set a question mark over their lives. The issue of Act Two becomes Liverpool, whether it's worth living there, and whether in particular the bride should chuck in her 'limiting' friends and stupefied fiancé, and take off with the band for London.

As a 'Liverpool play', on in London, one tends to watch it as it were vicariously. If the dramatic situation is not intrinsically all that interesting, one imagines it holding a particular interest for a Liverpool audience—the spectacle of the play comes to include the spectacle of its own, its proper, audience. "I dare say it meant more up there." To suspend one's judgement upon someone else's response is an awkward position—only a remove from the doubtful benevolence of the parent at the pantomime: "Well, at least *they* enjoyed it."— but odder, because the response deferred to is imaginary. The conclusion of the play, where by the bride does leave town, and before her fiancé recovers consciousness, seemed inconclusive. Within the play it was well (perhaps too well) motivated—she'd just been hit by the most intolerant of his friends, and her friends had simply stood by—but as a general statement? How was it supposed to go down in Liverpool? How did it go down? Ought it to have done? Who is to say? Instead of inventing someone else's opinion, why not invent your own. Or resign yourself (as the play reasonably but not quite satisfactorily does) to not quite knowing what to think. I'm sorry not to mention the players but it's just one of those not so rare plays in which the role of the audience is the most challenging. (p. 32)

> *Tom Lubbock, in a review of "Stags and Hens," in*
> Plays and Players, *No. 371, August, 1984, pp. 31-2.*

STELLA FLINT

Russell's new play [*Shirley Valentine*] is once again based on his conviction that inside everyone is a freedom loving spirit searching for a way out. Shirley, working-class with at least one foot on the middle-class ladder, (and the piece is emphatically not concerned with the difference), is, at 43, stranded in marriage, trammelled by not quite adult children. Attractive, especially when in animated converse with the walls of her fitted kitchen, she may have lost sight of her own identity, she has not lost her tongue and her ability to observe and comment. Her mimicry makes neighbours and family instantly recognisable.

At first as Shirley cooks egg and chips, the steak having, in a rebellious moment widened the horizon of a vegetarian dog, she speculates on her husband's reaction. The material is the stuff of women's magazines and club comedy. It continues so throughout: sentimental, romantic, improbable, even as Russell extrapolates an adventure, an encounter, a change far better than a rest. A sun-drenched Mediterranean beach witnesses the resurgence of Miss Shirley Valentine. Being more practical than the romantic poets, Shirley has more sense than to drown.

The unlikely, unexpected success of the one woman show lies in Russell's easy craftsmanship. Where *Educating Rita* follows a format, playing each character against its foil, now through a solo performance Russell stealthily catches Shirley's private musings and subjects them to her own caustic judgement. No-one is exempt, not even Shirley. No topic is raised but it is neatly rounded and dismissed, only to return in a new guise, another aspect, cleverly woven into the character's self discovery. The technique is disarmingly accomplished. Even the plot, a very simple little plot that others might have been tempted to expand, refuses to be strictly linear. No longer are we imprisoned in a time sequence, the mind ranges at liberty. . . .

Shirley belongs anywhere. Dario Fo's women would enjoy raising her political consciousness; Ibsen's Nora ought to have a long chat with her. She must at once mature and grow younger. Her holiday romance is without the starry-eyed gullibility which would threaten a fresh entanglement and risk renewed entrapment. The crisis is low key, humorous. Taking off the amiable Kostos, skilled in the sexual enlightenment of lonely ladies from chillier climes, Shirley persuades us that she has fallen for his spurious charms. Then 'Men, they're all full of shit', the ribald chuckle we have come to expect and Shirley, in bikini, cut-off jeans and a suntan is ready for husband and grown-up children to arrive and challenge her new life. She turns back for a job and liberty not a lover, declaring war on the loneliness and frustration, the waste of all the life that could have been, waste that weighs you down with a fatal presence.

> *Stella Flint, in a review of "Shirley Valentine," in*
> Plays and Players, *No. 391, April, 1986, p. 36.*

MEL GUSSOW

Educating Rita is a *Pygmalion* play with a slight *Equus* twist. A teacher educates—and elevates—a vulgar, waif-like student and, to his dismay, the student sheds her distinctive coloration and eagerly embraces conformity. This is, of course, taking *Educating Rita* too seriously. At its heart, the Willy Russell two-hander is a comedy about an odd couple who have nothing in common except for the fact that they are the only characters on stage. . . .

The play is filled with artificial banter, most of it deriving from the disparity between the characters. When the teacher refers to Eliot, he means T. S., whereas the pupil thinks first of Eliot Ness. Asked to write an essay on the staging difficulties of *Peer Gynt,* she writes, succinctly, "Do it on the radio." By the end of the play, of course, she has been indoctrinated in the ways of literary pretension and has demolished a fellow student who had the effrontery to suggest that *Lady Chatterley's Lover* was a better novel than *Sons and Lovers.*

Many of Mr. Russell's lines are still amusing. At the same time, the situation is contrived. The play seems rooted in the 1970's. . . . With its references to such people as Lawrence Ferlinghetti and Farrah Fawcett before she dropped the Majors, the "present" seems more than a decade at a remove. Today an uneducated Rita might bypass the open university system and start out as a fashion trendsetter. One thing has come full cycle: Rita's short skirts are back in vogue.

> *Mel Gussow, " 'Educating Rita,' with Laurie Metcalf," in* The New York Times, *May 8, 1987.*

EDITH OLIVER

[*Educating Rita* is set in a] professor's messy, bookish study in a university in the North of England. Rita . . . is a local hairdresser of twenty-six—tough, brazen, broad of speech and sharp of mind—who, having decided that she must change her circumstances and her life and start learning, comes to him for lessons. They are the only characters aboard. The action is a matter of brief scenes as we track her progress. Frank, a failed poet and disillusioned drunk, takes a quite romantic view of himself and of Eng. Lit. in general. At first, he is taken aback, not to say shocked, at her bald replies to his questions and her responses to the books he assigns her (her remarks are often very funny), but soon he comes to relish them. As time passes, he takes more and more delight in her—in her brain, that is—and as she changes before our eyes in dress and deportment, so does he. He pulls himself together; there are fewer nips at the bottle of Scotch that is always within reach, and less self-pity and cynicism about his career. When we leave them, he is about to embark for Australia and she, taking several steps back—she has long ago given up her job in the beauty shop—is about to give him a super haircut. There is no question of physical attraction between them, but he does ask her if she'd like to come along.

As presented, *Educating Rita* is very much the professor's play, although Miss Metcalf is believable as Rita, and amusing and attractive. The lines are witty and telling. . . . My single quibble is that the play goes on too long; when it was over, I couldn't believe that I'd spent only two and a quarter hours in the theatre. (p. 87)

> Edith Oliver, "Homework," in The New Yorker, *Vol. LXIII, No. 13, May 18, 1987, pp. 87-8.*

JIM MILEY

Willy Russell's *One for the Road* provides a West End showcase that's as felicitous as it is unapologetic. . . . [The play concerns] a Northern couple nearing mid-life crisis and possessed with upward mobility. During an archetypically disastrous dinner party—attended by their even more pretentious pals—Dennis is revealed as the mysterious vandal who's been decapitating everyone's garden gnomes and slipping bath foam into ornamental ponds. From his younger days, he nurtures a fantasy of hippie escape. Puzzlingly, he settles instead for wife-swapping, but only after an evening of manic delinquency.

At times, the play manages to be hopelessly nostalgic, and even xenophobic. What's more, in the character of Dennis, Russell keeps blurring the line between thinking rebel and overgrown schoolboy. But he pokes dazzlingly-observed fun at the Privatisation Generation, with excellent running gags about cordless telephones, Dennis's non-appearing parents, and—mercilessly—John Denver. (pp. 38-9)

> Jim Miley, "Chocks Away," in The Listener, *Vol. 118, No. 3035, October 29, 1987, pp. 38-9.*

JACK TINKER

There are several niggling reservations lurking in the back of my mind about Willy Russell's [*One for the Road,* a] blast-off at middle-class smugness and middle-age compromise.

But two factors ride roughshod over any lingering inhibi-

tions. Two forces demolish the last shreds of shame I might feel sniggering at other people's lifestyles (bad taste, after all, is only what you find on other people's walls).

First must be Mr. Russell's brave grasp of one of life's eternal truths: That the only things you end up regretting are the ones you didn't do.

His hero is about to celebrate his 40th birthday. A child of the sixties with only his Joni Mitchell records to remind him of his lost horizons, he has dwindled into a man with responsibilities—'a mortgage and a British Gas shareholder'.

The action revolves around his disastrous birthday party given by his wife for their best friends.

We are, as you can see, deep in Ayckbourn country. But Willy Russell has no time for subtleties. He makes his contempt obvious by full-blooded caricature.

> Jack Tinker, in a review of "One for the Road," in Daily Mail, *October 22, 1987. Reprinted in* London Theatre Record, *Vol. VII, No. 21, October 8-21, 1987, p. 1348.*

SUE JAMESON

Amid the debris of ordered suburbia, Willy Russell has set his play [*One for the Road*]. The outward veneer in the kitchen, the tinted glass concealing the staircase, the four-in-a-set pictures of boats and seascapes, and most importantly the cordless telephone no one can find when it rings. Beneath the collection of the niceties adorning one of the Dormer bungalows on the "Phase Two" estate, there are, of course problems. Afterall, no problems, no play. The bungalow is home to Dennis and Pauline, married long enough not to have to scratch the seven year itch anymore. . . .

The play is set on the eve of Dennis's 40th birthday (Russell actual wrote it as he neared his 30th!). Jane and Roger are coming for dinner. . . . A John Denver album is the final straw and renews all Dennis's secret longings for the open road and escape from the other racing rodents. . . . If only he could get to the M4! Now all this sounds promising, . . . but it is patchy. It's hard to put this play in the same stable as *Educating Rita* or *Blood Brothers.* This is at best just another farce with few distinguishing marks. The marks, as it happens, are pretty good when they do appear and the gusts of comedy flicker the flames, but for much of the time, the effort is more obvious than the effect.

I can see that Willy Russell has also tried hard to update the play ten years with lines like "Dennis, you're a mortgagee, you're a father, you're a British Gas Shareholder" and with references to Terry Wogan (come to think of it they were probably in the original!) but the piece is still disjointed. The stereotyping is a little heavy handed though not necessarily in the script. . . . They're exactly the sort of characters (and maybe even the sort of situation) that Ayckbourn would write about though he would have made far more of the real urge Dennis has to change his life. It needs that contrast.

> Sue Jameson, in a review of "One for the Road," in London Broadcasting, *October 22, 1987. Reprinted in* London Theatre Record, *Vol. VII, No. 21, October 8-21, 1987, p. 1349.*

EDWARD PEARCE

The ideas of the Liverpool playwright Willy Russell are calculated to win the scorn of Marxists and Right-wing fogies alike. In *Educating Rita* he showed working-class life as a boring ritual of pints and procreation. The escape from it for a bright girl comes from a yearning for books. The wife of a dull, unknowing lump finds Keats and Blake and her release. Such an approach would be regarded on the hortatory Left as unsound, escapist, and sentimental, while the fogies would probably say, "How sweet of her", and snigger.

Russell's outlook *is* sentimental in that it craves happiness for the protagonists, but in fact he looks at the same problem which initially preoccupied Raymond Williams, who died at the end of January. Working-class culture has come to nothing. It is at the lethargic, passive end of distribution, a devitalised body fed intravenously. What is the way out? (p. 76)

Willy Russell, first in *Rita* and now in *Shirley Valentine*, . . . speaks plainly for the gifted working-class individualist. . . . Shirley Bradshaw prepares egg-and-chips every night of the week for the tea of her husband, excepting only Thursdays when she prepares mince-and-chips. However, the routine has been fractured by a Vegan bloodhound to whom in a moment of scatty inspiration—on the principle that a bloodhound should taste meat at least once in its life—Shirley has fed half a pound of mince! Joe does the correct thing expected of his sex and class status, saying "What's this, woman?" before sweeping the affront to the social decencies clean off the table and going out for a Chinese takeaway. Up till now Shirley has spent her time quietly, in rational conversation with the wall. ("I like a glass of wine when I'm making his tea, don't I, wall?" is a line for the anthologies.) The protocols of the *Almanach de Gotha* shattered, her release becomes possible.

Shirley trawls her life so far. She talks hilariously about sex—dismal with thudding Joe. She rather likes the idea of "Clitoris" as a girl's name. "Why not? There's enough fellers around called Dick."

This is Shirley's way—bright and sardonic, not truly beaten down yet, despite the hermetic and oppressive ways of working-class life. But first-class music-hall wit is matched with melancholy introspection. Here and now she is Mrs Bradshaw, a no-account, immured mum, children grown up, life completed, as she contemplates her stretch marks and considers that at 42 she has hardly inhaled life at all. The prospects are of Merseyside in perpetuity, acceptance, duty, and talking to the wall. Before she was married, she had another name—the Shirley Valentine of the title—and everything had seemed possible. She remembers a question from a teacher at school—"What is the most important invention of all?" Shirley had known the answer, the wheel; her teacher had first ignored her ("No, Shirley, of course you couldn't know"), but after running through the class without success, condescendingly let her answer. She had been not pleased but appalled that Shirley should know.

The episode symbolises the entire Willy Russell outlook. It is broadly unpolitical; it involves kinship with the working class, and a deadly grasp of its limitations, together with a certainty that enlightenment and liberation are possible. In this he goes against current educational practice, which suffers hideously from many teachers' resentments and inadequacies, overlaid by the illiterating cant of much educational theory. Russell thinks that the best is good enough for anyone with a spark of talent, and rejoices when they find it.

The best for Shirley is to take the chance, offered by a slightly condescending friend, of a holiday in Greece. There is no point in talking about it to Joe ("He gets culture shock if we go to Chester"). We are left dangling at the interval; but when the curtain rises on a rock in Corfu, the audience burst into spontaneous applause. There is, of course, more gentle derision of the British abroad, fearful of foreign muck on their plates, crassly and uncomprehendingly rude to the locals (to a Greek waiter: "Hey you—Zorba. Come 'ere"). . . . When the time comes for luggage to go through the checks at the airport, she doubles back, passing the waiter with whom she has had a cool-headed, humorous fling. As he repeats his seduction formula to another tripper, Shirley tells him: "Carry on. It's not you I can't do without, but can I have a job at the taverna?" The possibility is wryly entertained that she may find herself cooking egg-and-chips for relays of Douggies and Jeanettes, but instead of talking to a wall in Kirby she will be talking to the Aegean. She is happy; she has rearranged the world on her own terms; and Joe, corresponding like an outraged reader of the *Daily Telegraph,* can accept or not.

Russell is an optimist preoccupied with a centrally important cultural problem. The failure of education to affect British working-class people and to alter what Ernest Bevin called "the terrible proverty of their expectations" is a permanent reproach to this country. We have universal education and a school-leaving age of 16, and we have joined the European Community, but it hardly shows. Narrowness, little-mindedness; the inability to be made interested, to light up with pleasure at the new and the beautiful, are all too evident. They are witnessed in the British habit—it might be termed "egg and chips with everywhere"—of taking "home" with them when they go abroad.

Yet Russell also runs the perpetual risk of being patronised by that audience for whom Skiathos and John Donne are a birthright. A clever, witty, unprivileged Liverpudlian, he still sees good things with pleasure and without a little shrug. The possibility exists that commentators who have had life easier will weary of his unsmart state of pleased surprise and smile him down. That would be one more affront. Russell, charting the liberalising enlightenment of books and places, while staying in touch with the upper end of popular entertainment (some of his lines remind me of the comedian Victoria Wood), is using a popular medium for a grave end. It is his genius to straddle two cultures and talk brilliant sense to both. (pp. 76-7)

Edward Pearce, "Grave Ends," in Encounter, *Vol. LXXX, No. 4, April, 1988, pp. 76-7.*

CLIVE BARNES

Russell, a Liverpudlian playwright, clearly believes that good things can come in small parcels. After his big stage hit . . . *Educating Rita,* he seems to have decided that that a two-character play represented a needless extravagance in cast costs.

[Russell recently] revealed his plan to double the cast efficiency by a 50 percent reduction in cast numbers—this new play [*Shirley Valentine*] positively exults in its huge cast of one!

Yet, like *Educating Rita* before it, this one-character new-comer is very definitely a play, and, in no real way, simply a one-woman show. It is a first-person play, a dramatic essay in fictional autobiography.

Shirley is a 42-year-old Liverpool housewife—moderately prosperous, immoderately bored. The kids have grown up and, more or less, flown the coop.

Shirley sits most of the day in her kitchen literally talking to the wall. She is not a feminist but she ponders on life's little inequalities, and wonders whether a day that finds its climax in placing her husband's dinner on the table at the precise moment his foot hits the Welcome mat by the door is really a fully fulfilled existence.

Things have changed. Her once romantic wooer has become a husband of monumental tediousness, a poor lover and a non-existent companion.

"I always said," she confides, "I'd leave him when the kids grew up, but when the kids had grown up, there was nowhere to go." So now Shirley is forced to admit: "If you described me to me, I'd say you were telling a joke."

But Shirley, thoughtfully sipping her glass of white wine in her labor-saved kitchen, and thinking earthy thoughts, has a dream. She sees herself "sitting by the sea drinking wine in a country where the grape is grown."

But with a husband who regards a trip to Manchester as an expedition, and suffers jet-lag even on the annual boat trip to holidays on the Isle of Man, her chances of wish-fulfillment seem slender.

Then life springs a miniature surprise. Her feminist girl-friend (whose "fella went off with the milkman," and who, to this day, does not take milk in her tea) wants company on a two-week holiday in Greece—and is so insistent on Shirley going along that she makes the arrangements and pays for her ticket.

Will she go? And will it make a difference if she does—or doesn't?

Russell has a way with women. Shirley, like that so educat-able Rita before her, is probably the dream child of half the women in the audience and the dream bride of half the men.

The rest of us will just have to take the play on its own clever-ly manipulative merits. The play is more fantasy than real-ism—Russell's jokes, for example take the story herein told of a highly unlikely but hilarious school performance of the Nativity, are unreal.

And always Shirley is a shade too cute to be true. Yet Russell has a way with a phrase. Listen to him on some British (and I suppose some American) tourists:

> They find the sun too hot, the sea too wet, Greece too Greek for them. If they had been at the Last Supper they would have asked for chips!

This is not just endearing—it has a well-rung tinkle of truth to it. And the story Russell has to tell us may be massaging and soothing, but it is not entirely unlikely. . . .

This is among the most entertaining evenings in town—and both funny and touching as an added bonus. . . .

Clive Barnes, "'Shirley' Soars in Solo Flight," in New York Post, *February 16, 1989.*

FRANK RICH

As a play, *Shirley Valentine* is feminism West End style; it intends to titillate and perhaps even shock matinee theatrego-ers with a mild level of ideological daring that will be familiar to those who have seen *Steaming, Song & Dance, Woman in Mind* or Mr. Russell's own *Educating Rita.* In these British plays, women discover that many men are pigs, children are ungrateful and autonomy is a birthright. A New York the-atergoer can fully agree with the message and still be per-plexed by the astonished cries of "Eureka!" with which it is presented at this late date. . . .

Shirley Valentine is an updated variant on the sentimental-ized, indomitable doormats once regularly assigned by Holly-wood to Shirley MacLaine. . . . The difference is that Mr. Russell's Shirley can free herself from subservience to a bad man (her callous husband, Joe)—as long as the catalyst for that liberation is a hot-blooded "good man" (a taverna waiter she meets during a two-week jaunt to Greece). Mr. Russell isn't about to risk offending customers of either gender. If he had written *A Doll's House,* Nora would have waltzed back through the door and asked Torvald out for a drink.

The playwright is a slick craftsman even so, and his first act, which Shirley delivers while preparing Joe's dinner, bubbles along professionally. Though the setups and punch lines fol-low a rhythmic formula—and though the mocking com-plaints about Joe are of Phyllis Diller bluntness—one laughs at Shirley's riesling-fueled explanations of why sex is like shopping at Safeway and why marriage resembles the Middle East. The Erma Bombeck-esque domestic anecdotes are jolly, and Miss Collins does a vibrant job of filling out the charac-ters who inhabit them: the kids in a school Nativity play, a patronizing headmistress, a braggart neighbor.

By Act II, Shirley has achieved her promised leap of rebel-lion: She has traveled to the foreign land of self-realization by running away to join her best friend on a Mediterranean vacation. The trip instantly accomplishes for Shirley what an education did for Mr. Russell's Rita, prompting her to deliver a fervent pitch for taking charge of one's unused (or wasted) life. "Why do we get all these feelings and dreams and hopes if we don't ever use them?" asks Shirley rhetorically. She an-nounces that she has "fallen in love with the idea of living" and that "it's nice to like yourself." These aren't postcards from Greece—they're inspirational greeting cards.

"It's the same for everyone; I know it is," Shirley says. Mr. Russell spells out his messages to advertise the universality of his heroine's plight and subsequent triumph. But . . . the universality and pathos of a wasted existence are most touch-ingly conveyed by that existence's specific details, not by su-perimposed sermons.

Frank Rich, "The Real Lowdown from an Old Friend," in The New York Times, *February 16, 1989.*

JOHN SIMON

Willy Russell's *Shirley Valentine* is a friendly puppy dog of a play that, all floppy ears and sloppy paws, jumps all over you, yapping and slobbering. Who could find enough hardness in his heart to kick it away just because it is an Old English sheepdog, unaware of its weight and muddiness, rather than a play? I suspect even of those great baby-and-dog-hating curmudgeons of the W. C. Fields school that their bark is worse than their kick.

Shirley Valentine is a one-character play (I don't think that inanimate objects, however frequently apostrophized but failing to respond, count) in which a 42-year-old middle-class housewife of that name—by now, actually, Shirley Bradshaw, housebroken mother of two grown children—soliloquizes about the middling woes and minuscule pleasures of Liverpudlian married monotony. She is preparing dinner for her husband, Joe, with some cooking wine of the kind that goes not into the dish but into the cook. She especially needs the sustenance today, when Joe, who expects the usual steak at the precise usual time will have to make do with eggs and chips: Shirley gave away the steak to a dog whose owners raised him to be a strict vegetarian. She just wanted the pleasure of seeing the expression on the dog's face as he discovered his true culinary heritage.

Shirley, you see, can still be whimsical. . . . What she isn't any longer, though, is the free spirit she once was, jumping off (low) roofs and such. And suddenly, at 42, she is handed this airline ticket by Jane and the invitation to come share a fortnight's holiday in Greece. Will Shirley have the courage to go despite the undoubted indignation of her smug husband, selfish daughter, and all those others who will assume that the only thing two middle-aged women would go looking for in Greece is, of course, sex?

I am giving away nothing if I tell you that the second act takes place not in the Bradshaws' crisply sterile kitchen but on a Greek island where our heroine is deliciously baking on a rock in the Aegean sun. What we want from the worm-will-turn plot is not suspense but the satisfaction of our appetites for the liberation of some and the comeuppance of others.

Shirley Valentine delivers these in a manner to thrill matinee ladies without unduly disturbing their complacent spouses.

For this is a feminist play that does not offend anti-feminists, and at times even an anti-feminist play that doesn't offend feminists. It is an anti-British play that had the British guffawing wholeheartedly, and a hymn to unconventionality that holds out hope even to the most hidebound. Prudes can smile at its sex jokes, slaves and slave drivers share a laugh at its advocacy of liberation. It is a play not written, like true comedies, in a mixture of soap bubbles and bile but propelled instead by a moist, warm puppy nose nudging you to do right by yourself and, coincidentally, the world.

Nothing reprehensible about that, but nothing remarkable either, especially when this is only a one-character play—the best way of shirking the real confrontations of drama—and when you consider that Russell has written it once before: *Shirley Valentine* is a sort of ***Educating Rita***. . . . [It may] be that two weeks in Greece for all concerned parties might end the Middle East crisis—but, somehow, I doubt it. (p. 99)

John Simon, "Our Funny Valentine," in New York Magazine, *Vol. 22, No. 10, March 6, 1989, pp. 99-100.*

FURTHER READING

Williams, Ian. "Russell's Road." *Plays and Players,* No. 409 (October 1987): 8-9.
   Combination of interview and critical commentary in which Russell discusses his plays, particularly an upcoming revival of *One for the Road.*

Paul Scott

1920-1978

(Born Paul Mark Scott) English novelist, poet, dramatist, and nonfiction writer.

An author of fiction that examines the effect of historical events upon individual lives, Scott is best known for *The Raj Quartet,* a tetralogy of novels chronicling the last days of British rule in India. Drawing from his experiences as an army intelligence officer in India during World War II, Scott portrayed British colonialists whose illusions about themselves and their work are destroyed by rapid political change. Making complex use of historical documents, flashbacks, alternating perspectives, and recurring symbols, Scott's works are often praised as highly inventive. Critics have also compared his meticulous development of character and panoramic presentation of history to that of such nineteenth-century authors as Charles Dickens and Leo Tolstoy. Although occasionally faulted as sentimental, Scott's novels are widely regarded as among the most comprehensive and revealing treatments of British colonialism in contemporary literature.

Scott's first two novels, *Johnnie Sahib* and *The Alien Sky,* earned critical accolades for their imaginative recreation of India during and immediately following World War II. *Johnnie Sahib* centers upon an unconventional British supply officer whose charismatic relationship with his Indian soldiers arouses the enmity of his fellow officers, while *The Alien Sky* presents a group of British civil servants and longstanding residents of India whose futures are suddenly jeopardized by the country's independence in 1947. Reviewers regarded both novels as amusing and poignant, commending Scott's insights on the precarious relationship that existed between British colonialists and Indians. While his next novel, *A Male Child,* forgoes exotic locales to portray a soldier's homecoming to postwar London, Scott returns to the Far East in his ensuing work, *The Mark of the Warrior.* Set in Burma, this novel focuses upon a British major who is haunted by the death in combat of a captain under his command. Hoping to cleanse his conscience, he reenacts the event and inadvertently causes the death of the captain's brother. Patricia Hodgart commented: "[In *The Mark of the Warrior*], Mr. Scott constructs a novel outstanding for its compassionate understanding of a subtle moral issue and for its formal precision." *The Chinese Love Pavilion* is Scott's last detailed examination of British soldiers in the Far East.

The Birds of Paradise, Scott's next novel, is a multilayered work of flashbacks and journal entries that focuses on William Conway, a dissatisfied London businessman who leaves his estranged wife and travels to the Far East hoping to recapture the intensity of feeling he experienced as a youth in India. He most vividly remembers an island where brilliant stuffed birds of paradise hung suspended in a large cage; to Conway, the birds symbolize the grandeur of the British Empire, yet when he returns to the island, he discovers that age and neglect have despoiled them. Although Scott received relatively little critical attention for his next novel, *The Bender: Pictures from an Exhibition of Middle Class Portraits,* his ensuing work, *The Corrida at San Feliu,* garnered praise for

its inventive interpretation of the novelistic form. The text contains various fragments written by Edward Thornhill, a novelist living in Spain who has died with his wife in a car wreck. Introduced by Thornhill's editor, the work incorporates the rough drafts of two short stories, set respectively in Africa and India; two alternative openings to a novel about India; and a novella titled *The Plaza de Toros.* Although some critics considered the novel overly complex, most praised *The Corrida at San Feliu* as a highly successful study of the creative process.

In the 1960s, Scott initiated a tetralogy chronicling the final days of India's subjugation under the British raj, or rule, that elaborately integrates numerous characters, symbolism, and historical events. Considered Scott's greatest achievement, *The Raj Quartet*—which includes *The Jewel in the Crown, The Day of the Scorpion, The Towers of Silence,* and *A Division of the Spoils*—is frequently compared to E. M. Forster's *A Passage to India* for its astute assessment of the disparate forces that characterized colonial India. K. Bhaskara Rao asserted: "The diversity of *The Quartet* is its strength. To the student of the novel, it is rich with the technique and craft of the novel. To the historian it is a valuable source, and for the humanist it is a highly perceptive commentary on interracial, intercultural relations. To the student of the performing arts there is a gallery of characters to bring to life, and to the general reader it is a series of novels within novels to read and enjoy. Its stature as a major work of fiction will grow and endure in the years to come."

The Jewel in the Crown, the first novel of *The Raj Quartet,* is set during the time of Britain's authoritarian response to the "Quit India" movement, an anti-colonial campaign initiated by the Indian Congress in 1942. The narrator uses letters, court reports, interviews, and newspaper clippings to reconstruct the suicide of Edwina Crane, an elderly British missionary, and the rape of Daphne Manners, a young English army nurse stationed in India during World War II. These two events are reexamined throughout the tetralogy and ultimately represent the relationship between India and Great Britain. Miss Crane emerges as a "widow" of colonial India when she commits *suttee,* or self-immolation, after witnessing the murder of her Indian assistant by young men she may have tutored. The print that Miss Crane and other missionaries used to teach English, which depicts Queen Victoria symbolically accepting India as the "Jewel in the Crown" of her Empire, appears periodically in *The Raj Quartet* as both an ironic and poignant comment upon the archaic ideals of colonialism. Scott devotes most of this novel, however, to the relationship between Daphne Manners and Hari Kumar, a Hindu whose British education has alienated him from Indian society. After Daphne is raped while secretly meeting Kumar, she becomes pregnant and must choose between a socially expedient abortion and the child she believes to be Kumar's. Kumar's arrest for the rape further polarizes the Indian and British communities and serves to introduce Ronald Merrick, the District Superintendent of Police, whose moralistic character is steadily undermined throughout *The Raj Quartet.* His racist attitudes and unjust conviction of Kumar on an unrelated charge of sedition inspires a hatred of him among Indians that reaches a climax in *A Division of the Spoils.*

The Day of the Scorpion takes place two years after *The Jewel in the Crown.* Daphne has died giving birth to a daughter now cared for by Lady Manners, Daphne's aunt. The child's only visitor is Sarah Layton, whose experiences and familial conflicts dominate the remainder of the tetralogy. Labeled "unsound" by the staid society of *memsahibs,* or women of the British ruling class, Sarah begins to defy racial barriers and to realistically assess the role of the British in India. After arriving in the Muslim princedom of Mirat for her sister's wedding, she becomes close friends with Ahmed Kasim, the apolitical son of an Indian Congress member. She is warned against the association by Merrick, who reappears at this point as an army captain and as the best man of Teddie Bingham, Sarah's future brother-in-law. Repulsed by Merrick's racist views and his disdain for the code of conduct underlying colonial rule, Sarah is also aware of his role in the now infamous Manners case. The circumstances surrounding that incident are further explored after the investigation is reopened at the request of Daphne's aunt. In the central episode of *The Day of the Scorpion,* Lady Manners travels to Kandipat Jail, where Kumar breaks his long silence to tell of his unprovoked arrest and sadistic treatment by Merrick. Although Kumar disappears after his release, the disclosure of the superintendent's behavior further exacerbates tensions between the British and Indians. Ironically, Merrick becomes a war hero after an unsuccessful attempt to save Bingham's life during combat leaves him grotesquely disfigured.

In *The Towers of Silence,* Scott concentrates primarily upon the women of the Layton family and the intricate society of *memsahibs* to which they belong. Barbie Batchelor, who first appears in *The Day of the Scorpion,* emerges as the central, tragic figure of this novel. A retired missionary schoolteacher, Barbie lives with Sarah's step-grandmother, Mabel Layton, the stalwart owner of Rose Cottage and the embodiment of the halcyon days of the British raj. Other *memsahibs* despise Barbie for her lower-middle-class background, however, including Sarah's mother, Mildred. When Mabel's unexpected death worsens the antagonistic relationship between the pair, Mildred evicts Barbie from the house. Upon returning to Rose Cottage to collect her belongings, Barbie unexpectedly encounters Merrick. Recently released from the hospital, he speaks obsessively about the Manners case and of Edwina Crane, whom Barbie knew as a young woman. Although she dislikes Merrick, Barbie, in a symbolic surrender of the Empire, gives him her print of "The Jewel in the Crown." She soon departs but is seriously injured in a road accident. The novel ends with Barbie alone in her hospital room, deliriously imagining that she is Miss Crane as the atomic bomb is dropped on Hiroshima, ending the war.

In *A Division of the Spoils,* the last volume of *The Raj Quartet,* Scott extensively examines the final retreat of the British and the partition of the colony into India and Pakistan in 1947. The novel's events are presented primarily through the perspective of Guy Perron, an intelligence officer and former schoolmate of Kumar who later marries Sarah Layton. An adjunct to Merrick who now interrogates deserters from the Indian army, Perron learns of the former policeman's latent homosexuality and his fascination with the social position of the Laytons. He also meets Sarah's father, a colonel recently released from a German prisoner-of-war camp, whose belief in the integrity of the British legacy in India is contrasted with the brutal yet realistic cynicism of Merrick. Violence escalates as independence draws near, resulting first in the murder of Merrick by a male prostitute for his role in the Manners case, and later in the graphic death of Ahmed Kasim, one of a group of Muslims taken from a train by Hindus and killed while the departing British helplessly watch. This scene and its bloody aftermath, in which Sarah and Perron futilely attempt to aid the wounded, serves to underscore Britain's responsibility for the chaos following the partition of the Indian subcontinent.

In his last novel, *Staying On,* Scott provides a postscript to *The Raj Quartet.* The winner of the Booker Prize in 1977, this novel focuses on Tusker and Lucy Smalley, peripheral characters in *The Day of the Scorpion,* who remained in India following its independence. Set in 1972, the novel opens with Tusker's death, then moves backwards from that moment as Lucy recalls their tedious existence in postcolonial India. Although Scott gently satirizes contemporary India by portraying the couple's association with an Indian middle class ironically steeped in the values of the British raj, he also acknowledges the enduring bond that exists between England and its former colony. Janis Tedesco observed: "The tone of [*The Raj Quartet*] is one of bitter lament, of a regret for the loss to both England and India because the two countries had not commingled in a union of equals. The tone of *Staying On* is quite different, as if Scott is at peace with what England and India actually gained from their experience together. We are all connected, Scott says in his final book. We are all united, perhaps even more than we feel."

(See also *CLC*, Vol. 9; *Contemporary Authors*, Vols. 77-80 [obituary], Vols. 81-84; and *Dictionary of Literary Biography*, Vol. 14.)

PRINCIPAL WORKS

NOVELS

Johnnie Sahib   1952
The Alien Sky   1953; also published as *Six Days in Marapore*, 1953
A Male Child   1956
The Mark of the Warrior   1958
The Chinese Love Pavilion   1960
The Birds of Paradise   1962
The Bender: Pictures from an Exhibition of Middle Class Portraits   1963
The Corrida at San Feliu   1964
The Jewel in the Crown   1966
The Day of the Scorpion   1968
The Towers of Silence   1971
A Division of the Spoils   1975
Staying On   1977

*These works were published as *The Raj Quartet* in 1976.

MARY JOHNSON TWEEDY

"They were stubborn, these Britishers on the point of departure, stubborn like the aged and the dying. About them was the smell of decay, the smell of the sickroom. They were clearing out of India and leaving the smell behind them. If you sniffed, now, it smarted in your nostrils. Decay. Death. An end to ambition. A burial of pride." This was the way it seemed to Joe MacKendrick [the protagonist of *Six Days in Marapore*] on his first day in Marapore.

It was a time for change in Marapore. Indians were eager, some ruthlessly so, for the equality and power so long denied them. The middle-class British who had spent their adult lives in India faced uneasy alternatives: to remain as something less than lords of creation, to return to a shadowy, almost forgotten "home" in England or to push off uncertainly to some unknown colonial way station.

When Joe arrived in Marapore he was immediately involved in the complex frustrations, jealousies and ambitions of the community in which the author has concentrated extreme but representative types. The army widow who supplemented her small pension with her wits and jaded charms was as representative as the sodden Major who stimulated his dull wits and jaded ambition with the charms of Anglo-Indian girls.

Scott's brief characterizations are as important to *Six Days in Marapore* as the basic plot, which traces the destruction of Tom Gower, idealist and real friend of India. Gower was destroyed in part by extreme nationalism and the country's desire to be rid of *all* Englishmen—and, finally, by his wife, who had lived in torment that the secret of her mixed blood would be known.

This is not primarily a novel of India, but rather more of

frightened foreigners living there at the end of their era. Certainly this is to be read along with such novels as *A Passage to India* and *Indigo*.

Mary Johnson Tweedy, "The End of Empire," in The New York Times Book Review, *September 20, 1953, p. 26.*

THE TIMES LITERARY SUPPLEMENT

[In *A Male Child,* Mr. Scott], rather than work out his discontent and project it on to a more or less symbolical set of people, turns in upon his characters, producing a deeply introspective study of depression, set within a narrow circle of personal relationships. . . .

Ian Canning, Mr. Paul Scott's hero, contracts some mysterious disease, never actually diagnosed, at the beginning of the book and the end of his war service in the Far East, and the attitude of mind reflected throughout *A Male Child* is that of the low, sub-normal state of illness, when trivialities assume enormous importance, and it is extremely hard to relate one's personal position and experience to that of the outside world. In this subdued, near-suicidal frame of mind, Ian Canning considers the gloomy facts of his broken marriage, his lack of stamina and consequently of success as a writer, the generally unsatisfactory lives of those he sees around him, and on the same level and at equal length such domestic matters as whether to turn the sub-tenants out of his flat or not. In this listless state he drifts down to the home of Alan, an Army friend, and there finds himself living in a weird household, of which Mr. Scott excellently conveys the seedy, slightly crazed atmosphere. " 'You think I ought to go to a nut house,' " says Ian Canning apprehensively to Alan, "Slowly he grinned at me. 'My dear old Ian,' he said, 'You're in one,' " and at times, when the mother takes to the bottle and the German woman downstairs starts conjuring up the ghost of the dead son of the house, it is all too clear he is right. The birth of a male child to Alan, however, is sufficient in Mr. Scott's eyes to wipe out the depressing thought of the past, the depressing evidence of the present, and to give hope for the future, to Ian Canning as well as to the actual members of the family. Mr. Scott in his writing shows plenty of signs of his continuing talent, but has this time chosen an inescapably drab subject in which it is hard to take interest.

"The Seamier Side," in The Times Literary Supplement, *No. 2820, March 16, 1956, p. 163.*

THE TIMES LITERARY SUPPLEMENT

The central figure of *The Birds of Paradise* is William Conway, a prosperous, unhappy city man who has taken a sabbatical year and is spending it on a tropical island (one of the New Guinea group?) called Manoba. Here, comforted occasionally by Kandy, a whore from the mainland who comes over especially to oblige, William Conway spends his time remembering things past, and writing these memories down, if not with the haunting elaborateness of a Proust, at any rate with admirable technical accomplishment for a city man, and with a flair for isolating all those remote and fleeting moments in his human history which can be invested with the authority of a symbol or an omen.

Conway is an Anglo-Indian, the son of a coldly ambitious civil servant and of a mother who died when he was an infant.

His childhood in the princedom of Tradura, where his father represented the British Crown, lies at the core of his memories. Mr. Scott evokes it with skill. The lonely boy, brought up first by Mrs. Canterbury, the governess, and then by Grayson-Hume, the tutor with homosexual tendencies heroically kept in check, is a real, unsentimentalized figure. His friendships—with Krishi, the son of a local princeling, and with Dora, the daughter of an Indian army man—are full of the intensity, and the steep ups-and-downs, which characterize childhood friendships everywhere. The boy's relationships with the grown-ups, with his father and with Ranjit Raosingh the old Maharajah particularly, are full of that bafflement lit by flashes of sudden insight which one might expect from a child in his situation. Incidents like the tiger-shoot and the symbolic entry by the children into the vast cage hung with dead birds of Paradise come especially to mind as having the pulse and throb of real things remembered.

Like most Anglo-Indian childhoods William Conway's suffers, alas, the executioner's sudden chop: he comes to England to school and stays with a childless uncle and aunt in stockbroker Surrey. About these memories, and indeed all subsequent ones, Mr. Scott writes with far less confidence. There is neither life nor conviction in the narrative of William Conway's unhappy marriage to the promiscuous Anne. Mr. Scott of course feels obliged to bring copulation right out into the open in the present-day manner. And he errs in so doing. . . .

Nor is William Conway made to appear quite at his ease as a memorialist of experiences in a Japanese prisoner-of-war camp. It is here that he meets Cranston, the dedicated doctor, the first encounter of Conway's adulthood in which he sees at close quarters a life having purpose and direction. It is a pity therefore that the imaginative insight which sustains Mr. Scott so well in the childhood scenes in India should fail him at this point, because Cranston is designed to contrast with Conway—the dried-up, loveless man striving to see ahead of him some bright destination worth setting a course for.

The book is beautifully composed. Mr. Scott quite masters a most difficult narrative method in which time's ever-rolling stream, and the tyranny of "and then ? and then ?" are put to defiance. The highlights are juxtaposed in such a way as to heighten their significance, not subject any more to the harsh imperatives of the time-sequence. Mr. Scott's *montage*, in fact, is first-class, and his book, with all its faults, extremely interesting: the work of a writer who clearly delights in the patient and scrupulous exercise of his craft and who has genuine, if intermittent, creativeness.

"Time Remembered," in The Times Literary Supplement, *No. 3137, April 13, 1962, p. 245.*

MAIA W. RODMAN

Books on bullfighting seem to suffer from the occupational hazard of bullfighters: unevenness. But just as a *matador* can be unforgivable with one bull, and that same afternoon unforgettable with another, so can the author redeem himself from page to page and chapter to chapter.

Paul Scott's *The Corrida at San Feliu* is an exciting novel as long as it keeps away from the bull ring. . . .

To Mr. Scott's great credit (and in spite of the insistence of the jacket copy), his book has precious little to do with tau-

romachy, which is used mainly to symbolize life in general and the plight of the novel's characters in particular. Since the author admits his inadequate knowledge of the subject, the reader should not only dismiss the bullfight references, but also forgive Mr. Scott for using *la fiesta brava* as an awkward allegorical prop.

The Corrida at San Feliu is purportedly a posthumously published book containing "papers," autobiographical notes, and manuscripts left by Edward Thornhill, a writer who died with his wife in a car accident in Spain. In the preface the publishers claim that death to be accidental, but ultimately one is certain it was, if not premeditated, then predestined.

Only the technicality of being part of *The Corrida at San Feliu* will prevent "Thornhill's" short story "The Leopard Mountain" from being anthologized. It is as fine a piece of writing as anything done on Africa by Hemingway. This is followed by three chapters of an unfinished novel with India for background.

These seemingly unrelated chapters are subsequently drawn upon in the book's principal part, *The Plaza de Toros*, where the characters of Lesley and Thelma, from the earlier section, are intermingled with Thornhill's wife Myra, forming a curiously effective, composite picture of an exciting and many-faceted woman. A similar technique is used with the male characters, those inhabiting the Indian landscape and rediscovered on the beach of the Costa Brava.

Detached, self-aware, Thornhill is a man obsessed with his wife, his past, the futility of the present and the obscurity of the future. A character both exasperating and noble. In him, and in the complex, somewhat abstract shape of the book, Mr. Scott has used his considerable gifts to excellent advantage. He wields beautiful passages with the grace with which an inspired *torero* wields the *muleta*. And the music of those passages seems to be as much a part of the novel's action as the *paso doble* during an exceptional *faena*.

Maia W. Rodman, "Blood on the Spanish Landscape," in Saturday Review, *Vol. XLVIII, No. 2, January 9, 1965, p. 55.*

ORVILLE PRESCOTT

Several months ago a novel [*The Jewel in the Crown*] was published that may well be the finest novel about India since E. M. Forster's *A Passage to India* and that will certainly be one of the finest novels of any kind published this year. . . . *The Jewel in the Crown* by Paul Scott is a major work, a glittering combination of brilliant craftsmanship, psychological perception and objective reporting. Too circuitous in its complex narrative structure and too leisurely in its contemplation of many aspects of its central theme for the taste of readers intent on drama only, *The Jewel in the Crown* demands the same kind of patient attention as do the major works of Joseph Conrad and rewards such attention equally.

For a number of years I have been reviewing the novels of Mr. Scott . . . with high praise and numerous reservations. The praise was for his blazing talent, his mastery of the English language and his sure knowledge of human character. The reservations were inspired by Mr. Scott's fondness for unnecessarily intricate methods of narration and for intrusive symbolism. Now in *The Jewel in the Crown* Mr. Scott has shunned all technical tricks and cryptic symbols and produced the novel of which he has always been capable.

This enormous, richly colored and densely populated novel comprises many parts, each told from the point of view of a representative English or Indian individual; some of the parts are in quotation from conversation, letters or memoirs, some in direct narration. All these parts are inspired by a crime that took place in August of 1942 in the City of Mayapore in northeastern India. The crime was the rape of an English girl in the Bibighar Gardens. So, to a certain extent, Paul Scott has boldly challenged comparisons with Forster.

But *The Jewel in the Crown* does not really resemble *A Passage to India.* It concerns a point in time much later and a far wider panorama of men and events. What *The Jewel in the Crown* is primarily about is empire, racial superiority and the many ways different individuals react to the fact of "white men in control of a black man's country." Such a theme is fashionable today, so fashionable that one might expect another bitter tirade about racial injustice.

But Mr. Scott is not bitter. He knows that he is not writing just about callous or insolent or arrogant English men and women, or about noble and resentful Indians. He is writing about many kinds of people involved in a situation they did not make themselves, conforming to traditions of long standing and acting according to their natures and their inmost convictions. There are some unpleasant individuals satirically viewed in *The Crown,* but there are no villains.

Rarely in modern fiction have so many interesting and even bizarre characters been brought to more intense life. Rarely has a time and a place and a political and social crisis been more brilliantly or more dispassionately described. Rarely have the sounds and smells and total atmosphere of India been so evocatively suggested. So comprehensive is Mr. Scott's scope, so detailed his focus, so intimately authoritative his knowledge that reading his novel becomes a major experience and a prolonged one.

In fact, the only way to read *The Jewel in the Crown* is to surrender to it, to immerse oneself in it for many days. Such amplitude, such elaborate circling around a given point, such deliberate pace may seem vexatious or intolerable to some readers. This is certainly a book that cannot be read in a hurry. But if one reads it on Mr. Scott's terms the effect is tremendous.

Unlike so many contemporary novels based upon topical events, *The Jewel in the Crown* is not just a dramatic or satirical comment in fictional terms. It is an illumination and a re-creation, sad, compassionate, wryly humorous. Mr. Scott seems to say that if people and history were different all might have been better; but given "the cycle of inevitability" this is the way it was.

Orville Prescott, "Empire, Race and 'The Cycle of Inevitability'," in The New York Times, *July 29, 1966, p. 29.*

THE TIMES LITERARY SUPPLEMENT

Mr. Paul Scott, in his writing middle-age, is going in for amplitude. *The Day of the Scorpion* has 484 large pages, and, even at that, forms only a part of the vast fictional structure he is erecting. This novel probes and elaborates themes already announced in *The Jewel in the Crown* . . . and there is a further volume still to come. Even the serious Victorian serialists would have no difficulty in thinking of Mr. Scott's present work-in-progress as coming well up to size.

Basically the novel is about the crumbling of an empire and about the changing attitudes discernible in those who—some of them for generations—have served it as soldiers and administrators. Mr. Scott writes of the twilight of the Kipling gods. England is still in command in India, but the war and its outcome are all that have to be lived through—or, in the case of Susan's soldier-husband, Teddie Bingham, not lived through—before the final withdrawal.

On the one side in this situation stand representatives of those waiting to take over: Mohammed Ali Kassim and Pandit Baba. Both of these portraits Mr. Scott makes splendidly alive. Kassim is serious, strong, idealistic, humane, not at all unmindful of the benefits conferred by the British on India during the long hegemony. In Pandit Baba, who is slippery, unscrupulous and bland, we see on display the more disreputable gadfly tactics favoured by certain elements in India's Congress Party.

On the other side are notably Merrick, the Indian Police officer who, in the earlier book *The Jewel in the Crown,* took drastic charge of the investigation into the suspected rape of an Englishwoman by young Indian hoodlums, and who has now, for the duration of the war, become an army officer; and also the Layton family, long established in India, together with their numerous connexions and branches, and in particular Sarah who is at the younger, self-questioning end of the line, and who has about her something of Forster's Adela Quested forty years on.

Between these mighty opposites the Nawab of Mirat, carefully groomed through the years for his role of unsubservient subservience by his Wazir, the homosexual White Russian Count Bronowsky, admirably plays his part. The subtlety and affection, the feeling for high comedy which Mr. Scott brings to his portrayal of these two are among the chief pleasures of this novel. In the middle also, but this time in a most uncomfortable no-man's land, Hari Kumar undergoes his interrogations and suffers physical violence. Kumar, brought up to be an Englishman at an English public school by an Indian father whose bankruptcy brought a sudden end to the process of anglicization, is the chief suspect in the affair of the rape of Daphne Manners who has by now died in giving birth to the half-caste child Parviti. Kumar has no place anywhere except perhaps in the heart of the dead girl whose child he is believed to have fathered.

The strength, assurance and stamina displayed in *The Day of the Scorpion* are quite outstanding. The characters, while they successfully represent aspirations and conflicts which are bigger than themselves, never cease to be individuals. The conversations have subtlety and a quality of plenteousness which is none the less welcome for being out of fashion. Above all, the reader is impressed, and given confidence, by the feeling which Mr. Scott can generate of a writer who has thoroughly mastered his material, and who can, because of this, work through a maze of fascinating detail without for a moment losing sight of distant, and considerable, objectives.

"Mighty Opposites," in The Times Literary Supplement, *No. 3472, September 12, 1968, p. 975.*

AUDREY C. FOOTE

[*The Towers of Silence*] is the third volume of an impressive tetralogy of the final days of the British Raj in India by Paul Scott, a superb writer who achieves a synthesis of Faulkner and Ford Madox Ford in depth and scope. While it is not indispensable to have read *The Jewel in the Crown* and *The Day of the Scorpion,* some readers may turn back to them to fit in the missing pieces, of motive and meaning rather than plot. For like Lawrence Durrell in the *Alexandria Quartet,* Scott employs a rather unusual technique, that of telling over and over certain central events through differing angles of vision. "In such a fashion human beings call for explanations of things that happen to them," he says of Daphne after she is raped, and then goes on as if to explain his own literary purpose, "and in such a way scenes and characters are set for exploration, like toys set out by kneeling children intent on pursuing their grim but necessary games."

The locale and time are a small province in India between 1939-1945; many of the huge cast of characters are the same as in the earlier volumes, though here Scott concentrates on the British rather than on his Indian subjects. The historical catalyst is the Indian Congress Party's "Quit India" declaration of August 1942, the immediate arrest by the British of Gandhi and others, and the resultant disorders. In the first book Scott created three fictional consequences around which this story still revolves: the suicide by suttee of an elderly English teacher who has seen her Indian colleague killed by a mob; the rape by Indians of a gentle English girl and her later death in childbirth; and the murder of a quixotic young British officer while trying to win back former Indians of his regiment, now fighting for the Japanese—deaths that seem a defeat of the brave, the loving, and the loyal.

These three events, previously explored as both human tragedies and political portents, are once more scrutinized, but almost on another plane—as if mythic episodes in a cosmic contest between love and evil, or to use Scott's preferred antithesis, love and despair. Barbie Batchelor, a retired mission schoolteacher, is a new Antigone in her unpopular and futile effort to arrange the proper burial of a friend. The English wives, widows, and daughters of absent officers, whose daily existence provides the narrative surface of the book, make up a classic chorus that comments on what happens and what it means. A mixed chorus, since while some of the women are mem sahib monsters, several are figures of love and compassion—a role only once bestowed on an Englishman by Paul Scott.

What these particular women have most in common is an infallible intuition of evil which, unlike the dispersed goodness, is personified by a single individual, the policeman Ronald Merrick. Merrick, curiously involved in the three tragedies, has until now seemed merely a symptom of the deterioration of British purpose and morale in India, but he now emerges as something even more sinister and universal. Admired by the officers and mem sahibs for his guts and efficiency, he repels such women as Daphne, Sister Ludmilla, Sarah, and Barbie. . . . [It] is through the vision of the ardent Christian Barbie that he is positively identified. As she first approaches him, she senses a miasma of sickness in the air, and finds him as she had earlier envisaged the Prince of Darkness, chin in hand, thoughtful, inconsolable, hungry for souls.

A fourth volume is to come. Scott is a complex, often cryptic writer, and there remain many symbols and mysteries we would like explained—but that as likely will not be. The cast may shift, but Merrick is bound to reappear. What more can be said or suggested about him? Scott's affection for the compassionate Barbie may be a clue. Pessimistic as he seems, he may yet, like the early heretic Origen, find ways in which even the devil may be saved.

Audrey C. Foote, "Way Out in the East," in Book World—Chicago Tribune, *February 20, 1972, p. 6.*

BENITA PARRY

In his four long and closely interrelated novels [*The Jewel in the Crown, The Day of the Scorpion, The Towers of Silence,* and *A Division of the Spoils*] Paul Scott unravels the knotted threads of the British-Indian association and reworks them into a pattern of his own making. He has written an elegy to the imperial dream which demystifies the myth and undermines the British claim to moral superiority, a lament for an aspiration which acknowledges that calculated self-interest, exploitation, obtuseness and indifference to the other's sensibilities were as central a part of the British reality as the better publicised mission, service and responsibility. To call these novels an elegy is to suggest that Scott is regretting the demise of what once was fine, or the doom of an ideal whose potential was never realised; only at the end of the quartet is it fully apparent that so enraptured is Scott by the idea of what the British-Indian relationship might have been that he has arranged his material, adjusted his focus and undermined his metaphors and analogues illuminating the association to produce a muted celebration of a concept rather than a critique of a reality.

Scott's novels are judicious, wise and well-informed; this is not to insinuate a tolerant aloofness which fails in passion, an equanimity of moral temper, or a blandness towards the ungainly, the confused and the anarchic, but to imply an intelligence rooted in a firmly-held body of values, beliefs and assumptions, and an imagination tied and always returning to this solid ground. His tone is of one who observes folly, error, misunderstanding and cruelty with the assurance that integrity and goodwill will endure, even if justice is not done and aspirations are not fulfilled; his method an exploratory debate on the historical retrospect of the raj and the difficulties besetting its last years. Political issues are meticulously discussed, impulses, motives, tensions and interactions distinctly stated, obscurities unveiled, mysteries ultimately exposed to strong light. The struggle of the Indian national movement against British rule is presented as a contention between two conflicting conceptions of right and between two aspirants to power; from a meeting between an Indian officer who had joined the Indian National Army to fight with the Japanese against the British and his father, a Muslim Congressman, two views of the same act emerge: to one it is patriotism, to the other treason. But there are areas where such apparent disengagement can be unsatisfactory and disturbing, for when political conflict and moral choices are opened to too many possible constructions, the definition of an author's own controlling intelligence is obscured. Again, while Scott knows the other side of the underneath, and uncovers the dubious inclinations nourished within the British-Indian association, the uneasy gratifications, the interplay of aggression and submission, of domination and rebellion, his treatment of the devious and the deviant is too clinical, as if he might be distancing himself from a source of contamination.

To accommodate the weight, significance and complexity which Scott attaches historically and analogically to the British-Indian encounter, he has mounted a vast panorama of events during the last years of British rule, analysing the historical dialectic and the dilemmas of those caught up in crisis and change. He has incorporated a mass of detailed information, a spectrum of white and Indian characters, and yards of exegeses, memoirs and recollections, some of which is presented in an all-purpose style rather than as the unique expression of an individual. The slow, even inexorable, pace of these books speaks of a confidence in reaching some sort of truth through the interplay of divergent viewpoints and the clearly stated revelation of character and motive. Yet where everything is spelt out, where so many possibilities are presented, the mind of the reader may be replete but the imagination is left undernourished; it is when Scott abandons the approach of explicitly defining people and situations, and discovers these through ellipses, metaphors and allegories, that his greater powers as a novelist are realised.

A writer who demonstrates his trust in the efficacy of lucid language to convey meaning and bring order to the chaos of experience, Scott knows also the power of silence; just as the Parsee dead are stripped by the vultures on the hill-tops, the Towers of Silence, so too can words be picked clean, losing their eloquence, their potency to communicate, and giving way to other means of attempting expression, making contact and listening. Silence can be that ecstatic state when selfhood is dissolved and the mystic enters a timeless dimension; it can also be the voice of despair, an announcement of withdrawal from human involvement where this seems futile. It is Scott's sibylline old white women who, in so acting out their personal disillusion, signal a larger social failure which for Scott is the ending of an era in which the British role in India had been viable and valuable. Edwina Crane, an agnostic mission-teacher, after the death of an Indian colleague in a riot, looks back on her failure to know and love those she had presumed to serve, and wearing a white sari incinerates herself as if becoming sati to join a dead belief. Barbara Batchelor, also a mission-teacher, whose compulsive garrulousness conceals a crisis of faith and unsought visionary insights . . . takes refuge in speechless madness. Mabel Layton, widow both of a civilian and an army officer, deaf and laconic, retreats from Anglo-India into a solitary inner resignation. Lady Manners, once a governor's wife, to whom British policy in the early 1940s seems an abdication of responsibility, herself postpones interceding for an Indian she knows to be falsely accused and detained. Ludmilla Smith, Sister Ludmilla, of obscure East European origins, who as atonement for her mother's unattended death devotes herself to bringing dignity to the dying, observes life with the composure and despair of a sage.

All these women had spent their adult years in India, none had borne children; they symptomise sterility, decay, and together with other whites in India whose acts and omissions, thoughts and sensations point up an individual sense of malaise, their stances converge in a pattern of more extensive significance. To Sarah Layton, a third-generation Anglo-Indian who knows that the British time in India has passed, it seems "as if we had built a mansion without doors and windows, with no way in and no way out. All India lies on our doorsteps and cannot enter to warm us or be warmed. We live in holes and crevices of the crumbling stone, no longer sheltered by the carapace of our history which is leaving us behind".

Scott draws the true Anglo-Indians—as distinct from refugees from European upheavals: the White Russian Count Bronowsky, secretary and grand-vizier to a Muslim prince, Sister Ludmilla, Dr. Anna Klaus—as a special community, snobbish, obsessed with status and rank, tightly closed against outsiders but without necessarily loving or even liking each other. India was the opportunity for ordinary English people to work and live as a ruling class, and however insistently they claimed their rights to be in India they were homeless transients, shut off socially and culturally from India, yet so altered by existence there that they were estranged from British life. If survival as exiles toughened, it also warped, and their untenable situation is considered by Sarah Layton, unillusioned, vulnerable, and shy of playing the roles expected of her as a colonel's daughter: "Their enemy was light, not dark, the light of their own kind, of their own people at home, from whom they had been too long cut off so that, returning there briefly, a deep and holy silence wrapped them and caused them to observe what was real as miniature. In India they had been betrayed by an illusion of topographical vastness into sins of pride that were foreign to their pygmy natures". The eye which Scott casts on Anglo-India can be cold or kindly or admiring. He recognises the comic dilemma of officials who believe in their own impartiality and integrity but whose instinct is to close ranks, to disbelieve anything discreditable about their peers when the accuser is an Indian and to act on this disbelief. In some of the British he sees rancour, smallness of sympathy, self-deceit, prejudice and fear; in others a hope that their work and actions will increase human dignity and happiness; in others an emotional attachment to India and empire. . . . (pp. 359-61)

An era is ending, making its sometimes whimpering, sometimes strident exit amidst political strife and bitter racial hostility. It is wartime; in the East the Japanese are victorious, within India the Quit India campaign is gaining momentum, Congress leaders are imprisoned, Muslims are agitating for a separate state, there are riots, civil disorder and British retribution. An inglorious raj; but was it ever resplendent? It is here, I think, that Scott's ambivalence unbalances his apparently dispassionate appraisal of British rule in India. In his recollections Robin White, CIE, ICS Retired, a serious and humane man, not given to bombast about morality, looks back on the raj as exploitation tempered by "the onus of moral leadership". But a more extravagant estimate of his significance as a servant of British policy is given by an elderly Indian lawyer who describes him as the tutor and conscience of India, a man whose relationship with Indians rested on his sense of responsibility for them which, in turn, "enabled him to accept his privileged position with dignity". Even more significant are the musings of Perron, an intellectual come to India because of the accident of war, who wonders whether there may not perhaps have been two continua which never coincided: "For at least a hundred years India has formed part of England's idea about herself and for the same period India has been forced into a position of being a reflection of that idea". He thinks too about "that liberal instinct which is so dear to historians that they lay it out like a guideline through the unmapped forests of prejudice and self-interest as though this line, and not the forest, is our history". But the poise of Perron's reflections is abandoned when he looks at the faces of urban Londoners recruited into the army and posted to India: "What could such a face know of India? And yet India was there, in the skull, and the bones of the body. Its possession had helped nourish the flesh, warm the blood of every man in the room, sleeping and waking". This is more than an acknowledgement of the benefits which may have filtered down to the British working-class because of imperialist exploitation, and if its meaning is to assert some psychic enrichment or involvement which possession of the British Empire brought to the British people, then its sense is dubious, and is an instance of that sentimentality which can cloud Scott's vision.

Whatever constructions are put on this "thin but integral association", at its core was paternalism: "Man-bap . . . It meant Mother-Father, the relationship of the Raj to India". . . . A banal allegorical picture once presented by the mission to Edwina Crane, entitled "The Jewel in Her Crown" and showing the old Queen receiving homage from her Indian subjects, who surround her like children, is a central and recurrent image in the novels. For Sarah Layton it illustrates a particular aspect of the imperial attachment, a combination of hardness and sentimentality, which intensifies her need to escape India "before it had quite finished with me, rusted me up, corroded me, corrupted me utterly with a false sense of duty and a false sense of superiority". What then is the essence of paternalism as Scott opens it to scrutiny? Robin White had found it uncongenial and corrupting; in his early days he had hated "the real India behind the pipe-puffing myth. I hated the loneliness and the dirt, the smell, the conscious air of superiority . . . I hated Indians because they were the most immediately available target, and couldn't hit back except in subtle ways that made me hate them more". But Scott moderates this assessment, suggesting another dimension. When Sarah Layton learns from Ronald Merrick, who is a stranger to the tradition, how her brother-in-law Teddy Bingham, an officer distinguished by his ordinariness, has died because of his concern with those Indian soldiers in his regiment who had joined the Indian National Army, she is moved to wonderment and respect. In an ashamed and humiliated soldier Teddy had been able to restore some dignity, some sense of still belonging. . . . Even Merrick, who is hostile to what he sees as amateurism and sentimental cant, is tempted to believe: "I fell for it . . . the whole thing, the idea that there really was this possibility. Devotion, Sacrifice, Self-Denial. A cause, an obligation. A code of conduct, a sort of final moral definition, I mean definition of us, what we're here for—people living among each other, in an environment some sort of God created, the whole impossible nonsensical dream". Because this comes from an outsider looking in and won over momentarily to awe and admiration at seeing a legend at work, this is a radical tempering of Scott's critical appraisal.

So we have the aspiration, the dream, and the recognition that the contemporary situation makes it irrelevant. When the widowed Susan Bingham, Sarah's sister, tries to kill her baby in a circle of flames—Scott repeatedly uses death by fire as a potent image of consuming destruction, one phase in Shiva's dance of creation, preservation and destruction within his cosmic circle of fire—her action reflects on the whole Anglo-Indian community, as if her madness were a larger statement about people doomed by the inadequacy of their armour, of the code, conduct, ideas and principles by which they lived. It is Sarah Layton, towards the close of the last novel, who in acting by the code knows that it signifies nothing. During the communal fighting at the time of independence her friend Ahmed Kasim, who is travelling with her and a group of English people, is called from the compartment and killed by the Hindus and Sikhs who had stopped the train to massacre the Muslims aboard it. The train moves on to a station and she rushes to help, kneeling at a tap in the

filth and muck so that water can be passed to the wounded and dying; but she sees her "brave little memsahib act" as useless, just as Ahmed's British travelling companions had been useless in protecting him from his assassins, just as Ahmed's act in quietly accompanying his murderers had been useless, all consequences of a code which, if it had ever had validity, was now meaningless. Scott transmits this experience of despair, but does he share in repudiating the ethic which the servants of British imperialism in India devised? In Ronald Merrick . . . Scott obliquely offers for reappraisal the whole tradition—man-bap, service, responsibility—for it is Merrick the outsider who is made the repository of racism's obscenities and the corruptions with which some individuals who served imperialism were infected. Because of who and what Merrick is—to which I will return—Scott's critique of the imperial relationship is subtly trimmed and the claims of the old tradition reaffirmed.

For Scott the deeply-rooted British fear and dislike of dark-skinned people deformed the British-Indian association; his statement recognises the strength of the taboos surrounding race, so that linked with the love between the English girl, Daphne Manners, and Hari Kumar is "the attraction to danger" in what they felt for each other. Daphne Manners knows too that because of a situation in which one race is dominant and the other subservient a love relationship could be perverted by the "inferior" using it to bolster the ego and the "superior" for the stimulation of a titillating fear. Merrick, whose racism finds elaborate outlets, makes an explicit connection between sex, race and white domination in asserting that unlike a white woman a white man because of his superior role both in society and in sexual associations would not be degraded by a relationship with a dark person: "There is this connotation paleness has of something more finely, more delicately adjusted. Well—superior. Capable of leading. Equipped mentally and physically to dominate. A dark-skinned man touching a white-skinned woman will always be conscious of the fact that he is—diminishing her. She would be conscious of it too". White and black are counterpoised, and the accretions forming upon these words, automatically accepted by most western sensibilities, are drawn on and inverted: to Sarah Layton it is Merrick, the efficient white policeman, who is the dark, arcane side of Anglo-India, inseparable in her mind from the image of Hari Kumar's aunt in her white sari pleading for alleviation of the suffering he was causing her nephew.

The separations and connections between white and black are symbolised by two houses in Mayapore: one the MacGregor House erected by a Scot in the nineteenth century on the foundations of a ruin where once had stood a home built by a prince for a singer he adored; the other the Bibighar, built for his courtesans by the prince's son, who had despised his father's unconsummated passion and left its monument to decay. It is in the MacGregor House that Daphne Manners is living with her aunt's Indian friend, Lady Lili Chatterjee; it is in the gardens of the Bibighar that she makes love with Hari Kumar and is then raped by a group of Indian youths. To Sister Ludmilla the new link made by Daphne Manner's experiences gives the traditional connection between the houses a special significance:

> It is as though across that mile that separates them there have flowed the dark currents of a human conflict . . . A current. The flow of an invisible river. No bridge was ever thrown across it and stood. You understand what I am telling you? That

MacGregor and Bibighar are the place of the white and the place of the black? To get from one to the other you could not cross by a bridge but had to take your courage in your hands and enter the flood and let yourself be taken with it, lead where it may. This is a courage which Miss Manners had.

And it is Sister Ludmilla, like some eternal spectator of the enactment of human tragedy, herself beyond grief, who observes the counterpart to the love between the Englishwoman and the Indian, and its negation, in the situation which Merrick creates between himself and Hari Kumar, his chosen victim, when he takes him into custody:

> To observe more closely the darkness that attracted the darkness in himself. A different darkness but still a darkness. On Kumar's part a darkness of the soul. On Merrick's a darkness of the mind and heart and flesh. And again, but in an unnatural context, the attraction of white to black, the attraction of an opposite, of someone this time who had never even leapt into the depths of his own private compulsion let alone into those of life or of the world at large, but had stood high and dry on the sterile banks, thicketed around with his own secrecy and also with the prejudice he had learned because he was one of the white men in control of a black man's country.

Despite the possible deterrent of an over-mannered style, I find that here Scott makes the richest connections between the historical and social situations and the psychological experiences of his characters, and he does so through images and metaphors which are more eloquent and suggestive than his many lengthy explanations.

The central event, the love and the rape, reverberates through the novels, and in the interconnections Scott finds an analogue of the British-Indian association, a relationship made up of love and hatred, consent and violation; but here the roles are reversed, with Indians as assailants and whites as vanquished. In the record which Daphne Manners leaves her aunt, written shortly before her death in childbirth, she connects her rape with the British conquest of India:

> I thought that the whole bloody affair of *us* in India had reached flashpoint. It was bound to because it was based on a violation. Perhaps at one time there was a moral as well as a physical force at work. But the moral thing had gone sour . . . You can't hide that any longer because the moral issue, if it ever really existed at all, is dead . . . Perhaps there was love. Oh, somewhere in the past, and now, and in the future, love as there was between me and Hari. But the spoilers are always there.

Both the rape and the British-Indian association are obscenely parodied by the eroticism of the "master and man" situation imposed by Merrick on Hari Kumar when he is interrogating him.

Through Sarah Layton, Sister Ludmilla, Count Bronowsky, Perron, and above all Hari Kumar, who know and observe Merrick, a composite picture is built up of a man troubled by his homosexuality, a sado-masochist whose needs cannot be met in sexual fantasy and its enactment, but infuse his whole being and are intertwined with his racism and his status as master; a person whom Sister Ludmilla discerns as one unable to love who seeks out others as prey, whom Perron sees as choosing people for the antagonism that will be generated. . . . Hari Kumar, the Indian educated at an En-

glish public school, is Merrick's consummate victim. During the interrogation Merrick invents an erotic game, a perverted ritual because Hari is an unwilling participant in the premeditated phases of degradation to which he is asked to submit. First he is subjected to Merrick's obscene remarks about his relations with Daphne Manners; then, naked and tied to an iron trestle, his genitals are fondled before he is beaten on the buttocks with a cane until he bleeds; when he is exhausted he is untied, and it is Merrick who bathes his lacerations, offers him water and exacts a statement of gratitude. But now, conscious of the relationship which Merrick is imposing, Hari disengages himself by non-participation: "the situation only existed on Merrick's terms if we both took part in it. The situation would cease to exist if I detached myself from it". Again the condition is analogous to the Indian movement for independence when Indians ceased to accede to the roles, functions and status assigned to them by the British. But there is another dimension, one which has emerged only in great literature which has had as its theme the colonial experience: the ultimately destructive psychological satisfactions of having power over subjugated peoples, which enslave the masters and paralyse their capacity for choice and the exercise of free will.

For the iniquities he inflicts on Hari Kumar, Merrick, the custodian of British justice, receives no punishment, but justice is done; the end, when his war-dismembered body is further mutilated as if to mirror the deformities of his personality, is a fitting one. Dressed as a Pathan warrior, his face darkened with dye, Merrick is found by his servant with a sash strangling him, his body hacked to pieces by his sword, and the floor covered in cabbalistic signs, a ceremonial death which may have afforded Merrick the pleasures of a last ritual. Over the months handsome Indian youths had come to the house as if seeking work, but in fact to tempt him, satisfy him, suffer his punishments and lure him to that death they were planning as a retribution for his part in the Bibighar Gardens case. It is Count Bronowsky's conjecture that one of the boys, Aziz, revealed something to Merrick about himself that appalled him:

> I don't mean the revelation of his latent homosexuality and his sado-masochism. These must have been apparent to him for many years and every now and again given some form of expression. What I mean by a revelation is revelation of the connexion between the homosexuality, the sado-masochism, the sense of social inferiority and the grinding defensive belief in his racial superiority. I believe . . . that Aziz was the first young man he had actually ever made love to, and that this gave him a moment of profound peace, but in the next the kind he knew he couldn't bear because to admit this peace meant discarding every belief he had. I think he realised that, when he woke up after his first night with the boy. And I think that when the boy turned up the following night he just found himself punished and humiliated. And I believe that when Merrick beat him with his fist he was inviting retaliation. I believe he knew why Aziz had arrived. I am sure that finally . . . he sought the occasion of his own death and grew impatient for it.

Yet while Scott goes on to create this powerful allegory of the British-Indian relationship, on the opening page of the first novel he suggests another analogy, one with very different connotations and which recurs across the quartet, where he sees the two nations as involved in a marriage strong enough to withstand strife and incompatibility. . . . I have tried to indicate that for me Scott's deeply ambiguous attitudes to the raj and the imperialist experience give his writings a double vision, on the one hand an unsparing critique of aspects of the British-Indian interaction which probes the spiritual corruptions visited on the rulers; on the other an honouring of its potentiality for benefiting India. To some this ambivalence will appear as an aid to establishing a complex truth, to others an incubus making for sentimentality and distortion; for me this latter is crystallised in Hari Kumar, alias Harry Coomer, whose deracination had been planned by his father, and who makes the journey from Chillingborough, a school famed as a training-ground for public service, to the Chillian-wallah bazaar in Mayapore.

Hari, who is destined to be the victim of Merrick's perversions, is from childhood the victim of his father's perverse ambition that he shall grow up English, free of Indian attitudes, customs, traditions, accent which he had experienced as handicaps leading to his own demoralisation and defeat. . . . Hari or Harry went to public school, spending many of his vacations with his close friend Colin Lindsey, and looking forward to a future at a university and then in the ICS. But when his father's financial enterprises collapse and he commits suicide, Hari is forced to return to India, to the modest home of his widowed Aunt Shalini. Here Hari finds himself a stranger, hating his situation and the people surrounding him, humiliated at discovering that to the British in India he is invisible as an individual, and greatly wounded when a few years later Colin Lindsey, now in India with the army, avoids and then encounters but fails to acknowledge him. This sends Hari reeling into despair and drunkeness, for he knows that for Colin he too is now India, a source of fear and revulsion. What pride Hari is able to retain comes from a sense of his Englishness. . . . Hari does not know how to be an Indian, and whereas Daphne Manners is curious about India, receptive to Indian art, music, religious practices, he clings to a remote disdain. At this stage his very dignity is undignified, resting as it does on a total repudiation of and alienation from India. As he is forced to recognise his membership of a subject race, to examine the false consciousness instilled in him, to question his identity, he lives for a time in a vacuum, and only after the experience of his love with Daphne, of wrongful arrest and long incarceration, does his estimate of his own person grow; and it is Merrick who forces him to come to terms with the unique being and value of Hari Kumar and to find a strength in discovering that no one has any rights over him. Yet what is Hari? After his belated release he retreats to an obscure existence as a private English tutor, sometimes writing pieces for the English-language Indian press, and in one such article—which moves Perron to compassion and admiration—he expresses a nostalgia for England which, although tempered by a realisation that his aspirations had been a fiction, is tinged with sentimental yearning. . . . (pp. 361-68)

In terms of the novels, the characterisation of Hari works; he is the actualisation of Macaulay's hope that the British influence would create persons who were Indian "in blood and colour, but English in taste, in opinions, in morals and in intellect". Where Hari might have raged or cringed, he keeps a stiff upper lip and a dignified reticence; where he might have looked to participating in India's future, he withdraws into solitude there to dream of his lost "home", for after the development of a new pride and sense of identity when in custody, he is assigned by Scott to permanent limbo. I have allowed my summary of Hari Kumar's person and dilemmas to be coloured by my own disbelief in his authenticity beyond these pages, for unless literature is to be regarded as totally self-validating, the question is raised of what Scott sees as essential to a consideration of the imperial connection and where he finds its failures and victories. And in so far as these novels have heroes, Hari is one.

Certainly Scott's novels are "about" India, yet this needs qualification, for they are centrally concerned with India in its interrelationships with Britain; indeed Scott's India is overwhelmingly British India, the transitory home of exiles, the alienated motherland of Indians. Here there are some affinities with other writers who took the British in India as their theme: some of Scott's characters and situations are inevitably from the old Anglo-Indian stockpile—chilly, predatory women, officials stiff with rectitude or disconcerted by their power and responsibilities, the drama of a token Indian violating the sanctity of The Club—but to these, as I have tried to indicate, Scott brings a particular critical viewpoint. Again, in his approach to racial barriers and the strains imposed by the imperialist relationship on communication and friendship between British and Indian, his writing could be likened to *A Passage to India;* yet this is a comparison which goes nowhere, for while Forster does re-invent the specific, peopled and historically situated sub-continent, his is essentially a speculative novel, moving backwards and forward in time to explore states of consciousness and versions of human nature as these were given form in the myths, symbols and philosophical traditions of India. As for the other and more powerful influence on British writing about India, Scott neither emulates nor overtly challenges the Kipling style and ethic. (p. 368)

Scott's India is more poetic than the weird and exotic land of squalor and romance which was the backdrop to heaps of novelettes produced earlier in the century, and it is more prosaic than that long-standing tradition in western writing which discovered there a mythic universe of the eternal, the archetypal and the paradoxical. Nevertheless Scott finds in India a sense of indefinable possibilities and the infinite, of the tangible as illusory—one of his principal locations is named Mayapore—and he uses Indian landscapes as a source and Indian iconography as the representation of a distinctive and coherent world of being; so that when Edwina Crane cannot find God in India, it seems that this is because she has been looking for a western deity and not seeing Shiva dancing in his cosmic circle of flames or the sleeping Vishnu looking as if he might at any moment awaken. Still, the mythological and the metaphysical, so central to serious western transcriptions of India, is on the margin of Scott's vision.

From these four long, dense and complex novels, thought about and put together over more than a decade, I have had to select continuities which seem to me of significance, and in doing so I have necessarily done an injustice to the many other themes and levels. For me Scott's novels are essentially a "tribute" to a segment of the British middle-class, a celebration whose interest lies in its eccentricity, its absence of self-glorification. In a retrospect which spans so much misunderstanding, conflict and disaster, a kind of promise radiates; dignity and integrity survive assaults calculated to reduce and degrade, bridges, even if they are to be destroyed, are thrown across the chasm of race by the friendship of Sarah Layton and Ahmed Kasim, by the love between Daphne Manners and Hari Kumar. And there is a symbolic victory in the child which Daphne Manners bears. . . . Perhaps this is Scott's affirmation that whatever the genesis of the raj, whatever its failures and defects, it did bear fruit which will seed and germinate and be fertile endlessly into the future, an affirmation which many will repudiate and find unacceptable. Again this symbolism works within the novel, but India's multiple realities, of which the British influence is only one, rob it of a total authenticity. (p. 369)

Benita Parry, "Paul Scott's Raj," in South Asian Review, Vol. 8, No. 4, July-October, 1974, pp. 359-69.

MALCOLM MUGGERIDGE

Paul Scott's latest novel, **Staying On,** provides a sort of post-script to his deservedly acclaimed **The Raj Quartet,** a series of four novels dealing with the closing stages of British rule in India in the 1940's. Although he is the author of nine other novels, poetry and plays, the quartet has made Scott's international reputation as the chronicler of the decline and fall of the Raj. He has, as it were, summoned up the Raj's ghost in **Staying On,** a novel set in April 1972, so that in it we may observe how the ghost continues to walk in some of its old haunts. It is the story of the living death, in retirement, and the final end of a walk-on character from the quartet.

The setting is a hill station, Pankot, where a few Raj derelicts have lingered on with their servants, the rest of the inhabitants being brown Sahibs who have inherited the position of the deposed white ones. India in the larger sense—with its 600 million and more population, the great majority of whom live in villages spread throughout the subcontinent and engage in subsistence agriculture—scarcely figures in the book. (p. 1)

Scott's two main characters are Colonel "Tusker" Smalley and his wife Lucy; relics of the old Indian Army, who when India became independent, opted for staying on rather than returning home or, as so many of the Raj's officials and officers did, settling in Kenya or the Riviera or some other sunny place. The Smalleys live in the decayed annex of Smith's Hotel, with their servant Ibrahim to look after them, and they carry on a running battle with the hotel's elephantine proprietress, Mrs. Bhoolabhoy, whose subdued husband is the Colonel's friend and crony. They are survivors, of whom in changing times like ours there are so many. . . .

The hill-station variety is well conveyed by Scott in the Smalleys—the looking backward at dubious past glories, with nothing to look forward to except, perhaps, under necessity creeping away to some suburban Shangri-la in Outer London, or to a pension with special terms in the back streets of Nice; the boredom of passing days varied only by a visit to the hair-dresser or a gossip with Mr. Bhoolabhoy. How quickly Burra Sahibs deprived of their status become Poor Whites. How quickly, too, their Indian successors acquire the ways of Burra Sahibs. Perhaps the most deplorable consequences of British rule in India has been the creation of a second-rate Anglo-Indian culture that has survived the Raj, and even flourished. Thus Colonel Smalley finds himself in the post-Independence Indian Army messes, where an Indianized version of the ceremonial and slang of Raj days lives on. . . .

Nothing much happens in **Staying On.** The row with Mrs. Bhoolabhoy turns on who is to be responsible for cutting the grass round the annex, and finally leads to the Colonel being informed that his tenancy is terminated, whereupon he has a heart attack and dies. We are introduced to the English church and Father Sebastian, Mr. Bhoolabhoy being a lay reader. Through Lucy Smalley's day-dreaming we get a notion of her life before she married Tusker, and of how disappointing and tiresome aspects of her life with him have been. We are even made privy to the Colonel's regular, but scarcely ardent, performance of his marital duties, as well as regaled with Mr. Bhoolabhoy's frantic efforts to mount and penetrate his spouse's vast carcass. I confess it surprised me that so accomplished a writer as Scott should have fallen into the error of supposing that descriptions of sexual encounters are made more convincing by being explicit.

The difficulty I found with **Staying On** was to work up sufficient sympathy with any of the characters to care about what happened to them. In any case, Mr. Scott's characters are doubtless intended to be dim figures belonging to a limbo between a dead empire and a nation not yet reborn. The triumph of Gandhi and his Swarajists has proved to be only the afterglow of imperial glory; before dawn can break, night must fall.

With **Staying On,** Scott has completed his task of covering in the form of a fictional narrative the events leading up to India's partition and the achievement of independence in 1947. It is, on any showing, a creditable achievement. . . . Present interest in the Raj, extending to appreciation of Kipling—formerly under a leftist anathema—should insure its success. A characteristic of our time is a passion to destroy anything that seems strong and reputable and then, when the destruction is complete, a nostalgic pleasure in viewing what has been destroyed. (p. 36)

Malcolm Muggeridge, in a review of "Staying On," in The New York Times Book Review, August 21, 1977, pp. 1, 36.

FRANCINE S. WEINBAUM

In his 1966 review of Paul Scott's **The Jewel in the Crown** [see excerpt above], Orville Prescott wrote that it "may well be the finest novel about India since E. M. Forster's *A Passage to India* and that [it] will certainly be one of the finest novels of any kind published this year." The considerable praise has been echoed by major reviewers of the novel's sequels: **The Day of the Scorpion** (1968), **The Towers of Silence** (1971), and **A Division of the Spoils** (1975). Yet aside from a discussion of the novels as historical enrichment and a view of them as ambivalent and unduly sentimental, no published criticism has appeared.

Scott's subject is the failure of British imperialism, the turmoil the British created and were caught by in pre-independence India. The novels dramatize the debacle of division, not only of India and Pakistan, but more centrally, the divorce of England from the Indian subcontinent in the years leading up to and including partition. Panoramic in scope and microscopic in detail, the books recreate the events, sights, sounds, and smells of British India in the 1940's. Scott presents a picture, politically, sociologically, and psychologically revealing, of how two nations came into tragic confrontation, and how and why British rule ended in failure and a sense of diminished stature.

The Raj Quartet is at once a series of objective historical novels, a philosophical tragedy, a moral detective story, and an illuminating psychological investigation of the mind's defenses. Its narrator, in the course of his 1964 travels, takes the reader on at least five journeys: an historical-temporal one going back to events that occurred in the turbulent India of the 1940's; a spatial passage through the imaginary Mayapore, Mirat, Ranpur, Pankot, in which the destinies of the characters are worked out; an ethical journey that is a search for the villain behind the related tragedies of the abandonment and division of India and the separation and sufferings of an English girl, Daphne Manners, and her English-bred Indian lover, Hari Kumar; a metaphysical quest for a resolution of the conflict of love and death in the world; and a journey into the mind investigating psychological defenses and mind-body dualism symbolized in *The Jewel in the Crown* by the divided city of Mayapore. Because Scott writes about the perpetual conflict of love and death in public and private affairs as well as in the mind, the journeys are interrelated, with complex unifying effect. Union is the aim: England and India, white and black, soul and body; but division and insularity are what finally remain of shattered political, sociological, and psychological ideals.

In his concern with British imperialism, Scott appears to have much in common with other writers of the colonial experience, but some striking differences in theme and tone heighten our perception of Scott's individuality. To contrast Scott with Kipling is to see each as a reflection of opposing values of their times. Kipling, writing shortly after the heyday of imperialism, captures a sense of pride in British accomplishment, a faith in the success of the imperial purpose whose failure Scott laments. Kipling writes of the marriage of East and West, a union of unequal partners since he takes for granted a national and racial superiority. Scott's ideal twentieth-century marriage of East and West, on the other hand, is not imperialistic but egalitarian, symbolized in the tragically thwarted union of Daphne Manners and Hari Kumar. Kumar represents the supposed imperial ideal, or Macaulay's brown-skinned Englishman come to life, to show how illusory were the good intentions of most Englishmen towards Indians, based on an implicit idea of superiority.

For Scott imperialism suggests the failure of an ideal and of an administrative structure that was for all its flaws essentially sound. The irony in Scott's vision of the Raj (one has the sense of its nineteenth-century grandeur having been primarily illusory) is restrained and subordinated to his sense of resigned sadness. Where Kipling imagines a British India of pride and legend, Scott mirrors his countrymen's lost moral purpose and self-definition. In *The Day of the Scorpion* Officer Teddie Bingham, oblivious of his own safety on the World War II battlefield in Burma, stands up in his jeep to call for his regiment's Indian National Army deserters to return. His extraordinary act is, as an observer realizes, the stuff of a legend where Teddie might well have succeeded; but even if he did not, Teddie's death rewritten in Kipling's manner would be viewed as a noble sacrifice. . . . In *The Raj Quartet* the British community and probably his regiment as well see Teddie's demise as a pointless and unnecessary death caused by the courage of a delusive belief in a loyalty that no longer existed, if it ever had.

George Orwell's Swiftian bitterness and irony at the Raj's injustice is Scott's disillusionment and sad resignation. Scott's view appears the more rounded and objective, for Orwell's Raj has no positive features but is a caricature of evil. It is exploitative and suppressive, arrogant and arbitrary, like

many of the characters in *Burmese Days*. . . . Scott has a much more beneficent view of the best of human nature, and his heroes and heroines find meaning in extending themselves regardless of personal risk.

E. M. Forster provides an interesting comparison as long as we remember that, despite a certain similarity in concern with the Anglo-Indian relation, the philosophies and styles of the two writers are different, even sometimes antithetical. Scott shares with Forster a concern with aspects of the imperialistic relationship that prevent friendship or union between the two peoples. Scott, however, converts the central dramatic incident of *A Passage to India,* the attempted rape in the Marabar Caves of foolish Adela Quested, an imaginary event which at length succeeds in preventing the development of the friendship between Aziz and Fielding, into an actual rape of an English girl, which is similarly causative in preventing her marriage with her Indian lover.

The dynamic Marabar symbolism, embodying the negative philosophy of *A Passage to India,* enjoys an emphatic role comparable to Scott's multilevel symbolism pointing to the frustration of union, but Forster's inability to transcend Marabar limits the philosophical appeal of his novel. . . . In *A Passage to India* a sense of inner emptiness is symbolically realized throughout the novel, in the "Boum" of the caves, the god-like vacuity of the non-thinking punkah wallah, the sunrise whose supreme moment reveals nothingness, the death of Mrs. Moore at sea, unredeemed from that dreadful state of unbelief in which Marabar has left her.

Despite the technical brilliance of *A Passage to India,* one may feel somewhat less than satisfied with the silly, tinny, Godbolean answer to the negativism of Marabar and unhappy with the weakness of Forster's positive values. Scott has metaphysical doubts, too, but the psychological core of his novels is solid; his philosophy is saddened rather than weakened by the ontological vacuum. While Scott finds illusory the belief that the forces of love will overwhelm those of destruction, he provides an answer to Marabar. Taking as his credo Eliot's lines in "East Coker," "We must be still and still moving / Into another intensity / For a further union, a deeper communion," Scott insists on the absolute human value of creative love.

Each of the characters embodying the values of *The Raj Quartet* attempts to cut across either communal, racial, political, or psychological barriers to achieve some form of union, usually with or for India and Indians. The missionary administrator, Edwina Crane, for example, has a mystical love for the country and yearns for spiritual union with an abstract Indian; Daphne Manners falls in love with the Anglicized Indian Hari Kumar; the Wazir (Chief Minister) Count Bronowsky wants equal privileges for Mirat's Hindus and Muslims, joined harmoniously under his prince; ex-Congress minister Mohammed Ali Kasim desires a united, independent India. Each is betrayed by a combination of political, social, and psychological forces. Tragically, the price of love or attempted union is often some form of diminishment, but these characters rarely doubt the rightness or value of their goals and remain, in Daphne's words, "imprisoned but free, diminished by everything that loomed from the outside, but not diminished from the inside."

Scott envisions a world of the "malign spirit," where only a few have the vision or the courage to act out of love or true principle, a quality which in any event often destroys its possessor. Since the authentic "hero" of the books is not the English-bred Indian Hari Kumar, as one would at first suppose, nor "India, as she passes from one epoch to another," nor even England in India, but creative, egalitarian love, the "villain" is not the British policeman Ronald Merrick so much as the forces of insularity which victimize protagonists and antagonists alike. Whether in politics or human relations, the enemies of love are self-interest and barriers to communication, insular forces apparent in "the white robot," the system of the British Raj that destroyed the union of Hari Kumar and Daphne Manners, and also in the psychological defenses against inner fears and desires.

Parochial forces are the crushing enemies that are often and memorably symbolized in Scott's novels. Like the recurrent image of the scorpion, which appears to sting itself to death when encircled by fire but is actually burned by the heat, the British Raj and the human condition are surrounded by indifferent and destructive forces. Such insular myopia in times of great emergency led General Dyer at Amritsar in 1919 (or Scott's fictional Brigadier-General Reid in 1942) to shoot into an unarmed crowd; or a British policeman, irrationally convinced of an innocent man's guilt, to incarcerate and torture him. These insularities are responsible, in Scott's view, for the general tragic failure of the British in India, the "thwarted, abortive human intention" to bring order, unity, and peaceful, prosperous self-government to a country whose people suffered as much from some of their own superstitions and religious practices (as in *suttee,* the Hindu practice of burning widows on their husbands' funeral pyres) as from poverty, humiliation, and death inflicted on them by autocratic despots, greedy *zemindars* (landlords), and warring factions. Narrow, detached interests were responsible for the imperceptive British policy and Indian over-reactions that led to the destruction of an admirable moral and political ideal. (pp. 100-04)

Even more than they express regret over policy errors, Scott's novels are concerned with the forces behind them. The books concentrate on British social attitudes towards Indians and the psychological defenses which led to the British alienation from India, symbolizing the body as England symbolizes the soul. (p. 104)

By the end of *A Division of the Spoils,* Scott clearly shows that the most admirable aspirations of the British for India were based on illusions. As a diminished Hari Kumar once wrote for the *Ranpur Gazette,* "I walk home, thinking of another place, of seemingly long endless summers and the shade of different kinds of trees, and then of winters when the branches of the trees were so bare, that recalling them now, it seems inconceivable to me that I looked at them and did not think of the summer just gone, and the spring soon to come, as illusions; as dreams, never fulfilled, never to be fulfilled."

Scott has steeped himself in the history of British India, and his view is close enough to that of reputable historians to suggest that *The Raj Quartet*'s portrayal of the scene and of British policy errors could be taken as an objective historical view, one that revitalizes history by making historical events "more directly intelligible than these events might otherwise be to us." This judgment reflects the fact that Scott's ideal is broadly humanist as well as historical; his convincing recreation of the bewilderment, frustration, and failure of the British living in India in the 1940's is a dramatization of the whole experience of the Raj and persuades not so much by

rational argument as by feelings and intuitive insights. The historical dimension is critical, but *The Raj Quartet,* like any fiction, is a metaphor for an author's view of life, and its history is subordinated to other components.

To criticize Scott for "a muted celebration of a concept rather than a critique of a reality" is to recognize that his broadly humanist ideal for the British never had much chance of becoming a reality. Such comments miss an important contribution of the novels—the tying of one historical failure to universal psychological shortcomings and metaphysical problems. Scott's novels transcend their tenor, or immediate historical picture, to say something about the limitations of the human condition. Their view of British failure in India is tied to general human deficiency; they lament in historical terms the failure of an ideal of love that, given the human condition, was never really possible.

This vision is most important, a conception which thematically and symbolically unites political with sociological and psychological components to create a transcendent or mystical vision of love, not as in Dante's *Paradiso,* fulfilled and infinitely fulfilling, but sadly, necessarily, and almost as infinitely thwarted. That the focus of the novels is subtly shifted from external to internal consequences is apparent when we consider that the relation of the rape victim, Daphne Manners, to *The Raj Quartet*'s center of values is more important than that of any political figure, and that even the considerable stature of a character like the Congress politician, Mohammed Ali Kasim, depends in a Dickensian fashion on his proximity to the mystical core of the novels rather than to the center of political and social power.

The mystical vision or core is revealed through insights which are shared, often telepathically, by those characters who embody the values of the novels. Sister Ludmila, a European woman who has devoted her life in India to the care of the destitute dying, declares to the narrator that Daphne had the courage to live deeply, to leap metaphorically from the MacGregor House, the place of the white, to the Bibighar, the place of the black:

> To get from one to the other you could not cross by a bridge but had to take your courage in your hands and enter the flood and let yourself be taken with it, lead where it may. This is a courage Miss Manners had. . . .
> It is as if she said to herself: Well, life is not just a business of standing on dry land and occasionally getting your feet wet. It is merely an illusion that some of us stand on one bank and some on the opposite. So long as we stand like that we are not living at all, but dreaming. So jump, jump in, and let the shock wake us up. Even if we drown, at least for a moment or two before we die we shall be awake and alive.

These values are admired by people like her aunt's charming Rajput friend, Lili Chatterjee, who tries to prevent her relationship with Hari Kumar because she fears the human consequences of Daphne's courage. Miss Manners' brave, sensitive, and creative approach to living is repeated in the army colonel's daughter, Sarah Layton, who speaks of her own and an Indian friend's refusal to play their traditional roles: "We recognized in each other the compulsion to break away from what I can only call a received life."

The insights are frequently symbolic or analogical and serve structurally to tie together levels of meaning by revealing the history of England in India incarnate in individual lives. Thus the historian Guy Perron, disturbed by a memory of Kumar playing cricket at Chillingboro, sees in Hari's face his own historical awareness "that to misjudge, to mistime, would lead to destruction." Bumbling, retired missionary, Barbara Batchelor, the novels' most explicit, sustained symbol of the British in India, hallucinates what she takes to be the Voice of God saying, "Nothing can bring you peace but yourself. Nothing can bring you peace but the triumph of principles." She cries out in fear, her knees unable to bend, symbolically fixed in this "proud and arrogant position" because "she could not remember what her principles were."

Scott employs a circular, partly repetitious writing style in *The Raj Quartet.* His narrator interviews those people still alive in 1964 who had some acquaintance with the Bibighar case, the sorry affair stemming from the rape of Daphne Manners in the Bibighar Gardens during the riots of August, 1942. The time lapse, the differing points of view, and the narrator's inability to interview even one of the three characters central to the affair—Daphne Manners, Hari Kumar, or the District Superintendent of Police Ronald Merrick—cause him to rely on diaries, letters, and second-hand, conflicting, and tangential accounts, establishing a distance and sense of perspective which seem to convey an objective truth. The narrator, who is physically present in his imaginative recreations of 1964, does not intrude his point of view (except to point, particularly through the heightened, restrained tone, to the tragedy involved) but concentrates on recreating the affair in its totality—and to all appearances, lets the reader reach his own conclusions.

Scott uses the narrative method to allow us to compare corresponding or conflicting views of the same character or event in part because he is writing about the painful limitations of human perception, the tragic failure of communication between men and nations (and between parts of ourselves). Besides permitting each novel its self-containment, the method creates an amazing verisimilitude—the sense of an entire world with its own dynamics—and allows us to apprehend the bridges of contact and the unfortunate gaps between them. The technique is most dramatically successful with strongly contrasting views of the same event. . . . The repetition—together with the sheer volume and emphasis on historical facts, contrasting views, and minute realistic details—has another, perhaps more important function in serving to balance the individual mystical insights which direct the reader by making the values of the novels explicit. Our sense of the real must be filled with a solid, comprehensive sense of life before we can accept a guiding mystical dimension, however individually and metaphorically realized.

Unlike the works of contemporary literature that portray the relationships of a few people in an empty universe, Scott's work has a nineteenth-century broadness of scope and solidity of value. Contemporary literature is depressing because it emphasizes the alienation of man from his universe and views life, where it is not comic, as absurd and meaningless. Scott's protagonists, on the other hand, though living in a dying world, possess a moral certainty and, despite their ordinariness, an heroic stature. From Ibsen Scott takes his sense of the tragic—of men like Dr. Stockman in *An Enemy of the People* caught in the grip of a fate that does not deny free will, and of the sacrifice of men for their ideals. To this he adds a Chekhovian sense of loss and nostalgia and a Jamesian subtlety of thought and feeling in human relations, perhaps most

movingly portrayed in *Staying On* (1977), a comic, sad comment about those British who remained in India after partition. Scott's chief claim to major stature in *The Raj Quartet,* however, is the novels' extraordinarily sustained unity of theme and form—their transcendent philosophical and symbolic vision of thwarted union. (pp. 105-08)

Francine S. Weinbaum, "Paul Scott's India: 'The Raj Quartet'," in Critique: Studies in Modern Fiction, *Vol. XX, No. 1, 1978, pp. 100-10.*

JACQUELINE BANERJEE

In retrospect it seems sadly prophetic that Paul Scott's prize-winning novel, *Staying On,* should have been so universally praised as a 'codicil' to his monumental work, *The Raj Quartet.* As in the case of another writer who has often been regarded and valued primarily as a social historian, true recognition came late, almost too late. John Galsworthy was never able to deliver the speech which he was composing for the acceptance of the Nobel Prize, awarded to him shortly before his death. Worlds of difference separate the two writers, but Scott, writing of the last days of the British in India, and Galsworthy, writing of late Victorian and Edwardian society, share an impressive range of subject matter, a grasp of the sweep of centuries and the passing of eras, and a gift for the evocation of the quality of living in times past. However, at the very end of his writing career, in the speech which he never had the chance to deliver, Galsworthy showed an awareness of the failures of insight and inspiration within the carefully reconstructed society of his novels: 'I have made a sort of world with my pen, but has it any resemblance to the world we live in, either in England or anywhere else?' Scott's powers of imaginative re-creation, on the other hand, have been used in an ambitious effort to analyse and present human emotions, ideas and relationships; his legacy to us is not simply a description, wide-ranging yet accurately detailed, of the lives of the British in India around the time of Independence, but much more than that, a deep analytical probing of the springs of human behaviour.

The complex society in which Scott was so keenly interested provided ideal material for such a probing. Among the English in India at the end of the Raj there were, of course, the regular Indian Army Officers and their wives, the 'bottled up and bottled in' Memsahibs whose strangely enclosed lives and attitudes exercise a fascination over us which grows with the years. But there were others: their children, educated 'at home' and returning from a changing society with much more liberal ideas; the Indian Civil Service officers, who might or might not have had considerably humbler origins than their counterparts in the army; the elderly missionaries, who might have had very humble origins indeed, and a variety of motives for coming out; and the first of a new generation of young people seeking not to impose their own values on the East, but rather to find something there which was clearly lacking in the West. What would make any study of these disparate elements of British society in India interesting is the fact that, added to the tensions produced by differences in class, there were those resulting from differences in attitude towards the Indians themselves, yet all were forced together in uneasy amalgam during times of crisis, and particularly during the time of which Scott was writing. On the other side, infinitely more complex, divided by religion as well as caste, politics as well as individual sensibilities, was the Indian society itself, which could only explode in the most horrible way when brought together under the pressure of Independence. Little wonder that Scott was drawn, time and again, to work this fruitful field of human conflict and flux. He shirks neither the issues which arise so clearly in the Indian context, nor their outcomes.

The Raj Quartet begins with the story of Edwina Crane. The ageing missionary, who is rather an oddity when seen among the cantonment ladies of Mayapore, dies by self-immolation after an Indian colleague has been battered to death by rioters while driving her to safety. Her final action, that of dressing herself in a white sari and setting light to herself, is not one of insanity, as the English District Superintendent would have it: it is a gesture symbolic of an absolute commitment to India, such as she now realized had proved impossible in her daily life in that country. The sequence of four novels ends with another unthinkable death, another courageous gesture of personal commitment which is also an admission of failure. This time the commitment is to values which transcend man-made divisions, and the failure is one which reflects on the future of the whole continent. Ahmed Kassim, the sensitive and uncommitted son of a Muslim leader himself still suffering the consequences of his decision to remain outside the Muslim League, courteously gives himself up to the band of Hindu rioters. . . . As a result, his English friends and their companions, including an Indian ayah, are quite unscathed, while he is brutally hacked to death by the Hindus. Two young people in the carriage, Sarah Layton and Guy Perron, go to do what they can to minister to the injured and dying. Sarah, who had had a special kind of empathy with Ahmed, helps to give water to them. The gesture seems utterly futile in the face of the terrible wounds inflicted on man by man, and with her characteristic self-detachment Sarah herself despises her 'brave little memsahib act' as much as she deplores what she sees as Ahmed's capitulation to an accepted code of conduct. But as she does what she can to alleviate pain, before returning, as she knows she must, to her own family duties, we may be justified in sensing the ultimate triumph of the human values Ahmed died for—even in the very midst of their apparent collapse. Lucy Smalley in *Staying On* calls it gratefully the 'continuity of civilized behaviour'.

It is tempting to see a deliberate progression from the purging fire of Edwina Crane's suicide to the young Sarah Layton's compassionate dispensation of water to the wretched victims of the Hindu/Muslim riots. Scott certainly makes use of symbolic episodes (most of his titles relate to them) but he seems less concerned than, say, Patrick White, to point up the symbolic pattern which emerges from his work. If this kind of symbolic development is intended, it is as just one aspect of the complex fabric of inter-woven events. Scott's skills are primarily those of a narrator with an amazing capacity for creating such a fabric. In an early novel, *The Mark of the Warrior* (1959), he had already shown different perceptions of reality constantly impinging on and inter-acting against each other: the remembered or guessed-at horrors of an incident in the Burma Campaign, the careful verisimilitude of a cadet's training exercise in the Indian jungle, and the psychological testing ground which the programme provides for a Major and the young cadet in temporary command. An accumulation of precise, authentic detail—one almost succumbs to the temptation to read certain passages as reportage—contributes to the building up of a relationship between the two areas of action, while each takes its toll on its chief participant. The parallels are so clear that all tensions arise from

the clash of personality between the two men; a tragic outcome seems so inevitable that suspense is concentrated less on the fate of the young cadet than on how he—and the Major—confront it. In a slightly later, more clearly experimental novel, *The Corrida at San Feliu,* Scott cleverly fits together three apparently unrelated episodes in the lives of different characters by showing their autobiographical reference to their author. After such preliminary exercises and the accomplishment, in particular, of *The Birds of Paradise,* the nature of his artistic achievement in *The Raj Quartet* should come as no surprise. His masterly handling of the multiple viewpoint technique is especially helpful in allowing him to illuminate each important 'situation', each character involved, each relationship, from a number of angles; and it is this too that enables him to link the four novels so naturally and intricately while maintaining (because of the inevitable repetition of basic facts) their self-sufficiency.

As might be expected, the significant confrontations are often, although by no means always, between the English and the Indians. The most striking and complex is that which takes place in *The Jewel in the Crown,* between Ronald Merrick, the District Superintendant who has also to deal with Edwina Crane's death, and Hari Kumar. . . . This young man, forced by the financial ruin and death of his father to return to a homeland from which he has become totally alienated, is accused of raping Daphne Manners, a young English visitor to Mayapore. We come to know the full truth of the matter from the girl's diary—how the two had made love before a band of youths came upon them, and held Hari away by force while they raped her themselves. But Merrick, who had also had some attachment to the girl, and had warned her of the consequences of 'crossing the barriers' between English and Indian; who has, perhaps, some inkling of what really happened, is determined to implicate the boy. The clash between these two troubled personalities is powerful, its full force only appreciated after Kumar's own account of his interrogation in *The Day of the Scorpion.* . . . The results of the confrontation, of the whole affair of the 'rape in the Bibighar Gardens', are extremely complex and have ramifications which spread through each novel, until finally Merrick is himself the victim of a shockingly gross revenge. It is as well to remember that Merrick's reasons for hounding down Kumar, and his handling of him—as of the defected Indian soldiers in *A Division of the Spoils*—are highly personal, and that Merrick himself is a singular personality, warped by the driving need to dominate which, though it gives him a kind of vitality, has diminished his humanity. But this most fully explored failure of sympathy does seem to epitomize not only the callous rejection of Kumar by all the British (except, of course, Daphne) to whom he is simply 'invisible' as an individual, but also the soul-destroying humiliation and bondage to which the Indians have been subject.

Are the paternalism of such men as Colonel Layton, Sarah's father, or the evangelism of such missionaries as Barbie Batchelor . . . any more valuable to the sections of Indian society towards which they are directed than the 'calm purity' of Merrick's contempt? Merrick himself does not think so, and the results do not suggest it. The defection of Indian troops to the Japanese-organized Indian National Army becomes a major problem; and Barbie wonders 'how many of those little Indian children really loved God and came to Jesus?' As for Daphne Manners, who dared to attempt a relationship with an Indian (albeit a very Anglicized one) on an equal footing—she and her aunt disappear from the picture, until she herself dies in childbirth, having obstinately borne the baby she believes to be Hari's. Has Forster said it all, after all? There is, however, the carefully traced emergence of Sarah Layton as a mature and objective observer of the Indian scene. She alone has the courtesy to visit the Manners baby, and there is a beautifully conceived and executed passage in which she and Ahmed ride out together at Mirat. Sensible enough to acknowledge the reasons for maintaining a certain distance, even as she deliberately exhibits her personal scorn for it, Sarah is able to establish a basis for real communication with Ahmed. The murders of both Merrick and Ahmed suggest the finality of the ending of the old ways, both of the rulers and the ruled, as the British make their exit from India, and the dream of a united India is shattered by the horrors of Partition. But the improved chances for successful human relationships are at least suggested.

Would such relationships really be possible for the generation actually involved in the events leading up to Independence? Sarah, we learn, marries Guy Perron, who returns to academic life in England. The central characters of *Staying On* are the elderly Smalleys, the couple who had succeeded the Laytons at their home in Pankot; the hotel which now caters for them employs the ayah who had escaped detection on that memorable train journey. For these people, who have chosen to remain behind, the tables have simply turned: they are not only much less wealthy, but also less 'international' than the smart set of Indian families among whom they have made acquaintances; by a new generation of Indian Officers at the Mess, they are treated with the politeness due to the 'defeated'; they depend on, rather than being depended on by, a servant born into the traditions of the Raj; worst of all, their future is in the unscrupulous hands of their gross landlady, insatiable, it seems, in all her appetites—a character of Dickensian proportions. Lucy Smalley is increasingly aware that in such a world she can no longer count on her white skin to act 'as a defensive armour', yet she cannot forget it either. . . . She feels herself to be surrounded by 'people who frankly do not care for me, not deeply, and for whom I do not deeply care either'.

Of course, there was no use pretending that it had been much better for them in the past, when Tusker Smalley's limited talents and lack of ambition, as well as her own unprepossessing background, had consigned her to a low rung in the very strict hierarchy of the original (that is, the English) Memsahibs. Nor would it have been much different for them in, say, 'bloody Stevenage', ekeing out their old age on Supplementary Benefits and private charities. In *The Raj Quartet,* the larger historical canvas does make special claims on our attention: but Lucy Smalley's reveries about the past, and Tusker Smalley's explanation of his decision to 'stay on' in India, make it quite clear in *Staying On* that India, however fascinating in itself, is only one of the countless possible contexts for the 'comedy of life' which, like it or not, we all have to share. Where Holi and Easter are celebrated with equal enthusiasm, what strikes us most is not the difference between the two cultures, nor even the problems of overcoming it, but the universality of the basic human condition. The breakdown of communication between the Smalleys is juxtaposed to the complete domination of Frank Bhoolabhoy ('Management' of the hotel) by his wife Lila ('Ownership' of the hotel), and the alternation of uproariously funny episodes between the two sets of marriage partners establishes their shared participation in a common lot.

When Lucy yearns to go 'home' with Tusker at the end, she is not using the word in the sense in which earlier Memsahibs have used it. As with Srinivas, the Indian immigrant in Kamala Markandaya's *The Nowhere Man,* a lonely life in another land has nevertheless cut her off effectively enough from her own country of origin. The only 'home' for her now is death, that final home for which we all, 'peering into the darkness', await transport. The restraint, self-control and endurance which this quite ordinary woman has learnt in the hard school of suffering, even from the rejections of her earliest childhood, as well as her searingly honest assessment of her generous response to the slightest glimmer of affection in her hot-tempered but taciturn husband, have already given Lucy a nobility which has blended tragedy with the comedy. As we close the novel, we are bound to feel, with Philip Larkin . . . that for all its many moments of laughter it is 'simply the most moving' of the novels which appeared in 1977. (pp. 97-103)

Anyone who has entered the world of *The Raj Quartet,* or stood with the Smalleys at the lowering of the Union Jack on an Indian parade ground, should be aware of the real nature of Paul Scott's achievement: it lies not in the depiction of great events, nor even in the analysis of their different effects on the different races involved, but in the presentation of human beings in all their infinite complexity. We mourn Scott's loss because of his qualities as a person, and because he was writing at the very height of his powers when he died; but we are deeply grateful for this living legacy. (p. 104)

Jacqueline Banerjee, "A Living Legacy," in London Magazine, *n.s. Vol. 20, Nos. 1 & 2, April & May, 1980, pp. 97-104.*

M. M. MAHOOD

'Popular history in a fictionalized form' is the kind of dismissive phrase used about Paul Scott's *Raj Quartet* by many who have not read the four-novel sequence and by a few who have. . . . [However], the sequence is very much more than an evocation of the last days of British India; . . . it aspires to be an imaginative creation of Tolstoyan breadth and depth, and as such demands a serious critical attention. What the rewards of such attention may be are for the most part left here as an open question. Some tentative valuations are attempted, but the important thing is that the enquiry should be seen as one which is worth pursuing, that the *Raj Quartet* should be understood to have not only size but magnitude as well.

A natural place to begin an investigation of Scott's objectives and achievements is his own beginning to the work, the story of Miss Crane: seventy-odd pages which are as powerfully disconcerting as the Dorothea Brooke episode of *Middlemarch* and to much the same purpose of startling us into a full receptivity of all that is to follow. The story is a kind of narthex in which, like medieval catechumens, we are put wise before we are admitted to the cathedral itself.

Edwina Crane is a mission-school supervisor of liberal views with high hopes for India's independence. She is more a Fielding than a Turton. But the instinctive closing of the ranks between English men and women of the most diverse opinions when the political temperature rises (something Forster remarks on before the end of *A Passage to India*) shows itself in Miss Crane's shocked reaction to Gandhi's Quit India resolutions of 1942. There is after all a war on, a war which the Japanese conquest of Burma has turned into a siege. The arrest of the Congress leaders as a consequence of the resolution builds up civil tension, but this Miss Crane sturdily ignores. She goes about her duties in a downright, business-as-usual manner, encouraged, we may fancy, by a low-pitched authorial murmur of 'Well done'.

The illusion that we hear such a murmur is necessary to Scott's purpose of playing upon the stock responses and prejudices that cause the readers to close their own ranks. It is a dangerous game to play, because the reader who is too clever by half may decide that this mixture of incipient violence and a prefabricated character is altogether too reminiscent of John Masters—and just drop out. Prefabrication, however, is the point Scott is making. Edwina Crane is a self-made woman. The approbation we at first fancied to come from the author soon reveals itself as emanating from the character. She has moulded for herself the persona of a capable woman with a divine mission to take charge of awkward situations as, in her finest hour, she once turned back an angry mob from a school building. The persona has been her refuge from a number of past stresses: the hostile immensity of India, the otherness of its people, the wounding condescension of the pukka Anglo-Indians. So Miss Crane continues in her old role, in a changed and highly charged situation. She is unaware that her mistrust of the man the newspapers will later refer to as 'her Indian subordinate' is rooted in unacknowledged arrogance and contempt: motives scarcely to be suspected in such a nice old lady, but strong enough to make her fend off his concern and protection. When she finally does go over the hump of traditional race relationships and trusts herself completely to Mr Chaudhuri, it is too late: he is able to save her life, but only at the expense of his own.

Most readers start **The Jewel in the Crown** with a more or less secret admiration for the proconsular ideal as it is set out in such a work as Percival Spear's *The Guardians.* The admiration can be mixed with nostalgia on the part of the proconsuls' descendants, but as often as is not it is the romantic reaction of those whose parents or grandparents, in 1947, relinquished India as an irrelevancy in the post-war world. Scott's art is to manipulate these attitudes and thus ensure that we are made wise with Edwina Crane, that we share her belated grasp of the truth as our own truth. In this way the work begins as it is to continue, in the enlargement of personal experience and understanding which fiction can bestow more immediately than can history. Yet history, too, offers applicable insights which Scott uses to the full in placing his story in North India between the years 1942 and 1947. For it was there and then, in Scott's own words, that the liberal philosophy last *excited* the British. Scott's wartime experiences of India, his study of Indian history, and his later visits, all convinced him that the British, in India, 'came to the end of themselves as they were' became the circumstances of the subcontinent tested the strength of the liberal philosophy and it could not take the strain. He read *A Passage to India* as the prophecy of this ultimate failure, which is what shocks Mrs Moore into her silence, her despairing withdrawal: a silence Forster himself was henceforward to share.

If the same failure shocked Scott into his loquacity of eighteen hundred pages (to say nothing of his earlier novels), his justification is that he not only needed to explore the grounds of that failure in a long and searching exposure of the moral springs of action in a society ostensibly committed to liberal values, but needed also, if his India was to be as he claimed a metaphor for a total view of life, to explore alternative motives to action. Action, of one kind or another, there has to be. [In his essay "India: A Post-Forsterian View," Scott] couples with his statement that 'Mrs Moore was before her time and sits motionless to draw attention to our own' an echo of T. S. Eliot: 'still as we sit we must still be moving'. But at this point, when we are asking for an indication of where we might move, Scott exasperatingly takes refuge in a very long quotation from 'East Coker', culminating in 'In my end is my beginning', and breaks off. What seems evasiveness may have been the reticence of a very reserved man about his own beliefs and values. It may also have been guided by a novelist's sound instinct to leave those beliefs intact in their fictional matrix, thereby encouraging the reader to trust the tale rather than the teller. But the overall effect of Scott's reticence is to leave out, as reviewers and critics generally have left out, the importance in the novels of motive forces quite other than the unrecognized self-interest of India's sometime rulers. Because even Scott's serious admirers tend to present the **Raj Quartet** as a relentless analysis of decline and ruin, the emphasis of this essay is upon Scott's recognition of the creative springs of action, his positive values. (pp. 244-46)

Contempt, the diminishment of the other so surprisingly revealed behind the behaviour of so admirable a character as Edwina Crane, finds its ultimate expression in rape. **The Jewel in the Crown** is 'the story of a rape'. But which one? The novel's central event, returned to and clarified in each of the three successive novels, is the rape of a young English nurse called Daphne Manners by five unknown men in the Bibighar Garden, a small park in Mayapore. Only at the end of the book, when we have learnt of the events leading up to and subsequent upon the assault from a number of people who were in Mayapore in 1942, do we get the whole truth from Daphne's journal, which has been bequeathed to Lady Manners. The rapists intruded upon Daphne's lovemaking with Hari Kumar. Daphne herself is the first explicitly to make the parallel between this sudden change from love to violation and the centuries-old relationship of Indian and British. She is thinking of the behaviour of Lady Manner's friend, Lady Chatterjee, with whom she has been living:

> There is that old, disreputable saying, isn't there? 'When rape is inevitable, lie back and enjoy it.' *Well, there has been more than one rape.* I can't say, Auntie, that I lay back and enjoyed mine. But Lili was trying to lie back and enjoy what we've done to her country. I don't mean done in malice. Perhaps there was love. Oh, somewhere, in the past, and now, and in the future, love as there was between me and Hari. But the spoilers are always there, aren't they?

As a political symbol this use of rape as Daphne has suffered it is far from satisfactory, if only because of the awkward reversal of black and white needed to make it work. But the italics in the above passage are not an authorial nudge. They are in a sense Daphne's italics, an interpretation by a character who, for all her perceptivity, does not know as much of the story as, by this stage, the reader knows. The really important image of contempt at its farthest has already been given to us in the 'deposition' of an otherwise insignificant character, Vidyasagar. He relates what happened at the police station after the rape. Hari Kumar, pulled in on suspicion and maintaining the silence agreed upon between him and Daphne, is tortured by the police officer Merrick whom we have already watched entering an involved triangular relationship with Daphne and with Hari: involved in that sex dominates in his feelings towards Hari and social ambition in his feelings towards Daphne.

Vidyasagar's statement is placed after two accounts of Mayapore's disturbances by the chief guardians of law and order, Brigadier Reid (an astonishingly skilful creation, owing something to General Dyer of the Amritsar Massacre) and the civil administrator Robin White. Both are men of integrity and goodwill. But the simplicity of the one and the subtlety of the other are at the mercy of the fundamental clannishness, intensified by the riots, which prevents their believing any ill of a man who is one of themselves. In this setting the deposition affords us a sudden terrifying glimpse of the truth which the second novel, *The Day of the Scorpion,* expands into its central episode, the judicial examination two years later of Kumar, who has been detained since the rape on a trumped-up political charge. In a literally glaring light, Kumar reveals the injustices done to him, injustices akin to rape. . . . (pp. 246-47)

Apart from this scene in the prison in the provincial capital, Ranpur, most of the action of *The Day of the Scorpion* takes place in the hill station called Pankot where the fortunes are followed of a typical Guardian family, the Laytons. Colonel Layton is a prisoner of war in Germany but it pleases him to think of his wife and two daughters as holding the fort. Yet as the story progresses it grows clear that the Layton family, far from holding the fort, are held by it; the real fort is held by the Congress leader M. A. Kasim, detained in the fortress of Premanagar on the edge of the Rajastan desert, and by Kumar in the jail in Ranpur. Images of fort and prisoner take on a *Little Dorrit* elaboration as we realize that the Layton women and all like them are captive to the collective self-image which also enthralled Edwina Crane: the image of imperial India as, in the Victorian phrase, one family, bound together by the filial loyalty of *manbap:* 'You are my father and my mother.' (pp. 247-48)

[It is Major Clark] who blends the prison image with another equally forceful one when he sees the Layton family as 'preserved by some sort of perpetual Edwardian sunlight that got trapped between the Indian Ocean and the Arabian Sea round about the turn of the century'. Such a perpetual light seems to Sarah to create the circle in which her family act out scenes of undisturbed security and happiness. But this is not the true *lux perpetua,* only a theatrical spotlight creating what Francis Hutchinson, writing in the same year as Scott, called *The Illusion of Permanence.* Part of that illusion is that the Pankot Rifles, English officers commanding Muslim tribesmen, think of themselves as the rightful guardians of the complex Hindu society in the plain below. Down there in Ranpur and at the centre of a story set for the most part in the Beulah light of the hills, there breaks upon us an elucidation which (someone will later say) is like radium in a mine: the blinding truth of Kumar's narrative to the two men appointed, on Lady Manners' request, to discover if he is wrongfully detained. The discovery is similar to that made by Orwell in the Burmese police, of the things that are done without the knowledge of the proconsuls, but in their name. Before Merrick's interpretation of the contemptuous exercise of naked power, which he calls 'the situation', the cardboard fort of the traditional faith in *manbap* crumbles for good.

Once this revelation has been made, the sustainedly neutral voice of *The Day of the Scorpion* somewhat loses its momentum among the book's elaborate images. Scott, whose narrative techniques, like those of many great novelists, were always exploratory, changes to a dramatic form in *The Towers of Silence.* The story moves back and forth between the choric chatter of the memsahibs and the thoughts of old Barbie Batchelor as she lives out her intense inner drama of evangelical piety. This metaphysical struggle takes place, as Muir and Auden and Greene see it taking place, in a corner; the action has narrowed still further to relations between the army bungalow occupied by Colonel Layton's wife and daughters, and Rose Cottage where his stepmother Mabel Layton fails even to consider turning out her ex-missionary companion Barbie to make room for her own half-family. Apart from Barbie's end, which belongs to the other part of our argument, this book, which is imaginatively the high point of the tetralogy, is concerned with two deaths: the death of the liberal ideal at its best, and the destruction of the flimsy structure that has taken its place. The falling of a tower and the crumbling of a façade: it is the difference between Mabel as Barbie sees her ('Rock of Ages: the seas pound and pound') and Susan's determination to be, like every good memsahib, 'a brick'.

By virtue of the generations of the Military and the Civil behind her, the old, deaf, and silent Mabel Layton is a 'symbol of distinction' to the chorus of memsahibs. Distinguished she is, but not in their sense, since she parted company with Anglo-India in 1919. The Gillian Waller she talks about in her sleep is of course Jallianwallah Bagh, the scene of the Amritsar Massacre. In the face of that revelation, Mabel retreated to Pankot to cultivate her garden. 'I shall not go to Ranpur until I am buried.' Perhaps the words express nothing more literal than regret that she could not have been involved with the real India rather than the artificial world of the hill station. But for Barbie they are the command Mildred Layton fails to carry out. Her resultant distress gives Mildred her chance to evict Barbie and take over Rose Cottage. For this is a book about the material interests behind the self-deceptions: the Silver of the Mess performs much the same function as Conrad's Silver of the Mine. Mildred's persecution of Barbie becomes as obsessional as Merrick's stalking of his victims. Now that the Anglo-Indians have nothing left to live by, now that their self-image has finally failed them, the way is open to pure rapine. (pp. 248-49)

[When Mabel dies] . . . the old ideals are buried. Their latter-day mockery dies quite literally with a whimper, in the gruesome death of Susan's dog which Sarah will not have put down because she herself is resisting the impending abortion which she must undergo if her mother is, as always, to keep up appearances, and remain a symbol of distinction. The death of the dog to the accompaniment of Mildred's tipsy laughter, with Susan segregated from the child she has tried to kill and Sarah facing the loss of the child she longs to bear, is a bitter image of the end of Anglo-India: of the British as they were.

A tetralogy closes with a comedy. With the arrival in Bombay at the end of the war of a British Other Rank (blessed relief), Guy Perron, a comic vision of the Anglo-Indians begins to prevail in *A Division of the Spoils.* Guy cannot take even the best of them (the Governor's aide, Nigel Rowan for example) as seriously as they take themselves. This ability to see that the Anglo-Indians have no clothes on is to endear him to Sarah. As a professional historian, however, Guy takes India very seriously. Two things appal him: the way that the policy of Divide and Rule has made Pakistan inevitable and is preventing the princely states from throwing in their lot with modern India (much of the book is set in the state of Mirat, south of Premanagar); and the eagerness with which Britain now seeks to jettison the jewel in the crown. Once again, it is a matter of a self-image. 'Getting rid of India', he records, 'will cause no qualm of conscience because it will be like getting rid of what is no longer reflected in our image of ourselves'.

The dangerous speed with which the English are pulling out is represented by all the train journeys of this novel. When in 1945 Nigel Rowan is sent on one of the diplomatic journeys that initiate the moves towards independence, he travels in the Governor's state coach, comforted 'by the way the coach absorbed and muffled the vibration and clatter of the wheels without diminishing the flattering sensation of a speed and movement forward that were absolutely effortless'. We recall that smooth movement in the second part of the book when, in 1947, the train in which Guy, Sarah, and others are leaving Mirat is ambushed, attacked, and then allowed to proceed. 'Suddenly', someone says afterwards, 'you had the feeling that the train, the wheels, the lines, weren't made of metal but of something greasy and evasive'. At Premanagar the train stops and the dead and dying are brought out. Guy, Sarah, and others try to tend them, mostly to discover, as Miss Crane did with Mr Chaudhuri, that it is too late. And from time to time Guy (whom we presume to be the eventual narrator of the whole sequence) looks into the shuttered first-class carriage where the last Anglo-Indians we are to meet, a couple called Peabody, are holding the fort: she taking a siesta and he, revolver at the ready, munching his tiffin. (pp. 250-51)

[Paul Scott] has characters who are 'after something', and the something becomes more and more definable as the sequence proceeds. Those of them who are old are watchers, wise and benevolent but largely powerless to give any material protection to the characters they watch. Those of them who are young are the watched, the victims; but the line drawn between guardians and victims is by no means clearcut. (p. 251)

[In] Scott's Anglo-India guardian angels are almost as ubiquitous as gin-and-fizzes. If the combination suggests *The Family Reunion,* well and good. A surprising number of the angels are aunts here also. They range from the tragic figure of Hari's aunt flinging herself at the feet of the unspeakable Merrick to Guy Perron's Wildeish Aunt Charlotte, who flutters down to rescue him from Merrick's clutches and to pay for his research in what, with a fine liberal abrogation, she always calls 'his' India.

Clear as is the distinction between the Platonic proconsular Guardians and the real guardian angels, there are characters on the side of the angels whose role, for one reason or another, stops short of full guardianship. The first part of *The Jewel in the Crown* leads us from the story of Miss Crane, who so tragically opted for the Anglo-Indian concept of guardianship, through the narrative of Daphne's protector Lady Chatterjee, the Rajput dowager educated at (it must be) Roedean, to the recollections of Sister Ludmila who is not a real nun but is certainly a real presence in Daphne's short life. Lili Chatterjee's position in the no-man's-land between the two societies gives her the sharp insight endured rather than enjoyed by the angelic guardians. . . . But in order to establish her small civilized world secure from racial attitudes, Lili Chatterjee has had to sever her roots. She can guide Daphne so far into India, but Sister Ludmila can take her much far-

ther. In the McGregor house, itself on the European side of the river, Lady Chatterjee's room faces the civil lines where, among others, Miss Crane is safe in her bungalow; Daphne's faces the river and the Indian city which is Sister Ludmila's sphere. (pp. 251-52)

Scott had real difficulty in giving Sister Ludmila a voice strong enough for the function she fulfils in Daphne's life. Unlike the articulate Lady Chatterjee, she is not a natural monologist. Prayer is her medium, but her talk with God has sometimes an embarrassing Don Camillo flavour. And to Scott's initial insecurity with the character we tend now to add our own groan of 'Oh not Mother Teresa *again*!'. This is unfair: Scott was writing nearly twenty years ago, long before Mother Teresa became a cult figure in the West. What he saw in her then is what strengthens and finally carries conviction for his portrayal of Sister Ludmila: the image of love without power, of a virtue that can in no way be self-regarding. Edwina Crane is a schools supervisor, a wielder of an authority that, like the paternalism of the Raj, aims at results. Sister Ludmila's care for the dying can scarcely be said to produce results, and it brings only the sense of powerlessness, of humility before an experience beyond experience. Paradoxically it is the deepest possible immersion in the life of the city, and as such helps Daphne through the last barriers of herd instinct and colour prejudice to her own love without power for Hari.

The true guardians are all seers. In 1964 the limits of Lady Chatterjee's shrewd intelligent vision are marked by a drive intended to give the narrator an overall view of Mayapore, where the more things change the more they remain the same. . . . But the real overall view has already been afforded to the narrator by Sister Ludmila, who in her blindness offers a much wider 'aerial' view of the historical pattern in Mayapore's topography. It is a vision of the recurring rhythm of destruction and renewal which in 1942 caught up Daphne and Hari in an event that 'telescoped time and dovetailed space'; an event in which Sister Ludmila the dancing Siva beside her, knows herself to have been inescapably involved, since though she made possible Daphne's love for Hari she also brought together Hari and Merrick.

The contrast between the would-be guardians and the true guardians operates in *The Jewel in the Crown* at the level of personal relations; the proconsuls are there and their shortcomings skilfully probed in the portraits of Reid and White, but the contrast as it operates at the political level is not fully shown until the later novels. In those the best, if not the most amiable, of the proconsuls is Nigel Rowan, whose duties bring him into contact and, for the reader, contrast with two of India's real guardians: the Congress leader M. A. Kasim, and Count Bronowski, chief minister to the Nawab of Mirat. The worldly influence of the angelic guardians is always limited, much as their literal vision tends to be impaired. Kasim finds he can best serve Congress and maintain its intercommunal nature by sharing the 1942 imprisonment of its leaders. Political longsightedness thus makes him reject the bait of special favour to Muslims. But there is also a deeply Islamic commitment to fidelity. (pp. 252-53)

Himself a tower of strength when held *incomunicado* in Premanagar, Kasim's strength is most tested when he is 'chucked out of the Fort' and faced by the Congress expectation that he will actively defend his son Sayed who has been captured after his defection to the Japanese. In his refusal the moral view (Sayed's pledged loyalty was as a commissioned officer of the Indian Army) is also the long political view, since with our hindsight over Pakistan's history we can see the verification of Kasim's belief that a choice between loyalties opens the way to military dictatorship. Kasim himself does not choose between loyalties but reconciles them; one of the most finely-written scenes in the tetralogy is that in which the astute old lawyer leads Sayed point by point through the defence that Sayed must now make for himself.

As 'Mak' watches over India's communal unity, so the one-eyed Bronowski, equally percipient of the dangers of partition and division, seeks to protect the relations of the princely state of Mirat with British India. Many years before, he fell in love with the state's ruler, and under his guidance this rackety little principality, very like Forster's Dewas State Senior, has attained communal peace and a measure of order and progress, so that post-independence union with India is feasible. Now his emotions and his hopes centre in the probable heir, Ahmed, who is Kasim's youngest son and the Nawab's protégé. Bronowski's homosexuality, unlike Merrick's, is constructive because it is self-acknowledged and self-understood. He is a Slav with a peculiarly Conradian sense of reality, for whom Merrick is 'one of your hollow men'.

The clearest vision into the darkness typified by Merrick is however afforded not by Bronowski but by Lady Manners, herself the most explicitly-defined angelic presence in the whole sequence. She is marginal to the first novel, though we are aware of her presence as the first legal guardian of Daphne's child Parvati and the guardian of the secret of Parvati's parentage. 'What a lot you know', Sarah says lightly to her in the second novel; but the full burden of knowledge comes only in the prison at Ranpur where, unknown to the prisoner, she listens and watches ('I shall put on my distance glasses') while Hari, in the proceedings she has herself initiated, recounts his treatment at Merrick's hands. She is left wishing only for her own release from the burden of this knowledge which undercuts so savagely the ideological structure of her generation. But more is asked of her. 'After such knowledge, what forgiveness?' Eliot is seldom far from Scott's imagination, and the veiled sister of 'Ash Wednesday', already glimpsed in the Muslim woman of the Prologue, becomes the upright old lady in solar topee and old-fashioned veil who appears later in the history in the church at Pankot—not at the jolly public rites of Anglo-India, but when she is needed, when Sarah and Barbara are each alone with distress. (pp. 253-54)

Mabel is seen by the memsahibs as another guardian, 'the guardian of a golden age', but this role she repudiates in her withdrawal and in her anger that after so many years nothing has changed in Anglo-India. Only in her garden there can be no illusion of permanence. So she is on the edge of the angelic company. The child Sarah, colouring her family tree to distinguish its English members from its Anglo-Indian, shows true insight when she underlines Mabel's name in the blue of the sky rather than in imperial red.

Mabel has her own protector in Barbie Batchelor. But the privilege of watching over Mabel's troubled sleep and the lives of the Layton girls is one of the things snatched from the old missionary in a concentrated tale of victimization and deprivation. Reduced to its outline, and so itself deprived of the surface relief of its social comedy, *The Towers of Silence* sounds like *King Lear* or the *Book of Job*. All that appears to make life liveable for Barbie (friends, reputation, security, health, finally even intellect) is taken from her, while the world round her affords glimpses of Bosch-like horror: Mabel being prepared for autopsy; the joyless coupling of Mildred Layton. It is all a tempering for the final encounter with Merrick in which Barbie, long tried in the fire so that she has become for us the most substantial of Scott's characters, confronts the hollowest of the hollow men. The encounter is low-keyed. . . . The only *bravura* passage occurs at the end, when Barbie puts Edwina's picture of the great illusion, *The Jewel in her Crown*, into Merrick's artificial hand before driving off protected from the weather by the christening shawl which, by all its associations, is the relic of her real life of both fidelity and faith. The drive ends in disaster and in Barbie's final breakdown which leaves her, sans everything, in the asylum in Ranpur. Now however we scarcely need the author's reassurance that hers has been a happy life. While her history ('my life in India') has been a dandelion clock, her life, to make use of Scott's central distinction, has cast a shadow. In August 1945 she is found sitting 'eternally alert, in sudden sunshine, her shadow burnt into the wall behind her': the shadow of a meaningful existence in a world aghast at its grossest act of meaningless destruction.

Barbara Batchelor then is more victim than guardian, and one with the younger victims of the sequence in that she loses her life to save it. In this respect Daphne, Hari, and Ahmed stand out from the alleged victims who are given martyr status by the alleged guardians, so that in the Bibighar affair Daphne is quickly forgotten, even condemned, and Anglo-India lavishes its sympathy upon Reid and Merrick (as it did upon Dyer in 1919), since it regards these men as having been made 'sacrifices' to political expediency by their superiors. But the real sacrifices bear fruit. For this reason the least effective to Scott's purpose is the one at the end, when Ahmed deliberately steps out of a railway carriage full of Anglo-Indians into the hands of his butchers. This leaves little but a sense of waste at the loss of a man who might have been another Nehru. The sense of waste outweighs Scott's careful preparation at the beginning of the novel: 'The victim chose neither the time nor the place of his death but in going to it as he did he must have seen that he contributed something of his own to its manner'; outweighs too the implication that Ahmed's sacrifice maintains the inviolability that the British so surprisingly kept throughout the 1947 bloodbath. In the previous novel (to move backwards) it is not nearly so difficult to understand that Barbie's is a good end. Before that again, in *The Day of the Scorpion,* the sense of waste is strong in Hari Kumar's disappearance from view. We have to wait until the fourth novel to learn that Hari, as the journalist 'Philoctetes', has found a voice that carries beyond the *bania* world that seems to have engulfed him. Yet in the novel to which he is central, Hari's oblivion is not obliteration. He retains his integrity and substance in his refusal to become Merrick's creature. . . . This negates Nigel Rowan's complacent description of Hari as 'a man who couldn't have existed without our help and deliberate encouragement'. Hari could not have existed without Daphne; he is the creation of love, not contempt. . . . From sensitivity to Hari's touchiness she moves forward in a relationship which gives Hari back his identity. Daphne's 'good' end not only brings to life Parvati; on its own that would be an altogether facile image of regeneration. More importantly she leaves Hari remade, a man who casts a shadow.

At the end of it all, the images of sacrifice are gathered together in the poem translated from the Urdu by Bronowski, which Guy is reading aboard the aircraft that carries him away from an independent but dismembered India. Philoctetes, the marooned and wounded archer, Ahmed, who once loved hawking, cut down by a mob of fanatics, and Daphne running in pain and terror from her assailants, are transformed in their association with the basic Eastern and Western image of renewal:

> The bowman lovingly choosing his arrow,
> The hawk outpacing the cheetah,
> (The fountain splashing lazily in the courtyard),
> The girl running with the deer.

By now, it is hoped, the *Raj Quartet* has been presented as a highly-wrought work, far beyond the intentions or capabilities of the 'women's magazine writer' that academics sometimes declare Scott to be (though most of them have not looked at a women's magazine since their childhood). From time to time, though, the possibility has been touched upon that things in the work are overwrought. The point at which misgiving becomes doubt can be indicated by a brief look at Scott's attention to articles of clothing, an attention he shares with most popular novelists and also with Shakespeare. . . . When Mabel and Barbie dress in their best for a regimental occasion, Mabel puts on an old black suit made in Bond Street, and Barbie a costume of the colour called heliotrope, which she has had made in the bazaar. The contrast is not a popular writer's chattiness nor the accurate social distinctions beloved of the semi-popular writer. Mabel's way of dressing reveals her as a being set apart from Anglo-India, whereas Barbie's, which is going to seem so comically vulgar to the memsahibs, reveals her response to the brilliance of India itself, to a warmth beyond the pale of tight-lipped good taste. And behind this response there is a longing revealed when she explains her pleasure in the colour to the old tailor who must be distinctly puzzled. ' "The name heliotrope", she said, "comes from the Greek words helios, meaning sun, and trepo meaning turn. Heliotropion. A plant that turns its flowers to the sun" '.

There could be no better emblem for Barbie, who for so long has felt only the hail of a religious despair, but who believes, once Merrick is put behind her, that 'God had shone his light on her at last by casting first the shadow of the prince of darkness across her feet', and who dies, the heliotrope by now ragged and egg-stained, in sunlight. Yet splendid as the image is, and however artful its introduction through Barbie's schoolmistressy instinct to inform, its employment is a little strained. In Barbie's favourite expression, the work 'can carry it', but only just. Other symbolic objects, notably the christening shawl which is important in Barbie's life, are altogether too complex and contrived. The manipulation of such symbols can produce imagistic passages which, even when we keep them where they belong, in a context of ordinary-sounding conversation or narrative, compel us to ask if such portentousness does not reveal the poet manqué rather than the born novelist. (pp. 254-57)

The powerful images of the *Raj Quartet* are the common currency of poetry: fire and rain, tower and river, rose and sunflower, dry bone and calling bird. The list brings us back to Eliot, a pervasive and lifelong influence on Scott not only in his literary technique, but even more perhaps in the world-view behind it. Like many who became adult on the verge of the Second World War, Scott reached back through his reading of Eliot to values more durable than those of nineteenth-century liberalism. The historical perspectives have changed after half a century, but the traditional bases of Eliot's

thought and of his poetic language check any complaint that Scott views India through the eyes of an Anglo-Catholic poet of a vanished generation. Rather Eliot helped Scott to view India, which calls for the largest vision, through the eyes of the seers: the single laser-beam vision of Bronowski, or the blind Ludmila's perception of the moment which is all time. . . .

[Today] we are on what Lady Manners sees as the vast dark plain between our history and our lives. The incongruity would be unendurable were it not for those other presences which, I have tried to suggest, assert so strong a counterstatement to the work of the spoilers in Scott's series of novels: grace and nature; Hermione and Perdita; the guardian figure above the church door and the tree now once again breaking, unbelievably, into its first leaf. (p. 258)

> *M. M. Mahood, "Paul Scott's Guardians," in* The Yearbook of English Studies, *Vol. 13, 1983, pp. 244-58.*

MARGARET SCANLAN

Not the least of the paradoxes of Paul Scott's *Raj Quartet* is that its two thousand pages of impeccably researched historical fiction end with a lyric poem. . . . [To] end a vast historical novel with a lyric is to do more than to unify diverse stories; it is to shift from a genre that demands commitment to social reality and political events to one that offers freedom from them. This movement from objective event to subjective regret, from panorama to image, from history to timelessness, is the novel's fundamental impulse. For as Scott's fiction explores the history of Anglo-India, it betrays a deep skepticism about the ways in which human beings understand, remember, and act on their history. This skepticism extends to the genre in which the *Quartet* is written, making its apparent conformity to the conventions of the historical novel a mask for its persistent subversion of them.

To be sure, the conventional elements are the most visible: pages of straightforward historical narration ("Hitler was dead . . . "), characters who go off to fight in Burma or North Africa or write letters to Gandhi. The brutal boredom of a wedding reception at the Mess, the cruelties of the bridge table, the heat and dust of a journey by train to Calcutta appear in striking period pieces. What distinguishes this novel from much historical fiction, however, is the constant tension between its realistic texture and its tendency to turn history into stories and stories into myths that seek to explain history. The process begins on the first page, when the narrator announces that his novel is "the story of a rape." This fictional story has a precise historical setting, "1942, the year the Japanese defeated the British army in Burma and Mr. Gandhi began preaching sedition," yet it is also a metaphor for a process that "ended with the spectacle of the two nations in violent opposition . . . still locked in an imperial embrace of such longstanding and subtlety that it was no longer possible for them to know whether they loved or hated one another." (pp. 153-54)

The "story of a rape" and the story of Edwina Crane's journey from Dibrapur are repeated, re-evaluated, and expanded through the four volumes. The narrator in the first volume describes himself as possessing a "lepidopteristic" intention to understand the story of Hari Kumar. He sets himself to work like a journalist or historian, visiting scenes, interviewing survivors, reading newspaper articles, letters, unpublished memoirs. From the beginning, even this modest exercise in butterfly-pinning proves problematic. Hari Kumar has disappeared; Daphne Manners and Ronald Merrick are dead; most of the British have returned to England and the Indians who remain do not remember. . . . Pictures and photographs are as lifeless as letters which "do not resurrect the dead. They are merely themselves." The biases of history-writing quickly become apparent: Laxminarayan, a Hindu publisher, "is writing a history of the origins of Indian nationalism that will probably never be finished, let alone published: his apologia for many years of personal compromise." To examine Brigadier Reid's unpublished memoirs, to listen to the mystical Sister Ludmilla and the incessant monologues of Lilli Chatterjee is to experience all of the distortions imposed by temperament and rhetoric. Some element is always missing: "History doesn't record the answer or even pose the question."

Yet if the rape story fails as scientific history—at least so far as the narrator fails to pin down its "historical" details, it begins to function as a myth with historical significance, explaining at least some of the history of Anglo-Indian relationships. Important themes are drawn into it: for example, the relationship between the English class system at home and colonial racism. In India a man of lower class origins like Merrick has the freedom, because he is white, to assimilate himself to the upper classes, but this freedom, depending as it does on color, makes him an ardent racist. We are meant to feel the power of Merrick's unacknowledged sexual feelings, but we also are meant to see his persecution of Kumar as exacerbated by his resentment of the Indian's public school accent. Educated by the English and then rejected by them in his own country, Kumar is like Nehru, whose "revolutionary" ideas are really only liberal British ideas made unacceptable because they are being advocated on behalf of India. Experiencing the shock of Kumar's return to India, we glimpse something of what Gandhi felt when he came back after spending almost twenty-five years abroad. Perhaps the distinctive contribution of Gandhi to politics, "to introduce the element of doubt into public life," is owed to that sense of estrangement from his own culture. The violent end of the love affair is a symbol too obvious to require comment; if there is any hope, it lies with Parvati, the next generation, "but she is another story." Quite similarly, Edwina Crane's story represents the failure of liberal progressive ideas unaccompanied by transcendent love.

The novel's first response to public history, then, is to distill it into its own stories, to which it attributes a core of stable meaning. Yet perhaps more crucially, the novel also demonstrates a distrust of stories and the kind of history they yield. The inaccuracies in stories and their seductiveness once they become myths can compel disaster. The most striking extended example is the story from which **The Day of the Scorpion** derives its title. The Laytons' Indian servants observe that a scorpion placed in a circle of fire will die before the flames reach it. Failing to understand that the scorpion is scorched because of its extreme sensitivity to heat, they make up a story that transforms him into a romantic suicide who kills himself, like a soldier falling on his sword in battle, because the odds are hopeless. Sarah Layton even at twelve seeks out the truth about scorpions and rejects the implications of the story: it is "more practical" and "braver" of the scorpion to try to sting the fire than to sting itself. Susan Layton, however, remains at the mercy of the story. Pregnant with her first

child, she believes that "people like us were finished years ago" and have nothing to offer the next generation. When her son is born she calls him Edward, a name with resonances suggested by another character's description of an Anglo-Indian family "preserved by some sort of perpetual Edwardian sunlight that got trapped between the Indian Ocean and the Arabian Sea. . . . " In the depths of depression following the deaths of her husband and her aunt, she places Edward on her parents' lawn and builds a fire around him, perhaps believing that this child who symbolizes the hopeless future of the raj will also commit suicide. Some of the members of the club offer another interpretation, which is based on a more accurate view of scorpions: "Susan had made a statement about her life or that somehow managed to be a statement about your own . . . which reduced you . . . to the size of an insect; an insect entirely surrounded by the destructive element . . . doomed . . . not by the forces ranged against you but by the terrible inadequacy of your own armour." We see the terrible price of such myths again in the career of Susan's second husband. Ronald Merrick, the "hollow man," was shaped by "all that Kiplingesque doubletalk that transformed India from a place where plain ordinary greedy Englishmen carved something out for themselves . . . into one where they appeared to go voluntarily into exile for the good of their souls and the uplift of the native." As sustaining fiction, the white man's burden gives a long-range historical purpose to present acts of cruelty and discourages introspection.

Moreover, the raw materials of history are endlessly vulnerable to interpretation. "The history of their relationship," says Guy Perron of Daphne and Hari, "could be made to fit almost any theory one could have of Kumar's character and intentions." . . . When Lady Manners has her vision of the disaster in which British India will end, she realizes that what history is likely to record will be the "actual deed," the granting of independence. But such a record will be false: "We must remember the worst because the worst is the lives we lead, the best is only our history and between our history and our lives there is this vast dark plain where the rapt and patient shepherds drive their invisible flocks in expectation of God's forgiveness." Elsewhere Robin White, former Deputy Commissioner of Mayapore, writes to the narrator of their shared fascination with the "beat" and "pulse," the "unrecorded moments of history." He wishes to relate this theory to his own life, but in doing so finds himself falsifying, for "even in attempting to relate it, I'm back in the world of describable events." As if to compensate for this tendency of written history to drift away from actual lives, the novel constantly seeks to establish an identity between public events and the private experiences of its characters.

Just as the novel draws historical panorama into the narrow circle of its own myths, it continually assimilates public events to the lives of the characters. For all their psychological verisimilitude, the major characters are in one way or another representative of political movements, or social strata: Mohammed Ali Kasim, the enlightened Muslim; Edwina Crane and Barbie Batchelor, earnest lower-middle class missionaries, women of liberal goodwill; Colonel John Layton, the flagging idealism of the officer caste; Aunt Charlotte, the English public's ignorance of Indian conditions, little Edward Bingham, the future of the raj. Place names move out of history into fiction: Chillianwallah Bagh, the section of Mayapore in which Hari Kumar lives with Aunt Shalini, recalls Jallianwallah Bagh, the scene of General Dyer's massacre which, as K. Bhaskara Rao observes [see Further Reading], becomes the Gillian Waller of Mabel Layton's uneasy sleep.

The same dates have public and private significance. Edwina Crane's journey from Dibrapur takes place on the afternoon of August 8, 1942; Daphne Manners is raped that night. August 8 was the day the All-India Congress Party voted in favor of Gandhi's Quit India resolution. T. Walter Wallbank summarizes: "Before the Congress could carry out its campaign of mass civil disobedience, the government of India acted and all Congress leaders—including Nehru, Gandhi, and Azad—were arrested on August 9. Immediately serious and widespread disorders broke out. . . . " Thus major actions of the fictional story tend to constellate around the landmarks of the historical one. Sometimes, of course, the process is inevitable, as when M. A. Kasim, fictional Congress Party leader, is jailed on the same day as his historical counterparts. But Scott carries the process of assimilating history to fiction to the point where history seems almost subsumed. (pp. 154-58)

These mechanisms not only allow Scott to draw diverse historical elements into a novelistic story; they allow him to explore an alternative idea of history. Such a view locates the meaning of public events in the lives and consciousness of single people. Emerson, in his famous essay on "History," assumes that historical facts are impossible to come by or inherently unstable. . . . He is undismayed by this prospect: "Who cares what the fact was, when we have made a constellation of it to hang in heaven an immortal sign?" The facts as external events do not matter because "there is one mind common to all individual men"; we can all experience history in our own lives, through our own self-knowledge: "We are always coming up with the emphatic facts of history in our private experience, and verifying them here." One must note how consoling Emerson's view of history as biography is to the historical novel's traditional claims, since it affirms the validity of imaginatively experienced history and its accessibility to the well-intentioned and reasonable reader.

The novel's examination of Emerson's theory centers around Barbie Batchelor, perhaps the most complicated and sympathetic of Scott's characters. Barbie becomes obsessed with Emerson when she comes across these lines in "History": "If the whole of history is one man . . . it is all to be explained from individual experience. There is a relation between the hours of our life and the centuries of time." Barbie "began to feel what she believed Emerson wanted her to feel: that in her own experience lay an explanation not only of history but of the lives of other living people." We might ask what sort of history she finds there and how finding it changes her.

Like other major characters in the **Quartet,** Barbie can be read as representative of a group—in her case the earnestly Protestant lower middle class. She comes to India as a missionary strongly motivated to convert Indian children and is disappointed when she discovers that official attitudes, even in the missions, are moderate and secular. . . . A story told about one of Barbie's experiences as a young teacher attributes to her the sort of cultural insensitivity one expects of zealous missionaries. A little girl in her class had colored the face of Jesus blue because that was the color of Krishna in the picture her parents had at home. To prevent a repetition Barbie took away all the blue crayons, "and then the children had no way of coloring the sky." As she is introduced to us in September 1939, she remains "a believer in the good will

and good sense of established authority." Yet inside Barbie is not the same: she has begun to feel that her life has been wasted doing something of which God disapproves.

Outward incidents in the remaining six years of her life are few. Barbie moves to Pankot, where she is a paying guest of Mabel Layton at Rose Cottage, and grows to love her; when Mabel dies Barbie is griefstricken because the family refuses to honor her wish to be buried in Ranpur. That grief worsens as Mabel's daughter-in-law Mildred rapidly evicts her. She attempts to give Susan Layton a set of apostle spoons as a wedding gift, but Mildred humiliates her by returning them; she walks miles in the rain to present them to the Mess, but her attempt fails when she discovers Mildred in bed with the officer in charge. The pneumonia that follows this walk leaves Barbie's voice weakened but she decides to accept a teaching post anyway. She returns to Rose Cottage for a last visit, meets Ronald Merrick there, and gives him her copy of the "Jewel in the Crown" picture. On the way home, her too-heavy trunk causes her tonga to overturn; the driver is killed and Barbie herself is pushed over the edge of madness.

We can read Barbie's life and private experiences as history. Her recognition that the civil authorities encourage the divisions between Hindu and Islamic communities, for example, is a crucial perception for the last volume, which ends with the religious massacres of 1947. Her Protestant zeal, however misguided, represents the idealistic hope that Britain can leave behind a unified India, and perhaps the more basic hope that the best of its civilization is a positive legacy for India. The symbolic value of Rose Cottage is already suggested by Patrick Swinden, who sees the loss of paradise as the subject of Scott's novels. The cottage is the Eden of Anglo-India. . . . Mabel herself represents much of the best of Anglo-India. The widow first of a British officer and then of a Deputy Commissioner, Mabel had rebelled against her class by contributing a hundred pounds to a fund for the victims of Jallianwallah Bagh when her friends were collecting for General Dyer, and insofar as possible dissociates herself from the Club. With her death the reader must sense that Anglo-India has lost her conscience, and that the English will soon be dispossessed forever. Mildred Layton's long antagonism for Barbie also has symbolic overtones. Mildred, who drinks heavily and sleeps with an ambitious junior officer while her husband is a prisoner of the Nazis, is always unattractive, but with Barbie she is ruthless. She despises her immediately for being Mabel's guest, and therefore keeping the Laytons out of Rose Cottage. Her first act on inheriting it is to have the fabled roses ripped out and replaced by a tennis court; her renovations strip the house of its "secluded, tentative" air, restore "its functional solidity, an architectural integrity which belonged to a time when the British built . . . with their version of India aggressively in mind and with a view to permanence." Yet ironically her restoration fails because "she had robbed the place of . . . the quality of survival and the idea behind it—that survival meant change." Twelve Upper Club Road, as Mildred calls the cottage, begins to look, even when the family is home, "like a place of historic interest, visited but not inhabited." The parallel with English attempts to return during the war to an earlier phase of colonialism and the consequences of doing so is readily drawn. Her success in keeping Barbie from giving her apostle spoons either to Susan or to the army is a desperate rejection of Christian values and of the lower-middle classes whose taste the spoons reflect. The picture of Queen Victoria accepting India, the jewel in the crown, is first given to Edwina Crane as a reward for facing down a rebellious Indian mob; both she and Barbie use it to teach the language and values of the English and jettison it when they have become disillusioned. For Barbie to give it to Ronald Merrick means conceding the colonial project to its most ruthless advocate. For her to see Ronald Merrick as the devil is to go little further than the novel does in seeing his racism and ruthlessness as "the dark side," the worst elements in British colonialism.

Yet although Barbie's life provides a good example of Scott's tendency to correlate private experience and public history, what happens to her as she embarks on the Emersonian search for history marks a separation between Emerson's optimism and Scott's deep pessimism, and in this respect the encounter between her consciousness and history is paradigmatic of the novel's. Under Emerson's spell, other people come alive for Barbie as they never have, and as they do so, her perception of them changes. Daphne Manners, for example, is transformed from the rape victim the Club imagines into her more essential identity: "the girl's hand was no longer pressed inverted against her forehead but held by another which was brown like the dead teacher's." Such moments in which the lives of other people are experienced truthfully in the imagination are not limited to Barbie: Sarah Layton has a similar revelation when she goes riding with Ahmed Kasim: "this morning as I rode home . . . she was alive for me completely. She flared up out of my darkness as a white girl in love with an Indian. And then went out because—in that disguise—she is not part of what I comprehend." Sarah, who finds Emerson "tiresome," is a survivor whose moments of intense sympathetic identification will always—mercifully—end in incomprehension. But Barbie's imagination is greater. Not only does she absorb the lives of other people into her own but she begins to confuse them:

> She was no longer sure of what she saw: Edwina guarding the body, Mabel kneeling to grub out weeds or inclining to gather roses; or herself, Barbie, surrounded by children she had presumed to bring to God; or Miss Manners in some kind of unacceptable relationship with a man of another race whom she was intent on saving. From these there emerged a figure, the figure of an unknown Indian: dead in one aspect, alive in another. And after a while it occurred to her that the unknown Indian was what her life in India had been about.

As Barbie watches him, the unknown Indian begins to howl. But after reading about Edwina Crane's suicide she understands who he is: "the dead body was the one Edwina guarded—her life in India come to nothing." For Barbie, who equates despair with the devil, this is an image of damnation, and "revelation of Edwina's despair uncovered her own, showed its depth, its immensity." In her consciousness every British life lived in India has "come to nothing."

Barbie's conflation of the lives of Daphne Manners and Hari Kumar, of Edwina and Mr. Chaudhuri, of Mabel and herself, replicates the process by which Scott draws history into his fictional stories. . . . Not only does the love story of Daphne Manners and Hari Kumar bear suggestive parallels with the story of Miss Crane on the road from Dibrapur; it looks back to the story of old Mr. MacGregor and the Indian girl he loved and forward to the never-realized story of Sarah Layton and Ahmed Kasim. The process of collapsing stories into each other blurs the identities of characters who never meet, or makes apparently random actions seem related.

Similarly, Ronald Merrick believes that Edwina Crane had committed suttee because she "felt that the India she knew had died"; Teddie Bingham's death in a burning jeep is a result of a foolishly outdated mixture of idealism and paternalism. . . . Sarah, who as we have seen thinks of Ronald Merrick as "one of us," "our dark side," extends the perception to Susan in her madness: "We sense from the darkness in you the darkness in ourselves, a darkness and a death wish." Doing so, she prepares us for their marriage and for Ronald's murder which, like Teddie Bingham's death in combat, is little more than a suicide. Such links are continually forged: Sister Ludmilla and Guy Perron might seem to have nothing in common, yet both see that Ronald Merrick "chooses" his victims. In Guy Perron's dream, "Purvis was Kumar, seated, looking up at me through the eyes of this other man who kept saying, I don't think I'll ever forgive it." Occasionally such links are bizarre, as when the narrator, bathing at MacGregor House, "closing the eyes against the contrary evidence of sex, attempts a reenactment of Miss Manners refreshing herself after a hard day. . . ."

Emerson believed that such links to the "common mind" liberate the understanding and free an ordinary person to possess the history of kings. . . . But in Scott's novel the history of Anglo-India is too terrible to liberate someone who reads it into his or her own life. As the stories collapse into each other, they become the same story, from which no escape is possible. Lady Manners watches Hari Kumar's interrogation and projects into the Indian future Barbie's vision of Edwina Crane's well-intentioned life "come to nothing": "It will end . . . in total and unforgivable disaster. . . . The reality of the actual deed would be a monument to all that had been thought for the best." Confusion of identity finally becomes a symptom of madness; in the asylum, the nurse greets Barbie, "Good morning, Edwina . . . or are we Barbie today?"

Not surprisingly, then, the novel comes to image history as a burden, a maze, a prison. To the actual prisons in which M. A. Kasim, his son Sayed, Hari Kumar, and Colonel John Layton are locked are added the nursing homes and hospitals in which Poppy Browning's daughter, Barbie Batchelor, and Susan Layton experience their madness. Guy Perron and Sarah Layton wander through the old summer residence of the British government in Pankot as through a "maze of imperial history." To Guy, Sarah seems to possess nothing but the "unreality" of Anglo-Indian history and "to belong to it like a prisoner would belong . . . to a cell his imagination had escaped but whose door he was not permitted to open." They move on to the Moghul Suite, which at first seems to offer release "from the stupefying weight of nearly a century of disconnexion from the source. But the Moghul suite was no less burdened by that weight; it was the inner box of a nest of boxes." Susan's christening dress is made of lace in which butterflies appear to shimmer, but the lacemaker, a blind woman who lives in a tower, calls them "prisoners" and regrets that they will never fly out of the lace. Susan dresses little Edward in the lace before trying to burn him; "Little prisoner," she murmurs, "Shall I free you?" Barbie wears a piece of it like a bridal veil when she sets out on the tonga ride that ends in death and madness. The too-heavy trunk that causes the accident is always identified as Barbie's life in India. It is "her history and without it according to Emerson she wasn't explained"; "without it she did not seem to have a shadow."

Experienced both as myth and biography, history is a shadow, a prison, a treacherous burden, a story with only one ending. Through Barbie the novel explores the possibility of escaping history by escaping language. All her life Barbie has been a compulsive talker, a teacher with a carrying voice. She dislikes her own chatter and admires Mabel's "gift for stillness." Shortly before Mabel's death, Barbie begins to experience "imaginary silences" in which she cannot hear her own voice talking. These leave her with a "vivid sense of herself as new and unused . . . no longer in arrears . . . because the account had not been opened yet." This sensation is so attractive that she thinks "Emerson was wrong, we're not explained by our history at all . . . it's our history that gets in the way of a lucid explanation of us." Barbie begins "to enjoy the sensation of her history and other people's history blowing away like dead leaves; but then it occurred to her that among the leaves were her religious principles and beliefs. . . ." She tries to re-shape her silence so that it will not "destroy contact but create it." Her silence is a mystical state of waiting for God to speak. . . . In death Mabel is imaged as a "fallen tower"; losing her and rejecting Babel, Barbie has no alternative but to drift toward the towers of silence that give the third volume of the *Quartet* its name.

When she is ill with pneumonia, Barbie tells Sarah that in her hospital bed "she has no history, just the hours of the day." Sarah argues that she does, the trunk still carefully stored at Rose Cottage; after the tonga accident, Barbie finally succeeds in living outside history. Claiming to be under a "vow of silence," Barbie communicates only in brief notes. Given a calendar turned to the first anniversary of D-Day (and of Mabel's death), Barbie rips it up; by August 6, 1945, the date of her own death, she has passed into a state where all dates are meaningless. . . . Sarah, coming to visit in late June, is distressed because Barbie seems to have lost her memory but more precisely what Barbie has lost is meaningful language: "She remembered a great deal. But was unable to say what it was. The birds had picked the words clean."

This image of language stripped clean is an image of death. The towers of silence are literal as well as metaphorical, a place visible from Barbie's barred window where vultures pick clean the bodies of the Ranpur Parsees. These birds perhaps associate themselves in her mind with the time when she had read the essay on "History": "She was not cut out for the philosophical life but through Emerson it impinged on her own like the shadow of a hunched bird of prey patiently observing below it the ritual of survival." The bird in turn associates itself with Barbie's devil, "not a demon but a fallen angel" who "was despair as surely as God was love." Sick and weeping over Edwina's suicide, Barbie had ordered him to leave, "then caught her breath at the sound of a slow ungainly winged departure as of a heavy carrion bird that had difficulty in overcoming the pull of gravity."

It is possible to see a mystical value in Barbie's patient waiting for God's voice; Barbie herself enters madness believing that she falls "like Lucifer but without Lucifer's pride and not . . . to his . . . destination." But her destination must be outside history and time, and almost outside language. Within historical time she dies on the same day as the victims of Hiroshima, virtually as one of them. . . . Remembering that shadow was one of the novel's words for history, the reader knows how complete that immolation is. It consumes Barbie's belief, secure in September 1939, in the good sense of established authority; it consumes Emerson, who believed we could understand ourselves and our history without going

mad; it consumes all missionary fervor, all belief that the West brings progress and humane values to the East.

As we have seen, the novel's metaphors for history suggest the futility of action: history is a shadow, a too-heavy trunk, a burden, a dead hand, a carapace. Edwina Crane imagines "the moral drift of history," a naive conception of a river flowing into a sea, losing as it runs on all the "debris" of prejudice and disharmony. Robin White tells the narrator that the impetus for this drift comes from "our consciences" which work in the "dangerous area" of personal risk, "with or without us, usually without." Thus changes occur almost without our knowledge or consent. . . . Ronald Merrick, however, explores the possibility of making one's participation in history more conscious. "History," he tells Hari Kumar, "is a sum of situations whose significance was never seen until long afterwards because people had been afraid to act them out. . . . They preferred to think of the situations they found themselves in as part of a general drift of events they had no control over. . . ." Binding Kumar to a trestle, beating him, then offering him a drink of water: for Merrick these are all elements of a "situation of enactment" that makes both men "for the moment . . . mere symbols." Merrick does not think one can necessarily "change the course of events by acting out situations" but believes that doing so "you'd understand better what that situation was and take what steps you could to stop things drifting in the wrong direction, or an unreal direction." In Merrick's view, he and Kumar are acting out not only the subjugation of colonial people, but its basis, "contempt," which is the "prime human emotion." . . . From the course of his career, it is easy to see how unproductive Merrick's enactment is for himself: he "takes steps" as a policeman, an army officer, and a special agent of the princely state, Mirat, but is brutally murdered on the eve of Indian independence.

But just as Sarah thinks of Merrick as the "dark side of [our] history," so his conception of the intractability of racial hatred is one of the novel's nightmares. Whether the luminous examples of interracial love the novel offers can ever be realized on the plane of its public history, whose most characteristic landmark is the genocidal massacre, is a question Scott leaves unanswered. For Hari Kumar the only response to Merrick is detachment. . . . In his detachment, Kumar joins his grandfather, who went *sannyasi,* that is, renounced family and property to wander India as a religious beggar; and seems linked to the many characters in the novel who detach themselves from history through exile, madness, and suicide.

The alternative to such detachment is positive action, and of this the *Raj Quartet* offers less than more traditional historical novels. Great battles and decisive meetings take place offstage; Merrick's description of Teddie Bingham's bungled attempt to encourage a former Muzzafirabad guide to desert from the Japanese-sponsored Indian National Army is as close as we come to combat in the Second World War. For action Scott substitutes the idea of action, which he embodies especially in M. A. Kasim and John Layton. These men devote their lives, respectively, to politics and the army; yet each—the bare fact already indicating Scott's bias—is a prisoner for most of the novel. Kasim is Scott's most admirable politician, an immensely attractive man who serves in Ranpur as provincial chief minister until 1939, when he resigns as part of the Congress Party's boycott of the English war effort. It becomes increasingly difficult for him to remain loyal to the Congress Party, which most of his fellow Muslims perceive as seeking to substitute a Hindu-*raj* for a British-*raj*. Kasim, however, foresees the violence that must accompany partition and resists all appeals to desert to Jinnah's pro-Pakistan Muslim League, even though he disagrees with all of the major decisions Congress has made since 1939, and regards its cap which he wears, as a "crown of thorns." The British first try to suborn, and then imprison him. Partly because of Kasim's imprisonment, his son Sayed, a British officer, deserts to the Indian National Army. Kasim is repelled by this breach of contract and by the INA generally; if allowed into the army of a free India, such men will represent a constant threat of military dictatorship. In Kasim's eyes Sayed has thrown away his future. Moreover, since he himself cannot expect to be elected to public office if he withholds support for the INA, he must move, at least temporarily, "hors de combat." Freed by the British, he must "cultivate his own garden," a skill he learned in prison. Kasim's apolitical son, Ahmed, brings his father a moment of happiness by supporting his decision to remain loyal to Congress. But in the novel's last major episode, Ahmed is killed by Hindus in one of the massacres that preceded partition. Thus in the moment of victory—the achievement of independence—Kasim appears defeated, deprived of a future and of the ability to act.

In John Layton, a less well-realized character, Scott similarly translates victory into defeat. Layton is the *Raj Quartet's* Ashley Wilkes, or, to be more charitable, its Mr. Compson—a gentleman whose code has become outdated, a man who cannot quite live up to his own conception of himself. Layton is taken prisoner in North Africa; he is imprisoned in Italy and then Germany and returns to India with a decimated regiment. He acquires prison habits, such as pocketing bits of food and cleaning his own bathroom, that are out of place in a country where an English gentleman never puts his own shoes on unaided. Scrupulously honorable, he refuses to return to Pankot before the last of his men is released from hospital in Bombay. Yet once in Pankot, Layton cannot bring himself to visit the family of Havildar Karim Muzzafirkhan, the only member of his regiment to go over to the German equivalent of the INA, the Frei Hind, who has committed suicide in British captivity. Every day for weeks he rides to the dead man's village but can go no further. . . . His daughter Sarah sees that he "believe[s] himself dishonoured—not by anything he had done but by his talent, which turning out limited had narrowed the whole area of his self-regard." He can no more prevent Susan's marriage to Ronald Merrick than he can prevent his wife from ripping out the roses in his garden; both are defeats that would have been unthinkable before the war. (pp. 158-67)

In John Layton and Mohammed Ali Kasim, Scott transforms the man of action into an honorable prisoner. Seen through the eyes of his Indian nationalist, the independence of 1947 is a defeat of Indian unity; through the eyes of his English colonel the allied victory signals the end of the British Empire and the beginning of the nuclear age. In India, "the British came to the end of themselves as they were." . . . To have lost world power and colonial possessions is not as important to Scott as losing one's belief in liberal humanism. Scott is convinced that England's rapid demission of power in India after the war was an abandonment of that nation to warfare between religious factions she herself had fostered. Well-meaning people like Guy Perron's Aunt Charlotte bear a responsibility for the massacres of 1947: her belief that only the Indians actually killing each other are to blame confirms his "impression of the overwhelming importance of the part that

had been played in British-Indian affairs by the indifference and the ignorance of the English at home. . . ." Those terrible massacres in turn exemplify the fate of England's colonies in the immediate postwar period. In his essay ["India: A Post-Forsterian View"] Scott comments on how, in the former colonies, "in most cases the opposite of what had been worked for had been achieved; and in other cases, where a hope had been fulfilled" one was led to suspect "that the fulfillment revealed flaws in the arguments in favour of it." In the novel's myth-making, Anglo-Indian history becomes a myth of its own, a story of the end of colonialism as a surrender of the third world to the violence and racism that are the real legacy of the colonizers. (pp. 167-68)

For all its sympathies with India and Indians, then, the *Raj Quartet* is a radically conservative novel that resonates with the conviction that human beings can do little to change their oppressive history. The genre in which Scott writes demands that he record their struggles, acknowledge their politics and ambitions and wars. But when it is all over, when the immediate price of India's freedom is at least a quarter of a million lives and a future of religious massacre, then Scott moves gracefully, almost with relief, to another genre. Time in the lyric is at last released, as Barbie was in her madness, from the constraints of the calendar. The Indian poet offers timeless images of mutability—the dying flower, the running deer, the flying hawks. So much history ends in a few images, "fleeting moments: these are held a long time in the eye / the blind eye of the aging poet." The last, most characteristic gesture of this historical novel is to empty itself of history, to turn to the beauty we "can imagine in this darkening landscape." The lyric asserts that human beings make an art that is better than their history, yet all that long history lies like a shadow over it. (pp. 168-69)

> *Margaret Scanlan, "The Disappearance of History: Paul Scott's 'Raj Quartet'," in* CLIO, *Vol. 15, No. 2, Winter, 1986, pp. 153-69.*

FURTHER READING

Boyer, Allen. "Love, Sex, and History in *The Raj Quartet*." *Modern Language Quarterly* 46, No. 1 (March 1985): 64-80.
    Examines how Scott in *The Raj Quartet* "deals with the imperial relationship that bound Britain and India by using love as a metaphor."

Giles, Frank. "Real Rubies of the Raj." *Sunday Times,* London (4 December 1977): 8.
    A brief article written upon learning that "Paul Scott now intends to give up writing about India."

Narayanan, Gomathi. "Paul Scott's Indian *Quartet:* 'The Story of a Rape'." *The Literary Criterion* XIII, No. 4 (1978): 44-53.
    Compares the rape of Miss Manners to the theme of interracial sexual assault in British literature.

Rao, K. Bhaskara. *Paul Scott.* Edited by Kinley E. Roby. Boston: Twayne Publishers, 1980, 167 p.
    A biographical and critical survey of Scott's career centering upon *The Raj Quartet*.

Ringold, Francine. "A Conversation with Paul Scott." *Nimrod* 21, No. 1 (Fall-Winter 1976): 16-32.

Interview in which Scott discusses his writing techniques.

Swinden, Patrick. *Paul Scott: Images of India.* New York: St. Martin's Press, 1980, 123 p.

A comprehensive examination of Scott's career.

Tedesco, Janis. "Staying On: The Final Connection." *Western Humanities Review* XXXIX, No. 3 (Autumn 1985): 195-211.

Compares and contrasts Scott's attitude toward history in *The Raj Quartet* and *Staying On.*

Weinbaum, Francine S. "Psychological Defenses and Thwarted Union in *The Raj Quartet.*" *Literature and Psychology* XXXI, No. 2 (1981): 75-87.

Discusses how Scott equates the relationship between India and England with the connection between body and soul and with the imperfect union of individuals.

Peter Shaffer

1926-

(Born Peter Levin Shaffer; has also collaborated with Anthony Shaffer under the joint pseudonym Peter Antony) English dramatist, scriptwriter, novelist, and critic.

The following entry presents criticism on Shaffer's play *Equus*. For an overview of Shaffer's career, see *CLC*, Vols. 5, 14, 18, 37.

Shaffer has earned a reputation for consistent craftsmanship in several theatrical genres, including those of domestic tragedy, farce, psychological thriller, and historical drama. Demonstrating his versatility with each new play, Shaffer has never been linked to a particular dramatic movement. His works often involve such themes as love, death, and salvation, and his most successful dramas explore humanity's moral dilemmas while examining the psychological motivations of his characters. Shaffer illuminates his thematic concerns through dissension, which he develops through strong characters who function as dramatic foils. In his dramas, Shaffer investigates, but does not attempt to resolve, the clash between the bizarre and the ordinary events of life. He is by his own admission "fascinated by the endless ambiguity of the human situation, of the conflict between two different kinds of right."

Shaffer's psychological drama, *Equus,* is among his best-known and most critically acclaimed works. Recipient of the New York Drama Critics Circle Award and the Tony Award, *Equus* explores the spiritually-based motivations of Alan Strang, a seventeen-year-old stable boy who embraces the pagan belief that horses are gods and is institutionalized after brutally blinding several of his charges. Intrigued with Alan's primitive passion, the youth's psychiatrist, Martin Dysart, faces a personal crisis when he becomes reluctant to strip the boy of his rare emotions and thus relegate him to the normal yet mundane life he himself leads.

Equus is based on a true story about a boy in rural England who inexplicably blinded twenty-six horses with an iron spike. In his play, Shaffer lowers the number of horses to six and improvises freely, suggesting complex reasoning behind the boy's actions. The play is set at Rokeby Psychiatric Hospital in southern England, where Dr. Dysart has been persuaded to take on Alan Strang as a patient. While the outraged community wants Alan imprisoned for life, a constable recognizes that the boy is deranged and believes Dysart can help him. As the drama progresses, Alan's past is slowly unveiled through therapy. Dysart often speaks directly to the audience in *Equus,* explaining the results of a session, which is then reenacted onstage. Although the boy initially refuses to respond to the doctor except by singing television jingles, Dysart learns crucial information about Alan through his parents, Frank and Dora Strang. Dora, a fanatical Catholic inordinately attached to her son, has constantly forced her beliefs on him. Frank is a vehement atheist and down-to-earth, working-class socialist with little patience for his wife's religion. The parents tell Dysart about Alan's obsession with horses and his tendency to whip himself while chanting a pseudo-biblical litany to a picture of a horse that hangs over

his bed. Dysart eventually learns that five years earlier, Frank had replaced a lurid painting of the crucifixion of Jesus Christ with this photograph. Describing the picture, Dora tells Dysart, "You very rarely see a horse taken from that angle—absolutely head-on. It comes out all eyes."

During his interviews with Frank and Dora, Dysart also learns about Alan's first horseback ride, which occurred during a seaside holiday when the boy was six. When Dysart later questions Alan about it, the youth describes his sexual excitement during the ride and his anger at his father for pulling him off the horse. Alan admits that he took the job at the stable to be around horses, and also confides to Dysart that he has ridden many more times than his parents realize. Every three weeks, he takes a midnight ride on a favorite horse that he has named Equus. Ritualistically, Alan gives Equus a lump of sugar for his "Last Supper," undresses, and rides until he sexually climaxes. Alan reenacts his ride for Dysart in the last scene of Act I, a segment considered an emotional high point of *Equus* for its convincing depiction of intense psychosexual passion. Dysart, a clinically sterile man who has not even kissed his wife in six years, is amazed at Alan's strong passions and becomes envious of him. Weary and repressed, Dysart admits that his only outlet is an annual vacation to Greece, but even that causes him nightmares.

In one dream, he imagines himself as a Homeric chief priest officiating at the ritual sacrifice of five hundred children. Although sickened, he disembowels each with a scalpel, afraid that the other priests will kill him if he stops. This recollection serves to demonstrate that even the pleasures of Dysart's life involve reticence and guilt.

Later in the play, Alan discloses to Dysart that on the night of the crime he had gone out on a date with Jill, a young woman from the stables. While attending a pornographic movie, they accidentally run into Alan's father. When Frank offers a feeble excuse for being there, Alan becomes furious at his father's hypocrisy and at the forced recognition of his parents' loveless marriage. Later, the young couple returns to the stables and Jill attempts to seduce Alan, who feels excited but is unable to perform sexually before the omniscient gaze of his gods, the horses. Humiliated, he frightens Jill away with an iron pick, then gouges out the eyes of the horses who witnessed his shame. Critics have lauded the reenactment of the crime as one of contemporary theater's most dramatic spectacles. Barry B. Witham observed: "[*Equus*] is an exhilarating play: a remarkable blend of delayed exposition and theatrical effect, of melodrama and circus. . . . And it is that increasingly rare serious drama which capitalizes on lurid events while maintaining a devotion to 'ideas.' " Alan's reverence is largely conveyed through the striking image of the horses themselves, who are usually portrayed in performance by actors in dark brown suits that allow their faces to protude beneath horse's heads constructed of wire. Onstage throughout the play as a kind of chorus, the horses remain motionless except during Alan's ride and the crime itself. They are silent apart from occasionally making the "Equus Noise," which Shaffer describes in the script as "a choric effect . . . composed of humming, thumping, and stamping—though never of neighing or whinnying. This Noise heralds or illustrates the presence of Equus the God." For Alan, this presence is ceaseless and determines his every action. Following Alan's revelation, Dysart determines that he must return the youth to normalcy. Loath to destroy Alan's passion, he curses the intolerance of his profession: "I need— more desperately than my children need me—a way of seeing in the dark. What way is this? . . . *What dark is this?* . . . I cannot call it ordained of God: I can't get that far. I will however pay it so much homage. There is now, in my mouth, this sharp chain. And it never comes out."

This irresolute ending is one of several elements cited by critics who compare *Equus* to classical Greek tragedy. As in Sophocles' *Oedipus,* for instance, a good character is brought to misery through an error of judgment; Dysart's agony arises from the realization that he has wasted his life. Critics often maintain that the psychiatrist is a fully-rounded character possessing the three qualities of character advocated by Aristotle: verisimilitude, appropriateness, and consistency. Frank and Dora act as the Greek messengers who bring vital, unpleasant news, and the *catharsis* of Greek tragedy is fulfilled by Alan's reenactment of the blinding as well as Dysart's subsequent monologue, in which he ponders both of their futures. Upon its initial performance, *Equus* was lauded as a landmark in contemporary psychological drama. However, reviewers have occasionally faulted the intangibility of Dysart's dilemma, finding it difficult to empathize with the doctor's concern for destroying emotion and disagreeing with Shaffer's presumed tendency to equate brutality with a lust for life. John Weightman commented: "While there may be no great harm . . . in a boy masturbating on horseback with

the impression that he is entering into communion with the equine divine, this is clearly a deviation he will have to grow out of if he is to enter the world of adult sexuality. . . . [Yet] is it likely that so intense and sensitive a boy will have nothing left when he has lost his illusions?" The character of Dysart has also been interpreted as an attack on the psychiatric profession. That this oppressed, antiseptic doctor represents reason and sanity is ironic, as Dysart's true dilemma lies in his personal envy of Alan's ferocious passion.

One of Shaffer's major themes in *Equus,* the search for identity, involves both Alan and Dysart, who, like characters from Shaffer's other works, are trapped in the roles ascribed to them by society. Alan and Dysart represent opposing currents of instinctive and rational thought, which Shaffer refers to respectively as the Dionysian and the Apollonian selves. Alan's dementia stems in part from his oppressive parents, who have pulled him in opposite directions since birth and insisted that he follow their chosen paths. Frank's tyrannical rule over the family unconsciously influences Alan, who shares elements of speech and gesture with his father. While Frank represses his sexuality, Alan's mother dispenses religious dogma. Dora first unknowingly distorts religion when she informs Dysart that she told Alan as a young boy: "Did you know that when the Christian cavalry first appeared in the New World, the pagans thought horse and rider was one person?" Dora continues, "Actually they thought it must be a god," concluding: "It was only when one rider fell off, they realized the truth." Alan's mistaken belief that the union of horse and human represents godhood, along with the bizarre photograph of the horse with which Frank replaces his son's graphic portrait of the Crucifixion, helps to fuse religion and sexuality in Alan's mind. The communion he seeks with Equus is actually masturbatory, and his parents' instruction on sex is damaging. Consequently, Alan creates his own code of ethics.

Critics often disagree as to whether Alan or Dysart functions as the protagonist of *Equus,* since both confront the necessity of change in their lives. Unlike Alan, Dysart lives by the doctrines of others. Skeptical of his profession, Dysart practices psychiatry to obtain a feeling of omnipotence, concealing his own myriad problems until Alan's volatile sense of free will forces him to confront his sterile existence and lack of a definable identity. Intrigued with the boy's emotional intensity, the doctor gradually understands, accepts, and envies Alan's strange worship for Equus. Nevertheless, at the play's end, it remains difficult for him to leave the security of his ennui. Gene A. Plunka asserted: "*Equus* is Shaffer's most complete attempt to unite an existential and sexual search for identity with a ritualistic representation of spiritual freedom." He added: "*[Equus]* incorporates many of Shaffer's previous themes; yet it is different from the earlier plays because of the ritualistic elements which tie together the sexual, sociological and psychological motifs. Without this sort of 'unconscious communication,' Shaffer would be prone to preaching; instead, *Equus* forces us to be our own psychiatrists exploring the real motives behind our 'normal' lives."

(See also *Contemporary Authors,* Vols. 25-28, rev. ed.; *Contemporary Authors New Revision Series,* Vol. 25; and *Dictionary of Literary Biography,* Vol. 13.)

PRINCIPAL WORKS

PLAYS

Five Finger Exercise   1958

The Private Ear and The Public Eye   1962
The Merry Rooster's Panto   1963
The Royal Hunt of the Sun: A Play Concerning the Conquest of Peru   1964
Black Comedy   1965
A Warning Game   1967
The White Liars   1967
It's About Cinderella   1969
Equus   1973
Shrivings   1974
Amadeus   1979
Yonadab: The Watcher   1985
Lettuce and Lovage   1987

SCREENPLAYS

Lord of the Flies   [with Peter Brook]   1963
The Pad (and How To Use It)   1966
Follow Me!   1971
The Public Eye   1972
Equus   1977
Amadeus   1984

NOVELS

Woman in the Wardrobe   [with Anthony Shaffer under joint pseudonym Peter Antony]   1951
How Doth the Little Crocodile?   [with Anthony Shaffer under joint pseudonym Peter Antony]   1952
Withered Murder   1955

OTHER

The Prodigal Father   (radio drama)   1955
The Salt Land   (television drama)   1955
Balance of Terror   (television drama)   1957

J. W. LAMBERT

[Peter Shaffer's *Equus* focuses on] a theme constant throughout human history, never resolved, always relevant, and very much in the air today: the clash between the Apollonian, or rational, and the Dionysian, or instinctive. Most representations of this clash push the opposing parties to extremes, so that the rational appears desiccated and the instinctive bloodcurdling—a regrettable over-simplification from which *Equus* is not free. Here is a boy, an unknown quantity except that he has, while employed in a stable, blinded six horses, confronting a psychiatrist in the institution to which he has been committed. Most skilfully Mr. Shaffer takes us through the skirmishing by which these two arrive at a relationship from which the reason for his appalling act may emerge—the weary patience of the doctor, the boy's sullen silences, or derisive throwing off of TV advertising jingles, the gradual opening up, the filling in of background from the boy's parents—the father a rational working-class radical, the mother a devout Catholic—the acting out of the boy's fantasies, the pressures upon him of inarticulate faith and gritty puritanism, then of the sheer brute beauty and sensual drive of the animals among which he works and dreams, and the crowning agony, not to say last straw, forced upon him by the attentions of a pretty girl. Well, a boy did in real life, though not necessarily for the same reasons, blind horses as did the central figure of the play; yet Mr Shaffer has not made his course of action seem inevitable. The act of gouging out the horses' eyes, when it comes, seems if not arbitrary then hardly less perverse than it would have done had we been given no reasons for it at all. And after all the purpose of the play's exposition is to offer us some reason for the irrational.

Then, turning to the psychiatrist whose task it is, in the hope of stabilizing the boy, precisely to find reasons for the irrational, we find a grey little man suffering from middle-aged malaise, his own irrational impulses locked up in a dim provincial world fed only by annual holidays in Greece, which in turn feed only nightmares in which he slices up his child patients. His case, we are I think meant to feel, is even worse than that of the boy. And when he dithers over the fact that even if he can do anything to fit the boy for everyday life, it must be at the cost of destroying some vital spark in him, we recognize gloomily a familiar contemporary sentimentality: never put out a fire, even if the consequence is letting the house burn down with all its people in it.

Mr. Shaffer is an honest, sometimes stiff writer; he does not attempt to disguise his theme with rhetoric. . . . (pp. 14-15)

J. W. Lambert, in a review of "Equus," in Drama, *London, No. 111, Winter, 1973, pp. 14-16.*

MOLLIE PANTER-DOWNES

[*Equus*] deals with a horrific theme that the English public, often accused by European neighbors of being so sentimental over animals that they would react more furiously to an ill-treated puppy than to a battered baby, might be supposed to shun with repugnance. The playwright tells us in a program note that he first had the compulsive urge to write it after a friend casually mentioned, without supplying any details other than the gruesome synopsis, the case of a mentally disturbed stableboy, devoted to horses, who some years before had unaccountably blinded six of his charges with an iron spike. Why? It was apparently never known. Shaffer tries to supply an answer through the long interviews that Dr. Dysart, a psychiatrist, has with the at first violently uncooperative youth, Alan, and through swift flashbacks to his childhood and discussions with his parents—an aggressive, down-to-earth printer and his pious wife. It seems that an early religious passion of Alan's, encouraged by his mother, was supplanted by a crazy fixation on horses, completed by a friendly rider who gave the little boy an intoxicating gallop one day along the sands. One of these twin deities—the Christian and the centaur—he melds a private god he calls Equus, worshipped in secret rites in his room and later in ecstatic midnight communion with the real horses in a stable where he works part time. . . . The horses are played by young men clad in dark brown, their own faces visible through skeletal silver-wire horses' heads, matched by high metal hooves strapped to their feet. With a very occasional restless stamp or toss of the head, these masked presences standing in the shadows of the stable manage to suggest the eeriness and power of "that terrific equine twilight," as D. H. Lawrence wrote of the old hoofed god. (p. 184)

Mollie Panter-Downes, "Letter from London," in The New Yorker, *Vol. XLIX, No. 38, November 12, 1973, pp. 181-84.*

CATHERINE HUGHES

Since *Equus,* something of a psychiatric detective story, relies considerably on suspense for its effect . . . , it would be unfair to give away too much about its plot and development. A few items, though, will serve to whet (or, for the squeamish, perhaps squelch) the appetite.

Alan is 17 and when he comes to the Rokeby Psychiatric Hospital in southern England, about all we or the psychiatrist, Martin Dysart, know about him is that for seemingly inexplicable reasons he has blinded six horses with a steel spike. The act has outraged the community, which wants him imprisoned, but Dysart is persuaded to seek its causes, to, perhaps, return the boy to "normal."

Gradually, after a series of abortive attempts, Alan's story begins to emerge, the story of growing up in a home where his mother's suffocating brand of Catholicism was matched and subverted by his father's atheism, where the lithograph of a suffering Christ, feet in chains, has been torn off his wall and replaced by the photograph of a horse, eyes staring.

Those staring eyes have come to obsess the boy. Equus, the horse, has become his new religion—Jesus-Equus, in chains—or a horse's bit—"for the sins of the world." The transference for Alan is complete: he not only loves horses, he idolizes, even adores them: they have become not only his myth but a source of sexual excitation.

What, then, has happened, what shattering event has caused him to commit his atrocity? Equally important, what will its exploration by Martin Dysart reveal about Dysart's own obsessions, his sense of failure and inadequacy?

A great deal, as it turns out, though to reveal it other than thematically would be less than cricket. By the time the play ends, Dysart will contend: "That boy has known a passion more ferocious than any I've ever felt at any moment in my life." He also will know that, although he is able to cure him, it will be at the sacrifice of the boy's ability for ecstasy, for passion; that from that time on he, like the doctor himself, will suffer the pains of the bland, his pallid, arid existence the penalty for his "normalcy."

On the level of theatricality, *Equus* is stunning. . . . Although Shaffer's philosophizing is too shallow, sometimes to the point of glibness, to be entirely convincing, one in the end forgives it in the wake of the play's brilliantly rendered imagery. (The stylized skeletal horses' masks and stomping silver horses' hooves as utilized by the neighing, snorting actors are but one of several striking effects.) Even when his writing is a trifle pat, Shaffer is that rarest of playwrights today: one who has something to say, one who can keep the audience continually absorbed and challenged while he is saying it. (pp. 443-44)

Catherine Hughes, "London's Stars Come Out," in America, Vol. 129, No. 19, December 8, 1973, pp. 443-44.

VOGUE

A friend told playwright Peter Shaffer a single, horrendous detail about an abominable crime—a stableboy, in rural England, had inexplicably blinded some horses. The friend's "complete mention of it," says Shaffer, "could barely have lasted a minute. . . ." But out of that minute and subsequent months of gestation came *Equus* with its incredibly alive Alan Strang, the boy, and his deeply troubled psychiatrist, Dr. Martin Dysart—a theater experience which devastated London audiences, now is flabbergasting Broadway audiences. "The play grew," says Shaffer, "from my own preoccupation with myth, with my own mental life." Here Peter Shaffer delves into his twin preoccupations.

"Equus [the Latin word for horse] is surely, among other things, the name one individual [Alan Strang] gives to his impulse for worship. I think that is the telegrammic statement about *Equus.* And like all gods of that kind, like almost all gods I've ever heard of, it is an ambiguous presence—both conquering and submissive, both judging and accusing on the one hand and accepting and gentle on the other. He wears a double aspect, and this double aspect is very important, and paralleled when Dr. Dysart, the psychiatrist, reflects on the normal. The magistrate has said to him, 'You know what I mean by a normal smile in the child's eye and one that isn't, and you have a duty to that.' The psychiatrist says, *'Touché,'* but left alone, he reflects that the normal is the indispensable murderous god of health. He has two aspects. It is, as he says, the ordinary made beautiful, but it is also the average made lethal. It's another example of a god or of an immense force that has two aspects, that enshrines its own opposites. The psychiatrist's perception of what the word 'normal' means parallels the ambiguous nature of his god Equus in the mind of the boy.

"I'm fascinated by the endless ambiguity of the human situation, of the conflict between two different kinds of right. As witnessed in *Equus,* particularly as witnessed in Dysart's reflections on the 'Normal' with a capital N, as witnessed in his own problem with the boy. There is no question that the boy has done a criminal act, and that something must be done about it. There's no question that the boy himself is in deep pain and distress. He has nightmares almost every night. He's in the hospital. And, there's no question that as a humane, working psychiatrist of skill and conscience, Dysart must do something about that, too.

"He's not pretending that you must allow people to continue in distress. He's not pretending that you must allow people just to do their own thing. If you're Jack the Ripper, or a mass murderer, you must be *stopped* from doing your own thing. There is a higher and more important priority sometimes at work than the individual's doing his own thing. However, that said, he cannot *but* be aware that in removing the source of the boy's distress and nightmares, and dealing with violent emotion that has resulted in this disgusting crime, he is also, very likely, removing the main source of the boy's ecstasy, individual passion, and his own glory in being himself.

"The boy has found, no matter how strange the ritual is— against a background of rather dreary and colorless provincial life, working with not much to look forward to in an electrical and kitchenware shop, with an unimaginative but kindly father and an unimaginative but kindly mother (they're much the same although one happens to believe in God and one does not), and no doubt surrounded by four-and six-lane highways going to the guts of cities, surrounded by concrete eggboxes and the dreary paraphernalia of modern life—his own source of ecstasy. Dysart has no choice but to remove that from him, with very little guarantee that he'll be able to find anything to put in its place.

"As he says, 'do you think that feelings like his can simply be reattached, like plasters, stuck onto other objects we select?' He says, 'No, I do not believe this. In some way, I am about to do him, I think, some damage in this area; but there is nothing else I can do about it.'

"That is a truly tragic situation. Because it's not, again, a conflict between easy courses; although rather arduous, it's not a conflict between leaving a boy as he is and *not* leaving a boy as he is. It's a conflict in having not to leave him as he is and, at the same time, possibly to eviscerate him. And this appears to me tragic.

"I think that audiences react to *Equus* the way they do partly because, I suspect, they collectively dislike their analysts immensely and want some way of showing this in public. I think that when they sigh, and groan, when they clap or shout at this play, it is because, although it sounds self-flattering to say so, they recognize when the play works and when the writing works. That some particular area of their own distress has been pinpointed for them. They're saying, 'Yes, we have felt this, we think this.' There's also an enormous area behind that which can't be put precisely into words. It is that area of experience which is a source of continuous distress. It's not neurotic; it's the distress of being alive at all. Jung, when talking about neurosis said, 'Neurosis is an escape from legitimate pain.' Until I read that, I hadn't quite been aware that there *was* such a thing as legitimate pain." (pp. 136, 192)

"I think Jung is one of the greatest minds of the twentieth century. And, to me, one of the most intelligible and accessible. Jung is so intensely grounded in myth.

"Most people do not realize—and by 'realize' I mean they do not feel intensely, from day to day, in any way that truly affects them—that we did not begin the world, that we are repositories, walking encyclopedias, of all human experience, that we contain, within us, within our heads and within our genes, the whole of human history. This sounds abstract and irrelevant to most people who just want to get on with living; but the more one comes to realize that the cells of one's brain contain endless archetypal images that stretch back beyond the Stone Age, the more one can come to an immense and important sense of who one is, for himself, instead of just a little worried package of responses and reflexes, sexual drives and frustrations. Jung is the poet of psychiatry. And by that I do not mean a lot of pretty words.

"I think it is impossible to conceive of the world except in terms of the immense concepts that he formulated. Not that he was the first to formulate them—great writers before him have always spoken of this.

"Today people have a tendency to know almost too much. That can be inhibiting to playwrights. An exact record of fact doesn't always help the imagination.

"The theater is, or has to be, an ecstatic and alarming experience. And a beautiful one. That doesn't mean that it's one continuous shout-out; it also must have great spaces of tranquillity and lyricism in it. And although it sounds pompous or pretentious to say it, and I hope it doesn't, that's one of the things I tried to do." (p. 192)

Peter Shaffer, " 'Equus': Playwright Peter Shaffer Interprets Its Ritual," in Vogue, *Vol. 165, February, 1975, pp. 136-37, 192.*

JOHN WEIGHTMAN

[In *Equus,* Peter Shaffer], as he explains in a programme note, started from a historical fact: a stable-boy actually did blind the horses in the stables where he worked. But since nothing more is known than the bare anecdote, Mr Shaffer was free to invent an explanation, and he has done so very ingeniously. His play is basically a suspense thriller in the form of an illustrated dialogue between the psychiatrist and the boy. . . . (p. 45)

We gradually learn that the boy has been brought up by a religious mother and an atheistic, literal-minded father. He has inherited his mother's religious temperament in an acute form, and from early childhood he is fascinated by a picture of the scourging of Christ, which he buys with his pocket-money and hangs at the foot of his bed. His father objects to this picture, just as he objects to Bible-reading and watching television, which he sees as similar forms of emotional indulgence. In fact, the father, a master-printer, thinks of himself as an upholder of artisan rectitude, and has no patience with the poetic confusions of life.

In a traumatic, pre-pubertal incident, the boy is given a ride on a horse by a stranger, and this establishes a link between his nascent sexuality, his religious feeling and horses. The picture of Christ is replaced by a picture of a horse, looking outwards with Christ-like eyes. The boy composes pseudo-biblical litanies with which to worship this horse. He becomes obsessed with horses in general, and attributes to them the ambiguity of Christ. They are god-like in their strength, but they allow themselves to be chained and scourged by men; inside all horses' eyes is the same equine Godhead. The obsession becomes so strong that the boy gets a job in some stables, where he can elaborate and complete his ritual. Once every three weeks, he takes a horse out in the middle of the night, strips naked, puts a stick between his teeth as a "man-bit", and rides round and round the field until he achieves orgasmic climax, i.e. *ejaculatio sacra,* or ecstatic communion with the God-beast. This ceremony makes an exciting piece of theatre, since the horses are excellently simulated by stalwart young men wearing chromium-wire heads and chromium *cothurni* as hooves.

The climax ends the first section, and at that point I guessed what the solution was going to be. The buxom blonde stable-girl is out to seduce our hero, in the nicest possible way; but when she gets him naked in the straw, he panics because of the sacrilegious need to transfer the ejaculation from the divine to the human, under the accusing gaze of many-eyed Equus. He picks up the legendary tool for removing stones from horses' hooves and stabs out all the eyes. This gives another fine frenzy when the scene is re-enacted as psychodrama.

All this sounds plausible enough. Although I am myself much too like the atheistic father for divine bestiality ever to occur spontaneously to me, the play made the possibility of it convincing. Here was a new and interesting example of the way sex can get mixed up with religion, or *vice versa*. But I was more and more astonished by the psychiatrist's running commentary or soliloquy, as he led the boy through the various stages towards self-understanding. He constantly established comparisons between himself and the boy, to his own disadvantage. He confessed he had a humdrum, non-sexual marriage, because he and his prosaic Scottish wife lived side by side without communion: she involved in her knitting and he fascinated by the primitiveness of Greek legends, with their centaurs and dionysiac revels. What good was his work, he asked, if his therapeutic efforts merely served to relieve young people of the particular pain which gave them their interesting identity? Now that he had "cured" this boy, what would the future hold for the ex-centaur who had known ecstasy in a Hampshire field? He would grow up into a drab, uncultured adult, whose only contact with the equine God would be to put a bet of 50p from time to time on "the geegees."

This part left me totally unconvinced, although it came over strongly as the author's point of view, since the female magistrate who countered it slightly was not allowed to develop any really cogent arguments. There is no necessity within the play for the psychiatrist to have a non-sexual, non-lyrical marriage; his maladjustment and self-pity are simply a device to produce an artificial contrast. While there may be no great harm, and possibly some temporary lyrical gain, in a boy masturbating on horseback with the impression that he is entering into communion with the equine divine, this is clearly a deviation he will have to grow out of if he is to enter the world of adult sexuality. It is distressing, rather than awesomely beautiful, that he should have blinded several horses through getting his instinct in a twist. In any case, is he a true centaur, or might there not be some other, more complex, explanation of the Greek mythical image? And is it likely that so intense and sensitive a boy will have nothing left when he has lost his illusions? And if certain aspects of myth or religion, whether Christian or pagan, do not survive full understanding, are we to be so sentimental as to cling to them, and to argue that muddled suffering is better than lucid vision? I hardly think so. If we are ever again, in any sense, to

> Have sight of Proteus rising from the sea;
> Or hear old Triton sound his wreathèd horn. . . .

we shall have to be as rigorous in our way as the Greeks were in theirs. (pp. 45-6)

> *John Weightman, "Christ as Man & Horse," in* En-
> *counter, Vol. XLIV, No. 3, March, 1975, pp. 44-6.*

RUSSELL VANDENBROUCKE

Camus tells us that myths are made for the imagination to breathe life into them. Peter Shaffer's most recent play, *Equus,* is a myth-like story with the integrity and rich overtones of the finest of artistic works. It is a modern myth, delicately probing a psyche formed by a mingling of modern forces and influences, yet reaching beyond to the concerns and problems of men of all ages. *Equus* is an arresting piece, a vast playground for the imagination.

The story is that of seventeen-year-old Alan Strang who has blinded six horses in a stable where he works and is placed in a psychiatric hospital under the care of Dr. Martin Dysart. It is clear, from the very beginning, that the play will move inexorably to the abreaction of Alan's outrageous act. In building to this conclusion Mr. Shaffer has created suspense and tension comparable with that of a mystery story. But, unlike the mystery story, the clues into Alan's background and psychology do not fit into a neat and tidy package. How can they? Mr. Shaffer provides no simple explication or pat lecture but a laboratory for inquiry; he clearly understands the complexities of the mind, understands that the motivation behind complex individual acts cannot be empirically delineat-

ed. Rather than providing the sharp lines of simplistic causal relationships, Mr. Shaffer has drawn the curves and parameters within which Alan acts. (p. 129)

The play is divided into two acts and thirty-five scenes indicating changes of time, location, or mood. Dysart acts as a narrator at times, explaining himself and the treatment of Alan to the court worker who has seen that Alan is admitted to the hospital rather than imprisoned. At other times Dysart addresses the audience directly—musing about himself or the development and unravelling of Alan's case. As Dysart begins to explain his sessions with Alan the "telling" of the scene shifts smoothly and skillfully to the actual portrayal of it. Similarly, in recounting an incident from his past, Alan may be joined by his parents for the dramatization of that actual moment. Repeated shifts in time are utilized: from present, to past, to further in the past, back to the present and so forth.

Dysart conducts his interviews of Alan methodically—urging, bribing, soothing, or tricking the boy as necessary. Bits and pieces of Alan's family and background are presented, impressed upon the mind, yet uneasily passed over. Each is important. But the way it fits into the puzzle that is Alan is unclear. The audience accompanies Dysart as he searches for clues and assembles them in his attempt to comprehend Alan. (pp. 129-30)

At their first interview Alan cannot speak but only sings jingles from advertisements and we learn that Alan's father refuses to allow a television in the home: "It's a dangerous drug. . . . Absolutely fatal mentally." Books, learning, industry, self-improvement are Mr. Strang's values and he is deeply disappointed in his son's lethargy: "It's a disgrace when you come to think of it. You the son of a printer, and never opening a book!" The father is vaguely Marxist and an atheist, much upset at his wife's religiosity and its influence on Alan. He tells Dysart, "If you want my opinion, it's the Bible that's responsible for all this." The remark seems simply reactionary and off-handed but sticks, uneasily, in one's mind. Alan's ex-school teacher mother is fond of reading her son stories from the Bible and stories about horses. . . . She allows Alan to visit a neighbor to watch television. Alan claims to know more history than Dysart and asks him a string of questions ending with "Who said 'Religion is the opium of the people'?" Dysart properly answers, "Karl Marx," but Alan says that's the wrong answer. The apothegm is Mr. Strang's?

At the age of six, playing on a beach, Alan is offered a ride by a young horseman. It is gratefully accepted but soon interrupted by the frantic shrieks and protestations of overprotective parents. It appears this is the only time Alan has ridden a horse. This is baffling, for one assumes that a boy who so loves, even adores, horses would like nothing better than to ride them. But no, Alan claims (and is supported by his parents) to have ridden only on the one occasion.

Alan once had in his room a picture of Jesus on his way to Calvary, chained and beaten mercilessly. Mr. Strang cannot tolerate the picture and replaces it with one of a horse: "A most remarkable picture, really. You very rarely see a horse taken from that angle—absolutely head-on. . . . It comes out all eyes."

Mr. Strang visits Dysart and tells of a most peculiar rite he has witnessed a year or two previously. Alan, kneeling before the horse picture in his bedroom begins to chant a litany of equine genealogy: "And Legwus begat Neckwus. And Neckwus begat Fleckwus, the King of Spit. And Fleckwus spoke out of his chinkle-chankle! . . . And he said 'Behold—I give you Equus, my only begotten son!' " Alan fashions a bridle from a piece of string, places it over his head, and beats himself with a wooden coat hanger.

From this point the pace quickens and the clues come more easily as Dysart probes deeper and deeper—not blindly now, but with some ideas as to areas for inquiry. Alan recounts the ride on the beach: it was sexy. (p. 130)

Persistently questioned, Alan reveals that he *does* ride horses: furtively, under cover of darkness he makes his secret pilgrimages to the stable-temple. He first puts sandals on the horse's feet/hooves, and then fixes the chinkle-chankle of bridle and bit. He gives the horse a lump of sugar—"His Last Supper." Alan leads the horse into Ha Ha (the open field? the march to Golgotha?) and, stripped of his clothes, mounts the horse-man: "His neck comes out of my body." He begins to ride, slowly at first, and the wooden platform, mounted on a giant ball bearing, is rotated by the attending horsemen: slowly, very slowly, gradually gaining speed as Alan and Equus race through the night, faster and faster as they achieve the most complete of physical, emotional, and sexual unions and Alan shrieks, "Equus, I love you! Now! Bear me away." The ride is over, sexual and spiritual communion achieved. Alan kisses the horse and whispers "Amen!" The first act ends, having achieved one of the most brilliant and arresting visual images ever staged.

On a date, perhaps his first, Alan is talked into seeing a blue movie where, of all people, he meets his father. Everyone has secrets. The girl entices Alan to walk to the stable, near her home. Excited by the movie and attracted by the girl's gentle seductive charm, he attempts to make love but is unable. "When I touched her, I felt *Him*. Under me. . . . His side waiting for my hand . . . His flanks . . . I refused him. I looked. I looked right at her . . . and I couldn't do it. When I shut my eyes, I saw Him at once." Mortified by his failure, he angrily, painfully, dismisses the girl. But Equus remains. "He'd seen everything—he was laughing . . . mocking." Alan reaches for a metal spike and blinds the horses. Shamed by his failure he lashes out, masochistically destroying a part of himself—the epicenter of his life, his god, his lover.

But while much of the focus has been on Alan, Dysart is no shadowy manipulator of the boy—no formal and precise automaton attempting to simply cure Alan. Or is he? Dysart seeks self-knowledge even as he strives to understand Alan. He must confront himself as he confronts Alan, cure his own ills and unhappiness with that of Alan.

> The thing is, I'm desperate. You see, I'm wearing that horse's head myself. That's the feeling. All reined up in old language and old assumptions, straining to jump clear-hoofed on to a whole new track of being I only suspect is there. I can't see it, because my educated, average head is being held at the wrong angle. I can't jump because the bit forbids it, and my own basic force—my horsepower, if you like—is too little.

He recounts a dream: he is an Hellenic chief priest officiating at the ritual sacrifice of a herd of five hundred children. Armed with a scalpel, he slits the stomachs and disembowels each child in turn. Somewhat nauseated after a time, he nonetheless fulfills his appointed task, fearful that any protest will result in his own sacrifice. Dysart dreams outrageous acts; Alan has committed one.

Dysart is undergoing "professional menopause." He has no children and, asked by Alan if he has sex with his wife, dismisses the boy from his office—obviously upset at Alan's pointed and perceptive question. He has not even kissed his wife in six years. He is sterile. "The lowest sperm count you could find." Is he sexually impotent as well? Perhaps. But is the patient's sexual impotence really any different from the doctor's vapid emotions and helpless inability to effect change in himself?

Dysart spends his evenings at home with his brisk and antiseptic wife, reading art books on Ancient Greece—the joys of which are completely beyond her comprehension. He exclaims, "I sit looking at pages of centaurs trampling the soil of Argos—and outside my window he is trying to *become one*." Dysart is jealous of the boy who has lived and experienced passion, life itself, with a fervor he can never possibly achieve. "That boy has known a passion more ferocious than I have felt in any second of my life. And let me tell you something: I envy it."

What finally are we to make of this collage?

Returning to the idea of *Equus* as myth: a myth may be considered to be a story which addresses basic problems and situations not limited in relevance or interest to one society or era. It fills a need by the presentation of a model which provides an explanation (or at least a delineation) of various human conditions and situations. It is always symbolic of something greater than the characters, incidents, and rhetoric of the story itself. Within such a broad definition, many works seem to aspire to these very ends. Indeed, it is easily argued that all art strives to be larger than the form itself—seeking to fathom and capture basic truths of man and nature. But a myth must also contain elements of ritual, religion, and ceremony. It is in this sense that *Equus* is truly mythical.

In his earlier *The Royal Hunt of the Sun*, Mr. Shaffer sought after the images and ritual to capture the essence of religious conflict, internal strife, and self-crucifixion. In *Equus* he has brilliantly found them, uniting subject and style: Hellenic-high-priest-Dysart's sacrifice of the herd of children, centaur-Alan's worship of his chinkle-chankle lord and ritualistic beating of himself, and, most perfectly of all, the communion of boy, horse, god, and lover in the Field of Ha Ha. Dysart might be speaking for any one of us when he states, "I've stared at such images before—or been stared at *by* them. But this one is the most alarming yet."

The Greek tragedies presented characters of superhuman, regal, stature. But modern would-be egalitarian Western men are bereft of larger-than-life heroes and models to emulate. The modern myth must present its middle-class audiences a hero of its own proportion with which it may identify—a Willy Loman, a Martin Dysart.

The stories of the Greek tragedies were well known to the Hellenic audience and while the story of *Equus* is not well known, its backdrop is. Alan and Dysart have been molded by a search for experience, self-fulfillment, and meaning in their lives, the pressures of sexual performance and its attendant anxieties, the conflicts of religion, and strivings for a greater purpose. (pp. 130-32)

Dysart has a fantasy of returning to a place by the seas—where gods *used* to live, before they died. "Gods don't die," asserts Alan; but for Dysart they do. We need not take this as a Nietzschean remark. The gods *have* died for Dysart: life itself and meaning have died. Robbed of the center of his life, the giver of meaning, and answerer of questions, Dysart is lost—searching ardently but without direction for order and intelligibility. "I need—more than my children need me—a way of seeing in the dark."

Without his gods, his heroes, his pat answers, modern man searches desperately—for meaning, for understanding of the world he would so like to behold as a real home. He longs to be assured of some basic congruence between his aspirations for intelligibility and the essential constitution of reality. "Can you think of anything worse one can do to anybody than take away their worship? . . . it's the core of his life. What else has he got? Think about him. . . . He's a modern citizen for whom society doesn't exist. . . . Without worship you shrink, it's as brutal as that."

Despite his reservations, Dysart *will* effect a cure: the illicit passions will be eliminated—replaced by the socially acceptable but loathsome *ennui* that consumes Dysart. Which is preferable? "My desire might be to make this boy an ardent husband—a caring citizen—a worshiper of an abstract and unifying God. My achievement, however, is more likely to make a ghost! . . . . Passion, you see, can be destroyed by a doctor. It cannot be created." Alan will be stripped of that which Dysart so earnestly desires.

The grace, delicacy, and restraint which Mr. Shaffer has called upon to perfect his statement must not be taken lightly. They are the marks of a master craftsman about his trade. *Equus* is an extraordinarily ambitious effort, movingly successful in its total impact. It is a finely wrought statement, redolent with meaning, certain to be performed and remembered for generations to come. (pp. 132-33)

> *Russell Vandenbroucke, " 'Equus': Modern Myth in the Making," in* Drama & Theatre, *Vol. 12, No. 2, Spring, 1975, pp. 129-33.*

OSCAR GRUSKY

The hit play *Equus,* by Peter Shaffer, which has now been turned into a movie, illustrates a tendency in the popular arts to idealize the mentally ill. The disturbed adolescent Alan, when he comes to psychiatrist Martin Dysart at first refuses to talk and then speaks in jingles from television commercials (one psychoanalyst has labeled him a borderline psychotic). The boy, whose passion for horses is both religious and psychosexual, has blinded six of them one night by driving a stake through their eyes. The psychiatrist's dilemma, as Dysart sees it, is that in curing Alan, he must excise the "ferocious" passion from his soul, even though Dysart himself laments the absence of such ecstasy in his own life.

Alan's illness becomes the embodiment of creativity in Shaffer's work, and the practitioners of psychiatry seem to have almost supernatural powers. In real life, neither the mentally ill nor their therapists are heroes. Therapy is frequently a mundane, bureaucratic encounter in which the moments of high drama are few, the involvement of patient and therapist is less than total (especially in the institutionalized settings of today), the fears and uncertainties of both often interfere with the outcome, and success is usually partial at best. Most

important, to picture therapy as posing a serious choice between creativity and conformity is to oversimplify and overdramatize.

To its credit, *Equus* is not dogmatic in its psychiatric explanations, but attempts to see Alan's illness against a broader canvas of family, religion, social class, law, and problems of social control. The deepest understanding of mental illness requires, as philosopher Michel Foucault asserts, knowledge not only of "the void that it hollows out, but also in the positive plenitude of the activities of replacement that fill that void." *Equus* suggests that a void hollowed out by sexual repression, social inequality, and modern technology is filled by a commitment to the supernatural.

Alan's parents, Frank and Dora, are pictured as the primary source of the boy's problems. The father, a printer and a socialist, has high ambitions for his son, hoping he will secure the college education and social acceptability he was unable to obtain himself. He is also an atheist and a man of strong views who will not permit his son to watch television because it is "fatal mentally" and will make him "stupid for life." Alan, however, rejects his father's influence and refuses to perform in school or even to read.

Dora Strang, the mother, is a very religious woman who is overindulgent and excessively attached to her son. Dora, who is from the upper or upper-middle class (she is described as moving in the "horsy" set), is also puritanical about sex, so much so that she even has difficulty talking about it. It is suggested that problems in her sex life with Frank have something to do with Alan's illness. Frank sees "bloody religion" as the root of the tensions in the Strang household and says most religion stems from "bad sex." He attributes Alan's illness to his wife's indoctrination of the boy into Christian lore, particularly its violent aspects. (pp. 21-2)

Alan's religious beliefs also interfere with his sexuality. One evening, he and Jill, a friend he works with at the stable, go to a porno movie, return to the barn, and undress. But Alan is unable to have intercourse; his impotence is triggered by the noises of the horses in the barn, the gods of his religious obsession. Jill leaves the barn when he threatens to attack her with a hoof pick, the same instrument he later uses to blind the horses.

Alan's horse worship serves as a bridge to his mother and alienates him from his father. When he blinds the six horses he has been secretly riding at night, he is symbolically killing part of himself, the part that believes in Equus the god—thereby completing the Oedipal plot. With the support of Dysart and the sympathetic understanding of Jill, Alan abandons Equus and thus frees himself from the Oedipal attachment to his mother.

Dysart himself is depicted as a troubled man whose marriage is devoid of passion and whose own chief pleasure comes from studying ancient Greece. He recounts one dream in which he is the high priest officiating at the sacrifice of 500 children. With a scalpel, he must carve up their insides—hating what he is doing but nevertheless carrying out the task lest his two assistants see his distaste and carve *him* up. Dysart sees the practice of psychiatry—the adjustment business, as he calls it—as "all reined up in . . . old assumptions" and therefore a discipline that is incapable of understanding people. By slicing up the insides of children, he believes he is acting as an instrument of social control.

The psychiatrist questions his role, pointing out some of the ironies of the industrialized society to which he is returning Alan, "the normal world where animals are treated properly, made extinct. . . ." He says, "I'll take away his Field of Ha Ha [a phrase the boy uses to describe his nightly revels that comes from the Book of Job—"He sayeth among the trumpets, Ha ha"] and give him normal places for his ecstasy—multilane highways driven through the guts of cities."

Dysart thus visualizes himself as the destroyer of Alan's essential life force and hence a godlike figure. His own pain—the chain in *his* mouth—stems from his inability to resolve the fundamental dilemma of modern psychiatry. In this view, society and religion function as both the creators and destroyers of individuality and emotion. (p. 22)

Oscar Grusky, "Equestrian Follies," in Psychology Today, *Vol. 11, No. 5, October, 1977, pp. 21-2.*

BARRY B. WITHAM

Peter Shaffer's *Equus* is neither great theatre nor bad psychology, but it has elements of both. It is an exhilarating play: a remarkable blend of delayed exposition and theatrical effect, of melodrama and circus, which has inspired huge ticket sales and adoring critical reviews. And it is that increasingly rare serious drama which capitalizes on lurid events while maintaining a devotion to "ideas." Yet, in spite of its wide popular acclaim, *Equus* is difficuilt to sort out even when all the clues have been discovered. Why does Alan make his slightly sadomasochistic leap from Jesus to horses? What specifically does the scene in the porno theatre have to do with Alan's confrontation with Jill and the horses? Is the climactic nude scene an organic part of the play's structure or simply a gratuitous bow to contemporary fashion?

These questions—and a variety of others—have been raised in the aftermath of the play's initial sensation. Sanford Gifford has criticized the drama for its faulty psychology and for its deceptive views of the patient-psychiatrist relationship. And John Simon has indicted it as a trumped-up plea for a homosexual life style [see Shaffer's entry in *CLC,* Vol. 5]. James Lee, on the other hand, has praised *Equus* for the fullness of its dramatic experience, and James Stacy has pointed out the strength of its religious passion, particularly in relation to Shaffer's earlier *Royal Hunt of the Sun* [see Shaffer's Further Reading]. What we are confronted with, then, is a major work of serious drama which continues to enthrall sophisticated (and not so sophisticated) audiences, but which leaves many viewers uneasy because they are uncertain what they are so enthusiastically applauding. . . . It is probable that the controversy will continue, and the purpose of this essay is to shed some light on the traditions which have given us *Equus* nearly twenty years after a similar work—[John Osborne's] *Look Back in Anger*—began changing the face of the contemporary English theatre.

The comparison is not so surprising as might be initially assumed. In its subject matter, its dramatic tradition, *Equus* is still infused with the same philosophical outlook which was so popular and controversial in 1956. And in spite of a variety of dramatic viewpoints carefully exhibited by two generations of English playwrights, we seem to be back almost where we began. Thus, being truly alive is synonymous with suffering an intensity of experience which frequently borders on the abnormal and which is repeatedly glamorized as "passion." Ali-

son Porter in *Look Back in Anger* can only be "saved," after all—as she herself comes to realize—if she grovels and suffers. (This despite the fact that she confides to Helena that she was very happy for the first twenty years of her life.) Jimmy Porter, whose passions we are sometimes invited to admire in much the same way that we are Alan Strang's, tells his wife that there is hope for her if she "could have a child and it would die." Indeed, Jimmy accuses everyone of wanting to avoid the discomfort of being alive, and he describes the process of living as a realization that you must wade in and "mess up your nice, clean soul." Routine is the enemy for Jimmy Porter, and those who are not willing to take part in his crusade of suffering are forced to desert him.

The same points and counterpoints are echoed in Shaffer's drama. Dr. Dysart's bland and colorless life is endlessly exhibited and catalogued. Like Alison and her brother, Nigel, Dysart is not a participant but a spectator. He has never ridden a horse. He experiences passion only vicariously. He is married to an antiseptic dentist whom he no longer even kisses. He travels to romantic climes with his suitcases stuffed with Kao-Pectate. And because he is acutely conscious of his normality, he feels accused by Alan just as Alison is attacked by Jimmy.

Alan Strang, on the other hand, experiences passion in its extremity; a passion which Dysart not only lacks but envies. Like Jimmy Porter, Alan has made a pain which is uniquely his, and uniquely part of his being alive.

> DYSART. His pain. His own. He made it. Look . . .
> to go through life and call it yours—your life—
> you first have to get your own pain. Pain that's
> unique to you. You can't just dip into the common bin and say, "That's enough!"

Dysart's description of Alan recalls Jimmy's complaint that, "They all want to escape from the pain of being alive," as well as Alison's cry, "Oh, don't try and take his suffering away from him—he'd be lost without it."

The pain that defines both Jimmy and Alan, of course, is always contrasted with the commonplace, the normal experiences of everyday life. Both of these plays explore, without ever resolving, the conflict between the abnormal and the ordinary events of our existence. Jimmy wants Alison to show some enthusiasm in order to experience the emotions of being alive. But it is always life by his terms, and his terms are demanding. He wants to "stand up in her tears." And ultimately he wins. "I was wrong," she admits. "I want to be a lost cause. I want to be corrupt and futile." She becomes a kind of victim-healer, because she is willing to give him his pain and reaffirm his vision of a world where "plundering" is equated with being alive.

Shaffer covers much of the same ground. Instead of Jimmy Porter, we now have the tormented Alan, whose horrible acts are translated by Dysart into a kind of enviable pain. The extremity of Alan's passions is what Dysart covets, and he is reluctant to remove Alan's pain because (like Alison) Dysart sees in the pain the source of a passionate life.

> You won't gallop any more, Alan. Horses will be
> quite safe. You'll save your pennies every week, till
> you can change that scooter in for a car, and put
> the odd fifty P on the gee-gees, quite forgetting that
> they were ever anything more to you than bearers
> of little profits and losses. You will, however, be

without pain. More or less completely without pain.

Dysart finally accepts his part as healer because any other alternatives are simply unacceptable. Alan's extremity—the blinding of the horses—is a shocking dramatic device, but no amount of theatrical trickery can enable Shaffer to equate barbarism with an enviable passion for life.

But what are we to make of all this? Is this stern indictment of the commonplace what is so compelling about *Equus?* Is it the core "idea" at the center of the drama? Or is it a metaphor for a more complex statement?

John Simon has examined the thematic issues in *Equus* and discovered a thinly disguised homosexual play beneath the surface of Shaffer's pseudo-psychology. [See Shaffer's entry, *CLC,* Vol. 5]. Simon claims that the depiction of Dysart's wife and marriage, the sexual imagery associated with the horses, and the inability of Alan to perform with Jill are all clear indications of a viewpoint which rejects heterosexuality—the ordinary—in favor of a homosexual world view. Simon additionally points out that the marriage of Jill's parents is also painted in a bad light, and that Jill, herself, is presented as a naughty seductress tempting Alan away from his Horse-Eden. Thus, for Simon the play abounds with dishonesty: ". . . toward its avowed purpose, the explication of 'a dreadful event,' by making that dreadfulness seem fascinating and even admirable. Dishonesty to the audiences, by trying to smuggle subliminal but virulent homosexual propaganda into them. Dishonesty toward the present state of the theatre, in which homosexuality can and has been discussed openly and maturely."

This point of view is particularly interesting in light of the comparison with *Look Back in Anger,* because Osborne's play has also been analyzed in terms of its strong homosexual overtones. Indeed, psychiatric criticism of the play addressed the *ménage à trois* implications of the Porter household two decades ago. How else, some critics believed, could you account for the characters' behavior? (pp. 61-4)

Uncovering homosexuality in literature, however, is often a shell game, and the degree of sleight of hand frequently vitiates the worth of the results. Once certain premises are established, almost anything is fair game. Perhaps Simon is accurate, . . . but there may be a more obvious answer to the apparent disdain with the ordinary which seems to infuse both *Look Back in Anger* and *Equus.*

Certainly the "angry young men" of the 1950's did not require a homosexual world view in order to see the failures of the welfare state, the outdated monarchy and the vanishing empire. Assaulting the commonplace was for Osborne and his contemporaries a thematic way of rejuvenating the English drama as well as tapping the *angst* that was so compelling in the surrealistic experiments of Beckett and Ionesco. And the normal represented everything from the inequalities of the class system to the blunders at Suez. In its world view, then, *Equus* is an extension not only of *Look Back in Anger,* but . . . numerous other dramatic ventures which contrasted the passion of the abnormal with the drabness of the postwar English world, and which, consequently, have led to an often misplaced admiration of violence and aberration.

In the final analysis, the thematic issues in *Equus* sometimes seem muddled and confused not because the play is disguised homosexuality, but because it is part of an ongoing fascina-

tion with life as "passion," a fascination which also has its counterparts in English films and popular music. The current extremity termed "punk rock," for example, owes its lineage to the grittiness of the early Rolling Stones just as much as *Equus* descends from *Look Back in Anger.* Iconoclasm has become institutionalized. The original "causes" are somewhat shrouded, but the rebellion goes on. Life as "passion" continues to be dramatic and highly theatrical, but after twenty years somewhat unsatisfactory as "IDEA."

Fortunately, like so many other English plays of the past two decades, *Equus* lives not by what it says but by the sparks that it ignites in its attempts to be articulate. And while Shaffer's dramatic traditions go back to *Look Back in Anger,* his theatrical tradition is closely linked to the experiments of a decade ago in the modes of Brecht and Artaud. For what is ultimately applauded in *Equus* is not its message but its packaging. Like spectators of *Marat-Sade,* audiences at Shaffer's play are frequently carried headlong into a vague kind of catharsis without a very clear knowledge of what they are experiencing or applauding. This is not, and has not been, an unusual occurrence in the contemporary theatre. It would be interesting to know, for instance, how many audience members have come away from *Marat-Sade* confused by the complex arguments of Peter Weiss's dialectic on revolution, yet enormously moved by the grotesque images in the play: the deranged inmates, the club-swinging nuns, the saliva, semen and revolutionary songs.

The "total theatre" of a decade ago was an exciting theatre. And it did play a large part in replacing a poetry of words with what Artaud called a poetry of the senses. *Marat-Sade* is the most famous of the total theatre experiments, because of the publicity surrounding its creation and its huge popular success outside the United Kingdom. (pp. 64-5)

It is from this theatrical tradition that *Equus* also draws, and it is this tradition which frequently convinces us that we are seeing and hearing something *important* because the images which bombard us are so exciting. *Equus* is an exciting play. The eerie music and equus noise are provocative and foreboding. The men as horses serve as a compelling theatrical invention which helps to intensify both the act-one curtain and the blinding sequence near the end of the play. The nude encounter between Jill and Alan is strikingly theatrical, as is the physical setting of the drama which allows one scene to flow rapidly into the next.

But ultimately *Equus* is a schizophrenic play, because its theatrical fireworks cannot mask its muddled logic and tired philosophy. After sorting through what Shaffer has to say, it is tempting to dispense with the intellectual straining and experience the play on a more visceral level. After all, Alan *will* be better once he is cured. And Dysart, too, may yet survive his menopause and move on to a time and place where he can admire his own great gifts as much as his patients' horrifying illnesses. (pp. 65-6)

Barry B. Witham, "The Anger in 'Equus'," in Modern Drama, *Vol. XXII, No. 1, March, 1979, pp. 61-6.*

HÉLÈNE L. BALDWIN

Equus was certainly the most popular serious drama of the 1974-75 season, fascinating and moving audiences with its presentation of a suffering boy's twisted notions of religion and of a weary, played-out psychiatrist who shudders at the supposed loss of passion consequent on a cure of the boy. Yet the play is controversial in its seeming anti-intellectualism, its implied criticism of psychiatry as a manipulative profession, and its apparent acceptance of sadism and bestiality as elements in religious worship. Can this play be defended as "theater of cruelty" in Antonin Artaud's sense of the word, or is it merely a sensational play seeking to attract audiences with eroticism and sadism?

To answer the question above we must first define exactly what "theater of cruelty" is. Much of what Artaud described in *The Theater and its Double,* his manifesto on theater of cruelty, is evident in **Equus.** Artaud's main point, reiterated over and over in the essays which are his main contribution to dramatic theory, is that the theater should be primarily a dynamic physical spectacle rather than verbal word-play uttered by rather static bodies. Artaud specified "a violent and concentrated action," an aim which **Equus** certainly fulfills, in both the "worship" ride of Alan on the horse and in the blinding scene itself. For Artaud, language should always be secondary to the *mise-en-scène,* which has its own language "of sounds, cries, lights, onomatopoeia." What he calls "sonorisation" is a basic aspect of the spectacle for Artaud: "sounds, noises, cries are chosen first for their vibratory quality, then for what they represent." **Equus** vividly demonstrates the quality of sonorisation. As Shaffer himself says, "I have in mind a Choric effect, made by all the actors sitting around Upstage, and composed of humming, thumping, and stamping—though never of neighing or whinnying." This weird sound, the **Equus** sound, is a vital aspect of the effect the play has upon audiences. (pp. 118-19)

In regard to lighting, Artaud suggests "new ways of spreading the light in waves, in sheets, in fusillades of fiery arrows." Whether lighting can work this way or not, the technology of lighting has certainly become far more sophisticated than it was in the thirties and forties when Artaud was working in the theater in Paris. The importance of lighting to **Equus** is amply demonstrated in the many stage directions, such as: "The light grows brighter," "Light grows warmer," " . . . the light decreases until it is only a fierce spotlight on horse and rider, with the overspill glinting on the other masks leaning in towards them." These various uses of light fulfill Artaud's emphasis on light as a means of playing upon the audience's emotions.

Most convincing evidence of the influence of Artaud on either playwright or director or both is the use of masks and other accessories for the horses. Artaud says: "Manikins, enormous masks, objects of strange proportions will appear with the same sanction as verbal images, will enforce the concrete aspect of every image and every expression—with the corollary that all objects requiring a stereotyped physical representation will be discarded or disguised." . . . Shaffer says in a note on "The Horses": "Any literalism which could suggest the cosy familiarity of a domestic animal—or worse, a pantomime horse—should be avoided." He specifies that the "track-suits of chestnut velvet" and the "light strutted hooves" and "masks made of alternating bands of silver wire and leather" should be supplemented by "animal effect . . . created entirely mimetically." (p. 119)

In regard to the set, Artaud says simply: "There will not be any set," and amplifies this later under "Spectacle," by saying: "The problem is to make space speak, to feed and furnish it like mines laid in a wall of rock, which all of a sudden turns into geysers and bouquets of stone." . . . In **Equus** there is no conventional setting; the "square" represents whatever is needed at the moment—the psychiatrist's office, the stables, etc. Yet . . . [the directing] and the acting "make space speak, . . . feed and furnish it." (pp. 119-20)

Two minor coincidences help to confirm Artaud as the master influence in the staging, if not the writing, of **Equus.** Shaffer's earlier success, **The Royal Hunt of the Sun,** and its staging resemble extraordinarily the scenario described by Artaud for his *The Conquest of Mexico,* except that, as in **Equus,** Shaffer is more concerned with the personal relationships between the leading characters than with the cosmic issues stressed by Artaud. Even more striking, Artaud describes admiringly Jean-Louis Barrault's "centaur-horse" in the mimed spectacle created by Barrault based on Faulkner's *As I Lay Dying:* "In Jean-Louis Barrault's spectacle there is a sort of marvellous centaur-horse, and our emotion before it was as great as if J. L. Barrault had restored magic itself to us with the entrance of his centaur-horse. . . . Barrault improvises the movements of a wild horse, and . . . one is suddenly amazed to see him turn into a horse. His spectacle demonstrates the irresistible expressiveness of gesture. . . . He fills the stage with emotion and life." One feels that Shaffer . . . had read Artaud's book and constructed **Equus** on the inspiration of the comments on Barrault's mime. (p. 120)

But in spite of the brilliant Artaudian staging, **Equus** falls short of Artaud's vision of the theater of cruelty in regard to costume, language, and theme. Artaud specifies: "modern dress will be avoided as much as possible without at the same time assuming a uniform theatrical costuming that would be the same for every play. . . . " We could explain this deficiency of **Equus** by stating that the modern subject matter necessitates modern costumes, but then we would immediately fall afoul of Artaud's concept of proper subject matter for the theater of cruelty, as will be discussed below.

In regard to language, Artaud says little, since for him language is the least important part of the *mise-en-scène.* He does assert, however, "I am trying to restore to the language of speech its old magic," and here Shaffer's play is very deficient. The best one can say of his prose is that it is serviceable, for example: "Do you know what it's like for two people to live in the same house as if they were in different parts of the world?" To be sure, there are some catchy phrases, such as "chinkle-chankle" in connection with Alan's horse-worship, but such phrases would be subsumed under the "sonorisation" aspect of the theater of cruelty. The dialogue and particularly the long speeches of Dysart are indubitably on the level of soap opera. Poetry or poetic language is particularly needed in the evocation of the Greek spirit so admired by Dysart, but it is sadly lacking:

> I wish there was one person in my life I could show. One instinctive, absolutely unbrisk person I could take to Greece, and stand in front of certain shrines and sacred streams and say, Look! Life is only comprehensible through a thousand local gods. And not just the old dead ones with names like Zeus—no, but living Geniuses of Place and Person! And not just Greece but modern England! Spirits of certain trees, certain curves of brick wall, certain fish and chip shops, if you like, and slate roofs . . .

If one compares this prose with that of, say, E. M. Forster in his beautiful short story *The Road from Colonus,* about the effect of Greece on an ordinary person, the flatness of Shaffer's prose is apparent.

Far more important, however, than language and costume in deciding whether or not *Equus* represents Artaud's theater of cruelty are the theme and scope of the play. Artaud is uncompromising in regard to personal problems and psychology as topics for plays: "Such preoccupation with personal problems disgusts me, and disgusts me all the more with nearly the whole contemporary theater which, as human as it is antipoetic, except for three or four plays, seems to me to stink of decadence and pus." Artaud attacks the use of psychology on stage, which he says, "works relentlessly to reduce the unknown to the known, to the quotidian and the ordinary, [and] is the cause of the theater's abasement and its fearful loss of energy, which seems to me to have reached its lowest point. And I think both the theater and we ourselves have had enough of psychology."

Shaffer's attack on psychiatry through Dysart may appear to correlate with Artaud's attack on psychology. But Artaud was attacking the use of psychology *on stage,* not the profession itself of which he unfortunately had to make much use in his tormented life. Shaffer attempts, weakly, to be fair to psychiatry, by putting in the mouth of the Juvenile Court judge Hesther some exceedingly brief protests, such as "It [psychiatry] still means something," or "All the same, they don't usually blind their wives," which Dysart counters with very long speeches. When Dysart talks about cutting from his patients "parts sacred to rarer and more wonderful gods," the implication is that both Christianity and normality require castration, a dubious view to which one cannot imagine psychiatrists Karl Menninger or Rollo May acceding. Dysart is an ailing psychiatrist, with a failed marriage and sadistic nightmares of disemboweling children—a case of "Physician, heal thyself" if there ever was one. The play might be justified for Artaud's view as Shaffer's revealing the sicknesses of psychiatrists, particularly had he made it clear that Dysart is not just thinking out loud but is himself talking to a psychiatrist. But there is no distance, no irony, and Dysart obviously speaks for Shaffer himself in condemning psychiatry as reductive and destructive. Dysart's final speech is loaded; he describes normality as plastic and shallow and implies that even destructive and distorted emotion is better than normality. (pp. 121-23)

Artaud rejects psychology but claims religion for the stage: "Everything in this active poetic mode of envisaging expression on the stage leads us to abandon the modern humanistic and psychological meaning of the theater, in order to recover the religious and mystic preference of which our theater has completely lost the sense." It may be argued that this is just what *Equus* does do—recover the religious and mystic preference. Yet the concept of religion in the play, whether it be that of Alan's mother or of Dysart, is limited and one-sided, and the concept of worship is simply and totally orgasmic—as John Weightman describes it: "a boy masturbating on horseback with the impression that he is entering into communion with the divine." [See Weightman's excerpt above]. The language used by Alan to describe his "religious" experience is frankly sexual: he puts the stick in his mouth "so's it won't happen too quick"; he touches the horse "All over. Everywhere. Belly. Ribs"; he cries to the horse, "Take me!"; and he speaks of the horse's coat as giving him "Little knives—all inside my legs," and of his mane as "stiff in the wind"; finally he ends his monologue with a scream of sexual pleasure. Even

though Dysart wants to preserve Alan's "worship," and wants to attain it himself, what he really appears to crave for both of them is sexual orgasm. One does not need to accept John Simon's interpretation of the play as covert homosexuality to see that Dysart's craving for passion has little to do with religion and everything to do with sex [see Shaffer's entry, *CLC,* Vol. 5]. Artaud's withering comment, "sexuality sugar-coated with an eroticism that has lost its mystery [has] nothing to do with the theater, even if [it] does belong to psychology. These torments, seductions, and lusts before which we are nothing but Peeping Toms gratifying our cravings . . ." seems to be written precisely about *Equus.*

Shaffer attempts to be fair to religion as intuitive and awesome rather than reasoned and intellectual. . . . But Shaffer's concept of worship, expressed through Dysart, is watery aestheticism, seasoned with eroticism: "I'm in some Doric temple—clouds tearing through pillars—eagles bearing prophecies out of the sky." He is actually unfair to religion, showing a limited and distorted form of Christianity in Alan's mother and ascribing to Christianity sadomasochistic qualities which properly belong either to Roman soldiers or to Alan himself in his flagellation ritual before his horse-god.

If Artaud does not want personal sexual problems or psychological analysis in the theater of cruelty, what does he want? What he said was that "the theater of cruelty proposes to resort to a mass spectacle," to "historic or cosmic themes, familiar to all," "to the preoccupations of the great mass of men, preoccupations much more pressing and disquieting than those of any individual whatsoever," to "the great preoccupations and great essential passions which the modern theater has hidden under the patina of the pseudocivilized man." Artaud stresses the use of myth: "These themes will be cosmic, universal, and interpreted according to the most ancient texts." (pp. 123-24)

True, Shaffer's play deals with the mythical figure of the centaur, but except for Chiron, the wise teacher-figure, centaurs do not play a major role in any of the Greek myths. Nor do Alan and his horse resemble Chiron, whose teaching was that man should balance passion and reason. Nor can *Equus* be said to be cosmic and universal; not many adolescents blind horses out of sexual-religious conflict. In our permissive age, not many adolescents still have sexual-religious conflicts. Nor do many psychiatrists feel that their profession is a failure and wish to abandon it. The problems of *Equus* are individual problems, though the author has attempted to give them some larger significance by relating them to the "plastic" culture.

Finally, the definition of cruelty must be assessed in relation to the theme of *Equus.* Cruel *Equus* certainly is. But what did Artaud mean by "theater of cruelty"? In defending his manifesto to a friend made uneasy by the term, Artaud states categorically: "cruelty is not synonymous with bloodshed, martyred flesh, crucified enemies." Further, he says: "death is cruelty, resurrection is cruelty, transfiguration is cruelty," which seems to imply that life itself, if rendered accurately, is cruelty. And indeed that is what he appears to mean, for he says:

> I have therefore said "cruelty" as I might have said "life" or "necessity." I employ it (the word "cruelty") not in an episodic, accessory sense, out of a taste for sadism and perversion of mind, out of love of sensationalism and unhealthy attitudes . . . it is not at all a matter of vicious cruelty, cruelty burst-

ing with perverse appetites and expressing itself in bloody gestures, sickly excrescences upon an already contaminated flesh, but on the contrary, a pure and detached feeling . . . the idea being that life . . . admits . . . evil.

In spite of this rather noble-sounding statement, which would justify every serious play from Shakespeare to O'Neill, the plays he actually proposed for his program, such as *The Cenci, The Conquest of Mexico,* and *Arden of Feversham,* are full of overt cruelty and bloodshed, much of which happens onstage. Artaud himself probably was unsure exactly how much cruelty was tolerable onstage. But the main question is: Would Artaud have felt the blinding of six horses by a sexually disturbed adolescent to be a theme sufficiently serious and cosmic for the theater of cruelty? Or would he have felt it to be a theme too individual, too personal, too "sugar-coated with eroticism," above all, too psychological to be acceptable? I believe Artaud would have rejected *Equus* as unworthy of the theater of cruelty.

What, then, can we conclude about *Equus?* Is it a serious, valid effort to create theater of cruelty along the lines sketched out by Artaud? Or is it merely a sensational play seeking to attract audiences with eroticism and sadism? (pp. 125-26)

According to Rollo May in *Love and Will,* the whole purpose of psychiatry, Shaffer and Dysart to the contrary notwithstanding, is not "helping the patient adjust to society, by offering him certain 'habits' which we think are better for him, or by making him over to fit the culture," as Shaffer appears to think it is. Rather, says May, it is "the confronting of [conflicts] in such a way that we rise to a higher level of personal and interpersonal integration." Shaffer's Dysart and Shaffer himself seem to have no faith in the possibility of constructive reintegration. In the play, psychiatry and religion both are whipping-boys for some possibly unworked-through feelings of Shaffer's own. As Steve Grant said in *Plays and Players:* ". . . this is the kind of Laingian pseudo-liberal manure in which the seeds of totalitarianism are often planted. Could the author report on the sense of wonder and worship felt by SS officers setting killer dogs at the throats of women and children . . . by Manson acolytes . . . ?"

The play is soap opera; the direction is theater of cruelty plastered on over the plot. Since the two are not fully integrated in expressing a cosmic, universal, mythic theme, the play must be regarded as theater of sensationalism, in which the audience's sensibilities are titillated by sexuality, both straight and deviant, spiced with cruelty. Let the last word be Artaud's: "But yet this performance is not the peak of theater, I mean the deepest drama, the mystery deeper than souls, the excruciating conflict of souls . . . where lives drink at their source." (pp. 126-27)

> *Hélène L. Baldwin, " 'Equus': Theater of Cruelty or Theater of Sensationalism?" in* West Virginia University Philological Papers, *Vol. 25, 1979, pp. 118-27.*

FRANK LAWRENCE

Peter Shaffer's *Equus* begins in darkness, in silence, with Doctor Dysart's enlightened Apollonian mind confronting his darker counterpart, the Dionysian, in Alan Strang, the boy who blinded six horses. The doctor seeks a cure; he wish-

es to forget that his healing art requires learning to see in both directions—both good and evil, light and dark. Consequently, one may view both Dysart's and Alan's problems as reflections of one another. The central conflict of the play is set. Dysart's name suggests some clues to his character and condition. In Greek, *Dy* is *two or double; dys* is *bad, hard, difficult, impaired, crippled, abnormal, morbid.* Both forms work for Dysart. And of course, there is the *art* in *Dys—art.*

Dysart probes his own psyche as the play proceeds, through moments of brightness to a final silence and blackout. The good doctor's Apollonian sense—his need for balance, order, and harmony—tells him he needs "a way of seeing in the dark." But he is frustrated by the voice out of the dark cave, the voice of the animal god, Equus. "He [Equus] opens his great square teeth, and says (*mocking*) '*Why? . . .* Why ME? . . . Why—ultimately—ME? Do you really imagine you can account for Me? . . . Poor Doctor Dysart!' "

Indeed, he covets the unbridled Dionysian freedom he can partially see and understand in Alan—freedom to run or ride naked through the night, freedom to love what one can love, freedom to love what one cannot love, freedom to love recognized disorder. Dysart cannot quite see that his sleeping dreams are all blood and guts and that his waking dreams are of a purified, ordered Apollonian Greece. That antique split between the Apollonian and the Dionysian is the play's burden—the doctor's, the boy's, and finally the audience's. Darkness and Light are at war, and victory over this chaos is an illusion. The Platonic ideal of reuniting the sundered halves remains an ideal. Chaos is the order of the play.

Shaffer makes us aware of this conflict through the theatrical experience as well as through dialogue. After the curtain rises, the audience and the stage are in darkness; the first stage direction is *Darkness.* The match flame from Dysart's lighting a cigarette is the first gleam, a tiny one at that. The first stage direction in Act One is as important as the last one. Act One climaxes with a sensual recreation of Alan's naked ride on the horse, Nugget, a ride which in its throbbing rhythm, its finally galloping pace and intensity, becomes an orgasm ending in *Blackout.* Thus we experience that "seeing in the dark" is at once a large part of Dysart's healing art and his terrifying dilemma, even his Hobson's choice. He knows he can heal Alan at the expense of making a "ghost." Dysart is ultimately unable to unite himself with his lost other and so ends in the darkness of his own tormented psyche. (pp. 13-14)

Dysart concludes . . . [his] opening speech in Act One: "I'm sorry. I'm not making much sense. Let me start properly: *in order* [italics mine]. It began one Monday last month with Hesther's visit." At this moment, the light becomes warmer; Doctor Dysart wishes to see whether he can discern some order, some "proper" order—even if that order is only a proper sequence to explain chaos. Yet, he can do no more, and so as a fallible god; doctor, healer, victim, co-sufferer, patient, he will try to enter his own psyche to get to his chained-up heart, to look at his own desires. Dysart is not even sure what these desires may be, specifically, in this waking nightmare.

Dysart's redescent into the cave's darkness is agonizing: finding only darkness, he must recognize that life moves from darkness to darkness and that the interstitial light is often very dim and very brief indeed. Dysart's lament in the last moment of the play completes his long wail begun out of Act

One's darkness. Dysart, as representative of the Apollonian, is limitedly successful: as a representative of mankind, he does his best by striking out in the darkness, sometimes with a metaphoric pick, still basically unarmed, uneyed, finally undone, and "with a sharp chain in [his] mouth." He has seen the vision of the boy, Alan, embracing the horse, Nugget. "Nonsensical," Dysart says, but "I keep thinking about the horse!"

Dysart, in agony at the close, believes he is wanting in the guts, in the Dionysian, which he has alternately admired and abhorred in Alan Strang. Dysart desires both the Apollonian and the Dionysian, but the doctor's pathos is that the Apollonian wins darkly: "Passion, you see can be destroyed by a doctor. It cannot be created." Hesther tries to convince Dysart that he will be curing the boy's pain and that this cure will have to solve the doctor's dilemma. Dysart counters with: "He [Alan] made it [pain]. . . . That boy has known a passion more ferocious than I have in any second of my life. And let me tell you something: I envy it."

Alan, the Dionysian self which Dysart envies, is a creator in the Nietzschean use of *Dionysian* in *The Birth of Tragedy*. Dysart, the impaired artist, envies Alan with a passion ironically so intense that he feels he must try to re-create, reorder his world. *Dys-art* representing that old split is here: between the purity of the Parthenon and the drunken, frenzied, mysterious Bacchae tearing up beasts and men alive, even their own god, Dionysus himself, in the hills beyond the ordered *polis*. Dysart desires the simplicity of the child's imagination and that control of the adult's mind—the delicate balance which has been not only mankind's dilemma but also the artist's own. There stands poor Doctor Dysart, where darkness wins in the land of the blind where no man is king.

The darkness motif, the cleavage between the Apollonian and the Dionysian, is reinforced by Alan's parents, Frank and Dora Strang. Each, with the rigidity their German name implies, tries to mold the son in the two very different visions of order into which they are chained. Frank, the old-line Marxist scoffing at his wife's ultra-religious zeal as so much "bad sex," replaces a gory representation of Christ's Passion with a calendar photograph of a white horse over Alan's bed. Dora, ironically, tells Alan of the Christian cavalry's first appearance in the New World: "The pagans thought horse and rider were one person. . . . Actually they thought it must be a god. . . . It was only when one rider fell off, they realized the truth." Dora does not recognize the awful, twisted truth of what she is doing to Alan in her attempt to rein him to her blind faith; so she helps him construct "The Field of Ha! Ha!" from her readings and Alan's learning by heart passages from The Book of Job. In this way, the Strangs helped their son become what he does not quite realize he has desired to be—a centaur, the Apollonian united with the Dionysian.

The Strangs present a splendid parallel to the conflict raging in Martin Dysart. However, his conflict runs deeper. What Dysart seeks in his semi-blindness is a way of seeing where the Golden Mean may be. Dysart *can* see the terrible irony in Alan's revelation that he has discovered his father has his own secret worship: Frank goes to pornographic movies.

Martin Dysart knows not only that he is no seer but also that he sees too much of what he can see with a limited horse-blinder's vision. Early in *Equus* Dysart speaks of his recurring, "very explicit dream" in which he sees himself as a chief priest in Homeric Greece, where he is sacrificing "about five hundred boys and girls. I can see them stretching in a long queue right across the plain of Argos." In his dream Dysart is wearing a pop-eyed mask which threatens to slip from his face and reveal to his two relentless assistants that he is revolted at what he is doing to these children and that he may become ill himself. He knows if these assistants see his real face, they will turn on him with his own knife. However, in this same dream, Dysart knows "It's this unique talent for carving that has got me where I am." Thus, Dysart, standing in the limited light of his profession of healing artist, priest, victim, and seeing his limitations, sees his patient-victims and is ill.

As chief priest of the God Normal, Dysart knows that each person must have a "worship," even if it is on the dark side of the psyche. He can contrast the dark and light worships: "Sacrifices to Zeus took at the most sixty seconds each. Sacrifices to the Normal can take as long as sixty months." Knowing he certainly cannot see entirely what he is doing, Dysart acknowledges," I do ultimate things . . . essential things." Neither can Dysart see for himself, see the cave of his own psyche or an answer to one of his own ultimate, essential questions: "What worship have I got?" With a "worship" the good doctor might heal himself. If he might become naked as a child, naked as a boy-priest mounting his god, then Dysart might find a way of seeing in the dark. This note sounds from early in the play: "You see, I'm lost." The "You see . . . " is in Dysart's opening speech to the audience. The clause is at once a statement of ironic fact, a challenge to the audience, and a moan when Dysart adds, "I'm lost" and later "*Extremity* is the point. . . . " Further on, he bitterly recounts his antiseptic-sounding "Three weeks a year" in Greece "every bed booked in advance, every meal paid for by voucher, cautious jaunts in hired Fiats, suitcase crammed with Kao-Pectate! Such a fantastic surrender to the primitive."

Dysart's world is sterile: unchangeable, pure, ordered, dead. In contrast, Alan's creation is that primitive one that Dysart would like to jump to had he the courage, but which his Apollonian side will not accept. Alan, on the other hand, sees in the nipples of the naked Jill, his potential seductress, the eyes of his God Equus, but he turns his back on the reality to plunge his spike into the eyes of his God. The Dionysian implications abound. Hence, both characters turn their backs; to learn to see both ways is the art which eludes them both, and Dysart laments, "I sit looking at pages of centaurs trampling the soil of Argos—and outside my window he [Alan] is trying to become one in a Hampshire field." The price each must pay is high; both Dysart and Alan are poor because each one's "art" is poor or *dys:* impaired, bad, crippled, and so on. The artist of living must look both ways, embrace both sides or remain a cave dweller. To embrace one side only, whether it be Apollonian or Dionysian, is psychic suicide; to see both sides yet deny one is also psychic suicide. Each character is a prisoner of self. One can no more embrace a horse solely than one can walk through life touching perfect reproductions of life.

The dark insanity of the entire situation compounds itself with Dysart's recognition of the insanity of his divided self; nevertheless, he returns to the hospital—"this dreary place" (symbolic of his own psyche) to perform his final act of clinical voyeurism on Dionysian Alan, whom he envies. "Act it out if you like," he tells Alan. Ironically, the replay of the nude seduction scene with Jill is an anti-climax compared to the structured climax of Act One.

However, what is revealing is Dysart's supreme act of voyeurism, which follows a middle ground between the Socratic question-and-answer and the analyst's clarifying questions. . . . In finding out what he both suspects and needs to know (that the boy did not have successful intercourse), Dysart has come, in the crescendoing of the climactic words, as close as he is able to embracing his denied Dionysian side. After Dysart's discovery, the two role-play, and Dysart takes the role of the God Equus completing the sequence with: "And you will fail! Forever and ever you will *fail!* You will see ME—and you will FAIL!" Although supposedly therapeutic, Dysart's last speech most certainly comes from his own torment; question marks fall away, and Dysart, not the god Equus, becomes the speaker. For one brief moment the role-switch occurs. However, role-playing is a safe game for Doctor Dysart in his healing art. He has broken Alan now and knows, "You [Alan] are going to be well."

At the same time, Doctor Dysart also fears and knows "[his] achievement, however, is more likely to make a ghost!" Dysart has picked Alan's brain as surely as Alan spiked the eyes of six horses, as certainly as the chief priest of his dream carved the children in Homeric Greece. The doctor then explains he will cure the boy as methodically as in his dream of being chief priest. Martin Dysart, with bitterness, does see that he is destroying in a patient what he himself desires but cannot (or will not) make the jump to reach: passion, the Dionysian. Yes, the operation will be successful: Alan will become a ghost; Dysart will remain a fragmented, crippled, tortured man with a chain in his mouth. "And it never comes out."

Dysart cannot "gallop." He is locked in his cave; his dim torch is guttering, but he (unlike Alan) will never forget. The poor doctor is cursed with a memory of a delight he could never have had. He sits finally staring, a prisoner of his psyche and his own healing art. Although the operation will be successful, both patient and doctor will die. The final stage directions read:

> A long pause.
> Dysart sits staring.
> Blackout.

(pp. 14-18)

Frank Lawrence, "The 'Equus' Aesthetic: The Doctor's Dilemma," in Four Quarters, *Vol. XXIX, No. 2, Winter, 1980, pp. 13-18.*

DENNIS A. KLEIN

References to the classical world abound throughout Peter Shaffer's work, from his detective novels of the 1950's through *Equus* (1973), in which the themes, spirit, and techniques of classical literature dominate. It is true that *Five Finger Exercise* (1958) and *Shrivings* (1974) were true to the spirit of the classical unities, but *Equus* goes beyond the surface to penetrate the substance of what Aristotle considered the essence of tragedy—translated by Shaffer into terms for today's audience. Shaffer seems to have assimilated thoroughly both *The Rhetoric* and *The Poetics. Equus,* in both its dramatic theory and in its execution, approximates true Aristotelian tragedy. The play imitates an actual event, modified to proportions suitable for the stage and interpreted in the in-

imitable manner of Peter Shaffer. The characters contrast the emotions of ecstasy and joylessness, and they experience suffering and catharsis; the incidents of the play inspire pity and fear for both Dysart and Alan; and each main character has the opportunity to express a general truth. Shaffer, like Aristotle, believes that the playwright's most important job is to construct a good plot, to tell a story that will hold the audience's interest.

The plot and theme of *Equus,* which has become something of a modern classic, are well known and need to be repeated here only in the most general terms. Magistrate Hesther Salomom comes to Dr. Martin Dysart and begs the overworked psychiatrist to take on one more patient, a seventeen-year-old boy who blinded a stableful of horses. Based on "vibrations" she feels, she believes that Dysart is the only doctor within a hundred miles of the provincial area of Southern England who can help the youth. He reluctantly consents. The body of the play is essentially a battle of wits between Apollo and Dionysus: the man of reason using his knowledge to cure the uninhibited fury of youth, which Aristotle characterizes in *The Rhetoric* as a time of hot tempers and lack of self-control over sexual appetites. In his heart, Dr. Dysart believes that he is doing the boy no favor by cutting away his individuality. The play reveals the discoveries that bring Dysart to an understanding of Alan's crime and of his own nature, and a peripety from Alan's psychotic state to a socially acceptable, normal state. *Equus* fulfills Aristotle's appraisal of what constitutes the ideal plot: Dysart, a man of basically good character, is brought to misery (i.e., acknowledgement of his emotional sterility) through an error of judgment—he has diminished his own life by not including in it an element of worship. The four parts of the plot in Aristotelian terms are the prologue, Dr. Dysart's opening monologue of self doubt; the episodes, the psychiatric sessions between doctor and patient; the exode, Dysart's final speech to the audience; and the choral portion, which Shaffer calls the "Equus Noise." The chorus is composed of all of the actors, who remain on stage throughout the play and when not acting are seated among the on-stage segment of the audience. The humming, thumping, and stamping herald the presence of Equus the god. Shaffer's crafting is meticulous, and he leaves no loose ends. If any of the information were omitted, there would be no play, at least not to the degree of perfection in which it now exists. Some critics find *Equus*'s construction to be *too* perfect, too pat; but Aristotle would have been pleased.

The plot of *Equus* is based on discoveries that Dr. Dysart makes into Alan's problem, often via information brought to him by characters who function as the messengers in Greek tragedy. Dora Strang, Alan's mother, tells the doctor of the picture of the horse that Alan had hanging in his room. Frank Strang, the father, tells of an incident that he witnessed, in which Alan was beating himself with a coat hanger in front of the picture and chanting a parody of biblical genealogy. . . . The final messenger, Mr. Dalton, is the owner of the stables at which the crime took place. He tells Dysart of Alan's midnight rides and of Jill Mason, the employee with whom Alan had a date on the night of his crime. Dalton thereby brings on the two climactic scenes: the orgasmic ride which ends the first act and the blinding scene of the second act. By relating the bits of information brought to him and by scrutinizing them with his knowledge and intuition, Dysart concludes that in Alan's mind Equus is a jealous god, and that when Alan turned from him to Jill for sexual fulfillment, his lover/god made him fail. Aristotle observed that anger is produced by mocking or jeering; Alan blinded Equus because he witnessed Alan in his moment of shame. (pp. 175-76)

Through the monologues in which Dysart describes his professional doubts and marital monotony, Shaffer arouses pity for his tragic hero. In the speeches in which he contrasts Alan's unleashed passion for horse flesh with his own intellectual interest in classical Greece, Shaffer depicts Dysart's envy of a psychotic boy guilty of a dreadful crime:

> Such wild returns I make to the womb of civilization. Three weeks a year in the Peleponnese [sic], every bed booked in advance, every meal paid for by vouchers, cautious jaunts in hired Fiats, suitcases crammed with Kao-Pectate! Such a fantastic surrender to the primitive, and I use that word endlessly: "primitive." "Oh, the primitive world,"I say. "What instinctual truths were lost with it!" And while I sit there, baiting a poor unimaginative woman with the word, that freaky boy tries to conjure the reality! I sit looking at pages of centaurs trampling the soil of Argos—and outside my window he is trying to *become one,* in a Hampshire field!. . . [sic] I watch that woman knitting, night after night—a woman I haven't *kissed* in six years—and he stands in the dark for an hour, sucking the sweat off his God's hairy cheek! *[pause]* Then in the morning, I put away my books on the cultural shelf, close up the Kodachrome snaps of Mount Olympus, touch my reproduction statue of Dionysus for luck—and go off to hospital to treat him for insanity.

(The New York audiences cheered this speech.) Throughout the play, Dysart uses his own extreme situation to prove his point that the life he lives is no pleasure. His speech is clear and he uses ordinary words that take on a metaphoric value. . . . If the audience fails to register fear and pity for Alan because his crime is in the past and his case is extreme, it does experience those emotions for Dr. Dysart, whose present and future are bleak and who could be any one of us.

Both writers knew that the events of a tragedy arouse fear and pity when they occur unexpectedly yet in consequence of one another. In *Equus* all of the action builds up to the blinding scene, an act which also fulfills the Aristotelian property of torture. The final monologue, which follows Alan's reenactment of his crime, is the equivalent of the catharsis in Greek tragedy. In it, Dysart tells the audience just what Alan's and his own future hold:

> My desire might be to make this boy an ardent husband—a caring citizen—a worshipper of abstract and unifying God. My achievement, however, is more likely to make him a ghost . . . ! I'll heal the rash on his body. I'll erase the welts cut into his mind by flying manes. When that's done, I'll set him on a nice mini-scooter and send him puttering off into the Normal world where animals are treated *properly:* made extinct or put into servitude, or tethered all their lives in dim light, just to feed it. . . ! He'll trot on his metal pony tamely through the concrete evening and one thing I promise you: he will never touch hide again! With any luck his private parts will come to feel as plastic to him as the product of the factory to which he will almost certainly be sent. Who knows? He may even come to find sex funny. Smirky funny. Bit of grunt funny. Trampled and furtive and entirely in control. Hopefully, he'll feel nothing at his fork but

Approved Flesh. *I doubt, however, with much passion. . . !* [sic] Passion, you see, can be destroyed by a doctor. It cannot be created. . . . And now for me it never stops: that voice of Equus out of the cave—"Why Me? . . . Why Me? . . . Account for Me!" . . . I stand in the dark with a pick in my hand, striking at heads. . . ! There is in my mouth, this sharp chain. And it never comes out.

Shaffer allows each of his main characters to pronounce a "general truth." Dysart's is on the values of passion and individuality; Alan's is a non-verbal accusation that the doctor believes is directed at him, that he never galloped. Mrs. Strang defends the religious rearing she provided for her son, while Mr. Strang extols the virtues of work and the development of the mind. Despite Dysart's own doubts, Mrs. Salomon is firm in her resolve that it is the psychiatrist's job to use his talents to return Alan to society in a conventionally normal state.

Right from the title, Shaffer fills his play with classical allusions. The word *equus* is meant to convey more than a horse, whose name has been translated into Latin; it stands for the very quality of "horseness," the object of Alan Strang's workshop and sexual desire. It is fitting that Dysart's interest be for classical Greece, where horses held an honored place in society, even to the point of being considered of godly origin, from the union of Poseidon and Demeter. Significantly, the first horse that Alan ever rode was called Trojan, reminding the audience of the wooden horse which the Trojans dragged to the Citadel in Book Eight of the *Odyssey.* . . . Alan regards horses as godly. They are for him a Jesus-substitute, and Alan's atheistic father blames his son's problem on Alan's religious mother, for reading him "kinky" stories about an innocent man who was whipped and made to drag a cross up a mountain. Alan had a picture of Jesus in his room, described even by his mother as "a little extreme. The christ was loaded down with chains, and the centurions were really laying on the stripes." When his father insisted that he remove the picture, Alan replaced it with one of a horse with huge eyes. The horse then became Alan's Christ, and he refers to it in just such terms. Alan tells Dysart that Equus was born in the straw, that he lives in chains for the sins of the world, and that he has come to save Alan. Like Xanthos of the *Iliad,* in Alan's private world, Equus is a "talking" horse.

The sexual association of horses is well established in literature, from D. H. Lawrence in England to García Lorca in Spain, to mention just two modern, European authors. At midnight, once every three weeks, Alan would take a horse from the stables at which he worked on weekends for a wild, ritualistic ride. First he offered Equus a lump of sugar as "His Last Supper;" then he took him out of his "Holy of Holies" for what began as a religious ceremony and ended as a sexual act. . . . (pp. 176-78)

Dr. Dysart's hobby is classical Greece, but his interest lacks all of the passion that Alan feels. In contrast to Alan's orgiastic rides, Dysart's studies are as sterile as is his marriage and as impotent as is his sperm. Dysart's character fulfills Aristotle's three qualities: appropriateness (he is a psychiatrist); verisimilitude (he is a fully-developed character who could exist); and consistency throughout the play: he proceeds to cure Alan, although he himself is not convinced of its advantages for the boy. He is a man of justice and virtue who is not yet convinced of his beneficence to those who need his healing talents.

Aristotle also mentions the elements of melody, spectacle, and poetry. Melody, the greatest of the pleasurable accessories of tragedy, is found in Alan's wild song to Equus-the-lover and Equus-the-god during his frantic ride. Spectacle is found in the stylized horse masks that some of the actors wear. Shaffer specifies that "great cure must also be taken that the masks [be] put on before the audience with very precise timing—the actors watching each other, so that the masking [has] an exact and ceremonial effect." There is also spectacle in the flaring eyes of the horses during the blinding scene. Shaffer evokes the emotions of fear and pity both through speech and through spectacle—in Dysart's monologues, and as a naked Alan stabs wildly at stylized horse-heads. Regarding the horses, Shaffer states that: "The actors wear track-suits of chestnut velvet. . . . On their heads are tough masks made of alternating bands of silver wire and leather blinkers." Although the blinding scene of the horses takes place on stage, the violence is directed against stylized masks and not against anything "which could suggest the cozy familiarity of a domestic animal. . . ." With regard to poetry, which Aristotle found to be a beautiful accessory of tragedy, it is found throughout Dysart's monologues as well as in Alan's chant to Nugget.

Both Dysart and Alan use a number of Aristotle's recommended enthymemes. Dysart attempts to prove how empty his life is without worship by contrasting it with Alan's, which has worship. He also plays on word modification, especially the word *normal*, to which he attaches all negative connotations. Applying *fortiori*, he tries to tell Alan that gods die, and if such is the case, then people are not perfect either. He does not have all the answers. Alan, on the other hand, applies to Dysart what Dysart uses on him. When the psychiatrist says that he continues to practice because people like Alan are unhappy, Alan turns around and tells the doctor that he is unhappy, too. Even Frank Strang applies one of Aristotle's enthymemes: publicly he disclaims interest in or approval of such places as pornographic cinemas, but on the sly he does go, as Alan learns on the night that they catch each other, the same evening that Alan blinds the horses.

One factor with which the modern critic must reckon with is the powerful role of the director in the contemporary theater. Many of the aspects that have become *Equus*'s trademarks are the inventions of the play's original director, John Dexter, and not of the playwright. Shaffer's original concept of the play was in accord with Aristotle's dictate that a tragedy have a beginning, a middle, and an end (presented in chronological order). Dexter was responsible for the suggestion that the play be presented in a series of flashbacks. Even (or perhaps especially) in its present form, there is sequence and consequence among the incidents, which create a dramatic crescendo from the introductory prologue to the cathartic final monologue. Dexter was also responsible for the stylized set, the exposed lighting, and the nudity, which has been condemned as a gratuitous attempt at sensationalism. Shaffer says that he did not know about the nude scene until the play was well into rehearsal. Manuel Collado, the director of the Spanish production in Madrid, achieved an effect of *torero* and bull in the first scene in which Dysart and Alan are together. Rather than using a pole as did Dexter to provide support for the actor who played the horse that Alan rides during his masturbation scene, he used a crucifix, thereby emphasizing the Equus/Jesus identification. Knowing that the Spanish audience might not have the patience for some of Dysart's lengthy monologues of self-exploration, he put one of them

on tape and used it as a counterpoint for the action on stage. The director of the German production was more faithful than others to Shaffer's text, in which Alan states: "The horse isn't dressed. It's the most naked thing you ever saw! More than a dog or a cat or anything." Accordingly, it was the horse-actors he undressed, except for the scantiest of covering.

But the director's job is to bring out the play's meaning—to use sets and properties in order to enhance the playwright's message. More than in his classical allusions and his adherence to many of the principals of the construction of a tragedy, it is in the creation of his characters that Shaffer touches the essence of what Aristotle called tragedy. He depicts envy, pity and inspires pity and fear. Early in the play, soon after Dysart meets Alan Strang, the doctor has a dream that he is chief priest in Homeric Greece, and behind his mask, which has the appearance of the Mask of Agamemnon, he is green with nausea over the sacrifices he has to perform on the boys and girls who are queued up, ready to be thrown across the sacrificial stone. While Dysart suspects that sacrifices to Zeus took sixty seconds, his sacrifices to the god of Normal can take sixty months. Dysart's doubts about his social utility (expressed by the two syllables of his name, dys-art) have been building steadily over the years, and his treatment of Alan Strang is the final blow to his professional commitment. He has to confess to the audience: "In an ultimate sense I cannot know what I do in this place—yet I do ultimate things. Essentially I cannot know what I do—yet I do essential things. Irreversible, terminal things. I stand in the dark with a pick in my hand, striking at heads." Both of these speeches serve as recognition scenes.

Modern playwrights do not write about the traditional heroes—the kings or the gods—but rather about those characters and subjects which are of interest to contemporary audiences. In his bid for constructing a tragedy, Shaffer turned to the Homeric priest's modern equivalent, object of much hero worship if not out and out adulation: the psychiatrist. And he suffers from what has become the tragic flaw of a relentless quest for self-understanding. (pp. 178-80)

Dennis A. Klein, "Peter Shaffer's 'Equus' as a Modern Aristotelian Tragedy," in Studies in Iconography, *Vol. 9, 1983, pp. 175-81.*

DOYLE W. WALLS

Nietzsche wrote *The Birth of Tragedy* not only to discuss the origin of tragic drama in Greece, but also to elucidate a form of madness, the madness of limited vision in the German culture of his day. . . . Peter Shaffer, like Nietzsche, is a student of psychology as well as culture, and he is very much interested in the idea of madness, certainly not in praising it . . . but rather in illustrating dramatically a particular strain of madness: the madness personified in *Equus* by the psychiatrist Martin Dysart. Everyone familiar with *Equus* understands that Alan Strang is mad. The challenge of the play—to those among us who are "normal" and "sane"—is to see what may be our own madness, a modern malady which has become so commonplace that we may fail to recognize it.

Speaking of *Equus,* Shaffer made the following comments:

> There is in me a continuous tension between what
> I suppose I could loosely call the Apollonian and

the Dionysiac sides of interpreting life, between, say, Dysart and Alan Strang.

> It immediately begins to sound high falutin', when one talks about it oneself—I don't really see it in those dry intellectual terms. I just feel in myself that there is a constant debate going on between the violence of instinct on the one hand and the desire in my mind for order and restraint. Between the secular side of me the fact that I have never actually been able to buy anything of official religion—and the inescapable fact that to me a life without a sense of the divine is perfectly meaningless.

The reading offered in this essay will run the risk of sounding "high falutin' " when it proceeds from a strict, rather than loose, definition of "those dry intellectual terms" Apollinian and Dionysian as they are used by Nietzsche in *The Birth of Tragedy.* And because the terms will be used in the Nietzschean sense, this reading will take the liberty of departing from the idea that Dysart schematically represents the Apollinian and Alan the Dionysian. Although Shaffer uses the terms "Apollonian" and "Dionysiac," he admits to using them "loosely." Consequently, Shaffer's remarks are too tenuous to prove a direct influence of Nietzsche's *The Birth of Tragedy* on *Equus.* However, the affinities between these two works do exist, and *The Birth of Tragedy* can be used to provide a framework for an approach to *Equus* which will illustrate a concern common to both men: health. (pp. 314-15)

In *The Birth of Tragedy,* Nietzsche provides a critique of what he believed to be the unhealthy German culture of his day; he writes of a "new opposition": the Dionysian vs. the Socratic, theoretical man. By comparing the case of Alan Strang (the Dionysian man) with *the extreme case of Martin Dysart* (the Socratic, theoretical man), one can illuminate the two characters around whom Shaffer's play is structured.

Alan Strang is the product of a mother who has—with the best of intentions—taken him through the paces of myth with her Christianity. Alan is also the product of a father who has—with noble intentions—encouraged his son to gain "Further Education." The father has done so by discouraging Alan from watching television (because it is a "swiz"; it takes away one's intelligence and concentration) and by discouraging Alan's orientation toward the Christian myth through his own atheism.

But Mrs. Strang is correct when she informs Dysart that Alan is much more than merely a product of his parents. She may have oversimplified the case by blaming what Alan has come to on the Devil; nevertheless, Alan has become possessed by a spirit—it just happens to be one of his own creation. Nietzsche writes that it was out of "a most profound need" "that the Greeks had to create . . . gods." Tutored enough to have a taste for myth and unlettered enough not to have to fight his way out of a web of abstractions (the modern malady), Alan moves instinctively to create his own myth surrounding the horse. By following his father's wishes, the boy would lose myth and become entangled in abstractions and optimism like a modern-day Laocoön. By following his mother's wishes, Alan would succumb to the naysaying of traditional Christianity that negates the will to power. In Christianity, Nietzsche sees "[h]atred of 'the world,' condemnations of the passions, fear of beauty and sensuality, a beyond invented the better to slander this life, at bottom a craving for the nothing, for the end, . . . "

Why does Alan's father pull him from the horse? Is it merely because the stranger who offered the ride might harm him, or because the boy might be hurt unintentionally? Or is it that the parents fear passion, fear beauty and sensuality? Is it a fear of these concepts, or is it a lack of appreciation for them, that has caused a rift between Alan's parents in their sex life? It may be that fear of these concepts led Alan's father to offer an excuse for being at a skinflick. Would Mr. Strang be embarrassed because a movie is a swiz, or because this particular kind of movie illustrates his unacknowledged desire for passion? Alan, on the other hand, creates a myth that allows for passionate worship. And if his myth is an abomination, at least it is an active abomination rather than a passive one. At least it is a myth that says yes to the present rather than placing its hope in a time to come, as the mother's Christianity and the father's socialism trust.

Nietzsche provides a definition of "the *mystery doctrine of tragedy*": it is "the fundamental knowledge of the oneness of everything existent, the conception of individuation as the primal cause of evil, and of art as the joyous hope that the spell of individuation as the primal cause of evil, and of art as the joyous hope that the spell of individuation may be broken in augury of a restored oneness." Alan seeks this union in his worship, that is, in the night rides he takes on his god—a horse—which culminate in sexual orgasm. Alan shouts "Make us One Person!" to "Equus," or Nugget, one of the horses from the stable. This attempt to create oneness, as Nietzsche explains, is sacrilege: "In the heroic effort of the individual to attain universality, in the attempt to transcend the curse of individuation and to become the *one* world-being, he suffers in his own person the primordial contradiction that is concealed in things, which means that he commits sacrilege and suffers." However, this very sacrilege is necessary in order to gain "[t]he best and highest possession mankind can acquire": it "must be paid for with consequences that involve the whole flood of sufferings and sorrows with which the offended divinities have to afflict the nobly aspiring race of men." Nietzsche claims that the sacrilege has "*dignity.*" Because of the sacrilege he has committed, the Dionysian man "feels himself a god." And Nietzsche claims that, consequently, the Dionysian man "is no longer an artist, he has become a work of art: . . . " That Alan becomes a work of art through sacrilege and suffering means that he is something instead of nothing. He is creator become creation. And as Nietzsche asserts: " . . . it is only as an *aesthetic phenomenon* that existence and the world are eternally *justified.* . . . " This is to say that Alan justifies his suffering in the world as an individual by creating a myth which unifies the totality of his existence in the world, and consequently, provides a place for himself inside that myth.

Alan's sacrilege is not the blinding of the horses. That is the crime he commits which almost sends him to prison rather than to the care of a psychiatrist. Alan's sacrilege is his destruction, momentarily through his artistic worship, of the division between individuation and oneness. This aspect of Alan's story links him to the Dionysian myth. This one aspect emphasizes the myth itself more than Alan. The passion involved emphasizes a pure passion. (pp. 315-17)

In the "un-Dionysian myth-opposing spirit" of tragedy since Sophocles, Nietzsche sees more attention to the individual and less attention to the myth, a "victory of the phenomenon over the universal." Yet for all the peculiar details which make Alan more than the "usual unusual" for Dysart, Alan's sexual episodes with the horse appear more as religious rites than attempts to reach sexual satisfaction. It is helpful at this point to visualize the nonhorse aspect of the actor playing the horse; that is, an idea—the idea of passion and its link to worship—is being communicated, not a vision. These very facts point to the conclusion that Alan represents much more than a young man whose sexual inclinations lean toward bestiality.

Such a view also makes it apparent that an intelligent and "normal" man such as Dysart could find himself attracted to some vital quality of spirit in a young man who has committed the horrific crime of stabbing the sight from the eyes of six horses. Clearly, Alan is not unequivocally the positive pole in the play. There can be no doubt in the spectator's mind that Alan Strang is a tortured soul who is unbalanced and dangerous; consequently, we, along with Hesther Salomon, hope that the doctor will be able to end Alan's suffering. Our first reaction may be similar to that of the stable owner, Harry Dalton: "In my opinion the boy should be in prison. Not in a hospital at the tax-payers' expense." However, it is just as clear that such initial responses of repulsion and fear will not do justice to the depth of Shaffer's play. Dalton can understand Alan's problem only as an isolated phenomenon; Dysart sees beyond the isolated phenomenon and understands Alan's problem as the absence of passion, worship, myth, and art in the modern world. Alan blinds six horses, and Dysart begins his struggle with new vision. The spectator of *Equus* must accept the paradox that a repulsive, horrific crime committed against innocent horses ignites a positive, poetic, spiritual fire within the deadened, timid soul of Dysart. It is, as Dysart says on more than one occasion, the "extremity" of Alan's case, one might say the Dionysian excess, which has started the struggle which Dysart faces.

Nietzsche writes that "the noblest *opposition* to the tragic world-conception—and by this I mean science" has "its ancestor Socrates at its head." The Socratic man is the man of logic rather than instinct. He has "the optimism of science." Nietzsche longs "for a rebirth of tragedy" and claims it will come about "only after the spirit of science has been pursued to its limits, and its claim to universal validity destroyed by the evidence of these limits. . . ."

Not quite eight decades after Nietzsche published *The Birth of Tragedy,* twelve men of letters who were affiliated with the American South published [*I'll Take My Stand: The South and the Agrarian Tradition*], a volume of essays that takes as its main subject the following dichotomy: "Agrarian *versus* Industrial." Their introduction states that " . . . the word science has acquired a certain sanctitude." One essay in the collection, "Remarks on the Southern Religion" by Allen Tate, contains a few paragraphs which will help to illustrate more clearly how Nietzsche's comments on the culture of his day can illuminate Dysart and his growing realization of not only the value of myth, but also the danger of the theoretical approach and its manifestations in the modern world:

> The reader must here be entreated to follow some pages of abstraction conducted in the interest of my religion, but partaking of that religion not an ounce. For abstraction is the death of religion no less than the death of anything else. Religion, when it directs its attention to the horse cropping the blue-grass on the lawn, is concerned with the whole horse, and not with (1) that part of him which he has in common with other horses, or that more general part which he shares with other quadrupeds or with the more general vertebrates; and not with (2) that power of the horse which he shares with horse-

power in general, of pushing or pulling another object. Religion pretends to place before us the horse as he is.

> Since this essay is not religion, but a discussion of it, it does not pretend to put before you the complete horse. It does pretend to do the following: to show that the complete horse may be there in spite of the fact that this discussion cannot bring him forth. In other words, there is a complete and self-contained horse in spite of the now prevailing faith that there is none simply because the abstract and scientific mind cannot see him.

> This modern mind sees only half of the horse—that half which may become a dynamo, or an automobile, or any other horsepowered machine. If this mind had much respect for the full-dimensioned, grass-eating horse, it would never have invented the engine which represents only half of him. The religious mind, on the other hand, has this respect; it wants the whole horse, and it will be satisfied with nothing less.

Reading *Equus* in light of the preceding paragraphs, one can say that Dysart has "the abstract and scientific mind," while Alan has "the religious mind." The modern mind has lost half the picture—and now another name, Allen Tate, is added to those of Nietzsche and Shaffer as one who is concerned with the idea of balance, not madness. In the Tate paragraphs, one can see that science is manifested in industrialism; modern man respects the half of the horse that drives cars up and down the highways. This passage provides the transition from Nietzsche's comments on science and optimistic knowledge to *Equus,* particularly the last speech Dysart makes: he realizes that he will replace Alan's horse with "a nice mini-scooter" and send him off "on his metal pony tamely through the concrete evening. . . . " Dysart also questions the concept of "Normal" during this speech: is it normal, "blinking our nights away in a nonstop drench of cathoderay . . . ?" Motor-driven appliances—by Hoover, Philco, Remington, Pifco, Volex, Croydex, and Robex—are labeled by Alan as foes he rides against with Equus. They are the unessential. They are the foes that separate human beings from the elemental forces of nature. Man, Nietzsche tells us, is the "lost son" of nature, and the Dionysian can bring about a "reconciliation" between man and nature.

Dysart has "the one great Cyclops eye of Socrates," an eye "denied the pleasure of gazing into the Dionysian abysses." In the last few lines of the play, Dysart states that he needs "a way of seeing in the dark." The limited vision of the Socratic view as opposed to the tragic view leaves one in weakness:

> And now the mythless man stands eternally hungry, surrounded by all past ages, and digs and grubs for roots, even if he has to dig for them among the remotest antiquities. The tremendous historical need of our unsatisfied modern culture, the assembling around one of countless other cultures, the consuming desire for knowledge—what does all this point to, if not to the loss of myth, the loss of the mythical home, the mythical maternal womb?

We may compare the preceding passage by Nietzsche with Dysart's ironic statement to Hesther: "Such wild returns I make to the womb of civilization." Modern man's state of weakness leaves him afraid: "It is certainly the sign of the 'breach' of which everyone speaks as the fundamental malady of modern culture, that the theoretical man, alarmed and dissatisfied at his own consequences, no longer dares entrust himself to the terrible icy current of existence: he runs timidly up and down the bank." We may compare Nietzsche's comment on weak and timid modern man to Dysart's growing knowledge of himself in the world and the admission that he makes by the end of the play: "Without worship you shrink, it's as brutal as that . . . I shrank my *own* life. No one can do it for you. I settled for being pallid and provincial, out of my own eternal timidity."

In this state of weakness, there are things which Dysart cannot do. We know that on the physical level Dysart cannot procreate; he has, by his own admission to Hesther, "[t]he lowest sperm count you could find." . . . Dysart's physical inability to reproduce or create is symptomatic of his inability to create in terms of his profession. There are two reasons for this professional impotence. The first reason is what Nietzsche calls "the delusion of being able . . . to heal the eternal wound of existence," the "delusion of limitless power." The second reason why Dysart is struggling while trying to treat Alan is paradoxical. Dysart experiences doubts concerning his work which are so severe that he reveals the following to himself, at last, through the dream where he envisions himself as a chief priest who sacrifices children: "It's obvious to me that I'm tops as chief priest. It's this unique talent for carving that has got me where I am. The only thing is, unknown to them, I've started to feel distinctly nauseous. And with each victim, it's getting worse. My face is going green behind the mask." Nietzsche explains this paradox of gaining knowledge and losing the ability to act:

> In this sense the Dionysian man resembles Hamlet: both have once looked truly into the essence of things, they have *gained knowledge,* and nausea inhibits action; for their action could not change anything in the eternal nature of things; they feel it to be ridiculous or humiliating that they should be asked to set right a world that is out of joint. Knowledge kills action; action requires the veils of illusion: that is the doctrine of Hamlet, not that cheap wisdom of Jack the Dreamer who reflects too much and, as it were, from an excess of possibilities does not get around to action. Not reflection, no— true knowledge, an insight into the horrible truth, outweighs any motive for action, both in Hamlet and in the Dionysian man.

Nietzsche proposes a remedy for this impotence: "When they see to their horror how logic coils up at these boundaries and finally bites its own tail—suddenly the new form of insight breaks through, *tragic insight* which, merely to be endured, needs art as a protection and remedy." When Dysart tells Hesther that he is jealous of Alan, he is saying that he is jealous of a passion which can create gods; he is jealous of a spiritual and artistic creativity which Alan, disturbed though he is, has illustrated. Even when Hesther mentions Alan's pain, Dysart responds: "His pain. His own. He made it." Without such creativity, Dysart lacks the "horsepower" which would enable him "to jump clean-hoofed on to a whole new track of being, . . . " Consequently, Dysart's one eye not only keeps him from seeing existence whole, but incapacitates him in terms of spiritual and artistic vision. Dysart has greater and greater difficulty in justifying himself. (pp. 317-20)

Socrates had "a divine voice" which spoke to him, and Nietzsche writes that the voice "always *dissuades.* In this utterly abnormal nature, instinctive wisdom appears only in order to *hinder* conscious knowledge occasionally." The instinctive voice Socrates heard could only dissuade, "[w]hile in all productive men it is instinct that is the creative-affirmative force, . . . " Similarly, Dysart cannot create and affirm anything for Alan; Dysart can only negate and deny a part of Alan's self. His only creation will be a form of desecration: "Can you think of anything worse one can do to anybody than take away their worship?" During Alan's final abreaction, Dysart rushes toward him to stop him from stabbing at his own eyes with the invisible pick. By instinct, Dysart sheds his new-found doubts and reassures the boy by repeating the line: "I'm going to make you well"; however, his new insights have taken hold, found root in the small plot of Grecian soil in his soul, and he immediately refutes his instinct and modern training by saying the following as "[t]he light brightens," as he moves "into the centre of the square":

> I'm lying to you, Alan. He won't really go that easily. Just clop away from you like a nice old nag. Oh, no! When Equus leaves—if he leaves at all—it will be with your intestines in his teeth. And I don't stock replacements . . . If you knew anything, you'd get up this minute and run from me fast as you could.

An analogy is made complete at this point in the play: if and when Equus leaves, he will take the intestines of Alan with him, that is, Alan's very being, just as Dysart's dream has told him he will, by "helping" Alan, carve out the inner Alan: "I part the flaps, sever the inner tubes, yank them out and throw them hot and steaming on to the floor."

Dysart realizes that he will not be able to accomplish what he wants to do for Alan: to make of him "an ardent husband—a caring citizen—a worshipper of abstract and unifying God." In fact, all he can do is replace ecstasy with "the Normal." In Nietzschean terminology, one could say that Dysart, the Alexandrian spirit, "substitutes for a metaphysical comfort an earthly consonance." He will try to ". . . confine the individual within a limited sphere of solvable problems, . . . " Dysart has a "reproduction statue of Dionysus" which he can "touch . . . for luck"; this detail illustrates that Dionysian power is only a force outside of Dysart, not an intoxication within.

By the end of *Equus,* we have Alan destroyed not because he has tried to break past individuation into the realm of oneness, but because he is finally torn between two myths: the classical, pagan one he created; and the Christian one he inherited from his mother, which saddled him with guilt and shame concerning his sexuality and its relation to an ultimate concept like God. And he is destroyed also because he is torn between the outlet his sensuality has found in horses and his burgeoning physical interest in Jill Mason, which indicates a desire for a more normal sexual relationship. Dysart should be giving birth through creation to this patient, Alan. But he finds that he is artistically and spiritually impotent because he is what Nietzsche would call the Socratic man, devoid of Dionysian passion, worship, and creativity. He realizes his delusions, and his nausea prevents action. There is a birth trying to happen within Dysart; this birth, given Dysart's background, must appear illegitimate. He had conceived the idea of the tragic world view before he met Alan, and now he cannot decide what to do. Should he abort the Dionysian wisdom growing inside him and, by so doing, "help" Alan, so that Alan can carry on as half a man, rather than as a mental case? Or should he give birth to a new world view, a tragic one, and set Alan free, leaving him the dignity of his myth and worship, yet leaving him with the corresponding pain?

Nietzsche explains "[t]he metaphysical joy in the tragic" as follows:

> . . . the hero, the highest manifestation of the will, is negated for our pleasure, because he is only phenomenon, and because the eternal life of the will is not affected by his annihilation. . . . the struggle, the pain, the destruction of phenomena, now appear necessary to us, in view of the excess of countless forms of existence which force and push one another into life, in view of the exuberant fertility of the universal will.

Whatever metaphysical joy in the tragic is apparent at the end of *Equus* stems from the idea that Dysart, a caretaker of people, gains some self-realization because he is faced directly with the passion of the Dionysian will. And perhaps he has been, in some sense, infused by this passion which cannot be annihilated. At the very least, he is more knowledgeable by the end of the play. And the struggle which he has begun could well be the catalyst for creation. When one considers the cultural criticisms which Shaffer makes, and the difficulty with which Dysart struggles between the tension of his modern, Socratic mind and his new-found Dionysian wisdom, one can find some joy in the fact that Shaffer, like Nietzsche, is engaging his public, so that it will realize that both science and art are necessary in our world. In *Equus,* Shaffer tells us that the age of the Socratic man is not over, but the idea of a healthy balance is still alive. (pp. 321-22)

> *Doyle W. Walls, " 'Equus': Shaffer, Nietzsche, and the Neuroses of Health," in* Modern Drama, *Vol. XXVII, No. 3, September, 1984, pp. 314-23.*

GENE A. PLUNKA

Equus is a controversial play, and because of its widespread appeal, it has also been criticized almost as much as it has been defended by Shaffer's supporters. Many conservative theatergoers have complained that the obvious sensationalism of the play, particularly the need to portray a young man's obsession with horses, is not suitable for the stage. These critics complain that the blinding of horses is too repulsive an event for any stage and is not an appropriate subject for a play. Yet many of the world's great tragedies deal with murder, patricide, revenge, lust, suicide, and other horrible themes. . . . *Equus* should not be criticized because of its serious thematic concerns. Even weak-hearted theater patrons should be able to recognize Shaffer's attempts to stylize the grotesque stable scene. When analyzed objectively, *Equus* can be viewed almost as a nonviolent play—certainly one that is much less brutal than the great tragedies of the Western world.

The second major criticism of the play concerns its religious theme. Although the play has been reviewed favorably in many publications that have a religious orientation, some critics insist that, as in *The Royal Hunt of the Sun,* Shaffer is attacking organized religion. In his reaction to the concept of "normal," Dysart, speaking through Shaffer, seems to support worship in any form regardless of whether or not it is organized and codified by society's rules and norms. Yet even the most casual reader will find numerous references that compare Alan's horse-god to Christ. . . . Shaffer has stated that the blinding of the horses, a scenic image with the power

to haunt, has affinities with the "extinction of divinity." Yet the religious motifs are no more the focus of Shaffer's attention in *Equus* than they were in *The Royal Hunt of the Sun;* instead, they are a means to an end. Even the psychological and sexual implications of the play serve only as surface material for the more important underlying issue that Shaffer is trying to explore: the dangers of role playing.

The third concern that critics had was that *Equus* was weak in content and relied mostly on sensationalism and theatrical gimmicks. Hélène L. Baldwin hints that the play is "sexuality sugar-coated with an eroticism" and calls it theater of sensationalism, not Theatre of Cruelty, as Artaud would have it. [See Baldwin's excerpt above]. (p. 149)

The sensationalism of the play is not contrived. *Equus* does deal quite graphically with psychoanalysis of a young man who has trouble sorting out his religious convictions and sexual inadequacies. The psychosexual and religious motifs are not gratuitous; instead, they are designed to release archetypes latent in the audience similar to what Artaud had in mind for his Theatre of Cruelty. . . . (p. 150)

The fourth major criticism of the play stems from psychiatrists who claim that Shaffer has distorted and maligned their sacred profession. In a now-famous article written for *The New York Times,* psychiatrist Sanford Gifford led the attack on the play, calling it a "pernicious fallacy." Dr. Gifford was alarmed that theatergoers could take this brand of psychotherapy seriously, because "by weaving together many clinical syndromes, therapeutic methods and psychoanalytic clichés, Shaffer presents us with a fictitious piece of psychopathology." Psychiatrists have a right to be concerned about the play's content because much of *Equus*'s popularity is the result of what Shaffer termed "the long-suppressed resentment of analysts." In an article for *Vogue,* Shaffer wrote, "I think that audiences react to *Equus* the way they do partly because, I suspect, they collectively dislike their analysts immensely and want some way of showing this in public." Gifford and his colleagues probably felt the need to hold on to dissenters who might abandon the long-established "wisdom" of their psychoanalysts. Shaffer is aware of the impact of his play on the New York audience in particular: "In London the play was performed before audiences of which only a very small percentage had been, or then was, in analysis; in New York it would have been hard to find anybody in the audience, in the first weeks of the run at any rate, who had *not* been or was not so still." Thus, Gifford's assumption is probably sound in that some of the success of the play can be attributed to our secret desire to know more about the private lives of our psychiatrists.

Shaffer has been defensive when critics, particularly psychiatrists, argue that the play is not scientifically accurate and that analysts would never doubt their professional integrity as Dysart does. In his preface, "A Note on the Play," Shaffer acknowledged that when he wrote *Equus,* he "enjoyed the advice and expert comment of a distinguished child psychiatrist. Through him I have tried to keep things real in a more naturalistic sense." The psychiatrist, who asked to remain anonymous, read the completed text and endorsed it emphatically. The play is scientifically valid, for Shaffer is a careful researcher who reads about his subject area thoroughly and explores his research topics with a meticulous obsession for details. Moreover, as Shaffer states in his preface to the play, "psychiatrists are an immensely varied breed, professing immensely varied methods and techniques. Martin Dysart is simply one doctor in one hospital."

Equus is not a critical examination of the psychiatric profession, and Shaffer insists that it is misleading to interpret the play in such a way: "It had never struck me that when I was drawing the part of Dr. Dysart I was making any disturbing comment about psychiatry. Obviously the creation of a doctor of some kind was inevitable if I was going to tell that story at all, but the doctor's part was originally a secondary preoccupation with me." Shaffer asserts that psychiatrists must entertain doubts about their profession all the time, just as many other professionals pose questions about the rewarding values of their own careers. (p. 150-51)

Equus was derived from a story that was told to Shaffer by his friend, James Mossman, the celebrated BBC television reporter. Shaffer and Mossman were driving through the English countryside, and as they passed a stable, Mossman recalled the story of a young man who, a number of years earlier, had blinded twenty-six horses. Shaffer remembers Mossman telling him that the youngster "was said to be the son of very 'thou shalt not' parents who were members of some peculiar religious sect. The boy was seduced on the floor of the stable by a girl under the eyes of the horses. They, presumably, in his distorted mind, would go off and tell his father and mother." A few months later, Mossman died, and Shaffer was stuck with a fascinating story that he could not verify. Shaffer spent the next two years trying to interpret Alan Strang's crime and what led up to it, often destroying thirty or forty pages of draft work per day. (p. 152)

Equus, like *The Royal Hunt of the Sun,* is Shaffer's attempt to unite an existential and sexual search for identity with a ritualistic representation of spiritual freedom. In an interview [in *The Listener*] with Peter Adam, Shaffer revealed that *Equus* was fundamentally concerned with "the envy of one man who hasn't experienced emotion, and the worship transcendentally of somebody whom he believes has." Dysart, insecure in his role playing, begins to learn from his patient, the primitive catalyst, Alan Strang. Through Alan, the psychiatrist becomes more aware that he must evade roles and adhere to his own values instead. Alan reveals the hypocrisy in Dysart's life as the primitive's brand of worship becomes more real to the psychiatrist than does his own preference for the "Normal." Dysart's new sense of consciousness will provide him with the first step in pursuing an identity that he will have created for himself, not for others.

Most of the play revolves around an exploration of Alan Strang's struggle for identity. The young man is caught between a religious mother and a father who is an atheist. Both parents push Alan in opposite directions as they demand that he become what *they* want him to be. Rejecting those values that he can only deem contradictory, Alan begins to explore various ways to establish an identity that will have its own intrinsic and rewarding value to him.

Frank Strang oppresses Alan more than anyone else does. He refuses to allow Alan to watch television and instead, directs his son into the "proper" norms of society—working in a certain electrical shop of which Mr. Strang approves. Frank Strang exerts an iron hand over Alan's lifestyle; the seventeen-year-old even adopts his father's vocabulary. Frank's favorite expression, "if you receive my meaning," is mockingly repeated by Alan, but even in more serious moments, Alan resorts to his father's terminology. This is most clearly shown by Alan's use of the word "swiz," a name he calls Dysart, or as Frank would have it, something that relieves you of "your intelligence and your concentration."

Frank Strang, as his first name implies, is quite candid when it comes to stamping his strong image on others. Cut in the same mold as his precursor, Stanley Harrington, Frank is the epitome of the old-guard socialist who has become successful on his own. He is a practical sort of man who preaches a work ethic and values his business acumen. According to Frank, religion has no practical value and is reduced to Marx's cliché, the "opium of the people." Thus, Frank "doesn't set much store by Sundays" and prefers working for profit rather than wasting his time in church. Frank reasons that the Bible will never make one rich; instead, it is "just bad sex." Shaffer, however, exposes Frank's hypocritical nature (an ironic use of his namesake) when later in the play we learn that he spends much of his time secretly visiting pornographic movie theaters to enjoy the "bad sex" that he so disdains.

Alan's father relieves the boy of the few pleasurable moments in his life, and as a prying Grand Inquisitor, the printer more than stamps his impression on his son and takes away his freedom. Alan, with his love for old westerns, is forced to sneak over to a neighbor's house to watch them on television because his father considers "the tube" to be "a dangerous drug." In addition, Mr. Strang discovers Alan's first sexual affair and then makes his son feel guilty about it. Frank also pulled Alan off a horse that he was riding on the beach, an incident that becomes a traumatic experience because Alan's sexual and spiritual freedom was disturbed. This disruption of Alan's freedom is made clear when we come to understand that this incident helped to form Alan's "strange" personality. The result of Mr. Strang's actions is that Alan fears his father, whom he associates with a godlike tyrant creating laws and rules for others to obey. It is no wonder that Alan feels insecure around Dysart, the epitome of the Grand Inquisitor resembling Frank Strang: "On and on, sitting there! Nosey Parker! That's all you are! Bloody Nosey Parker! Just like Dad. On and on and bloody on! Tell me, tell me, tell me! . . . Answer this, Answer that. Never Stop!—"

Equus contains an unusual number of images related to eyes, and much of this eye imagery focuses on Frank Strang's role as a godlike figure for his son. Alan, who compares himself to Christ, the son of God, associates himself with Equus, the son of the horse-god. During the scene of self-mutilation where Alan flagellates himself with a wooden coat hanger, he does so in his bedroom in front of the photograph of the "horse with the huge eyes." As he admonishes himself as "Equus, my only begotten son," Alan is unconsciously berating himself in front of his father, the horse-god. For Alan, Frank Strang has assumed the identity of the horse-god, and his eyes reflect God's judgment. Alan always feels so insecure around his father that he "lies under the blanket" when his father enters the acting square.

There are numerous references in the play to eyes, and these images serve to reinforce in Alan the stern, judgmental attitude of his father and Alan's subsequent blinding of the horses. Dora Strang used to repeat to Alan over and over again that " 'God sees you, Alan. God's got eyes everywhere—' ". She tells Dysart that she allowed Alan to sneak out of the house to watch television in spite of Frank's protests because "what the eye does not see, the heart does not grieve over." When Alan is knocked off the horse at the beach, Frank calls the animal dangerous: "Look at his eyes.

They're rolling," but the horseman makes the connection clear when he says, "So are yours!" At the age of six, Alan may not have intuitively made the comparison between the eyes of his godlike father and the eyes of his horse-god. However, he later becomes fascinated both with the horses' eyes in the photograph hanging in his bedroom and with Nugget's eyes, which he spends a great deal of time staring into. In addition, when Dysart asks Alan to name his favorite British monarch, Alan chooses King John because "he put out the eyes of that smarty little—", a reference to John's order to have Hubert de Burgh burn out the eyes of Arthur of Bretagne, the king's nephew.

On the night that Alan blinded the six horses, he spent the early part of the evening at a pornographic theater with Jill Mason. Guilt dominates the scene as Alan focuses his attention on the eyes of the pornographers: "All around me they were all looking. All the men—staring up like they were in church." When Frank enters, Alan's first reaction is, "Oh God," perhaps an unconscious reference to his father as the omnipotent individual who sees through all of the evil going on behind his back. Outside, while waiting an unbearably long time for a bus that would not come, Alan can only think of his father's eyes, "staring, straight ahead." Later during the same evening, Alan accompanies Jill to the stables. When Alan abreacts, he tells Dysart that he stared into her eyes, and she reciprocated, saying, "I love your eyes." By the time the two of them arrived at the stables, the eye imagery was well ingrained in Alan's consciousness. Dysart, already aware that Alan links eyes with his father's godlike control over his son, has only to say the right words to achieve catharsis: "The Lord thy God is a Jealous God. He sees you. He sees you forever and ever, Alan. He sees you! . . . *He sees you!*" Alan's response solidifies the association between father and god: "Eyes!. . . White eyes—never closed! Eyes like flames—coming—coming! . . . God seest! God seest! . . . NO. . . . " Alan, hoping to erase the guilt he has over his "romp in the hay" with Jill and evade his father's godlike aura that sees all evil, blinds the horses, thereby abandoning the tight "reins" of his father's authority.

It was Frank Strang's idea to have Alan work in an electrical shop rather than with him as a printer's apprentice because Frank believed that his son did not have "the aptitude," and "printing's a failing trade." Alan's job in the electrical shop does little to provide the confused lad with the spiritual freedom that he seeks. Instead, the young man becomes mesmerized by commercialism. When the customers enter the shop, they ask him, "Are you a dealer for *Hoover?*" or demand "the heat retaining *Pifco.*" Alan's response is always, "Sorry," and, as was true in his relationship with his father, Alan is made to feel guilty and is forced to succumb to the whims and wishes of others. Since this commercialization is a direct antithesis to Alan's freedom, it is not difficult to imagine that when Alan's liberty is destroyed by Dr. Dysart, the young man will return to his particular socialization process and therefore become no more than a series of television advertisements. Thus, it is not unbelievable for this restless primitive to regress to the state of repeating Doublemint gum jingles or other such advertisements.

Because Alan is in awe of his father and even fears him, much of his early childhood training is the result of his strong association with his mother. Alan's knowledge about sex and the Bible is based on the type of education Dora Strang, an ex-school teacher, wanted her son to receive. Mrs. Strang tells Dysart that in teaching Alan about life, "I told him the biological facts. But I also told him what I believed. That sex is not *just* a biological matter, but spiritual as well." Alan accepted his mother's religious values simply because his personality in the formative years was being shaped by the training he received from his parents.

Beginning with the ideas he learned from his mother, Alan searches for his identity—a quest that becomes a spiritual communion with a personal god. When he was twelve, Alan had in his bedroom a picture of Christ on his way to Calvary. Dora Strang acknowledges that "the Christ was loaded down with chains, and the centurions were really laying on the stripes." In a rage, Alan's father, who had previously insisted that "it's the Bible that's responsible for all this," ripped the picture from the wall; Alan then replaced the beaten Christ with a picture of a horse with the eyes staring straight ahead. Alan identified with Christ, not as a redeemer or as one who is resurrected, but as an individual who suffers and is beaten. The young primitive believed that the world was replete with oppression and felt that he was literally being strapped down with chains. Alan was most impressed with the idea that Christ was omnipotent and could transcend his slavery, thus controlling his own fate in the midst of external forces. Alan therefore wanted to become one with Christ in order to obtain complete control of his existence.

The spiritual quest is further complicated when Alan views the horse as his new god. Mrs. Strang used to tell Alan "that when Christian cavalry first appeared in the New World, the pagans thought horse and rider was one person." Alan is fascinated by the idea, especially when his mother reveals that the pagans "thought it must be a god." The story unconsciously reminds Alan of Christ, since the religious idea of "becoming one" is associated with the Holy Trinity. In short, Alan mistakenly compares cavalry with Calvary and identifies the concept of "becoming one" with Christ. Alan's vision of horses stems partly from his mother's reading of the horse imagery in the Book of Job. That particular biblical passage describes the horse as an animal with "strength" and a "neck of thunder," capable of pounding the ground "with fierceness and rage." To Alan, Equus, which Dora explains to Alan is the Latin word for "horse," represents omnipotence galloping freely in the field of "Ha! Ha!"

Alan internalizes the stories and tries to imitate Christ by uniting with Equus, the horse-god, thus becoming master and slave at the same time. One evening, when Alan was fifteen, Frank Strang noticed his son chanting prayers to his newly created god, then kneeling in reverence. After the biblical "begats" and Alan's resurrection as "Equus, my only begotten son," Alan takes out a string and coat hanger and begins to beat himself. The important point here is that the thrashing is self-imposed. Alan has taken on the sins of the world for himself and masochistically enjoys the idea that he is able to control this oppression. For the first time in his life, the thrashing is not external, and Alan is now pleased to have this new power that he can control.

Alan's spiritual quest to obtain a union with the horse-god continues throughout the play; it is most noticeable in reference to Alan's ride on the beach. Alan relates the experience to Dysart:

> ALAN.   It never comes out. They have me in chains.
>
> DYSART. Like Jesus?

ALAN. Yes!

DYSART. Only his name isn't Jesus, is it?

ALAN. No.

DYSART. What is it?

ALAN. No one knows but him and me.

DYSART. You can tell me, Alan. Name him.

ALAN. Equus.

Alan associates the horse's bit and bridle with Christ's chains, as the young man views himself as one who is bridled and suffers "for the sins of the world." More importantly, the horse conveys a sense of godlike omnipotence for Alan: "All that power going any way you wanted." Alan, recalling the ecstasy of that initial ride on the horse at the beach when he was only six years old, respects the power of the horse-god and expresses a desire to become a horse-rider—a cowboy: "I wish I was a cowboy. They're free. They just swing up and then it's miles of grass . . . I bet all cowboys are *orphans!*" This freedom seems to be a latent reference to Alan's family life. For Alan, an orphan represents freedom from societal, particularly familial, restraints and is someone who, by his very nature, must be in control of his own life.

Later, Alan gets a job in the stables, the Temple or "His Holy of Holies." Upon seeing the stable for the first time, Alan "starts almost involuntarily to kneel on the floor in reverence." Alan begins to take the horses out at night, for he can be with his personal god only when he is alone. In an effort to "become one" with the horse, Alan obeys "Straw Law": ride—or fall. He explains to Dysart that "Straw Law" means, "He was born in the straw, and this is the law," an obvious reference to the horse-god as a Christ-like figure.

The ritualistic exorcism that ends act 1, Alan's midnight ride on Nugget, is a visual representation of Alan's spiritual and existential relationship with the horse-god. The scene begins with symbolic communication between Alan and Nugget: "Alan first ritually puts the bit into his own mouth, then crosses, and transfers it into Nugget's." In the nude, Alan begins the ride but not before he bridles himself with the Manbit, his "sacred stick" which unites horse and rider. Alan, still unconsciously viewing the horse as Christ, gives Nugget a piece of sugar as "His Last Supper." Alan leads the horse out of the stable, riding Nugget without a saddle so as to achieve a flesh-to-flesh union between horse and rider. The scene presents Alan astride Nugget, riding in the sacred field of Ha-Ha. We see the primitive's fantasies come to life as he identifies with his god:

> *My* mane, stiff in the wind!
> *My* flanks! My hooves!
> Mane on my legs, on my flanks, like whips!
> Raw!
> Raw!
> *I'm raw! Raw!*
> Feel me on you! *On* you! *On* you! *On* you!
> I want to be *in* you.
> I want to BE you forever and ever!—

In a ceremonial chant, Alan calls out to "Equus the God-slave, Faithful and True" and mimes a symbolic ride on his god, reminiscent of Christ's ride on the white horse in Revelation. As Alan whips the horse, he cries out against his enemies, representing the commercialism of his father's world:

"The Hosts of Hoover. The Hosts of Philco. The Hosts of Pifco. The House of Remington and all its tribe!" These commercial industries are inessential to Alan's spiritual quest for an identity. In addition, Alan castigates "the Hosts of Jodhpur. The Hosts of Bowler and Gymkhana. All those who show him off for their vanity." Thus, Alan's midnight ride is also a break with his mother's values—principles that confine the young man to a role or codified behavior defined by others. Alan associates the word "hosts" with the Godhead, for these are the forces that destroy the Self and reduce his longed-for omnipotent spirit to nothing more than the state of being "sorry." As the horse-god at the end of act 1, Alan, like Christ, tramples his enemies. Alan "becomes one" with himself, and Shaffer reinforces this concept by ending act 1 with Alan's appropriate cry, "AMEN!"

Underlying Alan's existential search for an identity is the fact that Alan is also experiencing a type of sexual awakening. Mrs. Strang has assured Alan that sex has spiritual value, but it is obvious that Alan has had very little contact with any physical sexual activity. When Alan begins to identify with Equus, the horse-god, the relationship becomes sexual. During Alan's ride on the horse at the beach, it is evident that even at age six, the experience is remembered chiefly as sexual titillation. Shaffer aptly names the horse Trojan, a fitting reference to the sexual comfort the "ride" is about to give Alan. The horseman carries a riding crop, and the punishment doled out reminds us of Alan's masochistic flagellation with his own coat hanger. While Alan is on horseback, the dialogue becomes sexually oriented:

> Tight now. And grip with our knees. All right?
> All set? . . . Come on, then, Trojan. Let's go!

Alan, when speaking of that wonderful ride, recalls that "It was *sexy*" and is particularly aware of the sexual experience as a means of control: "The fellow held me tight, and let me turn the horse which way I wanted. All that power going any way you wanted . . . His sides were all warm, and the smell. . . . " Thus, when Mr. Strang pulls Alan from the mare, he seems in a sense to be interfering with Alan's sexual pleasure: "I could have bashed him," Alan states, while telling Dysart of the incident.

The implications of Alan's sexual union with the horse are seen throughout the play. John Simon notes that the horse is frequently associated with propagation, and certainly the image of "riding" has sexual connotations. During Alan's ride on Nugget, the ritualistic ceremony that ends act 1, the spiritual becomes entwined with the sexual. Alan's "I'm stiff! Stiff in the wind!" is phallic, as could be "Knives in his skin! Little knives—all inside my legs." The chanting of "I want to be *in* you" and "Make us One Person!" are obviously references to intercourse. Since Alan and Equus are one person, master-slave, or horse-rider, the sexual relationship is actually masturbatory. Alan's experience with the horse on the beach is frightening to him because the only image he can vividly recall is the cream dropping from the horse's mouth. Because this experience with horses is sexual as well as spiritual, Alan is particularly terrified at the unconscious sexual implications that the dripping cream has for him.

Working at the stables, Alan develops a sexual rapport with Nugget. Alan is so ashamed of his sexual activities that he refuses to ride Nugget when others are nearby. He takes Nugget out only in the secrecy of the evening and then, completely in the nude, he "rides" the horse. Alan's only piece of equipment is a Manbit, a stick that he places in his mouth to prevent ejaculation or, as Alan puts it, "So's it won't happen too quick." Alan then proceeds to whip Nugget, an act that exemplifies his newly gained power, possibly brought to life by the riding crop in the horseman's hand as he was whipping Trojan on the beach.

Alan refuses to see the horse as anything but a free and uncontrolled spirit, and his mother's insistence on putting bowler hats and jodhpurs on the horse suggests the repression of the powerful union of man and god, which represents an existential sense of Being for Alan. At the end of act 1, in his invocation against the foes of Equus, Alan cites "the Hosts of Jodhpur. The Hosts of Bowler and Gymkhana." The idea that Mrs. Strang wants to "clothe" or mask the horse interferes with Alan's sexual gratification: "The horse isn't dressed. It's the most naked thing you ever saw! More than a dog or a cat or anything. Even the most broken down old nag has got its *life!* To put a bowler on it is *filthy!*" This particular view that Mrs. Strang has toward horses is reminiscent of Frank Strang's refusal to let Alan ride freely and enjoy the sexual pleasure it gives him. Such sexual repression seems to force Alan to turn inward for his carnal desires.

One night, Jill Mason leads Alan into sexual experiences with another person. She begins the long evening by telling Alan that "I love horses' eyes. The way you can see yourself in them." Then she follows up with, "D'you find them sexy?" Alan covers his true feelings by insisting that Jill is "daft" for asking such questions. Not realizing that Alan can have sex only with his personal god, Jill escorts him on a date. They enter a pornographic movie theater, and Alan immediately associates the sexually oriented locale with a spiritual environment: "All the men—staring up like they were in church. Like they were a sort of congregation."

Jill tries to introduce Alan to what is considered to be the "normal" conception of sex. Alan begins to understand this when he sees his father in the porno theater, then he thinks to himself: "They're not just Dads—they're people with pricks! . . . And Dad—he's just not Dad either. He's a man with a prick, too. You know, I'd never thought about it." But Mr. Strang maintains that he was in the theater for business reasons only and instead castigates Alan for being there. Thus, Alan's father unconsciously represses the development of any mature sexual knowledge on Alan's part. This is confirmed when Alan returns to the stables with Jill and refuses to have intercourse with her. Alan is frigid because Equus, Alan's conscience, appearing in the form of his father's watchful eyes, is bothering him. When Alan removes his clothes, the nudity associated with his "mount" is too much for him to bear. In short, Alan suppresses the horse-god, an embodiment of his own superego that is guilty about sex. In a rage, Alan blinds the horses, thus striking out at his own sexual insecurities.

Mr. and Mrs. Strang have tried to raise Alan according to conflicting philosophies, so it is no wonder that Alan has developed sexual and spiritual anxieties that culminated in psychiatric treatment. Yet Alan is actually a character with a strong sense of self-awareness. By refusing to live by the superficial norms and values of others, Alan is envied as a person who creates his own identity. As critic Doyle W. Walls has noted, "At least it is a myth that says yes to the present rather than placing its hope in time to come, as the mother's Christianity and the father's socialism trust." [See Walls' excerpt below]. (pp. 152-60)

Alan may find that . . . "normal" individuals deem it necessary for him to seek psychiatric help, yet he cannot justify the hypocritical values that these people share. Alan sees his father as a role player whose strict moral values mask the fact that he is busy attending pornographic movies. . . . Alan realizes that his father lives in lies: "I kept thinking—all those airs he put on! . . . 'Receive my meaning. Improve your mind!' . . . All those nights he said he'd be in late. 'Keep my supper hot, Dora!' 'Your poor father: he works so hard!' . . . Bugger! Old bugger! . . . Filthy old bugger!" Mrs. Strang fills Alan's head with religious stories that become less acceptable when the young man sees that his parents contradict their own values. Everyone tries to be what they are not, but only Alan strives to understand and control his own life, free from the influence of others. Dysart understands that Alan has created his own sense of worship: "He can hardly read. He knows no physics or engineering to make the world real for him. No paintings to show him how others have enjoyed it. No music except television jingles. No history except tales from a desperate mother. No friends. Not one kid to give him a joke, or make him know himself more moderately. He's a modern citizen for whom society doesn't exist." Alan has rejected the sense of "vitality" that modern society offers; instead, he has created his own brand of worship, and he has constructed his own value system within this mythical code of ethics.

Even though much of the play concerns Alan's rehabilitation, the astute student of Shaffer's works will recognize Dysart as the protagonist of the play. Much of the drama deals with the education that Dr. Dysart receives from his patient. Dysart learns that Alan has created his own form of worship, while the psychiatrist is still searching for some semblance of a personal identity. Through his association with Alan, Dysart begins to understand the inability of modern society, a vapid band of role players, to invigorate our inner drives and impulses.

Dysart, the God of the Normal, is, in essence, a role player who lives up to immutable codes and regulations. He is fond of the fact that "the Normal is the indispensable, murderous God of Health, and I am his Priest," a position that enables him to control others and socialize them so that they can conform to society's expectations. Moreover, Dysart views psychiatry not just as a useful therapeutic tool, but also as a profession that gratifies his strong ego. When asked by Hesther Salomon whether or not he knows that he has done a fine job working with children, Dysart responds with an egotistical, "Yes, but do the children?" Almost in the next breath he proudly admits that "I feel the job is unworthy to fill me."

Dysart tries to believe that he is living a worthwhile life, but the truth is that illusions and lies control his existence. Dysart describes a typical evening at home as nothing more than sitting by the fireplace, watching his wife knit clothes for orphans. Meanwhile, Dysart, frustrated with his lackluster job and with his wife's predictable middle-class attitude, takes refuge in his own illusion—ancient Greek culture. Thumbing through his art books on ancient Greece, Dysart finds a world of adventure, wonder, ecstasy, and excitement to replace his midlife crisis. Dysart can never evade the real world; every time he confronts his wife Margaret with his lofty visions, she brings him back to reality. For example, when Dysart passes her a picture of Cretan acrobats, she can only remark that "the Highland Games, now there's *normal* [sic] *sport!*" In short, in both his work and home environments, Dysart is forever a prisoner and constant defender of the "Normal."

Dysart knows full well that his carefully regulated bourgeois existence prevents him from ever touching the bowels of Greek civilization, his true love. . . . Meanwhile, Alan, creating his own sense of worship—which is what Dysart would love to do—is being treated for insanity. Thus, it is not unusual for the psychiatrist to lose a certain amount of respect for a profession that seems more like a sham where, as he tells Alan, "Everything I do is a trick or a catch."

Dysart, the role player, realizes that his structured life is accompanied by sexual problems. . . . The psychiatrist is fooling everyone when he suggests that he cannot have children because his wife is a puritan. Alan hits a bit too close to home when he states that Dysart never has sex with his wife: "I bet you don't. I bet you never touch her. Come on, tell me. You've got no kids, have you? Is that because you don't fuck?" Actually, there is little contact between Dysart and his wife, whom the psychiatrist has not kissed in six years. They spend their evenings in the same room, but she is absorbed in her knitting while he sees visions of Doric temples. This lack of contact between the dentist and the psychiatrist—two professionals who ironically enough spend most of their time caring for others—on the surface appears to be a sterile relationship. Dysart acknowledges that beneath the surface, the marriage suffers from his own sterility: "I imply that we can't have children: but actually, it's only me. I had myself tested behind her back. The lowest sperm count you could find."

While treating Alan, Dysart begins to understand more about himself and comes to realize what freedom really means. Alan gradually exposes Dysart, but it is clear that Dysart . . . unconsciously wants to benefit from a cathartic stripping away of pretensions of which these two men are aware but cannot control. Dysart claims that he can learn from Alan because his patient is a free spirit, not a phony who lives by roles imposed on him by society. Alan controls his own fate; as Dysart says, his free will reflects "his pain. His own. He made it." The doctor laments to Hesther that Alan "has known a passion more ferocious than I have felt in any second of my life. And let me tell you something: I envy it." The psychiatrist can only dream of primitive cultures and their sacred rites and rituals; Alan lives them. (pp. 161-63)

Dysart's contact with Alan has changed the psychiatrist, who is now more conscious of his artificial existence and how his life contrasts with Alan's "primitive" sense of worship. Dysart begins to compete with Alan, his alter ego, and the resulting battle of wills becomes a struggle between a Dionysian youth (Alan) and the Apollonian man (Dysart). Dysart consciously identifies with his "twin" or alter ego, Alan, the horse-god:

> You see, I'm wearing that horse's head myself. That's the feeling. All reined up in old language and old assumptions, straining to jump clean-hoofed on to a whole new track of being I only suspect is there. I can't see it, because my educated, average head is being held at the wrong angle. I can't jump because the bit forbids it, and my own basic force—my horsepower, if you like—is too little.
>
> (p. 163)

During the play, Dysart gradually identifies with Alan, and as the drama progresses, he becomes more like his alter ego. Both Alan and Dysart are fascinated by myths; Dysart is im-

mersed in his art books on Greek civilization and dreams of mythology while Alan lives his myths. Both individuals have sadomasochistic tendencies: Alan blinds horses, stabbing at his conscience, and Dysart dreams of carving up children, expressing doubts about his profession as a psychiatrist. Dysart's last lines in the play relate to this identification with Alan's neuroses: "I stand in the dark with a pick in my hand, striking at heads!" In addition, the psychiatrist and his patient have sexual problems and are frigid around women. Together, Dysart and Alan function as a unit to solve their sexual and social difficulties. (p. 164)

Dysart's contact with Alan has changed the psychiatrist to the extent that he now suffers nightmares. Dysart has been disturbed by an explicit dream in which he acts as a priest in ancient Greece who officiates at the sacrifice of small children. Wearing the mask of King Agamemnon, Dysart asserts that "it's obvious to me that I'm tops as chief priest. It's this unique talent for carving that has got me where I am." Unfortunately, the "chief priest" has begun to have doubts about his work. In his dream, Dysart admits that "I've started to feel distinctly nauseous. And with each victim, it's getting worse." At the end of the dream, the mask slips, the knife is torn out of his hands, and then he awakens.

As a psychiatrist, Dysart has "tampered" with many children, but his face has remained hidden behind the role he must play. While treating Alan, he begins to identify with King Agamemnon, who lived under the curse of the House of Atreus and sacrificed his daughter, Iphigenia, to conquer Troy. Dysart sees himself as the cursed priest destroying the suffering patients brought before him. Images within the dream relating to knives and "pop-eyed masks" force Dysart anxiously and unconsciously to recall Alan's blinding of the horses with the sharp pick. In short, the psychiatrist has committed the ultimate crime of his profession: he has felt guilty about treating his patient. As the mask in the dream slips, green sweat runs down the doctor's face—a sign that nausea is the result of this guilt. Dysart, whose profession is based on [Freud's] *The Interpretation of Dreams,* fully understands why treating Alan will have serious repercussions for both individuals.

Gradually, Dysart begins to understand that Alan's brand of worship is not so abnormal, and a thousand local gods can be revered just as easily as one. Alan may not worship the proper gods, but at least he chooses his own fate, much like Dysart, who candidly acknowledges that "I shrank my *own* life. No one can do it for you. I settled for being pallid and provincial, out of my own eternal timidity." Dysart has chosen to uphold the "Normal," but his contact with Alan has forced him to have doubts about his role. . . . He tells Alan of his dislike for the role he must play, but the student of Shaffer's work will recognize the author speaking: "The Normal is the good smile in a child's eyes—all right. It is also the dead stare in a million adults. It both sustains and kills—like a God. It is the Ordinary made beautiful: it is also the Average made lethal." Dysart discovers that his life has held very little meaning for him, but his experience with Alan has forced him to question his existence and ask, "What am I doing here? I don't mean clinically doing or socially doing—I mean *fundamentally!*" The conversion is complete when Dysart remarks that "actually, I'd like to leave this room and never see it again in my life." Dysart wants to switch from his role of God of the Normal to a God unto Himself, existential-style. Therefore, when Alan tells Dysart that gods do not die, the doctor responds with, "Yes, they do." The reference here has a double meaning. Dysart has already told Hesther that "life is only comprehensible through a thousand local Gods. And not just the old dead ones with names like Zeus— no, but living Geniuses of Place and Person!" In other words, because of the multiplicity of the many varied forms of worship, man has dared to be different. Dysart also would like to be different by destroying his reverence for the "Normal" and substituting it with a more viable form of worship. In addition, as Shaffer explained to me during my interview with him, Dysart's response to Alan's suggestion that gods do not die is an assurance that the doctor plans to destroy Alan's sense of worship, or the deity within him.

However, as the psychiatrist's name implies, the doctor's old personality "dies hard," simply because it is not easy for him to free himself from the role. . . . It is not unusual to hear Dysart promise to shape Alan as a Disciple of the Normal, at the expense of the teenager's freedom: "I'll erase the welts cut into his mind by flying manes. When that's done, I'll set him on a nice mini-scooter and send him puttering off into the Normal world where animals are treated *properly:* made extinct, or put into servitude, or tethered all their lives in dim light, just to feed it!"

Shaffer seems to be saying that the band, society, and the institutions into which individuals must be properly assimilated destroy free will and worship. To "cure" Alan, Dysart must erase the young man's sense of mythology and replace it with a form of worship that society accepts as "normal." The essence of Shaffer's argument then is sociological; *Equus* is a treatise on the failure of modern society to provide appropriate channels for the blossoming of individuals. Shaffer laments the fact that the codes, rules, and mores of modern society help foster the attitude that the average be made desirable or the ordinary be made beautiful. In short, individuals who do not play roles—the primitives—will be destroyed by societal forces beyond their control in order to channel their mythological sense of worship into more socially acceptable attitudes and beliefs. (pp. 164-66)

Although Shaffer modeled *Equus* along the lines of classical Greek theater, the play is not a tragedy. *Equus* does not follow the unities: flashbacks interrupt any unity of time, and the diverse settings would be foreign to Greek tragedy. Dysart is obviously the protagonist, but is he a tragic figure? As a psychiatrist, he has no claims to nobility. He never mentions any wish to ascend to the pinnacle of his career à la Willy Loman, so there is no great fall from the heights. The audience is purged of the emotions of pity and fear, but it is Alan's abreaction that leads to the purification, not anything Dysart says or does. The abreaction cannot be a catharsis, which must come from Dysart. The psychiatrist recognizes his dilemma: he is a role player who establishes an identity through socially sanctioned channels. At the outset of the play, Dysart recognizes his shortcomings—his first speech of the play, the very first words uttered on stage, reflect his understanding of his "flaw." Dysart's insight therefore destroys any chance of peripeteia. (pp. 166-67)

Equus works well on stage because it is effective Theatre of Cruelty as Artaud suggested it should be performed. Dysart, the rational Apollonian man, is interested in studying primitive cultures; he would like nothing better than to live among them. Alan, a primitive, reflects the Dionysian spirit incapable of adjusting to the roles and norms of modern society. The rituals presented on stage become the vital link in the chain

that both binds the doctor with his patient and assists in reversing the learning process that normally occurs between the two. While observing Alan's ritualistic behavior, Dysart achieves symbolic communication from Alan's anthropomorphic sense of worship, and by doing so, he matures and begins to reach a new level of understanding. Most importantly, the ritualistic nature of the play serves to communicate intuitively to the audience the Apollonian-Dionysian struggle on stage.

Artaud, himself a frequent patient in mental asylums, viewed theater as a therapeutic cure for psychopathological disorders. In *Le théâtre et son double,* Artaud discussed theater as a therapeutic tool: "I propose to bring back into the theater this elementary magical idea, taken up by modern psychoanalysis, which consists in effecting a patient's cure by making him assume the apparent and exterior attitudes of the desired condition." Alan's treatment, an exorcism that is therapeutic for the audience as well, is the perfect theme for Artaud's Theatre of Cruelty. Furthermore, the dramatization of such a horrible crime as the blinding of six horses is the visceral, grotesque, and unnerving type of thematic nexus that will purge the audience's unconscious drives and impulses. Artaud again enlightens us with regard to the importance of shocking the spectators out of their mundane existence:

> After sound and light there is action, and the dynamism of action: here the theater, far from copying life, puts itself whenever possible in communication with pure forces. And whether you accept them or deny them, there is nevertheless a way of speaking which gives the name of "forces" to whatever brings to birth images of energy in the unconscious, and gratuitous crime on the surface.
>
> A violent and concentrated action is a kind of lyricism: it summons up supernatural images, a bloodstream of images, a bleeding spurt of images in the poet's head and in the spectator's as well.

Equus reflects the type of ritualistic drama that Artaud had in mind for his Theatre of Cruelty. Shaffer abides by Artaud's wish to abolish the stage and use a single space in which the audience can interact with the actors. The chorus provides a uniform rhythm, a constant pulsating effect in which the humming, thumping, and stamping produce vibratory sensations that work through the skin as well as on our minds. Noises, cries, and groans weave throughout the production, creating a constant rhythmic structure that covertly affects our inner drives, impulses, and archetypes. Particularly effective are the tape-recorded cries of "Ek" in Alan's nightmare (scene 8), the Equus Noise before and during Alan's ride on Trojan (scene 10), the constant humming of trade names that accompanies Alan's litany against commercialism (scene 15), the choric effect during Alan's first visit to Dalton's stables (scene 16), the reverberations of "TELL ME" as Alan reacts to Dysart's inquisition (scene 16), Dysart's hypnotism of Alan, captured by a loud metallic sound on tape (scene 19), the Equus Noise accompanying Alan's ride on Nugget (scene 20), the warning noises during Jill's seduction in the stable (scene 32), and the haunting vibratory effects, culminating in screaming and stamping of the horses' hooves as Alan blinds the horses (scene 34). (pp. 167-68)

Shaffer uses ritualistic drama to provide symbolic communication between Dysart, the protagonist, and his alter ego, Alan. In tragedy, the catharsis evokes a sense of pity and terror, but much of the "talking out" stage is verbal. Ritualistic theater goes beyond the verbal level to provide symbolic communication between the actors and the audience through a release of our latent drives and instincts. Such ritualistic communication is presented in primarily two scenes: Alan's ride on Nugget at the end of act 1 and the seduction scene that concludes the play.

Alan's ride on Nugget begins with the rhythmic humming of the chorus as Alan mimes leading Nugget out of his sacred stable. Alan reverently kneels to the horse as he puts on "sandals of majesty," kissing them devoutly. The ceremonious nature of the scene continues as Alan "first ritually puts the bit into his own mouth, then crosses, and transfers it into Nugget's." Alan then strips of all clothes and adornments before his god and becomes one with the animal as he rides Nugget without a saddle. The anthropomorphic ceremony continues as Alan offers Equus the talisman, the sacred Manbit. A symbolic piece of sugar, "his Last Supper," is offered to Nugget as Alan kneels before his godslave and says, "Take my sins. Eat them for my sake." Alan mounts Nugget, then he "whispers his God's name ceremonially." The horse-rider, Alan, begins a ritualistic chanting of a genealogical litany. As the audience is assaulted with the Equus noise and a rhythmic incantation against the foes of the godhead, the set begins to rotate. The increased speed of the turntable, the change of lighting, and the rhythmic dialogue all serve to create a terror that cuts directly through the skin to the bone. The Equus noise increases until Alan becomes one with his god. The "amen" concludes the religious ceremony.

The sexual connotations of the scene also relate to our inner urges, instincts, and impulses. Alan mimes stripping off his clothes so that he can ride Nugget in the nude. As was previously mentioned, Alan puts the Manbit in his mouth, "So's it won't happen too quick," a reference to ejaculation. Then Alan engages in a type of masturbatory foreplay, touching Nugget all over his body. Alan "mounts" the horse and engages in a "ride" at night when no one can see him. During the sexual seduction of the horse, Alan fills his litany with such phallic references as "knives in his skin" and "Stiff in the wind." Obviously, Alan's "Feel me on you! *On* you! *On* you! *On* you!" and "Make us One Person!" have strong sexual implications.

Speaking of the ride at the end of act 1, Shaffer noted that "I found it very difficult to write. I experimented with onomatopoeia, with keeping the frenzy verbal, but there must be a moment when the visceral takes over." Shaffer's efforts to create total theater—a complex interplay of language, mime, lighting, gesture, movement and intonation—to affect our unconscious libidinal urges proves that ritualistic drama can be as effective as classical tragedy in producing this sense of terror in the audience.

Equally impressive as ritualistic drama is Alan's attempted seduction of Jill in the stables. Again, the scene begins when the chorus initiates a faint hum and the actors "ceremonially put on their masks." The setting is like a temple, or as Alan puts it, "the Holy of Holies" for his sacred god. As Alan and Jill remove their clothes, the dialogue that describes the seduction becomes increasingly rhythmic, uniting the ritual with the sex act:

> ALAN. I put it in her!
>
> DYSART. Yes?
>
> ALAN. I put it in her.

DYSART. You did?

ALAN. Yes!

DYSART. Was it easy?

ALAN. Yes.

DYSART. Describe it.

ALAN. I told you.

DYSART. More exactly.

ALAN. I put it in her!

DYSART. Did you?

ALAN. All the way!

DYSART. Did you, Alan?

ALAN. All the way. I shoved it. I put it in her all the way.

DYSART. Did you?

ALAN. Yes!

DYSART. Did you?

ALAN. Yes! . . . Yes!

Alan, embarrassed by his unsuccessful sexual encounter, kneels on the stable floor to ask forgiveness of his god. The scene in which Alan blinds the horses develops into an Artaudian mélange of savage cries, slashing hooves, and rhythmic gestures superseded by the horses themselves: "archetypal images—judging, punishing, pitiless." The climax of the sexual ritual occurs when Dysart tries to comfort Alan but can only soothe the young man by urging him to breath "In . . . Out . . . In . . . Out . . . That's it . . . In. *Out* . . . *In* . . . *Out* . . . ", creating a rhythm which suggests that the sexual ceremony is over.

Through the use of ritualistic theater, Dysart, as well as the audience, is able to appreciate the freedom expressed in primitives such as Alan Strang. Shaffer uses total theater as a means to distinguish Alan's primitive existence from a more socialized means of worship. Theatre of Cruelty enables Shaffer to portray social communication between two people without having to resort either to a didactic or a naturalistic form of writing. The ritualistic elements of the play tie together the sexual, sociological, and psychological motifs effectively. Without this sort of "unconscious communication," Shaffer would be prone to preaching; the result might be a carbon copy of one of Ibsen's nineteenth-century plays—effective theater but not innovative. Instead, *Equus,* through a graceful fusion of form, content, and stage conventions, forces us to be our own psychiatrists exploring the real motives behind our "normal" existence. (pp. 169-71)

Gene A. Plunka, in his Peter Shaffer: Roles, Rites, and Rituals in the Theater, *Fairleigh Dickinson University Press, 1988, 249 p.*

FURTHER READING

Clum, John M. "Religion and Five Contemporary Plays: The Quest for God in a Godless World." *South Atlantic Quarterly* 77, No. 4 (Autumn 1978): 418-32.
    Examines Shaffer's fascination with religion in *Equus*. See excerpt in *CLC*, Vol. 14.

Greiff, Louis K. "Two for the Price of One: Tragedy and the Dual Hero in *Equus* and *The Elephant Man.*" In *Within the Dramatic Spectrum,* edited by Karelisa V. Hartigan, pp. 64-77. Lanham, Md.: University Press of America, 1986.
    Compares dramatic patterns and tragic heroes in the respective plays of Shaffer and Bernard Pomerance.

Hinden, Michael. "Trying to Like Shaffer." *Comparative Drama* 19, No. 1 (Spring 1985): 14-29.
    Discusses the dramatic language in Shaffer's plays.

Stacy, James R. "The Sun and the Horse: Peter Shaffer's Search for Worship." *Educational Theatre Journal* 28, No. 3 (October 1976): 325-37.
    Assesses Shaffer's exploration of humanity's spiritual needs in *The Royal Hunt of the Sun* and *Equus*.

Taylor, John Russell. *Peter Shaffer*. Harlow, Essex: Longman Group Ltd., 1974, 34 p.
    Discusses Shaffer's works up to 1974 and includes a select bibliography. See excerpt in *CLC*, Vol. 14.

Timm, Neil. "*Equus* as a Modern Tragedy." *Philological Papers* 25, No. 8 (February 1979): 128-34.
    Compares *Equus* to the Greek tragedies *Antigone, Oedipus,* and Racine's version of *Phèdre*.

Joshua Sobol

19??-

Israeli dramatist.

One of Israel's most controversial playwrights, Sobol often addresses the social and political issues of his country by examining pivotal events in Jewish history. According to Leonie Lichtenstein, "Sobol's concern . . . is with the effect of the past on identity in the present: how can Israel today cope not only with the past genocide of Jews, but with millennia of humiliation?" The former artistic director of Israel's internationally recognized Haifa Municipal Theater, Sobol is frequently compared with German dramatist Bertolt Brecht for his highly theatrical presentation of intellectual issues. Although some critics have objected to his portrayal of Jews as historically governed by self-hatred and xenophobia, most commend Sobol's provocative examination of the psychology underlying the moral dilemmas facing contemporary Israel.

The Wars of the Jews, Sobol's first play to garner international attention, was originally written in archaic Hebrew and presented among the excavated ruins of the Old City in Jerusalem. This work features the ghosts of Jews who lived during the first century and died either in the failed rebellion against Rome or in the ensuing Jewish civil war. By unfavorably comparing the violent nationalism of ancient zealots to the pacifism of the rabbinical students who surrendered to Rome, Sobol indirectly indicts contemporary Israelis who would sacrifice the integrity of their nation to ensure its survival. His next play, *The Soul of a Jew,* won widespread critical praise for its surrealistic portrayal of the last night in the life of Otto Weininger, a Jewish author who lived during the late nineteenth century. Referred to by Adolf Hitler as "my favorite Jew," Weininger remained fervently misogynous and antisemitic up to the time of his suicide at the age of twenty-three. Throughout the play, such figures as Sigmund Freud and the Swedish playwright August Strindberg visit Weininger in the rented room where he later kills himself. Before Weininger commits suicide, however, his female doppelgänger appears, embodying personality traits the young author had wished to destroy. According to Sobol, *The Soul of a Jew* is an examination of "what it means to be a victim of hatred, the ways one interiorizes it and becomes one's own enemy."

Ghetto, Sobol's best known play outside Israel, revolves around a theatre troupe that existed during World War II in the Nazi-occupied Jewish ghetto of Vilnius, Lithuania. Featuring authentic songs performed by the group, this play draws partly from Sobol's extensive interviews with Srulik, one of the two surviving members of the company whose memories and fantasies are realized on the stage. Among those Srulik remembers are Jacob Gens, the Jewish leader of the ghetto who bargains away the lives of some residents to save others; Hermann Kruk, the idealistic librarian who opposes any cooperation with the Germans; Hayyah, the troupe's leading female vocalist; and Kittel, the artistic yet sadistic Nazi commandant of the ghetto. While Kittel initially allows the company to flourish, he later orders all troupe members killed upon discovering that Hayyah has escaped before a performance. Although some critics contended that *Ghetto* inadequately conveyed the horror of the Holocaust,

others lauded the play as a celebration of those Jews who resisted the Nazis not through violence but through cultural and moral action. In addition to *Ghetto,* Sobol has also written *Shooting Magda,* which revolves around a controversial documentary film about a Palestinian woman, and *Jerusalem Syndrome,* which portrays the end of the world as brought about by a soldier's execution of a civilian.

PRINCIPAL WORKS

PLAYS

The Wars of the Jews   1981
The Soul of a Jew   1982
Ghetto   1983
Shooting Magda   1987
Jerusalem Syndrome   1988

EDWARD GROSSMAN

For some years now, Israelis have been warning one another

that they can't afford the luxury of civil war. These warnings sometimes have been accompanied by references, implicit or explicit, to the civil war in Jerusalem that preceded the fall of the city to the Romans. Until lately, the warnings and the implied analogies seemed far-fetched. Today they seem less so. It has become conceivable that the Israelis, like the Jews of 19 centuries ago, will shed one another's blood.

Such a possibility is indirectly suggested by a new play which opened in Jerusalem [*The Wars of the Jews*]. . . . [It] connects ancient fratricide and disaster with current events so dramatically that it might as well be doing it explicitly. Like the language in which it is cast, however, the drama and the timeliness of the play are readily understood only by insiders. Perhaps for this reason, few tourists are to be seen at performances.

The Hebrew spoken, chanted, and shouted in *The Wars of the Jews* is strictly archaic. It is suitable, and difficult. The sources for the words, and for the action, are the Bible, the Talmud, the Apocrypha, and especially the book by the first-century Jewish turncoat Josephus after which the play is named.

The production has been mounted very aptly in the ramparts and ruins of the Old City. The audience seats itself on the rocks as best it can, and the actors are picked out suddenly with torches as they crouch in holes or stand on the battlements, their robes flapping in the wind. . . . For those unfamiliar with classical Hebrew and with the Israeli scene, the power of the play might seem to derive just from this setting. Its popularity and the feelings it stirs up might seem puzzling. The ax that Sobol grinds throughout might go unnoticed.

The robed figures represent the ghosts of the Jews killed or starved in the rebellion against the Romans and during the civil war. They remember and mourn the greatness of Jerusalem, that wonder of the world with its prophets and crazy men and pilgrims and inhabitants "from all nations." Why has it been destroyed? They promise to show the audience how the Jews themselves brought destruction on the city—as Josephus wrote, "for our misfortunes we have only ourselves to blame."

And indeed, for those who can follow the Hebrew and have read Josephus, it's remarkable how closely the argument of *The Wars of the Jews* follows the account that this nobleman and general published in Rome after he switched sides. Sobol's villains, like Josephus's, are the Zealots. It is they whom we are shown in the course of the play murdering Jews who waver, it is they who are said to have forced the Romans to besiege the city and burn the Temple. On the other hand, the hero of the piece is Rabbi Yohanan Ben Zakkai, who, as Jewish tradition tells it, smuggled himself out of Jerusalem in a coffin, surrendered to the Romans, and got their permission to set up an academy where the Jews substituted the study of sacred texts for territory, statehood, and Zion.

Any Israeli who has stayed awake in school knows the outlines of the story and is acquainted with its controversy: who served the Jewish cause better after Jerusalem fell—the remnant of the Zealots who escaped to Masada to fight on, or the peaceful students of Ben Zakkai? This old debate has revived thanks to the excavation of Masada and the glorification, by some, of the suicide pact. Yet although most members of the audience at *The Wars of the Jews* undoubtedly know of this dispute, and probably don't buy the glorification of Masada, it isn't the relative merits of armed as against non-violent re-

sistance that Sobol leads them to weigh. He questions the necessity of rebellion against a tolerant Rome in the first place.

Sobol, like most of his audience, is liberal in outlook. His ideal Jerusalem, as the ghosts remember it, is a pluralistic, perhaps even a somewhat hedonistic city. Not for nothing are the villains, the Zealots, given speeches fulminating against foreign influence, against non-Jewish sacrifices at the Temple, against Jews who deal with non-Jews, against the very presence of non-Jews in the land. Here, in these illiberal speeches—which Sobol didn't invent but only lifted from historical and legendary sources—the play, for Israelis, becomes contemporary. (pp. 12-13)

The Wars of the Jews uses history to deliver a message about the present and a warning about the future. Its success with the theater-going segment of the Israelis and with liberal critics shouldn't be attributed solely to the play's energy and skillfulness. It also stems from the fact that Sobol's mood is the mood of many of those in Israel who don't wish to see the state become more theocratic and who still hope for an accommodation with Arabs closer to home than the Egyptians. Liberals are demoralized. They fear what the future holds. The portents, the signs that Israeli democracy may not be able to handle the strains that are coming, render Sobol's historical analogies believable, in spite of the fact that there is no famine, and that Israel—far from being a weak province—is the superpower of the Middle East. . . .

What kind of Jewish state should the Jewish state be? What are to be its boundaries, cultural and geographical? Is it to live in isolation always? These questions were only obscured for a generation by the national consensus on survival, and postponed by political arrangement. If they can't be postponed further, or answered democratically, it may go hard for Israel, and for its friends. (p. 13)

Edward Grossman, "A Play of Jewish Passions," in The New Republic, *Vol. 185, No. 3, July 18, 1981, pp. 12-13.*

JOSHUA SOBOL [INTERVIEW WITH CLIVE SINCLAIR]

[Sinclair:] *[Last June, Samih al-Qasim, the Palestinian poet, claimed that you] had been censored. I understood differently, but didn't want to contradict him until I had spoken to you. Have you?*

[Sobol]: Well, they sent a committee of censors to see *Soul of a Jew* and they decided not to cut it. Later we had a problem at a small theatre here in Tel Aviv where I put on a satirical play. The censors tried to ban it. There was a scandal. So they sent a committee to see the show again and they decided not to ban it after all. They were not brave enough to do it probably. I think it's mainly the Arab writers who suffer from the effects of censorship. (p. 25)

Can you see yourself ever becoming a dissident writer? Perhaps in a certain amount of danger.

It might happen. I can give you the scenario. If the Likud together with the right-wing parties take over and they rehabilitate the Jewish underground—give them an amnesty—I think that then the deeds of the terrorists will become a norm in Israel. By the way, I'm almost sure that the Israeli government knew of these deeds—I mean they knew who perpetrated them. In that case I think that the situation might develop into one where even Israeli leftists or doveish personalities might be persecuted.

By the government or by terrorists?

By extremists backed up by the government.

Your latest play about the last days of the Vilno ghetto recently opened in Haifa. . . . How did the critics respond to **Ghetto** *here?*

They liked it, but there was only one critic who really referred to the implications of the play for the present Israeli situation. That was Boaz Evron of *Yediot Ahronot.* He said that it dealt with the question of how we—Israelis—have been influenced in a very strange way by Nazi ideology, by its egoistic nationalism. He thought that this was the main issue of the play for an Israeli audience, and stated that the question was so important for us nowadays that it should be put on the table.

Why not write directly about contemporary Israel?

Because I think that if we want to understand what is happening in Israel today we have to go to the past and try to see where are the roots of it all. You know, when I wrote the play one of the things I found was an article written by Martin Buber in November 1939, a year after *Kristallnacht.* It seems that at that time there were Revisionists in the Zionist movement who said that Nazi ideology in itself is not bad, that it is almost the most effective ideology for a nation in a state of crisis. What was bad about the Nazi ideology, of course, was that it was directed against Jews. Apart from that unfortunate perversion they shared its belief in a policy based on national egoism. And Buber says in his article that this is the most terrible abomination he knows of assimilation, and he goes on to say that if a day comes when we adopt Hitler's god here in Palestine and only change its name into a Hebrew one then we are lost. Well, what I think now happens in Israeli society, at least with the extremists, is exactly this. According to the polls there are 14% of the population who believe that the Jewish underground was all right. To me it seems very significant and very dangerous that we have such a high percentage of people who find its ideology plausible. To answer your question, I feel the necessity to go back to the past in order to understand what happens here, what the hell is going on with our Zionism here in Israel.

So Israel is a continuation of diaspora history?

Yes it is, but in a very distorted way. What I tried to show in **Ghetto** was that the Jews in Vilno tried to resist the Nazis, not by using force against them, but by resisting spiritually and morally, by trying to survive not only as living creatures but mainly as human creatures. They wanted to survive and come out of this terrible hell as human beings. I think that's why they made the theatre and that's why they created the library and had all the cultural activity in the ghetto. For years this was not mentioned here in Israel. The consensus was that most of the people went as sheep to the slaughter, whilst there was a minority of heroes who stood up and resisted the Nazis gun in hand. Well, what I found out while making my research for the play was that resistance in the ghetto represented a very small minority, less than one percent of the population. The best people, I think, were involved in this kind of moral and cultural surviving.

Did any survivors see **Ghetto?**

That's exactly what I want to tell you. The theatre invited

survivors of two kinds, if I can put it that way; some were in the partisans and others were just survivors. Those who were in the resistance movement attacked the play, some of them. They said the play ignored the fact of the resistance in the ghetto by putting a very strong emphasis on the Jews who just survived. They asked me, what do you want to do with the play, what kind of an example do you set for youth? Then there were those who just survived. They came out with a very fierce attack on this tradition of glorifying the resistance and ignoring totally the fact the majority were just survivors—second-class survivors, they called themselves. They said they felt for the first time that justice was done to them and to their way of living through the Holocaust. It was very, very interesting and Israeli television tried to make something of it. In one of the meetings a woman came out with such an attack on the tradition of praising the armed resistance and ignoring the rest of them that everyone around started weeping. They couldn't go on. Filming stopped. They didn't want to show such grief on television. And this was one of the strongest moments in the whole symposium. Well, there was censorship, but of another kind, benign censorship.

It's ironic, isn't it, that the culture they were trying to salvage was more Western European than Jewish?

You are absolutely right that they were not trying to perpetuate the Jewish orthodox tradition. Those who were, let's say, Bundists believed in universal humanistic values, and that's what they tried to save. If you take the ghetto of Vilno I think that the most active people came from this non-religious tradition.

So, in one sense, the Zionist tradition isn't Jewish at all?

That's why I think there's a contradiction between Zionism and orthodox Judaism. Nowadays in Israel they try to make a whole mixture, a mish-mash of Zionism and messianism. I don't think that Zionism had anything to do with messianism originally. It was, as you said, a secular ideology, a nationalistic ideology, trying to reimplant the Jews in an historical context. It's only after the Six Day War that messianism all of a sudden started to become the expression both of Judaism and of Zionism and I think that this is our worst catastrophe.

But what was the alternative to winning?

Since there was a war we had to win it, but the outcome could be different. Immediately after the war we could have started to negotiate with the Palestinians, have offered them a solution. We could have offered them national independence at that time. I think that the moment this was not done we lost everything. That failure made us what we are now; a colonialistic society. (pp. 25, 54)

Joshua Sobol and Clive Sinclair, in an interview in Index on Censorship, *Vol. 14, No. 1, February, 1985, pp. 24-5, 54.*

GARY HEISSERER

Joshua Sobol's **Ghetto** . . . is an important contribution to the growing number of plays addressing the complex issues of the Jewish Holocaust. The play is based on the history of Lithuania's Vilna ghetto and explores the nature and potential for moral action by Jews who face the grim reality of ghetto existence.

Although many types of responses are theatrically catalogued in Sobol's play, the central conflict emerges between the course of "resistance" offered by Jacob Gens, the ghetto Chief of Police and most powerful Jew in Vilna, and Hermann Kruk, the ghetto librarian. Gens's response demonstrates a willingness to sacrifice some of the population in order to prolong the life of the ghetto's remaining inhabitants. This plan involves assisting in the selection of those to be executed in the neighboring woods of Ponar, as well as the attempt to make the ghetto economically vital to the Germans through efficient industry. In contrast Kurk attempts to apply the ancient lesson of Maimonides, maintaining that if necessary, all must be sacrificed to save the life of a single Jew. Kruk thus refuses to accept the authority of the *Judenrat,* and looks to the resistance of the underground. *Ghetto* . . . effectively argues the integrity and moral courage of both men, but perhaps more importantly, suggests the profound complexity of the decisions these men were forced to consider. (p. 477)

[Sobol's play possesses] an extraordinary theatricality. *Ghetto* is a memory play and Srulik, the sole survivor of a ghetto theatre company, looks back from his Tel Aviv apartment in the present and attempts to recreate in imagination the final performance of his troupe. As this internal play is actually a history of his company involving satirical production numbers from its repertoire, *Ghetto* in effect frequently operates as a play within a play within a play. The production's theatricality was evidenced by the presence of a small jazz ensemble, tango dancing, larger-than-life size puppets of the play's central characters, and a ventriloquist with a human "dummy." This broad visual style was reflected in . . . scenery that presented a montage of images both organically related to the specific action of the play as well as deeply rooted in Holocause iconography. . . . [The] montage included a silhouette view of the Ponar woods at the rear of the stage, several hangman's nooses suspended behind a high and snow-decked wall of the ghetto, a large library shelf of books used by Kruk, and most importantly, an enormous center-stage pile of clothing rising approximately ten feet in the air. Although this clothing belonged to those who were killed or wounded, and thus invoked a powerful quantitative image of death, it was also an important symbol of life and hope in a ghetto whose "livelihood" was dependent upon clothing to launder and mend. This collection of scenic images, juxtaposed with the stage action placed amidst them, often gave the production a strong expressionistic quality, a theatrical style obviously well-suited to reflect the horror of a nightmare reality.

It was, however, in the character of the S.S. officer Kittel . . . that the audience was confronted with the most striking images in the production. Kittel, historically brought to the ghetto shortly before its demise in 1943, and who came to Vilna with a reputation for liquidating ghettos, is present from the outset of the play's action in 1942. Kittel becomes quickly fascinated by the ghetto troupe, for he too fancies himself an artist. His particular artistic passion is jazz, forbidden as culturally contaminating by the Nazis, and it was the image of Kittel with his saxophone, singing, dancing, and playing Gershwin's "Swanee" with the ghetto actors and musicians that constituted the most powerful visual scene in the production. This image was of great importance for we saw in Kittel not a meticulous bureaucratic craftsman, but rather an ardent "liquidation specialist" whose approach toward atrocity most closely resembled the jazz he admired; it was free-form, improvisational, and highly-spirited.

It is possible, however, that the character of Kittel may be too powerful for the play in which he has been placed. It seems that the primary thematic focus—the complex nature of the choices facing the Jews in this ghetto environment, and their struggle to maintain their integrity, their "soul," and their lives—too often became overshadowed by the presence of this powerful character. Consequently . . . , it was Kittel, in his black S.S. uniform, carrying saxophone in one hand and submachine gun in the other, who claimed what in my assessment was a disproportionately large theatrical space. Even at the end of the play, when the memory form used by Sobol would seem to suggest a return to the present and to Srulik as narrator, and thus to the central question regarding Jewish survival and its cost, Kittel instead was given the final moment when he gunned down the Ghetto Troupe from atop the clothing heap. As a result the enduring images of this rich visual production too often centered on the perpetrator, and not the victims of the suffering.

This objection notwithstanding . . . , Sobol's *Ghetto* honored with distinction what is the implicit but elusive mandate of Holocaust art, namely, the imagistic recreation of a history whose reality some claim exceeds our capacity to imagine it. (pp. 477-78)

Gary Heisserer, in a review of "Ghetto," in Theatre Journal, *Vol. 38, No. 4, December, 1986, pp. 477-78.*

MARCIA J. WADE

Turning forty: perhaps no other act symbolizes the sober passage into the acceptance of limitation. This fall, a four-city tour of Israel's internationally acclaimed Haifa Municipal Theatre and its provocative, controversial production of Joshua Sobol's *The Soul of a Jew* offers American theater audiences a rare opportunity to see a remarkably similar process at work in a culture. Part of a year-long round of performance tours, residencies, festivals, and conferences organized . . . to commemorate the fortieth anniversary of the founding of the Jewish State, the Haifa Theatre's tour will doubtless generate heated debate in this country as well. The author of *Ghetto* and *The Wars of the Jews,* presents in *The Soul of a Jew* a man who believes "Women and Jews are zeros. But at least women believe in men. Jews don't believe in anything."

The company has cut its teeth on controversy, from 1972, when Moshe Dayan walked out of a performance of Hannoch Levin's biting satire *The Queen of the Bathtub,* to 1988, when Sobol's *Jerusalem Syndrome* . . . incited a demonstration that delayed its curtain ninety minutes while five hundred police struggled with the angry crowd ouside. (p. 37)

[With *The Soul of a Jew*] Americans will see just what it is about the Haifa Theatre that stirs up storms. A searing examination of Jewish conflict and angst, it is a memory play, in which Sobol has reconstructed the last night of Otto Weininger. Hitler called the brilliant, virulently misogynist and anti-Semitic young turn-of-the-century Jewish author of *Sex and Character* "my favorite Jew." In Sobol's work, we meet him on the evening he has rented the room in which Beethoven died seventy-six years earlier, in order to take his own life at the age of twenty-three. Against the rich backdrop of fin-de-siecle Vienna, the central figures in Weininger's life, from

Freud and Strindberg to friends and family members, to his own shadowy (and female) Double, parade through the small room.

The Soul of a Jew lays bare the inner conflict of a man who saw his own life, and that of his people as an irreconcilable struggle between contradictory principles: The law-creating reason which Weininger identified with Aryanism and the masculine, and the irrational, destructive chaos he saw in both Judaism and the feminine.

Volatile subject matter for an embattled country, and the censure it attracted is not surprising. Why, many detractors wondered, revive the ghost of a traitor? The Haifa Rabbinate denounced the work, first performed in October 1982, as "full of blasphemy and deformity, depravity and Jewish self-hatred." But it had more than three hundred stagings in Israel alone, and has drawn wide acclaim abroad. . . . "When I wrote it, I could hardly understand what I was doing," comments Sobol. . . . Seven years after the summer he sat down and penned *The Soul of a Jew* in three weeks, he says he realizes that he was exploring "what it means to be a victim of hatred, the ways one interiorizes it and becomes one's own enemy." The work's relentless, painful probing of the internal dynamics of self-hatred is, he believes, the reason for the attacks as well as the acclaim *The Soul of a Jew* has elicited.

Israeli literature has been increasingly preoccupied with questions of ideology and their psychological underpinnings over the last two decades. Sobol's career itself exemplifies a national trend. A member of Kibbutz Shamir from 1957 to 1965, he wrote fiction before going to Paris to study philosophy at the Sorbonne. He returned to Israel in the early seventies and became involved with the directors, writers, and actors of the Haifa Theatre. The company was struggling, Sobol says, "to come to grips with our reality." The crucial and decisive issues facing the nation, they felt, "had been abandoned to the newspapers, and given only superficial treatment. We thought that exactly by dealing with these topics we might come to grips with our reality." . . .

Eventually Sobol's own dramatic explorations took a backward turn, becoming a search for the origins of the conflicts facing the young nation. He found himself in turn-of-the-century Vienna. While he exhaustively researched Weininger's life and read everything he could on the fin-de-siecle Austrian milieu, Sobol soon realized that "I was writing about myself. It opened me up." Examining a subject matter so far removed in time and place from the circumstances of his own life, he explains, "helped me lose my defenses."

Audiences throughout Israel and Europe found themselves responding in a similar manner. "In a curious way," Sobol comments, "Otto Weininger is talking about us, about our anxieties today in Israel. He touches an insecurity." The twisted genius the playwright believes, touches a level of the national psyche "menaced by destruction—not from the outside, but from the inside. In the last ten years it's become very clear that dangerous forces are acting from within."

While writing the play, Sobol says he could not shake a terrible sense of foreboding that something tragic was about to happen. Shortly before *The Soul of a Jew* opened, Israel invaded Lebanon. "When the war broke out, Begin kept repeating, in order to justify it, 'What if Hitler was hiding in a shelter in Beirut? What would we do?' " Sobol sees Begin as a figure "manipulated by history," and the foreign policy he has

pursued as one in which the Jewish people "are not controlling history. We are not pulling the strings."

Controlling one's destiny, Sobol maintains, remains an impossibility for a person or a people until the shadowy forces of self-hatred and compulsion are pulled from the unconscious into the light. His own sober analysis of Israeli culture is that it has in recent months, become increasingly unwilling to do so. "The readiness to take responsibility and to think has diminished. People started to refuse to see what was on television, to read what was in the papers. They drew down a curtain, not wanting to know what was going on." He points to the violent reaction to the recent performances of *The Jerusalem Syndrome* by the press, political authorities, and the audiences. "A hundred to one hundred and fifty members of every audience would leave, shouting and cursing," he recalls. "Yet the play was not more provocative than the others" he's written for the company. "Something has changed." . . .

"My country is divided into two camps," Sobol offers. "On the one hand, there is a tendency to get in touch with ourselves and our motivations. But the culture is young. Everything calling for that kind of connection is threatening. Many writers, and poets are making a serious effort to create this kind of context. But it brings about a hostile reaction from those who are not ready for it." Nonetheless, the playwright believes "our future lies in our capacity to understand ourselves and our history." (p. 38)

Marcia J. Wade, "Soul in Conflict," in Horizon: The Magazine of the Arts, *Vol. XXXI, No. 8, October, 1988, pp. 37-8.*

CLIVE BARNES

Never understimate man's inhumanity to man, whether that inhumanity occurs in Central Park or in a Lithuanian ghetto. The savagery beneath the skin is still the mark of Cain, still the atavistic remembrance of tribes past.

What was horrific about the German solution to their self-styled Jewish problem during the days and years of Germany's Nazi philosophy was the coolness of its reasoning, the scientific deliberation of its execution.

This was violence by government, not by mob—this was genocide authenticated by law. Such cruelty was not unknown. Racism in general and anti-Semitism in particular was scarcely a novelty, but never before, at least not since Europe's Dark Ages, had it been so cynically validated and politically esteemed.

It is this horror—the sense of bureaucratic murder and orderly extinction—that comes over so strongly in Joshua Sobol's splendid, moving and provocative play *Ghetto*. . . .

The play, and its story, are painful, but this is not just a scream of agony from a dark place we are now only too anxious to forget.

Such a scream might be relevant, might even be timely, but screaming is not to Sobol's purpose. He has not written a play just about Germany's Nazi philosophy of murder, or even the political machinery and human madness behind it.

Death and genocide are made the backdrop, the practical environment, of a play about history, choice, expediency and morality. And, of course, survival—the survival of the human spirit, Abel's only revenge.

The play is subtitled "The Last Performance in the Vilna Ghetto," and it is nominally about a theatrical troupe that actually existed in the Vilna Ghetto under Lithuania's Nazi occupation, starting in September 1941 to its liquidation . . . two years later.

Life in the Ghetto—briefly caught as it was between the punctuation points of the death warrant and the firing squad—had to acquire a semblance of normality.

The Jews were eventually given some limited measure of self-government—there was a Jewish police, even a Jewish administration.

The deaths were constant—Jews being transported to the labor camps, or simply taken out into the woods and shepherded by bullets into mass graves.

Yet there were schools, and there were hospitals, there was even a library. And there was a theater company—which is itself the stage, or trampoline, for Sobol's play.

All drama, when you come to think of it, is about choice. And the precarious choices of the moral acrobats in the ghetto—those final fiddlers on a burning roof—were complex beyond the scope of morality.

Should one rebel, or should one bargain? If one rebelled, what would be the eventual consequences? If one bargained, how much survival was worth how much compromise . . . ?

To collaborate with the devil to buy time and bodies, more practical issues arise. Life-saving drugs are short—should they be issued fairly so that all die equally, or should the stronger, with best chance of life, be favored? The questions of survival never ceased.

Sobol has theatricalized this fragmentary morality play with great skill. He constructs it almost as scenes from this expressionist Vilna cabaret, remembered in the embroidered imagination of its sole survivor, its artistic director, a ventriloquist called Srulik.

Srulik, and his dummy, who had the satirical courage and license to shout out against the oppressors, and Kruk, the librarian who keeps a journal of these plague years, are, like the admired cabaret singer Hayyah, the oddly matched proponents of Jewish culture.

In the political arena are matched Kittel, the Nazi commandant, a smooth-snarling sadist who plays the saxophone and has leanings towards "degenerate" art, the Jewish Administrator, Gens, a master of compromise tempted by power, and Weiskopf, a Jewish capitalist governed by greed but a useful parasite.

I called this a drama about choice, it is also a play about juggling. Sobol juggles his issues and techniques of politics and art, morals and dialogue, character and characters with considerable skill.

These sharp-etched vignettes—Jews being compelled to plunder the clothes of their murdered brethren, or a ghastly party held at the jack-boot whim of the Nazi boss, even the inevitability of the final slaughter—are kept highly theatrical. . . .

[*Ghetto* is a] play of questions—and the answers, like this moving play itself, are very much worth your time.

Clive Barnes, "A Scream in the Dark," in New York Post, *May 1, 1989.*

FRANK RICH

At the bare minimum, dramatic works about the Holocaust have an obligation to restore vivid immediacy to horrors that scoundrels and the passing of time would have the world forget. As presented in good conscience but with scant competence . . . , Joshua Sobol's *Ghetto* is too lifeless to meet this minimal requirement. A tedious stage treatment of the Holocaust, however well intentioned, is a trivialization of the Holocaust. One need only look at all the dozing faces in the audience to see that *Ghetto* is aiding rather than combating historical amnesia.

Presumably something has happened to Mr. Sobol's play on its circuitous route from Israel to New York. *Ghetto* has received acclaim on several continents in other stagings. . . .

[In the present production, a] highly viable dramatic idea has been buried beneath the wreckage. Using a mixture of fact and justifiable poetic license, Mr. Sobol tells the story of the theater that incongruously flourished in the ghetto of Vilna, Lithuania, from 1942 to 1943. Though *Ghetto* takes place a few weeks after a majority of Vilna's 70,000 residents had been exterminated by the Nazis, the remaining Jews still "put on their finery and come to the show." Why? Mr. Sobol sees the survival of the theater at Vilna as a testament to the perseverance of the human spirit in the face of unfathomable evil and certain doom.

The point is well taken, but the dramatization of it is diffuse. *Ghetto* frequently breaks down into predictable soliloquies delivered by stereotyped ghetto residents. There's an austere socialist librarian who reads his diary entries to the recorded accompaniment of a pecking typewriter; an oily, ranting entrepreneur who puts his own survival before his community's, and the German-appointed Jewish leader who endlessly attempts to square his conscience with his collaborationist expediencies. The minor figures are even more anonymous. . . .

To an extent, *Ghetto* aspires to be a musical in the Brecht-Weill mode. Songs that survived Vilna's liquidation are intermingled with the dialogue scenes, both as ironic commentary and as a simulation of the shows presented in the ghetto. But this promising format is destroyed by the seeming arbitrariness of the songs' placement. . . .

Though it's to be assumed that Mr. Sobol's play would have more heft in a better production, some of the writing gives one pause. In David Lan's translation, at least, *Ghetto* is a fount of clichéd rhetoric, with speeches often beginning with constructions like "No one has the moral authority to decide . . ." and "History will judge . . ." Theatergoers can't be blamed if they tune out before the end of such sentences, or if they refuse to pay diligent attention to canned debates about the nature of art or the validity of the resistance movement. . . .

Ghetto is almost perverse in its ability to make the true nightmare of our century ring completely false.

Frank Rich, "Sobol's 'Ghetto,' a Holocaust Drama

with Music," in The New York Times, May 1, 1989,
p. C11.

PETER SHERWOOD

The theatre and the Final Solution have been uneasy bedfellows for more than a generation. His chance (re)discovery that they were by no means so at the time—the Warsaw ghetto, for example, had no less than five permanent theatres, as well as three choirs and a philharmonic orchestra—has given Joshua Sobol . . . a potent and apposite format for treating still problematic issues of the links of the Jewish past with the Israeli present.

Based on extensive research into the surprisingly rich record, [*Ghetto*] is organized around the hugely popular ghetto theatre of Vilno (to Germans and Poles Wilna, now the Lithuanian Vilnius) during the bleak days of 1942-3, when neither players nor audience knew if they would live to see the next show. With its selection of the troupe's songs . . . and fragmentary routines culminating in a virulent parody of a Nazi rally, *Ghetto* is certainly a worthy tribute to that theatre and its players. Sobol's virtuoso exploitation of the full panoply of theatrical device and techniques in dealing with a "difficult" subject continually invites us to celebrate theatre itself, as a life-affirming and life-enhancing bearer of culture triumphant over barbarism, evil and death.

No less persuasive is the presentation of moral issues. Anticipating divisions soon to resurface in Israel, several ghetto inhabitants skilfully present their case. The belief of the Socialist Kruk, ghetto librarian and diarist, in total resistance to the Germans is symbolized by his slogan "no theatre in a graveyard". Weiskopf the tailor makes a fortune out of repairing torn and bloody clothing, both Nazi and Jewish; well, why should the money go to some German, and don't you see, it's just *clothes?* Gens, chief of the ghetto's Jewish Police, carries out the Germans' orders, grimly accepting the label of collaborator in order to save lives whenever he can haggle with the SS officer Kittel, a saxophone-and-sub-machine-gun-toting young psychopath at whose whim the ghetto lives and dies. Though Sobol's sympathies clearly lie with Gens, most positions are convincingly argued; but doubts creep in when the necessary transformation from well-documented historical figure to representative of a particular moral stance sometimes gives a character a two-dimensional feel, as though merely an argument in Sobol's thesis.

In fact, the brilliance of the theatre topos and the outstanding professionalism of the writing have succeeded too well and kept not just emotionality but often even emotion at a safe distance. For example, the scene in which actors from the troupe, dressed as rabbi, judge and doctor, present the ethical dilemma posed by the ghetto hospital's limited stock of insulin is technically flawless, but it alienates at the emotional level through its format and its ridiculing of both rabbi and judge. Other dramatically effective scenes also seem designed to keep emotional triggers out of reach: the only children in the play are shown in silhouette behind a white screen; a perfunctory love interest is mediated by a life-size ventriloquist's dummy . . .; in the ghetto of a historic centre of traditional Judaism the only religious Jew depicted is a palm-reading charlatan.

That Israel is different is, of course, one of the points Sobol is making through his play; and what could be seen as over-

cautiousness on the banks of the Thames may well be no more than necessary prudence on a Mediterranean shore. Here, one can say only. that . . . the unexpected injection of pure schmaltz into a finale quite altered from David Lan's English text merely serves to point up the emotional insecurity of a play that is perhaps too easy to admire.

Peter Sherwood, "Going Dark," in The Times Literary Supplement, No. 4493, May 12-18, 1989, p. 514.

JOHN SIMON

Irresistible to drama lovers is a play that conjures up a fateful meeting between theater and history, as happens in *Hamlet*, Schnitzler's *The Green Cockatoo*, Günter Grass's *The Plebeians Rehearse the Uprising*. Such a play—with the added poignance of being based on fact—is Joshua Sobol's *Ghetto.* The Israeli playwright's 1983 work concerns the theater company that thrived in the Vilna ghetto during World War II under the ambiguous patronage of Kittel, the Nazi commandant, who, as saxophone player and art lover, encouraged the enterprise out of a mixture of connoisseurship and sadism.

The distinguished Yiddish theater of the Lithuanian capital had been disbanded long before. More recently, the Jewish population of 70,000 had been reduced by mass murder to 16,000. But, herded into the wartime ghetto, some gifted surviving actors, to keep life and hope going, put on a varied repertoire for SRO audiences of Jews, Germans, and Lithuanians. As the Russian armies approached, the Jews of Vilna, actors and nonactors alike, were liquidated along with Jacob Gens, the pragmatic Nazi-appointed Jewish ghetto overseer, who had saved—as well as, perforce, doomed—so many of them. From the few survivors' stories and such documents as the diary of Kruk, the Socialist ghetto librarian, the Vilna ghetto's swan song is reconstructed here—partly remembered, partly fantasized by Srulik, the surviving ventriloquist and director of that theater, whose every performance was potentially its last. Its plays and players perished, but its songs, used in *Ghetto,* survived, as did its legendary gallantry.

Sobol has the right idea: The super- and subhumanly monstrous cannot be tackled head-on. Hence he uses bits of absurdism (a ventriloquist's dummy with a life of its own), Brechtian alienation (the song numbers), Expressionism (the German army as a set of giant, seemingly uninhabited uniforms doing a dance of death), Pirandellism (a play within a play). But he doesn't use these devices enough; too much naturalism remains. Stylization and realism get into each other's hair and rebuke rather than reinforce each other.

There were two other factions in the Vilna ghetto or just outside it: the underground and a passive-resistance party; their interaction with the Nazis, Jews, and Jewish police is insufficiently examined. On the other hand, there are more principal characters than the author can fully humanize in his limited time. Weiskopf—the tailor turned entrepreneur who finds a way of saving some fellow Jews while indecently enriching himself—is conveyed adequately. But Hayyah, the beautiful singer-entertainer who becomes one of Kittel's chief antagonists, is not explored fully enough, neither are Kruk and Gens, whose antithetical modes of resistance—defying the devil and bargaining with him—must have taken a toll on them, underdeveloped here.

The Nazi officer, although verging on cliché, perhaps doesn't require further analysis, though a major playwright could have managed even that. But Srulik, the director-ventriloquist, hardly exists apart from his Dummy, and that is a serious loss. Minor characters are indeed reduced to puppetlike stereotypes; worst of all, the writing hovers between the pedestrian and the serviceable—where only genius could do justice to the enormousness and enormity of the subject. Finally, for a play about the life-affirming value of theater in the shadow of death, *Ghetto* doesn't have enough of that theater in it. (p. 123)

John Simon, "The Uses of Fantasy," in New York Magazine, *Vol. 22, No. 20, May 15, 1989, pp. 123-25.*

LEONIE LICHTENSTEIN

[*Ghetto*] investigated the relationship in 1942 between Jewish actors and musicians in the ancient Vilna ghetto, and a sadistic *Gestapo* chief who himself has musical leanings of a psychopathic kind, such that his machine-gun, his saxophone, and his creatures—the actors and musicians in the ghetto—are all equal to him as instruments to play upon. *Ghetto* uses the theatre to show "how an entire community tried to cope at the time by doing the best they could to remain a community" as a form of resistance in the shadow of the Nazi Holocaust. It explored the sensitive issue of Jewish collaboration. . . .

The playwright is an Israeli who repudiates "the ghetto mentality", feeling that this matter must be aired "in front of the *goyim*", so to speak, because trust between nations can only be restored by telling a true story. It then becomes the audience's problem how to receive it without exploiting what it shows of Jewish imperfections.

Sobol's work has not always found favour among his primary audience in Israel. . . . [His] concern, not unlike that of former colonial peoples, is with the effect of the past on identity in the present: how can Israel today cope not only with the past genocide of Jews, but with millennia of humiliation? (Other plays by Sobol have confronted Jewish-Arab relations.)

In *Ghetto,* Sobol distinguishes between Dessler, a Jewish police officer and unregenerate opportunist who collaborates with his captors (those in contact with oppression risk contamination), and Gens, the Jewish head of the ghetto, who was an authentic Jewish leader confronted by agonising choices in trying to serve his community. Gens bargains with Kittel, the SS officer, his intention being to save Jews by sacrificing others; ultimately, he chooses to die with those he has sacrificed. It is his energy which transforms the actors by providing them with an opportunity to exercise their creativity once more, thereby also enabling them to acquire work permits and consequently to be—temporarily—among the living.

The moral question of choosing who shall die is early introduced through the device of the ventriloquist's dummy, a licensed Fool. When his master, the ventriloquist Srulik (the play's narrator), begs Kittel for Hayyah's life, appealing to him as an artist to spare another artist, the dummy asks, "What if she had lost her voice? Would she have no right to live?"

Elsewhere the question is addressed by doctors, a judge and a rabbi, who debate how the insufficient supplies of insulin shall be deployed. The painful subtlety with which choice is explored in this discussion is counterpoised in montage with the Nazi's easy order to kill every third child in a family. But Kittel, mad *and* bad (how else to treat Nazis?), is no simple stereotype. He too asks crucial questions. He does not simply hate Jews; he is interested in their contribution to German glory. And Sobol is interested in him, as Shakespeare is in Iago, but also in what it is that the world wants from Jews.

First performed in Haifa in 1984, the play has been staged all over the Western world, and won the 1985 German Critics Award for Best Foreign Play. Sobol's inspiration was the discovery of a document, a diary recording the opening of a theatre in Vilna in the midst of the Holocaust. The diary was kept by Kruk, the ghetto librarian—for the library is another structure which was kept alive in the midst of the Final Solution.

Kruk, a member of the socialist *Bund* which opposed the Zionist position espoused by Gens, was implacably opposed to dealing with the Germans in any way. He rejected "theatre in a graveyard" even if it might save Jewish lives. The play suggests that, more profoundly, theatre might stave off spiritual corruption by enabling the Jews to keep their culture alive. The German scholar Dr Paul is recognisably played by the same actor who plays Kittel, and indeed they share an intense interest in Jews. Ironically, it is Dr Paul who, knowledgeable in the Jewish culture he is committed to rooting out, questions Kruk about his anti-Zionism and tries unsuccessfully to tempt him to replace Gens as Jewish leader.

All these people actually existed, and most of them died. Srulik survived—Sobol found him living nearby, in Tel Aviv. *Ghetto* is in no sense a dramatisation of Kruk's diary, as in plays and films derived from *The Diary of Anne Frank;* but though not in documentary mode, it is, like the Holocaust itself, realistically surreal. Distancing techniques—such as direct address to the audience and the use, as a central structuring device, of a form of play (in which music and dance play a large part) within the "play" directed and stage-managed by the Nazi—are brilliantly used as artistic resources, but are also naturalised by Sobol.

The artists put on cabarets and satirical sketches and plays to divert Kittel in order to pay him for their lives. Hayyah is obliged to sing for him to pay for a 60 gramme shortfall in the dried beans discovered on her at the outset of the play. Kittel, a connoisseur of both art and murder, measures the value of each performance against her "debt". Though art and atrocity are brought dangerously close together, aesthetic considerations are not allowed to blur the moral landscape of the play. The use of theatrical illusion, particularly the brilliantly expressionistic dummy—which, a puppet and outside the action, is played by a live person and is finally killed off—is offset by the awareness that these were real-life performers who are now "the characters" of the play. The potentially startling incorporation of music and dance in the presence of death offers affirmation of the humanity of those exterminated.

In their play-acting while awaiting their deaths, the ghetto's inmates use the gigantic mound of clothing left behind by those already dispatched as their "dressing-up box", with the encouragement of the *Gestapo* chief. The clothing dominates the set, both as eloquent symbol and fact: it is recyclable waste, which Weiskopf, the Jewish tailor/entrepreneur, turns into a business venture. At the end of the play, articles detach themselves from the grotesque mound in disembodied fashion and perform like manipulated puppets. This metaphorical *danse macabre* is also a realistic device of the inmates, who are actually inside the gyrating clothes, to disguise from the *Gestapo* chief who is being entertained the fact that one of their troupe has escaped. They do not succeed.

The escaper is the singer Hayyah, an object of particular attraction to Kittel. She borrowed a Russian book from the library, with the help of which her group has blown up a train. The massed chorus in the final satirical revue (which plays on Shylock's "Hath not a Jew" speech) sports Hitler moustaches and sings Beethoven's "Ode to Joy". This is all highly diverting to the Nazi. He exclaims: "Your artistry has saved your lives." But he has discerned the absence of Hayyah and divined her part in the blowing up of the train, and enjoys the artistic symmetry of implementing the Jewish credo that "each Jew is responsible for all others", gunning them all down as they fall upon the ceremonial Jewish *challah* bread with which he pretends to reward them for their revue—having first terrorised them by "pretending" that he is going to have them shot. Hindsight hovers in the form of our knowledge—which was not fully available to a man like Gens—that there was no possibility of dealing with any Nazis, for none of them required any motive for killing Jews, even the "darlings" among them. (pp. 40-1)

Leonie Lichtenstein, "Rushdie, Steiner, Sobol & Others: Moral Boundaries," in Encounter, *Vol. LXXIII, No. 3, September-October, 1989, pp. 34-42.*

William Styron

1925-

(Born William Clark Styron, Jr.) American novelist, critic, editor, and dramatist.

Styron is often identified with the Southern Gothic tradition as exemplified by William Faulkner. Writing in a style that John W. Aldridge described as alternately "rich, reckless, bombastic, melodramatic, poetical, rhetorical, metaphorical, and sentimental," Styron addresses such typical concerns among Southern writers as mortality and the effect of the past on the present while broadening his regional emphasis to include world issues, foreign locales, and non-southern characters in his works. Although occasionally faulted for verbosity and didacticism, Styron has garnered consistent acclaim for his willingness to examine difficult subjects and for his intelligent treatment of such moral dualisms as love and hatred, honor and shame, pride and guilt, and compassion and cruelty.

Styron was born in Newport News, Virginia, the son of William Clark Styron, a shipyard engineer, and Pauline Styron (neé Abraham), a Pennsylvanian whose father served as a Confederate army officer in the Civil War. During World War II, Styron trained as a candidate for officer in the Marine Corps while attending Duke University in North Carolina. After graduating in 1947 and working briefly as an associate editor for McGraw-Hill, a publisher in New York City, Styron joined Hiran Haydn's writing course at the New School for Social Research and began his first novel, *Lie Down in Darkness*. Described by Styron as "a mirror of the family life I myself put up with," this semiautobiographical work received the Prix de Rome from the American Academy of Arts and Letters. Set in Virginia during World War II, *Lie Down in Darkness* uses interconnecting flashbacks to recreate events leading up to the funeral of Peyton Loftis, a young woman who has committed suicide resulting from family problems involving a devoted father for whom she harbored incestuous feelings and a hostile and uncaring mother. Although Peyton's suicide coincides with the explosion of the atomic bomb at Hiroshima, a sign of humanity's fall from innocence and of the mutual guilt of her family, Styron presents Peyton's death as a redemptive act: "we lie down in darkness, and have our light in ashes." While comparing Styron to such authors as F. Scott Fitzgerald and William Faulkner, critics agreed that he convincingly transcends the deterministic sense of fate that characterizes the works of these writers. John W. Aldridge asserted: "[*Lie Down in Darkness* is] a first novel containing some of the elements of greatness, one with which the work of no other young writer of 25 can be compared, and . . . [Styron] has done justice to the southern tradition from which his talent derives."

In 1951, Styron was recalled to the Marine Corps and served for a year during the Korean War. This experience indirectly informs *The Long March*, a novella first published in the periodical *Discovery* in 1953 and republished in book form in 1956. Set in a Marine boot camp in the Carolinas, *The Long March* dramatizes both the dignity and absurdity of a rebellious captain's attempts to expose the idiocy of militarism by exceeding the patriotic zeal of his superiors. Styron's next

work, *Set This House on Fire*, which appeared nearly a decade after his first, was received unenthusiastically by American critics. Set primarily in Italy, this work focuses on the moral dilemma of Cass Kinsolving, a gifted American artist suffering from a creative block, who ironically returns to mental health after overcoming moral reservations regarding his murder of Mason Flagg, an evil and sadistic man whom Marc L. Ratner described as "a personification of all the defects of an anti-human society." Although faulted in the United States as rhetorical and didactic, *Set This House on Fire* was commended by French critics for its evocative style, observations, and dialogue.

Styron received a Pulitzer Prize for *The Confessions of Nat Turner*, a controversial novel that he described as a "meditation on history" about the slave revolt that occurred in 1831 in Southampton County, Virginia. This uprising, organized by Nat Turner, an intelligent and charismatic black slave and preacher, resulted in the deaths of at least fifty-five whites and the retaliatory slayings of over two hundred blacks, many of whom were not involved in the rebellion. Narrating the book from Turner's perspective, Styron begins with his confession, which is based on a twenty-page pamphlet Turner dictated to lawyer Thomas Gray prior to his hanging and continues with Turner's autobiographical reminiscences. Rather than attempt to convey the scope and complexity of Turner's reflections in a representative dialect, Styron presents the novel's narrative in the lush, intricate idiom of the Victorian novel. Although greeted with praise by such established critics as Alfred Kazin and Philip Rahv, *The Confessions of Nat Turner* aroused furious reactions from black leaders, critics, and intellectuals. In the essays collected by scholar John E. Clarke in *William Styron's "Nat Turner": Ten Black Writers Respond* (1968), Styron is variously charged with addressing a topic inappropriate to the experience of a white liberal southerner, with distorting historical fact, and with portraying Turner as an indecisive and neurotic amalgam of black stereotypes. In response, Styron and his defenders asserted that the book was not intended to portray Turner as an infallible hero; rather, he is meant to be a complex and tragic figure susceptible to human foibles and errors.

Styron's next novel, *Sophie's Choice,* is set primarily in the Brooklyn borough of New York City following World War II. This work, for which Styron received an American Book Award, portrays the coming of age of Stingo, a young Virginian who attains adulthood through his involvement with Sophie, a Polish gentile who survived the concentration camps of Nazi Germany but lost two of her children to her persecutors. Juxtaposed with Sophie's recollections of Nazi Germany is her relationship with a Jewish lover, Nathan, a brilliant but disturbed native New Yorker whose guilt over avoiding the Nazi past leads him to punish Sophie for having survived the concentration camps. Although some reviewers faulted Styron for examining a topic foreign to his experience, most concurred with Robert Towers: "The question is not whether Styron has a right to use alien experiences but whether his novel proves that he knows what he is writing about. In this instance, the overriding answer is yes."

In addition to his fiction, Styron has also written *In the Clap Shack,* a comic drama set in the urological ward of an American Navy hospital during World War II. *This Quiet Dust and Other Writings,* a collection of book reviews, essays, and other pieces published primarily during the 1960s and 1970s, features Styron's views on such topics as politics, the South, the military, and Nazi atrocities. A fellow at Silliman College, Yale University, Styron has served as an advisory editor of *The Paris Review,* as a member on the editorial board of *The American Scholar,* and as an Honorary Consultant in American Letters to the Library of Congress.

(See also *CLC,* Vols. 1, 3, 5, 11, 15; *Contemporary Authors,* Vols. 5-8, rev. ed.; *Contemporary Authors New Revision Series,* Vol. 6; *Dictionary of Literary Biography,* Vol. 2; and *Dictionary of Literary Biography Yearbook: 1980.*)

PRINCIPAL WORKS

NOVELS

Lie Down in Darkness   1951
Set This House on Fire   1960
The Confessions of Nat Turner   1967
Sophie's Choice   1979

OTHER

The Long March   1953   (novella)
In the Clap Shack   1972   (play)
This Quiet Dust and Other Writings   1982   (criticism)

THOMAS R. EDWARDS

This Quiet Dust, a collection of essays, reviews and occasional pieces mostly written during the 1960's and 70's, is William Styron's first book of nonfiction. The current novelists who are masters of nonfiction—Mailer, Vidal, Didion and the rest—needn't feel threatened. Mr. Styron's comments on literature are modest and unsurprising; his views of life, often eloquent and always decent-minded, seldom push us to the brink of a new understanding. This is, as the author says in a prefatory note, "a very personal book," and as such, despite its limitations, it holds considerable interest for readers of Mr. Styron's novels.

There are direct accounts here of the writing of *Lie Down in Darkness* and *The Long March,* vignettes of the youth in Tidewater Virginia that he shares with so many of his fictional characters, recurrent musings on the materials of his novels—war and the military mind (*The Long March*), American slavery (*The Confessions of Nat Turner*), the Nazi death camps (*Sophie's Choice*). There are essays, more elegiac than critical, on writers he learned from—Wolfe, Fitzgerald, Faulkner—and elegantly chiseled appreciations of literary friends, often in the form of funeral addresses. The volume draws its title from one of Emily Dickinson's fine mortuary verses—"This quiet dust was Gentlemen and Ladies, / And Lads and Girls; / Was laughter and ability and sighing, / And frocks and curls"—and in it one comes to see more clearly that death and loss are Mr. Styron's major subjects, nostalgia or grief the moods that most powerfully stir his rhetorical powers.

One also sees that his powers *are* largely rhetorical, that he often calls on eloquence and passion to do the work of thought. In an angry piece, for example, on the Democratic convention of 1968 and its attendant horrors, he calls Mayor Daley's brutality

> the triumphant end product of his style, and what else might one expect from this squalid person . . . howling "Kike!" at Abe Ribicoff, packing the galleries with his rabble, and muttering hoarse irrelevancies about conspiracy and assassination.
>
> (p. 9)

The vocabulary and tone of such a passage uncomfortably suggest that moral decisions are being derived from social or esthetic, not intellectual, discriminations, and a similar voice is raised against another figure who deserves the most intelligent censure possible, Lieut. William Calley of the Mylai massacre. For Mr. Styron, Lieutenant Calley is "fly-blown," "banal," "stunted in mind and body," "dreary," "loutish," "rancid," "charmless"—one of those products of bad genes and bad schooling, evidently, who are just not our sort at all. Mr. Styron's condescension obscures what is surely the most awful meaning of Lieutenant Calley's case, that he is just enough *like* the rest of us to be terrifying.

The person, or persons, projected by these "personal" writings is, however, not a simple one. Though Mr. Styron's qualities include certitude about his own values, a certain stiffness of manner and an unawareness of, or indifference to, his effect on another mind—an outlook, in short, for which the kindest word would be "aristocratic"—he is also anxious to serve humane causes (witness the moving and troubling pieces about convicts, guilty and innocent), to unpuzzle the complexities of social and moral justice, to express love and admiration for friends.

This is in many ways an appealing literary presence, perhaps all the more so for the problems Mr. Styron has in living up to his own best intentions. In a recent essay about a voyage up the Nile, for example, he worries about our passion for tourism, which may ruin the world by looking at it too hard. It is indeed depressing to hear that the temples and tombs of the Pharaohs are being damaged by the dust raised by tourist feet and the carbon dioxide exuded by sightseers who *will* (curse them!) persist in breathing. Yet, of course, Egypt needs tourist money, and, of course, one can't fully appreciate such a danger without going there, as Mr. Styron did, breathing and raising a little dust oneself, joining in the "aimless proliferation" of man's "own peripatetic self" that he so deplores.

Another writer might have made comedy of these cross-purposes. He observes the "bloated" boats in which hoteliers ship hordes of tourists up to Aswan, eroding the river banks all the while. Mr. Styron, however, travels on a smaller, more seemly craft . . . as the guest of Prince Sadruddin Aga Khan, along with such as Arthur Miller and Prince Nicholas Romanoff. And with only 13 in the party (there was a crew of 20 to care for them), it hardly seems like tourism at all. But Mr. Styron's sense of such ironies leads him, not to comedy, and certainly not to the international politics that concerns most travelers in the Middle East in the 1980's, but to a rich descriptive rhetoric appropriate to the pages of *Geo* magazine, where the article first appeared. . . . I find this insouciant fusing of Burton Holmes travelogue and S. J. Perelman rather breathtaking and admirable.

If Mr. Styron were more interested in self-questioning or self-mockery, these subjects would afford appropriate occasions. One of his worst moments at the Chicago convention came when Gov. Richard J. Hughes of New Jersey called him "Mr. Michener" in a Credentials Committee hearing. He wonders why Thomas Wolfe, unweaned until 3½ and unshorn until 9, didn't become homosexual. Answering the charges that *Nat Turner* ignored the work of black historians, he loftily asks, "When were writers of historical novels obligated in any way to acknowledge the work of historians?" And yet a few pages later he complains about two subsequent historical works that "studiously avoided all mention of my work." (Are historians obligated to acknowledge the work of novelists?) He then complains that one of the historians in question *did* mention his novel but in a "reductive way."

Upset by a foolish enough question on a TV talk show about why non-Jews should be concerned about the Holocaust, he points out that "vast numbers of gentiles" also died in the camps. Is *this* why gentiles should be concerned? Digging his hole deeper, he also argues that Auschwitz was not just a killing ground but also a seriously meant, if badly botched, attempt to put slave labor to productive economic use; the point permits a connection with another favorite theme, slavery in America, but I don't see how this clarifies the moral significance of the Holocaust.

But if *This Quiet Dust* is stronger on feeling than on thought, its heart is usually in the right place. These writings don't tell us as much as they might about the world, but they tell a good deal about William Styron and about the novels—often loose and murky but illuminated by flashes of impressive passion and humanity—that remain his chief claim on our attention. (pp. 9, 40-1)

Thomas R. Edwards, "Rhetoric Doing the Work of Thought," in The New York Times Book Review, *November 21, 1982, pp. 9, 40-1.*

JONATHAN YARDLEY

The three dozen essays and book reviews [collected in *This Quiet Dust and Other Writings*] are William Styron's occasional writings, the work to which he turns in order to divert and refresh his mind while more substantial enterprises are under way. Collected, they add up to what Styron describes as "a very personal book," in that "virtually all of the pieces are the offshoot of either my occasional crotchets or perennial preoccupations." Predictably, therefore, the themes upon which Styron dwells in these oddments of literary journalism . . . are the same ones that he has concentrated on in his long, passionate novels; though many of the essays are attractive and interesting, and all are most powerfully written, the overall impression they create is of a writer working in a medium in which he is less than comfortable.

What readers will find in *This Quiet Dust* is a large sampling of Styron's distinctive, arresting prose that manages to disguise the rather small body of ideas it discusses. At portraiture and landscape Styron has scarcely a rival, and when he summons himself to produce oceans of rolling paragraphs he can positively drown the reader in emotion; his tools are those of the novelist, and no American now living is capable of employing them to more stunning effect. But like the novelists to whom he is perhaps most usefully compared— Faulkner and Fitzgerald—he is more gifted at narrative than analysis; he speaks with striking force, but he does not always have that much to say.

This is not, in point of fact, a pejorative comment; ideas are not what we look for from novelists. The experimentalists and the academics notwithstanding, the novelist's task is to describe and reveal the world, to find coherence in human experience at whatever scale he chooses; with the rarest of exceptions, the "novel of ideas" is by its very nature a failure, because it invariably deprives fiction of the vitality that is its essence. To say that Styron is short on original and arresting ideas is not to say that he has an unoriginal or uninteresting mind, but that his strengths lie elsewhere.

Styron's essays on capital punishment are cases in point. The first of these, **"The Death-in-Life of Benjamin Reid,"** was originally published in 1962 and apparently played a significant role in the subsequent commutation of the death sentence of its subject, a Connecticut man of exceedingly limited education and opportunity who had killed a person in a moment of panic.

It is a pity that Styron chose to include this contemptible essay in the collection, for it nearly poisons everything around it. But immediately thereafter Styron dismounts from his high horse and returns to the business at which he is best. In a section called "Portraits and Farewells" he pays tribute to a number of literary figures who have influenced his life. These include the great teacher of writing at Duke University, William Blackburn, and, somewhat surprisingly but most agreeably, Philip Rahv:

> Strangers often found it hard to understand how one could become a good friend of this brusque, scowling, saturnine, sometimes impolite man with his crotchets and fixations, his occasional savage

outbursts and all the other idiosyncrasies he shared with Dr. Johnson. But I found it easy to be Philip's friend. For one thing, I was able almost constantly to relish his rage, which was a well-earned rage inasmuch as he was an erudite person—learned in the broadest sense of the word, with a far-ranging knowledge that transcended the strictly literary— and thus was supremely confident to sniff out fools. I discovered it to be a cleansing rage, this low, guttural roar directed at the frauds and poseurs of literature.

There is also much in *This Quiet Dust,* as would be expected, about Styron's native South and the many ways in which it has influenced his work. . . . It's a powerful piece; indeed, Styron confesses that if anything the writing now seems to him "overwrought." But this highly charged prose masks the predictability of Styron's arguments. Though he makes the usual and unexceptionable points in opposition to the death penalty, he simply does not demonstrate that capital punishment "is one of the few moral issues about which it is almost impossible to harbor mixed feelings, at least after one has studied the matter carefully," as he claims in a preface to the essay.

The same objections must be raised against Styron's occasional ventures into political commentary. In some cases he is either naive or ill-informed, as when he claims that "in the horrible dark night of racism at its worst in America, the 1930s, the Communists were among the few friends black people had." In others he is blinded by the emotions that surge through and about him. His piece on the 1968 Democratic Convention is a chaotic mixture of righteous passion and snobbery. . . .

All of these pieces are quite lovely and often nostalgic, but never sentimental or, in the familiar Southern manner, evasive; it is precisely because Styron has been willing to engage the harsh truths of Southern history that he has written about the region's past and present with such deep understanding.

Although Styron takes obvious pride in the pieces he has collected here, there is little evidence that he assigns most of them greater weight than they can hold. That is as it should be. The best of these essays are very good, but they bear only a passing resemblance to the novels that have been the true work of his life. His admirers, among whom I wish to be numbered, will be happy to have *This Quiet Dust* in the absence of something more substantial; but no one is likely to mistake it for the real thing.

> Jonathan Yardley, "Styron's Choice: Essays from Three Decades," in Book World—The Washington Post, *December 5, 1982, p. 3.*

MICHIKO KAKUTANI

As he struggles to write his first novel, Stingo, the young hero of *Sophie's Choice,* dreams of becoming "a writer—a writer with the same ardor and the soaring wings of the Melville or the Flaubert or the Tolstoy or the Fitzgerald who had the power to rip my heart out and keep a part of it and who each night, separately and together, were summoning me to their incomparable vocation." Stingo, of course, is an autobiographical version of his creator—a portrait of the author as a young man, innocent of history and hungry for artistry and fame—and, at 57, William Styron himself has now spent some three decades working at that vocation. . . .

"I feel I'm at a good point," he says.

> I feel healthier than I did years ago when I was drinking a lot, and I think I can write with somewhat more ease than I could long ago. Looking back, I think I see a growth and maturation— certainly in my style. What I'm saying is I think the style of a book like *Sophie's Choice* shows a kind of serenity that my earlier work does not have, and in that sense I'm pleased. It's the quality of not calling attention to one's own language. It was also very, very good to feel such a sense of having written a book that sort of worked on all the levels one wished it to work on and in these various incarnations.

Certainly one of the incarnations Mr. Styron is referring to is the movie version of *Sophie's Choice,* starring Meryl Streep, Kevin Kline and Peter MacNicol. . . . As readers of the novel recall, *Sophie's Choice* concerns the friendship that develops between Stingo and a couple he meets one summer in New York: Sophie, a beautiful but haunted survivor of Auschwitz, and Nathan, her darkly charming lover. (p. 3)

[Although Mr. Styron asserted that *Sophie's Choice* was] essentially a story about "the awakening of a young man from innocence into revelation," it is also a story played out against the historical background of World War II and, like Mr. Styron's previous novels, touches upon other ambitious themes. This penchant for creating novels with large canvases no doubt stems, in part, from a suspicion that his own life, in Mr. Styron's words, "has been rather ordinary—vast areas of it are just not dramatic or interesting enough to write about"; in part, from his philosophical sympathy with Melville's dictum that "to write a mighty book, you need a mighty theme."

"I think too many writers in recent years have been boring or insignificant because they haven't sought themes commensurate with their imaginations," he says.

> There's nothing wrong with the material of middle-class life—that's been the bread and butter of contemporary writing for centuries—but, again, I think one has to either establish a new theme around it or in some way invigorate this raw material. I think (John) Updike does it rather well. At his best, he's probably our best internist of middle-class life, its delights and diseases. But he's an immensely gifted writer, and I think others who have attempted this have come back with the same old tired stories.

There is, Mr. Styron believes, "some sort of poetic apprehension, an excitement, that comes when you're writing about the most important thing within your command." His own novels—as he notes in *This Quiet Dust,* his new collection of essays—tend to focus on one recurrent theme, namely "the catastrophic propensity on the part of human beings to attempt to dominate one another." Combined with a Southerner's heightened sense of history, this theme tends to result in a vision at once tragic and fatalistic.

A Gothic taste for violence frequently informs the novels: murder, suicide and rape are recurrent motifs—and, for all their differences, Mr. Styron's protagonists remain alike in one respect: All of them are victims, casualties of history and such social institutions as slavery as well as their own weaknesses and failings.

"There doesn't seem to be any rational order in existence," Mr. Styron says.

> This is certainly not an original view, but it seems to me that human beings are a hair's breadth away from catastrophe at all times—both personally and on a larger historical level, and this, perhaps, is why I've written the sort of books I have. I mean, I was never a slave nor was I at Auschwitz, but somehow these two modes of existence sort of grabbed me and became a kind of metaphor for what I believe a great deal of life is about.
>
> This theme has really found me. Why, I don't know. Perhaps it's a result of being in World War II—being a fairly sensitive boy of 18 and finding myself in a war which, however just it might have been, nonetheless threatened to kill me. I think something like that, which affected many men of my generation, caused me to wonder about human domination, about the forces in history that simply wipe you out. You're suddenly a cipher—you find yourself on some hideous atoll in the Pacific, and if you're unlucky you get a bullet through your head. And within the microcosm of the Marine Corps itself you're just a mound of dust in terms of free will, and I think this fact of being utterly helpless enlarges one's sensitivity to the idea of evil.

Just as Mr. Styron's preoccupation with evil stems from a particular episode in his life, his books, however ambitious, are also grounded in distinctly autobiographical concerns. In writing about Stingo in *Sophie's Choice*—"a fairly complicated and bedeviled person with a comical gift which saves him from his own miseries"—he says he was trying to rediscover his own past. Nat Turner, too, represented an effort to reinvent the slave leader in his own image, a means of fulfilling what Mr. Styron has called "the moral imperative of every white Southerner—to come to *know* the Negro.

> He was indeed a reflection of me, and I don't apologize to the blacks for that at all, because I think that any character of substance in a literary work is a product of the author's personality. I think that by turning my own residual Southern racial crotchets around—in effect, trying to view white men like me from Nat Turner's point of view—I was able to work out a lot of possible racial bigotries.

For Mr. Styron, in fact, writing represents a kind of therapy. It is a way of coming to terms with life through self-analysis and catharsis. "I look back on the characters in my books—and there are so many who are neurotic, unable to cope, frustrated and obsessed—as an attempt to get rid of my own frustrations and obsessions." It was Mr. Styron's first novel, *Lie Down in Darkness*—the story of Peyton Loftis's struggles with a heavy-drinking father and domineering mother—that explored, perhaps most intimately, his personal problems. Although he once spoke of modeling Peyton on a friend who committed suicide, he now points out that her plight was based more on his own adolescent gropings and struggles with "a stepmother who was as close to the wicked stepmother image as one can possibly imagine.

> Now that my father and stepmother are both gone, I think I can speak without hesitation. *Lie Down in Darkness* is a book which is really a mirror of the family life I myself put up with. Plainly, in writing this, I had brought resources of what I hoped was art to the whole thing. I wanted to be a writer, I was dying to write a book, and I saw, even then,

the necessity of embedding this in a sociological framework—to show a small town in the South in all its variety, to show the kind of rootless upper-middle-class country club life I'd seen. So I put it on a larger canvas, but the basic torment between Peyton and her family was really a projection of my own sense of alienation from my own tiny family—that is, my father, whom I really loved and this strange woman who had just come on the scene and who—I think I'm speaking as objectively as I can—was really trying to make my life a hell.

"The book was a form of self-psychoanalysis, which freed me of any need to go to a shrink," he continues.

> I was never in despair like Peyton, but at the age of 22, when I started that book, I remember being in a wildly unhappy state of neurotic *angst*. I had very few underpinnings. My emotional life was in upheaval. I'd lost what little faith I had in religion. I was just adrift, and the only thing that allowed me any kind of anchor was the idea of creating a work of literature which somehow would be a thing of beauty in the old-fashioned sense of the word and would also be a kind of freeing for me of these terrible conflicts that were in my soul. And by the time I got to the end of that tunnel I was a relatively happy young man.

Since then, Mr. Styron has found that writing helps him "keep an equilibrium," and he has shaped his life around his work. For the last 28 years, he and his wife Rose have lived quietly in rural Connecticut. Although they occasionally see such neighbors as Philip Roth and Arthur Miller, Mr. Styron says, "I don't feel myself caught up in the New York literary life or, God forbid, the academic literary life, which is my idea of living death."

Pinned to the wall of his study is a quotation from Flaubert—"Be regular and orderly in your life like a bourgeois, so that you may be violent and original in your work"—and these days Mr. Styron spends most afternoons in this room, working on his next book, a long novel about the Marine Corps, set during the Korean War. . . . Animated by such familiar Styron preoccupations as evil, guilt and domination, the novel is somewhat reminiscent of Conrad's *Lord Jim*. It focuses on the spiritual plight of a brave and intellectually gifted Marine colonel who is obsessed by memories of an atrocity he committed in Nicaragua years before. The book, says Mr. Styron, is intended to be a kind of "parable of the United States' nosy involvement in places like Latin America."

While the book once posed considerable difficulties—he put it aside to work on *Sophie's Choice*—Mr. Styron says that writing has actually become somewhat easier over the years. "I think that you no longer agonize, like Flaubert, over *le mot juste*. You still want to write a felicitous sentence, but it's not going to kill you if it's not the most beautiful thing in Christendom. So you're satisfied, not with second best but with the best you can do."

What's more, Mr. Styron says he no longer worries whether his next novel will exceed or approximate the success of his previous ones, for he thinks of writing not as "a series of mountain peaks, but as a plateau with a series of indentations." "It's a rolling landscape," he explains, "rather than one of these theatrical Wagnerian dramas with peak after peak, one being higher or bigger." (pp. 3, 26)

Michiko Kakutani, "William Styron on His Life

and Work," in The New York Times Book Review, December 12, 1982, pp. 3, 26.

BERNARD DUYFHUIZEN

[*This Quiet Dust and Other Writings*], which is largely comprised of book reviews, has been arranged topically, focusing on subjects that have preoccupied Styron in his fiction: the South, the military, and the Holocaust. . . . The collection shows Styron caught up in history, ceaselessly exploring its "most compelling theme . . . that of the catastrophic propensity on the part of human beings to attempt to dominate one another." But Styron highly personalizes the history he is caught up in by constantly including himself in nearly every piece.

In his opening note to the reader, Styron states that this collection "is held together by an autobiographical thread . . . [is] a partial record of a life." Readers will find this aspect of *This Quiet Dust* both interesting and disturbing: interesting because Styron reveals his literary debts and the thematic preoccupations that undergird his fiction; disturbing because, like Stingo in *Sophie's Choice,* his self-reflexiveness borders on self-indulgence and self-righteousness. In recalling the essays he wrote on behalf of Benjamin Reid, a convicted murderer, Styron compares his advocacy of Reid to Norman Mailer's advocacy of Jack Abbott, and, though Styron makes some telling points about society, crime, and capital punishment, he also reveals a Maileresque romanticizing of the criminal, titling this section of the collection "Victims." In more recent essays Styron looks at the Holocaust, taking a revisionist stand and focusing his perspective on the non-Jewish victims of the concentration camps. But this position has left him open to charges of anti-Semitism and of a willful blindness to the Nazis' main program of extermination. Styron's view of the Holocaust is not without merit, but ultimately one is left with the impression that Styron is only using history as a means to better understand "Styron" and his own relationship to his time. (p. 742)

> *Bernard Duyfhuizen, in a review of "This Quiet Dust and Other Writings," in* Modern Fiction Studies, *Vol. 29, No. 4, Winter, 1983, pp. 741-42.*

GENE BLUESTEIN

[*This Quiet Dust,* a] collection of William Styron's essays and reviews, is well worth having in print under one cover. It is always interesting to encounter the expository views of good writers, especially when they, like Styron, are determined to become involved in the critical and controversial issues of our time. I would have tried to talk him out of including several eulogies for some fellow writers (the tearful response to the death of James Jones is embarrassing), but his major essays are effective and felicitous insights into what he considers "the most compelling theme in history, including the history of our own time—that of the catastrophic propensity on the part of human beings to attempt to dominate one another."

Like most important writers who have emerged from the South, Styron first encountered this theme in the context of slavery, and that "peculiar institution" is never far from his mind. The title essay (from an Emily Dickinson poem— "This quiet Dust was Gentlemen and Ladies, / and Lads and Girls") is an intriguing discussion of the controversy raised by his novel *The Confessions of Nat Turner* (1967), an attempt to penetrate the mind and soul of Styron's fellow Virginian. Styron was first attacked for daring to write about a black man on the ground that no white Southerner could possibly depict the innermost thoughts of a Negro character, especially one like Nat Turner, whose insurrection in 1831 terrified slaveholders everywhere.

The criticism of Styron raises an underlying issue that has nothing to do with race, bearing rather on the relation between illusion and reality, imagination and experience, and ultimately the creative power of the writer. Can a man write effectively about a woman? Can a woman write accurately about a man? Could a great war novel be written by someone who never took part in it? (Stephen Crane wrote *The Red Badge of Courage* with absolutely no first-hand experience in the Civil War.) (pp. 35-6)

I have argued with people who insist that a man shouldn't sing a "woman's blues" and vice versa. Styron carefully subtitled his work "a meditation on history" to signal the fictional nature of his study of Turner's life and times. But the fact that a white man had made the attempt was bound to provoke an onslaught of ferocious criticism, especially in the midst of the 1960s' burgeoning of black consciousness. The issue remains almost as hot today although, as I have implied, there is no way to limit the scope of a writer's imagination.

Another major section of *This Quiet Dust* has to do with capital punishment. A Southerner and a former U.S. Marine Corps officer, Styron had taken a hard line and even publicly supported the execution of Caryl Chessman, the California rapist who was ultimately executed in the gas chamber. Styron's description of his conversion is instructive and moving. He cites the influence of "Camus's great essay, 'Reflections on the Guillotine,' " but the main change of heart came about through Styron's involvement in the case of a young Connecticut prisoner, Benjamin Reid, whose life Styron probably saved by bringing his case to the attention of the public. There is a close analogy to the more recent case involving Norman Mailer and Jack Henry Abbott, for after escaping the death penalty, Reid walked away from a work detail and raped a thirty-seven-year-old woman. . . . Agonizing over his defense of Reid, Styron gives a full and honest account of all the issues, but remains steadfast in his refusal to accept vengeance and official murder as a response to violence. It's not incidental that Reid is a black man, a "victim of foster homes and deprivation" who was inaccurately identified as a mental defective. . . .

There are other essays and reviews to savor: on the 1968 Democratic convention in Chicago, on the military, on the founding of *The Paris Review,* and on the sources of his own work. With the exception of the eulogies, they are all worth reading (or re-reading, if you know the originals). (p. 36)

> *Gene Bluestein, "Styron as Muse," in* The Progressive, *Vol. 48, No. 1, January, 1984, pp. 35-6.*

JOHN KENNY CRANE

Although Styron tells us, both in *Sophie's Choice* and in an essay entitled **"Lie Down in Darkness,"** that his inspiration to write his first novel [of the same title] came as the result of a letter he received from his father during the great blizzard of 1947—"telling me of the suicide of a young girl, my age, who had been the source of my earliest and most aching infatuation,"—the raw material of the book was derived elsewhere. In a December, 1982, interview in the *New York Times Book Review,* he mentions that his first novel "is a book which is really a mirror of the family life I myself put up with." Helen Loftis was modeled on his stepmother, "as close to the wicked stepmother image as one can possibly imagine," and, to an extent, Milton Loftis was modeled on his own father.

Yet this is not the whole story either. In each of Styron's four novels we can see a more idealized father-figure who does not drink, does not do battle with a shrewish wife, does not flounder in self-pity and inertia. . . . These seem to me more to represent the recollections Styron has of his own father who died in 1978 and to whose memory he dedicated *Sophie's Choice.* Because of his father's inability to control his stepmother, Styron for a time felt alienated from him "whom I really loved," and in his fiction he seems to attempt to repair his earlier attitudes.

This father-figure has crept into each of Styron's four novels in a very thematic role. While each is significantly different on the surface, . . . they are at bottom all built on the same model. Each has great affection and expectations for his son, each is moral and God-fearing, each is atuned to the decay of the modern world and the ambiguous glory of the past. Each is anxious to pass on his hard-learned worldly-wisdom to his son, both so the son will not have to learn it the hard way and so that he may carry a different standard into the future than his contemporaries have raised on their own poles. (pp. 117-18)

It is the contention of this [essay] that in one way or another each of the four father-figures lured the son on toward a future which was at least more humane and moral than the apparently preordained and destined one, whether or not this alternative were actually attainable. In doing so each is placed in sharp contrast to the "standard father" available to most young people of the materialistic, beautyless, amoral if not immoral age which Styron so frequently criticizes. Loftis's father, if ineffective, was superior to Loftis himself as a father and to other fathers in the book, such as Dick Cartwright's. . . . [By offering such a contrast, Styron] is placing the responsibility for the continued evolution of human evil squarely upon the shoulders of the progenitors of each new generation. . . . (p. 118)

Milton Loftis' father [in *Lie Down in Darkness*] comes equipped with the broad wisdom and measured loquaciousness of the other three and represents a dying ideal.

> *I only trust you will heed the warning of one who has seen much water pass as it were beneath the bridge one to whom I must admit the temptations of the flesh have been potent and manifold, and that you will perhaps in some measure renounce a way of life which even in its most charitable concept can lead only to grief and possibly complete ruination.*

(italics Styron's) If Milton on occasion "hates" his father, it is because the old fellow's message seems built upon platitudes (*"keep your chin up and your kilts down and let the wind blow"* [italics Styron's]), is invitingly ambiguous (*"Your first duty remember, son, is always to yourself"* [italics Styron's]), and is overly optimistic and, Milton feels, wrong (*"Believe me, my boy, you have a good woman"* [italics Styron's]). In retrospect Milton resents the fact that his father was too good to him, "lacked the foresight to avoid spoiling his son," and

in general did not prepare him for the disillusionment his middle age would bring.

David Galloway, in *The Absurd Hero in American Fiction,* makes much of Styron's creation of absurd universes early in each novel. The elder Loftis, perhaps more than any of the other father figures, is unable to recognize these absurdities or, at least, believes they can be effectively coped with. *"Most people . . . get on through life by a sophomoric fatalism. Only poets and thieves can exercise free will, and most of them die young"* (italics Styron's). The paradoxes of modern existence are, to him, a challenge rather than an obstacle. For instance, when he discusses the ironic position of the modern Southerner who seeks to do right, that "right" seems much more available to him than it ever will to Milton:

> *. . . being a Southerner and a Virginian and of course a Democrat you will find yourself in the unique position of choosing between (a) those ideals implanted as right and proper in every man since Jesus Christ and no doubt before and especially in Virginians and (b) ideals inherent in you through a socio-economic culture over which you have no power to prevail; consequently I strongly urge you my son to be a good Democrat but to be a good man too if you possibly can. . . .*

(italics Styron's). The guidance for proper behavior is in the past not the future ("If the crazy sideroads start to beguile you, son, take at least a backward glance at Monticello," but for Milton the past is irretrievable, the future inevitable, the present intolerable. His father's wisdom seems outdated, does not work. (pp. 119-20)

However ineffective he is and unrealizable is his message, the elder Loftis stands as a memory of a better, more noble, more moral, more hopeful time. Milton is never fully convinced that the road back to that time is irrevocably blocked, nor I think is Styron. . . . However ludicrous his father's verbiage occasionally is, Milton knows that his father was a better man than he is, and the reader can contrast him to the more regular and "acceptable" fathers who populate the book. Helen's father, Blood and Jesus Peyton, sits confidently at the right hand of God: " ' "We must stand fast with the good. The Army of the Lord is on the march. We'll lick the Huns and the devil comes next. Your daddy knows what's right." ' " Or there is Dick Cartwright who tries so hard to shape his son that he cuffs him overboard in thirty feet of water when the boy fails to handle the sailboat's mainsheet properly. Throughout his childhood Dick is torn between love and hate for him. He is occasionally surprised by moments of tenderness, but too often "there came foul weather . . . monsoon winds, smelling faintly of dollars, perilous transactions, heady enterprises to be sought on some distant hazardous shore."

The true father-figure in Styron is above all cautionary; the senior Peyton and Cartwright know no caution and proceed blindly into the future Styron fears, thereby creating it. They are men whose sense of Guilt is virtually undeveloped simply because they "know" what "right" is and, so, do it relentlessly.

In none of his books is Styron more critical of America than he is in *Set This House on Fire,* and some of the most articulate and damning remarks he places, early on, in the mouth of Alfred Leverett, father of the narrator. Much more bitter than the elder Loftis, old Leverett (still alive in this novel where Loftis' father has long been dead) also seems to believe that the tide can be stemmed if someone—preferably his son—would be on with the stemming. During the visit Peter makes to see him in Port Warwick on his way to Cass's home in South Carolina, Alfred Leverett plays the full keyboard range of things which are bothering him (and clearly bothering Styron and perhaps Styron's father as well).

While they ride together through the "new" Port Warwick, father tells son that they are witnessing the "decline of the West" as they recognize that their once sleepy Southern city now resembles Perth Amboy, Bridgeport, or Yonkers. He inveighs against the " 'California influence' " which will prevail in the end and will strip the nation of its leaves and greenery. Though not opposed to change *per se* (" 'Only fools lament change in itself' "), he objects to the "pillaging" that Americans perceive that change must amount to in modern times. (pp. 120-21)

[In another] discussion of the narrative structure of this novel I suggest, counter to some critics, that Peter Leverett does not belong as its narrator and perhaps has no meaningful reason to even be in it. Not so, however, his father, for Alfred Leverett keynotes the actions that Cass will eventually perform:

> What this country needs . . . what this great land of ours needs is something to happen to it. Something ferocious and tragic, like what happened to Jericho or the cities of the plain—something terrible I mean, son, so that when people have been through hellfire and the crucible, and have suffered agony enough and grief, they'll be men again, human beings, not a bunch of smug contented hogs rooting at the trough. Ciphers without mind or soul or heart. Soap peddlers!

In order to find his mind and soul and heart, Cass Kinsolving puts himself through hellfire both in lesser incidents with the dreary McCabes and larger ones with the sated and evil-doing Mason Flagg.

When Peter listens to his father's words he feels, he says, "jaded and depressed, . . . unaccountably weary and worn out—old before my time—and I had a sudden sharp pang of total estrangment, as if my identity had slipped away, leaving me without knowledge of who I was or where I had been and where I was ever going." Yet his father touches him to the heart with his "old sweetness and decency and rage, but also by whatever it was within me—within life itself, it seemed so intense—that I knew to be irretrievably lost." Once again, the father figure represents the lost time which was, if not ideal, much better and which serves to spur the son into dissatisfaction that he trusts will be constructive rather than demoralizing. (p. 122)

As in *Lie Down in Darkness,* the father-figure in [*Set This House on Fire*] represents the opposite direction from the one in which "things" are going. In terms of Styron's thematic pattern as a whole, he represents a purer time before the great attempt to realize supposed "promises" through the forcing of Fortune began. Or, to use Alfred's own words for it, before he got around to "trading (his) soul for a sawbuck, and forswearing (God's) love."

Perhaps ironically Samuel Turner [in *The Confessions of Nat Turner*] is a father-figure of the future, not of the past. The past is racist and slave-holding. Turner, if he is not ready to free his slaves or to believe that the Negro race is inferior only because of white repression, is in fact prepared to recognize the equality of at least one member of it. In so doing, he is ready to begin to emerge from the error of the past into the burgeoning possibilities for "right" in the future. If Turner is the only father-figure to look forward rather than backward, he is the only one of Styron's father-figures to live in the early nineteenth rather than the early twentieth century when things are beginning to collapse.

It is also ironic that forward-looking Sam Turner is also the only one of the four father-figures to create evil as a result of his words and actions. Not realizing that neither Nat nor the world may be ready for his own new awareness, he promises Nat something that he cannot eventually produce—he gives him "fanciful notions" of freedom. Though the possibilities are initially so staggering to Nat that he tries to refuse the opportunity—" 'But I don't want to go to any Richmond!' "— Nat begins to count on the realization of this promise, even on occasion brags about it to those less fortunate. But, not only does Turner's economic situation deteriorate before this can happen, he is also victimized by a "fetching ingenuousness and faith in human nature." A poor judge of people, he retains belief in the inherent goodness of the clergy and chooses the Reverend Eppes to carry out his promise to Nat. Eppes has no intention of doing so, and Nat as a result comes to hate Samuel Turner in his memory. His promise unrealized, Nat plans his ill-fated rebellion. In Styron, it seems, the father-figure is always "out of sync" with the times because the times are always at odds with the moral law, God's plan, the natural law, or whatever one might prefer to call it.

What are we to make of Nat's actual father, long since gone by the time Nat is old enough to inquire about him? On the one hand he was apparently a man who had some awareness of his own human dignity despite the propensity of bondage to dispel him of any such idea. Like Nat he was "too smart fo' dat kind of low nigger work'," and one day he simply walked off the plantation after his new master, Ben Turner, struck him in the mouth for insubordination. Local myth has it that he went to Pennsylvania to earn enough money to buy his wife and son out of slavery.

On the other hand that was quite a few years ago, and he has never come back. He was possibly captured or killed; but like Nat, he could simply have been seeing to his own needs, realizing his own promises. There are other women to have other sons by. Whatever Styron would have us infer, Nat's true father does not fit the role of father-figure that he uses so regularly in his fiction, most clearly in his failure to give his son guidance that is otherwise hard to come by. (pp. 123-24)

In terms of the father-figure type, [Stingo's Father in *Sophie's Choice*] is the most fully developed one. If he does still have his trouble with a cab driver in New York—and so seems out of control in the age in which he has been doomed to live— this is surely just Styron's way, once again, of calling our attention to the fact that he represents something different and more admirable than we are otherwise likely to find in that age.

Where the elder Loftis and Alfred Leverett seem to spout random bits of occasional wisdom, Stingo's father more resembles Samuel Turner in that he seems to have a "program" for his son's development away from the apparent destiny of his peers. In the Hampden-Sydney address Styron humorously recounts his own father's attempts to find a college for him where he would not drink himself into a useless adulthood.

Stingo's father does much the same by sending him to a "pleasant institution" to correct some defects that made him "difficult to handle after my mother died." As the novel progresses, Stingo's father sends him "enough" money but not too much to live on in New York. He keeps him up on the local news while Stingo labors in the North, "that no-good world," and even triggers his imagination to produce his first novel by informing him of the death of Maria Hunt (the model, here at least, for Peyton Loftis). He even offers him Frank Hobbs's property as a place to write it and to research his life-long interest in Nat Turner. Stingo at twenty-two may be an "adult," but his father has realized that he is still too young to be cast into a misdirected world, too likely to fall victim to the guiltless model I have been exploring.

In Chapter Two of *Sophie's Choice* Stingo delivers the encomium on his father that might best summarize both Styron's attitude toward his own father and, artistically, the role the father-figure plays in his four novels:

> I opened the letter from my father. I always looked forward to these letters, feeling fortunate to have this Southern Lord Chesterfield as an advisor, who so delighted me with his old-fashioned disquisitions on pride and avarice and ambition, bigotry, political skullduggery, venereal excess and other mortal sins and dangers. Sententious he might be, but never pompous, never preacherish in tone, and I relished both the letters' complexity of thought and feeling and their simple eloquence; whenever I finished one I was usually close to tears, or doubled over with laughter, and they almost always set me immediately to rereading passages in the Bible, from which my father had derived many of his prose cadences and much of his wisdom.

Stingo's father teaches him the essential concept of Transfer, both in his reminders about people like Hobbs and Maria Hunt who have fallen before the world's onslaughts and through his own example. And this latter form of instruction has always been double-edged. We have both the punishment of his son for . . . the choice to cultivate solitariness—as in his abandonment of his sick mother to an unheated house, and his own continued attempts to stay close to his son in letters and in visits. "His motive was sweet and patently uncomplicated: he said he missed me and since he hadn't seen me in so long (I calculated it had been nine months or more) he wanted to reestablish, face to face, eyeball to eyeball, our mutual love and kinship."

Sophie, on the other hand, had no such father: " 'I sometimes got to think that everything bad on earth, every evil that was ever invented had to do with my father.' " Stingo on another occasion refers to her father as "a presence oppressive and stifling which polluted the very wellsprings of her childhood and youth" to the point that "she loathed him past all telling." The evil his blindness and bigotry and hatred help to bring about will swallow not only those for whom he essentially cares little—Sophie would be one—but also those few mortals for whom he can truly feel love—Jan and Eva, for example: "It is impossible to speculate on the reaction of this tormented man had he survived to see Jan and Eva fall into that black pit which his imagination had fashioned for the Jews." Because he lacks even the potential to feel sympathy for all men, . . . he is able to sort out those whom he deems worthy to live and those to die. He assumes the role of God in his attempts to dominate the world of his solitary vision, loses his sense of guilt (if he ever had one), and so creates evil.

This evil will destroy, almost mechanistically, his family, his nation, nearly the world, definitely himself. He is the grotesque combination of all the vices Styron portrays in the "regular" fathers—Helen Loftis', Dick Cartwrights's, Mason Flagg's—of the first three novels. And perhaps Colonel Templeton belongs on this list as well.

Stingo's father, on the other hand, is the master father-figure, the polished blend of all the virtues of his three predecessors. To the extent that he is Styron's own father, this is a fine tribute; to the extent that he is a fictional character he is an example of Styron's belief that the fine and good man can continue to thrive in the twentieth-century world, however rarely he seems to appear. (pp. 124-27)

John Kenny Crane, in his The Root of All Evil: The Thematic Unity of William Styron's Fiction, *University of South Carolina Press, 1984, 168 p.*

SAMUEL COALE

Many of William Styron's strengths as a writer come from those that we associate with Southern fiction. Baroque rhetoric powers his narratives; Faulkner's ghost lingers in his language. He evokes the kind of doomed, guilt-ridden landscapes we associate with the Southern vision of the world. The problem of evil haunts him at all levels—social, psychological, metaphysical—and spawns the moral quest, the search for values of his heroes amid the stark realities of pain and suffering. Manichean conflicts ravage his prose, his outlook, his characters, as if an ultimate nihilism or irrevocable Greek fate savaged the vestiges of his own Christian faith or background. Such a war-torn spirit leads to certain death, to spiritual paralysis. He stalks the "riddles of personality" like the best romancers and sets up voices of "normalcy," moderate spokesmen, as clear-eyed witnesses to extraordinary events and persons: Culver to Mannix, Peter Leverett to Cass Kinsolving, Stingo to Sophie Zawistowska and Nathan Landau. A kind of existential, finally unexorcized sense of guilt relentlessly hounds him.

Styron writes in the tradition of the Southern gothic romance, moving from revelation to revelation, surprise to surprise, pacing his fiction as a series of building climaxes, each more shattering than the preceding one. He has written in this manner from the very first, as in *Lie Down in Darkness:* "it finally occurred to me to use separate moments in time, four or five long dramatic scenes revolving around the daughter, Peyton, at different stages in her life. The business of the progression of time seems to me one of the most difficult problems a novelist has to cope with." The secret remains "a sense of architecture—a symmetry, perhaps unobtrusive but always there, without which a novel sprawls, becomes a self-indulged octopus. It was a matter of form."

Styron's gothic architecture comes complete with its aura of damnation and doom, a dusky cathedral filled with omens and auguries, nightmares and demonic shadows. And at the end of labyrinthine corridors appear the inevitable horrors: Peyton's suicide, Cass's murder of Mason Flagg, Nat's murder of Margaret Whitehead, Sophie's surrendering her daughter Eva to the gas ovens of Birkenau. Sambuco, "aloof upon its precipice, remote and beautifully difficult of access," the enclosed white temple of Nat Turner's dreams, "those days" of the 1940s in *Sophie's Choice:* here are the removed, withdrawn settings for dark romances. Nathan Landau wonders, however, if such a structure for fiction could be "a worn-out tradition," and John Gardner, reviewing *Sophie's Choice* [see excerpt in *CLC,* Vol. 15], considered the ambiguous relationship between the evil of Auschwitz and "the helpless groaning and self-flagellation of the Southern Gothic novel." The suggestion is raised by both Styron and Gardner whether or not this kind of romance has outlived its usefulness, however passionately and grippingly re-created.

The ambiguous nature of Styron's vision may serve to undermine his gothic structures. For one thing, he often relies too heavily upon psychological explanations, a kind of rational reductionism that reduces metaphysical speculations to Freudian solutions. In *Lie Down in Darkness,* Styron deals with what his character, Albert Berger, calls, "this South with its cancerous religiosity, its exhausting need to put manners before morals, to negate all ethos . . . a *husk* of culture," in the new suburban middle-class South, a world hung up on its own narcissistic corruptions. These may be the result of the Old South gone dead, but a stronger case can be made for Oedipal tensions and familial dislocations along a purely psychological grid: nostalgia and self-indulgence, however alcoholic, however wounding, seem almost disconnected from any Southern past, or for that matter any past at all.

The trouble with the elegantly rendered and moving *The Confessions of Nat Turner* is that the religious fanatic cum prophet tells his own tale. All explanations and suggestions—psychological, tragic, Christian, heroic—tend to look like mere self-justifications. Nat as both interpreter and actor may see himself moving from Old Testament vengeance to New Testament charity and contrition, but within his own psychological maneuverings and suggestions, even this broadly mythic and religious design dissolves. The tidy psychology of the case study threatens to undermine the realities of any political action, any historical commitment. Manichean conflict—black vs. white, good vs. evil, master vs. slave—produces a kind of paralysis, a deeply felt and exquisitely written blank like the smooth white sides of that dreamed windowless enclosure.

Styron once suggested "that all my work is predicated on revolt in one way or another. And of course there's something about Nat Turner that's the ultimate fulfillment of all, this. It's a strange revelation." As he once described himself, [Styron] remains a "provisional rebel": his sufferers are witnessed at a distance. . . . If many of Styron's rebels participate in a kind of self-mutilation or self-flagellation, his witnesses experience this as well, but at a distance. As we shall see in both *Set This House on Fire* and *Sophie's Choice*—for me his most passionate and fierce romances—violence and revenge are just barely, if at all, transmuted into Christian symbols; at times, the Christian imagery seems itself "provisional," a literary laying on of uncertain hands. We get finally not tragedies but melodramas, exorcisms rendered "safe" by the remarkably unscathed witnesses.

The whole question of Styron's notion of evil remains ambiguous. In *Lie Down in Darkness* Styron writes: "Too powerful a consciousness of evil was often the result of infantile emotions. The cowardly Puritan . . ., unwilling to partake of free religious inquiry, uses the devil as a scapegoat to rid himself of the need for positive action." Evil becomes a dodge, an excuse for inaction, paralysis, as if Manichean polarities produced only stalemate, fashioned in a fierce baroque prose style. And Styron adds: "Perhaps the miseries of our century will be recalled only as the work of a race of strange and trou-

blous children, by the wise old men in the aeons which come after us." Infantile emotions: troublous children: a hint of adolescent angst sounded in a void? Evil as howling self? Is there something to Mailer's indictment of *Set This House on Fire* as the "magnum opus of a fat spoiled rich boy who could write like an angel about landscape and like an adolescent about people"? Does gothic doom become, then, rhetorical, a literary attitude, a Faulknerian mannerism laced with a fatal Fitzerald-like glamour, overwrought in a gothic style?

Jonathan Baumbach suggests that *Set This House on Fire* "attempts the improbable: the alchemical transformation of impotent rage into tragic experience. Styron's rage is the hellfire heat of the idealist faced by an unredeemably corrupt world for which he as fallen man feels obsessively and hopelessly guilty" [see excerpt in *CLC,* Vol. 1]. This suggests also Gardner's assessment of Styron's writing as "a piece of anguished Protestant soul-searching, an attempt to seize all the evil in the world—in his own heart first—crush it, and create a planet fit for God and man." The Manichean battles in this book reveal the passionate intensity of this alchemical urge.

The sacred and the profane, the prudish and the prurient, God and nothingness, being and nihilism, doom and nostalgia, Anglo-Saxon and Italian honesty battle it out in *Set This House on Fire.* Peter Leverett, the moderate realistic lawyer, confronts Cass Kinsolving, the guilt-ridden visionary artist. Each has been attracted and played sycophant to the "gorgeous silver fish . . . a creature so strange, so *new*" that is Mason Flagg. Flagg represents a Manichean vision in his "dual role of daytime squire and nighttime nihilist," a distinctively American Jekyll and Hyde, "able in a time of hideous surfeit, and Togetherness's lurid mist, to revolt from conventional values, to plunge into a chic vortex of sensation, dope, and fabricated sin, though all the while retaining a strong grip on his two million dollars." Is this Styron's "provisional rebel?" He celebrates the new frontier of sexual adventure as a gnostic libertine, corrupt in his faith, would and reveals "that slick, arrogant, sensual, impenitently youthful, American and vainglorious face": the spoiled, self-indulgent American child, filled with unfulfilled desire, itself desirous of further increase. He suggests Styron's America in the Fifties, "a general wasting away of quality, a kind of sleazy common prostration of the human spirit," in times "like these when men go whoring off after false gods" in a realm of "moral and spiritual anarchy." Is there any wonder that Peter Leverett's father cries out for "something ferocious and tragic, like what happened to Jericho or the cities of the plain," a promise to "bring back tragedy to the land of the Pespi-Cola"? (pp. 57-60)

Peter Leverett suffers a recurring nightmare of a shadow beyond the window in the dark, a friend bent on betrayal and murder but for no apparent reason. It is Cass who suggests "that whosoever it is that rises in a dream with a look on his face of eternal damnation is just one's own self, wearing a mask, and that's the fact of the matter." Evil becomes the self trapped in itself, a spirit at war with itself, a narcissistic and ineradicable sense of guilt that despite Cass's explanations of exile, orphanhood, ignorance, the war, his wife's Catholicism, his own "puddle of self" at the base of his artistic nature, his Anglo-Saxon background, his terror, his Americanness, his actions toward blacks, will not be overcome. "To triumph over self is to triumph over Death," Cass declares. "It is to triumph over that beast which one's self interposes between one's soul and one's God." Between that soul and God lurks the beast of the self, the solipsistic psychological center around which Styron's metaphysical and socio-cultural explanations of Manicheism pale. At one point Cass discusses "the business about evil—what it is, where it is, whether it's a reality, or just a figment of the mind," a cancer in the body or something "to stomp on like you would a flea carrying bubonic plague." He decides that "both of these theories are as evil as the evil they are intended to destroy and cure." Evil thus remains either "the puddle of self," which Styron belabors in the book, or the mystery of endless pain that knows no justification, a cruel beating down of the human spirit that in the end, like that puddle, suggests a perpetual entrapment. . . . (pp. 60-1)

Both Leverett and Kinsolving press on to make their personal nightmares make sense. "Passionately he tried to make the dream give up its meaning," Styron writes of Cass. He might just as well be writing about his use of the gothic romance to surrender up the significance of his own dark dreams of perpetual conflict and combat. "Each detail was as clear in his mind as something which happened only yesterday, yet when he tried to put them all together he ended up with blank ambiguous chaos." The details refuse to conjure up the overall design: we have reached a standstill, an impasse. "These various horrors and sweats you have when you're asleep add up to something," Cass maintains, "even if these horrors are masked and these sweats are symbols. What you've got to do is get behind the mask and the symbol." Kinsolving suggests Melville's Ahab who, in penetrating the mask, reduces ambiguity to palpable design and submits willfully to the Manichean fire-worshippers at his side. He becomes his own devil. Cass cannot.

Set This House on Fire cries out for tragedy to alleviate its pain. Styron instead settles for melodrama, the *deus ex machina,* the Fascist-humanist Luigi who will not allow Cass to wallow in any more of his guilt. Luigi to Cass plays the wise father to the angst-ridden American adolescent: Cass is "relieved" of his guilt.

Kinsolving and Leverett meet years later to talk in a fishing boat on the Southern river of their childhoods. If at first both seem like opposites, they in fact blend into one Southern sensibility: bewitched and entranced by Flagg, they succumb to a rampant unanchored nostalgia that swallows everything before it, an omniverous sentimentality, "the sad nostalgic glamor," the Southern mind's ravenous appetite for "a hundred gentle memories, purely summer, purely southern, which swarmed instantly through his mind, though one huge memory encompassed all." Nostalgia begets narcissism or vice-versa: intensity of feeling replaces knowledge as the keystone to awareness. This nostalgia is not seen as tragic, as a flight from adulthood: it survives "pure" in its sweeping intensities, its rhetorical sweep—and is the ominous flip-side of Cass's dread, of Styron's gothic plot and structure. Catastrophe, doom, guilt, phantoms, and diabolical enchantment draw Leverett to Flagg, Cass to Flagg, Leverett to Cass, but a rampant childhood nostalgia surmounts and floods them all, feeding upon itself.

As Flannery O'Connor suggested, "When tenderness is detached from the source of tenderness, its logical outcome is terror." That nostalgic tenderness cancels spiritual stalemate. As Joyce Carol Oates suggests in reference to Norman Mailer, "he has constructed an entire body of work around a Manichean existentialism [with] a firm belief in the absolute existence of Evil [and] a belief in a limited God, a God Who

is a warring element in a divided universe. . . . his energetic Manichaeanism forbids a higher art. Initiation . . . brings the protagonist not to newer visions . . . but to a dead end, a full stop." Melodrama deflates tragedy and for all its passion and power leaves a world split between suffering and sentimentality, a dark design of untransmuted spiritual impotence, mesmerized by a Manichean reality but unable or unwilling to succumb to its fatal power and terrifyingly realized inevitability. Perhaps "ultimate" rebellion would insist on such a vision. "Provisional" rebellion can only disguise it in Christian images and psychological explanations. The void which surrounds Cass's tirades, that outer world which dissolves in the wake of his internal cries, may reflect only his own narcissism, suggesting that Styron is intent upon withdrawing from the very Manichean vision he's so fiercely created into a safer hollow.

The Manichean vision of *Sophie's Choice* is announced in Styron's opening quotation from André Malraux's *Lazare:* "I seek that essential region of the soul where absolute evil confronts brotherhood." Nathan is both Sophie's savior and destroyer; love battles death; Calvinist Southerners are mesmerized by New York Jews; North and South fight over virtue or the lack of it; black and white, slave and master become both victims and accomplices of one another; out of the adversity Poland has suffered comes not compassion and charity but sustained anti-Semitic cruelty; sex in Stingo's 1940s at the age of twenty-two breeds both liberation and guilt; Sophie "could not bear the contrast between the abstract yet immeasurable beauty of music and the almost touchable dimensions of her own aching despair"; every choice is fraught with disaster; survival itself produces the ineradicable "toxin of guilt." (pp. 61-2)

The most "common norm of human values," Styron undermines is Christianity, at the same time he uses Christian imagery, apparently without irony, to describe the scope and mythic archetypes of his material: "I mean it when I say that no chaste and famished grail-tormented Christian knight could have gazed with more slack-jawed admiration at the object of his quest than I did at my first glimpse of Sophie's bouncing behind." A good line, but the Christian quest motif sticks to the entire form of Styron's use of the gothic romance: it is supposed to lead, however disastrously, to understanding, significance in ultimately religious terms. Stingo's own "Protestant moderation" invests sex with guilt and his "residual Calvinism" sparks his imagination with visions of doom and desecration. On the train, however, with the "dark priestess" toward the end of the book, the black woman, he "went into a bizarre religious convulsion, brief in duration but intense" and reads the Bible aloud with her, not the Sermon on the Mount, but "the grand old Hebrew woe seemed more cathartic, so we went back to Job," the archetypal victim, but one of residual faith, a kind the agnostic Stingo does not share. He disguises himself as the Reverend Entwistle to get a room with Sophie and admits that "the Scriptures were always largely a literary convenience, supplying me with allusions and tag lines for the characters in my novel," but what are we to make of Stingo's impression of Dr. Jemand von Niemand, the man who forces on Sophie her most chilling choice? He must have done so, Stingo speculates, because he thirsted for faith, and to restore God he first must commit a great sin: "All of his depravity had been enacted in a vacuum of sinless and businesslike godlessness, while his soul thirsted for beatitude." The great sin will shadow forth a greater faith "to restore his belief in God."

At the conclusion of the book, Stingo reads lines from Dickinson at the graves of Sophie and Nathan: "Ample make this bed. / Make this bed with awe; / In it wait till judgment break / Excellent and fair." After a night on the beach of Poesque dreams, being buried alive and awaking to find himself buried in sand like "a living cadaver being prepared for burial in the sands of Egypt," he welcomes the morning, blesses "my resurrection," and explains: "This was not judgment day—only morning. Morning: excellent and fair." The ironies are apparent, but so is the stab at symbolic resurrection, waking from the gothic nightmare, returned to the land of the living. It is as if Stingo/Styron wants it both ways again, provisionally damned, provisionally saved. (pp. 62-3)

Gothic romance usually demands the waking from the nightmare, a return to normalcy after the exorcism. But Stingo, like Peter Leverett and Cass Kinsolving before him, will not surrender to being exorcised; he clings to the very fallacious and out-moded Christian doctrines the narrative of the romance undermines. Perhaps the gothic romance cannot embrace absolute evil; the term itself curdles the narrator's will to embrace it. Others will die; they will survive because of the very harried faith they have been "taught" during the romance to outgrow. Stingo's attraction to a certain morbidity is not the same thing as being "called the 'tragic sense'." It is too guarded, too self-protected, too distanced from the real Manichean vision of things by splendid baroque rhetoric and vocabularies of doom and dark auguries. He loves the doom as he loves a nostalgic South; it is a feeling in his bones, shiveringly enjoyable, a *frisson* of the spirit. Within that emotional solipsism, absolute evil proves sheerest poppycock.

Yet ***Sophie's Choice*** works with its escalating confessions, its ominous rhetoric, its sheer dramatic scope and power, as we learn of the real nature of Sophie's father, the many lovers from the murderer Jozef to the lesbian Wanda, the incredible choice of surrendering her daughter to the ovens. Stingo's climax literally occurs in bed—at last—with the pale, radiant Sophie; hers occurs with her suicide pact with Nathan: sex and death, twin dark towers of Manichean castles: semen and cyanide brutally intermingled. "Everyone's a victim. The Jews are also the victims of victims, that's the main difference." There is the frightening core of ***Sophie's Choice,*** evaded or at least displaced by Stingo's awakening from premature burial to the possibility of morning and of resurrection. Sophie weaves tale after tale before her "patient confessor," each until the end "a fabrication, a wretched lie, another fantasy served up to provide a frail barrier, a hopeless and crumbly line of defense between those she cared for, like myself, and her smothering guilt." But the Christian fabrications, the literary allusions, are themselves frail barriers and should crumble completely before the overwhelming presence of guilt, even as "small" in comparison to Sophie's as is Stingo's in relation to his mother's death, his native region, the money he inherited from the slave sold down river, Artiste (appropriately named). Gothic romance, aligned to Christian images of demonic nightmare, the dark night of the soul, and resurrection, itself crumbles. . . . In Stingo's narrative, it does seem a "worn-out tradition."

Perhaps Styron writes at the end of Southern romance, or perhaps he has stretched the form to include a vision of the world that it cannot contain, that murky spurious mixture of Christian archetype and Manichean vision. Rational psychological explanations and Christian archetypes cannot encompass such a fierce conjuring up of guilt; they can only reduce and confine it. Styron's guilt will not be confined in any rational, religious scheme or design: it overwhelms every attempt to comprehend it, existing as some great Manichean "black hole" that can result only in ultimate withdrawal— the aescetics of suicide—or in sexual revelry—the libertinism of Mason Flagg, of Stingo's starving lust. Rhetoric, however intense and poetic, cannot transmute it into anything finally significant other than its own dark irrevocable existence, men and women entombed for life. As Rilke suggests in Styron's opening quote, "death, the whole of earth,—even before life's begun . . . this is beyond description!"

In Styron's world, we are really in Poe country. Faulkner transcended it by his genius, the depth of his complexity of vision; Flannery O'Connor surmounted it through an ultimate religious faith garbed in grotesque disguises, in the grim visages of serious clowns. Carson McCullers and Styron seem trapped within it, McCullers more certain of the Manichean shadows of her vision, setting it up as dark fable, as inevitable as death itself. Styron cautiously moves around it, hanging on to Christian images, archetypes, symbols despite the splendid proofs that they do not apply. Perhaps this is where the Southern tradition in American fiction ends, grappling with absolute evil outside its borders, serving up horrors as it would serve up childhood fantasies. Styron excels at it. . . . The line between paradox and paralysis is a thin one. Styron's marvelous conjurings up of the former leads finally to the latter, and perhaps this is the absolute evil in contemporary society that haunts him the most. (pp. 63-5)

> *Samuel Coale, "Styron's Disguises: A Provisional Rebel in Christian Masquerade," in* Critique: Studies in Modern Fiction, *Vol. XXVI, No. 2, Winter, 1985, pp. 57-65.*

FURTHER READING

Aldridge, John W. "The Society of Three Novels." In his *In Search of Heresy,* pp. 126-48. New York: McGraw-Hill Book Company, 1956.

> Overview of three major works of fiction in which Aldridge identifies Styron as the most established southern novelist of his generation and examines the theme of guilt in his novel *Lie Down in Darkness.*

Aptheker, Herbert. "Styron-Turner and Nat Turner: Myth and Truth." *Political Affairs* 46 (October 1967): 40-50.

> Negative appraisal of *The Confessions of Nat Turner* in which Styron is castigated for historical inaccuracies and for perpetuating racial stereotypes.

Barzelay, D., and Sussman, R. "William Styron on *The Confessions of Nat Turner.*" *Yale Literary Magazine* 137 (September 1968): 24-35.

> Informative interview in which Styron relates his intent in writing this controversial novel.

Bryant, Jerry H. "The Hopeful Stoicism of William Styron." *South Atlantic Quarterly* 42 (Autumn 1963): 539-50.

> Analysis of Styron's novels prior to *The Confessions of Nat Turner* in which Bryant contends that in each work Styron offers a different response to his major theme: "What must man endure?"

Clarke, John H., ed. *William Styron's "Nat Turner": Ten Black Writers Respond.* Boston: Beacon, 1968, 128 p.

Collection of essays by black writers such as Lerone Bennett and John A. Williams in which Styron's novel is faulted on social, racist, psychological, and historical grounds.

Core, George. "*The Confessions of Nat Turner* and the Burden of the Past." *Southern Literary Journal* 2 (Spring 1970): 117-34.

Asserts that while the novel's setting is both historic and contemporary, Styron's portrayal of Turner is intended as fictitious.

Crane, John Kenny. "Laughing Backward: Comedy and Morality in Styron's Fiction." *College Literature* XIV, No. 1 (Winter 1987): 1-16.

Examines Styron's use of humor as a means for his characters to attain moral insight.

Flanders, Jane. "William Styron's Southern Myth." *Louisiana Studies* 15 (Fall 1976): 263-78.

Analysis of southern elements in Styron's first three novels.

Forkner, Ben, and Schricke, Gilbert. "An Interview with William Styron." *Southern Review* 10 (Autumn 1974): 923-34.

Interview conducted with Styron while on a lecture tour in France in which he discusses his authorship of a work-in-progress, *Sophie's Choice.*

Friedman, Melvin J. *William Styron.* Bowling Green, Ohio: Bowling Green University Popular Press, 1974, 82 p.

Favorable biographical and critical study of Styron's fiction.

Gossett, Louise Y. "The Cost of Freedom." In her *Violence in Recent Southern Fiction,* pp. 117-31. Durham, N. C.: Duke University Press, 1965.

Discusses the conflict between freedom and discipline in Styron's fiction. A standard source.

Holman, C. Hugh. *The Immoderate Past: The Southern Writer and History.* Athens: The University of Georgia Press, 1976.

Analyzes the theme of history in southern fiction during the nineteenth and twentieth centuries.

Leon, Philip W. *William Styron: An Annotated Bibliography of Criticism.* Westport, Connecticut: Greenwood Press, 1978, 129 p.

Detailed bibliography, including a biographical chronology, primary and secondary sources, an index of critics' names, and a subject index.

Lawson, Lewis. "Cass Kinsolving: Kierkegaardian Man of De-

spair." *Wisconsin Studies in Contemporary Literature* 3 (Fall 1962): 54-6.

Explores the influence of Kierkegaard on the protagonist of Styron's novel *Set This House on Fire.*

Matthiessen, Peter, and Plimpton, George. "William Styron." In *Writers at Work: The "Paris Review" Interviews,* edited by Malcolm Cowley, pp. 267-82. New York: The Viking Press, 1959.

Reprinted interview in which Styron rejects the designation of southern writer and comments on his novel *Lie Down in Darkness.*

Mudrick, Marvin. "Mailer and Styron." In his *On Culture and Literature,* pp. 176-99. New York: Horizon Press, 1970.

Reprint of an appraisal of works by Mailer and Styron in which Mudrick asserts that the novel *Lie Down in Darkness* is an artistic failure due to Styron's initial desire to attain celebrity through its publication.

Ross, Daniel W. "A Family Romance: Dreams and the Unified Narrative of *Sophie's Choice.*" *Mississippi Quarterly* XLII, No. 2 (Spring 1989): 129-45.

Contrary to the common critical opinion that the stories of Stingo and Sophie in Styron's novel are disconnected from one another, Ross argues that the two plots are "unified and interrelated."

Shapiro, Herbert. "*The Confessions of Nat Turner:* William Styron and His Critics." *Negro American Literature Forum* 9 (1975): 99-104.

Posits that Styron's portrayal of Nat Turner may have been influenced by Stanley Elkin's hypothesis that slaves historically conformed to the "Sambo" stereotype.

Sullivan, Walter. "The New Faustus." In his *Death by Melancholy: Essays on Modern Southern Fiction,* pp. 97-113. Baton Rouge: Louisiana State University Press, 1972.

Reprinted essay in which Sullivan defends Styron's novel from attacks by black critics, asserting that Styron's character is intended as a modern rather than historical creation.

Urang, Gunnar. "The Broader Vision: William Styron's *Set This House on Fire.*" *Critique* 8 (Winter 1965-1966): 47-69.

Analysis in which the successes and failures of Styron's novel are judged against his intentions.

Kurt Vonnegut, Jr.

1922-

American novelist, short story writer, dramatist, scriptwriter, and essayist.

The following entry presents criticism on Vonnegut's novel *Slaughterhouse-Five; or, The Children's Crusade: A Duty-Dance with Death.* For an overview of Vonnegut's career, see *CLC,* Vols. 1, 2, 3, 4, 5, 8, 12, 22, 40.

Regarded by many as a master of contemporary literature, Vonnegut uses satire, irony, and iconoclastic humor in his work to raise philosophical questions about the meaning of modern existence. Although characterized at various times in his career as a science fiction writer, a black humorist, a fantasist, and a postmodernist, Vonnegut commonly utilizes elements from all of these genres in his fiction. He is particularly noted for his playful narrative style, which typically features puns, aphorisms, slapstick, running gags, and self-effacing humor. His protagonists are usually idealistic, ordinary people who struggle in vain to understand and effect change in a world beyond their control or comprehension. Vonnegut rejects any ideology claiming absolute truth, emphasizing the role of chance in human actions and the insensitivity of social institutions. He describes himself as a "total pessimist," asserting that humankind is inherently self-destructive and existence is a "higgledy-piggledy cultural smorgasbord" that ends only in death. Despite his caustic message, Vonnegut always tempers his commentary with compassion for his characters, suggesting that humanity's ability to love may partially compensate for its destructive tendencies.

Slaughterhouse-Five was Vonnegut's first novel to achieve wide critical and popular acclaim, and the book's antiwar sentiments immediately established him as a counterculture hero among American students. This is also his first work to directly confront personal experience. Like his protagonist, Billy Pilgrim, Vonnegut was a soldier captured by Germans in World War II and interned as a prisoner of war in Dresden, Germany. Sheltered in a meat storage cellar below a slaughterhouse, Vonnegut was among the few to survive the Allied fire-bombing of Dresden, a city of no military or strategic value, on February 13, 1945. The massacre, which is estimated to have claimed the lives of over 135,000 civilians, killed more people than the atomic bombing of Hiroshima in 1945. However, the bombardment has been largely ignored by American historians. *Slaughterhouse-Five* is Vonnegut's attempt to preserve this destructive event from obscurity and to reconcile his own feelings regarding the incident, which for him represents the epitome of humanity's meaningless barbarism.

In the opening chapter of *Slaughterhouse-Five,* Vonnegut, as narrator, directly addresses the reader on the difficulty of writing about the Dresden fire-bombing. For over twenty years, Vonnegut confesses, he had tried to write a novel about his World War II experience but found language insufficient to convey its impact. In preparation for *Slaughterhouse-Five,* Vonnegut visited Bernard O'Hare, an old friend with whom he had been incarcerated as a prisoner-of-war in Germany, hoping to recall specific memories. However, O'Hare's wife, Mary, interrupted their discussion to say that she objected to any book that would glamorize war rather than reveal how the young are usually sacrificed during wartime. This observation prompted Vonnegut to subtitle his novel "The Children's Crusade," by which he draws a parallel between all modern warfare and the original Children's Crusade of 1213, in which 30,000 youths died pointlessly. Throughout most of *Slaughterhouse-Five,* Vonnegut, as narrator, recedes into the background, only occasionally intruding in the narrative. In the book's final chapter, however, he reappears to ponder the value of the quietistic philosophy espoused by Billy Pilgrim. Although critics differ as to whether Vonnegut-as-narrator should be construed as Vonnegut the author, many commentators have suggested that this distancing technique enables him to approach his painful memories of the Dresden fire-bombing.

Slaughterhouse-Five is written as a fragmented, non-chronological narrative to emphasize the confusion and absurdity of contemporary life. Cyclical in structure, this work randomly shifts through time and space, chronicling Billy Pilgrim's grisly experiences in World War II, his loveless marriage and bland postwar life as an optometrist in Ilium, New York, his resulting nervous breakdown, and his visits to an alien planet known as Tralfamadore. Billy's past and present abound with incidents of violence and loss: a tormented childhood, the accidental hunting death of his father, the hardships as a prisoner-of-war, the Dresden fire-bombing, a plane crash in which he fractures his skull, and the death of his wife by carbon-monoxide poisoning. After suffering a nervous breakdown following the war, Billy voluntarily enters a veterans' hospital. There he meets Eliot Rosewater, who introduces him to the novels of Kilgore Trout, an unsuccessful science fiction author. These books help the two veterans cope with life, which had come to seem meaningless largely because of their war experiences. In one of Trout's novels, Billy reads about a man and woman who are kidnapped by extraterrestrials and displayed in a zoo on their planet. Billy soon begins experiencing mental "time-trips" to Tralfamadore, a paradisal planet on which he is mated with a former movie star, Montana Wildhack. On the distant planet, he learns about the Tralfamadorian philosophy of time and death, for which he becomes a spokesman on earth. While recovering from injuries he suffers in a plane crash, Billy decides to impart Tralfamadorian wisdom to the rest of the world despite his precognition that people will think him insane and that he will be assassinated.

Critics have generally interpreted Billy's Tralfamadorian fantasies as arising from his psyche and being related to specific events in his life on earth. This science fiction device allows Vonnegut to introduce the Tralfamadorian philosophy of time and death that is essential to understanding *Slaughterhouse-Five.* Billy learns from the Tralfamadorians that all moments in a person's life exist simultaneously and that it is therefore best to think only of pleasant things. This perspective permits Tralfamadorians to view death as merely another moment in life and thereby to render the event meaningless. The Tralfamadorians also teach Billy that there is no cosmic purpose to the universe; that all actions are predetermined and knowledge of the future does not enable one to change destiny; and that free will is only an earthling illusion. By adopting the Tralfamadorian response to death, "So it goes," Billy seeks to avoid the pain of human suffering. When using this reasoning to comfort a boy whose father has died in Vietnam, however, Billy only upsets the child further, leading to the realization that he cannot lessen his own misery, let alone that of others. "So it goes," he concludes, is an inadequate response to death. Although Vonnegut writes the phrase "So it goes" following every mention of death in *Slaughterhouse-Five,* many critics contend that he is not condoning a stoic acceptance of injustice and suffering. According to Thomas L. Wymer: "Far from championing passive or blind acquiescence, Vonnegut insists on the importance of awareness, the necessity of human beings understanding how they cause pain." While Billy may believe intellectually in Tralfamadorianism, he rejects the philosophy emotionally because he cannot eradicate the trauma of the fire-bombing.

The hapless, unheroic Billy Pilgrim has elicited diverse interpretations from critics. Thomas L. Wymer, for example, has categorized Billy "as a kind of Everyman . . . , the typical blind and insensitive western man who pays little attention to the suffering around him." On the other hand, Dolores K. Gros Louis has posited that Vonnegut employs Billy as an ironic Christ figure, "an ineffectual and immoral messiah" who preaches the dubious gospel of Tralfamadorianism. And according to Stanley Schatt, Billy is a fictional descendant of John Yossarian, the hero of Joseph Heller's novel *Catch-22;* Yossarian's attempts to erase recurrent memories of his co-

pilot's death resemble Billy's efforts to suppress thoughts regarding Dresden. Schatt observed: "Only when Yossarian and Billy Pilgrim learn to cope with mankind's inhumanity and the horrors of war are they able to describe the atrocities they have repressed."

While *Slaughterhouse-Five* is often justly classified as an anti-war novel, many critics maintain that the book is more properly viewed as a complex, experimental work that imaginatively treats a conventional subject. Charles B. Harris remarked: "Ultimately, [*Slaughterhouse-Five*] is less about Dresden than it is about the impact of Dresden on one man's sensibilities. More specifically, it is the story of Vonnegut's story of Dresden, how he came to write it and, implicitly, why he wrote it as he did." Vonnegut's greatest commercial success and perhaps his best-known work, *Slaughterhouse-Five* is widely regarded, with Heller's *Catch-22* and Thomas Pynchon's *Gravity's Rainbow,* as a classic of postmodern fiction.

(See also *Contemporary Authors,* Vols. 1-4, rev. ed.; *Contemporary Authors New Revision Series,* Vols. 1, 25; *Dictionary of Literary Biography,* Vols. 2, 8; *Dictionary of Literary Biography Yearbook: 1980; Dictionary of Literary Biography Documentary Series,* Vol. 3; and *Concise Dictionary of American Literary Biography: Broadening Views, 1968-1988.*)

PRINCIPAL WORKS

NOVELS

Player Piano 1952; republished as *Utopia 14,* 1954
The Sirens of Titan 1959
Mother Night 1962
Cat's Cradle 1963
God Bless You, Mr. Rosewater; or, Pearls before Swine 1965
Slaughterhouse-Five; or, The Children's Crusade: A Duty-Dance with Death 1969
Breakfast of Champions; or, Goodbye, Blue Monday! 1973
Slapstick; or, Lonesome No More! 1976
Jailbird 1979
Deadeye Dick 1982
Galápagos 1985
Bluebeard 1987

SHORT FICTION COLLECTIONS

Canary in a Cat House 1963
Welcome to the Monkey House 1968

PLAYS

Happy Birthday, Wanda June 1970
Between Time and Timbuktu; or, Prometheus-Five: A Space Fantasy 1972

OTHER

Wampeters, Foma, and Granfalloons: Opinions (essays) 1974
Palm Sunday: An Autobiographical Collage 1981

CHARLES B. HARRIS

When both love and lies prove futile as viable responses to the absurd human condition, all that remains—other than suicide—is resignation. True wisdom, Vonnegut implies in *Slaughterhouse-Five,* lies in recognizing the things man cannot change. In the novel Vonnegut also suggests that it would be nice to possess the courage to change the things we can, but the novel offers little indication as to what falls within man's power to reform. "Among the things [the protagonist] Billy Pilgrim could not change," for example, "were the past, the present, and the future." The main idea emerging from *Slaughterhouse-Five* seems to be that the proper response to life is one of resigned acceptance.

This resignation undercuts any anti-war sentiment found in the novel. One might as well write an anti-glacier book as an anti-war book, Vonnegut says early in the novel. "And," he continues, "even if wars didn't keep coming like glaciers, there would still be plain old death." In many ways, *Slaughterhouse-Five* is a book about death, an extension of the statement Vonnegut quotes from Celine: "The truth is death." Everytime someone dies in *Slaughterhouse-Five* Vonnegut writes, "So it goes." The phrase occurs over one-hundred times in a one-hundred-eighty-six page novel.

The flippancy of the phrase offers a clue to the effectiveness of *Slaughterhouse-Five.* That effectiveness depends upon the novel's tone, the same kind of tone that colors most of Vonnegut's novels. In these novels, a carefully controlled ironic tension exists between the horrible, often catastrophic, events that make up the content of Vonnegut's novels, on the one hand, and what Richard Schickel calls "the sardonic, unhysteric rationalism of [the narrative] voice" on the other. A second kind of tension also exists in many of his novels. Present in these novels are figures like Julian Castle and Eliot Rosewater, whose concern for humanity contrasts with the absurdity of their surroundings and the hopelessness of the novel's tone. In *Slaughterhouse-Five,* however, no such figure appears. "There are almost no characters in this story," Vonnegut explains, "and almost no dramatic confrontations, because most of the people in it are so sick and so much the listless playthings of enormous forces." So the pervasive hopelessness of the novel's tone remains unmitigated by any character who strives, no matter how futilely, to act in a meaningful manner.

Slaughterhouse-Five is based partially on Vonnegut's own experiences in World War II. Like Vonnegut, Billy Pilgrim is captured by the Germans and taken to Dresden, where he witnesses the destruction of the city by American fire-bombers. While in Germany, Billy first becomes "unstuck in time." For Billy, "all moments, past, present, and future, always have existed, always will exist." "Spastic in time," with "no control over where he is going next," Billy has "seen his birth and death many times, . . . and pays random visits to all the events in between." One of these events involves his kidnaping by Tralfamadorians, who take him via flying saucer to their planet where he lives in a zoo with Montana Wildhack, famous earthling movie star. One of the things the Tralfamadorians teach Billy is that "it is just an illusion we have here on Earth that one moment follows another one, like beads on a string, and that once a moment is gone it is gone forever." True time is like the Rocky Mountains, permanent, and one can "look at any moment that interests [him]." (pp. 69-70).

Completely resigned to the inevitability of events, Billy finds everything "pretty much all right." Even the destruction of Dresden, which claimed the lives of 135,000 German citizens, mostly civilians, draws the following response from Billy: "*Everything* is all right, and everybody has to do exactly what he does. I learned that on Tralfamadore."

The first thing Billy learns from the Tralfamadorians is the utter lack of any cosmic purpose. "Why *you?* Why *us* for that matter? Why *anything*" Billy is told upon being kidnapped. "Because the moment simply is. . . . There is no *why.*" One searches for meaning in vain. Time, say the Tralfamadorians, "does not lend itself to warnings or explanations. It simply *is.* Take it moment by moment, and you will find that we are all . . . bugs in amber." The world, in other words, is all that the case is, and attempts either to change or to understand it are foredoomed to failure.

The proper response to life, then, becomes resignation. "God grant me the serenity to accept the things I cannot change" becomes the prayer of relevance, one Vonnegut repeats several times throughout the novel. To enhance this serenity, one should "concentrate on the happy moments of . . . life, and . . . ignore the unhappy ones." Billy succeeds in this advice so well that a fitting epitaph for his tombstone, we are told, might read: "Everything was beautiful, and nothing hurt." This, despite a life filled with such violent events as the destruction of Dresden, his own capture by enemy troops, a plane crash in which his skull is fractured, the bizarre death of his wife by carbon monoxide poisoning, and his eventual assassination by a deranged killer!

Such bland acceptance of "things as they are" seems strange in a Vonnegut novel. Initially, one suspects the novel ridicules rather than recommends such passivity. Yet little in the novel supports this contention. In fact, when Vonnegut suggests the epigraph for Billy Pilgrim, he comments upon its appropriateness to his own life. A similar sentiment appears in his introduction to *Welcome to the Monkey House.* The "two main themes of my novels," he writes, "were stated by my siblings." Peter, Vonnegut's older brother, stated the first in a letter home shortly after the birth of his first child. "Here I am," he wrote, "cleaning shit off of practically everything." Vonnegut's sister stated the second theme. Dying of cancer, she uttered, "No pain." Together, the themes seem contradictory. Can one, aware of how polluted "practically everything" in life has become, remain content with life? Or, to put it another way, why would one able to view painlessly the conditions of life bother to protest those conditions?

The prayer repeated several times in *Slaughterhouse-Five* provides the answer to these questions. "God grant me the serenity," it reads, "to accept the things I cannot change, courage to change the things I can, and wisdom always to tell the difference." Certain things, then, lie within man's control. Included would be those illusions mentioned earlier that make man's life more tedious than necessary, the illusions that contribute to wars and poverty and prejudice. These illusions Vonnegut exposes and ridicules. Most things, however, exceed man's limited control, not to mention his equally limited understanding. True wisdom accepts this fact, acknowledging the lack of universal purpose or meaning or direction. All human activity is blighted by this pervasive absurdity. Since the blight is irremediable, acceptance of it may be the only sane response for man. Indeed, acceptance of absurdity may constitute the only logical extension of the absurdist vision. (pp. 70-2)

Charles B. Harris, "Illusion and Absurdity: The Novels of Kurt Vonnegut, Jr.," in his Contemporary American Novelists of the Absurd, *College & University Press, 1971, pp. 51-75.*

RAYMOND M. OLDERMAN

Because of our pride and bad illusions—which are the dragons in Vonnegut's fables—the quality of human life as he presents it is horrendous. The way we live influences the dark part of Vonnegut's vision, for, as Howard W. Campbell, Jr., puts it in **Mother Night,** anyone growing up in this world expecting peace and order will "be eaten alive." The texture of our lives is made clearest in **Slaughterhouse-Five**—a title that ostensibly refers to a real meat slaughterhouse in Dresden, but which reflects a sense of our world at its worst. When the Tralfamadorians tell Billy Pilgrim in **Slaughterhouse-Five** to live the way they do and ignore life's ugly moments, Vonnegut juxtaposes this advice with some of Billy's childhood moments: a trip to the Grand Canyon and one to Carlsbad Caverns—both are moments filled with fear, terror, and flirtation with death. The world he lives in does not offer Billy too many marvelous moments at all; the tone is set by World War II, by prison camps and prison trains, by incredible hatred between men—allies and enemies both—and finally by the outrageous fire-bomb destruction of Dresden. This is the moment that Vonnegut himself keeps coming back to, a moment he actually witnessed as a prisoner of war; it is the personal basis of the apocalyptic darkness in his vision, for if man is capable of a senseless and absolutely gratuitous slaughter like Dresden, then he is capable of total world destruction. (p. 196)

Slaughterhouse-Five goes the furthest of all Vonnegut's books in mixing fact with fiction. "All this happened, more or less," he tells us on the first page, and the voice of the narrator in the first chapter is decidedly and openly Vonnegut speaking about Vonnegut. The body of the book tells the story of Billy Pilgrim, a fictional someone who was at Dresden with Vonnegut the narrator. Billy too is clearly a ghost in Vonnegut's chamber of fears about himself. Billy has been deadened by his experience and is passive to the slaughters he continues to witness—to an airplane crash that kills everyone on board but himself; to Vietnam and his son, who, we are told repeatedly, has been straightened out by the Green Berets; to his wife's death and to his own death. Clearly, Billy can afford to be a little passive since he is "unstuck in time" and knows the past, the present, and the future. But the detached cool he develops obviously is too detached for Vonnegut the narrator, who in contrast tells us of himself:

> I have told my sons that they are not under any circumstances to take part in massacres, and that the news of massacres of enemies is not to fill them with satisfaction or glee.

> I have also told them not to work for companies which make massacre machinery, and to express contempt for people who think we need machinery like that.

There is, however, something about Billy's detachment that is attractive to Vonnegut. As narrator he too tries a small touch of it—a kind of *cosmic cool* that comes with looking at himself from some perspective, from an interplanetary vantage point, perhaps. In Vonnegut's novels a little cosmic cool, if it does not turn into indifference, helps some of his charac-

ters resist Lilliputian pride. It helps them cool off a little about their own deaths. Vonnegut has a running symbol for that kind of detachment—it appears in **Cat's Cradle, God Bless You, Mr. Rosewater,** and **Slaughterhouse-Five,** and is reminiscent of a symbol used by John Hawkes. Hovering above the abyss of total destruction, reminding us that there is little to say about massacres, and nothing to say about Purpose and Meaning, Vonnegut continually pictures a small bird asking eternally a small question: "Poo-tee-weet?" If such a question means anything, it probably means "so what"; but it also means "I see the dimensions of human life and I survive!"

A second device Vonnegut uses to convey a sense of proportion about the world he sees is the phrase "so it goes," which he uses after every mention of death in **Slaughterhouse-Five.** The death of a dog, of Christ, of a fictional character, of the bubbles in champagne, of 135,000 Germans and 6,000,000 Jews, of Robert Kennedy, of Martin Luther King, and of narrator-Vonnegut's father all rate the same response—"so it goes." Death of any kind is meaningless and all deaths are equal—Vonnegut tells us the term comes from the Tralfamadorians whose perspective on time allows them to see death as just another moment in life.

> "When a Tralfamadorian sees a corpse, all he thinks is that the dead person is in bad condition in that particular moment, but that the same person is just fine in plenty of other moments. Now, when I myself hear that somebody is dead, I simply shrug and say what the Tralfamadorians say about dead people, which is 'So it goes.' "

This kind of cosmic cool is of course an illusion, but as Vonnegut warns us, if we are to keep our heads and continue to live while we are looking into the abyss of possible cataclysm, we are going to have to learn some new lies—we are going to have to learn to say "Poo-tee-weet?" and "so it goes." It is what the fabulist says by containing his black vision in a form we usually connect with happy endings; it is what the black humorist says when he is laughing; it is very much the imagistic counterpart of what Pynchon says when he tells us "to keep cool but care." It is not said without compassion. If I may continue to use the term *cosmic cool,* I think it can help us understand the ideal way to live in Vonnegut's world. Without it we commit personal suicide like Howard W. Campbell, Jr., in **Mother Night,** public suicide like the cataclysm at the end of **Cat's Cradle,** spiritual suicide like Billy Pilgrim in **Slaughterhouse-Five**. . . . (pp. 197-200)

The process through which the illusion of fate can go too far and turn the cosmic cool into petrified inaction and indifference is . . . clearly demonstrated during a conversation in **Slaughterhouse-Five** between Billy Pilgrim and the Tralfamadorians. Billy has just finished cataloguing some of earth's brutalities, explaining in Lilliputian-like fashion that earthlings will be the terrors of the universe and destroy everyone unless they learn peace. The Tralfamadorians tone down Billy's pride and panic with a touch of cosmic perspective, but the result is to deaden Billy's already damaged will to live instead of giving him the balanced perspective of the cosmic cool. The universe will not be destroyed by earthlings, the Tralfamadorians tell Billy:

> "We know how the universe ends"—said the guide, "and Earth has nothing to do with it, except that *it* gets wiped out, too."
> "How—how does the universe end?" said Billy.

"We blow it up, experimenting with new fuels for our flying saucers. A Tralfamadorian test pilot presses a starter button, and the whole Universe disappears." So it goes.

"If you know this," said Billy, "isn't there some way you can prevent it? Can't you keep the pilot from *pressing* the button?"

"He has *always* pressed it, and he always *will*. We *always* let him and we always *will* let him. The moment is *structured* that way."

"So—" said Billy gropingly, "I suppose that the idea of preventing war on Earth is stupid, too." "Of course."

It is obvious that such an illusion leads to the toleration of button pressing, and Billy's will to live is not reinforced by these Tralfamadorian insights. (pp. 203-04)

Vonnegut seems to identify himself closely with his characters' confessions of guilt; we have already seen that the connection between Vonnegut the narrator and Billy Pilgrim in **Slaughterhouse-Five** reveals that Billy's living death—a death of the spirit caused in large part by his experience with the Dresden slaughter—is something Vonnegut fears possible for himself. . . . In **Slaughterhouse-Five,** I believe, Vonnegut purposely intrudes himself as a character appearing in the first and last chapters of the book, surrounding the story of Billy Pilgrim, in order to test his own personal ability to achieve the posture of the cosmic cool. Billy himself, as we have seen, *appears* both detached and compassionate enough to have achieved the ideal balance, but it is all an appearance. He is really a man whose will to live—never more than a precarious thing to begin with—has been deadened by Dresden and by the harmful illusion that all things are determined, that everything has always happened and nothing can change. And this *is* a harmful illusion, for while it allows Billy to exist physically, it also allows him to be absolved from the guilts of war without the cost of compassion. But Vonnegut the narrator believes man can still learn to be kind and end wars—he believes he himself can still write an antiwar novel where war is not glorified but labeled an obscene "Children's Crusade." Yet he does fear that the same detached perspective, the cosmic vantage point, which helps him recognize man's pride and the necessity for conscience and compassion could lead him to Billy Pilgrim's kind of deadness. It could do that because it is based on the memory of Dresden, which not only demands some detachment but provides a constant temptation to give up and withdraw. The writing of **Slaughterhouse-Five,** however, is a special act of love for Vonnegut; it is a fable, he tells us, he has been a long time trying to write, a fable that exorcises his own terrors and guilts and convinces him he is able to invent and therefore live and love under the illusion of the cosmic cool. "Sam—here's the book," he tells his publisher:

It is so short and jumbled and jangled, Sam, because there is nothing intelligent to say about a massacre. Everybody is supposed to be dead, to never say anything or want anything ever again. Everything is supposed to be very quiet after a massacre, and it always is, except for the birds. And what do the birds say? All there is to say about a massacre, things like *"Poo-tee-weet?"*

Vonnegut's fable proves that he is not dead, that—like T. S. Eliot's poet-prophets, also symbolized by birds—he can still say something, even if it is only the "Poo-tee-weet?" that

symbolizes the illusion of the cosmic cool. Like Pynchon's Fausto Maijstral, he has glimpsed annihilation in Dresden and come back from his view of the dead. Vonnegut tells us Lot's wife was turned to a pillar of salt for looking back on the destruction of Sodom and Gomorrah. He tells us **Slaughterhouse-Five** is a failure because it was written by a pillar of salt who looked back on Dresden. But the truth is, it is a success on some levels: it is one way of dealing with historical fact—an intensely personal way and a way that seems to be very popular in the late sixties; it is a confessional exorcism and an act of love for both the author and his reader. In it Vonnegut creates a true fable of someone managing to live in the world, coping with the agonies of massacre and the confusions of fabulous fact—true because that someone is Vonnegut himself. He is the someone who is able to achieve the balance of the cosmic cool, combining humility, compassion, love, and conscience with a detached control of these virtues, and the will to go on living. And because that someone is himself, he further perfects the concept of the cosmic cool, adding what is much needed in our world of guilt and terror—the dignity of self-respect. He need not fear that he is the spiritually dead Billy Pilgrim. . . .

"Poo-tee-weet?" the symbolic bird asks in the last line of **Slaughterhouse-Five,** and the nonsense words become especially moving because we are witnessing more than a black humorist's symbolic affirmation of life, and more than a fabulist's act of love—we are witnessing a moment of balance in Vonnegut's own life, when he finds himself capable of dealing with the intense pain of his Dresden experience and ready to go on with the delicate business of living. (pp. 211-14)

> *Raymond M. Olderman, "Out of the Waste Land and into the Fire: Cataclysm or the Cosmic Cool," in his* Beyond the Waste Land: A Study of the American Novel in the Nineteen-Sixties, *Yale University Press, 1972, pp. 189-219.*

NEIL D. ISAACS

[*Slaughterhouse-Five*] adapts itself to reduction to statements of essence better than most [novels], though there are three separate statements, like the voices of a fugue, in a tripartite essence and structure. First and foremost, it is an antiwar document, conceived in anguish for firebomb-destroyed Dresden and dedicated to the propositions that war is an absurd assertion of man's will, that it must be revealed in all its absurdity, and that all men must see the futility and desperate irony in all the manifestations of war, past, present and future. Vonnegut portrays himself, his friends, his characters—people, cities, countries, institutions—as all victimized, brutalized, dehumanized by war. And even the slightest, most ridiculously ironic loss is a measure of that self-destruction. *Slaughterhouse-Five* is a denunciation of war, written compulsively to denounce war, designed to denounce war, and fulfilled by the litany of that denunciation. This is the element that has won a large audience among the peace-seeking young.

Second, it is a science fiction that deals with the topic of free will versus fatalism and a related philosophical issue of the nature of time. If the self-assertiveness of humanity inevitably leads to war, the alternative is a kind of sublime acceptance of everything. This is the fatalistic message from Tralfamadore brought to earth by Billy Pilgrim. The Tralfamadorian response to death and destruction, however violent, pointless, mindless, brutal, or unnecessary, is, "So it goes." If you dwell only on the pleasant moments, your epitaph can read, "Everything was beautiful, and nothing hurt." And since all moments always exist, it is important to remember that each moment "is structured" the way it happens, to accept everything, and to desire nothing different.

That *Slaughterhouse-Five* does not itself preach the Tralfamadorian gospel is evident. Billy Pilgrim is as foolish a figure as his wife, as irrelevant as Kilgore Trout, as mad as Paul Lazzaro. Tralfamadorian fatalism and time concepts are as valid as the Tralfamadorian theory that all seven human sexes are necessary for reproduction of earthlings. That the alternative to war is acceptance of everything as structured—including war—is, then, a very bitter irony. The familiar prayer, repeated at strategic points in the book—

> God grant me the serenity
> to accept the things I cannot change,
> courage to change the things I can,
> and wisdom always to tell the difference—

delineates the ironic tensiveness between Vonnegut's need to condemn the destruction of Dresden and Billy's call to spread the Tralfamadorian word of fatalism. Billy has learned from his zoo-keeper that earth is the only one of 131 inhabited planets where there is any talk of free will. But that is precisely the point: earthlings are concerned with earthly humanity. Those who see the book as fatalistic have been either beguiled by its potential for humor directed at human society or seduced by the satirical nihilism it seems to share with [the film director Stanley] Kubrick. And they have not heard the tonal distinction between "So it goes" as uttered by Kurt Vonnegut and by Billy Pilgrim. Again, a considerable audience has been won by the conventional sci-fi treatment of contemporary institutions.

Third, *Slaughterhouse-Five* is a book about the writing of the book. The whole first section is a kind of foreword in which Vonnegut, in propria persona, talks about the conception of the book, the history of its composition, some of the research involved, the incident that supplied the subtitle, and the personal significance of the whole project. Then, throughout the narration, there are frequent interjections like "I was there" or "That was me, the author of this book" to remind us to distinguish the voices and to keep this element in mind. The theme is enlarged by discussions of writing with Rosewater, Trout, Rumfoord, and even the Tralfamadorian guide. Trout and his fiction play a role in this novel like Pursewarden in Durrell's *Alexandria Quartet* and even more like Morelli in Cortázar's *Hopscotch*. It is this element, then, that places *Slaughterhouse-Five* in one of the mainstreams of contemporary literature, though its audience seems largely unaware of it. (pp. 127-30)

> *Neil D. Isaacs, "Unstuck in Time: 'Clockwork Orange' and 'Slaughterhouse-Five'," in* Literature/Film Quarterly, *Vol. 1, No. 2, April, 1973, pp. 122-31.*

ARNOLD EDELSTEIN

The basic question for every reader of *Slaughterhouse-Five* is simple: how seriously are we to take Billy Pilgrim's Tralfamadorian theory of time? Is it happy fantasy, like the harmoniums in *The Sirens of Titan?* Is it fictionalized but serious speculation about the nature of time? Is it a large, philosophical metaphor of man's existential condition? (p. 128)

On first reading, at least, the theory of the simultaneity of all time and its implication of a thorough-going determinism in which man is totally incapable of changing his condition do seem to constitute either an avoidance of moral responsibility or a metaphysical horror story. The world is both real and totally determined from its beginning to its end. We are bugs trapped in the amber of an unalterable spacial display of simultaneous moments that only seem to succeed each other. Instead of vainly trying to free ourselves from the amber, we should take the Tralfamadorians' advice and "ignore the awful times, and concentrate on the good ones." This kind of first reading, which takes the time theory at face value, is encouraged by the similarities between Vonnegut's own experience and Billy Pilgrim's and by the presence in the novel of both Vonnegut in his own voice and characters from his earlier novels. Never the less, there is overwhelming evidence throughout *Slaughterhouse-Five* that every element of Billy's "sci-fi fantasy" can be explained in realistic, psychological terms.

Perhaps aware of the reader's temptation to identify the author with his central character after hearing the author speaking in his own voice in the first chapter, Vonnegut begins the second chapter with a clear assertion of narrative distance. Billy "has seen his birth and death many times, *he says,* and pays random visits to all the events in between. *He says.* . . . He is in a constant state of stage fright, *he says.* . . . " Two pages later, Vonnegut repeats this emphasis.

> He said, too, that he had been kidnaped by a flying saucer in 1967. The saucer was from the planet Tralfamadore, *he said.* He was taken to Tralfamadore, where he was displayed naked in a zoo, *he said.*

Vonnegut maintains the narrative distance that is established here throughout the novel by a rather complex formal structure which distinguishes, sometimes not too clearly, between four levels of narration: *Vonnegut's present tense* (chapters one and ten); *Billy's present tense* (his trip to New York and its aftermath); *a novelistic past tense of historical fact* (the war experiences, Billy's eighteenth wedding anniversary and the plance crash); *and Billy's travels in time and space,* which contain both historical events and the Tralfamadorian episodes (generally woven throughout the war experiences). Only the last level, the flash-forwards, raise any problems. Most of these problems vanish, however, when we reconstructed a chronological time-sequence from the bits and pieces that Vonnegut gives us. For then we discover that the flash-forwards are actually reinterpretations of Billy's past experience in the light of a time fantasy that takes twenty years to develop, but that achieves full form only a short while before he communicates it during his visit to New York City.

Such a chronological reconstruction would begin with the events that disturb the pattern of Billy's life in 1944: basic training and the death of his father. In quick succession after that, Billy is sent to Europe, is cut off from his unit, is taken prisoner by the Germans, and becomes a survivor of the firebombing of Dresden. Three years later, after the war and during his last year in optometry school, Billy breaks down and commits himself to a veterans' hospital. While in the hospital, he reads Kilgore Trout's science fiction novel *The Big Board,* "about an Earthling man and woman who were kidnaped by extra terrestrials" and "put on display in a zoo on a planet called Zircon-212." The seeds for the space-travel elements of Billy's fantasy, then, were planted as early as 1948, twenty years before Billy communicates the fantasy to anyone else (in the actual telling, Vonnegut withholds the information until the end of the novel).

Billy is released from the hospital, marries the daughter of the school founder and president, and, for eighteen years, lives an exemplary suburban life. He makes lots of money, invests his money wisely, owns a Cadillac that exhibits ultra-conservative bumper-stickers, attends Little League banquets, becomes an important member of the Lions Club, is unfaithful to his wife (but only once), and raises two children he really does not know or understand. On the night of his eighteenth wedding anniversary, however, the war returns to Billy's consciousness. In the middle of the hilarity of the celebration, he associates the optometrists' barbershop quartet with the four German guards who survived the fire-bombing of Dresden along with the American prisoners. Billy reacts to the memory called up by this association by having what seems to be a cardiac seizure. Kilgore Trout, whom Billy had accidentally met a few days earlier and had invited to the party, speculates that Billy has seen the past or the future through a time window. Billy denies it, but since he *has* seen the past, the time-travel element of his fantasy has been added to the idea of being kidnapped by extra-terrestrials. The entire incident is given authorial support by being described in novelistic past tense, not as one of Billy's travels in time.

After the anniversary party, Billy's world begins to crumble. He falls asleep in his office while taking care of his patients; he cannot care about the future of European optometry; the scene of a riot in Ilium's black ghetto frightens him and the scene of Ilium's attempt at urban renewal seems more desolate than Dresden; a pro-Vietnam war speaker at the Lions Club leaves him unmoved, although his own son is a Green Beret; seeing two cripples working a racket depresses him; and the loneliness of his house causes him to weep. Indeed, as only his doctor knows, "every so often, for no apparent reason, Billy Pilgrim would find himself weeping." This first stage of his breakdown climaxes in the absolute emptiness he feels on the night after his daughter's wedding—the night on which he chooses to be abducted by the Tralfamadorians.

Three earlier scenes help explain this emptiness; each relates to old age, and two are clearly associated with war. In 1965 his mother, recuperating from pneumonia in a nursing home, had asked him, "How did I get so *old*"—associated with the war because Billy thumbs through *The Execution of Private Slovik* a few minutes later in the waiting room. When he was sixteen, a man suffering horribly from gas had told him, "I knew it was going to be bad getting old. . . . I didn't know it was going to be *this* bad"—associated with the war because it is recalled while Billy is in bed next to Bertram Copeland Rumfoord, the official historian of the Air Force, and is discussing the bombing of Dresden. Finally, on one of the days that Billy falls asleep at the office, he notices the license plate of his Cadillac, dated 1967, and wonders: "Where have all the years gone?" His son a sergeant in Vietnam, his daughter married, his house empty, Billy has nothing to look forward to but old age and death—and nothing to look back to but Dresden.

Billy's collapse is completed by two accidents—when the plane taking him to a convention of optometrists crashes, killing everyone but Billy; and when his wife dies of carbon mon-

oxide poisoning after rushing to see him in the hospital. The plane crash is associated with Dresden in a number of ways. The barbershop quartet from the anniversary party is singing just before the plane goes down—although Vonnegut obscures the connection by having the crash precede the party in the telling. Rumfoord, the military historian, is in the bed next to Billy. When the Austrian ski instructors from Sugarbush are bending over Billy, he whispers "Schlachthof-fünf"—slaughterhouse-five—his address in Dresden. Finally, he is again a survivor.

Soon after his release from the hospital, Billy, possibly suffering the after effects of a broken skull, sneaks off to New York City to communicate his time theory and its source to the world. Before he can get on a talk show, however, he wanders into a bookstore that specializes in pornography and thumbs through two books by Kilgore Trout—including the one about being kidnaped by extra-terrestrials that he had read years earlier in the veterans' hospital. He also sees a girly magazine with the headline, "What really became of Montana Wildhack" and part of a blue movie that Montana had made as a teenager. The fantasy is now complete. The clearest indication that Vonnegut means us to see it as fantasy is his use of the same phrases, with the pronouns made singular in the second instance, to describe the photographs of Montana in the girly magazine and the photograph of Montana's mother on her locket, which Billy says he sees in the zoo on Tralfamadore: "They were grainy things, soot and chalk. They could have been anybody." Significantly, the message on the other side of the locket is the same as the prayer on the wall of Billy's office: "God grant me the serenity to accept the things I cannot change, courage to change the things I can, and wisdom always to tell the difference." It is clear at this point that all the significant details of Billy's life on Tralfamadore have sources in Billy's life here on Earth.

That night, Billy tells about Tralfamadore on a radio talk show. A month later, he writes a letter about Tralfamadore to the Ilium *News Leader* and is working on a second when his daughter interrupts him. A few days after that, he tries to comfort a boy whose father has been killed in Vietnam by telling him the Tralfamadorian's theory about death. The chronology ends with Billy's daughter taking him home and saying: "Father, Father, Father—what *are* we going to *do* with you?" The chronology ends, that is, if we do not include Billy's time-travel version of his death in 1976.

Billy is happy at the end of the novel, no matter what his daughter thinks. Significantly, however, the time-travel elements of his fantasy—those flash-forwards based on historial fact—bring Billy no peace at all. They cause that stage fright he feels at never knowing "what part of his life he is going to have to act in next." They are, then, an excellent metaphor for a man's inability to keep the horrible experiences of his past from invading the relative serenity of his present. They are more frightening in Vonnegut's version because the earlier experiences are not just remembered; they are *relived*. The space-travel to Tralfamadore and what Billy learns there about time provide him with a framework in which he can make peace with both the horrors of his past and the horrors of his impending old age, and in which his entire life has meaning—a framework that neither reality nor the time-travel elements alone could provide. Instead of a lost, little man whose life is empty and filled with horror, Billy becomes a saviour, "prescribing corrective lenses for Earthling souls." As a prophet of the Tralfamadorian "way," Billy can now forsee a life that has direction and significant meaning—and he can foresee a martyr's death that is completely antithetical to the painful meaninglessness of his mother in the nursing home and the old man afflicted with gas. These saviour elements of Billy's fantasy also have their source in his actual experience: the "ghastly crucifix" on his wall and Kilgore Trout's novel about a time-traveler who wants to see Jesus.

If Billy were an actual person, not a literary character, we could say that his resigned "so it goes," the leit-motif of the novel, is earned at a price terrible enough to be psychologically consistent with the horror of Billy's experiences. The only way he can live with his memories of the past and his fear of the future and find meaning in both is to withdraw from reality into a pleasant but neurotic fantasy. Vonnegut's restructuring of the chronological sequence prolongs our confusion about what is going on until the end of the novel and allows us to see in a single moment of insight—the scene in the bookstore—exactly what Dresden has done to Billy. This ending has a potentially enormous emotional impact.

The restructuring also gives Vonnegut an opportunity for some biting ironic juxtapositions that bring the war scenes and the suburban scenes into the same complex of influences on Billy's life and help explain the total emptiness that drives him away from reality. Billy packed into an orange and black cattle car in 1944, for example, flashes forward to his daughter's wedding in 1967, which takes place under an orange and black tent. How different are the two events and yet how similar—dehumanized flesh markets in Halloween colors. Or totally powerless Billy, about to be thrashed by Roland Weary, flashes forward to Billy the self-assured optometrist, about to speak as president of the Lions Club. Which is the real Billy? How self-assured can Billy the president be when he is built upon Billy the soldier?

Other juxtapositions relate causes and effects or problems and possible solutions. In the middle of the cattle-car episodes, we flash forward to Billy's malaise in 1967. The intensity of the experience is different in each incident, but Billy is equally unwanted and powerless in both. In the middle of the prison camp episode, which describes the further dehumanization of the American prisoners in ironic contrast to the fraternity heriocs of the British officers, Billy flashes forward to the veterans' hospital and his honeymoon, episodes in which we see his first withdrawal from reality in ironic contrast to both his mother's and his wife's inability to understand what he has been through in Dresden.

In short, Billy's fantasy provides him with a hard-won escape from the horrors of death—both the violent death of Dresden and the natural death that he faces in the future—and from the moral responsibility of having to do something about war, his meaningless existence, the generation gap, ghetto riots, cripples who work magazine rackets, and so on. (pp. 128-33)

Billy Pilgrim's withdrawal from reality is not a random one. Its pattern is obscured by Vonnegut's restructuring of the chronological sequence but becomes obvious when we take the Tralfamadorians' advice and look at only the pleasant moments in Billy's life. Oddly, Billy's most pleasant moments include the potentially terrifying incidents in which he is dropped into a pool by his father, is crammed into a cattle car with other prisoners of war, is stripped and scalded in a delousing station, is carried through Dresden after the bombing, and then is kidnaped by creatures that resemble green machines and displayed in a zoo. As we shall see, the pattern

is almost the same in all of these incidents: completely passive Billy is placed in a situation that is pleasant because it provides all the necessities of life and precludes anxiety but then is jolted back into reality.

Two of the incidents are very simple and indicate the direction of the entire group. At first, Billy's plunge into the pool is "like an execution," but then it changes:

> When he opened his eyes, he was on the bottom of the pool, and there was beautiful music everywhere. He lost consciousness, but the music went on. He dimly sensed that somebody was rescuing him. Billy resented that.

The scalding water of the delousing station brings on a flashback of Billy being bathed by his mother, but his gurgling and cooing is then interrupted by a flash-forward of Billy playing golf and Billy being told that he is "trapped in another blob of amber" and has no free will. In both incidents, Billy accepts the lure of infancy but is propelled back into adulthood.

The cattle car and the horse-cart take Billy back from infancy into the womb itself. Each cattle car

> became a single organism which ate and drank and excreted through its ventilators. It talked or sometimes yelled through its ventilators too. In went water and loaves of blackbread and sausage and cheese, and out came shit and piss and language.

But the womb of the cattle-car is pleasant: "When food came in, the human beings were quiet and trusting and beautiful. They shared." Later, Billy is delivered from the car and must face the horrors that await him.

The destruction of Dresden and its aftermath constitute the most complex example of this pattern. The American soldiers, who have been herded about like children and who have survived by eating syrup, are saved from the firebombing because they are being kept deep in the basement of a concrete slaughterhouse. A few days later, Billy is sleeping in the back of a "coffin-shaped green wagon . . . . He was happy. He was warm. There was food in the wagon, and wine . . ." We are told that this ride was Billy's "happiest moment." Complete with Billy's own tears and blood dripping from the horse's mouth, Billy is delivered from the wagon-coffin-womb by two obstetricians. Once again, Billy is reborn from a womb-like, pleasant death (the obstetricians look at the suffering of the horse as they would have looked at Christ being taken down from the cross) not into paradise but into a life that is filled with the horrors of actual death.

If Billy's escape from the horrors of reality is ultimately unsuccessful in each of these actual incidents, the final escape—into the fantasy of the zoo on Tralfamadore—is completely successful. The zoo is a geodesic dome that contains a simulated Earth environment, including a lounge chair which had been Billy's "cradle during his trip through space." Billy is appropriately naked within his geodesic womb; the necessities of life are provided by the Tralfamadorians; and Billy can not escape even if he wants to: "the atmosphere outside the dome was cyanide, and Earth was 446,120,000,000,000,000 miles away." While in the zoo, Billy is indoctrinated with the Tralfamadorians' theories, which seem designed to free him from his anxieties:

> On other days we have wars as horrible as you've ever seen or read about. There isn't anything we can do about them, so we simply don't look at

them. We ignore them. We spend eternity looking
at pleasant moments—like today at the zoo.

But Billy is not alone on Tralfamadore. He is mated with
Montana Wildhack, a pleasant, buxom, movie starlet with a
jaded past. Why is Montana in the fantasy at all? The easiest
answer is simply that Montana has apparently always lived
her life in accordance with the prayer on Billy's wall. She accepts what she cannot change and adapts to her condition
whether she is making pornographic movies, living high in
Hollywood as a starlet, or being held prisoner in a zoo on
Tralfamadore. She can be seen, then, as something of a contrast to Billy and we may take the contrast on its own terms
or see it as a terrible irony: only mindless movie starlets can
be happy in this world.

Montana as part of the general environment on Tralfamadore, however, is a contrast of another kind as well. She is
a twenty-year-old movie star whose naked body reminds
Billy of the "fantastic architecture in Dresden, before it was
bombed." In spite of the disparity in their ages and in physical attractiveness—Billy is "shaped like a bottle of Coca
Cola"—Montana "came to love and trust Billy Pilgrim."
Their first lovemaking was "heavenly." Further, she is a great
contrast to Valencia, Billy's wife—who had been pleasant,
but fat and ugly—and to Barbara, Billy's daughter—who is
not much older than Montana but who is described as a
"bitchy flibbertigibbet" who takes Billy's "dignity away in
the name of love." Montana—the big-breasted, yielding,
ideal woman of adolescent masturbation fantasies—
supplements the Tralfamadorians' theories as a defense
against Billy's feelings of impotence and his fear of death.

The frequent references to Eden indicate that, on one level,
we are meant to take Billy and Montana as another Adam
and Eve. Eden myths, however, frequently mask and attempt
to dignify escapist, regressive fantasies of the kind we have
been discussing here. Significantly, just before he is kidnaped
Billy is watching a war movie on television that moves backwards from the landing of a decimated squadron in England
after a bombing raid. Billy sees bullets being sucked out of
planes and bombs returning from the ground into the bellies
of the planes. Finally, in Billy's imagination, "everybody
turned into a baby, and all humanity, without exception, con-
spired biologically, to produce two perfect people named
Adam and Eve." This backwards movie may be one of Vonnegut's gems in the novel but it also indicates the function of
the Eden imagery and its relation to the womb imagery. In
the long run, Eden and the womb seem identical—places of
retreat beyond which Billy cannot regress.

Billy Pilgrim, Vonnegut's everyman-schlemiel-hero, reacts to
the horrors of the world around him by withdrawing totally
from reality. Billy is not merely an ostrich who hides his head
in the pleasant moments of his past rather than facing the difficulties of the present and the future; but one who crawls
back into the egg itself. (pp. 133-36)

As human beings, we may—perhaps must—ask ourselves
whether or not Vonnegut's response to World War II and to
the chaotic Nineteen-Sixties is adequate, but the standards
with which our judgment will be made are extra-literary. Politically, Vonnegut's solution may not get us anywhere, perhaps because it is based on a resigned and pessimistic, although loving, view of human nature; psychologically, like
the solution implied in so many other American novels, it attempts to deny the responsibilities of adulthood by escaping

into a pre-sexual, pre-fall past. Nevertheless, as readers, we
must recognize that *Slaughterhouse-Five* makes eloquent
sense within its own esthetic limits. Our objections, if any, are
to the limits, not to Vonnegut's achievement within them.
(pp. 138-39)

*Arnold Edelstein, " 'Slaughterhouse-Five': Time
Out of Joint," in* College Literature, *Vol. 1, No. 2,
Spring, 1974, pp. 128-39.*

DAVID L. VANDERWERKEN

The reader's central problem in comprehending Vonnegut's
Slaughterhouse-Five lies in correctly understanding the
source of Billy Pilgrim's madness. Vonnegut continually undercuts our willing suspension of disbelief in Billy's time travel by offering multiple choices for the origin of Billy's imbalance: childhood traumas, brain damage from his plane crash,
dreams, his shattering war experiences, and plain old fantasy.
Yet if, as F. Scott Fitzgerald once observed, only a "first-rate
intelligence" has the "ability to hold two opposed ideas in the
mind at the same time, and still retain the ability to function,"
an inquiry into the two opposed philosophical systems that
Pilgrim holds in his mind—Tralfamadorianism and Christianity—may lead us to the fundamental cause of Billy's
breakdown. Clearly, Billy is no "first-rate intelligence," and
he hardly can be said to "function"; he simply cracks under
the strain of his dilemma. For some critics, however, Vonnegut's method of juxtaposing two explanatory systems, seemingly without affirming one or the other, becomes a major
flaw in the novel. . . . I would argue that, on the contrary,
Vonnegut's position is clear; he rejects both Tralfamadorianism and divinely oriented Christianity, while unambiguously
affirming a humanly centered Christianity in which Jesus is
a "nobody," a "bum," a man.

In the autobiographical first chapter, Vonnegut introduces
the opposed ideas, which the narrative proper will develop,
evolving from his twenty-three-year attempt to come to terms
with the horror of Dresden. The Christmas card sent to Vonnegut's war buddy by a German cab driver, expressing his
hope for a "world of peace and freedom . . . if the accident
will," dramatizes, in miniature form, a central tension in the
novel. Human history is either divinely planned—Christmas
signifies God's entrance into human history—and historical
events are meaningful, or human history is a series of random
events, non-causal, pure "accident," having no ultimate
meaning as the Tralfamadorians claim. Both viewpoints deny
free will; man is powerless to shape events. . . . Either position allows one serenely to wash his hands of Dresden. Billy
Pilgrim washes his hands, so to speak, and becomes reconciled to his Dresden experience under the tutelage of the Tralfamadorians: " '[Dresden] was all right,' said Billy. *'Everything* is all right, and everybody has to do exactly what he
does. I learned that on Tralfamadore.' "

The Tralfamadorians provide Billy with the concept of non-
linear time, which becomes the foundation for a mode of living: " 'I am a Tralfamadorian, seeing all time as you might
see a stretch of the Rocky Mountains. All time is all time. It
does not change. It does not lend itself to warnings or explanations. It simply *is*. Take it moment by moment, and you
will find that we are all, as I've said before, bugs in amber.' "
Although men on earth are always " 'explaining why this
event is structured as it is, telling how other events may be
achieved or avoided,' " Billy learns that " 'there is no *why*.' "

In short, Tralfamadorianism is an argument for determinism. Yet, this is a determinism without design, where chance rules. The universe will be destroyed accidentally by the Tralfamadorians, and wars on earth are inevitable. . . . The upshot of the Tralfamadorian philosophy finds expression in a cliché: "Everything was beautiful, and nothing hurt."

When Billy, full of revelations, returns to Earth "to comfort so many people with the truth about time," the implications of Tralfamadorianism become apparent. Although Billy's first attempt to "comfort" someone, a Vietnam war widow's son, fails, Billy blossoms into a charismatic national hero at the time of his assassination in 1976. The public appeal of Tralfamadorianism is obvious. Simply, it frees man from responsibility and from moral action. If all is determined, if there is no why, then no one can be held accountable for anything, neither Dresden nor My Lai. In his personal life, Billy's indifference and apathy toward others are clearly illustrated. Chapter Three offers three consecutive examples of Billy's behavior: he drives away from a black man who seeks to talk with him; he diffidently listens to a vicious tirade by a Vietnam Hawk at his Lions Club meeting; he ignores some cripples selling magazine subscriptions. Yet the Tralfamadorian idea that we can do nothing about anything fully justifies Billy's apathy. When Billy preaches this dogma as part of his "calling," he does a great service for the already apathetic by confirming their attitude; he provides them with a philosophical base for their apathy. If one ignores the ghetto or the Vietnam War, neither exists. By exercising one's selective memory, by becoming an ostrich, one may indeed live in a world where everything is beautiful and nothing hurts. Perfect. No wonder Billy is a successful Comforter; he has fulfilled Eliot Rosewater's request that "new lies" be invented or "people just aren't going to want to go on living."

If Tralfamadorianism is a "new lie," it recalls an "old lie"—God. There is little difference between God's will and accident's will in the novel. For Vonnegut, man's belief in an all-powerful Creator, involved in human history, has resulted in two great evils: the acceptance of war as God's will; the assumption that we carry out God's will and that God is certainly on our side, which justifies all atrocities. Sodom, Gomorrah, Hiroshima, Dresden, My Lai IV—all victims of God's will. Vonnegut directs his rage in **Slaughterhouse-Five** at a murderous, supernatural Christianity that creates Children's Crusades, that allows men to rationalize butchery in the name of God, that absolves men from guilt. Since, for Vonnegut, all wars are, finally, "holy" wars, he urges us to rid ourselves of a supernatural God.

While Vonnegut indicts Tralfamadorianism and supernatural Christianity as savage illusions, he argues in **Slaughterhouse-Five** for a humanistic Christianity, which may also be an illusion, but yet a saving one.

Throughout the novel, Vonnegut associates Billy Pilgrim with Bunyan's Pilgrim and with Christ. A chaplain's assistant in the war with a "meek faith in a loving Jesus," Billy finds the war a vast Slough of Despond; he reaches Dresden, which "looked like a Sunday school picture of Heaven to Billy Pilgrim," only to witness the Heavenly City's destruction. Often, Vonnegut's Christian shades into Christ Himself. During the war, Billy hears "Golgotha sounds," foresees his death and resurrection, " 'it is time for me to be dead for a little while—and then live again,' " identifies himself fully with Christ: "Now his snoozing became shallower as he heard a man and a woman speaking German in pitying tones.

The speakers were commiserating with somebody lyrically. Before Billy opened his eyes, it seemed to him that the tones might have been those used by the friends of Jesus when they took His ruined body down from His cross." After his kidnapping in 1967 by the Tralfamadorians, Billy assumes the role of Messiah: "He was doing nothing less now, he thought, than prescribing corrective lenses for Earthling souls. So many of those souls were lost and wretched, Billy believed, because they could not see as well as his little green friends on Tralfamadore." Vonnegut has created a parody Christ whose gospel is Tralfamadorian, who redeems no one, who "cried very little although he often saw things worth crying about, and in *that* respect, at least, he resembled the Christ of the carol." Indeed, Pilgrim's dilemma is that he is a double Savior with two gospels—a weeping and loving Jesus and a Tralfamadorian determinist. His opposed gospels drive him mad, render him impotent, result in his crackpot letters to newspapers and in his silent weeping for human suffering. Possibly Billy could have resolved his dilemma if he had paid closer attention to the human Christ in the novels of Billy's favorite writer—Kilgore Trout.

While Vonnegut often mentions Trout's books and stories for satiric purposes, Trout, "this cracked messiah" who has been " 'making love to the world' " for years, also serves as Vonnegut's spokesman for a humanistic and naturalistic Christianity. In Trout's *The Gospel from Outer Space,* a planetary visitor concludes that Christians are cruel because of "slipshod storytelling in the New Testament," which does not teach mercy, compassion, and love, but instead: *"Before you kill somebody, make absolutely sure he isn't well connected."* Trout's visitor offers Earth a new Gospel in which Jesus is not divine, but fully human—"a nobody." When the nobody is crucified: "The voice of God came crashing down. He told the people that he was adopting the bum as his son, giving him the full powers and privileges of The Son of the Creator of the Universe throughout all eternity." What Vonnegut suggests here is that Christ's divinity stands in the way of charity. If the "bum" is Everyman, then we are all adopted children of God; we are all Christs and should treat each other accordingly. (pp. 147-50)

As mentioned earlier, both Tralfamadorian determinism and the concept of a Supreme Being calling every shot on Earth nullify human intention, commitment and responsibility. But Vonnegut's humanistic Christianity in the face of a naturalistic universe demands moral choice—demands that we revere each other as Christs, since all are sons and daughters of God. Not surprisingly, Vonnegut's position echoes that of Stephen Crane. . . . The correspondent's insight that we are all in the same boat adrift in an indifferent sea, and that once we realize that we have only each other, moral choice is "absurdly clear," is Kurt Vonnegut's insight as well. (Vonnegut mentions *The Red Badge of Courage*.) The courage, sacrifice, and selflessness in *The Red Badge* appear in **Slaughterhouse-Five** also. (pp. 150-51)

While Vonnegut offers several versions of ideal brotherhood in his works—the Karass, the Volunteer Fire Department, and, despite Howard W. Campbell, Jr.'s assessment of American prisoners, moments of brotherhood in **Slaughterhouse-Five**—he also suggests an alternative for the individual, a slogan that becomes a way of living. On the same page where Vonnegut says, "Billy was not moved to protest the bombing of North Vietnam, did not shudder about the hideous things he himself had seen bombing do," appears the following prayer and Vonnegut's comment:

GOD GRANT ME
THE SERENITY TO ACCEPT
THE THINGS I CANNOT CHANGE,
COURAGE
TO CHANGE THE THINGS I CAN,
AND WISDOM ALWAYS
TO TELL THE
DIFFERENCE

Among the things Billy Pilgrim could not change
were the past, the present, and the future.

The Serenity Prayer, sandwiched between episodes concerning Vietnam, is Vonnegut's savage indictment of Billy Pilgrim. In short, Billy lacks the "wisdom" to see that Dresden is of the past and cannot be changed, but that the bombing of North Vietnam lies in the present and can be changed. However, to protest the bombing requires moral "courage," a quality obviated by his Tralfamadorian education.

The seemingly innocuous Serenity Prayer, the motto of Alcoholics Anonymous, appears once more in a most significant location—on the last page of Chapter Nine. The truth of Raymond M. Olderman's observation in his *Beyond the Waste Land* [see excerpt above] that "Vonnegut is a master at getting inside a cliché" is verified when we consider that Vonnegut has transformed the AA motto into a viable moral philosophy. Vonnegut knows that we have to accept serenely those things that people cannot change—the past, linear time, aging, death, natural forces. Yet the Prayer posits that, through moral courage, there are things that can be changed. War, for example, is not a natural force like a glacier, as Harrison Starr would have it. While Billy believes that he cannot change the past, present, or future, Vonnegut suggests that in the arena of the enormous present, we can, with courage, create change: "And I asked myself about the present: how wide it was, how deep it was, how much was mine to keep."

If there is a broad moral implication in *Slaughterhouse-Five,* it is aimed at America. Vonnegut, like his science fictionist Kilgore Trout, "writes about Earthlings all the time and they're all Americans." Vonnegut's message for America is this: America has adopted the Tralfamadorian philosophy, which justifies apathy. We have lost our sense of individuality; we feel powerless, helpless, and impotent; we consider ourselves the "listless playthings of enormous forces." What Vonnegut would have us do is develop the wisdom to discriminate between what we can or cannot change, while developing the courage to change what we can. We have met Billy Pilgrim and he is us. (pp. 151-52)

David L. Vanderwerken, "Pilgrim's Dilemma: 'Slaughterhouse-Five'," in Research Studies, *Vol. 42, No. 3, September, 1974, pp. 147-52.*

THOMAS LeCLAIR

[In his] novels Vonnegut presents the by-products of twentieth-century violence, men deprived of normal responses and traditional purposes, men pitifully befuddled or insanely inspired by their survival of mass or individual death. *Slaughterhouse-Five* is the late paradigm of a virtual obsession, perhaps because it treats Vonnegut's own survival of the Dresden bombing. In the introductory chapter, Vonnegut pres-

ents himself as a "pillar of salt," a man whose responses to personal death have been scrambled by his knowledge of the filled "corpse mines" of smoldering Dresden. How does an accidental man, a sport of nature whose law seems premature death, write a novel about an experience that inspires only silence?—that is the question Vonnegut solves by using a tone of sepulchral bemusement and the artifice of Tralfamadore, a planet where death is just another experience. In his comments about himself and the Dresden experience, Vonnegut parallels the responses Robert Lifton found in the survivors of atomic attack. In the spell of a grotesque, unanticipated, and profoundly unnatural mass death, the survivor, says Lifton, is both attracted to and repelled by the experience he has illogically escaped. His guilt (for not dying) and his revulsion activate both a psychic numbing (Vonnegut's irony) and a search for a world-order (Tralfamadore) which will account for his suffering and the deaths of others. Lifton also states that such a death-focused imagination becomes painfully sensitized to the extremities of sadness and humor, a comment that applies directly to Vonnegut. Vonnegut uses irony and artifice as ways into the silence that follows massacre, but his hero, Billy Pilgrim, finds only in the delusion of Tralfamadore, with its denial of time and offering of sex, a way to cope with *his* survival of Dresden and the many deaths before and after. Confronted with an overwhelming quantitative and qualitative reality of death which fits no rational category, Billy progressively distorts time and space and seizes upon the impossible category of Tralfamadore. His knowledge and space travels set him apart from his contemporaries, but his isolation makes little difference. His delusions hurt no one, and, besides, this world with all its comforts could do little to mediate Billy's memory. Diminished by his knowledge and magnified by his delusions, Billy finally accedes to his murder by another survivor of Dresden as the ultimate affirmation of his Tralfamadorian faith in the irrelevance of death's finality.

The comedy in *Slaughterhouse-Five* issues from the futility and mechanical repetition of phrase and action. The torment of time and the cruelty of the scenes we and Billy are forced to see mount a picture of life so horrible and determined that laughter is our only response. Billy cannot laugh and so goes mad; the reader, encouraged by Vonnegut, finds the irrelevance of man's gestures and the stupidity of his errors so pervasive that crying or rage would be reactions affirming a dignity absent in Vonnegut's death-defiled creatures. To produce the head-shaking, mirthless laugh, Vonnegut says death is necessary: "you have to have death quite near, or terror, or you don't laugh out loud . . . you just sort of snicker to yourself." Or, as he quotes Celine in *Slaughterhouse-Five,* "no art is possible without a dance with death." *Slaughterhouse-Five* is the "Duty-Dance with Death" that Vonnegut had been working toward in his previous novels. Both *Player Piano* and *The Sirens of Titan* have dehumanized survivors of wars as heroes. In *Mother Night* Vonnegut presents the first of his artist-heroes, Howard Campbell, Jr., who cannot cope with a memory of death, which is also a collaboration with Nazism. *Cat's Cradle* has as its narrator a man who survives (underground, as Vonnegut survived Dresden) the end of the world, only to be attracted to a comically futile suicide. Eliot Rosewater, hero of *God Bless You, Mr. Rosewater,* works out a crazy plan of charity and benevolence to expiate his guilt for killing innocent German firemen. In *Breakfast of Champions,* one of the two protagonists, Dwayne Hoover, goes mad not long after his wife commits suicide by drinking Drano. Vonnegut's survivors do not explicitly worry much about their own deaths; they are too busy trying to cope with their awareness of others' unnatural and grotesque extinction. Unable "to re-invent themselves and their universe," they stumble along in a dance with a partner they did not choose until their consciousness of death brings them to madness or suicide. (pp. 23-5)

Thomas LeClair, "Death and Black Humor," in Critique: Studies in Modern Fiction, *Vol. XVII, No. 1, 1975, pp. 5-40.*

WAYNE D. McGINNIS

Surely the biggest question asked in Kurt Vonnegut, Jr.'s fiction—and asked almost consistently in his novels—is one patently unanswerable from without: "What is the purpose of life?" Like any good existentialist, Vonnegut, putting himself in league with writers like Barth and Borges, finally answers the question by affirming that man must arbitrarily make his own purpose. The real interest for the writer of fiction in *how* the purpose is made has resulted in an emphasis on the skill and intricacy involved in the process in both Vonnegut's fiction and that of his contemporaries who take the view of the arbitrary nature of fiction itself. Today, many of the best writers are indeed writing about art, primarily. *Slaughterhouse-Five,* Vonnegut's major achievement, is essentially different from Nabokov's *Pale Fire* or Borges's *ficciones,* however, because it insists on both the world of fiction or fantasy (Tralfamadore) and the world of brutal fact (Dresden). Vonnegut's novel urges the primacy of the imagination in the very act of facing one of history's most infamous "massacres," the firebombing of Dresden in World War II, the source of its great originality.

The poignancy and force of *Slaughterhouse-Five* derive largely from an attitude about art and life that Vonnegut apparently shares with Louis-Ferdinand Celine, whom he quotes in the first chapter as saying two things: "No art is possible without a dance with death" and "the truth is death." Taking his cue from Celine, Vonnegut calls his novel A DUTY-DANCE WITH DEATH on the title page. Ultimately, however, *Slaughterhouse-Five* goes beyond the fatalism implied in Celine's statements by stressing survival through the use of the imagination. Vonnegut has said that the novel "was a therapeutic thing. I'm a different person now. I got rid of a lot of crap." Although strikingly similar to Lawrence's notion that "one sheds one's sicknesses in books," the important thing is to *go on,* to escape the paralyzing emotional rigidity that can turn one into a pillar of salt. The ability to go on, to escape fixity by motion in time is precisely what *Slaughterhouse-Five* is about, and its success comes from being able to effect a regeneration in reader as well as writer.

In keeping with the theme of regeneration, the form of the novel avoids the climax and denouement typical of linear narration, as indicated by Vonnegut's rejection of the grid-like outline of the story he proposes in the first chapter, with its climax at Edgar Derby's execution for taking a teapot and its ending in a POW trade made after the destruction of Dresden. Essentially, Vonnegut avoids *framing* his story in linear narration, choosing a circular structure. Such a view of the art of the novel has much to do with the protagonist of *Slaughterhouse-Five,* the author's alter ego, Billy Pilgrim, an optometrist who provides corrective lenses for Earthlings. For Pilgrim, who learns of a new view of life as he becomes "unstuck in time," the lenses are corrective metaphorically as well as physically. Quite early in the exploration of Billy's life

the reader learns that "frames are where the money is," a statement which has its metaphorical equivalent, too, and helps to explain why Vonnegut chose a non-linear structure for his novel. Historical events like the bombing of Dresden are usually "read" in the framework of moral and historical interpretation. (pp. 55-6)

Vonnegut's decision to cast his Dresden experience in a "non-explainable" work of the imagination ("I don't know how people explain the imagination, anyway. My books are protests against explanations") is a movement away from framing and toward a more unresolved circular structure. Vonnegut supplies strong hints of the circular nature of *Slaughterhouse-Five* in Chapter One. He is reminded, he says, of a particular song when he thinks of "how useless the Dresden part of my memory has been, and yet how tempting Dresden has been to write about":

> My name is Yon Yonson,
> I work in Wisconsin,
> I work in a lumbermill there.
> The people I meet when I walk down the street,
> They say, "What's your name?"
> And I say,
> "My name is Yon Yonson,
> I work in Wisconsin . . ."
> And so on to infinity.

Vonnegut's own life (and memory) is a model of the Yon Yonson cycle: "And [our babies] are all grown up now, and I'm an old fart with his memories and his Pall Malls. My name is Yon Yonson. I work in Wisconsin, I work in a lumbermill there." The message of the song is that life is cyclical, self-renewable—at least part of the implication of Roethke's "The Waking," the first stanza of which Vonnegut quotes in Chapter One. The paradox of the villanelle (a form which, through complexity and artificiality, should give an impression of simplicity and spontaneity, like *Slaughterhouse-Five* itself) is its circularity, both in form and content. Vonnegut invokes the same sort of circularity when he begins the fictional part of his novel by writing at the end of the first chapter:

> This book is a failure, and had to be, since it was
> written by a pillar of salt. It begins like this:
> *Listen:*
> Billy Pilgrim has come unstuck in time.
> It ends like this:
> Poo-tee-weet?

The rather strange preamble, then, helps to create the essentially cyclical nature of the novel, for here we have beginning and end in one place, the cycle completed in a small space.

The cyclical nature is inextricably bound up with the large themes of *Slaughterhouse-Five,* time, death, and renewal. Once again, the first chapter, the autobiographical one, prepares the reader for the full exploration of these themes in the novel itself. Vonnegut uses Celine to start two of the themes when he writes,

> Time obsessed him. Miss Ostrovsky [author of *Celine and His Vision*] reminded me of the amazing scene in *Death on the Installment Plan* where Celine wants to stop the bustling of a street crowd [end of Chapter 123]. He screams on paper, *"Make them stop . . . don't let them move anymore at all . . . There, make them freeze . . . once and for all! . . . So that they won't disappear anymore!"*

What Celine would have as an antidote in the passage Vonnegut quotes is *fixity,* which would prevent the flow of time and the constant encroachment of death. The agonizing paradox here, of course, is that fixity or rigidity is also associated with death. Lot's wife is punished for looking back on the burning cities of Sodom and Gomorrah with death, the rigidity of a pillar of salt. While Vonnegut loves Lot's wife for looking back "because it was so human," obviously he, like anyone desiring life, wants *not* to be rigid. Stopping the flow of time is at once a solution and no solution.

The Tralfamadorian answer to the problem is hinted at from the very first page. After telling of the German taxicab driver, Gerhard Mueller, whose mother "was incinerated in the Dresden fire-storm," Vonnegut begins what will be a persistent refrain throughout the novel, the phrase "so it goes." The reader does not know until the second chapter, however, that this is what the Tralfamadorians, those mythical creatures who live on a distant planet in Billy Pilgrim's mind, say about dead people. The philosophy of Tralfamadore on time and death, as Billy explains it, is an escape from the concept of linear time, just as their novels are an escape from linear narration. . . . The Tralfamadorians . . . avoid the "duty-dance with death" by ignoring death as a finality. Their little formula "so it goes," said ritualistically throughout the novel whenever any death, no matter how trivial, is mentioned, is from the human point of view, the height of fatalism. The most important function of "so it goes," however, is its imparting a cyclical quality to the novel, both in form and content. Paradoxically, the expression of fatalism serves as a source of renewal, a situation typical of Vonnegut's works, for it enables the novel to *go on* despite—even because of—the proliferation of deaths. Once again we come upon a paradox: death keeps life in motion, even the life of the novel, but the movement is essentially unaided in Vonnegut's silent universe. . . . In a world where life must renew itself arbitrarily, the mental construct becomes tremendously important. The phrase "so it goes" is a sign of the human will to survive, and it recurs throughout the novel as an important aid to *going on.*

Vonnegut's fiction deals heavily with survival by the arbitrary imposition of meaning on meaningless reality, as demonstrated most forcefully in *Cat's Cradle.* Tralfamadore is another mental construct, like Bokononism, that goes beyond the question of true or false. As Eliot Rosewater says in *Slaughterhouse-Five* to the psychiatrists: "I think you guys are going to have to come up with a lot of wonderful *new* lies, or people just aren't going to want to go on living." The statement is certainly a clue to the meaning of Tralfamadore, since it comes right after the statement that Rosewater and Billy had found life meaningless, partly because of what they had seen in the war: "So they were trying to re-invent themselves and their universe. Science fiction was a big help." Vonnegut lets us know that an act of re-invention is going on within the novel, just as the novel is Vonnegut's own re-creation of his past and even of his other novels. Mental constructs like Bokononism and Tralfamadore, both re-inventive fictions, are models of Vonnegut's own fiction, throughout which one can see the pattern of meaninglessness/re-invention.

That Tralfamadore is ultimately a "supreme fiction," a product of the imagination, and that Vonnegut emphasizes using the imagination as a method of survival are obvious from his preoccupation with the value of works of art, especially in the novels from *Cat's Cradle* on. . . . Especially interesting is

Vonnegut's source for his idea of Tralfamadore; evidence shows that, characteristically, Vonnegut was inspired by modern science in creating his fiction. Shortly after *Slaughterhouse-Five* was published, Vonnegut wrote an article in which he quotes from another book arranged along the lines of a trip into space, Guy Murchie's popularization of the great body of science, *Music of the Spheres.* In his article Vonnegut writes, "I had lifted a comment Murchie made about time for a book of my own." (The book must surely be *Slaughterhouse-Five.*) The quotation from Murchie that Vonnegut cites occurs at the end of "Of Space, Of Time," a chapter on relativity—the part deleted by Vonnegut is placed in brackets:

> I sometimes wonder whether humanity has missed the real point in raising the issue of mortality and immortality [—whether perhaps the seemingly limited time span of an earthly life is actually unlimited and eternal—] in other words, whether mortality itself may be a finite illusion, being actually immortality and, even though constructed of just a few "years," that those few years are all the time there really is, so that, in fact, they can never cease.

Although Vonnegut does not quote further, Murchie goes on to ask, "Indeed, if time is the relation between things and themselves, how can time end while things exist? Or how can time have ever begun, since either a beginning or an end would logically and almost inevitably frame time in more of itself?"

Vonnegut, then, is apparently trying to get away from "framing" in *Slaughterhouse-Five* by means of circularity. Both the Tralfamadorian concept of time and the Murchie passage from which it is probably lifted imply a kind of cyclical "return," though, of course, Billy Pilgrim's *movement* in time embodies this return, rather than the Tralfamadorian idea of fixity expressed by the mountain range image. (pp. 57-61)

Billy Pilgrim . . . is engaged in a quest to make mortality (which he knows so well from Dresden) a guarantor of immortality; at least he has an affinity with [Friedrich Nietzsche] in believing that death is the ultimate challenge to the imagination. He essentially experiences circularity when he goes from life to death to life and then back to pre-birth in the novel. . . . Circularity is what Billy also affirms when, having "memories of the future," he talks of his own death while preaching his Tralfamadorian gospel: " 'If you protest, if you think that death is a terrible thing, then you have not understood a word I've said.' Now he closes his speech as he closes every speech—with these words: 'Farewell, hello, farewell, hello.' " His little ritual manifests the ever present possibility of renewal through the imagination.

The Tralfamadorian concept of time, with the suggestion of cyclical return embodied in Billy's time travels, reflects the fact that timelessness is a product of the irrational, the unconscious, the imagination itself. Although we might be tempted to see *Slaughterhouse-Five* as a "plotless" novel allied to the stream of consciousness novel, Billy's psyche is not as fully explored as, say, Mrs. Dalloway's or Benjy Compson's, for he is too effaced and manipulated by the author to have the kind of independent being required for the stream of consciousness novel. While *Slaughterhouse-Five* cannot fully employ the stream of consciousness technique because it simply does not deal with the internal psychic processes of a fully developed character, it does make a secondary use of the technique by providing certain signals to help predict time and space shifts in the "durational" world of the novel. Among these images or attitudes are feet of blue and ivory, the black and orange color of a POW train, nestling like spoons, sleeping and waking, and having tears in the eyes. With the use of these signals the reader gets a strong feeling that Billy's time travels are manipulated from outside—by Vonnegut. As the narrator rather mockingly says of Billy's becoming unstuck in time, "He has seen his birth and death many times, he says, and pays random visits to all the events in between. He says. Billy is spastic in time, has no control over where he is going next, and the trips aren't necessarily fun." The idea of being "spastic" captures the immediate quality of Billy's travels in the regenerative cycle. (pp. 61-3)

The form created in the novel is essentially circular, not spatial or linear; because its "sequence" is that of the circle, *Slaughterhouse-Five* is a novel without climaxes, since its real subject matter and formal arrangement is renewal. In this sense it is like the Tralfamadorian novel, a novel without beginning, middle, and end, without suspense and without a moral. Like the Roethke villanelle, it learns by going where it has to go. While the Tralfamadorian style implies an *indirect* statement of the novel's aesthetic, the real impression one is left with is based on its form, that of continual self-renewal. That the renewal is arbitrary is the thematic point of the novel, and even the novel's circular form shares the arbitrary quality. Aside from the specific question of how Tralfamadorian *Slaughterhouse-Five* is, its echo of cinematic technique is quite loose and appears especially loose when one considers how closely other novels have reflected their formal references—the echo of the fugue in the Sirens section of *Ulysses* or the echo of musical counterpoint in *Point Counter Point,* for example. The debt of *Slaughterhouse-Five* to cinema is enough to establish a general basis for considering its cinematic technique, but not enough to say that it does more than loosely borrow from the formal pattern that film has to offer the novel. Neither does the form of *Slaughterhouse-Five* share more than a certain affinity with the technique of the stream of consciousness novel. . . . The cyclical scheme of *Slaughterhouse-Five* . . . is "arbitrary" in that its continual self-renewal is essentially unaided by an echo of some general outside form.

What makes self-renewal possible in *Slaughterhouse-Five* is the human imagination, which is what the novel finally celebrates. Many critics have failed to perceive how strongly the novel affirms the value of the mental construct and have attacked it either for urging passivity or being hopelessly ambiguous about the Tralfamadorian ethic—which does, of course, deny free will and support Billy's passivity. Willed action is simply not stressed in Vonnegut's fictional world. In *Breakfast of Champions,* Vonnegut finally stresses that "our awareness is all that is alive and maybe sacred in any of us. Everything else about us is dead machinery." The imagination, then, beholds the immaterial core of every living thing, the "unwavering band of light" that the minimalist artist in that novel paints. Billy Pilgrim is a kind of artist, too, as Howard W. Campbell, Jr., Bokonon, and Eliot Rosewater have been before him. Like Vonnegut's other protagonists-artists, Billy must use an artistic stance to survive in a basically absurd world. As a *doer* Billy is ineffectual—thus, he simply drives through a burned-out ghetto, for example. Despite his lack of enthusiasm about living, Billy does go on, largely through the aid of his Tralfamadorian fiction. Neither he nor Vonnegut can change the fact of Dresden, but they both can survive it by the use of the imagination. Vonnegut's television

special, **"Between Time and Timbuktu,"** ended with a scene in heaven in which death (in the form of Hitler) fights the imagination and loses. The duel represents in stark outline the great theme of Vonnegut's work.

Finally, the fixity of death at Dresden, which reduces people to "seeming little logs lying around," is overcome in *Slaughterhouse-Five* by the novel's arbitrary cycle. Appropriately, the novel "ends" with a re-cycling back to the Dresden experience. Billy's liberation from his German captors is described:

> Billy and the rest wandered out onto the shady street. The trees were leafing out. There was nothing going on out there, no traffic of any kind. There was only one vehicle, an abandoned wagon drawn by two horses. The wagon was green and coffin-shaped.
> Birds were talking.
> One bird said to Billy Pilgrim, *"Poo-tee-weet?"*

Vonnegut's "famous Dresden book," then, comes to its open end with the symbol of renewal that had saved the narrator Jonah from suicide in *Cat's Cradle* and had awakened Eliot Rosewater in *God Bless You, Mr. Rosewater* to the potential of living a life of the absurd, the bird that asks, *"Poo-tee-weet?"* With the faint echo of the cycle of nature, the green and coffin-shaped wagon, we realize that the cycle itself reflects man's own nature as he experiences the regeneration of immortality in his mind. In using the idea of regeneration to integrate both theme and form, Vonnegut has written in *Slaughterhouse-Five* his best and even most hopeful novel to date. (pp. 65-7)

Wayne D. McGinnis, "The Arbitrary Cycle of 'Slaughterhouse-Five': A Relation of Form to Theme," in Critique: Studies in Modern Fiction, *Vol. XVII, No. 1, 1975, pp. 55-67.*

DOLORES K. GROS LOUIS

Novelists use the gospel story in many ways and for many different purposes. Some use it to structure their work of fiction. Some use it as an aid in characterization, either to elevate a protagonist or to deflate him by his contrast to Jesus. Others adapt the story to show how Jesus himself might exist and act in a particular modern situation. Some writers use only casual allusions and metaphors to broaden the meaning of certain incidents and events. Some create a Christ figure, either ironic or serious, to convey a contemporary religious, political, or social theme. Still others use the Christ story as a rhetorical device for indirect authorial comment.

In *Slaughterhouse-Five,* Kurt Vonnegut is using the Christ story in the last two ways. Through Billy Pilgrim's similarities to Jesus, Vonnegut creates a Christ figure who is a resurrected survivor with a philosophical message for the world. Vonnegut's own, contrasting message is conveyed indirectly, through his deflation of Billy Pilgrim as an ineffectual and immoral messiah. Vonnegut's implied moral is the antithesis of the gospel preached by his ironic Christ figure. (pp. 161-62)

In this compressed, complex novel, the Christ motif is not immediately apparent to a casual reader, nor even to some serious readers. My commentary concentrates on the descriptions, situations, and actions of Billy Pilgrim which parallel those of Jesus in the Gospels. When seen all at once—"many marvelous moments seen all at one time"—these parallels form a pattern which is, clearly, consciously intended by Vonnegut. I have not rearranged these parallels to follow the gospel story chronologically, because Vonnegut, as is well known, has not used the story of Jesus to order his time scheme. Thinking about this, one realizes a major ironic contrast between Billy Pilgrim and Jesus: when Billy Pilgrim lives again after having been shot, there is no change in his life nor in anyone else's; through time-travel, he simply repeats again and again various moments of his life.

There are, however, many similarities between Billy and Jesus. The epigraph, a quatrain from the carol "Away in the Manger," hints that in some way "the little Lord Jesus" is related to the meaning of the novel. Early in the novel, in two oblique references to the carol, "Billy Pilgrim would find himself weeping. . . . It was an extremely quiet thing Billy did, and not very moist." "But sleep would not come. Tears came instead. They seeped." The emphasis upon the moderateness of Billy's crying suggests that it is motivated by a profound and sincere grief. . . . Much later in the novel, after stating again that Billy "would weep quietly and privately sometimes, but never make loud *boohooing* noises," Vonnegut repeats the epigraph and explicates it explicitly:

> Which is why the epigraph of this book is the quatrain from the famous Christmas carol. Billy cried very little, though he often saw things worth crying about, and in *that* respect, at least, he resembled the Christ of the carol.

This authorial comment—"in *that* respect, at least, he resembled the Christ of the carol"—indicates that Vonnegut is certainly conscious of other possible resemblances between Billy and Jesus. We may note that here, as throughout the novel, it is only Vonnegut who is aware that Billy Pilgrim is a Christ figure. Billy himself is never conscious of any similarity between himself and Jesus.

A second major resemblance is Billy's compassionate desire to comfort people, "Billy's belief that he was going to comfort so many people with the truth about time." The solace he offers is in his extraterrestrial message, the essence of which is the negligibility of death—or, in Christian terms, the eternity of life. . . . The first part of Billy's Tralfamadorian message has to do with the true nature of time; that is, the fourth-dimension, omniscient, Godlike view of time: "All moments, past, present, and future, always have existed, always will exist. . . . How permanent all the moments are." The second part of the message follows from that: if all the moments always were, always are, and ever will be, then "we will all live forever, no matter how dead we may sometimes seem to be."

After learning this comforting truth on Tralfamadore, Billy develops a somewhat messianic sense of having a special mission to the poor souls on Earth:

> . . . he was devoting himself to a calling much higher than mere business.
> He was doing nothing less now, he thought, than prescribing corrective lenses for Earthling souls. So many of those souls were lost and wretched, Billy believed, because they could not see as well as his little green friends on Tralfamadore.

"He was going to tell the world about the lessons of Tralfamadore" on the New York City radio talk show, in his letters to the Illium newspaper, and later, in public lectures.

At the beginning of his teaching, Billy encounters the same reaction as Jesus did early in his ministry: "When his family heard it, they went out to seize him, for people were saying, 'He is beside himself'" (Mark 3:21). Billy's family, especially his daughter Barbara, and other people in Illium think "that Billy [is] evidently going crazy" when he teaches the lessons of Tralfamadore. On several occasions Barbara attempts to take charge of him. . . . Billy, like Jesus, persists nevertheless, with serenity and confidence. He maintains his sense of mission, his compassion for people, and his belief in his other worldly message about the eternal nature of time and the insignificance of death. And like Jesus, Billy will eventually gain a large following. At the time of his death, which he has foreseen happening on February 13, 1976, "Billy is speaking before a capacity audience in a baseball park. . . . There are police around him as he leaves the stage. They are there to protect him from the crush of popularity."

Billy's foreseeing his own death is one example of his belief that whatever happens to him had to be so; that since all time is all time, all the moments in his life have already been structured. This reminds us that Jesus frequently does certain things "so that the prophecies might be fulfilled," though Jesus, of course, freely chooses to fulfill the prophecies. Billy's foreknowledge of his own death is mentioned several times in the novel. . . . (pp. 162-65)

The description of Billy's death includes several gospel parallels. When the crowd protests his announcement of his imminent death, "Billy Pilgrim rebukes them. 'If you protest, if you think that death is a terrible thing, then you have not understood a word I've said.'" Not only the verb "rebukes" but also the rebuking statement recall Jesus' words: "Do you not yet perceive or understand? Are your hearts hardened? Having eyes do you not see, and having ears do you not hear? And do you not remember? . . . Do you not yet understand?" (Mark 8:17-18, 21). Then there are the offers to help save his life—"The police offer to stay with him. They are floridly willing to stand in a circle around him all night, with their zap guns drawn"—offers which Billy rejects. "'No, no,' says Billy serenely. 'It is time for you to go home to your wives and children, and it is time for me to be dead for a little while—and then live again.' . . . So Billy experiences death for a while." This passage echoes John 16:16-19, "A little while, and you will see me no more; again a little while, and you will see me. . . . A little while, and you will not see me, and again a little while, and you will see me."

Some thirty years before his death, Billy is compared several times to Jesus on the cross. First is the near-identification of Billy (a non-Catholic) with the "ghastly crucifix" which he had contemplated twice daily as a child:

> Billy, after all, had contemplated torture and hideous wounds at the beginning and the end of nearly every day of his childhood. Billy had an extremely gruesome crucifix hanging on the wall of his little bedroom in Illium. A military surgeon would have admired the clinical fidelity of the artist's rendition of all Christ's wounds—the spear wound, the thorn wounds, the holes that were made by the iron spikes. Billy's Christ died horribly. He was pitiful.

Just four pages later, "He was pitiful" is Roland Weary's evaluation of Billy as a footsoldier. As a war prisoner on a crowded boxcar, Billy is repeatedly described in terms of the crucifixion:

> Billy stood by one of these [ventilators], and, as the crowd pressed against him, he climbed part way up a diagonal corner brace to make more room.
>
> And Billy let himself down oh so gradually now, hanging onto the diagonal cross-brace in the corner in order to make himself seem nearly weightless to those he was joining on the floor. He knew it was important that he make himself nearly ghostlike when lying down. He had forgotten why, but a reminder soon came. . . . So Billy stood up again, clung to the cross-brace.
>
> Billy Pilgrim was lying at an angle on the corner-brace, self-crucified, holding himself there with a blue and ivory claw hooked over the sill of the ventilator.

Besides reinforcing the Christ parallel fairly early in the novel, these apparently conscious references to the crucifixion suggest that being a war prisoner is a crucifying experience.

After he is shot in 1976 and "experiences death for a while," Billy experiences a Tralfamadorian resurrection as "he swings back into life again." The first place he returns to is the stage setting of the prisoners' production of *Cinderella,* a story which is an analogue of the theme of rebirth. Vonnegut himself suggests a particular analogy when he describes *Cinderella* as the gospel story is usually described—"the most popular story ever told." In Cinderella's silver boots, Vonnegut tells us, "Billy Pilgrim was Cinderella, and Cinderella was Billy Pilgrim." Cinderella is reborn in her transformation from an abused, humble servant into a princess; Billy is reborn when he swings back into life again, to relive the moment when he discovered that Cinderella's boots "fit perfectly"; and man's servant, Jesus, arises from death to eternal life.

Later in the novel (though much earlier in his life), Billy experiences a miraculous survival which is almost a resurrection: after the firebombing of Dresden, he emerges from "an echoing meat locker which was hollowed in living rock under the slaughterhouse." Jesus rose, we recall, from a tomb "hewn in the rock" (Matt. 27:60). After climbing the staircase out of the tomblike meat locker, Billy Pilgrim sees a new kind of world he never could have imagined. Dresden after the firebombing is an apocalyptic scene of total destruction; everything organic has been killed, including 135,000 human beings. Under the city, Billy Pilgrim was very close to death; when he emerges, he sees nothing but death. Yet he goes on living. (pp. 166-68)

In addition to the major parallels between Billy and Jesus, further occasional biblical allusions reinforce the identification. First, before his capture by the Germans, Billy is "a dazed wanderer" in the wilderness "without food or maps." Second, in the German boxcar moving slowly toward the war prison, Billy is scorned and reviled by his fellow prisoners just as Jesus is "mocked," "derided," and "reviled" by soldiers, passersbys, chief priests, scribes, and even by the two robbers who were crucified with him (Mark 15:17-32). Billy is falsely accused, as Jesus is, and is made a scapegoat by Roland Weary; in 1976, he will be unjustly killed by Paul Lazzaro's hired murderer.

Fourth, as Billy leads the parade of prisoners to the Dresden-bound train, he had some resemblance to Jesus: "He had silver boots now, and a muff, and a piece of azure curtain which he wore like a toga. Billy still had a beard." His arrival in Dresden is an ironic parallel to the triumphal entry into Jerusalem:

> And then they saw bearded Billy Pilgrim in his blue toga and silver shoes, with his hands in a muff. . . . Billy Pilgrim was the star. He led the parade. Thousands of people were on the sidewalks, going home from work.

Finally, if Jesus is the new Adam, the New Testament Son of God who will atone for Adam's fall, Billy Pilgrim is the old Adam before his fall. Immediately after he sees Adam and Eve in the highly polished boots of a German corporal, he looks up into the face of "a blond angel . . . as beautiful as Eve"—a juxtaposition suggesting that Billy is Adam. More important, Billy resembles Adam in the zoo on Tralfamadore where he lives naked and innocently ("guilt-free") with his mate in the Tralfamadorian ideal of human paradise.

With these minor allusions and the major parallels to the gospel story, Vonnegut endows his time-traveling optometrist with many similarities to Jesus. In descriptions, he compares Billy to the infant Jesus, to Jesus in his triumphal entry into Jerusalem, and to the mocked and crucified Christ. Even more parallels exist in Billy's actions: he wanders in the wilderness, he acts out of a sense of mission to the world, he preaches a message about eternal life, he is thought by many people to be out of his mind, he preaches to crowds, he foresees his own death, he is mocked and scorned, he is falsely accused and unjustly killed, and he returns to life after death. This extensive pattern of parallels makes Billy Pilgrim a modern Christ figure.

The elaborate and conscious identification is undercut, however, by the important ways in which Billy Pilgrim differs from Jesus. By important differences I don't mean omitted gospel details such as the Last Supper but, rather, morally significant contrasts. First, Billy's death is not a sacrifice. Second, his death has no redemptive value for other people. And third, unless we believe the Tralfamadorian values taught by Billy, his teaching is unlike Jesus' in that it doesn't change our lives or suggest new values worth living by. Vonnegut clearly rejects—and wants us to reject—the Tralfamadorian view of time and its implications for human life.

Why, then, does Vonnegut make Billy Pilgrim a Christ figure of this sort? Isn't Billy Pilgrim a Vonnegut hero? What is the point of a savior who saves no one?

There are several answers to these questions. Since he is so ineffectual, Billy Pilgrim is an ironic Christ figure, that is, one resembling Jesus in many ways but ultimately lacking the all-important redemptive, sacrificial death. This irony is appropriate in a novel, and in a world, where there is such irony as Edgar Derby's being executed for stealing a teapot while no one is punished for the destruction of Dresden.

Then, too, an ironic Christ figure fits in with Vonnegut's pessimistic and satiric view of humanity in today's world. A poor imitation of Jesus may be all we can expect in a society which covers up and then justifies the needless firebombing of Dresden. Maybe an ironic Christ figure is appropriate in a society whose values are reflected in the American dream that is Billy's miserable life in Illium.

At the same time, Vonnegut's use of the gospel story, his allusions ranging from the first Christmas Eve to the resurrection, suggest a nostalgia, a kind of yearning that the Christ story might be true. This yearning is part of Vonnegut's search for meaning in an absurd world (he alludes to the Creator, Jesus, or God in his other novels). His use of the gospel story is nearly blasphemous; yet the fact that he does use it, doesn't ignore it, suggests that it has some appeal for him. [As Ernest W. Ranly has stated, (see *CLC*, Vol. 2)] "The question [of God] haunts Vonnegut at every turn."

The most important reason for Billy's being an ineffectual, ironic Christ figure, however, is that this allows Vonnegut indirectly to counter Billy's Tralfamadorian message with his own very different, very worldly message. Vonnegut is qualified to oppose Billy's teachings because, as he tells us several times, his experiences in the prison camp and in Dresden were the same as Billy's. Vonnegut is very conscious of this; Billy is a semi-autobiographical character, at least in the war parts of *Slaughterhouse-Five.* There are many similarities between Vonnegut and his protagonist: both were born in 1922; both have the same souvenir of war (a Luftwaffe ceremonial saber); both are interested in science fiction as a help in "trying to re-invent themselves and their universe"; both have messages to help mankind. Most important, both rise from near-death "in an echoing meat locker which was hollowed in living rock" and cannot understand why they were among the 105 survivors of the massacre of 135,000 people. Vonnegut comes close to identifying himself with Billy when he intrudes into the narrative four times to say, "I was there." Yet, though he was there, and though he had many of the same war experiences as Billy, Vonnegut's ultimate reaction to those experiences differs greatly from Billy's ultimate reaction. (pp. 168-71)

Through his Tralfamadorian lessons, Billy Pilgrim learns a resigned tolerance of war ("So—I suppose that the idea of preventing war on Earth is stupid, too" and an acceptance of whatever will be, will be (and always was, and always will be). Vonnegut, most obviously in his autobiographical first chapter but also throughout the novel, challenges Billy's postwar philosophy of serene acceptance. Billy's office sign and Montana Wildhack's locket say, "God grant me the serenity to accept the things I cannot change. . . ." According to Billy's view of time, he can change *nothing;* but Vonnegut, on the other hand, is only ironic when he says, "So it goes."

The Tralfamadorian lesson taught by Billy is "All moments, past, present, and future, always have existed, always will exist." Therefore, "we will all live forever, no matter how dead we may sometimes appear to be." Therefore, also, there is nothing we can do to prevent war, nothing we can do to prevent the end of the world ("A Tralfamadorian test pilot presses a starter button, and the whole Universe disappears. . . . He has *always* pressed it, and he always *will.*"). So the thing to do as we visit various moments during eternity is to select the happy moments, the pretty moments. The Tralfamadorian guide tells Billy, "On other days we have wars as horrible as any you've ever seen or read about. There isn't anything we can do about them, so we simply don't look at them. We ignore them. We spend eternity looking at pleasant moments. . . ." This is the gospel from outer space, the view of history that leads Billy Pilgrim to say about the destruction of Dresden, "It was all right. *Everything* is all right. . . ."

This complacent gospel, preached by the ironic Christ figure, is rejected by Vonnegut himself. The author's extensive research on Dresden, and his writing of this novel with its overt pacifism, show that for him everything is *not* all right. Unlike

the Tralfamadorians, Vonnegut the narrator looks back at many *horrible* moments: the destruction of Sodom and Gomorrah, the drowning or enslavement of the thousands of children in the Children's Crusade, the 1760 devastation of Dresden by the Prussians, the extermination of millions of Jews by the Nazis, the firebombing of Dresden, the atomic bombing of Hiroshima, the bombing of North Vietnam, the napalm burning of the Vietnamese, the assassination of Robert Kennedy, the assassination of Martin Luther King, the daily body count from Vietnam.

Like Billy Pilgrim, Kurt Vonnegut also has a message for the world. If we are to avoid another Dresden, if we are to break out of the Tralfamadorian inevitability of war and the end of the world, "we must not fight under any conditions." . . . Comparing himself to Lot's wife, Vonnegut says it is human to look back on a massacre; he implies that it is *inhuman* to forget or ignore it. Looking back in *Slaughterhouse-Five,* he reminds us that war is awful, that it is absurd, that it creates many grotesque ironies.

Slaughterhouse-Five is not a Christian book, but it is a compassionate and moral one in its concern for man and his fate. Through an ironic Christ figure, Vonnegut presents and rejects an extraterrestrial gospel which leads away from moral responsibility, away from guilt, away from active protest against war. As reborn survivor, Billy preaches a view of life which negates guilt, negates responsibility, negates active concern for the past or for the future. "*Everything* is all right." As reborn survivor, Vonnegut transcends Billy's Tralfamadorian vision of life. He transcends it by offering us his own earthly vision, a vision which has nothing to do with science fiction. Although he is skeptical about the success of his message, Vonnegut teaches the "impossible" pacifism to which he converted after his experience of Dresden: Do not kill. Do not burn. Do not fight in war. Do not condone war. Everything is *not* all right.

Although Billy Pilgrim ends up as a resurrected time-traveler whose gospel helps no one, there *is* a positive aspect to some of his other similarities to Jesus. Billy's genuine suffering, and his deeply sincere desire to help humanity, suggest that there may be something of Jesus even in a nobody. In *these* respects, at least, Billy seriously resembles the Christ of the Gospels. This identification extends the significance of Billy's role in the novel. He is, however, also a pilgrim traveling away from the city of destruction. The inverted parallels to Jesus, such as the negative quality of Billy's message and the inefficacy of his death, add an ironic dimension of meaning to his role. As an ironic Christ figure whose gospel is both untrue and ultimately immoral, Billy Pilgrim is opposed by the moral, real narrator, who travels *back* to the city of destruction and arrives at an active pacifism.

To understand Billy's ambivalent role as a modern version of Jesus, we and our students must be familiar with the gospel story. Knowledge of that story is necessary for the aesthetic pleasure of recognizing the biblical allusions in *Slaughterhouse-Five* and for the intellectual pleasure of recognizing both the serious and the ironic parallels between Billy Pilgrim and Jesus. Most important, however, we and our students need the gospel background in order to recognize Billy's *failure* as a *savior,* to recognize the immorality and the ineffectiveness of his serene vision of time and death. If we perceive Billy as a Christ figure, then we will perceive the important ways in which he is *unlike* Jesus: his death redeems no one; and his particular vision of eternal life leads to a passive acceptance of war, which if not unchristian is certainly immoral, inhuman, and uncompassionate. Only unfeeling and unthoughtful readers could find anything of positive value in the guilt-free, passive Tralfamadorian gospel. Vonnegut's pacifism and active moral concern are much closer to the teachings of Jesus as recorded in the Gospels. (pp. 172-75)

> Dolores K. Gros Louis, "The Ironic Christ Figure in 'Slaughterhouse-Five'," in Biblical Images in Literature, edited by Roland Bartel with James S. Ackerman and Thayer S. Warshaw, Abingdon Press, 1975, pp. 161-75.

CHARLES B. HARRIS

Carefully read, Chapter One [of Slaughterhouse-Five] emerges as a functional and illuminating part of the novel as a whole. For the chapter contains passages that suggest three important facts crucial to a proper understanding of Vonnegut's novel: (1) the novel is less about Dresden than about the psychological impact of time, death, and uncertainty on its main character; (2) the novel's main character is not Billy Pilgrim, but Vonnegut; and (3) the novel is not a conventional anti-war novel at all, but an experimental novel of considerable complexity.

Billy Pilgrim, the putative protagonist of Slaughterhouse-Five, does not even appear in this chapter. Instead, the focus is on Vonnegut, the author-as-character. Emerging is a portrait of the artist as an aging man, "an old fart with his memories and his Pall Malls, with his sons full grown." He is a man of nostalgia who makes late-night drunken phone calls to almost-forgotten acquaintances, calls that seldom make connection. He reminisces about his days as a university student and police reporter in Chicago, as a public relations man in Schenectady, and as a soldier in Germany. The wartime memories, particularly as they concern the mass deaths at Dresden, especially haunt his reveries and of course form the basis of plot for the subsequent nine chapters.

Yet for one so apparently obsessed with the fleeting nature of time—he even quotes Horace to that effect—Vonnegut seems at times curiously vague and indefinite about time. He cannot remember the exact year he visited O'Hare and, upon returning to bed after a night of drinking and telephoning, cannot tell his wife, who "always has to know the time," what time it is. "Search me," he answers. His forgetfulness seems a shield, a defense against a medium that oppresses him. (pp. 228-29)

The Vonnegut of Chapter One appears simultaneously obsessed with and oppressed by time, the past, and death—particularly death. His preoccupation with death is reflected in the various figures he employs in Chapter One and throughout the novel. Among the most prominent of these is the flowing-frozen water metaphor. Vonnegut has used this motif before, especially in Cat's Cradle, when ice-nine, dropped accidentally into the ocean, ossifies everything liquid. But it recurs in a subtler though perhaps more pervasive way in Slaughterhouse-Five. Early in the novel, Vonnegut, on his way to visit Bernard V. O'Hare in Philadelphia, crosses the Delaware, then appropriates the river as a metaphor in his reflections upon the nature of time. "And I asked myself about the present: how wide it was, how deep it was, how much of it was mine to keep." Even before this association of time and the river, however, Vonnegut associates death with ice, frozen water. "Even if wars didn't keep coming like glaciers," he writes, "there would still be plain old death." Extending this metaphor throughout the novel, Vonnegut repeatedly portrays living humanity as water flowing, dead humanity as water frozen. "They were moving like water," he describes a procession of Allied POW's, ". . . and they flowed at last to a main highway on a valley's floor. Through the valley flowed a Mississippi of humiliated Americans." One of the POW's, a hobo, is dead, therefore "could not flow, could not plop. He wasn't liquid anymore." Later, Billy Pilgrim sees the dead hobo "frozen stiff in the weeds beside the track," his bare feet "blue and ivory," the color of ice. The phrase "blue and ivory" occurs seven times in Slaughterhouse-Five, twice to describe the frozen feet of corpses, five times to describe the feet of Billy Pilgrim, who, though still in the land of the flowing, is marked as mortal.

A similar figure applies to Vonnegut himself. Twice in Chapter One he refers to his breath as smelling of "mustard gas and roses." The phrase appears again in Chapter Four when Billy Pilgrim receives a misdialed phone call from a drunk whose breath, like the drunken "telephoner" of Chapter One, smells of mustard gas and roses. The full implication of the image becomes clear only on the next-to-the-last page of the novel. In the "corpse mines" of Dresden, as the dead bodies begin to rot and liquify, "the stink (is) like roses and mustard gas." Like Billy Pilgrim's "blue and ivory" feet, Vonnegut's breath marks him as mortal. This, the image suggests, is what time does to us all, not only when we lie dead like the Dresden corpses, but while we breathe. Life is a state of gradual but perpetual decay.

Time, then, is the enemy harrowing the brow of the first character we meet in the novel. It is important to recognize that the Vonnegut of Chapter One is, indeed, a character in Slaughterhouse-Five. Of course he is very much like Vonnegut the author, has had the same experiences, but he remains nonetheless the author-as-character. Moreover, he becomes the first-person narrator for the remainder of the novel, a fact obscured by the Billy Pilgrim plot, which is often read as the novel proper rather than the novel-within-the-novel-proper. Vonnegut-as-character introduces himself in Chapter One, informs us of his procedures in gathering materials for his novel, and confesses the difficulties he has had over the past twenty-three years in writing his story. Then, starting with Chapter Two, he begins narrating his novel, that is, the novel by the author-as-character within the novel by Vonnegut the author. (pp. 229-30)

It is not until the Tenth and final chapter that Vonnegut-as-character again "appears." He has not changed much since Chapter One. He again remembers conversations with O'Hare, he is still confused about time, placing the assassinations of Robert Kennedy and Martin Luther King only a month apart; and he still harbors thoughts of death. The most significant aspect of this chapter, however, is that in describing the Dresden "corpse mines" the narrator shifts for the first time in the novel to first person plural:

> Now Billy and the rest were being marched into the ruins by their guards. I was there. O'Hare was there. We had spent the past two nights in the blind innkeeper's stable. Authorities had found us there. They told us what to do. We were to borrow picks and shovels and crowbars and wheelbarrows from our neighbors. We were to march with these implements to such and such a place in the ruins, ready to go to work. (italics added)

The shift in number insists, however subtly, that the story just related is not merely Billy Pilgrim's story, but the *narrator's* as well. He, too, had suffered capture and malnutrition and the devastating firebombing. He, too, worked in the corpse mines and saw a friend shot for "plundering" a teapot from the ruins.

And so, we realize, did Vonnegut the author. Indeed, many autobiographical similarities linking Billy Pilgrim to his "creator," Vonnegut-as-character, extend even more to Vonnegut himself. Both Pilgrim and Vonnegut were born in 1922, had fathers who hunted, are tall; both were captured in Luxembourg during the Battle of the Bulge, were sent to Dresden, where they stayed in *Schlachthof-funf,* worked in a plant that manufactured malt-syrup for pregnant women; both survived the Dresden holocaust and helped dig up the corpses afterwards; both were discharged in 1945, returned to college, and were married soon afterwards. Billy thus becomes a dual persona, a mask not only for Vonnegut-as-character (who is already a mask of sorts for Vonnegut), but for Vonnegut the author as well. Vonnegut has thus removed himself at least twice from the painful Dresden experience. By including himself as a character in his own novel, he achieves the distance that must exist between author and first person narrator, no matter how autobiographically based that narrator is. The further inclusion of Billy Pilgrim as protagonist of the novel-within-the-novel removes Vonnegut yet another step from the scenes he is recreating.

Nowhere is this need for distance more evident than when Vonnegut relates the actual firebombing itself. Since this scene constitutes the novel's *raison d'etre,* one might expect an extended and graphic presentation. The scene, however, is not only brief, but is couched in indirection, layered with multiple perspectives. At least one reviewer has criticized the scene's failure to describe more fully the Dresden catastrophe. But Vonnegut did not *see* the firebombing, he heard it, from within **Slaughterhouse-Five.** So does Billy Pilgrim.

> He was down in the meat locker on the night that Dresden was destroyed. There were sounds like giant footsteps above. Those were sticks of high explosive bombs. The giants walked and walked. . . . A guard would go to the head of the stairs every so often to see what it was like outside, then he would come down and whisper to the other guards. There was fire-storm out there. Dresden was one big flame. The one flame ate everything organic, everything that would burn.

Most significant about this scene is not its indirection, however, but the fact that it is a *remembered* scene. For the first time in the novel, Billy Pilgrim *remembers* a past event rather than time-travelling to it. Time-travel, it seems, would have made the event too immediate, too painful. Memory, on the other hand, supplies a twenty-year buffer. But if the firebombing, only indirectly witnessed, was distressing, the totally devastated city confronted the following day by the one-hundred prisoners and their four guards must have been almost overwhelming. To relate that scene Vonnegut-as-narrator requires even more distance than memory can provide. So the scene is revealed through a story Billy remembers having told Montana Wildhack on Tralfamadore. . . . Vonnegut-as-character removes himself as much as possible from the scene he narrates, cushioning it with multiple perspectives, constructing what is finally a story within a memory within a novel. (Vonnegut the author removes himself yet one step further, achieving a story within a memory within a novel within a novel.) Moreover, before relating this important scene, Vonnegut-as-narrator withdraws to the protective fantasy of Tralfamadore. Only from the perspective of that timeless planet can he at last come to artistic terms with a scene that has haunted him for twenty-three years.

The Tralfamadorian fantasy has generally been read as originating in Billy's consciousness. Much in the novel seems to support this reading. Once, after making love to Montana on Tralfamadore, Billy awakens in Ilium to discover he has had a wet dream. In Chapter Five, three different scenes—the zoo on Tralfamadore, the prison hospital in Germany, and the honeymoon apartment in Cape Ann, Massachusetts—are connected by Billy's urinating. Chapter Nine seems to provide much of the psychological source for Billy's Tralfamadorian fantasy: he reads a Kilgore Trout novel about an earthling man and woman kidnapped by extraterrestrials and kept in a zoo on an alien planet, he sees an article in an "old girly magazine" speculating about the whereabouts of the missing Montana Wildhack, and he looks at pictures of Montana described as "grainy things, soot and chalk," a description repeated three pages later but applied to a photograph of Montana's mother kept in a locket around Montana's neck on Tralfamadore. The prayer inscribed on that locket hangs as well in a frame on the wall of Billy's optometry office in Ilium. In short, the entire Tralfamadorian adventure can be traced back to certain incidents in Billy's life as an earthling. That life, incidentally, has been a harsh one, involving a series of personal catastrophes that include the accidental death by gunshot of Billy's father, the bizarre death of his wife in an automobile wreck, his own injury in an airplane crash, a troubled childhood, a nervous breakdown, troublesome children, and of course the Dresden experience—a life sufficiently painful to motivate escape fantasies.

Despite the fact that such evidence provides an apparent psychological basis for the Tralfamadorian "fantasy," the narrator clearly implies that the Tralfamadorian experiences are real. Billy often "visits" that planet through time-travel, which, we are told, unlike fantasy, really happens. In Chapter Two, the narrator refers to Pilgrim's "delightful hallucination" about skating on a ballroom floor. "This wasn't time travel," Vonnegut explains. "*It had never happened, never would happen.* It was the craziness of a dying young man with his shoes full of snow" (italics mine). The narrator again distinguishes between time-travel and fantasy when he describes Valencia's daydream: "Valencia wasn't a time-traveller, but she did have a lively imagination. While Billy was making love to her, she imagined that she was a famous woman in history." According to the narrator, then, time-travel results from neither "craziness" nor vivid imagination.

Nor does it result from dreaming. Of the fifty-six scene shifts accomplished via time-travel, thirty-one occur while Billy sleeps. Yet Vonnegut clearly distinguishes between dreams and time-travel. After his plane crash, for example, an unconscious Billy dreams "millions of things," but only the "true things" are time-travel. Moreover, his dreams—unlike time-travel—do involve wish-fulfillment. Once, for instance, he dreams under morphine that he is a giraffe placidly munching sugar pears and fully accepted "as one of their own by the other giraffes"—"harmless creatures," like Billy Pilgrim, whose natural weapons, their horns, are "covered with velvet." The dream obviously fulfills the longings of a miserable misfit POW for peace and acceptance. Billy, in other words, along with other characters in the novel indulges in wish-fulfillment fantasy. But the Tralfamadorian episodes, insists the narrator, are not included in these fantasies. They constitute actual experience.

Thus Vonnegut seems to supply internal evidence for a psychological explanation of Tralfamadore while at the same time denying that evidence with a contradictory narrative statement. (pp. 231-35)

At its deeper levels of meaning *Slaughterhouse-Five* . . . posits an uncertain world and, as such, may be perceived as a metaphor for an indeterminate universe. But uncertainty in the novel also reflects the artistic problems of Vonnegut-as-character, specifically his attempts over the years to reconstruct and formulate accurately the Dresden experience. For twenty-three years, the narrator tells us, he had been attempting to write his "famous Dresden book." "I thought it would be easy for me to write about the destruction of Dresden, since all I would have to do would be to report what I had seen. But perception, Vonnegut learns, consists only partially of "seeing." Over the years Dresden does not remain a mere historical event, but becomes all the emotion and anguish associated in Vonnegut's mind with that event as well as the symbolic values the firebombing has come to accrue. Ultimately, Dresden represents for Vonnegut the inevitability and ubiquity of death. (pp. 235-36)

In its obvious subjectivity *Slaughterhouse-Five* implies what historical relativists such as Carl Becker insist upon, that history is written "in the service of Mr. Everyman's emotional needs" and that "every generation, our own included, will, must inevitably, understand the past and anticipate the future in the light of its own restricted experience." Ultimately, Vonnegut's "famous book about Dresden" is less about Dresden than it is about the impact of Dresden on one man's sensibilities. More specifically, it is the story of Vonnegut's story of Dresden, how he came to write it and, implicitly, why he wrote it as he did. Again, the historical relativists provide an analogy for coming to terms with the meaning of *Slaughterhouse-Five.* As Maurice Mandelbaum points out, "the relativist believes that to understand a history we must not only understand what is said in it but also *why* this is said." Similarly, the meaning of *Slaughterhouse-Five* rests not so much in its content, its plot, but in its form, in the very tactics Vonnegut employs in telling the story of his story. (p. 236)

Critics have explained the Tralfamadorian experience as Billy Pilgrim's fantasy because certain patterns seem to link that experience to Billy's life on earth. That is, they have viewed Tralfamadore through the perspective provided by Billy Pilgrim. Overlooked, however, is the fact that many of the incidents in the Billy Pilgrim plot also can be traced back to Chapter One and to the perspective provided by Vonnegut-as-character, who, after all, is the "creator" of the Billy Pilgrim plot. Already mentioned are certain images—"mustard gas and roses," "blue and ivory," the flowing/frozen water motif—and the general concern with death and time, including Vonnegut's own experience of "time-travelling." But there are many others. Vonnegut's reference to The Children's Crusade, for example, is echoed by a British colonel in the German prison hospital. The Luftwaffe saber Billy takes as a souvenir of Dresden echoes the reference in Chapter One to Vonnegut's souvenir sabre. Like Billy Pilgrim, the Vonnegut of Chapter One has a favorite dog and listens to late-night radio talk shows. The woman reporter in Chapter One eats a Three-Musketeers candy bar, foreshadowing Valencia's eating one later in the novel as well as the name

Weary applies to himself and the two scouts trapped behind enemy lines. The quotation from Horace is echoed two chapters later when Billy wonders, "Where have all the years gone?" And Gerhard Muller's paradoxical "if the accident will" adumbrates the Tralfamadorian dictum that everything happens because it is supposed to happen, that the universe contains neither accident nor free will, but simply *is.*

As such patterns recur throughout the novel they direct attention back to their referents in Chapter One, thereby suggesting that all patterns in *Slaughterhouse-Five* have their origin in that chapter and in the artistic consciousness introduced there. The very fact that *Slaughterhouse-Five* is so carefully patterned serves as reminder that the Billy Pilgrim plot is an aesthetic construct produced by an ordering imagination. This includes the Tralfamadorian episodes, which, while they are fantasies, are not the fantasies of Billy Pilgrim but of Vonnegut-as-character. Like "his" characters Eliot Rosewater and Billy Pilgrim, Vonnegut-as-character is reinventing his universe and turning to science fiction for ideas. One of these ideas is Tralfamadore.

On one level, Tralfamadore is a sexual fantasy, since Billy spends much of this time abed with the luscious Montana Wildhack. More important to the general wish-fulfillment nature of the Billy Pilgrim plot, however, is the Tralfamadorian conception of time. As stated earlier, time—since it leads inevitably to death—is the real enemy of Vonnegut-as-character. Death seems too real for Vonnegut to omit from his reinvented cosmos, but by reinventing the nature of time, Vonnegut deprives death of its sting. According to the Tralfamadorians time is not linear but *simultaneous.* Everything that has happened or will happen exists in a vast omnipresent eternal Now. (pp. 237-38)

The concept of simultaneous time not only informs the theme of Vonnegut's novel but determines its structure as well. "This is a novel," the title page proclaims, "somewhat in the telegraphic schizophrenic manner of tales of the planet Tralfamadore . . ." While on the flying saucer Billy sees a Tralfamadorian book, "laid out . . . in brief clumps of symbols separated by stars." Each clump describes a situation, but the books are not read clump-by-clump, but "all at once." Without beginning, middle, or end, without suspense, moral, or cause-and-effect relationship, the Tralfamadorian books reflect "the depths of many marvelous moments seen all at one time."

Originally, Vonnegut planned a conventional novel about Dresden. "As a trafficker in climaxes and thrills and characterization and wonderful dialogue and suspense and confrontations," he writes, "I had outlined the Dresden story many times." According to early plans, the novel's climax would be the death of Edgar Derby. But the very presence of a climax requires a complication that develops *through time* toward some resolution. And it is the very notion of linear time Vonnegut wishes to reject in his novel. Ultimately, he turns to a structure that is not linear but *spatial.* As Sharon Spencer points out, "the spatialization of time in the novel is the process of splintering the events that, in a traditional novel, would appear in a narrative sequence and of rearranging them so that past, present, and future actions are presented in reversed, or combined, patterns." Events so arranged become spatial since their "orientation to reality" is not *when* but "the place *where* they occur" in the novel. The primary effect achieved by spatialization, Spencer continues, is *simultaneity,* "the representation of two or more actions in different places occurring at the same moment in time." By reflecting structurally his thematic concern with simultaneity, Vonnegut achieves a novel in which form and content merge.

The novel denies linear time in other ways, too. One of these ways involves the manipulation of the novel's chronology. Specific references to relative time fill the novel. Yet any attempt to link these references into a logical time sequence proves futile. For example, we are told that Billy marries Valencia six months after his release from the veterans hospital to which he had been committed in the spring of 1948. Since they honeymoon during Indian summer, the marriage must have occurred in the early fall of 1948. On that honeymoon, Robert Pilgrim is conceived, which, assuming a normal gestation period, would place his birth sometime in the summer of 1949. So far so good. But in Chapter Eight, Billy, after finally meeting Kilgore Trout, invites the writer to Billy and Valencia's *eighteenth* wedding anniversary party "two days hence." This event occurs in 1964, at least two years short of the eighteen years of marriage the party celebrates. Moreover, we are told that Robert is seventeen at this time. Yet if he was born in the summer of 1949 he could be no older than fifteen. (pp. 238-40)

The preponderance of such discrepancies—and many more could be cited—argues against dismissing them as careless errors. Indeed, they are perfectly consistent with the view of time that informs the novel's theme and structure. Chronological consistency would be paradoxically *inconsistent* with that theme and structure. Vonnegut ironically employs apparent contradiction to avoid actual contradiction. He does not merely deny the *relevance* of chronological order, as, say, Faulkner does through his temporal involutions in *The Sound and the Fury;* he denies its very *existence.* By making it impossible to link the novel's various dates into a coherent chronological sequence, Vonnegut effectively denies the pastness of Billy's past, the futureness of his future. Both past and future are now.

As Tony Tanner points out, "Pilgrim is not only slipping backwards and forwards in time; he is also astray in Vonnegut's own fiction." Every novel Vonnegut has written before *Slaughterhouse-Five* finds its way directly or indirectly into the Dresden novel. At least three characters—Eliot Rosewater and Kilgore Trout from *God Bless You, Mr. Rosewater,* and Howard Campbell, Jr. from *Mother Night*—as well as the Tralfamadorians, who first appear in *Sirens of Titan,* reappear in *Slaughterhouse-Five.* Each character therefore has a "past" supplied by the reader's memory of those previous fictions. Vonnegut, however, refuses to allow that past to remain fixed by changing the content of some of these previous novels. (p. 241)

Several possible explanations for these emendations exist. Such alterations deny metaphorically that the events alluded to remain preserved in permanent past and imbue them with the dynamic "live" quality of events in the process of occurring. Moreover, the appearance of uncertainty supplied by such apparent contradictions and inconsistencies contributes further to the novel as a metaphor of indeterminacy. But the most pertinent explanation seems a psychological one. We must remember that these "errors" occur in the novel-within-the-novel, hence are "made" by Vonnegut-as-character, the author of that novel-within-the-novel. Indeed, the entire novel represents the consciousness of Vonnegut-as-character in the same sense that *Moby Dick* represents the consciousness of its teller, Ishmael. The inconsistencies and errors

therein should be attributed not to the carelessness of Vonnegut the author, but to the *psychology* of Vonnegut the character. They should be read as clues to the state-of-mind of Vonnegut the character, as reflections of his desires and fears. If the Vonnegut of the first and last chapters *Slaughterhouse-Five* cannot keep his dates and other facts straight, it is because time, and the death time leads to, oppress him. The "novel" he narrates, the Billy Pilgrim plot, reflects (as it relieves) this oppression. Thus these very inconsistencies and errors—indeed, the entire mode of presentation in the novel—become the true locus of meaning in *Slaughterhouse-Five.* (pp. 242-43)

Somewhat in the tradition of Frost and Hemingway, Vonnegut conceals a complex texture beneath a deceptively simple surface. His use of contradiction and uncertainty as fictional devices alone represents a significant technical innovation. Vonnegut, we must come to understand, is a literary trickster, a Houdini of letters who escapes the straitjacket of intellectual conventions, swims deep beneath our frozen expectations, and, when he surfaces, comes up in several different places at the same time. But his literary sleight-of-hand is so skillful, so disarmingly simple, we often remain unaware a difficult trick has been performed. So we praise his themes while we ignore his artistry. (p. 243)

Charles B. Harris, "Time, Uncertainty, and Kurt Vonnegut, Jr.: A Reading of 'Slaughterhouse-Five'," in The Centennial Review, *Vol. XX, No. 3, Summer, 1976, pp. 228-43.*

STANLEY SCHATT

While money is a central character in *God Bless You, Mr. Rosewater,* death serves that role in this novel that is one without characters and, as Vonnegut admits, a book with "almost no dramatic confrontations, because most of the people in it are so sick and so much the listless playthings of enormous forces . . .". The subtitle "The Children's Crusade: A Duty-Dance with Death" clearly represents Vonnegut's most serious statements about both war and death. On the title page of *Slaughterhouse-Five,* Vonnegut describes the book as "a novel somewhat in the telegraphic schizophrenic manner of tales of the planet Tralfamadore," and this description might very well be the best one of a work that abandons the novel's conventional linear plot for a Gestalt approach that asks readers to observe a series of seemingly unrelated episodes and then to share Vonnegut's view of both war and death.

In his opening chapter Vonnegut describes his efforts to gather information about the fire-bombing of Dresden from a "war buddy" who shared the experience with him. He promises his friend's wife that *Slaughterhouse-Five* will not be just another war book with potential roles for John Wayne and Frank Sinatra. By subtitling his novel "The Children's Crusade," Vonnegut relates all modern warfare to the original Children's Crusade of 1213 when thirty thousand children volunteered to go to Palestine but half of them drowned in shipwrecks while the remaining half were sold as slaves in North Africa. He concludes that all wars are fought by the young—usually for causes they cannot understand.

Vonnegut's story centers on an awkward young chaplain's assistant named Billy Pilgrim who returns from World War II to Ilium, New York, where he marries the fat, unattractive daughter of a wealthy optometrist. As a result, Billy becomes a wealthy optometrist with two healthy children. But Vonnegut's updated version of the traditional Horatio Alger rags-to-riches story does not end at this point, for it is described in the first two pages of the novel's second chapter. Billy finds that he has no control over time, and without warning he is frequently hurled through time and space away from his lush surroundings to the desolate German front. He is kidnapped by some Tralfamadorian robots and taken to the planet Tralfamadore where he is placed in a zoo with the movie star and sex symbol, Montana Wildhack. But this episode is only a short segment of his life, for Billy learns from the Tralfamadorians that all moments in a person's life exist simultaneously and that the best philosophy is to enjoy the good moments and to ignore the bad ones. Like Malachi Constant, he also learns that the concept of free will is uniquely human. The Tralfamadorians with their cosmic vision are puzzled by Billy's concern about finding a cure for the wars that plague Earth and result in atrocities like the fire-bombing of Dresden; they know that the universe always has and always will be destroyed by an accident, the result of a Tralfamadorian's experiment with a new rocket fuel.

Slaughterhouse-Five is constructed much like Joseph Heller's *Catch-22*. Just as that novel's Yossarian is compelled to think about Snowden's death yet finds it too painful and tries to avoid the memory, so too is a reluctant Billy Pilgrim forced to return again and again to the fire-bombing of Dresden. Only when Yossarian and Billy Pilgrim learn to cope with mankind's inhumanity and the horrors of war are they able to describe the atrocities they have repressed. Billy consistently retreats from Dresden just before the atrocity is to take place until he hears a group of optometrists singing, for the barbershop quartet reminds him of the group of German soldiers who shared the protection of Slaughterhouse-five with the American prisoners during the bombing. When Kilgore Trout, Vonnegut's archetypal science-fiction prophet and writer, observes Billy's strange expression, he asks Billy if he is looking through a time window, if he is observing either the past or the present. While Billy denies it, he is doing that, and his observation or recall of the past incident represents the climax of Vonnegut's novel since it is only after Billy has faced the past that he is able to return to Dresden and live through the holocaust once more. Vonnegut himself had blotted out his memories of the actual fire-bombing of Dresden, for he has admitted that "there was a complete forgetting of what it was like . . . as far as my memory bank was concerned the center had been pulled right out of the story."

By naming the unheroic hero Billy Pilgrim, Vonnegut contrasts John Bunyan's *Pilgrim's Progress* with Billy's story. As Wilfrid Sheed has pointed out, Billy's solution to the problems of the modern world is to "invent a heaven, out of 20th century materials, where Good Technology triumphs over Bad Technology. His scripture is Science Fiction, man's last good fantasy." In a review of *Slaughterhouse-Five* entitled "Requiem to Billy Pilgrim's Progress," Sheed speculates that Vonnegut is unable to write a novel of conventional form about the fire-bombing of Dresden perhaps because "in a sense he has been blinded by the glare of the fire bombs." Instead, Vonnegut "has turned his back on the raid and written a parable." Although Sheed's title emphasizes the many similarities between *Slaughterhouse-Five* and *Pilgrim's Progress,* Vonnegut's novel is not a parable; indeed, the differences between these two works reveal Vonnegut's concern with his own personal reactions to his experience in Dresden.

While Bunyan's Christian begins a journey with Heaven as his goal, Vonnegut's Billy Pilgrim is a pilgrim who is not a Christian and who does not even think about Heaven. While Christian is warned that the City of Destruction will be burned by heavenly fire, Billy Pilgrim is shocked when he observes bombed Dresden, a city with a skyline that was "intricate and voluptuous and enchanted . . . like a Sunday School picture of Heaven . . . " that has been burned by a hellish fire-bombing. Finally, when Christian and Hopeful are about to leave the plain, they see "a pillar of salt with the inscription 'Remember Lot's Wife.' They marvel much at this monument that seems to warn them against covetousness." Vonnegut, on the other hand, interprets the action of Lot's wife as not covetousness, but as a very human concern for the welfare of the inhabitants of both Sodom and Gomorrah. He then goes one step farther and indicates that *Slaughterhouse-Five* in a sense does the same thing; it too looks back at a holocaust with feelings of human compassion and love.

The key to these differences between the views of Christian and Pilgrim becomes apparent when one realizes that, since *Pilgrim's Progress* is an allegory, a parable, it deals with "a re-examination of the objective norms of experience in the light of human ideality. It concludes the making of a new version of reality by means of an ideal which the reality of the fiction proves." In *Slaughterhouse-Five,* there is no idealism—only shock and outrage over the havoc and destruction man is capable of wreaking in the name of what he labels a worthy cause. (pp. 81-4)

Billy Pilgrim's reaction to the fire-bombing of Dresden is crucial to an understanding of Pilgrim's character. Because of the parallel in *Slaughterhouse-Five* between Vonnegut's experience in Dresden and that of Billy Pilgrim, Vonnegut creates a mask, a narrator who provides a certain distance between author and protagonist. Just as the first chapter of *Slaughterhouse-Five* is ending, Vonnegut introduces a note of science fiction when he tells his readers that "Somebody was playing with the clocks. . . . The second hand on my watch would twitch once, and a year would pass, and then it would twitch again. There was nothing I could do about it. As an Earthling I had to believe whatever clocks said—and calendars."

Vonnegut then quotes a stanza from Theodore Roethke's "The Waking" that describes how it is possible to "wake to sleep" and "dream by going where I have to go." The key word in the poem for Vonnegut is *sleep*. *Slaughterhouse-Five* in a way is a vision, a dream, Vonnegut's version of James Joyce's *Finnegans Wake* in which he and the reader both learn by "going where I have to go." The very process of making this journey is so painful for Vonnegut that he has labeled this novel a failure. After the quote from "The Waking," a masked narrator continues Vonnegut's story for the next eight chapters with occasional interruptions by Vonnegut himself. This narrator has a Tralfamadorian philosophy of life which makes it painless for him to describe the fire-bombing of Dresden and Billy's suffering in a cold, detached, objective manner. Tralfamadorians, it should be remembered, are machines devoid of all human feelings of love and compassion. In the final chapter Vonnegut reappears and speculates on whether or not he can accept such a view of life.

Often, when an author uses a mask, its reliability may be questionable. In *Slaughterhouse-Five* Vonnegut is careful to distinguish his viewpoint from both Billy Pilgrim's and his narrator's. In the first chapter Vonnegut, speaking as himself, is not using a mask; and he explains that he loves the wife of Lot for expressing her feelings of love and compassion by turning to look back at the inhabitants of Sodom and Gomorrah even though doing so means being transformed into a pillar of salt. What may be confusing is the fact that Vonnegut's view that man must try to ameliorate the suffering of his fellow man, or at least show some concern, is not shared consistently either by his narrator or by Billy Pilgrim. (pp. 84-5)

While Billy, like Vonnegut, is torn between a desire to forget Dresden and the pain this memory brings and an obsession about finding a way to reconcile the human suffering he observed there, the narrator pragmatically adopts the Tralfamadorian philosophy of "ignoring unpleasant times and concentrating on the good ones." He declares "so it goes" whenever he describes an unpleasant event such as the death of Billy's parents or the airplane crash that killed all the passengers except Billy. "So it goes" is a Tralfamadorian expression used by these robots to describe an unpleasant event which cannot be avoided since man and robot both live in a universe in which there is no such thing as free will.

While the novel's narrator reports that Billy turns away from a slight reminiscence of Dresden's fire-bombing, he does not appear to understand the motives behind such an action. Billy is not following the Tralfamadorian philosophy of indifference because, as a human filled with compassion, he cannot. Rather, his actions are a result of the equipoise between his painful memories of Dresden and his almost intolerable fixation about the suffering he observed there. While at one moment the memory of Dresden may make the urban renewal project in Ilium something he wants to pass through quickly—and the sight of a ghetto Negro equally unpleasant—he at other times marries a fat woman to alleviate her suffering and loneliness, and he also cries over the agony of a horse he has unwittingly mistreated. The question Vonnegut never answers in reference to Billy and his slogan is what young Pilgrim can and cannot change.

The major difficulty for the reader of *Slaughterhouse-Five* is that, while Vonnegut's narrator accepts the Tralfamadorian view of the universe wholeheartedly, Billy Pilgrim accepts this view intellectually but not emotionally. Emotionally, his view of the universe is much closer to Vonnegut's sentiments in the first chapter where the author speaks for himself: for Billy, like Vonnegut, cannot endure the sight of human suffering even though the Tralfamadorians tell him that there is nothing he can do about it. (p. 86)

Intellectually, at least, Billy tries to escape from the sight of human suffering by adopting the Tralfamadorian philosophy. When he meets a boy whose father died in Vietnam, he tells him "about his adventures on Tralfamadore," and assures the fatherless boy that his father "is very much alive still in moments that boy would see again and again." He then asks, "Isn't that comforting?" The boy and his mother flee the office convinced that Billy is insane. Eventually, Pilgrim realizes that he cannot comfort others with the Tralfamadorian philosophy; he cannot even ameliorate his own suffering. When Billy marries his fat wife Valencia, the narrator knows that "Billy didn't want to marry ugly Valencia. She was one of the symptoms of his disease. He knew he was going crazy when he heard himself proposing marriage to her, when he begged her to take the diamond ring and be his companion for life." Pilgrim's "disease" is his inability to accept human suffering; during their honeymoon night Valencia tells him "I'm so happy . . . I never thought anybody would marry

me." Billy does not feel any love for her, but he is reconciled to the marriage since he "had already seen a lot of their marriage, thanks to time-travel, knew it was going to be at least bearable all the way." A marriage that is "bearable" seems a small price for Billy to pay if it relieves the pangs he feels when he watches Valencia suffer as an unmarried, fat, unloved woman.

As noted, the Dresden holocaust made such an impression on Vonnegut that he devoted twenty-three years to trying to write a novel about it. It made such an impression on Billy Pilgrim that, as an optometrist who, by dint of his profession, should help people see more clearly, he frequently feels compelled to travel back in time and to relive the events leading up to the climactic day of the Dresden air raid. Although the novel's narrator can accept the destruction of this city with a Tralfamadorian "so it goes," Billy cannot because Vonnegut cannot. Both protagonist and author respond in characteristic Vonnegut fashion—ambivalently. While Billy and Vonnegut would very much like to purge themselves of the painful memory, they find themselves fixated on the needless suffering they observed there. This condition of dynamic equilibrium seems irreconcilable; both are confronted with the very human conflict between man's desire for personal comfort and his desire to ameliorate another's suffering.

Crucial to an understanding of *Slaughterhouse-Five* is the realization that Billy's feelings concerning human suffering are directly linked to his experience at the fire-bombing of Dresden. . . . The fire-bombing is at the center of Billy's consciousness and is much more real to him than his shallow life as an optometrist in Ilium, New York. Pilgrim frequently feels himself drawn to Dresden by what was by far the most traumatic experience of his life. When he does travel there, however, he utilizes the Tralfamadorian concept of time travel to jump away whenever he comes too close to the actual day of the bombing. On the night before the actual attack, for example, the narrator reveals that "Nothing happened that night. It was the next night that about one hundred and thirty thousand people in Dresden would die. So it goes. Billy dozed in the meat locker. He found himself engaged again, word for word, gesture for gesture, in the argument with his daughter with which this novel began." It is less painful for Billy to sustain his daughter's scolding than it is to endure the fire bombing once again.

Since Vonnegut has constructed *Slaughterhouse-Five* with the fire-bombing of Dresden at its center, all Billy's time travel and memories are linked to it by repression. Because Vonnegut apparently links the fire-bombing of Dresden with what to him is the very problem posed by man's seemingly unbounded proclivity for evil that he referred to in an earlier novel as the forces of "Mother Night," it is quite natural for him to show Billy trying to repress such a memory. Despite such efforts, however, Billy's repressed thoughts are part of his stream of consciousness though, even while in his sleep-like state, the actual holocaust is still too painful to face directly.

Vonnegut uses stream of consciousness, sensory impressions, and interior monologue to show that all of Billy's thoughts lead indirectly yet ultimately to Dresden and to the disturbing yet unanswerable question for him of why man destroys and kills. Billy begins one of his journeys through time as a German prisoner of war about to be given a shower in Dresden in 1944. When a German soldier turns on a master valve, the water is like "scalding rain." It "jangled Billy's skin without thawing the ice in the marrow of his long bones." This sensation of being showered with hot water causes young Pilgrim to go back in time to his infancy. Suddenly he "was a baby who had just been bathed by his mother." In order to powder him, his mother takes him into "a rosy room . . . filled with sunshine." The remembrance of that sunshine upon him causes Billy to jump forward in time to a point when he is a "middle-aged optometrist again, playing hacker's golf . . . on a blazing summer Sunday morning." When he bends down to retrieve his golf ball safely trapped in the cup, Billy suddenly travels in time to the moment when he finds himself trapped by the Tralfamadorians, "strapped to a yellow contour chair . . . aboard a flying saucer, which was bound for Tralfamadore."

The logic behind this time shift appears to be his association with the word *trapped*. A Tralfamadorian tells him that all men and all Tralfamadorians are like bugs trapped in amber, for "Only on Earth is there any talk of free will." Billy has moved from taking a shower in Dresden in 1944 to talking to aliens on the planet Tralfamadore in 1967, but his focus is still on man's inhumanity exemplified by the Dresden holocaust; for, when he ponders the question of human free will, what he really is asking is, if man does indeed have free will, what rationale can he possibly have to explain his actions during the war, particularly his fire-bombing of Dresden.

While Vonnegut's use of a narrator with a personality all his own, his use of stream of consciousness, and his manipulation of the novel's time scheme and esthetic distance makes *Slaughterhouse-Five* a difficult book to follow, his strong feelings about the Dresden holocaust made such techniques necessary. Without such artistic sleight-of-hand, the novel might have turned into a political diatribe or perhaps into a maudlin, introspective look at war. (pp. 87-9)

Since Vonnegut's novels usually are constructed around two diametrically opposed points of view, it is not surprising that *Slaughterhouse-Five* is built around the irreconcilable conflict between free will and determinism. While Vonnegut urges his sons to exercise their free will and do what is morally and ethically justified, his Tralfamadorian robots point to the utter meaninglessness of such human actions. The Tralfamadorian sections of the novel may also serve another function since they provide a form of comic relief from the unbearable tension that builds as Billy approaches the day of the actual fire-bombing. (p. 91)

Slaughterhouse-Five is proof that Vonnegut kept his promise to write a war novel that does not glorify or glamorize killing. His novel does repudiate most of the stereotyped characters and patriotic bilge that has become standard movie fare. One of Billy's companions after the Battle of the Bulge is Roland Weary; he is stupid, fat, mean, and smells like bacon no matter how often he bathes; and he enjoys romanticizing the war until his daydreams blot out the reality of the frozen German landscape. While he is in reality unpopular, he imagines himself to be one of the three close war comrades who call themselves the "Three Musketeers." Vonnegut describes how Weary confronted Billy Pilgrim and "dilated upon the piety and heroism of 'The Three Musketeers,' portrayed, in the most glowing and impassioned hues, their virtue and magnanimity, the imperishable honor they acquired for themselves, and the great services they rendered to Christianity."

Weary's fantasy is counterpointed by Vonnegut's earlier description about an early Christian crusade—by the shocking reality of a children's crusade in which young boys are butchered or sold into slavery because of a war they cannot even comprehend. Vonnegut further deflates the idea that war is glorious and fun by describing a group of English prisoners of war who live in a self-supervised camp that they keep immaculate and well stocked with goods. They exercise regularly, keep themselves well bathed and groomed, and manage to preserve an atmosphere of normalcy. It is not surprising that the German commander adores them because "they were exactly what Englishmen ought to be. They made war look stylish and reasonable, and fun." The British prisoners are unaware that the soap and candles they use were made from "the fat of rendered Jews and gypsies and fairies and communists, and other enemies of the state." It is more than coincidental that they entertain Billy Pilgrim's group of bedraggled American prisoners by performing an adult version of Cinderella. They reinforce the German commander's justification for the war by transforming the ugly, horrifying realities of war into something beautiful and magical. But midnight tolls, and Billy once again sees the real picture of warfare when he goes outside to move his bowels. He finds all his fellow Americans terribly sick with diarrhea and suddenly becomes snagged to a barbwire fence. (p. 94)

While *Slaughterhouse-Five* is about the Dresden air attack and about World War II, its major focus is on death. Many deaths in the novel are ironic, especially that of unfortunate school teacher Edgar Derby who survives the Battle of the Bulge only to be shot for plundering a teapot from the ruins of the smoldering city. Vonnegut offers another view of death when he describes the Tralfamadorian view that all moments always have and always will exist and that death is just one moment in anyone's life. The Tralfamadorians enjoy the good moments and ignore the bad moments, but this solution is unsatisfactory to Vonnegut who believes that death is far too important to ignore.

Vonnegut's view of death becomes clear in the final chapter of *Slaughterhouse-Five* in which he describes not his visit to Dresden in 1968 but Billy Pilgrim's efforts to dig up the bodies buried beneath the rubble of the fire-bombed city. When Billy is released from captivity, Vonnegut describes the scene as follows:

> And somewhere in there was springtime. The corpse mines were closed down. The soldiers all left to fight the Russians. . . . And then one morning, they got up to discover that the door was unlocked. World War Two in Europe was over.
> Billy and the rest wandered out onto the shady street. The trees were leafing out. There was nothing going on out there, no traffic of any kind. There was only one vehicle, an abandoned wagon drawn by two horses. The wagon was green and coffin shaped.
> Birds were talking.
> One bird said to Billy Pilgrim, "Poo-tee-weet?

Billy's world is filled with both life and death. Though it is spring and the trees are leafing out, the coffin-shape of the abandoned wagon serves as a reminder of the death surrounding him. The last word in the novel is the bird's message to Billy Pilgrim, and it is the same message Eliot Rosewater received as *God Bless You, Mr. Rosewater* concluded. As Raymond Olderman has pointed out in *Beyond the Wasteland*, [see excerpt above] "Poo-tee-weet represents a 'cosmic cool,' a way of viewing life with the distance necessary to cope with the horrors that both Billy Pilgrim and Eliot Rosewater experience." It is not callousness or indifference but merely a defense mechanism that allows Vonnegut to smile through his tears and to continue to live and to write.

Slaughterhouse-Five concludes with Vonnegut himself describing among other things the latest casualty lists in Vietnam, the death of his father, the assassination of Robert Kennedy, the execution of kindly Edgar Derby, and the end of World War II. Though Vonnegut sees the Dresden firebombing in the context of the political assassinations and of the unpopular war that overshadowed almost all other issues in the 1960's, he is able to smile through his tears and provide an affirmation of life. The message of **Slaughterhouse-Five** is the need for compassion; [Billy Pilgrim learns] that the purpose of life, no matter whether there is free will or not, is to love whomever is around to be loved. (pp. 95-6)

> *Stanley Schatt, in his* Kurt Vonnegut, Jr., *Twayne Publishers, 1976, 174 p.*

THOMAS L. WYMER

In **Slaughterhouse-Five** there are two central thematic concerns: first, the presentation of the horror of war and its dehumanization of man, for which theme the central character Billy Pilgrim serves as the major example of victim; second, a kind of solution to this problem, a world view associated with extraterrestrial beings called Tralfamadorians, for which Billy Pilgrim becomes the major spokesman. The first theme, the thesis layer, is quite clear and needs no explanation; the antithesis layer again offers major difficulties.

A Tralfamadorian explains to Billy that time does not change. "It does not lend itself to warnings or explanations. It simply *is*. Take it moment by moment, and you will find that we are all, as I've said before, bugs in amber." Free will is therefore nonsense. The Tralfamadorians, living in an eternal now with all time spread before them, know that the universe will suddenly disappear when one of their test pilots, experimenting with new fuels, presses a starter button. Why won't they prevent it? "He has *always* pressed it, and he always *will*. We *always* let him and we always *will* let him. The moment is *structured* that way." What can be done about wars? "There isn't anything we can do about them, so we simply don't look at them. We ignore them. We spend eternity looking at pleasant moments . . ."

Tony Tanner sees the issue clearly:

> Billy becomes completely quiescent, calmly accepting everything that happens as happening exactly as it ought to (including his own death). He abandons the worried, ethical, tragical point of view of western man and adopts a serene conscienceless passivity. . . . Here I think is the crucial moral issue in the book . . . how are we to regard his new vision?

Tanner goes on to point out the weakness of such a view, the question of whether we can afford to ignore the ugly moments in life, but he also sees the opposed question of whether conscience can "cope with events like the concentration camps and the Dresden air raid." Perhaps we need "fantasies to offset such facts." He tries to balance the two views:

> Vonnegut has, I think, a total sympathy with such quietistic impulses. At the same time his whole work suggests that if man doesn't do something

about the conditions and quality of human life on Earth, no-one and nothing else will. Fantasies of complete determinism, of being held helplessly in the amber of some eternally unexplained plot, justify complete passivity and a supine acceptance of the futility of all action. Given the overall impact of Vonnegut's work I think we are bound to feel that there is at least something equivocal about Billy's habit of fantasy, even if his attitude is the most sympathetic one in the book.

Tanner is an excellent reader whose sensitivity helps reveal the possible error which throws him off the track. The fact that "total sympathy" turns into "at least something equivocal" illustrates the disorienting effect of the Swiftian technique, but Swift's pattern is suggested even more clearly. Tanner's confusion turns on the opposition between the apparent judgment of Vonnegut the man and the "whole work," its "overall impact." That opposition is there, but how we understand it depends on whether or not we trust Vonnegut the artist. Tanner does not. Put the case that Vonnegut the artist knows what he is doing; then it follows that the work as a whole is the most reliable measure of Vonnegut's purpose, while any discrepancies between "the overall impact" and Vonnegut *the man in the novel* (his major appearances are not in preface or epilogue but in the first and last chapters) would have to be explained by seeing that man as a satiric persona. This suggestion is plausible enough on a purely theoretical level; how accurate it may be must depend again on close analysis of the ways in which irony operates in the novel.

For the portion of the novel that deals with the war experience Billy functions as the satiric persona of the *naïf*. Totally victimized, he bears effective mute witness to the insane and dehumanizing cruelty that is war. But his function as *naïf* wears thin. If we discount Billy's prediction of his own death in 1976, the portion of his life covered by the novel extends to 1968. Billy has reached the age of forty-six. By this time he has for some twenty years been married to the rich, fat daughter of the owner of the Ilium School of Optometry, "a girl nobody in his right mind would have married." From the Buick and $30,000 a year his father-in-law guaranteed him in 1948 he has moved up by 1967 to $60,000 a year and his own Cadillac, complete with right-wing bumper stickers. He is a president of the local Lions Club who applauds speeches by marine majors advocating "bombing North Vietnam back into the stone age," and he admits proudly that he is a veteran and has a son who is a sergeant in the Green Berets. "Everything was pretty much all right with Billy." In short, he blindly supports in every way consistent with his age and position all those forces which had brought him to Dresden. He is, in fact, a familiar Vonnegut type, the agent-victim. (pp. 241-43)

The process of undercutting and exposing the folly of the Pilgrim-Tralfamadorian position is built into the structure of **Slaughterhouse-Five**. It is constructed, we are told on the title page, "somewhat in the telegraphic schizophrenic manner of tales of the planet Tralfamadore." The technique is explained in greater detail later on by a Tralfamadorian: these tales are laid out "in brief clumps of symbols":

> [each] is a brief, urgent message—describing a situation, a scene. We Tralfamadorians read them all at once, not one after the other. There isn't any particular relationship between all the messages, except that the author has chosen them carefully, so

that, when seen all at once, they produce an image of life that is beautiful and surprising and deep. There is no beginning, no middle, no end, no suspense, no moral, no causes, no effects. What we love in our books are the depths of many marvelous moments seen all at one time.

Immediately following these lines we are told that Billy goes through a time warp and finds himself at the age of twelve quaking in fear on the edge of the Grand Canyon: "His mother touched him, and he wet his pants."

The connections between the two scenes are not particularly subtle. The "image of life that is beautiful and surprising and deep" takes us by way of the puns to the Grand Canyon, but Billy's terror hardly marks this as a marvelous moment. The point is carried further when little Billy next takes "a peewee jump of only ten days" to Carlsbad Caverns, where he is "praying to God to get him out of there"; a ranger turns out the lights in order to give the terrified child the beautiful surprise of total darkness. This instant undercutting of the Tralfamadorian concept of the novel should alert us to the fact that Vonnegut has chosen his messages carefully, but in a way which parodies the other-worldly form he has created. Tralfamadorians use the schizophrenic manner to build up impressions of beautiful, unrelated images; Vonnegut parodies the form by juxtaposing ironically contrasting scenes. And the irony directs us to read the novel's messages not like Tralfamadorians, who see them "all at once, not one after another," but like human beings. In fact, the center of the novel's satiric thrust is its exposure of the sad fact that most people behave more like Tralfamadorians than like human beings, while the fundamental "ought" is one repeated throughout Vonnegut's works since its initial statement in his first novel, *Player Piano:* "The main business of humanity is to do a good job of being human beings."

As soon as one begins reading the novel like a human being, the observable relationships between scenes become so numerous that only a few can be pursued here. One of the major relating devices is a series of recurrent images: colors like blue and ivory, orange and black, nacreous pink; images like roses and mustard gas; the first dirty photograph in the western world; a barbershop quartet. All these images are associated with Billy's war experiences. (pp. 245-46)

The color images serve to undercut not only the Tralfamadorian concept of the novel but the philosophical view which underlies that concept. The Tralfamadorians advise Billy "to concentrate on the happy moments of his life, and to ignore the unhappy ones—to stare only at pretty things as eternity failed to go by." It is a selective approach to time that emphasizes the unrelatedness of events, the discontinuity of time. The ironic effect of the novel, however, runs counter to that view, insisting instead that time past is contained within time present, that Dresden is still happening while we ignore it. The recurrent images illustrate how Billy's whole existence is shot through with reminders of the unhappy moments. The fact that Billy so seldom seems to recognize these reminders illustrates his monumental blindness, his incredible lack of moral awareness, characteristics which continually recur. . . . A major irony which Billy's behavior exhibits is that, except for the power to control time jumps, Billy had become an excellent practicing Tralfamadorian long before he ever heard of such creatures. And his embracing of their world view is rendered suspect by the fact that their view is an excuse for and justification of the way he has been living

all along, like a Tralfamadorian machine: "Tralfamadorians, of course, say that every creature and plant in the Universe is a machine." But the only reason he needs such a philosophical view is the fact that his mechanization began to break down; he began around 1964 to show increasingly disturbing symptoms of being human, symptoms which Tralfamadorianism manages to "cure."

The key scene is the wedding party of Billy's daughter. A barbershop quartet of optometrists sing "That Old Gang of Mine," and Billy finds himself weeping:

> . . . he could find no explanation for why the song had affected him so grotesquely. He had supposed for years that he had no secrets from himself. Here was proof that he had a great big secret somewhere inside, and he could not imagine what it was.

For one of the few times in his life Billy examines his own response and pursues it to a memory. He remembers four of his guards emerging from his slaughterhouse bomb shelter the morning after the Dresden holocaust, looking at the scene of utter desolation:

> The guards drew together instinctively, rolled their eyes. They experimented with one expression and then another, said nothing, though their mouths were open. They looked like a silent film of a barbershop quartet.

Shortly before this scene our narrator had described a story by Kilgore Trout about a robot whose occupation was dropping jellied gasoline on human beings. The robots, we are told, "had no conscience, and no circuits which would allow them to imagine what was happening to the people on the ground." In spite of Billy's mechanistic behavior, his memory of the quartet reveals the secret that, unlike the robots, he does have such circuits. His memory, however, stirs his conscience on a very elementary level, and it is at this point that the time warp theory is introduced to Billy by Trout, who notices Billy's upset and tells him he must have seen through a "time window": "Most of Trout's novels, after all, dealt with time warps and extra-sensory perception and other unexpected things. Trout believed in things like that, was greedy to have their existence proved." With the aid of Trout's theory Billy manages not to achieve anything like moral awareness. Billy's memory triggers a time jump to the Tralfamadorian zoo where he is telling Montana Wildhack about what it was like in Dresden just after the bombing—a very closely connected and unTralfamadorian time jump. He begins with the quartet of guards and describes the scene in cold detail. We are treated to the stunned odyssey of a hundred American POW's through the ruins, past charred bodies, the desolation momentarily relieved by a strafing run by American fighter planes trying "to hasten the end of the war," and we come to rest with the prisoners in an outlying inn where a blind German innkeeper feeds and beds them. The last line of the chapter quotes the innkeeper: " 'Good night, Americans,' he said in German. 'Sleep well.' " Billy is only telling a story. Vonnegut is addressing us, and doing so in a way designed to inspire most unTralfamadorian feelings of guilt.

Perhaps the most heavily loaded scene of the novel occurs appropriately enough near the end. It is a May afternoon two days after the end of the war. Billy, still in Dresden, is lying in "a coffin-shaped green wagon" which he and some friends had found abandoned with horses, and then ridden around in. The others leave, Billy falls asleep, and we are told that if he had had the Tralfamadorian power to choose his times, "he might have chosen as his happiest moment his sun-drenched snooze in the back of the wagon." But Billy's happiness has a price; he hears voices and looks over the edge of the wagon:

> A middle-aged man and wife were crooning to the horses. They were noticing what the Americans had not noticed—that the horses' mouths were bleeding, gashed by the bits, that the horses' hooves were broken, so that every step meant agony, that the horses were insane with thirst. The Americans had treated their form of transportation as though it were no more sensitive than a six-cylinder Chevrolet.

The scene becomes emblematic of the purpose of the novel:

> Billy asked them in English what it was they wanted, and they at once scolded him in English for the condition of the horses. They made Billy get out of the wagon and come look at the horses. When Billy saw the condition of his means of transportation, he burst into tears. He hadn't cried about anything else in the war.

By emblematic I mean that Billy functions as a kind of Everyman, perhaps the average reader, the typical blind and insensitive western man who pays little attention to the suffering around him and probably had no knowledge whatever of Dresden before reading Vonnegut's novel. The man and wife are identified as "doctors, both obstetricians," a detail which helps reveal the wagon's function as a perverse womb symbol, coffin-shaped to suggest the death to come from a false peace built upon indifference. The doctors, in attempting to deliver Billy from his indifference by making him look at the suffering horses, reflect Vonnegut's attempt to wake us to the world of suffering which we all ignore and to which we contribute.

The importance of this scene is reinforced by the reference to it at the conclusion of the novel which focuses on a scene two days before, the day the war ended:

> Billy and the rest wandered out into the shady street. The trees were leafing out. There was nothing going on out there, no traffic of any kind. There was only one vehicle, an abandoned wagon drawn by two horses. The wagon was green and coffin-shaped.
> Birds were talking
> One bird said to Billy Pilgrim, 'Poo-tee-weet?'

We end with symbols of rebirth centering on the bird's song; that song, however, is not a statement of rebirth but a question. We know how Billy will answer; he will climb into the womb, not out of it; the attempt to deliver him will result in the pointless sentimentality of his crying, and then he will forget the incident, remembering only the happy moment before. In short, Billy's birth will be aborted. The question that is not answered, however, is directed at us: is it possible for man to learn, in the terms the question was raised in *Sirens,* "the intricate tactics of causing less rather than more pain"; can man break out of the cruel self-destructive pattern in which he seems to be trapped?

How Western man will answer that question we can only speculate, but if some of the critics are any indication we have small basis for optimism. McNelly, for instance, maintains that "earthlings can find stoical, hopeful acceptance in the pattern presented by Tralfamadore." Somer sees Billy as the crowning success in Vonnegut's struggle to create "a hero who can survive with dignity in an insane world." In fact, Billy's stance of "heroic" acceptance is expressed in the situation of his being imprisoned with a voluptuous, guilt-free, sexually hyperactive movie queen, a classic adolescent wet dream.

A major thesis of the novel is that killing on a massive scale happens not simply because of the lovers of violence like Paul Lazzaro or Roland Weary, nor because of the rationalizers of violence like Professor Rumfoord, but also because of the Billy Pilgrims, the nice, plain, innocent, blind fools who lend passive support to that killing. Vonnegut builds up additional incidents to support this implication. The victims of his passive infliction of pain are not confined to horses; he has troubles on the prison train because his *sleep* is violent: "Nearly everybody, seemingly, had an atrocity story of something Billy Pilgrim had done to him in his sleep." Billy boards a plane in 1968 knowing it will crash, but says nothing because "he didn't want to make a fool of himself by saying so." Vonnegut also uses a real historian, British Air Marshal Sir Robert Saundby: speaking of Dresden, he says, "Those who approved it were too remote from the harsh realities of war to understand fully the appalling destructive power of air bombardment in the spring of 1945." Indeed, if we could imagine that Tralfamadorian test pilot who destroys the universe as having a "human" face, we would see neither the sadistic leer of a Roland Weary nor the insane hate of a Paul Lazzaro, but the vacant grin of Billy Pilgrim.

Far from championing passive or blind acquiescence, Vonnegut insists on the importance of awareness, the necessity of human beings understanding how they cause pain, how they commit atrocities in their sleep. (pp. 246-51)

There are a number of important functions which [the phrase "So it goes"] serves. It appears applied indiscriminately to such matters as dead champagne, dead lice, dead soldiers, the death of the Universe, of characters in Trout's novels, of 135,000 Dresden residents, of Jesus, and the death of the novel. This is not a simple expression of indifference; it is a *reduction ad absurdum* which parodies indifference, much as the description of the disarray on Belinda's dressing table in Pope's *Rape of the Lock,* "Puffs, powders, patches, Bibles, billetdoux," both expresses and parodies the disorder of her sense of values. Similarly "so it goes" functions ambiguously as the sign of the persona's indifference and as Vonnegut's ironic comment on Tralfamadorian indifference, a device of double irony common in Swift. Indeed, there is a bit of Billy Pilgrim in every man, and Vonnegut also uses the persona to acknowledge his own share of man's common inhumanity. And perhaps, as Tanner sensed, there is a certain degree of necessary distancing from the horror of war which the phrase provides; we have noted the necessity of both not being indifferent and not being sentimental. That balance is adroitly achieved when Vonnegut steps out of his satiric persona and gives his answer to the novel's question, thereby separating himself from Billy and the Tralfamadorians (it is analogous to Swift's practice when, after having presented his outrageous proposal as a modest one, he concludes, "Therefore let no man talk to me of other expedients," and proceeds to list a set of alternatives so practical and humane that it becomes clear that the ironic mask has been dropped). Vonnegut again uses the bird's song to set up the question. We know Billy's answer, but Vonnegut's is clearly different:

Everything is supposed to be very quiet after a massacre, and it always is, except for the birds.
And what do the birds say? All there is to say about a massacre, things like 'Poo-tee-weet?'

I have told my sons that they are not under any circumstances to take part in massacres, and that the news of massacres of enemies is not to fill them with satisfaction or glee.

I have also told them not to work for companies which make massacre machinery, and to express contempt for people who think we need machinery like that.

These two short paragraphs are set off not only by double-spacing but also by their style; free of irony or whimsy, they have the ring of an oracular declaration, a commitment. Still, as an answer it may strike some as insufficient, but its limitations are, I think, carefully considered. Billy Pilgrim demonstrates in one figure two major follies: the supposition that we can transcend the limitations of our humanity and the insistence that those limitations are necessarily so great as to deprive us of any responsibility for our humanity. Vonnegut's commitment demonstrates how moral responsibility operates within these extremes.

The moral vision suggested here is modern since it is derived from a conception of human freedom, but that conception, far from freeing us of moral norms, creates new ones. Being free in Vonnegut's existential terms becomes itself not a factual situation but a possibility that ought to be achieved; freedom is moreover characterized by its mutality: the deprivation of another's freedom ultimately victimizes oneself. One cannot therefore save or forcibly change another person or the world. But each person is responsible for what he himself does, both in directly denying and in lending active or passive support to those who deny the freedom of others. The sense of this obligation, however, in order to be consistent with freedom, must come from within, which means that the only way the world can be saved is the hard way, by the commitment of enough individual human beings to the task of finding a way to resist without destroying, of causing less pain without flying from responsibility; the task of becoming, in short, better human beings. That commitment is expressed in what Vonnegut says he has told his sons, his contribution to a modern children's crusade. No man can stop people from killing, but he can himself at least stop encouraging it. (pp. 259-61)

Essential to being human is the capacity to face oneself, to make moral judgments in the knowledge that one is without certainty, to create value through the agony of personal commitment. As difficult and even dangerous as it is to try to be decent, he says, in effect, human beings have to try, have to start somewhere. He sticks his own neck out early in *Slaughterhouse-Five* with his own commitment; the rest of the novel attempts to set us up to face the same question: "Poo-tee-weet?" (p. 262)

Thomas L. Wymer, "The Swiftian Satire of Kurt Vonnegut, Jr.," in Voices for the Future: Essays on Major Science Fiction Writers, *edited by Thomas D. Clareson, Bowling Green University Popular Press, 1976, pp. 238-62.*

ROBERT MERRILL AND **PETER A. SCHOLL**

It is safe to assume that novels of social protest are not written by cynics or nihilists. Surely protest implies the belief that man's faults are remediable. It is relevant, then, that Vonnegut's novels, early and late, were conceived in the spirit of social protest. Vonnegut has said that his motives as a writer are "political": "I agree with Stalin and Hitler and Mussolini that the writer should serve his society. I differ with dictators as to *how* writers should serve. Mainly, I think they should be—and biologically *have* to be—agents of change." This belief informs Vonnegut's first book, *Player Piano* (1952), a novel which deserves Leslie Fiedler's elegant complaint that it is excessively committed to "proving (once more?) that machines deball and dehumanize men." It is crucial to *Mother Night* (1961), a novel which has a rather unquietistic "moral" if the author's 1966 introduction is to be believed: "We are what we pretend to be, so we must be careful about what we pretend to be." And it is no less central to *God Bless You, Mr. Rosewater* (1965), a novel in which Vonnegut's attack on capitalistic practices is unrelenting. These books were all written by the man who once said that he admired George Orwell "almost more than any other man." They were written by the man who likes Utopian talk, speculation about what Earth should be, anger about what the planet is.

Therefore, it is hard to believe that *Slaughterhouse-Five* is a novel that recommends "resigned acceptance" as the proper response to life's injustices. Tony Tanner is the only critic who has used the term "quietism" in discussing *Slaughterhouse-Five,* but most of Vonnegut's critics seem intent on reading the book as if it *were* the work of a quietist. The problem concerns Vonnegut's "hero," Billy Pilgrim. *Slaughterhouse-Five* is about Pilgrim's response to the fire-bombing of Dresden. This response includes Billy's supposed space-travel to the planet Tralfamadore, where he makes the rather startling discovery about time that Winston Niles Rumfoord first made in Vonnegut's second novel, *The Sirens of Titan* (1959), "that everything that ever has been always will be, and everything that ever will be always has been." This proves immensely satisfying to Pilgrim, for it means "that when a person dies he only *appears* to die. He is still very much alive in the past, so it is very silly for people to cry at his funeral." Indeed, it is very silly for people to cry about anything, including Dresden. This is the "wisdom" Billy achieves in the course of Vonnegut's novel. It is, of course, the wisdom of quietism. If everything that ever has been always will be, and everything that ever will be always has been, nothing can be done to change the drift of human affairs. As the Tralfamadorians tell Billy Pilgrim, the notion of free will is a quaint Earthling illusion.

What is more disturbing, Vonnegut's critics seem to think that he is saying the same thing. For Anthony Burgess, "*Slaughterhouse* is a kind of evasion—in a sense like J. M. Barrie's *Peter Pan*—in which we're being told to carry the horror of the Dresden bombing and everything it implies up to a level of fantasy. . . ." For Charles Harris [see excerpt above], "The main idea emerging from *Slaughterhouse-Five* seems to be that the proper response to life is one of resigned acceptance." For Alfred Kazin, "Vonnegut deprecates any attempt to see tragedy that day in Dresden. . . . He likes to say with arch fatalism, citing one horror after another, 'So it goes.' " For Tanner, "Vonnegut has . . . total sympathy with such quietistic impulses." (pp. 66-7)

This view of Vonnegut's book tends to contradict what he has said in published interviews and his earlier novels. But of course the work itself must be examined to determine whether or not *Slaughterhouse-Five* is a protest novel. Such a study should reveal Vonnegut's complex strategy for protesting such horrors as Dresden. (p. 67)

The key to Vonnegut's strategy is his striking introduction of the Tralfamadorians into what he calls an antiwar novel. The fire-bombing of Dresden actually receives less emphasis than Billy Pilgrim's space and time travel, especially his visit with the Tralfamadorians. Vonnegut has played down the immediate impact of the war in order to make "a powerful little statement about the kinds of social attitudes responsible for war and its atrocities," as Harris has remarked of *Mother Night.* By transporting his hero to Tralfamadore, Vonnegut is able to introduce the Tralfamadorian notions about time and death which inevitably call attention to more "human" theories. The status of the Tralfamadorians is therefore the most important issue in any discussion of *Slaughterhouse-Five.*

It is the status of the Tralfamadorians themselves which is in question, not just their ideas. Vonnegut offers many hints that the Tralfamadorians do not exist. Just before he goes on a radio talk show to spread the Tralfamadorian gospel, Billy Pilgrim comes across several books by Kilgore Trout in a forty-second Street porno shop:

> The titles were all new to him, or he thought they were. Now he opened one. . . . The name of the book was *The Big Board.* He got a few paragraphs into it, and then realized that he *had* read it before—years ago, in the veterans' hospital. It was about an Earthling man and woman who were kidnapped by extra-terrestrials. They were put on display on a planet called Zircon-212.

It seems that the scenario of Billy's life in outer space is something less than original. Pilgrim gets his "idea" for Tralfamadore from Kilgore Trout, just as Dwayne Hoover gets his ideas from Trout in *Breakfast of Champions* (1973). Perhaps this is what Vonnegut had in mind when he said that "*Slaughterhouse* and *Breakfast* used to be one book." The parallel is instructive, for Hoover is clearly insane. Pilgrim may not literally be insane, but Vonnegut has undermined the reality of his experience on Tralfamadore. Indeed, the conclusion is irresistible that Pilgrim's space and time travel are modes of escape. Surely it is not coincidental that Billy first time-travels just as he is about to lie down and die during the Battle of the Bulge, nor that he begins to speak of his trip to Tralfamadore *after* his airplane crash in 1968. Faced with the sheer horror of life, epitomized by World War II and especially the fire-bombing of Dresden, Billy "escapes" to Tralfamadore.

If the very existence of Tralfamadore is in doubt, one might wonder about the ideas Billy Pilgrim encounters there. Billy takes great comfort in these ideas, but at first glance there would seem to be nothing very heartening in the Tralfamadorian philosophy. After all, the Tralfamadorians think of human beings as "bugs in amber." Like bugs, human beings are trapped in *structured* moments that have always existed and always will exist. For that matter, human beings are not really human: "Tralfamadorians, of course, say that every creature and plant in the universe is a machine." The Tralfamadorians would seem to be as jovial about life as the later Mark Twain.

But the Tralfamadorians have much to offer in the way of consolation. Most crucially, their theory of time denies the reality of death. Further, it allows man to pick and choose among the eternal moments of his existence. If everything that ever has been always will be, one can practice the Tralfamadorian creed and "ignore the awful times, and concentrate on the good ones." (pp. 67-9)

But all this can be done only by ignoring the wisdom embodied in Billy Pilgrim's prayer: "God grant me the serenity to accept the things I cannot change, courage to change the things I can, and wisdom always to tell the difference." This advice is meaningless for Billy himself, for "among the things Billy Pilgrim could not change were the past, the present, and the future." Billy is one of those people Vonnegut was referring to when he said "there are people, particularly dumb people, who are in terrible trouble and never get out of it, because they're not intelligent enough. And it strikes me as gruesome and comical that in our culture we have an expectation that a man can always solve his problems." Billy is a man who can only solve his problems by saying that they are insoluble.

The irony here is that the Billy Pilgrims of this world *are* better off saying that everything is beautiful and nothing hurts, for they truly cannot change the past, the present, or the future. All they can do is survive. Tralfamadore is a fantasy, a desperate attempt to rationalize chaos, but one must sympathize with Billy's need to create Tralfamadore. After all, the need for supreme fictions is a very human trait. As one of Vonnegut's characters tells a psychiatrist, "I think you guys are going to have to come up with a lot of wonderful *new* lies, or people just aren't going to want to go on living." The need for such "lies" is almost universal in *Slaughterhouse-Five.* Most obviously, it lies behind Roland Weary's pathetic dramatization of himself and two companions as The Three Musketeers. It is most poignantly suggested in the religiosity of Billy's mother, who develops "a terrible hankering for a crucifix" even though she never joins a church and in fact has no real faith. Billy's mother finally does buy a crucifix from a Sante Fe gift shop, and Vonnegut's comment is crucial to much else in the book: "Like so many Americans, she was trying to construct a life that made sense from things she found in gift shops." Billy Pilgrim's "lie" is no less human and a good deal more "wonderful."

But finally Billy Pilgrim is not Everyman. One may sympathize with his attempt to make sense of things, but the fact remains that some men have greater resources than others. Indeed, some men are like Kurt Vonnegut. By intruding into his own tale, Vonnegut contrasts his personal position with that of his protagonist. Billy Pilgrim preaches the Tralfamadorian theory of time until he becomes a latter-day Billy Graham; Vonnegut looks with anguish at a clock he wants to go faster and remarks, "There was nothing I could do about it. As an Earthling, I had to believe whatever clocks said—and calendars." Billy Pilgrim sends his sons to Vietnam and the Green Berets; Vonnegut tells his sons "that they are not under any circumstances to take part in massacres, and that the news of massacres of enemies is not to fill them with satisfaction or glee." Vonnegut even tells his sons "not to work for companies which make massacre machinery, and to express contempt for people who think we need machinery like that." Billy Pilgrim says that God was right when He commanded Lot's wife not to look back upon Sodom and Gomorrah; Vonnegut writes *Slaughterhouse-Five* and so becomes "a pillar of salt" himself. As Donald Greiner has said, "while Billy can come to terms with death and Dresden, Vonnegut cannot." Nor can anyone who would be fully human. (pp. 69-70)

It may seem that Vonnegut has contradicted himself, for Billy's "lie" apparently expresses a profoundly human need at the same time that it denies his humanity. In point of fact, the contradiction is Pilgrim's. Indeed, the pathos of Billy's story is captured in this paradox. Because he is one of those people who are in terrible trouble and not intelligent enough to get out of it, Billy is unable to imagine a saving lie except one that denies personal moral responsibility. Of course, for those who see Vonnegut as a quietist, this is as it should be. These critics see the Tralfamadorian message as an example of *foma,* or "harmless untruths," a concept advocated in an earlier Vonnegut novel, *Cat's Cradle* (1963). Whether this is indeed the case is crucial to any interpretation of the later novel. (p. 71)

So far as *Slaughterhouse-Five* is concerned, the question is whether the theories of Tralfamadore qualify as *foma.* In a very limited sense the answer is yes, for these theories do provide comfort for people like Billy Pilgrim. But what comforts Pilgrim will not do the job for everyone. Finally there is a great difference between the quietistic notions of Tralfamadore and the injunction not to kill. The latter is a truly comforting "lie": it implies that human life is inherently valuable, and it suggests that men are capable of *choosing* whether or not they will destroy their fellow human beings. The consequences of accepting this idea are altogether agreeable. The consequences of believing in Tralfamadore and its theorics are something else again. Vonnegut is careful to show that these consequences involve more than enabling Billy Pilgrim to achieve a sustaining serenity. They involve an indifference to moral problems which is the ultimate "cause" of events like Dresden.

Critics of *Slaughterhouse-Five* seem never to notice that it is filled with Tralfamadorians who look very much like human beings. An obvious example would be the German guards who brutalize Billy Pilgrim and his fellow prisoners of war. The connection with Tralfamadorian fatalism is suggested by an interesting parallel. When he is kidnapped by the Tralfamadorians, Billy inquires of his captors, "Why me?" The Tralfamadorians reply, "Why you? Why *us* for that matter? Why *anything?*" Later, one of Billy's fellow prisoners is beaten gratuitously by a German guard. "Why me?" the prisoner asks. "Vy you? Vy anybody?" the guard answers. This parallel exposes the inhumane consequences of adopting the Tralfamadorian point of view, for the denial of personal responsibility easily leads to the brutal excesses of the Nazis. Vonnegut hardly sees the problem as peculiarly Germanic, however. Early in Chapter One, he reminisces about his experiences as a police reporter for the Chicago City News Bureau. One day he covered the death of a young veteran who had been squashed in a freak elevator accident. The woman writer who took his report calmly asked him to contact the dead man's wife and pretend to be a police captain. He was to do this in order to get her response. As Vonnegut remarks, "World War II had certainly made everybody very tough." This sort of complacence might be termed quasi-Tralfamadorian. What is missing is an attempt to rationalize the status quo. This comes later from a Marine major at a Lions Club meeting: "He said that Americans had no choice but to keep fighting in Vietnam until they achieved victory or until the Com-

munists realized that they could not force their way of life on weak countries." It seems that America had "no choice" but to remain in Vietnam. But then the Allies had no choice but to destroy Dresden, either, or so Billy is told by Bertram Copeland Rumfoord, a retired brigadier general in the Air Force Reserve and the official Air Force historian. "It *had* to be done," Rumfoord tells Billy. "Pity the men who had to *do* it." Billy assures Rumfoord that he understands: "Everything is all right, and everybody has to do exactly what he does. I learned that on Tralfamadore." As this reply suggests, Rumfoord's statements are in the best spirit of Tralfamadore. The general has obviously read his Pope: Whatever is, is right.

The scene involving Rumfoord and Billy Pilgrim is positioned at the end of *Slaughterhouse-Five* because it is the real climax to Vonnegut's complex protest novel. The object of satiric attack turns out to be a complacent response to the horrors of the age. The horror of Dresden is not just that it *could* happen here, in an enlightened twentieth century. The real horror is that events such as Dresden continue to occur and no one seems appalled. *Slaughterhouse-Five* is filled with allusions to such postwar disasters as Vietnam, the assassinations of Bobby Kennedy and Martin Luther King, Jr, and the riots in American ghettos. Vonnegut stresses the kinship between these events and Dresden, most notably in the scene where Billy Pilgrim drives his Cadillac through a burned-down ghetto which reminds him "of some of the towns he had seen in the war." These are the problems Billy avoids in his life as Lions Club President, Tastee-Freeze entrepreneur, and Reagan supporter. These are the problems the Marine major and Professor Rumfoord would see as "inevitable." But it is one thing to say that human problems are insoluble if one has visited Tralfamadore. It is quite another to support this view from a strictly Earthling perspective. Vonnegut's point is that insofar as men are guided by the likes of Professor Rumfoord, they act as if the Tralfamadorians were real and their deterministic assumptions valid. Yet Rumfoord's assertion that Dresden *had* to be is obviously false. The distinguishing feature of the raid on Dresden is that there was no strategic advantage to it whatsoever. The assertion is not a true example of *foma* because the notion of harmless untruths implies that there are also *harmful* untruths. Man must judge his lies by their consequences, and the consequences are disastrous if people in power believe that Dresden was inevitable. In Vonnegut's view, the consequences are Vietnam, the ghettos, and a social order that seriously considers the election of Ronald Reagan as President of the United States. (pp. 71-3)

Vonnegut is not sanguine about the possibilities for this better world, for he believes that the people in power really determine the quality of life in any age. As he once told the graduating class at Bennington, "Another great swindle is that people your age are supposed to save the world. . . . It isn't up to you. You don't have the money and the power. . . . It is up to older people to save the world." Alas, the older people seem to respect men like Professor Rumfoord. Yet the effort can and must be made to "poison" the young with more humane values.

Vonnegut's Bennington speech has been grossly misrepresented by those who would characterize him as a quietist. Glen Meeter, for example, cites the passage just quoted as proof that Vonnegut is a Tralfamadorian at heart. In doing so, Meeter ignores what Vonnegut went on to tell the Bennington graduates: "When it really is time for you to save the world, when you have some power and know your way around, when people can't mock you for looking so young, I suggest that you work for a socialist form of government." He ignores Vonnegut's blunt rejection of the Tralfamadorian view of man: "Military science is probably right about the contemptibility of man in the vastness of the universe. Still—I deny that contemptibility, and I beg you to deny it."

Slaughterhouse-Five presents much the same argument. The book suggests that if there is any philosophical basis to the actions of men like Professor Rumfoord, it is a callous Social Darwinism. In this spirit Rumfoord tells his doctors "that people who were weak deserved to die." But the doctors disagree, for they are "devoted to the idea that weak people should be helped as much as possible." Vonnegut is devoted to the same idea. He has said again and again that whatever man's limitations he does have the power to change the conditions of human life. *Slaughterhouse-Five* defends this position so eloquently because it blinks at none of the attendant problems. Vonnegut's self-portrait is again crucial, for the depression he acknowledges in his own history testifies to the terrible effort men must make if they would commit themselves to an all but impossible task. No one knows better than Vonnegut that the vast majority of comforting lies are insufficient. He has recently redefined *foma* as "harmless untruths, intended to comfort simple souls. An example: 'Prosperity is just around the corner.'" It will take more than this sort of thing to defeat the "bad" illusions of Marine majors and Air Force historians. But for those who are not such simple souls, the alternative to concerted action is suicide.

Vonnegut's next novel, *Breakfast of Champions,* is about an unsimple soul named Kurt Vonnegut who does contemplate suicide as a viable option. It is about a man who seriously entertains the Tralfamadorian view of man as machine, who has "come to the conclusion that there was nothing sacred about myself or about any human being, that we were all machines, doomed to collide and collide and collide." It is a novel about a man who is "rescued" from this philosophical cul-de-sac by the assertion of one of his characters that most of man's parts may be "dead machinery," but there is still "an unwavering band of light" in man, his human *awareness,* which must be seen as sacred. Other men must see it this way, too, for as Vonnegut says, ". . . there is no order to the world around us. . . . We must adapt ourselves to the requirements of chaos instead." Having so adapted himself, Vonnegut can say, in the subtitle to *Breakfast of Champions,* "Goodbye Blue Monday!" This assertion is dramatically unimpressive, but it does suggest that the author of *Slaughterhouse-Five* knows very well that the requirements of chaos demand human vigilance and not "resigned acceptance." Indeed, they demand the insistence on humane practices which is the burden of everything Vonnegut has written. (pp. 73-5)

Robert Merrill and Peter A. Scholl, "Vonnegut's 'Slaughterhouse-Five': The Requirements of Chaos," in Studies in American Fiction, *Vol. 6, No. 1, Spring, 1978, pp. 65-76.*

ROBERT L. NADEAU

In *Slaughterhouse-Five,* concepts from the new physics not only provide justification, however slight, for the notion of time travel, but also inform the commentary on the nature of human perception in time. Billy Pilgrim, survivor like Vonnegut of the allied bombing of Dresden (13 February 1945) and prosperous optometrist in Vonnegut's fictional Illium, New York, learned during his captivity on the planet Tralfamadore that "all moments, past, present, and future, always have existed, always will exist." . . . If the energy represented in the equation $E = MC^2$ contains within itself all possibilities for the configuration of matter, then it is conceivable, although certainly not likely, that other aspects of its being configured at other moments in time could somehow be known to us. Vonnegut has, incidentally, made a similar but somewhat different claim in a short essay prepared for the collection of his non-fictional work entitled *Wampeters, Foma and Granfalloons:* "Anybody with any sense knows that the whole solar system will go up like a celluloid collar by-and-by. I honestly believe, though, that we are wrong to think that moments go away, never to be seen again. This moment and every moment lasts forever." Eliminate the notion that materializations at other nodes in space-time are possible, like those of Billy in the novel, and we should have little difficulty accepting, from the point of view of modern physics, the feasibility of Vonnegut's remarks.

Virtually all of Billy's realizations about the character of life in the universe closely resemble those of Vonnegut's other travellers in space-time. When Billy inquires, for example, of the Tralfamadorians what the ultimate cause or reason for his being chosen for the voyage to their planet might be, their reply is "Why you? Why us for that matter? Why anything? Because this moment simply is." A related bit of Tralfamadorian wisdom also offered in response to Billy's need for explanations is, "All time is all time. It does not change. It does not lend itself to warnings or explanations." The correspondences with the new physics are obvious and I will not belabor the subject by repeating them.

We do find in this novel, however, some fresh applications of ideas from physics in Vonnegut's metaphorical description of the manner in which received conceptions of the nature of time condition our view of experience in time. Since the Tralfamadorians could not begin to imagine what time looked like to Billy in his zoo-like enclosure on Tralfamadore, the guide asks the crowd to imagine the earthling's head "encased in a steel sphere which he could never take off. There was only one eyehole through which he could look, and welded to that eyehole were six feet of pipe." Further refinements in the metaphor have Billy strapped to a steel lattice, bolted to a flatcar on rails, with no way to turn his head or touch the pipe. Although the flatcar moves at various speeds, angles, directions, Billy can see only "the little dot at the end of the pipe"—just as most of us continue to conceive of time as a linear progression of events moving in causal fashion from an imagined future into the remembered past. Our tendency, in short, is to focus upon future time, directly in front of us—that metaphorical dot at the end of the pipe—and to ignore actual time which is the condition of our being in the space-time complex that is the cosmos. If we could somehow perceive our relationship in time, as the Tralfamadorians apparently can, we would sense our involvement in all space-time and hence our activity as every event, (past, present and future) everywhere in the cosmos. (pp. 42-3)

Robert L. Nadeau, "Physics and Metaphysics in the Novels of Kurt Vonnegut, Jr.," in Mosaic: A Journal for the Interdisciplinary Study of Literature, *Vol. XIII, No. 2, Winter, 1980, pp. 37-47.*

JEROME KLINKOWITZ

[Vonnegut] viewed *Slaughterhouse-Five* as a culmination in his own life of fiction. It was a coming to terms with a great traumatic event in his life, the World War II firebombing of Dresden which he experienced as a prisoner of the Germans, but which he was unable to express in fiction through twenty-five years of trying. One problem was in visualizing the firebombing itself. The conventions of his forties and fifties culture did not provide much latitude for portraying large military actions; they inevitably turned out as grand, heroic enterprises. Moreover, war stories became things neatly tucked away in the past, to be recalled with drinking buddies over beer and brandy, but offering no real threat to the comfortable life one now enjoyed. Before the 1960s, there seemed no sure way to capture the disorganizing effect war could have on one's notion of reality—until Joseph Heller found the syntax for it in *Catch-22*, and Kurt Vonnegut followed with a complementary restructuring of time and space in *Slaughterhouse-Five.*

Vonnegut's war novel is his most complete reinvention of the world. It encompasses his experience of four decades, for the book considers not just Billy Pilgrim's adventure in World War II, but his childhood before it and his adult life after it. Billy lives all these moments simultaneously, building his self-image much as any conventional American in the sixties might, having been raised on a diet of Saturday-afternoon movies and sustained with even greater doses of TV. Still, *Slaughterhouse-Five* was the first popular American novel to completely abandon the traditional notions of linear time and solidly fixable space, though people had been living in such imaginative modes for at least a decade. Once Billy learns this new secret of life, he is anxious to tell his countrymen the good news, for by living out of synchronization with the times their lives have become frustrating and disappointing. An optometrist by profession, "He was doing nothing less now, he thought, than prescribing corrective lenses for Earthling souls. So many of those souls were lost and wretched, Billy believed because they could not see as well as his little green friends on Tralfamadore."

The Tralfamadorian viewpoint, easily mistaken as a satirical piece of space opera, is nothing less than Vonnegut's reinvention of the contemporary American novel. Its notion that all time is continually present, that there is no linear progression to reality but that it all exists at once, to be absorbed completely and travelled in at will, is reflected in the form of the Tralfamadorian novel, a description which fits Vonnegut's work . . . as well:

> each clump of symbols is a brief, urgent message—describing a situation, a scene. We Tralfamadorians read them all at once, not one after the other. There isn't any particular relationship between all the messages, except that the author has chosen them carefully, so that, when seen all at once, they produce an image of life that is beautiful and surprising and deep. There is no beginning, no middle, no end, no suspense, no moral, no causes, no effects. What we love in our books are the depths of many marvelous moments seen all at one time.

A great deal of *Slaughterhouse-Five* is given over to speculations on novels and their therapeutic, recreative power. Billy Pilgrim and Eliot Rosewater have found life meaningless because of the horrors they have witnessed during the war, "So they were trying to reinvent themselves and their universe.

Science fiction was a big help." At one point in the evolution of human culture Dostoevsky's *The Brothers Karamazov* told everything one needed to know about life. " ' But that isn't enough any more,' said Rosewater." A new perspective is needed for the new cultural conditions of the sixties, Vonnegut knows, and so he spends a fair amount of time showing all the options. The sum total of those options would be his own life's work, but to get it all into one book Vonnegut calls on his mythical alter ego, Kilgore Trout, whose hundred-odd novels can be described in a few lines each. Like his contemporary, Jorge Luis Borges, Vonnegut appreciates how merely talking about a book as if it existed can be as good as writing the whole work himself. One is Kilgore Trout's *Maniacs in the Fourth Dimension,* about the need for broader perspectives in medicine. It turns out that many people suffering from incurable diseases are actually sick in the fourth dimension; "Earthling doctors couldn't see those causes at all, or even imagine them." Another is Trout's *The Gospel from Outer Space,* which argues that the Christian liturgy is confused, and that having God reveal Christ as His Son only teaches the people that *"Before you kill somebody, make absolutely sure he isn't well connected."* Trout reinvents the religion by making Christ a nobody, and the people are in this manner warned that God *"will punish horribly anybody who torments a bum who has no connections!"* People need new definitions, "wonderful *new* lies," as Eliot Rosewater calls them, "or people just aren't going to want to go on living." Novels are the handiest repository for such lies—especially novels which admit their own artificiality.

Vonnegut must also invent a new form for fiction, because the subject matter of Dresden—of death itself—simply cannot be handled within the old conventions. "Sam—Here's the book," Vonnegut tells his publisher in the first chapter. "It is so short and jumbled and jangled, Sam, because there is nothing intelligent to say about a massacre." Trying to say something, Vonnegut learned, too often results in false heroics or sentimentality. But then again there are times when one must speak, even when there is no answer. The moment is dramatized for us at the bedside of Billy's dying mother, who after several suspenseful moments of stuttering manages to voice the unanswerable question, "How did I get so old?" What in hell are people *for?* Vonnegut's fiction revolves in silence at these unanswered points.

The redefinitions Vonnegut offers are substantial: that the notion of free will has been a cruel swindle, that existence is in fact fully determined and utterly meaningless, that life and death coexist in one eternal moment. But it is not his purpose to be nihilistic. Quite the contrary, by relieving man of responsibility for the mechanical function of existence, Vonnegut frees him to construct whatever arbitrary meaning he desires, in full knowledge that whatever he invents is equally harmless and satisfying. Only because art itself is free of such responsibilities can it do its job. How we perceive reality is what matters, because imagination comes first. To show how, Vonnegut takes a World War II action movie and runs it backwards through the projector. All the destruction is reversed: bombs fall upwards, shrinking and containing the explosions and fires within them. The planes fly backwards to England, where the cannisters are removed and shipped back to the United States, so factory workers can dismantle them, separating the contents into minerals. "The minerals were then shipped to specialists in remote areas. It was their business to put them into the ground, to hide them cleverly, so they would never hurt anybody ever again."

There is a world possible beyond the tyrannies of linear time, cause and effect, and the awful responsibility of free will. Those factors only assume importance when the imagination makes them the almighty rulers of life. The human mind, Vonnegut tells us, is far richer than the body, and by giving it a role in keeping with its power, life can become a much more liveable affair. (pp. 54-7)

Jerome Klinkowitz, "Kurt Vonnegut and Donald Barthelme: The American Image," in his The American 1960s: Imaginative Acts in a Decade of Change, The Iowa State University Press, 1980, pp. 47-62.

C. BARRY CHABOT

There is a scene near the end of *Slaughterhouse-Five* which nicely captures Vonnegut's posture toward the world he would address. Having recently survived an airplane crash fatal to many acquaintances, including his father-in-law, and immediately thereafter suffering the accidental death of his wife, Billy Pilgrim journeys to New York City for the purpose of spreading the good news he has learned from the Tralfamadorians. While he has known this news for a considerable period, he had previously confined his missionary efforts to stray patients in need of comfort, such as a boy whose father had been killed in Vietnam. Now, however, the time is "ripe," and he comes to New York to address the populace at large. He checks into the Royalton Hotel and is assigned a room with a terrace overlooking Forty-fourth Street. As he prepares for his mission of mercy, he chances to look "down at all the people moving hither and yon. They were jerky little scissors. They were a lot of fun." The derision this passage directs against those whom Billy Pilgrim would succor compromises the comfort he would give, and this tangle of motives—concern and contempt—typifies not only Pilgrim's attitude toward his fellows, but Vonnegut's as well.

If the Tralfamadorian vision of things holds out for Pilgrim some relief from the harsh terms of his life, it must be recognized that to some extent Vonnegut himself concocted that vision in an attempt to come to terms with his experience of the bombing of Dresden and all that that experience had come to represent. The facts that they were both at Dresden, that both at least give mouth service to the Tralfamadorian vision, that both seek some comfort from it, and that both broadcast it to their fellows bespeak the extent to which Pilgrim stands in for his author. We need not question either the genuineness of their distress at the lot and the conduct of man or their sincerity in addressing their audiences in suggesting that that vision is cruelly inadequate, that its comforts are the comforts of indifference, that it is the opiate of the terminally weary, the defeated. Its solace is purchased only at the cost of accommodating oneself to the things one would otherwise regret, thereby insuring that they will multiply. If *Slaughterhouse-Five* urges such attitudes on us, it nonetheless provides us with an opportunity to understand the impasse they represent and to locate the slippage which transforms indignation into indifference, concern into taunt apathy.

Slaughterhouse-Five begins in pain and indignation. It is, we are told, Vonnegut's attempt to recount and come to terms with the trauma of witnessing the destruction of Dresden while a prisoner of war. He had initially assumed that it would be a comparatively simple undertaking, a recital of facts and observations. Of course he was mistaken; words

came slowly, seemed inadequate to the task, and he did not finish the novel for twenty-three years. . . . What can one say about wanton destruction on this scale? Is it sufficient simply to tot up the loses, so many buildings, so many casualties, men, women and children?

As if the bombing of Dresden were not enough, during the course of the novel Vonnegut makes it emblematic of the destruction wrought by war generally. Thus he makes references to the concentration camps, the destruction of European Jewry, the bombing of Hiroshima, and behind them, as if to insist that such murderousness is no historical anomaly, to the children's crusades of another era. Beside these instances of mass slaughter, he sets references to smaller events, such as the executions of Private Slovik and Edgar Derby, which would seem comically disproportionate were their consequences not so dire. Corpses litter his pages. Since these deaths are all the fruits of man's own murderousness, they suggest that we are all secretly Roland Weary's and Paul Lazzaro's who derive some immense compensatory pleasure in the torture and destruction of our fellows. Of course this sense of man as casually destructive fully warrants Vonnegut's rage at such acts, and partially accounts for the particular acerbity of his depiction of the species as a whole.

However, deaths of another order are also recounted in *Slaughterhouse-Five.* The final chapter begins with these brief paragraphs:

> Robert Kennedy, whose summer home is eight miles from the home I live in all year round, was shot two nights ago. He died last night. So it goes. Martin Luther King was shot a month ago. He died, too. So it goes.
> And every day my Government gives me a count of corpses created by military science in Vietnam. So it goes.
> My father died many years ago now—of natural causes. So it goes. He was a sweet man. He was a gun nut, too. He left me his guns. They rust.

While they extend the reign of murderousness both into the present and outside warfare, the first three paragraphs are nonetheless of a piece with the other incidents we have recounted: they offer further evidence of the murderousness of man. The final paragraph introduces another dimension; Vonnegut's father died of natural causes, not at the hands of others. However, the fact that it can be included as merely another item in this series, the fact that it too is punctuated by "So it goes," suggests that Vonnegut takes it to be loosely equivalent to the previous items in the series. This conflation of natural death with murders of various sorts is a consistent feature of *Slaughterhouse-Five.* Thus we are told early on in the novel that even were wars somehow eliminated (an unlikely eventuality, it is made clear), thus no longer being occasions for human misery and subsequent outrage, we would still be left with "plain old death." (pp. 45-7)

The extent to which death as such comes to replace human murderousness as the especial regret of *Slaughterhouse-Five* must qualify Vonnegut's rage at the latter. Even if men did not visit violence upon their fellows, they would still, one and all, be subject to the reign of "plain old death." If death itself is the outrage, then humans cannot be held accountable for it, since it is built into the very structure of things. While their actions might hurry it in any particular instance, human violence brings nothing to pass that would not occur in any event. Thus when Vonnegut broadens the scope of his complaint to include the mere fact of death—that is, when he equates gratuitous murder with passing away in one's sleep—he deprives himself of any reason for holding any special animus toward those who perpetrate the mass slaughters which so exercise him.

The novel actually carries this deflation one step further. Not only people die, but so do champagne, water, and the novel. The death of each is punctuated by "So it goes," thereby suggesting that they are all of a piece, roughly equivalent. Thus it is not just murder, not even the fact of human mortality, which outrages Vonnegut; it is rather the fact that all things in this universe apparently have some tropism toward death. Thus what began as an anguished outcry against particular atrocities becomes a lament at the manner in which the world happens to be put together. At this point one must ask if this does not trivialize the destruction of Dresden. Is there no difference among the items in this series: the bombing of Dresden, the assassinations of Kennedy and King, the executions of Slovik and Derby, the accidental death of Pilgrim's wife, and the deaths of champagne and water in a still glass? Are we to take each of them in the same way?

Vonnegut never lets us forget about death in *Slaughterhouse-Five.* The punctuation is insistent, relentless. By the time they have read any considerable portion of the novel, many readers find the reiterated phrase annoying, and I suspect that to some extent Vonnegut wants us to be annoyed. If the phrase "So it goes" insists that we attend to each and every death recounted in the novel, however, it also suggests a way to minimize its impact. We are told that the phrase, used by both Vonnegut and Pilgrim, originates with the Tralfamadorians, and if their version of things is accurate, death is not the terminal event we three-dimensional beings take it to be.

"The most important thing I learned on Tralfamadore," says Billy Pilgrim, "was that when a person dies he only *appears* to die." He continues:

> He is still very much alive in the past, so it is very silly for people to cry at his funeral. All moments, past, present, and future, always have existed, always will exist. . . . When a Tralfamadorian sees a corpse, all he thinks is that the dead person is in bad condition in that particular moment, but that the same person is just fine in plenty of other moments. Now, when I myself hear that somebody is dead, I simply shrug and say what the Tralfamadorians say about dead people, which is "So it goes."

This obviously spatializes time, transforms moments into points on an eternal landscape. The future has already happened; it is just that those of us in three dimensions are ignorant of what is there. And if the future has already happened, if the next moment has already occurred someplace else, there can be no question of free will: our actions are thoroughly determined, our lives laid down like railroad tracks we simply travel along. Let us consider several consequences of this view.

First, if everything has already happened, from some perspective there can be no suspense. In other words, suspense is a function of our ignorance of an already existent future, not the result of the structure of a world whose figure remains to be made. This accounts for the structure of Tralfamadorian novels:

> . . . the books were laid out . . . in brief clumps

of symbols separated by stars. . . . [Each] clump of symbols is a brief, urgent message—describing a situation, a scene. We Tralfamadorians read them all at once, not one after the other. There isn't any particular relationship between all the messages, except that the author has chosen them carefully, so that, when seen all at once, they produce an image of life that is beautiful and surprising and deep. There is no beginning, no middle, no end, no suspense, no moral, no causes, no effects. What we love in our books are the depths of many marvelous moments seen all at one time.

The subtitle announces that *Slaughterhouse-Five* is something of a Tralfamadorian novel, and it surely meets many of the specifications. While we cannot read them at once, the novel is built up out of a series of brief fragments or episodes, which are in turn organized in such a manner that terms such as beginning, middle, and end do not capture its sequence. More substantially, Vonnegut deliberately undercuts the development of any suspense: the first chapter ends by providing the reader with the final words of the novel, and Edgar Derby is never mentioned without reference to the fact that he is to be executed for stealing a teapot, an event which is not finally narrated until the final pages of the novel. Each mention of Derby's fate serves as a reminder that his fate is already an accomplished fact.

Secondly, if there can be no question of human volition—if, as it were, determinism goes all the way down—people are relieved of all responsibility for their actions, for in such circumstances it cannot make sense to hold human agents accountable for their various doings. If Paul Lazzaro is craven and vicious, if he is to kill Billy Pilgrim, so be it. In this view he cannot be blamed; he is, like his victim, merely another bug caught in a particular piece of amber. He suffers his actions in the same manner that Billy Pilgrim does: he is, so to speak, simply a conduit for behavior that passes through him. Thus, in the Tralfamadorian view of things, guilt is a meaningless and empty notion; it can play no formative role in the conduct of human life. Moreover, not only are men absolved from the consequences of their actions, but they are relieved as well from the responsibility for acting at all; that is, this view thrusts an individual into a passive relationship to his own actions. A life is something to be suffered or endured, not something one makes. Thus, although he cannot know it until much later, the utter passivity of Billy Pilgrim throughout his life comes to seem prescient once he has been schooled on Tralfamadore.

Finally, since all moments, happy and painful alike, already exist, and since the Tralfamadorians have access to a fourth dimension, on the principle of making the best of what is allotted them the Tralfamadorians attend only to the happy moments. While telling Pilgrim about the wars which mark their history, a Tralfamadorian guide tells him that "There isn't anything we can do about them, so we simply don't look at them. We ignore them. We spend eternity looking at pleasant moments—like today at the zoo. Isn't this a nice moment." The guide goes on to urge that earthlings too conduct their lives on such a policy, and a passing remark in the first chapter suggests that Vonnegut has taken the advice—at least he will try to forget the pain he has lived through. Such a policy obviously removes the sting from disappointment and suffering; events which occasion them now take place behind one's back, without one ever submitting to their duration. With this move we are effectively immunized against death in any form.

Actually, this final piece of Tralfamadorian view of things introduces a telling inconsistency into the putative fabric of the novel. If all one's actions are as thoroughly determined as claimed, how is it that one can choose to "ignore the awful times, and concentrate on the good ones"? One could not. The only way this contradiction could be redeemed would be to grant the existence of psychic freedom in the midst of a physically determined universe. One can think what one will, but of course one's thought cannot alter the course of events, which will be what it must be. Thus psychic freedom has been purchased only at the cost of rendering thought impotent, of severing it completely from the events which otherwise compose one's life. This impotence in turn suggests another: for all that he would avail himself of this psychic freedom, Vonnegut seems unable to talk himself into complete accommodation to the ways of the world. (pp. 47-9)

Were he successful, Vonnegut would be impervious to the stresses of events and the claims of those about him. However, he would achieve this peace only at the cost of trivializing the very events that make it necessary. If the destruction of Dresden (or of Vietnam) is on a par with natural deaths, much less with that of water in a still glass, there is no reason to single it out for special lament or comment. On this view, in fact, there is not even any viable reason to prefer peace (nor any means to achieve it) over distress; one should be indifferent even as regards such temporary mental states. The truth is, of course, that Vonnegut cannot sustain such indifference: his mask of indifference is repeatedly broached by his irrepressible rage at the events he documents. (p. 50)

The residual anger testifies to the futility of Vonnegut's cultivation of indifference. It is futile on several scores. To the extent that social life provides the impetus, such quietism can only insure the triumph of all that one regrets, for it leaves the issue uncontested. Further, even were human events as impervious to concerted intervention as Vonnegut seems to think, it is not at all clear that the mere shrug of one's shoulders is thereby the sole or most appropriate response. Might one not still comfort the hapless in ways more substantial than simply suggesting that they ignore their distress and think instead of happier times? that they are, in a way, wrong to feel pained at all? The cultivation of indifference is also futile in the sense of being finally impossible. Despite the human capacity for self-deception, its project can never reach completion, if only because of the vigilance with which one must guard against the encroachment of what one would forget. In **Slaughterhouse-Five** Vonnegut's rage—however now wide of its mark, however displaced—constitutes the last remnant of his concern; if its presence marks a failure, it is a failure that saves the novel from being an inhuman exercise. (pp. 50-1)

C. Barry Chabot, " 'Slaughterhouse-Five' and the Comforts of Indifference," in Essays in Literature, Vol. VIII, No. 1, Spring, 1981, pp. 45-51.

RUSSELL BLACKFORD

The novels of Kurt Vonnegut and Thomas Pynchon have often been distorted by naive critics purveying related brands of popular mysticism, rather than responding to the complexities and ironies of the texts. In particular, **Slaughterhouse-Five** and Gravity's Rainbow, the most well-known and intellectually exciting novels of Vonnegut and Pynchon respectively, have fallen victim to this approach. To invalidate such readings, some considerations of metaphysics are necessary; however, the argument can be pressed mainly on pure literary critical grounds. The particular form of the mystical approach which I will be considering, and which I hope to invalidate, is that these books are mystical documents whose visionary messages are stimulated by the findings of modern physics.

Such an interpretation is conveniently exemplified by two articles. One was published in Studies in the Novel and the other in Mosaic—both are by Robert L. Nadeau [see excerpt from latter essay above]. Nadeau's naive approach to criticism is shared by many other commentators on Vonnegut and Pynchon, although few demonstrate so explicitly his naive approach to metaphysics: what I consider a conflation of physics and fantasy. I am not conducting a vendetta against Nadeau in particular, but merely using his work and approach to focus my implicit objections to a wider range of critical approaches and conclusions.

Nadeau obviously believes his interpretation of **Slaughterhouse-Five** is given validation by his comments on an earlier work by Vonnegut, his second novel, **The Sirens of Titan** in which a metaphysical viewpoint similar to that of the Tralfamadonans is offered by Winston Niles Rumfoord. Rumfoord, having suffered a mysterious sea change in the depths of space, now has chrono-synclastic infundibulated vision. Experience appears to him as a four-dimensional space-time block rather than as spatial events unfolding in time. On a superficial reading, this vision necessitates fatalism; Rumfoord tells his wife Beatrice that, although he sees the future, he cannot use his foreknowledge to give her stock-market tips. The future is laid up in advance, according to Rumfoord. It cannot be changed.

All of this is hard to take seriously, mainly because Vonnegut uses every imaginable ironic device to show us Rumfoord's unreliability. Rumfoord is often manipulative, deceitful, or mistaken; his words should never be granted their face value. His fatalistic words to Beatrice in fact sit ill with the narrator's description of how Rumfoord gained the money to finance his Martian army:

> The elaborate suicide of Mars was financed by capital gains on investments in land, securities, Broadway shows, and inventions. Since Rumfoord could see into the future, it was as easy as pie for him to make money grow.

The narrator of **The Sirens of Titan** is far more authoritative than Rumfoord. Rumfoord's fatalistic claims are merely one of his many deceits. **The Sirens of Titan,** in fact, is not seriously concerned with physics or metaphysics at all. Its concerns are existential and moral. Centrally, the novel concerns the moral initiation of two people into humanity, an initiation which takes place only through a series of events which involve Malachi Constant and Beatrice Rumfoord in physical separation from their kind.

Far from suggesting that Vonnegut has an ongoing interest in the hypothetical implications of modern physics, this glance at **The Sirens of Titan** suggests that such an interest is unlikely to appear in later works such as **Slaughterhouse-Five.** Vonnegut is inclined to treat such matters with a mixture of casual comedy and disturbing irony. Given Vonnegut's earlier treatment of fatalism, we might expect him to be presenting the fatalism of Billy Pilgrim and the Tralfamadorians with some suspicion. Nadeau is inclined to accept the Tralfamadorian conspectus on affairs because he perceives it to correspond with Einstein's mass-energy relationship formula—in a way which seems puzzling:

> If the energy represented in the equation E equals MC² contains within itself all possibilities for the configuration of matter, then it is conceivable, although certainly not likely, that other aspects of its being configured at other moments in time could somehow be known to us.

This simply does not strike me as a logical proposition, whatever value there may be in its scientific content. The mere fact that mass and energy can be related by a constant tells us nothing about specific future and past events and suggests nothing about how such events may be known to us.

Einstein's theories provide a breeding ground for illogical propositions. Consider this Tralfamadorian-sounding claim made in a non-Vonnegutian context by Gary Zukav:

> In this static picture, the spare-time continuum, events do not develop, they just are. If we could view our reality in a four-dimensional way, we would see that everything that now seems to unfold before us with the passing of time, already exists *in toto,* painted, as it were, on the fabric of space-time. We would see all, the past, the present, and the future with one glance. Of course, this is only a mathematical proposition (isn't it?).

"Isn't it?" Zukav's aside challenges us to adopt what is, in fact a variety of facile mysticism. The issue here is not Zukav's physics; it is his logic. As a matter of fact, Zukav's entire description of the Einsteinian space-time continuum might be acceptable if he changed only one word. Logic demands that the word "already" be replaced by the word "tenselessly". The use of the word "static" is also slightly worrying; to call the space-time continuum itself either "static" or "dynamic" is surely a category mistake. Such words apply to objects which exist in time and which may or may not change intrinsically or relationally over time. To say this sort of thing of the space-time continuum itself is to speak nonsense.

However, the word "already" is much more worrying. When we use the word "already", we mean that affairs are configured in a certain way at an unexpectedly early time. To speak of events which unfold in the future as "already" existing is again to speak nonsense. From a four-dimensional point of view these events *exist,* but in a special tenseless way. They do not exist *now,* in the present. To speak of the four-dimensional space-time continuum's demanding that future events already exist or always existed is to forget the meanings of words.

This facile doctrine is precisely what Billy Pilgrim learns on Tralfamadore: "All moments, past, present, and future," Billy writes to the Ilium *News Leader,* "always have existed, always will exist." Billy could have written that all moments tenselessly *exist;* but this technical proposition of metaphysics, though true, would have comforted no one.

So far this essay has indicated some arguments for resisting the mystical fatalism advocated by Robert L. Nadeau, Gary Zukav, Billy Pilgrim, and the Tralfamadorians. Whether it is also advocated by Kurt Vonnegut can be answered on literary critical grounds rather than philosophical ones. One fairly obvious clue is to be found in an interview Vonnegut gave to *Playboy* magazine. There Vonnegut referred to the doctrine as "a useful, comforting sort of horseshit."

What about internal evidence from *Slaughterhouse-Five?* Again, Nadeau's critical approach appears naive. The narrator artfully presents affairs from Billy Pilgrim's viewpoint while dissociating himself from Billy's perceptions. Perhaps Nadeau is confused by the complex narrative viewpoint of the novel. In this he is not alone. I would argue that Billy Pilgrim is presented as at least possibly insane, the victim of hallucinations in his time-travelling and his Tralfamadorian adventure. However, some other readers of the novel have looked at him less skeptically, especially John Somer in one very well-known essay.

A number of earlier studies have shown that *Slaughterhouse-Five* is a far more complex and ironic document than Somer imagines. Thomas L. Wymer's study, "The Swiftian Satire of Kurt Vonnegut, Jr." [see excerpt above], is particularly devastating in this regard. However, no study has fully exposed the insupportable simplicity of Somer's concept of narrative viewpoint as he rejects the possibility that Billy is the victim of hallucinations:

> But that implication is simply not valid. Billy experiences three hallucinations in his story, and the narrator carefully distinguishes them from Billy's time travels.

Somer does not list all three of these hallucinations, but he does offer one example which is supposed to clinch the argument. The example actually does distinguish between "time-travel" and an unequivocal hallucination:

> Billy Pilgrim was having a delightful hallucination. He was wearing dry, warm, white sweatsocks, and he was skating on a ballroom floor. Thousands cheered. This wasn't time-travel. It was the craziness of a dying young man with his shoes full of snow.

Somer does not read this passage closely. He writes of Billy's dreaming that he is "ice-skating", but it is clear from the passage that Billy actually imagines he is sliding in his socks over the polished floor of a ballroom. More importantly, the criterion offered in the passage for this hallucination's not being time-travel is that it does not fit into the events of Billy's past or future. It is easy to imagine Billy's having hallucinations about his past and future, and accepting them as real because they are consistent with the rest of his experience, while also having hallucinations which do not have the same consistency.

In fact, though Somer's argument is expressed forcefully, it is this argument that is "simply not valid": the fact that somebody has a systematically distorted view of reality does not mean that some of his or her experiences may not be more obviously illusions than others. Such a person may even come to recognize some experiences as hallucinations, especially if they do not fit in with the larger distortion, but this does not automatically confer legitimacy on his or her view of reality.

As has been hinted, Somer does not seem to understand the narrative viewpoint of *Slaughterhouse-Five.* He simply announces, "The narrator says, 'Billy Pilgrim was having a delightful hallucination. . . .'"; he does not consider the role of the narrator. Rejecting Somer's simplistic concept of narrative viewpoint, we may legitimately distinguish between who speaks in a piece of narrative and who experiences, or is said to experience, what is spoken of. *Slaughterhouse-Five* is narrated by a character who is established from the first chapter as a version of Kurt Vonnegut himself. Accordingly, he might be expected to have the omniscience which Somer trustingly attributes to him. The fact is that he has not. The narrator's knowledge of Billy's story is largely limited by what Billy sees and experiences. In the first and last chapters, especially, he shows a considerable range of experience of his own, and he knows more about other characters than Billy does, but he never offers to correct Billy's perceptions, despite his occasional doubt. Doubt is suggested in the laconic fourth paragraph of the second chapter, "He says"; the presence of doubt here is a fact which Somer acknowledges but dismisses without any explanation.

The third paragraph of the chapter establishes much of the narrative viewpoint and tone of the book:

> Billy has gone to sleep a senile widower and awak-
> ened on his wedding day. He has walked through
> a door in 1955 and come out another one in 1941.
> He has gone back through that door to find himself
> in 1963. He has seen his birth and death many
> times, he says, and pays random visits to all the
> events in between.

The first three sentences, with their heavy parallelism, establish that a strong and unusual claim is being made. That sense reinforces the injunction, "Listen", just before. However, the paragraph is surrounded by short sentences with odd figurative phrases such as "unstuck in time", "spastic in time", and "He is in a constant state of stage fright". These phrases suggest that what is being asserted is not just unusual or even marvellous, but somehow grotesque. The sense of the grotesque is implicit in the phrase "random visits" in the fourth sentence of the paragraph, with its suggestion of something useless, meaningless, and uncontrolled. The long fourth sentence, which breaks the rhythm of the paragraph, offers itself as the culmination of the argument; but the sentence is broken neatly in half by the phrase "he says". It is established that what is being reported is Pilgrim's own claims, and that the story to come will be dependent on Pilgrim's suspect testimony. That fact is emphasized in the next two paragraphs, which both use the same phrase. The narrator's skeptical stance towards Billy's philosophy is made clear at the beginning of the tenth chapter as the book nears its end, in a passage where the narrator does not even find the philosophy consoling:

> *If* what Billy Pilgrim learned from the Tralfama-
> dorians is true, that we will all live forever, no mat-
> ter how dead we may sometimes seem to be, I am
> not overjoyed.
>
>   (My emphasis).

I could continue at length the detailed textual commentary to show how the narrative makes possible doubt about Billy Pilgrim's experiences and, by implication, the philosophy he bases on those experiences. Once this possibility of doubt is established, many arguments can be advanced to build a case that Billy Pilgrim is insane. Most obviously, many of Billy's claims sound as if they are put together from situations in the novels of Kilgore Trout—which Billy reads avidly. The arguments have been developed by Charles B. Harris among others. Vonnegut presents the mysticism of Billy Pilgrim and the Tralfamadorians as a comforting vision, quite likely that of an insane man, and having little probability of being true. It

is not the latest truth whose recognition is demanded of us by the new physics—though it does sound as if the Tralfamadorians have been reading philosophically slack popularizers of Einstein.

As with *The Sirens of Titan,* I would like to point out related passages from different parts of *Slaughterhouse-Five* to strengthen my point. Billy Pilgrim announces that he has come unstuck in time and has been kidnapped by a Tralfamadorian flying saucer only after an airplane crash which leaves him with "a terrible scar across the top of his skull," possibly suggesting brain damage. Billy supposedly returns to a particular moment in World War II just before the plane crash. That moment is the one in which Roland Weary shakes him and hits his head against a tree. Earlier in the novel, the narrator tells us that this was the very moment when Billy first came unstuck in time. The dovetailing of these two critical moments suggests to us a possible interpretation which is quite different from Billy's. It may be that Billy's time-travel hallucinations begin at the time of the plane crash and that he imagines them to have begun in 1944 because he was in fact thinking of that time just before the crash or because events of this period were the first that he imaginatively visited. (pp. 35-40)

> *Russell Blackford, "Physics and Fantasy: Scientific Mysticism, Kurt Vonnegut, and 'Gravity's Rainbow',"* in Journal of Popular Culture, *Vol. 19, No. 3, Winter, 1985, pp. 35-44.*

BARBARA WIEDEMANN

Advances in technology with a corresponding abdication of responsibility on the part of scientists and political leaders is a prime concern of Vonnegut. Vonnegut was a prisoner of war housed in Dresden during the bombing and resulting firestorms. As he relates it, "I was in Dresden when America dropped scientific truth on it." For twenty-five years in one form or another Vonnegut tried to come to terms with the Dresden experience. In early books such as *Mother Night* (1962) and *Cat's Cradle* (1963), Vonnegut developed themes related to war and destruction; however, he did not focus specifically on Dresden until *Slaughterhouse-Five.* In this novel the protagonist Billy Pilgrim has similar experiences to Vonnegut's. Like Vonnegut, Billy is in the Battle of the Bulge, gets lost searching for his own troops, is captured by the Germans, and is sent to Dresden in a cattle car. In Dresden as a prisoner of war he works in a factory making a dietary supplement for pregnant women, and he survives the bombing of Dresden by being in a meat storage locker. He then digs up and disposes of corpses described by Vonnegut as "pieces of charred firewood two or three feet long—ridiculously small human beings, or jumbo fried grasshoppers" (*Mother Night*). Then the parallels with Vonnegut end as Billy becomes a time traveler kidnapped by the inhabitants of Tralfamadore.

Vonnegut uses the fantasy as a means of distancing himself in order to observe the events more closely and as a means of commenting upon the madness and the cruelty in the world. The senselessness of the bombing of Dresden, a city with little strategic importance, can only be treated effectively through fantasy. Nothing else can transmit the horror of the experience. In *Slaughterhouse-Five* Vonnegut, as the narrator, discusses the problem of not being able to describe the event adequately and meaningfully:

"I would hate to tell you what this lousy little book cost me in money and anxiety and time. When I got home from the Second World War twenty-three years ago, I thought it would be easy for me to write about the destruction of Dresden, since all I would have to do would be to report what I had seen . . . But not many words about Dresden came from my mind then—not enough of them to make a book, anyway."

Vonnegut overcomes this writer's block by not relying solely on factual, realistic reporting but by incorporating fantasy and science fiction into his novel. (pp. 139-40)

Barbara Wiedemann, "American War Novels: Strategies for Survival," in War and Peace: Perspectives in the Nuclear Age, *edited by Ulrich Goebel and Otto Nelson, Texas Tech University Press, 1988, pp. 137-44.*

FURTHER READING

Gros Louis, Dolores K. "*Slaughterhouse-Five*: Pacifism vs. Passiveness." *Ball State University Forum* XVIII, No. 2 (Spring 1977): 3-8.
 Discusses the relationship between the attitudes of protagonist Billy Pilgrim, Vonnegut-as-narrator, and Vonnegut the author.

Kazin, Alfred. "The War Novel: From Mailer to Vonnegut." In his *Bright Book of Life: American Novelists & Storytellers from Hemingway to Mailer.* New York: Little, Brown, 1973. See excerpt in *CLC,* Vol. 3.
 Reprint in which Kazin asserts that *Slaughterhouse-Five* is marred by Vonnegut's unwillingness to directly portray the tragedy of the Dresden fire-bombing.

Ketterer, David. "Vonnegut's Spiral Siren Call: From Dresden's Lunar Vistas to Tralfamadore." In his *New Worlds for Old: The Apocalyptic Imagination, Science Fiction, and American Literature,* pp. 296-333. Bloomington: Indiana University Press, 1974.
 Analysis of science fiction elements in *Slaughterhouse-Five.*

Klinkowitz, Jerome. "Kurt Vonnegut, Jr." In his *Literary Disruptions: The Making of a Post-Contemporary American Fiction,* pp. 33-61. Urbana: University of Illinois Press, 1975.
 Overview of Vonnegut's career that includes a highly favorable appraisal of *Slaughterhouse-Five.*

Matheson, T. J. " 'This Lousy Little Book': The Genesis and Development of *Slaughterhouse-Five* as Revealed in Chapter One." *Studies in the Novel* 16, No. 2 (Summer 1984): 228-40.
 Outlines the importance of the book's first chapter in providing readers with clues to Vonnegut's changing attitude to the horrors of war and to the composition of *Slaughterhouse-Five.*

Meyer, William E. H., Jr. "Kurt Vonnegut: The Man with Nothing to Say." *Critique: Studies in Modern Fiction* XXIX, No. 2 (Winter 1988): 95-109.
 Rejects the notion that *Slaughterhouse-Five* is a satirical or anti-war novel, maintaining that it is instead a work written in the manner of Herman Melville's *Moby-Dick* about the protagonist's discovery of self.

☐ Contemporary Literary Criticism

Indexes

Literary Criticism Series
  Cumulative Author Index
Cumulative Nationality Index
Title Index, Volume 60

This Index Includes References to Entries in These Gale Series

Contemporary Literary Criticism

Presents excerpts of criticism on the works of novelists, poets, dramatists, short story writers, scriptwriters, and other creative writers who are now living or who have died since 1960. Cumulative indexes to authors and nationalities are included, as well as an index to titles discussed in the individual volume.

Twentieth-Century Literary Criticism

Contains critical excerpts by the most significant commentators on poets, novelists, short story writers, dramatists, and philosophers who died between 1900 and 1960. Cumulative indexes to authors, nationalities, and titles discussed are included in each new volume.

Nineteenth-Century Literature Criticism

Offers significant passages from criticism on authors who died between 1800 and 1899. Cumulative indexes to authors, nationalities, and titles discussed are included in each new volume.

Literature Criticism from 1400 to 1800

Compiles significant passages from the most noteworthy criticism on authors of the fifteenth through eighteenth centuries. Cumulative indexes to authors, nationalities, and titles discussed are included in each new volume.

Classical and Medieval Literature Criticism

Offers excerpts of criticism on the works of world authors from classical antiquity through the fourteenth century. Cumulative indexes to authors, titles, and critics are included in each volume.

Short Story Criticism

Compiles excerpts of criticism on short fiction by writers of all eras and nationalities. Cumulative indexes to authors, nationalities, and titles discussed are included in each new volume.

Children's Literature Review

Includes excerpts from reviews, criticism, and commentary on works of authors and illustrators who create books for children. Cumulative indexes to authors, nationalities, and titles discussed are included in each new volume.

Contemporary Authors Series

Encompasses five related series. *Contemporary Authors* provides biographical and bibliographical information on more than 92,000 writers of fiction, nonfiction, poetry, journalism, drama, motion pictures, and other fields. Each new volume contains sketches on authors not previously covered in the series. *Contemporary Authors New Revision Series* provides completely updated information on active authors covered in previously published volumes of *CA*. Only entries requiring significant change are revised for *CA New Revision Series*. *Contemporary Authors Permanent Series* consists of updated listings for deceased and inactive authors removed from the original volumes 9-36 when these volumes were revised. *Contemporary Authors Autobiography Series* presents specially commissioned autobiographies by leading contemporary writers. *Contemporary Authors Bibliographical Series* contains primary and secondary bibliographies as well as analytical bibliographical essays by authorities on major modern authors.

Dictionary of Literary Biography

Encompasses three related series. *Dictionary of Literary Biography* furnishes illustrated overviews of authors' lives and works and places them in the larger perspective of literary history. *Dictionary of Literary Biography Documentary Series* illuminates the careers of major figures through a selection of literary documents, including letters, notebook and diary entries, interviews, book reviews, and photographs. *Dictionary of Literary Biography Yearbook* summarizes the past year's literary activity with articles on genres, major prizes, conferences, and other timely subjects and includes updated and new entries on individual authors. A cumulative index to authors and articles is included in each new volume.

Concise Dictionary of American Literary Biography

A six-volume series that collects revised and updated sketches on major American authors that were originally presented in *Dictionary of Literary Biography*.

Something about the Author Series

Encompasses two related series. *Something about the Author* contains heavily illustrated biographical sketches on juvenile and young adult authors and illustrators from all eras. *Something about the Author Autobiography Series* presents specially commissioned autobiographies by prominent authors and illustrators of books for children and young adults.

Yesterday's Authors of Books for Children

Contains heavily illustrated entries on children's writers who died before 1961. Complete in two volumes.

Literary Criticism Series
Cumulative Author Index

This index lists all author entries in the Gale Literary Criticism Series and includes cross-references to other Gale sources. References in the index are identified as follows:

AAYA: *Authors & Artists for Young Adults,* Volumes 1-3
CAAS: *Contemporary Authors Autobiography Series,* Volumes 1-11
CA: *Contemporary Authors* (original series), Volumes 1-130
CABS: *Contemporary Authors Bibliographical Series,* Volumes 1-3
CANR: *Contemporary Authors New Revision Series,* Volumes 1-29
CAP: *Contemporary Authors Permanent Series,* Volumes 1-2
CA-R: *Contemporary Authors* (revised editions), Volumes 1-44
CDALB: *Concise Dictionary of American Literary Biography,* Volumes 1-6
CLC: *Contemporary Literary Criticism,* Volumes 1-60
CLR: *Children's Literature Review,* Volumes 1-21
CMLC: *Classical and Medieval Literature Criticism,* Volumes 1-4
DLB: *Dictionary of Literary Biography,* Volumes 1-92
DLB-DS: *Dictionary of Literary Biography Documentary Series,* Volumes 1-7
DLB-Y: *Dictionary of Literary Biography Yearbook,* Volumes 1980-1988
LC: *Literature Criticism from 1400 to 1800,* Volumes 1-13
NCLC: *Nineteenth-Century Literature Criticism,* Volumes 1-27
SAAS: *Something about the Author Autobiography Series,* Volumes 1-9
SATA: *Something about the Author,* Volumes 1-59
SSC: *Short Story Criticism,* Volumes 1-5
TCLC: *Twentieth-Century Literary Criticism,* Volumes 1-37
YABC: *Yesterday's Authors of Books for Children,* Volumes 1-2

A. E. 1867-1935 .... TCLC **3, 10**
See also Russell, George William
See also DLB 19

Abbey, Edward 1927-1989 ...... CLC **36, 59**
See also CANR 2; CA 45-48;
obituary CA 128

Abbott, Lee K., Jr. 19??- .... CLC **48**

Abe, Kobo 1924- .... CLC **8, 22, 53**
See also CANR 24; CA 65-68

Abell, Kjeld 1901-1961 .... CLC **15**
See also obituary CA 111

Abish, Walter 1931- .... CLC **22**
See also CA 101

Abrahams, Peter (Henry) 1919- ..... CLC **4**
See also CA 57-60

Abrams, M(eyer) H(oward) 1912-... CLC **24**
See also CANR 13; CA 57-60; DLB 67

Abse, Dannie 1923- .... CLC **7, 29**
See also CAAS 1; CANR 4; CA 53-56;
DLB 27

Achebe, (Albert) Chinua(lumogu)
1930- .... CLC **1, 3, 5, 7, 11, 26, 51**
See also CLR 20; CANR 6, 26; CA 1-4R;
SATA 38, 40

Acker, Kathy 1948- .... CLC **45**
See also CA 117, 122

Ackroyd, Peter 1949- .... CLC **34, 52**
See also CA 123, 127

Acorn, Milton 1923- .... CLC **15**
See also CA 103; DLB 53

Adamov, Arthur 1908-1970 ...... CLC **4, 25**
See also CAP 2; CA 17-18;
obituary CA 25-28R

Adams, Alice (Boyd) 1926- ... CLC **6, 13, 46**
See also CANR 26; CA 81-84; DLB-Y 86

Adams, Douglas (Noel) 1952- ... CLC **27, 60**
See also CA 106; DLB-Y 83

Adams, Henry (Brooks)
1838-1918 .... TCLC **4**
See also CA 104; DLB 12, 47

Adams, Richard (George)
1920- .... CLC **4, 5, 18**
See also CLR 20; CANR 3; CA 49-52;
SATA 7

Adamson, Joy(-Friederike Victoria)
1910-1980 .... CLC **17**
See also CANR 22; CA 69-72;
obituary CA 93-96; SATA 11;
obituary SATA 22

Adcock, (Kareen) Fleur 1934- ...... CLC **41**
See also CANR 11; CA 25-28R; DLB 40

Addams, Charles (Samuel)
1912-1988 .... CLC **30**
See also CANR 12; CA 61-64;
obituary CA 126

Adler, C(arole) S(chwerdtfeger)
1932- .... CLC **35**
See also CANR 19; CA 89-92; SATA 26

Adler, Renata 1938- .... CLC **8, 31**
See also CANR 5, 22; CA 49-52

Ady, Endre 1877-1919 .... TCLC **11**
See also CA 107

Agee, James 1909-1955 .... TCLC **1, 19**
See also CA 108; DLB 2, 26;
CDALB 1941-1968

Agnon, S(hmuel) Y(osef Halevi)
1888-1970 .... CLC **4, 8, 14**
See also CAP 2; CA 17-18;
obituary CA 25-28R

Ai 1947- .... CLC **4, 14**
See also CA 85-88

Aickman, Robert (Fordyce)
1914-1981 .... CLC **57**
See also CANR 3; CA 7-8R

Aiken, Conrad (Potter)
1889-1973 .... CLC **1, 3, 5, 10, 52**
See also CANR 4; CA 5-8R;
obituary CA 45-48; SATA 3, 30; DLB 9,
45

Aiken, Joan (Delano) 1924- .... CLC **35**
See also CLR 1; CANR 4; CA 9-12R;
SAAS 1; SATA 2, 30

Conner, Ralph   1860-1937 . . . . TCLC 31

Conrad, Joseph
    1857-1924 . . . . TCLC 1, 6, 13, 25
    See also CA 104; SATA 27; DLB 10, 34

Conroy, Pat   1945- . . . . CLC 30
    See also CANR 24; CA 85-88; DLB 6

Constant (de Rebecque), (Henri) Benjamin
    1767-1830 . . . . NCLC 6

Cook, Michael   1933- . . . . CLC 58
    See also CA 93-96; DLB 53

Cook, Robin   1940- . . . . CLC 14
    See also CA 108, 111

Cooke, Elizabeth   1948- . . . . CLC 55

Cooke, John Esten   1830-1886 . . . . . NCLC 5
    See also DLB 3

Cooper, J. California   19??- . . . . CLC 56
    See also CA 125, 127

Cooper, James Fenimore
    1789-1851 . . . . NCLC 1, 27
    See also SATA 19; DLB 3;
    CDALB 1640-1865

Coover, Robert (Lowell)
    1932- . . . . CLC 3, 7, 15, 32, 46
    See also CANR 3; CA 45-48; DLB 2;
    DLB-Y 81

Copeland, Stewart (Armstrong)
    1952- . . . . CLC 26
    See also The Police

Coppard, A(lfred) E(dgar)
    1878-1957 . . . . TCLC 5
    See also YABC 1; CA 114

Coppee, Francois   1842-1908 . . . . . . TCLC 25

Coppola, Francis Ford   1939- . . . . CLC 16
    See also CA 77-80; DLB 44

Corcoran, Barbara   1911- . . . . CLC 17
    See also CAAS 2; CANR 11; CA 21-24R;
    SATA 3; DLB 52

Corman, Cid   1924- . . . . CLC 9
    See also Corman, Sidney
    See also CAAS 2; DLB 5

Corman, Sidney   1924-
    See Corman, Cid
    See also CA 85-88

Cormier, Robert (Edmund)
    1925- . . . . CLC 12, 30
    See also CLR 12; CANR 5, 23; CA 1-4R;
    SATA 10, 45; DLB 52

Corn, Alfred (Dewitt III)   1943- . . . . . CLC 33
    See also CA 104; DLB-Y 80

Cornwell, David (John Moore)
    1931- . . . . CLC 9, 15
    See also le Carre, John
    See also CANR 13; CA 5-8R

Corso, (Nunzio) Gregory   1930- . . . CLC 1, 11
    See also CA 5-8R; DLB 5, 16

Cortazar, Julio
    1914-1984 . . . . . CLC 2, 3, 5, 10, 13, 15,
                               33, 34
    See also CANR 12; CA 21-24R

Corvo, Baron   1860-1913
    See Rolfe, Frederick (William Serafino
    Austin Lewis Mary)

Cosic, Dobrica   1921- . . . . CLC 14
    See also CA 122

Costain, Thomas B(ertram)
    1885-1965 . . . . CLC 30
    See also CA 5-8R; obituary CA 25-28R;
    DLB 9

Costantini, Humberto   1924?-1987 . . . CLC 49
    See also obituary CA 122

Costello, Elvis   1955- . . . . CLC 21

Cotter, Joseph Seamon, Sr.
    1861-1949 . . . . TCLC 28
    See also DLB 50

Couperus, Louis (Marie Anne)
    1863-1923 . . . . TCLC 15
    See also CA 115

Courtenay, Bryce   1933- . . . . CLC 59

Cousteau, Jacques-Yves   1910- . . . . . . CLC 30
    See also CANR 15; CA 65-68; SATA 38

Coward, (Sir) Noel (Pierce)
    1899-1973 . . . . CLC 1, 9, 29, 51
    See also CAP 2; CA 17-18;
    obituary CA 41-44R; DLB 10

Cowley, Malcolm   1898-1989 . . . . CLC 39
    See also CANR 3; CA 5-6R; DLB 4, 48;
    DLB-Y 81

Cowper, William   1731-1800 . . . . . . NCLC 8

Cox, William Trevor   1928- . . . . . . CLC 9, 14
    See also Trevor, William
    See also CANR 4; CA 9-12R

Cozzens, James Gould
    1903-1978 . . . . CLC 1, 4, 11
    See also CANR 19; CA 9-12R;
    obituary CA 81-84; DLB 9; DLB-Y 84;
    DLB-DS 2; CDALB 1941-1968

Crabbe, George   1754-1832 . . . . NCLC 26

Crace, Douglas   1944- . . . . CLC 58

Crane, (Harold) Hart
    1899-1932 . . . . TCLC 2, 5
    See also CA 104; DLB 4, 48

Crane, R(onald) S(almon)
    1886-1967 . . . . CLC 27
    See also CA 85-88; DLB 63

Crane, Stephen
    1871-1900 . . . . TCLC 11, 17, 32
    See also YABC 2; CA 109; DLB 12, 54, 78;
    CDALB 1865-1917

Craven, Margaret   1901-1980 . . . . CLC 17
    See also CA 103

Crawford, F(rancis) Marion
    1854-1909 . . . . TCLC 10
    See also CA 107; DLB 71

Crawford, Isabella Valancy
    1850-1887 . . . . NCLC 12

Crayencour, Marguerite de   1903-1987
    See Yourcenar, Marguerite

Creasey, John   1908-1973 . . . . CLC 11
    See also CANR 8; CA 5-8R;
    obituary CA 41-44R

Crebillon, Claude Prosper Jolyot de (fils)
    1707-1777 . . . . LC 1

Creeley, Robert (White)
    1926- . . . . CLC 1, 2, 4, 8, 11, 15, 36
    See also CANR 23; CA 1-4R; DLB 5, 16

Crews, Harry (Eugene)
    1935- . . . . CLC 6, 23, 49
    See also CANR 20; CA 25-28R; DLB 6

Crichton, (John) Michael
    1942- . . . . CLC 2, 6, 54
    See also CANR 13; CA 25-28R; SATA 9;
    DLB-Y 81

Crispin, Edmund   1921-1978 . . . . CLC 22
    See also Montgomery, Robert Bruce

Cristofer, Michael   1946- . . . . CLC 28
    See also CA 110; DLB 7

Croce, Benedetto   1866-1952 . . . . . . TCLC 37
    See also CA 120

Crockett, David (Davy)
    1786-1836 . . . . NCLC 8
    See also DLB 3, 11

Croker, John Wilson   1780-1857 . . NCLC 10

Cronin, A(rchibald) J(oseph)
    1896-1981 . . . . CLC 32
    See also CANR 5; CA 1-4R;
    obituary CA 102; obituary SATA 25, 47

Cross, Amanda   1926-
    See Heilbrun, Carolyn G(old)

Crothers, Rachel   1878-1953 . . . . . . TCLC 19
    See also CA 113; DLB 7

Crowley, Aleister   1875-1947 . . . . TCLC 7
    See also CA 104

Crowley, John   1942-
    See also CA 61-64; DLB-Y 82

Crumb, Robert   1943- . . . . CLC 17
    See also CA 106

Cryer, Gretchen   1936?- . . . . CLC 21
    See also CA 114, 123

Csath, Geza   1887-1919 . . . . TCLC 13
    See also CA 111

Cudlip, David   1933- . . . . CLC 34

Cullen, Countee   1903-1946 . . . . . TCLC 4, 37
    See also CA 108, 124; SATA 18; DLB 4,
    48, 51; CDALB 1917-1929

Cummings, E(dward) E(stlin)
    1894-1962 . . . . CLC 1, 3, 8, 12, 15
    See also CA 73-76; DLB 4, 48

Cunha, Euclides (Rodrigues) da
    1866-1909 . . . . TCLC 24
    See also CA 123

Cunningham, J(ames) V(incent)
    1911-1985 . . . . CLC 3, 31
    See also CANR 1; CA 1-4R;
    obituary CA 115; DLB 5

Cunningham, Julia (Woolfolk)
    1916- . . . . CLC 12
    See also CANR 4, 19; CA 9-12R; SAAS 2;
    SATA 1, 26

Cunningham, Michael   1952- . . . . CLC 34

Currie, Ellen   19??- . . . . CLC 44

Dabrowska, Maria (Szumska)
    1889-1965 . . . . CLC 15
    See also CA 106

Dabydeen, David   1956?- . . . . CLC 34
    See also CA 106

Dacey, Philip   1939- . . . . CLC 51
    See also CANR 14; CA 37-40R

Dagerman, Stig (Halvard)
    1923-1954 . . . . TCLC 17
    See also CA 117

Author Index

Shaw, (George) Bernard
1856-1950 . . . . TCLC **3, 9, 21**
See also CA 104, 109, 119; DLB 10, 57

Shaw, Henry Wheeler
1818-1885 . . . . NCLC **15**
See also DLB 11

Shaw, Irwin 1913-1984. . . . . . CLC **7, 23, 34**
See also CANR 21; CA 13-16R;
obituary CA 112; DLB 6; DLB-Y 84;
CDALB 1941-1968

Shaw, Robert 1927-1978 . . . . CLC **5**
See also CANR 4; CA 1-4R;
obituary CA 81-84; DLB 13, 14

Shawn, Wallace 1943- . . . . CLC **41**
See also CA 112

Sheed, Wilfrid (John Joseph)
1930- . . . . CLC **2, 4, 10, 53**
See also CA 65-68; DLB 6

Sheffey, Asa 1913-1980
See Hayden, Robert (Earl)

Sheldon, Alice (Hastings) B(radley)
1915-1987
See Tiptree, James, Jr.
See also CA 108; obituary CA 122

Shelley, Mary Wollstonecraft Godwin
1797-1851 . . . . NCLC **14**
See also SATA 29

Shelley, Percy Bysshe
1792-1822 . . . . NCLC **18**

Shepard, Jim 19??- . . . . CLC **36**

Shepard, Lucius 19??- . . . . CLC **34**

Shepard, Sam
1943- . . . . CLC **4, 6, 17, 34, 41, 44**
See also CANR 22; CA 69-72; DLB 7

Shepherd, Michael 1927-
See Ludlum, Robert

Sherburne, Zoa (Morin) 1912- . . . . . . CLC **30**
See also CANR 3; CA 1-4R; SATA 3

Sheridan, Frances 1724-1766. . . . . LC **7**
See also DLB 39

Sheridan, Richard Brinsley
1751-1816 . . . . NCLC **5**

Sherman, Jonathan Marc 1970?- . . . . CLC **55**

Sherman, Martin 19??- . . . . CLC **19**
See also CA 116

Sherwin, Judith Johnson 1936- . . . CLC **7, 15**
See also CA 25-28R

Sherwood, Robert E(mmet)
1896-1955 . . . . TCLC **3**
See also CA 104; DLB 7, 26

Shiel, M(atthew) P(hipps)
1865-1947 . . . . TCLC **8**
See also CA 106

Shiga, Naoya 1883-1971. . . . . CLC **33**
See also CA 101; obituary CA 33-36R

Shimazaki, Haruki 1872-1943
See Shimazaki, Toson
See also CA 105

Shimazaki, Toson 1872-1943 . . . . TCLC **5**
See also Shimazaki, Haruki

Sholokhov, Mikhail (Aleksandrovich)
1905-1984 . . . . CLC **7, 15**
See also CA 101; obituary CA 112;
SATA 36

Sholom Aleichem 1859-1916 . . . . TCLC **1, 35**
See also Rabinovitch, Sholem

Shreve, Susan Richards 1939- . . . . . . CLC **23**
See also CAAS 5; CANR 5; CA 49-52;
SATA 41, 46

Shue, Larry 1946-1985. . . . . CLC **52**
See also obituary CA 117

Shulman, Alix Kates 1932- . . . . . . CLC **2, 10**
See also CA 29-32R; SATA 7

Shuster, Joe 1914- . . . . CLC **21**

Shute (Norway), Nevil 1899-1960 . . . CLC **30**
See also Norway, Nevil Shute
See also CA 102; obituary CA 93-96

Shuttle, Penelope (Diane) 1947- . . . . . CLC **7**
See also CA 93-96; DLB 14, 40

Siegel, Jerome 1914- . . . . CLC **21**
See also CA 116

Sienkiewicz, Henryk (Adam Aleksander Pius)
1846-1916 . . . . TCLC **3**
See also CA 104

Sigal, Clancy 1926-. . . . . CLC **7**
See also CA 1-4R

Sigourney, Lydia (Howard Huntley)
1791-1865 . . . . NCLC **21**
See also DLB 1, 42, 73

Siguenza y Gongora, Carlos de
1645-1700 . . . . LC **8**

Sigurjonsson, Johann 1880-1919 . . . TCLC **27**

Silkin, Jon 1930- . . . . CLC **2, 6, 43**
See also CAAS 5; CA 5-8R; DLB 27

Silko, Leslie Marmon 1948- . . . . CLC **23**
See also CA 115, 122

Sillanpaa, Franz Eemil 1888-1964. . . CLC **19**
See also obituary CA 93-96

Sillitoe, Alan
1928- . . . . CLC **1, 3, 6, 10, 19, 57**
See also CAAS 2; CANR 8, 26; CA 9-12R;
DLB 14

Silone, Ignazio 1900-1978 . . . . CLC **4**
See also CAAS 2; CANR 26; CAP 2;
CA 25-28, 11-12R,; obituary CA 81-84

Silver, Joan Micklin 1935- . . . . CLC **20**
See also CA 114, 121

Silverberg, Robert 1935- . . . . CLC **7**
See also CAAS 3; CANR 1, 20; CA 1-4R;
SATA 13; DLB 8

Silverstein, Alvin 1933- . . . . CLC **17**
See also CANR 2; CA 49-52; SATA 8

Silverstein, Virginia B(arbara Opshelor)
1937- . . . . CLC **17**
See also CANR 2; CA 49-52; SATA 8

Simak, Clifford D(onald)
1904-1988 . . . . CLC **1, 55**
See also CANR 1; CA 1-4R;
obituary CA 125; DLB 8

Simenon, Georges (Jacques Christian)
1903-1989 . . . . . . CLC **1, 2, 3, 8, 18, 47**
See also CA 85-88; DLB 72

Simenon, Paul 1956?-
See The Clash

Simic, Charles 1938-. . . . . . . CLC **6, 9, 22, 49**
See also CAAS 4; CANR 12; CA 29-32R

Simmons, Charles (Paul) 1924- . . . . . CLC **57**
See also CA 89-92

Simmons, Dan 1948-. . . . . CLC **44**

Simmons, James (Stewart Alexander)
1933- . . . . CLC **43**
See also CA 105; DLB 40

Simms, William Gilmore
1806-1870 . . . . NCLC **3**
See also DLB 3, 30

Simon, Carly 1945-. . . . . CLC **26**
See also CA 105

Simon, Claude (Henri Eugene)
1913- . . . . CLC **4, 9, 15, 39**
See also CA 89-92

Simon, (Marvin) Neil
1927- . . . . CLC **6, 11, 31, 39**
See also CA 21-24R; DLB 7

Simon, Paul 1941- . . . . CLC **17**
See also CA 116

Simonon, Paul 1956?-
See The Clash

Simpson, Louis (Aston Marantz)
1923- . . . . CLC **4, 7, 9, 32**
See also CAAS 4; CANR 1; CA 1-4R;
DLB 5

Simpson, Mona (Elizabeth) 1957- . . . CLC **44**
See also CA 122

Simpson, N(orman) F(rederick)
1919- . . . . CLC **29**
See also CA 11-14R; DLB 13

Sinclair, Andrew (Annandale)
1935- . . . . CLC **2, 14**
See also CAAS 5; CANR 14; CA 9-12R;
DLB 14

Sinclair, Mary Amelia St. Clair 1865?-1946
See Sinclair, May
See also CA 104

Sinclair, May 1865?-1946 . . . . . . TCLC **3, 11**
See also Sinclair, Mary Amelia St. Clair
See also DLB 36

Sinclair, Upton (Beall)
1878-1968 . . . . CLC **1, 11, 15**
See also CANR 7; CA 5-8R;
obituary CA 25-28R; SATA 9; DLB 9

Singer, Isaac Bashevis
1904- . . . . CLC **1, 3, 6, 9, 11, 15, 23, 38;**
SSC **3**
See also CLR 1; CANR 1; CA 1-4R;
SATA 3, 27; DLB 6, 28, 52;
CDALB 1941-1968

Singer, Israel Joshua 1893-1944 . . . TCLC **33**

Singh, Khushwant 1915-. . . . . CLC **11**
See also CANR 6; CA 9-12R

Sinyavsky, Andrei (Donatevich)
1925- . . . . CLC **8**
See also CA 85-88

Sirin, V.
See Nabokov, Vladimir (Vladimirovich)

Sissman, L(ouis) E(dward)
1928-1976 . . . . CLC **9, 18**
See also CANR 13; CA 21-24R;
obituary CA 65-68; DLB 5

Sisson, C(harles) H(ubert) 1914-. . . . . CLC **8**
See also CAAS 3; CANR 3; CA 1-4R;
DLB 27

Sitwell, (Dame) Edith 1887-1964. . . CLC **2, 9**
See also CA 9-12R; DLB 20

Author Index

CLC Cumulative Nationality Index

Nationality Index

Nationality Index

Nationality Index

CLC-60 Title Index

Title Index